THE WORLD OF
ECONOMICS

D0875874

THE NEW PALGRAVE

THE WORLD OF ECONOMICS

EDITED BY

JOHN EATWELL · MURRAY MILGATE · PETER NEWMAN

W · W · NORTON

NEW YORK · LONDON

© The Macmillan Press Limited, 1987, 1991

First published in
The New Palgrave: A Dictionary of Economics
Edited by John Eatwell, Murray Milgate and Peter Newman
in four volumes, 1987

The New Palgrave is a trademark of
The Macmillan Press Limited.

First American Edition, 1991
All rights reserved.

ISBN 0-393-02973- 5

W. W. Norton & Company, Inc.
500 Fifth Avenue
New York, NY 10110

W. W. Norton & Company, Ltd.
10 Coptic Street
London WC1A 1PU

Printed in Hong Kong

1   2   3   4   5   6   7   8   9   0

Contents

v

Contents

Acknowledgments

The following contributors (articles shown in parentheses) acknowledge support from public bodies or permission to reprint copyright material:

Andrew B. Abel (Ricardian Equivalence Theorem), financial support from the Amoco Foundation Term Professorship in Finance, the National Science Foundation and the Sloan Foundation. Kenneth J. Arrow (Economic Theory and the Hypothesis of Rationality), support from the Office of Naval Research; originally published as 'Rationality of Self and Others in an Economic System' in *Rational Choice: The Contrast between Economics and Psychology*, (eds R.M. Hogarth and M.W. Reder) © University of Chicago Press. John C. Harsanyi (Value Judgements), financial support from the National Science Foundation (SES82-18938) administered by the Center for Research in Management, University of California, Berkeley. R. Wilson (Exchange), support from Stanford University, Stanford; research support from the National Science Foundation (SES83-08723) and the Office of Naval Research (N00014-79C0685).

Preface

Most of us remember learning how to ride a bicycle, the struggle it was to stay on, to steer straight, to turn without falling to one side. Then, after minutes or hours or even days of practice we suddenly got the hang of it, and learned that almost miraculous sense of balance which makes riding on two wheels so easy, and which never goes away.

A similar experience in learning their subject is often reported by economists, even by some of the most famous. For weeks or months or even years they listen to the lectures, read the textbooks, even pass the examinations with flying colours; yet they still do not really understand what economic analysis is all about. Then quite suddenly the clouds disperse, the sun shines brightly and they realise just how economics, with its own particular vision of the way in which society allocates resources and organizes production and distribution, can and does illuminate the world around them.

That vision was created at the end of the 18th century. In 1776 Adam Smith, building on the work of François Quesnay, set out in *The Wealth of Nations* his understanding of the workings of a competitive economy, in which production and distribution are organized through market exchange. In such economies, he claimed, the decisions of all individuals and firms respond to the same price signals and to the calculation of profit and loss reckoned at those prices. But in all other ways those agents make decisions entirely independently of one another. In the first great insight of modern economics, Smith argued that such an economy would not collapse into chaos but would instead constitute a *system*, with its own patterns of operation and its own 'laws' of behaviour; and it was the job of the economist to discover those laws, what they are and how they work.

Smith then showed how the economist should proceed on the path towards that discovery. From the infinite complexity of daily life one should extract the connected skeleton of the market system, which supports the whole structure. This analytical abstraction is then to be taken and used as the fundamental representation of the major forces shaping the economy. The science of economics is not merely descriptive, but instead consists both of abstract analysis and of description that is informed and structured by that analysis.

It was David Ricardo's *Principles of Political Economy and Taxation* (1817) that firmly established *deductive* reasoning as the central method of economics. The workings of the economy were to be inferred logically from a few fundamental presumptions: that individuals and firms pursue specified objectives through markets which function in particular ways, most especially through freely competitive markets over which no individual agent has any control.

Thus, by 1817 the key components of the discipline of economics were in place. An economy was to be seen as a system which operates through market exchange and so through a price mechanism. Individuals in society, pursuing their own interests, interact in their economic relations both with nature and with each other. Both aspects of this vision are important, the interests of the individuals – not necessarily narrowly selfish or 'economic' – and the ways they interact in society. It is precisely their combination by deductive analysis which characterizes the way in which economists perceive the world.

All coherent bodies of economic thought share this vision of the way in which economies operate, even though they may differ – and differ quite profoundly – in many other respects. Non-economists in the media and elsewhere seldom understand this, and as a result that acceptance of scientific difference which is routinely extended to such controversial sciences as biology and cosmology is seldom extended also to economics. Almost every day, for example, many econometric forecasts are proved false by the actual realization of events; and the same is true of innumerable meteorological forecasts. Yet unlike economic forecasters weather forecasters are seldom sacked, and when they are it is usually for lack of media presence rather than lack of accuracy. The fact that most economists, like most physicists, have a well-defined vision of their world does not imply that they also have to agree about how it actually works, any more than physicists have to agree about the nature of the fundamental particles which constitute their universe.

Perhaps John Maynard Keynes put the point best, in a famous quotation: 'The Theory of Economics does not furnish a body of settled conclusions immediately applicable to policy. It is a method rather than a doctrine, an apparatus of the mind, a technique of thinking, which helps its possessor to draw correct conclusions.'

The New Palgrave: A Dictionary of Economics was published in four large volumes in late 1987, and has rapidly become a standard reference work in economics. Its name is explained by the fact that it is the modern successor to the *Dictionary of Political Economy*, edited by R.H. Inglis Palgrave and published by Macmillan in three volumes in 1894, 1896 and 1899. A second and slightly modified version, edited by Henry Higgs, appeared during the mid-1920s.

As editors of *The New Palgrave* we asked its contributors not to write surveys of current literature nor to adhere to a prescribed point of view. Instead, each was asked – while remaining accurate in discussing the work of others – to make clear his or her own views on the subject concerned. Moreover, the contributions were to be written from an historical perspective wherever possible, to describe not only present problems but also past growth and future prospects. For we believe that knowledge of the historical development of any theory enriches both its present understanding and the possibilities for better theories in the future. Even though not all the nearly 2000 topics covered in the *Dictionary* lent themselves to such historical treatment, the authors' responses to this request were generally positive.

All one hundred essays in this volume are taken from *The New Palgrave*, and appear essentially as they did there. They have been chosen to show how that 'technique of thinking' to which Keynes referred can be applied so as to illuminate a wide range of diverse topics. However, those readers quite new to economics will inevitably encounter certain terms and tools of the trade – such as *elasticity*, *Pareto optimality, substitutes and complements* – that are unfamiliar. Such readers should be undeterred. With the guidance of the index, help can often be found elsewhere in the collection; and in the last resort there are always the textbooks of the subject, for which *The World of Economics* is a complement, not a substitute.

John Eatwell
Murray Milgate
Peter Newman

Agricultural Growth and Population Change

E. BOSERUP

The macroeconomic theory of the relationship between demographic and agricultural change was developed by Malthus and Ricardo in the early stage of demographic transition in Europe, and interest in classical theory was revived in the middle of this century, when economists became aware of the unfolding demographic transition in other parts of the world. Ricardo (1817) distinguished between two types of agricultural expansion in response to population growth. One is the extensive margin, the expansion into new land which he supposed would yield diminishing returns to labour and capital because the new land was presumed to be more distant or of poorer quality than the land already in use. The other type, the intensive margin, is more intensive cultivation of the existing fields, raising crop yields by such means as better fertilization, weeding, draining, and other land preparation. This also was likely to yield diminishing returns to labour and capital. Therefore Ricardo assumed, with Malthus (1803), that population increase would sooner or later be arrested by a decline in real wages, increase of rents, and decline of per capita food consumption.

This theory takes no account of a third type of agricultural expansion in response to population growth: using the increasing labour force to crop the existing fields more frequently. This was in fact what was happening in England in Ricardo's time, when the European system of short fallow was being replaced by the system of annual cropping. Fallows are neither more distant nor of poorer quality than the cultivated fields, but if fallow periods are shortened or eliminated, more labour and capital inputs are needed, both to prevent a decline of crop yields and to substitute for the decline in the amount of fodder for animals, which was previously obtained by the grazing of fallows. Therefore this type of intensification is also likely to yield diminishing returns to labour and capital, but the additions to total output obtained by increasing the frequency of cropping are much larger than those obtainable by use of more labour and capital simply

1

to raise crop yields. In fact, the Ricardian type of intensification is better viewed as a means not to raise crop yields, but more to prevent a decline of those yields as fallow is shortened or eliminated. When this third type of agricultural expansion by higher frequency of cropping is taken into account, elasticities of food supply in response to population growth are different from those assumed in classical theory.

The failure to take differences in frequency of cropping into account renders the classical theory unsuitable for the analysis of agricultural changes which accompany the demographic transition in developing countries in the second half of this century. Differences in population densities between developing countries are very large, and so are the related differences in frequency of cropping. The relevant classification for analysis of agricultural growth is not between new land and land which is sown and cropped each year, but the frequency at which a given piece of land is sown and cropped. Both in the past and today, we have a continuum of agricultural systems, ranging from the extreme case of land which is never used for crops, to the other extreme of land which is sown as soon as the previous crop is harvested. Increasing populations are provided with food and employment by gradual increase of the frequency of cropping.

In large, sparsely populated areas of Africa and Latin America, the local subsistence systems are pastoralism and long fallow systems of the same types as those used in most of Europe in the first millennium AD and earlier. In areas with extremely low population densities, twenty or more years of forest fallow alternate with one or two years of cropping, while four to six years of bush fallow alternate with several years of cropping in regions where population densities have become too high to permit the use of longer fallow periods. Methods of subsistence agriculture in developing countries with even higher population densities include short fallow systems (i.e. one or two crops followed by one or two years' fallowing) or systems of annual cropping. In countries with very high population densities, including many Asian countries, some of the land is sown and cropped two or three times each year without any fallow periods.

If these differences in frequency of cropping are overlooked, or assumed to be adaptations to climatic or other permanent natural differences, the prospects for agricultural expansion in response to the growth of population and labour force look either more favourable, or more unfavourable, than they really are. In sparsely populated areas with long fallow systems, the areas which bear secondary forest or are used for grazing may be assumed incorrectly to be new land in the Ricardian sense, it being overlooked that they have the functions of recreating soil fertility or humidity, preventing erosion or suppressing troublesome weeds before the land is again used for crops. If neither the local cultivators nor their governments are aware of the risks of shortening fallow periods, and are not taking steps to avoid them, such shortening may damage the land, and erosion, infertility or desertification may result. In such cases, the scope for accommodating increasing populations will prove to be less than expected, and later repair of the damage will become costly, if possible at all. On the other hand, if land presently used as fallow in long fallow systems is assumed to be of inferior quality, in accordance with Ricardian theory, the large possibilities for accommodation of increasing populations by shifting from long fallow to shorter or no fallow, will be overlooked or underestimated.

LABOUR SUPPLIES. When population growth accelerated in the developing countries in the middle of this century, economists applied Ricardo's distinction between expansion of cultivation to new land and attempts to raise crop yields by additional inputs of labour and capital. They therefore focused on the most densely populated countries in Asia, in which there was little new land. Since the possibilities for multicropping were not taken into account, it was assumed that the elasticity of food production in response to population growth would be very low in these countries, and that the acceleration of population growth would soon result in food shortages, high food prices, reduction of real wages, and steep increase of Ricardian rent.

Lewis (1954) suggested that in densely populated countries with little, if any, uncultivated land, marginal returns to labour were likely to be zero or near to zero, and that a large part of the agricultural labour force was surplus labour, which could be transferred to non-agricultural employment without any diminution of agricultural output, even if there were no change in techniques. So Lewis recommended that rural-to-urban migration should be promoted, as a means of increasing marginal and average productivity in agriculture and of raising the share of the population employed in higher productivity occupations in urban areas. He confined his recommendation to densely populated countries, but many other economists made no distinction between densely and sparsely populated countries, assuming with Ricardo that uncultivated land must be of low quality so that a labour surplus would exist in all developing countries. The labour surplus theory contributed to create the bias in favour of industrial and urban development and the neglect of agriculture which has been a characteristic feature of government policy in many developing countries.

However, the labour surplus theory underestimates the demand for labour in agricultural systems with high frequency of cropping, based on labour intensive methods and use of primitive equipment. If population density in an area increases, fallow eliminated and multicropping introduced, then more and more labour-intensive methods must be used to preserve soil fertility, reduce weed growth and parasites, water the plants, grow fodder crops for animals, and protect the land. Some of the additional labour inputs are current operations, but others are labour investments. Before intensive cropping systems can be used, it may be necessary to terrace or level the land, build irrigation or drainage facilities, or fence the fields in order to control domestic animals. If these investments are made with human and animal muscle power, the necessary input of human labour is large. Even draught animals cannot reduce the work burden much, if fallows and other grazing land have been reduced so much that the cultivator must produce their fodder.

Part of the investments which are needed in order to increase the frequency of cropping are made by the cultivator with the same tools, animals and equipment

3

that are used for current operations. Estimates of investments and savings in agricultural communities with increasing population are seriously low if they fail to include such labour investments. Due to the larger number of crops, the additional operations with each crop, and the labour investments, the demand for labour rises steeply when intensive land use is introduced. This contrasts with the assumptions of the labour supply theory, which expects that the effect of population growth is always to add to the labour surplus.

When the theory of low supply elasticity and labour surplus in agriculture is combined with the theory of demographic transition, the prospects for densely populated countries with the majority of the population in agriculture look frightening. With the prospect of prolonged rapid growth of population (as forecast by the demographers) and with the poor prospects for expansion of food production and agricultural employment (implied by the labour surplus theory), it seemed obvious that sufficient capital could not be forthcoming for the enormous expansion of non-agricultural employment and output that was needed. So, because the possibilities for adapting food production to population were underestimated, many economists suggested that the best, or even the only means to avoid catastrophe was the promotion of rapid fertility decline by family planning. This in turn overlooked the links between the level of economic development and the motivations for restriction of family size.

The motivation for adopting an additional work load in periods of increasing population, and the means to shoulder it, are different as between agricultural subsistence economies and communities of commercial farmers. In the former, the need to produce enough food to feed a larger family may be sufficient motivation for adopting a new agricultural system which, at least for a time, raises labour input more steeply than output. The way to shoulder a larger work load is to increase the labour input of all family members. In some regions most of the agricultural work is done by men, and in other regions, by women; but when the work load becomes heavier, women become more involved in agricultural work in the former regions, and men more involved in the latter; in both, children and old people have more work to do. For all members of agricultural families, average work days become longer and days of leisure fewer. The whole year may become one long busy season in areas with widespread multicropping, labour-intensive irrigation, and transplanting from seed beds.

For commercial producers, the motivation for intensification of agriculture emerges when population growth or increasing urban incomes increase the demand for food, and push food prices up until more frequent cropping becomes profitable, in spite of increasing costs of production or need for more capital investment. By this change in sectoral terms of trade, a part of the burden of rural population increase is passed on to the urban population. The increase of agricultural prices is by no means all an increase of Ricardian rent, but is in good part a compensation for increasing costs of production. If the increase of food prices is prevented by government intervention or by imports of cheap food, the intensification will not take place.

Moreover, in regions with commercial agriculture, work seasons become longer when crop-frequency increases in response to population growth. Therefore the decline of real wages per work hour is at least partially compensated for by more employment in the off-seasons, and by more employment opportunities for women and children in the families of agricultural workers. The discussion of low or zero marginal productivity in agriculture suffers from a neglect of the seasonal differences in employment and wages. Many off-season operations are in fact required in order to obtain higher crop-frequency through labour-intensive methods alone, and so may well appear to be of very low productivity if viewed in isolation from their real function. Wages for these operations, or indeed off-season wages generally, may be very low, but the seasonal differences in wages are usually larger. Therefore, accumulation of debt in the off-seasons with repayment in the peak seasons is a frequent pattern of expenditure in labouring families.

Low off-season wages are an important incentive for intensification of the cropping pattern in commercial farms, since much of the additional labour with multicropping, irrigation, labour-intensive crops and feeding of animals falls in these seasons. But, when the same land is cropped more frequently in response to population growth, the demand for labour in the peak season also rises steeply, perhaps more than the supply of labour. In many cases, a large share of the agricultural population combines subsistence production on small plots of owned or rented land with wage labour for commercial producers in the agricultural peak seasons, and this contributes to considerable flexibility in the labour market. If real wages decline, because population increase pushes food prices up, full-time agricultural workers have no other choice than to reduce their leisure and that of their spouse and children, and offer to work for very low wages in the off-season periods. But workers who have some land to cultivate may choose to limit their supply of wage labour, and instead cultivate their own land more intensively with family labour. Since they took wage labour mainly in the peak seasons, their limitation of the supply of wage labour may prevent a decline of, or cause an increase of, real wages in the peak seasons, and thus put a floor below the incomes of the full-time workers.

The flexibility of the rural labour market is enhanced if not only labour but also land is hired in and out. A family that disposes of an increasing labour force may either do some work for other villagers, or rent some land from them, while a family that disposes of a reduced labour force may either hire some labour, or lease some land to others. With such a flexible system, prices for lease of land and wages will rapidly be adjusted to changes in labour supply. But the smooth adaptation of the system to population change will be hampered or prevented if, for political reasons, either hiring of labour or lease of land is made illegal, or changes in agricultural prices are prevented by government action.

TRANSPORT COST AND URBANIZATION. In Ricardian theory, marginal returns to labour and capital decline in response to population growth, partly because agricultural production is intensified, partly because it is expanded to inferior

5

land, and partly because more distant land is taken into cultivation, thus increasing costs of transport. Thus, when population is increasing, producers have a choice between increasing costs of production, or increasing costs of transport between fields and consumers. However, there is a third possibility, which is to move the centre of consumption closer to land which is of similar quality to that which was used before the population became larger. Communities who use long fallow periods often move their habitations after long-term settlement in a forested area, and move to another area where the fertility of forest land has become high after a long period of non-use. Such movement of villages is likely to become more frequent, as population increases.

In other cases it is not the whole village which is moved, but an increasing number of villagers move their habitation to new lands, where they build isolated farmsteads or new hamlets. This may accommodate additional populations until all the space between the villages is filled up with habitations, and the choice in case of further population growth is between more frequent cropping, or use of inferior land, or long-distance migration of part of the population.

The combination of shorter fallow periods and filling up of the space between the villages helps to create the conditions for emergence of small urban centres. Costs of transport are inversely related to the volume of transport, and roads, even primitive ones, are only economical, or feasible, with a relatively high volume of traffic. If fallow periods are very long, and distances between villages are large, there will be too few people in an area to handle both the production and transport which are necessary to supply a town with agricultural products. Urbanization and commercial agricultural production are only possible when population densities are relatively high, and fallow periods short. So when population in an area continues to increase, a point may be reached when small market towns emerge, served by road and water transport, as happened in large parts of Europe in the beginning of this millennium.

With further growth of population it will again be necessary to choose between further intensification of agriculture at increasing costs, or moving the additional consumers (or some of them) to another location, where they can be supplied by less intensive agriculture, and with shorter distances of transport. So at this stage of development, new small market towns may emerge in between the old towns, or in peripheral areas together with agricultural settlement. In other words, instead of agricultural products moving over longer and longer distances, thus creating Ricardian rent in the neighbourhood of existing consumer centres, new centres of consumption may appear closer to the fields. In most of Europe, such a gradual spread of decentralized urbanization made it possible to delay the shift from short fallow agriculture to annual cropping to the late 18th or the 19th century. Areas with such a network of market towns have better conditions for development of small-scale and middle-sized industrialization than sparsely populated areas with a scattered population of subsistence farmers.

The long-distance migration from Europe to North America in the 19th century can be viewed as a further step in this movement of European agricultural producers and consuming centres to a region with lower population density, less intensive agriculture, and much lower agricultural costs. The urban centres in America were supplied by extensive systems of short fallow agriculture at a time when production in Western Europe had shifted to much more intensive agriculture with annual cropping and fodder production.

TECHNOLOGY. From ancient times, growth of population and increase of urbanization have provided incentives to technological improvements in agriculture, either by transfer of technology from one region to another, or by inventions in response to urgent demand for increase of output, either of land, labour, or both. Until the 19th century, technological change in agriculture was a change from primitive technology, that is, human labour with primitive tools, to intermediate technology, that is, human labour aided by better hand tools, animal-drawn equipment, and water power for flow irrigation. In the classical theory of agricultural growth, such changes are means to promote population growth and urbanization, but they are assumed to be fortuitous inventions, and are not viewed as technological changes induced by population growth and increasing urbanization.

In the course of the 19th century, the continuing increase of the demand for agricultural products, and the increasing competition of urban centres for agricultural labour, induced further technological change in European and North American agriculture. The technological innovations of the industrial revolution were used to accomplish a gradual shift from intermediate to high-level technologies, that is, human labour aided by mechanized power and other industrial inputs. The chemical and engineering industries contributed to raise productivity of land, labour and transport of agricultural products, and scientific methods were introduced in agriculture as a means of raising yields of crops and livestock.

The existence of such high-level technologies improves the possibilities for rapid expansion of agricultural production in developing countries as well, but because in North America and Europe these technologies were used to reduce direct labour input in agriculture, those economists who believed in the labour surplus theory feared that they would further increase labour surplus. However, the idea of a general labour surplus in agriculture in developing countries had never been unanimously agreed, and under the influence of empirical studies of intensive agriculture in densely populated regions, Schultz (1964) suggested that labour was likely to be fully occupied even in very small holdings, when primitive technology was used. Therefore output and income in such holdings could only be increased by introduction of industrial and scientific inputs, and human capital investment of the types used in industrialized countries.

Although the proponents and the opponents of the labour surplus theory had different views concerning the relationship between the demand for and supply of labour, they agreed in suggesting a low supply elasticity of output in response to labour inputs, because they overlooked, or underestimated, the large effects on output and employment which can be obtained by using high-level

7

technologies to increase the frequency of cropping. The availability of new varieties of quickly maturing seeds, of chemical fertilizers, and of mechanized equipment for pumping water and land improvements, permits the use of multicropping on a much larger scale, and in much drier and colder climates than was possible before these new types of inputs existed. The new high-level technologies have changed the constraints on the size of the world population from the single one of land area to those of energy supply and costs, and of capital investment.

The new inputs permit a much more flexible adaptation of agriculture to changes in population and real wages. Intensive agriculture is no longer linked to low real wages, and it is possible, by changing the composition of inputs, to vary the rates of increase of employment and real wages for a given rate of increase of total output. By using a mixture of labour-intensive and high-level techniques, adapted to the man–land ratio and the level of economic development, first Japan, and later many other densely populated countries, obtained rapid increases in agricultural employment, output per worker, and total output. This 'Green Revolution' is an example of a technological change in agriculture induced by population change. The research which resulted in the development of these methods and inputs was undertaken and financed by national governments and international donors concerned about the effects of rapid population growth on the food situation in developing countries. Therefore, it focused mainly on improvement of agriculture in densely populated countries, where both governments and donors considered the problem to be most serious.

Agricultural producers who use high-level technologies are much more dependent upon the availability of good rural infrastructure than producers who use primitive or intermediate technologies. Transport and trade facilities are needed not only for the commercial surplus but also for the industrial inputs in agriculture; repair shops, electricity supply, technical schools, research stations, veterinary and extension services, are also needed. Therefore short-term supply elasticities differ between those regions which have and those which do not have the infrastructure needed for use of industrial and scientific inputs in agriculture. In the former, a rapid increase of output may be obtained by offering more attractive prices to the producers, while in the latter, increase of prices may have little effect on output, until the local infrastructure has been improved. Improvement of infrastructure may, on the other hand, be sufficient to obtain a change from subsistence production to commercial production, if it results in a major reduction in the difference between the prices paid to the local producers and those obtained in the consuming centres.

In densely populated regions with a network of small market towns, it is more feasible to introduce industrial and scientific inputs in agriculture, than in regions inhabited only by a scattered population of agricultural producers. Because per capita costs of infrastructure are lower in the first mentioned regions, they are more likely to have the necessary infrastructure, and if not, governments may be more willing to supply it. Thus sparsely populated regions are handicapped compared with densely populated ones, when high-level technologies are taken into use.

TENURE. Changes in output may also be prevented if the local tenure system is ill-adapted to the new agricultural system. Land tenure is different in regions with different frequency of cropping. In regions with long fallow agriculture, individual producers have only usufruct rights in the land they use for cultivation, and the land, the pastures, and the forested land are all tribally owned. Before a plot is cleared for cultivation it is usually assigned by the local chief, and when large investments or other large works are needed the producers are organized by the chief as mutual work parties. If population increases and with it the demands for assignment of land, a stage may be reached when either the chief or the village community will demand a payment for such assignments, thereby changing the system of land tenure. Payments to the chief for assignment of land may turn him into a large-scale landowner, and this payment may tip the balance and make more frequent cropping of land more economical than use of new plots, or settlement in new hamlets.

When frequency of cropping becomes sufficiently high that major permanent investments in land improvement are necessary, a change to private property in land may provide security of tenure to the cultivator, and make it possible for him to obtain credits. If at this stage no change of tenure is made by legal reform, a system of private property in land is likely to emerge by unlawful action and gradual change of custom; but in such cases the occupants, who have no legal rights to the land, may hesitate (or be unable) to make investments and land may remain unprotected against erosion and other damage.

In more densely populated areas, with more frequent cropping and need for large-scale irrigation and other land improvement, these investments may be organized by big landlords as labour service or by local authorities as wage labour, financed by local or general taxation. In order to change from a particular fallow system to another that is more intensive, it is likely that not only the ownership system in the cultivated plots but also that for uncultivated land must be changed, as must responsibility for infrastructure investment. Because of the links between the fallow system, the tenure system, and the responsibility for infrastructure investment, attempts to intensify the agricultural system by preservation (for political reasons) of the old tenure system and rural organization are likely to be unsuccessful, as are attempts to introduce new tenure systems that are unsuitable for the existing (or the desired, future) level of intensity and technology. Therefore, government policy is an important determinant of the agricultural response to population growth.

During fallow periods, the land is used for a variety of purposes: for gathering fuel and other wood, for hunting, for gathering of fertilizer, for grazing and browsing by domestic animals. Therefore, a change of the fallow system may create unintended damage to the environment unless substitutes are introduced for these commodities, or the pattern of consumption is changed. When hunting land becomes short, the right to hunt may be appropriated by the chiefs

9

(or others), forcing the villagers to change their diet. When grazing land becomes short, enclosures may prevent the villagers (or some of them) from using it, or the village community may ration the right to pasture animals in the common grazing land and fallows, in order to prevent overgrazing and erosion, or desertification. These measures will impose a change of diet, and perhaps a change to fodder production in the fields.

NUTRITION. Both production and consumption change from land-using to less land-using products when population increases and agriculture is intensified. There may be a shift from beef and mutton to pork and poultry, from animal to vegetable products, from cereals to rootcrops for human consumption, and from grazing to production of fodder for animals. Under conditions of commercial farming, the changes in consumption and production are induced by increasing differentials between the prices of land-saving and land-using products. If the process of population growth is accompanied by decline of real wages, the changes in consumption patterns for the poorest families may be large. This may result in protein deficiencies and malnutrition with spread of the disease-malnutrition syndrome; this causes high child mortality because disease prevents the child from eating and digesting food, and malnutrition reduces the resistance to disease.

The classical economists had suggested that continuing population growth would result in malnutrition, famine and disease, which would re-establish the balance between population and resources by increasing mortality. But they also envisaged the possibility of an alternative method, in which population growth was prevented by voluntary restraint on fertility. Malthus (1803) talked of moral restraint and Ricardo (1817) of the possibility that the workers would develop a taste for comforts and enjoyment, which would prevent a superabundant population. However, it was not ethical or psychological changes but the economic and social changes resulting from increasing industrialization and urbanization which induced a deceleration of rates of population growth, first in Europe and North America, and later in other parts of the world.

GOVERNMENT POLICIES. The deceleration of rates of population growth in Europe and North America coincided with a decline in the income elasticity of demand for food due to the increase in per capita incomes. As a result the rate of increase in the demand for food slowed down, just as the rate of increase of production accelerated due to the spread of high-level technologies and scientific methods in agriculture. If it had not been for government intervention in support of agriculture these changes would have led to abandonment of production in marginal land, and use of less industrial inputs in the land that was kept in cultivation. But this process of adjustment was prevented by attempts to preserve the existing system of family farming. Large farms could utilize high-level technologies (especially mechanized inputs) better than smaller ones, but governments wanted to prevent the replacement of small or middle-sized farms by larger capitalist farms, or company farming. Therefore both Western Europe and North America gradually developed comprehensive systems of agricultural protection and subsidization of agriculture, agricultural research, and other rural infrastructure. In spite of this support a large proportion of the small farms disappeared and much marginal land went out of cultivation, while the support actually encouraged large farms, and farms in the most favoured regions, to expand their production; they increased their use of fertilizer and other inputs, and invested in expansion of capacity for vegetable and animal production. So supply still continued to outrun demand, and protection against imports and subsidies to exports still continued to increase, while the industrialized countries turned from being net importers to net exporters of more and more agricultural products.

In the discussions about labour surplus and low elasticity of agricultural production in non-industrialized countries, Nurkse (1953) had suggested that an increase in agricultural production could be obtained if the surplus population was employed in rural work projects. In the period until such a programme, in conjunction with industrialization and a deceleration of population growth, could re-establish the balance between demand for and supply of food, he recommended that temporary food imports (preferably as food aid) should be used to prevent food shortage. Because of the increasing costs of financing and disposing of the food surplus, Nurkse's suggestion of food aid was well received by Western governments, and transfer of food, as aid or subsidized exports, reached larger dimensions.

Some governments in developing countries did use food aid and commercial imports of the food surpluses of the industrialized countries as stop-gap measures, until their own promotion of rural infrastructure and other support to agriculture would make it possible for production to catch up with the rapidly increasing demand for food. But for many other governments the availability of cheap imports and gifts of food became a welcome help to avoid the use of their own resources to support agriculture and invest in rural infrastructure. Even in those developing countries with a large majority of the population occupied in agriculture, the share of government expenditure devoted to agriculture and related rural infrastructure is small, and within this small amount priority is usually given to development of non-food export crops, which often supply a large share of foreign exchange earnings. Exports of food crops are unattractive because of the surplus disposal of the industrialized countries, which exerts a downward pressure on world market prices. Therefore, both producers and governments in developing countries focus on the types of crops which do not compete with these subsidized exports. In regions in which the necessary infrastructure was available, employment and output of such export crops increased rapidly, not only in countries with abundant land resources but also in many densely populated countries, which shifted in part from food to non-food crops. This general shift from food to non-food crops contributed to a downward pressure on export prices of the latter crops in the world market.

Food imports can have important short-term advantages for the importing country. Rapidly increasing urban areas can be supplied at low prices and without the need to use government resources to obtain expansion of domestic production.

11

Moreover, counterpart funds from food aid can be used to finance general government expenditure, and in countries with high levies on export crops, government revenue increases when production is shifted from food to export crops. However, although there might be short-term advantages of food imports and food aid, the long-term cost of neglecting agricultural and rural development can be very high. The lack of transport facilities and local stocks, and the lack of irrigation in dry and semi-dry areas, may transform years of drought to years of famine. When governments do not invest in rural infrastructure and fail to provide the public services which are necessary for the use of high technology inputs, the latter can be used only by large companies (who can themselves finance the necessary infrastructure) or in a few areas close to large cities.

Without cost reduction by improvement of the transport network and agricultural production, commercial food production may in many areas be unable to compete with imports. Commercial production will decline and subsistence producers will not become commercial producers. Instead, the most enterprising young villagers will emigrate in order to earn money incomes elsewhere. A larger and larger share of the rapidly increasing urban consumption must be imported, and food imports become a drug on which the importers become more and more dependent. The increasing dependency of many developing countries on food imports and food grants is often seen as a confirmation of the classical theory of inelastic food supply, and an argument for continuation of the policy of production subsidies and surplus disposal in America and Western Europe. Food imports are seen as gap fillers, bridging over increasing differences between food consumption and national food production in developing countries; but in many cases the gap is actually created by the food imports, because of their effect on local production and rural development.

FERTILITY. Contrary to the expectations prevalent in the middle of this century, government policy has proved to be a more important determinant of agricultural growth than the man–resource ratio, and the response to rapid population growth has often been better in densely populated countries than in sparsely populated ones with much better natural conditions for agricultural growth. The differences in agricultural growth rates and policies have in turn contributed to create differences in demographic trends, partly by their influence on industrial and urban development and partly by the effects on rural fertility, mortality and migration.

Because of their preoccupation with the man–land ratio, governments in densely populated countries not only devoted more attention and financial resources to agriculture than governments in sparsely populated countries, they also more often devoted attention and financial resources to policies aimed at reducing fertility. Moreover, tenure systems in densely populated countries usually provided less encouragement to large family size than tenure systems in sparsely populated countries.

In many densely populated countries with intensive agricultural systems, much of the rural population consists of small and middle-sized landowners, and such people are more likely to be motivated to a smaller family size than are landless labour and people with insecure tenure. They are less dependent upon help from adult children in emergencies and old age, because they can mortgage, lease, or sell land, or cultivate with hired labour. They may also have an interest in avoiding division of family property among too many heirs. If they live in areas where child labour is of little use in agriculture, they may have considerable economic interest in not having large families, and be responsive to advice and help from family planning services.

In sparsely populated regions with large landholdings, the rural population seldom has access to modern means of fertility control, and motivations for family restrictions are weak. A large share of the rural population tends to be landless or nearly landless workers, and if not, they may be without security in land. So they are much more dependent upon help from adult children in emergencies and old age than are landowners, or tenants with secure tenure. If, moreover, their children work for wages in ranches, farms and plantations, the period until a child contributes more to family income than it costs is too short to provide sufficient economic motivation for family restriction.

People who use long fallow systems in regions with tribal tenure have even more motivation for large family size than landless workers. The size of the area they can dispose of for cultivation is directly related to the size of their family, and most of the work, at least with food production, is done by women and children. So a man can become rich by having several wives and large numbers of children working for him. Moreover, unless he has acquired other property, a man's security in old age depends on his adult children and younger wives, since he cannot mortgage or sell land in which he has only usufruct rights. Because of the differences in motivations for family size provided by individual and tribal tenure systems, the start of the fertility decline in regions with long fallow systems is likely to be linked to the time when population increase induces the replacement of the tribal tenure system by another system of tenure, and a decline is then more likely if it is replaced by small-scale land ownership than if it is replaced by large-scale farming.

In addition to the tenure system, changes in technological levels in agriculture and the availability of economic and social infrastructure may influence the timing of fertility decline in rural areas. The heavy reliance upon female and child labour in those densely populated areas in which agriculture is intensified by means of labour alone, may provide motivation for large families in spite of the shortage of land. Introduction of higher-level technologies may then, in such cases, reduce a man's motivation to have a large family because it reduces the need for female and child labour. Use of intermediate and high-level technologies is nearly always reserved for adult men, while women and children do the operations for which primitive technologies are used. So when primitive technologies are replaced by higher-level ones in more and more agricultural operations, men usually get more work to do and the economic contributions of their wives and children decline, thus reducing their economic interest in large family size. Moreover, in regions with little rural development high rates of child mortality may delay fertility decline, and the large-scale migration of youth from such areas may have a similar effect if parents can count on receiving remittances from emigrant offspring.

However, the relationship between rural development and fertility is complicated. Parents may want a large family for other than economic reasons, and increases in income due to rural development or to better prices for agricultural products make it easier for them to support a large family, thus preventing or delaying fertility decline. Other things being equal, fertility is positively related to income; but in developing societies most increases in income are caused and accompanied by technological, occupational and spatial changes that tend to encourage fertility decline, and the operation of these opposing effects may result in a relatively long time-lag between rural modernization and fertility decline.

BIBLIOGRAPHY
Boserup, E. 1965. *The Conditions of Agricultural Growth*. London: Allen & Unwin; Chicago: Aldine Publishing Company, 1966.
Boserup, E. 1981. *Population and Technological Change*. Chicago: Chicago University Press.
Lewis, W.A. 1954. Economic development with unlimited supplies of labour. *Manchester School of Economic and Social Studies* 22(2), May, 139–91.
Malthus, T.R. 1803. *An Essay on the Principle of Population*. London: J.M. Dent, 1958; New York: Dutton.
Nurkse, R. 1953. *Problems of Capital Formation in Underdeveloped Countries*. Oxford and New York: Oxford University Press.
Ricardo, D. 1817. *The Principles of Political Economy and Taxation*. Ed. P. Sraffa, Cambridge: Cambridge University Press, 1951; New York: Cambridge University Press, 1973.
Schultz, T.W. 1964. *Transforming Traditional Agriculture*. New Haven: Yale University Press.
Schuttjer, W. and Stokes, C. (eds) 1984. *Rural Development and Human Fertility*. New York and London: Macmillan.

Bribery

SUSAN ROSE-ACKERMAN

The economic analysis of political and bureaucratic institutions can productively begin with the study of bribery, not because it is necessarily pervasive but because it highlights the conflict between the public interest and the market. Widespread bribery can transform a governmental procedure ostensibly based on democratic or meritocratic principles into one based on willingness-to-pay.

Most work on bribery is descriptive and taxonomic. While this makes for interesting reading and is an important source of background information on the range and diversity of corrupt deals, such research does not systematically examine the economic bases of bribery. When the latter are recognized, they are frequently treated in a cursory fashion so that either the underlying forces of supply and demand are seen as justifying payoffs or else the same forces are taken as reason to condemn the practice. Some of the best of this descriptive work appears in Clarke (1983), Gardiner and Olson (1974) and Heidenheimer (1970); other relevant books and articles are listed in the bibliography.

The theory of perfect competition emphasizes the impersonality of all market dealings. A manufacturer will sell to all customers irrespective of their race, gender, or inherent charm. Similarly, the ideal bureaucrat makes decisions on the basis of objective, meritocratic criteria and is not influenced by personal, ethnic or family ties. Bribes can replace an impersonal meritocratic procedure with an impersonal willingness-to-pay procedure, or can help to support a system of personalized favours based on close personal relations; conversely, payoffs may be a way for newcomers or members of pariah groups to obtain influence in the society. It follows that bribery can only be evaluated relative to a system without bribery. Then one's evaluation of the payoffs that occur will depend not only upon one's moral scruples concerning bribery as such, but also upon whether payoffs produce a more or a less impersonal, objective set of decisions and whether one values such a shift positively or negatively. The difficulties of analysis here are indicated, on the one hand, by those who see payoffs to officials in some underdeveloped countries as an extension of well-entrenched tribal customs, and on the other, those who see similar payoffs as a way of circumventing traditional attitudes and helping the country develop economically (see e.g. Heidenheimer, 1970; Clarke, 1983).

LEGISLATIVE CORRUPTION. Elected representatives care about being re-elected but they are also likely to care about their incomes. Consider a simple world in which voters are well informed about the votes of legislators but cannot observe bribes directly. Assume that politicians run for re-election on their voting record and that no campaign spending is needed. Then a bribe designed to change a vote in the legislature will cost the politician some constituency support since otherwise no payoff would be necessary. Thus at a minimum, even if politicians have no moral qualms about accepting payoffs, the bribe must be sufficient to compensate the politician for the reduced chance of re-election. *Ceteris paribus* we would expect that the politicians with the lowest reservation bribes are those who are either quite certain of being elected or quite sure of defeat, for in each case a decline in electoral support can affect the ultimate outcome very little. It follows that, given the salience of the issue to the electorate, the closer the race, the higher will be the politician's reservation bribe.

In this simple model there is no need for campaign contributions, so bribes can be used only for personal gain, and there is a direct trade-off between bribes and the probability of re-election. But if payoffs *can* be spent either on a re-election campaign or used as personal income, then all types of politicians may be corruptible, depending on differences between legislators in moral scruples and in the salience to the voters of the issues of interest to the briber (see Rose-Ackerman, 1978, pp. 15–58).

PURCHASING AGENTS. In both public and private sectors and in both capitalist and socialist economies, purchasing agents are likely to have the opportunity either to pay or receive bribes. No bribes occur in a perfectly competitive market, where suppliers can sell and demanders can buy all they wish at the going price. Corruption requires market imperfections. For example, the government may be so large a purchaser that economies can be realized in filling its order; it may need products not available 'off-the-shelf' so that a negotiated contract is necessary. In short, if bribes are offered there must be some prospective excess profits out of which to pay them, and if bribes are accepted, it must be because the agent's superiors are either privy to the deal themselves or else cannot monitor the agent's behaviour adequately by such simple devices as comparing market prices with contract prices.

One might argue that in these situations corruption furthers efficiency, since the most efficient firm will have the highest prospective profits and so be willing to pay the highest bribe. This is simplistic. First, a firm may gain advantage by lowering quality in subtle ways not immediately obvious to government inspectors. Secondly, if managers of firms differ in respect for the law, the most unscrupulous have an advantage. Thirdly, keeping payoffs secret both wastes resources and causes the market to operate poorly because of the low level of available information. In short, the correspondence between efficiency and the size of the bribe is likely to be imperfect.

In other economic contexts purchasing agents may pay bribes to obtain supplies, instead of being paid to choose particular suppliers. This can happen when shortages of particular products develop and prices do not rise to reflect market conditions. This is especially important in planned economies. Indeed, discussions of corruption in the Soviet Union frequently point to this form as endemic (Grossman, 1977; Simis, 1978). Here again bribes can serve economic functions but have no advantage over prices, except the ideological one of hiding the pervasiveness of market-like processes from public view (see Montias and Rose-Ackerman, 1981).

The establishment of a legal and flexible price system is not always a realistic option. For example, the military purchases many complex and highly specialized weapons that cannot be effectively obtained through sealed bids. In such situations one must consider the role of detection and punishment. Here basic work on the economics of crime is relevant and, in fact, Becker and Stigler (1974) have themselves made the application to corrupt payments. They stress the importance of giving each employee a stake in his or her job by, for example, providing non-vesting pensions. This will make workers less likely to take risks that could lead to their dismissal. More generally, the expected punishment for bribery should be tied to the marginal gain from marginal increases in the payoff (Rose-Ackerman, 1978, pp. 109–35). Otherwise only some bribes will be deterred. Thus the marginal expected penalty for the bribe-taker, that is, the probability of apprehension and conviction times the penalty if convicted, must rise by at least one dollar for every dollar increase in expected payoff. If it does not, then even if a large lump-sum penalty is levied only relatively small bribes may be prevented. The bribe-payer's marginal penalty should be tied, not to the size of the bribe, but to the marginal increase in profit that a bribe makes possible. Penalties set at a multiple of the bribe paid may thus have little deterrent effect on bribe-payers, if the expected profits are many times larger.

DISPENSERS OF BENEFITS AND BURDENS. Low-level officials frequently have considerable discretion to decide who should receive a scarce benefit such as a unit of public housing, expedited access to an important person, a liquor licence, assignment to a particular judge. Others, such as health and safety inspectors and the police, have the power to impose costs and the discretion to refuse to exercise that power. While legal pricing systems can sometimes substitute for payoffs here, in many cases there is a strong public policy reason for opposing a market solution.

Given such programmes where market tests are undesirable, how can corruption be controlled? One option, explored in Rose-Ackerman (1978, pp. 137–66), is to introduce competitive pressures as a way of lowering the payoffs that people are willing to make and hence discouraging officials from accepting bribes which are low relative to the risk of detection and punishment. When a bureaucracy dispenses a scarce benefit, competition can be introduced by permitting an applicant to reapply if he has been turned down by one official. Then if the cost of reapplication is small, the first official cannot demand a large bribe in return for approving the application; in fact the offered bribe may be forced down so low that the official may turn it down and instead behave honestly. A few honest officials in this system may thus produce honesty in the others. Notice, however, that unqualified applicants will still wish to make payoffs and their willingness-to-pay increases if they expect that most other officials to whom they could apply are honest.

The case for competition among inspectors or police is somewhat different and depends upon the feasibility and cost of overlapping authority. Thus, the operator of a gambling parlour will not pay much to a corrupt policeman if a second independent policeman is expected to come along shortly. The whole precinct must be on the take, that is, monopolized, to make high bribes worthwhile.

In short, the role of competitive pressures in preventing corruption may be an important aspect of a strategy to deter the bribery of low-level officials, but requires a broad-based exploration of the impact of both organizational and market structure on the incentives for corruption facing both bureaucrats and their clients.

BIBLIOGRAPHY

Banfield, E. 1975. Corruption as a feature of governmental organization. *Journal of Law and Economics* 18(3), December, 587–605.

Becker, G.S. and Stigler, G.J. 1974. Law enforcement, malfeasance, and compensation of enforcers. *Journal of Legal Studies* 3(1), January, 1–18.

Benson, B.L. and Baden, J. 1985. The political economy of governmental corruption: the logic of underground government. *Journal of Legal Studies* 14(2), June, 391–410.

Clarke, M. (ed.) 1983. *Corruption: Causes, Consequences and Control.* New York: St Martin's Press.

Darby, M.R. and Karni, E. 1973. Free competition and the optimal amount of fraud. *Journal of Law and Economics* 16(1), April, 67–88.

Gardiner, J. 1970. *The Politics of Corruption: Organized Crime in an American City.* New York: Russell Sage Foundation.

Gardiner, J.A. and Lyman, T.R. 1978. *Decisions for Sale: Corruption in Local Land-Use Regulations.* New York: Praeger.

Gardiner, J.A. and Olson, D.J. (eds) 1974. *Theft of the City.* Bloomington: Indiana University Press.

Grossman, G. 1977. The 'second economy' of the USSR. *Problems of Communism* 26(5), September–October, 25–40.

Heidenheimer, A.J. (ed.) 1970. *Political Corruption: Readings in Comparative Analysis.* New York: Holt, Rinehart & Winston.

Jacoby, N., Nehemkis, P. and Eels, R. 1977. *Bribery and Extortion in World Business.* New York: Macmillan.

Johnson, O.E.G. 1975. An economic analysis of corrupt government with special application to less developed countries. *Kyklos* 28(1), 47–61.

Krueger, A.O. 1974. The political economy of the rent-seeking society. *American Economic Review* 64(3), June, 291–303.

LeVine, V.T. 1975. *Political Corruption: The Ghana Case*. Stanford: Hoover Institution Press.

Lui, F.T. 1985. An equilibrium queuing model of bribery. *Journal of Political Economics* 93(4), August, 760–81.

Montias, J.M. and Rose-Ackerman, S. 1981. Corruption in a Soviet-type economy: theoretical considerations. In *Economic Welfare and the Economics of Soviet Socialism: Essays in Honor of Abram Bergson*, ed. S. Rosefielde, Cambridge: Cambridge University Press.

Noonan, J. 1984. *Bribes*. New York: Macmillan.

Pashigan, B.P. 1975. On the control of crime and bribery. *Journal of Legal Studies* 4(2), June, 311–26.

Rashid, S. 1981. Public utilities in egalitarian LDCs: the role of bribery in achieving Pareto efficiency. *Kyklos* 34(3), 448–60.

Rose-Ackerman, S. 1975. The economics of corruption. *Journal of Public Economics* 4(2), February, 187–203.

Rose-Ackerman, S. 1978. *Corruption: A Study in Political Economy*. New York: Academic Press.

Rose-Ackerman, S. 1986. Reforming public bureaucracy through economic incentives. *Journal of Law, Economics and Organization* 2(1), 131–61.

Scott, J.C. 1972. *Comparative Political Corruption*. Englewood Cliffs, NJ: Prentice-Hall.

Sherman, L. (ed.) 1974. *Police Corruption*. Garden City, New York: Doubleday, Anchor Books.

Simis, L. 1978. The machinery of corruption in the Soviet Union. *Survey* 23(4), Autumn, 35–55.

Wraith, R. and Simkins, E. 1963. *Corruption in Developing Countries*. London: George Allen & Unwin.

19

Bubbles

CHARLES P. KINDLEBERGER

A bubble may be defined loosely as a sharp rise in price of an asset or a range of assets in a continuous process, with the initial rise generating expectations of further rises and attracting new buyers – generally speculators interested in profits from trading in the asset rather than its use of earning capacity. The rise is usually followed by a reversal of expectations and a sharp decline in price often resulting in financial crisis. A boom is a more extended and gentler rise in prices, production and profits than a bubble, and may be followed by crisis, sometimes taking the form of a crash (or panic) or alternatively by a gentle subsidence of the boom without crisis.

Bubbles have existed historically, at least in the eyes of contemporary observers, as well as booms so intense and excited that they have been called 'manias'. The most notable bubbles were the Mississippi bubble in Paris in 1719–20, set in motion by John Law, founder of the *Banque Générale* and the *Banque Royale*, and the contemporaneous and related South Sea bubble in London. Most famous of the manias were the Tulip mania in Holland in 1636, and the Railway mania in England in 1846–7. It is sometimes debated whether a particular sharp rise and fall in prices, such as the German hyperinflation from 1920 to 1923, or the rise and fall in commodity and share prices in London and New York in 1919–21, the rise of gold of $850 an ounce in 1982 and its subsequent fall to the $350 level, were or were not bubbles. Some theorists go further and question whether bubbles are possible with rational markets, which they assume exist (see e.g. Flood and Garber, 1980).

Rational expectations theory holds that prices are formed within the limits of available information by market participants using standard economic models appropriate to the circumstances. As such, it is claimed, market prices cannot diverge from fundamental values unless the information proves to have been widely wrong. The theoretical literature uses the assumption of the market having one mind and one purpose, whereas it is observed historically that market participants are often moved by different purposes, operate with different wealth and information and calculate within different time horizons. In early railway investment, for example, initial investors were persons doing business along the rights of way who sought benefits from the railroad for their other concerns. They were followed by a second group of investors interested in the profits the railroad would earn, and by a third group, made up of speculators who, seeing the rise in the railroad's shares, borrowed money or paid for the initial instalments with no intention of completing the purchase, to make a profit on resale.

The objects of speculation resulting in bubbles or booms and ending in numerous cases, but not all, in financial crisis, change from time to time and include commodities, domestic bonds, domestic shares, foreign bonds, foreign shares, urban and suburban real estate, rural land, leisure homes, shopping centres, Real Estate Investment Trusts, 747 aircraft, supertankers, so-called 'collectibles' such as paintings, jewellery, stamps, coins, antiques, etc. and, most recently, syndicated bank loans to developing countries. Within these relatively broad categories, speculation may fix on particular objects – insurance shares, South American mining stocks, cotton-growing land, Paris real estate, Post-Impressionist art, and the like.

At the time of writing, the theoretical literature has yet to converge on an agreed definition of bubbles, and on whether they are possible. Virtually the same authors who could not reject the no-bubbles hypothesis in the German inflation of 1923 one year, managed to do so a year later (Flood and Garber, 1980). Another pair of theorists has demonstrated mathematically that rational bubbles can exist after putting aside 'irrational bubbles' on the grounds not of their non-existence but of the difficulty of the mathematics involved (Blanchard and Watson, 1982).

Short of bubbles, manias and irrationality are periods of euphoria which produce positive feedback, price increases greater than justified by market fundamentals, and booms of such dimensions as to threaten financial crisis, with possibilities of a crash or panic. Minsky (1982a, 1982b) has discussed how after an exogenous change in economic circumstances has altered profit opportunities and expectations, bank lending can become increasingly lax by rigorous standards. Critical exception has been taken to his taxonomy dividing bank lending into hedge finance, to be repaid out of anticipated cash flows; speculative finance, requiring later refinancing because the term of the loan is less than the project's payoff; and Ponzi finance, in which the borrower expects to pay off his loan with the proceeds of sale of an asset. It is objected especially that Carlo Ponzi was a swindler and that many loans of the third type, for example those to finance construction, are entirely legitimate (Flemming, Goldsmith and Melitz, 1982). Nonetheless, the suggestion that lending standards grow more lax during a boom and that the banking system on that account becomes more fragile has strong historical support. It is attested, and the contrary rational-expectations view of financial markets is falsified, by the experience of such a money and capital market as London having successive booms, followed by crisis, the latter in 1810, 1819, 1825, 1836, 1847, 1857, 1866, 1890, 1900, 1921 – a powerful record of failing to learn from experience (Kindleberger, 1978).

BIBLIOGRAPHY

Blanchard, O. and Watson, M.W. 1982. Bubbles, rational expectations and financial markets. In *Crises in the Economic and Financial Structure*, ed. P. Wachtel, Lexington, Mass.: Heath.

Flemming, J.S., Goldsmith, R.W. and Melitz, J. 1982. Comment. In *Financial Crises: Theory, History and Policy*, ed. C.P. Kindleberger and J.-P. Laffargue, Cambridge: Cambridge University Press.

Flood, R.P. and Garber, P.M. 1980. Market fundamentals versus price-level bubbles: the first tests. *Journal of Political Economy* 88(4), August, 745–70.

Kindleberger, C.P. 1978. *Manias, Panics and Crashes: A History of Financial Crises*. New York: Basic Books.

Minsky, H.P. 1982a. *Can 'It' Happen Again?: Essays on Instability and Finance*. Armonk: Sharpe.

Minsky, H.P. 1982b. The financial instability hypothesis. In *Financial Crises: Theory, History and Policy*, ed. C.P. Kindleberger and J.-P. Laffargue, Cambridge: Cambridge University Press.

Burden of the Debt

ROBERT EISNER

Public debt constitutes private assets. The deficit of one sector of the economy is the surplus of another.

Thus, for a closed economy, internally held public debt is not the obvious burden it is to an individual. If the private sector pays taxes to service the debt, it is also the private sector which receives the proceeds of these taxes in payments of interest and principal. If taxes could be lump-sum, with no marginal effect upon economic behaviour, and were anticipated with certainty, and if public and private borrowing costs were the same, it could be argued that the public debt would be irrelevant, except for distributional effects.

This would imply that it would make no difference whether public expenditures were financed by current taxes or by borrowing (which would create a public debt that would be serviced by future taxes). This proposition, considered but dismissed by Ricardo, was labelled by Buchanan (1976; see also 1958) the Ricardo Equivalence Theorem after being refurbished by Barro (1974).

The public debt is not considered neutral, even with lump-sum taxation, if only because people are mortal. Those currently holding debt and receiving interest will escape some taxation by death. Barro's answer was to postulate agents with preference functions in which the assets and liabilities of their descendants were arguments. Hence the current generation's holdings of public debt in excess of the present value of their own consequent tax liabilities would be matched by their need to adjust their bequests to leave their heirs uninjured by future taxes necessary to service the debt.

To this there are many objections, including such obvious ones as the fact that some current agents have no heirs, that others do not care about their heirs, and that still others are at 'corner solutions', so that the amount that they give to (or receive from) their children will not be affected. There are further objections in terms of uncertainty as to life span, both for current agents and their children, and even with regard to the number of their heirs and of their heirs' heirs for whom provision should be made. These objections to the effective assumption

23

of immortality, along with differences in public and private borrowing costs, and of course the fact that most taxation is not and cannot reasonably be expected to be of a lump-sum variety, have led to considerable rejection of the equivalence theorem (see Buiter and Tobin, 1979).

Whether (and if so, in what way) the public debt is a burden then becomes a highly conditional issue. While most theoretical discussions have apparently accepted the premise of full, market-clearing equilibrium, the more relevant circumstance is frequently one of underemployment related to insufficient aggregate demand. In this situation, public debt, far from being a burden, is likely to induce greater consumption, as is made particularly clear by Modigliani's life-cycle hypothesis (Modigliani and Brumberg, 1954; Ando and Modigliani, 1963). Those with greater wealth, in the form of public debt or other assets, will consume more now and plan to consume more in the future as well. Within a framework of rational expectations (without market-clearing), firms should then complement the increased consumption with increased investment to meet current and future consumption demand. Current output and employment would thus be higher, and a greater capital stock would be available for the future.

The existence of public debt, including non-interest-bearing debt in the form of government money, also facilitates inter-generational contracts. It permits the current working generation to save and exercise a claim for retirement support from the next generation in the absence of the ability to accumulate non-depreciating capital.

This possible benefit of widening available choices to saving and consumption leads some to view public debt as a burden. For if the public debt increases current consumption, it is argued that there must be less saving and hence a lesser accumulation of capital. Public debt proves a replacement for assets in the form of productive capital. The economy then suffers a lesser capital stock and hence less production, and, in equilibrium, less consumption as well. This argument has been extended by Feldstein (1974) to implicit government debt in the form of 'social security' or pension commitments.

While this argument, as indicated above, is clearly reversed in a situation of underemployment, where added consumption is likely to mean added investment as well, its macroeconomic applicability even in a condition of full-employment equilibrium, is questionable. For an increase in the public debt, in an economy already in full-employment equilibrium, would generate excess demand which would raise prices. If government non-interest-bearing debt in the form of money were increased in proportion to the increase in interest-bearing debt, the economy could then move to a new equilibrium in which prices would be higher but the *real* value of the public debt, the real value of the quantity of money, the rate of interest and all other real variables, including the rates of investment and consumption would be unchanged. If, again under conditions of full employment, the government imposes a permanent nominal deficit on a no-growth economy, it will generate a rate of inflation corresponding to the rate of increase of nominal debt. Hence real debt will not rise, and once more none of the presumed burden of increased debt will develop.

This suggests the existence of considerable confusion between real and nominal magnitudes. It is essentially the real public debt that matters. The nominal, par value of public debt has risen in many countries while rising interest rates and rising prices have caused substantial declines in its real, market values. It is hence important to correct measures of budget surpluses and deficits so that they correspond to *real* changes in the public debt. Suppose, for example, a nominal deficit of $100 billion and interest and price effects on the real value of an outstanding public debt of $2000 billion such that its real, market value, aside from the current deficit, declines to $1850 billion. In relevant, real terms the budget may then be viewed as in *surplus* by $50 billion, which is equal to the $150 billion 'capital gain' or 'inflation tax', minus the $100 billion nominal deficit (see Eisner and Pieper, 1984; Eisner, 1986).

Whether a burden or a blessing, public debt may, along these lines, be better evaluated in terms of its relation to the income or product of the economy. The debt may thus be viewed as rising, in a relative sense, only when it increases more rapidly than gross national product. In an economy with a debt-to-GNP ratio of 0.5, for example, this would mean that with a growth rate of, say, 8 per cent per annum (consisting, approximately, of 3 per cent real growth and 5 per cent inflation), the debt could grow at 8 per cent per year, implying a deficit equal to 4 per cent of GNP, with no change in the ratio of debt to GNP. A corollary of this is that, in a growing economy, there is always some equilibrium debt-to-GNP ratio consistent with any deficit-to-GNP ratio, that is

$$[\text{Debt}/\text{GNP} = (\text{DEF}/\text{GNP}) \div (\Delta\text{GNP}/\text{GNP})].$$

If public debt is related to public assets, financial and tangible, the net public debt is likely to prove considerably less than the gross public debt, and the net worth or net assets of the public sector are likely to prove positive even in economies with large public debts. In a larger sense, public debt may well be related to total wealth of the economy, private as well as public, and human as well as non-human. A larger public debt may then be associated with greater public wealth. The public debt may properly be viewed as a burden on the economy, however, to the extent that it diminishes total real wealth. It may do so, if it does not increase public capital, by reducing the supply of private capital and/or the supply of labour.

That public debt would reduce the supply of private capital is, as already pointed out, questionable. With regard to the supply of labour, the force of the argument would depend upon agents finding their wealth in the form of public debt so great that their supply of labour to secure additional income or wealth would be significantly curtailed. The real magnitudes of public debt, or ratios of public debt to gross national product, are nowhere sufficient to make this a serious concern. In the United States, for example, interest payments on the federal debt in 1986, despite half a decade of presumably huge deficits, represent no more than 3 per cent of gross national product. The real interest received by bondholders, after adjusting for the inflation loss in the principal of their bonds, is less than 2 per cent of gross national product. The public debt would have to be many times as large before private income from holding of the debt would be sufficient to have an appreciable effect in reducing the supply of labour (or other factors of production). Indeed, it may not be *possible* for the real debt to be sufficiently high to impinge significantly upon the supply of labour. For the necessary increases in nominal debt would generate such excess demand and consequent increases in the price level that an upper bound to the real debt would be reached before its effects upon supply could be significant.

All of this relates to internally or domestically held public debt. Public debt held by other countries or their nationals is another matter. If that debt is denominated in a country's own currency, it too can always be paid off by money creation and depreciated by inflation. If there is an external debt in foreign currencies, however, there is a real burden, which can, if the debt is sufficiently large, prove overwhelming. In the case of such external debt, this burden must be carefully balanced against any benefits in terms of income from the wealth or assets which the debt may have financed.

BIBLIOGRAPHY

Ando, A.K. and Modigliani, F. 1963. The 'life cycle' hypothesis of saving: aggregate implications and tests. *American Economic Review* 53, March, 55–84.

Barro, R.J. 1974. Are government bonds net wealth? *Journal of Political Economy* 82, November–December, 1095–117.

Buchanan, J.M. 1958. *Public Principles of Public Debt*. Homewood, Ill.: Irwin.

Buchanan, J.M. 1976. Barro on the Ricardian equivalence theorem. *Journal of Political Economy* 84, April, 337–42.

Buiter, W.H. and Tobin, J. 1979. Debt neutrality: a brief review of doctrine and evidence. In *Social Security versus Private Saving*, ed. George M. von Furstenburg, Cambridge, Mass.: Ballinger.

Eisner, R. 1986. *How Real Is the Federal Deficit?* New York: Free Press, Macmillan.

Eisner, R. and Pieper, P.J. 1984. A new view of the federal debt and budget deficits. *The American Economic Review* 74, March, 11–29.

Feldstein, M. 1974. Social security, induced retirement, and aggregate accumulation. *Journal of Political Economy* 82, September–October, 905–25.

Modigliani, F. and Brumberg, R. 1954. Utility analysis and the consumption function: an interpretation of cross-section data. In *Post-Keynesian Economics*, ed. K.K. Kurihara, New Brunswick: Rutgers University Press.

Ricardo, D. 1817. *On the Principles of Political Economy and Taxation*. In *The Works of David Ricardo*, ed. J.R. McCulloch, London: John Murray, 1846.

Ricardo, D. 1820. Funding system. In *The Works and Correspondence of David Ricardo*, Vol. IV, ed. Piero Sraffa, Cambridge: Cambridge University Press, 1951.

Bureaucracy

MANCUR OLSON

The study of bureaucracy has to deal with an elemental paradox. The role of bureaucracy has obviously increased dramatically in modern times. This is true not only of government bureaucracies but business bureaucracies as well. Though there were a few bureaucracies of significant size in pre-industrial times, such as the hierarchy of the Roman Catholic Church and the civil services of various Chinese empires, they were clearly exceptional. By contrast, a very large proportion of the total resources in the developed nations are controlled by either governmental or private bureaucracies. The role of governmental bureaucracies, at least, has increased with some rapidity within the last few decades. The increase in the use of bureaucracies has occurred in so many countries that it could hardly be due entirely to chance, and thus must be due to what are, in some sense, social choices to use more bureaucracy.

Normally, when there are great increases in the demand for or use of some product or instrumentality, this is accompanied by independent evidence of enthusiasm for the product or instrumentality in question. When a society experiences a great increase in the demand for automobiles or for personal computers, there is at the same time a considerable amount of favourable commentary about whatever product is experiencing the boom in demand. There is pride in automobile ownership or awe at the power or compactness of personal computers. Nothing is more natural than that people's choices should be influenced by enthusiasms.

But where is the enthusiasm for bureaucracy that might have been expected to accompany the dramatic increase in the use of bureaucratic mechanisms? Any such enthusiasm is difficult to discern, and there are many conspicuous examples of dislike (or even contempt) of bureaucracy. Some of this negativism may be traced to particular ideological traditions, but this is not sufficient to explain the negativism; the problem is not only that the prevalence of the relevant ideology needs to be explained, but also that the lack of enthusiasm for bureaucracy prevails in a wide variety of ideological and cultural contexts and tends to apply (at least to some extent) to business as well as to governmental bureaucracies. There is no doubt that 'red tape' is viewed negatively by almost everyone, and that it is associated with bureaucracy, and especially governmental bureaucracy; the phrase is derived from the colour of the ribbons that were once used to tie folders of papers in the British government.

Some strands of the literature on bureaucracy are called into question by the paradox. Much of the admiring literature on bureaucracy is difficult to reconcile with the negative popular image of bureaucracy, whereas much of the negative literature suffers from the lack of any explanation of why virtually all societies, at least implicitly, keep choosing to use the instrumentality that is alleged to be so faulty.

Perhaps the most influential scholarly analysis of bureaucracy is not by an economist, but rather by the sociologist and historian, Max Weber. According to Weber:

> ... the fully developed bureaucratic mechanism compares with other organizations exactly as does the machine with the non-mechanical modes of production ...
>
> Precision, speed, unambiguity, knowledge of the files, continuity, discretion, unity, strict subordination, reduction of friction and of material and personal costs – these are raised to the optimum point in the strictly bureaucratic administration (1946, p. 214).

Although also critical of 'bureaucratic domination', Weber's more positive view of bureaucracy has been influential in sociology and political science. Yet it does not appear to have generated systematic or quantitative empirical studies that have tended to provide any confirmation for it, and it surely is not in accord with the popular image of bureaucracy. Weber himself fails to identify any strong incentives in bureaucracies that would lead to efficient allocations of resources or to high levels of innovation.

Similarly, the popular pejorative view of bureaucracy is inadequate to the extent that it offers no explanation why modern societies choose or accept an increasing degree of bureaucratization. There is, admittedly, a rapidly growing economic literature on the growth of government that attempts to identify incentives that lead to a supra-optimal size of government. Examining this large literature would take us a long way from bureaucracy, and it has not in any case yet advanced to the point of generating a professional consensus on any incentive that would systematically bring about the overuse of government and thus of governmental bureaucracy, though some contributions (e.g. Mueller and Murrell, 1985) are extremely promising. But even dramatic success in the literature on the growth of government would not be sufficient to solve the problem, as it would leave us with no explanation of the growth in modern times of business and other private bureaucracies.

Since an explanation of the growth of private bureaucracies is needed, and since an inquiry which begins with the growth of private bureaucracies may obtain some modest degree of detachment from the ideological controversies about the appropriate role of government, it may be best to consider private bureaucracies first. Here the basic question that must be answered is, 'Why do firms with hierarchies of employees exist?' Familiar economic theory explains that markets can, under the appropriate conditions, allocate resources efficiently, so we must ask why individuals in the business hierarchy, and owners of the buildings and equipment that a typical corporation uses, do not use the price signals of the market to coordinate their everyday interaction. As Ronald Coase pointed out in somewhat different language in his seminal article on 'The Nature of the Firm' (1937), the survival of firms with hierarchies of long-run employees and long-term ownership of complementary fixed capital can only be explained by a kind of market failure. The type of market failure that Coase, and Williamson (1964, 1975 and 1985) and the other economists that have developed the very important literature on private hierarchies have emphasized is 'transactions costs'. It would cost too much to contract out each day each of the very many separate tasks that are usually needed in any complex productive process, so in many cases it pays to forego the use of the market and to make long-term deals with employees who will perform such tasks each day as their superiors instruct them to do and receive in turn a regular salary. Though most of the literature in this tradition emphasizes only transactions costs, it is important to note that any market failure, such as that arising from an externality, could provide the incentive for the establishment of a firm that would internalize the externality, and all but the smallest firms have bureaucracies.

Though the foregoing argument also applies to small firms of the kind that predominated in pre-industrial times, there have been some changes since the industrial revolution that, within this Coasian–Williamson framework, can provide important insights into the growth of business bureaucracies. One factor that made for larger and more bureaucratic firms was the discovery of technologies subject to indivisibilities that only a large enterprise can profitably exploit.

But the extraordinary improvement in the technologies of transportation and communication was probably far more important. Reductions in transportation and communication costs make it economic for firms to draw factors of production from farther away and also make it profitable for a firm to sell its output over a wider area. When transportation and communication technologies make it profitable for many firms to operate at a global rather than a village level, some very large firms can emerge. The improved transportation and communication also make it possible to coordinate the activities of a firm over a larger area. Superficial observers of the emergence of large firms have supposed that this growth of firm size entails a reduction in competition and a growth of monopoly. In fact, the dramatic reductions in transportation and communication costs have, of course, also increased the opportunities for market transactions over great distances, so the size of the market and the number of firms to which the typical consumer has access have (in the absence of extra trade barriers) also increased. At least in the Common Market or the United States, the average consumer, even if purchasing a product such as automobiles that is produced under greater-than-average economies of scale, has more firms competing for his business than did the average consumer in the typical rural village before the industrial revolution. Thus we see that the growth of business bureaucracy and the expansion of competitive markets are by no means necessarily obverse tendencies, but rather the kinds of things that often happen together.

The technologies that facilitated larger markets and larger firms also gradually led to the discovery of better methods of governing large-scale business organizations, as the historian Alfred D. Chandler has shown in some seminal historical studies of what he has called *The Visible Hand* (1977; see also 1962 and 1980). Several of these innovations occurred in the unprecedently large and geographically scattered railroads in the 19th-century United States, and many involved the creation of separate 'profit centres' and other devices that enabled larger firms to use market mechanisms to fulfill some functions within the firm (Williamson, 1985). This suggests that the costs and control losses in bureaucracies are still very considerable, so that business bureaucracy can only be explained in terms of rather substantial costs of using markets. The same conclusion emerges from the observation that activities that are highly space-intensive, such as most types of agricultural production, are quite resistant to bureaucratization, even after the development of modern technologies of transportation and administration; the firms that succeed in surviving in most types of farming are normally too small to have bureaucracies (Olson, 1985).

By contrast, in activities in which the transfer of new technologies and other information is especially important, market failure is likely to be fairly extensive, mainly because new information would only be rationally purchased by those who did not already have this information, and from this it follows that the market for new information is particularly handicapped by the asymmetrical information of the parties to any transaction. Thus, as J.C. McManus (1972), Buckley and Casson (1976) and, especially, Hennart (1982) have shown, the emergence of the multinational firms with bureaucracies that transcend national borders can be explained in this framework; capital can cross national borders through portfolio investment (almost all British and other foreign investment in the 19th century was portfolio investment), but the rise in the relative importance of firms with new technologies and methods that were often not well suited to market transfer via licensing of patents, gave rise to the multinational corporation.

The foregoing emphasis on the business bureaucracies that are generally neglected in discussions of bureaucracy makes possible a brief and unified explanation of governmental bureaucracy as well. Governmental bureaucracies are similarly necessary only because markets fail, at least to some degree; the theory of market failure is readily capable of being generalized to include all functions for which governments are an efficient response (Olson, 1986). Since governmental as well as market mechanisms are obviously imperfect, it does not follow from the presence of market failure that government intervention is normatively appropriate, since the government might fail even worse than the market, but market failures are nonetheless often important and always a necessary condition for optimal governmental intervention. Of course, it would be absurd to suppose that actual government intervention is always optimal or that governments always intervene when it is Pareto-efficient for them to do so. It is nonetheless instructive to look at the existence of government bureaucracy, as of business bureaucracy, in terms of market failure.

Among other reasons, it is instructive because the very conditions that give rise to market failure inevitably generate, in governments, and to a considerable degree also in firms, exactly those inefficiencies and rigidities that are popularly and correctly attributed to bureaucracies. Some of these inefficiencies also occur when either governmental or business bureaucracy is used inappropriately, but the problem is most easily evident, and most serious, in precisely those cases where market failure makes bureaucratic mechanisms indispensable.

The reasons why the same conditions that make markets fail also generate difficulties and inefficiencies in bureaucracies unfortunately do not lend themselves to brief exposition. But perhaps a faint and intuitive sense of the matter will be evident from a moment's reflection about what could make a bureaucracy necessary. If, say, the fruits or vegetables grown on a farm are best picked by hand and the best way to pay each worker is by the number of bushels picked, there is no need to have any bureaucratic mechanism for getting the work done. When piece-rate or commission systems of reward work well, the market gives each worker a more or less optimal incentive to work and to be as efficient as the worker knows how to be. In essence, the reason is that the output is highly divisible into more or less homogeneous units or the revenue attributable to each worker is known, and so the output of different workers can be measured with reasonable accuracy.

Let us now shift to an opposite extreme. Consider a typical civil servant in the foreign ministry of a government. Even supposing that the only purpose of the foreign ministry in question was peacefully to maintain the country's independence, there would still be a stupendous difficulty in rewarding the civil servant on a piece-rate or commission basis, or in any way that is proportional to his productivity. The security of the country in question would normally depend in large part on what might loosely be described as the state of the international system – on worldwide indivisible or public good for which no one country could be entirely responsible. But even if the country in question were the only producer of this indivisible good, the foreign ministry would not be the only part of the government or the country that was relevant. Even in the foreign ministry, the typical civil servant is only one among thousands. How is his individual output to be measured, or even distinguished from that of his co-workers? The civil servant obviously cannot be paid in proportion to the revenue he generates, because if there really is market failure, the output cannot be sold in a market in the first place. Thus in practice, the remuneration of civil servants involved in producing public goods is not even a close approximation to each civil servant's true output; rewards in civil services will depend dramatically on proxy variables for performance such as seniority, education, and the fidelity of the employee to the interests of his superior and to the 'culture' or ideology of that bureaucracy. The peculiarities of civil service personnel systems, competitive bidding rules, and red tape are mainly explained by this logic (Olson, 1973, 1974).

The knowledge of the 'social production function' of a government bureaucracy producing public goods will also be limited by the same indivisibility that has been described; there are fewer countries, or even airsheds for pollution abatement, than there are farms (or experimental plots at agricultural experiment stations), so in general less is known about how to run countries or control pollution than about agriculture or about production processes in other competitive industries (Olson, 1982). The same indivisibility that obscures the social production function and the productivity of individual civil servants and other public inputs also insures that there cannot be even an imperfectly competitive market, so there is also no direct information on what an alternative bureaucracy could have achieved in the same circumstances.

In large part, it is the lack of information due to the indivisibilities described above that allows some of the bureaucratic pathologies described in Niskanen (1971) and Tullock (1965) to occur. In Niskanen's widely cited formal model, it is assumed that only the government bureaucrats know how many resources are required to produce a given public output. These bureaucrats are assumed to gain from growth of the bureaucracy, because an official's power, opportunities for promotion and other perquisites are assumed to be an increasing function of the budget the bureaucrat administers. An agency faces the constraint, however, that the electorate will not sustain any government programme whose total costs exceed the total value of its output. The optimization of government bureaucrats therefore leads to a bureaucracy far larger than is Pareto-efficient; in essence the bureaucracy takes all of the surplus under the society's demand curve for the government output at issue. Critics of Niskanen's model have pointed out that it neglects the subordination of bureaucrats to politicians, and that politicians whose opportunities for re-election are positively correlated with the government's performance will endeavour to prevent bureaucracies from taking all of the surplus (see, for example, Breton and Wintrobe, 1975). These criticisms have substantial empirical support, but it is also true that there are many known cases where officials who fear a lower budget allocation than anticipated for their agency will eliminate or threaten to eliminate their politically most cherished activity rather than a marginal activity; this is precisely what Niskanen's model predicts. Though any final conclusion must await further research, the evidence available so far appears to suggest that the lack of information due to the indivisibilities described above does often allow bureaucracies to appropriate some of the surplus that consumers might otherwise be expected to receive, but that the incentives faced by politicians tend to keep bureaucracies from getting anything resembling the whole of this surplus.

Bureaucracies operating in a market environment share some of the information problems that confront government agencies providing public goods, but not others. The divisions of a large corporation that handle personnel, accounting, finance or public relations for the entire corporation provide collective goods to the corporation as a whole. They are in many ways in a situation analogous to the foreign ministry described above when deciding how much of the total profits of the firm to attribute to a given corporate employee; this accounts for the many similarities of large corporate and civil service bureaucracies. But the corporation as a whole, and even the nationalized firm producing private goods in a market, does not, when it sells its output, have as great a difficulty as the government agency that produces a collective of public output that is indivisible and unmarketable. The firm produces a good or service that is divisible in that it may be provided to purchasers and denied to non-purchasers. This means that the output is directly measurable in some physical units or at least that the revenue obtained from this output is measurable. Since consumers, even in the absence of any high degree of competition, will have alternative uses for their money, the private corporation or nationalized firm in a market economy will get some feedback about how much value it is providing. If there is no legal barrier to the operation of a competitive enterprise and the market is contestable, the society will also have at least potential information about what value an alternative organization could provide. An enterprise in the market produces an output from which non-purchasers may be excluded, and this also means there is normally better knowledge of the production functions for private goods than of production functions for public goods. All this implies that the problems of bureaucracy are less severe in private business than in government agencies producing public goods. Interestingly, they are also less severe in government enterprises that unnecessarily produce private goods that private firms would readily provide than they are in agencies that produce public goods that would not have been provided by the market. The more flexible personnel policies in some nationalized firms than in classical civil service contexts thus provide support for the conception offered here.

The paradox of a vast growth of both public and private bureaucracy at the same time that there is almost a consensus that bureaucracies are not very efficient or flexible, thus appears to have a resolution. There are fundamental reasons, arising from the inherent conditions causing market failure, that make both public and private bureaucracies inevitable. These same reasons also explain why bureaucracies lack the information needed for high levels of efficiency. But these same market failures show that (though the existing degree of bureaucracy may of course be far from optimal), it should not be surprising that societies choose to use more private and public bureaucracy even as they condemn such bureaucracy.

BIBLIOGRAPHY
Breton, A. and Wintrobe, R. 1975. The equilibrium size of a budget maximizing bureau. *Journal of Political Economy* 83(1), February, 195–207.
Buckley, P. and Casson, M. 1976. *The Future of the Multinational Enterprise.* London: Macmillan.
Chandler, A.D. 1962. *Strategy and Structure: Chapters in the History of American Industrial Enterprise.* Cambridge, Mass.: MIT Press.
Chandler, A.D. 1977. *The Visible Hand: The Managerial Revolution in American Business.* Cambridge, Mass.: Harvard University Press.

Chandler, A.D. and Daems, H. (eds) 1980. *Managerial Hierarchies: Comparative Perspectives on the Rise of Modern Industrial Enterprise.* Cambridge, Mass.: Harvard University Press.

Coase, R.H. 1937. The nature of the firm. *Economica* 4, November, N.S., 386–405.

Hennart, J.-F. 1982. *A Theory of the Multinational Enterprise.* Ann Arbor: University of Michigan Press.

McManus, J.C. 1972. The theory of the international firm. In *The Multinational Firm and the Nation State*, ed. Gilles Paquet, Donn Mills, Ontario: Collier Macmillan.

Mueller, D.C. and Murrell, P. 1985. Interest groups and the political economy of government size. In *Public Expenditure and Government Growth*, ed. F. Forte and A. Peacock, Oxford: Basil Blackwell.

Niskanen, W.A. 1971. *Bureaucracy and Representative Government.* Chicago: Aldine-Antherton.

Olson, M.L. 1973. Evaluating performance in the public sector. In *The Measurement of Economic and Social Performance*, ed. M. Moss, Studies in Income and Wealth, Vol. 38, National Bureau of Economic Research, New York: Columbia University Press.

Olson, M.L. 1974. The priority of public problems. In *The Corporate Society*, ed. R. Marris, London: Macmillan.

Olson, M.L. 1982. Environmental indivisibilities and information costs: fanaticism, agnosticism, and intellectual progress. *American Economic Review, Papers and Proceedings* 72, May, 262–6.

Olson, M.L. 1985. Space, agriculture, and organization. *American Journal of Agricultural Economics* 67, December, 928–37.

Olson, M.L. 1986. Toward a more general theory of governmental structure. *American Economic Review, Papers and Proceedings* 76, May, 120–5.

Tullock, G. 1965. *The Politics of Bureaucracy.* Washington, DC: Public Affairs Press.

Weber, M. 1946. Bureaucracy. In *From Max Weber: Essays in Sociology*, ed. H. Gerth and C.W. Mills, New York: Oxford University Press.

Williamson, O.E. 1964. *The Economics of Discretionary Behavior: Managerial Objectives in a Theory of the Firm.* Englewood Cliffs, NJ: Prentice-Hall.

Williamson, O.E. 1975. *Markets and Hierarchies: Analysis and Anti-trust Implications.* New York: The Free Press.

Williamson, O.E. 1985. *The Economic Institutions of Capitalism.* New York: The Free Press.

Capital Gains and Losses

E. MALINVAUD

National accounting has made the definition of capital gains and losses rather precise in practice, but fundamentally their distinction from income raises quite subtle issues, about which great economists have long been wavering. Whenever it becomes important, inflation gives to some of these issues a fresh relevance. Much remains to be learned, moreover, on how capital gains affect economic behaviour and how the allocation of resources ought to deal with the capital losses resulting from current activity.

DEFINITION. Although the reference books such as United Nations (1969) are not explicit enough about this basic notion, national accounting systematically applies the following

$$\Delta W = Y + CT + CG - C, \tag{1}$$

where ΔW is the variation of wealth between the beginning and end of the period under consideration, Y is income, CT the net capital transfer received (gifts, bequests, capital taxes and subsidies), CG the net capital gain and C consumption. The identity applies to any agent or group of agents. This identity may be taken as the *de facto* definition of net capital gains (i.e. gains *minus* losses), to the extent that well-defined rules are used for the flows Y, C and CT, which appear in the current accounts, and to the extent that wealth is assumed to be unambiguously determined.

Looking carefully at the existing rules, one realizes, however, that the distinction between income and net capital gain is conventional to a large extent. It is precisely on the choice of this convention that some important questions about the definition of incomes lie.

Chapter 7 of Fisher (1906) shows that defining the concept of income was not an easy task for economists. Fisher's own preferred definition, 'the services of capital', may not seem quite clear, but it can be identified with consumption. This would make the whole of investment belong to capital gains, a solution that

35

was seriously discussed by Samuelson (1961) but has hardly any advocate today. At the other extreme, the 'comprehensive definition of income', also called the Haig–Simons definition, was proposed by economists studying income taxes (Haig, 1921; Simons, 1938); income would be equal to the sum of consumption and wealth increase, thus leaving neither capital gains, nor capital transfers, in equation (1). One now most commonly refers to the definition introduced by Hicks (1939), 'A man's income is the maximum value which he can consume during a week, and still expect to be as well off at the end of the week as he was at the beginning' (p. 172).

National accountants, however, measure income as the sum of the value of production and net current transfers. Production is essentially computed from physical outputs and inputs, valued at current prices and aggregated. This means that stock revaluations that explain part of the change of wealth are not incomes but capital gains or losses. Hicks's definition, on the contrary, implies that expected stock revaluations belong to income. In equation (1) only windfalls would be true capital gains. But whether the change of value of an asset should be classified as expected or not is most often not clear. (How long in advance should it have been expected? Should an outside observer be able to make sure that the asset holder had expected the change?) The distinction between expected and unexpected capital gains or losses, however, remains essential in economic analysis.

INFLATION. The most sizeable asset revaluations result from changes of the price level. When inflation is important, a good proportion of these revaluations are, moreover, expected by all agents. Their occurrence then plays a role in the determination of the equilibrium of all exchanges and economic operations, inducing in particular high interest rates. On the other hand, the change of nominal wealth becomes of little interest in comparison with the change of real wealth; 'real capital gains' should then be distinguished from nominal ones. Hence, inflation perturbs the significance of normal accounting rules; new measurements are required for correct assessments of income flows (Jump, 1980).

This applies first to business accounting, in which reference to historical costs underestimates physical assets and depreciation of fixed capital, while it overestimates net returns from financial assets. This explains the search for new or alternative accounting rules that would be better suited in cases of fast inflation and would more correctly draw the line between income and capital gains or losses. This search went as far as the stage of implementation in the United Kingdom (see Walton, 1978).

At the level of the whole economy, when the rules of national accounting are applied, real capital gains and losses resulting from variations of the general level of prices are important. Typically they benefit enterprises and government, which are net debtors, whereas they mean large losses for households. When all these capital gains and losses are imputed to incomes, on the ground that they must have been expected, the current accounts of firms and government appear substantially more favourable, whereas sizeable redistribution is also found as between groups of households (see Bach and Stephenson, 1974; Babeau, 1978; Wolff, 1979).

The question has been considered whether national account practices should not be revised so as to better record true incomes in times of inflation (see Hibbert, 1982). A prerequisite is the regular production of national balance sheets. When this is done, important capital gains and losses, due for instance to booms in real estate or share prices, also appear beyond those due to changes of the general price level.

CAPITAL GAINS IN ECONOMIC BEHAVIOUR. Most econometric studies tend to neglect capital gains as flows, although wealth and indebtedness are often taken into account. The role of capital gains on the consumption behaviour of households has, however, been studied. Up to now the results have been rather inconclusive (Bhatia, 1972; Peek, 1983; Pesaran and Evans, 1984).

In all likelihood the difficulty comes from the fact that some capital gains are purely transitory, whereas most of them have some degree of permanence, but this degree varies widely from one to the other. A pure windfall is comparable to an exceptional gift; accidental losses, or war damages occur once for all, whereas capital losses due to an inflation that is expected to last may appear to be as permanent as interest incomes, even sometimes as wage incomes. But to classify capital gains according to their supposed permanence is far from being an obvious operation.

Gains on the value of corporate shares have a permanent component following from the firms' policy of retaining part of their profits. This is why increases of retained earnings have been considered as likely to increase household consumption, but not as much as an increase of permanent income would, since the size of undistributed profits varies a good deal with business conditions (Feldstein and Fane, 1973; Malinvaud, 1986).

The problem becomes still more complex when capital gains are correlated with cost changes for items of household wealth. An extreme case occurs when prices of residential real estate increase: owners of houses make a capital gain, but simultaneously the cost of housing increases by the corresponding amount; whether houses are let or used by their owners, a stimulating effect on real consumption is doubtful.

CAPITAL LOSSES, CONSERVATION AND WELFARE. The existence of capital gains and losses raises a number of issues for the theory of allocation of resources, for instance what should be the taxation of capital gains (David, 1968; Green and Sheshinski, 1978), or how best to organize insurance against capital losses. But particular attention nowadays concerns the damages that economic activity causes to the environment and to reserves of exhaustible resources (Fisher, 1981).

Not all environmental effects mean capital losses; many of them are just externalities in the normal course of economic activity. But irreversible damages to the forests, the soil or even the climate must also be recognized and are usually not recorded as consumption or as inputs to production. Depletion of non-renewable reserves are similarly often treated as capital losses.

The detrimental effects of many of these losses will appear mainly in a rather distant future. Whether or not losses should be accepted – what for instance should be the optimal speed of depletion of natural resources – raises difficult questions of intergenerational equity, on which economists have uncomfortably to enter the field of social philosophy.

The problem cannot be discarded here on the ground that proper discounting makes the distant future negligible. Indeed, in the purest case, the shadow discounted price of an exhaustible resource is as high in the future as it is now, for as long as the resource will remain used (Hotelling, 1931). The remote future must then be taken into account for present decisions.

It is moreover notorious that enormous uncertainties affect the purely physical estimation of the consequences involved. Neither the effects of carbon dioxide emission on the climate, nor the existing reserves of fossil fuels, nor the future emergence of appropriate technologies for the wider use of renewable energy can be securely assessed. Under such circumstances, the emergence of an objective methodology for economic decisions is particularly difficult.

BIBLIOGRAPHY

Babeau, A. 1978. The application of the constant price method for evaluating the transfer related to inflation: the case of French households. *Review of Income and Wealth* 24(4), December, 391–414.

Bach, G. and Stephenson, J. 1974. Inflation and the redistribution of wealth. *Review of Economics and Statistics* 56(1), February, 1–13.

Bhatia, K. 1972. Capital gains and the aggregate consumption function. *American Economic Review* 62(5), December, 866–79.

David, M. 1968. *Alternative Approaches to Capital Gains Taxation*. Washington, DC: Brookings Institution.

Feldstein, M. and Fane, G. 1973. Taxes, corporate dividend policy and personal savings: the British experience. *Review of Economics and Statistics* 55(4), November, 399–411.

Fisher, A. 1981. *Resource and Environmental Economics*. Cambridge: Cambridge University Press.

Fisher, I. 1906. *The Nature of Capital and Income*. New York: Macmillan.

Green, J. and Sheshinski, E. 1978. Optimal capital-gains taxation under limited information. *Journal of Political Economy* 86(6), 1143–58.

Haig, R. 1921. The concept of income: economic and legal aspects. In *The Federal Income Tax*, ed. R. Haig, New York: Columbia University Press.

Hibbert, J. 1982. *Measuring the Effects of Inflation on Income, Saving and Wealth*. Paris: OECD.

Hicks, J. 1939. *Value and Capital*. 2nd edn, Oxford: Oxford University Press, 1946.

Hotelling, H. 1931. The economics of exhaustible resources. *Journal of Political Economy* 39, 137–75.

Jump, G. 1980. Interest rates, inflation expectations, and spurious elements in measured real income and saving. *American Economic Review* 70(5), December, 990–1004.

Malinvaud, E. 1986. Pure profits as forced saving. *Scandinavian Journal of Economics* 88(1), 109–30.

Peek, J. 1983. Capital gains and personal saving behaviour. *Journal of Money, Credit and Banking* 15(1), February, 1–23.

Pesaran, M. and Evans, R. 1984. Inflation, capital gains and UK personal savings: 1953–81. *Economic Journal* 94, June, 237–57.

Samuelson, P. 1961. The evaluation of 'social income': capital formation and wealth. In *The Theory of Capital*, ed. F. Lutz and D. Hague, London: Macmillan.

Simons, H. 1938. *Personal Income Taxation*. Chicago: University of Chicago Press.

United Nations. 1969. *A System of National Accounts*. New York: United Nations.

Walton, J. 1978. Current cost accounting: implications for the definition and measurement of corporate income. *Review of Income and Wealth* 24(4), December, 357–90.

Wolff, E. 1979. The distributional effects of the 1969–75 inflation on holdings of household wealth in the United States. *Review of Income and Wealth* 25(2), June, 195–208.

Chicago School

M.W. REDER

To identify a Chicago School of economics requires some demarcations, both of ideas and persons, that may not be universally accepted. Justification for these decisions must be heuristic, that is, they facilitate the story to be told. But it is not denied that there may be alternative accounts that would entail different demarcations. In this account, the 'Chicago School' is and has been centred in the University of Chicago's Economics Department from about 1930 to the present (1985). However, it is convenient to define the School so as to include many members of the large contingent of economists in the Graduate School of Business and the group of economists and lawyer-economists in the Law School. Largely because of the intellectual loyalty of former students, the influence of the Chicago School extends far beyond the University of Chicago to the faculties of other universities, the civil service, the judiciary and private business. Moreover, this influence is not confined to the United States.

To restrict the retrospective horizon of the School to 1930 implies exclusion of a number of famous economists who had been on the University of Chicago faculty before that time; for example, Thorstein Veblen, Wesley C. Mitchell, J.M. Clark, J. Laurence Laughlin, C.O. Hardy. However, none of these shared the intellectual characteristics that have typified members of the Chicago School as defined here.

In a nutshell, the two main characteristics of Chicago School adherents are: (1) belief in the power of neoclassical price theory to explain observed economic behaviour; and (2) belief in the efficacy of free markets to allocate resources and distribute income. Correlative with (2) is a tropism for minimizing the role of the state in economic activity.

Before discussing these characteristics in detail, let me give a brief historical account in which it is convenient to divide the history of the School into three periods: (1) a founding period, in the 1930s; (2) an interregnum, from the early 1940s to the early 1950s; and (3) a modern period, from the 1950s to the present.

40

During the founding period, the Chicago Economics Department contained a wide diversity of views both on methodology and public policy. Institutionalist views were well represented among the senior faculty, and institutionally oriented students constituted a large part of the graduate student population. Among the prominent Institutionalists were the labour economists H.A. Millis and (one side of) Paul H. Douglas, the economic historians John U. Nef and C.W. Wright, and Simeon E. Leland, a Public Finance specialist and long-time department chairman.

Like other social science departments at Chicago, economics was actively engaged in developing the (then) embryonic 'quantitative techniques'. The leading figures in quantitative methods were Henry Schultz, a pioneer student of statistical demand curves, who taught the graduate courses in mathematical economics and mathematical statistics, and Paul Douglas who was (during the 1920s and 1930s) a leader in the estimation of production functions and the measurement of real wages and living costs.

However, it is generally agreed that the progenitors of the Chicago School were Frank H. Knight and Jacob Viner. These two scholars shared an intense interest in the history of economic thought and both were, broadly speaking, devotees of neoclassical price theory. However, their intellectual styles and temperaments were quite different, and their personal relations were not close. Apart from his interest in the history of thought, Viner was primarily an applied theorist working on problems in international trade and related issues in monetary theory. Knight's work was focused on the conceptual underpinnings of neoclassical price theory, and his main concerns were to clarify and improve its logical structure.

Temperament and intellectual focus combined to make Knight a formidable critic, both of ideas and their protagonists. This led to a good deal of friction between him and both Douglas and Schultz. Personalities aside, Knight was strongly averse to the quantification of economics and was very outspoken on this, as on most other matters. (For further details, see Reder, 1982, pp. 362–5.)

By contrast, Viner was rather sympathetic to the aspirations of 'quantifiers', though sceptical of their prospects for success, at least in the near future. Viner's sympathy for quantitative work was prompted by the strong empirical bent of his own research, although friendship for Douglas and Schultz may also have been involved. On the other hand, Knight's purely theoretical studies of capital theory, risk, uncertainty, social costs, and so on, generated neither need for empirical verification nor exposure to research that might have offered it. As a result, Knight's relations with Douglas and Schultz were ridden with conflict, and theoretical disagreements with Viner spilled over into barbed comments to graduate students and kept personal relations (between Knight and Viner) from becoming more than merely correct (Reder, 1982, p. 365).

What Knight and Viner had in common was a continuing adherence to the main tenets of neoclassical price theory and resistance to the theoretical innovations of the 1930s, Monopolistic Competition and Keynes's *General Theory*. This theoretical posture paralleled an antipathy to the interventionist aspects of the New Deal and the full employment Keynesianism of its later years. Viner, who was actively consulting the government throughout the period, was much less averse to New Deal reforms than Knight and his protégés. However, there was a sharp contrast between the views of Knight and Viner, on the one hand, and those of avowed New Deal supporters such as Douglas, Schultz and some of the Institutionalists.

As a result of the division of faculty views, on both economic methodology and public policy, the graduate student body was exposed to a diversity of thought patterns and did not exhibit a great degree of conformity to any particular one. But despite their many disagreements, an effective majority of the Chicago faculty concurred in a set of degree requirements (for the PhD) that stressed competence in the application of price theory. These requirements were quite unusual in the 1930s and the process of satisfying them exercised a great influence in forming a (common) view of the subject among the students, in which price theory was of major importance.

The most important of the requirements was that all PhD candidates, without exception, pass preliminary examinations in both price theory and monetary theory. These examinations were difficult and attended with an appreciable failure rate. Even on second and third trials, there was a non-negligible probability of failure, with the result that some students were (and are) unable to qualify for the doctorate. For most students, the key to successful performance on the examinations was mastery of the material presented in relevant courses, especially the basic price theory course (301) and study of previous examinations.

For over half a century, the need to prepare for course and preliminary examinations, especially in price theory, has provided a disciplinary–cultural matrix for Chicago students. Examination questions serve as paradigmatic examples of research problems and 'A' answers exemplify successful scientific performance. The message implicit in the process is that successful research involves identifying elements of a problem with prices, quantities, and functional relations among them as these occur in price theory, and obtaining a solution as an application of the theory.

Although the specific content of examination questions has evolved with the development of the science, the basic paradigm remains substantially unchanged: economic phenomena are to be explained primarily as the outcome of decisions about quantities made by optimizing individuals who take market prices as data with the (quantity) decisions being coordinated through markets in which prices are determined so as to make aggregate quantities demanded equal to aggregate quantities supplied.

Of course, students vary in the degree to which they assimilate price theoretic ideas to their thought processes, and resistance to these ideas was probably greater in the 1930s than later. Nevertheless, regardless of their special field of interest, all students were compelled to absorb and learn to use a considerable body of economic theory. In the 1980s these skills are very widespread, but in the 1930s they were rarely found and served to distinguish Chicago-trained PhD's – especially in applied fields – from other economists.

Despite the common elements of their training, as in other institutions, doctoral students tended to identify themselves with one or another particular faculty member, usually their dissertation supervisor. Thus each of the major figures in the department was associated with a cluster of advanced students. One such cluster, associated with Knight in the mid-1930s, became of very great importance in the history of the Chicago School. Key members of this cluster were Milton Friedman, George Stigler and W. Allen Wallis. The group established close personal relations with two junior faculty members, Henry Simons and Aaron Director, who were also protégés of Knight. Another member of the group was Director's sister, Rose, who later married Milton Friedman.

It was this group that provided the multigenerational linkage in intellectual tradition that is suggested by the term 'Chicago School'. Although they admired Knight, and were devoted to him, the intellectual style of Friedman, Stigler, et al. was very different from Knight's. They were thoroughgoing empiricists with a distinct bias toward application of quantitative techniques to the testing of theoretical propositions. In their empirical bent and concern with 'real world' problems, they were much closer to Viner than to Knight, but, whatever the reason, they identified with the latter.

Partly because of his important role in the teaching of theory to undergraduates and (less well-prepared) beginning graduates, in the 1930s and until his untimely death in 1946, Henry Simons exercised an important influence on Chicago students. But he is remembered mainly for his essays on economic policy (collected in Simons, 1948) which constituted the principal statement of Chicago *laissez-faire* views during this period.

Simons's view had a distinctly populist flavour that is absent from those more recently associated with Chicago economics. For example, he favoured use of government power to reduce the size of large firms and labour unions. Where such policies would lead to unacceptable losses of efficiency (e.g. 'natural monopolies'), Simons favoured outright public ownership. In sharp contrast to more recent Chicago statements on the matter, Simons emphatically supported progressive income taxation to promote a more egalitarian distribution of income (Simons, 1938).

Finally, Simons proposed a requirement of 100 per cent reserves against demand deposits and restriction of Federal Reserve discretion in monetary policy in favour of fixed rules designed to stabilize the price level (Simons, 1948). In this he was the direct forbear of Chicago monetarism, as later developed by Friedman and Friedman's students.

Historically, Friedman, Stigler and Wallis were both the intellectual and the institutional heirs of Knight and Viner. The story of Chicago economics would be less convoluted if the succession had been a matter of the older generation appointing their best students to succeed them. But it was not that simple. On the eve of World War II there was great concern, within the Economics Department and (probably) in the central administration as well, that Chicago had none of the leading figures in the new theoretical developments of the period, that is, in nonperfect competition and Keynesian macroeconomics.

To rectify this, in 1938, they appointed Oscar Lange as assistant professor. In addition to his credentials as a contributor to the literature of Keynes's *General Theory*, especially in relation to general equilibrium theory, Lange was a leading participant in the current debate on the possibility of market socialism and its (alleged) advantages relative to *laissez-faire* capitalism in terms of efficiency. Further, he had made a number of contributions to mathematical economics and was able to provide backup support for Henry Schultz in that subject area, and in mathematical statistics as well.

As an outspoken and politically active socialist, Lange's views were diametrically opposed to *laissez-faire*. That he managed to stay on friendly terms with virtually all of his colleagues was a testimonial both to his own tact and to their tolerance of dissent. Of course, it was no accident that the principal socialist in the Chicago tradition should have been a *market* socialist.

Within a few months of Lange's appointment, Henry Schultz was killed in an automobile accident and Lange became the sole mathematical economist in the Chicago department. Within a year the loss of Schultz was compounded by the partial withdrawal of Douglas from academic life to pursue a political career. Still further, with the outbreak of World War II, Viner became increasingly involved in Washington and, ultimately, in 1945, he resigned to accept an appointment at Princeton.

As a result of these losses, the Department had to be rebuilt. The process of reconstruction began during the war years, with Lange taking a leading role. He was very anxious to recruit colleagues who were leaders in current theoretical developments, especially in mathematical economics. Failing to obtain his first choice, Abba Lerner, he readily accepted Jacob Marschak and, for a short period, collaborated with the latter in making further appointments both to the Department and to the Cowles Commission, which had been based at the University of Chicago in 1938. The collaboration ended abruptly in 1945 when Lange resumed Polish citizenship to become ambassador to the United States and, subsequently, to fill many other high positions in the socialist government of Poland.

During the war years, T.W. Schultz was attracted from Iowa State. A leading figure in agricultural economics, Schultz soon became chairman, a position from which he exercised much influence for over two decades. In addition to Schultz, in 1946 the Department acquired Lloyd Metzler to teach international trade and a number of younger theorists and econometricians associated mainly with the Cowles Commission. Whatever was the intention, these appointments served as a counterweight to the more or less contemporaneous appointments of Friedman (to the Economics Department) and Wallis (to the Business School).

There then ensued a struggle for intellectual pre-eminence and institutional control between Friedman, Wallis and their adherents on one side, and the Cowles Commission and its supporters on the other. The struggle persisted into the early 1950s, ending only with the partial retirement of Lloyd Metzler (due to ill health) and the departure of the Cowles Commission (for Yale) in 1953. While not monolithic, the Chicago economics department that emerged from this conflict had a distinctive intellectual style that set it apart from most others.

In positive economics, this style involves de-emphasizing the role of aggregate effective demand as an explanatory variable and stressing the importance of relative prices and 'distortions' thereof. In economic policy, it involves stressing the beneficial effects of allowing prices to be set by market forces rather than by government regulation. In an important sense, 'Chicago economics' in the 1950s and 1960s was simply an extension of the ideas of the Knight coterie of the 1930s. Indeed, some of the key figures – notably Friedman, Stigler and Wallis – of that group were leading Chicago economists in the later period as well. Moreover, they were consciously concerned with explicating the continuity of the tradition and preserving it (see below).

The close personal relations of the members of the Knight coterie, maintained for over a half century, has reinforced the strong common elements in their idea-systems and made it easy to ignore the (important) points of disagreement, both among themselves and with others. As already mentioned, Friedman, Stigler and Wallis, like most Chicago economists of their own and subsequent cohorts, believe strongly in use of statistical data and techniques for testing economic theories. In this they differ from Knight, Simons, James Buchanan, Ronald Coase (1981) and a significant minority of other economists associated with Chicago, either as graduate students or faculty, who believe (on various grounds) that the validity of an economic theory lies in its intuitive appeal and/or its compatibility with a set of axioms, rather than in the conformity of its implications with empirical observation.

A second disagreement concerns the consistency of policy advocacy in any form, with the methodology applied in positive economics. (The most influential general description of this methodology is chapter 1 of Friedman, 1953.) This methodology recommends that explanations of economic behaviour be based on a model of (individual) decisions of resource allocation (among alternative uses) designed to maximize utility subject to the constraints of market prices and endowments of wealth. Market prices are presumed to be set so as to equate quantities supplied with those demanded, for all entities traded.

As traditionally applied by neoclassical economists with a predilection for *laissez-faire* solutions, this methodology coexists with advocacy of government policies designed to promote that objective. But in the late 1960s one group of Chicago economists led by Stigler (who had returned to Chicago in 1958 as Walgreen Professor in both the Economics Department and the Business School) began to apply the tools of economic analysis to the investigation of the determinants of political activity, especially government intervention in resource allocation. Thus study of the regulatory and taxing activities of the state became directed not simply at demonstrating their adverse effects upon economic efficiency, but primarily to explaining their occurrence as an outcome of the operation of 'political markets' for such activities.

So analysed, interventions traditionally viewed as efficiency impairing, such as tariffs, require reinterpretation. An individual's resources include not only his command over goods and services acquired through conventional markets, but also his political influence (however measured). Government interventions are considered to be endogenous outcomes of a political-economic process, reflecting the political as well as the economic wealth of decision-making units, and not as aberrations of an exogenous state (e.g. see Stigler, 1982). So viewed, criticism of political outcomes is no more warranted than criticism of the expenditure behaviour of sovereign consumers; both are outcomes of the free choice of resource owners.

This is not to suggest that the 'political economy' wing among Chicago economists has become indifferent to *laissez-faire*. On the contrary, opposition to government intervention (e.g. regulation) among Stigler and his allies is quite as strong as it ever has been. During the past decade many economists and lawyers at some time affiliated with the Law and Economics group at Chicago have been prominent advocates of deregulation. However, tension between advocacy of reform, and positive analysis of the political process through which reform must be achieved, presents a continuing existential problem to the heirs of the Chicago tradition. Although they are well aware of the problem, thus far they have refrained from divisive dispute and treat exercises in political advocacy as a consumption activity by those engaged.

Political science is only one of the fields into which Chicago economics has expanded during the past quarter century. Beginning in the early 1940s and accelerating in the last two decades under Richard Posner's leadership, the economic analysis of legal institutions has become an important area of research both for economists and for legal scholars. Further, using the theory of labour supply as a point of departure, the economic analysis of the family has become an important part of the study of population, marriage, divorce and family structure. This development has challenged sociological and psychological modes of explanation in fields that had long been considered provinces of these other disciplines. Still further, the theory of human capital has had a major impact on the study of education.

It is convenient to date the 'disciplinary imperialist' phase of the Chicago School as beginning in the early 1960s and continuing to the present. However, its roots go back into the 1930s; since that time there has been, at least in the oral tradition, a tropism for application of the tools and concepts of price theory to (seemingly) alien situations, and for taking delight in confronting conventional wisdom with the results. Correlatively, there has been a strong tendency to resist explanations of behaviour that do not run in terms of utility maximization by individual decision-makers coordinated by market clearing prices.

However, until well into the 1950s, the disciplinary imperialist aspect of the Chicago paradigm was overshadowed by the struggle to defend the integrity of neoclassical price theory from the attacks of Keynesians at the macro level and the attempts of various theorists of nonperfect competition to provide alternatives at the micro level. The counterattack on the *General Theory* produced a revival of neoclassical monetary theory in a refined and empirically implemented form; this revival is associated with the work of Milton Friedman (1956).

The struggle to re-establish the competitive industry as the dominant model for explaining relative prices was led by Stigler (1968, 1970), and generated much of the theoretical and empirical literature of the field of Industrial Organization. Both in Industrial Organization and Money-Macro, the earlier debates continue, with Chicago-based participants being identifiable as partisans of the standpoints of Friedman and Stigler a quarter of a century ago. However, in the 1970s and 1980s the topics related to these debates have been forced to share centre stage with newer subjects.

The expansion of Chicago economics beyond the traditional boundaries of the discipline began in the middle and late 1950s; two early examples were H.G. Lewis's application of price theory to the 'demand and supply of unionism' (Lewis, 1959) and Gary Becker's dissertation on racial discrimination (Becker, 1957). These were followed in the 1960s and 1970s by a number of others, as already mentioned. Many of these are more or less straightforward applications of conventional price theory to new problems. However, the analysis of time as an economic resource (Becker, 1965) has led to important improvements in the theory of household behaviour.

The analysis of time is also related to a methodological tendency to reject differences in tastes (including attitudes, opinions and beliefs in 'tastes') as a source for explanations of cross-individual differences in behaviour (Stigler and Becker, 1977; Becker, 1976). The rejection is based on the contention that (1) seeming differences of taste are usually reducible to differences of cost and (2) statements about cost differences are much more amenable to empirical test. While this methodological principle has met with resistance, at Chicago as elsewhere, it is reflected in a great deal of ongoing research, especially where cost of time is an important variable.

A separate path of disciplinary expansion has arisen in the field of Finance. Whether, prior to the 1960s, this field was a province of Economics, is a point that it is convenient to bypass. But unquestionably, prior to the theoretical developments initiated by Modigliani and Miller's famous paper (1958) on the (non-) relation of stock prices and dividends, the theory of corporate finance, asset prices, risk-bearing and related topics had at best only a tenuous relationship with the theory of price. Subsequent developments have completely reversed that situation, so that in the mid-1980s, the 'capital asset pricing model' has become an integrating matrix for the theories of security prices, asset structure of the firm, and, via the study of executive compensation, wages.

The dominant idea underlying these developments is that, save for transaction costs, *on average* no opportunity for arbitrage gains goes unexploited. One implication of this is the proposition that there is 'no free lunch'; another implication is that no specifiable algorithm can be found that will enable a resource owner to utilize publicly available information to predict movements of asset prices well enough to gain by trading. The latter implication is tantamount to the 'hypothesis of efficient markets'.

While not formally identical with rational expectations, efficient markets will support any behaviour conforming to rational expectations, but will be compatible with other models of expectations only where one or another set of correlated forecast errors (across individuals) is assumed. Moreover, so long as expectations are rational, and regardless of how they are generated, there is no way in which variables operating through expectations can improve upon the neoclassical explanation of relative prices and quantities. This obviates any need for augmenting economic theory by variables reflecting psychological or sociological factors that operated upon individual decision-making via expectations. Obviously, such a theory of expectations is strongly supportive of the claims of economic theory in interdisciplinary competition.

The interrelated ideas of rational expectations and efficient markets originated at Carnegie-Mellon in the work of Muth (1961) and Modigliani and Miller (1958) rather than at Chicago. However, their consonance with the Chicago paradigm is such that they have found a home in the Chicago Business School under the leadership of Miller and his students, and (since the mid-1970s) in the Economics Department under Robert Lucas, rather than in their place of origin. While the claim of Chicago to be the primary locus for research in these fields is a strong one, it is a claim more subject to challenge than analogous claims in some other fields.

A third Chicago innovation of the late 1950s is the 'Coase Theorem' (Coase, 1960). In essence this theorem states that, ignoring transaction costs, if there is any reallocation of goods, claims, rights (especially property) or alteration of institutions that – after making compensating side payments to losers – increases the utility of everyone, the said reallocation will occur. If rationality is a maintained hypothesis and transaction costs are negligible, the theorem becomes a tautology. Thus the empirical content of the theorem will vary inversely with the importance attributed to transaction costs, which serve as a conceptual receptacle for all forces bearing upon decision-making other than those explicitly incorporated in the theory of price. To consider the Coase Theorem empirically important is to believe that transaction costs and departures from rationality are unimportant.

Put differently, the Coase Theorem suggests that the real world tends towards a position of Pareto optimality. Of course, for given tastes and technology, there may be a different Pareto optimum for each distribution of wealth. Therefore, to the extent that the distribution of wealth is exogenous and has important behavioural consequences, the predictive implications of both Pareto optimality and the Coase Theorem are less salient. Thus the rise in influence of the Coase Theorem at Chicago has more or less paralleled a decline in the marked concern with income distribution that existed in the 1930s and 1940s, especially in the work of Henry Simons (Reder, 1982, p. 389).

When objects of exchange are taken to include legislation and other political variables, the Coase Theorem strongly suggests that the forces of decentralized decision-making that govern production and exchange also control changes in laws and institutions. Thus belief in the Coase Theorem is – or should be – conducive to political passivity. Nevertheless, not all Chicago economists are politically quiescent. But with few exceptions, they are generally conservative, though with considerable differences of shading and intensity of belief, and in taste for political controversy. Probably these differences parallel differences in the degree to which they accept economic explanations of political behaviour.

Perhaps the most common characteristic of Chicago economists is distrust of the state. This distrust, together with the belief that, given time, voluntary exchange will usually generate truly desirable reforms, acts as a powerful brake on wayward impulses to improve society through political action.

The saga of the Chicago School is at once the story of the evolution of a set of ideas – a paradigm – and of a particular institution with which its leading protagonists have been associated. In this essay I have emphasized certain central theoretical ideas and historical events to the exclusion of detailed coverage of applied work and mention of the individuals responsible for it. However, it is the association of these central ideas with an identifiable, multigenerational group of individuals located at a particular institution that justifies the title of this article. Many of the key individuals in this history – Director, Friedman, Stigler, Wallis – are still alive, intellectually active and in close touch with their successors on the Chicago faculty. This continuity, both of personalities and ideas, is a distinctive feature of the intellectual tradition called the Chicago School.

In the mid-1980s the vitality of this tradition is threatened more by the growing acceptance of many of its key ideas than by resistance to them. A quarter century ago, Chicago economics was distinguished by its emphasis on the importance of competition and money supply. Arguably, in 1985, these views and their extensions have become mainstream economics, leaving the story of the Chicago School as a nearly closed episode in the history of economic thought. While such an argument may prove valid, it is too soon to tell.

BIBLIOGRAPHY

Becker, G.S. 1957. *The Economics of Discrimination*. Chicago: University of Chicago Press.

Becker, G.S. 1965. A theory of the allocation of time. *Economic Journal* 75, September, 493–517.

Becker, G.S. 1976. *The Economic Approach to Human Behavior*. Chicago: University of Chicago Press.

Coase, R.H. 1960. The problem of social cost. *Journal of Law and Economics* 3(1), October, 1–44.

Coase, R.H. 1981. How should economists choose? Washington, DC: American Enterprise Institute for Public Policy Research.

Friedman, M. 1953. *Essays in Positive Economics*. Chicago: University of Chicago Press.

Friedman, M. 1956. *Studies in the Quantity Theory of Money*. Chicago: University of Chicago Press.

Lewis, H. Gregg. 1959. Competitive and monopoly unionism. In *The Public Stake in Union Power*, ed. P.D. Bradley, Charlottesville: University of Virginia Press.

Modigliani, F. and Miller, M.H. 1958. The cost of capital, corporation finance and the theory of investment. *American Economic Review* 48, June, 261–97.

Muth, J.F. 1961. Rational expectations and the theory of price movements. *Econometrica* 29, July, 315–35.

Reder, M.W. 1982. Chicago economics: permanence and change. *Journal of Economic Literature* 20(1), March, 1–38.

Simons, H.C. 1938. *Personal Income Taxation*. Chicago: University of Chicago Press.

Simons, H.C. 1948. *Economic Policy for a Free Society*. Chicago: University of Chicago Press.

Stigler, G.J. 1968. *The Organization of Industry*. Homewood, Ill.: Richard D. Irwin.

Stigler, G.J. 1982. Economists and public policy. Washington, DC: American Enterprise Institute for Public Policy Research.

Stigler, G.J. and Becker, G.S. 1977. De gustibus non est disputandum. *American Economic Review* 67(2), March, 76–90.

Stigler, G.J. and Kindahl, J.K. 1970. *The Behavior of Industrial Prices*. New York: Columbia University Press for the National Bureau of Economic Research.

Coase Theorem

ROBERT D. COOTER

Anyone who has taught the Coase Theorem to fresh minds has experienced first hand the wonder and admiration which it inspires, yet Coase never wrote it down, and, when others try, it probably turns out to be false or a tautology. The proposition, or propositions, called the Coase Theorem was originally developed through a series of examples (Coase, 1960). Like a judge, Coase steadfastly refused to articulate broad generalizations in his original paper. Like a judge's opinion, for every interpretation of his paper there is a plausible alternative. Instead of trying to arrive at the ultimate answer, I will offer several conventional interpretations of the Coase Theorem and illustrate them with one of his examples. After more than twenty years of debate the conventional interpretations appear to have exhausted its meanings.

A central insight in microeconomics is that free exchange tends to move resources to their highest valued use, in which case the allocation of resources is said to be Pareto efficient. Besides ownership of resources, the law creates many other entitlements, such as the right to use one's land in a certain way, the right to be free from a nuisance, the right to compensation for tortuous accidents, or the right to performance on a contract. Coase can be regarded as having generalized propositions about the exchange of resources to cover propositions about the exchange of legal entitlements. Under this interpretation, the Coase Theorem states that *the initial allocation of legal entitlements does not matter from an efficiency perspective so long as they can be freely exchanged.* In other words, misallocation of legal entitlements by law will be cured in the market by free exchange.

This interpretation suggests that insuring the efficiency of law is a matter of removing impediments to the free exchange of legal entitlements. Legal entitlements often suffer from vagueness, which makes their value difficult to assess. Furthermore, the courts are not always willing to enforce contracts for the sale of legal entitlements. Consequently, under the 'free exchange

51

interpretation', the efficiency of law is to be secured by defining entitlements clearly and enforcing private contracts for their exchange.

Besides freedom of exchange, there are other conditions which economists usually regard as necessary for markets to allocate resources efficiently. One such condition concerns the elusive, but unavoidable, concept of transaction costs. Narrowly conceived, transaction costs refer to the time and effort required to carry out a transaction. In some circumstances these costs can be very high, as when a deal involves several parties at different locations. High transaction costs can block the workings of markets which would otherwise be efficient. Broadly conceived, transaction costs refer to any use of resources required to negotiate and enforce agreements, including the cost of information needed to formulate a bargaining strategy, the time spent higgling, and the cost of preventing cheating by the parties to the bargain. Stressing the 'transaction cost interpretation', the Coase Theorem can be regarded as stating that *the initial allocation of legal entitlements does not matter from an efficiency perspective so long as the transaction costs of exchange are nil.*

Like a frictionless plane in physics, a costless transaction is a logical construction, rather than something encountered in life. Keeping this fact in mind, the policy prescription following from the transaction cost interpretation of the Coase Theorem is to use law to minimize transaction costs, not eliminate them. According to this line of reasoning, rather than allocating legal entitlement efficiently in the first place, lawmakers are more likely to achieve efficiency by lubricating their exchange. Legal procedure is rife with devices whose purpose is to avoid litigation by encouraging private agreements involving an exchange of legal entitlement.

The 'transaction costs' interpretation focuses attention on some obstacles to exchanging legal entitlement, specifically the cost of negotiating and enforcing private agreements. When 'transaction costs' are given a reasonably circumspect definition, there are additional obstacles to private exchange besides transaction costs. The theory of regulation has developed a finer, richer classification based upon deviations from perfect competition (Schultze, 1977). To illustrate, a monopolist can increase his profits by supplying less than the competitive amount of the good and forcing the price up. Thus monopoly is a form of market failure which is usually distinguished from transaction costs. Stressing this 'market failures interpretation', the Coase Theorem can be regarded as stating that *the initial allocation of legal entitlements does not matter from an efficiency perspective so long as they can be exchanged in a perfectly competitive market.*

This interpretation suggests that ensuring the efficiency of law is a matter of ensuring the existence of perfectly competitive markets for legal entitlements. The conditions of perfect competition include the existence of many buyers and sellers, the absence of external effects, full information about price and quality by the participants in the market and no transaction costs.

The three interpretations can be illustrated by an historical example which Coase made famous. Wood- and coal-burning locomotives emit sparks that set fire to farmers' fields from time to time. Each of the parties can take precautions to reduce the damage caused by fires. To illustrate, the farmers can avoid planting and storing crops along the margins of the railroad tracks, and the railroad can install spark arresters or run fewer trains.

Upon first inspection, it seems that the law controls the incentives for precaution by the parties, and, consequently, determines the amount of damage from fires. To illustrate, injunction is the conventional remedy in property law for a nuisance. If the farmers have a right to enjoin the railroad and shut it down until it stops emitting sparks, it seems that there will be little or no damage from sparks. Conversely, if the railroad has the right to operate trains with impunity, it seems that there will be a lot of damage. According to the Coase Theorem, these appearances are misleading, because while the law creates the initial allocation of entitlements, the market determines the final allocation. To illustrate, if farmers have a right to enjoin the railroad, they can sell this right. Specifically, the railroad could pay a sum of money to the farmers in exchange for a legally binding promise not to enjoin the railroad. Conversely, if the railroad has the right to emit sparks with impunity, it can sell this right. Specifically, farmers could pay a sum of money to the railroad in exchange for a legally binding promise to reduce spark emissions.

Whatever the initial allocation of rights, the farmer and the railroad have an incentive to continue trading entitlements so long as there are potential gains from trade. As with ordinary goods, the gains from trading legal entitlements are not exhausted until each entitlement is held by the party who values it the most. To illustrate, if, say, farmers have a right to be free from sparks, and if the entitlement to emit sparks is worth more to the railroad than the right to be free from sparks is worth to farmers, both parties will benefit from the farmers selling their rights to the railroad. The potential gains from trade are exhausted when entitlements are allocated efficiently. Thus, when the market works, the equilibrium allocation of legal entitlements will be efficient.

The three interpretations of the Coase Theorem give different accounts of the conditions that must be satisfied in order for this market to work. According to the 'free exchange' interpretation, the equilibrium allocation of entitlements will be efficient if entitlements are clearly defined and contracts for their exchange are enforceable. In the example, the conditions of the 'free exchange' interpretation are apparently met when the farmers have the right to enjoin the nuisance, or when the railroad has the right to emit sparks with impunity. Thus, according to the free exchange interpretation of the Coase Theorem, it does not matter from an efficiency perspective whether farmers have the right to enjoin the railroad or the railroad has the right to pollute with impunity.

The conclusion about efficiency is different under the 'transaction cost' interpretation. If there are many farmers, the cost of negotiating and enforcing an agreement among them would be high, especially since individual farmers might hold out for a larger share of the surplus, so inefficiencies in the initial allocation of entitlements would probably persist in spite of opportunities for private agreements. On the other hand, if there are just a few farmers, the cost of negotiating and enforcing an agreement between them and the railroad would be low, so the theorem predicts that the equilibrium allocation of entitlements would be efficient.

Turning to the third version, according to the 'perfect competition' interpretation, the equilibrium allocation of entitlements will be efficient if the conditions of perfect competition are satisfied in the market for legal entitlements. In the example of the railroad and the farmers, there is only one railroad, so the market is characterized by monopoly rather than perfect competition. Furthermore, there may be other types of failure in the conditions of perfect competition. For example, farmers may have more information than the railroad about the harm caused by sparks, whereas the railroad may have more information than the farmers about the technology for reducing spark emissions. In view of these facts, the exchange of legal entitlements between the farmers and the railroad would depart far from the conditions of perfect competition, so the market might fail to cure inefficiencies in the initial allocation of legal entitlements.

Of course, the initial allocation of rights always matters from the perspective of income distribution. To illustrate, if efficiency requires the railroad to be free from injunction, granting the farmers the right to injunctive relief will motivate the railroad to try to buy this right. The purchase is a cost to the railroad and income to the farmers. Conversely, granting impunity to the railroad will save it the cost of purchasing the right and deprive farmers of the income from selling it. Like scarce resources, scarce legal rights are valuable.

IS THE COASE THEOREM TRUE OR FALSE? In economics, a 'proof' is a derivation from generally accepted behavioural assumptions. As I will show, attempts to formulate the Coase Theorem in any of its three interpretations encounter obstacles, which suggests that it is probably false or a mere tautology.

The weakest form of the theorem asserts that legal entitlements will be allocated efficiently under perfect competition. When Arrow (1969) examined externalities similar to those discussed by Coase, he showed that the efficiency conditions can be interpreted as the equilibrium conditions in a competitive market for the exchange of externality rights. But, as indicated by Arrow and others (Starrett, 1972), this formal demonstration has little practical value because externalities by their nature have characteristics which prevent the formation of competitive markets.

To illustrate, suppose that pollution is forbidden except by holders of resaleable pollution coupons issued by the government. Each pollutee who holds a coupon thereby prevents pollution from occurring, whereas each polluter who acquires a coupon uses it to increase the amount of pollution. Obviously, the social benefits of an individual pollutee retaining a coupon exceed his private benefits, so pollutees will sell too many of them. Equivalently, the social cost of a polluter acquiring a coupon exceeds his private cost, so polluters will acquire too many of them. This divergence between private and social costs is itself an externality. So the attempt to eliminate externalities by setting up a market for pollution coupons just gives rise to a new type of externality (for details, see Cooter, 1982). In reality, there are no perfectly competitive markets for externalities of the type discussed by Coase, and it seems impossible for them to arise spontaneously by private agreement. There might be some way for the government to create a pseudo-market (e.g. Groves, 1976), but none has been implemented.

Turning from the perfectly competitive market interpretation to the transaction cost interpretation of the Coase Theorem, observe that a private solution is likely to be efficient in cases affecting only a few parties, as, say, when contiguous land owners negotiate concerning a nuisance caused by one of them. If only a few parties are involved, the prices of entitlements will be negotiated instead of the parties acting as price-takers, which violates an assumption of perfect competitition, but such negotiations often succeed anyway. According to the transaction cost interpretation of the Coase Theorem, externality problems affecting small numbers of people should have efficient solutions.

Although accurate as a rule of thumb, the transaction cost interpretation is not strictly true. It rests upon the proposition that bargaining reaches an efficient conclusion when the cost of negotiating and enforcing agreements is nil (Regan, 1972). In reality, bargaining among small numbers of people sometimes breaks down – unions strike, hijackers kill hostages, realtors lose sales because of disagreements over the price, disputes go to trial, and so forth. The essential obstacle, which has nothing to do with the cost of communicating or enforcing agreements, is the strategic character of bargaining. By definition, a bargaining situation has the characteristic that a surplus can be achieved by agreement, but there is no settled way for dividing it up among the beneficiaries. A self-interested negotiator will press his claim to a share of the surplus as far as he dares without destroying the basis for cooperation. In economic jargon, the rational negotiator demands an additional dollar so long as the resulting increase in the probability of noncooperation creates an expected loss of less than a dollar. When negotiators underestimate an opponent's resolve, they press too hard and the negotiations fail to reach an agreement. Thus bargaining situations are inherently unstable.

Seen in this light, the transaction cost interpretation of the Coase Theorem errs in the direction of optimism by assuming that cooperation will always occur when bargaining is costless. The polar opposite viewpoint, which has been called the 'Hobbes Theorem' (Cooter, 1982), errs in the direction of pessimism by assuming that the problem of dividing the surplus can only be solved by coercive forces, not by cooperation. Reality lies in between the poles of optimism and pessimism, because strategic behaviour causes bargaining to fail in some cases, but not in every case.

The challenge to theory and empirical research raised by this interpretation of the Coase Theorem is to predict when legal entitlements will be allocated efficiently by private agreements. To advance this debate, broad labels such as 'transaction costs' and 'free exchange' must yield to substantive, detailed descriptions of the conditions under which private bargaining about legal entitlements succeeds. Fortunately, a more satisfactory bargaining theory has begun to emerge in recent years which adheres more closely to reality. According to this account, bargaining will break down for strategic reasons in a percentage of cases, but in equilibrium no-one is surprised by the frequency with which breakdowns occur. (The key concept is the Bayesian Nash equilibrium; see Harsanyi, 1968, and Cooter and Marks, 1982.)

In economics, an 'empirical test' is a comparison between a prediction and facts. Recently, attempts have been made to test the Coase Theorem, for example, by determining the conditions under which bargaining in small groups reaches an efficient conclusion (Spitzer, 1982). The new developments in game theory, combined with the associated empirical research, hold the promise of finally establishing a scientific account of the conditions under which inefficient allocations of legal entitlements will be cured by private agreements.

WHAT IS THE SIGNIFICANCE OF THE COASE THEOREM? Pigou used economics to defend the common law principle that a party who causes a nuisance should be enjoined or required to pay damages. According to Pigou, the common law rules tend to promote economic efficiency by internalizing social costs. In some cases, he found gaps in the common law which require supplementary legislation, such as imposing a tax upon polluters equal to the social cost of pollution.

Coase's paper was framed as an attack upon Pigou's analysis of the law of nuisance. Coase disagreed with the conclusion that government action, through nuisance law or taxation, is typically required to achieve efficiency. The Coase Theorem suggests that the externalities represented by nuisances will sometimes, or perhaps usually, be self-correcting. I have argued that the forms of market failure are too diverse to be subsumed under a reasonably circumspect concept of transaction costs, and, consequently, the transaction cost interpretation of the Coase Theorem should be regarded as false or as a tautology whose truth is achieved by inflating the definition of transaction costs. Although the obstacles to spontaneous, private solutions of externalities are broader than suggested by the Coase Theorem, the role of government in lubricating private agreements, rather than issuing commands, is much favoured in the contemporary economic understanding of regulation.

In the event that government action is required to correct a nuisance, Coase denied Pigou's claim that the common law concept of causality is a useful guide to assigning responsibility. In Coase's view, the fact that someone 'causes' a nuisance, as judged by common law principles, does not imply that holding him liable or enjoining him is efficient. For Coase, the question of efficiency is to be decided by a balancing of cost and benefits in which the role of causality is not decisive. Coase's suggestion that causality should have little bearing upon legal responsibility contradicts countless court decisions and appears to have had little impact upon the practice or theory of law.

Whatever the merits of his arguments, Coase offered a challenge to widely accepted views in public finance. Before his article appeared, not much attention was paid to the possibility that externalities could be cured by private bargains. Thus Coase's claim went to the heart of a major debate in economics. Furthermore, the publication of Coase's article can be regarded as a breakthrough for the subject which has acquired the name of 'law and economics'. Before publication of Coase's article, economic *analysis* (as opposed to economic thought) had received little application to the common law, which is at the core of legal theory and method as taught in law schools. By analysing cases from property law in a lawyerly style, yet drawing upon microeconomics to guide the analysis, Coase demonstrated the fruitfulness of the economic analysis of the common law. He inspired a generation of scholars who pioneered the economic analysis of law, although he did not use the mathematical tools which have come to characterize the subject twenty years later.

BIBLIOGRAPHY

Arrow, K. 1969. The organization of economic activity: issues pertinent to the choice of market versus non-market allocation. In *The Analysis and Evaluation of Public Expenditure: the PPB System*. US Congress, Joint Economic Committee, Washington, DC: GPO. Reprinted in *Public Expenditure and Policy Analysis*, ed. R. Haveman and J. Margolis, Chicago: Rand McNally, 1977.

Coase, R. 1960. The problem of social cost. *Journal of Law and Economics* 3(1), October, 1–44.

Cooter, R. 1980. How the law circumvents Starrett's nonconvexity. *Journal of Economic Theory* 22(3), June, 145–9.

Cooter, R. 1982. The cost of Coase. *Journal of Legal Studies* 11(1), January, 1–34.

Cooter, R. and Marks, S. 1982. Bargaining in the shadow of the law; a testable model of strategic behavior. *Journal of Legal Studies* 11(2), 225–52.

Groves, T. 1976. Information, incentives, and the internalization of production externalities. In *Theory and Measurement of Economic Externalities*, ed. Steven A.Y. Lin. London and New York: Academic Press.

Harsanyi, J.C. 1967–8. Games with incomplete information played by 'Bayesian' players, I–III. *Management Science*, Part I, 14(3), November 1967, 159–82; Part II, 14(5), January 1968, 320–34; Part III, 14(7), March 1968, 486–502.

Pigou, A.C. 1920. *The Economics of Welfare*. London: Macmillan. 4th edn, 1932; New York: St Martin's Press, 1952.

Regan, D. 1972. The problem of social cost revisited. *Journal of Law and Economics* 15(2), October, 427–37.

Schultze, C. 1977. *The Public Use of Private Interest*. Washington, DC: Brookings.

Spitzer, M. 1982. The Coase Theorem: some experimental tests. *Journal of Law and Economics* 25(1), 73–98.

Starrett, D. 1972. Fundamental non-convexities in the theory of externalities. *Journal of Economic Theory* 4(2), April, 180–99.

Cobweb Theorem

B. PETER PASHIGIAN

The persistent fluctuations of prices in selected agricultural markets have attracted the attention of economists from time to time, and the theory of the cobweb was developed to explain them. The theory is applicable to those markets where production takes time, where the quantity produced depends on the price anticipated at the time of sale and where supply at time of sale determines the actual market price.

One strand of the cobweb literature (the term was coined by Kaldor, 1934) concentrates on how expectations are formed and the effect of the price expectations mechanism on the stability of equilibrium. Cobweb theory was first developed under static price expectations where the predicted price equalled actual price in the last period. The cobweb theorem proved that the market price would (not) converge to (long-run) equilibrium price if the absolute value of the price elasticity of demand was greater (smaller) than the price elasticity of supply. This stability condition was modified later as more sophisticated expectations models were adopted. Early articles by Tinbergen, Ricci and Schultz appeared in German in 1930 (see Waugh, 1964, for a review of this literature). Ezekiel's important article (1938) spells out in greater detail the conditions for convergence, divergence or perpetual oscillation and shows how cycles of different lengths could be generated under static expectations.

Why the theory was developed in the 1930s and not earlier is a bit of mystery, for recurring price cycles for some agricultural products had been reported by agricultural economists for some time. Economists may have been attracted to the cobweb theory in the 1930s because of the events of the Depression. A theory that explained both oscillation and long departures from stationary equilibrium was more attractive after the events of the Depression. The fact that Ezekiel's paper was reprinted in the 1944 American Economic Association volume on business cycles lends credence to this view.

The impression left by Ezekiel and subsequent contributors is that the cobweb theory is a valuable tool for explaining price cycles. Ezekiel was aware of the simplicity of static expectations and not unmindful of the importance of shocks on the demand and the supply sides of the market in causing aberrant price fluctuations (e.g. weather and the randomness of yields). Even so, agricultural economists, who were presumably more familiar with price fluctuations in agricultural markets have been more prone to accept the theory, while theorists have given the theory more of a mixed reception.

The price expectations mechanism has undergone many refinements over the years. In 1958 Nerlove proposed the use of adaptive expectations. This suggestion is motivated by the findings of econometric studies which showed the price elasticity of demand to be less than the price elasticity of supply for many agricultural goods. Under these conditions the static expectations version of the cobweb model predicts a price cycle of increasing amplitude. However, the observed price cycles in agricultural markets showed no sign of being explosive. Nerlove attempted to reconcile theory with evidence and to show that convergence is possible under a broader set of conditions provided expectations are adaptive. During the 1930s the attractiveness of the cobweb model seemed to be in its ability to explain persistent or even explosive price cycles. By the late 1950s these were no longer attractive features, and Nerlove felt compelled to offer an explanation of why price cycles of increasing amplitude are not observed even when demand elasticities are smaller than supply elasticities. Waugh (1964) took a different tack and attempted to reconcile the theory with the evidence of stable price cycles by suggesting that the price elasticity of supply becomes smaller (larger) than the price elasticity of demand at prices well above (below) the long-run equilibrium price. Under this assumption, a stable price cycle will eventually be reached.

The length of the cobweb price cycle is determined by the length of the production process. If it takes one year to bring a fattened hog to the market, then the complete price cycle should take two years. At first, little attention and superficial explanations were given to explain why the predicted length is often shorter than the actual length of the price cycle. It was left to the critics to point out these discrepancies.

The critics are responsible for the other strand of the literature. Their contributions appeared early but were not very influential at first although their criticisms were ultimately given more weight. The critics questioned the rationality of using an arbitrary expectations mechanism by otherwise profit-maximizing agents, and pointed out that the theory implies that producers would expect to lose wealth if they entered and remained in an industry with a cobweb price cycle. In a perceptive article on the pig cycle in England, Coase and Fowler (1935) questioned the realism of static expectations. They showed that the price of a bacon (mature) pig less the cost of feeding for the next five months and less the cost of a feeder (young) pig, which would be stable in a competitive market if farmers had static expectations, fluctuated over time. Hence the empirical evidence contradicted the assumption of static expectations. They presented evidence that pig breeders reacted quickly to a change in expected profits, and this implied that the pig price cycle should be only two years instead of the observed four-year period. The fluctuations in the profits per pig were attributed to the difficulty of predicting both demand and foreign imports. The Coase–Fowler paper advanced, if only in faint outline, the essence of the rational expectations hypothesis which was to blossom some 35 years later. They hinted that anticipated prices would not be formed in a mechanistic way because profits would be higher the more accurate the forecasts were. Prediction errors were due to the difficulty of predicting shifts in demand and in foreign supply.

Buchanan's paper (1939) criticized the cobweb model because it implied that producers suffer aggregate losses over the price cycle when output is determined by the long-run supply curve. He pointed out that the theory was based on the dubious assumption of a continued supply of entrepreneurs standing ready to dissipate their capital. The critics were also disturbed by the ambiguity of whether the supply curve is of the short- or long-run variety, and the failure to clarify how the adjustment from the short-run to the long-run supply curve is made. These early criticisms and ambiguities aside, references to the cobweb theory continued to appear in textbooks.

Nerlove's paper (1958) briefly rekindled the controversy. His purpose was to resurrect the theory and show that it could explain price behaviour if adaptive expectations were employed. Mills (1961) criticized the use of adaptive and other autoregressive expectations mechanisms in the deterministic model because they implied a simple pattern of forecast errors that producers could detect, incorporate into their forecasts and thereby improve the accuracy of their price forecasts. While Nerlove's suggestion did rectify one limitation of the cobweb theory, it did not address the critical issue of why producers relied on any particular forecasting mechanism. Muth (1961) developed the implications of rational expectations for cobweb theory in his now famous paper. He postulated that expectations were the predictions of the economic structure of the market and incorporated all available information. Under certain conditions the predicted price equals the conditional expectation of price, given currently available information. Adaptive expectations can be rational only under special conditions, and the coefficient of adaptation is determined by the values of the slopes of the demand and supply curves.

The rational expectations formulation has powerful implications for cobweb theory. If the price forecasts incorporate all available information and are on average correct, then forecast errors will not be serially correlated and the pattern of past forecast errors cannot be used to improve the accuracy of the forecasts. Moreover, what is then left of the supposed ability of the cobweb theory to explain the cyclical behaviour of prices? Price fluctuations would have to be explained either by the cyclical pattern of exogenous variables or by the summation of random shocks (Slutsky, 1937). Muth's paper represents a frontal attack on the traditional cobweb model. He notes that the traditional model tends to predict a shorter price cycle than is observed and indicates that the rational expectations version predicts a longer price cycle.

Interest in the cobweb model has ebbed in recent years and few articles on it have appeared in the major journals. Economists have found it more rewarding to apply the rational expectations hypothesis to areas like monetary or business-cycle theory than to the study of particular markets, even though the analysis of markets with inventories raises issues that are just as difficult and subtle. The question of whether the cobweb does or does not explain price cycles has not really been resolved. Freeman (1971) has suggested that the traditional cobweb model explains cycles in the markets for lawyers, physicists and engineers. Tests of the rational expectations hypothesis have been suggested by Pashigian (1970) when expectations data are available and by Hoffman and Schmidt (1981) when expectations data are unavailable. So the methodology exists for distinguishing between the competing hypotheses. Few econometric tests have been made of the rational expectations hypothesis in markets where the assumptions of the cobweb model apply. The fundamental question of whether observed price cycles are better explained by systematic errors in price forecasts or by the cumulative impact of unpredictable shocks, has not as yet been definitively addressed.

BIBLIOGRAPHY

Buchanan, N. 1939. A reconsideration of the cobweb theorem. *Journal of Political Economy* 47, February, 67–81.

Coase, R.H. and Fowler, R.F. 1935. Bacon production and the pig-cycle in Great Britain. *Economica* 2, May, 142–67.

Ezekiel, M. 1938. The cobweb theorem. *Quarterly Journal of Economics* 52, February, 255–80.

Freeman, R.B. 1971. *The Market for College-Trained Manpower.* Cambridge, Mass.: Harvard University Press.

Hoffman, D.L. and Schmidt, P. 1981. Testing the restrictions implied by the rational expectations hypothesis. *Journal of Econometrics* 15(2), February, 265–87.

Kaldor, N. 1934. A classificatory note on the determinateness of equilibrium. *Review of Economic Studies* 1, February, 122–36.

Mills, E.S. 1961. The use of adaptive expectations in stability analysis: comment. *Quarterly Journal of Economics* 75, May, 330–35.

Muth, J.F. 1961. Rational expectations and the theory of price movements. *Econometrica* 29, July, 315–35.

Nerlove, M. 1958. Adaptive expectations and cobweb phenomena. *Quarterly Journal of Economics* 72, May, 227–40.

Pashigian, B.P. 1970. Rational expectations and the cobweb theory. *Journal of Political Economy* 78(2), March–April, 338–52.

Slutsky, E.S. 1937. The summation of random causes as the source of cyclical processes. *Econometrica* 5, April, 105–46.

Waugh, F.V. 1964. Cobweb models. *Journal of Farm Economics* 46, November, 732–50.

Codetermination and Profit-sharing

D.M. NUTI

The contract regulating labour employment by capitalist firms usually embodies three basic elements: a fixed money wage rate per unit of time, the subjection of workers to the employer's authority in the workplace and the short-term nature of the hiring commitment. Explicit or implicit departures from this standard can be observed; they are the result of individual or collective negotiations in the labour market, which balance out their advantages and disadvantages for each party, either directly or through accompanying changes in other parameters of the labour contract. Government legislation and economic policy set limits or fix actual values for some of these parameters and stipulations; within these bounds the market determines the rest.

Long tenure, i.e. the employee's option on continued employment, like all options, has a value (for the employee) and a cost (for the employer), which is matched by correspondingly lower pay than that associated with shorter-term contracts. The partial and delayed indexation of money wages to a consumer price index for the period between successive rounds of wage negotiations favours employees when inflation decelerates and employers when it accelerates. Piece-rates, i.e. wages related to *individual* performance, give employees a short-term reward (penalty) for supply of effort higher (lower) than that which otherwise could be contractually fixed, as well as automatic participation in productivity gains due to learning by doing, subject to a ratchet effect on the determination of subsequent rates; employers save on the costs of recruitment, supervision, and contractual enforcement, lose short-term productivity gains but can use more fully their contractual power in exacting effort and speeding up progress when rates are reviewed. Government policy influences directly or indirectly market choice, in the pursuit of policy targets such as distributive fairness, employment, price stability, efficiency and growth.

The same combination of private interest and government policy determines the degree of workers' participation in decision-making processes (codetermination) and in the performance (profit-sharing) of enterprises (for a bibliographical survey, see Bartlett and Uvalic, 1985).

CODETERMINATION. Employee participation in enterprise decision-making in cooperatives amounts to full entrepreneurship through participation in assemblies, the election of representative organs and involvement in the appointment of managers. In other enterprises it takes the form of access to information and right to consultation, participation in decisions on conditions and organization of work and on internal social questions, through a workers' council or similar organ, right up to minority (or even parity) participation and vote on the board of directors of a joint-stock company (as in German *Mitbestimmung*; see Nutzinger, 1983) with a possibility of influencing decisions about employment, the level and structure of investment and other crucial factors, were the other board members to be sufficiently divided.

The effects of codetermination are three-fold:

(i) The reduction in labour disutility obtainable when workers have a say in the division of labour and work organization, since enterprises may neglect workers' preferences about the specific uses to which their labour is put or at any rate respond to the needs of a hypothetical average worker: if the number of enterprises is not large enough, workers' control is necessary to reduce disutility and alienation. The effect of workers' control on productivity has an indeterminate sign (Pagano, 1984).

(ii) The reduction of the number and intensity of conflicts in the workplace in general and, in particular, the more likely acceptance by workers of unpopular decisions by management, when workers receive detailed and credible information and participate in decision-making, identifying themselves partly with the enterprise and above all lengthening their time horizon in view of continued participation in decision-making (Aoki, 1984; Cable, 1984; Fitzroy and Mueller, 1984). Of course conflicts within the firm are made more tractable by the *introduction* of codetermination but *afterwards* are bound to reappear over time (Furobotn, 1985); also there remains a basic conflict between employed and unemployed workers which may even be exacerbated by the employment protection policies conceivably encouraged by those already employed in their exercise of codetermination.

(iii) The greater correspondence between workers' powers and responsibilities, codetermination being the counterpart of workers' exposure to enterprise risks. The very fact that workers, unlike capitalists, cannot diversify between different enterprises when selling their services exposes them to an employment and income risk which induces them to make a claim to control, a claim which up to a point the employer may prefer to accept instead of granting higher wages or longer tenure.

PROFIT-SHARING. In pre-capitalist systems workers' participation in the results of their enterprise took the forms – now little used – of sharecropping in agriculture and of sliding scales (indexing wage rates to the price of the product), for instance, in English coal mines. In modern capitalism such participation – for which 'profit-sharing' is a shorthand label – takes the form of cooperatives' net revenue-sharing, production prizes based on group or overall performance, participation in gross/net revenue/profit, share options, participation in investment funds and pay increases graded according to productivity growth.

The effects of an element of profit-sharing in labour earnings are three-fold:

(i) An expected increase in labour productivity. This is not due to workers gaining from the product of *individual* extra-effort (as in the case of piece-rates) since each of n workers employed will only get at most $1/n$ of the product of his own extra-effort (Samuelson, 1977) and on the contrary may *reduce* effort if he can, being exposed to at most only $1/n$ of the output loss from his own lower effort. The productivity gain can be expected from workers, costlessly to themselves, gaining from intelligent and effective use of any given individual level of effort, from cooperating with other workers and management and from monitoring and supervising each other's effort, efficiency and cooperation (Reich and Devine, 1981; Fitzroy and Kraft, 1985).

(ii) Cyclical flexibility of labour earnings and therefore greater stability of profit levels and rates. Employment will not be stabilized during the cycle by labour earnings flexibility obtained through profit-sharing because the marginal cost of labour to firms – i.e. the fixed component of pay – does not vary automatically. Workers, who are normally risk-averse, will prefer a fixed sum of money to a profit-sharing formula of equivalent amount, while employers, who are normally risk-lovers, may or may not prefer greater stability of profit rates (according to their actual attitude to risk and the alternative cost of reducing risk through diversification) to the point of granting higher average earnings on a profit-sharing formula than a fixed wage to mutual advantage. Therefore profit-sharing is favoured primarily in risky ventures; otherwise on this ground alone profit-sharing would be favoured by firms only in a recession (when workers would only accept it as an alternative to a permanent wage cut) and by workers only during a boom (when firms would only accept it as an alternative to a permanent wage increase).

(iii) Higher level of labour employment, for a given level of labour earnings with respect to a fixed wage regime, due to the lower marginal cost of labour to profit-sharing firms. Vanek (1965) finds that higher employment will be associated with higher aggregate income, lower prices (because of higher output), higher export volume and domestic import substitution (with undetermined effects on the balance of payments depending on price and income elasticities), lower after-tax and after-labour-share profits and higher labour-share in national income.

Rediscovering Vanek's macroeconomic benefits from profit-sharing (though not its impact on net profits and relative income shares), Weitzman (1983, 1984) claims that these benefits are neglected by individual firms, as in other instances of 'public goods', 'externalities' and 'market failures', therefore necessitating public policy measures. However, there is no reason why a firm should object to granting a given increase in earnings under the guise of a profit-share instead of an equivalent fixed amount unless that represents forced insurance against profit variability, and why workers – at least at the level of nation-wide collective bargaining – should not take into account the potential employment and price stability benefits of this formula and offset them against the greater variability of their earnings in between negotiations, due to both cyclical factors and random factors affecting their firm's performance.

Contrary to Weitzman's belief, in fact, profit-sharing is not absolutely superior to wage contracts. For workers, profit-sharing transforms the probability distribution of uncertain employment at a fixed and certain income into a probability distribution of employment with a higher mean (because of lower marginal cost of labour) but no less variable over the cycle, at a more variable income (both over the cycle and for other factors affecting dispersion of enterprise performance) and at a higher (real) mean. For firms it transforms a more into a less variable probability distribution of money profit rates around the same mean (or a lower mean if workers are protected from actual losses; the effect on real profit rates depending on accounting conventions and choice of *numéraire*). In the pursuit of greater employment and price stability of course a government may grant tax relief to shared profits, just as effectively and with just as much reason as it may subsidize the marginal cost of labour to firms under a wage regime. Otherwise there is no reason why profit-sharing should be forced upon unwilling workers and firms by well-meaning reformers, beyond the extent they are prepared to consider in their market transactions. These propositions are developed further below (see also Nuti, 1985 and 1986).

INTERDEPENDENCE BETWEEN CODETERMINATION AND PROFIT-SHARING. The respective effects of codetermination and of profit-sharing are not independent. The productivity increase expected from profit-sharing can be raised by workers having collective discretion over the organization of labour; or the productivity fall which might derive from workers' control over labour organization might be tempered by profit-sharing. Greater variability of earnings – during the cycle and across firms – strengthens under profit-sharing the case for codetermination already present in workers' exposure to employment risk in the wage régime. The income premium required by risk-averse workers to replace some of their fixed wage with a variable profit-share can be reduced by their involvement in the decisions which expose them to income variability in the first place. The reduction in conflict frequency and intensity expected from codetermination is enhanced by profit-sharing because for each worker it partly internalizes the conflict between 'us' and 'them' otherwise manifested and enacted externally; in any case it is a requirement of any effective incentive system that power and responsibility should not be separated.

The quantification of degrees of 'codetermination' and to a lesser extent of 'profit-sharing' raises conceptual and practical difficulties (though see Cable, 1984). By and large we can observe a certain correlation between the two: both codetermination and profit-sharing are zero in the pure capitalist enterprises and unity in cooperatives and other forms of partnerships of capital and labour; minor forms of codetermination (or conversely of profit-sharing) tend to go hand in hand with minor forms of profit-sharing (or of codetermination); a high degree of one without the other is virtually unknown.

The combination of 100 per cent codetermination (= self-determination) and 100 per cent profit-sharing (= net revenue-sharing) obtained in cooperative firms, according to conventional literature, is subject to economic stimuli of a somewhat 'perverse' kind. These are primarily: restrictive employment (= membership) policies; destabilizing and Pareto-inefficient reactions (or at best inelasticities) to price changes and technical progress; a low propensity towards self-financed investment (Ward, 1958; Vanek, 1970). In empirical studies of cooperative firms there is no incontrovertible evidence of these phenomena, which are probably partly offset by other economic (job security, growth-mindedness, etc.) and non-economic stimuli; but there is a presumption that – albeit in a weak form – the same tendencies and, in particular, employment restrictive policies might be associated with codetermination. We can also presume that workers' eagerness to press and ability to assert demands for codetermination, as in the case of other demands, increase as unemployment diminishes. Hence the employment-generating benefits of profit-sharing can be at least partly offset by the restrictive employment policies possibly associated with codetermination brought about by profit-sharing and by greater proximity to full employment. Recent empirical studies suggest modest but sizeable improvements in economic performance from codetermination and profit-sharing (Cable and Fitzroy, 1980; Estrin et al., 1984) when and where they occur but there may have been costs that remained unobserved and, in any case, the improvements cannot be generalized.

MARKETS AND POLICY. Degrees of codetermination and profit-sharing may well be regarded as desirable on 'political' (as opposed to 'purely technical') grounds such as equity and social peace. They may also be the best policy instruments in the pursuit of public objectives such as stability, employment and growth, in the sense of having the least cost in terms of public funds or offering the most attractive trade-offs between alternative targets. Otherwise, as Jensen and Meckling (1979, p. 474) argue for codetermination and one can also argue for profit-sharing, if it is truly beneficial to both stockholders and labour no laws would be needed to force firms to undertake reorganization. Yet renewed and insistent calls for public intervention in favour of *profit-sharing without codetermination* have been put forward by M.L. Weitzman in recent writings (1983, 1984, 1985a, 1985b, 1986). The proposal has been enthusiastically received in certain academic and political circles and hailed as a breakthrough in the specialist press.

Weitzman's novelty, the foundation for this renewed fascination with profit-sharing, is the rash assertion of two propositions. First, that long-run full employment equilibrium under profit-sharing is associated with permanent but non-inflationary excess demand for labour, which cushions off the economy from contractionary shocks and gives new dignity and status to labour. In adman's language we are told, for instance:

> A share system has the hard-boiled property of excess demand for labour, which turns into a tenacious natural enemy of stagnation and inflation. The share economy possesses a built-in, three-pronged assault on unemployment, stagnant output, and the tendency of prices to rise. This is a hard combination to beat (Weitzman, 1984, p. 144).

Second, that even in the short run the share economy can achieve and maintain full employment. For instance:

> The share system ... has a strong built-in mechanism that automatically stabilizes the economy at full employment, even before the long-run tendencies have had the chance to assert their dominance ... a share economy has the direct 'strong force' of positive excess demand for labour ... pulling it towards full employment ... the strong force of the share system will maintain full employment (Weitzman, 1984, p. 97).

Were these claims well founded an enlightened government possessing these truths would be justified in forcing profit-sharing on to a yet unconverted and disbelieving public, thus achieving full employment, price stability and growth at a stroke. Unfortunately miracles exist only for the uninformed and the faithful, but do not bear the weight of sober scrutiny. First, excess demand for labour at full employment cannot be sustained and can only be a temporary disequilibrium. Second, permanent excess demand for labour is inconsistent with lack of codetermination, and when this is introduced restrictive employment policies will alter the picture. Third, and most important, there is no guarantee that full employment can necessarily be achieved. Without these benefits the alleged 'public good' merits of the sharing contract disappear.

EXCESS DEMAND FOR LABOUR AT FULL EMPLOYMENT. Suppose that the share economy reaches a state of full employment. Weitzman (1983) maintains the presence and persistence of excess demand for labour in long-run equilibrium on the basis of the following argument:

$$\text{labour total pay} = \text{marginal revenue value of labour productivity at full employment} \quad (1)$$

because long-run equilibrium must be full-employment equilibrium and because of the underlying homomorphism of profit-sharing and wage contracts in long-run equilibrium. By definition of profit-sharing

$$\text{labour total pay} = \text{fixed pay} + \text{share of net profits} \quad (2)$$

where fixed pay is greater than or equal to zero, and the share of net profits is greater than zero. It follows from (1) and (2) that

$$\text{marginal revenue value of labour productivity at full employment} > \text{fixed pay} = \text{marginal cost of labour to firms} \quad (3)$$

67

i.e. firms will wish to employ more workers than are available. A permanent state of excess demand for labour will exist, which will protect full employment from contractionary shocks, as long as shocks do not reduce the marginal revenue value of labour productivity at full employment below the fixed element of pay, in which case the maintenance of over-full employment requires a reduction of the fixed element without cutting earnings as much as necessary in the wage regime.

There are three grounds for refuting this syllogism. First, firms should be well aware that, whatever their pay formula, they can only attract workers by offering the going rate for labour total pay and should regard this, and not the fixed element of pay, as marginal cost of labour. If firms behave as they should, excess demand for labour disappears.

Second, if firms regard the fixed element of pay as the marginal cost of labour they should find its being lower than the marginal revenue value of labour productivity disquieting enough to experiment with alternative combinations of pay parameters without raising total pay above labour productivity. Risk-averse workers preferring fixed pay to potentially variable earnings of identical mean, risk-neutral or risk-loving employers will reduce their labour cost by raising the fixed element of pay at the expense of workers' profit share; even without taking into account attitude to risk it is plausible to expect managers to experiment with alternative pay parameters and not to rest until they have equalized their marginal cost and marginal value of labour, i.e.

$$\text{marginal revenue value of labour productivity at full employment} = \text{fixed pay} \tag{3'}$$

which can only be reconciled with the definition (2) of a profit-sharing contract if the workers' share of net profit is zero: with the sharing component of earnings the 'share economy' also vanishes and reverts to the fixed wage economy without any excess demand for labour.

Third, workers perceiving excess demand for labour are likely to reduce their supply of effort and/or increase turnover – as they have done in the only known instances of permanent excess demand for labour, i.e. Soviet-type economies (see Lane, 1985) – if not right down to the point where their marginal product equals fixed pay at least as close to that level as they are allowed to get by monitoring and supervising arrangements. This is another mechanism which can reduce and eliminate excess demand for labour if it occurred.

CODETERMINATION AND EMPLOYMENT. The lack of codetermination is an explicit precondition of Weitzman's claims (though not of Vanek's, who does not claim full and over-full employment of labour and does not need this restriction). (In the earlier version of his analysis Weitzman takes a sanguine view of the possibility of keeping codetermination in check: '... the bargaining power of labor unions is not a natural right ...' (1984a, p. 109); '... the decisions on output, employment and pricing are essentially made by capitalists' in his model (p. 132); 'I can see no *compelling* reason why a capitalist firm should be more prone to allow increased worker participation in company decision making under one contract form than under another' (p. 133, emphasis added). His latest version is more open-minded: workers' participation in decision-making becomes not only possible but desirable as 'a question of justice and practical politics' as long as it excludes *employment* decisions (1986). It is extremely hard to imagine *any* major decision, in which workers might have a voice, that would *not* directly or indirectly also affect employment. Either this limitation or workers' participation would have to give way.) We know that it is possible to exclude workers from codetermination in the presence of persistent unemployment; such exclusion might be difficult at full employment, and it would certainly be very difficult with excess demand for labour, but the *persistent state* of excess demand for labour postulated by Weitzman should make the exclusion of codetermination, whether or not employment questions are directly involved, impossible without an authoritarian or military regime. This is not a moral, or legal, or legalistic proposition; it is a question of 'practical politics'.

Once workers have a say on output, employment and pricing and related questions (investment, innovation, etc.) they will try and resist the very possibility of dilution of their own shares just as shareholders usually resist the dilution of share capital; for better or worse they are likely to adopt, or are tempted to adopt, other things being equal, restrictive employment policies in the possibly misguided and self-defeating purpose of raising or maintaining individual earnings. This is not a case *against* profit-sharing, but an argument for not expecting that over-full employment, if achievable, can necessarily be sustained, i.e. an argument against the plausibility of Weitzman's model (see Nuti, 1985).

PROFIT-SHARING AND FULL EMPLOYMENT. The foundation of Weitzman's claims on behalf of profit-sharing is the assertion that, even in the short run, the share economy 'delivers' full employment of labour. ('Resources are always fully utilised in a share system' (Weitzman, 1985b, p. 949); real world frictions, inertias and imperfections are mentioned only to be exorcised, and to reassert the full employment claim at least as a 'natural tendency' (p. 949, p. 952) of the share economy which, we are told, 'delivers full employment' (1986); see also Weitzman, 1984, p. 97.)

For a share economy to 'deliver' full employment three necessary conditions must be satisfied simultaneously:

(i) the physical marginal productivity of labour at full employment must be positive;

(ii) the marginal revenue obtained by firms from that physical marginal product of labour must also be positive;

(iii) the fixed element of pay in share contracts must be flexible enough to fall down to the level of the marginal revenue product of labour at full employment, positive as it may be.

The first condition rules out the possibility of *classical* unemployment, i.e. due to lack of equipment, land or other resources in the quantities necessary to employ all workers efficiently. Yet, after over a decade of deep and protracted recession, deindustrialization and decapitalization, even advanced industrialized countries such as Britain or France today cannot be expected to be able to satisfy this condition as a matter of course, not to speak of Italy, or, say, Spain, or of less developed countries. In his formal model Weitzman (1985b) postulates constant physical productivity of labour; this is a plausible assumption *up to near-full capacity* but Weitzman gives no reason why the capacity should be constrained by labour instead of other resources.

The second condition rules out the possibility of *Keynesian* unemployment, i.e. aggregate demand constraints making the marginal product of labour valueless before full employment is reached. Even if the first condition was satisfied, imperfect competition – which in all of Weitzman's work provides the environment in which the share contract is to operate – provides an excellent reason why firms might not give to additional physical products a positive value. Weitzman can assert that '... a "pure" sharing system not having any base wage would possess an infinite demand for labor' (1985b, p. 944), which implies positive marginal revenue for any level of output, because of the very special assumption that the elasticity of demand is *greater than unity* (p. 938), which makes demand curves absurdly and indefinitely elastic even for imperfectly competitive firms. The proposition cannot have any claim to general validity.

Even if demand for labour *were* to be infinite in the pure share economy, i.e. with a zero fixed element of pay, it would not necessarily be infinite, or even large enough to reach full employment, for a positive fixed element of pay. Weitzman neglects the determination of the relative weight of the fixed and variable components of the share contract but recognizes the impossibility of total dependence of pay on profit; yet he takes for granted, for no good reason, that the fixed element of pay can be compressed down to whatever is the full employment marginal revenue product of labour, which we do not even know for sure is positive.

It is a non-controversial feature of the sharing contract, known from Vanek (1965), that the replacement of part of the wage by a profit-share of identical average cost to firms will lead to greater employment, higher output and lower prices – in the absence of large-enough adverse feedback on investment (which Weitzman recognizes as a possible short-run effect of the introduction of sharing) and in the absence of large-enough feedbacks of accompanying codetermination on firms' employment policy. But there is a world of difference between higher employment and full employment and another world of difference between full employment and persistent over-full employment; no serious work can afford to switch indifferently and cavalierly from one to the other.

SHARE CONTRACTS AND PUBLIC GOOD. If the share economy could really guarantee, as general and necessary consequences of its establishment, the achievement and stability of full employment without adverse drawbacks there would be a case for public policy treating the share contract as 'public good' to be pressed on an unenlightened public still largely unaware of potential benefits, as in the case of safe vaccination against infectious disease. The case for the share economy would not be much greater than that for enforced wage flexibility, which would also guarantee full employment and stability under the same circumstances. A downward flexible wage would not deliver excess demand for labour but this is a questionable achievement and would not be necessary to absorb contractionary shocks if wages were flexible; downward flexible wages would also require a greater fall of money earnings to achieve full employment in the short run and may be more likely to bring about adverse effects on aggregate demand; otherwise there is little to choose between the two, except for the lower degree of public resistance that can be expected for share contracts with respect to wage cuts.

In fact if the share contract could really deliver and maintain full employment, while a wage economy could not, the greater variability of workers' earnings associated with profit-sharing over the cycle would disappear and, between firms, could be eliminated by labour freely redeploying itself at will across labour-hungry firms; the variability of employment would also disappear; workers would have *de facto* free access to a job in any firm of their choice, as in forgotten utopias (Hertzka, 1980; Chilosi, 1986). Thus it could be said that '... a move towards profit sharing represents an unambiguous improvement for the working class' (Weitzman, 1985b, p. 954). But we have seen that profit-sharing cannot guarantee full (let alone over-full) employment. Without full employment, the higher variability of earnings associated with profit-sharing remains and it may or may not be compensated by the higher mean value of employment probability and perhaps real earnings. Outside over-full employment, in fact, the share economy is just as vulnerable to contractionary shocks as the wage economy, because in spite of flexibility of labour earnings in the share regime, the marginal cost of labour to firms (which is the fixed component of workers' pay) remains constant just as does the wage. Thus the higher stability of employment to be found in Japan simply cannot be the result of profit-sharing, as Weitzman firmly believes, seeing that Japan has never known a state of over-full employment; higher employment stability would require workers' shares in GNP instead of their enterprise's profits.

The fact that the adoption of a share contract, without the guarantee of stable full employment, has a cost for workers, eliminates the necessity, but not the possibility, of the share contract having 'public good' features. A vaccine may be somewhat unsafe, its degree of unsafety acceptable to all if vaccination is universal and all benefit from reduced exposure to infection, yet individuals benefit from free-riding strategies and the enforcement of universal vaccination as 'public good' can still be beneficial to all. If labour contracts were negotiated exclusively at the level of individuals or firms the external beneficial effects of the share contract might be lost from sight; but these external benefits – unlike the case of genuine 'public goods' – are completely internalized in nationwide negotiations between associations of employers and employees. Admittedly, the benefits, such as they are, of profit-sharing may be still unknown to the public at large and deserve wider publicity. But it is counterproductive to foist a good medicine on a sceptical public by claiming that it can guarantee longevity or

immortality. At the first signs that such excessive claims are unfounded it may
be thrown away despite its real lesser benefits.

BIBLIOGRAPHY

Aoki, M. 1984. *The Co-operative Game Theory of the Firm.* Oxford: Oxford University Press.

Bartlett, W. and Uvalic, M. 1985. Bibliography on labour-managed firms and employee participation. European University Institute Working Paper, No. 85/198, Florence.

Cable, J.R. 1984. Employee participation and firm performance: a prisoners' dilemma framework. European University Institute Working Paper, No. 84/126, Florence.

Cable, J.R. and Fitzroy, F.R. 1980. Productive efficiency, incentives and employee participation: some preliminary results for West Germany. *Kyklos* 33(2), 100–121.

Chilosi, A. 1986. The right to employment principle and self-managed market socialism: a historical account and an analytical appraisal of some old ideas. European University Institute Working Paper, No. 86/214, Florence.

Estrin, S., Jones, D.C. and Svejnar, J. 1984. The varying nature, importance and productivity effects of worker participation: evidence for contemporary producer cooperatives in industrialised Western societies. CIRIEC Working Paper, No. 84/04, University of Liège.

Fitzroy, F.R. and Kraft, K. 1985. Profitability and profit-sharing. *Discussion Papers of the International Institute of Management,* WZB, Berlin, IIM/IP 85–41, December.

Fitzroy, F.R. and Mueller, D.C. 1984. Cooperation and conflict in contractual organisations. *Quarterly Review of Economics and Business* 24(4), Winter, 24–49.

Furobotn, E.G. 1985. Codetermination, productivity gains and the economics of the firm. *Oxford Economic Papers* 37, 22–39.

Hertzka, T. 1980. *Freiland. Ein soziales Zukunftsbild.* Dresden: Pierson. English translation, London: Chatto & Windus, 1981.

Jensen, M.C. and Meckling, W.H. 1979. Rights and production functions: an application to labor-managed firms and codetermination. *Journal of Business* 52, October, 469–506.

Lane, D. (ed.) 1985. *Employment and Labour in the USSR.* London: Harvester Press.

Nuti, D.M. 1985. The share economy: plausibility and viability of Weitzman's model. European University Institute Working Paper, No. 85/194, Florence. Italian translation in *Politica ed Economia* 1, January, 1986.

Nuti, D.M. 1986. A rejoinder to Weitzman. (In Italian.) *Politica ed Economia* 4, April.

Nutzinger, H.G. 1983. Empirical research into German codetermination: problems and perspectives. *Economic Analysis and Workers' Management* 17(4), 361–82.

Pagano, U. 1984. Welfare, productivity and self-management. European University Institute Working Paper, No. 84/128, Florence.

Reich, M. and Devine, J. 1981. The microeconomics of conflict and hierarchy in capitalist production. *Review of Radical Political Economics* 12(4), Winter, 27–45.

Samuelson, P.A. 1977. Thoughts on profit-sharing. *Zeitschrift für die Gesamte Staatswissenschaft.* (Special issue on profit-sharing.)

Vanek, J. 1965. Workers' profit participation, unemployment and the Keynesian equilibrium. *Weltwirtschaftliches Archiv* 94(2), 206–14.

Vanek, J. 1970. *The General Theory of Labor-Managed Market Economies.* Ithaca: Cornell University Press.

Ward, B.M. 1958. The firm in Illyria: market syndicalism. *American Economic Review* 48(4), 566–89.

Weitzman, M.L. 1983. Some macroeconomic implications of alternative compensation systems. *Economic Journal* 93(4), 763–83.
Weitzman, M.L. 1984. *The Share Economy*. Cambridge, Mass.: Harvard University Press.
Weitzman, M.L. 1985a. Profit sharing as macroeconomic policy. *American Economic Review, Papers and Proceedings* 75(2), May, 41–5.
Weitzman, M.L. 1985b. The simple macroeconomics of profit sharing. *American Economic Review* 75(5), December, 937–53.
Weitzman, M.L. 1986. Reply to Nuti. (In Italian.) *Politica ed Economia* 4, April.

Common Law

P.S. ATIYAH

Common law is a system of law and legal processes which originated in England shortly after the Norman Conquest and after several centuries of continuous development was exported to the English colonies, and so came to be the basis of the law of the greater part of the United States, as well as of Australia, New Zealand, most of Canada and (to a lesser degree) also of India, Pakistan, Bangladesh and many parts of Africa. The chief characteristic of the common law has always been that its development has lain largely in the hands of the judges, and that it has therefore grown and changed incrementally, case by case, in the course of actual litigation.

In modern times the term 'common law' is used in a variety of senses. In the broadest sense, it continues to be used to refer to the entire system of law originating in England which now forms the basis of the law in the greater part of the former British Empire, often nowadays called the 'common law world'. In this sense the common law is often contrasted with the 'civil law' which derives from the law of ancient Rome, and today operates in most of Western Europe, as well as in a number of other countries (such as Japan and Egypt) which have borrowed their law from European countries. One of the chief characteristics of the modern civil law is that it derives its authority from one or more basic Codes of law; and it remains a principal distinction between common law and civil law countries that the former have not generally codified their law. And even in common law jurisdictions (such as California, for example) where there does today exist a kind of common law Code, it differs fundamentally in nature from the civil law Codes; in particular the system of precedent, and the authority of the judges to interpret and develop such common law Codes are quite different from those recognised in civil law countries.

The term 'common law' is also often used in various narrower senses. In the most important of these narrower senses, the common law is often contrasted with legislation, so that the lawyer in a common-law country still thinks of legislation as a type of law different from the 'common law', which is basically judge-made law. The term 'common law' is sometimes used in yet a third relevant sense in which it is distinguished from a body of law, known technically as 'Equity' which was originally supplementary to the common law, and was developed in the separate Court of Chancery. Today common law (in this narrow sense) and 'Equity' are almost everywhere merged and administered by a single set of courts.

The common law (in the first two senses identified above) has traditionally been associated with the economics of the free market in at least two different ways. First, there is a strain of thought, represented in particular by Hayek (1973), which seems to suggest that a system of law, like the common law, which is largely judge-made, is inherently more likely to favour and protect individual freedoms, and among them (or especially) economic freedoms. But this is an implausible and indeed eccentric claim, which seems to involve confusion of the first two senses of the term 'common law' referred to above. Because most redistribution is accomplished in modern democracies by legislative measures, it is easy to assume that a legal system which owes little to legislation will be more likely to recognize and protect the freedom of the market, but the amount of redistribution which occurs in a legal system does not necessarily depend upon whether that society is part of the common law world. There is no *a priori* reason to suppose that judges left to themselves by a legislature will necessarily favour the economics of the market. In the last analysis, the policies favoured by judges will depend upon their own preferences, their culture and traditions.

But there is a second way in which the common law has traditionally been associated with the freedom of the market, and this association rests upon the historical facts of the last three centuries. The concept of the Rule of Law which came to be recognized and defended in England after the revolution of 1688 has been seen by many as having favoured the development of a free market economy in England prior to and during the early years of the industrial revolution. Because of this historical fact it was for a long time almost an article of faith among English writers that the common law and the freedom of the market were closely associated. This view is today less strongly held in England, as a result no doubt of the fact that, while Englishmen still like to believe in the Rule of Law (despite grave doubts in some quarters as to whether this concept has much meaning), they are by no means so wedded to the free market as they were. In America, where the Constitution of 1788 substantially embodied the English traditions as to the Rule of Law, as well as the then accepted ideology of the free market, the association between the two has survived rather more strongly.

The reasons for the traditional belief in the close association between the common law and the freedom of the market must therefore be sought in history, and in particular in English history during the period from approximately 1770 to 1870, when the free market economy was largely in process of being established. And of all parts of the common law, none was more important for this purpose than the law of contract, because this was the part of the law most intimately relaed to the economic system. Indeed, the story of English law between 1770 and 1870 was to a large degree the story of how the law of contract was converted into the law of the free market, and of how the ideology of freedom of contract became one of the great intellectual movements of history (Atiyah, 1979).

The first three-quarters of the 18th century was a period of transition in England, during which many older ideas about contract and the market were being displaced by the newer ideas which gradually became dominant towards the end of the century. Among the older ideas at least three can be identified as particularly hostile to the laws needed to serve the emerging free market economy. First, there was a regulatory element in the law and the economy dating back to Tudor times, represented for instance by statutory controls of wages and prices of many commodities, and by the apprenticeship laws which controlled entry to many trades with outdated and largely unnecessary restrictions. Secondly, there was a paternalistic element in much contract law at this time, with the courts still being willing to relieve various classes of persons from the consequences of bad bargains which they had made. This paternalism was particularly pronounced under various doctrines of Equity, such as rules for the relief of mortgagors, rules against the enforcement of contractual penalties and forfeitures, rules for the protection of seamen and 'expectant heirs', and so forth. Thus, in the third sense of the term the 'common law' identified above, it can be said that the common law was always more market-oriented than Equity. Thirdly, there was a traditional moralistic element in the contract law of the 18th century, and this also took different forms, such as the general hostility to usury (as to which see Simpson, 1975, pp. 510–18), and the attempts to regulate the way in which essential foods and drinks were sold by use of the traditional marketing offences. The 'moral' roots of older law were also related to ideas about 'just prices' which, though rarely openly recognized in the common law, seem to have been influential at least in some of the cases in Equity, where there are signs that the Chancellors did have some vague sense of unease if they were asked to enforce contracts at prices which seemed to them very unfair, or on terms which were (in the language of the law) 'unconscionable'.

In addition to these specific instances of interference with the binding force of private contracts, there were important respects in which the whole concept of a general contract law remained relatively undeveloped at this time. Thus, while the law recognized and enforced specific types of contracts, such as contracts for the sale of land, contracts of insurance and so forth, there was, as yet, little sign of a general law of contract governing all types of transaction. Then also, it remains unclear how far the contract law of this period actually recognized and enforced wholly executory contracts, in the sense of awarding damages for breach of a contract prior to any acts of performance or detrimental reliance by any of the parties. And finally, it is clear that, from the standpoint of today, the law of contract in the 18th century had not yet freed itself from dependence on the law of property. Of course, in one sense contract law can never be free from a dependence on property entitlements, because contract law is the mechanism by which entitlements are exchanged; but there are clear signs in the 18th century that contract law was still closely tied to property law in another sense, in the sense (for instance) that the proprietary aspects of many transactions were still regarded as more important than the promissory or contractual aspects. So, for instance, the right of a mortgagor to redeem the mortgaged property was protected by the courts, even when by the terms of the mortgage documents he had forfeited that right to delay in repaying the loan. It was assumed that if the mortgagee received back his money, with interest and costs, he was adequately protected by the law, even though the contract itself would have given him more extensive rights.

During the century beginning around 1770 these older ideas and traditions gradually gave way before the ideology of freedom of contract; but it would be wrong to think that this ideology did not have long roots and antecedents in still earlier periods. There are, even in the 16th and 17th centuries, many signs of incipient economic liberalism among the lawyers such as Coke, who bequeathed to the common law a hatred of monopolies as well as a passion for individual liberties (Wagner, 1935). And Thomas Hobbes, in a well-known passage in *Leviathan*, swept away all the medieval learning about 'just prices' and declared that 'the value of all things contracted for, is measured by the Appetite of the Contractors; and therefore the just value, is that which they be contented to give' (Hobbes [1651] 1968, p. 208). So the ideology of freedom of contract certainly had origins going back well beyond the 18th century. Nevertheless, it does seem (though the matter remains controversial) that major changes in the law began during the course of that century which gathered pace as the century progressed.

Certainly, a great deal occurred to change the character of contract law from the last quarter of the 18th century until well into the 19th century, and there is much evidence that many of these changes in the law were profoundly influenced by classical economic theory, and perhaps still more by popular versions of classical economic theory. First, the relics of the Tudor regulatory economy gradually disappeared. Wage regulation had become increasingly obsolete in practice during the 18th century, and a major challenge to the older laws in the name of freedom of contract had taken place in the celebrated case of the Gloucestershire Weavers (1756–7), (Atiyah, 1979, pp. 73–4). By the early 19th century most of the legislation authorizing the fixing of wages had been repealed. So too was the Statute of Apprentices, after many years during which its operation had been gradually whittled down by the judges. Secondly, the signs of paternalism which are still found in 18th-century Equity seem to have disappeared gradually as the judges hardened their hearts and toughened their minds. For example, signs of an attempt to introduce implied warranties on the sale of goods for the protection of buyers, which can be detected in the 18th century, were largely scotched, and the principle of *caveat emptor* reasserted with full vigour. The equitable doctrines allowing the courts to relieve various unfortunates from the effects of hard bargains were gradually whittled down, although they never disappeared altogether. Third, the moralistic elements in the law were also gradually whittled down. The law of contract came increasingly to be seen to be neutrally enforcing agreements which must be presumed to be beneficial to both parties. The only moral component left in the law of contract during the 19th century seemed to derive from the binding nature of promises.

The subjective theory of value also seems to have been largely accepted by the judges even before it had been wholly accepted by economists. Although the common law had always insisted that a promise be supported by some 'consideration', some reason, before it would be enforced (and to that extent at least contained a paternalist element), the growing acceptance of the subjective theory of value meant that the doctrine of consideration became much less important during the 19th century. So for instance, in *Haigh* v. *Brooks* (1840, 113 English Reports 124) the judges enforced a promise to pay £9000 in return for the giving up of a guarantee previously given by the promisor, even though it now appeared that the guarantee might be unenforceable and legally worthless. The promisor had valued it at £9000, said the judges; it was not for them to say that the document was worthless. For similar reasons, the prejudice against usury had gradually been overcome, and the usury laws were totally repealed in England in 1854.

In these ways, then, the principle that contracts are binding and must be strictly enforced had been greatly strengthened, and exceptional cases had been whittled down by the middle of the 19th century. In addition, other changes had occurred in the general nature of contract law, which were closely related to the growing trend to see contract law as the law of the free market. First, it was during this period that a general law of contract came into existence for the first time in the common law world. And the process of generalization was important to the ideology of the law in a number of respects. In particular, the generalizing of contractual ideas meant that the law had to become more abstract, more broadly principled. Principles had to be developed which could be applied equally to (say) commercial contracts for the sale of wheat, to contracts of employment, and (for instance) to personal contracts such as the contract to marry. This abstraction may have helped the law become more neutral, less inclined to pursue any redistributive tendencies, such as may exist where (say) there is a separate body of legal doctrine dealing with contracts of employment, or with residential leases, or with loan transactions.

Next, it seems clear that another major development during this period was the gradual shift in emphasis in contract law away from treating contracts as present, or partly performed exchanges, and towards treating them as private planning devices, made in advance to allocate risks. The wholly executory contract became clearly recognized by the law, so that it now became possible for a person to sue for damages for breach of a pure promise, even where no performance or detrimental reliance had taken place. The justification for requiring damages to be paid in such circumstances was never clearly enunciated, and indeed, specific justification was rarely seen to be necessary. It was widely assumed that the broad principle of freedom of contract required, not only that parties be left free to make their own exchanges, but that the law should be available in aid of a party to enforce his claim to damages where the other failed to perform. John Stuart Mill was the first economist to point out that a policy of *laissez-faire* could not be used to justify the enforcement of executory contracts (Mill, 1848, vol. 2,

p. 386), but even modern economists do not generally pursue this line of thought, though some libertarians have done so.

And finally, 19th-century contract law increasingly freed itself from its dependence on property law. Although obviously entitlements still remain the subject matter of all contracts, contract law has become much less concerned with specific items of property, and is more concerned with wealth as a kind of fungible property. The reason for this was basically that 19th-century contract law was dominated by the needs of merchants and traders, to whom all property is in principle replaceable with money. A merchant can be assumed to be indifferent between a piece of property, and the value of that property. Similarly, as contracts came to be increasingly seen as fundamentally risk-allocation devices, the particular entitlements or property to which the risks attached became less important.

By the last quarter of the 19th century, the process of developing a mature body of general contract law had largely been completed in England, and although a similar process took place in America (Horwitz, 1977), there is ground for believing that that was not completed for another fifty years or so. Freedom of contract had, apparently, reached its highest point. But although this was true of the ideology of freedom of contract among lawyers and judges, it was not really true of the views of economists or of the politicians, or of the public. By the late 19th century, neoclassical economists were already beginning to write sceptically about the sweeping effects of freedom of contract which had been attributed to the classical economists, and were pointing out the many possible causes of market failure such as information difficulties, externalities and monopoly. And although most of the older regulatory legislation had been repealed in the first half of the 19th century, Parliament had at the same time been gradually building up a completely new body of regulatory enactments dealing with new industrial problems – factories, coal mines, safety at sea for seamen and emigrant passengers, public health, the adulteration of food and drink, regulation of the weights and measures used for sales, and so on. Much of this new legislation had been a pragmatic response to perceived evils, and though some of it could have been justified economically by arguments concerning misinformation or externalities, much of it would have been difficult to justify except on the assumption of paternalistic or redistributive motives. Some of it may have been inspired by sheer impatience, an unwillingness to give the market time to work, or a belief that the short-term costs of market failures were so severe that legislative correction was necessary without regard to the long-term distortions this might produce.

What is quite clear is that by the time the English common law and common lawyers had accepted the teachings (as they were thought to be) of the classical economists on freedom of contract, these teachings were already somewhat out of date. The result was that the mature common law of contract was seriously deficient in a number of respects. It was first of all deficient in its almost total neglect of the problem of externalities. Contracting parties were entitled to pursue their own interests, regardless of the effect of their contract on third parties, or the public. Only in the most extreme cases of actual illegality would the courts generally refuse to uphold a contract. Secondly (although this certainly could not be laid at the door of the classical economists), there had been, during the 19th century, a serious neglect by common lawyers of the problem of monopoly. This may well have been largely due to the fact that for the greater part of this period the British economy was itself highly competitive, and in little danger from monopolies. But the complacent assumption that cartels were unstable and were always vulnerable to internal or external competition was in England (though not in America) carried over by lawyers and courts into new conditions towards the end of the 19th century, and well into the present century, when it was utterly out of date. A second result of this failure of the common law to keep pace with economic theory and political reality, was the growing gulf between the common law and legislation. Once again, extensive legislative intervention with freedom of contract began to become commonplace, and much of it was increasingly redistributive in character.

During the course of the present century this process continued at an increasing pace until 1980 or thereabouts, since when there are signs that history has virtually reversed itself. Disillusion with the free market, particularly in England, increased during the great depression in the 1930s until, by the end of World War II, a Labour Government was elected to power with a massive majority and with a mandate to lay the foundations for a socialist state and a socialist economic system. Since then England has increasingly learned to live with a 'mixed economy', to a large part of which the traditional law of contract seems irrelevant because the public sector is often controlled by public laws rather than by contract law. But even in areas where private law continues to operate, the common law of contract has become increasingly affected by legislative intervention. Virtually all types of consumer transactions are today controlled or affected to some degree by legislation, including consumer credit contracts, contracts of employment, residential leases, and insurance contracts. Unconscionable or unfair contracts are increasingly subjected to judicial control. Many areas of law which were formerly controlled largely by contract, such as family law, are now subject to extensive judicial discretionary control. Even business and commercial contracts are subject to vast bodies of legislative and regulatory laws, some, such as the modern monopoly or anti-trust laws, being designed to preserve the operation of a competitive market, but much of it still being designed to restrict competition or the operation of the free market.

America has not gone so far down this road as Britain and other common-law countries, and indeed, for a long time, in the late 19th and early 20th centuries, constitutional decisions of the United States Supreme Court in the name of freedom of contract, actually prevented similar developments. Much legislative intervention with freedom of contract was, during this period, declared unconstitutional, frequently over the dissent of Justice Holmes. By the late 1930s, however, the majority of the court had largely accepted Holmes's view, and since then, legislative intervention with freedom of contract has not been regarded as *per se* unconstitutional. The shift in the court opened the door to the same kind of regulation and intervention which had already been taking place in Britain, and although America has not, like Britain, brought large-scale industries within the public sector and therefore partially outside the control of contract law, most of the other legislative developments of the British type certainly have their parallel in America. No doubt some contracts are more regulated in Britain, but conversely there are plenty of examples of legislative interference with freedom of contract in America which are not to be found in Britain.

These vast changes in the operation of the common law have accompanied or brought with them a change in ideology once again. Paternalism and redistribution were, at least until around 1980, increasingly favoured by many writers and teachers of contract law, as well as large sectors of the electorate. Even the judges became much more sympathetic to arguments based on concepts like unconscionability and inequality of bargaining power. In America, unconscionability was given express legitimacy as a device for overturning unfair contracts by the Uniform Commercial Code, and was increasingly used by the judges as a matter of common law as well. Many relationships of a contractual character (for instance, that of physician and patient) and others of a virtually contractual character (for instance, that between manufacturers of products and ultimate purchasers and consumers) are, both in America and Britain, increasingly regulated by tort law rather than contract law, at least where things go badly wrong and legal actions for damages are brought based on negligent conduct, or on defects in the goods. In such malpractice or products liability actions the appropriate standards of care or quality are set by judges and juries and not by the contracting parties, and contractual exculpatory clauses are often denied legal validity.

Since about 1980 there have been increasing signs that the tide has turned yet again, both in Britain and America. Obviously, and visibly, British and American governments have since then been trying to reassert the virtues of the free market and roll back the frontiers of regulation, and in this they are being vigorously supported by some lawyers and law teachers in America, though not to any real extent in Britain. It is not yet clear what the impact of this is going to be on the future of the common law of contract. One possible scenario is that, as in the late 19th century, the courts will be behind the times, but that on this occasion they will be hostile to the reasserted belief in the free market and will continue to defend paternalist and redistributive intervention in free contracts, particularly where one of the parties to the contract is a consumer or 'small man' thought to be weak in bargaining power. But another possible scenario is that the new enthusiasm for the free market will prove but a short-lived hiccup in the long-term trend towards paternalist and redistributive policies. In either event it seems unlikely that for many years to come British or American courts will be enforcing contracts according to the full rigour of the common law.

BIBLIOGRAPHY
Atiyah, P.S. 1979. *The Rise and Fall of Freedom of Contract.* Oxford: Oxford University Press.

Hayek, F.A. 1973. *Law, Legislation and Liberty*, Vol. 1, *Rules and Orders*. London: Routledge & Kegan Paul; 3 vols. Chicago: University of Chicago, 1979.

Hobbes, T. 1651. *Leviathan*. Ed. C.B. Macpherson, Harmondsworth: Penguin Books, 1968.

Horwitz, M.J. 1977. *The Transformation of American Law 1780–1860*. Cambridge, Mass. and London: Harvard University Press.

Mill, J.S. 1848. *Principles of Political Economy*. From the 5th London edn, New York: D. Appleton & Co., 1908.

Simpson, A.W.B. 1975. *A History of the Common Law of Contract*. Oxford: Clarendon Press; New York: Oxford University Press.

Wagner, D.O. 1935. Coke and the rise of economic liberalism. *Economic History Review* 6(1), October, 30.

Common Property Rights

STEVEN N.S. CHEUNG

In a society where individuals compete for the use of scarce resources, some rules or criteria of competition must exist to resolve the conflict. These rules, known as property rights, may be established in law, in regulation, in custom or in hierarchy ranking. The structures of rights may take a variety of forms, ranging from private property rights at one extreme to common property rights at the other. Most fall somewhere in between: either set of rights would be rare in its purest form.

In a private property, the delimitation of the right to its use is expressed in dimensions or characteristics inherent in the property itself. These rights are exclusive to some private party, are freely transferable, and the income derived from them is not attenuated, restrained or infringed by laws or regulations. Hence price control, taxation, and social restriction of transferability may be regarded as violations of private property rights. In a common property, there is no delimitation or delineation of its use rights to any private party. No one has the right to exclude others from using it, and all are free to compete for its use. Hence there are no exclusive use rights, no rights to be transferred, and in the limiting case, no net income can be derived from using the common property.

This last condition rests on an economic proposition known as the dissipation of rent. It argues that because of the lack of exclusive use rights, individuals competing for the use of a common property will reduce its rental value or net worth to zero. The reason is that if no one has an exclusive claim to the value (i.e. rent) of that property, its use will invite competition to the point that each and every competing user can earn no more than the alternative earning of his own resources required in the exploitation of that common property. In other words, under competition and with no one having a special advantage, a 'prize' that has no exclusive claimant will be dissipated or absorbed by the costs of other resources which must be dedicated to its winning. Hence the net value of the prize won is zero.

The usual examples of common property rights cite a public beach and marine fisheries, and the dissipation of rent typically implies excessive use or over-exploitation. However, the dissipation may take the form of under-exploitation. For example, a piece of fertile land under common ownership may be used for herd grazing, or left idle, instead of being planted as an orchard.

In the real world, the complete dissipation of rent is rare indeed. This is because the supply curve of labour or of other inputs may be rising (some intramarginal rent may be captured), the competing users may have different opportunity costs (the non-marginal users may be enjoying rent), or entry may be restricted by regulations, by customs or by information costs. Still, with common property rights some dissipation of rent is inevitable, and no society can afford to surrender a large portion of its valuable resources to this structure of property rights.

A property may be held in common because its capturable rent is lower than the cost of enforcing exclusivity. In this case, the dissipation of rent is no waste. However, to the extent that rent dissipation is viewed as a waste, its occurrence must be attributable to the omission of some constraints in the analysis. Attempts to reduce rent dissipation go far to explain why common property in its 'pure' form is seldom observed. In marine fisheries, for example, numerous regulations govern the fishing season, the size of fish caught, the boat size and the mesh size, and various licensing arrangements restrict the number of boats and fishermen. The market value of a fishing licence, sometimes enormous, is one measure of the ocean rent captured. Even for public beaches, regulations of some type will often be found to govern the use of those most in demand.

Whereas regulations and restrictions on entry in the use of a common property often serve to reduce dissipation, the rent that can be captured is usually less than if the property were privately owned. To reconcile this observation with constrained maximization, we must infer that, enforcement costs aside, other transaction costs associated with the changing of institutional arrangements must restrain the formation of private property rights.

No economy can survive if the majority of its scarce resources are commonly owned. Regulations may indeed reduce rent dissipation, but in the process they not only distort the use of the resources but also invite corruption and the emergence of special interests. An unrestrained common property, strictly speaking, is propertyless in ownership; if its structure is extended to all resources, starvation for all must result. If one rules out private property rights, then to avoid the imposition of an infinite array of regulations the remaining alternative is the communal system or the communist state.

In a communist state there is no private owner of productive resources: each constituent is propertyless, in the literal sense of the word. Since the dissipation of rents associated with common properties will guarantee starvation, in a communist state the rights to use resources, and to derive income therefrom, are defined in terms of rank. That is, stripped of all ownership rights over valuable and productive resources, the citizens of a communist state hold differing rights to use resources and to obtain income according to their status. In the people's communes in China under the Great Leap Forward, for example, no one owns the productive resources (i.e. everyone is propertyless), but comrades of different ranks enjoy different rights and privileges. 'Rank' as such has value and is subject to competition, therefore a system of 'property' rights is implicit. However, the valuable rights are now defined in terms other than the inherent properties of the productive resources.

This is, in fact, the key distinction between a private property system and a communist state: the former delineates rights in terms of certain dimensions of the productive resources themselves; the latter delineates rights in terms of a characteristic (rank) of people deprived of productive human capital. In the communist state, the competition for and protection of rank will draw on the use of valuable and productive resources (another form of rent dissipation). Moreover, the lack of market prices increases the cost of information, and the lack of contractual choices increases the cost of enforcing performance. What is saved in return are the costs of delineating and enforcing rights in properties.

It is among these varied costs – broadly defined as transaction costs – that we find the key divergence in economic performance between the communist and the private property systems. If one ignores transaction costs, the delineation of rights in terms of rank will produce the same use of resources as would the delineation of rights in properties. However, it can be convincingly argued that the broadly defined transaction costs are generally higher with communal than with private rights. Communism fails, not because it does not work in theory, but precisely because in practice its costs of transaction are higher than those in a system of private property rights. Still, the delineation of rights in ranks is a way to reduce rent dissipation in a propertyless state.

Strictly speaking, the dissipation of rent associated with common property is no 'theory' at all, because dissipating rent merely to produce an equilibrium does not explain behaviour. Worse, to stand aside and simply permit rent to dissipate is inconsistent with the postulate of constrained maximization.

What is useful and important from the standpoint of economic explanation is to view whatever rent dissipation does occur as necessarily a constrained minimum because, under the maximization postulate, each and every individual has an incentive to reduce that dissipation. Behaviour associated with the dissipation of rent must therefore be regarded as attempts to reduce that loss, and this altered view explains many observations. That some dissipation remains must then be attributable to the constraints of transaction costs. The challenge to the economist is to specify and identify what these costs are and how they will vary under differing circumstances.

BIBLIOGRAPHY

Alchian, A.A. 1965. Some economics of property rights. *Il Politico* 30(4), 816–29.
Bottomley, A. 1963. The effect of the common ownership of land upon resource allocation in Tripolitania. *Land Economics* 39, February, 91–5.
Cheung, S.N.S. 1970. The structure of a contract and the theory of a non-exclusive resource. *Journal of Law and Economics* 13, April, 49–70.

Cheung, S.N.S. 1974. A theory of price control. *Journal of Law and Economics* 17, April, 53–71.

Cheung, S.N.S. 1982. *Will China Go 'Capitalist'?* Hobart Paper 94, London: IEA.

Coase, R.H. 1960. The problem of social cost. *Journal of Law and Economics* 3, October, 1–44.

Demsetz, H. 1964. The exchange and enforcement of property rights. *Journal of Law and Economics* 7, October, 11–26.

Gordon, H.S. 1954. The economic history of a common property resource: the fishery. *Journal of Political Economy* 62, April, 124–42.

Knight, F.H. 1924. Some fallacies in the interpretation of social cost. *Quarterly Journal of Economics* 38, August, 582–606.

Communications

ROGER G. NOLL

The economics of communications is a loose, somewhat vaguely defined amalgam of topics in applied microeconomics. Although having close ties to the microeconomic theory of the economics of information, it is probably best characterized as a subfield of industrial organization, regulation and public enterprise that deals with the communications sector: telecommunications, broadcasting, the print media, the performing arts and the postal system. Of course, the activities that constitute this list are somewhat arbitrary, but they reflect what is both taught and studied by people in the subfield as well as some important economic realities that make specialized studies of the communications sector a valid category among distinct intellectual pursuits. First among these realities is that the industries in the communications sector are closely linked. Broadcasting competes with the performing arts for both audience and inputs, and telecommunications competes with the postal service. Moreover, tele-communications networks are capable of delivering broadcast services, and vice versa. Among the products over which the postal system, telecommunications and cable television compete is the delivery of the output of the print media.

Another unifying theme across communications industries is the connection of the study of the sector to the economics of public goods and externalities. Communications is the production and dissemination of information. Some aspects of the production of information are public goods, and the dissemination and use of information can have important external effects. Moreover, most of these external effects are non-economic phenomena such as political participation, the cultural values held by members of a society or the level of violence. Because of the unique character of these externalities, the motives for public policy in communications are closely linked with a society's fundamental political and social values. Thus, freedom of speech and the extent of the right to privacy, as well as the use of control of communications to manipulate the political process, are at the heart of debates over communications policy.

87

RATIONALES FOR GOVERNMENT INTERVENTION. Not surprisingly, the role of the public sector is very large in the communications sector in nearly every nation. Subsidization, nationalization and extremely detailed regulation of prices and attributes of the product are common. In market-orientated societies, tele-communications and mail are nationalized or subject to economic regulation for much the same reasons that underpin the same policies in other infrastructural industries: that these industries are natural monopolies and that their performance and pattern of development profoundly affect the development of much of the rest of the economy. But even here, unique externality arguments are brought forth as additional factors to be taken into account by policy-makers. First, subscription to the telecommunications network or access to mail delivery creates the capability to receive communication from others. A person who decides to mail a letter or place a telephone call presumably considers only his or her net benefits from the communication; the willingness to pay of the recipient (positive or negative) is not taken into account. Thus, for example, the extent of phone service and the pattern of calling can be expected to be inefficient if each person bears the full cost of, first, subscribing to the network, and then placing telephone calls. In particular, if some potential customers have too low a willingness to pay to become subscribers, but are also desired objects of communications by others, the number of subscribers will be too low if subscribers must bear the full cost of connecting them to the network. This argument constitutes the foundation for the 'universal service' objective, that is, a policy of maximizing the number of subscribers to the telephone network, and the policy practised nearly everywhere of adopting a price structure for telephone services that subsidizes installation charges, pay-telephone prices and/or monthly access charges to the local network, especially for customers in high-cost areas such as rural communities.

A second externality of the telecommunications system is said to be its contribution to national security. A joint product of a private telecommunications network is a ready resource that can be commandeered and used by government in times of national emergency, such as foreign attack, natural disasters or accidents. The use of communications to coordinate a response to such an event, then, should play a role in affecting the capacity and design of the tele-communications system, and often is the basis of an argument for building into the system more redundancy and interconnectability than might otherwise be optimal and than independent private concerns would undertake on their own. These contingent needs by government have been said to constitute a separate natural-monopoly argument, an example of 'economies of scope' between private and public uses that can only be captured if the private system is a single, integrated whole. In the United States, for example, the Department of Defense was a consistent critic of proposals to relax regulation and increase competition in the telecommunications industry during the 1960s and 1970s.

The externalities associated with the mass media have to do with the social, political and psychological consequences of the content of information, and for the most part are dealt with by scholars from disciplines other than economics.

(The main exception is research on the effects of advertising, where an inconclusive debate has raged for decades as to whether the informational value of advertising exceeds the sum of its direct costs and possible resource misallocation owing to manipulation and misperceptions of consumers.) The analytical foundation for the belief in the importance of informational externalities is the proposition that people's behaviour as citizens, parents, consumers, workers, friends, and so on, can be significantly affected, at least in the short run, by the informational content of the mass media. Once one accepts this proposition, the next logical step is to entertain the idea that censorship by the state, at least in principle, can prevent some of the external diseconomies of destructive content, while proactive state interventions to channel the content of the media towards greater educational and otherwise uplifting content can provide additional social benefits.

The most obvious manifestations of these ideas are in broadcasting. The British Broadcasting Corporation was founded on openly paternalistic principles about the potential of radio broadcasts for educational and other uplifting purposes. Until the recent move towards decentralization through cable television and towards private, commercial television, a core principle of French broadcasting policy was to preserve French culture and values by limiting and censoring programmes from other nations. In Germany, decentralized, regional quasi-public broadcast monopolies were created after World War II to protect simultaneously against capture by the national government or by the national print media barons, either of which, it was feared, might use broadcasting to arouse nationally destructive political passions. And in the United States, broadcast licensing has, until recently, enforced a long set of standards for evaluating competitors for a given licence, including personal characteristics and other business holdings of the licensee and both performance and promise about the extent of 'public service' programming offered by commercial as well as non-commercial (educational) outlets.

Of course, other mass media are not free of similar policy constraints, although the print media and the arts are usually accorded greater freedom in the content of their messages than are broadcasters. The areas of policy controversy are the definition of the liability for slanderous attacks and the concomitant definition of privacy rights, the boundaries between pornography and legitimate expression, and the principles separating sedition from reasonable political discourse.

The core economic issue in this debate is whether the 'market place for ideas' works well without intervention, or at least better than is the case with active political intervention by the very government authorities whose security and power can be affected by the content of communications. The argument for non-intervention is twofold. Positively, it is that in the end people's tastes in ideas should be accorded the same status as their tastes in other goods as long as the consumption of communications produces no external diseconomies. If communications cause bad behaviour, then if people are informed about this fact – and about the punishments exacted if that behaviour is manifest – they will efficiently anticipate this in making decisions about which communications to receive and how to treat those that are received. And, as with goods, ideas about how the world works that prove correct will be perceived, at least eventually, as superior to less correct ideas. Negatively, the argument for an unregulated marketplace for ideas is a pessimistic forecast of how political intervention is likely to work: a combination of orientation towards propaganda to serve the interests of preserving the status quo and an extreme sensitivity to either vocal, organized single-issue groups seeking to impose their values on others or a tyranny of the majority that persecutes those who stray too far from current norms.

The other side of the dispute, usually advocated more by non-economists, is rooted in observed relationships between communications and behaviour, perhaps best documented in the study of the effects of television on violence (especially by children) and on the manipulation of the news for short-term political objectives. This position regards the efficiency of the market place for ideas as demonstrably poor, at least in the short run; implicitly, it accords less credence to the proposition that individuals are as rational – indeed, are even proactive – in selecting among competing communications as economic theory assumes. Proponents of intervention especially emphasize the unformed and manipulable attitudes of children.

The final pervasive feature in the communications sector that deserves further elaboration is the partially non-rivalrous nature of the consumption of information. All information is a public good in the sense that once a new information product has been created for a first user, it does not have to be created again for subsequent users: in principle, at least, the first use of information does not preclude its use by others. In practice, this characteristic may be unimportant. Information must be disseminated in some way to subsequent users, and the cost of dissemination may exceed the cost of secondary creation – as for example can be the case for a simple computer program. Or, information may be very cheaply privatized so that the public goods characteristic introduces no significant inefficiency to a private market system of distribution. Nevertheless, the publicness of information is a serious issue in an assessment of the performance of allocational institutions in the communications sector, and in the design of private market processes for allocating resources the problems of publicness must be addressed. Whether the product is a written news report, a novel, a theatrical production, a television broadcast, or 'Dial-A-Joke' on the telephone, the problem is fundamentally the same: producers will not supply a product unless they can recover the opportunity cost for creating it, yet the marginal cost of providing the product to one more consumer does not include any of the production costs of the information. Hence, efficient provision of information requires one of the following: subsidies of the production of information, or price discrimination with protection against arbitrage so that consumers with relatively low willingness to pay for information will not be inefficiently excluded. In practice, both are common. Governments subsidize broadcasting and performing arts by direct payments, and certain users of the postal and telecommunications system either directly or by engaging in price discrimination (e.g. the differences in basic monthly service rates of telephones between residences and businesses, and the lower postal rates for circulating the print media). Of course, neither direct subsidies nor discriminatory prices are explicitly designed in a quantitative sense to offset the inefficiencies of private provision of public goods, so that the issue of optimal pricing of communications services is an active and still-developing field of research. The focus here is on the two fields in which most of the work has been done: telecommunications and broadcasting. Moreover, the discussion includes research on market structure issues because of their close connection with the implications of alternative pricing policies.

PRICING AND MARKET STRUCTURE IN TELECOMMUNICATIONS. The telecommunications industry in the United States offers an array of services that until very recently were provided as joint products by a legally protected monopoly. When the monopoly was secure and unquestioned, the pricing problem was to devise a price structure that recovered joint and fixed costs with minimal loss of efficiency. As the natural monopoly presumption came to be called into question, the pricing problem began to incorporate another dimension, to provide appropriate signals to potential competitors so that the market structure would evolve efficiently.

To understand the rudiments of the telephone pricing problem requires some basic knowledge about the technical characteristics of the telecommunications network. The traditional telephone system is best conceptualized as having four components: customer terminal equipment (a telephone, a computer terminal, a switchboard); a pair of copper wires connecting each terminal device to a central switch; the central switch that serves the local community; and a hierarchy of transmission conduits and additional switches that serve to connect the local switches. Typically the telephone price structure has three elements: an installation charge for activating a customer's copper wire pairs; a basic monthly service charge for renting terminal equipment and the copper wire pairs; and a message toll for placing telephone calls. The common practice is for the installation charge to cover only a fraction of installation costs as a means of encouraging universal service, and for the basic monthly charge to entitle the subscriber to unlimited local calling – sometimes not confined to other telephones connected to the same local switch, but also including calls through adjacent local switches. Usually the basic monthly charge is much higher (by a factor of two or three) for business than for residences, but within each of these categories it tends to be approximately the same over wide geographic areas regardless of differences in cost of service.

Until about 1960, the revenues from installation charges and the basic monthly rate approximately covered the cost of local service (including local switches). But as long-distance toll calls became more important, telephone companies increasingly used toll revenues to cover part of the cost of the local system. This required no increase in toll prices; indeed, long-distance prices generally were falling because technological change was extraordinarily rapid in this segment of the system. By simply letting prices fall a little more slowly than costs, a large and growing fraction of local network costs could be paid for by toll. These revenues could be used to construct systems in high-cost rural areas without causing increased prices for basic service elsewhere, again to encourage universal service.

Since toll calls pass through local switches they impose a cost on the local network because local switches must be designed to be large enough and complex enough to accommodate them. Consequently, toll prices would bear some local system costs in an efficient pricing structure. In addition, however, toll calls also contributed to 'non-traffic sensitive' (NTS) costs – the terminals and copper wire – even though, by definition, the magnitude of investment required for this equipment was unrelated to the amount of calling.

Obviously, this pricing structure not only encouraged universal service but encouraged local calling (with a zero price at the margin) while discouraging long-distance calling compared to an efficiency standard. Encouraging subscriptions to the system may be warranted on efficiency grounds, although the magnitude of the subscription externality has not been quantified, and so it is not possible to tell whether the amount of the subsidy is justified. Likewise, a subsidy of local calls may be desirable, but the method of subsidization is of doubtful validity. The external benefit (or cost) of a call falls on the person being called, not on society generally.

Hence, the optimal pricing structure involves a sharing of the costs of calling between the parties to a conversation, where the costs involve the operating costs of the system and the effect of calls on the required capacity of the switching system. Only if metering costs were large in comparison with the costs of calling would it make sense not to charge for calls, but with modern electronic switching metering costs are not significant, so that one cannot justify a subsidy for local calls. Moreover, even if one could, there is no justification for taxing long-distance calls to pay the subsidy unless one believes that the externality of a local call is substantially more important than the externality of a long-distance call.

The general structure of an optimal price structure for the telephone network, given important externalities and natural monopoly, can be derived as follows. Begin with a basic monthly charge that would pay the marginal cost of terminals and copper wire connections to the local switch, and toll charges on all calls that pay the marginal cost of the switching and transmission facilities that are traffic-sensitive. These prices need further adjustment, for they may collect too much or too little total revenue. But prior to this adjustment they must also be uniformly adjusted downwards to account for the externality of subscribing and calling (assuming that people like to receive phone calls). The adjustment for the toll rate can simply be passed on to the recipient of the call; however, the basic monthly rate must come down for everyone. At this point the likely case is that the basic monthly rate does not cover the NTS costs, so that further adjustments must be made. One possibility is a subsidy paid from an economy-wide tax, but more likely the additional revenues will come from the rate structure of the telephone company. The first-best solution is to raise infra-marginal prices, such as the cost of the first few calls made per month, producing what amounts to quantity discounts for all types of calls. Alternatively, one could adopt Ramsey pricing, raising the price the most for services with relatively inelastic demand.

The resulting price structure would have a number of very interesting features. Call recipients would pay a share of the price of a call. To implement this so as only to charge for calls with a positive benefit, the shared cost would start a decent interval after the call is answered, and subscribers who desired it could be permitted to designate in advance that they would bear the full cost of their calls. All prices would be built on marginal costs, which means peak-load pricing of calling and prices for both basic access and calling that are higher in high-cost areas. To the extent that Ramsey prices were invoked, they would most certainly rely primarily on basic monthly charges, for this has by far the lowest demand elasticity: estimates range between -0.02 and -0.10. Thus, even if there is a significant externality associated with subscribing to the network, the Ramsey pricing method for paying for it involves raising the price of basic access. Or, putting the matter another way, ignoring this externality in setting prices will have very little effect on subscriptions to the system, and hence very little effect on efficiency. Finally, differences between residential and business basic monthly charges would exist only if their externality value differed, they imposed different costs on the system or they had different price elasticities.

Obviously, the pricing structure of telephone service has never reflected these principles. Until the 1970s, government officials perceived the extent of inefficiency of the pricing structure as something of an academic issue and largely ignored it. But technological change and the false signals to entrants from the price structure have led to strong pressures for competitive entry into the formerly secure telephone monopoly. Computer technology has vastly diversified the demand for telecommunications, as well as vastly increased its magnitude, and computers and other advances in microelectronics have altered the technology of supply. Examples of the broad range of new computer-based services include on-line connections to mainframes and data bases for technical and business use, automatic teller machines, remote sensing for protection against fires and burglars, and reservation services. Each of these uses has somewhat different technical requirements, so that the optimal market structure for the industry may well be to have a product-differentiated oligopoly, even if each has unexploited economies of scale. Moreover, the greater demand created by these technical advances allows considerable exploitation of scale economies even in a segmented system.

On the supply side, advances in electronics have changed the basic character of the local network. No longer are high-density networks built of dedicated copper wire pairs for each terminal. Instead, micro-electronic technology allows multiple signals on the same wires, and small-scale switches distributed throughout the local network that serve to concentrate lines from many terminals into a smaller number of active circuits, taking advantage of the fact that not all terminals are in use simultaneously. This reduces the unit cost of capacity and hence the significance of scale economies in the local network. Moreover, it undermines a cornerstone of the optimal-pricing structure that was developed above by eliminating most of the NTS costs. If, as is becoming the case, customers own their terminal equipment, and if line concentration begins when a small number of terminals are aggregated into a single pathway to the first switch, then nearly all of the system that is owned by the local telephone company consists of traffic-sensitive investment. Hence, the trend should be away from reliance on the basic monthly charge and towards greater reliance on message tolls for calling.

The failure to adjust the pricing system to the realities of costs and technology adds to the pressure for competitive entry in the parts of the system where prices are higher than the costs of service. Specifically, the attempt to tax long-distance service in order to subsidize local calling makes relatively intense users of long-distance service ripe candidates for a competitive long-distance supplier. Large companies with many telephone lines who can provide their own concentrated connections between their facilities have a strong incentive to bypass subscriptions to the local network. And other electronic pathways for communications, such as cable television and point-to-point uses of the radio spectrum, can be exploited to bypass the telecommunications network.

Thus far, government officials responsible for telecommunications policy whether as operators of public enterprises or regulators of private utilities, have focused more on the structural aspects of the problem than on pricing issues. Even in the United States, which has perhaps the greatest commitment to competition, government policy regarding entrants has been the binding constraint on the growth of competition, and the price structure is still replete with inefficiencies. The likely explanation for this phenomenon is the belief by political actors that the cost of local service to residences is the price that is most visible politically and that rationalized pricing will cause residential service to become more expensive, either from raising basic monthly charges or from message toll for local calls. To avoid raising residential prices, political actors therefore believe that they have to keep some other prices above the cost of service, and to maintain these prices in the face of diminished or perhaps even non-existent natural monopoly they must erect barriers to competitive entry aimed at the overcharged customers.

PRICES AND MARKET STRUCTURE IN BROADCASTING. The most common way to pay for broadcasting is to provide signals to the audience at no charge, and to rely on either advertising or government subsidies as the source of revenues. In one sense such an arrangement seems to fit the fact that broadcasts are a classic public good; the marginal cost to the broadcaster of one more person receiving a broadcast is zero, and consumption among members of the audience is completely non-rivalrous. Hence, any attempt to charge a viewer for a programme can introduce inefficiency to the extent that anyone is thereby excluded from participation who also has a positive willingness to pay to join the audience.

The difficulty with free broadcasting, however, is that it does not necessarily result in programmes that maximize the net willingness of the audience to pay. Ignoring for a moment the frictions in the political process and the incentives of political actors to manipulate programme content to their private benefit, both subsidized and advertiser-supported television lead broadcasters to measure their

94

success primarily on the basis of the size of audience. In a subsidized system, the objective would be to make certain that political support is as high as possible, and in an advertising system, in which the broadcaster is selling the attention of viewers, revenues are more or less proportional to audience size. The issue in both cases is not whether audience satisfaction is maximized but whether it is kept high enough for a large enough number of people to maximize revenues from a payment system that is not based on the intensity of preferences but on the number of satisfied customers. In particular, small groups with intense willingness to pay for an unusual type of programming material will generally not have their preferences satisfied even if their aggregate willingness to pay exceeds that of a large audience for the traditional mass-audience programme.

Three means are available for coping with this state of affairs. One is to expand the number of broadcast options until all groups are satisfied. Suppose that there is a large mass audience and a series of small, specialized ones. As the number of stations expands, the audience for mass programmes each can expect will be the total mass audience divided by the number of stations. Eventually, there will be enough stations so that the largest specialized taste will constitute a larger audience than the share of the mass audience the next station could expect to capture, so that a strategy to maximize audience will lead to specialization. In the United States, this is more or less the policy with respect to radio broadcasting. In the early years of radio, the Federal Communications Commission tried to assure diversity in commercial broadcasting by specifying the format (e.g. type of programmes) that a station could broadcast. Recently, station formats have been deregulated, yet the multiplicity of categories remains, in much the same fashion that there is a broad spectrum of magazines and books by type of material.

In television, the strategy of increasing the number of stations is more difficult to follow. Television stations consume far more radio frequency space than radio stations, and no nation has thus far been willing to allocate enough high-quality radio spectrum to television to provide much of a test as to whether specialization might take place in a more extensive industry. An unplanned test, however, is under way in Italy, where in the 1970s the courts declared that the government had no constitutional right to limit the number of television stations, and largely unregulated entry has taken place on a massive scale. It is too soon to tell what the ultimate outcome of this system will be.

The second mechanism to produce more diversity in television is to allow the audience to express a willingness to pay, commonly by installing cable television with much higher capacity than off-air television and charging customers on the basis of the number and type of channels that they elect to receive. The inefficiency inherent in this system is the cost of privatizing broadcasts so that on either a per programme or per channel basis they can be sold. Prior to the extensive development of cable television in the United States, the common speculation was that privatization of broadcasts would cause a diversion from traditional mass-audience programming, with more activity in cultural programmes, educational broadcasting and public affairs. The expectation was based upon the belief that higher-income groups were more interested in diversity and would have more influence in determining the content of for-pay systems. In practice, this expectation has not been realized. The new cable-oriented networks for the most part offer programming that is like that provided by off-air broadcasters, such as movies, sports events and regular series. The principal exception is in public affairs, where national cable news and public events networks have succeeded. Educational and cultural programming, however, has been largely unsuccessful. The inference to be drawn is that scarcity in television stations caused an excess demand for television, but primarily for programmes that were much like those featured by off-air stations, largely oriented towards the mass audience.

The third means of increasing diversity is to create a single, multi-outlet monopoly broadcasting entity. If such an entity seeks to maximize total audience, it will not have as much incentive to duplicate mass programming, because audience substitution from one channel to the next will have no value. A second or third mass-audience station will increase the size of the total audience, but the evidence indicates that the effect is small compared with audience diversion. For example, in the United States the first television station captures a little less than half of the potential audience available in prime evening viewing time. No matter how many additional stations are added, the maximum viewing share appears to be about 80 per cent, and this is almost totally achieved after three or four stations are operating. This suggests that a multi-channel monopolist would either diversify programming on the second or third channel, or simply elect not to broadcast on more than one or two channels, depending on the relationship between the value of a net increment to the audience and the costs of adding another channel.

American public television provides an example of a novel method of support, for it is one of the few attempts to implement a decentralized decision process for acquiring a public good (here programmes). The first component of the system is the method of public financing, which involves multiple year, advance funding to erect some barrier to political manipulation of programmes. The public funds are then divided into three components: a budget for experimental programming that is spent by an independent, quasi-public entity (the Corporation for Public Broadcasting); a budget for the technical operation of the national network (Public Broadcasting Service); and a direct subsidy of local stations. This subsidy is based in part on the success of the station in obtaining private contributions from its audience. Thus the station subsidy amounts to an attempt to overcome the free-rider problem faced by viewers by providing matching funds for their contributions.

The second component of the system is the mechanism by which stations decide which programmes will appear on the network. This is accomplished by a combination voting and price system. The price of a programme for each station is determined by the size of the community it serves, and stations then vote on each programme proposal. If some stations vote against the proposal, the prices faced by the supporters are increased by an amount necessary to allow the programme to cover its costs, and voting proceeds again. The process continues until programmes are either purchased or discarded; usually fewer than a dozen iterations are required to reach a decision. Stations voting against a programme are excluded from broadcasting it; however, stations may later join the group paying for it by paying a premium price.

The programme acquisition process decentralizes network programming to the stations, thereby serving two ends. First, because the station budgets depend on contributions, or the voluntary willingness to pay of the audience, there exists a feedback mechanism from the audience to the network that is similar to a pay-TV system. Second, the network schedule becomes less vulnerable to political attack, for centralized government officials who might seek to control it face a collective of over 150 station licensees, who, in turn, are actively using contributions patterns to make decisions about which programmes to acquire.

The American system of financing public television does not, of course, have pristine efficiency properties; neither the voluntary audience contributions nor the mechanism whereby stations select programmes is an incentive-compatible mechanism. Nevertheless, in the inherently imperfect world of public goods acquisition, they appear to perform remarkably well, and experimental investigations in a laboratory setting suggest that the method of acquiring programmes can be productively employed in a variety of settings for collective decisions.

REMAINING ISSUES. Two aspects of the communications sector make it a ripe area for continuing study. First is the rapidly evolving technology of supply and demand, and the second is the pervasive and changing influence of political processes on the structure and performance of the sector.

With changing technology has come a significant change in the pattern of demand for services. This suggests that historical patterns of use and estimates of service-specific demand are unreliable predictors of the future. Yet relatively little research has investigated how changing technology – lower costs, greater possibilities of use, more technical capabilities – has affected key aspects of demand: the rate of growth by service and customer category and the own and cross-elasticities of demand.

Changing technical possibilities and demand should also feed back into the political forces that guide the development of the sector. Most advanced industrialized nations are in the midst of transition in at least some policies regarding communications, such as the privatization and introduction of competition in telecommunications in Japan and Great Britain, and the elimination of the state broadcasting monopolies in France and Italy. These changes deserve study on two counts: how these dramatic policy changes affect performance, and what political forces they may be creating that will shape policy and industry structure in the future.

A period of rapid change is one in which important new knowledge is likely to be forthcoming. One can anticipate that a summary of the economics of communications a decade or two hence will contain significant and surprising new insights.

BIBLIOGRAPHY

Bloch, H. and Wirth, M. 1984. The demand for pay services on cable television. *Information Economics and Policy* 1(4), 311–32.

Brock, G. 1981. *The Telecommunications Industry: The Dynamics of Market Structure.* Cambridge, Mass.: Harvard University Press.

Coase, R. 1959. The Federal Communications Commission. *Journal of Law and Economics* 2(1), 1–40.

Courville, L., de Fontenay, A., Dobell, R. 1983. *Economic Analysis of Telecommunications.* Amsterdam: North-Holland.

Evans, D. (ed.) 1971. *Breaking Up Bell.* Amsterdam: North-Holland.

Levin, H. 1971. *The Invisible Resource.* Baltimore: Johns Hopkins Press.

Machlup, F. 1980. *The Production and Distribution of Knowledge in the United States.* Princeton: Princeton University Press.

Mitchell, B. 1978. Optimal pricing and local telephone services. *American Economic Review* 68(4), September, 517–37.

Network Inquiry Special Staff. 1980. *New Television Networks: Entry, Jurisdiction, Ownership and Regulation.* Washington, DC: Federal Communications Commission.

Noll, R. 1985. 'Let them make toll calls': a state regulator's lament. *American Economic Review* 75(2), May, 52–6.

Noll, R., Peck, M.J. and McGowan, J.J. 1973. *Economic Aspects of Television Regulation.* Washington, DC: Brookings.

Owen, B. 1975. *Economics and Freedom of Expression.* Cambridge, Mass.: Ballinger.

Owen, B., Beebe, J. and Manning, W. 1974. *Television Economics.* Lexington, Mass.: D.C. Heath.

Park, R.E. 1972. Prospects for cable in the 100 largest television markets. *Bell Journal of Economics* 3(1), Spring, 130–50.

Park, R.E. 1975. New television networks. *Bell Journal of Economics* 6(2), Autumn, 607–20.

Rosse, J. 1967. Daily newspapers, monopolistic competition, and economies of scale. *American Economic Review* 52(2), May, 522–33.

Rosse, J., Dertouzos, J., Robinson, M. and Wildman, S. 1979. Economic issues in mass communications industries. *Proceedings of the Symposium on Media Concentration.* Washington, DC: Federal Trade Commission. Vol. I, 40–192.

Snow, M. 1986. *Marketplace for Telecommunications: Regulation and Deregulation in Industrialized Democracies.* White Plains, NY: Longman.

Spence, A.M. and Owen, B. 1977. Television programming, monopolistic competition and welfare. *Quarterly Journal of Economics* 91(1), February, 103–21.

Steiner, P. 1952. Program patterns and preferences, and the workability of competition in radio broadcasting. *Quarterly Journal of Economics* 66(2), May, 194–223.

Spitzer, M. 1985. Controlling the content of print and broadcast. *Southern California Law Review* 58(6), September, 1349–405.

Taylor, L. 1980. *Telecommunications Demand: A Survey and Critique.* Cambridge, Mass.: Ballinger.

von Weiszacker, C. 1984. Free entry into telecommunications? *Information Economics and Policy* 1(3), 197–216.

Comparative Advantage

RONALD FINDLAY

The modern economy, and the very world as we know it today, obviously depends fundamentally on specialization and the division of labour, between individuals, firms and nations. The principle of comparative advantage, first clearly stated and proved by David Ricardo in 1817, is the fundamental analytical explanation of the source of these enormous 'gains from trade'. Though an awareness of the benefits of specialization must go back to the dim mists of antiquity in all civilizations, it was not until Ricardo that this deepest and most beautiful result in all of economics was obtained. Though the logic applies equally to inter*personal*, inter*firm*, and inter*regional* trade, it was in the context of inter*national* trade that the principle of comparative advantage was discovered and has been investigated ever since.

What constituted a 'nation' for Ricardo were two things – a 'factor endowment', of a specified number of units of labour in the simplest model, and a 'technology'; the productivity of this labour in terms of different goods, such as cloth and wine in his example. Thus labour can move freely between the production of cloth and wine in England and in Portugal, but each labour force is trapped within its own borders. Suppose that a unit of labour in Portugal can produce 1 unit of cloth or 1 unit of wine while in England a unit of labour can produce 4 units of cloth or 2 units of wine. Thus the opportunity cost of a unit of wine is 1 unit of cloth in Portugal while it is 2 units of cloth in England. Assuming competitive markets and free trade, it follows that *both* goods will never be produced in *both* countries since wine in England and cloth in Portugal could always be undermined by a simple arbitrage operation involving export of cloth from England and import of wine from Portugal. Thus wine in England or cloth in Portugal must contract until at least one of these industries produces zero output. If both goods are consumed in positive amounts, the 'terms of trade' in equilibrium must lie in the closed interval between 1 and 2 units of cloth per unit of wine. Which of the two countries specializes completely will depend upon the relative size of each country (as measured by the labour force *and* its productivity in each industry) and upon the extent to which each of the two goods is favoured by the pattern of world demand. Thus Portugal is more likely to specialize the smaller she is compared to England in the sense defined above and the more world demand is skewed towards the consumption of wine relative to the consumption of cloth.

Viewed as a 'positive' theory, the principle of comparative advantage yields *predictions* about (a) the *direction* of trade, that each country exports the good in which it has the lower comparative opportunity cost ratio as defined by the technology in each country, and about (b) the *terms* of trade, that it is bounded by these comparative cost ratios. From a 'normative' standpoint the principle implies that the citizens of each country become 'better off' as a result of trade, with the extent of the gains from trade depending upon the degree to which the terms of trade exceed the domestic comparative cost ratio. It is the 'normative' part of the doctrine that has always been the more controversial, and it is therefore necessary to evaluate it with the greatest care.

In Ricardo's example the labour force is presumably supplied by different households, each of which has the same *relative* productivity in the two sectors as the national average. Thus *all* households in *each* country must become better off as a result of trade if the terms of trade lie strictly in between the domestic comparative cost ratios. The import-competing sector in each country simply switches over instantaneously and costlessly to producing the export good (moving to the opposite corner of its linear production-possibilities frontier, in terms of the familiar geometry), obtaining the desired level of the other good by imports, raising utility in the process. When one country is incompletely specialized, then all households in that country remain at unchanged utility levels, all of the gain from trade going to the individuals in the 'small' country. Thus we have a situation in which *everybody gains*, in at least one country, while *nobody loses* in either country, as a result of trade.

This very strong result depends upon Ricardo's assumption of perfect occupational mobility in each country. Suppose we take the opposite extreme of completely *specific* labour in each sector, so that each country produces a fixed combination of cloth and wine, with no possibility of transformation. In this case labour in the import-competing sector in each country must necessarily *lose*, as a result of trade, while labour in each country's export sector must gain. It can be shown, however, that trade will improve *potential* welfare in each country in the Samuelson sense that the utility-possibility frontier with trade will dominate the corresponding frontier without trade, so that no one need be worse off, and at least someone better off, if lump-sum taxes and transfers are possible (Samuelson, 1962).

Another very important normative issue is the question of the relationship between the free-trade equilibrium and *world* efficiency and welfare. In the Ricardian model world welfare in general will *not* be maximized by free trade. In the numerical example considered here Ricardo stresses the fact that England can still gain from trade even though she has an *absolute* advantage in the production of *both* goods, her productivity being greater in both cloth and wine, though comparatively greater in cloth. Suppose that labour in Portugal could produce at English levels, *if it moved to England*; i.e. the English superiority is based on climate or other 'environmental' factors and not on differences in aptitude or skill. Then, if labour were free to move, and in the absence of 'national' sentiment, all production would be located in England, and Portugal would cease to exist. The former Portuguese labour would be better off than under free trade, since their real wage in terms of wine will now be 2 units instead of 1. English labour would be worse off, if the terms of trade were originally better than 0.5 wine per 1 cloth, but it is easy to show that they could be sufficiently compensated since the utility-possibility frontier for the world economy as a whole is moved out by the integration of the labour forces.

The case when each country has an absolute advantage in one good is more interesting. As is easy to see (see Findlay, 1982), this case will involve a movement of labour to the country with the higher real wage under free trade, increasing the production of this country's exportable good and reducing that of the lower-wage country under free trade. The terms of trade turn against the higher-wage country until eventually the real wage is equalized. The terms of trade that achieve this equality of real wages will be equal to the ratio of labour productivities in each country's export sector; i.e. the 'double factoral' terms of trade will be unity. This solution of free trade *combined* with perfect labour mobility will achieve not only efficiency for the world economy but equity as well. 'Unequal exchange' would not exist, while liberal, Utilitarian and Rawlsian criteria of distributive justice would be satisfied as well, as pointed out in Findlay (1982). Despite all this, it still seems utopian to expect a policy of 'open borders', in *either* direction, for the contemporary world of nation-states.

The two-country, two-good Ricardian model was extended to many goods and countries by a number of subsequent writers, whose efforts are described in detail by Haberler (1933) and Viner (1937). In the case of two countries and n goods the concept of a 'chain of comparative advantage' has been put forward, with the goods listed in descending order in terms of the *relative* efficiency of the two countries in producing them. It is readily shown that with a uniform wage in each country all goods from 1 to some number j must be exported, while all goods from $(j + 1)$ to n must be imported. The number j itself will depend upon the relative sizes of the two countries and the composition of world demand. An analogous chain concept applies to the case of two goods and countries, this time ranking the countries in terms of the ratio of their productivities in the two goods, with country 1 having the greater *relative* efficiency in cloth and country n in wine. World demand and the sizes of the labour forces will determine the 'marginal' country j, with countries 1 to j exporting cloth and $(j + 1)$ to n exporting wine.

The simultaneous consideration of comparative advantage with many goods and many countries presents severe analytical difficulties. Graham (1948) considered several elaborate numerical examples, his work inspiring the Rochester theorists McKenzie (1954) and Jones (1961) to apply the powerful tools of activity analysis to this particular case of a linear general equilibrium model. It is interesting'to note in connection with mathematical programming and activity analysis that Kantorovich (1965) in his celebrated book on planning for the Soviet economy worked out an example of optimal specialization patterns for factories that corresponds *exactly* to the Ricardian model of trade between countries.

While most of the literature on the Ricardian trade model has concentrated on the model of chapter 7 of the *Principles*, in which it appears that labour is the sole scarce factor, his more extended model in the *Essay on Profits* has been curiously neglected, though the connections between trade, income distribution and growth which that analysis explores are quite fascinating. The formal structure of the model was laid out very thoroughly in Pasinetti (1960). The economy produces two goods, corn and manufactures, each of which has a one-period lag between the input of labour and the emergence of output. Labour thus has to be supported by a 'wage fund', an initially given stock that is accumulated over time by saving out of profits. Corn also requires land as an input, which is in fixed supply and yields diminishing returns to successive increments of labour. The wage-rate is given exogenously in terms of corn, and manufactures are a luxury good consumed only by the land-owning class, who obtain rents determined by the marginal product of land. Profits are the difference between the marginal product of labour and the given real wage, which is equal to the marginal product 'discounted' by the rate of interest, in this model equal to the rate of profit, defined as the ratio of profits to the real wage that has to be advanced a period before. Momentary equilibrium determines the relative price of corn and manufactures, the rent per acre and the rate or profit, as well as the output levels and allocation of the labour force between sectors. The growth of the system is at a rate equal to the product of the rate of profit and the propensity to save of the capitalist class. It is shown that the system approaches a stationary state, with a monotonically falling rate of profit and rising rents per acre.

The opportunity to import corn more cheaply from abroad will have significant distributional and growth consequences. Just as Ricardo argued in his case for the repeal of the Corn Laws, cheaper foreign corn will reduce domestic rents and raise the domestic rate of profit, and thus the rate of growth. The approach to the Ricardian stationary state is postponed, though of course it cannot be ultimately averted. The growth consequences for the corn exporter, however, are adverse (Findlay, 1974).

The main doctrinal significance of this wider Ricardian model, however, is to reveal the extent to which the subsequent 'general equilibrium' or 'neoclassical' approach to international trade is already present within the Ricardian framework. For one thing, the pattern of comparative advantage itself depends upon the complex interaction of technology, factor proportions and tastes. In the chapter 7 analysis the pattern of comparative advantage is *exogenous*, simply given by the four fixed technical coefficients indicating the productivity of labour in cloth and wine in England and Portugal. The production-possibility frontiers for each country are linear, and comparative advantage is simply determined by the magnitude of the slopes. As demonstrated in Findlay (1974), however, the *Essay on Profits* model implies a concave production-possibilities frontier at any moment, since there are diminishing returns to labour in corn even though the marginal productivity of labour in manufactures is constant. With two countries the pattern of comparative advantage will depend upon the slopes of these curves at their autarky equilibria, which are *endogenous* variables depending upon the sizes of 'wage fund' in relation to the supply of land and the consumption pattern of landowners, as well as the technology for the two goods.

As Burgstaller (1986) points out, however, the steady-state solution of the model restores the linear structure of the pattern of comparative advantage. The zero profit rate in the steady state requires the marginal product of labour to be equal to the given real wage, and this implies a fixed land–labour ratio and hence output per unit of labour in corn. Thus we once again have two fixed technical coefficients, so that the slope of the linear production-possibilities frontier is again an exogenous indicator of comparative advantage.

The 'neo-Ricardian' approach of Steedman (1979a, 1979b) considers more general time-phased structures of production. Technology alone determines negatively sloped wage–profit or factor–price frontiers, any point on which generates a set of relative product prices and hence a pattern of comparative advantage relative to another such economy.

While J.S. Mill, Marshall and Edgeworth all made major contributions to trade theory, the concept of comparative advantage did not undergo any evolution in their work beyond the stage at which Ricardo had left it. They essentially concentrated on the determination of the terms of trade and on various comparative static exercises. The interwar years, however, brought fundamental advances, stemming in particular from the work of the Swedes Heckscher (1919) and Ohlin (1933). The development of a diagrammatic apparatus to handle general equilibrium interactions of tastes, technology and factor endowments by Haberler (1933), Leontief (1933), Lerner (1932) and others culminated in the rigorous establishment of trade theory and comparative advantage as a branch of neoclassical general equilibrium theory.

The essentials of this approach can be expounded in terms of the familiar two-country, two-good, two-factor model (see Jones (1965) for an algebraic and Findlay (1970) for a diagrammatic exposition). The given factor supplies and constant returns to scale technology define concave production-possibility frontiers, assuming that the goods differ in factor intensity. This determines the 'supply side' of the model, which is closed by the specification of consumer preferences. Economies that have identical technology, factor endowments and tastes will have the same autarky equilibrium price-ratio and so will have no incentive to engage in trade. Countries must therefore differ with respect to at least one of these characteristics for differences in comparative advantage to emerge. With identical technology and factor endowments, a country will have a comparative advantage in the good its citizens prefer *less* in comparison to the foreign country, since then this good will be cheaper at home. Similarly, if factor endowments and tastes are identical, differences in comparative advantage will

103

be governed by relative technological efficiency; i.e. a country will have a comparative advantage in the good in which its relative technological efficiency is greater, just as in the Ricardian model. These differences in technological efficiency could be represented, for example, by the magnitude of multiplicative constants in the production functions; i.e. 'Hicks-neutral' differences.

In keeping with the ideas of Heckscher and Ohlin, however, it is differences in factor proportions that have dominated the explanation of comparative advantage in the neoclassical literature. The Heckscher–Ohlin Theorem, that each country will export the commodity that uses its relatively abundant factor most intensively, has been rigorously established and the necessary qualifications carefully specified. Among the more important of these is the requirement that factor-intensity 'reversals' do not take place; i.e. that one good is always more capital-intensive than the other at all wage-rental ratios or at least within the relevant range defined by the factor proportions of the trading countries.

Associated with the Heckscher–Ohlin Theorem is the Stolper–Samuelson Theorem (1941), that trade benefits the scarce factor, and the celebrated Factor Price Equalization Theorem of Lerner (1952, though written in 1932) and Samuelson (1948, 1949, 1953), which states that under certain conditions free trade will lead to complete equalization of factor rewards even though factors are not mobile internationally. The normative significance of this theorem is that free trade alone can achieve world efficiency in production and resource allocation, unlike the case of the Ricardian model. The requirements for the theorem to hold, however, are very stringent. In particular it requires factor proportions to be sufficiently close to each other in the trading partners so that the production patterns are fairly similar. Thus it would be far-fetched to expect the price of unskilled labour to be equalized between Bangladesh and the United States, for example.

One limitation of the Heckscher–Ohlin model was that the stock of 'capital', however conceived, should be an endogenous variable determined by the propensity to save or time preference of each trading community. The model has been extended by Oniki and Uzawa (1965) to a situation where the labour force is growing in each country at an exogenous rate and capital is accumulated in response to given propensities to save in each country. One of the goods is taken to be the 'capital' good, conceived of as a malleable 'putty-putty' instrument. They demonstrate that the system will converge in the long run to a particular capital–labour ratio for each country, which will be higher for the country with the larger saving propensity. As the capital–labour ratios evolve, the pattern of comparative advantage for a given 'small' country in an open trading world will also shift over time towards more capital-intensive goods in the process of economic development. Thus comparative advantage should not be conceived as given and immutable, but evolving with capital accumulation and technological change. Much of the loose talk about 'dynamic' comparative advantage in the development literature, however, is misconceived since it attempts to change the pattern of production by protection *before* the necessary changes in the capacity to produce efficiently have taken place. Other models which endogenize the capital stocks of the trading countries are Stiglitz (1970) and Findlay (1978), which utilize a variable rate of time preference and an 'Austrian' point-input/point-output technology, which implies a continuum of capital goods as represented by the 'trees' of different ages.

Empirical testing of the positive side of the theory of comparative advantage only begins in a systematic way with the work of MacDougall (1951) on the Ricardian theory and the celebrated article of Leontief (1954) which uncovered the apparent paradox that US exports were more labour-intensive than her imports. Leontief's dramatic finding spurred considerable further empirical research motivated by the desire to find a satisfactory explanation. The role of natural resources, the increasing scarcity of which in the US caused capital to be substituted for it in import-competing production, was stressed by Vanek (1963). The role of 'human' capital was stressed by Kenen (1965) and a number of empirical investigators, who found that US exports were considerably more skill-intensive than her imports, even though physical capital-intensity was only weakly correlated with exports and imports. This pointed to the need to reinterpret the simple Heckscher–Ohlin model in terms of skilled and unskilled labour as the two factors, rather than labour of uniform quality and physical capital. Since the formation of skill through education is an endogenous variable, a function of a wage differential that is itself a function of trade, we need a general equilibrium model that can simultaneously handle both these aspects, a task that was attempted in Findlay and Kierzkowski (1983).

Many other extensions of the Heckscher–Ohlin theory are surveyed in Jones and Neary (1984), while Deardorf (1984) gives a very incisive account of the attempts at empirical testing of the theory of comparative advantage in its different manifestations. Ethier (1984) is a very helpful guide to the intricacies of comparative advantage with many goods and factors. Finally, the crucially important role of increasing returns to scale in specialization and international trade has only recently been rigorously investigated since it implies departures from perfect competition. Helpman and Krugman (1985) is a thorough treatment of the present state of knowledge in this area.

BIBLIOGRAPHY

Burgstaller, A. 1986. Unifying Ricardo's theories of growth and comparative advantage. *Economica*.

Deardorf, A. 1984. Testing trade theories. In *Handbook of International Economics*, ed. R.W. Jones and P.B. Kenen, Vol. 1, Amsterdam: North-Holland.

Ethier, W. 1984. Higher dimensional issues in trade theory. In *Handbook of International Economics*, ed. R.W. Jones and P.B. Kenen, Vol. 1, Amsterdam: North-Holland.

Findlay, R. 1970. *Trade and Specialization*. Harmondsworth: Penguin.

Findlay, R. 1974. Relative prices, growth and trade in a simple Ricardian system. *Economica* 41, February, 1–13.

Findlay, R. 1978. An 'Austrian' model of international trade and interest equalization. *Journal of Political Economy* 86(6), December, 989–1007.

Findlay, R. 1982. International distributive justice. *Journal of International Economics* 13, 1–14.

Findlay, R. and Kierzkowski, H. 1983. International trade and human capital: a simple general equilibrium model. *Journal of Political Economy* 91(6), December, 957–78.

Graham, F. 1948. *The Theory of International Values*. Princeton: Princeton University Press.

Haberler, G. 1933. *The Theory of International Trade*. Trans. by A. Stonier and F. Benham, London: W. Hodge, 1936; revised edn 1937.

Heckscher, E. 1919. The effects of foreign trade on the distributions of income. *Ekonomisk Tidskrift*. English translation in *Readings in the Theory of International Trade*, ed. H.S. Ellis and L.A. Metzler, Philadelphia: Blakiston, 1949.

Helpman, E. and Krugman, P. 1985. *Market Structure and Foreign Trade*. Cambridge, Mass.: MIT Press.

Jones, R.W. 1961. Comparative advantage and the theory of tariffs. *Review of Economic Studies* 28, 161–75.

Jones, R.W. 1965. The structure of simple general equilibrium models. *Journal of Political Economy* 73, December, 557–72.

Jones, R.W. and Neary, P. 1984. Positive trade theory. In *Handbook of International Economics*, ed. R.W. Jones and P.B. Kenen, Vol. 1, Amsterdam: North-Holland.

Kantorovich, L. 1965. *The Best Use of Economic Resources*. Cambridge, Mass.: Harvard University Press.

Kenen, P.B. 1965. Nature, capital and trade. *Journal of Political Economy* 73, October, 437–60; Erratum, December, 658.

Leontief, W.W. 1933. The use of indifference curves in the analysis of foreign trade. *Quarterly Journal of Economics* 47, May, 493–503.

Leontief, W.W. 1954. Domestic production and foreign trade: the American capital position re-examined. *Economia Internazionale* 7, February, 9–38.

Lerner, A.P. 1932. The diagrammatic representation of cost conditions in international trade. *Economica* 12, August, 345–56.

Lerner, A.P. 1952. Factor prices and international trade. *Economica* 19, February, 1–15.

MacDougall, G.D.A. 1951. British and American exports. *Economic Journal* 61, December, 697–724.

McKenzie, L.W. 1954. Specialisation and efficiency in world production. *Review of Economic Studies* 21(3), 165–80.

Ohlin, B. 1933. *Inter-regional and International Trade*. Cambridge, Mass.: Harvard University Press.

Oniki, H. and Uzawa, H. 1965. Patterns of trade and investment in a dynamic model of international trade. *Review of Economic Studies* 32, 15–38.

Pasinetti, L. 1960. A mathematical formulation of the Ricardian system. *Review of Economic Studies* 27, 78–98.

Ricardo, D. 1951. *The Works and Correspondence of David Ricardo*. Ed. P. Sraffa, Vols I and IV, Cambridge: Cambridge University Press.

Samuelson, P.A. 1948. International trade and the equalization of factor prices. *Economic Journal* 58, June, 163–84.

Samuelson, P.A. 1949. International factor price equalization once again. *Economic Journal* 59, June, 181–97.

Samuelson, P.A. 1953. Prices of factors and goods in general equilibrium. *Review of Economic Studies* 21, 1–20.

Samuelson, P.A. 1962. The gains from international trade once again. *Economic Journal* 72, December, 820–29.

Steedman, I. 1979a. *Trade Amongst Growing Economies*. Cambridge: Cambridge University Press.

Steedman, I. (ed.) 1979b. *Fundamental Issues in Trade Theory*. London: Macmillan.

Stiglitz, J. 1970. Factor-price equalization in a dynamic economy. *Journal of Political Economy* 78(3), May–June, 456–88.

Stolper, W. and Samuelson, P.A. 1941. Protection and real wages. *Review of Economic Studies* 9, 58–73.

Vanek, J. 1963. *The Natural Resource Content of US Foreign Trade 1870–1955*. Cambridge, Mass.: MIT Press.

Viner, J. 1937. *Studies in the Theory of International Trade*. New York: Harper.

Competition and Selection

SIDNEY G. WINTER

Under competitive conditions, a business firm must maximize profit if it is to survive – or so it is often claimed. This purported analogue of biological natural selection has had substantial influence in economic thinking, and the proposition remains influential today. In general, its role has been to serve as an informal auxiliary defence, or crutch, for standard theoretical approaches based on optimization and equilibrium. It appeared explicitly in this role in a provocative passage in Milton Friedman's famous essay on methodology (Friedman, 1953, ch. 1), and it seems that many economists are familiar with it in this context only.

There is, however, an alternative role that the proposition can and does play. It serves as an informal statement of the common conclusion of a class of theorems characterizing explicit models of economic selection processes. A model in this class posits, first, a range of possible behaviours for the firm. This range must obviously extend beyond the realm of profit maximization if the conclusion of the argument is to be non-trivial, and it must include behaviour that is appropriately termed 'profit maximizing' if the conclusion is to be logically attainable at all. The model must also characterize a particular dynamic process that in some way captures the general idea that profitable firms tend to survive and grow, while unprofitable ones tend to decline and fail. A stationary position of such a process is a 'selection equilibrium'.

Models of this type occupy an important but non-central position in evolutionary economic theory (Nelson and Winter, 1982). They establish that the equilibria of standard competitive theory can indeed be 'mimicked' (in several different senses) by the equilibria of selection models. More importantly, by making explicit the strong assumptions that apparently are required to generate this sort of result, they are the basis for a critique of its generality and an appraisal of the strength of the crutch on which standard theory leans. They also provide a helpful entry-way to the much broader class of evolutionary models in which mimicry results fail to hold. This entry-way has the convenient feature that the return path to standard theory is well marked; the sense in which evolutionary theory subsumes portions of standard theory becomes clear.

The concept of competition need not, of course, be considered only in the context of perfectly competitive equilibrium. In a broader sense of the term, any non-trivial selection model in which the 'fit' prosper and the 'unfit' do not is a model of a 'competitive' process. The process need not have a static equilibrium, or any equilibrium, and it may easily lead to results that are clearly non-competitive by the standards of industrial organization economics.

The remainder of this essay first considers in more detail the theoretical links between selection processes and competitive equilibrium outcomes. It then examines a more interesting and less well-explored area that involves selection and, in a broad sense, competition – Schumpeterian competition.

COMPETITIVE EQUILIBRIUM AS A SELECTION OUTCOME. The intention here is to describe the heuristic basis of existing examples of this type of theorem, or, alternatively, to describe the basic recipe from which an obviously large class of broadly similar results could be produced. There may be other basic recipes, as yet unknown. There certainly are ways to ignore individual instructions of the recipe and yet preserve the result, though at the cost of delicately contrived adjustments in other assumptions.

(To avoid confusion, it should be noted at the outset that the word 'equilibrium' is used in two different senses in this discussion, the 'no incentives to change behaviour' sense employed in economic theory and the 'stationary position of a dynamic process' sense that is common outside of economics. The point of the discussion is, in fact, to relate these two equilibrium ideas in a particular way.)

(1) Constant returns to scale must prevail in the specific sense that the supply and demand functions of an individual firm at any particular time are expressible as the scale (or 'capacity') of that firm at that time multiplied by functions depending on prices, but not directly on scale or time. Increasing returns to scale must be excluded for familiar reasons. Decreasing returns must be excluded because they will in general give rise to equilibrium 'entrepreneurial rents' which could be partially dissipated by departures from maximization without threatening the survival of the firm. Thus, for example, the U-shaped long-run average cost curve of textbook competitive theory does not provide a context in which selection necessarily mimics standard theory if competitive equilibrium would require some firms to be on the upward sloping portion of the curve.

(2) Firms must increase scale when profitable and decrease scale (or go out of business entirely) when unprofitable. Alternatively, profitability of a particular firm must lead to entry by perfect imitators of that firm's actions. In the absence of such assumptions, it is plain that there will in general be equilibria with non-zero profit levels, which under assumption (1) cannot mimic the competitive result. While the 'decline or fail' assumption is a plausible reflection of long-run breakeven constraints characteristic of actual capitalist institutions, no such realistic force attaches to the requirement that profitability lead to expansion. If firms do not pursue profits in the long-run sense of expanding in response to

positive profitability, stationary positions may involve positive profits. Such stationary positions fail to mimic competitive equilibria for that reason alone (given constant returns), but they also introduce once again the possibility that the short-run behavioural responses of surviving firms may dissipate some of the positive profit that is potentially achievable at selection equilibrium scale.

In standard theory, expansion in response to profitability may be seen as an aspect of the firm's profit-seeking on the assumption that it regards prices as unaffected by its capacity decisions. In turn, this ordinarily requires that the firm in question be but one of an indeterminately large number of firms that all have access to the same technological and organizational possibilities.

While the assumption that firms have identical production sets and behavioural rules is common and appears inoffensive in orthodox theorizing, it is very much at odds with evolutionary theory. The orthodox view comes down to the assertion that all productive knowledge is freely available to one and all – perhaps it is all in the public library. By contrast, evolutionary theory emphasizes the role of firms as highly individualized repositories of productive knowledge, not all of which is articulable. From the evolutionary perspective, the fact that mimicry theorems rely on assumptions of unimpaired access to a public knowledge pool is by itself sufficient to make it clear that the selection argument can provide only a weak and shaky crutch for standard competitive theory.

(3) A firm that is breaking even with a positive output at prevailing prices must not alter its behaviour; a potential entrant that would only break even at prevailing prices must not enter. This assumption is needed to assure that the competitive equilibrium position is in fact a stationary position of the selection process.

Models of natural selection in biology do not typically involve this sort of assumption, but neither do they conclude that only the fittest genotypes survive – the biological analogue of the proposition discussed here. Rather, they show how constant gene frequencies come to prevail as the selection forces that tend to eliminate diversity come into balance with mutation forces that constantly renew it. A strictly analogous treatment of economic selection would be much more appealing than the sort of result discussed here. It would admit that occasional disruptions may arise from random behavioural change, or from over-optimistic entrants. Thus, potentially at least, it could better serve the purpose of establishing the point that the results of standard competitive theory are in some sense robust with respect to its behavioural assumptions. Unfortunately, standard theory offers no clue as to what this sense might be. It is plain that the adjustment processes of the system are centrally involved, and there is no behaviourally plausible theory of adjustment that is the dynamic counterpart in the disciplinary paradigm of static competitive equilibrium theory.

Within the limits defined by the requirement for a strictly static competitive outcome, the most plausible approach combines the idea of characterizing the firms in the selection process by their 'rules of behaviour' – an idea advanced in a seminal paper by Armen Alchian (1950) – with Herbert Simon's idea of satisficing (1955). In the simplest version, each firm simply adheres unswervingly to its own deterministic behavioural rule (or 'routine', in the language of Nelson and Winter, 1982). Such a rule subsumes or implies the firm's supply and demand functions, and given the conditions set forth in (1) and (2) above, a constant environment evokes a constant response. Satisficing may be introduced as a complication of this picture by an assumption that a firm that sustains losses over a period of time will search for a better behavioural rule; this adds behavioural plausibility to the adjustment process but does not introduce the possibility that random rule change might disrupt an otherwise stationary competitive equilibrium position.

(4) The final requirement can be succinctly but inadequately stated as 'some firms must actually be profit maximizers'. Although this formulation does adequately cover some simple cases, it does not suggest the depth and subtlety of the issues involved.

Two points deserve particular emphasis here. The first is the distinction between profit maximizing *rules of behaviour* (functions) and profit maximizing *actions*. In general, a selection equilibrium that mimics a particular competitive equilibrium must clearly be one in which some firms take actions that are profit maximizing in that competitive equilibrium, and in this sense are profit maximizers. But this observation does not imply that the survivors in the selection equilibrium possess maximizing *rules*, and in general it is not necessary that survivors be maximizers in this stronger sense. (Proof: Consider a competitive equilibrium with constant returns to scale. Restrict the firms's supply and demand functions to be constant up to a scale factor at the values taken in the given equilibrium. Embed this static equilibrium in a dynamic adjustment system in which firms' scales of output respond to profitability in accordance with assumption (2). Then the given competitive equilibrium becomes a selection equilibrium – since the only techniques in use make zero profit – but the firms are not profit maximizers in the stronger sense.)

The second point extends the first. The notion of profit maximizing behavioural rules itself rests on the conceptual foundation of a production set or function that is regarded as a given. In evolutionary theory, however, it is the rules themselves that are regarded as data and as logically antecedent to the values (actions) they yield in particular environments. Thus, in this context, a problem arises in interpreting the basic idea of a selection equilibrium mimicking a standard competitive one: there is no obvious set of 'possibilities' to which one should have reference.

The most helpful approach here emphasizes internal consistency. Assumptions about the structure of what is 'possible' can be invoked without the additional assumption that there is a given set of possibilities – for example, additivity and divisibility may be assumed without implying that the set of techniques to which these axioms apply is a given datum of the system. Such an approach provides a basis for discussing whether a particular selection equilibrium is legitimately *interpretable* as a competitive equilibrium given the other assumptions in force. Along this path one can explore a rich variety of selection equilibrium situations that may be thought of as competitive equilibria. Precisely because the variety is so rich, to know only that an outcome is interpretable in this fashion is to know very little about it.

In the light of formal analysis of selection models of the sort described above, how strong is the crutch that selection provides to standard theory? For many analytical purposes, it is a crucial weakness that the crutch relates only to equilibrium actions and not to behavioural rules; it is from the knowledge that the rules are maximizing that the results of comparative statics derive. A selection system disturbed by a parameter change from a 'mimicking' equilibrium does not necessarily go to a new 'mimicking' equilibrium, let alone to one that is consistent, in standard theoretical terms, with the information revealed in the original equilibrium. More fundamentally, selection considerations cannot compensate for the inadequacies of standard theory that arise from the basic assumption that production possibilities are given data of the system.

SCHUMPETERIAN COMPETITION. In two great works and in many other writings, Joseph Schumpeter proclaimed the central importance of innovative activity in the development of capitalism. His early book, *The Theory of Economic Development*, focused on the role and contribution of the individual entrepreneur. From today's perspective the work remains enormously insightful and provocative but may seem dated; the image of the late 19th-century captains of industry lurks implicitly in the abstract account of the entrepreneur. The late work, *Capitalism, Socialism and Democracy*, is likewise insightful, provocative and a bit anachronistic. In this case, the anachronism derives from the predictions of a future in which the innovative process is bureaucratized, the role of the individual entrepreneur is fully usurped by large organizations, and the sociopolitical foundations of capitalism are thereby undercut. Present reality does not correspond closely to Schumpeter's predictions, and it seems increasingly clear that he greatly underestimated the seriousness of the incentive problems that arise within large organizations, whether capitalist corporations or socialist states.

Substantial literatures have accumulated around a number of specific issues, hypotheses and predictions put forward in Schumpeter's various writings. Regardless of the verdicts ultimately rendered on particular points, everyday observation repeatedly confirms the appropriateness of his emphasis on the centrality of innovation in contemporary capitalism. It confirms, likewise, the *in*appropriateness of the continuing tendency of the economics discipline to sequester topics related to technological change in sub-sectors of various specialized fields, remote from the theoretical core.

The purpose of the present discussion is to assess the relationships of selection and competition from a Schumpeterian viewpoint, that is, to extend the discussion above by considering what difference it makes if firms are engaged in inventing, discovering and exploring new ways of doing things. Plainly, one difference it makes is that 'competition' must now be understood in the broad sense that admits a number of additional dimensions to the competitive process, along with price-guided output determination. In particular, costly efforts to innovate, to imitate the innovations of others, and to appropriate the gains from innovation are added to the firm's competitive repertoire.

Selection now operates at two related levels. The organizational routines governing the use made of existing products and processes in every firm interact through the market place, and the market distributes rewards and punishments to the contenders. These same rewards and punishments are also entries on the market's scorecard for the higher level routines from which new products and processes derive – routines involving, for example, expenditure levels on innovative and imitative R&D efforts. Over the longer term, selection forces favour the firms that achieve a favourable balance between the rents captured from successive rounds of innovation and the costs of the R&D efforts that yield those innovations.

In formal models constructed along these lines, it is easy to see how various extreme cases turn out. One class of cases formalizes the cautionary tale told by Schumpeter (1950, p. 105), in which competition that is 'perfect – and perfectly prompt' makes the innovative role non-viable. Sufficiently high costs of innovation and low costs of imitation (including costs of surmounting any institutional barriers such as patents) will lead to the eventual suppression of all firms that continue to attempt innovation, and the system will settle into a static equilibrium. (The character of this equilibrium may, however, depend on initial conditions and on random events along the evolutionary path; the production set ultimately arrived at is an endogenous feature of the process.) One can also construct model examples to illustrate the cautionary message 'innovate or die', the principal requirement being simply a reversal of the cost conditions stated above.

With the exception of some extreme or highly simplified cases, models of Schumpeterian competition describe complex stochastic processes that are not easily explored with analytical methods. Of course, the activity of writing down a specific formal model is often informative by itself in the sense that it illuminates basic conceptual issues and poses key questions about how complex features of economic reality can usefully be approximated by a model. Some additional insight can then be obtained using simulation methods to explore specific cases (Nelson and Winter, 1982, Part V; Winter, 1984). One of the most significant benefits from simulation is the occasional discovery of mechanisms at work that are retrospectively 'obvious' and general features of the model.

The discussion that follows pulls together a number of these different sorts of insights, emphasizing in particular some issues that do not arise in the related theoretical literature that explores various Schumpeterian themes using neoclassical techniques. (For the most part these neoclassical studies explore stylized situations involving a single possible innovation, and thus do not address issues relating to the cumulative consequences of dynamic Schumpeterian competition. See Kamien and Schwartz (1981) and Dasgupta (1985) for references and perspectives on this literature.)

A fundamental constituent of any dynamic model of Schumpeterian competition is a model of technological opportunity. Such a model establishes the linkage between the resources that model firms apply to innovative effort and their innovative achievements. The long-run behaviour of the model as a whole depends critically on the answers provided for a set of key questions relating to technological opportunity. Does the individual firm face diminishing returns in innovative achievement as it applies additional resources over a short period of time? If so, from what 'fixed factors' does the diminishing returns effect arise, and to what extent are these factors subject to change over time either by the firm's own efforts or by other mechanisms? Are selection forces to be studied in a context in which technological opportunity presents more or less the 'same problem' for R&D policy over an extended period, or is the evolutionary sorting out of different policies for the firm a process that proceeds concurrently with historical change in the criteria that govern the sorting?

Technological opportunity is said to be *constant* if R&D activity amounts to a search of an unchanging set of possibilities – in effect, there is a meta-production set or meta-production function that describes what is ultimately possible. *Increasing* technological opportunity means that possibilities are being expanded over time by causal factors exogenous to the R&D efforts in question – implying that, given a level of technological achievement and a level of R&D effort, the effort will be more productive of innovative results if applied later. With constant technological opportunity, returns to R&D effort must eventually be decreasing, approaching zero near the boundary of the fixed set of possibilities.

It is all too obvious that it may be very difficult to develop an empirical basis for modelling technological opportunity in an applied analysis of a particular firm, industry or national economy. There is no easy escape from the conundrum that observed innovative performance reflects both opportunity and endogenously determined effort, not to mention the fact that neither performance nor effort is itself easily measured or the even more basic question of whether analysis of the past can illuminate the future. These difficulties in operationalizing the concept of technological opportunity do not, unfortunately, in any way diminish its critical role in Schumpeterian competition.

The evolutionary analysis of Schumpeterian competition has not, thus far, produced any counterpart for the sorts of mimicry theorems that can be proved for static equilibria. That is, there is no model in which it can be shown that selection forces, alone or in conjunction with adaptive behavioural rules, drive the system asymptotically to a path on which surviving firms might be said to have solved the remaining portion of the dynamic optimization problem with which the model situation confronts them – except in the cases where the asymptotic situation is a static equilibrium with zero R&D. The list of identified obstacles to a non-trivial positive result is sufficiently long, and the obstacles are sufficiently formidable, so as to constitute something akin to an impossibility theorem. It seems extremely unlikely that a positive result can be established within the confines of an evolutionary approach – that is, without endowing the model firms with a great deal of correct information about the structure of the total system in which they are embedded.

The most formidable obstacle of all derives from the direct clash between the future-oriented character of a dynamic optimization and the fact that selection and adaptation processes reflect the experience of the past. If firms cannot 'see' the path that technological opportunity will follow in the future, if their decisions can only reflect past experience and inferences drawn therefrom, then in general they cannot position themselves optimally for the future. They might conceivably do so if the development of technological opportunity were simple enough to validate simple inference schemes. Such simplicity does not seem descriptively plausible; who is to say that it is implausible that in a particular case technological opportunity might be constant, or exponentially increasing, or following a logistic, or some stochastic variant of any of these? And without some restriction on the structural possibilities, how are model firms to make inferences to guide their R&D policies?

This obstacle is not featured prominently in the simulations reported by Nelson and Winter, which are largely confined to very tame and stylized technological regimes in which opportunity is summarized by a single exponentially increasing variable, called 'latent productivity'. Such an environment, reminiscent in some ways of neoclassical growth theory, seems at first glance to be a promising one for the derivation of a balanced growth outcome in which actual and latent productivity are arising at the same rate; the problem facing the firms is in a sense constant, and selection and adaptation might bring surviving firm R&D policies to optimal values.

In fact, such a result remains remote even under the very strong assumption just described. Demand conditions for the product of the industry (or the economy) affect the long-run dynamics, and in this area also assumptions must be delicately contrived to avoid excluding a balanced growth outcome. For example, consider an industry model with constant demand in which demand is (plausibly) less than unit elastic at low prices. Then, cost reduction continued indefinitely would drive sales revenue to zero. Zero sales revenue will not cover the cost of continuing advance. What is involved here is a reflection of the basic economics of information; costs of discovery are independent of the size of the realm of application, and on the assumption stated the economic significance of that realm is dwindling to nothing. The implication is that demand conditions may check progress even if technological opportunity is continually expanding. Indeed, this may well be the pattern that is typically realistic for any narrowly defined sector.

This difficulty too can be dispatched by an appropriately chosen assumption. Beyond it lie some further problems. A model that acknowledges the partially stochastic nature of innovative success will display gradually increasing concentration (Phillips, 1971), unless some opposing tendency is present. A good candidate for an opposing tendency is the actual exercise of market power that has been acquired by chance (Nelson and Winter, 1982, ch. 13). But this market power can, presumably, also shelter various departures from present value maximization, including departures from dynamically optimal R&D policy.

To reiterate, the quest for mimicry theorems in the context of Schumpeterian competition seems foredoomed to failure. Since models of Schumpeterian competition plainly provide a much better description of the world we live in than do models of static equilibrium, the overall conclusion with regard to the strength of the selection crutch is distinctly more negative than the conclusion

115

for static models alone. Assumptions that firms maximize profit or present value
will have to stand on their own, at least until somebody invents a better crutch
for them. In the meantime, it will continue to be the case that predictions based
on these assumptions are sometimes sound and sometimes silly, and standard
theory does not offer a means of discriminating between the cases. More direct
attention should be paid to the mechanisms of selection, adaptation and learning,
which among them probably account for as much sense as economists have
actually observed in economic reality, and also leave room for a lot of readily
observable nonsense.

BIBLIOGRAPHY

Alchian, A.A. 1950. Uncertainty, evolution and economic theory. *Journal of Political Economy* 58, June, 211–21.

Dasgupta, P. 1985. The theory of technological competition. In *New Developments in the Analysis of Market Structure*, ed. J. Stiglitz and G.F. Mathewson, Cambridge, Mass.: MIT Press.

Friedman, M. 1953. *Essays in Positive Economics*. Chicago: University of Chicago Press.

Kamien, M. and Schwartz, N. 1981. *Market Structure and Innovation*. Cambridge: Cambridge University Press.

Nelson, R. and Winter, S. 1982. *An Evolutionary Theory of Economic Change*. Cambridge, Mass.: Belknap Press of The Harvard University Press.

Phillips, A. 1971. *Technology and Market Structure: a Study of the Aircraft Industry*. Lexington, Mass.: D.C. Heath.

Schumpeter, J.A. 1912. *The Theory of Economic Development*. Trans. Redvers Opie, Cambridge, Mass.: Harvard University Press, 1934.

Schumpeter, J.A. 1950. *Capitalism, Socialism and Democracy*. 3rd edn, New York: Harper.

Simon, H. 1955. A behavioral model of rational choice. *Quarterly Journal of Economics* 69, February, 99–118.

Winter, S.G. 1964. Economic 'natural selection' and the theory of the firm. *Yale Economic Essays* 4(1), Spring, 225–72.

Winter, S.G. 1971. Satisficing, selection and the innovating remnant. *Quarterly Journal of Economics* 85(2), May, 237–61.

Winter, S.G. 1984. Schumpeterian competition in alternative technological regimes. *Journal of Economic Behavior and Organization* 5(3–4), September–December, 287–320.

Conflict and Settlement

JACK HIRSHLEIFER

All living beings are competitors for the means of existence. Competition takes the more intense form we call *conflict* when contenders seek to disable or destroy opponents, or even convert them into a supply of resources. Conflict need not always be violent; we speak, for example, of industrial conflicts (strikes and lockouts) and legal conflicts (law suits). But physical struggle is a relevant metaphor for these ordinarily non-violent contests.

THE STATICS OF CONFLICT. Involved in a rational decision to engage in conflict, economic reasoning suggests, will be the decision-maker's *preferences*, *opportunities* and *perceptions*. These three elements correspond to traditional issues debated by historians and political scientists about the 'causes of war': Is war mainly due to hatred and ingrained pugnacity (hostile preferences)? Or to the opportunities for material gain at the expense of weaker victims? Or is war mainly due to mistaken perceptions, on one or both sides, of the other's motives or capacities?

Of course it is quite a leap from the choices of individuals to the war-making decisions of collectivities like tribes or states. Group choice-making processes notoriously fail to satisfy the canons of rationality, most fundamentally owing to disparities among the interests of the individual members. Thus the internal decision-making structures of the interacting groups may also be implicated among the causes of war.

Setting aside this last complication, Figures 1 and 2 are alternative illustrations of how preferences, opportunities and perceptions might come together in a simple dyadic interaction. In each diagram the curve QQ bounds the 'settlement opportunity set' – what the parties can jointly attain by peaceful agreement or compromise – drawn on axes representing Blue's income I_B and Red's income I_R. The points P_B and P_R, in contrast, indicate the parties' separate *perceptions* of the income distribution resulting from conflict. The families of curves labelled U_B and U_R are the familiar utility indifference contours of the two agents.

117

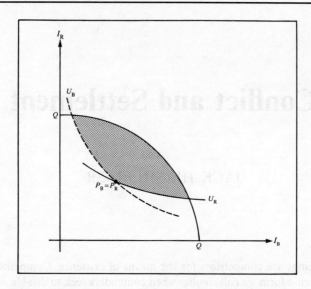

Figure 1   Statics of conflict – large potential settlement region.

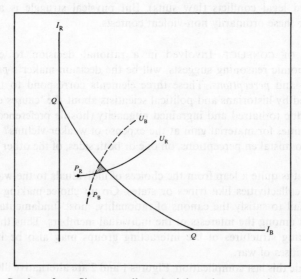

Figure 2   Statics of conflict – small potential settlement region.

Figure 1 shows a relatively benign situation: settlement opportunities are complementary, so there is a considerable mutual gain from avoiding conflict; the respective preferences display benevolence on each side; and the perceptions of returns from conflict are conservative and agreed (P_B and P_R coincide). The

118

'Potential Settlement Region' PSR (shaded area in the diagram), that is, the set of income distributions such that *both* parties regard themselves as doing better than by fighting, is therefore large – which plausibly implies a high probability of coming to an agreement. Figure 2 shows a less pleasant situation: antithetical opportunities, mutually malevolent preferences, and divergently optimistic estimates of the returns from conflict. The PSR is therefore small, and the prospects for settlement much poorer.

What might be called the *materialistic theory* attributes conflict, ultimately, to competition for resources. Primitive tribes attack one another for land, for hoards of consumables, or for slaves. Similar aims evidently motivated barbarian invasions of civilized cities and empires in ancient times, and European colonial imperialism in the modern era. Yet, between contending parties there will almost always be some element of complementary interests, an opportunity for mutual gain represented by the potential settlement region PSR. Orthodox economics has always emphasized the scope of mutual benefit, even to the point of losing sight of conflict; certain dissident schools, notably the Marxists, have committed the opposite error. While a detailed analysis cannot be provided here, among the factors underlying the relative material profitability of fighting versus negotiating are wealth differentials, Malthusian pressures, military technology and the enforceability of agreements.

In contrast with the materialistic approach, *attitudinal theories* of conflict direct attention to the respective preference functions. An issue which has excited considerable interest concerns the relative weights assignable to genetic versus cultural determinants of attitudes. One extreme viewpoint, for example, regards xenophobic wars of family against family, of tribe against tribe, or nation against nation, as biologically 'normal' in the human species. An opposite interpretation pictures man as an innately compliant being, who has to be culturally indoctrinated into bellicosity.

Finally, what might be termed *informational theories* of conflict emphasize differences of perceptions or beliefs. Neoclassical economics tends to minimize the importance of such divergences – partly because they tend to cancel out from a large-numbers point of view, partly because incorrect beliefs are adjusted by experience in the process of establishing an economic equilibrium. But conflict and war are pre-eminently small-numbers, disequilibrium problems. Indeed, conflict may be regarded, in a sense, as an *educational process*. The school of actual struggle teaches the parties to readjust their perceptions to more realistic levels. Wars end by mutual consent when the potential settlement opportunities are seen as more attractive than continued fighting.

THE DYNAMICS OF CONFLICT. Static and dynamic elements are both importantly involved in conflict or settlement processes. In game theory terms, the *payoff environment*, represented by the familiar normal-form matrix, is the static element. The dynamic element may be called the *protocol of play*; as pictured in the game tree, the protocol specifies the allowable step-by-step moves in the light of the players' information at each stage.

A few very simple payoff environments are shown in Matrices 1 to 4. The numbers in each cell indicate ordinally ranked payoffs for each player, 1 being the poorest outcome in each case. In Matrix 1, 'Land or Sea', the environment is characterized by completely antithetical (constant-sum) payoffs. The other three matrices – 'Chicken', 'Reciprocity' and 'Prisoner's Dilemma' – represent several of the many different possible mixed-motive situations combining an element of opposition of interests with an opportunity for mutual gain.

Matrix 1
LAND OR SEA

	Defend by land	Defend by sea
Attack by land	1,2	2,1
Attack by sea	2,1	1,2

Matrix 2
CHICKEN

	Soft	Tough
Soft	3,3	2,4
Tough	4,2	1,1

Matrix 3
RECIPROCITY

	Soft	Tough
Soft	4,4	1,3
Tough	3,1	2,2

Matrix 4
PRISONER'S DILEMMA

	Co-operate	Defect
Co-operate	3,3	1,4
Defect	4,1	2,2

The simplest protocol to analyse is *one-round sequential play*: first Row selects one of his options, then Column makes his move in the light of Row's choice, and the game ends. In a sequential-play protocol it is always possible to find a 'rational' solution. If Column can be relied upon to choose his best final move then Row, knowing this, can calculate his best first move accordingly. (This process results in what is called a 'perfect equilibrium'.) In contrast, where the protocol dictates that players in a single-round game choose *simultaneously* – or, equivalently, where each chooses in ignorance of the other's move – solution concepts are harder to justify. The most commonly employed is called the 'Nash equilibrium' (or 'equilibrium point'), a pair of strategies from which neither player would want to diverge unilaterally.

In the 'Land or Sea' payoff environment, under the one-round *sequential-move* protocol, it is the second-mover or defender who has the advantage. If Row moves first, for example, Column can always successfully counter; e.g. if Row attacks by land, Column will defend by land. Hence the (1, 2) payoff-pair is the outcome regardless of Row's initial move. In military terms the defence has an intrinsic advantage whenever the attacker must visibly commit his forces to one or another line of attack. And, of course, where the defence has such an advantage neither party is motivated to initiate warfare through aggression. But if 'Land or Sea' is played under the *simultaneous-move* protocol, both parties are groping in the dark and little can be said with confidence. (Here the Nash equilibrium would have each side choosing its move at random, in effect tossing a coin.)

In the payoff environment of 'Chicken' (Matrix 2), while the opportunities remain highly antithetical there is now a mutual interest in avoiding the disastrous (1, 1) outcome that comes about when both play Tough. In contrast with 'Land or Sea', in the 'Chicken' payoff environment the advantage lies with the *first-mover*. Specifically, Row should rationally play Tough, knowing that Column then has to respond with Soft. For, Column must accept the bad (payoff of 2) to avoid the worst (payoff of 1). If the protocol dictates simultaneous moves, however, once again the players are groping in the dark. Under the Nash equilibrium concept they choose probabilistically, which implies that the disastrous (1, 1) outcome will indeed occur a percentage of the time. There is a suggestive application of this model to industrial conflict. If union (or management) becomes committed to play Soft, it will be at a disadvantage in negotiations – the other side will then surely play Tough. But if both play Tough, there is no hope for peaceful settlement. Hence each side should rationally adopt a 'mixed' strategy, with the consequence that strikes and lockouts will occur in a certain fraction of the dealings.

The 'Reciprocity' payoff environment (Matrix 3) is more rewarding to cooperative behaviour. The idea is that each player would answer Soft with Soft – leading to the mutually preferred (4, 4) payoffs – but failing this, would respond to Tough with Tough. If the *sequential-move* protocol applies, the first-mover would then always rationally choose Soft, and so the ideal (4, 4) payoff-pair should be achieved. But under the *simultaneous-move* protocol, with each party in the dark about the other's move, again the outcome is quite unclear. In fact there are three Nash equilibria: pure-strategy solutions at (4, 4) and (2, 2), and a mixed-strategy solution as well.

Finally, in the famous 'Prisoner's Dilemma' payoff environment (Matrix 4) the parties are likely to find themselves in the Defect–Defect 'trap' with (2, 2) payoffs, even though (3, 3) could be achieved were each to play Cooperate. Here the 'trap' takes hold under both sequential-move and simultaneous-move protocols.

Limited as it was to 2-player single-round games, the preceding discussion could only be suggestive within that category of a few 2-strategy symmetrical payoff environments and finally to the very simplest protocols – excluding, for example, all negotiations and communications between the parties. Space limitations permit comment upon only a few additional points.

Perceptions. Standard game models assume that players know not only their own payoffs but also their opponents'. Unintentional error on this score, or else deliberate deception, may play a crucial role. Suppose two parties in the 'Reciprocity' payoff environment of Matrix 3 find themselves initially playing Tough–Tough with outcome (2, 2). Imagine now they are given a chance to shift strategies under a *sequential-move* protocol. As first-mover, Row would be happy to change from Tough to Soft if only he could rely upon Column to respond in kind. But Row may, mistakenly, believe that Column's payoffs are as in 'Chicken', from which he infers that Column would stand pat with Tough. Row would therefore not shift from Tough, hence Column in his turn would not change either. (Some authors have gone so far as to attribute all or almost all of human conflict to such mistaken 'self-fulfilling beliefs' about the hostility of opponents, but of course this pattern is only one of many possibilities.)

Commitment and deterrence. In some circumstances the second-mover in point of time (Column) may be able to *commit* himself to a given response strategy before Row makes his first move. While Column thereby surrenders freedom of choice, doing so may be advantageous. Consider threats and promises. A *threat* is a commitment to undertake a second-move punishment strategy even where execution thereof is costly. A *promise* similarly involves commitment to a costly reward strategy. Matrices 5 and 6 illustrate how a threat works. Row's choices are Attack or Refrain, while Column's only options are to Retaliate or Fold if Row attacks. Column's problem, of course, is to deter Row's attack. In Matrix 5, Column prefers to Retaliate if attacked, a fact that – given Row's preferences – suffices for deterrence. Commitment is not required. (Since Column prefers to Retaliate, there is no need to *commit* himself to do so.) In Matrix 6 the Column player prefers to turn the other cheek; if attacked, he would rather Fold than Retaliate. Unfortunately, this guarantees he will be attacked! (Note that here it is not excessive hostility, but the reverse, that brings on conflict.) But if Column could *commit* himself to Retaliate, for example by computerizing the associated machinery beyond the possibility of his later reneging, then deterrence succeeds. In short, if a pacific player can reliably *threaten* to do what he does not really want to do, he won't have to do it! (Needless to say, so dangerous an arrangement is not to be recommended casually.)

	Matrix 5 DETERRENCE WITHOUT COMMITMENT			*Matrix 6* DETERRENCE REQUIRING COMMITMENT	
	Fold	Retaliate		Fold	Retaliate
Refrain	2,3	2,3	Refrain	2,3	2,3
Attack	3,1	1,2	Attack	3,2	1,1

THE TECHNOLOGY OF STRUGGLE. Conflict is a kind of 'industry' in which different 'firms' compete by attempting to disable opponents. Just as the economist, without being a manager or engineer, can apply certain broad principles to the process of industrial production, so, without claiming to replace the military commander, he can say something about the principles governing how desired results are 'produced' through violence.

Battles typically proceed to a definitive outcome – victory or defeat. *Wars* on the whole tend to be less conclusive, often ending in a compromise settlement. These historical generalizations reflect the working of increasing versus decreasing returns applied to the production of violence.

(1) Within a sufficiently small geographical region such as a battlefield, there is a critical range of increasing returns to military strength – a small increment of force can make the difference between victory and defeat.

(2) But there are decreasing returns in projecting military power away from one's base area, so that it is difficult to achieve superiority over an enemy's entire national territory. The increasing-returns aspect explains why there is a 'natural monopoly' of military force *within* the nation-state. The diminishing-returns aspect explains why a multiplicity of nation-states have remained militarily viable to this date. (However, there is some reason to believe that the technology of attack through long-range weapons has now so come to prevail over the defence that a single world-state is indeed impending.)

Going into the basis for increasing returns, at any moment the stronger in battle can inflict a more than proportionate loss upon his opponent, thus becoming progressively stronger still. Important special cases of this process are modelled via Lanchester's equations. In combat, in the ideal case where all the military units distribute their fire equally over the enemy's line, the process equations are:

$$dB/dt = -k_R R$$

$$dR/dt = -k_B B.$$

Here B and R are the given force sizes for Blue and Red, and the per-unit military efficiencies are given by the k_B and k_R coefficients. It follows that military strengths are equal when:

$$k_B B^2 = k_R R^2.$$

But even where military strength varies less sensitively than as the square of force size, it remains quite generally the case that in the combat process the strong become stronger and the weak weaker, leading to ultimate annihilation unless flight or surrender intervene. (Of course, a skilful commander finding himself with an adverse force balance will attempt to change the tactical situation – by timely withdrawal, deception or other manoeuvre.)

One implication of increasing returns may be called the 'last-push principle'. In the course of a conflict each side will typically not be fully aware of the force size and strength that the opponent is ultimately able and willing to put in the field. Hence the incentive to stand fast, even at high cost, lest a potentially won battle be lost. (Foch: 'A battle won is a battle in which one will not confess oneself beaten.') This valid point unfortunately tends to lead to battlefield carnage beyond all reasonable prior calculations, as experienced for example at Verdun.

On the other hand, an effective substitute for force size is superior *organization*. An integrated military unit is far more powerful than an equally numerous conglomeration of individual fighters, however brave. Organizational superiority, far more than superiority in weapons, explains why small European expeditionary contingents in early modern times were even able to defeat vast indigenous forces in America, Africa and Asia. Battles are thus often a contest of organizational forms; the army whose command structure first cracks under pressure is the loser.

As for diminishing returns, in the simplest case an equilibrium is achieved at a geographical boundary such that:

$$M_B - s_B x_B = M_R - s_R x_R.$$

Here M_B and M_R are military strengths at the respective home bases, s_B and s_R are decay gradients, and x_B and x_R are the respective distances from base. The condition of equality determines the allocation of territory.

The 'social physics' of struggle is of course far more complex than these simplistic initial models suggest. There are more or less distinct offence and defence technologies, first-strike capability is not the same as retaliatory strength, countering insurgency is a different problem from central land battle, etc.

CONFLICT, SOCIETY AND ECONOMY. Conflict theory can help explain not only the size and shape of nations, but also the outcomes of competition in all aspects of life: contests among social classes, among political factions and ideologies, between management and labour, among contenders for licences and privileges ('rent-seeking'), between plaintiffs and defendants in law suits, among members of cartels like OPEC, between husband and wife, and sibling and sibling within the family, and so on. Whenever resources can be seized by aggression, invasion attempts can be expected to occur. Invasive and counter-invasive effort absorb a very substantial fraction of society's resources in every possible social structure, whether egalitarian or hierarchical, liberal or totalitarian, centralized or decentralized. Furthermore, every form of human social organization, whatever else can be said for or against it, must ultimately meet the survival test of internal and external conflict.

Notes on the literature of conflict (of special relevance for economists). Classical military thought from Machiavelli to Clausewitz to Liddell Hart, though rarely analytical in the economist's sense, remains well worth study. An excellent survey is Edward Mead Earle (1941). Modern work in this classical genre understandably concentrates upon the overwhelming fact of nuclear weaponry and the problem of deterrence; the contributions of Herman Kahn (1960, 1962) are notable. There is of course a huge historical literature on conflict and war. An interesting economics-oriented interpretive history of modern warfare is Geoffrey Blainey (1973). William H. McNeill (1982) examines the course of military organization and technology from antiquity to the present, emphasizing the social and economic context. On a smaller scale John Keegan (1976) provides a valuable picture of how men, weapons and tactics compete with and complement one another on the battlefield. There is also a substantial body of statistical work attempting in a variety of ways to summarize and classify the sources and outcomes of wars; the best known is Lewis F. Richardson (1960b). Mathematical analysis of military activity, that is, quantifiable modelling of the clash of contending forces, is surprisingly sparse. The classic work is Frederick William Lanchester (1916 [1956]).

The modern analysis of conflict, typically combining the theory of games with the rational-decision economics of choice, is represented by three important books by economists: Thomas C. Schelling (1960), Kenneth E. Boulding (1962) and Gordon Tullock (1974). Works by non-economists that are similar in spirit include Glenn H. Snyder and Paul Diesing (1977) and Bruce Bueno de Mesquita (1981). A tangentially related literature, making use of the rather mechanical psychologistic approach of Richardson (1960a), includes a very readable book by Anatol Rapoport (1960).

BIBLIOGRAPHY

Blainey, G. 1973. *The Causes of War*. New York: The Free Press.
Boulding, K.E. 1962. *Conflict and Defense: A General Theory*. New York: Harper & Brothers.
Bueno de Mesquita, B. 1981. *The War Trap*. New Haven and London: Yale University Press.
Earle, E.M. (ed.) 1941. *Makers of Modern Strategy: Military Thought from Machiavelli to Hitler*. Princeton, NJ: Princeton University Press.
Kahn, H. 1960. *On Thermonuclear War*. Princeton, NJ: Princeton University Press.
Kahn, H. 1962. *Thinking About the Unthinkable*. New York: Avon Books.
Keegan, J. 1976. *The Face of Battle*. New York: Viking Press.
Lanchester, F.W. 1916. *Aircraft in Warfare: The Dawn of the Fourth Arm*. London: Constable. Extract reprinted in *The World of Mathematics*, ed. James R. Newman, Vol. 4, New York: Simon & Schuster, 1956.
McNeill, W.H. 1982. *The Pursuit of Power: Technology, Armed Force, and Society since AD 1000*. Chicago: University of Chicago Press.
Rapoport, A. 1960. *Fights, Games, and Debates*. Ann Arbor: University of Michigan Press.
Richardson, L.F. 1960a. *Arms and Insecurity: A Mathematical Study of the Causes and Origins of War*. Pittsburgh: Boxwood; Chicago: Quadrangle.
Richardson, L.F. 1960b. *Statistics of Deadly Quarrels*. Pittsburgh: Boxwood; Chicago: Quadrangle.
Schelling, T.C. 1960. *The Strategy of Conflict*. Cambridge, Mass.: Harvard University Press.
Snyder, G.H. and Diesing, P. 1977. *Conflict Among Nations: Bargaining, Decision Making, and System Structure in International Crises*. Princeton, NJ: Princeton University Press.
Tullock, G. 1974. *The Social Dilemma: The Economics of War and Revolution*. Blacksburg, Virginia: University Publications.

Congestion

A.A. WALTERS

With ambient conditions of scarcity, congestion (like 'shortages') appears either when the property rights are not well defined or when mutual trading and contracting is excluded. Thus, consider an elevator with a capacity of ten persons when fifteen people appear to demand a ride, so that at least five people must incur the costs of a wait for the next available space. In most modern societies there is no inherent investiture of the right to a place in the first elevator. However, social behaviour sometimes recognizes a rule of convenience or status – such as that of the elderly, the handicapped, the chief executive officer and women to take priority. But to avoid all possibility of conflict, such rules would have to be enormously complex. In practice, most societies recognize a simple rule of the queue, first come first served. It is remarkable that queuing rules are to be found ubiquitously and that very different societies appear to find that rule fair, although rather wasteful; seemingly, equity is worth the cost.

Even with the rule, however, there is considerable scope for making mutually advantageous trades. The eleventh man in the queue might offer to buy the place of one of the first ten, and someone with an assured place may be willing to trade his place and wait for the next elevator in exchange for the offer of the eleventh man. Deals may be struck so that those who value a speedy lift highly may buy the places of those who do not. Since all contracts are freely negotiated, people must be at least as well off and so there is Pareto improvement. However, the queue is still an inefficient rationing device; clearly, it would have been better if no more than ten people had arrived for the lift, and that those ten had been the people who valued most highly the service at that time. The queue involves waste in waiting. Yet, in principle, it is easy to devise alternative schemes for the allocation of property rights which do not involve the waste of time and resources in queuing. For example, a lottery might allocate the ten places in the elevator, and indeed such a system was used at the London School of Economics to allocate parking places, but, of course, only to the faculty.

126

Suppose the ownership of the right to designate the qualifications for travel in the elevator to be vested in its owner. Then, assuming that the owner wants to maximize his profits, he will find it profitable – transactions costs and stochastic variations aside – to *sell* the right to travel on the elevator directly to the travelling public. There will be no queue and no evidence of congestion. Well-specified property rights, zero transactions costs, profit maximization and freedom to contract are sufficient, but clearly not necessary, to banish congestion. The private provision of elevators, often by the users themselves, ensures that there is in fact no persistent or structural congestion.

Persistent or structural congestion, as distinct from accidental or transitory stochastic congestion, is normally to be found in the lack of specification of a property right, usually involving the public sector. For example, it is widely believed that there is considerable congestion in many fishing grounds – too many fishermen chasing too few fish. The number of fish is limited and so for a particular boat the marginal cost of fishing should reflect the fact that additional fish netted will increase the costs of other vessels catching fish; there are fewer fish and less spawn, etc. The point is that the fish are not *owned* by a profit-maximizing entity which extracts a royalty for each fish caught. They are nominally in the ownership of the state, if in national waters, but the state charges no royalty per fish caught. Scarce fish are not priced but treated as free. Thus the fishing grounds are congested and over-fished.

HIGHWAY CONGESTION. The most important form of congestion is on the highways, particularly on city streets, normally owned and operated by the state. If the state authorities were profit-seeking entities then they would charge prices for the use of the city streets that reflect the intensity of demand relative to the scarce capacity available. They would levy tolls in order to maximize their net revenue from the street system. But traditionally the state has not charged for the use of city streets prices or tolls that reflect their scarcity. The urban roads are 'free' for all users; provided they have paid their licence duty and acquired the right to use any of the roads in the national network as intensively as they wish. Thus people try to make too much use of the road network in areas where road capacity is scarce relative to demand. The urban streets become overcrowded, vehicle speeds slow as they get in one another's way, and the costs of a journey rise. Congestion is rather different from queuing; one cannot buy a place up front of a traffic jam as one can with negotiable positions in the disciplined queue. But in other respects – for example the waste of resources involved – queuing and congestion have the same characteristics.

The formal economic modelling of congestion can proceed either by analysing the phenomenon in terms of demand, or in the form of supply and cost conditions. Following the historical precedent of Dupuit (1844) and Pigou (1912) the approach is usually from the cost and supply side. The first assumption is that traffic consists of homogeneous vehicles with identical technical characteristics and cost functions. Each vehicle is operated by people with the same utility functions and the same levels of income, and so the same valuation of time. In

127

order to avoid problems at the end or beginning of the road, we might conveniently assume that the road is a circle, with traffic going round and round. Let $c(x)$ be the cost incurred for travelling one kilometre, where x is the number of kilometres travelled by all the vehicles on the circular route of k kilometres in circumference. The density of vehicles is then x/k. Thus the total cost of the x vehicle-trips of 1 kilometre each is then $C(x) = x \cdot c(x)$.

As the number of trips on the road increases, the density of vehicles on the road rises, and so the speed of the traffic flow falls, and $c(x)$ rises. These are the familiar conditions of increasing congestion on the road. An individual deciding whether to make another trip will reckon the cost involved as $c(x)$ per kilometre, and will make that trip if his valuation of the worth of the trip is at least as great as $c(x)$ per kilometre. But the addition of another vehicle on the road will slow down all existing vehicles and so increase the costs of all other road users. Consequently the marginal costs of the additional trip consist not merely of the private costs of the particular motorist but the additional costs he inflicts on others by adding to the congestion of the highway. With C defined as the total cost of x trips, the marginal costs of the trip are $dC/dx = c + x \cdot dc/dx$, where c measures the private marginal cost of the individual and $x \cdot dc/dx$ measures the increase in cost to each user (dc/dx), multiplied by the number of user-trips (x). Clearly, if (as we have assumed) no price is levied for the use of the highway, then private marginal costs are less than the true marginal costs. Private decisions will then result in too much traffic on the road.

This state may be conveniently defined as the condition of *congestion*. In common usage, congestion may be used to denote circumstances where there is *some* interaction and slowing of vehicles below their traffic-free speed. With this wider definition, some congestion is virtually always efficient and actually there may be too little congestion on some highways. In this essay the common usage definition will be eschewed and throughout the technical definition, denoting *too much* traffic and too dense a traffic flow, will be employed.

The underlying reason for congestion is that the authorities do not charge an appropriate rent for the use of the highway. Were the highway to be owned by a profit-seeking agent, a toll would be levied for the use of the road at least as high as the cost which the marginal motorist imposes on other $(x \cdot dc/dx)$. (If the road owner were to enjoy some monopoly power, rather than be a member of a large number of agents competing to supply the services of roads, then he would exact a monopoly rent in excess of $(x \cdot dc/dx)$. But we shall continue with the fiction of a large number of privately owned competitive road suppliers so that the analogue with private business is clear.) In his classic work, Pigou (1912) used the priceless road illustration as a paradigm for competitive industry and thereby concluded that the competitive industry would always overexpand and degenerate into conditions of congestion. As Knight (1924) pointed out, under conditions of private ownership of resources, including roads, there would be no such overuse (congestion), since the road-owners would charge a competitive price for their services. Pigou was correct in the particular illustration of the 'free' road, but it was a distortion introduced by the public sector which would not have appeared under conditions of private ownership.

The normative conclusion is that it would be best, or at least better, if the authorities adopted a pattern of road pricing that simulated the behaviour of a competitive, privately owned road system. For a specified level of traffic, say $x = x_i$, the authorities should charge a toll for the use of the road of $x \cdot (dc/dx)$ evaluated at $x = x_i$. This can be interpreted as the product of the private cost of a trip (c) multiplied by the elasticity of that cost with respect to the number of trips $[(x/c) \cdot (dc/dx)]$, evaluated at $x = x_i$.

This calculation gives the optimum supply price of road space when the traffic is at the level x_i. If, however, the level x_i represents the traffic equilibrium when there is a zero charge for the road service, as shown in Figure 1, then one must take into account the fact that raising the price of the total trip from $c(x_i)$ to $[c(x_i) + x \cdot (dc/dx)]$ will give rise to a reduction of traffic along the demand curve. As traffic falls, both cost and the optimum toll also decline. The new equilibrium toll will be $x_0 \cdot (dc/dx)$ for the optimum level of traffic x_0 and private cost $c(x_0)$. The optimum toll will always be below that calculated for the existing level of toll-free equilibrium traffic flow.

A rising value for the $c(x)$ function is intuitively plausible and fits in well with corresponding notions of the theory of the firm and industry. In Figure 1, however, the $c(x)$ function becomes vertical at a level of trips shown as *max*, but instead of the cost curve staying vertical for all values exceeding $c(\text{max})$, it is shown as backward-bending, eventually becoming asymptotic to the vertical cost axis. The rationalization for the backward-bending segment is best considered in terms of the flow/density/speed relationship by which trips are produced. Clearly the flow of vehicles past any given point of our circular road represents the number of trips completed. But the flow per hour is equal to the product of the density of vehicles (number per kilometre) and the speed of those vehicles (kilometres per hour). As vehicles join the road, density increases and speed is reduced. At low densities the reduction in speed is small, so that additional vechicles and increases of density will increase flow. However, as more vehicles jam into the existing road-space the effects of the additional density on speed will be so important that the slower speeds reduce the flow of trips. Ultimately one can imagine the bumper to bumper conditions of the complete jam. Then flow is zero and costs approach very high values indeed.

In this description of traffic flow, there is an obvious analogue with the theory of fluid dynamics (Walters, 1961). In the simplest form of the steady state flow theory:

$$s = b[\log D(s = 0) - \log D(s)],$$

where s is the speed and D is the density at which that specified speed is attained, and $x = sD$. This gives a very simple form to the elasticity of speed with respect to traffic flow, namely $d \log s / d \log x = b/(b - s)$. The parameter b measures the critical speed at which flow is maximized. In statistical studies of traffic flow one finds values of b ranging from about 12 kph for city streets to 26 to 30 kph for

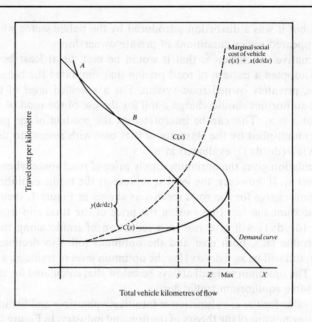

Figure 1 Demand and supply on a congested highway

urban freeways and motorways. There is thus some evidence that the fluid-dynamic model is useful for interpreting conditions of very dense traffic.

There is obviously considerable difficulty in dealing with such backward-bending curves. For any given level of trips there are two conceivable levels of cost – one high level associated with a high density, and one low level corresponding to the light density. In any rational arrangement of affairs one would expect that the backward-bending high-density conditions would be avoided by some system of exclusion, by pricing or other means. But it would be foolhardy to assume that such rational arrangements would be the norm; clearly the observed frequent traffic jams are not consistent with economic rationality. The possibility of a high-density, high-cost equilibrium being stable, a point such as A in Figure 1, cannot be dismissed. There is however also another locally stable equilibrium at point C, on the rising part of $c(x)$. There may be many such locally stable equilibria and some unstable ones, such as that represented by point B in Figure 1. The chaotic nature of traffic flow in many cities suggests that it would not be entirely wise to ignore such phenomena – although one might argue that such conditions are likely to be transitory and of limited interest. Very little analytical or empirical attention has been paid to such problems of multiple equilibria and stability.

Various other models derived from the theory of thermodynamics and the statistical theory of queues have been used to model the congested aspects of road traffic. Although useful for simulating the interaction of congestion and flows in networks, the thermodynamic analogue has not been of much use in

130

understanding the economics of congestion (Haight, 1963). The theory of queues and the stochastic processes derived to model lightly congested traffic have not been notably successful in producing theoretical simulations of observed processes, so again little has been done to interpret them in economic terms.

The empirical study of congestion has, however, found that the studies by traffic engineers of the relationship between speed, flow and density have been an invaluable basis for the economic assessment of the costs of congestion and the levels of the appropriate road tolls. Regression analysis of speed on flow has been the staple of analysis, sometimes using a rather unsatisfactory linear approximation for the rising section of the cost curve (and the falling section of the speed curve), and occasionally using the logarithmic form of the fluid dynamics analogue. The job of the economist was to translate a speed–flow relationship into a cost–flow form. The simplest approximation for very congested traffic is that cost is inversely proportional to speed. For less congested traffic, however, the approximation usually adopted is $c = m + n/s$, where m and n are constants which depend on the currency of measurement, and c is cost per kilometre (Smeed, 1968).

Since the speed–flow relationships conform to theoretical expectation (with the exception of those with light flow and low density), the cost–flow version of the relationship is also consistent with the form displayed in Figure 1. Taking observed levels of flow, density, speed and cost on urban highways, one may calculate the gap between marginal social cost and private cost (i.e. a measure of $x \cdot (dc/dx)$). For cost inversely proportional to speed and with the fluid dynamic model, the optimum toll $t(s)$ at speed s is then $(cb)/(s - b)$. For some urban highways, however, the situation is clearly on the backward-bending part of the cost curve. Formally, the optimum toll at that point is infinite. But such a conclusion takes no account of the reaction of demand; one may merely take it as a reminder that it is patently wasteful to have so highly congested a road. Even if the demand curve lies to the right of the whole of the rising section of the cost curve, the optimum arrangement will always be to bring traffic down so that the equilibrium flow is on the rising section of the cost curve. This makes it important to know the shape of the demand curve and the values of the elasticities of demand over the relevant ranges of flow.

Unfortunately we know much less about the elasticity of demand for trips than we do about the cost functions. Substitution of elasticities between one road and another can be adduced from minimum cost (usually minimum time) routings by programming models, but substitutions between modes and the long-run development of urban areas and movement are more intractable. Nevertheless some work by John Tanner, reported in Smeed (1968), showed that the level of optimum tolls was not very sensitive to different assumptions about elasticities of demand, but this result has not been fully explored and explained.

The empirical studies suggest that the optimum toll for town and city traffic during peak periods is probably at least 50 per cent – and in many cases as much as 100 per cent – of the private cost of the journey. Off-peak, the appropriate tolls are perhaps nearer to 10 to 40 per cent of the private cost. Note that in many cities, particularly those in the Third World such as Bangkok, Lagos and Sao Paulo, the peak can last for more than eight hours. The main implication for policy is that the wastes of congestion are very high and that there is a good *prima facie* case for reducing the demand for trips, probably by some sort of pricing mechanism.

The best policy to deal with urban road congestion is likely to be some form of road pricing. However, road pricing is the exception rather than the rule. Most governments have simply stood idly by as the wastes of congestion mount. When the traffic jams become quite unacceptable, the normal procedure is to impose regulations to ration the use of the streets. In Lagos, for example, odd-numbered licence plates were allowed on odd days and even numbers on even days. The most ubiquitous policy is to discourage the private motorist, with a particularly low occupancy to road space ratio, and to promote mass transit by rail or bus. Various priority systems with special bus lanes and impediments for cars have been the usual policy. A proper application of road pricing has been practised in only one case – Singapore. There the private motorist pays a daily or a monthly fee to enter the restricted area of downtown Singapore during the morning rush hours. The scheme was instituted in 1975 and has been judged by both the government and independent observers as a considerable success on economic and political criteria (World Bank, 1985). Rather similar schemes have been considered for London, Washington DC, and many other cities, but political considerations have prevented their implementation. The development of information technology has made feasible many sophisticated systems of computer-controlled pricing. One such system has been introduced on an experimental basis in Hongkong (World Bank, 1985). The technical objections to road pricing have been largely overcome, but the distributional, vested interests and political hurdles have yet to be surmounted.

CONGESTION IN AIRPORTS AND PORTS. After highways, perhaps the most important examples of congestion are to be found in airports and ports. Both differ from the urban road congestion in so far as it is the normal practice to charge fees for landing aircraft and for harbouring ships. The problem of congestion arises when such fees do not reflect the scarcity of the facilities. (For some examples in ports, see Bennathan and Walters, 1979, and in airports, Park, 1971.) Landing fees or port dues may be subject to legal limitations or political pressure. Yet in practice it has been much easier to adjust airport and port fees to reflect scarcity, including seasonal or diurnal peaks, than to introduce congestion tolls on the highways.

CONCLUSION. The economic analysis of congestion has made some useful progress and the ideas and the policy measures that flow from those notions have a firm place in the economics of public policy. However, the policy of congestion tolls has been resisted by most governments, presumably because it is believed that there is not sufficient electoral support for such measures. In that sense, the political economy of congestion pricing has been largely a failure. It is difficult to see what changes would ensure its success.

BIBLIOGRAPHY

Bennathan, E. and Walters, A.A. 1979. *Port Pricing and Investment Policy for Developing Countries*. New York: Oxford University Press.

Dupuit, J. 1844. On the measurement of the utility of public works. Reprinted in *Transport*, ed. Dennis Munby, London: Penguin, 1968.

Demsetz, H. 1982. *Economic, Legal, and Political Dimensions of Competition*. Amsterdam: North-Holland.

Haight, F. 1963. *Mathematical Theories of Traffic Flow*. New York: Academic Press.

Knight, F. 1924. Some fallacies in the interpretation of social cost. *Quarterly Journal of Economics* 38, August, 582–606.

Park, R. 1971. Congestion tolls for commercial airports. *Econometrica* 39, September, 683–94.

Pigou, A.C. 1912. *Wealth and Welfare*. London: Macmillan.

Smeed, R. 1968. Traffic studies and urban congestion. *Journal of Transport Economics and Policy* 2, January, 33–70.

Vickrey, W. 1969. Congestion theory and transport investment. *American Economic Review* 59, May, 251–60.

Walters, A.A. 1961. The theory of measurement of private and social costs of highway congestion. *Econometrica* 29, October, 676–99.

World Bank. 1985. *Urban Transport*. Washington, DC: World Bank.

Constitutional Economics

JAMES M. BUCHANAN

The term 'Constitutional Economics' (Constitutional Political Economy) was introduced to define and to classify a distinct strand of research inquiry and related policy discourse in the 1970s and beyond. The subject matter is not new or novel, and it may be argued that 'constitutional economics' is more closely related to the work of Adam Smith and the classical economists than its modern 'non-constitutional' counterpart. Both areas of inquiry involve positive analysis that is ultimately aimed at contributing to the discussion of policy questions. The difference lies in the level of or setting for analysis which, in turn, implies communication with different audiences.

Orthodox economic analysis, whether this be interpreted in Marshallian or Walrasian terms, attempts to explain the choices of economic agents, their interactions one with another, and the results of these interactions, within the existing legal–institutional–constitutional structure of the polity. Normative considerations enter through the efficiency criteria of theoretical welfare economics, and policy options are evaluated in terms of these criteria. The policy analyst, building on the analysis, presents his results, whether explicitly or implicitly, to the political decision-makers, who then make some ultimate determination from among the available set. In this role the policy analyst directly, and the theorist indirectly, are necessarily advising governmental decision-makers, whoever these may be.

By both contrast and comparison, constitutional economic analysis attempts to explain the working properties of alternative sets of legal–institutional– constitutional rules that constrain the choices and activities of economic and political agents, the rules that define the framework within which the ordinary choices of economic and political agents are made. In this sense, constitutional economics involves a 'higher' level of inquiry than orthodox economics; it must incorporate the results of the latter along with many less sophisticated subdisciplines. Normative considerations enter the analysis in a much more complex manner than through the artificially straightforward efficiency criteria.

Alternative sets of rules must be evaluated in some sense analogously to ranking of policy options within a specified institutional structure, but the epistemological content of the 'efficiency' criteria becomes more exposed.

The constitutional economist, precisely because the subject matter is the analysis of alternate sets of rules, has nothing to offer by way of policy advice to political agents who act within defined rules. In this sense, constitutional economics is not appropriately included within 'policy science' at all. At another level, however, the whole exercise is aimed at offering guidance to those who participate in the discussion of constitutional change. In other words, constitutional economics offers a potential for normative advice to the member of the continuing constitutional convention, whereas orthodox economics offers a potential for advice to the practising politician. In a real sense, constitutional economics examines the *choice of constraints* as opposed to the *choice within constraints*, and as this terminology suggests, the disciplinary attention of economists has almost exclusively been placed on the second of these two problems.

A preliminary illustration of the distinction may be drawn from the economics of monetary policy. The constitutional economist is not directly concerned with determining whether monetary ease or monetary restrictiveness is required for furthering stabilization objectives in a particular setting. On the other hand, he is directly concerned with evaluating the properties of alternative monetary regimes (e.g. rule-directed versus discretionary, fiat versus commodity standards). The ultimate objective of analysis is the choice among the institutions within which political agents act. The predicted behaviour of these agents is incorporated in the analysis of alternative sets of constraints.

I CONSTITUTIONAL ECONOMICS AND CLASSICAL POLITICAL ECONOMY. As suggested, Constitutional Economics is related to classical political economy and it may be considered to be an important component of a more general revival of the classical emphasis, and particularly as represented in the works of Adam Smith. (The closely related complementary components are discussed briefly in section III.) One obvious aim of the classical political economists was to offer an explanation and an understanding of how markets operate without detailed political direction. In this respect, orthodox neoclassical economics follows directly in the classical tradition. But the basic classical analysis of the working of markets was only a necessary step toward the more comprehensive purpose of the whole exercise, which was that of demonstrating that, precisely because markets function with tolerable efficiency independently of political direction, a powerful normative argument for constitutional structure exists. That is to say, Adam Smith was engaged directly in comparing alternative institutional structures, alternative sets of constraints within which economic agents make choices. In this comparative analysis, he found it essential to model the working properties of a non-politicized economy, which did not exist in reality, as well as the working properties of a highly politicized mercantilist economy, which could be directly observed.

There is no need here to enter the lists on either side of the 'ideas have consequences' debate. We know that the economy of Great Britain was effectively de-politicized in the late 18th and early 19th centuries, and from the analysis of Smith and his classical fellow travellers there emerged both positive understanding of economic process and philosophical argument for a particular regime. The normative argument for *laissez-faire* was, perhaps inevitably, intermingled with the positive analysis of interaction within a particular structure of constraints, essentially those that describe the minimal, protective, or night-watchman state. Economics, as a social science, emerged, but in the process attention was diverted from the institutional structure. Even the predicted normative reaction against the overly zealous extension of the *laissez-faire* argument was couched in 'market failure' terms, rather than in the Smithian context of institutional comparison. The early socialist critique of market order, both in its Marxist and non-Marxist variants, was almost exclusively negative in that it elaborated putative failures of markets within an unexamined set of legal–political rules while it neglected analysis of the alternative rules that any correction of the alleged failures might require. Only with the debates on socialist calculation in the decades prior to World War II did the issues of comparative structure come to be examined.

It was only in the half-century after these debates that political economy, inclusively defined, returned, in fits and starts, to its classical tradition. Given the legal order of the protective state (the protection of property and the enforcement of contracts), we now know that under some conditions 'markets fail' when evaluated against idealized criteria, whether these be 'efficiency', 'justice' or other abstract norms. We also know that 'politics fails' when evaluated by the same criteria. Any positive analysis that purports to be of use in an ultimate normative judgment must reflect an informed comparison of the working properties of alternative sets of rules or constraints. This analysis is the domain of Constitutional Economics.

II CONSTITUTIONAL ECONOMICS AND SOCIAL PHILOSOPHY. Classical political economy emerged from moral philosophy, and its propounders considered their efforts to fall naturally within the limits of philosophical discourse. As a modern embodiment, Constitutional Economics is similarly located, regardless of disciplinary fragmentation. How can persons live together in liberty, peace and prosperity? This central question of social philosophy requires continuing contributions from many specialists in inquiry, surely including those of the constitutional economists. By their focus directly on the ultimate selection of a set of constraining rules within which ordinary social interaction takes place, constitutional economists remove themselves at least one stage further from the false position of 'social engineer' than their counterparts in orthodox economics. Precisely because there is no apparently simple evaluative criterion analogous to 'allocative efficiency' at hand, the constitutional economist is less tempted to array alternatives as if an unexamined criterion commands universal assent. The artificial abstraction of 'social utility' is likely to be less appealing to those who concentrate on choices among constraints than to those who examine choices within constraints.

If, however, there is no maximand, how can ultimate normative consequences emerge? In this respect, one contribution lies at the level of positive analysis rather than in a too-hasty leap into normative evaluation. Classical political economy contains the important principle of spontaneous coordination, the great discovery of the 18th century. This principle states that, within the legal umbrella of the minimal state and given certain conditions, the market 'works'. Even if in the principle's modern embellishment we must add 'warts and all', we still have come a long way toward a more comprehensive understanding of the alternatives for social order. To the extent that his efforts expand the public understanding of this principle, in application to all institutional settings, the constitutional economist remains under less apparent compulsion to advance his own privately preferred 'solutions' to the ultimate choice among regimes.

III THE NEW POLITICAL ECONOMY. Care should be taken not to claim too much for Constitutional Economics, especially if a narrow definition is used. As noted earlier, this research programme, by designation, emerged in the 1970s to describe efforts at analysing the effects of alternative sets of rules, as opposed to analyses of choices made within existing and unexamined structures. In a more comprehensive overview of developments after World War II, Constitutional Economics takes its place among an intersecting set of several research programmes, all of which have roots in classical political economy. Critical emphases differ as among the separate programmes, but each reflects efforts to move beyond the relatively narrow confines of orthodox neoclassical economics.

In continental Europe, the whole set of subdisciplines is included under the rubric 'The New Political Economy'. Within this set we can place (1) Public Choice, from which Constitutional Economics emerged; (2) Economics of Property Rights; (3) Law and Economics or Economic Analysis of Law; (4) Political Economy of Regulation; (5) the New Institutional Economics, and (6) the new Economic History. Defined imperialistically, Constitutional Economics would parallel the inclusive term and embrace all of these programmes, since some attention is drawn in each case to the legal–political constraints within which economic and political agents choose. Differences can be identified, however, and it may be useful to summarize some of these here, even if detailed discussion of the other research programmes cannot be attempted.

Public Choice, in its non-constitutional aspects of inquiry, concentrates attention on analyses of alternative political choice structures and on behaviour within those structures. Its focus is on predictive models of political interactions, and is a preliminary but necessary stage in the more general constitutional inquiry. The economics of property rights, law and economics, and the political economy of regulation remain somewhat closer to orthodox economic theory than Constitutional Economics or Public Choice. The standard efficiency norm remains central to these subdisciplines, both as an explanatory benchmark and as a normative ideal. The new institutional economics is directed more toward the interactions within particular institutional forms rather than toward the comprehensive structure of political rules (Furubotn and Richter, 1980; Frey,

1984). Some elements of the new economic history closely parallel Constitutional Economics, with, of course, an historical rather than a comparative emphasis (North and Thomas, 1973).

IV PRESUPPOSITIONS. Constitutional Economics, along with the related research programmes mentioned above, shares a central methodological presupposition with both its precursor, classical political economy, and its counterpart in modern neoclassical microeconomics. Only individuals choose and act. Collectivities, as such, neither choose nor act and analysis that proceeds as if they do is not within the accepted scientific canon. Social aggregates are considered only as the results of choices made and actions taken by individuals. The emphasis on explaining non-intended aggregative results of interaction has carried through since the early insights of the Scottish moral philosophers. An aggregative result that is observed but which cannot, somehow, be factored down and explained by the choices of individuals stands as a challenge to the scholar rather than as some demonstration of non-individualistic organic unity.

Methodological individualism, as summarized above, is almost universally accepted by economists who work within mainstream, or non-Marxian, traditions. A philosophical complement of this position that assumes a central role in Constitutional Economics is much less widely accepted and is often explicitly rejected. A distinction must be drawn between the methodological individualism that builds on individual choice as the basic unit of analysis and a second presupposition that locates the ultimate sources of value exclusively in individuals.

The first of these presuppositions without the second leaves relatively little scope for the derivation of constitutional structures from individual preferences. There is no conceptual normative bridge between those interests and values that individuals might want to promote and those non-individualistic values that are presumed to serve as ultimate normative criteria. The whole constitutional exercise loses most if not all of its *raison d'être* in such a setting. If the ultimate values which are to be called upon to inform the choices among institutions are non-individualistic, then there is, at best, only an instrumental argument for using individually expressed preferences in the process of discovering those values.

On the other hand, if the second presupposition concerning the location of the ultimate sources of value is accepted, there is no *other* means of deriving a 'logic of rules' than that of utilizing individually expressed interests. At base, the second presupposition implies democracy in governance, along with the accompanying precept that this structure of decision-making only takes on normative legitimacy with the prefix 'constitutional' appended to it.

V WICKSELL AS PRECURSOR. The single most important precursor to Constitutional Economics in its modern variant is Knut Wicksell, who was individualist in both of the senses discussed above. In his basic work on fiscal theory (*Finanztheoretische Untersuchungen*, 1896) Wicksell called attention to the significance of the rules within which choices are made by political agents, and he recognized that efforts at reform must be directed towards changes in the rules for making decisions rather than toward modifying expected results through influence on the behaviour of the actors.

In order to take these steps, Wicksell needed some criterion by which the possible efficacy of a proposed change in rules could be judged. He introduced the now-familiar unanimity or consensus test, which is carried over into Constitutional Economics and also allows the whole research programme to be related closely to the contractarian tradition in political philosophy. The relationship between the Wicksellian and the Paretian criteria is also worthy of note. If only individual evaluations are to count, and if the only source of information about such evaluations is the revealed choice behaviour of individuals themselves, then no change could be assessed to be 'efficient' until and unless some means could be worked out so as to bring all persons (and groups) into agreement. If no such scheme can be arranged, the observing political economist remains silent. The Wicksellian contribution allowed the modern economist to bring the comparative analysis of rules or institutions within a methodological framework that utilizes and builds on the efficiency criterion, which, when interpreted as indicated, does not require departure from either of the individualistic presuppositions previously discussed.

VI *Homo Economicus* IN CONSTITUTIONAL CHOICE. Constitutional Economics, as distinct from the complementary research programme on political constitutions that are within the boundaries of law, political science, sociology and other disciplines, goes beyond the logical presuppositions of individualism to incorporate non-tautological models of individual utility maximization. *Homo economicus* takes a central role in comparative institutional inquiry. Individuals are assumed to seek their own interests, which are defined so as to retain operational content.

Two quite different arguments can be made in support of this postulate in Constitutional Economics. The first is based simply on methodological consistency. To the extent that individuals are modelled as utility maximizers as they participate in market relationships, there would seem to be no basis for postulating a shift in motivation as they behave within non-market constraints. There is at least a strong presumption that individuals do not undergo character transformation when they shift from roles as buyers or sellers in the market place to roles as voters, taxpayers, beneficiaries, politicians or bureaucrats in the political process. A more sophisticated reason for postulating consistency in behaviour lies in the usefulness of the model for the whole exercise of institutional comparison. If the purpose is to compare the effects of alternative sets of constraints, some presumption of behavioural consistency over the alternatives is necessary in order to identify those differences in results that are attributable to the differences in constraints.

A second argument for introducing *homo economicus* in Constitutional Economics is both more complex and more important. It is also the source of confusion because it is necessary to distinguish carefully between the use of *homo economicus* in predictive social science, specifically in positive Public Choice and

139

in neoclassical economics, and in Constitutional Economics. There is an argument for using the construction in the latter, even if there are demonstrated empirical limits on the explanatory power of the model in the former.

The argument is implicit in the work of the classical economists. It was stated as a methodological principle by both David Hume and J.S. Mill:

> In constraining any system of government, and fixing the several checks and controls of the constitution, each man ought to be supposed a knave, and to have no other end, in all his actions, than private interest (Hume [1741], 1963, pp. 117–18).

> The very principle of constitutional government requires it to be assumed that political power will be abused to promote the particular purposes of the holder; not because it is always so, but because such is the natural tendency of things, to guard against which is the special use of free institutions (Mill [1861], 1977, p. 505).

The ultimate purpose of analysing alternative sets of rules is to inform the choice among these sets. The predicted operating properties of each alternative must be examined, and these properties will reflect the embodied models of individual behaviour within the defined constraints. Behavioural departures from the presumptive models used in deriving the operating properties will, of course, be expected. But the costs of errors may not be symmetrically distributed around the single best predictive model. The predicted differential loss from behavioural departures from a model that involves 'optimistic' motivational assumption may be much larger than the predicted differential gain if the model is shown to be an accurate predictor. Hence, comparative evaluation of an institution based on an altruistic model of behaviour should take into account the possible non-linearity in the loss function that describes departures from the best estimates. (In legal practice, formal contracts include protections against worst-case behaviour patterns.) In constitutional choice, therefore, there is an argument for incorporating models of individual behaviour that presume more narrowly defined self-interest than any empirical record may warrant (Brennan and Buchanan, 1985).

VII APPLICATIONS. Applications of Constitutional Economics, as a research programme, have emerged in several settings. First, consider taxation. Post-Marshallian economic theory, either in its partial or general equilibrium model, was often applied to tax incidence. Analysis was directed toward predicting the effects of an exogenously imposed tax on the private economizing behaviour of persons in their varying capacities as demanders and suppliers of goods and services in the market place. Building on this base of positive analysis, normative welfare economics allows a ranking among alternative equi-revenue tax instruments in terms of the Paretian standard. In both the positive and normative aspects, neoclassical tax theory embodies the presumption that taxes, as such, are exogenous to the choice process.

The major contribution of modern Public Choice, as a subdiscipline in its own right, has been that of endogenizing political decision-making. In its direct emphasis, public choice theory examines the political decision rules that exist with a view toward making some predictions about just what sort of tax institutions or tax instruments will emerge. Constitutional Economics, as an extended research programme that emerges from Public Choice, goes a step further and uses the inputs from both neoclassical economics and public choice theory to analyse how alternative political rules might generate differing tax rules.

The relevant constitutional choice may be that of granting government authority to levy taxes on Tax Base A or Tax Base B. Suppose that under the neoclassical equi-revenue assumption, analysis demonstrates that the taxing of A generates a lower excess burden than the taxing of B. Analysis of the political choice process may demonstrate, however, that government, if given the authority to tax A, will tend to levy a tax that will generate *more* revenue than would be forthcoming under an authority to tax B. The equi-revenue alternatives may not be effective political alternatives under any plausibly acceptable modelling of the behaviour of political agents. Once this simple point is recognized, the normative significance of the neoclassical ranking of tax instruments is reduced. Discussion shifts necessarily to the level of interaction between political decision structures and fiscal institutions.

A second application of Constitutional Economics is found in the post-Keynesian discussion of budgetary policy. The Keynesian advocacy of the use of governmental budgets to accomplish macroeconomic objectives was based on a neglect of the political decision structure. The proclivity of democratic governments to prefer spending over taxing, and hence to bias budgets toward deficit, is readily explained in elementary public choice theory (Buchanan and Wagner, 1977). This essential step in public choice reasoning leads naturally to inquiry into the relationships between the constraints that may be placed on political choice and predicted patterns of budgetary outcomes. Out of this intensely practical, and important, application of Constitutional Economics emerged the intellectual bases for the normative argument that, in the post-Keynesian era when moral constraints on political agents have lost much of their previous effectiveness, formal rules limiting deficit financing may be required to insure responsible fiscal decisions. In the modern setting, such rules would limit spending rates. But it is perhaps worth noting that, in the political environment of Sweden in the 1890s, Wicksell advanced analytically similar proposals for reform in the expectation that, if the suggested reforms should be implemented, public sector outlay would increase.

The analysis of alternative rules for 'the transfer constitution' represents a third application of constitutional economics. With the 1971 publication of John Rawls's *A Theory of Justice*, renewed attention came to be placed on principles of distributive justice. Although explicitly pre-constitutional, Rawls's work has a close relationship with the efforts to derive criteria for political and economic rules of social interaction. Economists, as well as other social scientists and social philosophers, have come increasingly to recognize that the untrammelled interplay of interest-group politics is unlikely to further objectives for distributive justice. Analysis of how this politics operates in the making of fiscal transfers suggests that principled adjustments in the post-tax, post-transfer distribution of values is only likely to be achieved if the institutional rules severely restrict the profitability of investment in attempts to subvert the transfer process.

Further applications include the regulatory constitutions, along with the organization of public enterprises. In its inclusive definition, Constitutional Economics becomes the analytical route through which institutional relevance is reintroduced into a sometimes sterile social science. In its less inclusive definition, Constitutional Economics, along with its related and complementary research programmes, restores 'political' to 'economy', thereby bringing a coherence that was absent during the long hiatus during which 'economics' made putative claims to independent status.

BIBLIOGRAPHY

Brennan, G. and Buchanan, J.M. 1980. *The Power to Tax*: *Analytical Foundations of the Fiscal Constitution*. Cambridge: Cambridge University Press.
Brennan, G. and Buchanan, J.M. 1985. *The Reason of Rules*: *Constitutional Political Economy*. Cambridge: Cambridge University Press.
Buchanan, J.M. 1974. *The Limits of Liberty*: *Between Anarchy and Leviathan*. Chicago: University of Chacago Press.
Buchanan, J.M. and Tullock, G. 1962. *The Calculus of Consent*: *Logical Foundations of Constitutional Democracy*. Ann Arbor: University of Michigan Press.
Buchanan, J.M. and Wagner, R.E. 1977. *Democracy in Deficit*: *The Political Legacy of Lord Keynes*. New York: Academic Press.
Frey, B. 1984. A new view of economics: comparative analysis of institutions. *Scelte Pubbliche* 1, 17–28.
Furubotn, E.G. and Richter, R. (eds) 1980. The New Institutional Economics – a symposium. *Zeitschrift für die gesamte Staatswissenschaft*, 140.
Hayek, F.A. 1973–9. *Law, Legislation, and Liberty*. 3 vols, Chicago: University of Chicago Press.
Hume, David, 1741. On the interdependency of Parliament. In *Essays, Moral, Political and Literary*, London: Oxford University Press, 1963.
McKenzie, R. 1982. *Bound to Be Free*. Palo Alto: Hoover Press.
McKenzie, R. (ed.) 1984. *Constitutional Economics*. Lexington, Mass.: Lexington Books.
Mill, J.S. 1861. Considerations on representative government. In *Essays on Politics and Society*, Vol. XIX of *Collected Works of J.S. Mill*, Toronto: University of Toronto Press, 1977.
North, D.C. and Thomas, R.P. 1973. *The Rise of the Western World*: *A New Economic History*. Cambridge: Cambridge University Press.
Rawls, J. 1971. *A Theory of Justice*. Cambridge, Mass.: Harvard University Press.
Wicksell, K. 1896. *Finanztheoretische Untersuchungen*. Jena: Gustav Fischer. Central portions of this work were published in English translation as 'A new principle of just taxation' in *Classics in the Theory of Public Finance*, ed. R.A. Musgrave and A.T. Peacock, London: Macmillan, 1959.

Continuity in Economic History

DONALD N. McCLOSKEY

Continuity and discontinuity are devices of story-telling, telling the story of monetary policy over the past few months or the story of modern economic growth. They raise certain questions in philosophy and lesser matters, such as precedence and politics.

It is well to have a case in mind. The most important is that of the British industrial revolution.

If it was a 'revolution', as it surely was, it happened sometime. There was a discontinuity, a before and after. When? Various dates have been proposed, down to the day and year: 9 March 1776, when the *Wealth of Nations* provided an ideology for the age; the five months in 1769 when Watt took out a patent on the high pressure steam engine and Arkwright on the cotton-spinning water frame; or 1 January 1760, when the furnaces at Carron Ironworks, Stirlingshire, were lit.

Such dating has of course an amateur air. A definite date looks handsome on a plaque or scroll but the precision does not fit well with sophisticated story-telling. The discontinuity is implausibly sharp, drawing attention to minor details. The Great Depression did not start on 24 October 1929; the deregulation of American banking was not completed with the fall of Regulation Q. Nicholas Crafts (1977) has pointed out that the detailed timing of the industrial revolution should not anyway be the thing to be studied, because small beginnings do not come labelled with their probabilities of developing into great revolutions. He is identifying a pitfall in story-telling. Joel Mokyr identifies another (1985, p. 44): rummaging among the possible acorns from which the great oak of the industrial revolution grew 'is a bit like studying the history of Jewish dissenters between 50 BC and 50 AD. What we are looking at is the inception of something which was at first insignificant and even bizarre', though 'destined to change the life of every man and woman in the West'.

What is destined or not destined to change our lives will look rather different to each of us. Each historian therefore has his or her own dating of the industrial revolution. Each sees another discontinuity. E.M. Carus-Wilson (1941, p. 41) spoke of 'an industrial revolution of the 13th century': she found that the introduction of the fulling mill was 'due to scientific discoveries and changes in technique' and 'was destined to alter the face of medieval England'. A.C. Bridbury (1975, p. xix–xx) found in the late middle ages 'a country travelling slowly along the road ... that [it] travelled so very much more quickly in Adam Smith's day'. In the eyes of Marxist writers, the 16th century was the century of discontinuity, when capitalism set off into the world to seek its fortune. John U. Nef, no Marxist, believed he saw an industrial revolution in the 16th century, centred on coal (1932), though admittedly slowed in the 17th century. A student of the 17th century itself, such as D.C. Coleman (1977), finds glimmerings of economic growth even in that disordered age. The most widely accepted period for the industrial revolution is the late 18th century, especially the 1760s and 1770s (Mantoux, 1928; Landes, 1969), but recent students of the matter (Harley, 1982; Crafts, 1984) have found much to admire in the accomplishments of the early 18th century. W.W. Rostow (1960) placed the 'takeoff into self-sustained growth' in the last two decades of the 18th century, but others have observed that even by 1850 the majority of British people remained in traditional sectors of the economy. And later still there was a second industrial revolution (of chemicals, electricity, and internal combustion) and a third (of electronics and biology).

Wider perspectives are possible, encouraging the observer to see continuity instead. Looking at the matter from 1907, the American historian Henry Adams could see a 'movement from unity into multiplicity, between 1200 and 1900, ... unbroken in sequence, and rapid in acceleration' (p. 498). The principal modern student of the industrial revolution, R.M. Hartwell, appealed for continuity against the jostling throng of dates (1965, p. 78): 'Do we need an *explanation* of the industrial revolution? Could it not be the culmination of a most unspectacular process, the consequence of a long period of economic growth?'

Such questions of continuity and discontinuity are asked widely in economics, though sometimes half consciously. They should not be left to historians. Economics is mainly contemporary history, and faces the problem of deciding when a piece of history has been continuous or not. For instance the crucial discontinuity in the growth of big government, as Robert Higgs (1987) points out, might be placed when the institutions of centralized intervention were conceived (1900–1918) or made (1930–45) or expanded (1960–70). Even recent history faces this narrative problem. When, if ever, did purchasing power parity break down in the 1970s? When did policy on antitrust alter to favour mergers? When did monetary policy last become expansionary? Where is the break?

The difficulty in answering the question has often been misconstrued as philosophical. The philosophical difficulty was first articulated in the 5th century BC by Parmenides and his student Zeno: that if everything is perfectly continuous, change is impossible (Korner, 1967). Everything is so to speak packed too tightly to move. The economist will recognize the point as analogous to an extreme form of economic equilibrium, or to the physicist's maximum entropy. If human nature doesn't 'really' change, then history will be a string of weary announcements that the more things change the more they stay the same. If the economy is 'really' in equilibrium all the time, then nothing remains to be done.

Alexander Gerschenkron, the economic historian who has contributed most to the understanding of continuity and discontinuity in economics, noted that such a metaphysics would close the book of history (1962, p. 12). A history of economics that began with the Parmenidean continuum would never speak.

For purposes of social science Gerschenkron rejects the transition from the connectedness of all change to an absence of change. True, if you squint and fit a curve then no economic change looks discontinuous in the mathematical sense; but it is wrong then to deduce that 'really' there is no change at all, or that the industrial revolution is a mirage. 'Continuity' in the strict mathematical sense must be kept distinct from 'continuity' in the story-telling sense.

Economists have often been muddled about this philosophical distinction, drawing surprising ideological implications from it. Alfred Marshall enshrined on the title page of his *Principles* the motto 'natura non facit saltum' (nature does not make a jump; Leibnitz had invented it as 'la nature ne fait jamais des sauts'). Marshall himself perhaps believed that the ability to represent behaviour with differentiable functions implies that marginalism is a good description of human behaviour. It is less certain that he believed that the lack of jumps in nature (this on the eve of quantum physics) implies people should not jump either, and should change society only gradually. Anyway, both implications are non sequiturs. Though both have been attributed to neoclassical economics, neither is necessary for it. Much bitter controversy has assumed that neoclassical economics depends on smooth curves and in consequence must advocate smooth social policies. The peculiar alliance between discrete mathematics and Marxian economics has this origin, as does the enthusiasm of some conservative writers for continuities in economic history. Gerschenkron cursed both their houses; the social scientist should study change and continuity 'unbothered by the lovers and haters of revolutions who must find themselves playgrounds and battlegrounds outside the area of serious scholarship' (p. 39).

In one sense of 'continuity' it is trivial that economic history is continuous. History has causes (the fourth of five historically relevant definitions that Gerschenkron distinguishes). Continuity, then, can be viewed as being merely an impressively long causal chain. The exploitation of Scottish iron deposits in the 18th century was caused by bold investments, but these depended on a reliable law of property and commerce, which depended on certain legal developments in the 16th century, and on the growth of political stability in the early 18th century, which in turn depended on all manner of earlier events. Establishing continuities, as Gerschenkron remarks, is the historian's purpose – or, one might add, the economist's, who is doing the historian's work when he is not doing the philosopher's. The purpose might be to find a cause of, say, the Great Depression. It would be to find a chain of events the absence of which would have made a difference: the international irresponsibility of the United States, for instance, as Kindleberger argued; or the domestic irresponsibility of the Federal Reserve, as Friedman and Schwartz argued. Finding such chains has its own philosophical difficulties (see the essay in this book on Counterfactuals).

The main problems of continuity and discontinuity, however, are not solvable in seminars on philosophy. They are practical problems in the uses of measurement, and must be solved in the economic or historical workshop. When shall we say that the industrial revolution happened? Gerschenkron gives an answer confined to industry, for in common with most economic historians he regards agriculture and services as laggards in economic growth.

> In a number of major countries of Europe ... after a lengthy period of fairly low rates of growth came a moment of more or less sudden increase in the rates, which then remained at the accelerated level for a considerable period. That was the period of the great spurt in the respective countries' industrial development.... The rates and the margin between them in the 'pre-kink' and the 'post-kink' periods appear to vary depending on the degree of relative backwardness of the country at the time of the acceleration (pp. 33–4).

The level at which such discontinuity is to be observed is at choice. As Gerschenkron remarks,

> If the seat of the great spurt lies in the area of manufacturing, it would be inept to try to locate the discontinuity by scrutinizing data on large aggregate magnitudes such as national income.... By the time industry has become bulky enough to affect the larger aggregate, the exciting period of the great spurt may well be over (pp. 34–5).

In a footnote to these sentences he remarks that 'Walt Rostow's failure to appreciate this point has detracted greatly from his concept of the take-off, which in principle is closely related to the concept of the great spurt as developed by this writer.'

The point is a good one, and applies to all questions of continuity in aggregate economics. Small (and exciting) beginnings will be hidden by the mass until well after they have become routine. Joel Mokyr has put it as a matter of arithmetic: if the traditional sector of an economy is growing at a slow one per cent per annum, and starts with 90 per cent of output, the modern sector growing at four per cent per annum will take three-quarters of a century to account for as much as half of output (1985, p. 5). We may call it the Weighting Theorem (or the Waiting Theorem, for the wait is long when the weight is small to begin with). There are parallel points to be made elsewhere in economics and in social science generally. In growth theory, for instance, as was noticed shortly after its birth, a century of theoretical time is needed in most models for a shift to yield growth as much as 90 per cent of its steady state. More generally, economists have long recognized the tension between microeconomic explanations and the macroeconomic things to be explained. And sociologists have been quarrelling along similar lines for a century, using even the same jargon of micro and macro.

In other words, the search for discontinuity in an aggregate time series raises the question of the level at which we should do our social thinking, the aggregation

146

problem. Yet Gerschenkron himself did not answer the question well, and was hoist by his own petard. Calculating Italian industrial output he placed his 'big spurt' in 1896–1908, and wished to explain it with big banks founded in the 1890s. Stefano Fenoaltea, once his student, applied the Weighting Theorem to the case (Fenoaltea, 1987). Surely, Fenoaltea reasoned, the components of the industrial index – the steel output and the chemical output – are the 'real' units of economic analysis (note the similarity of this rhetoric to that advocating a micro foundation for macroeconomics). If the components started accelerating *before* the new banks appeared, becoming bulky only later, then the new banks could not have been the initiating force. Alas, the components did just this. They spoil Gerschenkron's bank-led story: the components accelerated not in the 1890s but in the 1880s, not after but before the banks. To paraphrase Gerschenkron on Rostow, by the time the progressive components of industry had become bulky enough to affect the larger aggregate, the exciting period was well over.

Yet the moral is still Gerschenkron's: that continuity and discontinuity are tools 'forged by the historian rather than something inherently and invariantly contained in the historical matter.... [A]t all times it is the ordering hand of the historian that creates continuities or discontinuities' (p. 38). Gerschenkron nodded, but in nodding made the point. The multiple datings of the industrial revolution make it, too. So does any choice of smoothness or suddenness in economic story-telling.

The point is that history, like economics, is a story we tell. Continuity and discontinuity are narrative devices, to be chosen for their story-telling virtues. Niels Bohr said once that 'It is wrong to think that the task of physics is to find out how nature is. Physics concerns what we can say about nature.' It is *our* say. We can choose to emphasize the continuous: 'Abraham begat Isaac; ... begat ... begat ... and Jacob begat Joseph the husband of Mary, of whom was born Jesus.' Or the discontinuous: 'There was in the days of Herod, the king of Judea, a certain priest named Zacharias.' It is the same story, but its continuity or discontinuity is our creation, not God's. That it is out of God's hands does not make it arbitrary. Scholars speak of the industrial revolution as early or late, gradual or sudden. Other scholars believe or disbelieve their stories on the usual grounds.

BIBLIOGRAPHY

Adams, H. 1907. *The Education of Henry Adams.* New York: Modern Library, 1931.

Bridbury, A.C. 1975. *Economic Growth: England in the Later Middle Ages.* Brighton: Harvester.

Carus-Wilson, E.M. 1941. An industrial revolution of the thirteenth century. *Economic History Review* 11(1), 39–60. Reprinted in *Essays in Economic History,* Vol. I, ed. E.M. Carus-Wilson, London: Edward Arnold, 1954.

Coleman, D.C. 1977. *The Economy of England 1450–1750.* Oxford: Oxford University Press.

Crafts, N.F.R. 1977. Industrial revolution in England and France: some thoughts on the question 'Why was England first?' *Economic History Review,* 2nd series 30(3), August, 429–41.

Crafts, N.F.R. 1984. *Economic Growth During the British Industrial Revolution*. Oxford: Oxford University Press.

Fenoaltea, S. 1987. *Italian Industrial Production, 1861–1913: A Statistical Reconstruction*. Cambridge: Cambridge University Press.

Gerschenkron, A. 1962. On the concept of continuity in history. *Proceedings of the American Philosophical Society*, June. Reprinted in A. Gerschenkron, *Continuity in History and Other Essays*, Cambridge, Mass.: Harvard University Press, 1968.

Harley, C.K. 1982. British industrialization before 1841: evidence of slower growth during the industrial revolution. *Journal of Economic History* 42(2), June, 267–90.

Hartwell, R.M. 1965. The causes of the industrial revolution: an essay in methodology. *Economic History Review*, 2nd series 18, August, 164–82. Reprinted in *The Causes of the Industrial Revolution in England*, ed. R.M. Hartwell, London: Methuen, 1967.

Higgs, R. 1987. *Crisis and Leviathan: Critical Episodes in the Growth of American Government*. New York: Oxford University Press.

Korner, S. 1967. Continuity. In *The Encyclopedia of Philosophy*, New York: Macmillan and Free Press.

Landes, D.S. 1969. *The Unbound Prometheus*. Cambridge: Cambridge University Press.

Mantoux, P. 1928. *The Industrial Revolution in the Eighteenth Century*. New York: Harper, 1961.

Mokyr, J. (ed.) 1985. *The Economics of the Industrial Revolution*. Totowa, NJ: Rowman and Allanheld.

Nef, J.U. 1932. *The Rise of the British Coal Industry*. 2 vols, London: Routledge.

Rostow, W.W. 1960. *The Stages of Economic Growth*. Cambridge: Cambridge University Press.

Counterfactuals

DONALD N. MCCLOSKEY

Counterfactuals are what ifs, thought experiments, *Gedankenexperimenten*, alternatives to actual history; they imagine what would have happened to an economy if, contrary to fact, some present condition were changed; in the philosophical literature therefore they are known also as 'contrary-to-fact conditionals'.

The notion has been used most self-consciously in historical economics. For example: 'If railroads had not been invented the national income of the United States in 1890 would have been at most 5 per cent lower.' Counterfactuals are implied, however, in many other parts of economics, such as macroeconomics: 'If a monetary rule with a small growth rate of M_1 were adopted then the rate of inflation would fall.' Or industrial organization: 'If the instant camera industry had 100 suppliers it would be competitive.'

The philosophical problem that counterfactuals raise, and part of the reason they have attracted the attention of modern philosophers, can be seen in the last example. We wish to contrast the present monopoly of instant cameras with (nearly) perfect competition. Perhaps we wish to do so in order to measure the welfare cost of the monopoly and to advise a judge. Now of course if somehow the instant camera industry were to have 100 sellers then each seller would be small relative to the whole demand or supply. Speaking mechanically, the usual formulas for elasticities imply that the elasticity of individual demand facing any one of them would be large, roughly 100 times the elasticity of total supply plus 100 times the elasticity of total demand. Such calculations are the heart of applied economics: If the cigarette tax were lowered what would be the new relative price of cigarettes? If the money supply were increased what would happen to the price level? If foreign doctors could practise freely in the United States what would happen to the cost of American medical care?

Such questions involve looking into a world having, say, an instant camera industry with 100 sellers rather than one. It would not be our world, which saw the miraculous birth of Polaroid, the struggle with Kodak, and the final triumph

149

of patent over antitrust law. So much is clear. But how then is the counterfactual world to be imagined? A world in which the conditions of technology, personality, and law resulted in 100 Edwin Lands and 100 miniature Polaroid companies would be a different one – there's the condition contrary to fact.

The problems which can afflict counterfactuals are two: vagueness and absurdity. The vagueness arises when the model has not been fully specified. The world could arrive at 100 companies in many different ways, each with different implications for the original question about welfare. One can imagine getting 100 Polaroid companies, for example, by fragmenting edict now, well after the invention, in the style of the American Telephone and Telegraph case. Whatever the advantages, there might be inefficiencies in this. It would certainly change the future patent law. The change in law would in turn change things for good or ill elsewhere in the economy. A world in which patents are granted and then prematurely abrogated differs from the present world. Alternatively one might imagine subsidies in the 1940s that would have resulted originally in 100 alternative technologies of instant cameras (though actually only two were invented). This counterfactual likewise would have its costs, though different ones, changing for example the expectations of inventors about subsidies. A counterfactual requires a model broad enough to do the job.

Vagueness is solved by explicitness. The conditions required for various counterfactuals are made explicit, and being explicit can be tested for plausibility. Historical economists have been making counterfactuals explicit since the 1960s, using them to explore the causes of the American revolution and the consequences of American slavery (the counterfactual work is well surveyed by McClelland, 1975).

In the most famous use of counterfactuals Robert W. Fogel (1964) calculated what the transport system of the United States in 1890 would have looked like without railroads. He argued that evaluating the 'indispensability' of the railroads entailed calculating what American life would have been like without them. Some historians were reluctant to talk about such a counterfactual, saying that it was "'as if" history, quasi-history, fictitious history – that is not really history at all ..., a figment' (Redlich, 1968, in Andreano (ed.), pp. 95f). But economists find the notion natural, and philosophers accept it as routine. Indeed, the philosophers point out that the following are nearly equivalent (Goodman, 1965, p. 44):

Scientific Law: All inflations arise from money growth.

Causal Assertion: Money growth alone causes inflation.

Factual Conditional: Since inflation has changed, money growth has changed.

Dispositional Statement: Inflation is controllable with money growth.

Parallel Worlds: In a world identical (or sufficiently similar) to ours except that money growth differed, inflation would be different.

Counterfactual: If money growth were to be held at zero, inflation would be zero.

The philosophy of counterfactuals revolves around the translation of one of these into another. Historians, not realizing that one is translatable into the other, flee the counterfactual in terror and cling to the causal statement. Yet economists have on this score no cause for smugness, since they have parallel philosophical fears. Economists flee the causal statement as historians flee the counterfactual, and believe as historians do that the thing itself can be avoided by suppressing its name.

Fogel's calculations stirred great controversy, but were robust (Fogel, 1979). Since he was interested in long-term economic growth he did not imagine a sudden closure of the railroads in 1890: that clearly would have resulted in a very large drop in national income. Mental experiments like this commonly lie behind claims that railroads (or airlines or postal services or garbage collection) are 'essential'. Fogel imagined instead what the American economy would have looked like without access to railroads from the beginning, forced from the 1830s onward to rely on substitutes.

Such an economy would have invested more in canals and roads (Fogel introduced some of these into his counterfactual world, using contemporary engineering studies proposing them). It would have been an economy closer to waterways, with a bigger St Louis and a smaller Denver. It would doubtless have invented more improvements in road transport, arriving at internal combustion a little earlier than the world we know.

Fogel could not specify every feature of the 'true' counterfactual world. But he suspected anyway that the true counterfactual would give a national income only a little below the actual. To test the suspicion, therefore, he biased the case against himself, choosing a 'practical' counterfactual world in which income would be if anything lower than in the true counterfactual: he did not introduce the internal combustion engine before its time; and he did not shift the location of the population to accommodate the non-railroad transportation. He forced his practical counterfactual to carry supplies by river, canal and horse cart (not by the motor trucks that might have been) to a Denver no smaller than it actually became at the height of the railroad age. The result was a calculable upper bound on the true impact on national income: since the 'true' counterfactual would have economized relative to the clumsy 'practical' counterfactual, a use of the practical counterfactual biases the case against a large impact. Fogel reckoned that the impact was at most five per cent of 1890 income, a couple of years of economic growth.

He was merely applying in a bold way the usual methods of economics. The usual method is to imagine an explicit economic model, M, with parameters, P, and initial conditions (or exogenous variables), I, and results by way of endogenous variables, R. The counterfactual varies some element of the setup, the simplest being a variation in I – where I might be a tax rate in a model of cigarette consumption or the number of firms in a naive model of instant camera pricing – and examines the results. Fogel removed from the initial conditions one of the technologies of transportation. In similar fashion a 500-equation model of the American economy permits experimentation in counterfactual worlds:

What would happen if the price of oil fell? What would be the effect of a tax change? (The main empirical attack on Fogel's finding, indeed, was an highly explicit general equilibrium model of the Midwest and East (Williamson, 1974).)

Counterfactuals are one of the two main ways that economists at present explore the world (the third, controlled experiment, is still not common). The first is regression, or the comparative method, asking how *in fact* results have varied with initial or exogenous conditions. The second is the counterfactual, or simulation, asking how the results *would* vary. The regression infers parameters P from data on initial conditions I and results R and from arguments about the model, M; the counterfactual simulation infers R from data on P and from arguments about M and I.

But in solving the vagueness of counterfactuals by positing explicit models the economist runs against the other philosophical problem of counterfactuals: absurdity. Consider again the counterfactual of a 100-firm industry selling instant cameras. The problem is that the initial conditions that would lead to such an industry may themselves be absurd. Indeed, they may violate the very model used. The counterfactual assertion 'If the instant camera industry were perfectly competitive then price would be lower than it is now' takes on the character of the proverbial line 'If my grandmother had wheels she'd be a tram'. The model may be true (wheeled grandmothers may indeed be trams) but the counterfactual may be impossible – that is, a contradiction of the model itself or of some other, wider model felt to be persuasive.

It is possible to argue on these grounds that *all* counterfactuals are absurd. One might argue, as did Leibniz, that a world that did not invent the railroad would strictly speaking have to be a world different from ours right back to the big bang. Such a world might be one in which the seas were boiling hot or pigs had wings, with different transportation problems. The theory being violated by the counterfactual is the theory that the world hangs tightly together. As J.S. Mill remarked in attacking counterfactual comparison of free trade and protection, 'Two nations which agreed in everything except their commercial policy would agree also in that' (1872, p. 575).

A less intense scepticism on the matter has figured widely in economics. The theory of games, for example, can be viewed as an inquiry into counterfactuals, which sometimes violate wider theories (Selten and Leopold, 1982); the usual criticisms of the Cournot solution made by students of industrial organization involve the same point. Most notably, the Lucas Critique of econometric policy evaluation (Lucas, 1976) can be restated as a criticism of the usual counterfactual. The usual counterfactual imagines the effects of a change in the initial conditions I on a model M with given parameters P, fitted under the old regime. A new monetary policy would change the regime under which people believed they operated, changing P and M as much as I. Some broader model of how people adjust to regime changes is necessary to decide which would change: a new policy believed to be temporary would have very different effects from one believed to signal a revolution in government. The usual counterfactual violates the broader model, by supposing that people do not anticipate changes of regime or understand them when they occur. A broader model of rational expectations shows the counterfactual to be absurd.

John Elster, in a penetrating discussion of the role of counterfactuals in the economic sciences, posed the Basic Paradox of Counterfactuals: the less vague the theory, the more likely is a counterfactual using the theory to encounter absurdity. If Fogel had developed a theory of invention to draw a less vague picture of road transport without railroads he would have faced the problem that the very theory would predict the existence of railroads. After all, railroads were actually invented and therefore should be predicted by a sound theory of innovation. Elster wrote, 'If he attempted to strengthen his conclusion ... he would be sawing off the branch he is sitting on. In this kind of exercise it is often the case that more is less and that ignorance is strength' (1978, p. 206). The counterfactual must be 'capable of insertion into the real past'.

The Basic Paradox illuminates the discussion in economics about simplicity of models. A simpler model is harder to believe in its simulation because it is not so rich, but because of its lack of richness it is more likely to be insertable into the real past. A 500-equation model of the economy will more tightly constrain the past from which it comes than will a 10-equation model. Model selection has its own type I and type-II errors.

Many of the meta-criticisms of economics, then, reduce to remarks about a counterfactual. This is scarcely odd, since counterfactuals are equivalent to causal statements and the point of economics is to make causal statements. The philosophical literature on counterfactuals is illuminating, though large, technical, and mainly inconclusive (Lewis, 1973; Goodman, 1965). It comes to a position more sophisticated than mere scepticism. Counterfactuals are a way in which economists speak, and philosophers wish usually to assist the speaking, not end it. Self-aware or not, economists will go on speaking counterfactually about non-cooperative games, macroeconomic policy, and the retrospective welfare calculations of historical economics. The task of a philosophy of the economic counterfactual would be to understand the practice, not to change it.

BIBLIOGRAPHY

Elster, J. 1978. *Logic and Society: Contradictions and Possible Worlds*. New York: Wiley.

Fogel, R.W. 1964. *Railroads and American Economic Growth: Essays in Econometric History*. Baltimore: Johns Hopkins Press.

Fogel, R.W. 1979. Notes on the social saving controversy. *Journal of Economic History* 39(1), March, 1–54.

Goodman, N. 1965. *Fact, Fiction and Forecast*. 2nd edn, Indianapolis: Bobbs-Merril.

Lewis, D. K. 1973. *Counterfactuals*. Cambridge, Mass.: Harvard University Press.

Lucas, R.E. 1976. Econometric policy evaluation: a critique. *Journal of Monetary Economics*, Supplementary Series 1, 19–46.

McClelland, P.D. 1975. *Causal Explanation and Model Building in History, Economics and the New Economic History*. Ithaca, NY: Cornell University Press.

Mill, J.S. 1872. *A System of Logic*. 8th edn, London: Longmans; reprinted, 1956.

Redlich, F. 1968. Potentialities and pitfalls in economic history. *Explorations in Entrepreneurial History* II, 6(1), 93–108. Reprinted in *The New Economic History: Recent Papers on Methodology*, ed. R.L. Andreano, New York: Wiley, 1970.

Selten, R. and Leopold, U. 1982. Subjective conditionals in decision and game theory. In *Studies in Contemporary Economics*, Berlin: Springer-Verlag.

Williamson, J.G. 1974. *Late Nineteenth-Century American Development: A General Equilibrium History*. Cambridge: Cambridge University Press.

Crowding Out

OLIVIER JEAN BLANCHARD

'Crowding out' refers to all the things which can go wrong when debt-financed fiscal policy is used to affect output. While the initial focus was on the slope of the LM curve – the equilibrium curve of the money market – 'crowding out' now refers to a multiplicity of channels through which expansionary fiscal policy may in the end have little, no or even negative effects on output.

DIRECT CROWDING OUT AND RICARDIAN EQUIVALENCE. A first line of argument questions whether fiscal policy will have any effect at all on spending.

Changes in the pattern of taxation which keep the pattern of spending unaffected do not affect the intertemporal budget constraint of the private economy and thus may have little effect on private spending. This argument, known as the 'Ricardian equivalence' of debt and taxation, holds only if taxes are lump sum. Some taxes which induce strong intertemporal substitution, such as an investment tax credit on firms, will have stronger effects if they are temporary; for most others, such as income taxes, changes in the intertemporal pattern may only have a small effect on the pattern of spending. The Ricardian equivalence argument is not settled empirically and its validity surely depends on the circumstances: a change in the intertemporal taxation of assets such as housing or firms, leaving the present value of taxes the same, will have little effect on their market value, and thus on private spending; an explicitly temporary income tax increase may have little effect on spending while the anticipation of long prolonged deficits may lead taxpayers to ignore the eventual increase in tax liabilities. Evidence from specific episodes, such as the 1968 temporary tax surcharge in the US, suggests partial offset at best.

Changes in the pattern of government spending obviously have real effects. But here again, various forms of direct crowding out may be at work. Public spending may substitute perfectly or imperfectly for private spending, so that changes in public spending may be directly fully or partially offset by consumers or firms. Even if public spending is on public goods, the effect will depend on

155

whether the change in spending is thought to be permanent or transitory. Permanent changes, financed by a permanent increase in taxes, will, as a first approximation, lead to a proportional decrease in private spending, with no effect on total spending. Temporary changes in spending, associated with a temporary increase in taxes, lead to a smaller reduction in private spending and thus to an increase in total spending.

Thus one should not expect any change in taxation or government spending to have a one-for-one effect on aggregate demand. An eclectic reading of the discussion above may be that only sustained decreases in income taxation, or the use of taxes which induce strong intertemporal substitution, or temporary increases in spending, can reliably be used to boost aggregate demand. The focus will be on these forms of fiscal expansion in what follows.

CROWDING OUT AT FULL EMPLOYMENT. Not every increase in aggregate demand translates into an increase in output. This is clearly the case if the economy is already at full employment. While tracing the effects of fiscal expansion at full employment is of limited empirical interest, except perhaps as a description of war efforts, it is useful for what follows.

If labour supply is inelastic, output is fixed and any increase in aggregate demand must be offset by an increase in interest rates, leaving output unchanged. In the case of an increase in public spending, private spending will decrease; in the case of a decrease in income taxation, private spending will in the end be the same, but its composition will change as the share of interest-sensitive components decreases. To the extent that labour supply is elastic, intertemporal substitution of labour in response to a temporary change in interest rates may lead to temporarily more output and employment.

But this is just the beginning of the story. Over time, changes in capital and debt lead to further effects on output. The decrease in investment in response to higher interest rates leads to a decline in capital accumulation and output, reducing the supply of goods. If fiscal expansion is associated with sustained deficits, the increase in debt further increases private wealth and private spending at given interest rates, further increasing interest rates and accelerating the decline in capital accumulation. How strong is this negative effect of debt on capital accumulation likely to be? One of the crucial links in this mechanism is the effect of government debt on interest rates; empirical evidence, both across countries and from the last two centuries, shows surprisingly little relation between the two.

Allowing for uncertainty, and recognizing that debt and capital have different return characteristics, complicates the story in a potentially interesting way. Depending on the relation between human wealth and debt on the one hand, and human wealth and capital on the other, an increase in the share of debt in portfolios may increase or decrease the rate of return on capital. It is therefore conceivable that while the increase in the level of debt increases the overall level of interest rates, the increase in the share of debt in portfolios decreases the required rate of return on capital relative to that on debt; if this is the case, the steady increase in debt may have a small net effect on the required rate of return on capital, and on capital accumulation. Theoretical and empirical evidence suggest however that this portfolio effect is small and can probably be ignored.

Worse can happen: it may be that the fiscal programme becomes unsustainable. There is no reason to worry about a fiscal programme in which debt grows temporarily faster than the interest rate. But there is reason to worry when there is a positive probability that, even under the most optimistic assumptions, debt will have to grow forever faster than the interest rate. When this is the case, this implies that the government can only meet its interest payments on existing debt by borrowing more and more. What happens then may depend on the circumstances. Bond holders may start anticipating repudiation of government debt and require a risk premium on the debt, further accelerating deficits and the growth of the debt. If they instead anticipate repudiation through inflation, they will require a higher nominal rate and compensation for inflation risk in the form of a premium on all nominal debt, private and public. What is sure is that there will be increased uncertainty on financial markets and that this will further contribute to decreases in output and in welfare. The historical record suggests that it takes very large deficits and debt levels before the market perceives them as potentially unsustainable. England was able in the 19th century to build debt-to-GNP ratios close to 200 per cent without apparent trouble. Some European countries are currently running high deficits while already having debt to GNP ratios in excess of 100 per cent, without any evidence of a risk premium on government debt. Sustainability seems in fact rarely to be an issue.

But even if one excludes this worst case scenario, fiscal expansion can clearly have adverse effects on output at full employment. The relevant issue is however whether the same dangers are present when fiscal expansion is implemented to reduce unemployment, which is presumably when it is most likely to be used.

CROWDING OUT AT LESS THAN FULL EMPLOYMENT. The historical starting point of the crowding out discussion is the fixed price IS–LM model. In that model, a fiscal expansion raises aggregate demand and output. The pressure on interest rates does not come from the full-employment constraint as before but from the increased demand for money from increased output. Thus the fiscal multiplier is smaller the lower the elasticity of money demand to interest rates, or the larger the elasticity of private spending to interest rates. Fiscal expansion crowds out the interest-sensitive components of private spending, but the multiplier effect on output is positive. As output and interest rates increase, it is quite possible for both investment and consumption to increase.

What happens however when the model is extended to take into account dynamics, expectations and so on? Can one overturn the initial result and get full crowding out or even negative multipliers?

Even within the static IS–LM, one can in fact get zero or negative multipliers. This is the case for example if money demand by agents is higher than by the government and the change in policy redistributes income from the government to agents. While this case is rather exotic, a much stronger case can be made if the economy is small, open, with capital mobility and flexible exchange rates, as in the 'Mundell–Fleming' model. In this case, with the interest rate given from outside, and fixed money supply, money demand determines output; fiscal policy only leads to exchange rate appreciation. Exchange rate sensitive components are now crowded out by fiscal expansion. The multiplier is equal to zero.

When dynamic effects are taken into account, other channels arise for crowding out. The analysis of these dynamic effects, taking into account the dynamics of debt accumulation, was initially conducted under the maintained assumption of fixed prices and demand determination of output. Then, as debt was accumulating, private wealth and spending increased, leading to even larger effects of fiscal policy on output in the long run than in the short run. But the assumption of fixed prices, while debt and capital accumulation are allowed to proceed, is surely misleading; when prices are also allowed to adjust, the effects of fiscal policy become more complex and crowding out more likely; this is because some of the full-employment effects come back into prominence.

If fiscal expansion is maintained even after the economy has reached full employment, then the perverse effects of higher interest rates on capital accumulation and full employment output come again into play. This is true even if deficits disappear before the economy returns to full employment; the economy inherits a larger level of debt, and thus must have higher interest rates and lower capital accumulation than it would otherwise have had. The fiscal expansion trades off a faster return to full employment for lower full-employment output.

Anticipations of these full-employment effects are likely to feed back and modify the effects of fiscal policy at the start, when the economy is still at less than full employment. Faced with an increase in deficits, agents now anticipate not only faster return to full employment, but also higher interest rates for the foreseeable future. Depending on the strength of the two effects, the multiplier associated with fiscal policy may be larger or smaller than in the simple IS–LM. If the interest rate effect dominates, the effect of fiscal policy on output may be small.

The recent US experience has also brought into focus another but related perverse anticipation effect, that of anticipated future deficits on output. Anticipated deficits lead to expectations of higher interest rates, higher output and, if the economy is open, exchange rate appreciation. This in turn leads to high long rates and exchange rate appreciation today. If the interest rate and exchange rate effects dominate, the anticipation of deficits will decrease aggregate demand and lead to a recession. This negative multiplier is however transitory and disappears when fiscal expansion actually takes place.

Finally, confidence effects may again come into play. Fiscal programmes which eventually imply government bankruptcy, debt repudiation or monetization may well introduce sufficient additional uncertainty to decrease or change the sign of the fiscal multiplier. But such a scenario requires a fiscal expansion of very large magnitude, much in excess of what is likely to be needed to get the economy back to full employment.

CROWDING OUT: AN ASSESSMENT. Should one conclude from this that fiscal policy is an unreliable macroeconomic tool, with small and sometimes negative effects on output? The answer is clearly negative. Fiscal policy is likely to partly crowd out some components of private spending, even in the best circumstances, but there is little reason to doubt that it can help the economy return to full employment.

Ricardian equivalence and direct crowding out warn us that not any tax cut or spending increase will increase aggregate demand. But there is little question that temporary spending or sustained income tax cuts will do so.

Results of full crowding out at less than full employment, such as the Mundell–Fleming result, are simply a reminder that the monetary–fiscal policy mix is important. In all cases, monetary accommodation of the increased demand for money removes the negative or the zero multipliers.

That fiscal expansion affects capital accumulation and output adversely at full employment, and that unsustainable fiscal programmes may lead to crises of confidence is a reminder that fiscal expansion should not be synonymous with steady increases in the debt-to-GNP ratio even after the economy has returned to full employment. This shows one of the difficulties associated with fiscal expansion: if done through tax cuts, it has to be expected to last long enough to affect private spending, but not lead to expectations of runaway deficits in the long run. The room for manoeuvre is however substantial. Some taxes, such as the investment tax credit, work best when temporary. The historical record shows how large the margin of safety is before a fiscal programme becomes truly unsustainable.

Declining Industries

LESTER C. THUROW

Logically, there are two meanings to the term declining industries. Industries can
decline because their products have been replaced by new and better products,
or industries can decline because what used to be most cheaply produced in
country A is now most cheaply produced in country B and exported to country A.
In the first case, the word processor replaces the typewriter. In the second
case, steel production moves from the United States to Brazil and American
needs are met with imports from Brazil.

In economic discussions the term 'declining industries' is almost always used
in conjunction with the shift of industries from one country to another. This
occurs because there is little public controversy about the first type of decline
and much public controversy about the second.

With a shift from one product to another it is immediately obvious to everyone
that to prevent such declines is to hold one's standard of living below where it
otherwise would be. New products and the better jobs that go with them have
to be held back to maintain a market for old products and old jobs. To do so
is to retard progress and no one seriously proposes such actions.

It is equally true that to prevent the second type of decline is to hold one's
standard of living below where it might otherwise be, but this conclusion is not
as immediately obvious. Everyone can see in the first type of decline that additional
new jobs serve as a counterbalance to the loss of old jobs and that the consumers
get a better product. In the second type of decline the lost jobs are politically
visible at home and the new jobs are politically invisible abroad. The home gain
in real income comes via lower costs for consumers who replace expensive
domestic products with cheap foreign products.

Most often the producers who lose their jobs suffer large immediate reductions
in their incomes but are small in number, while the consumers are large in number
but reap only small gains in their real incomes. The aggregate gains exceed the
aggregate loss but the losses are highly visible while the gains are so small on a
per capita basis as to be almost invisible politically. Combine this with a world

where producer interests almost always have more political clout than consumer interests, and you have the political ingredients for policies to protect declining industries despite the fact that a country lowers its rate of growth by so doing.

Almost all countries protect their declining industries to some extent. Steel, for example, benefits from various forms of protection in Europe, the United States and Japan since none of them is today the low-cost producer for basic steel products. The more extensive the protection, however, the more harm a country does to its economic future.

The pattern of events is well known. Given protection in the home market, cheap foreign producers first drive the home industry out of its unprotected export markets. After World War II, the American steel industry first lost its export markets. Without those export markets home production falls. The home producers of unsophisticated metal products then find that they cannot compete against foreign producers who can buy cheap foreign steel while they have to buy expensive domestic steel. Products such as nails and wire start to be produced abroad and imported into the United States. Home production again falls. Eventually, foreign producers of sophisticated metal-using products such as cars find that their lower cost of materials is one of their advantages in competing against the American auto industry with its high material costs. The steel that is not exported as steel is exported as cars. As the case of steel indicates, protection can serve to slow down the rate of decline, but it is almost never possible to stop it.

To protect a declining industry is to weaken related industries and set in motion spreading waves of decline and protection. As a result, protecting declining industries is much like poking a balloon: for every successful indentation there is an equal expansion somewhere else.

While it is clear that a country should not seek to delay declines in industries where comparative advantage has shifted abroad, it is often not clear as to whether comparative advantage really has shifted. This occurs since currency values have not moved smoothly to maintain national balances between exports and imports as they should have done if they had operated as expected from textbook models. They have often in the past 15 years given very misleading signals – and very rapidly changing signals – as to where a country's real comparative advantage lies.

Thus in February 1985 the value of the dollar was so high that foreign wheat could be sold for less in the United States than American wheat; yet it is clear that the United States still has a comparative advantage in the production of wheat. It just does not seem to be so because of the temporarily high value of the dollar and the markets, such as the Common Market, that have rules and regulations essentially closing them to American exports.

Since the transition costs of closing an industry when the value of the dollar is high and reopening the industry when the dollar falls are very large, it may not make sense to allow the market to operate as it would without government interference. The question then becomes one of whether the right solution is protection or subsidies for the affected domestic industries, or international actions to moderate the movements between major currencies and to open closed foreign markets. Given that protection once in place is difficult to remove politically, international actions to moderate currency movements and open markets would seem to be the preferable solution.

When one analyses a declining industry, one seldom finds an industry in total decline without competitively viable parts. In the steel industry, for example, there are parts – mini-steel mills using electric furnaces and low-cost scrap iron, speciality high-tech alloy steels – that could be competitively operated in the United States given a value of the dollar that would balance exports and imports. To say that an industry is a declining industry is not to say that it will disappear.

A declining industry also need not lead to declining firms. While it is certainly true that modern industrial economies need less steel per unit of GNP produced, it is also true that there is a new growing high-tech industry in new materials – powdered metals, composites, pressed graphite – that is the new steel industry of tomorrow. Today's declining steel firms could be tomorrow's expanding new material firms. But most often they are not.

If one asks why not, it is clear that firms find it very difficult to develop new products that will destroy large old markets that they dominate. The firm has a large vested interest in the old market and entrenched forces within the firm make it very difficult for it to move into these new areas quickly. Thus IBM, the dominant force in the office typewriter business, was slow to develop a word processor despite the fact that it was the world's leader in computers. At General Electric, the dominant vacuum tube division sat on the transistor and prevented General Electric from becoming a leader in transistors. The classic example is of course the railroads, which saw themselves as railroads rather than as transportation companies.

While decline is the flip side of progress, real costs are involved. Most of these costs come in the form of human resources that are not easily transferred to new areas. An unemployed 55-year-old Pennsylvania steel worker is not apt to be retrained to be a California computer assembler. Such an individual faces a large cut in expected income over the remainder of his working life and society may well find itself burdened with higher social welfare costs.

Economic theory has little to say about these transition problems and costs, since it assumes that mobility is easy and that transition costs either do not exist or are very marginal. With its concept of equilibrium, wage workers forced out of work in old industries quickly find jobs in new industries with closely comparable wages. In contrast, those who have actually followed workers forced out of work in declining industries in the United States find that most of them find work only with a long time-lag and then only with much lower wages. The losses in real incomes are not the marginal ones assumed by economic theory.

As a result there is a real issue in how a nation manages decline. A nation cannot and should not prevent declining industries from shrinking, but it still has to face the issue of how it manages the transition of human resources from old sunset industries to new sunrise industries and what it does about those human resources that are essentially junked in the transition.

BIBLIOGRAPHY

Borrus, M., Millstein, J. and Zysman, J. 1982. U.S. Japanese competition in the semiconductor industry. *Policy Papers in International Affairs*, No. 17, Berkeley: Institute of International Studies, University of California.

Eckstein, O., Caton, C., Brinner, R. and Duprey, P. 1984. *The DRI Report on U.S. Manufacturing Industries*. New York: McGraw-Hill.

Hatsopoulos, G.N. 1983. *High Cost of Capital: Handicap of American Industry*. Waltham, Mass.: American Business Conference, Thermo Electron Corp.

Konaga, K. 1983. Industrial policy: the Japanese version of a universal trend. *Journal of Japanese Trade and Industry* 4, 21f.

Krist, W.K. 1984. The U.S. response to foreign industrial policies. In *High Technology Public Policies for the 1980s*, Washington, DC: a National Journal Issues Book.

Krugman, P. 1984. The United States response to foreign industrial targeting. *Brookings Papers on Economic Activity* 1, 77–121.

Labor-Industry Coalition for International Trade. 1983. *International Trade, Industrial Policies, and the Future of American Industry*. Washington, DC: Labor-Industry Coalition for International Trade, 40f.

Lawrence, R.A. 1984. *Can America Compete?* Washington, DC: Brookings.

Magaziner, I. 1983. New policies for wealth creation in the United States. In *Growth with Fairness*, Institute on Taxation and Economic Policy.

McKenna, R., Borrus, M. and Cohen, S. 1984. Industrial policy and international competition in high technology – Part I: blocking capital formation. *California Management Review* 26(6), Winter, 15–32.

Melman, S. 1984. The high-tech dream won't come true. *INC Magazine*, August.

Office of Technology Assessment. 1981. *US Industrial Competitiveness: A Comparison of Steel, Electronics and Automobiles*. Washington, DC: Congress of the US, Office of Technology Assessment.

Phillips, K. 1984. *Staying on Top: The Business Case for a National Industrial Strategy*. New York: Random House.

Piore, M.J. 1982. American labor and the industrial crisis. *Challenge* 25, March–April, 5–11.

Reich, R.B. 1982. Why the United States needs an industrial policy. *Harvard Business Review* 60(1), January, 74–80.

Schultze, C. 1983. Industrial policy: a dissent. *The Brookings Review* 2, Fall, 3–12.

Zysman, J. 1983. *Governments, Markets, and Growth*. Ithaca: Cornell University Press.

Distributive Justice

EDMUND S. PHELPS

Social justice is justice in all of the relationships occurring in society: the treatment of criminals, children and the elderly, domestic animals, rival countries, and so forth. Distributive justice is a narrower concept for which another name is economic justice. It is justice in the economic relationships within society: collaboration in production, trade in consumer goods, and the provision of collective goods. There is typically room for mutual gain from such exchange, especially voluntary exchange, and distributive justice is justice in the arrangements affecting the distribution (and thus generally the total production) of those individual gains among the participants in view of their respective efforts, opportunity costs, and contributions.

In earlier times the discussion of distributive justice tended to focus upon the obligations of the individual toward those with whom he or she had exchanges. So an employer was expected to be just or not to be unjust, and the problem was to demarcate employer injustice. With the rise of governments capable of redistribution and the spread of economic liberalism, the focus shifted to the distributional obligations of the central government. Let enterprises and households pursue their self-interests while the government attends to distribution (within the limits of its just powers). Distributive justice is largely about redistributive taxation and subsidies. The latter may take many forms such as public expenditures for schooling and vocational training (beyond the point justified only by the Pareto principle from the *status quo ante*) as well as cash subsidies for the employment of labour or low-wage labour (whether paid to employer or employee).

Note that the so-called negative income tax, whatever the claims for or against it as a tool of social justice, does not appear to be an instrument for distributive justice unless restricted somehow to those participating (more than some threshold amount?) in the economy (and thus in the generation of the gains to be (re)distributed). In any case, it will not be discussed here, although some propositions about subsidies apply also to the negative tax.

164

The suggestion that distributive justice might (at least in principle) require subsidies, not merely tax concessions or tax forgiveness for the working poor, tends to raise the eyebrows of some and accounts for the fact that distributive justice raises the hackles of a few. As long as the Iroquois and the Sioux have no contact, there are no gains to be distributed and distributive justice does not apply; if they are let free to engage in bilateral inter-tribal exchanges, however, the payment of a subsidy to pull up the wage of the lowest earners, who are Sioux, say, would come partly or wholly at the expense of the Iroquois. Now some commentators object to the notion that the Sioux, whose exchanges with the Iroquois are entirely voluntary and all of whom have benefited (or could have), we may suppose, might deserve an additional payment from the Iroquois, perhaps through some supra-tribal authority. Ayn Rand (1973), for example, argues that it is one thing to require of a poor person a fare for riding a bus with empty seats that the other riders can finance out of the benefits they receive from the bus – she has no qualms about such a free ride – and another thing for the poor person to tax the other riders. But she has got the economics wrong in the application of her (actually rather Rawlsian) ethical premise. Up to a point, a subsidy to the poorest-earning group (the Sioux in the above example) would leave the others (the Iroquois) still with a net gain – a gain after the tax needed to pay the subsidy. This is because of diminishing returns: when the group of Sioux workers is added to the fixed pool of Iroquois labour and land, the extra product added by the first arrivals – and, more generally, the average of the extra products added by the succession of Sioux workers – is larger than the extra product resulting from the last of these workers, which is the 'marginal product' of Sioux labour; the Iroquois could afford a subsidy equal to the excess of the average extra product over the marginal product. Correctly applied, then, the Randian objection is to a gain-erasing or, at any rate, a gain-reversing subsidy, not to *any* subsidy whatsoever.

Another objection to the concept of distributive justice and to the admissibility of subsidies argues that if these notions were sound it would make sense, by analogy, to apply them to marriage allocation, to the matching of husbands and wives; since we never hear of such applications the ideas are presumably unsound. Of course, it would strike us as novel and foreign to see a proposal for a tax on marriage with Iroquois men and a subsidy to marriage to Sioux men on the ground that the former were apparently more attractive to women (from either tribe) and the resulting inequality of benefits unjust and demanding correction. But the reasons might be other than the supposed unacceptability of the ideas of distributive justice. Maybe the impracticality of deciding on the taxes and subsidies stands in the way. Perhaps a marriage subsidy would be demeaning while employment subsidies would not, being graduated or even a flat amount per hour. Yet the key observation may be that, although there is economic exchange here and although racial discrimination or racial prejudices could cause real injustices, the Sioux and Iroquois men in this example are not cooperating for mutual gain and so no problem about the just division of such gains can arise; they are competing, or contesting, for partners, not forming partnerships with one another. Thus distributive justice cannot apply here.

The terms offered to the working poor, as already implied, are the locus classicus to which notions of distributive justice have been applied. However, two other arenas in which issues of justice are being fought out should be mentioned. One of these is the problem of intergenerational justice. It was first addressed in a celebrated paper in 1928 by Frank Ramsey, who adopted as the criterion of optimality the standard associated with utilitarianism – the sum of utilities over time. This conception of intergenerational justice encountered difficulties when in the 1960s it was applied to optimum saving of a society in which the population is to grow without bound, although that odd demographic case may have put utilitarianism to an unfair (and absurd) test. In 1971 John Rawls struggled with the problem of intergenerational justice in a famously problematic section of his, only to conclude that '... the difference principle [i.e., Rawls's maximin or, more accurately, leximin principle, which judges states of affairs by the well-being of the worst-off individual] does not apply to the savings problem. There is no way for later generations to improve the situation of the least fortunate first generation.' This seems to say that intergenerational justice, if there is such a thing, is not a problem of distributive justice, since there is no cooperation for mutual gain among generations, not even between adjacent ones in the chain. But the premise that the current generation cannot be helped by succeeding generations appears, on the face of it, to be a slip in Rawls's economics. In a closed economy, we can help future generations by providing them with more capital – even in an open economy enjoying perfect capital mobility, we can provide them with social overhead capital that the world capital market would not provide (or not so cheaply) – and, if overlapping with us, they can help us by meeting consumption claims we make through our issue of public debt and pension entitlements. Thus distributive justice does apply here, with a precision fit. What Rawls may be interpreted to mean is that if, being the least fortunate owing to heaven-sent technological discoveries over the future, the present generation were permitted to invest nothing (not even gross of depreciation!) – rather as we can imagine the poorest in the static problem to begin by sullenly asking for equality – the future generations could not bribe the present one to do something in their mutual interest – unlike the static problem in which the rich can explain the benefits of trickle-down. But in fact the next generation *can* bribe the present one with some old-age consumption in return for some investment. It may be conjectured that a maximin-optimal growth path would still exist in a model along the lines of the Phelps–Riley (1978) model notwithstanding the introduction of technological progress.

The other arena in which we find a debate over distributive justice is the international trade field. When a giant nation trades with a small number of pygmy countries, not large enough even in the aggregate to influence relative prices in the giant state, the latter receive all the gains from trade and the former gets nothing and loses nothing; this is exactly the Rawlsian maximin solution if perchance the pygmy countries are poorer (in some suitably defined way) than the giant. But if these tiny countries 'spoil the market', worsening their terms of trade in the course of exporting to and importing from the giant, because they are not of negligible size at least in the aggregate, then the Rawlsian solution is not obtained by the free market. The recent North–South problem of which the 'Southern' countries complain can be understood as the tendency of the 'Northern' countries that are already the richest countries, such as the North American and European countries, to retain the gain from trade resulting from the aforementioned change in the terms of trade caused by the 'Southern' countries through their trade with the 'Northern' ones. The 'Southern' countries believe justice to require that the 'Northern' countries arrange to give back that gain through some appropriate international transfer mechanism.

There are able and serious philosophers who would be happy to see distributive justice left to the economists. In fact, the history of philosophy has been seen as a process of divesting itself of a sub-field as soon as it could thrive independently. Likewise, there are economists who would leave the subject to philosophers. But, whichever group receives the lion's share of the contract to work on it, it seems that the economics (as well as philosophy) of the problems being studied is an essential element of the subject. In this sense and for this reason, the necessary cross-listing notwithstanding, distributive justice is an important field under economics.

BIBLIOGRAPHY

Phelps, E.S. and Riley, J.G. 1978. Rawlsian growth: dynamic programming of capital and wealth for intergeneration 'maximin' justice. *Review of Economic Studies* 45(1), February, 103–20.

Ramsey, F.P. 1928. A mathematical theory of saving. *Economic Journal* 38, December, 543–59.

Rand, A. 1973. Government financing in a free society. In *Economic Justice*, ed. E.S. Phelps, Harmondsworth: Penguin.

Rawls, J. 1971. *A Theory of Justice*. Cambridge, Mass.: Harvard University Press; Oxford: Oxford University Press, 1972.

Dividend Policy

JAMES A. BRICKLEY AND JOHN J. McCONNELL

There are two major ways in which a firm can distribute cash to its common stockholders. The firm can either declare a cash dividend which it pays to all its common stockholders or it can repurchase stock. Stock repurchases may take the form of registered tender offers, open market purchases, or negotiated repurchases from a large shareholder. By far the most common method of distributing cash to shareholders is through the payment of cash dividends. For example, in 1985, US corporations paid over $83 billion in cash dividends.

Most firms pay cash dividends on a quarterly basis. The dividend is declared by the firm's board of directors on a date known as the 'announcement date'. The board's announcement states that a cash payment will be made to stockholders who are registered owners on a given 'record date'. The dividend checks are mailed to stockholders on the 'payment date' which is usually about two weeks after the record date. Stock exchange rules generally dictate that the stock is bought or sold with the dividend until the 'ex-dividend date' which is a few business days before the record date. After the ex-dividend date, the stock is bought and sold without the dividend.

Dividends may be either labelled or unlabelled. Most dividends are not given labels by management. Unlabelled dividends are commonly referred to as 'regular dividends'. At times, managers will give a special label to the dividend. The most common label is the word, 'extra'. About 30 per cent of the *increases* in the dividend from the previous quarter are given some special label by management.

AN HISTORICAL PERSPECTIVE. Prior to 1961, academic treatments of dividends were primarily descriptive in nature, as, for example, in Dewing (1953). To the extent that economists considered corporate dividend policy, the commonly held view was that investors preferred high dividend payouts to low payouts (see, for example, Graham and Dodd, 1951). The only question was how much value was attached to dividends relative to capital gains in valuing a security (Gordon,

1959). This view was concisely summarized with the saying that a dividend in the hand is worth two (or some multiple) of those in the bush. The only question was – what is the multiple?

In 1961, scientific inquiry into the motives and consequences of corporate dividend policy shifted dramatically with the publication of a classic paper by Miller and Modigliani. Perhaps the most significant contribution of the Modigliani–Miller paper was to spell out in careful detail the assumptions under which their analysis was to be conducted. The most important of these include the assumption that the firm's investment policy is fixed and known by investors, that there are no taxes on dividends or capital gains, that individuals can costlessly buy and sell securities, that all investors have the same information and that investors have the same information as the managers of the firm, and, finally, that there are no contracting or agency costs associated with stock ownership. With this set of assumptions, Modigliani and Miller demonstrated that a firm's dividend policy is a matter of indifference to stockholders. That is, the value of the firm is independent of the dividend policy adopted by management.

The essence of the Modigliani–Miller proof is that investors can create their own dividends by selling shares of stock. If earnings are retained by the firm and invested in new projects, existing shareholders can sell stock and consume the proceeds, leaving themselves in the same position as if the firm had paid a dividend. Alternatively, if management elects to pay a dividend, new stock must be issued to undertake new projects. If shareholders prefer to reinvest rather than consume, they can do so by buying a pro rata share of the new stock issue with the dividends paid. In this instance, shareholders would be in the same position that they would have been had no dividend been paid. Thus, regardless of corporate dividend policy, investors can costlessly create their own dividend position. For this reason, stockholders are indifferent to corporate dividend policy, and, as a consequence, the value of the firm is independent of its dividend policy.

The conclusion that the market value of the firm is independent of its dividend policy means that corporate investment decisions can be made without regard to dividend policy. It is the case, though, that total cash inflows to and outflows from the firm do depend upon its investment decision. If the level of funds required for investment purposes exceeds internally generated funds, then new shares must be issued (or dividends retained) in order for firm value to be maximized. If internally generated funds exceed investment requirements, then shares must be repurchased or a cash dividend must be paid. Under the Modigliani–Miller assumptions though, the value of the firm is independent of the method used to distribute the cash.

After a brief flurry of debate, the Modigliani–Miller irrelevance proposition was essentially universally accepted as correct under their set of assumptions. There nevertheless remained an underlying notion that dividend policy must 'matter' given that managers and security analysis spend time worrying about it. If so, and if the Modigliani–Miller proposition is accepted, it must be due to violation of one or more of the Modigliani–Miller assumptions in the real world.

Since the early 1960s, the dividend debate has been lively and interesting as economists have analysed the effect on the value of the firm of relaxing the various Modigliani–Miller assumptions and have explored the data for evidence that dividend policy affects security prices and investor behaviour. Economists have focused on three related questions. First, does the *level* of dividends paid by the firm affect the value of the firm? That is, are high dividend-paying firms valued differently by the market than low dividend-paying firms, holding other factors constant? Second, do *changes* in an established dividend level affect the value of the firm? Third, does the method of cash payout affect the value of the firm? For example, are cash dividends valued differently than share repurchases and are labelled dividends valued differently than unlabelled dividends? We organize our discussion around these three questions.

FIRM VALUE AND THE LEVEL OF DIVIDEND PAYOUT. *Taxes.* Perhaps the obvious starting point for an investigation into the effect of relaxing the Modigliani–Miller assumptions is to introduce taxes. In the US, dividend payments by a corporation do not affect that firm's taxes. However, at least historically, dividends have been taxed at a higher rate than capital gains at the personal level. Thus, superficially, the US tax code appears to favour a low dividend payout policy.

Under the assumption that dividends and capital gains are taxed differentially, Brennan (1970) derived a model of stock valuation in which stocks with high payouts have higher required before-tax returns than stocks with low payouts. However, empirical tests of Brennan's model by Black and Scholes (1974), Litzenberger and Ramaswamy (1979) and Miller and Scholes (1982) have yielded ambiguous results, in which support for a dividend tax effect in stock returns appears to depend heavily upon the definition of dividend yield employed. In a provocative case study, Long (1978) has examined the prices of two classes of stock of Citizens Utility, which differ only in terms of dividends and tax treatments, and finds support for the notion that investors favour a high dividend payout.

As a counterpoint to Brennan, Miller and Scholes (1978) argue that the assumption that dividends are taxed disadvantageously relative to capital gains is inaccurate. They argue that, at least historically, under the US tax code there exist sufficient loopholes so that investors may shelter dividend income so as to drive the effective tax rate on dividends to zero. However, Feenberg (1971) and Peterson, Peterson and Ang (1985) examine data from actual tax returns which indicate the various methods of avoiding taxes described by Miller and Scholes are not used by investors who receive dividends.

Empirical investigation into the effects of taxes on the level of stock prices has not been limited to US data. For example, Poterba and Summers (1984) examine British stock returns and Morgan (1980) examines Canadian stock returns with no more definitive conclusion than has been reached with US data.

Suffice it to say that, at this point, empirical studies on the relation among dividends, taxes and firm value are inconclusive. Interestingly, the most recent US tax legislation taxes dividends and capital gains at the same rate. The introduction of this legislation holds forth the prospect of providing an opportunity for a before-and-after examination of the data.

Agency costs. A second potentially important real world violation in the Modigliani–Miller assumptions is the existence of agency costs associated with stock ownership. In particular, managers of firms maximize their own utility, which is not necessarily the same as maximizing the market value of common stock. The costs associated with this potential conflict of interest include expenditures for structuring, monitoring and bonding contracts between shareholders and managers, and residual losses due to imperfectly constructed contracts (Jensen and Meckling, 1976).

Several authors have argued that dividends may be important in helping to resolve manager/shareholder conflicts. If dividend payments reduce agency costs, firms may pay dividends even though these payments are taxed disadvantageously.

Easterbrook (1984) and Rozeff (1982) argue that establishing a policy of paying dividends enables managers to be evaluated periodically by the capital market. By paying dividends, the managers are required to tap the capital market more frequently to obtain funds for investment projects. Periodic review by the market is one way in which agency costs are reduced, which, in turn, raises the value of the firm. If so, the value of the firm is no longer independent of dividend policy. It is still the case, however, that even in these models an 'optimal' dividend payout level is far from obvious.

At this point, no direct (or even indirect) tests of the agency cost explanations of corporate dividend policy have been reported. The dearth of empirical tests of these models is due, in part, to their recent development and, in part, to the relative lack of specificity of the theories.

FIRM VALUE AND CHANGES IN THE PAYOUT. While the evidence on whether the level of dividend payouts affects firm value is mixed, studies have consistently documented that stock returns around the announcement of a dividend change are positively correlated with the change in the dividend (Aharony and Swary, 1980; Asquith and Mullins, 1983; Brickley, 1983; Pettit, 1972). The leading explanation of this phenomenon is that dividend changes convey information about current or future earnings of the firm.

Contrary to the Modigliani–Miller assumption that investors have the same information as managers, the information content of dividends hypothesis is based on the assumption that managers possess more information about the prospects of the firm than individuals outside the firm. The hypothesis asserts that dividend changes convey managers' inside information to outsiders. This idea was suggested by Miller and Modigliani (1961) and has roots in Lintner's (1956) classic study on dividend policy. Lintner interviewed a sample of corporate managers. One of the primary findings of the interviews was that a high proportion of managers attempt to maintain a stable regular dividend. In Lintner's words, managers demonstrate a 'reluctance (common to all companies) to reduce regular

171

rates once established and a consequent conservatism in raising regular rates' (p. 84). Lintner's argument is provided additional empirical support by Fama and Babiak (1968). If managers change regular dividends only when the earnings potential of the firm has changed, changes in regular dividend changes are likely to provide some information to the market about the firm's prospects.

More recently, formal models of dividends and information signalling have been developed. Models in which dividends convey information to outsiders include Bhattacharya (1979, 1980), John and Williams (1985) and Miller and Rock (1985). The assumptions under which these models are developed differ across the models. The major common feature is that managers are presumed to have information not available to outside investors. Typically, the information has to do with the current or future earnings of the firm.

The accumulated empirical evidence indicates that dividend announcements provide information to the market. As such, the evidence is consistent with the asymmetric information models of dividend changes. Whether these models actually capture the information to which the market is responding when dividend changes are announced is still an open question and which of the models best characterizes the process of information dissemination is still open to debate.

FIRM VALUE AND THE FORM OF THE PAYOUT. As with increases in regular cash dividends, specially labelled cash dividends and shares repurchases have been shown to be accompanied by permanent increases in stock prices (Brickley, 1983; Dann, 1981; Vermaelen, 1981). However, the factors that lead managers to choose one method over another are not well understood.

Given the Modigliani–Miller assumptions, the choice of the payout mechanism, like the choice of dividend policy itself, does not affect the value of the firm. Therefore, if the form of the payout is to matter, it must be due to violation of one or more of the Modigliani–Miller assumptions.

Economists have just begun to explore possible explanations as to why a particular form of payout is chosen. To develop a theory to explain the choice of payout mechanism, it must be that there are differential costs and/or benefits associated with the alternative payout methods. Given the preponderance of regular cash dividends relative to stock repurchases and specially-labelled dividends, a convincing explanation must credit regular cash dividends with substantial benefits or debit the alternatives with substantial costs. Furthermore, the relative benefits and/or costs must be especially significant because, at least historically, dividends have been tax-disfavoured (at the personal level) relative to share repurchases.

Two recently developed theories that attempt to explain the choice between cash dividends and share repurchases assume that managers have information not available to outside stockholders. Barclay and Smith (1986) and Offer and Thakor (1985) assume that managers can use this inside information to benefit themselves by means of share repurchases. In both cases, however, there are costs associated with the opportunistic use of the information. When the costs to the managers outweigh the benefits, dividends will be used to distribute cash instead of share repurchases.

As with various other hypotheses regarding corporate dividend policy, those explaining the choice between cash dividends and share repurchases have been developed only recently. As a consequence, they also have not yet undergone rigorous empirical testing. As regards the choice between regular cash dividends and specially labelled cash dividends, reasonable explanations are even more scarce. However, Brickley (1983) does provide evidence that specially-labelled dividends convey a less positive message about firm value than do increases in regular cash dividends.

CONCLUSION. After twenty-five years of rigorous consideration, what is known about dividend policy is far outweighed by what is not known. We know that firms annually pay out to stockholders substantial amounts of cash and that the vast majority of this payout is in the form of regular cash dividends. Intermittently, firms also make specially labelled cash dividend payments and large-scale share repurchases. We also know that stock prices increase permanently when regular dividends are increased, when special dividends are declared, and when shares are repurchased and that stock prices decline when regular dividends are reduced. There is a growing consensus that the stock price changes come about because the dividend changes reflect information available to managers that is not otherwise available to outside investors. There is, however, little agreement as to what information management is providing to the market through the dividend payment and there is little agreement as to the linkage between the information released and the value of the firm. There is also little agreement as to whether the level of cash payout affects the value of the firm and there is little agreement as to whether the choice of the payout method matters and, if it matters, what factors favour one method relative to another.

It is tempting to conclude this essay on a disappointing note of frustration. But twenty-five years is a very short period of investigation for most economic phenomena. While what we do know about dividend policy is far less than we would like to know, we clearly know more about dividend policy now than we did twenty-five years ago. Undoubtedly, the next twenty-five years will witness further significant progress in understanding the determinants of corporate dividend policy.

BIBLIOGRAPHY

Aharony, J. and Swary, I. 1980. Quarterly dividends, earnings announcements, and stockholder returns. *Journal of Finance* 35(1), March, 1–12.

Asquith, P. and Mullins, D. 1983. The impact of initiating dividend payments on shareholders' wealth. *Journal of Business* 56, January, 77–96.

Barclay, M. and Smith, C.W. 1986. Corporate payment policy. Cash dividends vs. share repurchases. Unpublished ms., August.

Bhattacharya, S. 1979. Imperfect information, dividend policy, and the 'Bird in the hand' fallacy. *Bell Journal of Economics* 10(1), Spring, 259–70.

Bhattacharya, S. 1980. Nondissipative signalling structures and dividend policy. *Quarterly Journal of Economics*, December 95, August, 1–24.

Black, F. and Scholes, M.S. 1974. The effects of dividend yield and dividend policy on common stock prices and returns. *Journal of Financial Economics* 1(1), May, 1–22.

Brennan, M.J. 1970. Taxes, market valuation, and corporate financial policy. *National Tax Journal* 23(4), December, 417–27.

Brickley, J.A. 1983. Shareholder wealth, information signalling, and the specially designated dividend: an empirical study. *Journal of Financial Economics* 12, August, 187–209.

Dann, L.Y. 1981. Common stock repurchases: an analysis of the returns to bondholders and stockholders. *Journal of Financial Economics* 9(2), June, 113–38.

Dewing, A.S. 1953. *The Financial Policy of Corporations*. 5th edn, New York: Ronald Press.

Easterbrook, F.H. 1984. Two agency-cost explanations of dividends. *American Economic Review* 74(4), September, 650–59.

Fama, E.F. and Babiak, H. 1968. Dividend policy: an empirical analysis. *Journal of the American Statistical Association* 63, December, 1132–61.

Feenberg, D. 1971. Does the investment interest limitation explain the existence of dividends? *Journal of Financial Economics* 9, September, 265–9.

Gordon, M.J. 1959. Dividends, earnings, and stock prices. *Review of Economics and Statistics* 41, May, 99–105.

Graham, B. and Dodd, D. 1951. *Security Analysis: Principles and Techniques*. New York: McGraw-Hill.

Jensen, M.C. and Meckling, W. 1976. Theory of the firm: managerial behavior, agency costs, and capital structure. *Journal of Financial Economics* 3(4), October, 305–60.

John, K. and Williams, J. 1985. Dividends, dilution and taxes: a signalling equilibrium. *Journal of Finance* 40(4), September, 1053–70.

Lintner, J. 1956. The distribution of incomes of corporations among dividends, retained earnings, and taxes. *American Economic Review, Papers and Proceedings* 46, May, 97–113.

Litzenberger, R.H. and Ramaswamy, K. 1979. The effect of personal taxes and dividends on capital asset prices: theory and empirical evidence. *Journal of Financial Economics* 7(2), June, 163–95.

Long, J.B. 1978. The market valuation of cash dividends: a case to consider. *Journal of Financial Economics* 6(2/3), June/September, 235–64.

Miller, M.H. and Modigliani, F. 1961. Dividend policy, growth, and the valuation of shares. *Journal of Business* 34, October, 235–64.

Miller, M.H. and Rock, K. 1985. Dividend policy under asymmetric information. *Journal of Finance* 40(4), September, 1031–51.

Miller, M.H. and Scholes, M.S. 1978. Dividends and taxes. *Journal of Financial Economics* 6(4), December, 333–64.

Miller, M.H. and Scholes, M.S. 1982. Dividends and taxes: some empirical evidence. *Journal of Political Economy* 90(6), December, 1118–41.

Morgan, I. 1980. Dividends and stock price behavior in Canada. *Journal of Business Administration*, Fall.

Offer, A. and Thakor, A. 1985. A theory of stock price response to alternative corporate cash disbursement methods: stock repurchases and dividends. Unpublished ms., December.

Peterson, P.P., Peterson, D.R. and Ang, J.S. 1985. Direct evidence on the marginal rate of taxation on dividend income. *Journal of Financial Economics* 14(2), June, 267–82.

Pettit, R.R. 1972. Dividend announcements, security performance, and capital market efficiency. *Journal of Finance* 27(5), December, 993–1007.

Poterba, J.M. and Summers, L.H. 1984. New evidence that taxes affect the valuation of dividends. *Journal of Finance* 39(5), December, 1397–1415.

Rozeff, M.S. 1982. Growth, beta and agency costs as determinants of dividend payout ratios. *Journal of Financial Research* 2, Fall, 249–59.

Schleifer, A. and Vishny, R.W. 1986. Large stockholders and corporate control. *Journal of Political Economy* 94(3) Part 1, June, 461–88.

Vermaelen, T. 1981. Common stock repurchases and market signalling: an empirical study. *Journal of Financial Economics* 9(2), June, 139–83.

Economic Integration

BELA BALASSA

In everyday parlance integration is defined as bringing together of parts into a whole. In the economic literature the term 'economic integration' does not have such a clear-cut meaning. At one extreme, the mere existence of trade relations between independent national economies is considered as a form of economic integration; at the other, it is taken to mean the complete unification of national economies.

Economic integration is defined here as process and as a state of affairs. Considered as a process, it encompasses measures designed to eliminate discrimination between economic units that belong to different national states; viewed as a state of affairs, it represents the absence of various forms of discrimination between national economies.

Economic integration may take several forms that represent various degrees of integration. In a free trade area, tariffs (and quantitative import restrictions) among participating countries are eliminated, but each country retains its own tariffs against non-members. Establishing a customs union involves, apart from the suppression of intra-area trade barriers, equalizing tariffs on imports from non-member countries.

A common market goes beyond a customs union, inasmuch as it also entails the free movement of factors of production. In turn, an economic union combines the suppression of restrictions on commodity and factor movements with some degree of harmonization of national economic policies, so as to reduce discrimination owing to disparities in these policies. Finally, total economic integration means the unification of economic policies, culminating in the establishment of a supra-national authority whose decisions are binding for the member states.

HISTORY. The first importance case of economic integration was the German Zollverein in the 19th century, which subsequently led to total economic integration through the unification of the German states with the establishment

176

of the Deutsches Reich. In the 20th century, the creation of the Benelux customs (1948) and subsequently economic (1949) union, comprising Belgium, Luxemburg and the Netherlands, represented the first step towards European economic integration. It was followed by the establishment of the European Coal and Steel Community (1953) and the European Economic Community or EEC (1958), both comprising Belgium, France, Italy, Luxemburg, the Netherlands, and West Germany.

Austria, Denmark, Norway, Portugal, Sweden, Switzerland, and the United Kingdom founded the European Free Trade Association or EFTA in 1960, with Finland participating first as an associate and later as a full member. In turn, Denmark and the United Kingdom left EFTA and, together with Ireland, entered the European Economic Community in 1968; Greece became a member of the EEC in 1978, and Portugal and Spain joined in 1986.

In Eastern Europe, the Council for Mutual Economic Assistance or CMEA was established in 1948, with the participation of the Soviet Union, Bulgaria, Czechoslovakia, Hungary, Poland, and Romania. Albania and East Germany joined shortly thereafter; subsequently, Cuba and Mongolia became full members while Albania ceased to participate in CMEA activities.

There have been a number of attempts at economic integration in developing countries. Some were to involve the establishment of a free trade area, such as the Latin American Free Trade Association (1960) comprising Argentina, Bolivia, Brazil, Chile, Colombia, Ecuador, Mexico, Peru, Uruguay, and Venezuela; others were designed to become customs unions, such as the West African Customs Union (1959), including the Ivory Coast, Mali, Mauritania, Niger, Senegal, and Upper Volta. In 1960, the Central American Common Market was established, with Costa Rica, Guatemala, Honduras, Nicaragua, and El Salvador as members; in turn, the East African Common Market, comprising Kenya, Tanzania, and Uganda and subsequently transformed into the East African Economic Community (1967), was designed to become an economic union. None of these attempts has come to fruition, however, as barriers to intra-area trade have not been fully eliminated or have subsequently been restored.

TRADE CREATION AND TRADE DIVERSION. Viner's *The Customs Union Issue* (1950) was the first important contribution to the theory of economic integration. Viner investigated the impact of a customs union on trade flows and distinguished between the 'trade-creating' and the 'trade-diverting' effects of a union. In the first case, there is a shift from domestic to partner country sources of supply of a particular commodity; in the second case, the shift occurs from non-member country to partner country sources of supply.

Trade creation increases economic welfare, inasmuch as higher-cost domestic sources of supply are replaced by lower-cost imports from partner countries that were previously excluded by the tariff. In turn, trade diversion has a welfare cost since tariff discrimination against non-member countries, attendant on the establishment of the customs union, leads to the replacement of lower-cost sources of supply in these countries by higher-cost partner country sources.

177

The net welfare effects of the customs union will depend on the amount of trade created and diverted as well as on differences in unit costs. In a partial equilibrium framework, under constant costs, there will be a welfare gain (loss) if the amount of trade created, multiplied by differences in unit costs between the home and the partner countries, exceeds (falls short of) the amount of trade diverted, multiplied by differences in unit costs between the partner and the non-member countries.

Meade (1955) further considered the effects of a customs union on inter-commodity substitution, involving the replacement of domestic products by partner country products (trade creation) and the replacement of products of non-member countries by partner country products (trade diversion). As in the case of substitution among the sources of supply of a particular commodity (production effects), trade creation involves a welfare improvement, and trade diversion the deterioration of welfare, in the event of substitution among commodities (consumption effects).

The separation of production and consumption effects does not imply the absence of interaction between the two. Substitution among sources of supply will affect the pattern of consumption through changes in the prices paid by the consumer. Also, intercommodity substitution will lead to modifications in the pattern of production by changing the prices received by producers.

At the same time, as Lipsey and Lancaster (1956–7) first noted, production and consumption effects – and the theory of customs unions in general – should be considered as special cases of the theory of the second best. Assuming that the usual conditions for a Pareto optimum are fulfilled, free trade will lead to efficient resource allocation while pre-union, as well as post-union, situations are sub-optimal because tariffs exist in both cases. In the abstract, then, one cannot make a judgement as to whether establishing a customs union will increase or reduce welfare. Nevertheless, a consideration of certain factors may provide a presumption as to the possible direction of the welfare effects of a union.

FACTORS INFLUENCING THE WELFARE EFFECTS OF A CUSTOM UNION. Lipsey (1960) suggested that the welfare effects of a customs union will depend on the relative importance in home consumption of goods produced domestically and imported from non-member countries prior to the establishment of the union. *Ceteris paribus*, the larger the share of domestic goods and the smaller the share of goods imported from non-member countries, the greater is the likelihood of an improvement in welfare following the union's establishment. Such will be the case since substitution of partner country products for domestic products entails trade creation and their substitution for the products of non-member countries involves trade diversion.

These propositions are consistent with Tinbergen's (1957) conclusion that increases in the size of a customs union will augment the probability of favourable welfare effects; in the limiting case, the customs union includes the entire world, which is equivalent to free trade. Applying the argument that gains are obtained through the enlargement of a union because of increased possibilities for the reallocation of production, it also follows that the gains are positively correlated with increases in the market size of the participating countries (e.g. small countries will gain more from participation in a customs union than large countries).

Viner further considered the implications that differences in production structures among the member countries have for the welfare effects of a customs union. He suggested that the more competitive (the less complementary) is the production structure of the member countries, the greater is the chance that a customs union will increase welfare.

This proposition reflects the assumption that countries with similar production structures tend to replace domestic goods by competing imports from partner countries following the establishment of a customs union, while differences in the production structure within the union lead to substitution of partner country products for lower-cost products originating in non-member countries (the latter conclusion does not hold if the union includes the low-cost producer).

The welfare effects of a customs union will also depend on transportation costs. *Ceteris paribus*, the lower are transport costs among the member countries, the greater will be the gains from their economic integration. Thus, the participation of neighbouring countries in a union, with greater possibilities for trade creation across their borders, will offer advantages over the participation of faraway countries that tends to promote trade diversion.

The height of tariffs will further affect the potential gains and losses derived from a customs union. High pre-union tariffs against the future member countries will increase the possibility of trade creation, and hence gains in welfare, following the establishment of the union while low tariffs against non-member countries will reduce the chances for trade diversion. But, these conclusions have little relevance under the application of the most-favoured-nation clause that entails providing equal tariff treatment to all countries before the customs union is established.

CUSTOMS UNIONS VS. UNILATERAL TARIFF REDUCTIONS. In the Viner–Meade–Lipsey analysis, participation in a trade-creating customs union was considered as a means to reduce the distorting effects of the country's own tariffs. This argument was carried to its logical conclusion in contributions by Cooper and Massell (1965a) and Johnson (1965) who suggested that participation in a customs union is inferior to the unilateral elimination of tariffs, which leads to greater trade creation without giving rise to trade diversion.

The same authors claimed that the reasons for the establishment of customs unions lie in the gains participating countries may obtain in furthering non-economic objectives, and considered preference for industry as such an objective. They further assumed that this objective can be pursued at a lower cost in the framework of the larger market of a customs union than in the country's own domestic market.

As Johnson noted, the formation of a customs union in the pursuit of the stated objective presupposes that the member countries are at a comparative disadvantage in the production of industrial goods vis-à-vis the rest of the world.

179

Cooper and Massell (1965b) identified such countries with developing countries, further suggesting that the economic planners of these countries are willing to accept some reduction in national income in order to assure increases in industrial production.

The question remains as to why there is a preference for industry. Johnson (1965) expressed the view that such preference may reflect nationalist aspirations and rivalry with other countries; the power of industrial firms and workers to increase their incomes; or the belief that industrial activity involves beneficial externalities. The last point, however, implies that there is no need to introduce non-economic considerations to obtain the Cooper–Massell–Johnson result; the desirability of a customs union may be established in economic terms, provided that it permits obtaining externalities that cannot be achieved otherwise.

A further question is if unilateral tariff reductions will be superior to a customs union in the absence of a preference for industry or beneficial externalities. The Wonnacotts (1981) showed that this may not be the case if one admits the existence of tariffs in partner and in non-member countries prior to the formation of the customs union.

The elimination of tariffs by partner countries will provide benefits to the home country as it can now sell at a higher price in partner country markets. This gain will be larger the higher is the pre-union tariff in the partner countries and will further be affected by tariffs in the non-member countries. This is because, in selling in partner country markets free of duty, home country producers avoid paying the tariff in non-member countries.

Finally, Cooper and Massell (1965b) noted that a subsidy union, with each participating country subsidizing its own industrial production, is superior to a customs union. This conclusion follows since the consumption cost of the tariff can be avoided if the prices of industrial products in the union are maintained at the world market level through subsidies. However, production subsidization may be done by each country individually, with the attendant welfare benefits, without participating in a union.

MULTI-COUNTRY ANALYSIS OF A CUSTOMS UNION. Traditionally, the welfare effects of a customs union were considered from the point of view of a single country. Yet these effects may differ among member countries, depending on their production structure, location, the height of pre-union tariffs, and other characteristics. In fact, one member country may obtain a gain and another a loss, when any attempt to aggregate gains and losses encounters the well-known difficulties of international welfare comparisons.

The distribution of welfare gains and losses in a customs union will be further affected by changes in the terms of trade. The establishment of a union may give rise to price changes in trade between the member countries, even if the prices at which trade takes place with non-member countries remain unchanged (the case of the 'small' union).

In the more general case, prices in trade with non-member countries will also vary. Now, while trade diversion involves a welfare loss to the member countries of a customs union under unchanged terms of trade, this loss may be offset by a welfare gain due to improvements in the terms of trade attendant on trade diversion. Conversely, whereas under the assumption of unchanged terms of trade the welfare of non-member countries is unaffected by the establishment of a customs union, non-member countries will lose owing to the adverse impact of trade diversion on their terms of trade. This may be interpreted as the result of a shift in the union members' reciprocal demand curve for products originating in non-member countries.

Improvements in the terms of trade thus provide reasons for the establishment of a customs union even in the absence of non-economic objectives and beneficial externalities. Such improvements also favour a customs union over unilateral tariff reductions, which would lead to the deterioration of the terms of trade of the country concerned.

Other things being equal, the larger the union the greater will be its gain, and hence the loss to non-member countries, through terms of trade changes. This is because, *ceteris paribus*, the larger the union the higher will be the elasticity of its reciprocal demand for foreign products and the lower the elasticity of reciprocal demand on the part of non-member countries for the union's products.

The extent of terms-of-trade effects will further depend on the height of tariffs before and after the establishment of a customs union. As Vanek (1965) first showed, a customs union will not involve a loss to non-member countries, while benefiting its own members, if the union's external tariff level is sufficiently lower than the pre-union tariffs of the member countries.

Vanek's proposition was formulated in a three-country, two-commodity (3 × 2) model. It has subsequently been extended to a general case, under which compensatory payments to non-member countries were also introduced (Kemp and Wan, 1976). At the same time, these propositions indicate a theoretical possibility rather than a likely outcome, since customs unions have shown little inclination to compensate non-member countries for losses attendant upon the union's establishment.

3 × 3 models represent an intermediate case between 3 × 2 and $m \times n$ models. They permit introducing a greater number of possible trade patterns, differential tariffs, complementarity and substitution in consumption, with a large number of marginal conditions in production and consumption, as well as intermediate products (Lloyd, 1982). The 3 × 3 model is thus richer in content than the 3 × 2 model. Despite attempts made at introducing new terminology (Collier, 1979), however, adding a third commodity does not appear to have materially affected the basic propositions of customs union theory. This conclusion may also find application to $m \times n$ models.

FREE TRADE AREAS. In a free trade area, maintaining different tariffs among member countries on the products of non-members introduces the possibility of trade deflection. Furthermore, production and investment deflection may occur if one admits trade in intermediate products.

There will be trade deflection if imports enter the free trade area via the member country which applies the lowest tariff. Transportation costs apart, this is equivalent to adopting a tariff equal to the lowest tariff for each commodity in any of the member countries. Under the assumption of unchanged terms of trade, the deflection of trade will increase welfare in the member countries by limiting the extent of trade diversion. Removing this assumption, trade deflection will affect the distribution of welfare between member and non-member countries by reducing the terms of trade gain (loss) for the former (latter).

Production deflection will occur if the manufacture of products containing imported inputs shifts to countries which have lower tariffs on these inputs, because differences in tariffs outweigh differences in production costs. The deflection of production will have unfavourable effects on welfare, since the pattern of productive activity will not follow lines of comparative advantage but rather differences in duties.

The deflection of production may also affect the pattern of investment. Other things being equal, investors will establish factories in countries with lower tariffs on imported inputs. Again, adverse welfare effects will ensue because investments respond to tariff differences rather than to differences in production costs.

The deflection of trade, production, and investment represent unintended effects of free trade areas. To avoid such an eventuality member countries of free trade areas have imposed country of origin rules. These rules limit the freedom of intra-area trade to commodities that incorporate a certain proportion of domestic products or undergo a particular process of transformation in one of the member countries. The application of origin rules limits, but does not entirely eliminate, trade, production and investment deflection in a free trade area. Other things being equal, then, their self-interest would tend to encourage member countries to reduce their own tariffs.

FACTOR MOVEMENTS. The deflection of investment may occur within a country or may involve international capital movements. In the first case, it affects the allocation of the country's own capital among industries; in the second case, it influences the international allocation of capital.

The last point leads to the case of common markets where, by definition, the full mobility of factors is assured. Meade (1953) first analysed the welfare effects of the movement of factors of production in an integrated area. He concluded that free factor movement will increase the gains obtained in a union by reducing the relative scarcities of the factors of production. This conclusion reflected the assumption that the conditions for factor price equalization through trade are not fulfilled.

If factors of production were not free to move between member and non-member countries, there will be no welfare loss due to factor movements among member countries to correspond to trade diversion in commodity trade. In the event of such factor movements, however, an analogous case to trade creation and trade diversion occurs if the movement of factors were subject to taxes prior to the establishment of a union and these taxes have been removed among union members. And, in any case, there will be indirect effects on welfare to the extent that factor movements substitute for trade. These effects may involve welfare losses to non-member countries as the newly established productions substitute for imports from them.

ECONOMIES OF SCALE. Economic integration may lead to lower costs through increases in the volume of plant output. For various types of equipment, such as containers, pipelines, and compressors, cost is a function of the surface area whereas capacity is related to volume; per unit costs decline with increases in output in the case of bulk transactions as well as for nonproportional activities such as design production planning, research, and the collection and channelling of information; inventory holdings do not need to increase proportionately with output; larger output warrants the application of technological methods that call for the use of specialized equipment or assembly-line production; and large-scale production may be necessary to ensure the optimum use of various kinds of indivisible equipment.

Corden (1972) showed that the traditional concepts of trade creation and trade diversion will be relevant in the case of economies of scale on the plant level but new concepts are added: the cost-reduction effect and the trade-suppression effect. The former refers to reductions in average unit costs as domestic output expands following the establishment of the union; the latter refers to the replacement of cheaper imports from non-member countries by domestic production under economies of scale. In Corden's view, a net benefit is likely to ensue as the cost-reduction effect tends to outweigh the trade-suppression effect.

Plant size and unit costs are not necessarily correlated in the case of multiproduct firms. In such instances, costs may be lowered by reducing product variety through specialization in an integrated area, which permits lengthening production runs for individual products.

The advantages of longer production runs derive from improvements in manufacturing efficiency along the 'learning curve' as cumulated output increases; the lowering of expenses involved in moving from one operation to another that involves the resetting of machines, the shifting of labour, and the reorganization of the work process; and the use of special-purpose machinery in the place of general purpose machinery.

Apart from product or horizontal specialization, there are possibilities for vertical specialization by subdividing the production process among individual establishments in an integrated area. As the sales of the final product increase, parts, components, and accessories may be manufactured in separate plants, each of which enjoys economies of scale, thereby resulting in cost reductions.

COMPETITION AND TECHNOLOGICAL CHANGE. Economic integration will also create the conditions for more effective competition (Scitovsky, 1958). By increasing the number of firms each producer considers as his competitors, the opening of national frontiers will contribute to the loosening of monopolistic and oligopolistic market structures in the individual countries. At the same time, there is no contradiction between gains from economies of scale and increased competition, since a wider market can sustain a larger number of efficient units (Balassa, 1961).

Greater competition may have beneficial effects through improvements in manufacturing efficiency as well as through technological change. While the former has no place in traditional theory, which postulates the choice of the most efficient production methods among those available to the firm, it may assume considerable importance in countries whose markets have been sheltered from foreign competition.

The stick and the carrot of competition also provides inducement for technological progress in the member countries. In particular, increased competition may stimulate research activity aimed at developing new products and improving production methods. Finally, economic integration may contribute to the transmission of technological knowledge by increasing the familiarity of producers with new products and technological processes originating in the partner countries.

It has been suggested, however, that gains from competition, and from economies of scale, may be obtained through unilateral trade liberalization and that the gains are predicated on the response of economic agents to the stimulus provided by competition (Krauss, 1972). While the validity of the second point depends on factors which are particular to each country, the first neglects the gains obtained through the increases in output associated with sales in the markets of partner countries.

POLICY HARMONIZATION. Policy differences among the member countries may influence trade flows and factor movements, thereby modifying the welfare effects of economic integration. Industrial policies, social policies, fiscal policies, monetary policies, and exchange rate policies are relevant in this context (Balassa, 1961).

Industrial policies may involve granting credit preferences and/or tax benefits across the board or to particular activities. 'Horizontal' policies that are applied across the board do not create distortions, unless the conditions under which they are provided favour one activity over another. By contrast, 'vertical' measures are granted to particular activities and thereby introduce distortions, which may counteract the effects of the elimination of intra-area tariffs.

Intercountry differences in social policies will not give rise to distortions, provided that social benefits are financed from the contributions of employers and employees. Nor are these conclusions affected if factor mobility is introduced into the analysis as long as the employees regard the resulting social benefits as part of their compensation.

The situation is different if social benefits are financed from general tax revenue. This case is equivalent to a wage subsidy that favours labour-intensive activities. Correspondingly, differences in the mode of financing social security among the member countries will introduce distortions in resource allocation. This conclusion is strengthened if consideration is given to factor movements that respond to international differences in labour costs.

184

The elimination of vertical measures of industrial policy and the equalization of the conditions of financing social security will reduce distortions in resource allocation as well as differences in tax burdens among the member countries. Differences in the tax burden may remain, however, owing to national preferences as to the provision of collective goods. The effects of such differences on factor movements will depend on the spending of the tax proceeds. But, there may be 'supply-side' effects, with a lower tax burden providing incentives for work effort and risk taking.

A further question is if, for a given tax burden, intercountry differences in reliance on indirect taxes and income taxes will distort competition. Under the destination principle, indirect taxes are rebated on exports and imposed on imports without such adjustments occurring in regard to income taxes. Nevertheless, distortions in the conditions of competition will not ensue as flexibility in exchange rates will offset differences in rates of indirect taxes.

The application of the origin principle, with indirect taxes levied on production irrespective of the country of sale, in one country and that of the destination principle in another will similarly be offset through exchange rate flexibility. Such will not be the case, however, if cascade-type taxation applied in one country and value added taxation in another, with the former raising the tax burden on industries that go through several stages of fabrication, each of which is subject to tax. Eliminating this source of distortion would necessitate the adoption of value added taxation in all member countries of a union.

While exchange rate flexibility is necessary to offset intercountry differences in systems of taxation, it has been proposed that fixed exchange rates be established following the creation of a union. But such an action is predicated on the coordination – and eventual unification – of monetary and fiscal policies, since otherwise pressures are created for exchange rate changes. The fixity of exchange rate should thus be considered as the final outcome of policy coordination rather than an intermediate step in economic integration (Balassa, 1975).

BIBLIOGRAPHY

Balassa, B. 1961. *The Theory of Economic Integration.* Homewood, Ill.: Richard D. Irwin.

Balassa, B. 1975. Monetary integration in European Common Market. In *European Economic Integration*, ed. B. Balassa, Amsterdam: North-Holland, 175–220.

Collier, P. 1979. The welfare effects of a customs union: an anatomy. *Economic Journal* 83, 84–7.

Cooper, C.A. and Massell, B.F. 1965a. A new look at customs union theory. *Economic Journal* 75, 742–7.

Cooper, C.A. and Massell, B.F. 1965b. Towards a general theory of customs unions for developing countries. *Journal of Political Economy* 73, 461–76.

Corden, W.M. 1972. Economies of scale and customs union theory. *Journal of Political Economy* 80, 465–75.

Johnson, H.G. 1965. An economic theory of protectionism, tariff bargaining, and the formation of customs unions. *Journal of Political Economy* 73, 256–83.

Kemp, M.C. and Wan, H.Y., Jr. 1976. An elementary proposition concerning the formation of customs unions. *Journal of International Economics* 6, 95–7.

Krauss, M.B. 1972. Recent developments in customs union theory: an interpretative survey. *Journal of Economic Literature* 10, 413–36.

Lipsey, R.G. 1960. The theory of customs unions: a general survey. *Economic Journal* 70, 496–513.

Lipsey, R.G. and Lancaster, K.J. 1956–7. The general theory of second best. *Review of Economic Studies* 24, 11–32.

Lloyd, P.J. 1982. The theory of customs unions. *Journal of International Economics* 12, 41–63.

Meade, J.E. 1953. *Problems of Economic Union*. London: Allen & Unwin.

Meade, J.E. 1955. *The Theory of Customs Union*. Amsterdam: North-Holland.

Scitovsky, T. 1958. *Economic Theory and Western European Integration*. London: Allen & Unwin.

Tinbergen, J. 1957. Customs unions: influence of their size on their effect. *Zeitschrift der gesamten Staatswissenschaft* 113, 404–14.

Vanek, J. 1965. *General Equilibrium of International Discrimination. The Case of Customs Unions*. Cambridge, Mass.: Harvard University Press.

Viner, J. 1950. *The Customs Union Issue*. New York: Carnegie Endowment for International Peace.

Wonnacott, P. and Wonnacott, R. 1981. Is unilateral tariff reduction preferable to a customs union? The curious case of the missing foreign tariffs. *American Economic Review* 71, 704–14.

Economic Interpretation of History

ERNEST GELLNER

Marxism does not possess a monopoly of the economic interpretation of history. Other theories of this kind can be formulated – for instance that which can be found in the very distinguished work of Karl Polanyi, dividing the history of mankind into three stages, each defined by a different type of economy. If Polanyi is right in suggesting that reciprocity, redistribution and the market each defined a different kind of society, this is, in a way, tantamount to saying that the economy is primary, and thus his work constitutes a species of the economic interpretation of history. Nevertheless, despite the importance of Polanyi's work and the possibility of other rival economic interpretations, Marxism remains the most influential, the most important and perhaps the best elaborated of all theories, and we shall concentrate on it.

One often approaches a theory by seeing what it denies and what it repudiates. This approach is quite frequently adopted in the case of Marxism, where it is both fitting and misleading. We shall begin by adopting this approach, and turn to its dangers subsequently.

Marxism began as the reaction to the romantic idealism of Hegel, in the ambience of whose thought the young Karl Marx reached maturity. This no doubt is the best advertised fact about the origin of Marxism. The central point about Hegelianism was that it was acutely concerned with history and social change, placing these at the centre of philosophical attention (instead of treating them as mere distractions from the contemplation of timeless objects, which had been a more frequent philosophical attitude); and secondly, it taught that history was basically determined by intellectual, spiritual, conceptual or religious forces. As Marx and Engels put it in *The German Ideology*, 'The Young Hegelians are in agreement with the Old Hegelians in their belief in the rule of religion, of concepts, of an abstract general principle in the existing world' (Marx and Engels, [1845–6], p. 5).

187

Now the question is – why did Hegel and his followers believe this? If it is interpreted in a concrete sense, as a doctrine claiming that the ideas of men determined their other activities, it does not have a great deal of plausibility, especially when put forward as an unrestricted generalization. If it is formulated – as it was by Hegel – as the view that some kind of abstract principle or entity dominates history, the question may well be asked: what evidence do we have for the very existence of this mysterious poltergeist allegedly manipulating historical events? Given the fact that the doctrine is either implausible or obscure, or indeed both, why were intelligent men so strongly drawn to it?

The answer to this may be complex, but the main elements in it can perhaps be formulated simply and briefly. Hegelianism enters the scene when the notion of what we now call *culture* enters public debate. The point is this: men are not machines. When they act, they do not simply respond to some kind of push. When they do something, they generally have an idea, a concept, of the action which they are performing. The idea or conception in turn is part of a whole system. A man who goes through the ceremony of marriage has an *idea* of what the institution means in the society of which he is part, and his understanding of the institution is an integral part of his action. A man who commits an act of violence as part of a family feud has an idea of what family and honour *mean*, and is committed to those ideas. And each of these ideas is not something which the individual has excogitated for himself. He took it over from a corpus of ideas which differ from community to community, and which *change* over time, and which are now known as *culture*.

Put in this way, the 'conceptual' determination of human conduct no longer seems fanciful, but on the contrary is liable to seem obvious and trite. In various terminologies ('hermeneutics', 'structuralism', and others) it is rather fashionable nowadays. The idea that conduct is concept-saturated and that concepts come not singly but as *systems*, and are carried not by individuals but by on-going historic communities, has great plausibility and force. Admittedly, those who propose it, in Hegel's day and in ours, do not always define their position with precision. They do not always make clear whether they are merely saying that culture in this sense is important (which is hardly disputable), or claiming that it is the prime determinant of other things and the ultimate source of change, which is a much stronger and much more contentious claim. Nonetheless, the idea that culture is important and pervasive is very plausible and suggestive, and Hegelianism can be credited with being one of the philosophies which, in its own peculiar language, had introduced this idea. It is important to add that Hegelianism often speaks of 'Spirit' in the singular; our suggestion is that this can be interpreted as *culture*, as the spirit of the age. This made it easy for Hegelianism to operate as a kind of surrogate Christianity: those no longer able to believe in a personal god could tell themselves that this had been a parable of a kind of guiding historical spirit. For those who wanted to use it in that way, Hegelianism was the continuation of religion by other means.

But Hegelianism is not exhausted by its sense of culture, expressed in somewhat strange language. It is also pervaded by another idea, fused with the first one, and one which it shares with many thinkers of its period: a sense of *historical plan*. The turn of the 18th and 19th centuries was a time when men became imbued with the sense of cumulative historical change, pointing in an upward direction – in other words, the idea of Progress.

The basic fact about Marxism is that it retains this second idea, the 'plan' of history, but aims at inverting the first idea, the romantic idealism, the attribution of agency to culture. As the two founders of Marxism put it themselves in *The German Ideology* (pp. 14–15),

> In direct contrast to German philosophy which descends from heaven to earth, here we ascend from earth to heaven ... We set out from real active men, and on the basis of their real life-process we demonstrate the development of the ideological reflexes and echoes of this life-process ... Morality, religion, metaphysics, all the rest of ideology and their corresponding forms of consciousness, thus no longer retain the semblance of independence. They have no history, no development; but men, developing their material production and their material intercourse, alter, along with their real existence, their thinking and the products of their thinking. Life is not determined by consciousness, but consciousness by life.

Later on in the same work, the two founders of Marxism specify the recipe which, according to them, was followed by those who produced the idealistic mystification. First of all, ideas were separated from empirical context and the interests of the rulers who put them forward. Secondly, a set of logical connections was found linking successive ruling ideas, and their logic is then meant to explain the pattern of history. (This links the concept-saturation of history to the notion of historic *design*. Historic pattern is the reflection of the internal logical connection of successive ideas.) Thirdly, to diminish the mystical appearance of all this, the free-floating, self-transforming concept was once again credited to a person or group of persons.

If this kind of theory is false, what then is true? In the same work a little later, the authors tell us:

> This sum of productive forces, forms of capital and social forms of intercourse, which every individual and generation finds in existence as something given, is the real basis of ... the ... 'essence of man'.... These conditions of life, which different generations find in existence, decide also whether or not the periodically recurring revolutionary convulsion will be strong enough to overthrow the basis of all existing forms. And if these material elements of a complete revolution are not present ... then, as far as practical developments are concerned, it is absolutely immaterial whether the 'idea' of this revolution has been expressed a hundred times already ... (p. 30).

The passage seems unambiguous: what is retained is the idea of a plan, and also the idea of primarily internal, endogenous propulsion. What has changed is the identification of the propulsion, of the driving force of the transformation. Change continues to be the law of all things, and it is governed by a plan, it is not random;

but the mechanism which controls it is now identified in a new manner.

From then on, the criticisms of the position can really be divided into two major species: some challenge the identification of the ruling mechanism, and others the idea of historic *plan*. As the most dramatic presentation of Marxist development, Robert Tucker's *Philosophy and Myth in Karl Marx* (1961, p. 123) puts it:

> Marx founded Marxism in an outburst of Hegelizing. He considered himself to be engaged in ... [an] ... act of translation of the already discovered truth ... from the language of idealism into that of materialism. ... Hegelianism itself was latently or esoterically an economic interpretation of history. It treated history as 'a history of production' ... in which spirit externalizes itself in thought-objects. But this was simply a mystified presentation of *man* externalizing himself in *material* objects.

This highlights both the origin *and* the validity or otherwise of the economic interpretation of history. Some obvious but important points can be made at this stage. The Hegel/Marx confrontation owes much of its drama and appeal to the extreme and unqualified manner in which the opposition is presented. This unqualified, unrestricted interpretation can certainly be found in the basic texts of Marxism. Whether it is the 'correct' interpretation is an inherently undecidable question: it simply depends on which texts one treats as final – those which affirm the position without restriction and without qualification, or those which contain modifications, qualifications and restrictions.

The same dilemma no doubt arises on the Hegelian side, where it is further accompanied by the question as to whether the motive force, the spirit of history, is to be seen as some kind of abstract principle (in which case the idea seems absurd to most of us), or whether this is merely to be treated as a way of referring to what we now term culture (in which case it is interesting and contentious).

One must point out that these two positions, the Hegelian and the Marxist, are contraries, but not contradictories. They cannot both be true, but they can perfectly well both be false. A world is easily conceivable where neither of them is true: a world in which social changes sometimes occur as a consequence of changes in economic activities, and sometimes as a consequence of strains and stresses in the culture. Not only is such a world conceivable, but it does really rather look as if that is the kind of world we do actually live in. (Part of the appeal of Marxism in its early days always hinged on presenting Hegel-type idealism and Marxism as two contradictories, and 'demonstrating' the validity of Marxism as a simple corollary of the manifest absurdity of strong versions of Hegelianism.) In this connection, it is worth noticing that by far the most influential (and not unsympathetic) sociological critic of Marx is Max Weber, who upholds precisely this kind of position. Strangely enough, despite explicit and categorical denials on his own part, he is often misrepresented as offering a return to some kind of idealism (without perhaps the mystical idea of the agency of abstract concepts which was present in Hegel). For instance, Michio Morishima, in *Why has Japan 'Succeeded'?* (1982, p. 1), observes: 'Whereas Karl Marx contended that ideology and ethics were no more than reflections ... Max Weber ... made the case for the existence of quite the reverse relationship.' Weber was sensitive to both kinds of constraint; he merely insisted that, on occasion, a 'cultural' or 'religious' element might make a crucial difference.

Connected with this, there is another important theoretical difference to be found in Weber and many contemporary sociologists. The idea of the inherent historical plan, which had united Hegel and Marx, is abandoned. If the crucial moving power of history comes from one source only, though this does not strictly speaking entail that there should be a plan, an unfolding of design, it nevertheless does make it at least very plausible. If that crucial moving power had been *consciousness*, and its aim the arrival at self-consciousness, then it was natural to conclude that with the passage of time, there would indeed be more and more of such consciousness. So the historical plan could be seen as the manifestation of the striving of the Absolute Spirit or humanity, towards ever greater awareness. Alternatively, if the motive force was the growth of the forces of production, then, once again, it was not unreasonable to suppose that history might be a series of organizational adjustments to expanding productive powers, culminating in a full adjustment to the final great flowering of our productive capacity. (Something like that is the essence of the Marxist vision of history.)

If on the other hand the motive forces and the triggers come from a *number* of sources, which moreover are inherently diverse, there is no clear reason why history should have a pattern in the sense of coming ever closer to satisfying some single criterion (consciousness, productivity, congruence between productivity and social ethos, or whatever). So in the Weberian and more modern vision, the dramatic and unique developments of the modern industrial world are no longer seen as the inevitable fulfilment and culmination of a potential that had always been there, but rather as a development which only occurred because a certain set of factors happened to operate at a given time simultaneously, and which would otherwise not have occurred, and which was in no way *bound* to occur. Contingency replaces fatality.

So much for the central problem connected with the economic interpretation of history. The question concerning the relative importance of conceptual (cultural) and productive factors is the best known, most conspicuous and best advertised issue in this problem area. But in fact, it is very far from obvious that it is really the most important issue, the most critical testing ground for the economic theory of history. There is another problem, less immediately obvious, less well known, but probably of greater importance, theoretically and practically. That is the relative importance of productive and *coercive* activities.

The normal associations which are likely to be evoked by the phrase 'historical materialism' do indeed imply the downgrading of purely conceptual, intellectual and cultural elements as explanatory factors in history. But it does not naturally suggest the downgrading of force, violence, coercion. On the contrary, for most people the idea of coercion by threat or violence, or death and pain, seems just as 'realistic', just as 'materialistic' as the imperatives imposed by material need for sustenance and shelter. Normally one assumes that the difference between coercion by violence or the threat of violence, and coercion by fear of destitution, is simply that the former is more immediate and works more quickly. One might even argue that *all* coercion is ultimately coercion by violence: a man or a group in society which coerces other members by controlling the food supply, for instance, can only do it if they control and defend the store of food or some other vital necessity by force, even if that force is kept in reserve. Economic constraint, it could be argued (as Marxists themselves argue in other contexts), only operates because a certain set of rules is enforced by the state, which may well remain in the background. But economic constraint is in this way parasitic on the ultimate presence of enforcement, based on the monopoly of control of the tools of violence.

The logic of this argument may seem persuasive, but it is contradicted by a very central tenet of the Marxist variant of the economic theory of history. Violence, according to the theory, is not fundamental or primary, it does not initiate fundamental social change, nor is it a fundamental basis of any social order. This is the central contention of Marxism, and at this point, real Marxism diverges from what might be called the vulgar image possessed of it by non-specialists. Marxism stresses economic factors, and downgrades not merely the importance of conceptual, 'superstructural' ones, but equally, and very significantly, the role of coercive factors.

A place where this is vigorously expressed is Engels's 'Anti-Dühring' (1878):

> ... historically, private property by no means makes its appearance as the result of robbery or violence. ... Everywhere where private property developed, this took place as the result of altered relations of production and exchange, in the interests of increased production and in furtherance of intercourse – that is to say, as a result of economic causes. Force plays no part in this at all. Indeed, it is clear that the institution of private property must be already in existence before the robber can *appropriate* another person's property ... Nor can we use either force or property founded on force to explain the 'enslavement of man for menial labour' in its most modern form – wage labour.... The whole process is explained by purely economic causes; robbery, force, and the state of political interference of any kind are unnecessary at any point whatever (Burns, 1935, pp. 267–9).

Engels goes on to argue the same, specifically in connection with the institution of slavery:

> Thus force, instead of controlling the economic order, was on the contrary pressed into the service of the economic order. *Slavery* was invented. It soon became the predominant form of production among all peoples who were developing beyond the primitive community, but in the end was also one of the chief causes of the decay of that system (ibid., p. 274).

Engels a little earlier in the same work was on slightly more favourable ground when he discussed the replacement of the nobility by the bourgeoisie as the most powerful estate in the land. If physical force were crucial, how should the peaceful merchants and producers have prevailed over the professional warriors? As Engels puts it: 'During the whole of this struggle, political forces were on the side of the nobility...' (ibid., p. 270).

One can of course think of explanations for this paradox: the nobility might have slaughtered each other, or there might be an alliance between the monarchy and the middle class (Engels himself mentioned this possibility, but does not think it constitutes a real explanation) and so forth. In any case, valid or not, this particular victory of producers over warriors would seem to constitute a prima facie example of the non-dominance of force in history. The difficulty for the theory arises when the point is generalized to cover all social orders and all major transitions, which is precisely what Marxism does.

Engels tries to argue this point in connection with a social formation which one might normally consider to be the very paradigm of the domination by force: 'oriental despotism'. (In fact, it is for this very reason that some later Marxists have maintained that this social formation is incompatible with Marxist theory, and hence may not exist.) Engels does it, interestingly enough, by means of a kind of functionalist theory of society and government: the essential function, the essential role and duty, of despotic governments in hydraulic societies is to keep production going by looking after the irrigation system. As he puts it:

> However great the number of despotic governments which rose and fell in India and Persia, each was fully aware that its first duty was the general maintenance of irrigation throughout the valleys, without which no agriculture was possible (Burns, 1935, p. 273).

It is a curious argument. He cannot seriously maintain that these oriental despots were always motivated by a sense of duty towards the people they governed. What he must mean is something like this: unless they did their 'duty', the society in question could not survive, and they themselves, as its political parasites, would not survive either. So the real foundation of 'oriental despotism' was not the force of the despot, but the functional imperatives of despotically imposed irrigation systems. Economic need, as in the case of slavery, makes use of violence for its own ends, but violence itself initiates or maintains nothing. This interpretation is related to what Engels says a little further on. Those who use force can either aid economic development or accelerate it, or go against it, which they do rarely (though he admits that it occasionally occurs), and then they themselves usually go under: 'Where ... the internal public force of the country stands in opposition to economic development ... the contest has always ended with the downfall of the political power' (Burns, 1935, p. 277).

We have seen that Engels's materialism is curiously functional, indeed teleological: the economic potential of a society or of its productive base somehow seeks out available force, and enlists it on its own behalf. Coercion is and ought to be the slave of production, he might well have said. This teleological element is found again in what is perhaps the most famous and most concise formulation of Marxist theory, namely certain passages in Marx's preface to *A Contribution to 'The Critique of Political Economy'* (1859):

A social system never perishes before all the productive forces have developed for which it is wide enough; and new, higher productive relationships never come into being before the material conditions for their existence have been brought to maturity within the womb of the old society itself. Therefore, mankind always sets itself only such problems as it can solve; for when we look closer we will always find that the problem itself only arises when the material conditions for its solution are already present, or at least in the process of coming into being. In broad outline, the Asiatic, the ancient, the feudal, and the modern bourgeois mode of production can be indicated as progressive epochs in the economic system of society (Burns, 1935, p. 372).

The claim that a new order does not come into being before the conditions for it are available, is virtually a tautology: nothing comes into being unless the conditions for it exist. That is what 'conditions' mean. But the idea that a social system never perishes before it has used up all its potential is both strangely teleological and disputable. Why should it not be replaced even before it plays itself out to the full? Why should not some of its potential be wasted?

It is obvious from this passage that the purposive, upward surge of successive modes of production cannot be hindered by force, nor even aided by it. Engels, in 'Anti-Dühring', sneers at rulers such as Friedrich Wilhelm IV, or the then Tsar of Russia, who despite the power and size of their armies are unable to defy the economic logic of the situation. Engels also treats ironically Herr Dühring's fear of force as the 'absolute evil', the belief that the 'first act of force is the original sin', and so forth. In his view, on the contrary, force simply does not have the capacity to initiate evil. It does however have another 'role in history, a revolutionary role'; this role, in Marxist words, is midwifery:

> ... it is the midwife of every old society which is pregnant with the new, ... the instrument by the aid of which social movement forces its way through and shatters the dead, fossilized, political forms... (Burns, 1935, p. 278).

The midwifery simile is excellent and conveys the basic idea extremely well. A midwife cannot create babies, she can only aid and slightly speed up their birth, and once the infant is born the midwife cannot do much harm either. The most one can say for her capacity is that she may be necessary for a successful birth. Engels seems to have no fear that this sinister midwife might linger after the birth and refuse to go away. He makes this plain by his comment on the possibility of a 'violent collision' in Germany which 'would at least have the advantage of wiping out the servility which has permeated the national consciousness as a result of the humiliation of the Thirty Years War'.

There is perhaps an element of truth in the theory that coercion is and ought to be the slave of production. The element of truth is this: in pre-agrarian hunting and gathering societies, surrounded by a relative abundance of sustenance but lacking means of storing it, there is no persistent, social, economic motive for coercion, no *sustained* employment for a slave. By contrast, once wealth is systematically produced and stored, coercion and violence or the threat thereof acquire an inescapable function and become endemic. The surplus needs to be guarded, its socially 'legitimate' distribution enforced. There is some evidence to support the view that hunting and gathering societies were more peaceful than the agrarian societies which succeeded them.

One may put it like this: in societies devoid of a stored surplus, no surplus needs to be guarded and the principles governing its distribution do not need to be enforced. By contrast, societies endowed with a surplus face the problem of protecting it against internal and external aggression, and enforcing the principles of its distribution. Hence they are doomed to the deployment, overt or indirect, of violence or the threat thereof. But all of this, true though it is, does not mean that surplus-less societies are necessarily free of violence: it only means that they are not positively obliged to experience it. Still less does it mean that within the class of societies endowed with a surplus, violence on its own may not occasionally or frequently engender changes, or inhibit them. The argument does not preclude coercion either from initiating social change, or from thwarting change which would otherwise have occurred. The founding fathers of Marxism directed their invective at those who raised this possibility, but they never succeeded in establishing that this possibility is not genuine. All historic evidence would seem to suggest that this possibility does indeed often correspond to reality.

Why is the totally unsubstantiated and indeed incorrect doctrine of the social unimportance of violence so central to Marxism?

The essence of Marxism lies in the retention of the notion of an historical plan, but a re-specification of its driving force. But the idea of a purposive historical plan is not upheld merely out of an intellectual desire for an elegant conceptual unification of historical events. There is also a deeper motive. Marxism is a salvation religion, guaranteeing not indeed individual salvation, but the collective salvation of all mankind. Ironically, its conception of the blessed condition is profoundly bourgeois. Indeed, it constitutes the ultimate apotheosis of the bourgeois vision of life. The bourgeois preference for peaceful production over violent predation is elevated into the universal principle of historical change. The wish is father of the faith. The work ethic is transformed into the essence, the very species-definition of man. Work is our fulfilment, but work patterns are also the crucial determinants of historical change. Spontaneous, unconstrained work, creativity, is our purpose and our destiny. Work patterns also determine the course of history and engender patterns of coercion, and *not* vice versa. Domination and the mastery of techniques of violence is neither a valid ideal, nor ever decisive in history. All this is no doubt gratifying to those imbued with the producer ethic and hostile to the ethic of domination and violence: but is it true?

Note that, were it true, Marxism is free to commend spontaneously cooperative production, devoid of ownership and without any agency of enforcement, as against production by competition, with centrally enforced ground rules. It is free to do it, without needing to consider the argument that only competition keeps away centralized coercion, and that the attempt to bring about propertyless and total cooperation only engenders a new form of centralized tyranny. *If* tyranny *only* emerges as a protector of basically pathological forms or organization of work, then a sound work-pattern will on its own free us for ever from the need for either authority or checks on authority. Man is held to be alienated from his true essence as long as he works for extraneous ends: he finds his true being only when he indulges in work for the sake of creativity, and chooses his own form of creativity. This is of course precisely the way in which the middle class likes to see its own life. It takes pride in productive activity, and chooses its own form of creativity, and it understands what it does. Work is not an unintelligible extraneous imposition for it, but the deepest fulfilment.

On the Marxist economic interpretation of history, mankind as a whole is being propelled towards this very goal, this bourgeois-style fulfilment in work without coercion. But the guarantee that this fulfilment will be reached is only possible if the driving force of history is such as to ensure this happy outcome. If a whole multitude of factors, economic, cultural, coercive, could all interact unpredictably, there could hardly be any historic plan. But if on the other hand only one factor is fundamental, and that factor is something which has a kind of vectorial quality, something which increases over time and inevitably points in one direction only (namely the augmentation of the productive force of man), then the necessary historical plan does after all have a firm, unprecarious base. This is what the theory requires, and this is what is indeed asserted.

The general problem of the requirement, ultimately, of a *single-factor theory*, with its well-directed and persistent factor, is of course related to the problems which arise from the plan that Marxists discern in history. According to the above quotation from Marx, subsequent to primitive communism, four class-endowed stages arise, namely the Asiatic, the ancient, the feudal and the modern bourgeois, which is said to be the last 'antagonistic' stage (peaceful fulfilment follows thereafter). Marxism has notoriously had trouble with the 'Asiatic' stage because, notwithstanding what Engels claimed, it *does* seem to exemplify and highlight the autonomy of coercion in history, and the suspension of progress by a stagnant, self-maintaining social system.

But leaving that aside, in order to be loyal to its basic underlying intuition of a guaranteed progression and a final happy outcome, Marxism is not committed to any particular number or even any particular sequence of stages. The factual difficulties which Marxist historiography has had in finding all the stages and all the historical sequences, and in the right order, are not by themselves necessarily disastrous. A rigid unilinealism is not absolutely essential to the system. What it *does* require (apart from the exclusiveness, in the last analysis, of that single driving force) is the denial of the possibility of stagnation, whether in the form of absolute stagnation and immobility, or in the form of circular, repetitive developments. If this possibility is to be excluded, a number of things need to be true: all exploitative social forms must be inherently unstable; the number of such forms must be finite; and circular social developments must not be possible. *If* all this is so, then the alienation of man from his true essence – free fulfilment in unconstrained work – *must* eventually be attained. But if the system can get stuck, or move in circles, the promise of salvation goes by the board. This would be so even if the system came to be stuck for purely economic reasons. It would be doubly disastrous for it if other factors, such as coercion, were capable of freezing it. The denial of any autonomous role for violence in history is the most important, and most contentious, element in the Marxian economic theory of history.

So what the Marxist economic interpretation of history really requires is that no non-economic factor can ever freeze the development of society, that the development of society itself be pushed forward by the continuous (even if on occasion slow) growth of productive forces, that the social forms accompanying various stages of the development of productive forces should be finite in number, and that the last one be wholly compatible with the fullest possible development of productive forces and of human potentialities.

The profound irony is that a social system marked by the prominence and pervasiveness of centralized coercion, should be justified and brought about by a system of ideas which denies autonomous historical agency both to coercion and to ideas. The independent effectiveness both of coercion and of ideas can best be shown by considering a society built on a *theory*, and one which denies the effectiveness of either.

BIBLIOGRAPHY
Burns, E. 1935. *A Handbook of Marxism*. London: Victor Gollancz.
Engels, F. 1878. 'Anti-Dühring'. In Burns (1935).
Marx, K. 1859. A Contribution to 'The Critique of Political Economy'. In Burns (1935).
Marx, K. and Engels, F. 1845–6. *The German Ideology*. London: Lawrence & Wishart, 1940.
Morishima, M. 1982. *Why has Japan 'Succeeded'? Western Technology and the Japanese Ethos*. Cambridge: Cambridge University Press.
Tucker, R.C. 1961. *Philosophy and Myth in Karl Marx*. Cambridge: Cambridge University Press.

Economic Theory and the Hypothesis of Rationality

KENNETH J. ARROW

In this essay I want to disentangle some of the senses in which the hypothesis of rationality is used in economic theory. In particular, I want to stress that rationality is not a property of the individual alone, although it is usually presented that way. Rather, it gathers not only its force but also its very meaning from the social context in which it is embedded. It is most plausible under very ideal conditions. When these conditions cease to hold, the rationality assumptions become strained and possibly even self-contradictory. They certainly imply an ability at information processing and calculation that is far beyond the feasible and that cannot well be justified as the result of learning and adaptation.

Let me dismiss a point of view that is perhaps not always articulated but seems implicit in many writings. It seems to be asserted that a theory of the economy must be based on rationality, as a matter of principle. Otherwise, there can be no theory. This position has even been maintained by some who accept that economic behaviour is not completely rational. John Stuart Mill (1848, Book 2, ch. 4) argued that custom, not competition, governs much of the economic world. But he adds that the only possible theory is that based on competition (which, in his theories, includes certain elements of rationality, particularly shifting capital and labour to activities that yield higher returns); 'Only through the principle of competition has political economy any pretension to the character of science' ([1848] 1909, p. 242).

Certainly, there is no general principle that prevents the creation of an economic theory based on hypotheses other than that of rationality. There are indeed some conditions that must be laid down for an acceptable theoretical analysis of the economy. Most centrally, it must include a theory of market interactions, corresponding to market clearing in the neoclassical general equilibrium theory. But as far as individual behaviour is concerned, any coherent theory of reactions to the stimuli appropriate in an economic context (prices in the simplest case) could in principle lead to a theory of the economy. In the case of consumer demand, the budget constraint must be satisfied but many theories can easily be devised that are quite different from utility maximization. For example, habit formation can be made into a theory; for a given price–income change, choose the bundle that satisfies the budget constraint and that requires the least change (in some suitably defined sense) from the previous consumption bundle. Though there is an optimization in this theory, it is different from utility maximization; for example, if prices and income return to their initial levels after several alterations, the final bundle purchased will not be the same as the initial. This theory would strike many lay observers as plausible, yet it is not rational as economists have used that term. Without belabouring the point, I simply observe that this theory is not only a logically complete explanation of behaviour but one that is more powerful than standard theory and at least as capable of being tested.

Not only is it possible to devise complete models of the economy on hypotheses other than rationality, but in fact virtually every practical theory of macroeconomics is partly so based. The price- and wage-rigidity elements of Keynesian theory are hard to fit into a rational framework, though some valiant efforts have been made. In the original form, the multiplier was derived from a consumption function depending only on current income. Theories more nearly based on rationality make consumption depend on lifetime or 'permanent' income and reduce the magnitude of the multiplier and, with it, the explanatory power of the Keynesian model. But if the Keynesian model is a natural target of criticism by the upholders of universal rationality, it must be added that monetarism is no better. I know of no serious derivation of the demand for money from a rational optimization. The loose arguments that substitute for a true derivation, Friedman's economizing on shoe leather or Tobin's transaction demand based on costs of buying and selling bonds, introduce assumptions incompatible with the costless markets otherwise assumed. The use of rationality in these arguments is ritualistic, not essential. Further, the arguments used would not suggest a very stable relation but rather one that would change quickly with any of the considerable changes in the structure and technology of finance. Yet the stability of the demand function for money must be essential to any form of monetarism, not excluding those rational expectations models in which the quantity theory plays a major role.

I believe that similar observations can be made about a great many other areas of applied economics. Rationality hypotheses are partial and frequently, if not always, supplemented by assumptions of a different character.

So far, I have argued simply that rationality is not in principle essential to a theory of the economy, and, in fact, theories with direct application usually use assumptions of a different nature. This was simply to clear the ground so that we can discuss the role of rationality in economic theory. As remarked earlier, rationality in application is not merely a property of the individual. Its useful and powerful implications derive from the conjunction of individual rationality and the other basic concepts of neoclassical theory – equilibrium, competition, and completeness of markets. The importance of all these assumptions was first made explicit by Frank Knight (1921, pp. 76–79). In the terms of Knight's one-time student, Edward Chamberlin (1950, pp. 6–7), we need not merely pure, but perfect competition before the rationality hypotheses have their full power.

It is largely this theme on which I will expand. When these assumptions fail, the very concept of rationality becomes threatened, because perceptions of others and, in particular, of their rationality become part of one's own rationality. Even if there is a consistent meaning, it will involve computational and informational demands totally at variance with the traditional economic theorist's view of the decentralized economy.

Let me add one parenthetic remark to this section. Even if we make all the structural assumptions needed for perfect competition (whatever is needed by way of knowledge, concavity in production, absence of sufficient size to create market power, etc.), a question remains. How can equilibrium be established? The attainment of equilibrium requires a disequilibrium process. What does rational behaviour mean in the presence of disequilibrium? Do individuals speculate on the equilibrating process? If they do, can the disequilibrium be regarded as, in some sense, a higher-order equilibrium process? Since no one has market power, no one sets prices; yet they are set and changed. There are no good answers to these questions, and I do not pursue them. But they do illustrate the conceptual difficulties of rationality in a multiperson world.

RATIONALITY AS MAXIMIZATION IN THE HISTORY OF ECONOMIC THOUGHT. Economic theory, since it has been systematic, has been based on some notion of rationality. Among the classical economists, such as Smith and Ricardo, rationality had the limited meaning of preferring more or less; capitalists choose to invest in the industry yielding the highest rate of return, landlords rent their property to the highest bidder, while no one pays for land more than it is worth in product. Scattered remarks about technological substitution, particularly in Ricardo, can be interpreted as taking for granted that, in a competitive environment, firms choose factor proportions, when they are variable, so as to minimize unit costs. To be generous about it, their rationality hypothesis was the maximization of profits by the firm, although this formulation was not explicitly achieved in full generality until the 1880s.

There is no hypothesis of rationality on the side of consumers among the classicists. Not until John Stuart Mill did any of the English classical economists even recognize the idea that demand might depend on price. Cournot had the concept a bit earlier, but neither Mill nor Cournot noticed – although it is obvious from the budget constraint alone – that the demand for any commodity must depend on the price of all commodities. That insight remained for the great pioneers of the marginalist revolution, Jevons, Walras and Menger (anticipated, to be sure, by the Gregor Mendel of economics, H.H. Gossen, whose major work, completely unnoticed at the time of publication (1854), has now been translated into English (1983)). Their rationality hypothesis for the consumer was the maximization of the utility under a budget constraint. With this formulation, the definition of demand as a function of all prices was an immediate implication, and it became possible to formulate the general equilibrium of the economy.

The main points in the further development of the utility theory of the consumer are well known. (1) Rational behaviour is an ordinal property. (2) The assumption that an individual is behaving rationally has indeed some observable implications, the Slutsky relations, but without further assumptions, they are not very strong. (3) In the aggregate, the hypothesis of rational behaviour has in general no implications; that is, for any set of aggregate excess demand functions, there is a choice of preference maps and of initial endowments, one for each individual in the economy, whose maximization implies the given aggregate excess demand functions (Sonnenschein, 1973; Mantel, 1974; Debreu, 1974; for a survey, see Shafer and Sonnenschein, 1982, sec. 4).

The implications of the last two remarks are in contradiction to the very large bodies of empirical and theoretical research, which draw powerful implications from utility maximization for, respectively, the behaviour of individuals, most especially in the field of labour supply, and the performance of the macroeconomy based on 'new classical' or 'rational expectations' models. In both domains, this power is obtained by adding strong supplementary assumptions to the general model of rationality. Most prevalent of all is the assumption that all individuals have the same utility function (or at least that they differ only in broad categories based on observable magnitudes, such as family size). But this postulate leads to curious and, to my mind, serious difficulties in the interpretation of evidence. Consider the simplest models of human capital formation. Cross-sectional evidence shows an increase of wages with education or experience, and this is interpreted as a return on investment in the form of foregone income and other costs. But if all individuals are alike, why do they not make the same choice? Why do we observe a dispersion? In the human capital model (a particular application of the rationality hypothesis), the only explanation must be that individuals are not alike, either in ability or in tastes. But in that case the cross-sectional evidence is telling us about an inextricable mixture of individual differences and productivity effects. Analogously, in macroeconomic models involving durable assets, especially securities, the assumption of homogeneous agents implies that there will never be any trading, though there will be changes in prices.

This dilemma is intrinsic. If agents are all alike, there is really no room for trade. The very basis of economic analysis, from Smith on, is the existence of differences in agents. But if agents are different in unspecifiable ways, then remark (3) above shows that very few, if any, inferences can be made. This problem, incidentally, already exists in Smith's discussion of wage differences. Smith did not believe in intrinsic differences in ability; a porter resembled a philosopher more than a greyhound did a mastiff. Wage differences then depended on the disutilities of different kinds of labour, including the differential riskiness of income. This is fair enough and insightful. But, if taken seriously, it implies that individuals are indifferent among occupations, with wages compensating for other differences. While there is no logical problem, the contradiction to the most obvious evidence is too blatant even for a rough approximation.

I have not carried out a scientific survey of the uses of the rationality hypothesis in particular applications. But I have read enough to be convinced that its apparent force comes only from the addition of supplementary hypotheses. Homogeneity across individual agents is not the only auxiliary assumption, though it is the deepest. Many assumptions of separability are frequently added. Indeed, it has become a working methodology to start with very strong assumptions of additivity and separability, together with a very short list of relevant variables, to add others only as the original hypotheses are shown to be inadequate, and to stop when some kind of satisfactory fit is obtained. A failure of the model is attributed to a hitherto overlooked benefit or cost. From a statistical viewpoint, this stopping rule has obvious biases. I was taught as a graduate student that data mining was a major crime; morality has changed here as elsewhere in society, but I am not persuaded that all these changes are for the better.

The lesson is that the rationality hypothesis is by itself weak. To make it useful, the researcher is tempted into some strong assumptions. In particular, the homogeneity assumption seems to me to be especially dangerous. It denies the fundamental assumption of the economy, that it is built on gains from trading arising from individual differences. Further, it takes attention away from a very important aspect of the economy, namely, the effects of the distribution of income and of other individual characteristics on the workings of the economy. To take a major example, virtually all of the literature on savings behaviour based on aggregate data assumes homogeneity. Yet there have been repeated studies that suggest that saving is not proportional to income, from which it would follow that distributional considerations matter. (In general, as data have improved, it has become increasingly difficult to find any simple rationally based model that will explain savings, wealth, and bequest data.)

The history of economic thought shows some other examples and difficulties with the application of the rationality hypothesis. Smith and the later classicists make repeated but unelaborated references to risk as a component in wage differences and in the rate of return on capital (e.g., Mill, [1848] 1909, pp. 385, 406, 407, 409). The English marginalists were aware of Bernoulli's expected-utility theory of behaviour under uncertainty (probably from Todhunter's *History of the Theory of Probability*) but used it only in a qualitative and gingerly way (Jevons, [1871] 1965, pp. 159–60; Marshall, 1920, pp. 842–3). It was really not until the last 30 years that it has been used systematically as an economic explanation, and indeed its use coincided with the first experimental evidence against it (see Allais, 1979). The expected-utility hypothesis is an interesting transition to the theme of the next section. It is in fact a stronger hypothesis than mere maximization. As such it is more easily tested, and it leads to stronger and more interesting conclusions. So much, however, has already been written about this area that I will not pursue it further here.

Economic Theory and the Hypothesis of Rationality

RATIONALITY, KNOWLEDGE, AND MARKET POWER. It is noteworthy that the everyday usage of the term 'rationality' does not correspond to the economist's definition as transitivity and completeness, that is, maximization of something. The common understanding is instead the complete exploitation of information, sound reasoning, and so forth. This theme has been systematically explored in economic analysis, theoretical and empirical, only in the last 35 years or so. An important but neglected predecessor was Holbrook Working's random-walk theory of fluctuations in commodity futures and securities prices (1953). It was based on the hypothesis that individuals would make rational inferences from data and act on them; specifically, predictability of future asset prices would be uncovered and used as a basis for current demands, which would alter current prices until the opportunity for gain was wiped out.

Actually, the classical view had much to say about the role of knowledge, but in a very specific way. It emphasized how a complete price system would require individuals to know very little about the economy other than their own private domain of production and consumption. The profoundest observation of Smith was that the system works behind the backs of the participants; the directing 'hand' is 'invisible'. Implicitly, the acquisition of knowledge was taken to be costly.

Even in a competitive world, the individual agent has to know all (or at least a great many) prices and then perform an optimization based on that knowledge. All knowledge is costly, even the knowledge of prices. Search theory, following Stigler (1961), recognized this problem. But search theory cannot easily be reconciled with equilibrium or even with individual rationality by price setters, for identically situated sellers should set identical prices, in which case there is nothing to search for.

The knowledge requirements of the decision may change radically under monopoly or other forms of imperfect competition. Consider the simplest case, pure monopoly in a one-commodity partial equilibrium model, as originally studied by Cournot in 1838. The firm has to know not only prices but a demand curve. Whatever definition is given to complexity of knowledge, a demand curve is more complex than a price. It involves knowing about the behaviour of others. Measuring a demand curve is usually thought of as a job for an econometrician. We have the curious situation that scientific analysis imputes scientific behaviour to its subjects. This need not be a contradiction, but it does seem to lead to an infinite regress.

From a general equilibrium point of view, the difficulties are compounded. The demand curve relevant to the monopolist must be understood *mutatis mutandis*, not *ceteris paribus*. A change in the monopolist's price will in general cause a shift in the purchaser's demands for other goods and therefore in the prices of those commodities. These price changes will in turn affect by more than one channel the demand for the monopolist's produce and possibly also the factor prices that the monopolist pays. The monopolist, even in the simple case where there is just one in the entire economy, has to understand all these repercussions. In short, the monopolist has to have a full general equilibrium model of the economy.

203

The informational and computational demands become much stronger in the case of oligopoly or any other system of economic relations where at least some agents have power against each other. There is a qualitatively new aspect to the nature of knowledge, since each agent is assuming the *rationality* of other agents. Indeed, to construct a rationality-based theory of economic behaviour, even more must be assumed, namely, that the rationality of all agents must be *common knowledge*, to use the term introduced by the philosopher David Lewis (1969). Each agent must not only know that the other agents (at least those with significant power) are rational, but know that each other agent knows every other agent is rational, know that every other agent knows that every other agent is rational, and so forth (see also Aumann, 1976). It is in this sense that rationality and the knowledge of rationality is a social and not only an individual phenomenon.

Oligopoly is merely the most conspicuous example. Logically, the same problem arises if there are two monopolies in different markets. From a practical viewpoint, the second case might not offer such difficulties if the links between the markets were sufficiently loose and the monopolies sufficiently small on the scale of the economy that interaction was negligible; but the interaction can never be zero and may be important. As usually presented, bargaining to reach the contract curve would, in the simplest case, require common knowledge of the bargainer's preferences and production functions. It should be obvious how vastly these knowledge requirements exceed those required for the price system. The classic economists were quite right in emphasizing the importance of limited knowledge. If every agent has a complete model of the economy, the hand running the economy is very visible indeed.

Indeed, under these knowledge conditions, the superiority of the market over centralized planning disappears. Each individual agent is in effect using as much information as would be required for a central planner. This argument shows the severe limitations in the argument that property rights suffice for social rationality even in the absence of a competitive system (Coase, 1960).

One can, as many writers have, discuss bargaining when individuals have limited knowledge of each other's utilities (similarly, we can have oligopoly theory with limited knowledge of the cost functions of others: see, e.g., Arrow, 1979). Oddly enough, it is not clear that limited knowledge means a smaller quantity of information than complete knowledge, and optimization under limited knowledge is certainly computationally more difficult. If individuals have private information, the others form some kind of conjecture about it. These conjectures must be common knowledge for there to be a rationality-based hypothesis. This seems to have as much informational content and to be as unlikely as knowing the private information. Further, the optimization problem for each individual based on conjectures (in a rational world, these are probability distributions) on the private information of others is clearly a more difficult and therefore computationally more demanding problem than optimization when there is no private information.

RATIONAL KNOWLEDGE AND INCOMPLETE MARKETS. It may be supposed from the foregoing that informational demands are much less in a competitive world. But now I want to exemplify the theme that perfect, not merely pure, competition is needed for that conclusion and that perfect competition is a stronger criterion than Chamberlin perhaps intended. A complete general equilibrium system, as in Debreu (1959), requires markets for all contingencies in all future periods. Such a system could not exist. First, the number of prices would be so great that search would become an insuperable obstacle; that is, the value of knowing prices of less consequence, those of events remote in time or of low probability, would be less than the cost so that these markets could not come into being. Second, markets conditional on privately observed events cannot exist by definition.

In any case, we certainly know that many – in fact, most – markets do not exist. When a market does not exist, there is a gap in the information relevant to an individual's decision, and it must be filled by some kind of conjecture, just as in the case of market power. Indeed, there turn out to be strong analogies between market power and incomplete markets, though they seem to be very different phenomena.

Let me illustrate with the rational expectations equilibrium. Because of intertemporal relations in consumption and production, decisions made today have consequences that are anticipated. Marshall (1920, bk 5, chs 3–5) was perhaps the first economist to take this issue seriously. He introduced for this purpose the vague and muddled concepts of the short and long runs, but at least he recognized the difficulties involved, namely, that some of the relevant terms of trade are not observable on the market. (Almost all other accounts implicitly or explicitly assumed a stationary state, in which case the relative prices in the future and between present and future are in effect current information. Walras (1874, lessons 23–25) claimed to treat a progressive state with net capital accumulation, but he wound up unwittingly in a contradiction, as John Eatwell has observed in an unpublished dissertation. Walras's arguments can only be rescued by assuming a stationary state.) Marshall in effect made current decisions, including investment and savings, depend on expectations of the future. But the expectations were not completely arbitrary; in the absence of disturbances, they would converge to correct values. Hicks (1946, chs 9–10) made the dependence of current decisions on expectations more explicit, but he had less to say about their ultimate agreement with reality.

As has already been remarked, the full competitive model of general equilibrium includes markets for all future goods and, to take care of uncertainty, for all future contingencies. Not all of these markets exist. The new theoretical paradigm of rational expectations holds that each individual forms expectations of the future on the basis of a correct model of the economy, in fact, the same model that the econometrician is using. In a competitive market-clearing world, the individual agent needs expectations of prices only, not of quantities. For a convenient compendium of the basic literature on rational expectations, see Lucas and Sargent (1981). Since the world is uncertain, the expectations take the form of probability distributions, and each agent's expectations are conditional on the information available to him or her.

As can be seen, the knowledge situation is much the same as with market power. Each agent has to have a model of the entire economy to preserve rationality. The cost of knowledge, so emphasized by the defenders of the price systm as against centralized planning, has disappeared; each agent is engaged in very extensive information gathering and data processing.

Rational expectations theory is a stochastic form of perfect foresight. Not only the feasibility but even the logical consistency of this hypothesis was attacked long ago by Morgenstern (1935). Similarly, the sociologist Robert K. Merton (1957) argued that forecasts could be self-denying or self-fulfilling; that is, the existence of the forecast would alter behaviour so as to cause the forecast to be false (or possibly to make an otherwise false forecast true). The logical problems were addressed by Grunberg and Modigliani (1954) and by Simon (1957, ch. 5). They argued that, in Merton's terms, there always existed a self-fulfilling prophecy. If behaviour varied continuously with forecasts and the future realization were a continuous function of behaviour, there would exist a forecast that would cause itself to become true. From this argument, it would appear that the possibility of rational expectations cannot be denied. But they require not only extensive first-order knowledge but also common knowledge, since predictions of the future depend on other individuals' predictions of the future. In addition to the information requirements, it must be observed that the computation of fixed points is intrinsically more complex than optimizing.

Consider now the signalling equilibrium originally studied by Spence (1974). We have large numbers of employers and workers with free entry. There is no market power as usually understood. The ability of each worker is private information, known to the worker but not to the employer. Each worker can acquire education, which is publicly observable. However, the cost of acquiring the education is an increasing function of ability. It appears natural to study a competitive equilibrium. This takes the form of a wage for each educational level, taken as given by both employers and workers. The worker, seeing how wages vary with education, chooses the optimal level of education. The employer's optimization leads to an 'informational equilibrium' condition, namely, that employers learn the average productivity of workers with a given educational level. What dynamic process would lead the market to learn these productivities is not clear, when employers are assumed unable to observe the productivity of individual workers. There is more than one qualitative possibility for the nature of the equilibrium. One possibility, indeed, is that there is no education, and each worker receives the average productivity of all workers (I am assuming for simplicity that competition among employers produces a zero-profit equilibrium). Another possibility, however, is a dispersion of workers across educational levels; it will be seen that in fact workers of a given ability all choose the same educational level, so the ability of the workers could be deduced from the educational level *ex post*.

Attractive as this model is for certain circumstances, there are difficulties with its implementation, and at several different levels. (1) It has already been noted that the condition that, for each educational level, wages equal average productivity of workers is informationally severe. (2) Not only is the equilibrium not unique, but there is a continuum of possible equilibria. Roughly speaking, all that matters for the motivation of workers to buy education are the relative wages at different educational levels; hence, different relations between wages and education are equally self-fulfilling. As will be seen below, this phenomenon is not peculiar to this model. On the contrary, the existence of a continuum of equilibria seems to be characteristic of many models with incomplete markets. Extensive non-uniqueness in this sense means that the theory has relatively little power. (3) The competitive equilibrium is fragile with respect to individual actions. That is, even though the data of the problem do not indicate any market power, at equilibrium it will frequently be possible for any firm to profit by departing from the equilibrium.

Specifically, given an equilibrium relation between wages and education, it can pay a firm to offer a different schedule and thereby make a positive profit (Riley, 1979). This is not true in a competitive equilibrium with complete markets, where it would never pay a firm to offer any price or system of prices other than the market's. So far, this instability of competitive equilibrium is a property peculiar to signalling models, but it may be more general.

As remarked above, the existence of a continuum of equilibria is now understood to be a fairly common property of models of rational market behaviour with incomplete information. Thus, if there were only two commodities involved and therefore only one price ratio, a continuum of equilibria would take the form of a whole interval of price ratios. This multiplicity would be nontrivial, in that each different possible equilibrium price ratio would correspond to a different real allocation.

One very interesting case has been discussed recently. Suppose that we have some uncertainty about the future. There are no contingent markets for commodities; they can be purchased on spot markets after the uncertainty is resolved. However, there is a set of financial contingent securities, that is, insurance policies that pay off in money for each contingency. Purchasing power can therefore be reallocated across states of the world. If there are as many independent contingent securities as possible states of the world, the equilibrium is the same as the competitive equilibrium with complete markets, as already noted in Arrow (1953). Suppose there are fewer securities than states of the world. Then some recent and partly still unpublished literature (Duffie, 1985; Werner, 1985; Geanakoplos and Mas-Colell, 1986) shows that the prices of the securities are arbitrary (the spot prices for commodities adjust accordingly). This is not just a *numéraire* problem; the corresponding set of equilibrium real allocations has a dimensionality equal to the number of states of nature.

A related model with a similar conclusion of a continuum of equilibria is the concept of 'sunspot' equilibria (Cass and Shell, 1983). Suppose there is some uncertainty about an event that has in fact no impact on any of the data of the economy. Suppose there is a market for a complete set of commodity contracts contingent on the possible outcomes of the event, and later there are spot markets.

However, some of those who will participate in the spot markets cannot participate in the contingent commodity markets, perhaps because they have not yet been born. Then there is a continuum of equilibria. One is indeed the equilibrium based on 'fundamentals', in which the contingencies are ignored. But there are other equilibria that do depend on the contingency that becomes relevant merely because everyone believes it is relevant. The sunspot equilibria illustrate that Merton's insight was at least partially valid; we can have situations where social truth is essentially a matter of convention, not of underlying realities.

THE ECONOMIC ROLE OF INFORMATIONAL DIFFERENCES. Let me mention briefly still another and counterintuitive implication of thoroughgoing rationality. As I noted earlier, identical individuals do not trade. Models of the securities markets based on homogeneity of individuals would imply zero trade; all changes in information are reflected in price changes that just induce each trader to continue holding the same portfolio. It is a natural hypothesis that one cause of trading is difference of information. If I learn something that affects the price of a stock and others do not, it seems reasonable to postulate that I will have an opportunity to buy or sell it for profit.

A little thought reveals that, if the rationality of all parties is common knowledge, this cannot occur. A sale of existing securities is simply a complicated bet, that is, a zero-sum transaction (between individuals who are identical apart from information). If both are risk averters, they would certainly never bet or, more generally, buy or sell securities to each other if they had the same information. If they have different information, each one will consider that the other has some information that he or she does not possess. An offer to buy or sell itself conveys information. The offer itself says that the offerer is expecting an advantage to himself or herself and therefore a loss to the other party, at least as calculated on the offerer's information. If this analysis is somewhat refined, it is easy to see that no transaction will in fact take place, though there will be some transfer of information as a result of the offer and rejection. The price will adjust to reflect the information of all parties, though not necessarily all the information.

Candidly, this outcome seems most unlikely. It leaves as explanation for trade in securities and commodity futures only the heterogeneity of the participants in matters other than information. However, the respects in which individuals differ change relatively slowly, and the large volume of rapid turnover can hardly be explained on this basis. More generally, the role of speculators and the volume of resources expended on informational services seem to require a subjective belief, at least, that buying and selling are based on changes in information.

SOME CONCLUDING REMARKS. The main implication of this extensive examination of the use of the rationality concept in economic analysis is the extremely severe strain on information-gathering and computing abilities. Behaviour of this kind is incompatible with the limits of the human being, even augmented with artificial aids (which, so far, seem to have had a trivial effect on productivity and the efficiency of decision making). Obviously, I am accepting the insight of Herbert Simon (1957, chs 14, 15), on the importance of recognizing that rationality is bounded. I am simply trying to illustrate that many of the customary defences that economists use to argue, in effect, that decision problems are relatively simple break down as soon as market power and the incompleteness of markets are recognized.

But a few more lessons turned up. For one thing, the combination of rationality, incomplete markets, and equilibrium in many cases leads to very weak conclusions, in the sense that there are whole continua of equilibria. This, incidentally, is a conclusion that is being found increasingly in the analysis of games with structures extended over time; games are just another example of social interaction, so the common element is not surprising. The implications of this result are not clear. On the one hand, it may be that recognizing the limits on rationality will reduce the number of equilibria. On the other hand, the problem may lie in the concept of equilibrium.

Rationality also seems capable of leading to conclusions flatly contrary to observation. I have cited the implication that there can be no securities transactions due to differences of information. Other similar propositions can be advanced, including the well-known proposition that there cannot be any money lying in the street, because someone else would have picked it up already.

The next step in analysis, I would conjecture, is a more consistent assumption of computability in the formulation of economic hypotheses. This is likely to have its own difficulties because, of course, not everything is computable, and there will be in this sense an inherently unpredictable element in rational behaviour. Some will be glad of such a conclusion.

BIBLIOGRAPHY

Allais, M. 1979. The so-called Allais paradox and rational decisions under uncertainty. In *Expected Utility Hypothesis and the Allais Paradox*, ed. M. Allais and O. Hagen, Boston: Reidel.

Arrow, K.L. 1953. Le rôle des valeurs boursières dans la répartition la meilleure des risques. In *Econométrie*, Paris: Centre National de la Recherche Scientifique.

Arrow, K.J. 1979. The property rights doctrine and demand revelation under incomplete information. In *Economics and Human Welfare*, ed. M.J. Boskin, New York: Academic Press.

Aumann, R.J. 1976. Agreeing to disagree. *Annals of Statistics* 4, 1236–9.

Cass, D. and Shell, K. 1983. Do sunspots matter? *Journal of Political Economy* 91, 193–227.

Chamberlin, E. 1950. *The Theory of Monopolistic Competition*. 6th edn, Cambridge, Mass.: Harvard University Press.

Coase, R. 1960. The problem of social cost. *Journal of Law and Economics* 3, 1–44.

Cournot, A.A. 1838. *Researches into the Mathematical Principles of the Theory of Wealth*. Translated by N.T. Bacon, New York: Macmillan, 1927.

Debreu, G. 1959. *Theory of Value*. New York: Wiley.

Debreu, G. 1974. Excess demand functions. *Journal of Mathematical Economics* 1, 15–23.

Duffie, J.D. 1985. Stochastic equilibria with incomplete financial markets. Research Paper No. 811, Stanford: Stanford University, Graduate School of Business.

Geanakoplos, J. and Mas-Colell, A. 1986. Real indeterminacy with financial assets. Paper No. MSRI 717–86, Berkeley: Mathematical Science Research Institute.

Gossen, H.H. 1854. *The Laws of Human Relations*. Cambridge, Mass.: MIT Press, 1983.

Grunberg, E. and Modigliani, F. 1954. The predictability of social events. *Journal of Political Economy* 62, 465–78.

Hicks, J.R. 1946. *Value and Capital*. 2nd edn, Oxford: Clarendon.

Jevons, W.S. 1871. *The Theory of Political Economy*. 5th edn; reprinted, New York: Kelley, 1965.

Knight, F. 1921. *Risk, Uncertainty, and Profit*. Boston: Houghton Mifflin.

Lewis, D. 1969. *Convention*. Cambridge, Mass.: Harvard University Press.

Lucas, R. and Sargent, T. 1981. *Rational Expectations and Econometric Practice*. 2 vols, Minneapolis: University of Minnesota Press.

Mantel, R. 1974. On the characterization of excess demand. *Journal of Economic Theory* 6, 345–54.

Marshall, A. 1920. *Principles of Economics*. 8th edn; reprinted, New York: Macmillan, 1948.

Merton, R.K. 1957. The self-fulfilling prophecy. In R.K. Merton, *Social Theory and Social Structure*, revised and enlarged edn, Glencoe, Ill.: Free Press.

Mill, J.S. 1848. *Principles of Political Economy*. London: Longmans, Green, 1909.

Morgenstern, O. 1935. Vollkommene Voraussicht und wirtschaftliches Gleichgewicht. *Zeitschrift für Nationalökonomie* 6, 337–57.

Riley, J.G. 1979. Informational equilibrium. *Econometrica* 47, 331–60.

Shafer, W. and Sonnenschein, H. 1982. Market demand and excess demand functions. In *Handbook of Mathematical Economics*, Vol. 2, ed. K.J. Arrow and M. Intriligator, Amsterdam: North-Holland.

Simon, H. 1957. *Models of Man*. New York: Wiley.

Spence, A.M. 1974. *Market Signaling*. Cambridge, Mass.: Harvard University Press.

Sonnenschein, H. 1973. Do Walras's identity and continuity characterize the class of community excess demand functions? *Journal of Economic Theory* 6, 345–54.

Stigler, G.J. 1961. The economics of information. *Journal of Political Economy* 69, 213–25.

Walras, L. 1874. *Elements of Pure Economics*. Translated by W. Jaffé, London: Allen & Unwin, 1954.

Werner, J. 1985. Equilibrium in economics with incomplete financial markets. *Journal of Economic Theory* 36, 110–19.

Working, H. 1953. Futures trading and hedging. *American Economic Review* 43, 314–43.

Efficient Market Hypothesis

BURTON G. MALKIEL

A capital market is said to be efficient if it fully and correctly reflects all relevant information in determining security prices. Formally, the market is said to be efficient with respect to some information set, ϕ, if security prices would be unaffected by revealing that information to all participants. Moreover, efficiency with respect to an information set, ϕ, implies that it is impossible to make economic profits by trading on the basis of ϕ.

It has been customary since Roberts (1967) to distinguish three levels of market efficiency by considering three different types of information sets:

(1) The weak form of the Efficient Market Hypothesis (EMH) asserts that prices fully reflect the information contained in the historical sequence of prices. Thus, investors cannot devise an investment strategy to yield abnormal profits on the basis of an analysis of past price patterns (a technique known as technical analysis). It is this form of efficiency that is associated with the term 'Random Walk Hypothesis'.

(2) The semi-strong form of EMH asserts that current stock prices reflect not only historical price information but also all publicly available information relevant to a company's securities. If markets are efficient in this sense, then an analysis of balance sheets, income statements, announcements of dividend changes or stock splits or any other public information about a company (the technique of fundamental analysis) will not yield abnormal economic profits.

(3) The strong form of EMH asserts that all information that is *known* to any market participant about a company is fully reflected in market prices. Hence, not even those with privileged information can make use of it to secure superior investment results. There is perfect revelation of all private information in market prices.

WEAK FORM MARKET EFFICIENCY AND THE RANDOM WALK HYPOTHESIS. If markets are efficient, the (technical) analysis of past price patterns to predict the future will be useless because any information from such an analysis will already have

211

been impounded in current market prices. Suppose market participants were confident that a commodity price would double next week. The price will not gradually approach its new equilibrium value. Indeed, unless the price adjusted immediately, a profitable arbitrage opportunity would exist and could be expected to be exploited immediately in an efficient market. Similarly, if a reliable and profitable seasonal pattern for equity prices exists (e.g. a substantial Christmas rally) speculators will bid up prices sufficiently prior to Christmas so as to eliminate any unexploited arbitrage possibility. Samuelson (1965) and Mandelbrot (1966) have proved rigorously that if the flow of information is unimpeded and if there are no transactions costs, then tomorrow's price change in speculative markets will reflect only tomorrow's 'news' and will be independent of the price change today. But 'news' by definition is unpredictable and thus the resulting price changes must also be unpredictable and random.

The term 'random walk' is usually used loosely in the finance literature to characterize a price series where all subsequent price changes represent random departures from previous prices. Thus, changes in price will be unrelated to past price changes. (More formally, the random walk model states that investment returns are serially independent, and that their probability distributions are constant through time.) It is believed that the term was first used in an exchange of correspondence appearing in *Nature* in 1905 (see Pearson and Rayleigh, 1905). The problem considered in the correspondence was the optimal search procedure for finding a drunk who had been left in the middle of a field. The answer was to start exactly where the drunk had been placed. That point is an unbiased estimated of the drunk's future position since he will presumably stagger along in an unpredictable and random fashion.

The earliest empirical work on the random walk hypothesis was performed by Bachelier (1900). He concluded that commodities prices followed a random walk, although he did not use that term. Corroborating evidence from other time series was provided by Working (1934 – various time series), Cowles and Jones (1937 – US stock prices) and Kendall (1953 – UK stock and commodities prices). These studies generally found that the serial correlation between successive price changes was essentially zero. Roberts (1959) found that a time series generated from a sequence of random numbers had the same appearance as a time series of US stock prices. Osborne (1959) found that stock price movements were very similar to the random Brownian motion of physical particles. He found that the logarithms of price changes were independent of each other.

More recent empirical work has used alternative techniques and data sets and has searched for more complicated patterns in the sequence of prices in speculative markets. Granger and Morgenstern (1963) used the powerful technique of spectral analysis but were unable to find any dependably repeatable patterns in stock price movements. Fama (1965) not only looked at serial correlation coefficients (which were close to zero) but also corroborated his investigation by examining a series of lagged price changes as well as by performing a number of nonparametric 'runs' tests. Fama and Blume (1966) examined a variety of filter techniques – trading techniques where buy (sell) signals are generated by some upward (downward) price movements from recent troughs (peaks) – and found they could not produce abnormal profits. Other investigators have done computer simulations of more complicated techniques of technical analysis of stock price patterns and found that profitable trading strategies could not be employed on the basis of these techniques. Solnik (1973) measured serial correlation coefficients for daily, weekly and monthly price changes in nine countries and also concluded that profitable investment strategies could not be formulated on the basis of the extremely small dependencies found.

While the empirical data are remarkably consistent in their general finding of randomness, equity markets do not perfectly conform to the statistician's ideal of a random walk. As noted above, while serial correlation coefficients are always found to be small, there are some small dependencies that have been isolated. While 'runs' tests found only slight departures from randomness, there is a slight tendency for runs in daily price changes to persist. Merton (1980) has shown that changes in the variance of a stock's return (price) can be predicted from its variance in the recent past. Such departures from a pure random walk do not violate the weak form of EMH, which states only that unexploited trading opportunities should not exist in an efficient market. Still, the formal random walk model does not strictly hold. The probability distributions of stock returns are not constant through time and thus the appropriate model for stock prices may be a submartingale rather than a random walk.

In addition, some disturbing seasonal patterns have been found in stock price series. Keim (1983) and others have documented a January effect, where stock returns are abnormally high during the first few days of January (especially for small firms) and French (1980) and others have also documented a so-called 'weekend effect' where average returns to stocks are negative from the close of trading on Friday to the close of trading on Monday. Seasonal patterns appear to exist in several international markets as documented by the Gultekins (1983) and by Jaffé and Westerfield (1984). But departures from randomness are generally remarkably small and an investor who pays transaction costs cannot choose a profitable investment strategy on the basis of these anomalies. Thus, while the random-walk hypothesis is not strictly upheld, the departures from randomness that do exist are not large enough to leave unexploited investment opportunities. Consequently, the empirical evidence presents strong evidence in favour of the weak form of the efficient market hypothesis. The history of stock price movements does not offer investors any information that permits them to outperform a simple buy-and-hold investment strategy.

SEMI-STRONG FORM EFFICIENCY. The weak form of EMH has found general acceptance in the financial community, where technical analysts have never been held in high repute. The stronger assertion that all publicly available information has already been impounded into current market prices has proved far more controversial among investment professionals, who practise 'fundamental' analysis of publicly available information as a widely accepted mode of security analysis.

In general, however, the empirical evidence suggests that public information is so rapidly impounded into current market prices that fundamental analysis is not likely to be fruitful.

A variety of tests have been performed to ascertain the speed of adjustment of market prices to new information. Fama, Fisher, Jensen and Roll (1969) looked at the effect of stock splits on equity prices. While splits themselves provide no economic benefit, splits are usually accompanied or followed by dividend increases that do convey to the market information about management's confidence about the future progress of the enterprise. Thus, while splits usually do result in higher share prices, the market appears to adjust to the announcement fully and immediately. Substantial returns can be earned prior to the split announcement, but there is no evidence of abnormal returns after the public announcement. Indeed, in cases where dividends were not raised following the split, firms suffered a loss in price, presumably because of the unexpected failure of the firm to increase its dividend. Similarly, while merger announcements, especially where premiums are being paid to the shareholders of the acquired firm, can raise market prices substantially, it appears that the market adjusts fully to the public announcements. Dodd (1981) finds no evidence of abnormal price changes following the public release of the merger information.

Scholes (1972) studied the price effects of large secondary offerings. The general belief among market professionals is that such offerings will depress prices temporarily so as to facilitate a large distribution relative to normal trading volume. Such a *temporary* decline would be inconsistent with market efficiency. Scholes hypothesized that the decline would be permanent, however, reflecting release of privileged information (since block traders are usually insiders) of an expected decline in the company's performance. Scholes found that the declines were permanent, especially when sales were by insiders, and thus consistent with the temporary price-pressure hypothesis. However, Kraus and Stoll (1972) used intraday prices and did find some evidence of a price reversal and an arbitrage opportunity. But these reversals took place within a 15-minute period – a speed of adjustment that suggests the market is remarkably efficient.

While the vast majority of studies support the semi-strong version of EMH, there have been some that do not. Ball (1978) found that stock-price reactions to earnings announcements are incomplete. Abnormal risk-adjusted returns are systematically non-zero in the period following the announcement. Ball attributed this to inadequacies in the capital asset pricing model (CAPM) used to adjust for risk differentials and suggested several steps to reduce the estimation bias. Watts (1978), however, performed the steps suggested by Ball and still found systematic abnormal returns. Rendleman, Jones and Latané (1982) also find a relationship between unexpected quarterly earnings and excess returns for common shares subsequent to the announcement date. Roll (1984) found that orange-juice futures prices were made informationally inefficient over short periods by the existence of exchange-imposed maximum daily price moves. Apart from this constraint, however, prices did fully reflect all known information. Moreover, the other abnormalities have not been shown to exist *consistently* over time, and when they did occur, they have usually been small enough that only a professional broker–dealer could have earned economic profits. Thus, it remains to be seen how robust these anomalies are as compared with the vast body of evidence supporting the semi-strong EMH. The evidence in favour of the market's rapid adjustment to new information is sufficiently pervasive that it is now a generally, if not universally, accepted tenet of financial econometric research.

THE STRONG FORM OF THE EFFICIENT MARKET HYPOTHESIS. As the previous studies indicated, stock splits, dividend increases and merger announcements can have substantial impacts on share prices. Consequently insiders trading on such information can clearly profit prior to making the announcement, as has been documented by Jaffé (1974). While such trading is generally illegal, the fact that the market often at least partially anticipates the announcements suggests that it is certainly possible to profit on the basis of privileged information. Thus, the strongest form of the EMH is clearly refuted. Nevertheless, there is considerable evidence that the market comes reasonably close to strong-form efficiency.

Several studies have been performed on the records of professional investment managers. In general they show that randomly selected portfolios or unmanaged indices do as well or better than professionally managed portfolios after expenses. Cowles (1933) examined the records of selected financial services and professional investors. He failed to find any evidence of performance superior to that which could be achieved by investing in the market as a whole. Friend et al. (1962) concluded that the performance of the average mutual fund was insignificantly different from the performance of an unmanaged portfolio with similar asset composition. Jensen (1969) measured the risk-adjusted performance of mutual funds utilizing the capital asset pricing model to measure the appropriate risk return trade-off. Jensen found that while the funds tended to earn *gross* positive abnormal returns, any relative advantage of the professional managers was lost in management fees. Note that the EMH would not rule out small gross abnormal returns as an incentive to acquire information. Grossman and Stiglitz (1980) and Cornell and Roll (1981) have shown that a sensible market equilibrium should leave some incentive for analysis. Those who acquire costly information would have superior gross returns but only average net returns. And the overwhelming evidence on the performance of professional investors is that net returns are only average or below average. For example, during the 20 years to 1984, two-thirds of US professional pension fund managers were out-performed by the unmanaged Standard and Poor's 500 stock index. Moreover, there seems to be little consistency to whatever exceptional performance one finds. It appears that a professional manager who has achieved exceptional performance in one period is just as likely to underperform the market in the next period. It is clear that while superior investment managers may well exist, they are extremely rare.

SOME FURTHER ANOMALIES. In general, the empirical evidence in favour of EMH is extremely strong. Probably no other hypothesis in either economics or finance has been more extensively tested. Thus, it is not surprising that along with general support for EMH there have been scattered pieces of anomalous evidence inconsistent with the hypothesis in its strongest forms. Basu (1977, 1983) found that stocks with low price–earnings (P/E) multiples have higher average risk-adjusted returns than stocks with high P/E's. Banz (1981) found that substantial abnormal (risk-adjusted) long-run rates of return could be earned by investing in portfolios of smaller firms. As was noted above, a large part of this higher return occurs early in January. We know that transactions costs are higher for smaller firms but this factor does not seem to explain the size effect. This size effect appears to persist in varying degrees over time and is related to the evidence regarding higher returns for stocks with low P/E multiples. Of course, we must always keep in mind that these findings of abnormal returns are always joint tests of market efficiency and the particular form of the asset pricing model involved. Thus, it is impossible to distinguish if the abnormal returns are truly due to inefficiencies or result instead because of inadequacies of the capital asset pricing model as a method of measuring risk.

In another empirical study rejecting the concept of market efficiency, Shiller (1981) argued that variations in aggregate stock market prices are much too large to be justified by the variation in subsequent dividend payments. This apparent rejection of the Efficient Market Hypothesis for the entire stock market goes far beyond the narrow issue of whether or not some investors or some trading schemes can beat the market. Shiller's tests, however, are joint tests of market efficiency and the correctness of his model of the dividend process. Marsh and Merton (1983) derive an alternative model for dividend and stock price behaviour. They conclude that Shiller's findings that stock prices are 'too volatile' is a result of his misspecification of the dividend process rather than a result of market inefficiency. A similar conclusion was reached by Kleidon (1986). Nevertheless, the history of fads and excesses in speculative markets I have reviewed (Malkiel, 1985), from tulip bulbs to blue-chip growth stocks, gives me some doubts that we should always consider that the current tableau of market prices represents the best estimates available of appropriate discounted present value.

There have been other scattered instances of inefficiencies as summarized by Jensen (1978) and Ball (1978). I have argued (Malkiel, 1980), that closed-end funds (even those holding essentially 'market' portfolios) were inefficiently priced over many years so that they would provide investors with abnormal returns over and above those involved in buying and holding directly the well-diversified portfolios owned by the funds.

But this last illustration, rather than convincing me of substantial areas of market inefficiency, actually drives me to the opposite conclusion. If there is *truly* some area of pricing inefficiency that can be discovered by the market and dependably exploited, then profit-maximizing traders and investors will eventually through their purchases and sales bring market prices in line so as to eliminate the possibility of extraordinary return. In time, investors recognized that closed-end funds at discounts represented extraordinary value and the discounts on these funds were eventually largely eliminated.

So we are again driven back to the position of the EMH. Pricing irregularities may well exist and even persist for periods of time, and markets can at times be dominated by fads and fashions. Eventually, however, any excesses in market valuations will be corrected. Undoubtedly with the passage of time and with the increasing sophistication of our data bases and empirical techniques, we will document further departures from efficiency and understand their causes more fully. But I suspect that the end result will not be an abandonment of the profession's belief that the stock market is remarkably efficient in its utilization of information.

BIBLIOGRAPHY

Bachelier, L. 1900. *Théorie de la speculation. Annales de l'Ecole Normale Supérieure,* 3rd series, 17, 21–86. Trans. by A.J. Boness in *The Random Character of Stock Market Prices,* ed. P.H. Cootner, Cambridge, Mass.: MIT Press, 1967.

Ball, R. 1978. Anomalies in relationships between securities' yields and yield-surrogates. *Journal of Financial Economics* 6(2–3), 103–26, June–September, 1981.

Banz, R. 1981. The relationship between return and market value of common stocks. *Journal of Financial Economics* 9(1), March, 3–18.

Basu, S. 1977. Investment performance of common stocks in relation to their price earnings ratios: a test of the efficient markets hypothesis. *Journal of Finance* 32(3), June, 663–82.

Basu, S. 1983. The relationship between earnings' yield, market value and the return of NYSE common stocks: further evidence. *Journal of Financial Economics* 12(1), June, 129–56.

Cornell, B. and Roll, R. 1981. Strategies for pairwise competitions in markets and organizations. *Bell Journal of Economics* 12(1), Spring, 201–13.

Cowles, A. 1933. Can stock market forecasters forecast? *Econometrica* 1(3), July, 309–24.

Cowles, A. and Jones, H. 1937. Some posteriori probabilities in stock market action. *Econometrica* 5(3), July, 280–94.

Dodd, P. 1981. The Effect on Market Value of Transactions in the Market for Corporate Control. *Proceedings of Seminar on the Analysis of Security Prices,* CRSP. Chicago: University of Chicago, May.

Fama, E. 1965. The behavior of stock market prices. *Journal of Business* 38(1), January, 34–105.

Fama, E. and Blume, M. 1966. Filter rules and stock market trading. *Security Prices: A Supplement, Journal of Business* 39(1), January, 226–41.

Fama, E., Fisher, L., Jensen, M. and Roll, R. 1969. The adjustment of stock prices to new information. *International Economic Review* 10(1), February, 1–21.

French, K. 1980. Stock returns and the weekend effect. *Journal of Financial Economics* 8(1), March, 55–69.

Friend, I., Brown, F., Herman, E. and Vickers, D. 1962. *A Study of Mutual Funds.* Washington, DC: US Government Printing Office.

Granger, D. and Morgenstern, O. 1963. Spectral analysis of New York Stock Market prices. *Kyklos* 16, January, 1–27.

Grossman, S. and Stiglitz, J. 1980. On the impossibility of informationally efficient markets. *American Economic Review* 70(3), June, 393–408.

Gultekin, M. and Gultekin, N. 1983. Stock market seasonality, international evidence. *Journal of Financial Economics* 12(4), December, 469–81.

Jaffé, J. 1974. The effect of regulation changes on insider trading. *Bell Journal of Economics and Management Science* 5(1), Spring, 93–121.

Jaffé, J. and Westerfield, R. 1984. The week-end effect in common stock returns: the international evidence. Unpublished manuscript, University of Pennsylvania, December.

Jensen, M. 1969. Risk, the pricing of capital assets, and the evaluation of investment portfolios. *Journal of Business* 42(2), April, 167–247.

Jensen, M. 1978. Some anomalous evidence regarding market efficiency. *Journal of Financial Economics* 6(2–3), June–September, 95–101.

Keim, D. 1983. Size related anomalies and stock return seasonality: further empirical evidence. *Journal of Financial Economics* 12(1), June, 13–32.

Kendall, M. 1953. The analysis of economic time series. Part I: Prices. *Journal of the Royal Statistical Society* 96(1), 11–25.

Kleidon, A. 1986. Variance bounds tests and stock price valuation models. *Journal of Political Economy* 94(5), October, 953–1001.

Kraus, A. and Stoll, H. 1972. Price impacts of block trading on the New York Stock Exchange. *Journal of Finance* 27(3), June, 569.

Malkiel, B. 1980. *The Inflation-Beater's Investment Guide*. New York: Norton.

Malkiel, B. 1985. *A Random Walk Down Wall Street*. 4th edn, New York: Norton.

Mandelbrot, B. 1966. Forecasts of future prices, unbiased markets, and martingale models. *Security Prices: A Supplement, Journal of Business* 39(1), January, 242–55.

Marsh, T. and Merton, R. 1987. Aggregate dividend behavior and its implications for tests of stock market rationality. *Journal of Business* 60(1), January, 1–10.

Merton, R. 1980. On estimating the expected return on the market: and exploratory investigation. *Journal of Financial Economics* 8(4), December, 323–61.

Osborne, M. 1959. Brownian motions in the stock market. *Operations Research* 7(2), March/April, 145–73.

Pearson, K. and Rayleigh, Lord. 1905. The problem of the random walk. *Nature* 72, 294, 318, 342.

Rendleman, R., Jones, C. and Latané, H. 1982. Empirical anomalies based on unexpected earnings and the importance of risk adjustments. *Journal of Financial Economics* 10(3), November, 269–87.

Roberts, H. 1959. Stock market 'patterns' and financial analysis: methodological suggestions. *Journal of Finance* 14(1), March, 1–10.

Roberts, H. 1967. Statistical versus clinical prediction of the stock market. Unpublished manuscript, CRSP, Chicago: University of Chicago, May.

Roll, R. 1984. Orange juice and weather. *American Economic Review* 74(5), December, 861–80.

Samuelson, P. 1965. Proof that properly anticipated prices fluctuate randomly. *Industrial Management Review* 6(2), Spring, 41–9.

Scholes, M. 1972. The market for securities; substitution versus price pressure and the effects of information on share prices. *Journal of Business* 45(2), April, 179–211.

Shiller, R.J. 1981. Do stock prices move too much to be justified by subsequent changes in dividends? *American Economic Review* 71(3), June, 421–36.

Solnik, B. 1973. Note on the validity of the random walk for European stock prices. *Journal of Finance* 28(5), December, 1151–9.

Thompson, R. 1978. The information content of discounts and premiums on closed-end fund shares. *Journal of Financial Economics* 6(2–3), June–September, 151–86.

Watts, R. 1978. Systematic 'abnormal' returns after quarterly earnings announcements. *Journal of Financial Economics* 6(2–3), June–September, 127–50.

Working, H. 1934. A random difference series for use in the analysis of time series. *Journa of the American Statistical Association* 29, March, 11–24.

Entitlements

HILLEL STEINER

In the strong sense, an entitlement is something owed by one set of persons to another. The thing owed is either a performance of a certain kind, such as a dental extraction, or a forbearance from interfering from some aspect of the title-holder's activity or enjoyment, such as not trespassing on someone's land. Strong entitlements imply the presence of a right in the person entitled and a corresponding or *correlative* obligation in the person owing the performance or forbearance. Typically, the person entitled is further vested with ancillary powers to waive the obligation or, alternatively, to initiate proceedings for its enforcement. A secondary (and contested) instance of a strong entitlement arises with respect to the position of a third-party beneficiary of a right–obligation relation between two other parties, such as the beneficiary of an insurance policy. Third parties usually lack powers of waiver and enforcement, for it is not strictly to them that fulfilment of the obligation is owed.

A weaker form of entitlement may be said to pertain to those of a person's activities which, while not specifically protected by obligations in others not to interfere, are nevertheless indirectly and extensively protected by their other forbearance obligations. Thus, while persons may be under no obligation specifically to allow someone to use a pay telephone, they probably do have forbearance obligations with respect to assault, theft, property damage, etc., the joint effect of which is to afford some high (but incomplete) degree of protection to someone using a pay telephone. However, such an entitlement amounts to less than the full protection afforded by a right, inasmuch as it does not, for example, avail against anyone who may already be using that telephone.

Beyond strong and weak entitlements, one may also possess many largely unprotected liberties. These consist in those activities from which one has no obligation to refrain, but with which, equally, one has no direct or extensive indirect claims to non-interference. So, broadly speaking, persons' strong entitlements may be construed as conjunctively constituting their spheres of ownership, while their weak entitlements and their unprotected liberties constitute the fields of activity within which they exercise the powers and privileges of ownership. Normally, it is persons' strong entitlements that are of primary normative concern, with weak entitlements and unprotected liberties being determined residually.

Entitlements may be either legal or moral. Sets of legal entitlements tend to reflect the multifarious demands of various customs, moral principles, judicial decisions and state policy. A set of moral entitlements, on the other hand, is commonly derived from some basic principle embedded in a moral code. The nature of this derivation varies with the type of code involved. In many single-value codes (such as utilitarianism), entitlements are instrumental in character: whether and what sort of an obligation is owed, by one person to another, depends upon the relative magnitude of the contribution that fulfilment of that obligation would make to realizing that value. Changing causal conditions of maximization warrant alterations in the content and distribution of entitlements. Codes containing a plurality of independent values characteristically generate entitlements from a principle of justice. The set of entitlements thus derived possesses intrinsic and not merely instrumental value, though its normative status depends upon the ranking of justice in relation to the code's other values. In such codes, the chief distinction between moral obligations that (like kindness) are not correlative to any entitlement and those of justice that are, lies in the fact that only the latter are waivable and permissibly enforceable.

Much of the philosophical treatment of entitlements is located in discussions of rival theories of justice. These theories differ according to the various norms they propose for determining who owes what to whom. Endorsing the classical formal conditions of justice – 'rendering to each what is due to him' and 'treating like cases alike' – they diverge widely in their interpretation of what is due to a person and what count as like cases. Procedural and substantive criteria that have been offered for determining individuals' entitlements include: relative need, productivity, equal freedom, equal utility, personal moral worth, interpersonal neutrality, personal inviolability, initial contract and so forth. As is immediately obvious, the nature and distribution of the entitlements mandated by each of these criteria are by no means self-evident, and their identification thus requires supplementary postulates that are variously drawn from psychological theories, from theories of moral and rational choice, and from conceptual analyses of the criteria themselves. It is also true that not all of these criteria are mutually exclusive: given a plausible set of premises, some can be derived from others.

There are other dimensions, apart from their distributive norms, in which theories of just entitlements differ. Some of these differences are logically implied by the nature of the norms themselves, while others are independent of them. One such dimension is the kinds of object to be distributed in conformity with a proposed criterion. Proffered items include all utility-producing goods, means of production, natural resources, the rents of superior skills or talents, and even human body parts. What one may do with the things to which one has strong entitlements – what weak entitlements and unprotected liberties one possesses – is largely a function of the sorts of thing to which others are strongly entitled.

The intricate structure of permissibility, jointly formed by the rights one has against others and the rights others have against oneself, constitutes the fields of activity within which each person exercises those rights. It thereby also determines the respective spheres of market, state and charitable activities.

A third differentiating dimension is the range of subjects to be counted as having entitlements. Generally accepting the membership of all adult human beings in the class of title-holders, theories differ over whether their distributive norms extend to minors, members of other societies, deceased persons (in respect of bequest), persons conceived but not yet born (in respect of abortion), persons not yet conceived (in respect of capital accumulation and environmental conservation) and non-human animals. Again, the nature and interpretation of a theory's distributive criterion often work to delimit its class of title-holders.

In the light of this multiplicity of differentiating dimensions, the classification – let alone assessment – of theories is no simple task. One, but by no means the only, important respect in which many of them can be compared is in terms of the scope they allow for unconstrained individual choice. Thus theories might be ranged along a spectrum from those that prescribe only an initial set of entitlements (permitting persons thereafter to dispose of these as they choose), to those that require constant enforceable adjustment of the content and distribution of entitlements to conform to certain norms. However, even this way of arraying competing theories is somewhat underspecified, inasmuch as it fails to capture the varied ramifications of the restrictions implied by different initial entitlements.

Hence it is an open question as to where on this spectrum one would locate theories that (via a unanimity requirement) construe each person's initial entitlement as a veto on a social or constitutional contract. Such an entitlement may in turn be derived from some interpretation of equal freedom, personal inviolability or interpersonal neutrality. Or it may itself be taken as an intuitively acceptable foundational postulate for deriving a more complex set of entitlements. Whether an initial contract theory is permissive or restrictive of wide individual choice depends upon its account of the terms of that contract. The derivation of these terms usually proceeds from some conception of human nature – of human knowledge and motivation – along with some meta-ethical theory about the nature of moral reasoning. Contractual terms generated by these premises may extend only to the design of political institutions, thereby leaving the determination of individuals' substantive entitlements to the legislative process. Alternatively, such contracts may stipulate a set of basic individual rights that are immune to legislative encroachment. In either case, the resultant scope for individual choice remains underdetermined. In the first case it depends upon the extent of legislation, while in the second it depends upon the size and nature of the stipulated set of rights. Laws and constitutional rights imply both restrictions on each person's conduct but also, *ipso facto*, restrictions on the extent of permissible interference with others' conduct.

Dispensing with the initial contract device and hypothetical unanimous agreement, some theories derive a set of entitlements directly (non-procedurally) from a substantive foundational value. Among such theories, one type assigns entitlements according to the differential incidence of some stipulated variable in the population of title-holders. Need and productivity are particularly prominent variables in this field, often acquiring their normative import from the values of welfare equalization and maximization. Clearly, applications of these distributive criteria respectively presuppose accounts of essential human requirements and of economic value. Although, for such theories, any shift in the incidence of the stipulated variable occasions a corresponding adjustment of entitlements, the issue of whether this adjustment must be imposed or occurs spontaneously partly turns on the model of interactive behaviour employed. In general, models indicating spontaneous adjustment generate that conclusion by ascribing dominance to altruistic (need) or income-maximizing (productivity) behaviour. To the extent that these ascriptions are empirically unrealistic, such theories mandate enforceable restrictions on the scope for individual choice.

Another type of directly derived (non-contract-based) entitlement set is drawn from foundational values like equal freedom, personal inviolability or interpersonal neutrality, which, by definition, are of uniform non-differential incidence in the population of title-holders. Varying interpretations of these concepts tend nonetheless to converge on the Kantian injunction that persons must be treated as ends in themselves and, more specifically, that no person's ends may be systematically subordinated to those of another. Here the theoretical task is to design a set of entitlements that is independent of any particular conception of 'the good' – independent of particular preferences and (other) moral values – and that is such as to ensure that the consequences of persons' actions, whether harmful or beneficial, are not imposed on others. A typical, though by no means invariable, structural feature of such an entitlement set is its extensive use of a threefold classification of things in the world as selves, raw natural resources and objects which are combinations of these. While title-holders are each vested with ownership of themselves (their bodies and labour), such theories often contain some sort of egalitarian constraint on individual entitlements to raw natural resources. The precise form of this constraint determines the nature of the encumbrances that may be imposed on the ownership of objects in the third category. But since these encumbrances exhaust the restrictions on what persons may do with what they own, such theories are presumed to allow considerable scope for individual choice.

It is hardly worth remarking that many theories of entitlement combine aspects of the three types outlined above. The assessment of competing theories – a complex task, as stated previously – commonly consists in testing for internal coherence and in appraising the interpretations placed on core concepts in the theory. Thus, if it is supposed that the moral principle underpinning a set of entitlements is that of justice, and that justice is analytically linked to the concept of rights, there is room for dispute as to whether the first (initial contract) and second (needs, productivity) types of theory are properly viewed as theories of entitlement. A distinctive normative feature of rights is that they are held non-contingently to confer an element of individuated discretion on their owners.

It is unclear whether possession of a veto in a collective-choice procedure amounts to a sufficiently individuated sphere of discretion. On the other hand, the entitlements generated by considerations of need or productivity, while sufficiently individuated, appear to lack any necessarily discretionary character. A difficulty besetting the first and third types of theory arises with regard to the notion of initial entitlements. Specifically, it seems clear that the identification of each person's initial entitlement – either in a collective-choice procedure or under an egalitarian constraint on natural resource ownership – cannot be interpreted as an historically 'one-off' determination, in the face of an undecidable number and size of partially concurrent future generations. These are among the more salient problems commanding attention in current work on theories of entitlement.

BIBLIOGRAPHY

Buchanan, J.M. 1974. *The Limits of Liberty*. Chicago: University of Chicago Press.
Demsetz, H. 1964. Toward a theory of property rights. *American Economic Review, Papers and Proceedings* 57, 347–59.
Dworkin, R. 1981. What is equality? *Philosophy and Public Affairs* 10, 185–246 and 283–345.
Hohfeld, W.N. 1919. *Fundamental Legal Conceptions*. New Haven: Yale University Press.
Lyons, D. (ed.) 1979. *Rights*. Belmont: Wadsworth Publishing Company.
Nozick, R. 1974. *Anarchy, State and Utopia*. Oxford: Blackwell; New York: Basic Books.
Rawls, J. 1971. *A Theory of Justice*. Cambridge, Mass.: Harvard University Press; Oxford: Oxford University Press, 1972.
Sen, A.K. 1981. Rights and agency. *Philosophy and Public Affairs* 11, 3–39.
Steiner, H. 1987. *An Essay on Rights*. Oxford: Blackwell.

Equilibrium: an Expectational Concept

EDMUND S. PHELPS

Economic equilibrium, at least as the term has traditionally been used, has always implied an outcome, typically from the application of some inputs, that conforms to the expectations of the participants in the economy. Many theorists, especially those employing the 'economic man' postulate, have also required the further condition for equilibrium that every participant be optimizing in relation to those correct expectations. However, it is the former condition, correct expectations, that appears to be the essential property of equilibrium, at least in the orthodox use of the term. Economic equilibrium is therefore not defined in the same terms as physical equilibrium. The rest positions or damped oscillations of pendulums cannot be economic equilibria nor disequilibria since pendulums have no expectations.

Yet it is natural and obvious that the first applications of the equilibrium idea identified some position of rest, or stationary state, as being the equilibrium in the problem at hand. Undoubtedly the term equilibrium, referring to an 'equal weight' of forces pushing capital or what-not *in* as pulling it *out*, owes its origins to the balance of forces prevailing in a stationary situation. But there can also be a *sequence* of positions in which there is a new balance with each new position. There was no reason why equilibria might exist only among stationary states or balanced-growth paths.

Once efforts began to extend economic theory to the case of moving equilibrium paths the expectational meaning of equilibrium began to be explicit. Two of the pioneers here are Myrdal and Hayek. In his 1927 book on price determination and anticipations (in Swedish) Myrdal addresses the two-way interdependency arising in a dynamic analysis of an on-going economy: present disturbances influence future prices and anticipations of future disturbances affect present prices (the latter relation being Myrdal's main subject). In a 1928 article (in German) on what he called intertemporal equilibrium, Hayek drew the analogy between intertemporal trade and international (or interspatial) trade: prices of the same thing at two different places or times are not generally equal, though they may be pulled up or down together. In a 1929 article (in Swedish) Lindahl studied what is considered to be the first mathematical model of intertemporal equilibrium. This literature is surveyed in Milgate (1979).

The English-speaking world was slow to take up the new line of research. In his *General Theory* of 1936, Keynes speaks grandly of having shown the existence of an (implicitly moving) equilibrium with underemployment, and argues that the expectation of falling wages and thus prices makes the slump worse, which suggests he had an expectational notion of equilibrium in mind; but he gives no clues as to what he means by equilibrium, so both the nature and the basis of his claim are left unclear. The new topic of intertemporal equilibrium and the explicit expectational treatment of equilibrium make their English debut in Hicks's *Value and Capital* in 1939. (In the same year Harrod's expectational notion of 'warranted growth', alias equilibrium, and the translation of Lindahl's writings appear.) Hicks makes clear the analytical problem that the analyst and the economic agents alike must solve to find equilibrium: in view of the dependence of future endogenous variables, such as next period's price, on present actions of firms and households, and the dependence of such actions on expectations of those future variables, what expectation would cause the actual outcome to coincide with the expectation? For example, if the actual price P is a function f of the expected price P^e, find the value of P^e such that $P^e = f(P^e)$. Thus the fixed-point character of equilibrium from a mathematical standpoint has a human, or real, interpretation. One might say, semi-jocularly, that pendulums have no economic equilibria since their motions, unlike those of trapeze artists, are not a function of expectations, if they have any.

In the postwar period the notion of equilibrium turns up in contexts quite different from that of the inter-war economic theorists. In game theory, begun by von Neumann and Morgenstern, the term equilibrium is used to refer to the theoretical solution to the policies, or play, of two or more players in strategic interaction. If the model postulates optimizing, or expected-utility-maximizing, behaviour by all players, as game theorists' models invariably do, the equilibrium necessarily has the feature that no player can do better acting alone; but lying behind this feature is the essential property that each player has correctly expected the strategy of the others and hence optimized relative to those correct expectations.

In the late 1960s the notion of equilibrium began to take root in the new territory of non-classical markets – markets without costless and thus complete information. An economy may have markets – the resort hotel market is perhaps a suitable example – in which there are costs in the acquisition or processing of information about prices (and perhaps product specifications) so that arbitrage tendencies are delayed and the classical law of one price operates only with a lag. One well-known portrait of such a market imagines that the national market is composed of Phelpsian islands lacking current-period information about one another's prices. Another image visualizes each firm as an island unto itself with its own stock of customers, who are not knowledgeable about the policies (and perhaps even the whereabouts or existence) of other firms. In such non-Walrasian markets the prevailing prices can be (and usually are) supposed to be market-clearing: no buyer or seller is subjected to rationing (sometimes called non-price rationing by overfastidious writers). However the market will be in *equilibrium* if and only if the prices (and other variables) reflect correct expectations on the part of suppliers and buyers about the prices prevailing elsewhere – at other islands or other firms; otherwise there is *dis*equilibrium.

An economy may also have markets – one may think of labour markets or markets for rental housing – in which, although information is immediate, the wage or rental setters have to make decisions of some durability, however short-lived, and without advance information about the similar decisions of the other firms. In such quasi-Walrasian markets there may be reasons – having to do with incentives, or efficiency – why wages tend to exceed and rentals lie below the market-clearing level. Yet the market will be in *equilibrium* in the case (if such exists) in which no wage setter or rental setter experiences surprise at the corresponding decisions being made simultaneously (or perhaps somewhat later within the period of the commitment) by the other wage or rental setters; otherwise the market must be in disequilibrium, however long or brief (see Phelps et al., 1970).

Thus the analogy between intertemporal equilibrium and interspatial equilibrium, which was drawn by Hayek and others in their analysis of the former, now seems deeper than it could have at first. The expectational meaning of equilibrium, which is so unavoidably clear in the context of intertemporal equilibrium, where future prices are generally expected future prices, turns out to be just as natural and inevitable in the interspatial context as soon as one gives up the fictive device of the Walrasian auctioneer and thus admits that there are 'other' prices elsewhere, about which there must be expectations, not merely a single market-wide price.

The 1970s witnessed the formal analysis of equilibrium in terms of expectations, or forecasts, of the probability distributions of prices. Lucas, adopting the device of separate market-clearing islands, analysed a model in which there is non-public, or local, information (later called asymmetric information), namely local prices, and these price observations are used to update people's conditional forecasts of the currently unobserved prices elsewhere. There may exist a *rational-expectations* equilibrium in which everyone knows and uses the correct *conditional* expectations of the unobserved prices – that is, the statistically optimal forecasts conditional upon his particular information set. This is equilibrium with a qualification.

In surveying the meaning of equilibrium Grossman has remarked that, in Hicks, 'perfect foresight is an equilibrium concept rather than a condition of individual rationality'. A similar comment applies, with even greater weight, to statistical equilibrium and to its rational-expectations variant. The agents of equilibrium models are not simply rational creatures; they have somehow come to possess fantastic knowledge. The equilibrium premise raises obvious problems of knowledge: why should it be supposed that all the agents have hit upon the true model, and how did they manage to estimate it and conform to it more and more closely? There has always been a strand of thought, running from Morgenstern in the 1930s to Frydman in the present, that holds that we cannot hope to understand the major events in the life of an economy, and perhaps also its everyday behaviour, without entertaining hypotheses of disequilibrium.

BIBLIOGRAPHY

Frydman, R. and Phelps, E.S. (eds) 1983. *Individual Forecasts and Aggregate Outcomes.* Cambridge: Cambridge University Press.

Grossman, S.J. 1981. An introduction to the theory of rational expectations under asymmetric information. *Review of Economic Studies* 54, June, 541–60.

Harrod, R.F. 1939. An essay in dynamic theory. *Economic Journal* 49, March, 14–33. Errata, June 1939, 377.

Hayek, F.A. 1928. Das intertemporale Gleichgewichtssystem der Preise und die Bewegungen des Geldwertes. *Weltwirtschaftliches Archiv* 28(1), July, 33–76.

Hicks, J.R. 1939. *Value and Capital.* Oxford: Clarendon Press; 2nd edn, New York: Oxford University Press, 1946.

Keynes, J.M. 1936. *General Theory of Employment, Interest and Money.* London: Macmillan.

Lindahl, E. 1929. Prisbildningproblemets uppläggning från kapitalteoretisk synpunkt. (The formulation of the theory of prices from the viewpoint of capital theory). *Ekonomisk Tidskrift* 31(2), 31–81.

Lucas, R.E., Jr. 1972. Expectations and the neutrality of money. *Journal of Economic Theory* 4(2), April, 103–24.

Milgate, M. 1979. On the origin of the notion of 'intertemporal equilibrium'. *Economica* 46(1), February, 1–10.

Morgenstern, O. 1935. Vollkommene Voraussicht und wirtschaftliches Gleichgewicht. *Zeitschrift für Nationalökonomie* 6(3), 337–57.

Myrdal, G. 1927. *Prisbildningsproblemet och föränderligheten.* Uppsala and Stockholm: Almqvist and Wiksell.

Phelps, E.S. et al. 1970. *Microeconomic Foundations of Employment and Inflation Theory.* New York: W.W. Norton.

Von Neumann, J. and Morgenstern, O. 1944. *The Theory of Games.* Princeton: Princeton University Press.

Equilibrium: Development of the Concept

MURRAY MILGATE

From what appears to have been the first use of the term in economics by James Steuart in 1769, down to the present day, equilibrium analysis (together with its derivative, disequilibrium analysis) has been the foundation upon which economic theory has been able to build up its not inconsiderable claims to 'scientific' status. Yet despite the persistent use of the concept by economists for over two hundred years, its meaning and role have undergone some quite profound modifications over that period.

At the most elementary level, 'equilibrium' is spoken about in a number of ways. It may be regarded as a 'balance of forces', as when, for example, it is used to describe the familiar idea of a balance between the forces of demand and supply. Or it can be taken to signify a point from which there is no endogenous 'tendency to change': stationary or steady states exhibit this kind of property. However, it may also be thought of as that outcome which any given economic process might be said to be 'tending towards', as in the idea that competitive processes tend to produce determinate outcomes. It is in this last guise that the concept seems first to have been applied in economic theory. Equilibrium is, as Adam Smith might have put it (though he did not use the term), the centre of gravitation of the economic system – it is that configuration of values towards which all economic magnitudes are continually tending to conform.

There are two properties embodied in this original concept which when taken into account begin to impart to it a rather more precise meaning and a well-defined methodological status. Into this category enters the formal definition of 'equilibrium conditions' and the argument for taking these to be a useful object of analysis.

There are few better or more appropriate places to isolate the first two properties of 'equilibrium' in this original sense than in the seventh chapter of the first book of Adam Smith's *Wealth of Nations*. The argument there consists of two steps. The first is to define 'natural conditions':

> There is in every society ... an ordinary or average rate of both wages and profits.... When the price of any commodity is neither more nor less than what is sufficient to pay ... the wages of the labour and the profits of the stock employed ... according to their natural rates, the commodity is then sold for what may be called its natural price (Smith, 1776, I.vii, p. 62).

The key point here is that 'natural conditions' are associated with a general rate of profit – that is, uniformity in the returns to capital invested in different lines of production under existing best-practice technique. In the language of the day, this property was thought to be the characteristic of the outcome of the operation of the process of 'free competition'.

The second step in the argument captures the analytical status to be assigned to 'natural conditions':

> The natural price ... is, as it were, the central price, to which the prices of all commodities are continually gravitating. Different accidents may sometimes keep them suspended a good deal above it, and sometimes force them down even somewhat below it. But whatever may be the obstacles which hinder them from settling in this centre of repose and continuance, they are constantly tending towards it (I.vii, p. 65).

This particular 'tendency towards equilibrium' was held to be operative in the *actual* economic system at any given time. It is not to be confused with the familiar question concerning the stability of competitive equilibrium in modern analysis. There the question about convergence to equilibrium is posed in some *hypothetical* state of the world where none but the most purely competitive environment is held to prevail. It is also essential to observe that in defining 'natural conditions' in this fashion, nothing has yet been said (nor need it be said) about the forces which act to determine the natural rates of wages and profits, or the natural prices of commodities. It will therefore be possible to refrain from discussing the *theories* offered by various economists for the determination of these variables in most of what follows. Similarly, there will be no discussion here of existence or uniqueness of equilibrium.

'Natural conditions' so defined and conceived are the formal expression of the idea that certain systematic or persistent forces, regular in their operation, are at work in the economic system. Smith's earlier idea, that 'the co-existent parts of the universe ... contribute to compose one immense and connected system' (1759, VII.ii, 1.37), is translated in this later formulation into an analytical device capable of generating conclusions with a claim to general (as opposed to a particular, or special) validity. These general conclusions were customarily referred to as 'statements of tendency', or 'laws' or 'principles' in the economic literature of the 18th and 19th centuries. It is worth emphasizing that there was no implication that these general tendencies were either swift in their operation or that they were not subject at any time to interference from other obstacles.

Like sea level, 'natural conditions' had an unambiguous meaning, even if subject to innumerable cross-currents.

To put it another way, the distinction between 'general' and 'special' cases (like its counterpart, the distinction between 'equilibrium' and 'disequilibrium'), refers neither to the immediate practical relevance of these kinds of cases to actual existing market conditions, nor to the prevalence, frequency, or probability of their occurrence. In fact, as far as simple observation is concerned, it might well be that 'special' cases would be the order of the day. John Stuart Mill expressed this idea especially clearly when he held that the conclusions of economic theory are only applicable 'in the *abstract*', that is, 'they are only true under certain suppositions, in which none but general causes – causes common to the *whole class* of cases under consideration – are taken into account' (Mill, 1844, pp. 144–5). Marshall, of course, understood their application as being subject not only to this qualification (which he spoke about in terms of 'time'), but also to the condition that 'other things are equal' (1890, I.iii, p. 36). There will be cause to return to this matter below.

To unearth these regularities, one has to inquire behind the scene, so to speak, to reveal what otherwise might remain hidden. Adam Smith had set out the basis of this procedure in an early essay on 'The Principles which Lead and Direct Philosophical Enquiries':

Nature, after the largest experience that common observation can acquire, seems to abound with events which appear solitary and incoherent ... by representing the invisible chains which bind together all these disjointed objects, [philosophy] endeavours to introduce order into this chaos of jarring and discordent appearances (Smith, 1795, p. 45).

In short, 'equilibrium', if we may revert to the modern terminology for a moment, became the central organizing category around which economic theory was to be constructed. It is no accident that the formal introduction of the concept into economics is associated with those very writers whose names are closely connected with the foundation of 'economic science'. It could even be argued that its introduction marks the foundation of the discipline itself, since its appearance divides quite neatly the subsequent literature from the many analyses of individual problems which dominated prior to Smith and the Physiocrats.

Cementing this tradition, Ricardo spoke of fixing his 'whole attention on the permanent state of things' which follows from given changes, excluding for the purposes of general analysis 'accidental and temporary deviations' (1817, p. 88). Marshall, though substituting the terminology 'long-run normal conditions' for the older 'natural conditions', excluded from this category results upon which 'accidents of the moment exert a preponderating influence' (1890, p. vii). J.B. Clark followed suit and held that 'natural or normal' values are those to which 'in the long run, market values tend to conform' (1899, p. 16). Jevons (1871, p. 86), Walras (1874–7, p. 380), Böhm-Bawerk (1899, II, p. 380) and Wicksell (1901, I, p. 97) all followed the same procedure.

Not only was the status of 'equilibrium' as the centre of gravitation of the system (the benchmark case, so to speak) preserved, but it was defined in the manner of Smith. The primary theoretical object of all these writers was to explain that situation characterized by a uniform rate of profit on the supply price of capital invested in different lines of production. Walras, whose argument is quite typical, stated the nature of the connection forcefully:

> uniformity of ... the price of net income [rate of profit] on the capital goods market ... [is one] condition by which the universe of economic interests is governed (1874–7, p. 305).

From an historical point of view, the novelty of these arguments which were worked out in the 18th century by Smith and the Physiocrats, is not that they recognized that there might be situations which could be described as 'natural', but that they associated these conditions with the outcome of a specific process common to market economies (free competition) and utilized them in the construction of a general economic analysis of market society. Earlier applications of 'natural order' arguments were little more than normative pronouncements about some existing or possible state of society. They certainly made no 'scientific' use of the idea of systematic tendencies, even if these might have been involved. This is particularly apparent in the case of the 'natural law' philosophers, but is also true of the early liberals like Locke and Hobbes. Even Hume, who to all intents and purposes had in his possession all of the building blocks of Smith's position, drew back from the one crucial step that would have led him to Smith's 'method' – he was just not prepared to admit that thinking in terms of regularities, however useful it might prove to be in dispelling theological and other obfuscations (and thus in advancing 'human understanding'), was anything more than a convenient and satisfying way of thinking. The question as to whether the social and economic world was actually governed by such regularities, so central to Smith and the Physiocrats, just did not concern Hume.

Yet the earlier normative connotations of ideas like 'natural conditions', 'natural order', and the like, quite rapidly disappeared when the terminology was appropriated by economic theory. Nothing was 'good' simply by virtue of its being 'natural'. This, of course, is not to say that once the theoretical analysis of the natural tendencies operating in market economies had been completed, and the outcomes of the competitive process had been isolated in abstract, an individual theorist might not at that stage wish to draw some conclusions about the 'desirability' of its results (a normative statement, so to speak). But such statements are not implied by the concept of equilibrium – they are value judgements about the characteristics of its outcomes.

Indeed, contrary to the view sometimes expressed, even Smith's use of Deistic analogies and metaphors in the *Theory of Moral Sentiments*, where we read about God as the creator of the 'great machine of the universe', and where we encounter for the first time the famous 'invisible hand', is no more than the extraneous window-dressing which surrounds a well-defined *theoretical* argument based upon the operation of the so-called 'sympathy' mechanism. Thus, as

W.E. Johnson noted when writing for the original edition of Palgrave's *Dictionary*, 'the confusion between scientific law and ethical law no longer prevails', and he observes that 'the term normal has replaced the older word natural' – to be understood by this terminology as 'something which presents a certain empirical uniformity or regularity' (1899, p. 139).

While 'natural conditions' or 'long-run normal conditions' represent the original concept of 'equilibrium' utilized in economic theory, John Stuart Mill's *Political Economy* seems to have been the source from which the actual term equilibrium gained widespread currency (though, like so much else, it is also to be found in Cournot's *Recherches*). More significant, however, is the fact that in Mill's hands the meaning and status of the concept undergoes a modification. While maintaining the idea of equilibrium as a long-period position, Mill introduces the idea that the equilibrium theory is essentially 'static'. The relevant remarks appear at the beginning of the fourth book:

> We have to consider the economical condition of mankind as liable to change
> ... thereby adding a theory of motion to our theory of equilibrium – the
> Dynamics of political economy to the Statics (Mill, 1848, IV.i, p. 421).

Since he retained the basic category of 'natural and normal conditions', Mill's claim had the effect of adding a property to the list of those associated with the concept of equilibrium. However, over the question of whether this additional property was necessary to the concept of equilibrium there was to be less uniformity of opinion. Indeed, this matter gave rise to a debate in which at one time or another (until at least the 1930s) almost all theorists of any repute became contributors. The problem was a simple one – are natural or long-period normal conditions the same thing as the 'famous fiction' of the stationary or steady state? Much hinged upon the answer; a 'yes' would have limited the application of equilibrium to an imaginary stationary society in which no one conducts the daily business of life.

On this question, as might be expected, Marshall vacillated. The thrust of his argument (as well as those of his major contemporaries, with the important exception of Pareto) seems to imply that such a property was not essential to his purpose, but as was his habit on so many occasions, in a footnote he qualified that position (1890, p. 379, n.1). In the final analysis, the answer seems to have depended rather more on the explanation given for the determination of equilibrium values, than upon the concept of equilibrium proper. It was not until the 1930s that the issue seems to have been resolved to the general satisfaction of the profession. But then its 'resolution' required the introduction of a new definition of equilibrium (the concept of intertemporal equilibrium) due in the main to Hicks.

However, some further embellishments and modifications were worked upon the concept of equilibrium before the 1930s. Here, two developments stand out. The first concerns the distinction between partial equilibrium analysis and general equilibrium analysis. The second concerns a trend that seems to have developed consequent upon Marshall's treatment of the element of time, which led him to his threefold typology of periods ('market', 'short', and 'long' – we shall leave to one side the further category of 'secular movement'). The upshot of this trend which is decisive, is that it became common to speak of the possibility of 'equilibrium' in each of these Marshallian periods.

The analytical basis for partial equilibrium analysis was laid down in 1838 by Cournot in his *Recherches*. Mathematical convenience, more than methodological principle, seems to have been responsible for his adopting it (see, for example, 1838, p. 127). Though this small volume failed to exercise any widespread influence on the discipline much before the present century, it was known and read by Marshall (who spoke of Cournot as his 'gymnastics master'), from whose *Principles* the popularity of partial equilibrium analysis is largely derived (though it would be remiss to overlook Auspitz, Lieben and von Mangoldt). Unlike the case of Cournot, however, it would be difficult to argue that Marshall came across the method in anything other than a roundabout way (though some have argued that its principal attraction for him lay in its facility in allowing him to express his theory in a manner which required little recourse to mathematics).

When Marshall first introduced the idea of assuming 'other things equal' in the *Principles*, the *ceteris paribus* condition which is taken as the hallmark of the partial equilibrium approach, he seems to have done so not in order to justify the procedure of analysing 'one bit at a time', but in order to make a quite different point – that a long-run normal equilibrium would only *actually* emerge if none but the most general causes were allowed to operate without interference (see, for example, 1890, p. 36, p. 366, and pp. 369–70). In other words, the 'other things' that were being held 'equal' were the given data of the theory and the external environment – if the data remained the same and the external environment was freely competitive, then a long-run normal equilibrium would result. Indeed, Walrasian general equilibrium holds 'other things equal' in this sense. To put it another way, in Marshall's initial argument nothing was said about the possibility of assuming the interdependencies between long-run variables themselves to be of secondary importance, as is customary in partial equilibrium analysis.

This latter requirement of Marshallian analysis, the idea of the negligibility of indirect effects when one looks at individual markets (1919, p. 677ff.), seems to have sprung from his habit of presenting equilibrium *theory* in terms of *particular* market demand and supply curves (with their attendant notions of representative consumers and firms). It is here, in fact, that Marshall's presentation of demand and supply theory differs so markedly from its presentation by Walras. To the extent that this is so, it would seem to be better to recognize that the idea of 'partial' versus 'general' equilibrium has more to do with the presentation of a particular theory, and Marshall's propensity to consider markets one at a time, than it has to do with the abstract category of equilibrium with which this discussion is concerned. This view would accord, incidentally, with the fact that the great disputes over the relative merits of these two modes of analysis (for example, that between Walras on the one hand, and Auspitz and Lieben on the other) were fought over the specification of demand and cost functions.

Another modification to the concept of equilibrium that has become more significant in recent literature also makes an appearance in Marshall, though it is not carried as far as it has been in recent literature. The second, third and fifth chapters of the fifth book of Marshall's *Principles* set out the conditions for the determination of what he calls the 'temporary equilibrium', the 'short-run equilibrium' and the 'long-run equilibrium' of demand supply. The last of these categories, as Marshall makes perfectly clear in the text, corresponds to Adam Smith's 'natural conditions' (1890, p. 347). The first two are to a greater or lesser degree 'more influenced by passing events, and by causes whose action is fitful and short lived' (p. 349). What is striking about Marshall's terminology is the fact that situations which from an analytical point of view would traditionally have been regarded as 'deviations' from long-period normal equilibrium (that is, disequilibria) are explicitly referred to as different cases of 'equilibrium'. This trend has taken on an entirely new significance in recent literature, and has had dramatic consequences for the meaning and status of the concept of equilibrium in economic theory. But just as important in comprehending this development is the introduction of the notion of intertemporal equilibrium into theoretical discourse.

The notion of intertemporal equilibrium (introduced by Hayek, Lindahl and Hicks in the inter-war years and developed in the 1950s by Malinvaud, Arrow and Debreu) warrants special consideration since 'equilibrium conditions' under this notion are defined quite differently from 'natural' or 'long-run normal' conditions. Intertemporal equilibrium defines as its object the determination of nt market-clearing prices (for n commodities over t elementary time periods commencing from an arbitrary short-period starting point). The chief implication of this definition of equilibrium conditions, and that which sets it apart from long-run normal conditions, is that not only will the price of the same commodity be different at different times but also that the stock of capital need not yield a uniform return on its supply price.

This fundamental change in the concept of equilibrium did not mean that intertemporal equilibrium positions were immediately divested of the status that had been given to 'equilibrium' ever since Adam Smith. In certain circles they continued to be regarded as positions towards which the economic system could actually be said to be 'tending' (or as benchmark cases).

However, once the *sequential* character of this equilibrium concept came to be better understood, it became apparent that there could be no 'tendency' towards it – at least not in the former meaning of that idea. One was either in it, in which case the sequence was 'inessential', or one was not, in which case the sequence was 'essential' (see Hahn, 1973, p. 16). And the probabilities overwhelmingly suggested the latter. Attention was thus turned to the individual points in the sequence; the temporary equilibria, as Hicks had dubbed them (applying the terminology of Marshall in a new context). A whole new class of cases, disequilibrium cases from the point of view of full intertemporal equilibrium, began to be examined. The discipline has now accumulated so many varieties that it is impossible to document them all here. Instead, two broad features of this development may be noted here, the first concerning the role that expectations were thereby enabled to play, the second the common designation now uniformly applied to all such cases: 'equilibrium'.

When equilibrium is interpreted as a solution concept in the sense that *all* solutions to *all* models (for which solutions exist) enjoy equal analytical status and differ only in that they become 'significant', as von Neumann and Morgenstern put it, when they are 'similar to reality in those respects which are essential in the investigation at hand' (1944, p. 32), it is sometimes said that economics has availed itself of a very powerful notion of equilibrium. On this line of argument, Walrasian equilibrium and, say, conjectural equilibrium compete with one another not for the title 'general' (since, in the traditional sense at least, there is no such category), but for the title 'significant'. Furthermore, at any given time they are competing for this title with as many other models as are available to the profession.

It seems to be the case that the status of equilibrium in economic analysis has come full circle since its introduction in the late 18th century. From being derived from the idea that market societies were governed by certain systematic forces, more or less regular in their operation in different places and at different times, it now seems to be based on an opinion that nothing essential is 'hidden' behind the many and varied situations in which market economies might actually find themselves. In fact, it seems that these many cases are to be thought of as being more or less singular from the point of view of modern theory. From being the central organizing category around which the whole of economic theory was constructed, and therefore the ultimate basis upon which its practical application was premissed, equilibrium has become a category with no meaning independent of the exact specification of the initial conditions for *any* model. Instead of being thought of as furnishing a theory applicable, as Mill would have said, to the whole class of cases under consideration, it is increasingly being regarded by theorists as the solution concept relevant to a particular model, applicable to a limited number of cases. The present fashion for replacing economic theory proper by game theory, an approach which could be regarded by no less a theorist than Professor Arrow as contributing only 'mathematical tools' to economic analysis not many years ago (1968, p. 113), seems to exemplify the trend of modern economics.

BIBLIOGRAPHY

Arrow, K.J. 1968. Economic equilibrium. In *International Encyclopedia of the Social Sciences*, as reprinted in *The Collected Papers of Kenneth J. Arrow*, Vol. 2, Cambridge, Mass: Harvard University Press.

Böhm-Bawerk, E. von. 1899. *Capital and Interest*. 3 vols; reprinted, Ill: Libertarian Press, 1959.

Clark, J.B. 1899. *The Distribution of Wealth*. London: Macmillan.

Cournot, A.A. 1838. *Researches into the Mathematical Principles of the Theory of Wealth*. Translated by N.T. Bacon with an introduction by Irving Fisher, 1897; 2nd edn, London and New York: Macmillan, 1927.

Garegnani, P. 1976. On a change in the notion of equilibrium in recent work on value. In *Modern Capital Theory*, ed. M. Brown et al., Amsterdam: North-Holland.

Hahn, F.H. 1973. *On the Notion of Equilibrium in Economics*. Cambridge: Cambridge University Press.

Hicks, J.R. 1939. *Value and Capital*. 2nd edn, Oxford: Clarendon Press, 1946.

Jevons, W.S. 1871. *Theory of Political Economy*. Edited from the 2nd edition (1879) by R.D.C. Black, Harmondsworth: Penguin, 1970.

Marshall, A. 1890. *Principles of Economics*. 9th (variorum) edition, taken from the text of the 8th edition, 1920, London: Macmillan; New York: Macmillan, 1948.

Marshall, A. 1919. *Industry and Trade*. 2nd edn, London: Macmillan.

Mill, J.S. 1844. *Essays on Some Unsettled Questions of Political Economy*. 2nd edn, 1874; reprinted, New York: Augustus M. Kelley.

Mill, J.S. 1848. *Principles of Political Economy*. 6th edn, 1871 (reprinted 1909), London: Longmans, Green & Company; New York: A.M. Kelley, 1965.

Palgrave, R.H.I. (ed.) 1899. *Dictionary of Political Economy*. Vol. III, London: Macmillan.

Pareto, V. 1909. *Manual of Political Economy*. Translated from the French edition of 1927 and edited by A.S. Schwier and A.N. Page, New York: Augustus M. Kelley, 1971.

Ricardo, D. 1817. *The Principles of Political Economy and Taxation*. Edited from the 3rd edition of 1821 by P. Sraffa with the collaboration of M. Dobb, Vol. I of *The Works and Correspondence of David Ricardo*, 11 vols, Cambridge: Cambridge University Press, 1951–73; New York: Cambridge University Press, 1973.

Smith, A. 1759. *The Theory of Moral Sentiments*. Edited by D.D. Raphael and A.L. Macfie from the 6th edn of 1790, Oxford: Oxford University Press, 1976.

Smith, A. 1776. *An Inquiry into the Nature and Causes of the Wealth of Nations*. 2 vols, ed. E. Cannan, London: Methuen, 1961; Chicago: University of Chicago Press, 1976.

Smith, A. 1795. *Essays on Philosophical Subjects*. Edited by W.P.D. Wrightman and J.C. Bryce, Oxford: Oxford University Press, 1980.

Von Neumann, J. and Morgenstern, O. 1944. *Theory of Games and Economic Behavior*. 3rd edn, Princeton: Princeton University Press, 1953.

Walras, L. 1874–7. *Elements of Pure Economics*. Translated and edited by W. Jaffé from the definitive edition of 1926, London: Allen & Unwin, 1954; Homewood, Ill.: R.D. Irwin.

Wicksell, K. 1901. *Lectures on Political Economy*. 2 vols, ed. L. Robbins, London: Routledge and Kegan Paul, 1934; New York: A.M. Kelley, 1967.

Exchange

ROBERT B. WILSON

The accepted purview of economics is the allocation of scarce resources. Allocation comprises production and exchange, according to a division between processes that transform commodities and those that transfer control. For production or consumption, exchange is essential to efficient use of resources. It allows decentralization and specialization in production; and for consumption, agents with diverse endowments or preferences require exchange to obtain maximal benefits. If two agents have differing marginal rates of substitution then there exists a trade benefiting both. The advantages of barter extend widely, e.g. to trade among nations and among legislators ('vote trading'), but it suffices here to emphasize markets with enforceable contracts for trading private property unaffected by externalities. In such markets, voluntary exchange involves trading bundles of commodities or obligations to the mutual advantage of all parties to the transaction.

In a market economy using money or credit, terms of trade are usually specified by prices. Besides purchases at prices posted by producers and distributors, exchange occurs in bargaining, auctions, and other contexts with repeated or competitive offers. In institutionalized 'exchanges' for trading commodities, brokers offer bid and ask prices; and for trading financial instruments, specialists cross orders and maintain markets continually by trading for their own accounts.

Records of transaction prices and quantities are the raw data of many empirical studies of economic activity, and explanation of these data is a major purpose of economic theory. Theories of exchange attempt to predict the terms of trade and the resulting transactions, depending on the market structure and the agents' attributes, including such features as each agent's endowment, productive opportunities, preferences and information. Also relevant are the markets accessible, the trading rules used and the contracts available; these may depend on property rights, search or transaction costs and on events observable or verifiable to enforce contracts. If a particular trading rule is used, it specifies the actions allowed each agent in each contingency, and the trades resulting from

237

each combination of the agents' actions. These features are the ingredients of experimental designs to test theories, and they motivate models used for empirical estimates of market behaviour. Normative considerations are also relevant, and welfare analyses emphasize the distributional consequences of alternative trading procedures and contracts.

Most theories hypothesize that each agent acts purposefully to maximize (the expected utility of) gains from trade. Some behaviour may be erratic, customary, or reflect dependency on a *status quo*, but experimental and empirical evidence substantially affirms the hypothesis of 'rational' behaviour, at least in the aggregate. Although more general theories are available, the main features are explained by preferences that are quite regular, as assumed here: monotone, convex, as smooth as necessary, and possibly allowing risk aversion.

Typically there are many efficient allocations of a fixed endowment: any allocation that equates all agents' marginal rates of substitution is efficient. In the case of risk sharing, for example, an allocation is efficient if all agents achieve the same marginal rates of substitution between income in every two states. The distribution of endowments among agents evidently matters, however, and a major accomplishment has been the identification of a small set of salient efficient allocations. Named for Léon Walras, this set is a focus of nearly all theories, in the sense that other allocations are explained by departures from the Walrasian model. An important issue is to elaborate the special role of the Walrasian allocations.

An allocation is Walrasian if it is obtainable by trading at prices such that it would cost each agent more to obtain a preferable allocation. That is, items are bought at uniform prices available to all, and each agent chooses a preferred trade within a budget constraint imposed by the value of goods sold. A Walrasian allocation is necessarily efficient to the extent that markets are complete; for another allocation preferred by every agent would cost each agent more at the current prices and therefore more in total, which cannot be true if the preferred allocation is a redistribution of the present one. Conversely, each efficient allocation is Walrasian without further trade, since the agents' common marginal rates of substitution serve as the price ratios. The basic formulation considers trade for delivery in all future contingencies, but refined formulations elaborate the realistic case that markets reopen continually and trade is confined to a limited variety of contracts for spot and contingent future delivery.

Sufficient conditions for Walrasian allocations to exist have been established. Mainly these require that agents' preferences be convex and insatiable, and that each agent has an endowment sufficient to obtain a positive income. For 'most' economies the number of Walrasian allocations is finite; strong assumptions on substitution and income effects are required to ensure uniqueness.

Walrasian allocations and prices for specified models can be computed by solving a fixed-point problem and general methods have been devised. The task is complex (e.g. linear models with integer data can yield irrational prices) but an important simplifying feature is that the Walrasian prices depend only on the distribution of agents' attributes, and in particular only on the aggregate excess demand function. Essentially, any continuous function satisfying Walras's Law and homogeneity in prices is the excess demand for some economy.

The key requirement for a Walrasian allocation is that each agent's benefit be maximized within the budget imposed by the assigned prices; and that markets clear at those prices. Complete exploitation of all gains from trade may be precluded, however, by incomplete markets, pecuniary externalities (such as absence of necessary complementary goods), or insufficient contracts; or by strategic behaviour. If producers with monopoly power restrain output to elevate prices, or practise any of the myriad forms of price discrimination, then the resulting allocation is not Walrasian. Much discrimination segments markets via quality differentiation or bundling, but equally common is discriminatory pricing of the various conditions of delivery (e.g. spatial, temporal, service priority) or nonlinear pricing of quantities (e.g. two-part and block declining tariffs) if purchases can be monitored and resale markets are absent.

The Walrasian model of exchange is substantially defined by the absence of such practices affecting prices. It also relies on a fixed specification of agents, products, markets and contracts. The theory of economies with large firms having power to influence prices and to choose product designs is significantly incomplete. The deficiencies derive partly from inadequate formulations, and partly from technical considerations: characterizations and even the existence of equilibria (in non-randomized strategies) depend on special structural features. For example, the simplest models positing simultaneous choices of qualities and prices by several firms lack equilibria; models with sequential choices encounter similar obstacles but to lesser degrees. In addition, if firms have fixed costs and must avoid losses then efficiency may require nonlinear pricing and other discriminatory practices if lump-sum assessments imposed on customers are precluded.

Market clearing is also essential to the Walrasian model and prices are determined entirely by the required equality of demand and supply. In contrast, successive markets with overlapping generations of traders need not clear 'at infinity'. Such markets can exhibit complicated dynamics even if the underlying data of the economy are stationary. Similarly, continually repeated markets, where buyers and sellers arrive at the same rate that others depart from after completing transactions, admit non-Walrasian prices or may have persistent excess on one side of the market if search or dispersed bargaining prevents immediate clearing.

When it is that among the feasible allocations the best prediction might be one of the Walrasian allocations, has been answered in several ways.

Competition is the first answer. On the supply side, for instance, with many sellers each one's incentive to defect from collusive pricing arrangements is increased. Absent collusion, if prices reflect supplies offered on the market and each seller chooses an optimal supply in response to anticipations of other sellers' supplies, then each seller's optimal percentage profit margin declines inversely with the number of sellers offering substitutes. Price discrimination, such as nonlinear pricing, is inhibited if there are many sellers, resale markets are available, or customers' purchases are difficult to monitor. Without capacity limitations, direct price competition among close or perfect substitutes erodes profits since undercutting is attractive. Although these conclusions are weakened to the extent that buyers incur search or switching costs, easy entry incurring no sunk costs remains important to ensure that markets are contestable and monopoly rents are eliminated. Monopoly rents are often substantially dissipated in entry deterrence, price wars and other competitive battles to retain or capture monopoly positions. This is true both when entrants bring perfect substitutes and more generally, since entrants tend to fill in the spectra of quality attributes and conditions of delivery.

Arbitrage is important in commodity markets with standardized qualities, and especially in financial markets; to the extent that the contingent returns from one asset replicate those from a bundle of other assets, or from some trading strategy, its price is linked to the latter. Also, repeated opportunities to trade contingent on events enable a few securities to substitute for a much wider variety of absent contingent contracts.

One form of the competitive hypothesis emphasizes the option that each subset of the traders has to redistribute their endowments among themselves. For example, a seller and those who purchase from him are a coalition redistributing their resources among themselves. A core allocation is one such that no coalition can redistribute its endowment to the greater advantage of each member. The core allocations include the Walrasian allocations. A basic result first explored by F.Y. Edgeworth establishes that as the economy is enlarged by adding replicates of the original traders, the set of core allocations shrinks to the set of Walrasian allocations.

Another form emphasizes the view that in an economy so large that each agent's behaviour has an insignificant effect on the terms of trade, every trader's best option is to maximize the gains from trade at the prevailing prices. For example, any one trader's potential gain from behaviour that influences the terms of trade becomes insignificant (generically) as the set of traders expands, providing the limit distribution is 'atomless'. Similar results obtain for various models of markets with explicit price formation via auctions. Generally, an efficient allocation is necessarily Walrasian if each agent is unnecessary to attainment of others' gains from trade. An idealized formulation considers an atomless measure space of agents in which only measurable sets of agents matter and the behaviour of each single agent is inconsequential. In this case the Walrasian allocations are the only core allocations. Similarly, the allocation obtained from the Shapley value, in which each agent shares in proportion to his expected marginal contribution to a randomly formed coalition, is a Walrasian allocation.

Structural features of trading processes suggest an alternative hypothesis. Matching problems (e.g. workers seeking jobs) admit procedural rules that with optimal play yield core allocations, and for a general exchange economy an appropriately designed auction yields a core allocation. Other games have been devised for which optimal play by the agents produces a Walrasian allocation. Continual bilateral bargaining among dispersed agents (with sufficiently diverse preferences), in which agents are repeatedly matched randomly and one designated to offer some trade to the other, also results in a Walrasian allocation with optimal play. In a related vein, several methods of selecting allocations create incentives for agents to falsify reports of their preferences, and if they do this optimally than a Walrasian allocation results. Quite generally, any process that is fair in the sense that all agents enjoy the same opportunities for net trades yields essentially a Walrasian allocation. In one axiomization, some 'signal' is announced publicly and then based on his preferences, each agent responds with a message that affects the resulting trades: if a core allocation is required, and each signal could be the right signal for some larger economy, then the signal must be essentially equivalent to the announcement of a Walrasian price to which each agent responds with his preferred trade within his budget specified by the price.

Traders' impatience can also affect the terms of trade. In the simplest form of impatience, agents discount delayed gains from trade. Dynamic play is assumed to be sequentially rational in the sense that a strategy must specify an optimal continuation from each contingency; this is a strong requirement and severely restricts the admissible equilibria. For example, if a seller and a buyer alternate proposing prices for trading an item, then in the *unique* equilibrium, trade occurs immediately at a price dependent on their discount rates. As the interval between offers shrinks the seller's share of the gains from trade becomes proportional to the relative magnitude of the buyer's discount rate; for example, equal rates yield equal division. Extensions to multilateral contexts produce analogous results. A monopolist with an unlimited supply selling to a continuum of buyers might plausibly extract favourable terms, but actually in any equilibrium in which the buyers' strategies are stationary, as the interval between offers shrinks the seller's profit disappears an all trade occurs immediately at a Walrasian price. Similarly, a durable-good manufacturer lacking control of resale or rental markets has an incentive to increase the output rate as the production period shrinks; or, to pre-commit to limited capacity. This emphasizes that monopoly power depends substantially on powers of commitment stemming from increasing marginal costs, capacity limitations, or other sources.

Impatience and sequential rationality can, however, produce inefficiencies in product design, as in the case of a manufacturer's choice of durability, or in market structure, as in a preference to rent rather than sell durable goods.

Complete information is a major factor justifying predictions of Walrasian prices. With complete information and symmetric trading opportunities among agents, many models predict a Walrasian outcome, but incomplete information often produces departures from the Walrasian norm.

Although information may be productively useful, in an exchange economy the arrival of information may be disadvantageous to the extent that risk-averse agents forgo insurance against its consequences. A basic result considers an exchange economy that has reached an efficient allocation before some agents receive further private information, and where this fact is common knowledge: the predicted response is no further trade, though prices may change.

241

Each efficient allocation has 'efficiency prices' that reflect the marginal rates of substitution prevailing; in the Walrasian case all trades are made at these prices. They summarize a wealth of information about technology, endowments and preferences. Prices (and other endogenous observables) are therefore not only sufficient instruments for decentralization but also carriers of information. If information is dispersed among agents then Walrasian prices are signals, possibly noisy, that can inform an agent's trading. Models of 'temporary equilibrium' envision a succession of markets, in each of which prices convey information about future trading opportunities. 'Rational expectations' models assume that each agent maximizes an expected utility conditioned on both his private information and the informational content of prices. In simple cases, prices are sufficient statistics that swamp an agent's private information, whereas in complex real economies the informational content of prices may be elusive; nevertheless, markets are affected by interferences from prices (e.g. indices of stock and wholesale prices) and various models attempt to include these features realistically. Conversely, responses of prices to events and disclosures by firms are studied empirically.

The privacy of each agent's information about his preferences and endowment affects the realized gains and terms of trade. Many procedures require that the relative prices of 'qualities' provide incentives for self-selection. An example is a product line comprised of imperfect substitutes, in which price increments for successive quality increments induce customers to select according to their preferences. Several forms of discrimination in which prices depend on the quality (e.g. the time, location, priority or other circumstances of delivery) or, if resale is prevented, the quantity purchased, operate similarly.

Absence of the relevant contingent contracts is implicitly a prime source of inefficiencies and distributional effects. Trading may fail if adverse selection precludes effective signalling about product quality: without quality assurances or warranties, each price at which some quality can be supplied attracts sellers offering lesser qualities. Investments in signals, possibly unproductive ones, that are more costly for sellers supplying inferior qualities induce signal-dependent schedules in which the price paid depends on the signal offered. For example, to signal his ability a worker may over-invest in education or work in a job for which he would be underqualified on efficiency grounds. If buyers make repeat purchases based on the quality experienced from trying a product, then the initial price itself, or even dissipative expenditures such as uninformative advertising, can be signals used by the seller to induce initial purchases.

Principal–agent relationships in which a risk-averse agent has superior information and his actions cannot be monitored completely by the principal require complex contracts. For example, in a repeated context with perfect capital markets and imperfect insurance, the optimal contract provides the agent with a different reward for each measurable output, and the total remuneration is the accumulated sum of these rewards. Contracting is generally affected severely by limited observation of contingencies (either events or actions relevant to incentives) and in asymmetric relationships nonlinear pricing is often optimal.

Insurance premia may vary with coverage, for example, to counter the effects of adverse selection or moral hazard.

Labour markets are replete with complex incentives and forms of contracting, partly because workers cannot contract to sell labour forward and partly because labour contracts substitute for imperfect loan markets and missing insurance markets (e.g. against the risk of declining productivity). Workers may have superior information about their abilities, technical data, or effort and actions taken; and firms may have superior information about conditions affecting the marginal product of labour. Incentives for immediate productivity may be affected by conditioning estimates of ability on current output, or by procedures selecting workers for promotion to jobs where the impact of ability is multiplied by greater responsibilities. The complexity of the resulting incentives and contracts reflects the multiple effects of incomplete markets and imperfect monitoring.

In the context of trading rules that specify price determination explicitly, analyses of agents' strategic behaviour emphasize the role of private information. The trading rule and typically the probability distribution of agents' privately known attributes are assumed to be common knowledge; consequently, formulations pose games of incomplete information. An example is a sealed-bid auction in which the seller awards an item to the bidder submitting the highest price: suppose that each bidder observes a sample, independently and identically distributed (i.i.d.) conditional on the unknown value of the item. With equilibrium bidding strategies, as the number of bidders increases the maximal bid converges in probability to the expectation of the value conditional on knowing the maximum of all the samples; for the common distributions this implies convergence to the underlying value. Alternative auction rules are preferred by the seller according to the extent that the procedures dilute the informational advantages of bidders (e.g. progressive oral bidding has this effect) and exploit any risk aversion. Rules can be constructed that maximize the seller's expected revenue: if bidders' valuations are i.i.d., then for the common distributions awarding the item to the highest bidder at the first or second highest price is optimal, subject to an optimal reservation price set by the seller. In such a second-price or oral progressive auction with no reservation price, bidders offer their valuations, so the price is Walrasian.

Another example is a double auction, used in the London gold and Japanese stock markets, in which multiple buyers and sellers submit bid and ask prices and then a clearing price is selected from the interval obtained by intersecting the resulting demand and supply schedules. For a restricted class of models, requiring sufficiently many buyers and sellers with i.i.d. valuations, a double auction is incentive efficient, in the sense that there is no other trading rule that is sure to be preferred by every agent; also, as the numbers increase the clearing price converges to a Walrasian price.

The effects of privileged information held by some traders have been studied in the context of markets mediated by brokers and specialists, as in most stock markets. The results show that specialists' strategies impose all expected losses from adverse selection on uninformed traders. On the other hand, specialists may profit from knowledge of the order book and immediate access to trading opportunities.

Private information severely affects bargaining. With alternating offers even the simplest examples have many equilibria, plausible criteria can select different equilibria, and a variety of allocations are possible. In most equilibria, delay in making a serious offer (one that has some chance of acceptance) is a signal that a seller's valuation is not low or a buyer's is not high; or the offers made limit the inferences the other party can make about one's valuation. When both valuations are privately known, signalling must occur in some form to establish that gains from trade exist. Typically all gains from trade are realized eventually, but significant delay costs are incurred.

In a special case, a seller with a commonly known valuation repeatedly offers prices to a buyer with a privately known valuation: assume that the buyer's strategy is a stationary one that accepts the first offer less than a reservation price, depending on his valuation. As mentioned previously for the monopoly context, as the period between offers shrinks the seller's offers decline to a price no more than the least possible buyer's valuation and trade occurs quickly: the buyer captures most of the gains. Even with alternating offers, the buyer avoids serious offers if his valuation is high and the periods short. Thus, impatience, frequent offers, and asymmetric information combine to skew the terms of trade in favour of the informed party.

The premier instance of exchange is the commodity trading 'pit' in which traders around a ring call out bid and ask prices or accept others' offers. These markets operate essentially as multilateral versions of bargaining but with endogenous matching of buyers and sellers: delay in making or accepting a serious offer can again be a signal about a trader's valuation, but with the added feature that 'competitive pressure' is a source of impatience. That is, a trader who delays incurs a risk that a favourable opportunity is usurped by a competing trader. These markets have been studied experimentally with striking results: typically most gains from trade are realized, at prices eventually approximating a Walrasian clearing price, especially if the subjects bring experience from prior replications. However, if 'rational expectations' features are added, subjects may fail to make the required inferences from information revealed by offers and transactions.

Trading rules can be designed to maximize the expected realized gains from trade, using the 'revelation principle'. Each trading rule and associated equilibrium strategies induce a 'direct revelation game' whose trading rule is a composition of the original trading rule and its strategies; in equilibrium each agent has an incentive to report accurately his privately known valuation. In the case that a buyer and a seller have valuations drawn independently according to a uniform distribution, the optimal revelation rule is equivalent to a double auction in which trade occurs if the buyer's bid exceeds the seller's offer, and the price used is halfway between these. More generally, with many buyers and sellers and an optimal rule, the expected unrealized gains from trade declines quickly as the numbers of buyers and sellers increase. Such static models depend, however, on the presumption that subsequent trading opportunities are excluded.

Enforceable contracts facilitate exchange, and most theories depend on them, but they are not entirely essential. Important in practice are 'implicit contracts' that are not enforceable except via threats of discontinuing the relationship after the first betrayal. Similarly, in an infinitely repeated situation, if a seller chooses a product's quality (say, high or low) and price before sale, and a buyer observes the quality only after purchasing, then the buyer's strategy of being willing to pay currently only the price associated with the previously supplied quality suffices to induce continual high quality.

Studies of exchange without enforceable contracts focus on the Prisoner's Dilemma game: both parties can gain from exchange but each has an incentive to defect from his half of the agreement. In any finite repetition of this game with complete information the equilibrium strategies predict no agreements, since each expects the other to defect. Infinite repetitions can sustain agreements enforced by threats of refusal to cooperate later. With incomplete information, reputational effects can sustain agreements until near the end. For example, if one party thinks the other might automatically reciprocate cooperation, then he has an incentive to cooperate until first betrayed, and the other has an incentive to reciprocate until defection becomes attractive near the end. Reputations are important also in competitive battles among firms with private cost information: wars of attrition select the efficient survivors.

Continuing studies of exchange are likely to rely on game-theoretic methods. This approach is useful to study strategic behaviour in dynamic contexts; to elaborate the roles of private information, impatience, risk aversion and other features of agents' preferences and endowments; to describe the consequences of incomplete markets and contracting limited by monitoring and enforcement costs; and to establish the efficiency properties of the common trading rules. It also integrates theories of exchange with theories of product differentiation, discriminatory pricing and other strategic behaviour by producers. Technically, the game-theoretic approach enables a transition from theories of a large economy with a specified distribution of agents' attributes, to theories of an economy with few agents having private information but commonly known probability assessments; further realism may depend on reducing the assumed common knowledge and developing better formulations of competition among large firms. Grand theories of general economic equilibrium incorporating all these realistic aspects are unlikely until the foundations are established.

In sum, the Walrasian model remains a paradigm for efficient exchange under 'perfect' competition in which equality of demand and supply is the primary determinant of the terms of trade. Further analysis of agents' strategic behaviour with private information and market power elaborates the causes of incomplete or imperfectly competitive markets that impede efficiency, and it delineates the fine details of endogenous product differentiation, contracting and price formation essential to the application of the Walrasian model.

245

BIBLIOGRAPHY

Arrow, K.J. and Debreu, G. 1954. Existence of an equilibrium for a competitive economy. *Econometrica* 22, 265–90.

Arrow, K.J. and Hahn, F.H. 1971. *General Competitive Analysis*. San Francisco: Holden-Day.

Aumann, R.J. 1964. Markets with a continuum of traders. *Econometrica* 32, 39–50.

Debreu, G. 1959. *Theory of Value*. New York: John Wiley & Sons.

Debreu, G. 1970. Economies with a finite set of equilibria. *Econometrica* 38, 387–92.

Debreu, G. and Scarf, H. 1963. A limit theorem on the core of an economy. *International Economic Review* 4, 235–46.

Gresik, T. and Satterthwaite, M.A. 1984. The rate at which a simple market becomes efficient as the number of traders increases: an asymptotic result for optimal trading mechanisms. Discussion Paper 641, Northwestern University; *Journal of Economic Theory* (1987).

Grossman, S.J. and Perry, M. 1986. Sequential bargaining under asymmetric information. *Journal of Economic Theory* 39, 120–54.

Gul, F., Sonnenschein, H. and Wilson, R.B. 1986. Foundations of dynamic monopoly and the Coase conjecture. *Journal of Economic Theory* 39, 155–90.

Hildenbrand, W. 1974. *Core and Equilibria of a Large Economy*. Princeton: Princeton University Press.

Hölmstrom, B.R. and Milgrom, P.R. 1986. Aggregation and linearity in the provision of intertemporal incentives. Report Series D, No. 5, School of Organization and Management, Yale University.

Hölmstrom, B.R. and Myerson, R.B. 1983. Efficient and durable decision rules with incomplete information. *Econometrica* 51, 1799–820.

Kreps, D.M., Milgrom, P.R., Roberts, D.J. and Wilson, R.B. 1982. Rational cooperation in the finitely repeated prisoners' dilemma. *Journal of Economic Theory* 27, 245–52.

McKenzie, L. 1959. On the existence of general equilibrium for a competitive market. *Econometrica* 27, 54–71.

Milgrom, P.R. 1979. A convergence theorem for competitive bidding with differential information. *Econometrica* 47, 679–88.

Milgrom, P.R. 1985. The economics of competitive bidding: a selective survey. In *Social Goals and Social Organization*, ed. L. Hurwicz, D. Schmeidler and H. Sonnenschein, Cambridge: Cambridge University Press.

Milgrom, P.R. and Stokey, N. 1982. Information, trade, and common knowledge. *Journal of Economic Theory* 26, 17–27.

Myerson, R.B. and Satterthwaite, M.A. 1983. Efficient mechanisms for bilateral trading. *Journal of Economic Theory* 29, 265–81.

Radner, R. 1972. Existence of equilibrium of plans, prices and price expectations in a sequence of markets. *Econometrica* 40, 289–303.

Roberts, D.J. and Postlewaite, A. 1976. The incentives for price-taking behavior in large exchange economies. *Econometrica* 44, 115–28.

Roberts, D.J. and Sonnenschein, H. 1977. On the foundations of the theory of monopolistic competition. *Econometrica* 45, 101–13.

Rubinstein, A. 1982. Perfect equilibrium in a bargaining model. *Econometrica* 50, 97–109.

Scarf, H. (with T. Hansen.) 1973. *The Computation of Economic Equilibria*. New Haven: Yale University Press.

Schmeidler, D. 1980. Walrasian analysis via strategic outcome functions. *Econometrica* 48, 1585–93.

Schmeidler, D. and Vind, K. 1972. Fair net trades. *Econometrica* 40, 637–42.

Smith, V. 1982. Microeconomic systems as experimental science. *American Economic Review* 72, 923–55.

Sonnenschein, H. 1972. Market excess demand functions. *Econometrica* 40, 549–63.

Sonnenschein, H. 1974. An axiomatic characterization of the price mechanism. *Econometrica* 42, 425–34.

Spence, A.M. 1973. *Market Signalling: Information Transfer in Hiring and Related Processes.* Cambridge, Mass.: Harvard University Press.

Wilson, R.B. 1985. Incentive efficiency of double auctions. *Econometrica* 53, 1101–16.

Family

GARY S. BECKER

In virtually every known society – including ancient, primitive, developing, and developed societies – families have been a major force in the production and distribution of goods and services. They have been especially important in the production, care and development of children, in the production of food, in protecting against illness and other hazards, and in guaranteeing the reputation of members. Moreover, parents have frequently displayed a degree of self-sacrifice for children and each other that is testimony to the heroic nature of men and women.

Of course, families have changed radically over time. The detailed kinship relations in primitive societies traced by anthropologists contrast with the predominance of nuclear families in modern societies, where cousins often hardly know each other, let alone interact in production and distribution. The obligation in many societies to care for and maintain elderly parents is largely absent in modern societies, where the elderly either live alone or in nursing homes.

Nevertheless, families are still much less prominent in economic analysis than in reality. Although the major economists have claimed that families are a foundation of economic life, neither Marshall's *Principles of Economics*, Mill's *Principles of Political Economy*, Smith's *Wealth of Nations* nor any of the other great works in economics have made more than casual remarks about the operation of families.

One significant exception is Malthus's model of population growth. Malthus was concerned with the relation between fertility, family earnings, and age at marriage, and he argued that when economic circumstances are less favourable couples usually do (or should) marry later. However, this important insight (see Wrigley and Schofield, 1981, for evidence that prior to the 19th century, marriage rates in England did increase when earnings rose) had no cumulative effect on the treatment of the family by economists.

During the last 40 years, economists have finally begun to analyse family behaviour in a systematic way. No aspect of family life now escapes interpretation with the calculus of rational choice. This includes such esoteric subjects as why some contraceptive techniques are preferred to others, and why polygamy declined, as well as more 'traditional' subjects such as what determines age at marriage, number of children, the amount invested in the human capital of children, and the amount spent by children on the care of elderly parents. This essay sets out the 'economic approach' to various aspects of family behaviour. Detailed discussions of particular aspects can be found in the bibliography.

I FERTILITY. Let us start with the Malthusian problem: how is the number of children, or fertility, of a typical family determined? Crucial to any discussion is the recognition, taken for granted by Malthus, that men and women strongly prefer their own children to children produced by others. This preference to produce one's children eventually helped stimulate economists to recognize that families, and households more generally, are important producers as well as consumers.

The desire for own children means that the number of children in a family is affected by supply conditions. Supply is determined by knowledge of birth control techniques, and by the capacity to produce children, as related to age, nutrition, health, and other variables.

The demand side emerges through maximization of the utility of a family that depends on the quantity of children (n) and other commodities (z), as in

$$U = U(n, z). \tag{1}$$

Utility is maximized subject not only to household production functions for children and other commodities, but also to constraints on family resources. Money income is limited by wage rates and the time spent working, and the time available for household production is limited by the total time available. These constraints are shown by the following equations where λ is the marginal utility of family income. The total net cost of rearing a child (Π_n) equals the value of the goods and services that he consumes, plus the value of the time spent on him by family members ($\Sigma w_i(t_{n_i})$), minus his earnings that contribute to family resources.

$$\left. \begin{array}{l} p_n n + p_z z = \sum w_i t_{w_i} + v \\ t_{n_i} + t_{z_i} + t_{w_i} = t \end{array} \right\} \text{ all } i \in f, \tag{2}$$

where t_{w_i} is the hours worked by the ith family member, w_i is his or her hourly wage, v is non-wage family income, t_{n_i} and t_{z_i} are the time allocated to children and other commodities by the ith member, and t is the total time available per year or other time unit.

By substituting the time constraints into the income constraint, one derives the family's full income (S):

$$\left(p_n + \sum w_i t_{n_i} \right) n + \left(p_z + \sum w_i t_{z_i} \right) Z = \sum w_i t + v = S,$$

$$\Pi_n n + \Pi_z Z = S. \tag{3}$$

If utility is maximized subject to full income, the usual first order conditions follow:

$$\frac{\partial U}{\partial n} = \lambda \Pi_n, \tag{4}$$

and

$$\frac{\partial U}{\partial Z} = \lambda \Pi_z. \tag{5}$$

The basic theorem of demand states that an increase in the relative price of a good reduces the demand for that good when real income is held constant. If the qualification about income is ignored, then, in particular, an increase in the relative price of children would reduce the children desired by a family. The net cost of children is reduced when opportunities for child labour are readily available, as in traditional agriculture. This implies that children are more valuable in traditional agriculture than in either cities or modern agriculture, and explains why fertility has been higher in traditional agriculture (see the evidence in Jaffe, 1940; Gardner, 1973).

Production and rearing of children have usually involved a sizeable commitment of the time of mothers, and sometimes also that of close female relatives, because children tend to be more time intensive than other commodities, especially in mother's time (i.e. in equation (3), $p_n/\Pi_n < p_z/\Pi_z$). Consequently, a rise in the value of mother's time would reduce the demand for children by raising the relative cost of children. In many empirical studies for primitive, developing, and developed societies, the number of children has been found to be negatively related to vaious measures of the value of mother's time (see e.g. Mincer, 1962; Locay, 1987).

Women with children have an incentive to engage in activities that are complementary to child care, including work in a family business based at home, and sewing or weaving at home for pay. Similarly, women who are involved in complementary activities are encouraged to have children because children do not make such large demands on their time. This explains why women on dairy farms have more children than women on grain farms: dairy farming inhibits off-farm work because that is not complementary with children.

During the past one hundred years, fertility has declined by a remarkable amount in all Western countries; as one example, married women in the US now average a little over two live births compared with about five-and-a-half live births in 1880 (see US Bureau of the Census, 1977). Economic development raised the relative cost of children because the value of parents' time increased, agriculture declined, and child labour became less useful in modern farming. Moreover, parents substituted away from number of children toward expenditures on each child as human capital became more important not only in agriculture, but everywhere in the technologically advanced economies of the 20th century (for a further discussion, see Becker, 1981, ch. 5).

II 'QUALITY' OF CHILDREN. The economic approach contributes in an important way to understanding fertility by its emphasis on the 'quality' of children. Quality refers to characteristics of children that enter the utility functions of parents, and has been measured empirically by the education, health, earnings, or wealth of children. Although luck, genetic inheritance, government expenditures and other events outside the control of a family help determine child quality, it also depends on decisions by parents and other relatives.

The quality and quantity of children interact not because they are especially close substitutes in the utility function of parents, but because the true (or shadow) price of quantity is partly determined by quality, and vice versa. To show this, write the utility function in equation (1) as

$$U = U(n, q, Z), \tag{6}$$

where q is the quality of children. Also write the family budget equation in equation (3) as

$$\Pi_n n + \Pi_q q + \Pi_c nq + \Pi_z Z = S, \tag{7}$$

where Π_n is the fixed cost of each child, Π_q is the fixed cost of a unit of quality, and Π_c is the variable cost of children.

By maximizing utility subject to the family income constraint, one derives the following first order conditions:

$$\frac{\partial U}{\partial n} = \lambda(\Pi_n + \Pi_c q) = \lambda \Pi_n^*, \tag{8}$$

$$\frac{\partial U}{\partial q} = \lambda(\Pi_q + \Pi_c n) = \lambda \Pi_q^*, \tag{9}$$

$$\frac{\partial U}{\partial Z} = \lambda \Pi_z. \tag{10}$$

Quantity and quality interact because the shadow price of quantity (Π_n^*) is positively related to the quality of children, and the shadow price of quality (Π_q^*) is positively related to the quantity of children.

To illustrate the nature of this interaction, consider a rise in the fixed cost of quantity (Π_n) that raises the shadow price of quantity (Π_n^*), and thereby reduces the demand for quantity. A reduction in quantity, however, lowers the shadow price of quality (Π_q^*), which induces an increase in quality. But the increase in quality, in turn, raises further the shadow price of quantity, which reduces further the quantity of children, which induces a further increase in quality, and so on until a new equilibrium is reached. Therefore, a modest increase in the fixed cost of quantity could greatly reduce the quantity of children, and greatly increase their quality, *even when quantity and quality are not good substitutes in the utility function.*

The interaction between quantity and quality can explain why large declines in fertility are usually associated with large increases in the education, health, and other measures of the quality of children (see the evidence in Becker, 1981, ch. 5). It also explains why quantity and quality are often negatively related among families: evidence for many countries indicates that years of schooling and the health of children tend to be negatively related to the number of their siblings (see e.g. De Tray, 1973; Blake, 1981).

The influence of parents on the quality of their children links family background to the achievements of children, and hence links family background to inequality of opportunity and intergenerational mobility. Sociologists have dominated discussions of intergenerational mobility, but in recent years economists have emphasized that the relation between the occupations, earnings, and wealths of parents and children depends on decisions by parents to spend time, money and energy on children. Economists have used the concepts of investment in human capital and bequests of nonhuman wealth to model the transmission of earnings and wealth from parents and children (see e.g. Conlisk, 1974; Loury, 1981; Becker and Tomes, 1986). These models show that the relation between, say, the earnings of parents and children, depends not only on biological and cultural endowments 'inherited' from parents, but also on the interaction between these endowments, government expenditures on children, and investments by parents in the education and other human capital of their children.

III ALTRUISM IN THE FAMILY. I have followed the agnostic attitude of economists to the formation of preferences, and have not specified how quality of children is measured. One analytically tractable and plausible assumption is that parents are altruistic toward their children. By 'altruistic' is meant that the utility of parents depends on the unity of children, as in

$$U_p = U(z_p, U_1, \ldots, U_n), \tag{11}$$

where z is the consumption of parents, and $U_i, i = 1, \ldots, n$ is the utility of the ith child.

Economists have generally explained market transactions with the assumption that individuals are selfish. In Smith's famous words,

> It is not from the benevolence of the butcher, the brewer, or the baker, that we expect our dinner, but from their regard to their own interest. We address ourselves, not to their humanity but to their self-love, and never talk of our own necessities but of their advantages.

252

The assumption of selfishness in market transactions has been very powerful, but will not do when trying to understand families. Indeed, the main characteristic that distinguishes family households from firms and other organizations is that allocations within families are largely determined by altruism and related obligations, whereas allocations within firms are largely determined by implicit or explicit contracts. Since families compete with governments for control over resources, totalitarian governments have often reached for the loyalties of their subjects by attacking family traditions and the strong loyalties within families.

The preference for *own* children mentioned earlier suggests special feelings toward one's children. Sacrifices by parents to help children, and vice versa, and the love that frequently binds husbands and wives to each other, are indicative of the highly personal relations within families that are not common in other organizations (see also Ben-Porath, 1980; Pollak, 1985).

Although altruism is a major integrating force within families, the systematic analysis of altruism is recent, and many of its effects have not yet been determined. One significant result has been called (perhaps infelicitously) the Rotten Kid theorem, and explains the coordination of decisions among members when altruism is limited. In particular, if one member of a family were sufficiently altruistic toward other members to spend time or money on each of them, they would have an incentive to consider the welfare of the family as a whole, *even when they are completely selfish.*

The proof of this theorem is simplest when the utility of an altruist (called the 'head') depends on the combined resources of all family members. Consider a single good (x) consumed by all members: the head and n beneficiaries (not only children but possibly also a spouse and other relatives). The head's utility function can be written as

$$U_h = U(x_h, x_1, \ldots, x_n). \tag{12}$$

The budget equation would be

$$x_h + \sum_{i=h}^{h} g_i = I_h, \tag{13}$$

where I_h is the head's income, g_i is the gift to the ith beneficiary, and the price of x is set at unity. With no transactions costs, each dollar contributed would be received by a beneficiary, so that

$$x_i = I_i + g_i, \tag{14}$$

where I_i is the income of the ith beneficiary. By substitution into equation (13),

$$x_h + \sum x_i = I_h + \sum I_i = S_h. \tag{15}$$

The head can then be said to maximize the utility in (12), subject to family income (S_h).

To illustrate the theorem, consider a parent who is altruistic toward her two children, Tom and Jane, and spends, say, $200 on each. Suppose Tom can take

an action that benefits him by \$50, but would harm Jane by \$100. A selfish
Tom would appear to take that action if his responsibility for the changed
circumstances of Jane were to go undetected (and hence not punished). However,
the head's utility would be reduced by Tom's action because family income would
be reduced by \$50. If altruism is a 'superior good', the head will reduce the utility
of each beneficiary when her own utility is reduced. Therefore, should Tom take
this action, she would reduce her gift to him from \$200 to less than \$150, and
raise her gift to Jane to less than \$300. As a result, Tom would be made worse
off by his actions.

Consequently, a selfish Tom who anticipates correctly the response from his
parent will not take this action, even though the parent may not be trying to
'punish' Tom because she may not know that Tom is the source of the loss to
Jane and the gain to herself. This theorem requires only that the head know the
outcomes for both Tom and Jane and has the 'last word' (this term is due to
Hirshleifer, 1977).

The head has the 'last word' when gifts depend (perhaps only indirectly) on
the actions of beneficiaries. In particular, if gifts to the ith beneficiary depend
both on his income and on family income, as in

$$g_i = \psi_i(S_h) - I_i, \quad \text{with} \quad \frac{\mathrm{d}\psi_i}{\mathrm{d}S_h} > 0, \tag{16}$$

then by substitution into equation (14),

$$x_i = I_i + g_i = \psi_i(S_h). \tag{17}$$

The head would then have the 'last word' because x_i would be maximized by
maximizing S_h; for further discussion of the Rotten Kid theorem, see Becker
(1981, ch. 5), Hirshleifer (1977), and Pollak (1985).

Although this theorem is applicable even when beneficiaries are envious of
each other or of the head, it does not rule out conflict in families with altruistic
heads. Sibling rivalry, for example, is to be expected when children are selfish
because they each want larger gifts from the head, and each would try to convince
the head of his or her merits. Conflict also arises when several members are
altruistic to the same beneficiaries, but not to each other. For example, if parents
are altruistic to their children but not to each other, each benefits when the other
spends more on the children. Married parents might readily work out an
agreement to share the burden, but divorced parents have more serious conflict.
Noncustodial parents (usually fathers) fall behind in their child support payments
partly to shift the burden of support to custodial parents (see the discussion in
Weiss and Willis, 1985).

Altruism provides many other insights into the behaviour of families. For
example, an efficient division of labour is possible in altruistic families without
the usual principal–agent conflict because selfish as well as altruistic members
consider the interests of other members. Or contrary to some opinion, bequests
and gifts to children are not perfect substitutes even in altruistic families.

Bequests not only transfer resources to children but also give parents the last word, which induces children to take account of the interests of elderly parents (see Becker, 1981, ch. 5; and also Bernheim, Schleiffer and Summers, 1986). Moreover, if public debt or social security were financed by taxes on succeeding generations that are anticipated by altruistic parents who make bequests, they would raise their bequests to offset the higher taxes paid by their children. Such compensatory reactions negate the effect of debt or social security on consumption and savings (see the detailed analysis in Barro, 1974).

IV THE SEXUAL DIVISION OF LABOUR. A sharp division of labour in the tasks performed by men and women is found in essentially all societies. Women have had primary responsibility for child care, and men have had primary responsibility for hunting and military activity; even when both men and women engaged in agriculture, trade, or other market activities, they generally performed different tasks (see the discussion in Boserup, 1970).

Substantial division of labour is to be expected in families, not only because altruism reduces incentive to shirk and cheat (see section III), but also because of increasing returns from investments in specific human capital, such as skills that are especially useful in child rearing or in market activities. Specific human capital induces specialization because investment costs are partially (or entirely) independent of the time spent using the capital. For example, a person would receive a higher return on his medical training when he puts more time into the practice of medicine. Similarly, a family is more efficient when members devote their 'working' time to different activities, and each invests mainly in the capital specific to his or her activities (see Becker, 1981, 1985; for developments of this argument outside families, see Rosen, 1981).

The advantages of a division of labour within families do not alone imply that women do the child rearing and other household tasks. However, the gain from specialized investments implies the traditional sexual division of labour if women have a comparative advantage in child-bearing and child-rearing, or if women suffer discrimination in market activities. Indeed, since a sexual division of labour segregates the activities of men and women, and since segregation is an effective way to avoid discrimination (see Becker, 1981), even small differences in comparative advantage, or a small amount of discrimination against women, can induce a sharp division of labour.

Until recently, the sexual division of labour in Western countries was extreme; for example, in 1890, less than five per cent of married women in the United States were in the labour force. In 1981, by contrast, over 50 per cent even of married women with children under six were in the labour force (see Smith and Ward, 1985). However, the occupations of employed men and women are still quite different, and women still do most of the child rearing and other household chores (see *Journal of Labour Economics*, January 1985).

The large growth in the labour force participation of married women during the 20th century is mainly explained by the economic development that transformed Western economies. Substitution toward market work was induced by the rise in the potential earnings of women (see Mincer, 1962). Moreover, the growth in clerical jobs, and in the services sector generally, gave women more flexibility in combining market work and child rearing (see Goldin, 1983). In addition, the large decline in fertility during this period (see section I) greatly facilitated increased labour force participation by married women. The converse is also true, however, because the rise in participation of women discouraged child-bearing.

V DIVORCE. Since women specialize in child care, they have been economically vulnerable to divorce and the death of their mates. All societies recognized this vulnerability by requiring long-term contracts, called 'marriage', between men and women legally engaged in reproduction. Often in Christian societies these contracts could not be broken except by adultery, abandonment or death. In Islam and Asia they could be broken for other reasons as well, but husbands were required to pay compensation to their wives when they divorced without cause.

The growth of divorce during this century in Western countries has been remarkable. Essentially no divorces were granted in England prior to the 1850s (see Hollingsworth, 1965), whereas now almost 30 per cent of marriages there will terminate by divorce, and the fraction is even larger in the United States, Sweden and some other Western countries (see US Bureau of the Census, 1977). What accounts for this huge growth in divorce over a relatively short period of time?

The utility-maximizing rational choice perspective implies that a person wants to divorce if the utility expected from remaining married is below the utility expected from divorce, where the latter is affected by the prospects for remarriage; indeed, most persons divorcing in Western countries now do remarry eventually (see e.g. Becker, Landes and Michael, 1977). This simple criterion is not entirely tautological because several determinants of the gain from remaining married can be evaluated.

Some persons become disappointed because their mates turn out to be less desirable than originally anticipated. That new information is an important source of divorce is suggested by the large fraction occurring during the first few years of marriage. Although disappointment is likely to be involved in most divorces, the large growth in divorce rates, especially the acceleration during the last 20 years, is not to be explained by any sudden deterioration in the quality of information. Instead, we look to forces that reduced the advantages from remaining in an imperfect marriage.

The strong decline in fertility over time discouraged divorce because the advantages from staying married are greater when young children are present. Conversely, fertility declined partly because divorce became more likely since married couples are less likely to have children when they anticipate a divorce (see Becker, Landes and Michael, 1977, for supporting evidence). The rise in the labour force participation of married women also lowered the gain from remaining married because the sexual division of labour was reduced, and women became more independent financially. At the same time, the labour force participation of married women increased when divorce became more likely since married women want to acquire skills that would raise their incomes if they must support themselves after a divorce.

Legislation certainly eased the legal obstacles to divorce, but empirical investigations have not found significant permanent effects on the divorce rate (see e.g. Peters, 1983). Moreover, economic analysis suggests that even no-fault divorce and other radical changes in divorce legislation would not significantly affect the rate of divorce because bargaining between husbands and wives about the terms of staying married or divorcing offsets even sharp changes in divorce laws.

To show this, let income be I_h^d and I_w^d respectively, if h and w decide to divorce, and I_h^m and I_w^m, respectively, if they remain married. The budget equation is

$$x_h^d + x_w^d = I_h^d + I_w^d = I^d \tag{18}$$

when divorced, and

$$x_h^d + x_w^m = I_h^m + I_w^m = I^m \tag{19}$$

when married. I suggest that the decision to divorce is largely independent of divorce laws, and depends basically on whether $I^d \gtreqless I^m$, because both h and w can be made better off by divorce when $I^d > I^m$ and by remaining married when $I^m > I^d$.

Consider, for example, a comparison between unilateral or no-fault divorce, and divorce only by mutual consent. Assume that the husband appears to gain from divorce ($I_h^d > I_h^m$), but the apparent loss to the wife is greater, so that $I^d < I^m$. If divorce were unilateral, he might be tempted to seek a divorce even when she would be greatly harmed. However, she could change his mind by offering a bribe (b_h) that would make both of them better off by staying married:

$$x_h^m + b_h > I_h^d, \quad \text{and} \quad I_w^m - b_h > I^d. \tag{20}$$

This bribe is feasible because $x_h^m + x_w^m = I^m > I^d$. He would then prefer to remain married, even if he could divorce without her consent. Note that they would also decide to remain married if divorce required mutual consent because at least one of them must be made worse off by divorce.

Divorce rates have been affected less by legislation that has regulated the conditions for divorce than by legislation that has affected the gains from divorce. For example, aid to mothers with dependent children and negative income taxes encourage divorce by providing poorer women with child support and 'alimony' (see Hannan, Tuma and Groeneveld, 1977).

VI MARRIAGE. Marriages can be said to take place in a 'market' that 'assigns' men and women to each other or to remain single until better opportunities come along. An optimal assignment in an efficient market with utility-maximizing participants has the property that persons not assigned to each other could not be made better off by marrying each other.

In all societies, couples tend to be of similar family background and religion, and are positively sorted by education, height, age and many other variables. The theory of assignments in efficient markets explains positive assortative mating by complementarity, or 'superadditivity', in household production between the traits of husbands and wives. Efficient assignments also partly explain altruism between husbands and wives: persons 'in love' are likely to marry because, at the detached level of formal analysis, love can be considered one source of 'complementarity'.

Associated with optimal assignments are imputations that determine the division of incomes or utilities in each marriage. Equilibrium incomes have the property that

$$I_{ii}^m + I_{ii}^f = I_{ii},\qquad(21)$$

and

$$I_{ii}^m + I_{ij}^f \geqslant I_{ij},\qquad i \neq j,\qquad(22)$$

where I_{ij} is the output from a marriage of the ith man (m_i) to the jth woman (f_j), and I_{ii}^m and I_{jj}^f are the incomes of m_i and f_j, respectively. The inequality in equation (22) indicates that $\{ii\}$ is an optimal assignment because m_i and f_j, $j \neq i$, could not be made better off by marrying each other instead of their assigned mates (f_i and m_j, respectively). Equilibrium incomes include dowries, bride prices, leisure and 'power' (further discussion can be found in Becker, 1974, 1981; the analysis of optimal assignments in Gale and Shapley, 1962, and Roth, 1984, is less relevant to marriage because equilibrium prices – i.e. incomes – are not considered).

Many of the forces in recent decades that reduce the gain from remaining married (see section V) have also raised the gain from delaying first marriage and remarriage. These include the decline in fertility and the rise in labour force participation of married women. The reduced incentive to marry in Western societies is evident from the rapid increase in the number of couples living together without marriage, and in the number of births to unmarried women. Nevertheless, even in Scandinavia, where the trend toward cohabitation without marriage has probably gone furthest, married persons are still far more likely to remain together and to produce children than are persons who cohabit without marriage (for Swedish evidence, see Trost, 1975).

VII SUMMARY AND CONCLUDING REMARKS. Families are important producers as well as spenders. Their primary role has been to supply future generations by producing and caring for children, although they also help protect members against ill health, old age, unemployment, and other hazards of life.

Families have relied on altruism, loyalty, and norms to carry out these tasks rather than the contracts found in firms. Altruism and loyalty are concepts that have not been utilized extensively to analyse market transactions, and our understanding of their implications is only beginning. Yet a much more complete understanding is essential before the behaviour and evolution of families can be fully analysed.

Firms and families compete to organize the production and distribution of goods and services, and activities have passed from one to the other as scale economies, principal–agent problems and other forces dictated. Agriculture and many retailing activities have been dominated by family firms that combine production for the market with production for members. Presumably, such hybrid organizations are important when altruism and loyalty are more effective than contracts in organizing market production (see Becker, 1981, ch. 8; Pollak, 1985), and when the production and care of children complements production for the market.

Families in Western countries have changed drastically during the past thirty years; fertility declined below replacement levels, the labour force participation of married women and divorce soared, cohabitation and births to unmarried women became common, many households are now headed by unmarried women with dependent children, a large fraction of the elderly either live alone or in nursing homes, and children from first and second, sometimes even third, marriages frequently share the same household.

Nevertheless, obituaries for the family are decidedly premature. Families are still crucial to the production and rearing of children, and remain important protectors of members against ill health, unemployment, and many other hazards. Although the role of families will evolve further in the future, I am confident that families will continue to have primary responsibility for children, and that altruism and loyalty will continue to bind parents and children.

BIBLIOGRAPHY

Barro, R.J. 1974. Are government bonds net wealth? *Journal of Political Economy* 82(6), November–December, 1095–117.

Becker, G.S. 1974. A theory of marriage: Part II. *Journal of Political Economy* 82(2), Part II, S11–26.

Becker, G.S. 1981. *A Treatise on the Family.* Cambridge, Mass.: Harvard University Press.

Becker, G.S. 1985. Human capital, effort, and the sexual division of labor. *Journal of Labor Economics* 3(1), Part II, 533–58.

Becker, G.S., Landes, E.M., and Michael, R.T. 1977. An economic analysis of marital instability. *Journal of Political Economy* 85(6), December, 1141–87.

Becker, G.S. and Tomes, N. 1986. Human capital and the rise and fall of families. *Journal of Labor Economics* 4(2, Part 2), S1–39.

Ben-Porath, Y. 1980. The F-connection: families, friends, and firms and the organization of exchange. *Population and Development Review* 6(1), 1–30.

Bernheim, B.I., Schleiffer, A. and Summers, L.H. 1986. Bequests as a means of payment. *Journal of Labor Economics* 4(3), Part 2, S151–82.

Blake, J. 1981. Family size and the equality of children. *Demography* 18(4), 421–42.

Boserup, E. 1970. *Woman's Role in Economic Development.* London: Allen & Unwin; New York: St. Martin's Press.

Conlisk, J. 1974. Can equalization of opportunity reduce social mobility? *American Economic Review* 64(1), March, 80–90.

De Tray, D.N. 1973. Child quality and the demand for children. *Journal of Political Economy* 81(2), Part II, March–April, S70–95.

Gale, D. and Shapley, L.S. 1962. College admissions and the stability of marriage. *American Mathematical Monthly* 69(1), January, 9–15.

Gardner, B. 1973. Economics of the size of North Carolina rural families. *Journal of Political Economy* 81(2), Part II, March–April, S99–122.

Goldin, C. 1983. The changing economic role of women: a quantitative approach. *Journal of Interdisciplinary History* 13(4), 707–33.

Hannan, M.T., Tuma, N.B. and Groeneveld, L.P. 1977. Income and marital events: evidence from an income maintenance experiment. *American Journal of Sociology* 82(6), 611–33.

Hirshleifer, J. 1977. Shakespeare vs Becker on altruism: the importance of having the last word. *Journal of Economic Literature* 15(2), 500–502.

Hollingsworth, T.H. 1965. *The Demography of the British Peerage.* Supplement to *Population Studies* 18(2).

Jaffe, A.J. 1940. Differential fertility in the white population in early America. *Journal of Heredity* 31(9).

Locay, L. 1987. *Population Density of the North American Indians.* Cambridge, Mass.: Harvard University Press.

Loury, G.C. 1981. Intergenerational transfers and the distribution of earnings. *Econometrica* 49(4), 843–67.

Malthus, T.R. 1798. *An Essay on the Principles of Population.* Reprinted, London: J.M. Dent, 1958; New York: Modern Library, 1960.

Marshall, A. 1890. *Principles of Economics.* London: Macmillan; 5th edn, New York: Macmillan, 1946.

Mill, J.S. 1848. *Principles of Political Economy, with some of their applications to Social Philosophy.* Reprinted, New York: Colonial Press, 1899.

Mincer, J. 1962. Labor force participation of married women. In *Aspects of Labor Economics,* Princeton: Princeton University Press.

Peters, E. 1983. The impact of state divorce laws on the marital contract: marriage, divorce, and marital property settlements. Discussion Paper No. 83–19. Economics Research Center/NORC.

Pollak, R.A. 1985. A transactions cost approach to families and households. *Journal of Economic Literature* 23(2), 581–608.

Rosen, S. 1981. Specialization and human capital. *Journal of Labor Economics* 1(1), 43–9.

Roth, A. 1984. The evolution of the labor market for medical interns and residents: a case study in game theory. *Journal of Political Economy* 92(6), 991–1016.

Smith, A. 1776. *An Inquiry into the Nature and Causes of the Wealth of Nations.* Reprinted, New York: Modern Library, 1937.

Smith, J.P. and Ward, M.P. 1985. Time series growth in the female labor force. *Journal of Labor Economics* 3(1) Part II, 559–90.

Trost, J. 1975. Married and unmarried cohabitation: the case of Sweden and some comparisons. *Journal of Marriage and the Family* 37(3), 677–82.

US Bureau of the Census. 1977. *Current Population Reports.* Series P-20, No. 308, Fertility of American Women: June, 1976.

Weiss, Y. and Willis, R. 1985. Children as collective goods and divorce settlements. *Journal of Labor Economics* 3(3), 268–92.

Wrigley, E.A. and Schofield, R.S. 1981. *The Population History of England 1541–1871.* Cambridge, Mass.: Harvard University Press.

Financial Intermediaries

JAMES TOBIN

The tangible wealth of a nation consists of its natural resources, its stocks of goods, and its net claims against the rest of the world. The goods include structures, durable equipment of service to consumers or producers, and inventories of finished goods, raw materials and goods in process. A nation's wealth will help to meet its people's future needs and desires; tangible assets do so in a variety of ways, sometimes by yielding directly consumable goods and services, more often by enhancing the power of human effort and intelligence in producing consumable goods and services. There are many intangible forms of the wealth of a nation, notably the skill, knowledge and character of its population and the framework of law, convention and social interaction that sustains cooperation and community.

Some components of a nation's wealth are appropriable; they can be owned by governments, or privately by individuals or other legal entities. Some intangible assets are appropriable, notably by patents and copyrights. In a capitalist society most appropriable wealth is privately owned, more than 80 per cent by value in the United States. Private properties are generally transferable from owner to owner. Markets in these properties, *capital markets*, are a prominent feature of capitalist societies. In the absence of slavery, markets in 'human capital' are quite limited.

A person may be wealthy without owning any of the assets counted in appropriable *national wealth*. Instead, a personal wealth inventory would list paper currency and coin, bank deposits, bonds, stocks, mutual funds, cash values of insurance policies and pension rights. These are paper assets evidencing claims of various kinds against other individuals, companies, institutions or governments. In reckoning personal *net worth*, each person would deduct from the value of his total assets the claims of others against him. In 1984 American households' gross holdings of financial assets amounted to about 75 per cent of their net worth, and their net holdings to about 55 per cent (Federal Reserve, 1984). If the net worths of all economic units of the nation are added up, paper claims

261

and obligations cancel each other. All that remains, if valuations are consistent and the census is complete, is the value of the national wealth.

If the central government is excluded from this aggregation, *private net worth* – the aggregate net worth of individuals and institutions and subordinate governments (included in the 'private' sector because, lacking monetary powers, they have limited capacities to borrow) – will count not only the national-wealth assets they own but also their net claims against the central government. These include coin and currency, their equivalent in central bank deposit liabilities, and interest-bearing Treasury obligations. If these central government debts exceed the value of its real assets, *private net worth* will exceed national wealth. (However, in reckoning their net worth, private agents may subtract something for the future taxes they expect to pay to service the government's debts. Some economists argue that the subtraction is complete, so that public debt does not count in aggregate private wealth (Barro, 1974) while others give reasons why the offset is incomplete (Tobin, 1980). The issue is not crucial for this essay.)

OUTSIDE ASSETS, INSIDE ASSETS AND FINANCIAL MARKETS

Private net worth, then, consists of two parts: privately owned items of national wealth, mostly tangible assets, and government obligations. These *outside* assets are owned by private agents not directly but through the intermediation of a complex network of debts and claims, *inside* assets.

Empirical magnitudes. For the United States at the end of 1984, the value of tangible assets, land and reproducible goods, was estimated at $13.5 trillion, nearly four times the Gross National Product for the year. Of this, $11.2 trillion were privately owned. Adding net claims against the rest of the world and privately owned claims against the federal government gives private net worth of $12.5 trillion, of which only $1.3 trillion represent outside financial assets. The degree of intermediation is indicated by the gross value of financial assets, nearly $14.8 trillion; even if equities in business are regarded as direct titles to real property and excluded from financial assets, the outstanding stock of inside assets is $9.6 trillion. Of these more than half, $5.6 trillion, are claims on financial institutions. The $9.6 million is an underestimate, because many inside financial transactions elude the statisticians. The relative magnitudes of these numbers have changed very little since 1953, when private net worth was $1.27 trillion, gross financial assets $1.35 trillion ($1.05 excluding equities) and GNP was $0.37 trillion (Federal Reserve, 1984).

Raymond Goldsmith, who has studied intermediation throughout a long and distinguished career and knows far more about it than anyone else, has estimated measures of intermediation for many countries over long periods of time (1969, 1985). Here is his own summary:

The creation of a modern financial superstructure, not in its details but in its essentials, was generally accomplished at a fairly early stage of a country's economic development, usually within five to seven decades from the start of modern economic growth. Thus it was essentially completed in most now-developed countries by the end of the 19th century or the eve of World War I, though somewhat earlier in Great Britain. During this period the financial interrelations ratio, the quotient of financial and tangible assets, increased fairly continuously and sharply. Since World War I or the Great Depression, however, the ratio in most of these countries has shown no upward trend, though considerable movements have occurred over shorter periods, such as sharp reductions during inflations; and though significant changes have taken place in the relative importance of the various types of financial institutions and of financial instruments. Among less developed countries, on the other hand, the financial interrelations ratio has increased substantially, particularly in the postwar period, though it generally is still well below the level reached by the now-developed countries early in the 20th century.

Goldsmith finds that a ratio of the order of unity is characteristic of financial maturity, as is illustrated by the figures for the United States given above (1985, pp. 2–3).

Goldsmith finds also that the relative importance of financial institutions, especially non-banks, has trended upwards in most market economies but appears to taper off in mature systems. Institutions typically hold from a quarter to a half of all financial instruments. Ratios around 0.40 were typical in 1978, but there is considerably more variation among countries than in the financial interrelations ratio. The United States, at 0.27, is on the low side, probably because of its many well-organized financial markets (1985, Table 47, p. 136).

The volume of gross financial transactions is mind-boggling. The GNP velocity of the money stock in the United States is 6 or 7 per year; if intermediate as well as final transactions for goods and services are considered, the turnover may be 20 or 30 per year. But demand deposits turn over 500 times a year, 2500 times in New York City banks, indicating that most transactions are financial in nature. The value of stock market transactions alone in the United States is one third of the Gross National Product; an average share of stock changes hands every nineteen months. Gross foreign exchange transactions in United States dollars are estimated to be hundreds of billions of dollars every day. 'Value added' in the financial services industries amounts to 9 per cent of United States GNP (Tobin, 1984).

Outside and inside money. The outside/inside distinction is most frequently applied to money. *Outside money* is the monetary debt of the government and its central bank, currency and central bank deposits, sometimes referred to as 'base' or 'high-powered' money. *Inside money*, 'low-powered', consists of private deposit obligations of other banks and depository institutions in excess of their holdings of outside money assets. Just which kinds of deposit obligations count as 'money' depends on definitions, of which there are several, all somewhat arbitrary. Outside money in the United States amounted to $186 billion at the end of 1983, of which

$36 billion was held as reserves by banks and other depository institutions; the remaining $150 billion was held by other private agents as currency. The total money stock M1, currency in public circulation plus checkable deposits, was $480 billion. Thus inside M1 was $294 billion, more than 60 per cent of the total.

Financial markets, organized and informal. Inside assets and debts wash out in aggregative accounting; one person's asset is another's debt. But for the functioning of the economy, the inside network is of great importance. *Financial markets* allow inside assets and debts to be originated and to be exchanged at will for each other and for outside financial assets. These markets deal in paper contracts and claims. They complement the markets for real properties. Private agents often borrow to buy real property and pledge the property as security; households mortgage new homes, businesses incur debt to acquire stocks of materials or goods-in-process or to purchase structures and equipment. The term *capital markets* covers both financial and property markets. *Money markets* are financial markets in which short-term debts are exchanged for outside money.

Many of the assets traded in financial markets are promises to pay currency in specified amounts at specified future dates, sometimes conditional on future events and circumstances. The currency is not always the local currency; obligations denominated in various national currencies are traded all over the world. Many traded assets are not denominated in any future monetary unit of account: equity shares in corporations, contracts for deliveries of commodities – gold, oil, soy beans, hog bellies. There are various hybrid assets: preferred stock gives holders priority in distributions of company profits up to specified pecuniary limits; convertible debentures combine promises to pay currency with rights to exchange the securities for shares.

Capital markets, including financial markets, take a variety of forms. Some are highly organized auction markets, the leading real-world approximations to the abstract perfect markets of economic theory, where all transactions occurring at any moment in a commodity or security are made at a single price and every agent who wants to buy or sell at that price is accommodated. Such markets exist in shares, bonds, overnight loans of outside money, standard commodities and foreign currency deposits, and in futures contracts and options for most of the same items.

However, many financial and property transactions occur otherwise, in direct negotiations between the parties. Organized open markets require large tradable supplies of precisely defined homogeneous commodities or instruments. Many financial obligations are one of a kind, the promissory note of a local business proprietor, the mortgage on a specific farm or residence. The terms, conditions and collateral are specific to the case. The habit of referring to classes of heterogeneous negotiated transactions as 'markets' is metaphorical, like the use of the term 'labour market' to refer to the decentralized processes by which wages are set and jobs are filled, or 'computer market' to describe the pricing and selling of a host of differentiated products. In these cases the economists' faith is that the outcomes are 'as if' the transaction occurred in perfect organized auction markets.

FINANCIAL ENTERPRISES AND THEIR MARKETS

Financial intermediaries are enterprises in the business of buying and selling financial assets. The accounting balance sheet of a financial intermediary is virtually 100 per cent paper on both sides. The typical financial intermediary owns relatively little real property, just the structures, equipment and materials necessary to its business. The equity of the owners, or the equivalent capital reserve account for mutual, cooperative, nonprofit, or public institutions, is small compared to the enterprises' financial obligations.

Financial intermediaries are major participants in organized financial markets. They take large asset positions in market instruments; their equities and some of their liabilities, certificates of deposit or debt securities, are traded in those markets. They are not just middlemen like dealers and brokers whose main business is to execute transactions for clients.

Financial intermediaries are the principal makers of the informal financial markets discussed above. Banks and savings institutions hold mortgages, commercial loans and consumer credit; their liabilities are mainly checking accounts, savings deposits and certificates of deposit. Insurance companies and pension funds negotiate private placements of corporate bonds and commercial mortgages; their liabilities are contracts with policy-holders and obligations to future retirees. Thus financial intermediaries do much more than participate in organized markets. If financial intermediaries confined themselves to repackaging open market securities for the convenience of their creditors, they would be much less significant actors on the economic scene.

Financial businesses seek customers, both lenders and borrowers, not only by interest rate competition but by differentiating and advertising their 'products'. Financial products are easy to differentiate, by variations in maturities, fees, auxiliary services, office locations and hours of business, and many other features. As might be expected, non-price competition is especially active when prices, in this case interest rates, are fixed by regulation or by tacit or explicit collusion. But the industry is by the heterogeneous nature of its products monopolistically competitive; non-price competition flourishes even when interest rates are free to move. The industry shows symptoms of 'wastes of monopolistic competition'. Retail offices of banks and savings institutions cluster like competing gasoline stations. Much claimed product differentiation is trivial and atmospheric, emphasized and exaggerated in advertising.

Financial intermediaries cultivate long-term relationships with customers. Even in the highly decentralized financial system of the United States, local financial intermediaries have some monopoly power, some clienteles who will stay with them even if their interest rates are somewhat less favourable than those elsewhere. Since much business is bilaterally negotiated, there are ample opportunities for price discrimination. The typical business customer of a bank is both a borrower and a depositor, often simultaneously. The customer 'earns' the right for credit accommodation when he needs it by lending surplus funds to the same bank when he has them. The same reciprocity occurs between credit unions and mutual savings institutions and some of their members. Close ties frequently develop between a financial intermediary and non-financial businesses whose sales depend on availability of credit to their customers, for example between automobile dealers and banks. Likewise, builders and realtors have funded and controlled many savings and loan associations in order to facilitate mortgage lending to home buyers.

Financial intermediaries balance the credit demands they face with their available funds by adjusting not only interest rates but also the other terms of loans. They also engage in quantitative rationing, the degree of stringency varying with the availability and costs of funds to the intermediary. Rationing occurs naturally as a by-product of lending decisions made and negotiated case by case. Most such loans require collateral, and the amount and quality of the collateral can be adjusted both to individual circumstances and to overall market conditions. Borrowers are classified as to riskiness and charged rates that vary with their classification.

United States commercial banks follow the 'prime rate convention'. One or another of the large banks acts as price leader and sets a rate on six-month commercial loans for its prime quality borrowers. If other large banks agree, as is usually the case, they follow, and the rate becomes standard for the whole industry until one of the leading banks decides another change is needed to stay in line with open-market interest rates. Loan customers are rated by the number of half-points above prime at which they will be accommodated. Of course, some applications for credit are just turned away. One mechanism of short-term adjustment to credit market conditions is to stiffen or relax the risk classifications of customers, likewise to deny credit to more or fewer applicants. Similar mechanisms for rationing help to equate demands to supplies of home mortgage finance and consumer credit.

THE FUNCTIONS OF FINANCIAL MARKETS AND INTERMEDIARY INSTITUTIONS

Intermediation, as defined and described above, converts the outside privately owned wealth of the economy into the quite different forms in which its ultimate owners hold their accumulated savings. Financial markets alone accomplish considerable intermediation, just by facilitating the origination and exchange of inside assets. Financial intermediaries greatly extend the process, adding 'markets' that would not exist without them, and participating alone with other agents in other markets, organized or informal.

What economic functions does intermediation in general perform? What do inside markets add to markets in the basic outside assets? What functions does institutional intermediation by financial intermediaries perform beyond those of open markets in financial instruments? Economists characteristically impose on themselves questions like these, which do not seem problematic to lay practitioners. Economists start from the presumption that financial activities are epiphenomena, that they create a veil obscuring to superficial observers an underlying reality which they do not affect. The celebrated Modigliani–Miller theorem (1958), generalized beyond the original intent of the authors, says so. With its help the sophisticated economist can pierce the veil and see that the values of financial assets are just those of the outside assets to which they are ultimately claims, no matter how circuitous the path from the one to the other.

However, economists also understand how the availability of certain markets alters, usually for the better, the outcomes prevailing in their absence. For a primitive illustration, consider the functions of inside loan markets as brilliantly described by Irving Fisher (1930). Each household has an intertemporal utility function in consumptions today and at future times, a sequence of what we now would call dated 'endowments' of consumption, and an individual 'backyard' production function by which consumption less than endowment at any one date can be transformed into consumption above endowment at another date. Absent the possibility of intertemporal trades with others, each household has to do its best on its own; its best will be to equate its marginal rate of substitution in utility between any two dates with its marginal rate of transformation in production between the same dates, with the usual amendments for corner solutions. The gains from trade, i.e., in this case from auction markets in inter-household lending and borrowing, arise from differences among households in those autarkic rates of substitution and transformation. They are qualitatively the same as those from free contemporaneous trade in commodities between agents or nations.

The introduction of consumer loans in this Fisherian model will alter the individual and aggregate paths of consumption and saving. It is not possible to say whether it will raise or lower the aggregate amount of capital, here in the sense of labour endowments in the process of producing future rather than current consumable output. In either case it is likely to be a Pareto-optimal improvement, although even this is not guaranteed *a priori*.

Similar argument suggests several reasons why ultimately savers, lenders and creditors prefer the liabilities of financial intermediaries not only to direct ownership of real property but also to the direct debt and equity issues of investors, borrowers and debtors.

Convenience of denomination. Issuers of securities find it costly to cut their issues into the variety of small and large denominations savers find convenient and commensurate to their means. The financial intermediary can break up large-denomination bonds and loans into amounts convenient to small savers, or combine debtors' obligations into large amounts convenient to the wealthy. Economies of scale and specialization in financial transactions enable financial intermediaries to tailor assets and liabilities to the needs and preferences of both lenders and borrowers. This service is especially valuable for agents on both sides whose needs vary in amount continuously; they like deposit accounts and credit lines whose use they can vary at will on their own initiative.

Risk pooling, reduction and allocation. The risks incident to economic activities take many forms. Some are nation-wide or world-wide – wars and revolutions, shifts in international comparative advantage, government fiscal and monetary policies, prices and supplies of oil and other basic materials. Some are specific to particular enterprises and technologies – the capacity and integrity of managers, the qualities of new products, the local weather. A financial intermediary can specialize in the appraisal of risks, especially specific risks, with expertise in the gathering and interpretation of information costly or unavailable to individual savers. By pooling the funds of its creditors, the financial intermediary can diversify away risks to an extent that the individual creditors cannot, because of the costs of transactions as well as the inconvenience of fixed lumpy denominations.

According to Joseph Schumpeter ([1911] 1934, pp. 72–4), bankers are the gatekeepers – Schumpeter's word is 'ephor' – of capitalist economic development; their strategic function is to screen potential innovators and advance the necessary purchasing power to the most promising. They are the source of purchasing power for investment and innovation, beyond the savings accumulated from past economic development. In practice, the cachet of a banker often enables his customer also to obtain credit from other sources or to float paper in open markets.

Maturity shifting. A financial intermediary typically reconciles differences among borrowers and lenders in the timing of payments. Bank depositors want to commit funds for shorter times than borrowers want to have them. Business borrowers need credit to bridge the time gap between the inputs to profitable production and their output and sales. This source of bank business is formally modelled by Diamond and Dybvig (1983). The bank's scale of operations enables it to stagger the due dates of, say, half-year loans so as to accommodate depositors who want their money back in three months or one month or on demand. The reverse maturity shift may occur in other financial intermediaries. An insurance company or pension fund might invest short term the savings its policy-owners or future pensioners will not claim for many years.

Transforming illiquid assets into liquid liabilities. Liquidity is a matter of degree. A perfectly liquid asset may be defined as one whose full present value can be realized, i.e., turned into purchasing power over goods and services, immediately. Dollar bills are perfectly liquid, and so for practical purposes are demand deposits and other deposits transferable to third parties by check or wire. Liquidity in this sense does not necessarily mean predictability of value. Securities traded on well-organized markets are liquid. Any person selling at a given time will get the same price whether he decided and prepared to sell a month before or on the spur of the moment. But the price itself can vary unpredictably from minute to minute. Contrast a house, neither fully liquid nor predictable in value. Its selling proceeds at this moment are likely to be greater the longer it has been on the market. Consider the six-month promissory note of a small business proprietor known only to his local banker. However sure the payment on the scheduled date, the note may not be marketable at all. If the lender wants to realize its value before maturity, he will have to find a buyer and negotiate. A financial intermediary holds illiquid assets while its liabilities are liquid, and holds assets unpredictable in value while it guarantees the value of its liabilities. This is the traditional business of commercial banks, and the reason for the strong and durable relations of banks and their customers.

SUBSTITUTION OF INSIDE FOR OUTSIDE ASSETS

What determines the aggregate liabilities and assets of financial intermediaries? What determines the gross aggregate of inside assets generated by financial markets in general, including open markets as well as financial intermediaries? How can the empirical regularities found by Goldsmith, cited above, be explained?

Economic theory offers no answers to these questions. The differences among agents that invite mutually beneficial transactions, like those discussed above, offer opportunities for inside markets. Theory can tell us little *a priori* about the size of such differences. Moreover, markets are costly to operate, whether they are organized auction markets in homogeneous instruments or the imperfect 'markets' in heterogeneous contracts in which financial intermediaries are major participants. Society cannot afford all the markets that might exist in the absence of transactions costs and other frictions, and theory has little to say on which will arise and survive.

The macroeconomic consequence of inside markets and financial intermediaries is generally to provide substitutes for outside assets and thus to economize their supplies. That is, the same microeconomic outcomes are achievable with smaller supplies of one or more of the outside assets than in the absence of intermediation. The way in which intermediation mobilizes the surpluses of some agents to finance the deficits of others is the theme of the classic influential work of Gurley and Shaw (1960).

Consider, for example, how commercial banking diminishes the need of business firms for net worth invested in inventories, by channelling the seasonal cash surpluses of some firms to the contemporaneous seasonal deficits of others. Imagine two firms A and B with opposite and complementary seasonal zigzag patterns. A needs $2 in cash at time zero to buy inputs for production in period 1 sold for $2; the pattern repeats in 3, 4,... B needs $2 in cash at time 1 to buy inputs for production in period 2 sold for $2 in period 3, and so on in 4, 5,... In the absence of their commercial bank, A and B each need $2 of net worth to carry on business; from period to period each alternates holding it in cash and in goods-in-process, so between them the two firms are always holding $2 of currency and $2 of inventories. B enters the bank and lends A half the $2 he needs to carry his inventory in period 1; A repays the loan from sales proceeds the next period, 2; the bank now lends $1 to B, ... A and B now need only $1 of currency; each has on average net worth of $1.50 – $2 and $1 alternating; as before they are together always holding $2 of inventories. Moreover, with a steady deposit of $2 from a third party, the bank could finance both businesses completely; they would need no net worth of their own. The example is trivial, but commercial banking proper can be understood as circulation of deposits and loans among businesses and as a revolving fund assembled from other sources and lent to businesses.

As a second primitive example, consider the effects of introducing markets that enable risks to be borne by those households more prepared to take them. Suppose that of two primary outside assets, currency and tangible capital, the return on the latter has the greater variance. Individuals who are risk neutral will hold all their wealth (possibly excepting minimal transactions balances of currency) in capital as long as its expected return exceeds the expected real return on currency. If these more adventurous households are not numerous and wealthy enough to absorb all the capital, the expected return on capital will have to exceed that on currency enough to induce risk-averse wealth-owners to hold the remainder. In this equilibrium the money price of capital and its mean real return are determined so as to allocate the two assets between the two kinds of households. Now suppose that the risk-neutral households can borrow from the risk-averse types, most realistically via financial intermediaries, and that the latter households regard those debts as close substitutes for currency, indeed as inside money if intermediation by financial intermediaries is involved. The inside assets do double duty, providing the services and security of money to those who value them while enabling the more adventurous to hold capital in excess of their own net worth. As a result, the private sector as a whole will want to hold a larger proportion of its wealth in capital at any given expected real return on capital. In equilibrium, the aggregate capital stock will be larger and its expected return, equal to its marginal productivity in a steady state, will be lower than in the absence of intermediation.

Intermediation can diminish the private sector's need not just for outside money but for net worth and tangible capital. These economies generally require financial markets in which financial intermediaries are major participants, because they involve heterogeneous credit instruments and risk pooling. In the absence of home mortgages, consumer credit and personal loans for education, young households would not be able to spend their future wages and salaries until they receive them. Constraints on borrowing against future earnings make the age-weighted average net non-human wealth of the population greater, but the relaxation of such liquidity constraints increases household welfare. Financial intermediaries invest the savings of older and more affluent households in loans to their younger and less wealthy contemporaries; otherwise those savings would go into outside assets. Likewise insurance makes it unnecessary to accumulate savings as precaution against certain risks, for example the living and medical expenses of unusual longevity. It is an all too common fallacy to assume that arrangements that increase aggregate savings and tangible wealth always augment social welfare.

DEPOSIT CREATION AND RESERVE REQUIREMENTS

The substitution of inside money for outside money is the familiar story of deposit creation, in which the banking system turns a dollar of base or 'high-powered' money into several dollars of deposits. The extra dollars are inside or 'low-powered' money. The banks need to hold only a fraction k, set by law or convention or prudence, of their deposit liabilities as reserves in base money. In an equilibrium in which they hold no excess reserves their deposits will be a multiple $1/k$ of their reserves; they will have created $(1 - k)/k$ dollars of substitute money.

A key step in this process is that any bank with excess reserves makes a roughly equal amount of additional loans, crediting the borrowers with deposits. As the borrowers draw checks. these new deposits are transferred to other accounts, most likely in other banks. As deposits move to other banks, so do reserves, dollar for dollar. But now those banks have excess reserves and act in like manner. The process continues until all banks are 'loaned up', i.e. deposits have increased enough so that the initial excess reserves have become reserves that the banks require or desire.

The textbook fable of deposit creation does not do justice to the full macroeconomics of the process. The story is incomplete without explaining how the public is induced to borrow more and to hold more deposits. The borrowers and the depositors are not the same public. No one borrows at interest in order to hold idle deposits. To attract additional borrowers, banks must lower interest rates or relax their collateral requirements or their risk standards. The new borrowers are likely to be businesses that need bank credit to build up inventories of materials or goods in process. The loans lead quickly to additional production and economic activity. Or banks buy securities in the open market, raising their prices and lowering market interest rates. The lower market rates may encourage businesses to float issues of commercial paper, bonds or stocks, but the effects of investment in inventories or plant and equipment are less immediate and less potent than the extension of bank credit to a business otherwise held back by illiquidity. In either case, lower interest rates induce other members of the public, those who indirectly receive the loan disbursements or those who sell securities to banks, to hold additional deposits. They will be acquiring other assets as well, some in banks, some in other financial intermediaries, some in open financial markets. Lower interest rates may also induce banks themselves to hold extra excess reserves.

Interest rates are not the only variables of adjustment. Nominal incomes are rising at the same time, in some mixture of real quantities and prices depending on macroeconomic circumstances. The rise in incomes and economic activities creates new needs for transactions balances of money. Thus the process by which excess reserves are absorbed entails changes in interest rates, real economic activity and prices in some combination. It is possible to describe scenarios in which the entire ultimate adjustment is in one of these variables. Wicksell's cumulative credit expansion, which in the end just raises prices, is a classic example.

Do banks have a unique magic by which asset purchases generate their own financing? Is the magic due to the 'moneyness' of the banks' liabilities? The preceding account indicates it is not magic but reserve requirements. Moreover,

271

a qualitatively similar story could be told if reserve requirements were related to bank assets or non-monetary liabilities and even if banks happened to have no monetary liabilities at all. In the absence of reserve requirements aggregate bank assets and liabilities, relative to the size of the economy, would be naturally limited by public supplies and demands at interest rates that cover banks' costs and normal profits. If, instead of banks, savings institutions specializing in mortgage lending were subject to reserve requirements, their incentives to minimize excess reserves would inspire a story telling how additional mortgage lending brings home savings deposits to match (Tobin, 1963).

RISKS, RUNS AND REGULATIONS

Some financial intermediaries confine themselves to activities that entail virtually no risk either to the institution itself or to its clients. An open-end mutual fund or unit trust holds only fully liquid assets traded continuously in organized markets. It promises the owners of its shares payment on demand at their pro rata net value calculated at the market prices of the underlying assets – no more, no less. The fund can always meet such demands by selling assets it holds. The shareowners pay in one way or another an agreed fee from the services of the fund – the convenience and flexibility of denomination, the bookkeeping, the transactions costs, the diversification, the expertise in choosing assets. The shareowners bear the market risks on the fund's portfolio – no less and, assuming the fund is honest, no more. Government regulations are largely confined to those governing all public security issues, designed to protect buyers from deceptions and insider manipulations. In the United States regulation of this kind is the province of the federal Securities and Exchange Commission.

Most financial intermediaries do take risks. The risks are intrinsic to the functions they serve and to the profit opportunities attracting financial entrepreneurs and investors in their enterprises. For banks and similar financial intermediaries, the principal risk is that depositors may at any time demand payments the institution can meet, if at all, only at extraordinary cost. Many of the assets are illiquid, unmarketable. Others can be liquidated at short notice only at substantial loss. In some cases, bad luck or imprudent management brings insolvency; the institution could never meet its obligations no matter how long its depositors and other creditors wait. In other cases, the problem is just illiquidity; the assets would suffice if they could be held until maturity, until buyers or lenders could be found, or until normal market conditions returned.

Banks and other financial intermediaries hold reserves, in currency or its equivalent, deposits in central banks, or in other liquid forms as precaution against withdrawals by their depositors. For a single bank, the withdrawal is usually a shift of deposits to other banks or financial intermediaries, arising from a negative balance in interbank clearings of checks or other transfers to third parties at the initiative of depositors. For the banking system as a whole, withdrawal is a shift by the public from deposits to currency.

'Withdrawals' may in practice include the exercise of previously agreed borrowing rights. Automatic overdraft privileges are more common in other countries, notably the United Kingdom and British Commonwealth nations, than in the United States. They are becoming more frequent in the United States as an adjunct of bank credit cards. Banks' business loan customers often have explicit or implicit credit lines on which they can draw on demand.

Unless financial intermediaries hold safe liquid assets of predictable value matched in maturities to their liabilities – in particular, currency or equivalent against all their demand obligations – they and their creditors can never be completely protected from withdrawals. The same is true of the banking system as a whole, and of all intermediaries other than simple mutual funds. 'Runs', sudden, massive and contagious withdrawals, are always possible. They destroy prudent and imprudent institutions alike, along with their depositors and creditors. Of course, careful depositors inform themselves about the intermediaries to which they entrust their funds, about their asset portfolios, policies and skills. Their choices among competing depositories provide some discipline, but it can never be enough to rule out disasters. What the most careful depositor cannot foresee is the behaviour of other depositors, and it is rational for the well-informed depositor of a sound bank to withdraw funds if he believes that others are doing so or are about to do so.

Governments generally regulate the activities of banks and other financial intermediaries in greater detail than they do nonfinancial enterprises. The basic motivations for regulation appear to be the following:

It is costly, perhaps impossible, for individual depositors to appraise the soundness and liquidity of financial institutions and to estimate the probabilities of failures even if they could assume that other depositors would do likewise. It is impossible for them to estimate the probabilities of 'runs'. Without regulation, the liabilities of suspect institutions would be valued below par in check collections. Prior to 1866 banks in the United States were allowed to issue notes payable to bearers on demand, surrogates for government currency. The notes circulated at discounts varying with the current reputations of the issuers. A system in which transactions media other than government currency continuously vary in value depending on the issuer is clumsy and costly.

The government has an obligation to provide at low social cost an efficient system of transactions media, and also a menu of secure and convenient assets for citizens who wish to save in the national monetary unit of account. Those transactions media and savings assets can be offered by banks and other financial intermediaries, in a way that retains most of the efficiencies of decentralization and competition, if and only if government imposes some regulations and assumes some residual responsibilities. The government's role takes several forms.

Reserve requirements. An early and obvious intervention was to require banks to hold reserves in designated safe and liquid forms against their obligations, especially their demand liabilities. Left to themselves, without such requirements, some banks might sacrifice prudence for short-term profit. Paradoxically, however, required reserves are not available for meeting withdrawals unless the required ratio is 100 per cent. If the reserve requirement is 10 per cent of deposits, then withdrawal of one dollar from a bank reduces its reserve holdings by one dollar but its reserve requirement by only ten cents. Only excess reserves or other liquid assets are precautions against withdrawals. The legal reserve requirement just shifts the bank's prudential calculation to the size of these secondary reserves. Reserve requirements serve functions quite different from their original motivation. In the systems that use them, notably the United States, they are the fulcrum for central bank control of economy-wide monetary conditions. (They are also an interest-free source of finance of government debt, but in the United States today this amounts to only $45 billion of a total debt to the public of $1700 billion.)

Last-resort lending. Banks and other financial intermediaries facing temporary shortages of reserves and secondary reserves of liquid assets can borrow them from other institutions. In the United States, for example, the well-organized market for 'federal funds' allows banks short of reserves to borrow them overnight from other banks. Or banks can gain reserves by attracting more deposits, offering higher interest rates on them than depositors are getting elsewhere. These ways of correcting reserve positions are not available to troubled banks, suspected of deep-rooted problems of liquidity or solvency or both, for example bad loans. Nor will they meet a system-wide run from liabilities of banks and other financial intermediaries into currency.

Banks in need of reserves can also borrow from the central bank, and much of this borrowing is routine, temporary and seasonal. Massive central bank credit is the last resort of troubled banks which cannot otherwise satisfy the demands of their depositors without forced liquidations of their assets. The government is the ultimate supplier of currency and reserves in aggregate. The primary *raison d'être* of the central bank is to protect the economy from runs into currency. System-wide shortages of currency and reserves can be relieved not only by central bank lending to individual banks but by central bank purchases of securities in the open market. The Federal Reserve's inability or unwillingness – which it was is still debated – to supply the currency bank depositors wanted in the early 1930s led to disastrous panic and epidemic bank failures. No legal or doctrinal obstacles would now stand in the way of such a rescue.

Deposit insurance. Federal insurance of bank deposits in the United States has effectively prevented contagious runs and epidemic failures since its enactment in 1935. Similar insurance applies to deposits in savings institutions. In effect, the federal government assumes a contingent residual liability to pay the insured deposits in full, even if the assets of the financial intermediary are permanently inadequate to do so. The insured institutions are charged premiums for the service, but the fund in which they are accumulated is not and cannot be large enough to eliminate possible calls on the Treasury. Although the guarantees are legally limited to a certain amount, now $100,000, per account, in practice depositors have eventually recovered their full deposits in most cases. Indeed the guarantee seems now to have been extended *de facto* to all deposits, at least in major banks.

Deposit insurance impairs such discipline as surveillance by large depositors might impose on financial intermediaries; instead the task of surveillance falls on the governmental insurance agencies themselves (in the United States the Federal Deposit Insurance Corporation and the Federal Savings and Loan Insurance Corporation) and on other regulatory authorities (the United States Comptroller of the Currency, the Federal Reserve and various state agencies). Insurance transfers some risks from financial intermediary depositors and owners to taxpayers at large, while virtually eliminating risks of runs. Those are risks we generate ourselves; they magnify the unavoidable natural risks of economic life. Insurance is a mutual compact to enable us to refrain from *sauve qui peut* behaviour that can inflict grave damage on us all. Formally, an uninsured system has two equilibria, a good one with mutual confidence and a bad one with runs. Deposit insurance eliminates the bad one (Diamond and Dybvig, 1983).

One hundred per cent reserve deposits would, of course, be perfectly safe – that is, as safe as the national currency – and would not have to be insured. Those deposits would in effect *be* currency, but in a secure and conveniently checkable form. One can imagine a system in which banks and other financial intermediaries offered such accounts, with the reserves behind them segregated from those related to the other business of the institution. That other business would include receiving deposits which required fractional or zero reserves and were insured only partially, if at all. The costs of the 100 per cent reserve deposit accounts would be met by service charges, or by government interest payments on the reserves, justified by the social benefits of a safe and efficient transactions medium. The burden of risk and supervision now placed on the insuring and regulating agencies would be greatly relieved. It is, after all, historical accident that supplies of transactions media in modern economies came to be byproducts of the banking business and vulnerable to its risks.

Government may insure financial intermediaries loans as well as deposits. Insurance of home mortgages in the United States not only has protected the institutions that hold them and their depositors but has converted the insured mortgages into marketable instruments.

Balance sheet supervision. Government surveillance of financial intermediaries limits their freedom of choice of assets and liabilities, in order to limit the risks to depositors and insurers. Standards of adequacy of capital – owners' equity at risk in the case of private corporations, net worth in the case of mutual and other nonprofit forms of organization – are enforced for the same reasons. Periodic examinations check the condition of the institution, the quality of its loans and the accuracy of its accounting statements. The regulators may close an institution if further operation is judged to be damaging to the interests of the depositors and the insurer.

Legislation which regulates financial intermediaries has differentiated them by purpose and function. Commercial banks, savings institutions, home building societies, credit unions and insurance companies are legally organized for different purposes. They are subject to different rules governing the nature of their assets. For example, home building societies – savings and loan associations in the United States – have been required to keep most of their asset portfolios in residential mortgages. Restrictions of this kind mean that when wealth-owners shift funds from one type of financial intermediary to another, they alter relative demands for assets of different kinds. Shifts of deposits from commercial banks to building societies would increase mortgage lending relative to commercial lending. Regulations have also restricted the kinds of liabilities allowed various types of financial intermediary. Until recently in the United States, only banks were permitted to have liabilities payable on demand to third parties by check or wire. Currently deregulation is relaxing specialized restrictions on financial intermediary assets and liabilities and blurring historical distinctions of purpose and function.

Interest ceilings. Government regulations in many countries set ceilings on the interest rates that can be charged on loans and on the rates that can be paid on deposits, both at banks and at other financial intermediaries. In the United States the Banking Act of 1935 prohibited payment of interest on demand deposits. After World War II effective ceilings on savings and time deposits in banks and savings institutions were administratively set, and on occasion changed, by federal agencies. Under legislation of 1980, these regulations are being phased out.

The operating characteristics of a system of financial intermediaries in which interest rates on deposits of various types, as well as on loans, are set by free competition are quite different from those of a system in which financial intermediary rates are subject to legal ceilings or central bank guidance, or set by agreement among a small number of institutions. For example, when rates on deposits are administratively set, funds flow out of financial intermediaries when open market rates rise and return to financial intermediaries when they fall. These processes of 'disintermediation' and 're-intermediation' are diminished when financial intermediary rates are free to move parallel to open market rates. Likewise flows between different financial intermediaries due to administratively set rate differences among them are reduced when they are all free to compete for funds.

A regime with market-determined interest rates on moneys and near-moneys has significantly different macroeconomic characteristics from a regime constrained by ceilings on deposit interest rates. Since the opportunity cost of holding deposits is largely independent of the general level of interest rates, the 'LM' curve is steeper in the unregulated regime. Both central bank operations and exogenous monetary shocks could be expected to have larger effects on nominal income, while fiscal measures and other shocks to aggregate demand for goods and services would have similar effects (Tobin, 1983).

Entry, branching, merging. Entry into regulated financial businesses is generally controlled, as are establishing branches or subsidiaries and merging of existing institutions. In the United States, charters are issued either by the federal government or by state governments, and regulatory powers are also divided. Until recently banks and savings institutions, no matter by whom chartered, were not allowed to operate in more than one state. This rule, combined with various restrictions on branches within states, gave the United States a much larger number of distinct financial enterprises, many of them very small and very local, than is typical in other countries. The prohibition of interstate operations is now being eroded and may be effectively eliminated in the next few years.

Deregulation has been formed by innovations in financial technology that made old regulations either easy hurdles to circumvent or obsolete barriers to efficiency. New opportunities not only are breaking down the walls separating financial intermediaries of different types and specializations. They are also bringing other businesses, both financial and nonfinancial, into activities previously reserved to regulated financial institutions. Mutual funds and brokers offer accounts from which funds can be withdrawn on demand or transferred to third parties by check or wire. National retail chains are becoming financial supermarkets – offering credit cards, various mutual funds, instalment lending and insurance along with their vast menus of consumer goods and services; in effect, they would like to become full-service financial intermediaries. At the same time, the traditional intermediaries are moving, as fast as they can obtain government permission, into lines of business from which they have been excluded. Only time will tell how these commercial and political conflicts are resolved and how the financial system will be reshaped (*Economic Report of the President*, 1985, ch. 5).

PORTFOLIO BEHAVIOUR OF FINANCIAL INTERMEDIARIES

A large literature has attempted to estimate econometrically the choices of assets and liabilities by financial intermediaries, their relationships to open market interest rates and to other variables exogenous to them. Models of the portfolio behaviour of the various species of financial intermediary also involve estimation of the supplies of funds to them, and the demands for credit, from other sectors of the economy, particularly households and nonfinancial businesses. Recent research is presented in Dewald and Friedman (1980).

Different econometric problems arise in using time series for these purposes because of regime changes. For example, when deposit interest rate ceilings are effective, financial intermediaries are quantity-takers in the deposit markets; when the ceilings are non-constraining or non-existent, both the interest rates and the quantities are determined jointly by the schedules of supplies of deposits by the public and of demands for them by the financial intermediary. Similar problems arise in credit markets where interest rates, even though unregulated, are administered by financial intermediaries themselves and move sluggishly. The prime commercial loan rate is one case; mortgage rates in various periods are another. In these cases and others, the markets are not cleared at the established rates. Either the financial intermediary or the borrowers are quantity-takers,

277

or perhaps both in some proportions. Changes in the rates follow, dependent on the amount of excess demand or supply. These problems of modelling and econometric estimation are discussed in papers in the reference above. The seminal paper is Modigliani and Jaffee (1969).

BIBLIOGRAPHY

Barro, R. 1974. Are government bonds net wealth? *Journal of Political Economy* 82(6), November–December, 1095–117.

Dewald, W.G. and Friedman, B.M. 1980. Financial market behavior, capital formation, and economic performance. (A conference supported by the National Science Foundation.) *Journal of Money, Credit, and Banking*, Special Issue 12(2), May.

Diamond, D.W. and Dybvig, P.H. 1983. Bank runs, deposit insurance, and liquidity. *Journal of Political Economy* 91(3), June, 401–19.

Economic Report of the President. 1985. Washington, DC: Government Printing Office, February.

Federal Reserve System, Board of Governors. 1984. *Balance Sheets for the US Economy 1945–83.* November, Washington, DC.

Fisher, I. 1930. *The Theory of Interest.* New York: Macmillan.

Goldsmith, R.W. 1969. *Financial Structure and Development.* New Haven: Yale University Press.

Goldsmith, R.W. 1985. *Comparative National Balance Sheets: A Study of Twenty Countries, 1688–1978.* Chicago: University of Chicago Press.

Gurley, J.G. and Shaw, E.S. 1960. *Money in a Theory of Finance.* Washington, DC: Brookings Institution.

Modigliani, F. and Miller, M.H. 1958. The cost of capital, corporation finance and the theory of investment. *American Economic Review* 48(3), June, 261–97.

Modigliani, F. and Jaffee, D.M. 1969. A theory and test of credit rationing. *American Economic Review* 59(5), December, 850–72.

Schumpeter, J.A. 1911. *The Theory of Economic Development.* Trans. from the German by R. Opie, Cambridge, Mass.: Harvard University Press, 1934.

Tobin, J. 1963. Commercial banks as creators of 'money'. In *Banking and Monetary Studies*, ed. D. Carson, Homewood, Ill.: Richard D. Irwin.

Tobin, J. 1980. *Asset Accumulation and Economic Activity.* Oxford: Blackwell; Chicago: University of Chicago Press.

Tobin, J. 1983. Financial structure and monetary rules. *Kredit und Kapital* 16(2), 155–71.

Tobin, J. 1984. On the efficiency of the financial system. *Lloyds Bank Review* 153, July, 1–15.

Fine Tuning

FRANCIS M. BATOR

'Fine Tuning' was Walter Heller's phrase for fiscal and monetary actions by government aimed at countering deviations in aggregate demand – forecast or actual – from some *target* path of output and associated inflation. The idea marked an important change in doctrine. The goal was not merely to smooth out fluctuations, but to track an output–employment/inflation path chosen from the set of attainable paths according to the preferences of the policymaker.

Hyperbole aside, advocates of 'tuning' believe that (1) the economy does not adequately tune itself; and (2) we know enough about its dynamic structure – the lags and multipliers – to achieve better results than a policy unresponsive to unwanted movements in aggregate demand, e.g., a regime of fixed money growth and a 'passive' fiscal policy. (To clinch the case, one has to suppose that politicians will not mess things up – that they will not produce worse results than would a policy of 'non-tuning'.)

Both technical premises have drawn sharp attack.

IF THE ECONOMY IS 'CLASSICAL'. New Classical Macroeconomics (NCM) – much in favour during the past fifteen years among young macro theorists – teaches that, if only the macroeconomic managers would stop meddling, the economy would perform in about the way that the stochastic version of the perfectly competitive, instantly convergent NCM model predicts it will perform: prices and wage rates would keep all markets more or less continuously cleared, and allocation would remain in the neighbourhood of its quasi-efficient Walrasian (moving) equilibrium. If that is so – an empirical question, and not a matter of methodological aesthetics or political preference – attempts by government to manage aggregate demand are at best an irrelevance, or more likely, the principal cause of macroeconomic inefficiency. Business cycles, insofar as they do not reflect feasibly efficient adjustment to changes in endowments, technology and tastes, are caused by capricious fiscal and monetary policies. Private agents make socially erroneous decisions because they are unable to decipher the behaviour of the government.

279

The money managers in such an NCM economy, at least in the canonical monetarist version of the story, cannot affect *real* economic magnitudes except by acting capriciously. They control the price level and only that, and should concentrate on making it behave. The fiscal managers, in turn, should stick to the neoclassical business of making the budget conform to the preferences of the electorate with respect to income redistribution and the division of output between private use and public services, present and future. As long as the government and the central bank both behave predictably, aggregate demand, total output and employment will take care of themselves. (The meaning of efficiency in a macro context is problematic. I use the phrase quasi-efficient to allow for some microeconomic distortions, and for the virtual nonexistence of state-contingent futures markets. Quasi-efficiency is, of course, relative to given information sets.)

IF THE ECONOMY IS KEYNESIAN. Suppose, however, that prices and nominal wage rates (or their rates of change) react to excess supply and demand only sluggishly. Real disturbances give rise to cumulative, self-multiplying quantity responses that are both inefficient and slow to dissipate. Even an anticipated nominal event, for example an increase in money supply brought about by a costless airdrop of currency, causes *real* effects. Then, *in principle*, a disturbance-responsive policy could improve matters.

Not so in practice, opponents say. The coefficients (indeed, the equations) of Keynesian models are too unreliable, and the lags are too variable and too long. As a result, an activist policy – even if free of political constraint – is more likely to do harm than good. As evidence, they cite the poor performance of the US economy during the late 1960s and 1970s. (On one extreme, NCM view, Keynesian models are no good at all. What appears to be quantitative 'structure' in such models is a mirage; it reflects not durable, exploitable regularities but behaviour that is specific to private agents' expectations of government policy. Any anticipated change in policy will cause rational agents to alter their behaviour; the coefficients will shift the way the Phillips wage–inflation/unemployment relationship shifted in response to the government's attempt during 1962–8 to exploit it. On still another view, Keynesian econometric methodology is inefficient in identifying the economy's true structure. Auto-regressive methods that infer structural relations among the variables entirely from the evolving pattern of leads and lags, and make no use of prior theory, are, it is alleged, more likely to reveal robust regularities.)

Pro-activists are quick to acknowledge that Keynesian econometric regularities are approximate and impermanent, and that large shifts in policy regimes may cause them to change. But they read the evidence to say that such 'structural' change is apt to be episodic or gradual or both – that the coefficients are durable enough to be *cautiously* usable. They favour large policy actions only when the gap between aggregate demand and its target is already large, or when the odds are good that it is about to become large. Against small gaps or small disturbances, they would take only small actions or none. Even then, they say, mistakes will occur. But they emphasize how singular the structure of the economy would have to be, and how special the pattern of disturbances, to justify reliance on a 'passive' policy (e.g. trying to keep the various measures of money supply growing at constant rates, and the fiscal instruments fixed in their neoclassically warranted baseline settings).

THE 1965–81 US EVIDENCE. Opponents of an activist policy make much of the American experience between 1965 and 1981. But the lesson to be learned from that experience depends critically on whether the US economy is classical or Keynesian. If in fact the economy is Keynesian, then the 1965–81 history provides little or no support for the opponents' case.

In the United States, the acceleration of inflation during 1965–8 was caused not by an overresponsive policy, but by exactly the opposite – the government's failure to heed Keynesian pleas that it counter the excessive thrust of aggregate demand by increasing taxes and making money tight. Plausibly, also, it was that failure, and the resulting rise in the pace of inflation experienced by employers and employees, that caused the Phillips unemployment/ wage–inflation regularity of 1946–65 to come unstuck (thus validating the Phelps/Friedman accelerationist prediction, though not necessarily its narrowly expectations-based rationale). That the excess demand of 1965–8 was caused by a large increase in government spending, and not by an unforeseen shift in private spending propensities, made the error of non-tuning the more egregious.

To blame activist policy for the spurts of rapid inflation during the 1970s, or for the simultaneous increase in inflation and unemployment during 1973–5 and 1979–81, is to miss a crucial implication of modern Keynesian models with their lagged-inflation augmented Phillips wage equation, and raw-material price-sensitive price equation. If the recently experienced rate of inflation is unacceptably high, or if the economy is subjected to a large upward supply-price shock (such as the dramatic increase in the price of oil in 1973–4 and again during 1979) then, modern Keynesian models assert, there will not exist *any* conventional fiscal and monetary actions that would produce cheerful results with respect to both (1) output and employment and (2) inflation. The entire slate of output–employment/inflation choices faced by the Federal Reserve, and Presidents Ford, Carter and Reagan was uninviting. Lacking an effective policy of direct price and wage restraint, Ford and Carter (and the Fed) could have achieved lower rates of inflation only at the cost of still more lost output and more (transient) unemployment. Reagan and Volcker could have achieved the President's ambitious 1981 output and employment objectives only at the cost of persistently rapid inflation. (The NCM model's only explanation for the acceleration of inflation during the mid- and late 1970s is that the Federal Reserve became unhinged. A determined, well-publicized policy of monetary restraint could have prevented any speed-up in inflation at virtually no cost in output and employment. That same model says that the Fed can near-costlessly stop inflation. Keynesian models assert that the cure is costly, as in fact it turned out to be during 1981–4.)

REMARKS. Trade-offs involving inflation and unemployment will plague policy-makers even in an accelerationist, natural rate, lagged-inflation augmented Phillips/Keynes world, especially one beset by upward supply-price shocks. The slate of inflation–unemployment choices in such a Phelps/Friedman/Phillips/Keynes economy is more complicated than in an old-fashioned Phillips/Keynes economy of the sort that Walter Heller had in mind in the early 1960s (perhaps correctly, for the range of rates of change of prices ($\dot{P}$) actually experienced during 1958–64 – there is no way to know). But only if prices instantaneously clear all markets, and, secondarily, if expectations are entirely free of inertia and strategic interdependence – that is if the economy is NCM in its structure–will the aggregate supply curve in $\dot{P}$–Q space be vertical in what may otherwise be a long-protracted short-run. (In NCM models, only capricious, unpredictable government actions give rise to an inflation–unemployment trade-off.)

One can espouse an actively responsive policy of demand management without condoning inflation. Preferences with respect to $\dot{P}$, $\ddot{P}$,..., Q and U bear on the choice of an aggregate demand target, not on how actively responsive the government should be in pursuing that target. There is no presumption that managers instructed to minimize inflation in a cost-effective manner would enjoy a quieter life than if they were told to favour output at the expense of faster inflation.

In a non-classical, Keynesian world, policy should aim at *both* nominal and real magnitudes, in a way that recognizes their interactions. An exclusively *nominal* strategy designed to yield a given year-to-year increase in nominal GNP (ΔPQ), no matter how it divides between increased prices (ΔP) and increased output (ΔQ) makes no sense whatever. The point is especially important if supply–price disturbances are important. *Real* targeting, if interpreted to mean that one should ignore inflation, is not acceptable either, unless one simply does not care about inflation *per se*, and about whatever microeconomic inefficiency it causes.

Theoretical considerations bearing on sensible portfolio behaviour, and evidence concerning the interest-responsiveness of the demand for money, make, I think, untenable the old monetarist claim that, even in the short run, *only* money matters – that fiscal action has no independent effect on total spending. With respect to the very long run, one has to be open-minded. The answer depends on the effect of the interest rate on the demand for wealth, i.e. on saving, and the effect of wealth on the demand for money. But that long-run, equilibrium-to-equilibrium outcome seems to be of no practical significance.

The selection of a policy mix – from among the many combinations of budget settings and base-money growth compatible with one's preferred output and inflation target – should reflect the community's preferences with respect to the distribution of income and the division of output between consumption and investment, private and public. In other ways, too, policy should pay attention to supply as well as demand – how to get more output out of given capital and labour, and whether and how to upgrade and augment the former and enhance the performance and pleasure of the latter.

Sensible managers will make tactical use of *any* intermediate indicator (e.g. free reserves, help wanted ads, Michigan surveys, whatever), as long as it exhibits sufficient short-run predictive power to improve their performance. But they will never waste degrees of freedom by treating such auxiliary aiming points as though they were objectives. They will avoid shibboleth goals like budget balance. Instruments are scarce enough, even relative to true objectives.

Because the American economy has become much more 'open', demand management in the US is more complicated than it was two decades ago. The causal interconnections are more uncertain, and instruments are scarcer relative to targets. But that is not an argument for setting the controls on 'automatic'. Rather, it strengthens the case for an eclectic, regret-minimizing activism.

BIBLIOGRAPHY

Bator, F.M. 1982. Fiscal and monetary policy: in search of a doctrine. In *Economic Choices*: *Studies in Tax/Fiscal Policy*. Washington, DC: Center for National Policy.

Blinder, A.S. and Solow, R.M. 1984. Analytical foundations of fiscal policy. In *Economics of Public Finance*, Washington: Brookings Institution.

Council of Economic Advisers. 1962. Annual Report of the Council of Economic Advisers. *Economic Report of the President*. Washington, DC: US Government Printing Office.

Friedman, M. 1948. A monetary and fiscal framework for economic stability. *American Economic Review* 38, June, 245–64.

Friedman, M. 1968. The role of monetary policy. *American Economic Review* 58(1), March, 1–17.

Heller, W.W. 1967. *New Dimensions of Political Economy*. New York: Norton.

Lerner, A.P. 1941. The economic steering wheel. *University Review*, Kansas City, June, 2–8.

Lucas, R. 1976. Econometric policy evaluation: a critique. *Journal of Monetary Economics BTX Supplement*, Carnegie-Rochester Conference Series 1, 19–46.

Lucas, R. 1977. Understanding business cycles. *Journal of Monetary Economics*, Supplement, Carnegie-Rochester Conference Series 5, 7–29.

Lucas, R. 1980. Methods and problems in business cycle theory. *Journal of Money, Credit, and Banking* 12(4), Part II, November, 696–715.

Modigliani, F. 1977. The monetarist controversy, or, should we foresake stabilization policies? *American Economic Review* 67(2), March, 1–19.

Okun, A.M. 1971. Rules and roles for fiscal and monetary policy. In *Issues in Fiscal and Monetary Policy: The Eclectic Economist Views the Controversy*, ed. James J. Diamond, Chicago: DePaul University Press. Reprinted in *Economics for Policymaking, Selected Essays of Arthur M. Okun*, ed. Joseph Pechman, Cambridge, Mass.: MIT Press, 1983.

Okun, A.M. 1980. Rational-expectations-with-misperceptions as a theory of the business cycle. *Journal of Money, Credit, and Banking* 12(4), Part II, November, 817–25.

Phelps, E.S. 1968. Money-wage dynamics and labor-market equilibrium. *Journal of Political Economy* 76(4), Part II, July–August, 678–711.

Samuelson, P.A. 1951. Principles and rules of modern fiscal policy: a neo-classical reformulation. In *Money, Trade and Economic Growth: Essays in Honor of John Henry Williams*, ed. Hilda L. Waitzman, New York: Macmillan.

Samuelson, P.A. and Solow, R.M. 1960. Analytical aspects of anti-inflation policy. *American Economic Review* 50, May, 177–94.

Sargent, T.J. and Wallace, N. 1975. 'Rational' expectations, the optimal monetary instrument, and the optimal money supply rule. *Journal of Political Economy* 83(2), April, 241–54.

Sims, C. 1980. Macroeconomics and reality. *Econometrica* 48(1), January, 1–48.

Solow, R.M. 1976. Down the Phillips curve with gun and camera. In *Inflation, Trade and Taxes,* ed. David A. Belsey et al., Columbus: Ohio State University Press.

Solow, R.M. 1979. Alternative approaches to macroeconomic theory: a partial view. *Canadian Journal of Economics* 12(3), August, 339–54.

Solow, R.M. 1980. What to do (macroeconomically) when OPEC comes? In *Rational Expectations and Economic Policy,* ed. Stanley Fischer, Chicago: University of Chicago Press.

Tobin, J. 1977. How dead is Keynes? *Economic Inquiry* 15(4), October, 459–68.

Tobin, J. 1980. Are new classical models plausible enough to guide policy? *Journal of Money, Credit, and Banking* 12(4), Part II, November, 788–99.

Tobin, J. 1980. Stabilization policy ten years after. *Brookings Papers on Economic Activity* No. 1, (10th Anniversary Issue), 19–71.

Tobin, J. 1982. Steering the economy then and now. In *Economics in the Public Service,* ed. Joseph A. Pechman, New York: W.W. Norton & Co.

Tobin, J. 1985. Theoretical issues in macroeconomics. In *Issues in Contemporary Macroeconomics and Distribution,* ed. George Feiwel, New York: State University of New York.

Free Lunch

ROBERT HESSEN

'There's no such thing as a free lunch' dates back to the 19th century, when saloon and tavern owners advertised 'free' sandwiches and titbits to attract mid-day patrons. Anyone who ate without buying a beverage soon discovered that 'free lunch' wasn't meant to be taken literally; he would be tossed out unceremoniously.

'Free lunch' passed over into political economy during the New Deal era, and is loosely credited to various conservative journalists, including H.L. Mencken, Albert Jay Nock, Henry Hazlitt, Frank Chodorov and Isabel Paterson. (All efforts to identify the true originator proved unavailing.) The phrase signified that the welfare state is an illusion: government possesses no wealth of its own, so it can only redistribute wealth it has seized by taxation.

During the Vietnam war era, 'free lunch' took on a libertarian cast. When defenders of the draft argued that young men *owed* military service because they had accepted free tuition and subsidized school lunches as youngsters, the 'free lunch' expression became a libertarian shorthand to denote that citizens never get something for nothing, that sooner or later they are presented with a bill for all the favours or 'freebies' they accepted from government.

'Free lunch' would have passed into oblivion if it had not been able to pass a crucial test of its viability in the marketplace of ideas. In the early 1970s, every political or philosophical idea had to be able to fit on a T-shirt or automobile bumpersticker. The new version, TANSTAAFL (there ain't no such thing as a free lunch), was popularized in a science fiction bestseller by Robert Heinlein (*The Moon is a Harsh Mistress*) and in Milton Friedman's widely read columns in *Newsweek* magazine.

285

Full Employment

G.D.N. WORSWICK

An expression which came into general use in economics after the Depression of the 1930s, full employment applies to industrially developed economies in which the majority of the economically active are the employees of firms or public authorities as wage and salary earners.

There has always been some unemployment in the course of development of capitalist economies and views have differed as to its causes and as to the extent to which it was a matter of public concern. In the first part of the 20th century three principal strands of thought about unemployment can be distinguished. Firstly, the followers of Marx believed that cycles were an integral part of capitalist development and would lead to ever deepening crisis: the attempt to evade this by colonial expansion would only lead to conflict between imperialist powers. A second group of analysts paid particular attention to the measurement and dating of business cycles, distinguishing cycles of different periodicity, but they did not, as a rule, offer systematic theories. The third strand consisted of those economists who argued that in capitalist economies, if the forces of the market were left to work themselves out, there would always be a tendency towards an equilibrium, in modern parlance towards full employment.

Table 1 shows average rates of unemployment in six developed countries for various periods of the 20th century. National estimates of unemployment are obtained either by sample survey or as the by-product of administration, such as a system of unemployment insurance. There are many problems in counting both the numbers unemployed and the labour force, whose ratio is to constitute the 'rate' of unemployment. There have been attempts to standardize rates obtained in different countries by different methods and over different periods. The figures in Table 1, taken from Maddison (1982) and OECD *Main Economic Indicators* are thought to be reasonably comparable. Only in two cases was it feasible to give estimates before World War I. We have four countries for the interwar years and all six after 1950. It will be seen that in the Depression years 1930–34 the average rates of unemployment were far higher than in any earlier

286

TABLE 1
Unemployed as a Percentage of the Total Labour Force

	France	Germany	Japan	Sweden	UK	USA
1900–1913	—	—	—	—	4.3	4.7
1920–1929	—	3.8	—	3.1	7.5	4.8
1930–1934	—	12.7	—	6.3	13.4	16.5
1935–1938	—	3.8	—	5.4	9.2	11.4
1950–1959	1.4	5.0	2.0	1.8	2.5	4.4
1960–1969	1.6	0.7	1.3	1.7	2.7	4.7
1970–1979	3.8	2.2	1.7	2.0	4.3	6.1
1980–1989	9.1	6.1	2.5	2.5	10.0	7.2

Sources: 1900–1969 A. Maddison, *Phases of Capitalist Development*, Oxford University Press, 1982. 1970–1989 OECD, *Main Economic Indicators*, Paris.

period in the 20th century and that even in the later 1930s the rates remained abnormally high except in Germany.

The time was ripe for a theory which could account for the persistence of large-scale unemployment and it was provided by John Maynard Keynes in *The General Theory of Employment, Interest and Money* (1936), which the author himself said was all about 'my doctrine of full employment'. The self-equilibrating tendencies expounded by those whom Keynes called 'classical' economists did not necessarily function in the manner prescribed for them and capitalist economies could get stuck with persistent unemployment. According to orthodox theory, unemployment should entail falling wages which would eliminate any 'involuntary' unemployment. Similarly, interest rates would fall, bringing about a recovery of investment. Keynes argued that money wages might be 'sticky', and even if they were not, falls in money wages would not entail corresponding falls in real wages, since prices would also fall. As to rates of interest, there was no guarantee that such falls as could occur would give a strong enough impetus to recovery. The analysis points clearly to the idea, which others developed more explicitly, that fiscal policy – the adjustment of the budget balance between revenue and expenditure – could prove a more powerful lever to bring about full employment.

Within less than ten years, the British wartime coalition government, in a famous White Paper, had accepted 'as one of their primary aims and responsibilities' the maintenance of 'a high and stable level of employment', and other governments, in Australia, Canada and Sweden, for instance, made similar affirmations. Article 55 of the United Nations Charter called on members to promote 'higher standards of living, full employment, and conditions of economic and social progress and development'. This remarkable change in public policy cannot be attributed simply to the 'Keynesian Revolution' in economic thought. More powerful was the observation that twice in a generation full employment had only been realized in war. How far the new principles were responsible for the performance of economies in the postwar period is a disputed question. The facts are that for the twenty-five years after 1945 the growth rates of productivity in European countries were much higher, and the average levels of unemployment much lower than they had ever been. Fluctuations in output and employment were smaller than in the past. A group of OECD experts reporting in 1968 said that the results of using fiscal policy to maintain economic balance had been encouraging, though there was room for further improvement. In the United States, the government's attitude towards the new ideas was initially somewhat cooler. By its own past standards, productivity growth was not exceptional, and unemployment, though much lower than in the Depression, was much the same as in the 1920s and before 1914. The Keynesian battle was not truly joined in the USA until the 1960s. In the majority of countries, the era of exceptional growth and full employment came to an end in the early 1970s, since when longer spells of high unemployment have been experienced.

Full employment does not mean zero unemployment. There can be dislocations where large numbers of workers are displaced from their present employment, and time is needed before new workplaces can be created. This can happen at the end of a war, or following some major technological change. Apart from such special cases, regular allowance must be made for frictional and seasonal unemployment. Policy would not aim, therefore, at zero but at the elimination of unemployment attributable to demand deficiency. Governments targeting full employment would like to know the level of measured unemployment to which this corresponds. Three attempts to answer this question deserve mention. (1) The definition given by Beveridge (1944) was that the number of unemployed (U) should equal the number of unfilled vacancies (V). When U is very high, we would expect to find V low, and vice versa. If, over a number of fluctuations, U and V trace out a fairly stable downward sloping curve, we could pick the point on it where U = V as indicating full employment. (2) Phillips (1958) claimed that for Britain there was a good statistical relationship between the level of unemployment and the rate of change of money wages. By choosing the level of unemployment delivering zero wage inflation, or when labour productivity was rising, the slightly higher level delivering zero price inflation, we could pinpoint full employment. (3) Friedman (1968) objected that in the long run there was no trade-off between unemployment and inflation: instead he argued that there was a 'natural' rate of unemployment, such that if the actual level was pushed below this, there would be not only inflation, but accelerating inflation. If this theory could be substantiated, one could choose the 'non-accelerating inflation rate of unemployment' (NAIRU) as the target. It is evident that the usefulness of each of the above approaches turns on the closeness and stability of the statistical relationship actually observed. Experience in different countries has varied, and the British evidence should be regarded as illustrative. For the period from the early 1950s to the later 1960s econometric analysis produced reasonably stable relationships for all three approaches, yielding estimates of the full employment level of unemployment of the order of 2–3 per cent. But in the 1970s any stability of the Phillips curve crumbled, and estimates of NAIRU shot up from below two to over ten per cent, but without any clear indication of the institutional or structural changes which must have occurred to bring about so large a shift in so short a time. The UV relationship did not escape entirely unscathed either, but a plausible story can be told in terms of an outward shift of the UV curve. Brown (1985) reckoned that the United States, the United Kingdom and France suffered increases in the imperfections of the labour market in the period from the early 1960s to 1981 which might account in full employment ($U = V$) conditions for extra unemployment of two per cent or less. It would seem that the substantial rises in unemployment, especially in Europe, in the 1970s and 1980s can only be accounted in a smaller part by a rise in 'full employment' unemployment and that a greater part denotes an excess beyond it.

If the growth of output of developed economies after 1945 was exceptional, so also was the rate of price increase: in Britain, for example, such a sustained and substantial rise (3–4 per cent a year on average) had not been seen in peacetime for more than two centuries. Some countries had faster rises, but, in most cases, there was no clear sign of acceleration. A marked change of gear in price inflation occurred between the 1960s and the 1970s, precipitated by two large cost impulses. Around 1969 there was in many countries a distinct surge in wage increases which Phelps Brown (1983) has called 'the Hinge' and in 1973 there was the first of the great OPEC oil price rises. Confronted with these spontaneous boosts in costs, the authorities had to choose between allowing their consequences to be worked out within the bounds of the existing monetary and fiscal stance and adjusting that stance to accommodate them, which would mean that final prices would also jump. They began increasingly to opt for the former course. In doing so they received intellectual support from the first wave of the 'monetarist' counter-revolution against the now orthodox Keynesian demand management. Firstly, it was said that to push unemployment below the 'natural rate' would cause accelerating inflation. In any case, too little was known about the structure of the economy, in particular its time lags, for fine tuning to be a sensible policy. Better to adopt simple rules, such as fixed targets for the growth of the supply of money, which would keep inflation under control, and output and employment would adjust to the level indicated by the 'natural rate' of unemployment. Later developments in the new classical economics went further and denied altogether the possibility that governments, by loan-financed expenditure, for instance, could effect lasting changes in employment. Instead, it was suggested, the only way to bring down unemployment was to reduce the monopoly power of trade unions, and to take other steps to free labour markets, such as abolishing minimum wage legislation and reducing unemployment benefit. Though not supported by any substantial body of evidence, these new ideas undoubtedly helped to persuade central banks to adopt fixed monetary targets, or rules, and after the second OPEC price rise in 1979, most governments followed restrictive monetary policies with more severe budgets. Calculations of 'constant employment' budget balances show a tightening equivalent to several percentage points of GNP in some cases, especially in Europe where unemployment rose considerably after 1980. On the other hand the United States broke ranks in 1983, allowing both actual and 'constant employment' deficits to rise, and it was the one major economy to experience falling unemployment.

If there is little evidence of a unique 'natural rate' of unemployment, it is nevertheless clear that to bring down a cost-induced inflation by demand restriction may involve high unemployment for a great many years. A wide range of 'incomes policies' has been attempted, and others canvassed, to secure that firms and workers would settle for lower prices and wages than they would seek if they were acting alone, provided others would do the same. It is unlikely that full employment of the kind experienced in Europe in the 1950s and 1960s could return without the aid of such policies. Throughout the great postwar expansion world trade grew at an unprecedented rate. Fixed exchange rates, with permission to change parities if needed, worked well enough for most countries to maintain their external balance. However, the Bretton Woods system crumbled and was succeeded by generally floating exchange rates, while at the same time controls over capital movements were being dismantled. Exchange rates came to be determined as much by capital movements as by trade, and they can diverge widely and for long periods from any level suggested by purchasing power parity. Thus full employment is also seen to depend increasingly on the joint action of all, or of a large number, of countries.

Employment policy has been linked with the welfare state in contradictory ways. On the one hand, higher unemployment is tolerated on the grounds that welfare provision mitigates the economic hardship involved; on the other hand, higher welfare costs are perceived as a growing burden on economies with high unemployment.

BIBLIOGRAPHY
Beveridge, W. 1944. *Full Employment in a Free Society*. London: George Allen & Unwin.
Brown, A.J. 1985. *World Inflation since 1950*. Cambridge: Cambridge University Press.
Friedman, M. 1968. The role of monetary policy. *American Economic Review* 58(1), March, 1–17.
Keynes, J.M. 1936. *The General Theory of Employment, Interest and Money*. London: Macmillan; New York: Harcourt, Brace.
Maddison, A. 1982. *Phases of Capitalist Development*. Oxford: Oxford University Press.
OECD. 1968. *Fiscal Policy for a Balanced Economy*. Paris: Organization for Economic Cooperation and Development.
Phelps Brown, E.H. 1983. *The Origins of Trade Union Power*. Oxford: Clarendon Press.
Phillips, A. W. 1958. The relation between unemployment and the rate of change of money wage rates in the United Kingdom. *Economica* 25, November, 283–99.

Gender

FRANCINE D. BLAU

The term gender has traditionally referred, as has sex, to the biological differences between men and women. More recently a movement has arisen both in social science writings and in public discourse to expand this definition to encompass also the distinctions which society has erected on this biological base, and further to use the word gender in preference to sex to refer to this broader definition. In this essay, we describe the relationship of this expanded concept of gender to economic theory.

Historically, gender has not been perceived to be a central concept in economic analysis, either among the classical and neoclassical schools or among Marxist economists. However, as the force of current events has thrust gender-related issues to the fore, economists have responded by seeking to analyse these issues. The outcome of this process has been not only a better understanding of the nature of gender differences in economic behaviour and outcomes, but also an enrichment of the discipline itself.

While, as noted above, the mainstream of economic analysis paid scant attention to gender-related issues, the 19th-century campaign for female suffrage did focus some attention on gender inequality. Among classical economists, J.S. Mill (1869) eloquently argued for the 'principle of perfect equality' (p. 91) between men and women. Not only did he favour equality of the sexes within the family, but also women's 'admissibility to all the functions and occupations hitherto retained as the monopoly of the stronger sex'. He also expressed the belief 'that their disabilities elsewhere are only clung to in order to maintain their subordination in domestic life' (p. 94). In the Marxist school, Engels (1884) tied the subjection of women to the development of capitalism and argued that women's participation in wage labour outside the home, as well as the advent of socialism, was required for their liberation. The belief in the emancipating effects of a fuller participation in employments outside the home was shared not only by Mill and Engels, but also by such contemporary feminist writers as Gilman (1898).

The passage of time has proved these views oversimplified. As Engels and Gilman correctly foresaw, there has been an increase in the labour force participation of women, particularly of married women, in most of the advanced industrialized countries. This has undoubtedly altered both the relationship between men and women and the very organization of society in many ways. However, while women's labour force participation has in many instances risen dramatically, it nonetheless remains the case that the types of jobs held by men and women, as well as the earnings they receive, continue to differ markedly.

The contribution of modern neoclassical analysis, which comprises the main focus of this essay, has been to subject to greater scrutiny and more rigorous analysis both women's economic roles within the family and the causes of gender inequality in economic outcomes. We examine each of these areas below. However, the interrelationships between the family and the labour market, most importantly the consequences of labour market discrimination against women for their roles and status in the family, have tended to be neglected. Nonetheless, the possible existence of such feedback effects is an important issue which is also considered here.

TIME ALLOCATION IN THE FAMILY CONTEXT

Prompted in part by their desire to understand the causes of the rising labour force participation of married women in the post-World War II period, economists extended the traditional theory of labour supply to consider household production more fully. The consequence was not only a better understanding of the labour supply decision, but also the development of economic analyses of the related phenomena of marriage, divorce and fertility.

The traditional theory of labour supply. The traditional theory of labour supply, also known as the labour–leisure dichotomy, was a simple extension of consumer theory. In this model, individuals maximize their utility, which is derived from market goods and leisure, subject to budget and time constraints. Where an interior solution exists, utility is maximized when the individual's marginal rate of substitution of income for leisure is set equal to the market wage.

Since in this model all time not spent in leisure is spent working, a labour supply (leisure demand) function may be derived with the wage, non-labour income and tastes as its arguments. The well-known results of consumer theory are readily obtained. An increase in non-labour income, all else equal, increases the demand for all normal goods including leisure, inducing the individual to consume more leisure and to work fewer hours (the income effect). An increase in the wage, *ceteris paribus*, has an ambiguous effect on work hours due to two opposing effects. On the one hand, the increase in the wage is like an increase in income and in this respect tends to lower work hours due to the income effect. On the other hand, the increase in the wage raises the price (opportunity cost) of leisure inducing the individual to want to consume less of it, i.e. a positive substitution effect on work hours.

292

The theory sheds light on the labour force participation decision when it is realized that a corner solution will arise if the marginal rate of substitution of income for leisure at zero work hours is greater than the market wage. In this case, the individual maximizes utility by remaining out of the labour force. The impact of an increase in the wage is unambiguously to raise the probability of labour force participation, since, at zero work hours, there is no off-setting income effect of a wage increase.

Household production and the allocation of time. While the simple theory is sufficient for some purposes, it has limited usefulness for understanding the determinants of the gender division of labour in family and the factors influencing women's labour force participation, both at a point in time and trends over time. The key to addressing these issues is a fuller understanding and analysis of the household production process.

The first step in this direction was taken by Mincer (1962) who pointed out the importance, especially for women, of the three-way decision among market work, non-market work and leisure. He argued that the growth in married women's labour force participation was due to their rising real wages which increased the opportunity cost of time spent in non-market activities. But since, during the same period, the real wages of married men were also increasing, this must mean that the substitution effect associated with women's own real wage increases dominated the income effect associated with the growth in their husbands' real wages. While this part of the analysis could be accommodated in the framework of the traditional model, the next question Mincer raised could not. Why should the substitution effect dominate the income effect for women when such time series evidence as the declining work week suggested a dominance of the income effect over the substitution effect for men? The answer, according to Mincer, lay in women's responsibility for non-market production. The opportunities for substituting market time (through the purchase of market goods and services) are greater for time spent in home work than for time spent in leisure. Thus, since married women spend most of their non-market time on household production while men spend most of theirs on leisure, the substitution effect of a wage increase would be larger for married women than for men.

Becker (1965) advanced this process considerably by proposing a general theory of the allocation of time to replace the traditional theory of labour supply. In this and other work (summarized in Becker, 1981), he laid the foundations of what has become known as the 'new home economics', and spearheaded the development of economic analyses of time allocation, marriage, divorce and fertility. Interestingly, while Mincer opened a window on household production by distinguishing non-market work from leisure where the traditional labour supply theory had not done so, Becker was able to provide a further advance by again eliminating the distinction. However, while in the traditional labour supply model all non-market time is spent in leisure, in Becker's model all non-market time is spent in household production.

Specifically, Becker assumes that households derive utility from 'commodities' which are in turn produced by inputs of market goods and non-market time. It is interesting to note that Becker's 'commodities', produced and consumed entirely in the home, are the polar opposite of Marx's (1867) 'commodities', produced and exchanged in the market. Examples of Becker's commodities range from sleeping, which is produced with inputs of non-market time and of market goods like a bed, sheets, a pillow and a blanket (and in some cases, perhaps, a sleeping pill); to a tennis game that is produced by inputs of non-market time combined with tennis balls, a racquet, an appropriate costume and court time; to a clean house produced with inputs of non-market time and a vacuum cleaner, a bucket and a mop and various cleaning products.

In this model the production functions for the commodities are added to the constraints of the utility maximization problem. Utility can still be expressed as a function of the quantities of market goods and non-market time consumed; however, market goods and non-market time now produce utility only indirectly through their use in the production of commodities. Relative preferences for market goods versus home time depend on the ease with which the household can substitute market goods for non-market time in consumption and production. Substitution in consumption depends on their preferences for 'goods-intensive' commodities – those produced using relatively large inputs of market goods in comparison to non-market time – relative to 'time-intensive' commodities – those produced using relatively large inputs of non-market time in comparison to market goods. Substitution in production depends on the availability of more goods-intensive production techniques for producing the same commodity.

The usefulness of these ideas may be illustrated by considering the relationship of children to women's labour force participation. Children (especially when they are small) may be viewed as a time-intensive 'commodity'. Traditionally, it has been the mother who has been the primary care-giver. Moreover, while it is possible to substitute market goods and services for home time in caring for children (in the form of babysitters, day care centres, etc.), these alternative production techniques tend to be costly and it is sometimes difficult to make suitable alternative arrangements (in terms of quality, scheduling, etc.). Thus, at a point in time, the probability that a woman will participate in the labour force is expected to be inversely related to the number of small children present. Over time, the increase in women's participation rates has been associated with decreases in birthrates, as well as increases in the availability of various types of child care facilities, formal and informal. Changes in social norms (Brown, 1984) making it more acceptable to substitute for the time of parents in the care of young children may also have been a factor, although it is difficult to know, in this case as in others, the extent to which attitude change precedes or follows change in the relevant behaviour.

The relationship between labour force participation and fertility is reinforced by the impact of the potential market wage on women's fertility decisions. Greater market opportunities for women have increased the opportunity cost of children (in terms of their mothers' time inputs) and induced families to have fewer of them. Similarly, the greater demand for alternative child care arrangements (also due to the increased value of women's market time) has made it profitable for more producers to enter this sector.

The gender division of labour. In our discussion of children, we simply assumed that women tend to bear the primary responsibility for child care. However, the gender division of labour in the family is also an issue which the new home economics addresses. According to Becker (1981), the division of labour will be dictated by comparative advantage. To the extent that women have a comparative advantage in household and men in market production, it will be efficient for women to specialize to some extent in the former while men specialize in the latter. In this view, the increased output corresponding to this arrangement constitutes one of the primary benefits to marriage. Thus, women's increasing labour force participation is seen to have reduced the gains from marriage thereby contributing to the trend towards higher divorce and lower marriage rates.

The notion that, where families are formed, it is generally efficient and thus optimal for one member, usually the wife, to specialize to some extent in household production, while the husband specializes in market work, has important consequences for women's status in the labour market. As we shall see in greater detail below, human capital theorists expect such a division of labour to lower the earnings of women relative to men, due to workforce interruptions and smaller investments in market-oriented human capital. For this and other reasons, it is important to consider in greater detail whether such specialization is indeed as desirable for the family as the model suggests, and, by implication, whether it is apt to continue into the future. There are three points to be made in this regard.

First, such a division of labour may not be as advantageous for women as it is for men (Ferber and Birnbaum, 1977; Blau and Ferber, 1986). Thus, even if such a specialization is efficient in many respects, it may not maximize the family's utility. Indeed, when there are conflicts of interest or even pronounced differences in tastes between the husband and wife, the concept of the family utility function itself becomes less meaningful, since the way in which the preferences of family members can meaningfully be aggregated to form such a utility function has not been satisfactorily specified.

What are the disadvantages to women of their partial specialization in household production? First, in a market economy, such an arrangement makes them to a greater or lesser degree economically dependent on their husbands (see also Hartmann, 1976). This is likely to reduce their bargaining power relative to their husbands' in family decision-making, as well as to increase the negative economic consequences for them (and frequently for their children) of a marital break-up. In the face of recent increases in the divorce rate, such specialization has become a particularly risky undertaking. Second, as more women come to value their careers in much the same way as men do, both in terms of achievement and earnings, their specialization in housework to the point where it is detrimental to their labour market success is not apt to be viewed with favour by them. The utility-maximizing family will take these disadvantages into account in

295

conjunction with the efficiency gains of specialization in allocating the time of family members.

If specialization is indeed considerably more productive than sharing of household responsibilities, it may be possible for this higher output to be used in part to compensate women for the disadvantages detailed above. However, it is likely that the gains to such specialization will shrink over time relative to the disadvantages of such an arrangement. As women anticipate spending increasingly more of their working lives in the labour market, their investments in market-oriented capital may be expected to continue to grow and their comparative advantage in home work relative to men to decline. Moreover, as the quality of the opportunities open to women in the labour market continues to improve, the disadvantages of specialization in home work in the form of foregone earnings and possibilities for career advancement will also rise. Thus greater sharing of household responsibilities between men and women is likely to become increasingly prevalent, even if women in general retain a degree of comparative advantage in household production for some time to come.

A second point to be made with regard to women's specialization in household production is that comparative advantage does not comprise the only economic benefit to family or household formation (Ferber and Birnbaum, 1977; Blau and Ferber, 1986). Families and households also enjoy the benefits of economies of scale in the production of some commodities, as well as the gains associated with the joint consumption of 'public' goods. These benefits of collaboration would be unaffected by a reduction in specialization, even if those based on comparative advantage would be diminished. Other benefits of marriage or household formation may actually be increased by a more egalitarian division of household responsibilities. For example, two-earner families are in a sense more diversified and thus enjoy greater income security than families which depend on only one income. It may also be the case that the enjoyment derived from joint consumption is enhanced when the members of a couple have more in common, as when both participate in market and home activities. Thus, the incentives of couples to adhere to the traditional division of labour in order to enjoy the economic benefits of marriage may not be as strong as suggested when only the gains to comparative advantage are considered.

Finally, it is important to point out that women's comparative advantage for household production may stem not only from the impacts of biology and gender differences in upbringing and tastes, but also from the effect of labour market discrimination in lowering women's earnings relative to men's. Decisions based to some extent on such market distortions are not optimal from the perspective of social welfare even though they may be rational from the perspective of the family. The importance of such feedback effects are considered in greater detail below.

GENDER DIFFERENCES IN LABOUR MARKET OUTCOMES

We turn now to the contribution of economic analysis to an understanding of the causes of gender inequality in economic outcomes. Here, the consideration of gender issues has been accommodated principally through the development of new and interesting applications of existing theoretical approaches. The particular challenge posed to the theories by women's economic status is the existence of occupational segregation as well as earnings differentials by sex. Occupational segregation refers to the concentration of women in one set of predominantly female jobs and of men in another set of predominantly male jobs. The reasons for such segregation and its relationship to the male–female pay differential are two key questions to be addressed.

As in the case of the analysis of women's roles in the family, the catalyst for the development of these approaches was provided by external events. Some moderate degree of interest in this issue was generated in England by the World War I experience. Pursuant to the war effort, there was some substitution of women into traditionally male civilian jobs, although not nearly to the degree that there would be during World War II. Questions of the appropriate pay for women under these circumstances arose and stimulated some economic analyses of the gender pay differential – all of which gave a prominent causal role to occupational segregation. These included the work of Fawcett (1918) and Edgeworth (1922) (which provided the antecedents for Bergmann's (1974) overcrowding model, discussed below) and Webb (1919).

The analysis of gender differentials in the labour market received another impetus in the early 1960s, this time in the United States, with the development of the women's liberation movement and the passage of equal employment opportunity legislation. Two broad approaches to the issue have since evolved. First is the human capital view which lays primary emphasis on women's own voluntary choices in explaining occupation and pay differences. Second are a variety of models of labour market discrimination which share the common characteristic of placing the onus for the unequal outcomes on differential treatment of equally (or potentially equally) qualified men and women in the labour market. While these two approaches may be viewed as alternatives, it is important to point out that they are in fact not mutually exclusive. Both may play a part in explaining sex differences in earnings and occupations and the empirical evidence suggests that this is the case (see, e.g., Treiman and Hartmann, 1981). Indeed, as we shall see, their effects are quite likely to reinforce each other. We now consider each of these approaches in turn.

The human capital explanation. The human capital explanation for gender differences in occupations and earnings, developed by Mincer and Polachek (1974), Polachek (1981) and others, follows directly from the analysis of the family described above. It is assumed that the division of labour in the family will result in women placing greater emphasis than men on family responsibilities over their life cycle. Anticipating shorter and more discontinuous work lives as a consequence of this, women will have lower incentives to invest in market-oriented formal education and on-the-job training than men. Their resulting smaller human capital investments will lower their earnings relative to those of men.

297

These considerations are also expected to produce gender differences in occupational distribution. It is argued that women will choose occupations for which such investments are less important and in which the wage penalties associated with workforce interruptions (due to the skill depreciation that occurs during time spent out of the labour force) are minimized. Due to their expected discontinuity of employment, women will avoid especially those jobs requiring large investments in firm-specific skills (i.e. skills which are unique to a particular enterprise), because the returns to such investments are reaped only as long as one remains with the firm. The shorter expected job tenure of women in comparison with that of men is also expected to make employers reluctant to hire women for such jobs, since employers bear some of the costs of such training. Thus, to the extent that it is difficult to distinguish more from less career-oriented women, the former may be negatively affected (see the discussion of statistical discrimination below).

More recently, Becker (1985) has further argued that, even when men and women spend the same amount of time on market jobs, women's homemaking responsibilities can still adversely affect their earnings and occupations. Specifically, he reasons that since child care and housework are more effort intensive than are leisure and other household activities, married women will spend less effort than married men on each hour of market work. The result will be lower hourly earnings for married women and, to the extent that they seek less demanding jobs, gender differences in occupations.

Thus, the human capital analysis provides a logically consistent explanation for gender differences in market outcomes on the basis of the traditional division of labour by gender in the family. An implication generally not noted by those who have developed this approach is that, to the extent that the human capital explanation is an accurate description of reality, it serves to illustrate graphically the disadvantages for women of responsibility for (specialization in) housework which we discussed above. To the extent that gender differences in economic rewards are not fully explained by productivity differences, we must turn to models of labour market discrimination to explain the remainder of the difference.

Models of labour market discrimination. As noted earlier, models of discrimination were developed to understand better the consequences of differences in the labour market treatment of two groups for their relative economic success. The starting point for models of labour market discrimination is the assumption that members of the two groups are equally or potentially equally productive. That is, except for any direct effects of the discrimination itself, male and female labour (in this case) are perfect substitutes in production. This assumption is made not because it is necessarily considered an accurate description of reality, but rather because of the question which discrimination models specifically address: why do equally qualified male and female workers receive unequal rewards? Such models may then be used to explain how discrimination can produce pay differentials between men and women in excess of what could be expected on the basis of productivity differences.

Theoretical work in this area was initiated by Becker's (1957) model of racial discrimination. Becker conceptualized discrimination as a taste or personal prejudice. He analysed three cases, those in which the tastes for discrimination were located in employers, co-workers and customers, respectively. As Becker pointed out, for such tastes to affect the economic status of a particular group adversely, they must actually affect the behaviour of the discriminators.

One may at first question whether such a model is as applicable to sex as to race discrimination in that, unlike the case of racial discrimination, men and women are generally in close contact within families. However, the notion of socially appropriate roles, not explicitly considered by Becker, both sheds light on this question and establishes a link between his theory and occupational segregation. Thus, employers may be quite willing to hire women as secretaries, receptionists or nursery school teachers but may be reluctant to employ them as lawyers, college professors or electricians. Co-workers may be quite comfortable working with women as subordinates or in complementary positions, but feel it is demeaning or inappropriate to have women as supervisors or as peers. Customers may be happy to have female waitresses at a coffee shop, but expect to be served by male waiters at an elegant restaurant. They may be delighted to purchase women's blouses or even men's ties from female clerks, but prefer their appliance salesperson, lawyer or doctor to be a man. Such notions of socially appropriate roles are quite likely a factor in racial discrimination as well.

Employers with tastes for discrimination against women in particular jobs will be utility rather than profit maximizers. They will see the full costs of employing a woman to include not only her wages but also a discrimination coefficient ($d_r \geqslant 0$) reflecting the pecuniary value of the disutility caused them by her presence. Thus, they will be willing to hire women only at lower wages than men ($w_f = w_m - d_r$). If men are paid their marginal products, employer discrimination will result in women receiving less than theirs. When employers differ in their tastes for discrimination, the market-wide discrimination coefficient will be established at a level which equates supply and demand for female labour at the going wage. Thus the size of the male–female pay gap will depend on the number of women seeking work, as well as on the number of discriminatory employers and on the magnitude of their discrimination coefficients.

One of the particularly interesting insights of Becker's (1957) analysis is that profit-maximizing employers who do not themselves have tastes for discrimination against women will nonetheless discriminate against them if their employees or customers have such prejudices. Male employees with tastes for discrimination against women will act as though their wage is reduced by $d_e (\geqslant 0)$, their discrimination coefficient, when they are required to work with women. Thus, they will consent to be employed with women only if they receive a higher wage – in effect a compensating wage differential for this unpleasant working condition.

The obvious solution to this problem from the employer's point of view is to hire a single-sex workforce. If all employers followed such a strategy, male and female workers would be segregated by firm, but there would be no pay differential. Yet, as Arrow (1973) has noted, employers who have made a personnel investment in their male workers, in the form of recruiting, hiring or training costs, may not find it profitable to discharge all their male employees and replace them with women, even if the latter become available at a lower wage. While such considerations cannot explain how occupations initially become predominantly male, it can shed light on one factor – the necessity of paying a premium to discriminatory male workers to induce them to work with women – contributing to the perpetuation of that situation. Further, where women do work with discriminating male workers, a pay differential will result.

Some extensions of Becker's (1957) analysis of employee discrimination are also of interest. Bergmann and Darity (1981) point out that employers may be reluctant to hire women into traditionally male jobs because of adverse effects on the morale and productivity of the existing male workforce. Given the replacement costs discussed above this would be an important consideration. As Blau and Ferber (1986) note, employee discrimination may also directly lower women's productivity relative to that of men. For example, since much on-the-job training is informal, if male supervisors or co-workers refuse or simply neglect to instruct female workers in these job skills, women will be less productive than men workers. Similarly, the exclusion of women from informal networks and mentor-protégé relationships in traditionally male occupations can diminish their access to training experiences and even to the information flows needed to do their jobs well.

Customer discrimination can also reduce the productivity of female relative to male employees. Customers with tastes for discrimination against women will act as if the price of a good or service provided by a woman were increased by their discrimination coefficient, $d_c (\geq 0)$. Thus, at any given selling price, a female employee will bring in less revenue than a male employee. Women either will not be hired for such jobs or will be paid less. The potential applicability of this model is not only to conventional sales jobs. In our 'service economy', a large and growing number of jobs entail personal contact between workers and customers/clients.

Models based on the notion of tastes for discrimination are consistent with occupational segregation, but do not necessarily predict it. If wages are flexible, it is altogether possible that such discrimination will result in lower pay for women, but little or no segregation. However, if discriminatory tastes against women in traditionally male pursuits (on the part of employers, employees and/or customers) are both strong and prevalent, women may tend to be excluded from these areas. On the other hand, even if such segregation occurs, it may or may not be associated with gender pay differentials. In the presence of sufficient employment opportunities in the female sector, equally qualified women may earn no less than men.

The relationship between occupational segregation and earnings differentials is further clarified in Bergmann's (1974) overcrowding model. If for whatever reason – labour market discrimination or their own choices – potentially equally qualified men and women are segregated by occupation, the wages in male and female jobs will be determined by the supply and demand for labour in each sector. Workers in male jobs will enjoy a relative wage advantage if the supply of labour is more abundant relative to demand for female than for male occupations. Such 'crowding' of female occupations can also widen differentials between male and female jobs that would exist in any case due to women's smaller human capital investments or to employers' reluctance to invest in their human capital.

Perhaps the most serious question that has been raised about the Becker analysis, particularly of the case of employer discrimination, is its inability to explain the persistence of discrimination in the long run. Assuming that tastes for discrimination vary, the least discriminatory firms would employ the highest proportion of lower-priced female labour. They would thus have lower costs of production and, under constant returns to scale, could in the long run expand and drive the more discriminatory firms out of business (Arrow, 1973).

This issue has provided the rationale, at least in part, for the elaboration of alternative models of discrimination, including the statistical discrimination model discussed below. Others, not considered here, have emphasized non-competitive aspects of labour markets (e.g. Madden, 1973). However, this criticism of the Becker model is a double-edged sword in that it has led some economists to doubt that labour market discrimination is responsible, in whole or part, for gender inequality in economic rewards. Yet it is important to recognize that the phenomenon which we seek to understand is intrinsically complex. From this perspective it is not surprising that no easy solution has been found to the question of why discrimination has persisted. Similarly, the various models of discrimination, each emphasizing different motivations and different sources of this behaviour, need not be viewed as alternatives. Rather, each may serve to illuminate different aspects of this complex reality.

As noted above, models of statistical discrimination were developed by Phelps (1972) and others to shed light on the persistence of discrimination. They do so by imputing a motive for employer discrimination which, in an environment of imperfect information, is consistent with profit maximization. Statistical discrimination occurs when employers believe that, all else equal, women are on average less productive or less stable workers than men. The common perception that women are more likely to quit their jobs than men would be an example of this.

As in the employer taste for discrimination model, statistical discrimination would cause employers to prefer male workers and to be willing to hire women only at a wage discount. A difference is, however, that in this case male and female workers are not perceived to be perfect substitutes. Further, if women are viewed as less stable workers, there will tend to be substantive differences between male and female jobs, with the former emphasizing firm-specific skills to a greater extent. This is essentially the picture painted by the dual market model (Piore, 1971; Doeringer and Piore, 1971). In this view, women tend to be excluded from the 'primary sector', jobs requiring firm-specific skills and thus characterized by relatively high wages, good promotion opportunities and low turnover rates, and to find employment in the 'secondary sector', comprised of low-paying, dead-end jobs in which there tends to be considerable turnover.

Like the human capital model, the notion of statistical discrimination provides a link between women's roles in the family and gender differences in market outcomes. However, the connection is in terms of differences in the treatment of men and women, rather than differences in the choices they make.

One crucial issue is of course whether employers' perceptions are indeed correct. If they are, as Aigner and Cain (1977) have pointed out, then in some sense labour market discrimination as conventionally defined does not exist: women's lower wages are due to their lower productivity. Nonetheless, the employer's inability to distinguish between more and less career-oriented women certainly creates an inequity for the former vis-à-vis their male counterparts.

On the other hand, employer perceptions may be incorrect or exaggerated. Differentials based on such erroneous views undoubtedly constitute discrimination as economists have defined it. However, as Aigner and Cain (1977) have persuasively argued, gender differentials based on employers' mistaken beliefs are even less likely to persist in the long run than those based on employers' tastes for discrimination. Nonetheless, in times of rapid changes in gender roles, there may be considerable lags in employers' perceptions. Employers' incorrect views could also magnify the impact of employee or customer discrimination, as when such discrimination is either less extensive or more susceptible to change than employers believe.

A potentially more powerful role for statistical discrimination is provided in models which allow for feedback effects, for example Arrow's (1973) model of perceptual equilibrium. In this case, men and women are assumed to be potentially perfect substitutes in production, but employers believe that, for example, women are less stable workers (Arrow, 1976). They thus allocate women to jobs where the cost of turnover is minimized and women respond by exhibiting the unstable behaviour employers expect. The employers' assessments are correct *ex post*, but are in fact due to their own discriminatory actions. This equilibrium will be stable even though an alternative equilibrium is potentially available in which women are hired for jobs which are sufficiently rewarding to inhibit instability. More generally, any form of discrimination can adversely affect women's human capital investments and labour force attachment by lowering the market rewards to this behaviour (see also, Blau, 1984; Blau and Ferber, 1986; Ferber and Lowry, 1976; and Weiss and Gronau, 1981).

CONCLUSION

We have considered the contributions of neoclassical economic theory to our understanding of women's labour supply decisions, the gender division of labour within the family, and male–female differences in labour market outcomes. With the introduction of feedback effects, the separate strands of neoclassical theory analysing women's economic roles in the family and their labour market outcomes may be more tightly woven together. The causation runs not only from women's roles within the family to their resulting economic success, as human capital theorists emphasize, but also from their treatment in the labour market to their incentives to invest in market-oriented human capital and to participate in the labour force continuously. Thus, even a small amount of discrimination at an early stage of the career can have greatly magnified effects over the work life. While it is unlikely that labour market discrimination created the traditional division of labour between men and women in the family, it could certainly help to perpetuate it.

However, it is also the case that increasing opportunities for women in the labour market create powerful incentives to reduce gender differences in family roles and labour market behaviour. At the same time, women's increased attachment to the labour force, due not only to these increased opportunities but also to changes in household technology and in tastes, may be expected to increase their market productivity and hence their earnings directly, and also to reduce statistical discrimination against them. Similarly, the movement of women into traditionally male jobs has the potential not only to increase the wages of those who become so employed, but to reduce overcrowding and increase wages in female jobs as well. Thus, just as a fuller understanding of the interrelationships between women's roles in the family and their status in the labour market helps us to understand the persistence of gender inequality in economic outcomes, it also enables us to appreciate how changes in either one of these spheres, or both, can induce a mutually reinforcing process of cumulative change. Recent signs of progress in reducing the pay gap in many of the advanced industrialized countries may well signal the beginnings of such a process.

In our emphasis upon the interdependence of women's status within the family and the labour market, we have in some respects returned to our starting point, for this conclusion bears a close resemblance to the views of the 19th-century observers which we reviewed at the outset. However, it is also clear that neoclassical economic theory has enhanced our understanding of the causes of gender differences in both the family and the labour market, as well as allowing us to comprehend better the links between the two sectors.

BIBLIOGRAPHY

Aigner, D. and Cain, G. 1977. Statistical theories of discrimination in labour markets. *Industrial and Labor Relations Review* 30(2), January, 175–87.

Arrow, K. 1973. The theory of discrimination. In *Discrimination in Labor Markets*, ed. O. Ashenfelter and A. Rees, Princeton: Princeton University Press.

Arrow, K. 1976. Economic dimensions of occupational segregation: comment I. *Signs* 1(3), Part II, 233–7.

Becker, G. 1957. *The Economics of Discrimination.* 2nd edn, Chicago: University of Chicago Press, 1971.

Becker, G. 1965. A theory of the allocation of time. *Economic Journal* 75, September, 493–517.

Becker, G. 1981. *A Treatise on the Family.* Cambridge, Mass.: Harvard University Press.

Becker, G. 1985. Human capital, effort, and the sexual division of labor. *Journal of Labor Economics* 3(1), January, 533–58.

Bergmann, B. 1974. Occupational segregation, wages and profits when employers discriminate by race or sex. *Eastern Economic Journal* 1, April/July, 103–10.

Bergmann, B. and Darity, W., Jr. 1981. Social relations in the workplace and employer discrimination. In *Proceedings of the Thirty-Third Annual Meeting of the Industrial Relations Research Association*. ed. B.D. Dennis, New York: Industrial Relations Research Association, 155–62.

Blau, F. 1984. Discrimination against women: theory and evidence. In *Labor Economics: Modern Views*, ed. W. Darity, Boston: Kluwer-Nijhoff Publishing.

Blau, F. and Ferber, M. 1986. *The Economics of Women, Men, and Work*. Englewood Cliffs, NJ: Prentice-Hall.

Brown, C. 1984. Consumption norms, work roles, and economic growth. Paper presented at the conference on Gender in the Workplace, Washington, DC: Brookings Institution, November.

Doeringer, P. and Piore, M. 1971. *Internal Labor Markets and Manpower Analysis*. Lexington, Mass.: D.C. Heath and Co.

Edgeworth, F. 1922. Equal pay to men and women for equal work. *Economic Journal* 32, December, 431–57.

Engels, F. 1884. *The Origin of the Family, Private Property and The State*. New York: International Publishers, 1972.

Fawcett, M.G. 1918. Equal pay for equal work. *Economic Journal* 28, March, 1–6.

Ferber, M. and Birnbaum, B. 1977. The 'new home economics': retrospects and prospects. *Journal of Consumer Research* 4(1), June, 19–28.

Ferber, M. and Lowry, H. 1976. The sex differential in earnings: a reappraisal. *Industrial and Labor Relations Review* 29(3), April, 377–87.

Gilman, C. 1898. *Women and Economics: a study of the economic relation between men and women as a factor of social evolution*. New York: Harper & Row, 1966.

Hartmann, H. 1976. Capitalism, patriarchy and job segregation by sex. *Signs* 1(3), Part II, 137–69.

Madden, J. 1973. *The Economics of Sex Discrimination*. Lexington, Mass.: D.C. Heath and Co.

Marx, K. 1867. *Capital: A Critique of Political Economy*, Vol. I. New York: International Publishers, 1967.

Mill, J.S. 1869. *The Subjection of Women*. 4th edn, London: Longmans, Green, Reader & Dyer, 1878; New York: Stokes, 1911.

Mincer, J. 1962. Labor force participation of married women. In *Aspects of Labor Economics*, National Bureau of Economic Research, Princeton: Princeton University Press.

Mincer, J. and Polachek, S. 1974. Family investments in human capital: earnings of women. *Journal of Political Economy* 82(2), Part II, S76–S108.

Phelps, E. 1972. The statistical theory of racism and sexism. *American Economic Review* 62(4), September, 659–61.

Piore, M. 1971. The dual labor market: theory and implications. In *Problems in Political Economy: an urban perspective*, ed. D. Gordon, Lexington, Mass.: D.C. Heath and Co.

Polachek, S. 1981. Occupational self-selection: a human capital approach to sex differences in occupational structure. *Review of Economics and Statistics* 63(1), February, 60–69.

Treiman, D. and Hartmann, H. (eds) 1981. *Women, Work, and Wages: equal pay for jobs of equal value*. Washington, DC: National Academy Press.

Webb, B. 1919. *The Wages of Men and Women: should they be equal?* London: Fabian Bookshop.

Weiss, Y. and Gronau, R. 1981. Expected interruptions in labour force participation and sex-related differences in earnings growth. *Review of Economic Studies* 48(4), October, 607–19.

Gifts

C.A. GREGORY

A gift, according to the *Concise Oxford Dictionary*, is a 'voluntary transference of property; thing given, present, donation'. For most economists, especially those familiar only with industrial capitalist economies, this is all that need be said on the matter: it is obvious what gift exchange is and there is nothing to be explained. The only problem the phenomenon of exchange poses for the economist is that of 'value' and this arises in the context of commodity exchange.

For the anthropologist, however, the phenomenon of exchange poses questions about the nature of gift exchange. These lie at the centre of the discipline and the topic has been the subject of much theoretical debate. Anthropologists stress that while gifts appear to be voluntary, disinterested and spontaneous, they are in fact obligatory and interested. It is this underlying obligation that anthropologists seek to understand: What is the principle whereby the gift received has to be repaid? What is there in the thing given that compels the recipient to make a return?

It is clear that the one economic category – exchange – means fundamentally different things to different people and that these contrary perceptions of the exchange process have given rise to quite distinct theoretical traditions. The reasons for this are to be found in the historical conditions which gave rise to the development of the academic disciplines of economics and anthropology. The history of economic thought must be understood with reference to the development of mercantile and industrial capitalism in Europe; the development of anthropological theorizing, on the other hand, must be situated in the context of the imperialist expansion of European capitalism and especially the colonial conquest of Africa and the Pacific towards the end of the 19th century. The fact that economists have been preoccupied with commodity exchange whilst anthropologists have been primarily concerned with gift exchange simply reflects the fact that the modern European economy is organized along very different lines from the indigenous economies of Africa, the Pacific and elsewhere. The data that anthropologists have collected from these countries over the past one

305

hundred years have revolutionized our understanding of tribal economy and the theory of the gift; their theoretical reflections on these data constitute a major contribution to the theory of comparative economic systems and also to the theory of development and underdevelopment. This anthropological literature takes us far beyond the superficial dictionary definition of the gift and raises important questions about the seemingly unrelated issue of shell money; interestingly it also brings us back to the original meaning of the word as 'payment for a wife' and 'wedding' found in *The Oxford Dictionary of English Etymology*.

Anthropological accounts of gift giving first began appearing towards the end of the 19th century; by the end of World War I a large quantity of data had been collected. The most spectacular accounts came from the Kwakiutl Indians of the northwest cost of America and from the Melanesian Islanders of the Milne Bay District of Papua New Guinea. Among the Kwakiutl vast amounts of valuable property (mainly blankets) are ceremonially destroyed in a system called 'potlatch' (Boas, 1897). In the potlatch system the prestige of an individual is closely bound up with giving: a would-be 'big-man' or 'chief' is constrained to give away or to destroy everything he possesses. The principles of rivalry and antagonism are basic to the system and people compete with one another, each trying to outgive the other in order to gain prestige. The status and rank of individuals and clans are determined by this war of property. In Papua New Guinea, the classic home of competitive gift exchange, the instruments of 'gift warfare' are food (Young, 1971) and shells of various shapes and sizes (Leach and Leach, 1983). These are not destroyed but transacted by status seekers according to complicated sets of rules which we are only now beginning to understand. Most Papua New Guinean societies are without any form of ascribed status and the egalitarian ideology of these societies means that competitive gift giving is primarily concerned with the maintenance of equal status rather than dominance. Staying equal is, as Forge (1972) has pointed out, an extremely onerous task requiring continual vigilance and effort: perfect balance is impossible to achieve as the temporal dimension of gift exchange necessarily introduces status inequalities. Perhaps the most complicated gift exchange system in Melanesia is the Rossel Island 'monetary system'. This was first described by Armstrong (1924) and has recently been restudied by Liep (1983). On Rossel Island there are two kinds of 'shell money' – *ndap* and *ko*. A single unit of *ndap* is a polished piece of *spondylus* shell a few millimetres thick, having an area varying from 2 to 20 square centimetres and roughly triangular in shape. A single unit of *ko* consists of ten pieces of *chama* shell of roughly the same size and thickness with a small hole in the centre for binding them together. Each shell group contains some forty-odd hierarchical divisions. What is unusual about these divisions is that they have rank rather than value, that is, they are ordinally related rather than cardinally related. For example, the relationship of a big *ndap* shell to a small one is analogous to that between an ace of hearts and a two of hearts rather than that between a dollar and a cent.

The publication of Armstrong's (1928) ethnography of Rossel Island and Malinowski's (1922) now classic description of an inter-island gift exchange system called *kula* sparked off a debate about the nature of 'shell money' which still rages today. This debate is kept alive not from an antiquarian interest in 'archaic' money systems but because these gift exchange systems are still flourishing despite their incorporation into the world capitalist economy (MacIntyre and Young, 1982; Gregory, 1980, 1982). On Rossel Island, for example, not only are the *ndap* and *ko* shells still transacted as gifts according to the complicated rules of old, but the demand for Rossel Island *chama* shells for use in the flourishing *kula* gift exchange system of neighbouring islands has transformed Rossel Island into a major commodity producer and exporter of *chama* shells (Liep, 1981, 1983).

These facts raise conceptual questions about the difference between gift exchange and commodity exchange, and theoretical and empirical questions about the nature of the interaction between them. Neoclassical economics answers these questions within a framework that employs the universalist and subjectivist concept 'goods', a category which, by definition, cannot explain the particularist and objective nature of gift and commodity exchange (Gregory, 1982). A 'gift' therefore becomes a 'traditional good' and highly questionable psychological criteria are used to distinguish this from a 'modern good'. For example, Einzig argues that 'the intellectual standard' of people in tribal societies 'is inferior and their mentality totally different from ours' (1948, p. 16); Stent and Webb (1975, p. 524) argue that 'traditional' consumers in Papua New Guinea are on the bliss point of their indifference curves. A further difficulty economists have with the problem of contrasting economic systems – and this is not restricted to neoclassical economic thought – is the habit of beginning an argument with an analysis of barter in an 'early and rude state of society'. The barter economies of these theories are figments of a Eurocentric imagination that bear no resemblance at all to actual tribal economies. Economic anthropologists have been making this point for over fifty years but without much success (Malinowski, 1922, pp. 60–61; Polanyi, 1944, pp. 44–5). What is needed, then, is an empirically based theory of comparative economy. The foundations of such a theory were laid by Marx (1867) but the rise to dominance of neoclassical theory precluded any further development of the theory of comparative economy within the economics discipline. The theoretical advances have come from without and have been made by anthropologists, sociologists and economic historians.

The outstanding contribution to the 20th-century literature is undoubtedly Mauss's *The Gift: Forms and Functions of Exchange in Archaic Societies*, first published in French in 1925 as 'Essai sur le don, forme archaique de l'echange' in Durkheim's journal, *L'Année Sociologique*. Mauss (1872–1950) was Durkheim's nephew and became a leading figure in French sociology after his uncle's death. His essay on the gift is a remarkable piece of scholarship. Not only did he survey all extant ethnographic data on gift giving from Melanesia, Polynesia, northwest America and elsewhere, he also examined the early literature from Ancient Rome, the Hindu classical period and the Germanic societies. His essays conclude with a critique of western capitalist society by drawing out the moral, political, economic and ethical implications of his analysis.

The key to understanding gift giving is apprehension of the fact that things in tribal economies are produced by non-alienated labour. This creates a special bond between a producer and his/her product, a bond that is broken in a capitalist society based on alienated wage-labour. Mauss's analysis focused on the 'indissoluble bond' between things and persons in gift economies and argued that 'to give something is to give a part of oneself' (1925, p. 10). Gifts therefore become embodied with the 'spirit' of the giver and this 'force' in the thing given compels the recipient to make a return. This does not exist in our system of property and exchange which is based on a sharp distinction between things and persons, that is, alienation (1925, p. 56). The wage-labourer in a capitalist society gives a 'gift' which is not returned (1925, p. 75). Capitalism for Mauss, then, was a system of non-reciprocal gift exchange, a system where the recipients of a gift were under no obligation to make a return gift.

This analysis of the wage-labour contract under capitalism has a Marxian ring about it. However, Mauss was no revolutionary and he drew very different policy conclusions from his analysis of the wage–labour relation. He argued for a welfare capitalism where the state, through its social legislation, provided recompense to the workers for their gifts.

A feature of Mauss's work, and indeed a feature of much early theorizing about the gift, was the evolutionary framework within which the ethnographic data were analysed. The tribal economies studied by anthropologists were seen as living fossils from European prehistory, hence the use of terms such as 'archaic' and 'primitive'. These early theorists, then, were only concerned with the intellectual contribution these data could make to the study of comparative economy. To the extent that they were concerned with the welfare of living people it was the welfare of their European countrymen and women; they were not concerned with policies for the development of tribal peoples.

The other outstanding theorist in this evolutionary tradition was another Frenchman, Claude Lévi-Strauss. His theory of the gift is contained in his *The Elementary Structures of Kinship* (1949). Like Mauss's *The Gift*, Lévi-Strauss's book is an encyclopaedic survey of the ethnographic literature. Its central focus is marriage. In line with a long tradition in anthropology he conceptualizes this as an exchange of women. However, Lévi-Strauss's innovation is to argue that women are the 'supreme gift' and that the incest taboo is the key to understanding gift exchange. The virtually universal prohibition on marriage between close kin, he argues, is the basis of the obligation to give, the obligation to receive, and the obligation to repay.

Lévi-Strauss's theory is an analytical synthesis of literally thousands of ethnographic accounts from the Australian Aborigines, the Pacific and Asia. The original or most elementary form of gift exchange, according to Lévi-Strauss, is 'restricted' exchange where the moieties of a population exchanged sisters at marriage; the second form is 'delayed' exchange where a women is given this generation and her daughter returned the next; the most advanced form is 'generalized' exchange where one clan gives women to another clan but never receives any in return, the closure of the system being brought about by a circle of giving. In the movement from one stage to another, extra spheres of gift exchange are developed as symbolic substitutes for women. These are needed to maintain the ever widening marriage alliances brought about by the shift from restricted to generalized exchange. This movement from marriage to exchange is an aspect of an opposing movement from exchange to marriage. Lévi-Strauss sees a continuous transition from war to exchange, and from exchange to intermarriage as effecting a transition from hostility to alliance, and from fear to friendship.

Lévi-Strauss's theory has attracted considerable critical attention and has been described by his principal opponent as 'in large measure fallacious' (Leach, 1970, p. 111). Whatever its shortcomings his theory nevertheless manages to establish the important link between gift giving and the social organization of kinship and marriage. In other words, he has established a relationship between the obligation to give and receive gifts and the biological and social basis of human reproduction.

While Lévi-Strauss was developing his theory of the gift, an economic historian, Karl Polanyi, was approaching the problem from an altogether different perspective in his classic study, *The Great Transformation* (1944). His problem was the analysis of the emergence of the 'self-regulating market' and in order to grasp the 'extraordinary assumptions' underlying such a system he developed a theory of comparative economy based on ethnographic and historical evidence.

Polanyi correctly identified the Smithian 'paradigm of the bartering savage', which is accepted as axiomatic by many social scientists, as a barrier to an adequate understanding of non-market economy. In a tribal economy, notes Polanyi, the propensity to truck, barter and exchange does not appear: there is no principle of labouring for remuneration, the idea of profit is banned and giving freely is acclaimed a virtue. How, then, is production and distribution ensured, he asks. Polanyi devoted only ten pages of his book to answering this question but his insights have had a significant impact on anthropological thought (see e.g. Dalton and Köcke, 1983). Tribal economy, he argued, is organized in the main by two principles; *reciprocity* and *redistribution*. Reciprocity works mainly in regard to the sexual organizations of society, that is, family and kinship, and it is that broad principle which helps to safeguard both production and family sustenance. Redistribution refers to the process whereby a substantial part of all the produce of the society is delivered to the chief who keeps it in storage. This is redistributed at communal feasts and dances when the villagers entertain one another as well as neighbours from other districts.

Reciprocity and redistribution are able to work because of the institutional patterns of *symmetry* and *centricity*. Tribes, says Polanyi, are subdivided along a symmetrical pattern and this duality of social organization forms the 'pendant' on which the system of reciprocity rests. (Lévi-Strauss's restricted exchange model of gift exchange also presupposes dual social organization.) The institution of territorial centricity forms the basis of redistribution.

To these two principles, Polanyi adds a third – *householding*, production for use with *autarky* as its basis – and argues that all economic systems known to us up to the end of feudalism were organized on either the principle of reciprocity,

309

or redistribution, or householding, or some combination of the three. These made use of the patterns of symmetry, centricity and autarky, with custom, law, magic and religion cooperating to induce the individual to comply with the rules of behaviour.

Capitalism, in Polanyi's view, implies the wholesale destruction of these principles and the establishment of free markets in land, money and labour run according to the profit principle. Like Marx, Polanyi sees the emergence of free wage-labour as a commodity as the crucial defining characteristic of capitalism. Labour was the last of the markets to be organized in England and both Marx and Polanyi saw the enclosure movements, especially those at the time of the industrial revolution, as central to this process. Polanyi is more precise in his historiography however. He sees the Poor Law Reform of 1834, which did away with the final obstruction to the functioning of a free labour market, as the beginning of the era of the self-regulating market.

Postwar developments in the theory of the gift have built on the foundations laid by Mauss, Lévi-Strauss and Polanyi. The influential contributions of Godelier (1966, 1973), Meillassoux (1960, 1975) and Sahlins (1972) in particular, are heavily indebted to these theorists whose ideas they attempt to develop in the light of Marx's theory of comparative economy. Recent empirical research (e.g. Strathern, 1971; Young, 1971; Leach and Leach, 1983) has provided, and will continue to provide, the basis for new comparative insights into the theory of the gift (Forge, 1972).

An important postwar development in the theory of the gift has been the analysis of the impact of colonization and capitalist imperialism on tribal societies.

For the early contributors to this literature the problem was how to explain the process of destruction brought about by capitalism. Paul Bohannan (1959), an American anthropologist with fieldwork experience in West Africa, developed a theory of the impact of money on a tribal economy based on Polanyi's ideas. Commodity exchange, according to Polanyi, is a 'uni-centric economy' because of the nature of 'general-purpose money' which reduces all commodities to a common scale. In a tribal society, by way of contrast, the economy is 'multi-centric': there are multiple spheres of exchange, each with 'special-purpose' money that could only circulate within that sphere. Among the Tiv of West Africa, for example, there were three spheres of exchange. The first sphere contained locally produced foodstuffs, tools and raw materials; the second sphere contained non-market 'prestige' goods such as slaves, cattle, horses, prestige cloth (*tuguda*) and brass rods; the third sphere contained the 'supreme gift', women. Bohannan's argument was that the general-purpose money introduced by the colonial powers reduced all the various spheres to a single sphere, thereby destroying them.

Bohannan's theory was applied to the analysis of the impact of colonization in other parts of the world, Papua New Guinea among others (e.g. Meggitt, 1971). While Bohannan's theory makes an important conceptual advance in comparative economy it is now recognized that his theory of the impact of colonization has a number of shortcomings as a description of what happened in West Africa (see Dorward, 1976); furthermore, it does not pose the problem to be explained. Today, it is now realized, the problem is not, 'How was the tribal gift economy destroyed?' but rather, 'Why has it flourished under the impact of colonization?'

Take the famous potlatch system, for example. The establishment of a canning industry in the area in 1882 led to a rapid increase in the per capita income of the Kwakiutl, a rapid increase in the number of blankets that could be purchased, and hence a rapid increase in the number of blankets given away in potlach ceremonies. Before the canning industry was established the largest potlatch consisted of 320 blankets, but during the period 1930–1949 potlatch ceremonies involving as many as 33,000 blankets were recorded (Codere, 1950, p. 94). This rapid growth in potlatch occurred despite the institution in 1885 of a law prohibiting the ceremonies. The system has not retained its pristine form, however. Legal and other influences have brought about a variety of outward changes in form but the original purpose of the system still persists: the presentation of a claim to a specific social status (Drucker and Heizer, 1967, pp. 47–52).

In Papua New Guinea, to take another example, the establishment of one of the world's largest copper mines in Bougainville has stimulated a flourishing import of shells into the island. The shells are manufactured by the Langalanga people of western Malaita in the Solomon Islands some 1550 kilometres away. The mine has given the people of Bougainville income-earning opportunities unavailable to other islanders and they are able to outbid other purchasers for the Langalangan shells. The Langalangans, for their part, have oriented all their production away from local purchasers to the Bougainville market. In Bougainville the shells are used mostly by the Siwai people who give them as marriage gifts and traditional gift exchanges involving land and pigs; they are also used as ornaments (see Connell, 1977).

This symbiosis between commercialization and gift exchange is found elsewhere in Papua New Guinea. The famous *kula* gift exchange system in the Milne Bay District still persists despite more than one hundred years of colonization (Leach and Leach, 1983). Milne Bay is now something of an economic backwater, its heyday of commercial development being the gold mining era early in this century. Labour is probably one of the area's most important exports today. These migrants maintain close contact with their villages and often send home money, some of which is channelled into *kula* transactions. The migrants, who are senior public servants, entrepreneurs, and politicians, also take their culture with them to the urban areas. The result is that the *kula* ring now extends to Port Moresby, where Mercedes cars and telephones have replaced outrigger canoes and conch shell horns as the principal means of communication.

There is some empirical evidence that appears to contradict the theses that gift exchange has effloresced under the impact of colonization. Prior to the European colonization of West Africa and India these countries were part of a flourishing international cowrie-shell economy. The shells (*cyprae moneta*) were produced in the Maldive Islands of the Indian Ocean and were shipped to West Africa and India where they were used primarily as instruments of exchange but also for religious and ornamental purposes (Heimann, 1980). The cowrie shells were an important and profitable item of international trade in the mercantile era. They were purchased very cheaply in the Maldives – where they grow in great profusion – and exported to India or Europe. The merchants of Europe re-exported them to West Africa where they used them to purchase slaves.

This international shell economy, which had persisted for many centuries, began to collapse around the middle of the 18th century. The supply of shells began to increase rapidly and their price began to fall. For example, in 1865, 1636 tons of cowries were imported into Lagos; by 1878 imports totalled 4472 tons, which was the peak; ten years later imports had fallen to a mere ten tons. Cowrie shell prices (measured in pounds sterling) collapsed over this period. In 1851 two thousand cowries cost 4s. 9d. but by 1876–79 the price had fallen to 1s. 0d. (Hopkins, 1966; Johnson, 1970). By the beginning of the 20th century cowrie shells were no longer current; their place had been taken by the fiat money of the respective colonial government.

This evidence of the destructive impact of colonization only appears to contradict the 'efflorescence of gift exchange' thesis however. The reality is otherwise and the evidence demonstrates the point that exchange is a social relationship which varies depending upon the political and historical context. Objects, such as shells, have many uses, and the historical fact that they have been used as instruments of gift exchange here, as objects of commodity exchange there, and as currency in other places has caused great confusion in the literature. The issue is further confused by the fact that in contemporary Papua New Guinea for example, a shell may be used in all three roles during the same day. The issue can be clarified somewhat by inquiring into the primary role of an exchange object and situating this historically and comparatively in terms of the mode of reproduction of a society. The uniqueness of a place such as Papua New Guinea becomes apparent from this perspective. Papua New Guinea, unlike West Africa or India, was not part of an international mercantile economy prior to European colonization, and as a result commercial exchange transactions were a subordinate and insignificant part of total exchange. Pre-colonial India and West Africa, on the other hand, were highly commercialized: land and labour were freely transacted as commodities with gold and silver commodity monies being used as the principal instruments of exchange. The colonization of West Africa transformed it from being a stateless commodity economy to a state controlled one. This involved a suppression of the stateless commodity monies and their substitution by state fiat money. In India a similar process occurred as the British Government established strong centralized administrative control over numerous weak, corrupt princely states. The destruction of the cowrie shell economy must be seen as part of this process of transition from stateless commodity money to state fiat money. Cowries were the small change of gold and silver. The relationship of cowries to gold and silver, then, finds its counterpart in the relationship of pennies to shillings and pounds. However, whereas the relationship between gold and cowries is determined by production conditions and changes from day to day, the relationship between pounds and pennies is set by government decree and never changes. Where a stable government exists, and the value of money remains constant, it is obvious that a merchant or consumer will prefer to use the latter.

The shells used in West Africa and India, then, were used primarily as instruments of commodity exchange and the term 'shell money' is correct in this context. However, the shells used in the exchange systems of Melanesia and elsewhere were not used as the small change of commodity monies in pre-colonial times. They were used primarily as instruments of gift exchange and the term 'shell gifts' is more appropriate in this context. Colonization has resulted in the efflorescence of gift exchange in Melanesia because the colonial state brought an end to tribal warfare and facilitated a transition from fighting with weapons to fighting with gifts. These gifts take the form of women, shells, food and even money nowadays. These gifts do not involve a 'voluntary transference of property' as the *Oxford English Dictionary* would have it. They are the results of obligations imposed on people struggling to achieve status and wealth in a situation where indigenous systems of land tenure, kinship and marriage are being incorporated into an international economic and political order, over which tribespeople and peasants have little control.

BIBLIOGRAPHY

Armstrong, W.E. 1924. Rossel Island money: a unique monetary system. *Economic Journal* 34, 423–9.

Armstrong, W.E. 1928. *Rossel Island: An Ethnological Study*. Cambridge: Cambridge University Press.

Boas, F. 1897. *Kwakiutl Ethnography*. Ed. H. Codere, Chicago: University of Chicago Press, 1966.

Bohannan, P. 1959. The impact of money on an African subsistence economy. *Journal of Economic History* 19(4), 491–503.

Codere, H. 1950. *Fighting with Property*. New York: Augustin.

Connell, J. 1977. The Bougainville connection: changes in the economic context of shell money production in Malaita. *Oceania* 48(2), December, 81–101.

Dalton, G. and Köcke, J. 1983. The work of the Polanyi group: past, present and future. In S. Ortiz (ed.), 1983.

Dorward, D.C. 1976. Precolonial Tiv trade and cloth currency. *The International Journal of African Historical Studies* 9(4), 576–91.

Drucker, P. and Heizer, R.F. 1967. *To Make My Name Good: A Reexamination of the Southern Kwakiutl Potlatch*. Los Angeles: UCLA Press.

Einzig, P. 1948. *Primitive Money*. London: Eyre and Spottiswoode.

Forge, A. 1972. The Golden Fleece. *Man* 7(4), 527–40.

Godelier, M. 1966. *Rationality and Irrationality in Economics*. London: New Left Books, 1972.

Godelier, M. 1973. *Perspectives in Marxist Anthropology*. Cambridge: Cambridge University Press, 1977.

Gregory, C.A. 1980. Gifts to men and gifts to god: gift exchange and capital accumulation in contemporary Papua. *Man* 15(4), 626–52.

Gregory, C.A. 1982. *Gifts and Commodities*. London: Academic Press.

Heimann, J. 1980. Small change and ballast: cowry trade and usage as an example of Indian Ocean economic history. *South Asia* 3(1), 48–69.

313

Hopkins, A.G. 1966. The currency revolution in south-west Nigeria in the late nineteenth century. *Journal of the Historical Society of Nigeria* 3(3), 471–83.

Johnson, M. 1970. The cowrie currencies of West Africa. *Journal of African History* 11(1), 17–49; 11(3), 331–53.

Leach, E.R. 1970. *Lévi-Strauss.* London: Fontana.

Leach, J.W. and Leach, E. (eds) 1983. *The Kula.* Cambridge: Cambridge University Press.

Lévi-Strauss, C. 1949. *The Elementary Structures of Kinship.* Trans., London: Eyre and Spottiswoode, 1969.

Liep, J. 1981. The workshop of the Kula: production and trade of shell necklaces in the Louisade Archipelago. *Folk og Kultur* 23, 297–309.

Liep, J. 1983. Ranked exchange in Yela (Rossel Island). In *The Kula*, eds J.W. Leach and E. Leach, Cambridge: Cambridge University Press.

MacIntyre, M. and Young, M. 1982. The persistence of traditional trade and ceremonial exchange in the Massim. In *Melanesia: Beyond Diversity*, ed. R.J. May and Hank Nelson, Canberra: Australian National University.

Malinowski, B. 1922. *Argonauts of the Western Pacific.* New York: E.P. Dutton, 1961.

Marx, K. 1867. *Capital.* Vol. 1: *A Critical Analysis of Capitalist Production.* Moscow: Progress Publishers, n.d; New York: International Publishers, 1967.

Mauss, M. 1925. *The Gift.* London: Routledge and Kegan Paul, 1974.

Meggitt, M.J. 1971. From tribesmen to peasants: the case of the Mae-Enga of New Guinea. In *Anthropology in Oceania*, ed. L.R. Hiatt and C.J. Jayawardena, Sydney: Angus and Robertson.

Meillassoux, C. 1960. Essai d'interprétation du phénomène économique dans les sociétés traditionelles d'auto-subsistance. *Cahiers d'Etudes Africaines* 4, 38–67.

Meillassoux, C. 1975. *Maidens, Meal and Money.* Cambridge: Cambridge University Press, 1981.

Ortiz, S. (ed.) 1983. *Economic Anthropology: Topics and Theories.* New York: University Press of America.

Polanyi, K. 1944. *The Great Transformation.* New York: Rinehart.

Sahlins, M. 1972. *Stone Age Economics.* Chicago: Aldine.

Stent, W.R. and Webb, L.R. 1975. Subsistence, affluence and market economy in Papua New Guinea. *Economic Record* 51, 522–38.

Strathern, A.J. 1971. *The Rope of Moka.* Cambridge: Cambridge University Press.

Young, M.W. 1971. *Fighting with Food: Leadership, Values and Social Control in a Massim Society.* Cambridge: Cambridge University Press.

Gold Standard

MARCELLO DE CECCO

For nearly three thousand years coined weights of metal have been used as money and for just as long, gold, silver and copper have been the preferred metals for minting coins. Currencies consisting of coins whose value is expressed by the weight of the metal contained in them at market prices, however, have seldom been used.

Until the inception of metallist reforms, the necessary amounts of the metals required for coinage were brought to the Mint by the sovereign or by the public. The sovereign's monetary prerogative consisted in fixing the Mint price of the metal, i.e. how many coins of a certain denomination could be coined from a given weight of metal. The Mint price was established with reference to a money of account, and it could diverge, and very often did, from the market price of the metal. When the sovereign deemed it necessary to devalue his coinage, he could change the parity between the coins and an 'ideal' currency, usually one which had circulated in the past. This made it unnecessary to resort to recoinage operations. The latter were also available but were considered as more radical policies, while changing the relative value of coins in terms of the 'ideal' currency was a more gradual instrument, which could be used almost daily if need be. But it was only very rarely that the sovereign would renounce his prerogative of giving coins a face value by law. Indeed, for many students of money this sovereign prerogative was what transformed a coined metal into money. Theodor Mommsen wrote some unforgettable passages (*Histoire de la Monnaie Romaine*, 1865, vol. 3, p. 157) on Emperor Constantine's decision, in the 4th century AD, to resort to free minting of gold coins whose value was given by their weight at market prices. To Mommsen this was the lowest point reached in the degradation of Roman monetary sovereignty. A Roman coin had always been taken at its face value, whatever its weight. Indeed, this had been the chief testimony of the credibility of the Roman State.

After the fall of the Roman Empire, none of the successor states can be said to have enjoyed, in the following centuries, an equivalent degree of monetary sovereignty. The plurality of successor states implied a plurality of currencies, with ample possibility of speculating and arbitraging between currencies. Citizens learned to defend themselves when the sovereign's privilege became exorbitant. Seignorage tended to be inversely correlated with the commercial openness of States. The less truck subjects had with foreigners, the greater the divergence between the legal and intrinsic value of coins could be. A trading nation very soon found that it had to have a currency whose value corresponded to its metallic content. With the rise of the absolute state, the sovereign's monetary privilege tended again to become exorbitant. The ratio of internal to international trade increased, in spite of the rise of mercantilism, and the fiscal use of money by the State became greater. It is obvious that this sovereign prerogative, when it became exorbitant, made life very difficult for the sovereign's subjects, who could only defend themselves by changing prices, provided that this had not been declared illegal by the sovereign. Metallist reforms were an expression of the new power acquired by the subjects vis-à-vis the State. At the core of these reforms was the actual coinage of the 'ideal' money as a real full-bodied coin, whose weight and fineness were decreed, and this coin became the 'standard' of the national monetary system. The sovereign, by these reforms, saw his monetary prerogatives diminished to that of a keeper of weights and measures. In the intentions of the reform's advocates, it was a way of constitutionalizing the sovereign, so that he would be compelled to resort openly to his fiscal powers, which had been constitutionalized long before.

The Gold Standard was just one of the possible metallic standards. It was adopted in England, while the French preferred to choose a silver standard. In the course of the following centuries intellectual debate centred around the choice of metal, and economists, statesmen, intellectuals, declared themselves in favour of or against silver or gold, in favour of or against bimetallism or monometallism. But the basic choice in favour of a pure metallic standard, where an actual coin whose value as given by the weight of its metal content at market prices was the only money of account available, was not seriously discussed again for a long time, until the development of banking and the integration of world commodity and financial markets gave reason to challenge existing institutions.

The great metallist reforms were the outcome of the intellectual movement which would later take the name of 'political economy'. This is now used to define an academic subject, taught in universities, but between the second half of the 17th century and the first decades of the 19th century, it became an intellectual, almost a political movement. It was composed of men who, in many countries, believed that human society was organized according to natural principles, which could be studied by the same methods used to inquire into the world of nature. By scientific inquiry the laws which governed society could be discovered and the action of the state could be made to agree with them. In particular, the laws governing the production and distribution of commodities could be discovered, and the principles according to which value was conferred upon goods and services. The political economists soon found themselves considerably disturbed by the existence of a human institution, Money, which continually interfered with the progress of commodity valuation. As hinted above, they tried to devise a solution which would allow society to enjoy the advantages of using money while being spared the problems which the creation and use of money entailed. The solution was a commodity money, a monetary regime whose standard would be a coin made of metal of fixed weight and fineness. They hoped that a commodity money would free the economic world from the uncertainties induced by the raids of those who exercised or usurped monetary sovereignty. A pure metallic money would be subject to the same laws of value to which other commodities were subject; its demand and supply would be determined strictly by the needs of trade.

By advocating the adoption of a pure metallic standard, the political economists were thus killing two birds with one stone. They were putting a stop to the exorbitant privilege of the State, which used its monetary prerogative to tax people without asking for the powers to do so, and were also recommending a type of money which would not disturb the functioning of economic laws, since it obeyed those laws. By the adoption of a pure metallic standard, a truly neutral money could be relied upon.

If the desires of political economists were important in actually pushing forward the adoption of metallic standards, however, it was more because both governing circles and public opinions were anxious to put an end to the previous system, which was based on uncertainty and sovereign privilege, than because of a widely felt need to put economic theory on a sounder theoretical footing.

In this respect British experience is different from the French. In England, a metallic standard had been in use since soon after the great recoinage of the end of the 17th century. At the turn of the next century, Sir Isaac Newton, the Master of the Mint, had established the canonical weight for the Pound sterling in gold, at 123.274 grains of gold at 22/24 carats (corresponding to 7.988 grammes at the title of 0.916). Free minting remained possible but, as very little silver was coined, silver coins were soon demoted by the public to the role of subsidiary currency, as they were still of the old sort, without milled edges, and were badly worn, because of the repeated clipping. Thus, early in the 18th century, England went on the Gold Standard.

In France, metallist reform had to wait until the Revolution. After an early attempt to introduce the Gold Standard, and a gigantic outflow of gold under the Terror government, in the year XI of the Revolution the free minting of both gold and silver was declared. One franc was given a weight of 5 grammes of silver at 9/10 title. A fixed parity was also established between gold and silver, although the French legislators, in the Report of the Comité de Monnayes in 1790, had declared that a permanently fixed parity between the metals was impossible, and had quoted Newton and Locke to corroborate their declaration. Bimetallism was thus instituted in France, and would last almost as long as the Gold Standard in England, but from the beginning it was understood that the parity between gold and silver would have to be changed when necessary, even if it was to be done by law each time. The French lawmakers gave life, therefore, to a system which we would call today of fixed but adjustable parity between gold and silver.

Contemporary literature devoted much attention to the relative virtues of mono- and bimetallism. Modern economic literature, however, starting from the end of World War I, has almost exclusively focused on Gold Monometallism. From the point of view of monetary history this is a pity, because what commonly goes under the name of the International Gold Standard was, on the contrary, a complex system composed of a monometallist and a bimetallist part, where the importance of the former was not greater, for the functioning of the whole system, than that of the latter. We shall see, in what follows, how the smooth functioning of the Gold Standard essentially required the existence if a bimetallist periphery which surrounded the monometallist centre.

Let us first concentrate on the British Gold Standard. After it had been in existence for close to a century it had to be suspended in 1797, because of the difficulties which the Napoleonic wars entailed for monetary management. In the period of over twenty-five years in which cash payments remained suspended, a very lively debate took place among political economists, politicians, bankers, and industrialists on how suspension affected internal and international economic relations. Some of the best pages in the history of political economy were written as contributions to that debate.

Specie payments had been suspended by an Order in Council in February 1797. The same decree had undertaken that they be resumed, at par, six months after a definitive peace treaty had been signed. In the intervening period of open hostilities, the currency had depreciated, the Government had incurred a huge debt which was largely in the hands of City financiers, and war demand for all sorts of commodities had favoured the amassing of great fortunes by a bevy of '*homines novi*'. As peace approached, it was found that a resumption at the old parity would enhance the postwar slump which already appeared after Waterloo. This prospect united landowners and industrialists, who had been natural enemies heretofore, against creditors, Government Debt holders and, in general, people with fixed incomes. Because of its huge debt, the Government ought to have been on the same side as the debtors. It had, however, muddled through the war by putting up a system by which it held bond prices up and kept the financial market favourable to new debt issues. The system consisted of redeeming old long-term debt and replacing it by floating debt. Pascoe Grenfell and David Ricardo were quick to chastise the Government's debt management policy. In 1816 and 1817 the Government's balancing act was successful but in 1818 it came unstuck, as the Government had to buy stock dear and sell it cheap. Meanwhile, the ratio of funded to floating debt had fallen, and this precluded the possibility of reducing the main debt.

Resumption was as highly political a measure as Restriction had been. The Whig opposition railed against Restriction, calling the Government a committee of the Bank of England. And, indeed, the Bank did its best to make the accusation credible. It tried to blackmail the Government into a continuation of Restriction by threatening to stop its support of the Government's debt management policy.

It also threatened to stop accommodating Meyer Nathan Rothschild, who was the principal holder of Government Stock. But Resumption had also its advocates within the Cabinet; Huskisson, for instance, who with Parnell, Henry Thornton, and Francis Horner, had drafted the Bullion Report in 1810 and had thus permanently alienated traditional City interests. He had advocated a prompt resumption in a memorandum he submitted in 1816, and again, early in 1819, he submitted a memorandum calling for prompt resumption accompanied by fiscal deflation. The Government then appointed a Secret Committee to consider resumption, which soon became dominated by opinion in favour. When the Committee's Report was discussed in Parliament, Ricardo's vehement advocacy of resumption definitively swung parliamentary opinion. Payments were resumed, at the old parity, in May 1819. Ricardo called the decision to resume 'a triumph of science, and truth, over prejudice, and error'. It certainly was a triumph of new City blood over old financial interests, who had thrived in the easy days of inflationary finance, lending to financially weak Governments, at rates they themselves pushed up by manipulating the money market.

After resumption at the old parity, a shock wave went through all British economic circles. The Gold Standard did seem to have no advocates left among manufacturers and financiers. The Bank of England had been against it all along, and so menacing had been its representations that the Government had been driven by such impudence to breaking its useful wartime alliance with it, which had rested, it now appeared, on easy money. Landowners, on the contrary, were pleased. A measure that made them poorer in capital values, gave them, at the same time, a greater real value for their rents. It also represented a restoration of old values against the encroachment of industry and its social evils, which had occurred during Restriction. If the Gold Standard was bad for industry, which had flourished under the Paper Pound, then the relative power of the Old Order, which Agriculture represented, would grow again.

The Bullionists, who had campaigned for a resumption at the old parity, believed that a deflation would purge society of the most glaring speculators, of unsound industrialists, and, more generally, of upstarts who had grown rich on easy money. At the same time they believed that the Gold Standard would transform Britain – and we have Huskisson's testimonial to this belief – into the chief bullion market of the world. London would become the 'settling house of the money transactions of the world'. The intention was thus to favour the New City, to be 'Mart and Banker' to the world, rather than its workshop.

Finally, Resumption was seen as an instrument of social justice. Deflation would give back to creditors, who had lent their money to their country in wartime, the full value of what they had lent. To politicians, an automatic Gold Standard looked like a relief from the heavy responsibilities of managing the economy. It would restore them to true political activity, and mark the final transition to Peace.

The French monetary reform was very different. It was aimed directly against the Ancien Régime, seen however in its fiscal capacity, and not as an unholy alliance of politicians and financiers. It ended up by establishing a long-lasting bimetallic system, which did not overlook the interests of those whose prices were fixed in silver, like wage earners and petty traders. The Reform thus did not represent a clearly determined social choice, like the Resumption in Britain. A more neutral system was devised, which tried to accommodate both the third and the fourth estate. The revolutionary experience was too recent to invite, by a deflationist monetary regime, new social disorders. It is somewhat ironic to see how the country, on the verge of defeat, opted for a regime much less radically deflationist than the one the victorious country would choose. In both countries money was constitutionalized, but in Britain the coalescence of interests of the New City and the landowners made the country the world pivot of monetary radicalism. It is fair to say that the expectations of those who had favoured the Gold Standard in Britain were not fulfilled. Deflation brought in its wake unemployment and social disorder. It also induced British industrial producers to invade world markets, as home demand shrank. The benefits the New City interests had expected did indeed materialize, but only a few decades later. The Gold Standard induced export-led growth in Britain, and to become 'mart and banker' to the world she first had to become the workshop of the world. The mechanisms the bullionists had set working thus functioned in reverse. But it would be unfair to say that Huskisson's expectations were representative of those of all bullionists. David Ricardo, for one, expected the Gold Standard to bring about industrial expansion. And he wanted industrial growth to employ the labour made available by the working of the Law of Population, in which he firmly believed.

The Gold Standard was supposed to check the power of the Bank of England, which seemed to have become so great under the Paper Pound as to represent a threat to a truly constitutional institution like Parliament. But its actual functioning enhanced that power even further. As Britain became the workshop of the world and Sterling was more and more widely used as an international currency, the importance of London as a financial centre grew apace. The Bank of England thus became pivot of an international payments system founded on Britain's industrial and financial supremacy. The Bank of England's importance as a commercial bank was enhanced by its monopoly position as a joint stock bank. Just as it had flourished as the chief source of Government finance under restriction, the Bank flourished as a commercial bank as a result of Britain's ascent to industrial and commercial leadership.

Its international pre-eminence was always dependent on its domestic primacy. Under the auspices of the Bank's monopoly, the centralized reserve system, which remained for a long time unique to Britain, was developed. It was a very lean and efficient system, which minimized the amount of cash needed to oil the wheels of the domestic payments network. But it was also highly unstable, since its leanness did not tolerate any serious obstacle which might appear in the national and international flow of cash and capital. The fact that it could carry on for such a long time, until World War I, is explained by a series of fortunate circumstances which occurred in succession. We shall examine them in some detail.

We must, however, strongly underline the fact that, under the Gold Standard, Britain experienced very strong cyclical swings. The hundred years after resumption were marked by commercial and financial crises which recurred about every ten years, even if the last part of the period saw crises appear at longer intervals than before. The regularity of crises gave rise to much monocausal theorizing, and the Gold Standard was often indicted as one of the chief culprits. It was, by contemporary opinion, accused of being a monetary regime too inflexible to allow for the smooth growth of the economy. Critics invariably quoted the French and then the German monetary systems as preferable, since they were supposed to possess a greater degree of flexibility and made possible better management of the economy.

Yet, in spite of a very lean centralized reserve, and of recurrent financial crises, Britain never abandoned the Gold Standard. One of the most important reasons why she was not compelled to do so under the pressure of crisis must be found, as we noted earlier, in the peculiar features the international financial system possessed in the combination of a monometallic and a bimetallic part. Since oldest antiquity, silver was the metal preferred by the Far East for coinage. And for almost as long as history goes, the Western trade balance with the Far East has shown a deficit. A structural trade imbalance with the Far East meant a continuous support of silver towards the East. Around the middle of the 19th century, this structural trend combined with gold discoveries to depress the price of gold. In the last thirty years of the century, however, the trend was reversed, as silver started to be abandoned by most developed countries as a monetary standard. The gold–silver parity rose accordingly.

Throughout the century, London retained a quasi-monopoly of gold and silver transactions. And it maintained, without any interruption, a free gold market. It is certain that it could not have afforded to do so, had not first France and, later on, the Indian Empire come to the rescue.

The Anglo-French financial connection is one of the most fascinating, and least researched, features of the 19th-century international payments system. From what we know, however, it appears that the much greater liquidity the French monetary system retained throughout the 19th century was skilfully exploited by Britain. Bank rate would be raised when pressure was felt on the Bank of England's reserve, but the expectation was that gold would flow mainly from Paris. Why did it flow? First of all, because there was a lot there, because of both the wealth of the French economy and of the underdevelopment of the French banking system, which rendered the use of gold coins for large transactions necessary (whereas in Britain cheques were commonly used). We must not forget, however, the essential role played by the House of Rothschild in connecting the French and British money markets. The archival evidence available shows that, in most British financial crises, the reserves of the Bank of England were refurbished with gold procured by Rothschild from France. The House of Rothschild intermediated between the gold and silver sides of the international monetary system. They were the super arbitrageurs who had the huge reserves and prestige necessary to play successfully a role which remains to be described in full detail, but whose importance it is possible to detect even in the present state of research. They were the 'protectors' of Bank Rate. It is not without importance that a Rothschild sat in the Court of Directors of the Bank of England and a French Rothschild occupied an equivalent position in the Directorate of the Banque de France.

Towards the end of the century, however, the precipitous fall of silver, induced by, and in turn determining, the abandonment of silver as a monetary standard in the whole developed world, reduced the role played by the French monetary system as a stabilizer of the Gold Standard. France had herself to close the mints to silver, to avoid being flooded by a metal nobody seemed to want any more. In the remaining period, commonly referred to as the 'heyday of the Gold Standard', the Bank of England's balancing act could continue with the help of two other shock absorbers, the Indian monetary system, still based on silver, and South African gold production. The Empire of India was kept by the British on a silver standard even when silver was fast depreciating against gold. This made exports of primary commodities and raw materials easy and was undoubtedly responsible to a large extent for the large export surplus India earned in the last part of the pre-war period. It is in the management of this surplus in a way conducive to the stablity of the Gold Standard that the British financial elite proved most imaginative and successful. The Indian surplus was invested in London, in Government bonds or in deposits with the banking system. The 'Council Bills' system, which had been devised to effect financial transfers between India and the Metropolis, was managed so as to keep the Rupee's value stable. The whole system, called the 'Gold Exchange Standard', was extolled as a paragon of skill and efficiency by J.M. Keynes, in the book that first gave him notoriety, *Indian Currency and Finance* (1913). Indeed, the young Keynes was right, as far as the functioning of the Gold Standard was concerned. Whether it was also efficient from the point of view of promoting Indian economic development is entirely another matter, and one with which Indian economic historians have seldom concerned themselves.

South African gold production also helped to stabilize the Gold Standard. All the gold mined there was commercialized in London, and the proceeds invested there, at least in the short run. It is easy to imagine how important the British monetary authorities considered the control of that huge flow. This became evident, after World War I, when an attempt was made to revive the Gold Standard. Following Professor Kemmerer's advice, South Africa decided in favour of the Gold Standard, and against pegging its currency to Sterling. The connection with London was cut, to the great discomfort of Montagu Norman, who saw one of the main props of Sterling suddenly disappear.

If France, India and South Africa contributed to making the Gold Standard stable, the United States represented, throughout the century in which the Gold Standard lasted, one of the great, perhaps the single greatest, disturbing elements to its smooth functioning. After the political and economic forces which stood for an orderly financial development of the Republic had been routed in the first decades of the 19th century, the growth of the American economy took the spasmodic features it would keep until World War II. The United States was deliberately deprived of the Central Bank that Alexander Hamilton, imitating the Bank of England, had designed. Banks proliferated everywhere, following a model of wildcat finance which, if it promoted the phenomenal growth of the US economy, also gave it a very strong cyclical pattern. For the whole Gold Standard period, the Bank of England was called to play the difficult role of being the lender of last resort to the American financial system. The growth of American farm exports, coupled to local industrial growth and the peculiar development-underdevelopment of the US banking system, gave rise to a notorious seasonal pattern of financial difficulties, which was called the 'autumn drain'. This recurred every year, when American crops were sold on world markets and the proceeds disappeared into the entrails of the completely decentralized American banking system, and, more generally, into the hands of American farmers. A gold drain was felt first in New York, the main US financial centre. Interest rates rose violently, as there was no centralized banking reserve in New York, and the US Treasury, which kept a very large gold reserve, knew only very imperfectly how to use it for stabilization purposes. The rise of New York rates would thus be transmitted to London, which kept the only free gold market. Gold would thus flow to New York and it would be months before it could be seen again, as farmers spent the proceeds of crop sales and US local banks recycled the money back to New York.

To this seasonal drain, to which the Bank of England was never able to find a remedy, other sudden drains would be added, when the peculiar American banking system went into one of its recurrent panics. After the most violent of them had, in 1907, brought chaos to the whole international economy, the US Congress decided to move and in 1913 the Federal Reserve System was established. But it took another twenty years, and another huge crisis, that of 1929–33, before it really began to work as a central bank.

We have dedicated considerable space to a summary of US financial history because it must be fully appreciated what the peculiar structure of American finance meant for the world financial system in the age of the Gold Standard. The country which by the end of the century had become both the largest industrial producer and largest agricultural exporter, was still importing huge financial resources from the rest of the world. It lacked a central bank and had developed a thoroughly decentralized banking system which, if it was functional to rapid economic growth, had also a strong vocation for recurrent instability. The US Congress and Government also did their part to enhance instability by unwise and partisan policies concerning, for instance, silver prices, and the management of fiscal revenues.

In the last decade of the 19th century the crisis of silver induced a veritable stampede by Governments and Parliaments, in most countries, to adopt the Gold Standard. More than the unidirectional movement of silver, it was its wild oscillations, made deeper by the inconsiderate silver policies of the United States, that convinced most interested parties to opt for gold. Even European farmers, who were fighting a desperate war against cheap New World imports, were

323

reduced to favouring the Gold Standard by the impossibility of forecasting a price for their harvest at sowing time. Industrialists in developing countries who had started import substitution activities were in favour of a strong currency to repay foreign loans without problems, and preferred protection as a means of keeping out foreign industrial products. Most countries, when they went on the Gold Standard, also started a centralized gold reserve, which they intended as an exchange stabilization fund. Very often they surrounded this reserve by an outward layer in foreign currency reserves, which they called upon under pressure in order to keep their gold reserve intact.

Contrary to what British monetary authorities thought and did after World War I, their pre-war predecessors were extremely worried by the universal trend in favour of Central Banking and of the Gold Standard. They very correctly understood that Britain had succeeded in staying at the centre of the system as long as it remained a free-flow system, where the only stock of gold was the one kept by the Bank of England. French gold accumulation had been seen favourably, as it enhanced the *masse de manoeuvre* of the Bank of England at almost no cost. But already German gold accumulation was a threat, as Germany did not believe in a free gold market and Bank Rate found obstacles in attracting gold from there. The German pattern was, unfortunately for Britain, the one that found the largest number of followers among countries that established a Central Bank and a central reserve to manage the Gold Standard. The result was the increasing seclusion of previously free-flowing gold into large stocks, over which the British traditional control instrument, Bank Rate, scarcely exercised any leverage and which dwarfed in size the reserves of the Bank of England.

To these external difficulties with which British monetary authorities were greatly concerned, others of a more domestic nature had to be added.

The British financial system had emerged from the turmoil of the Napoleonic wars apparently unscathed. It was formed by a cluster of merchant banks and other financial institutions, like the discount house, and by the great commodity and service exchanges, and it had the Bank of England at its centre. The composition of the governing body of the Bank of England ensured that most City voices would get a fair hearing. It is impossible to exaggerate its internal homogeneity and cohesion (especially at a time like the present, when the system is being definitively demolished). A good study of the City in the years of the Gold Standard ought to be conducted by structural anthropologists, rather than by economists. A very serious threat to this semi-tribal system, which had succeeded in controlling world trade and payments for many decades, was developing fast in the late years of the Gold Standard. It was represented by the rapid concentration of British deposit banking, which resulted in the survival of only a handful of giant joint-stock banks. The Clearing Banks – as they came to be called – provided the City with a large part of the short-term funds which were used as raw material to finance world commodity trade. They had huge branch networks which channelled savings from the remotest corners of Britain to London, and thence to all parts of the world through City intermediation. Thus the Clearing Banks provided the base for the whole British financial system.

But their power was not constitutionalized by any matching responsibility. They had no say in the conduct of monetary policy. They were not represented in the Court of Directors of the Bank of England. Moreover, as concentration increased, the Clearing Banks thought they might as well invade some of the markets traditionally reserved to merchant banks and, in particular, they started invading the field of commodity trade financing. Finally, they began to lay the foundations for their own centralized gold reserve, alternative to that kept by the Bank of England.

Speaking more generally, a trend can be noticed in the last 25 years of the pre-war Gold Standard, away from homogeneity and towards decentralization, in the British financial system. The Clearing Banks increasingly baulked at being disciplined by the Bank of England. Often, especially in times of crisis, they pulled the rug from under the financial establishment, by withdrawing their short-term deposits with City houses. By this behaviour they showed their muscle and demanded recognition. This pattern is clearly detectable in the 1890, 1907 and 1914 crises. It was a trend that greatly disturbed the financial elite and contributed, with the exogenous factors we have mentioned before, to making the Gold Standard more unstable. It could even be said that the loss of cohesiveness and homogeneity of the British financial system brought the Gold Standard to its demise, in July 1914. The system collapsed long before Britain entered the conflict.

THE GOLD STANDARD AND THE ECONOMISTS. The development of Gold Standard theory coincides with the development of economic theory. We have already mentioned the role played by commodity money in the theoretical apparatus of the classical economists. A commodity money would obey the rules dictated by Nature (of which even human behaviour was part) as far as its supply, demand, and price were concerned. Thus a monetary economy based on a pure metallic standard would enjoy all the advantages afforded by the presence of money, without being subject to the many disadvantages induced by a man-made currency not tied to a metal. For David Ricardo, the recommendation to adopt the Gold Standard meant not only preventing the Bank of England from usurping monetary sovereignty, which he recognized as a Parliamentary prerogative, it also meant giving the economic system a standard, like gold, which had the virtue of being a good approximation to his invariant measure of value. He wanted to see the price system uninfluenced by political power, so that Nature would be free to play her game and gold would be distributed among the 'different civilized nations of the earth, according to the state of their commerce and wealth, and therefore according to the number and frequency of the payments which they had to perform' (Ricardo [1811], 1951, p. 52). If freedom of gold movements existed, this redistribution would soon bring about a state of rest, when gold had been allotted to each nation according to its needs and would not move again. If all countries promoted metallist reforms, fixing a gold weight for their currencies, arbitrageurs would operate, within the gold points, to keep gold prices uniform. Gold would function as the *numéraire* of the world economic system and it would be enough to ensure gold arbitrage to guarantee uniformity of all the world price systems. There would be no need for arbitrage to involve other, bulkier commodities, whose transportation would imply greater costs. This, of course, did not mean that international trade would not take place. Commodities would move across countries according to the Law of Comparative Advantage, and the Gold Standard would make sure that this law did not suffer perturbations because of 'unregulated' money supplies. 'Regulation', of course, meant that fiduciary money would depend, for its supply, on the dynamics of the gold reserve of the issuing agency. Ricardo's view of how the world economy worked, based on his analysis of commodity currency systems, rapidly conquered not only the economics profession but also politicians and intellectuals. It was a scientific system of political economy, whose core was the Gold Standard. John Stuart Mill and Alfred Marshall were to refine and qualify that world view.

Mill analysed with great care the implications of a commodity money, whose exchange value would be equal to its cost of production. He did, however, clearly point out the importance of the existing stock of gold relative to its current or even potential flow. The gold stock/flow ratio made full adjustment a lengthy process, so that, in the short run, the price level would be determined by the demand for, and supply of, money. He never doubted, however, that a commodity money would not be able to change the international production relations as they existed under barter. To him money was, like oil in the wheels of moving mechanisms, 'a contrivance to reduce friction'. He fully trusted that David Hume's adjustment mechanism would have only nominal consequences in the case of a discovery of a hoard of treasure in one country. This would raise prices there, discourage exports and induce imports. The resulting balance of payments deficit would redistribute the hoard to the rest of the world and lower prices in the original country to their previous level. In Mill's opinion, real effects would, however, result in the case of a loan from one country to another. Then a real transfer would have to be effected.

Neither Mill nor Marshall considered the Gold Standard a perfect system. Both of them opposed bimetallism at fixed rates. They believed that relative changes in the costs of production of the two metals would be likely, and that would involve a scarcity of the dearer metal and a shift in favour of the monetary use of the cheaper one. Instability was therefore built into the bimetallist system. Mill preferred a 'limping' gold standard, where gold would be the only legal tender, and silver would be coined at market prices. John Locke's tradition obviously lived on.

Marshall's creative thinking in the field of monetary standards included 'symetallism' and the 'Tabular standard'. According to the first scheme, vaguely reminiscent of the oldest currency, the Lydian 'Elektron', if the public wanted to give paper currency and receive metals it could only get gold and silver together, in bars of fixed proportions. Marshall thought this would link the paper currency to the mean of the values of the two metals and make possible, by this more stable currency, a world monetary area including both the gold and silver countries. It is easy to recognize in Marshall's scheme a forerunner of the contemporary European Monetary System's ECU.

Marshall's Tabular standard, on the other hand, reintroduced the concept of a money of account separate from the medium of exchange. The money of account would serve for long-term contracts and would be tied to an 'official index number, representing average movements of the prices of important commodities' (Marshall, 1923, p. 36).

As far as the adjustment mechanism under a gold standard regime was concerned, Marshall clearly saw the growing integration of capital markets replacing traded goods, arbitrage and gold movements as the chief instrument of adjustment. This of course meant recognizing the importance of interest rate differentials and interest arbitrage, and, in turn, giving a great role to play to banks and Central Banks.

With J.S. Mill, Marshall, and, in particular, Irving Fisher, we begin to get out of the 'naturalist' world view which permeates the writings of Ricardo, his inspirers, and his followers. The world is not run solely according to forces of nature, which it is the economist's role to discover and which cannot be violated without meeting an inevitable punishment. The Gold Standard is not a 'scientific method' of organizing a monetary regime. Like Marshall, Irving Fisher thinks of it more in historical rather than scientific terms. It is something the world embraced by historical accident. Supply and demand conditions for gold and silver are unstable. The system is not perfect and is perfectible, justifying proposals to make it work better.

As we advance toward what has been called the 'heyday' of the Gold Standard, in the eyes of contemporary economists its virtues seem to pale and its vices to come into relief. To Knut Wicksell, under a commodity standard there is no guarantee that a causal link will be able to exist between money supply and price level movements. Such a link can be seen to exist only if we take a very long view. Like the practitioner-theorists who staffed the British Treasury before 1914, Wicksell noticed that central banks, by keeping large gold reserves, had interposed themselves between gold supply and price movements. The price stabilization function of central banks is recognized and the new institutional set-up is in any case superior to a pure metallic standard, which in Wicksell's eyes would be totally at the mercy of the vagaries of demand for and supply of gold.

The 'heyday of the Gold Standard' which (as we hope to have shown above) was in historic reality the beginning of its decline, were thus also days of decline as far as Gold Standard theory was concerned. A growing scepticism begins to engulf Hume's price–specie flow mechanism. Commodity arbitrage is seen as prevailing over gold arbitrage. Adjustment must involve real, not just nominal changes. International capital movements are brought increasingly into the picture. Stock adjustment in all sorts of markets is a phenomenon which fascinates the economic theorists of this age. From recognizing stock adjustments to advocating stock management is a short intellectual distance and most of these theorists cover it at great speed.

Ironically, in the theoretical cycle the pendulum had swung, in the 25 years before World War I, away from Ricardo and Locke and towards Lowndes and Thornton. The pure metallic standard has lasted only '*l'espace d'un matin*' both in theory and practice. Economists had not been able to ignore the giant strides of banking and of world economic and financial integration. From Ricardo's golden rules, simple and infallible, we move to Mill, Marshall, Wicksell, and Fisher and their inventive recipes for national and international monetary management. Doubts prevail over certainties. We cannot accept J.M. Keynes's post-war strictures about the pre-war perception of the Gold Standard. It was *not* seen as immutable, frictionless, and automatic by its contemporaries. The seeds of post-war criticism and disenchantment were firmly sown before the war. In fact, we might go as far as to say that pre-war learned opinion was much less apologetic of the pure metallic standard than would be the post-war economists and politicians. Pre-war observers had realized that the Gold Standard was a game which had become increasingly hard to play, precisely because everybody had learned – and wanted – to play it.

BIBLIOGRAPHY

Ashton, T.S. and Sayers, R.S. 1953. *Papers in English Monetary History*. Oxford: Clarendon Press.
Bagehot, W. 1873. *Lombard Street*. Reprint of the 1915 edn, New York: Arno Press, 1969.
Bloomfield, A.I. 1959. *Monetary Policy under the International Gold Standard*. New York: Federal Reserve Bank of New York.
Bordo, M. and Schwartz, A.J. (eds) 1984. *A Retrospective of the Classical Gold Standard 1821–1931*. Chicago: University of Chicago Press.
Clapham, J.H. 1944. *A History of the Bank of England*. 2 vols, Cambridge: Cambridge University Press.
Cottrell, P.L. 1980. *Industrial Finance 1830–1914*. London: Methuen.
De Cecco, M. 1984. *The International Gold Standard: Money and Empire*. 2nd edn, London: Frances Pinter.
Fanno, M. 1912. *Le banche e il mercato monetario*. Roma: Loescher.
Feaveryear, A. 1963. *The Pound Sterling*. 2nd edn, Oxford: Clarendon Press.
Fetter, F.W. 1965. *Development of British Monetary Orthodoxy 1717–1875*. Cambridge, Mass.: Harvard University Press.
Ford, A.G. 1962. *The Gold Standard 1880–1914: Britain and Argentina*. Oxford: Clarendon Press.
Goodhart, C.A.E. 1972. *The Business of Banking 1891–1914*. London: Weidenfeld & Nicholson.
Hilton, B. 1977. *Cash, Corn and Commerce: the Economic Policies of the Tory Governments 1815–1830*. Oxford: Oxford University Press.
Ingham, G. 1984. *Capitalism Divided? The City and Industry in British Social Development*. London: Macmillan.
Keynes, J.M. 1913. *Indian Currency and Finance*. In Vol. 1 of *The Collected Writings of J.M. Keynes*, London: Macmillan, 1971.
Lindert, P.H. 1969. *Key Currencies and Gold 1890–1913*. Princeton Studies in International Finance, No. 24, Princeton: Princeton University Press. ·
Marshall, A. 1923. *Money, Credit and Commerce*. London: Macmillan.
McCloskey, D.N. and Zecher, J.R. 1976. How the Gold Standard worked. In *The Monetary Approach to Balance of Payments Theory*, ed. J. Frenkel and H.G. Johnson, Toronto: University of Toronto Press.

Mommsen, T. 1865. *Histoire de la monnaie romaine*. Paris: Rollin et Feuardent.

Morgan, E.V. 1965. *The Theory and Practice of Central Banking 1797–1913*. London: Frank Cass.

Nogaro, B. 1908. L'expérience bimétalliste du XIXe siècle. *Revue d'Economie Politique* 22(10), October, 641–721.

Report from the Select Committee on the High Price of Bullion 1810. New York: Arno Press, 1978.

Ricardo, D. 1811. *The High Price of Bullion: A Proof of the Depreciation of Bank Notes*. In *The Works and Correspondence of David Ricardo*, ed. P. Sraffa, Vol. 3, Cambridge: Cambridge University Press, 1951.

Sayers, R.S. 1936. *Bank of England Operations 1890–1914*. London: P.S. King & Son.

Supino, C. 1910. *Il mercato monetario internazionale*. Milano: Hoepli.

Thornton, H. 1802. *An Inquiry into the Nature and Effects of the Paper Credit of Great Britain*. New York: Augustus Kelley, 1978.

Triffin, R. 1964. *The Evolution of the International Monetary System*. Princeton Essays in International Finance No. 12, Princeton: Princeton University Press.

Williams, D. 1968. The evolution of the sterling system. In *Essays in Honour of R.S. Sayers*, ed. C.R. Wittlesley and J.S.G. Wilson, Oxford: Clarendon Press.

Hunting and Gathering Economies

VERNON L. SMITH

Men and women (*Homo erectus*) who were culturally and biologically distinguishable from other hominoids have lived on the planet Earth for about 1.6 million years (Pilbeam, 1984). It is likely that the biological changes since that time form a microevolutionary continuum: archaic *H. sapiens*, including the Neanderthal, appeared 125,000 years ago and anatomically modern *H. sapiens* appeared about 45,000 years ago. The record suggests that *H. erectus* fabricated and used tools, and his use of fire may have begun by 700,000 years ago. The changes identified in the prehistoric period appear only to distinguish less advanced from more advanced stone age technology. Consequently, the dominating message seems to be that over almost the whole of man's epoch on earth he lived successfully as an exceptionally well-adapted hunter. It is only recently, in the last 8–10,000 years (less than one per cent of his time on Earth), that man abandoned the nomadic life of the hunter to begin growing crops, husbanding domesticated animals and living in villages. It is difficult to exaggerate the importance of this agricultural or first economic revolution (North and Thomas, 1977) in understanding who we are, and what we have become. Once man opted for the farmer–herder way of life it was but a short step to mankind's much more sophisticated development of specialization and exchange, greatly enlarged production surpluses, the emergence of the State, and finally the industrial revolution. Our direct knowledge of early man is confined to the record of the durables he left behind. Yet when combined with anthropological evidence from the study of recent hunter–gatherer economies the evidence can be intepreted as demonstrating that all the ingredients associated with the modern wealth of nations – investment in human capital, specialization and exchange, the development of property right or contracting institutions, even environmental 'damage' – had their development in the course of that vast prehistorical, pre-agricultural period.

330

What accounts for this sudden abandonment of the nomadic hunting life? We do not know for we have no direct observations on the transformation from hunting to agriculture. This transformation is perhaps the pre-eminent scientific mystery, since all of that which we have called civilization, all the great achievements of industry, science, art and literature stem from that momentous event within the last few minutes of man's day on Earth. Yet there are common factors that dominated the evolution of man from his earliest form to modern *H. sapiens* and his primary intellectual and social development, and which suggest an underground continuity between the pre-agricultural, Paleolithic hunting period, and the agricultural and subsequent periods.

MAN THE HUNTER–GATHERER. There are many widely held beliefs concerning the characteristic features of the hunter–gatherer way of life that stretch back several hundred years in academic writings, and persist as part of the folklore of contemporary man's misperception of his own prehistoric past; until recently these benefits dominated even the anthropological view of hunter–gatherer 'subsistence'. These beliefs tend to obscure the striking continuity in man's ability to respond to changes in his environment by substituting new inputs (labour, capital and knowledge) for old, and develop new products to replace the old when effort prices were altered by the environment.

Ever since Hobbes there has prevailed the perception that life in the state of nature was 'solitary, poor, nasty, brutish and short'. A more accurate representation (if not strictly correct in all aboriginal societies) would argue that the hunter culture was the original affluent society (Lee and DeVore, 1968). Extensive earlier data on extant hunter–gatherers show that with rare exceptions (such as the Netsilik Eskimos) their food base was at minimum reliable, at best very abundant. The African Kung Bushman inhabited the semi-arid northwest region of the Kalahari Desert, an inhospitable environment, characterized by drought every second or third year. These conditions had served more to isolate the Kung from their agricultural neighbours than to condemn them to a brutish existence. Adults typically worked 12–19 hours per week in getting food. As with all such societies for the most part the women gathered, the men hunted. The caloric-protein returns exceeded several measures of nutritional adequacy. Gathering was the more reliable and productive activity with women producing over twice as many edible calories per hour as men. Both men and women bought leisure with this work schedule – resting, visiting, entertaining and (for the men) trance dancing. About 40 per cent of the population were children, unmarried young adults (15–25 years of age) or elderly (over 60 years of age), who did not contribute to the food supply and were not pressured to contribute.

A comparable macroeconomic picture applied to the Hazda in Tanzania. Large and small animals were numerous and all – with the exception of the elephant – were hunted and eaten by Hazda. Hunting was the speciality of men and boys, conducted as an individual pursuit that relied primarily on poisoned arrows. The Hazda spent on average no more than two hours a day hunting. The principal leisure activity of the men was gambling which consumed more time than hunting.

331

Other hunting (or fishing) peoples of Africa, Australia, the Pacific Northwest, Alaska, Malaya and Canada have shown comparably effective adaptation to this form of livelihood. Malnutrition, starvation and chronic diseases were rare or infrequent, although accidental death was high in certain cases such as the Eskimo.

The argument that life in the Paleolithic must have been intolerably harsh is simply not borne out by the many ethnographic studies of extant hunting societies in the past century. With few exceptions such societies have fared well, and did not leap to embrace the agricultural or pastoral pursuits of their neighbours. Whether life in the Paleolithic mirrored this modern experience cannot be known with any assurance, but certainly there is no support for the proposition that hunting, *per se*, means an intolerably harsh existence. In fact the Paleolithic hunting economy had demonstrably high survival value in a world far more plentifully endowed with game than has existed since the great megafaunal extinctions of the late Pleistocene, and therefore a world which might indeed have been marked by numerous original affluent economies.

Although it is natural to suppose that man's uniqueness derived from his intellectual superiority, what is more likely is that man's physical superiority was also important in giving him a superpredator's advantage over other species. His endowment of physical human capital would probably have been of significance even in the absence of his investment in tools and the human capital required to produce and use tools. As noted by J.B.S. Haldane, only man can swim a mile, walk twenty, and then climb a tree. Add to this observation the four-minute mile, unsurpassed long-distance endurance running, the ability to carry loads in excess of body weight, high altitude performance, American Indian capacity literally to run down a horse or deer by pacing the animal, the incredible accomplishments of acrobats and gymnasts, and finally the finger agility and coordination required to milk a cow, and you are left with the physical portrait of an astonishingly superior species. It appears that man's basic foundation of physical superiority was laid by his upright stance, to which of course the addition of knowledge made him truly formidable, even in the presence of the various giant proboscidea (mastodon, mammoth, elephant) which early man did not hesitate to hunt and to kill on three continents.

The idea that primitive man was too puny and too few in number to have had a significant influence on his environment underestimates man's uniqueness as a tool-using, fire-using, highly mobile species who, with minor exceptions (Madagascar, New Zealand and Antarctica), had populated the world by 8000 BC. The archaeological record suggests that man was a big game hunter *par excellence*. He hunted mammoth, mastodon, horse, bison, camel, sloth, reindeer, shrub oxen, red deer, aurochs (wild cattle), and other large mammals, for perhaps a minimum of 30–40,000 years, ceasing only with the great megafaunal extinctions throughout much of the world some 8–12,000 years ago. Paul Martin (1967) has argued the case for the overkill hypothesis that man was a significant causative factor in these extinctions. Essentially, the argument is that the alternatives to overkill, principally the climate hypothesis, fail to account for the worldwide pattern of these extinctions which appear to have begun in Africa and perhaps southeast Asia 40–50,000 years ago, spread north through Eurasia 11–13,000 years ago, jumped to Australia perhaps 13,000 years ago, and entered North America in the last 11,000 years, followed by South America 10,000 years before the present. The most recent extinctions are in New Zealand (numerous species of flightless moa birds) 900 years ago and in Madagascar 800 years ago, shortly after the remarkably late migration of man to those islands.

Man's use of fire as a tool in the management and control of natural resources must be counted as having a profound effect on his ecological environment. Numerous authors who have studied patterns of land burning by primitive peoples have concluded that most of the greatest grasslands of the world represent fire-vegetation that is manmade (see Heizer, 1955, for a summary). Where tree growth is strongly favoured by climatic conditions, regular burning will select for certain species of tree such as the pine stands of southern New York and to the West, which have been attributed to Indian burning. Contemporary man's attempts to prevent fires, which today are almost entirely caused by lightning, has probably produced far more ecological damage than the controlled use of fire that has characterized aboriginal cultures. Recurrent fire prevents the accumulation of brush which then fuels the holocaust wildfire that destroys all forest vegetation.

A third source of ecological change produced by primitive peoples was their transportation of seed, in their migrations as hunter–gatherers, which introduced numerous botanical exotics into new regions. Archaeologists have frequently observed the association of various plants with ancient campsites and dwellings. For example, the wide distribution of wild squash, gathered for its seed, appears to be associated with man. The introduction of exotics can and has produced significant environmental changes in modern times, but the phenomenon has ancient origins and may have been considerably more disruptive as the first men moved from one 'pristine natural' region to another.

Success as a hunter–gatherer requires human capital usually associated only with agricultural and industrial man: learning, knowledge transfer, tool development and social organization. Comprehensive studies of the aboriginal use of fire for game and plant management show clearly that primitive men demonstrated extensive knowledge of the reproductive cycles of shrubs and herbaceous plants, and used fire to encourage the growth and flowering of the plants used in gathering, and to discourage the growth of undesirable plants (Lewis, 1973). This required one to know when, where, how and with what frequency to apply the important tool of controlled burning for managing the resources that allow gathering to make an efficient, productive and sustainable contribution to living. Primitive men knew that the growing season can be advanced by spring burns designed to warm the earth, that in dry weather fires should be set at the top of hills to prevent wild fires, but in damp air they should be set in depressions to avoid being extinguished, that the burning of underbrush aided the growth of the oak whose acorns were eaten and attracted moose which avoid underbrush, and that deer and other animals congregate to feed on the proliferation of tender new plants that sprout following a fall burn.

To live by hunting is to be committed to an intellectually and physically demanding activity that requires technology, skill, social organization, some division of labour, knowledge of animal behaviour, the habit of close observation, inventiveness, problem solving, risk bearing and high motivation, since the rewards are great and the penalties severe. Such exceptional demands could have been highly selective in man's long evolution, and disciplined the development of the intellectual and genetic equipment that facilitated his subsequent rapid creation of modern civilization. This natural selection could have been intensified by the widespread practice among aboriginals of rewarding superior hunters with many wives.

It was as a hunter that man learned to learn. In particular he understood that young boys must be imbued with the habit of goal-oriented observations, and with knowledge of animal behaviour and anatomy. To know that many ungulates travel in an arc meant that tracking success could be improved by transversing the chord. Knowledge of animal behaviour was a substitute for weapon development. Even the weapons of the later pre-agricultural period (spears, bow and arrow, harpoon) required the hunter to approach the prey within ten yards for a best shot. This might require hours crouched on the ground waiting for a shift in the wind, for just the right change in the animal's position, or for the mammoth to get deeper into the bog in a watering hole. The weapons changed with shifts to new prey. Thus the Clovis fluted point, widely distributed throughout North America, was used to kill mammoth and mastodon 11–12,000 years ago. The Folsom point was then developed and used to kill the large, now extinct *Bison antiquus*, and then gave way to the Scottsbluff point associated with the killing of the slightly smaller, now extinct *Bison occidentalis* (Haynes, 1964; Wheat, 1967). These observations suggest high specialization which required new forms of human and physical capital to meet the specialized demands of new prey.

The organizational requirements of the hunt are illustrated at the Olsen–Chubbuck site in Colorado, where the excavated remains of bones and projectile points of the Scottsbluff design show that about 8500 years ago some two hundred *Bison occidentalis* were stampeded into an arroyo 5–7 feet deep. Armed hunters in the arroyo on each side of the stampede then slaughtered the injured or escaping animals with their weapons (Wheat, 1967).

Primitive man has often been modelled as 'cultural' not 'economic' man, but the power and importance of the opportunity cost principle in conditioning the choice of all peoples was perceptively stated by the Kung Bushman, who, when asked why he had not turned to agriculture, replied, 'Why should we plant, when there are so many mongongo nuts in the world?' (Lee and DeVore, 1968, p. 33). This Bushman, I would hypothesize, stated the answer to the scientific question: why did man the hunter tend to abandon that which appeared to serve him so well for 1.6 million years and to which he seems to have adapted ever more successfully, as indicated by the growing complexity of his tools and weapons as he evolved from *H. erectus* to anatomically modern *H. sapiens*? Man would not have given up the hunter–gatherer life had there not been a change in the terms of trade between man and nature that made the hunting way of life more costly relative to agriculture. This *hypothesis* does not leave 'culture' out of the equation. Thus to describe hunter–gatherers as directly seeking the cultural goal of prestige does not contradict the hypothesis that man, like nature, ever economizes. Attaching prestige to the hunt may simply be an astute means of advertising, teaching and propagating the discovery that hunting and its attendant technology is the best means of livelihood, with the result that each new generation does not have to rediscover this knowledge. Myths of the great hunter, of great rewards, of great penalties for lost technique, of killing the goose that lays golden eggs, are part of the oral tradition by which the economy preserve this human capital.

The hypothesis that the agricultural revolution was due to a major decrease in the productivity of labour in hunting–gathering relative to agriculture (Smith, 1975; North and Thomas, 1977) is consistent with the observations that this cultural shift (a) occurred at different times in different parts of the world, with small aboriginal hunting enclaves still in existence, and (b) did not occur once and for all in every such tribe. With respect to (a), the great wave of terrestrial animal extinctions occurred over a period of several thousand years, and therefore the relative increase in the cost of hunting struck different regions at different times. Also different peoples in different environments with different opportunity costs would be expected to provide different mechanisms of adaptation, with some persisting as gatherers and small game hunters, and others turning to or perhaps persisting as fisherman (e.g. the Aleutian Eskimos and the Pacific Northwest Indians) in regions unsuitable for agriculture. With respect to (b) the reintroduction of the horse in North America by the Spanish (in the hardy form of *Equus caballus* just 8000 years after other members of the genus became extinct in the Americas) had a major modifying impact on the economy of the plains Indians. In the northern plains the 'fighting' Cheyenne, as they were later to be termed by the Europeans, and the Arapahoe quickly abandoned their villages along with their pottery arts and horticulture to become nomadic bison hunters (see the references in Smith, 1975). Apparently, agricultural productivity was dominated by the enormous increase in the bison harvest made possible by a technological change that combined the horse with the bow and arrow. To the south, where the growing season was longer and the climate more favourable, the Pawnee preserved their maize agriculture when they turned to bison hunting, creating a mixed agricultural–hunting economy. The southwestern Apache, reported by Coronado in 1541 to be subsisting as bison hunters, simply adapted the horse to their pre-existing hunter culture. The vast bison-hide tepee encampments witnessed by the first Europeans to cross the plains were already the product of technologically transformed native Americans, many of whom had only recently abandoned their agricultural economies.

PLEISTOCENE EXTINCTIONS AND THE RISE OF AGRICULTURE. Here then is a model of the epoch of man: he arrives 1.6 million years ago as a hunter among hunters, but distinguishable in terms of his human capital endowment and his ability to invest in the development of human and physical capital. His tools become more complex and knowledge of the use of fire, perhaps his most significant tool, is added to his stock of human capital. There is a gradual improvement in weapons technology – clubs, stones, stone axes, spears, stone projectile points, the atlatl (which applies the leverage principle) and, in the late pre-agricultural period, the bow (which combines the leverage principle with temporary storage of energy for increased mechanical advantage). The combination of his physical superiority, tools and fire make him a superpredator without equal. At some unknown point this success brings relative affluence, and the important commodity 'leisure', which might have contributed to the development of language and other forms of investment in human and physical capital.

Although *H. erectus* and archaic *H. sapiens* were advanced hunters who apparently spread from Africa to Eurasia and Asia, it remained for modern *H. sapiens* to establish himself as a big-game hunter *par excellence*, who populated most of the world by 8000 BC. Associated with this radiation is recorded a wave of extinction that was largely confined to the large terrestrial herbivores and their dependent carnivores and scavengers. (Other extinction episodes in the Earth's history had affected plants and marine life, as well as animals.) There appear to be no continents or islands where these accelerated late Pleistocene extinctions precede man's invasion (Martin, 1967). Whether men caused these extinctions cannot be known with any certainty, but Martin's overkill hypothesis is clearly consistent with a common property resource model of the economics of megaherbivore hunting (Smith, 1975). Thus the large gregarious animals that suffered extinction provided low search cost and high kill value. The lack of appropriation (branding or domestication) provided disincentives for conservation and sustained yield harvesting. There are numerous stampede kill sites (pitfalls and cliffs) in Russia, Europe and North America that indicate wastage killing in excess of immediate butchering requirements. Considering the complex of suitabilities necessary for the remains of such a site to have been preserved, it is likely that only the tip of such phenomena has been observed. Finally, the slow growth, long lives and long maturation of the megafauna made them more vulnerable than other animals to extinction by hunting pressure.

But our model of economizing man need not sustain such a controversial hypothesis as overkill. It is sufficient that the easy, valuable prey disappeared, precipitating a decline in the productivity of hunting. Substitution is to be expected, given a change in relative effort 'prices'. Hence, it is in this late pre-agricultural period that the archaeological record shows the appearance of bows and arrows, seed-grinding stones, boiling vessels, boats, more advanced houses, even 'villages' (probably clan group abodes), animal-drawn sledges and the dog (almost certainly derived from domesticating the wolf). These developments strongly suggest the substitution of new tools and techniques for the old, which allowed new products to substitute for the loss of big game that could be harvested by stampeding and/or dispatch with thrusting or throwing weapons. Now the bow and arrow becomes adaptive, and gathering becomes more crucial to maintaining overall food productivity. Whereas formerly, gathering emphasized seeds and plants that could be eaten on the run, now some of the seeds gathered were inedible without grinding, soaking, boiling.

All this paraphernalia implies more sedentary, less nomadic, hunting and gathering.

Hence the incentive to invest in facilities such as utensils, sledges and houses. The boat allows fishing, sealing and whaling. The wolf, also characterized by its capacity to apply organization to the hunt, is now enlisted with man in the hunting of the game still available. Perhaps more important, the wolf may have been the model for domesticating other animals since the dog was a companion and pet that enabled children to learn about domesticated animal behaviour. With a more sedentary life, and the accumulation of personal property and real estate, would come more complex property right and contracting arrangements. The study of precolonial aboriginal societies in Northwest America and Melanesia reveals the existence of elaborate *multilateral contracting* arrangements in the form of 'ceremonial exchanges' such as the potlatch, kula, moka and abutu (Dalton, 1977). The use of valuables or commodity money (bracelets, pearl shells, cowries, young women) in these primitive societies was much more complex than the use of cash in nation-states with their well-defined legal environments for exchange. These valuables not only bought other valuables in ordinary internal or external market exchange, they bought kinship ties with the exchange of women, military assistance when attacked, the right of refuge if invasion required the abandonment of homes, and emergency aid in times of poor harvest, hunting or fishing. In short they brought political stability, and a property-right environment that made ordinary exchange and specialization possible. Property was owned by corporate descent lineages and included land, fishing sites, cemetery plots and livestock, but, interestingly, also public goods like crests, names, dances, rituals and trade routes, that could be assigned to many groups or individuals. These practices, which characterize stateless hunter–gatherer aboriginals, demonstrate that the phenomenon of multilateral contracting (Williamson, 1984), so common to the market economy in nation-states, has ancient origins which antedate the State and the agricultural revolution.

Man's long existence as a hunter had brought knowledge of animals; extinction brought a change in relative costs; gathering brought knowledge of seeds and eggs; life became more sedentary, with property, contracting and exchange becoming more important. Under these more stable conditions it was a short step for mankind to plant for harvest, and/or to husband some of the more docile game that had been hunted previously. With agriculture and herding came a more sophisticated development of the earlier hunter–gatherer institutions of contract, property, exchange and specialization; and ultimately the continuing industrial–communication revolution. But long before these sweeping changes can be seen the dim outline of continuity in the development of man's capacity to adapt, by creating cheaper products and techniques to substitute for dearer ones.

BIBLIOGRAPHY

Dalton, G. 1977. Aboriginal economies in stateless societies: interaction spheres. In *Exchange Systems in Prehistory*, ed. T.K. Earle and J.E. Ericson, New York: Academic Press.

Haynes, C.V. 1964. Fluted projectile points: their age and dispersion. *Science* 145, 25 September, 1408–13.

Heizer, R. 1955. Primitive man as an ecological factor. *Krober Anthropological Society Papers* No. 13.

Lee, R.B. and DeVore, I. 1968. *Man the Hunter*. Chicago: Aldine.

Lewis, H. 1973. *Patterns of Indian Burning in California: Ecology and Ethnohistory*. Ballena Press, Anthropological Papers, No. 1.

Martin, P. 1967. Prehistoric overkill. In *Pleistocene Extinctions*, ed. P.S. Martin and H.E. Wright, Jr., New Haven: Yale University.

North, D.C. and Thomas, R.P. 1977. The first economic revolution. *Economic History Review* 30(2), May, 229–41.

Pilbeam, D. 1984. The descent of hominoids and hominids. *Scientific American* 250(3), 60–69.

Smith, V.L. 1975. The primitive hunter culture, pleistocene extinction, and the rise of agriculture. *Journal of Political Economy* 83(4), August, 727–55.

Wheat, J.B. 1967. A Paleo-Indian bison kill. *Scientific American* 216(1), January, 44–52.

Williamson, O. 1984. Credible commitments: using hostages to support exchange. *American Economic Review* 74(3), September, 488–90.

Hyperinflation

PHILLIP CAGAN

Hyperinflation is an extremely rapid rise in the general level of prices of goods and services. It typically lasts a few years or in the most extreme cases much less before moderating or ending. There is no well-defined threshold. It is best described by a listing of cases, which vary enormously. The numerous cases have provided a testing ground for theories of monetary dynamics reported in a vast literature.

HISTORICAL SURVEY. The world's record occurred in Hungary after World War II when an index of prices rose an average 19,800 per cent per month from August 1945 to July 1946 and 4.2×10^{16} per cent in the peak month of July. Also in the aftermath of World War II extreme price increases occurred in China, Greece, and Taiwan. Hyperinflations followed World War I in Austria, Germany, Hungary, Poland and Russia. If we measure the total increase in prices from the first to last month in which the monthly increase exceeded 50 per cent and afterwards stayed below that rate for a year or more, a price index rose from 1 to 3.8×10^{27} in the record Hungarian episode, 10^{11} in China, 10^{10} in Germany, and ranged down to 70 in Austria and 44 in the first Hungarian episode after World War I. In the last, the mildest of those cited above, the rise in prices averaged 46 per cent per month.

Prior to World War I extreme inflations were rare. A price index rose from 1 to about 18 from mid-1795 to mid-1796 at the height of the *assignats* inflation in France, from 1778 to 1780 in the American War of Independence, to 12 from 1863 to 1865 in the Confederacy during the American Civil War, and comparable inflation rates were reported for Columbia in 1902. The oft-cited currency depreciations of the ancient and medieval world and of Europe in the 17th century from the influx of precious metals were mild by modern experience. Earlier extreme inflations were rare because of the prevalence of commodity monies and convertibility. Only inconvertible paper currencies can be expanded rapidly without limit to generate hyperinflation.

339

Although the greatest hyperinflations have occurred in countries devasted by war, non-war-related inflation rates of several hundred per cent per year were reached briefly in 1926 in Belgium and France. Since World War II to the time of writing (1985) the frequency of both mild and extreme inflations unrelated to war has increased throughout the world. While rates of several hundred per cent per year or more for short periods have become common since World War II, few cases have exceeded 1000 per cent per year for even a few months (Meiselman, 1970), and hence they fall far short of the great hyperinflations. The rate of over 10,000 per cent per year in Bolivia in 1985 is a major exception.

MONETARY CHARACTERISTICS. Extreme increases in the price level cannot occur without commensurate increases in the money stock, which are usually less than proportionate because of decreases in the demand for real money balances. Governments resort to issuing money rapidly when they are unable to contain expanding budget expenditures and to raise sufficient funds by conventional taxation and borrowing from the public. Money creation is a special form of taxation which is levied on the public's holdings of money. It is administratively easy to impose and collect. Excessive money issues to finance the government budget add to aggregate spending and raise prices; the resulting depreciation in the purchasing power of outstanding money balances imposes the tax. Bailey (1956) finds the social costs of this tax to be high compared with other forms of taxation.

Escalations of inflation at any level tend to stimulate economic activity temporarily. Since high rates of inflation tend to distort relative prices, however, much of the economic activity is socially wasteful. Many businesses and workers are dependent on prices and wages that lag behind the general inflation, and thus suffer severe declines in real income. In addition, unanticipated depreciations in financial and monetary assets in real terms produce major redistributions of wealth. These effects are socially and politically disruptive (Bresciani-Turroni, 1931). Yet the de-escalation of inflation temporarily contracts aggregate demand, which is also disruptive and therefore politically difficult to undertake.

THEORETICAL ISSUES. The depreciation of money during inflation greatly increases the cost of holding it. Although depreciating currencies are not abandoned completely, testifying to the great benefits of a common medium of exchange, the public undertakes costly efforts to reduce holdings of a rapidly depreciating money, including barter arrangements and the use of more stable substitutes such as foreign currencies (Barro, 1970). These efforts result in a large reduction in money balances in real terms and a large rise in monetary velocity.

A study of this result by Cagan (1956) estimated the demand for real money balances in hyperinflation as inversely dependent on the *expected* rate of inflation. Expectations about future developments can differ from concurrent conditions and determine the public's response to inflation. Cagan hypothesized that expectations are formed adaptively, whereby expected values are adjusted in proportion to their discrepancy from actual values. The theoretical implication is that expected inflation can be estimated as an exponentially weighted average of past inflation rates.

Such adaptive expectations lag behind the changes in actual values, which can explain why hyperinflations characteristically tend to escalate. As the inflation tax extracts revenue from real money balances, the expected inflation rate increases to match the higher actual rate and the revenue declines in real terms, but with a lag. The real revenue can be increased by speeding up money creation, but only until expectations adjust to the higher inflation rate. If the inflation rate were to remain constant so that the expected rate eventually matched it, the real revenue from money creation would be sustainable at a constant level. Among such constant levels a maximum real revenue is obtainable by a particular constant inflation rate, which depends on the elasticity of demand for real money balances with respect to the inflation rate. This revenue can be raised further by continually increasing monetary growth and the inflation rate. The hyperinflations kept escalating well beyond the maximizing constant rate to obtain more revenue.

Inflation also usually reduces the real value of other tax revenues because of lags between the imposition of a tax and its collection. A tax on money balances must exceed the reduced real collections of other taxes in order to prevent a decline in total government real revenue. This is often true initially under civil disorder, but hyperinflation reduces all taxes in real terms and in a short time largely destroys its revenue justification.

Adaptive expectations can be a 'rational' way for people to distinguish between transitory and one-time permanent changes in a variable (Muth, 1960). But if the inflation rate is continually rising, adaptive expectations as a weighted average of past rates are always too low, and such a series of correlated expectational errors is inconsistent with rational behaviour. The theory of rational expectations argues that the public uses all available information in predicting the inflation rate, including economic models of the process. This implies in particular that expectations of inflation, taking into account the importance of money, will focus on the money-creating policies of the monetary authorities. If the government is after a certain amount of revenue, the public may be able to estimate the rate of money creation, which can be translated into a path for prices. Usually, however, the amount of money issued may change unpredictably or otherwise not be knowable with much precision.

Rational expectations have two important empirical implications for hyperinflation. First, if money is consistently issued to raise a certain revenue in real terms, monetary growth will depend on the inflation rate (Webb, 1984). The money stock is then statistically endogenous to the inflationary process. Sargent and Wallace (1973) and Frenkel (1977) presented statistical evidence that money depends on prices in the German hyperinflation, though such evidence has been contested (Protopapadakis, 1983).

To find that the money supply is endogenous does not mean that money demand is no longer dependent on the expected rate of inflation. But the finding discredits econometric regressions of real money balances on inflation rates. Other variables are needed to measure the expected cost of holding money.

Frenkel (1977) used the forward premium on foreign exchange in the German hyperinflation, which reflected the market's estimate of future depreciation of the foreign exchange rate and presumably was dominated by expectations of inflation. (This also helps avoid possible spurious correlation when a price series for calculating real money balances is used in the same regression to derive the rate of price change.) The forward premium does explain movements in real money balances and confirms as a proxy the effect of the expected inflation rate. The forward premium in Germany was also found to be uncorrelated with past inflation, which satisfies the rational expectations requirement that the premium should not depend on past information and not involve lagged adjustments. This leaves unexplained, however, why the German inflation rate escalated beyond the revenue-maximizing constant rate, since rational expectations prevent anticipated escalation from increasing the revenue. Sargent (1977) suggests that the revenue-maximizing rate, when properly estimated under the hypothesis of rational expectations, was not exceeded by actual inflation rates. Another possibility is that public behaviour did not fully anticipate the successive increases in inflation rates, which thus temporarily added to the government's inflation revenue.

STABILIZATION REFORM. Hyperinflation, if driven by rising expectations of inflation rather than rising money growth, can become a self-generating process. This has never occurred, however, except conceivably for very brief periods. Hyperinflations can always be stopped, therefore, by ending the monetary support. But the revenue from money creation is often difficult for governments to replace or survive without, explaining why some countries are subjected to high inflation for long periods.

Yet many hyperinflations have been stopped all at once with a programme of reform and without prolonged economic disruption. After a short period the economy usually recovers and prospers. These stabilization programmes have been studied to determine the necessary conditions for success (Sargent, 1982; Bomberger and Makinen, 1983). Some attempted reforms have failed, notably twice in Greece after World War II (Makinen, 1984). First of all, it is critical to gain control over monetary growth, and this requires an end to the government's dependence on money creation to finance its budget. Successful reforms involve a reorganization of government finances, both to cut expenditures and to raise taxes, and legal authority for the central bank to refuse to create money to lend to the government. Although a new currency unit is often issued to replace the depreciated one, this is symbolic only. Foreign loans or financial aid to bolster foreign exchange reserves and to finance government deficits for a while help to inspire confidence in the success of stabilization, but have not always been necessary. Convertibility of the new currency into gold or a key foreign currency assures the reform but is not always introduced immediately. Such convertibility to end a severe inflation has proven difficult in the post-Bretton Woods environment in which the key foreign currency (usually the dollar) floats in value. Fixing the foreign exchange rate can then produce massive trade deficits (if the key currency appreciates) which are impossible to maintain. Chile in the early 1980s is a notable example (Edwards, 1985).

Most reforms are initially popular, promising to bring back the benefits of a well-functioning monetary system. A resurgence of public confidence in the currency usually occurs, which produces a substantial increase in money demand from low hyperinflation levels. This allows a one-time increase in the money supply without raising prices. The monetary expansion must not continue beyond the demand increase, however, or it will set off a new round of inflation, and the stabilization will fail. Many reforms that eventually failed gained credibility initially and had an increase in money demand, but then subsequently over-issued money and returned to high inflation rates. To avoid this outcome there must be a commitment to maintain a stable price index or convertibility.

Stabilization reforms that have achieved an immediate end to hyperinflations contrast with the protracted efforts to subdue many moderate inflations. One difference is that in hyperinflations, long-term contracts specifying prices or interest rates and wage agreements are no longer entered into because of great uncertainty over the inflation rate. Consequently, few parties are injured by such contracts when hyperinflation suddenly ends, and inflexibilities in the price system do not impede the required substantial readjustment of relative prices. Contracts that index financial and wage contracts to previous price movements impart a momentum to inflation that makes it more disruptive to end the process. The wide use of indexing, as in Brazil and Israel in the early 1980s, reduces differential price and wage movements but creates an obstacle to successful reform.

Hyperinflations of the order of those following the two World Wars remain rare and, when they occur, soon escalate to levels that necessitate an ending by drastic measures. Inflations of the order of 50 to several hundred per cent a year have been difficult to end, though they often subside for varying periods. These inflations despite their serious economic consequences give no indication of disappearing.

BIBLIOGRAPHY

Bailey, M. 1956. The welfare cost of inflationary finance. *Journal of Political Economy* 64, April, 93–110.

Barro, R.J. 1970. Inflation, the payments period and the demand for money. *Journal of Political Economy* 78, November/December, 1228–63.

Bomberger, W.A. and Makinen, G.E. 1983. The Hungarian hyperinflation and stabilization of 1945–46. *Journal of Political Economy* 91, October, 801–24.

Bresciani-Turroni, C. 1931. *The Economics of Inflation: A Study of Currency Depreciation in Post-War Germany: 1914–1923*. Trans., London: Allen & Unwin, 1937.

Cagan, P. 1956. The monetary dynamics of hyperinflation. In *Studies in the Quantity Theory of Money*, ed. M. Friedman, Chicago: University of Chicago Press.

Edwards, S. 1985. Stabilization with liberalization: an evaluation of ten years of Chile's experiment with free-market policies, 1973–1983. *Economic Development and Cultural Change* 33, January, 223–54.

Frenkel, J.A. 1977. The forward exchange rate, expectations, and the demand for money: the German hyperinflation. *American Economic Review* 67, September, 653–70.

Makinen, G.E. 1984. The Greek stabilization of 1944–46. *American Economic Review* 74, December, 1067–74.

Meiselman, D. (ed.) 1970. *Varieties of Monetary Experience.* Chicago: University of Chicago Press.

Muth, J. 1960. Optimal properties of exponentially weighted forecasts. *Journal of the American Statistical Association* 55, June, 299–306.

Protopapadakis, A. 1983. The endogeneity of money during the German hyperinflation: a reappraisal. *Economic Inquiry* 21, January, 72–92.

Sargent, T.J. 1977. The demand for money during hyperinflation under rational expectations I. *International Economic Review* 18, February, 59–82.

Sargent, T.J. 1982. The ends of four big inflations. In *Inflation: Causes and Effects*, ed. R. Hall, Chicago: University of Chicago Press.

Sargent, T.J. and Wallace, N. 1973. 'Rational' expectations and the dynamics of hyperinflation. *International Economic Review* 14, June, 328–50.

Webb, S.B. 1984. The supply of money and Reichsbank financing of government and corporate debt in Germany, 1919–1923. *Journal of Economic History* 44, June, 499–507.

Import Substitution and Export-led Growth

JOHN EATWELL

In an economy in which expansion is limited by a balance of payments constraint, action must be taken either to boost exports or to limit imports. This truism takes on an added dimension when the trade strategy adopted is part of a general development strategy. In these circumstances the evaluation of any particular trade strategy must include not only the implications for the allocation of resources, but also the consequences for the rate of accumulation and of technological progress.

In the 1950s and early 1960s, the years of the dollar shortage, the balance of payments constrained industrial countries adopted quite different trade and industrial strategies. West Germany pursued a strategy of export expansion by means of an undervalued Deutschmark and subsidies to export industries. With world trade in manufactures growing rapidly, and West Germany's share of that trade growing too, the rapid growth of manufactured exports provided the foundation for domestic expansion (Shonfield, 1962). Italy pursued a similar strategy by means of regular devaluation of the lira, devaluations often being associated with a surplus on Italy's current account.

These two examples of export-led growth contrast markedly with the strategies adopted by France and by Japan. Both countries vigorously protected their home markets, using industrial expansion within the home market as a springboard for the capture of export markets. The rationale behind this policy of import substitution was spelt out by Vice-Minister Ojimi, of the Japanese Ministry of International Trade and Industry:

> After the war, Japan's first exports consisted of such things as toys or other miscellaneous merchandise and low-quality textile products. Should Japan have entrusted its future, according to the theory of comparative advantage, to these industries characterized by intensive use of labour? That would perhaps

be rational advice for a country with a small population of 5 or 10 million. But Japan has a large population. If the Japanese economy had adopted the simple doctrine of free trade and had chosen to specialise in this kind of industry, it would almost permanently have been unable to break away from the Asian pattern of stagnation and poverty...

The Ministry of International Trade and Industry decided to establish in Japan industries which require intensive employment of capital and technology, industries that in consideration of comparative cost should be the most inappropriate for Japan, industries such as steel, oil refining, petro-chemicals, automobiles, industrial machinery of all sorts, and electronics, including electronic computers. From a short-run, static viewpoint, encouragement of such industries would seem to be in conflict with economic rationalism. But from a long-range viewpoint, these are precisely the industries where income elasticity of demand is high, technological progress is rapid, and labour productivity rises fast ... (Ojimi, 1970).

Ojimi's argument encapsulates the dispute over import substitution or export-led growth as development strategies. The orthodox theory of international trade suggests that resources are most efficiently allocated in a regime of free trade. Efficient development would therefore require the adoption of free trade, with variation in exchange rates being used as the means of balancing trade.

This argument rests on a number of strong assumptions, in particular the assumptions that all countries have access to the same technologies, that factor markets clear (labour is fully employed), and that all countries have equal access to all markets – including equal access to all financial markets. If these, and other well-known assumptions, are not fulfilled, then the argument for free trade *on these grounds* no longer stands and is superseded by the uncertainties of the second best.

Rejection of arguments for the efficiency of the price mechanism, for example on Keynesian grounds, also lead to the rejection of the efficiency of free trade. It was Keynesian arguments that underpinned the so-called ECLA strategy for structural change in Latin America. If expansion of domestic demand could be prevented, by protective measures, from leaking abroad then savings and fiscal revenues at home would finance domestic investment and government expenditure. Moreover, the profitability of protected domestic production would encourage further investment. The process of expansion would be self-sustaining.

The application of import-substitution strategies in Latin America in the 1950s met initially with considerable success. Output of domestically produced manufactured goods grew rapidly, as did industrial employment. Later the policy fell into disrepute. It was argued that import substitution took place primarily in 'soft' consumer goods industries, whereas investment goods continued to be imported. Hence after the early growth associated with import substitution in consumer goods, growth was once again constrained by the necessity of importing machinery. Moreover, it was argued that protected domestic industry was relatively inefficient, and unable to compete on world markets. These matters are the subject of considerable dispute, particularly as they involve not only questions of economic efficiency, but also issues of national sovereignty, since the IMF has responded to the difficulties in which some Latin American countries have found themselves by demanding the removal of the trade protection on which the earlier development strategy was based.

These criticisms of import substitution extend beyond the traditional case for free trade to consideration of the implication of different trade strategies for structural development and technological change. It was on exactly these grounds that Ojimi sought to justify Japan's strategy of import substitution. The Japanese case suggests that the traditional dichotomy between import substitution and export-led growth is invalid. Whilst Japanese industry was developed within a rapidly growing and protected home market, that growth proved to be a springboard for expansion into world markets. Exports were domestic-growth led.

The performance of the successful Japanese (and French) examples of import substitution, and the problems encountered in Latin America, cannot be evaluated using static conceptions of allocative efficiency. Success (and lack of it) have clearly been associated with technological progress and industrial modernization. The case for free trade must be made on the ground that it encourages the most rapid adoption of the new techniques which determine competitive advantage.

Nicholas Kaldor's version of Verdoorn's Law (Kaldor, 1966), whereby it is argued that the rate of productivity growth in manufacturing industry is a function of the rate of growth of demand for manufactured products, provides a framework within which trade strategies may be evaluated (see, for example, Brailovsky, 1981).

The growth of demand for a country's manufactures is a function of the rate of growth of its home market, the rate of growth of its export markets and the rate of change of its share of those markets. Changing market shares is a slow and uncertain business. It is growth of markets which is the major determinant of growth of demand. Since all countries are competing for shares of (roughly) the same export market, it is growth of the home market which typically differentiates the growth of demand for the manufactures of one country from those of another. This would suggest that manipulation of growth of the home market, using whatever means are necessary to relax the balance of payments constraint, is the most efficient development strategy.

However, the Verdoorn argument does not encompass the scale of productivity response to any given growth of demand. The implementation of industrial policies which ensure that the expansion of industrial structure is 'balanced', and hence not overly dependent on imports, and that it directs demand toward those sectors which have both greatest competitive potential and the highest ratio of domestic value-added to import content, are more likely to produce a greater response than if these issues are neglected.

The efficiency of any given trade strategy is not independent of the performance of the world economy as a whole. All countries cannot achieve export-led growth at once. Moreover, the success of the West Germany recovery strategy was undoubtedly enhanced by the fact that it was implemented in a period of rapid growth in world trade. In an era in which world trade is expanding relatively slowly, reliance on export demand is unlikely to prove a successful foundation for rapid growth of demand and hence for rapid technological progress.

BIBLIOGRAPHY

Brailovsky, V. 1981. Industrialisation and oil in Mexico: a long-term perspective. In *Oil or Industry?*, ed. T. Barker and V. Brailovsky, London: Academic Press.

Kaldor, N. 1966. *The Causes of the Slow Rate of Growth of the UK*. Cambridge: Cambridge University Press.

Ojimi, V. 1970. Japan's industrialisation strategy. In OECD, *Japanese Industrial Policy*, Paris: OECD.

Shonfield, A. 1962. *Modern Capitalism*. Oxford: Oxford University Press.

Interests

ALBERT O. HIRSCHMAN

'Interest' or 'interests' is one of the most central and controversial concepts
in economics and, more generally, in social science and history. Since coming
into widespread use in various European countries around the latter part of the
16th century as essentially the same Latin-derived word (*intérêt*, *interesse*,
etc.), the concept has stood for the fundamental forces, based on the drive
for self-preservation and self-aggrandizement, that motivate or should motivate
the actions of the prince or the state, of the individual, and later of groups
of people occupying a similar social or economic position (classes, interest
groups). When related to the individual, the concept has at times had a very
inclusive meaning, encompassing interest in honour, glory, self-respect, and even
after-life, while at other times it became wholly confined to the drive for economic
advantage. The esteem in which interest-motivated behaviour is held has also
varied drastically. The term was originally pressed into service as a euphemism
serving, already in the late Middle Ages, to make respectable an activity, the
taking of interest on loans, that had long been considered contrary to divine law
and known as the sin of usury. In its wider meanings, the term at times
achieved enormous prestige as a key to a workable and peaceful social order.
But it has also been attacked as degrading to the human spirit and corrosive of
the foundations of society. An inquiry into these multiple meanings and
appreciations is in effect an exploration of much of economic history and in
particular of the history of economic and political doctrine in the West over the
past four centuries.

The concept, moreover, still plays a central role in contemporary economics
and political economy: the construct of the self-interested, isolated individual
who chooses freely and rationally between alternative courses of action after
computing their prospective costs and benefits to him or herself, that is, while
ignoring costs and benefits to other people and to society at large, underlies
much of welfare economics; and the same perspective has yielded important, if
disturbing, contributions to a broader science of social interactions, such as the

349

Prisoner's Dilemma theorem and the obstacles to collective action because of free riding.

Two essential elements appear to characterize interest-propelled action: *self-centredness*, that is, predominant attention of the actor to the consequences of any contemplated action for himself; and *rational calculation*, that is, a systematic attempt at evaluating prospective costs, benefits, satisfactions and the like. Calculation could be considered the dominant element: once action is supposed to be informed only by careful estimation of costs and benefits, with most weight necessarily being given to those that are better known and more quantifiable, it tends to become self-referential by virtue of the simple fact that each person is best informed about his *own* satisfactions and disappointments.

INTEREST AND STATECRAFT. Rational calculation also played the chief role in the emergence of the concept of interest-motivated action on the part of the prince in the 16th and 17th centuries. It accounts for the high marks interest-governed behaviour received during the late 16th- and early 17th-century phases of its career in politics. The term did duty on two fronts. First, it permitted the emergent science of statecraft to assimilate the important insights of Machiavelli. The author of *The Prince* had almost strained to advertise those aspects of politics that clashed with conventional morality. He dwelt on instances where the prince was well advised or even duty-bound to practise cruelty, mendacity, treason, and so on. Just as, in connection with money lending, the term interest came into use as a euphemism for the earlier term usury, so did it impose itself on the political vocabulary as a means of anaesthetizing, assimilating and developing Machiavelli's shocking insights.

But in the early modern age, 'interest' was not only a label under which a ruler was given *new latitude* or was absolved from feeling guilty about following a practice that he had previously been taught to consider as immoral: the term also served to impose *new restraints* as it enjoined the Prince to pursue his interests with a rational, calculating spirit that would often imply prudence and moderation. At the beginning of the 17th century, the interests of the sovereign were contrasted with the wild and destructive passions, that is, with the immoderate and foolish seeking of glory and other excesses involved in pursuing the by then discredited heroic ideal of the Middle Ages and the Renaissance. This disciplinary aspect of the doctrine of interest was particularly driven home in the influential essay *On the Interest of Princes and States of Christendom* by the Huguenot statesman the Duke of Rohan (1579–1638).

The interest doctrine thus served to release the ruler from certain traditional restraints (or guilt feelings) only to subject him to new ones that were felt to be far more efficacious than the well-worn appeals to religion, morals or abstract reason. Genuine hope arose that, with princely or national interest as guide, statecraft would be able to produce a more stable political order and a more peaceful world.

INTEREST AND INDIVIDUAL BEHAVIOUR. The early career of the interest concept with regard to statecraft finds a remarkable parallel in the role it played in shaping behaviour codes for individual men and women in society. Here also a new licence went hand in hand with a new restraint.

The new licence consisted in the legitimation and even praise that was bestowed upon the single-minded pursuit of material wealth and upon activities conducive to its accumulation. Just as Machiavelli had opened up new horizons for the Prince, so did Mandeville two centuries later list a number of 'don'ts' for the commoner, in this case primarily in relation to money making. Once again, a new insight into human behaviour or into the social order was first proclaimed as a startling, shocking paradox. Like Machiavelli, Mandeville presented his thesis on the beneficial effects on the general welfare of the luxury trades (which had long been strictly regulated) in the most scandalous possible fashion, by referring to the activities, drives and emotions associated with these trades as 'private vices'. Here again, his essential message was eventually absorbed into the general stock of accepted practice by changing the language with which he had proclaimed his discovery. For the third time, euphemistic resort was had to 'interest', this time in substitution for such terms as 'avarice', 'love of lucre', and so on. The transition from one set of terms to the other is reflected by the first lines of David Hume's essay 'On the Independency of Parliament':

> Political writers have established it as a maxim, that, in contriving any system of government and fixing the several checks and balances of the constitution, every man ought to be supposed a *knave*, and to have no other end, in all his actions, than private interest. By this interest we must govern him, and, by means of it, make him, notwithstanding his insatiable avarice and ambition, cooperate to public good (Hume, 1742, vol. I, pp. 117–18, emphasis in the original).

Here interest is explicitly equated with knavishness and 'insatiable avarice'. But soon thereafter the memory of these unsavoury synonyms of interest was suppressed, as in Adam Smith's famous statement about the butcher, the brewer and the baker who are driven to supply us with our daily necessities through their interest rather than their benevolence. Smith thus did for Mandeville what the Duke of Rohan had done for Machiavelli. His doctrine of the Invisible Hand legitimated total absorption of the citizen in the pursuit of private gain and thereby served to assuage any guilt feelings that might have been harboured by the many Englishmen who were drawn into commerce and industry during the commercial expansion of the 18th century but had been brought up under the civic humanist code enjoining them to serve the public interest *directly* (Pocock, 1982). They were now reassured that by pursuing gains they were doing so *indirectly*.

In fact, Adam Smith was not content to praise the pursuit of private gain. He also berated citizens' involvement in public affairs. Right after his Invisible Hand statement he wrote 'I have never known much good done by those who affected to trade for the public good' (1776, p. 423). Ten years before, Sir James Steuart had supplied an interesting explanation for a similar aversion toward citizens' involvement in public affairs.

> ... were everyone to act for the public, and neglect himself, the statesman would be bewildered ... were a people to become quite disinterested, there would be no possibility of governing them. Everyone might consider the interest of his country in a different light, and many might join in the ruin of it, by endeavouring to promote its advantages (1767, vol. I, pp. 243–4).

In counterpart to the new area of authorized and recommended behaviour, these statements point to the important *restraints* that accompanied the doctrine of interest. For the individual citizen or subject as for the ruler, interest-propelled action meant originally action informed by rational calculation in any area of human activity – political, cultural, economic, personal and so on. In the 17th century and through part of the 18th, this sort of methodical, prudential, interest-guided action was seen as vastly preferable to actions dictated by the violent, unruly and disorderly passions. At the same time, the interests of the vast majority of people, that is of those outside of the highest reaches of power, came to be more narrowly defined as economic, material or 'moneyed' interests, probably because the non-elite was deemed to busy itself primarily with scrounging a living with no time left to worry about honour, glory and the like. The infatuation with interest helped bestow legitimacy and prestige on commercial and related private activities, that had hitherto ranked rather low in public esteem; correspondingly, the Renaissance ideal of glory, with its implicit celebration of the public sphere, was downgraded and debunked as a mere exercise in the destructive passion of self-love (Hirschman, 1977, p. 31–42).

THE POLITICAL BENEFITS OF AN INTEREST-BASED SOCIAL ORDER. The idea that the interests, understood as the methodical pursuit and accumulation of private wealth, would bring a number of benefits in the political realm took various distinct forms. There was, first of all, the expectation that they would achieve at the macrolevel what they were supposed to accomplish for the individual: hold back the violent passions of the 'rulers of mankind'. Here the best-known proposition, voiced early in the 18th century, says that the expansion of commerce is incompatible with the use of force in international relations and would gradually make for a peaceful world. Still more utopian hopes were held out for the effects of commerce on domestic politics: the web of interests delicately woven by thousands of transactions would make it impossible for the sovereign to interpose his power brutally and wantonly through what was called '*grands coups d'autorité*' by Montesquieu or 'the folly of despotism' by Sir James Steuart. This thought was carried further in the early 19th century when the intricacies of expanding industrial production compounded those of commerce: in the technocratic version of Saint-Simon the time was at hand when economic exigencies would put an end, not just to *abuses* of the power of the state, but to any power whatsoever of man over and man – politics would be replaced by administration of 'things'. As is well known this conjecture was taken up by Marxism with its prediction of the withering away of the state under communism. An argument that a century earlier had been advanced on behalf of emergent capitalism was thus refurbished for a new, *anti*-capitalist utopia.

Another line of thought about the political effects of an interest-driven society looks less at the constraints such as society will impose upon those who govern than at the difficulties of the task of governing. As already noted, a world where people methodically pursue their private interests was believed to be far more predictable, and hence *more governable*, than one where the citizens are vying with each other for honour and glory.

The stability and lack of turbulence that were expected to characterize a country where men singlemindedly pursue their material interests were very much on the minds of some of the 'inventors' of America, such as James Madison and Alexander Hamilton. The enormous prestige and influence of the interest concept at the time of the founding of America is well expressed in Hamilton's statement:

> The safest reliance of every government is on man's interests. This is a principle of human nature, on which all political speculation, to be just, must be founded (Hamilton [1784], cited in Terence Ball, 1983, p. 45).

Finally, a number of writers essentially extrapolated from the putative personality traits of the individual trader, as the prototype of interest-driven man, to the general characteristics of a society where traders would predominate. In the 18th century, perhaps as a result of some continuing disdain for economic pursuits, commerce and money-making were often described as essentially innocuous or 'innocent' pastimes, in contrast no doubt with the more violent or more strenuous ways of the upper or lower classes. Commerce was to bring 'gentle' and 'polished' manners. In French, the term innocent appended to commerce was often coupled with *doux* (sweet, gentle) and what has been called the thesis of the *doux commerce* held that commerce was a powerful civilizing agent diffusing prudence, probity and similar virtues within and among trading societies (Hirschman, 1977, 1982a). Only under the impact of the French Revolution did some doubt arise on the direction of the causal link between commerce and civilized society: taken aback by the outbreak of social violence on a large scale, Edmund Burke suggested that the expansion of commerce depended itself on the *prior* existence of 'manners' and 'civilization' and on what he called 'natural protecting principles' grounded in 'the spirit of a gentleman' and 'the spirit of religion' (Burke, 1790, p. 115; Pocock, 1982).

THE INVISIBLE HAND. The capstone of the doctrine of self-interest was of course Adam Smith's Invisible Hand. Even though this doctrine, being limited to the economic domain, was more modest than the earlier speculations on the beneficent *political* effects of trade and exchange, it soon came to dominate the discussion. An intriguing paradox was involved in stating that the *general* interest and welfare would be promoted by the self-interested activities of innumerable decentralized operators. To be sure, this was not the first nor the last time that such a claim of identity or coincidence or harmony of interests of a part with

353

those of a whole has been put forward. Hobbes had advocated an absolute monarchy on the ground that this form of government brings about an identity of interest between ruler and ruled; as just noted, the writers of the Scottish Enlightenment saw an identity of interest between the general interests of British society and the interests of the middle ranks; such an identity between the interests of one class and those of society became later a cornerstone of Marxism, with the middling ranks having of course been supplanted by the proletariat; and finally, the American pluralist school in political science returned essentially to the Smithian scheme of harmony between many self-interests and the general interest, with Smith's individual economic operators having been replaced by contending 'interest groups' on the political stage.

All these *Harmonielehren* have two factors in common: the 'realistic' affirmation that we have to deal with men and women, or with groups thereof, 'as they really are', and an attempt to prove that it is possible to achieve a workable and progressive social order with these highly imperfect subjects, and, as it were, behind their backs. The mixture of paradoxical insight and alchemy involved in these constructs makes them powerfully attractive, but also accounts for their ultimate vulnerability.

THE INTERESTS ATTACKED. The 17th century was perhaps the real heyday of the interest doctrine. Governance of the social world by interest was then viewed as an alternative to the rule of destructive passions; that was surely a lesser evil, and possibly an outright blessing. In the 18th century, the doctrine received a substantial boost in the economic domain through the doctrine of the Invisible Hand, but it was indirectly weakened by the emergence of a more optimistic view of the passions: such passionate sentiments and emotions as curiosity, generosity and sympathy were then given detailed attention, the latter by Adam Smith himself in his *Theory of Moral Sentiments*. In comparison to such fine, newly discovered or rehabilitated springs of human action, interest no longer looked nearly so attractive. Here was one reason for the reaction against the interest paradigm that unfolded toward the end of the 18th century and was to fuel several powerful 19th-century intellectual movements.

Actually the passions did not have to be wholly transformed into benign sentiments to be thought respectable and even admirable by a new generation. Once the interests appeared to be truly in command with the vigorous commercial and industrial expansion of the age, a general lament went up for 'the world we have lost'. The French Revolution brought another sense of loss and Edmund Burke joined the two when he exclaimed, in his *Reflections on the Revolution in France*, 'the age of chivalry is gone; that of sophisters, economists and calculators has succeeded; and the glory of Europe is extinguished for ever' (1790, p. 111). This famous statement came a bare 14 years after the *Wealth of Nations* had denounced the rule of the 'great lords' as a 'scene of violence, rapine and disorder' and had celebrated the benefits flowing from everyone catering to his interests through orderly economic pursuits. Now Burke was an intense admirer of Adam Smith and took much pride in the identity of views on economic matters between himself and Smith (Winch, 1985; Himmelfarb, 1984). His 'age of chivalry' statement, so contrary to the intellectual legacy of Smith, therefore signals one of those sudden changes in the general mood and understanding from one age to the next of which the exponents themselves are hardly aware. Burke's lament set the tone for much of the subsequent Romantic protest against an order based on the interests which, once it appeared to be dominant, was seen by many as lacking nobility, mystery, and beauty.

This nostalgic reaction merged with the observation that the interests, that is, the drive for material wealth, were not nearly as 'innocuous', 'innocent' or 'mild', as had been thought or advertised. To the contrary, it was now the drive for material advantage that suddenly loomed as a subversive force of enormous power. Thomas Carlyle thought that all traditional values were threatened by 'that brutish god-forgetting Profit-and-Loss Philosophy' and protested that 'cash payment is not the only nexus of man with man' (1843, p. 187). This phrase – cash-nexus – was taken over by Marx and Engels who used it to good effect in the first section of the *Communist Manifesto* where they painted a lurid picture of the moral and cultural havoc wrought by the conquering bourgeoisie.

Many other critics of capitalist society dwelt on the destructiveness of the new energies that were released by a social order in which the interests were given free rein. In fact, the thought arose that these forces were so wild and out of control that they might undermine the very foundations on which the social order was resting, that they were thus bent on self-destruction. In a startling reversal, feudal society, which had earlier been treated as 'rude and barbarous' and was thought to be in permanent danger of dissolution because of the unchecked passions of violent rulers and grandees, was perceived in retrospect to have nurtured such values as honour, respect, friendship, trust and loyalty, that were essential for the functioning of an interest-dominated order, but were relentlessly, if inadvertently, undermined by it. This argument was already contained in part in Burke's assertion that it is civilized society that lays the groundwork for commerce rather than vice versa; it was elaborated by a large and diverse group of authors, from Richard Wagner via Schumpeter to Karl Polanyi and Fred Hirsch (Hirschman, 1982a, pp. 1466–70).

THE INTERESTS DILUTED. While the interest doctrine thus met with considerable opposition and criticism in the 19th century, its prestige remained nevertheless high, particularly because of the vigorous development of economics as a new body of scientific thought. Indeed, the success of this new science made for attempts to utilize its insights, such as the interest concept, for elucidating some non-economic aspects of the social world. In his *Essay on Government* (1820), James Mill formulated the first 'economic' theory of politics and based it – just as was later done by Schumpeter, Anthony Downs, Mancur Olson etc. – on the assumption of rational self-interest. But this widening of the use of the concept turned out to be something of a disservice. In politics, so Mill had to recognize, the gap between the 'real' interest of the citizen and 'a false supposition [i.e., perception] of interest' can be extremely wide and problematic (1820, p. 88).

This difficulty provided an opening for Macaulay's withering attack in the *Edinburgh Review* (1829). Macaulay pointed out that Mill's theory was empty: interest 'means only that men, it they can, will do as they choose ... it is ... idle to attribute any importance to a proposition which, when interpreted, means only that a man had rather do what he had rather do' (p. 125).

The charge that the interest doctrine was essentially tautological acquired greater force as more parties climbed on the bandwagon of interest, attempting to bend the concept to their own ends. As so many key concepts used in everyday discourse, 'interest' had never been strictly defined. While individual self-interest in material gain predominated, wider meanings were never completely lost sight of. An extremely wide and inclusive interpretation of the concept was put forward at a very early stage in its history: Pascal's Wager was nothing but an attempt to demonstrate that belief in God (hence, conduct in accordance with His precepts) was strictly in our (long-term) self-interest. Thus the concept of *enlightened* self-interest has a long history. But it received a boost and special, concrete meaning in the course of the 19th century. With the contemporary revolutionary outbreaks and movements as an ominous backdrop, advocates of social reform were able to argue that a dominant social group is well advised to surrender some of its privileges or to improve the plight of the lower classes so as to insure social peace. 'Enlightened' self-interest of the upper classes and conservative opinion was appealed to, for example, by the French and English advocates of universal suffrage or electoral reform at mid-century; it was similarly invoked by the promoters of the early social welfare legislation in Germany and elsewhere toward the end of the century, and again by Keynes and the Keynesians who favoured limited intervention of the state in the economy through countercyclical policy and 'automatic stabilizers' resulting from welfare state provisions. These appeals were often made by reformers who, while fully convinced of the intrinsic value and social justice of the measures they advocated, attempted to enlist the support of important groups by appealing to their 'longer-term' rather than short-term and therefore presumably *short-sighted* interests. But the advocacy was not only tactical. It was sincerely put forward and testified to the continued prestige of the notion that interest-motivated social behaviour was the best guarantee of a stable and harmonious social order.

Whereas enlightened self-interest was something the upper classes of society were in this manner pressed to ferret out, the lower classes were similarly exhorted, at about the same epoch but from different quarters, to raise their sights above day-to-day pursuits. Marx and the Marxists invited the working class to become aware of its *real interests* and to shed the 'false consciousness' from which it was said to be suffering as long as it did not throw itself wholeheartedly into the class struggle. Once again, the language of interests was borrowed for the purpose of characterizing and dignifying a type of behaviour a group was being pressed to adopt.

Here, then, was one way in which the concept of interest-motivated behaviour came to be diluted. Another was the progressive loss of the sharp distinction an earlier age had made between the passions and the interests. Already Adam Smith had used the two concepts jointly and interchangeably. Even though it became abundantly clear in the 19th century that the desire to accumulate wealth was anything but the 'calm passion' as which it had been commended by some 18th-century philosophers, there was no return to the earlier distinction between the interests and the passions or between the wild and the mild passions. Money-making had once and for all been identified with the concept of interest so that all forms of this activity, however passionate or irrational, were automatically thought of as interest-motivated. As striking new forms of accumulation and industrial or financial empire-building made their appearance, new concepts were introduced, such as entrepreneurial leadership and intuition (Schumpeter, 1911) or the 'animal spirits' of the capitalists (Keynes, 1936, pp. 161–3). But they were not contrasted with the interests, and were rather assumed to be one of their manifestations.

In this manner the interests came to cover virtually the entire range of human actions, from the narrowly self-centred to the sacrificially altruistic, and from the prudently calculated to the passionately compulsive. In the end, interest stood behind anything people do or wish to do and to explain human action by interest thus did turn into the vacuous tautology denounced by Macaulay. At about the same time, other key and time-honoured concepts of economic analysis, such as utility and value, became similarly drained of their earlier psychological or normative content. The positivistically oriented science of economics that flourished during much of this century felt that it could do without any of these terms and replaced them by the less value- or psychology-laden 'revealed preference' and 'maximizing under constraints'. And thus it came to pass that interest, which had rendered such long and faithful service as a euphemism, was now superseded in turn by various even more neutral and colourless neologisms.

The development of the self-interest concept and of economic analysis in general in the direction of positivism and formalism may have been related to the discovery, toward the end of the 19th century, of the instinctual-intuitive, the habitual, the unconscious, the ideologically and neurotically driven – in short, to the extraordinary vogue for the nonrational that characterized virtually all of the influential philosophical, psychological and sociological thinking of the time. It was out of the question for economics, all based on rationally pursued self-interest, to incorporate the new findings into its own apparatus. So that discipline reacted to the contemporary intellectual temper by withdrawing from psychology to the greatest possible extent, by emptying its basic concepts of their psychological origin – a survival strategy that turned out to be highly successful. It is of course difficult to prove that the rise of the non-rational in psychology and sociology and the triumph of positivism and formalism in economics were truly connected in this way. Some evidence is supplied by the remarkable case of Pareto: he made fundamental contributions both to a sociology that stressed the complex 'non-logical' (as he put it) aspects of social action and to an economics that is emancipated from dependence on psychological hedonism.

CURRENT TRENDS. Lately there have been signs of discontent with the progressive evisceration of the concept of interest. On the conservative side, there was a return to the orthodox meaning of interest and the doctrine of enlightened self-interest was impugned. Apart from the discovery, first made by Tocqueville, that reform is just as likely to unleash as to prevent revolution, it was pointed out that most well-meant reform moves and regulations have 'perverse' side effects which compound rather than alleviate the social ills one had set out to cure. It was best, so it appeared, not to stray from the narrow path of narrow self-interest, and it was confusing and pointless to dilute this concept.

Others agreed with the latter judgement, but for different reasons and with different conclusions. They also disliked the manoeuvre of having every kind of human action masquerade under the interest label. But they regarded as relevant for economics certain human actions and activities which cannot be accounted for by the traditional notion of self-interest: actions motivated by altruism, by commitment to ethical values, by concern for the group and the public interest, and, perhaps most important, the varieties of non-instrumental behaviour. A beginning has been made by various economists and other social scientists to take these kinds of activities seriously, that is, to abandon the attempt to categorize them as mere variants of interest-motivated activity (Boulding, 1973; Collard, 1978; Hirschman, 1985; Margolis, 1982; McPherson, 1984; Phelps, 1975; Schelling, 1984; Sen, 1977).

One important aspect of these various forms of behaviour which does not correspond to the classical concept of interest-motivated action is that they are subject to considerable variation. Take actions in the public interest as an example. There is a wide range of such actions, from total involvement in some protest movement down to voting on Election Day and further down to mere grumbling about, or commenting on, some public policy within a small circle of friends or family – what Guillermo O'Donnell has called 'horizontal voice' in contrast to the 'vertical' voice directly addressed to the authorities (1986). The actual degree of participation under more or less normal political conditions is subject to constant fluctuations along this continuum, in line with changes in economic conditions, government performance, personal development and many other factors. As a result, with total time for private *and* public activity being limited, the intensity of citizens' dedication to their private interests is also subject to constant change. Near-total privatization occurs only under certain authoritarian governments, for the most repressive regimes do not only do away with the free vote and any open manifestation of dissent, but also manage to suppress, through their display of terrorist power, all *private* expressions of nonconformity with public policy, that is, all those manifestations of 'horizontal voice' that are actually important forms of public involvement.

An arresting conclusion follows. That vaunted ideal of predictability, that alleged idyll of a privatized citizenry paying busy and exclusive attention to its economic interests and thereby serving the public interest indirectly, but never directly, becomes a reality only under wholly nightmarish political conditions!

More civilized political circumstances necessarily imply a less transparent and less predictable society.

Actually, this outcome of the current inquiries into activities not strictly motivated by traditional self-interest is all to the good: for the only certain and predictable feature of human affairs is their unpredictability and the futility of trying to reduce human action to a single motive – such as interest.

BIBLIOGRAPHY

Ball, T. 1983. The ontological presuppositions and political consequences of a social science. In *Changing Social Science*, ed. D.R. Sabia, Jr. and J.T. Wallulis, Albany: State University of New York Press.

Boulding, K.E. 1973. *The Economy of Love and Fear: A Preface to Grants Economics*. Belmont, California: Wadsworth.

Burke, E. 1790. *Reflections on the Revolution in France*. Chicago: Regnery, 1955.

Carlyle, T. 1843. *Past and Present*. New York: New York University Press, 1977.

Collard, D. 1978. *Altruism and Economy: A Study in Non-selfish Economics*. Oxford: Robertson.

Collini, S., Winch, D. and Burrow, J. 1983. *That Noble Science of Politics: A Study in Nineteenth-century Intellectual History*. Cambridge: Cambridge University Press.

Hamilton, A. 1784. Letters from Phocion, Number I. In *The Works of Alexander Hamilton*, ed. John C. Hamilton, New York: C.S. Francis, 1851, Vol. II, 322.

Himmelfarb, G. 1984. *The Idea of Poverty: England in the Early Industrial Age*. New York: Knopf.

Hirschman, A.O. 1977. *The Passions and the Interests: Political Arguments for Capitalism Before its Triumph*. Princeton: Princeton University Press.

Hirschman, A.O. 1982a. Rival interpretations of market society: civilizing, destructive, or feeble? *Journal of Economic Literature* 20(4), December, 1463–84.

Hirschman, A.O. 1982b. *Shifting Involvements: Private Interest and Public Action*. Princeton: Princeton University Press.

Hirschman, A.O. 1985. Against parsimony: three easy ways of complicating some categories of economic discourse. *Economics and Philosophy* 1, 7–21.

Hume, D. 1742. *Essays Moral, Political and Literary*. Ed. T.H. Green and T.H. Grose, London: Longmans, 1898.

Keynes, J.M. 1936. *The General Theory of Employment, Interest and Money*. London: Macmillan; New York: Harcourt, Brace.

Macaulay, T.B. 1829. Mill's Essay on Government. In *Utilitarian Logic and Politics*, ed. J. Lively and J. Rees, Oxford: Clarendon, 1978.

McPherson, M.S. 1984. Limits on self-seeking: the role of morality in economic life. In *Neoclassical Political Economy*, ed. D.C. Colander, Cambridge, Mass.: Ballinger.

Margolis, H. 1982. *Selfishness, Altruism and Rationality*. Cambridge: Cambridge University Press.

Meinecke, F. 1924. *Die Idee der Staatsräson in der neueren Geschichte*. Munich: Oldenburg.

Mill, J. 1820. *Essay on Government*. In *Utilitarian Logic and Politics*, ed. J. Lively and J. Rees, Oxford: Clarendon, 1978.

O'Donnell, G. 1986. On the convergences of Hirschman's *Exit, Voice and Loyalty* and *Shifting Involvements*. In *Development, Democracy and the Art of Trespassing: Essays in Honor of A.O. Hirschman*, ed. A. Foxley et al., Notre Dame, Ind.: University of Notre Dame Press.

359

Phelps, E.S. (ed.) 1975. *Altruism, Morality and Economic Theory*. New York: Russell Sage Foundation.

Pocock, J.G.A. 1982. The political economy of Burke's analysis of the French Revolution. *Historical Journal* 25, June, 331–49.

Rohan, H., Duc de. 1638. *De l'interêt des princes et états de la chrétienité*. Paris: Pierre Margat.

Schelling, T.C. 1984. *Choice and Consequence*. Cambridge, Mass.: Harvard University Press.

Schumpeter, J.A. 1911. *The Theory of Economic Development*. Cambridge, Mass.: Harvard University Press, 1951.

Sen, A. 1977. Rational fools: a critique of the behavioral foundations of economic theory. *Philosophy and Public Affairs* 6(4), Summer, 317–44.

Smith, A. 1776. *An Inquiry into the Nature and Causes of the Wealth of Nations*. Ed. E. Cannan, New York: Modern Library, 1937.

Steuart, J. 1767. *Inquiry into the Principles of Political Oeconomy*. Ed. A.S. Skinner, Chicago: University of Chicago Press, 1966.

Winch, D. 1985. The Burke–Smith problem and late eighteenth century political and economic thought. *Historical Journal* 28(1), 231–47.

Interpersonal Utility Comparisons

JOHN C. HARSANYI

Suppose I am left with a ticket to a Mozart concert I am unable to attend and decide to give it to one of my closest friends. Which friend should I actually give it to? One thing I will surely consider in deciding this is which friend of mine would enjoy the concert *most*. More generally, when we decide as private individuals whom to help, or decide as voters or as public officials who are to receive government help, *one* natural criterion we use is who would derive the greatest benefit, that is, who would derive the *highest utility*, from this help. But to answer this last question we must make, or at least attempt to make, *interpersonal utility comparisons*.

At the common-sense level, all of us make such interpersonal comparisons. But philosophical reflection might make us uneasy about their meaning and validity. We have direct introspective access only to our *own* mental processes (such as our preferences and our feelings of satisfaction and dissatisfaction) defining our *own* utility function, but have only very indirect information about other people's mental processes. Many economists and philosophers take the view that our limited information about other people's minds renders it impossible for us to make meaningful interpersonal comparisons of utility.

COMPARISONS OF UTILITY LEVELS VS. COMPARISONS OF UTILITY DIFFERENCES. In any case, if such comparisons are possible at all, then we must distinguish between interpersonal comparisons of utility *levels* and interpersonal comparisons of utility *differences* (i.e. utility increments or decrements).

It is one thing to compare the utility level $U_i(A)$ that individual i enjoys (or would enjoy) in situation A, with utility level $U_j(B)$ that another individual j enjoys (or would enjoy) in situation B (where A and B may or may not refer to the same situation). It is a very different thing to make interpersonal comparisons between utility differences, such as comparing the utility increment

$$\Delta U_i(A, A') = U_i(A') - U_i(A) \tag{1}$$

that individual i would enjoy in moving from situation A to situation A', with the utility increment

$$\Delta U_j(B, B') = U_j(B') - U_j(B) \tag{2}$$

that individual j would enjoy in moving from B to B'. Either kind of interpersonal comparison might be possible without the other kind being possible (Sen, 1970).

Some ethical theories would require one kind of interpersonal comparison; others would require the other. Thus, *utilitarianism* must assume the interpersonal comparability of utility *differences* because it asks us to maximize a social utility function (social welfare function) defined as the *sum* of all individual utilities. (There are arguments for defining social utility as the *arithmetic mean*, rather than the *sum*, of individual utilities (Harsanyi, 1955). But for most purposes – other than analysing population policies – the two definitions are equivalent because if the number of individuals can be taken for a *constant*, then maximizing the sum of utilities is mathematically equivalent to maximizing their arithmetic mean.) Yet, we cannot add different people's utilities unless all of them are expressed in the same utility units; and in order to decide whether this is the case, we must engage in interpersonal comparisons of utility *differences*. (On the other hand, utilitarianism does not require comparisons of different people's utility *levels* because it does not matter whether their utilities are measured from comparable zero points or not.)

Likewise, the interpersonal utility comparisons we make in everyday life are most of the time comparisons of utility *differences*. For instance, the comparisons made in our example between the utilities that different people would derive from a concert obviously involve comparing utility differences.

In contrast, the utility-based version of Rawls's *Theory of Justice* (1971) does require interpersonal comparisons of utility *levels*, but does not require comparisons of utility *differences*. This is so because his theory uses the *maximin principle* (he calls it the *difference principle*) in evaluating the economic performance of each society, in the sense of using the well-being of the *worst-off* individual (or the worst-off social group) as its principal criterion. But to decide which individuals (or social groups) are worse off than others he must compare different people's utility levels. (In earlier publications, Rawls seemed to define the worst-off individual as one with the lowest utility level. But in later publications, he defined him as one with the smallest amount of 'primary goods'. For a critique of Rawls's theory, see Harsanyi, 1975.)

ORDINALISM, CARDINALISM AND INTERPERSONAL COMPARISONS. In studying comparisons between the utilities enjoyed by *one* particular individual i, we again have to distinguish between comparisons of utility *levels* and comparisons of utility *differences*. The former would involve comparing the utility levels $U_i(A)$ and $U_i(B)$ that i assigns to two different situations A and B. The latter would involve comparing the utility increment

$$\Delta U_i(A, A') = U_i(A') - U_i(A) \tag{3}$$

that i would enjoy in moving from situation A to situation A', with the utility increment

$$\Delta U_i(B, B') = U_i(B') - U_i(B) \tag{4}$$

that he would enjoy in moving from B to B'.

If i has a well-defined utility function U_i at all, then he certainly must be able to compare the utility *levels* he assigns to various situations; and such comparisons will have a clear behavioural meaning because they will correspond to the preference and indifference relations expressed by his choice behaviour. In contrast, it is immediately less obvious whether comparing utility *differences* as defined under (3) and (4) has any economic meaning (but see below).

A utility function U_i permitting meaningful comparisons *only* between i's utility levels, but *not* permitting such comparisons between his utility differences, is called *ordinal*; whereas a utility function permitting meaningful comparisons *both* between his utility levels and his utility differences is called *cardinal*.

As is well known, most branches of economic theory use only ordinal utilities. But, as von Neumann and Morgenstern (1947) have shown, cardinal utility functions can play a very useful role in the theory of risk taking. In fact, utility-difference comparisons based on von Neumann–Morgenstern utility functions turn out to have a direct behavioural meaning. For example, suppose that U_i is such a utility function, and let Δ_i^* and Δ_i^{**} be utility differences defined by (3) and by (4). Then the inequality $\Delta_i^* > \Delta_i^{**}$ will be algebraically equivalent to the inequality

$$\tfrac{1}{2}U_i(A') + \tfrac{1}{2}U_i(B) > \tfrac{1}{2}U_i(B') + \tfrac{1}{2}U_i(A). \tag{5}$$

This inequality in turn will have the behavioural interpretation that i *prefers* an equi-probability mixture of A' and of B to an equi-probability mixture of B' and of A. Of course, once von Neumann–Morgenstern utility functions are used in the theory of risk taking, they become available for possible use also in other branches of economic theory, including welfare economics as well as in ethical investigations. (It has been argued that von Neumann–Morgenstern utility functions have no place in ethics (or in welfare economics) because they merely express people's attitudes toward *gambling*, which has no moral significance (Arrow, 1951, p. 10; and Rawls, 1971, pp. 172 and 323. But see Harsanyi, 1984.)

Note that by taking an ordinalist or a cardinalist position, one restricts the positions one can consistently take as to interpersonal comparability of utilities.

(1) An *ordinalist* is logically free to *reject* both types of interpersonal comparisons. Or he may *admit* comparisons of different people's utility *levels*. But he *cannot* admit the interpersonal comparability of utility differences without becoming a cardinalist. (The reason is this: if the utility differences experienced by one individual i are comparable with those experienced by *another* individual j, this will make the utility differences experienced by *one* individual (say) i

likewise indirectly comparable with one another, which will enable us to construct a *cardinal* utility function for each individual.)

(2) A *cardinalist* is likewise logically free to *reject* both types of interpersonal comparisons. Or he may *admit* both. Or else he may admit interpersonal comparisons only for utility *differences*. (Though it is hard to see why anybody might want to reject interpersonal comparisons for utility levels if he admitted them for utility differences.) But he *cannot* consistently admit interpersonal comparisons for utility *levels* while rejecting them for utility *differences*. (This can be verified as follows. If utility levels are interpersonally comparable, then we can find four situations A, A', B and B' such that $U_i(A) = U_j(B)$ and $U_j(A') = U_j(B')$. But then we can conclude that

$$\Delta_i^* = U_i(A') - U_i(A) = \Delta_j^* = U_j(B') - U_j(B),$$

which means that at least the utility differences Δ_i^* and Δ_j^* are interpersonally comparable. But since U_i and U_j are *cardinal* utility functions, any utility difference Δ_i^{**} experienced by i is comparable with Δ_i^*, and any utility difference Δ_j^{**} experienced by j is comparable with Δ_j^*. Yet this means that *all* utility differences Δ_i^{**} experienced by i are comparable with *all* utility differences Δ_j^{**} experienced by j. Thus, cardinalism together with interpersonal comparability of utility levels *entails* that of utility differences.)

EXTENDED UTILITY FUNCTIONS. In what follows, I will use the symbols A_i, B_i,... to denote the economic and non-economic resources available to individual i in situations A, B, ... Moreover, I will use the symbol A_j to denote an arrangement under which j has the same resources available to him as were available to individual i under arrangement A_i. These entities A_i, B_i, ..., A_j, B_j,... I will call *positions*.

Interpersonal utility comparisons would pose no problem if all individuals had the *same* utility function. For in this case, any individual j could assume that the utility level $U_i(A_i)$ that another individual i would derive from a given position A_i should be the *same* as he himself would derive from a similar position. Thus, j could write simply

$$U_i(A_i) = U_j(A_j). \tag{6}$$

Of course, in actual fact, the utility of different people is rather *different* because people have different *tastes*, that is, they have different abilities to derive satisfactions from given resource endowments. I will use the symbols R_i, R_j,... to denote the vectors listing the personal psychological characteristics of each individual i, j,... that *explain* the differences among their utility functions U_i, U_j,.... Presumably, these vectors summarize the effects that the genetic make-up, the education, and the life experience of each individual have on his utility function. This means that any individual j can attempt to assess the utility level $U_i(A_i)$ that another individual j would enjoy in position A_i as

$$U_i(A) = V(A_i, R_i), \tag{7}$$

where the function V represents the psychological laws determining the utility functions $U_i, U_j, \ldots$ of the various individuals $i, j, \ldots$ in accordance with their psychological parameters specified by the vectors $R_i, R_j, \ldots$. Since, by assumption, all differences among the various individuals' utility functions $U_i, U_j, \ldots$ are fully explained by the vectors $R_i, R_j, \ldots$, the function V itself will be the same for all individuals. We will call V an *extended utility function*. (See Arrow, 1978, and Harsanyi, 1977, pp. 51–60, though the basic ideas are contained already in Arrow, 1951, pp. 114–15.)

To be sure, we know very little about the psychological laws determining people's utility functions and, therefore, know very little about the true mathematical form of the extended utility function V. This means that, when we try to use equation (7), the best we can do is to use our – surely very imperfect – personal *estimate* of V, rather than V itself. As a result, in trying to make interpersonal utility comparisons, we must expect to make significant errors from time to time – in particular when we are trying to assess the utility functions of people with a very different cultural and social background from our own. But even if our judgements of interpersonal comparisons can easily be *mistaken*, this does not imply that they are *meaningless*.

Ordinalists will interpret both the functions U_i and the function V as *ordinal* utility functions and will interpret (7) merely as a warrant for interpersonal comparisons of utility *levels* (cf. Arrow, 1978). In contrast, cardinalists will interpret all these as *cardinal* utility functions and will interpret (7) as a warrant for *both* kinds of interpersonal comparison (cf. Harsanyi, 1977).

LIMITS TO INTERPERSONAL COMPARISONS. It seems to me that economists and philosophers influenced by *logical positivism* have greatly exaggerated the difficulties we face in making interpersonal utility comparisons with respect to the utilities and the disutilities that people derive from ordinary commodities and, more generally, from the ordinary pleasures and calamities of human life. (A very influential opponent of the possibility of meaningful interpersonal utility comparisons has been Robbins, 1932.) But when we face the problem of judging the utilities and the disutilities that other people derive from various *cultural* activities, we do seem to run into very real, and sometimes perhaps even unsurmountable, difficulties. For example, suppose I observe a group of people who claim to derive great aesthetic enjoyment from a very esoteric form of abstract art, which does not have the slightest appeal to me in spite of my best efforts to understand it. Then, there may be no way for me to decide whether the admirers of this art form *really* derive very great and genuine enjoyment from it, or merely *deceive themselves* by claiming that they do.

Maybe in such cases interpersonal comparisons of utility do reach unsurmountable obstacles. But, fortunately, very few of our personal moral decisions and of our public political decisions depend on such exceptionally difficult interpersonal comparisons of utility. (References additional to those listed below will be found in Hammond, 1977, and in Suppes and Winet, 1955.)

BIBLIOGRAPHY

Arrow, K.J. 1951. *Social Choice and Individual Values*. 2nd edn, New York: Wiley, 1963.

Arrow, K.J. 1978. Extended sympathy and the possibility of social choice. *Philosophia* 7, 223–37.

Hammond, P.J. 1977. Dual interpersonal comparisons of utility and the welfare economics of income distribution. *Journal of Public Economics* 7, 51–71.

Harsanyi, J.C. 1955. Cardinal utility, individualistic ethics, and interpersonal comparisons of utility. *Journal of Political Economy* 63, 309–21. Reprinted as ch. 2 of Harsanyi (1977).

Harsanyi, J.C. 1975. Can the maximum principle serve as a basis for morality? A critique of John Rawls' theory. *American Political Science Review* 69, 594–606. Reprinted as ch. 4 of Harsanyi (1977).

Harsanyi, J.C. 1976. *Essays on Ethics, Social Behavior and Scientific Explanation*. Dordrecht: Reidel.

Harsanyi, J.C. 1977. *Rational Behaviour and Bargaining Equilibrium in Games and Social Situations*. Cambridge: Cambridge University Press.

Harsanyi, J.C. 1984. Von Neumann–Morgenstern utilities, risk taking, and welfare. In *Arrow and the Ascent of Modern Economic Theory*, ed. G.R. Feiwel, New York: New York University Press.

Rawls, J. 1971. *A Theory of Justice*. Cambridge, Mass.: Harvard University Press.

Robbins, L. 1932. *An Essay on the Nature and Significance of Economic Science*. London: Macmillan.

Sen, A.K. 1970. *Collective Choice and Social Welfare*. San Francisco: Holden-Day.

Suppes, P. and Winet, M. 1955. An axiomatization of utility based on the notion of utility differences. *Management Science* 1, 259–70.

Von Neumann, J. and Morgenstern, O. 1947. *Theory of Games and Economic Behavior*. 2nd edn, Princeton: Princeton University Press.

Keynesianism

JOHN EATWELL

The impact of Keynes's *General Theory* was felt not only in macroeconomic analysis, in national income accounting and in applied economics, but also in economic doctrine. 'Keynesianism' became a distinctive approach to economic affairs. The label was applied both to the conclusions of the *General Theory*, and to propositions which although not found in the *General Theory* were felt, often wrongly, to derive from its arguments.

The distinctive characteristics of Keynesianism are, in analysis a tendency to downplay the role of price effects in the determination of overall output and employment, giving priority to income effects, and in the formation of policy a tendency to emphasize the interventionist role of the state, most particularly in the determination of satisfactory levels of aggregate demand and, more generally, in taking responsibility for the management of economic growth.

The emphasis on income effects follows directly from the analysis of the *General Theory*. The principle of effective demand, which Keynes himself regarded as the essential novelty of his approach, is innocent of the price mechanism, being solely a relationship between investment ('autonomous' expenditure) and output. The power of the multiplier analysis was readily extended from the simple model in which variation in output maintains the equality of desired saving and investment, to more general analyses of 'injections' and 'leakages' which include fiscal stance and the balance of trade, to produce a family of 'Keynesian' income and expenditure models.

Similarly, the central conclusion of the *General Theory*, that there is no automatic tendency in a market economy which ensures that the level of output corresponds to that which will sustain full employment, leads naturally to the idea that it should be the responsibility of the state to manage the overall level of expenditure in pursuit of that objective. Keynes himself argued that 'a somewhat comprehensive socialisation of investment will prove the only means of securing an approximation to full employment; though this need not exclude

367

all manner of compromises and devices by which public authority will co-operate with private initiative' (Keynes, 1936, p. 378).

Both theoretical proposition and policy stance might have been derived from a rejection of the idea that the market mechanism ensures an efficient allocation of resources, a rejection, that is, of the fundamental theory of welfare economics. And since this rejection stems not from the presence of imperfections in the market mechanism, but from the assertion that even in the best of all possible worlds the market economy does not operate that way, acceptance of Keynes's argument implied rejection of the neoclassical theory of value and distribution *in toto*.

However, these 'income effect' and 'interventionist' interpretations of the significance of the *General Theory* were modified, if not submerged, by Keynes's assertion that 'if our central controls succeed in establishing an aggregate volume of output corresponding to full employment as nearly as is practicable, the classical theory comes into its own again from this point onwards' (Keynes, 1936, p. 378). Keynes appears to rehabilitate the price mechanism as an efficient means of allocation, whilst at the same time denying its efficiency as a means of assuring full utilization of available factor services, *even though these are two aspects of the same phenomenon.*

This seductive (if contradictory) position was reinforced by the development of the neoclassical synthesis version of Keynes's analysis (Hicks, 1937; Modigliani, 1944), in which Keynes's conclusions were said to rest on the assumption of rigid (or sticky) money wages, given the supply of money, so that it 'is the fact that money wages are too high relative to the quantity of money that explains why it is unprofitable to expand employment to the "full-employment" level' (Modigliani, 1944, p. 255).

Confining the significance of Keynes's analysis to short-run rigidities inhibiting the operation of the labour market restored the conception of the long-run efficiency of the market mechanism which had been threatened by the argument of the *General Theory*, and placed the label 'Keynesian' on policies of macroeconomic management which eschewed microeconomic intervention, and certainly did not incorporate any 'comprehensive socialisation of investment'. Economic management became a search for the appropriate mix of monetary and fiscal policies – the relative weight placed on one or the other being based on assumptions concerning the relative elasticities of the IS and LM curves, these in turn being based, in part, on the degree of faith placed in the presumed efficiency of the market mechanism.

Thus, instead of superseding neoclassical analysis and the policy perspectives which are derived from that system of thought – perspectives which had been discredited in the Thirties – Keynesianism preserved free-market economics at the microeconomic and industrial level, as if in aspic, until such time as those ideas were reasserted with the revival of monetarism and its associated free-market policies.

The revival of monetarism was facilitated by the empirical failure of a device which had been grafted onto the neoclassical synthesis version of Keynes, even though it had played no role in the *General Theory* – this device was the Phillips curve. The Phillips curve provided, in dynamic form, a solution to the neoclassical synthesis puzzle of how the sticky money wage was to be determined (or, more accurately, how *changes* in the sticky money wage were to be determined). The Phillips curve filled the fourth quadrant of the familiar textbook diagrams, matching the requisite extra equation to the number of unknowns, and so closing the model.

The very obvious absence of any inverse relationship between the rate of money wage inflation and the level of unemployment in the early 1970s was then, extraordinarily, portrayed as clear evidence of the 'failure' of Keynes's economics, even though there is nothing in the *General Theory* which suggests that such a relationship exists, and even though the analysis of the *General Theory* is quite independent of such a relationship. (The ideas on inflation outlined in *How to Pay for the War* were certainly not regarded by Keynes as a constituent part of his theory of employment.)

The dilution of the theoretical implications of the *General Theory* in 'Keynesianism' resulted in a neglect of microeconomic issues by those who perceived the need for interventionist policies to ensure economic efficiency. The demand-management policies pursued in Britain after 1951, for example, proved to be inadequate to the task of industrial reconstruction, or to the maintenance of a competitive manufacturing industry. These policies contrast strongly with the industrial policies pursued in France, Germany and Japan, where active microeconomic intervention was pursued as the predominant method of economic management, and where 'Keynesianism' played a less prominent role in the formulation of economic policy.

The intellectual failure of Keynesianism, or, more accurately, the intellectual failure of the neoclassical synthesis version of Keynes's analysis, was cruelly exposed by the perfectly reasonable argument that the theoretical underpinnings of that synthesis are exactly the same Walrasian foundations upon which monetarist ideas are erected. This was conceded by Modigliani in his presidential address to the American Economic Association, in which he declared that the proposition that 'in the long run money is neutral ... by now does not meet serious objection from non-monetarists' (Modigliani, 1977, p. 119). The difference between monetarism and Keynesianism thus degenerated into an argument over elasticities in the short and long run – nothing fundamental was at stake (see the papers in Gordon, 1974).

Thus in both theory and policy 'Keynesianism' has, paradoxically, tended to reinforce the opinions which Keynes anticipated in the preface to the *General Theory*:

Those, who are strongly wedded to what I shall call 'the classical theory', will fluctuate, I expect, between a belief that I am quite wrong and a belief that I am saying nothing new.

The current disarray of macroeconomic theory and macroeconomic policy suggests the need to assess whether, as Keynes put it, 'the third alternative is right'.

369

BIBLIOGRAPHY

Gordon, R.J. (ed.) 1974. *Milton Friedman's Monetary Framework*. Chicago; University of Chicago Press.

Hicks, J.R. 1937. Mr Keynes and the 'classics': a suggested interpretation. *Econometrica* 5, April, 147–59.

Keynes, J.M. 1936. *The General Theory of Employment, Interest and Money*. London: Macmillan.

Keynes, J.M. 1940. *How to Pay for the War*. London: Macmillan.

Modigliani, F. 1944. Liquidity preference and the theory of interest and money. *Econometrica* 12, January, 45–88.

Modigliani, F. 1977. The monetarist controversy, or should we foresake stabilization policies? *American Economic Review* 67(2), March, 1–19.

Law and Economics

DAVID FRIEDMAN

The economic analysis of law involves three distinct but related enterprises. The first is the use of economics to predict the effects of legal rules. The second is the use of economics to determine what legal rules are economically efficient, in order to recommend what the legal rules ought to be. The third is the use of economics to predict what the legal rules will be. Of these, the first is primarily an application of price theory, the second of welfare economics and the third of public choice.

PREDICTING THE EFFECT OF LAWS. Of the three enterprises, the least controversial is the first – the use of economic analysis to predict the effect of alternative legal rules. In many cases, the result of doing so is to show that the effect of a rule is radically different from what a non-economist might expect.

Consider the following simple example. A city government passes an ordinance requiring landlords to give tenants three months notice before evicting them, even if the lease agreement provides for a shorter period. At first glance, the main effect is to make tenants better off, since they have greater security of tenure, and to make landlords worse off, since they now find it more difficult to evict undesirable tenants.

The conclusion is obvious; it is also false. The new ordinance raises the demand curve; the price at which tenants choose to rent any given quantity of housing is higher, since they are getting a more attractive good. It also raises the supply curve, since the cost of producing rental housing is now higher. If both the supply and the demand curve rise, so does the price. In the short run, the regulation benefits the tenant at the expense of his landlord. Once rents have had time to adjust, the tenant is better off by the improved security of his apartment but worse off by the higher rent he pays for it; the landlord is worse off by the increased difficulty of eviction and better off by the increased rent he receives.

One can easily construct specific examples in which such a regulation makes both landlords and tenants worse off, by adding to the lease terms which increase the landlord's costs by more than they are worth to the tenant and increase the

371

market rent by more than enough to eliminate the tenants' gain but too little to compensate the landlords' loss. One can also construct examples in which both parties are better off, because the regulation saves them the cost of negotiating terms which are in fact in their mutual interest. Thus economic analysis radically alters the grounds on which the regulation can be defended or attacked, eliminating the obvious justification (helping tenants at the expense of landlords) and replacing it with a different and much more complicated set of issues.

In this example, and in many similar ones, the two parties are linked by a contract and a price. In such cases, the first and most important contribution of economics to legal analysis is the recognition that a legally imposed change in the terms of the contract will result in a change in the market price. Typically, the result is to eliminate the transfer that would otherwise be implied by the change.

This is not true for cases, such as accidents and crimes, where there is no contract and no price. In analysing such situations, the essential contribution of economics is to include explicitly the element of rational choice involved in producing outcomes that are commonly regarded as either irrational or not chosen.

Consider automobile accidents. While a driver does not choose to have an accident, he does make many choices which affect the probability that an accident will occur. In deciding how fast to drive, how frequently to have his brakes checked, or how much attention to devote to the road and how much to his conversation with the passenger next to him, he is implicitly trading off the cost of an increased risk of accident against the benefit of getting home sooner, saving money, or enjoying a pleasant conversation. The amount of 'safety' the driver chooses to 'buy' will then be determined by the associated cost and benefit functions. Thus, for example, Peltzman (1975) demonstrated that safer autos tend to result in more dangerous driving, with the reduction in death rates per accident being at least partly balanced by more accidents, as drivers choose to drive faster and less carefully in the knowledge that the cost of doing so has been lowered.

This way of looking at accidents is important in analysing both laws designed to prevent accidents, such as speed limits, and liability laws designed to determine who must pay for accidents when they occur. From the economic perspective, the two sorts of laws are alternative tools for the same purpose – controlling the level of accidents.

A driver who knows he will be liable for the costs of any accidents he causes will take that fact into account in deciding how safely he should drive. Elizabeth Landes, in a study of the shift to no-fault auto insurance, concluded that one effect of the reduction in liability was to increase highway death rates by about 10–15 per cent.

The advantage of liability over direct regulation is that the knowledge that if he causes an accident he must pay for it gives the driver an incentive to modify his behaviour in any way that will reduce the chance of an accident, whether or not others can observe it. Regulations such as speed limits control only those elements of driver behaviour which can be easily observed from the outside –

speed but not attention, for example. The disadvantage of liability is that it forces drivers, who may well be risk averse, to participate in a lottery – one chance in two thousand, say, of causing an accident and having to pay all of its cost.

An accident is one example of an involuntary interaction; a crime is another. Economic analysis of crime starts with the assumption that becoming a criminal is a rational decision, like the decision to enter any other profession. Changes in the law which alter either the probability that the perpetrator of a crime will be punished for it or the magnitude of the punishment can be expected to affect the attractiveness of the profession, hence the frequency with which crimes occur – as demonstrated empirically in Ehrlich (1972). Similarly, changes in crime rates will, via the rational decisions of potential victims, affect expenditures on defending against crime.

Another area of law, in which the application of economic analysis is less novel, is anti-trust. One important contribution of economic analysis has been to suggest that some elements of anti-trust law may be based on an incorrect perception of how firms get and maintain monopoly power.

McGee (1958) used arguments originally proposed by Aaron Director to show that if, as commonly alleged, Standard Oil had attempted to maintain its market position by predatory pricing – cutting the price of oil below cost in order to drive out smaller but equally efficient rivals – the effort would probably have failed. Standard's larger assets would be balanced by a larger volume of sales, and hence larger losses when those sales were at a price below cost. Even if the smaller firm had gone bankrupt first, its physical plant would have remained, to be purchased by some new competitor. Based on a study of the record of the Standard Oil anti-trust case McGee concluded that predatory pricing was a myth: Rockefeller had in fact maintained his position by buying out rivals, usually at high prices.

The argument, if correct, implies that some conventional anti-trust activity is misplaced. Pricing policies which are attacked as predatory may in fact be ways in which new firms break into existing markets, using low prices to induce potential customers to try their products. If so, prohibiting such policies reduces competition and encourages the monopoly that the law is intended to prevent.

EFFICIENCY: PRESCRIBING LAWS. The use of economic analysis to determine what the law ought to be starts with one simple and controversial premise – that the sole purpose of law should be to promote economic efficiency. There are two problems with this premise. The first is that it depends on the utilitarian assumption – that the only good is human happiness, defined not as what people should want but as what they do want. The second is that economic efficiency provides at best a very approximate measure of what most of us understand by 'total human happiness', since it assumes away the problem of interpersonal utility comparisons by, in effect, treating people as if they all had the same marginal utility of income.

One reply to this criticism is that while few people believe that economic efficiency is all that matters, most people who understand the concept would

373

agree that it is either an important objective or an important means to other objectives. Hence while maximizing economic efficiency may not be the only purpose of laws, it is an important one – and one that economic theory can, in principle, tell us how to achieve. Further, economic theory suggests that an improvement in efficiency may be something that courts can achieve, whereas redistribution, for reasons suggested in the discussion of landlord–tenant relations, may not be.

Once one accepts economic efficiency as the objective, the standard tools of welfare economics can be used to analyse a wide variety of legal issues. Consider, for example, the eviction regulation discussed earlier. If the additional security of tenure is worth more to the tenant than it costs the landlord to produce, then landlords will find it in their interest to include that condition in the lease contract whether or not the law requires them to; the additional rent they will be able to charge will more than make up for the cost of delays in evicting undesirable tenants. If, on the other hand, security of tenure costs the landlords more than it is worth to the tenants, then they will not choose to offer it – and, viewed from the standpoint of economic efficiency, a regulation compelling them to do so is undesirable.

So one conclusion suggested by such analysis is a strong case for freedom of contract – allowing the parties to a lease, or any other contract, to include any terms mutually agreeable. To the extent that one accepts that argument, the function of legal rules is simply to specify a default contract – a set of terms that apply unless the parties specify otherwise. If the default contract closely approximates what the parties would agree to if they did specify all the details of their agreement, it serves the useful purpose of reducing the cost of negotiating contracts.

An important example of such analysis occurs in the case of product liability law. Just as with lease contracts, the first step is to observe that changes in who bears the liability for product defects will produce corresponding changes in market price, so that shifting liability from, say, buyer to seller will not in general result in the buyer being better off and the seller worse off. Changes in liability law will, however, change the incentives facing both buyer and seller with regard to decisions they make that effect the damage produed by defects. To the extent that a buyer cannot judge the quality of a product before he buys it, a rule of *caveat emptor* gives the seller an inefficiently weak incentive to prevent defects, since he pays the cost of quality control and receives no corresponding benefit. On the other hand, a rule of *caveat venditor* provides the seller with the appropriate incentive, since he ends up paying, via damage suits, for the cost of defects, but it gives the buyer an inefficiently low incentive to try to use the product in a way that will minimize the damage from defects – by, for example, driving an automobile in a way that does not rely too heavily on the brakes always working perfectly.

This suggests that different legal rules may be appropriate for different sorts of goods. It also suggests that some intermediate rule, such as contributory negligence, in which the producer of a defective good may defend himself against a damage suit by showing the accident was in part the result of imprudent use by the purchaser, may be superior to both *caveat emptor* and *caveat venditor*.

Just as in the case of tenant and landlord, the analysis suggests that while the law may set a default rule, it ought to permit freedom of contract. Sellers can then convert *caveat emptor* into *caveat venditor* by offering a guarantee, and buyers can convert *caveat venditor* into *caveat emptor* by signing a waiver.

Another area of interest is corporate law. Here the central problem is that of structuring the contract which defines the corporation so as to control the principal–agent problem resulting from the separation of ownership and management. One solution, missed in Smith's classic statement of the problem (Smith, 1776), is the takeover bid, used to discipline managers who do not maximize the value of the assets they manage. The question of whether the law should assist or oppose managers in their attempt to prevent takeovers has been a lively issue in the recent literature.

Freedom of contract is of no use where there is no voluntary agreement among the parties. The law must somehow specify who is responsible under what conditions for the cost of accidents, and what the punishment is to be for crimes. One traditional approach to this problem is the 'Hand formula', according to which someone is judged negligent, hence legally responsible for an accident, only if he could have prevented it by precautions that would have cost less than the expected cost (probability times damage) of the accident. This seems to fit very neatly into the economic analysis of law, since it punishes someone only if he has acted inefficiently by failing to take a cost-justified precaution.

It has, however, two serious difficulties. One is that 'accidents' are usually the result of the joint action of two or more parties. My bad brakes would not have injured you if you had not chosen to ride a bicycle at night wearing dark clothing – but your bicycle riding would not have put you in the hospital if my car had had good brakes. In such a situation, the efficient solution is to have precautions taken by whichever party can take them more cheaply – even if the other party could prevent the accident at a cost lower than the resulting damage. This suggests that the Hand formula should be interpreted as making the party liable who could have avoided the accident at the lower cost. Situations in which the probability and cost of accidents are continuous functions of both my level of precaution and yours require additional elaborations of the formula.

A second problem is that the Hand formula requires the court to make judgements, both about the probability of accidents given various levels of precaution and about the cost of both precautions and accidents to the parties involved, which it may not be competent to make. This suggests the desirability of legal rules which are sufficiently general so that they do not depend on a court making case-by-case evaluations of cost and benefits, but which give the parties incentives to use their private knowledge of costs and benefits to produce efficient outcomes. The attempt to construct such rules, for a wide variety of legal problems, makes up a considerable part of the law and economics literature.

Crimes, like accidents, involve involuntary interactions. The economic analysis of crime focuses on two related issues – the incentives facing the criminal and the incentives facing the system of courts and police. The first leads to the question of what combination of punishment and probability of apprehension would be applied, for any crime, in an efficient system; the answer involves trading off costs and benefits to criminals, victims and the enforcement system. The second leads to questions about the procedures used by the court system to determine guilt or innocence (also an issue in other parts of the law), and of the relative advantages of private enforcement of law, as in our civil system, in comparison to public enforcement, as in our criminal system.

ECONOMISTS LEARNING FROM LAW: THE COASE THEOREM. So far, all of the examples of economic analysis of law have involved using existing economic theory to analyse the law. There is at least one area, however, where the interaction of law and economics has resulted in a substantial body of new economic theory. This is the set of ideas originating in the work of Ronald Coase and commonly referred to as the Coase Theorem.

According to the traditional analysis of externalities associated with Pigou, an externality exists where one party's actions impose costs on another, for which the first need not compensate him. This leads to an inefficient outcome, since the first party ignores the costs to the second in making his decision. Thus, for example, a railroad company may permit its locomotives to throw sparks, even though they cause occasional fires in the neighbouring corn fields. The cost of modifying the engine to prevent sparks would be borne by the company; the cost of the fires is an externality imposed on the adjacent farmers. The traditional solution is a Pigouvian tax. The railroad company is charged for the damage done, and can either pay or stop doing the damage, whichever costs less.

Coase pointed out that in this and many other cases, the cost is not simply imposed by one party on the other, rather, it arises from incompatible activities by two parties. The fires are the result both of the railroad company using a spark-throwing locomotive and of the farmers choosing to grow inflammable crops near the rail line. The efficient solution might be to modify the locomotive, but it also might be to grow different crops. In the latter case, a Pigouvian tax on the railroad leads to an inefficient outcome.

Hence the first step in Coase's analysis suggests that there is no general solution to the problem of externalities. The legislature, in setting up general laws, cannot know which party, in any specific case, will be able to avoid the problem at the lowest cost. If it attempts to solve the problem by a law making whichever party can avoid the problem at the lower cost liable, the court is left with the problem of estimating the costs. Each party has an incentive to misrepresent the cost of its potential precautions, in order to make the other party liable for preventing the damage.

The second step is to observe that both this argument and the traditional analysis of externalities ignore the possibility of agreements between the parties. If the law makes the railroad liable for the damage when the farmers can prevent it at a lower cost, it will be in the interest of both farmers and railroad to negotiate an agreement in which the railroad pays the farmers to grow clover rather than corn along the rail line. Hence this line of analysis leads to the conclusion that whatever the initial definition of rights – whether the railroad has the right to throw sparks or the farmers to enjoin the railroad or collect damages – market transactions among the participants will lead to an efficient outcome.

The final step in the argument is to observe that inefficient outcomes do in fact occur, and that the reason is transaction costs. If, for example, any farmer can enjoin the railroad from throwing sparks, then the railroad, in dealing with the farmers, is faced by a hold-out problem. A single farmer may try to collect a large fraction of what the railroad saves by not modifying its locomotive, using the threat that if his demands are not met he can enjoin the railroad, whatever the other farmers do. If, on the other hand, the railroad is free to throw sparks and it is up to the farmers to offer to pay for the modifications, then in raising the money to do so they face a public good problem; a farmer who does not contribute still benefits. Transaction cost problems of this sort may prevent the process by which bargaining among participants would otherwise lead to an efficient outcome.

The conclusion of all of this is the Coase Theorem, which states that in a world of zero transaction costs any initial definition of rights will lead to an efficient outcome. It is important not because we live in such a world, but because it shows us a different way of looking at a large range of problems – as resulting from the transaction costs that prevent the parties affected from bargaining their way to an efficient outcome.

This approach represents both an important change in the traditional economic analysis of externalities and a powerful tool for analysing legal institutions. Many such issues can be seen as questions of how property rights are to be bundled. When I acquire a piece of land, does what I buy include the right to make loud noises on it? To prevent passing locomotives from throwing sparks on it? To leave objects lying about that might be hazardous to neighbours who accidentally trespass? From the perspective of the Coase Theorem, all such questions can be approached by asking first what bundling of rights would lead, under various circumstances, to an efficient outcome, and second, if a particular initial bundling of rights leads to inefficient outcomes, how easy will it be for the parties to negotiate a change, with the party who has a greater value for one of the rights in a bundle purchasing it from its initial owner.

One example is the law of attractive nuisance. Does the ownership of a piece of land include the right to put on it open cement tanks full of deadly chemicals, protected only by large signs – which are no barrier at all to the trespasser too young to read? The immediate answer is that the right to decide whether the tanks are fenced is worth more to the neighbourhood parents than to the owner of the property. The further answer is that if the law gives the right to the owner, including it in the bundle labelled 'ownership of land', it will be difficult for the parents to buy it, since the parents face a public good problem in purchasing an agreement from the owner to put high fences around his tanks. Hence we have an argument for the existing law of attractive nuisance, under which the parent can enjoin the property owner from leaving the tanks unfenced, or sue for damages if his child is injured. This is one example of the way in which the Coase Theorem approach helps illuminate a wide range of legal issues.

PREDICTION: WHAT THE LAW WILL BE. Economic analysis, of law or anything else, can be viewed either as an attempt to learn what should be or as an attempt to explain what is and predict what will be. In the case of the economic analysis of the law, attempts to explain and predict have taken two rather different forms.

On the one hand, there is the argument of Richard Posner, according to which the common law tends, for a variety of reasons, to be economically efficient. The analysis of what legal rules are efficient thus provides an explanation of what legal rules exist – and the observation of what legal rules exist provides a test of theories about what rules are efficient.

On the other hand, there is the approach associated with public choice theory which views legislated, administrative and perhaps even common law as outcomes of a political market on which interest groups seek private objectives by governmental means. Since the amount a group is willing to spend in order to get the laws it favours depends not only on the value of the law to that group but also on the group's ability to solve the public good problem of inducing its members to contribute, expenditures in the political market will not accurately represent the value of the law to those affected, hence inefficient laws – laws which injure the losers by more than they benefit the gainers – may well pass, and efficient laws m._y well fail. The most obvious implication of this line of analysis is that laws will tend to favour concentrated interests at the expense of dispersed interests, since the former will be better able to raise money from their members to lobby for the laws they prefer.

CONCLUSIONS. In looking at economic analysis of law, one striking observation is the way in which economists tend to convert issues from disputes about equity, justice, fairness or the like into disputes about efficiency. In part, this is because economists do, and traditional legal scholars often do not, take account of the effect of legal rules on market prices. The result of taking these effects into account is frequently to eliminate the distributional effects of changes in such rules. In part, it is because economists do, and legal scholars sometimes do not, assume that rules modify behaviour. If so, then in evaluating the rules we must ask not only whether they produce a just outcome in a particular case, but whether their effects on the behaviour of those who know of the rules and modify their actions to take account of them is in some sense desirable.

A second observation is that economic analysis frequently demonstrates the existence of efficiency arguments for rules usually thought of as based entirely on considerations of justice. One simple example is the law against theft. At first glance, theft appears to involve no question of economic efficiency at all; the thief is better off by the same amount by which the victim is worse off, hence the transaction, however unjust, is not inefficient.

That conclusion is wrong. The opportunity to gain by stealing diverts resources to that activity. In equilibrium, the marginal thief receives the same income from stealing (net of risk of imprisonment, cost of tools, etc.) as he would in some alternative productive activity; there is no gain to the marginal thief to balance the cost to the victim. Hence theft can be condemned as inefficient with no reference to issues of justice.

A third observation is the degree to which the examination of real legal issues and real cases forces the economist to take account of some of the complexities of real-world interactions which he might otherwise never notice, and thus provides him with the opportunity to increase the depth and power of his analysis.

A final, and important, observation is that economics provides a unity among disparate fields of law which is lacking in much traditional legal analysis. In the words of one of the field's leading practitioners:

> Almost any tort problem can be solved as a contract problem, by asking what the people involved in an accident would have agreed on in advance with regard to safety measures if transaction costs had not been prohibitive.... Equally, almost any contract problem can be solved as a tort problem by asking what sanction is necessary to prevent the performing or paying party from engaging in wasteful conduct, such as taking advantage of the vulnerability of a party who performs his side of the bargain first. And both tort and contract problems can be framed as problems in the definition of property rights; for example, the law of negligence could be thought to define the right we have in the safety of our persons against accidental injury. The definition of property rights can itself be viewed as a process of figuring out what measures parties would agree to, if transaction costs weren't prohibitive, in order to create incentives to avoid wasting valuable resources (Posner, 1986).

Any note as short as this can provide only a very incomplete description of the field, and one heavily biased towards the author's own interests. The references cited below, and the references in Posner (1986) and Goetz (1984), provide a much more extensive survey.

BIBLIOGRAPHY

Becker, G. 1968. Crime and punishment: an economic approach. *Journal of Political Economy* 76, March, 169–217.

Becker, G. 1976. *The Economic Approach to Human Behavior*. Chicago: University of Chicago Press.

Calabresi, G. 1961. Some thoughts on risk distribution and the law of torts. *Yale Law Journal* 70, March, 499–553.

Calabresi, G. and Melamed, A.D. 1972. Property rules, liability rules, and inalienability: one view of the cathedral. *Harvard Law Review* 85(6), 1089–182.

Coase, R.H. 1960. The problem of social cost. *Journal of Law and Economics* 3, October, 1–44.

Demsetz, H. 1967. Toward a theory of property rights. *American Economic Review, Papers and Proceedings* 57(2), May, 347–59, especially 351–3.

Ehrlich, I. 1972. The deterrent effect of criminal law enforcement. *Journal of Legal Studies* 1(2), 259–76.

Goetz, C.J. 1984. *Cases and Materials on Law and Economics*. St Paul, Minn.: West.

Landes, E.M. 1982. Insurance, liability, and accidents: a theoretical and empirical investigation of the effect of no-fault on accidents. *Journal of Law and Economics* 25(1), April, 49–65.

Landes, W. and Posner, R. 1978. Salvors, finders, good samaritans, and other rescuers: an economic study of law and altruism. *Journal of Legal Studies* 7(1), 83–128.

McGee, J.S. 1958. Predatory price cutting: the Standard Oil (N.J.) case. *Journal of Law and Economics* 1, October, 137–69.

Peltzman, S. 1975. The effects of automobile safety regulations. *Journal of Political Economy* 83(4), 677–725.

Posner, R. 1986. *Economic Analysis of Law*. Boston: Little, Brown.

Smith, A. 1776. *An Inquiry into the Nature and Causes of the Wealth of Nations*. London: W. Strahan & T. Cadell.

Tullock, G. 1971. *The Logic of the Law*. New York: Basic Books.

Leisure

GORDON C. WINSTON

Leisure came into economic analysis by the back door. Even Veblen, in whose primary title (1899) leisure had the primary place, was not much interested in it except insofar as leisure embodied the idleness and waste of resources in 'pecuniary emulation' that were the motive and the trophy of the moneyed class. In the subsequent and more serious analytical business of sorting out the response of labour supply to changing real wages begun by Knight (1921) and Pigou (1920) and continued by Robbins (1930), leisure was introduced but only as a residual; the time left over when time spent working had been accounted for. Leisure became a consumption good. It needed only simple characteristics; to be sufficiently (if vaguely) pleasing that, when set against income, as all other consumption goods, it would generate a nicely behaved indifference curve in time–income space and hence a determinate allocation of time to work.

With Gary Becker's 1965 article in the *Economic Journal* and Staffan Linder's *Harried Leisure Class* (1970), recognition of the fact that consumption takes time changed all that. Leisure was no longer simply non-work, it was the time needed by the individual or 'household' to consume the goods and services bought with the money income earned by work. Leisure, no less than work, became an integral part of the economic system.

But this leisure was also less clearly 'leisure' in the sense of Veblen or Knight – time spent in idle or nonpecuniary activities. If the very act of consuming – of deriving the utility from the economic system that is its ultimate justification – is what people do during their leisure time, then the word had to carry new and different connotations.

Linder and Becker had somewhat different objectives, despite the analytical similarity of their models. Both saw utility as derived not from goods and services directly, but from the 'commodities' (Becker) or 'consumption' (Linder) the individual could produce by combining his own reified time with purchased goods and services. Time and goods, together, were necessary to the creation of utility – a cup of coffee yields little satisfaction if there isn't time to drink it. Becker set

381

out to integrate the results of an individual's activities over the day, showing them to be the outcome of an implicitly intertemporally coherent, even optimal, choice; Linder set out to identify the large (and many small but entertaining) social implications of a secularly increasing relative scarcity of time.

The driving force of Linder's analysis was the rising real wage rates that result from historical increases in labour productivity. While most commentators had seen such increasing material affluence as a source of increased well-being, Linder argued that because 'the supply of time' was fixed, *time* and not material income would increasingly affect welfare. As material goods and services became cheaper, time would become relatively more valuable. And the result of this would be a systematic change in the things people do – an abandonment of the leisurely and contemplative activities that require a lot of time and few goods and services in favour of those frenetic activities that need a lot of goods and services and can be done in little time.

Linder's story was well told. Shortly before its US publication, *The Harried Leisure Class* was reviewed by *Time Magazine* (1969) – an honour denied to most books in economic theory – and three years later it was the focus of a special issue of the *Quarterly Journal of Economics* (1973), edited by Thomas Schelling, that included articles by Hirschman, Spence and Baumol, among others.

Time was attracted by Linder's irreverent assertions that gourmet cooking and attendance at the opera were casualties of the growing scarcity of time and that even the easy virtue of women that Linder saw in the late 1960s was the result of the time pressures that induced them to make love quickly and get on with other things. The quality of decision-making – rationality – would suffer as people, quite rationally, spent less time backing their decisions with careful and time-intensive search, investigation, and thought. But the most serious casualty was loss of the sense of a leisurely and controlled pace that produces genuine satisfaction:

> A slower tempo constitutes one way of spending time that, perhaps, is the best example of an activity, the yield of which cannot be increased through any addition of consumption goods. This is so by definition. 'Peace and quiet' is thus an 'inferior' way of passing time (Linder, 1970, p. 152).

Linder's leisure paradox was thus implied: rational actors were increasingly unhappy under the increasing relative scarcity of time, because they maximized utility. Linder described the hapless consumer as a Sorcerer's Apprentice who has to absorb an ever increasing volume of goods and services in a fixed amount of time – more and more and more things have to be dealt with because goods are becoming cheaper and cheaper. Those activities that use up the most goods per unit time are the ones into which he is relentlessly driven.

But though Linder's vision was powerful, it left the uneasy sense that his leisure paradox might not survive careful scrutiny; that the analysis might be flawed in some fundamental way if utility maximizing behaviour fails to maximize utility. Misery through utility maximization would appear to have problems. And it does, of three sorts.

The first problem is that it neglects the household's durable capital and with it, the most tranquil of all ways to absorb goods and services – buying and owning things that simply aren't used much of the time. His implicit Sorcerer's Apprentice assumption that *using* goods and services must take time and effort misses the fact that the consumer is in sovereign control of the prices he pays for capital service flows from the household capital stocks he owns. At will, he can vary that price-per-hour-of-use from minimum values to infinity by the simple expedient of letting things sit idle more of the time (Winston, 1982).

Instead of being compelled frantically to dash from opera to stereo store to football game to work, the affluent consumer can follow a more Veblenesque pattern and let his expensive Nikon camera sit in the glove compartment of his Ferrari even while he spends the rare weekend on his sailboat tied up at the Newport condominium, rather than going to either his New York apartment or the empty cabin in Colorado. Rarely utilized household capital provides generous, and certainly relaxed and mellow, opportunities to absorb vast amounts of the fruits of increasing productivity.

Linder's second analytical problem lay in his classification of activities as immutably 'goods-intensive' or 'time-intensive' – a problem he shares with Becker's similar analysis. He neglected the way these input proportions would, themselves, respond to increasing incomes. So 'peace and quiet' need not be – and often is not – produced with a lot of time and little input of goods and services. Certainly it is not produced that way in mid-town Manhattan or in other urban settings, even in underdeveloped countries, where a considerable expenditure on air-conditioning and devices that control light and noise are essential to producing that peace and quiet. Shift workers' low levels of night-time labour productivity in poor countries reflect meagre endowments of housing capital that deny them peace and quiet during the day. And a contemplative stroll along the beach is not an inexpensive activity if the beach is thousands of miles from home and peak-season rates apply to air fare and cottage.

With growing material well-being, the activities that will endure are those that best absorb increases in goods and services in their production of utility, not those that initially have the highest goods intensities. And they may well include activities with a considerable component of leisurely relaxation. Veblen would never have suggested that the rich are inadequately provided with chances to get away from it all.

But finally and most basically, Linder's formal model told us that the source of utility is only the things people *do* – activities and their durations – but then his verbal descriptions told us that utility has much to do also with the *temporal density* of those activities; that we care very much about the pace of our lives and we feel harried and unhappy if that tempo is too fast. But if that aspect of our activity choices matters to us, then it surely has to be an argument of our utility functions. If it doesn't enter our utility functions, then in a coherent model we can't feel frazzled and dissatisfied because our activities are increasingly so densely packed. He slipped an implicit density variable into the verbal version of the model that didn't appear in its formal, utility-maximizing statement. The result, not surprisingly, was that we maximize utility in the misspecified formal model and make ourselves miserable in the process.

But even if the logic of the leisure paradox cannot be sustained, the enduring legacy of Linder's analysis – and of Becker's – is that 'work' and 'leisure' will not again be seen by economists as an exhaustive dichotomy of human activities. Relatively few of the things people do are pure leisure activities with no extrinsic rewards; relatively few are all work, devoid of immediate intrinsic pleasures. Instead, the richer theory of activity choice that comes after Linder and Becker can recognize in most of the things we do a more complex motivational structure that combines, in different measure for different activities, some of the inherent pleasures we used to associate only with leisure and some of the extrinsic rewards attributed to work.

BIBLIOGRAPHY

Becker, G. 1965. A theory of the allocation of time. *Economic Journal* 75, September, 493–517.

Knight, F. 1921. *Risk, Uncertainty and Profit*. Chicago: University of Chicago Press, 1971.

Linder, S. 1970. *The Harried Leisure Class*. New York: Columbia University Press.

Pigou, A. 1920. *The Economics of Welfare*. London: Macmillan; 4th edn, New York: Macmillan, 1938.

Quarterly Journal of Economics. 1973. Symposium: Time in economic life. *Quarterly Journal of Economics* 87(4), November, 627–75.

Robbins, L. 1930. On the elasticity of demand for income in terms of effort. *Economica* 10, June, 123–9.

Time Magazine. 1969. Leisure. August.

Veblen, T. 1899. *The Theory of the Leisure Class: An Economic Study of Institutions*. New York: New American Library, 1953.

Winston, G. 1982. *The Timing of Economic Activities: Firms, Households, and Markets in Time-Specific Analysis*. New York: Cambridge University Press.

Liberalism

RALF DAHRENDORF

Liberalism is the theory and practice of reforms which has inspired two centuries of modern history. It grew out of the English Revolutions of the 17th century, spread to many countries in the wake of the American and French Revolutions of the 18th century, and dominated the better part of the 19th century. At that time, it also underwent changes. Some say it died, or gave way to socialism, or allowed itself to be perverted by socialist ideas; others regard the social reforms of the late 19th and 20th centuries as achievements of a new liberalism. More recently, interest in the original ideas of liberals has been revived. Thus, classical liberals, social liberals and neoliberals may be distinguished.

Classical liberalism is a simple, dramatic philosophy. Its central idea is liberty under the law. People must be allowed to follow their own interests and desires, constrained only by rules which prevent their encroachment on the liberty of others. Early liberals before and after John Locke liked to use the metaphor of a social contract to express this view. Society can be thought of as emerging from an agreement among its members to protect themselves against the selfish desires of others. Man's 'unsociable sociability' (Kant) makes rules necessary which bind all, but requires also the maximum feasible space for competition and conflict.

In fact, of course, early liberals were not concerned with building societies from scratch. They were concerned with forcing absolute rulers to yield to demands for liberty. The rule of law envisaged by liberals was a revolutionary force which heralded the enlightened phase of modernity.

The notion of the rule of law is not without ambiguity. It is, in the first instance, largely formal. One thinks of rules of the game applying to all and regulating the social, economic and political process. In theory, such rules are intended not to prejudge the outcome of the game itself. Still, even their formal conditions, equality before the law and due process, involved fundamental changes which justify speaking of a movement of reform. Throughout the history of liberalism, however, the question of certain substantive rights of man has been an issue. The inviolability of the person and the rights of free expression have been liberal causes along with constitutional rules. Liberals have rarely found it easy to reach for such substantive rights to their own satisfaction. A certain tension between liberal thought and the notion of natural rights is unmistakable.

The modern debate of these issues began in Scotland and England. John Locke, David Hume and Adam Smith are but three of the many names to consider. From Britain, the ideas spread to the United States and to continental Europe. Montesqieu and Kant borrowed some of their ideas from British liberals. The American Declaration of Independence and the Constitution and the Declaration of the Rights of Man three years after the French Revolution are only two practical illustrations of the effect of the new ideas. If one wants to, one can distinguish, with Friedrich von Hayek, between a British 'evolutionary' and a continental 'constructivist' concept of liberalism. Either or both, however, became the dominant reform movements of the early 19th century and determined the dynamics of Europe and North America between the 1780s and the 1840s or 1850s.

Liberalism had consequences for economic, social and political thought. Its economic application was the most obvious and remains the most familiar. If rules of the game are all that can be justified whereas otherwise interests should be allowed a free reign, the scene is set for the operation of the market. It is the forum where equal rights of access and participation but divergent and competing interests lead, through the operation of an 'invisible hand' (Adam Smith), to the greatest welfare for all. Liberalism and market capitalism are inseparable, much as later European theorists (notably in Germany and Italy) have tried to dissociate the two.

The social application of liberalism analogously leads to the emergence of the public, if by 'public' we understand the meeting place of divergent views from which a 'public opinion' emerges. On the continent, a more emphatic language is often preferred; here one likes to speak of the emergence of society from under the state. Either way, the basic idea involves the same departure from an all-embracing system of domination by traditional authorities to one in which public authority is confined to certain tasks of regulation, and thus bound to grant and defend the freedom of individuals to express their views.

This is the point at which classical liberalism was not only instrumental for the promotion of market capitalism and social participation, but also for the development of what is today called democracy. Again, the term is anything but clear. It can be understood to mean a system of government which is based on the competition of divergent views – individual views or group views – for power, constrained by rules which limit the instruments used in the process, and stipulate the possibility for change. In this sense, a variety of constitutional forms of democracy respond to liberal views, including versions of representative government as well as forms of plebiscite. Liberalism is not anarchism, but anarchism is in some ways an extreme form of liberalism. The law has a key role in liberal thinking, but for a long time the prevalent interest of liberals was that of liberating people from the fetters of control imposed by the tangible force of the state (and the church) or the abstract force of tradition. Not surprisingly, some authors took this attention of liberation to its extreme. If they believed in the essential goodness of man, they advocated the abolition of all social restraint; at times, Jean-Jacques Rousseau seems to argue this way. If, on the other hand, they believed in the ambivalence of human nature, they were not afraid to demand unlimited room for manoeuvre for 'the singular one and his property' (Max Stirner).

Perhaps this anarchist strain in early liberal thinking can be said to have been one of the reasons for the counter-reaction of the 19th century. Marx was the first to point out the historical advance brought about by 'bourgeois' equality before the law, including the contractual basis of economic action, but also the price paid by many for the 'anarchic' quality of the resulting market. The market – it was increasingly argued – was in fact not neutral, but favoured certain players to the systematic disadvantage of others. Mass poverty, conditions of labour, the state of industrial cities were cited as examples. Nor was this merely a view of anti-liberals. The great ambiguities in the thinking of John Stuart Mill tell the same story.

There are two ways of describing the resulting history of thought and of social movements. One is to say that as the 19th century progressed, and certainly in the early decades of the 20th century, liberalism was replaced by socialism as a dominant force. People began to shrink back from the unconstrained market and sought new kinds of intervention. Today, authors would add that the 'structural change of the public' (J. Habermas) and the bureaucratization of democracy followed suit. Liberalism died a 'strange death'; it ceased to be a source of reform and became a defence of class interest.

Another view ascribes the new reforms to liberals also, albeit to a different kind of liberalism. In his Alfred Marshall Lectures of 1949, T.H. Marshall argued that the progress of citizenship rights had to involve, from a certain point onwards, their extension from the legal and the political to the social realm. Social citizenship rights turned out to be a necessary prerequisite for the exercise of equality before the law and universal suffrage. Thus the social, or welfare, state was no more than a logical extension of the process which began with the revolutions of the 18th century.

There is much to be said for this line of argument if one considers that the two men who above all determined the climate of political thought and action from the 1930s to the 1970s, John Maynard Keynes and William Beveridge, were both self-declared Liberals. In effect if not in intention, they advanced ideas which led to restrictions on the operation of markets. One will be remembered as the author of economic policy as a deliberate effort by governments, the other has contributed much to the creation of transfer systems which are operated by governments in the light of an assumed common interest. In other words, these were liberals who pursued policies which led to strengthening rather than limiting the power of public authorities. Theirs was a substantive, a social liberalism.

Liberal parties have found it difficult to follow the twists of theoretical liberalism. Before World War I, when socialist parties were still in their infancy and unable to determine policy in any major country, they were often the spokesmen of the deprived and underprivileged. At least one strand of the liberal tradition continued to be reformist. However, after World War I, socialists or social democrats came to form governments in many countries. Their gain was the Liberals' loss. Liberal parties declined to the point of insignificance, unless they merely kept the name and changed their policies out of recognition, either in the direction of social democracy (Canada) or in that of conservatism (Australia). Indeed, as a practical political movement, liberalism came to present such a confused picture that Hayek could argue that liberalism had become a mere intellectual, and not a political, force.

The experience of totalitarianism interrupted this process without stopping it altogether. To the dismay, but also to the surprise of many, basic human rights and the rules of the game of civil government became an issue again in the 1930s and 1940s. This gave rise to an important literature in which the underlying values of liberal thought were spelt out anew. Hayek's *Road to Serfdom* is one example, but the most important one is probably Karl Popper's *Open Society and its Enemies*. Popper developed above all what might be called the epistemology of liberalism. We are living in a world of uncertainty. Since no one can know all answers, let alone what the right answers are, it is of cardinal importance to make sure that different answers can be given at any one time, and especially over time. The path of politics, like that of knowledge, must be one of trial and error. The principle can be applied to economy and society as well.

The liberal revolt against totalitarianism waned with the memory of totalitarianism itself. While the term 'social market economy' was coined for Germany in the 1950s, the quarter-century of the economic miracle was in fact a social-democratic quarter-century. In it, economic growth was combined almost everywhere with a growing role of government and with the extension of the social state. Entitlements came to matter as much as achievements. Consensus counted for more than competition or conflict. Despite variations, this was a very successful period in the countries of the First World. But in the 1970s, the side-effects of success had become major problems in their own right. These were not only obvious problems like environmental and social 'limits to growth', but systematic ones arising from the role of the state. Both Keynes and Beveridge gave rise to new questions. Neither stagflation in the 1970s, nor boom unemployment in the 1980s seemed amenable to government intervention. The social state had got out of hand; it became harder and harder to finance, and its bureaucracies robbed it of much of its plausibility. There were demands for a reversal of trends.

Where such a reversal happened, it remained bitty, halting and inconsistent. However, the new climate also gave rise to elements of a new theory of liberalism. In one sense this was, and is, a return to the original project of asserting society against the state, the market against planning and regulation, the right of the individual against overpowering authorities and collectivities. American authors in particular re-stated the theory. Milton Friedman tried to show in a series of arguments that the role of government is usually contrary to the interests of people. Robert Nozick made a strong case for the 'minimal state' and against the arrogance of modern state power. James Buchanan and the 'constitutional economists' reconstructed the social contract and argued for severely limited rules and regulations, using the fiscal system as one of their main examples. This trend, more than the notion of supply-side economics (which in some ways is merely Keynes stood on his head) signifies the revival of liberalism.

There are other facets of the many-faceted term. For many, the extension of civil rights to hitherto disadvantaged groups is a liberal programme. Others still concentrate on the separation of church and state and the reduction of church influence. Again others regard liberalism as an advocacy of cultural values, including pluralism and creativity. It is not difficult to see the connection of such preferences with the mainstream of liberal thought.

This mainstream has three elements. Liberalism is a theory and a movement of *reform* to advance *individual liberties* in the horizon of *uncertainty*. This means by the same token that the prevailing theme of liberalism cannot be the same at all times. In the face of absolutism, it is liberty under the law; in the face of market capitalism, it is the full realization of citizenship rights; in the face of the 'cage of bondage' (Max Weber) of modern bureaucratic government, it is the optimal, if not the minimal state. The struggle for the social contract has become virulent in the advanced free societies. The crisis of the social state, the new unemployment, issues of law and order all raise basic questions of what is Caesar's and what are therefore the proper limits of individual desires. It is no accident that constitutional questions have come to the fore in several countries. At such a time, liberalism is gaining new momentum. It will not solve all issues, but it will remain a source of dynamism and progress towards more life chances for more people.

BIBLIOGRAPHY

Buchanan, J. 1975. *The Limits of Liberty*. Chicago: University of Chicago Press.
Habermas, J. 1962. *Strukturwandel der Öffentlichkeit*. Neuwied: Luchterhand.
Hayek, F. von. 1944. *The Road to Serfdom*. Chicago: University of Chicago Press.
Hume, D. 1740. *A Treatise of Human Nature*. Ed. L.A. Selby-Bigge, Oxford: Clarendon Press, 1888.
Kant, I. 1784. Idee zu einer allgemeinen Geschichte in weltbürgerlicher Absicht. In *Kants Populäre Schriften*, ed. P. Menzer, Berlin: Georg Reimer, 1911.
Locke, J. 1690. *Second Treatise of Government*. Ed. T.P. Peardon, New York: Liberal Arts Press, 1952.
Marshall, T.H. 1950. *Citizenship and Social Class*. Cambridge: Cambridge University Press.
Popper, K.R. 1952. *The Open Society and its Enemies*. 2nd edn, London: Routledge & Kegan Paul.
Smith, A. 1776. *An Inquiry into the Nature and Causes of the Wealth of Nations*. Oxford: Oxford University Press,1976.
Stirner, M. 1845. *Der Einzige und sein Eigentum*. Leipzig: D. Wigand.
Weber, M. 1922. *Wirtschaft und Gesellschaft*. 4th edn, Tübingen: Mohr/Siebeck, 1956.

Liberalism

Limits to Growth

WILFRED BECKERMAN

During the 1950s and the 1960s economic growth became one of the central preoccupations of economists and economic policy makers. This was probably the result mainly of the unprecedented rates of economic growth being achieved by the advanced countries of the world, together with significant differences in the growth rates of individual countries. Hence there was considerable interest in explaining the overall acceleration of growth and the causes of the inter-country differences.

However, during the 1960s the view emerged that perhaps the high growth rate of the advanced countries was not necessarily adding commensurately to the welfare of their populations. The various reasons for this concern were first set out brilliantly, in comprehensive and persuasive terms, by E.J. Mishan (1967). Mishan enumerated various alleged disamenities of economic growth, such as pollution, congestion of travel facilities and desirable holiday resorts, and other forms of externality, as well as more spiritual effects, such as the subordination of other social values to the pursuit of commercial objectives and the consequent deterioration in society's moral standards. Mishan's highly sophisticated and articulate attack on the mindless pursuit of economic growth corresponded to growing social awareness of some of the undesirable externalities associated with economic growth – of which obvious visible pollution of various kinds, and the rise of urban violence, made an impact on many sections of the public in the more affluent countries.

At the same time concern was being expressed in some quarters about the viability of continuing high rates of growth on account of the possible resource constraints faced by the world as a whole. These concerns, together with the alleged association between economic growth and pollution, were formulated precisely in *The Limits of Growth*, a study commissioned by the 'Club of Rome' (Meadows et al., 1972). This study purported to show that on any reasonable assumptions continuation of high rates of growth would mean that (i) the world would run out of resources of key materials; (ii) increasing pollution would have serious effects; and (iii) population would outrun the world's potential food supplies. This report was at first accepted by many sections of the public as constituting a scientific demonstration of the need for governments to take action to slow down growth rates.

Whilst the basic methodology used in *The Limits to Growth* was derived from that developed by Jay Forrester (1961, 1968) in that it employed a computerized 'systems dynamics' model that enabled the emphasis to be placed on the inter-relationships and 'feed-backs' between different parts of a complex model, serious defects in its particular application of the Forrester techniques were immediately apparent and as soon as it appeared *The Limits to Growth* was subjected to sharp criticism by some expert commentators (see The *Economist*, 1972; Sir (now Lord) Eric Ashby, 1972; Mellanby, 1973; a World Bank task force 1972; H.S.D. Cole et al. on behalf of the Science Policy Research Unit of Sussex University, 1973). Its main defects included:

(1) Failure to allow for the fact that changes in the balance between demand and supply for any materials had, over the past, eventually led to changes in price which provided the stimulus, where necessary, to the discovery of new resources, to the development of substitutes, to the technological improvements in methods of exploration, extraction and refinement, to substitution in the products in which they are embodied and so on. History is full of dire predictions that if the demand for a certain product continued to grow as before the known resources would be used up in x years time, and all of them have been shown by events to have been absurd. The concept of 'known resources' is a misleading one; society only 'knows' of the resources that it is worth discovering given present and prospective demands, costs and prices.

(2) Thus the technique of inserting fixed supplies – even with some assumptions concerning eventual finite increases in these supplies – into a computer and then confronting them with indefinitely expanding demands, which must eventually overtake the supplies, bears no resemblance to the way demands and supplies have developed over the past and has no foundation in economic analysis or the particular analysis of technological innovation.

(3) Furthermore, even if the concept of 'finite resources' made sense, slower growth would not enable society to continue indefinitely: it would merely postpone the fateful day of reckoning. If resources were really 'finite' the only way the indefinite existence of society could be ensured would be to cut standards of living to infinitesimally low levels, and this did not seem to be politically feasible in democratic countries.

(4) Pollution per unit of output was being reduced and could be reduced very much more if the correct pricing policies were introduced to internalize the externalities that pollution represented. This was a problem of resource allocation at any point of time and has nothing to do with resource misallocation over time, which is what the claim that growth was excessive amounted to. Indeed, pollution tended to be worst in the poorest countries and less resources were made available to reduce pollution to optimal levels in conditions of low and slowly rising incomes.

391

(5) World food supplies had been rising faster than population for several decades and faster economic growth seemed to lead to slower population increases, rather than the reverse. The acute food shortages of many parts of the world reflected gross maldistribution of world food supplies. Slowing down the growth rate of the USA was not likely to increase availability of food in those parts of Africa constantly threatened by famine. If anything, insofar as it meant less aid to such countries, it would only aggravate their condition.

These and various other serious defects in *The Limits to Growth* were analysed in detail by Wilfred Beckerman (1972, 1974). As well as demonstrating fully the technical errors in the Club of Rome report, Beckerman also emphasized the elitist middle-class nature of much of the anti-growth movement. It was the middle class, he maintained, that was most conscious of losing its privileges in a rapidly growing society, and the middle classes had always been adept at presenting their own interests as a crusade for social morality fought by people of moral refinement and exquisite aesthetic sensibility, by contrast with the crass materialism of the pro-growth lobby. This appeal made some impression on idealistic youth, and on radical members of society who saw the harmful effects of growth as evidence of the evils of a profit-dominated capitalist society (in spite of the evidence that Beckerman produced concerning the even greater neglect of the environment in Soviet bloc countries). In much of this Beckerman was, of course, developing points that had been anticipated by Anthony Crosland (Crosland, 1956, 1962).

The glaring errors in the Club of Rome report and the obvious partiality of the Mishan-type attack on affluence, some of which were exposed at a UN Conference on the Environment in Stockholm in 1972 by the poorer countries whose citizens were more worried about how to get a square meal next day than about the possible accumulation of sulphur dioxide in the atmosphere by the year 2050, gradually weakened the impact of the anti-growth movement. Furthermore, it had already begun to run out of steam when world economic growth was brought to a sudden halt by the first oil shock of 1973/74. Since then the rates of economic growth in the world have been very much lower than previously. One of the consequences of this has been the emergence of mass unemployment in most of the advanced countries of the world and economic crises in many of the developing countries. Government policies to restrain demand and to reduce budget deficits in the face of increased social security payments and lower tax revenues have meant, *inter alia*, that expenditures on safeguarding the environment now have much lower priority than had hitherto been the case. Those sections of the population whose social consciences are most active, therefore, are now amongst those who complain most vociferously about the failure of governments to take action to accelerate economic growth. Some people are just hard to please.

BIBLIOGRAPHY

Ashby, E. 1972a. Lecture on Pollution in Perspective, to *The Times* 1000 Conference. *The Spectator*, 27 May.

Limits to Growth

Ashby, E. 1972b. *Pollution and the Public Conscience: fifty-first Earl Gray memorial lecture.* Newcastle upon Tyne: University of Newcastle.

Beckerman, W. 1972. Economists, scientists and environmental catastrophe. *Oxford Economic Papers* 24(3), November, 327–44.

Beckerman, W. 1974. *In Defence of Economic Growth.* London: Jonathan Cape. Reprinted as *Two Cheers for the Affluent Society,* New York: St Martins, 1975.

Cole, H.S.D. et al. (eds) for the Science Policy Research Unit of Sussex University. 1973. *Thinking About the Future: A Critique of the Limits of Growth.* London: Chatto and Windus.

Crosland, A. 1956. *The Future of Socialism,* London: Jonathan Cape.

Crosland, A. 1962. *The Conservative Enemy.* London: Jonathan Cape. The *Economist,* 11 March, 1972.

Forrester, J.W. 1961. *Industrial Dynamics.* Cambridge, Mass.: MIT Press.

Forrester, J.W. 1968. *Principles of Systems.* Cambridge, Mass.: Wright Allen Press.

Meadows, D.H. et al. 1972. *The Limits to Growth: a report for the Club of Rome's project on the predicament of mankind.* New York: Universe.

Mellanby, K. 1973. The phoney crisis. *Minerva* 10(3), July.

Mishan, E.J. 1967. *The Costs of Economic Growth.* London: Staples Press.

World Bank. 1972. Report on the Limits to Growth. Report by a special task force of the International Bank for Reconstruction and Development (known as the World Bank), Washington, DC, September, Mimeo.

Macroeconomics: Relations with Microeconomics

PETER HOWITT

The lack of clear connection between macroeconomics and microeconomics has long been a source of discontent among economists. Arrow (1967) called it a 'major scandal' that neoclassical price theory cannot account for such macro-economic phenomena as unemployment. Lucas and Sargent (1979) argued that Keynesian macroeconomics is 'fundamentally flawed' by its lack of a firm microfoundation. Countless students and practitioners alike have complained of the schizophrenic nature of a discipline whose two major branches project such radically different views of the world.

It is not hard to see why this lack of unity should bother economists. Fragmentary explanations are intellectually unsatisfying in any discipline, and are rightly labelled *ad hoc*. Theories that must be altered when moving from one application to another do not provide general covering laws and are liable to break down when new applications are tried or when new data arise.

The urge to close the micro–macro gap has been particularly strong among macroeconomic theorists, whose general desire for unity has been reinforced by at least three special factors. First, there is the reductionist methodological predisposition that economists of almost all persuasions share to some degree, according to which no explanation of economic phenomena is truly satisfactory if it does not reduce the phenomena to a question of individual actions by basic decision-making units. Second, the lack of decisive empirical tests or experiments in economics has precluded demonstrations that macroeconomic theory is valid within a well-delineated domain of applicability, despite the difficulty of reconciling it with micro principles. This same factor has also forced economists to rely to a large extent upon introspection as a criterion and source of new ideas, a reliance which enhances their reductionist tendencies, since introspection is easier to apply if a theory is cast in terms of individual actions rather than in terms of broad social forces or primitive relationships

394

among aggregate variables. Third, microeconomics was codified and given a well-articulated mathematical structure when macroeconomics was just emerging from its pre-analytical stage. Historically, one of the most fruitful strategies for macro theorists has been to borrow and apply the principles, conventions and techniques that have succeeded in the theoretically more advanced branch of the discipline.

Thus the quest for microfoundations has been a mainspring of development in macro theory. However, this does not mean that macro has been developing into a branch of applied micro. The forces tending to make macro theory conform more closely with micro principles have been opposed by equally important forces requiring those principles to be modified radically before being applied to macro questions.

More specifically, what has restrained the urge to apply micro principles is a widespread recognition that some of the most important macroeconomic phenomena manifest defects in the economic system that standard micro theory rules out with its basic assumption of equilibrium. In a state of general equilibrium, as traditionally conceived by micro theorists, all trading plans are costlessly coordinated by 'the market', whose operation is often heuristically personified by the Walrasian auctioneer. The auctioneer establishes prices such that plans are collectively compatible, with demand and supply equated for each commodity. He also ensures that, given this compatibility condition, all trading plans can be executed at no cost.

With the auctioneer at work, one individual's decisions interfere with another's only to the extent that they affect the vector of equilibrium prices. Thus the only constraint that social interactions are assumed to impose on the formation of trading plans is the single budget constraint requiring the value of purchases not to exceed the value of sales. No one need concern himself beyond this with the possibility of selling less than he had planned, with the difficulty of finding potential trading partners or with the possibility that a collapse of credit markets might make it impossible for him to transform future sales into present purchases at any price.

There has been a natural reluctance among most macroeconomists to use a theory based on this conception of ideal coordination for purposes of explaining business-cycle fluctuations, large-scale unemployment and credit crises. These phenomena are obviously characterized by a gross lack of coordination between different agents' economic activities, and by a widespread concern for just those problems which general equilibrium analysis implies can safely be ignored by all agents.

The story of the development of macroeconomic theory beginning with the Keynesian Revolution is largely a story of the struggle between these two opposing forces: the quest for a microfoundation and the recognition that existing micro theory is inadequate for dealing with macro problems. The major innovations in macro theory have consisted of new ways to use the powerful organizing concepts of micro theory, equilibrium and rational choice, to explain phenomena that have traditionally eluded micro theory.

The main analytical innovation of Keynes's *General Theory* was to develop an alternative concept of equilibrium that allowed modified versions of supply and demand analysis to be applied to macroeconomic questions without assuming a state of ideal coordination. The key to this innovation was the recognition that prices were not the only equilibrating variables. In Keynes's equilibrium, the quantity of aggregate output did the equilibrating. Instead of determining employment by the condition that the supply and demand for labour were equal, Keynes imposed the condition that the quantity of output produced equal the quantity demanded, the equilibrium condition of the familiar Keynesian Cross diagram. Hicks (1937) showed how Keynes's analysis could be formulated as two equations in the two equilibrating variables – output and the rate of interest – a formulation that became the standard paradigm of macro theory for the next 30 years.

With this new concept of equilibrium, Keynesian economics achieved the immediate goal of having a short-run macroeconomic theory with enough equations to determine the variables of interest. Rather than having to treat fluctuations in output and employment as disequilibrium phenomena, using the cumbersome and problematic dynamic techniques available at the time, macroeconomists after Keynes could use the much simpler methods of comparative statics. Furthermore, with the equilibrium concept in hand, they could begin applying choice theory to the analysis of aggregate demand. From Hicks's essay through the 1960s, the main developments in macro theory consisted of the rationalization and modification of the aggregate behavioural relationships postulated by Keynes, through the application of principles of optimization.

Although there was considerable disagreement over whether a Keynesian equilibrium should really be called an equilibrium, and whether it adequately captured Keynes's central ideas, there was a broad consensus among macro-economists following the Keynesian Revolution concerning the relative domain of applicability of Keynesian macroeconomics and Walrasian micro theory. Modigliani (1944) had shown how Keynesian results could be derived from an otherwise classical model if the money-wage rate were fixed. Since it was widely believed that wages were less than fully flexible in the short run, it seemed natural to see Keynesian theory as applying to short-run fluctuations and general equilibrium theory as applying to long-run questions in which adjustment problems could safely be ignored. This view came to be known as the 'neoclassical synthesis'.

By the 1960s, however, serious doubts were being raised about the logical consistency of this division. Most notably Clower (1965) pointed out that the Keynesian consumption function, a key concept in Keynes's quantity-equilibrating multiplier process, was incompatible with Walrasian general equilibrium analysis. In particular, it was based on the notion that the typical household takes its income, whether current or prospective, as given, whereas in general equilibrium analysis a household is supposed to choose its income, by choosing how many factor-services to sell. Clower raised the question of how a theory with this kind of consumption function could possibly be reconciled with standard microeconomic theory.

The answer proposed by Clower was that Keynesian 'effective' demands would be transmitted by agents in a Walrasian world when the system was not in equilibrium. If general equilibrium prices have not yet been established, then excess demands and supplies will make it impossible for all agents successfully to execute the trading plans that they had formulated on the basis of a single budget constraint. Once they see that this is the case, they will begin to take into account not just their budget constraint but also the quantity limitations implied by non-price rationing. The unemployed worker will base his demands not on the amount of labour he would like to sell at the going wage but on the amount he is selling or expects to sell.

Clower's suggestion was further developed by Barro and Grossman (1971), who also integrated it with Patinkin's (1956, ch. 13) similar analysis of how the demand for labour would be affected by the quantity of output demanded when the system was not in a general equilibrium. Barro and Grossman showed how these ideas could be combined to generalize Keynes's concept of quantity equilibrium. If prices are held fixed at levels that create excess supplies of labour and output, then the equilibrium will generally be a set of quantities that are demanded when agents take into account the sales constraints implied by those quantities.

To many writers, the Barro–Grossman analysis presented a microfoundation for macro theory that confirmed the neoclassical synthesis. Barro and Grossman labelled their contribution a 'general disequilibrium' analysis to emphasize that it generated Keynesian results only if prices were away from their Walrasian equilibrium values. As the subsequent literature emphasized, this analysis could be combined with the *tâtonnement* mechanism of general equilibrium theory, according to which the price of any good out of equilibrium rises or falls as a function of excess demand or supply of the good. As prices changed, the quantity equilibrium would change with them. The only long-run rest-point to such a system was a Walrasian equilibrium. In the short run, the system would generally be in a Keynesian fixed-price equilibrium.

The major problem with this microfoundation is that it relies on what is generally regarded as the weakest part of micro theory – the *tâtonnement* mechanism. No one has yet successfully integrated that mechanism with the main part of micro theory – the theory of equilibrium. The problem with attempted integrations was posed forcibly by Arrow (1959), who noted that since all agents are assumed to act as price-takers in general equilibrium theory, there is no one who can change prices that are not at equilibrium values. The heuristic device of the 'auctioneer' does more to evade this problem than to solve it.

This problem led several authors in the 1960s and 1970s to turn to the economics of information for a microfoundation. In general equilibrium analysis, the *tâtonnement* can be thought of as the mechanism through which the market collates and disseminates the information required to achieve a coordinated state. When an economy is disturbed by a change in tastes or technology that is at first apparent only to a limited subset of agents, the excess demands and supplies created by this change act as a signal to the rest of society that a changed allocation of resources is called for. The message is passed on to other individuals in the form of a change in relative prices. The neoclassical synthesis pictured macroeconomic problems as arising because this process takes time. The difficulty noted by Arrow was that the informational aspects underlying this process were not present in the decision problems faced by the individuals in the theory. Thus it seemed to many that the way out of the difficulty lay in a more explicit treatment of the role of less than perfect information in individual decision-making.

Considerable progress along these lines was made by various contributors to the famous 'Phelps volume' (Phelps et al., 1970). This volume contained a variety of different approaches to the problem, but the most lasting contribution was the 'island parable' presented in Phelps's introductory essay. According to this parable, the typical transactor trades on a succession of 'informational islands'. Prices on each island always equate demand and supply on that island, but people are unaware of prices and quantities simultaneously prevailing on other islands.

This parable seemed to offer a microfoundation for the neoclassical synthesis without relying on the problematical *tâtonnement* mechanism. In particular, consider an unanticipated purely nominal fall in aggregate demand. According to Phelps's parable, the system would react with a decrease in output and employment and a less than proportional fall in prices in the short run, as in Keynesian theory, but with fully proportional price declines that neutralized any real effects in the long run, as in general equilibrium analysis. The reason for the short-run non-neutrality is that sellers who saw their selling prices fall would tend to read this as a fall in the relative price of their wares, not realizing until later that prices elsewhere in the economy were also falling, and would therefore be induced to sell less. This withdrawal of supply would soften the initial fall in prices. Eventually the realization that this was an aggregate phenomenon, and not just local, would persuade people to supply the same amount as before, and prices would fall all the way to their new equilibrium values.

This apparent microfoundation did not rely on the *tâtonnement* mechanism, but it relied heavily upon the theory of expectation formation. In particular, it postulated that the only impediment to achievement of long-run equilibrium was the slowness with which people formed accurate expectations of the general price level. This postulate left several writers unsatisfied because it implied an incongruity between the formation of trading plans, which agents were assumed to undertake rationally, and the formation of expectations, which they were assumed to do according to a mechanical rule. This dissatisfaction led the way to the rational expectations revolution in macroeconomics.

The seminal paper in this revolution was Lucas (1972). In this paper Lucas presented an exact model of the island parable, in which agents formed subjective expectations that were the mathematical expectations of the model itself. This expectation scheme was not derived from any explicit optimization scheme; nevertheless, it became known as 'rational' due to the belief that people who formed expectations in any other way must be leaving unexploited some opportunities for increasing their well-being. Lucas's model became the analytical paradigm of the school of new classical economics in the 1970s and 1980s, whose research programme was explicitly to base all of macroeconomics upon firm microeconomic principles.

By the early 1980s new classical economics had become the dominant approach in macroeconomic theory. But it was strongly resisted by Keynesian economists, who argued that although it had firm microfoundations it was based on a notion of equilibrium that was too close to the frictionless ideal of Walrasian theory. Among other arguments, they objected that the price of avoiding the problems of *tâtonnement* by means of the Phelps island parable was giving up the fundamental Keynesian notion of quantities and other non-price signals as equilibrating variables; hence giving up hope of explaining many of the obvious coordination problems faced by people in the trough of a business cycle.

In the mid 1980s, however, there has been a resurgence of theoretical support for Keynesian ideas. Specifically, authors like Diamond (1982) and Howitt (1985) have derived models in which all agents are explicitly rational and in which the equilibrium states exhibit Keynesian phenomena. The unifying feature of these models is the assumption that even with perfect price-flexibility, people respond to non-price signals. Specifically, an increase in economic activity on one side of the market (e.g. an increase in aggregate demand) will reduce the costs of trading by making potential trading partners easier to find, and hence will affect the trading decisions on the other side of the market (e.g. will induce an increase in aggregate supply), even if it does not affect market prices. These models are still, however, in their infancy.

It is interesting to speculate on whether or not the quest for a microfoundation will continue to play as important a role in the future development of macroeconomics. The disunity between micro and macro that has motivated so many contributors is shrinking rapidly on the frontiers of research, where micro theory is being transformed by the explicit consideration of informational problems like those so often adduced by macroeconomists and where macroeconomics without explicit reference to individual transactors, their decision problems and conditions of equilibrium, is becoming increasingly rare.

It is also questionable whether the microeconomic principles of equilibrium and rationality that have been applied so fruitfully in the development of macroeconomics can be of more service. By themselves they are no more than organizing devices; they yield no meaningful empirical propositions in the absence of a great many supporting hypotheses.

BIBLIOGRAPHY

Arrow, K.J. 1959. Towards a theory of price adjustment. In *The Allocation of Economic Resources*, ed. M. Abramovitz et al., Stanford: Stanford University Press.
Arrow, K.J. 1967. Samuelson collected. *Journal of Political Economy* 75, October, 730–37.
Barro, R.J. and Grossman, H.I. 1971. A general disequilibrium model of income and employment. *American Economic Review* 61(1), March, 82–93.

399

Clower, R.W. 1965. The Keynesian counter-revolution: a theoretical appraisal. In *The Theory of Interest Rates*, ed. F.H. Hahn and F.P.R. Brechling, London: Macmillan.

Diamond, P.A. 1982. Aggregate demand management in search equilibrium. *Journal of Political Economy* 90(5), October, 881–94.

Hicks, J.R. 1937. Mr Keynes and the 'classics': a suggested interpretation. *Econometrica* 5, April, 147–59.

Howitt, P. 1985. Transaction costs and the theory of unemployment. *American Economic Review* 75(1), March, 88–100.

Lucas, R.E. 1972. Expectations and the neutrality of money. *Journal of Economic Theory* 4(2), April, 103–24.

Lucas, R.E. and Sargent, T.J. 1979. After Keynesian macroeconomics. *Federal Reserve Bank of Minneapolis Quarterly Review* 3(2), Spring, 1–16.

Modigliani, F. 1944. Liquidity preference and the theory of interest and money. *Econometrica* 12, January, 45–88.

Patinkin, D. 1956. *Money, Interest, and Prices*. New York: Harper & Row.

Phelps, E.S. et al. (eds) 1970. *Microeconomic Foundations of Employment and Inflation Theory*. New York: Norton.

Malthus's Theory of Population

D.R. WEIR

It is often said that Malthus was a better historian than prophet. He would be disappointed in that verdict because his intention in formulating his Theory of Population was to create a scientific basis for predicting the future state of mankind, in opposition to the speculations of utopian writers, especially Godwin. His failure to predict the Industrial Revolution is the evidence most often brought against him. But even with the benefit of hindsight, economic historians today still find it difficult to predict the Industrial Revolution from its antecedents. The crucial contribution of Malthus's theory was not its pessimism about innovation but rather its prediction of the demographic consequences of technological change and the inevitable effect of population on the standard of living. Malthus's Theory of Population continues to influence economic thought from popular discussion to policy-making, to model-building – long after many of its classical contemporaries, like the labour theory of value, have passed from the scene.

This essay will focus on the population side of Malthus's theory. We begin with a distillation of his ideas into a simple model in the modern sense of the term. Our intention is not to treat in detail all the nuanced and sometimes contradictory aspects of Malthus's writing. The *Essay on Population*, first published in 1798, was revised six times before the final seventh edition was published in 1872, some 38 years after his death. The model used here aims to portray the most essential and durable aspects of the theory. It also provides an organizational framework for discussing the evidence for and against its predictions from time periods both before and after Malthus wrote.

THE MODEL. Figure 1 portrays the essential elements of Malthusian equilibrium. There are three curves, representing three functional relationships. In the first panel is an aggregate production function showing the standard of living (or real wage, or income per capita) produced by a population of a given size. Its main feature is diminishing returns to labour – a tenet of classical economics not unique to Malthus. The second panel describes demographic behaviour.

401

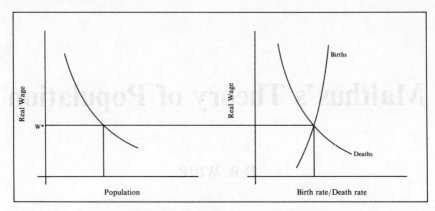

Figure 1   Malthusian equilibrium

Mortality (here, the crude death rate, which is the number of deaths per 1,000 persons) rises as the standard of living falls. This is the positive check. Fertility (here, the crude birth rate) falls as the standard of living falls. This is the preventive check. Population grows when births exceed deaths and falls when deaths exceed births. A rising population lowers the standard of living (through the production function), which in turn raises mortality and lowers fertility, eventually bringing population growth to a halt. Equilibrium in this simple version of the model is attained at zero population growth. At that point wages do not change, and consequently the birth and death rates do not change. The equilibrium is stable, since any disturbance sets in motion compensating changes.

The stability of the equilibrium is the source of Malthusian pessimism. Imagine an expansion of land area for cultivation. The production function would shift out, raising the standard of living for the current population. Fertility would rise and mortality fall; population growth would continue to devour the gains until the wage fell to its original level. Demographic behaviour is the forge of the Iron Law of Wages. Permanent change in the standard of living can arise only from restraint of fertility (a lower birth rate at each wage) or a worsening of mortality (more deaths at each wage).

The smooth curves drawn above describe the long-run tendencies as envisaged by Malthus. He saw the process of adjustment, however, as anything but smooth. Population growth would tend to overshoot the equilibrium. The positive check, working through disasters like major famines or disease, would be slow to respond but would then overadjust when it did, setting off a new cycle. Malthus offered no specifics on the periodicity or amplitude of the cycle, only the prediction of oscillations around a long-run equilibrium level.

THE EVIDENCE. In discussing in detail the component parts of the model, there are three aspects of each to be considered. First is the evolution of Malthus's own ideas on the functional relationship; second, the historical evidence for or against it; and third, its relevance to the major economic and demographic transformations of the last two centuries. The importance of empirical verification was strongly emphasized by Malthus himself. Criticizing the utopians, Malthus wrote:

A writer may tell me that he thinks man will ultimately become an ostrich. I cannot properly contradict him. But before he can expect to bring any reasonable person over to his opinion, he ought to show that the necks of mankind have been gradually elongating, that the lips have grown harder and more prominent, that the legs and feet are daily altering their shape, and that the hair is beginning to change into stubs of feathers (Malthus, 1798).

Much of the work of the later editions of the *Essay on Population* was devoted to amassing evidence on the Principle of Population at work.

A central problem with using this or any other equilibrium framework to explain co-variations in economic and demographic variables (across time or space), or with using empirical observations to 'test' the model, is the identification of exogenous shocks as distinct from endogenous responses. Malthus himself was vaguely aware of the problem as early as the first edition of his *Essay*. David Hume, noting the early age at marriage of women in China, had deduced that the population must as a consequence be very large. Malthus, taking age at marriage as endogenous rather than exogenous, concluded that the population must on the contrary be rather small and wages relatively high to induce such early marriage.

MORTALITY. Malthus gave to mortality's response to wages the name 'positive' check because it was certain and unavoidable once population had grown too large. Fertility offered a 'preventive' check in the sense that if low fertility held back the growth of population, the mortality response could be postponed.

Malthus envisaged two modes of action for the positive check. Associated with declining wages would be increasing 'misery and vice'. Misery and vice included some conditions that would raise mortality as well as lower mortality. This would yield a smooth continuous relationship like that in the diagram. The second mode of action would be sudden mortality crises to reduce a population greatly in a year or two. To put it in modern terms, the probability of a mortality crisis of any given magnitude should increase as the standard of living falls. The expected value of the death rate would show the smooth relationship to wages pictured above. Actual events would be much less regular. Adjustment to equilibrium was inevitable but not constant.

Historical studies of the positive check have approached it from two very different perspectives. One sort examines great crises to determine whether they resulted from population pressure. The other attempts to specify the extent of population pressure on resources over time and look for mortality consequences.

The Black Death of 1347 and 1348 killed between one-third and one-half of Europe's population in a single massive epidemic of bubonic plague. Hatcher (1977) concludes for England that the Black Death was 'not Malthusian', by which he means not a response to population pressure. Evidence abounds that population had been growing: rents and the relative price of basic foods had been rising for two centuries or more. There had been major famines in the 1320s. The 'anti-Malthusian' conclusion is based on the absence of a logical connection between standard of living and the scale of epidemic bubonic plague and on the fact that the mortality response was disproportionate to the population pressure. Economic responses to the Black Death were clearly Malthusian (Hatcher, 1977, pp. 101–94). It is certainly consistent with the subtler Malthus to find that an induced (endogenous) mortality response would overreact and become an exogenous disturbance driving population below its equilibrium. The study of a single episode cannot determine whether the probability of its occurrence was raised by the economic conditions preceding it. The persistence of the plague and continued population declines of the next century or more, clearly were not a consequence of the improved standard of living after the first outbreak.

Half a millennium later the Irish Potato Famine provided a tragic forum for debate over the new Malthusian ideas. Mokyr (1983) traces reliance on the potato to population pressure, through the unique funnel of Irish institutions. As was the case with the plague, the element of chance looms large in the timing and location of the potato blight itself. Unlike the Black Death, however, the means were available to alleviate the heavy mortality consequences. One wonders what might have been the fate of the Irish had not English policy-makers of the 1840s been educated in the science of Malthus's Theory of Population.

The main supporting evidence for the positive check comes from the study of subsistence crises: short-run mortality increases following harvest failures. Meuvret (1946) drew attention to the close association of grain prices and deaths in specific incidents in France. Subsequent studies have shown a regular statistical association over long periods in several countries. Improved marketing and production methods appear to have been successful in nearly eliminating the relationship in England by the end of the 16th century and in France by the middle of the 18th century.

Since Malthus wrote, life expectancy has increased from well under 40 to well over 70 in most of the now developed world. Since the standard of living has also increased, it would appear that Malthus's theory of mortality has been a better prediction than it was a description of prior history. Some scepticism on that point is voiced by Preston (1976), who finds that life expectancy across countries is not closely related to their level of per capita income at any point in time. He concludes that medical and public health technology are more important than income. Since medical technology may well be a function of per capita income in the leading country, or in the average of leading countries, his finding may indicate only that Malthus no longer applies within national boundaries.

There is, in sum, only limited evidence of the income–mortality relation postulated by Malthus. Evidence abounds that most of the variation in mortality cannot be accounted for by so simple a framework.

FERTILITY. In the first edition of the *Essay on Population* Malthus claimed that 'passion between the sexes was necessary and will remain nearly in its present state'; that is, that fertility was roughly constant and did not vary with living standards. On our diagram, the fertility curve would be vertical. He subsequently advocated delayed marriage as a check to population growth. Being a vicar of the Anglican Church, he condemned both contraception and never-marrying as 'vice'. It is one of the greatest misattributions in human history that associates the name of Malthus with the birth-control movements of the late 19th century. Nevertheless, since fertility restraint offers the only means of raising both the standard of living and length of life within his system, it is not surprising that those who believed his model but not his morals would eventually invoke his science to promote their cause.

The evidence for endogenous fertility responses is growing but is not yet convincing. Wrigley and Schofield (1981) find that long-run trends in English fertility followed long-run trends in real wages from 1541 to 1871. The lag, however, was 40 years, and the two moved in opposite directions for approximately 140 of the 330 years. Moreover, in England, as in the rest of early modern Europe, age at marriage and fertility within marriage were fairly constant, leaving changes in proportions ever-married as the main source of changes in English fertility before the Industrial Revolution (Weir, 1984).

The greatest failure of Malthus's Theory of Population is in explaining the fertility transition from high, mostly uncontrolled fertility within marriage to modern low fertility. The process began first in France at the time Malthus was writing. Parts of the United States and Hungary also began at about that time. The rest of Europe followed sometime between 1870 and 1914. In no case was the long-run downward trend in fertility caused by a downward trend in national income. In today's developing countries fertility decline has sometimes been induced by policy measures without economic development, but sustained economic growth continues to be a prescription for contraception.

Neoclassical theories of fertility, as in the work of Becker (1981), salvage Malthus's theory as an income effect in a model of the demand for children. Substitution effects from a rising price of children relative to other consumption goods may be a more important determinant of fertility trends during development, overwhelming the income effect. Such a model does help explain why the Malthusian model seems to explain cyclical fluctuations in fertility both before (Lee, 1981) and after (Easterlin, 1973) the fertility transition. Relative prices may not fluctuate as much as income. Marx, a harsh critic of Malthus, would not be surprised. He claimed that Malthus's laws of population were specific to the particular mode of production of pre-industrial Europe. Other modes of production would have other modes of reproduction. Unfortunately, he left no better guide to predicting the changes than did Malthus.

It is perhaps ironic that Malthus's Theory of Population, conceived as a prediction of long-run equilibrium, should be consistent with short-run fluctuations but not with long-run movements. Humankind has not reached the idyllic state anticipated by Malthus's utopian adversaries. Neither have we fulfilled Malthusian predictions. The separation of reproduction from 'passion between the sexes' has led the wealthiest of nations to fertility below the level

405

needed to replace their populations while in the poorest of nations great numbers of children are born into short lives of poverty. Theories of population must acknowledge their debt to Malthus and move on.

BIBLIOGRAPHY

Becker, G.S. 1981. *A Treatise on the Family*. Cambridge, Mass.: Harvard University Press.

Easterlin, R.A. 1973. Relative economic status and the American fertility swing. In *Family Economic Behavior: Problems and Prospects*, ed. E.B. Sheldon, Philadelphia: J.B. Lippincott.

Hatcher, J. 1977. *Plague, Population, and the English Economy, 1348–1530*. London: Cambridge University Press.

Lee, R.D. 1981. Short-term variation: vital rates, prices, and weather. In Wrigley and Schofield (1981), ch. 9.

Malthus, T.R. 1798. *An Essay on the Principle of Population, as it affects the future improvement of society. With remarks on the speculations of Mr Godwin, M. Condorcet, and other writers*. Harmondsworth: Penguin, 1970; 7th edn, New York: Kelley 1970.

Meuvret, J. 1946. Les crises des subsistances et la démographie de la France de l'Ancien Régime. *Population* 1(4), November, 643–50.

Mokyr, J. 1983. *Why Ireland Starved*. London: Allen & Unwin.

Preston, S.H. 1976. *Mortality Patterns in National Populations*. New York: Academic Press.

Weir, D.R. 1984. Rather never than late: celibacy and age at marriage in English cohort fertility, 1541–1871. *Journal of Family History* 9(4), Winter, 340–54.

Wrigley, E.A. and Schofield, R. 1981. *The Population History of England, 1541–1871: A Reconstruction*. Cambridge, Mass.: Harvard University Press.

Market Failure

JOHN O. LEDYARD

The best way to understand market failure is first to understand market success, the ability of a collection of idealized competitive markets to achieve an equilibrium allocation of resources which is Pareto optimal. This characteristic of markets, which was loosely conjectured by Adam Smith, has received its clearest expression in the theorems of modern welfare economics. For our purposes, the first of these, named the First Fundamental Theorem of welfare economics, is of most interest. Simply stated it reads: (1) if there are enough markets, (2) if all consumers and producers behave competitively, and (3) if an equilibrium exists, then the allocation of resources in that equilibrium will be Pareto optimal (see Arrow, 1951, or Debreu, 1959). Market failure is said to occur when the conclusion of this theorem is false; that is, when the allocations achieved with markets are not efficient.

Market failure is often the justification for political intervention in the market place (for one view, see Bator, 1958, section V). The standard argument is that if market allocations are inefficient, everyone can and should be made better off. To understand the feasibility and desirability of such Pareto-improving interventions, we must achieve a deeper understanding of the sources of market failure. Since each must be due to the failure of at least one of the three conditions of the First Theorem, we will consider those conditions one at a time.

The first condition requires there to be enough markets. Although there are no definitive guidelines as to what constitutes 'enough', the general principle is that if any actor in the economy cares about something that also involves an interaction with at least one other actor, then there should be a market for that something; it should have a price (Arrow, 1969). This is true whether the something is consumption of bread, consumption of the smoke from a factory, or the amount of national defence. The first of these examples is a standard private good, the second is an externality and the third is a public good. All need to be priced if we are to achieve a Pareto-optimal allocation of resources; without these markets, actors may be unable to inform others about mutually beneficial trades which can leave both better off.

The informational role of markets is clearly highlighted by a classic example of market failure analysed by Scitovsky (1954). In this example, a steel industry, which must decide now whether to operate, will be profitable if and only if a railroad industry will begin operations within five years. The railroad industry will be profitable if and only if the steel industry is operating when the railroad industry begins its own operations. Clearly each cares about the other and it is efficient for each to operate; the steel industry begins today and the railroad industry begins later. Nevertheless, if there are only spot markets for steel, the railroad industry cannot easily inform the steel industry of its interests through the market place. This inability to communicate desirable interactions and to coordinate timing is an example of market failure and has been used as a justification for public involvement in development efforts; a justification for national planning. However, if we correctly recognize that there are simply too few markets, we can easily find another solution by creating a futures market for steel. If the railroad industry is able to pay today for delivery of steel at some specified date in the future then both steel and railroad industries are able to make the other aware of their interests through the market place. It is easy to show that as long as agents behave competitively and equilibrium exists the addition of futures markets will solve this type of market failure.

A completely different example of the informational role of markets arises when actors in the market place are asymmetrically informed about the true state of an uncertain world. The classic example involves securities markets where insiders may know something that outsiders do not. Even if it is important and potentially profitable for the uninformed actor to know the information held by the informed actor, there may not be enough markets to generate an efficient allocation of resources. To see this most clearly, suppose there are only two possible states of the world. Further suppose there are two consumers, one of whom knows the true state and one of whom thinks each state is equally likely. If the only markets that exist are markets for physical commodities then the equilibrium allocation will not in general be Pareto optimal. One solution is to create a contingent claims market. An 'insurance' contract can be created in which delivery and acceptance of a specified amount of the commodity is contingent on the true state of the world. Assuming both parties can, *ex post*, mutually verify which is indeed the true state of the world, if both behave competitively and an equilibrium allocation exists, it will be Pareto optimal, given the information structure. A more general and precise version of this theorem can be found in Radner (1968).

Analysing this example further, we note that in equilibrium the prices of commodities in the state which is not true will be close to or equal to zero, since at positive prices the informed actor will always be willing to supply an infinite amount contingent on the false state, knowing delivery will be unnecessary. If the uninformed actor is clever and realizes that prices will behave this way in equilibrium then he can become informed simply by observing which contingency prices are zero. If he then uses this information which has been freely provided by the market, the equilibrium will be Pareto optimal under full information. In a very simple form, this is the idea behind rational expectations (see Muth, 1961). With clever competitive actors, it may not be necessary to create all markets in order to achieve a Pareto-efficient equilibrium allocation.

Completing markets seems to be an easy technique to correct market failure. The suggestions that taxes and subsidies (Pigou, 1932) or property rights reassignments (Coase, 1960) can cure market failure follow directly from this observation. However, an unintended consequence can sometimes occur after the creation of these markets. In some cases, adding more markets may cause conditions (2) and (3) of the First Theorem to be false. Curing one form of market failure can lead to another. To understand how this happens and how the second condition requiring competitive behaviour can be affected, consider the informed consumer in our previous example. If he realizes that the uninformed consumer is going to make inferences based indirectly on his actions, then he should not behave competitively because he could do better by pretending to be uninformed. He can, by strategically limiting the supply of information of which he is the monopoly holder, do better than if he behaved competitively. It is only his willingness to supply infinite amounts of the commodity in the false state that gives away his knowledge. Supplying only a little commodity contingent on that (false) state in return for a small payment today would not allow the uninformed agent to infer anything, and would allow the informed agent to make a profit from his monopoly position. This is not very different from the standard example of a violation of condition (2), monopoly supply of a commodity.

A different example of this phenomenon of unintended outcomes arises when markets are created to allocate public goods. It is now well known that the introduction of personal, Lindahl prices to price individual demands for a public good (i.e. prices such that there is unanimity in the amount of the public good demanded under voluntary exchange) does indeed lead to Pareto-optimal allocations if consumers behave competitively (see Foley, 1970). However, under this scheme, each agent becomes a monopsonist in one of the created markets and, therefore, has an incentive to understate demand and not to take prices as given. This is the phenomenon of 'free riding', often alluded to as the reason why the creation of markets may not be a viable solution to market failure. To understand why, let us now examine the second condition of the First Theorem in more detail.

The second condition of the First Theorem about market success is that all actors in the market place behave competitively. This means that each must act as if they cannot affect prices and, given prices, as if they follow optimizing behaviour. Consumers maximize preferences subject to budget constraints and producers maximize profits, each taking prices as fixed parameters. This condition will be violated when actors can affect the values of equilibrium prices take and in so doing be better off. The standard example of market failure due to a violation of this condition is monopoly in which one actor is the sole supplier of an output. By artificially restricting supply, this actor can cause higher prices and make himself better off even though the resulting equilibrium allocation will be inefficient.

Can we correct market failure due to non-competitive behaviour? To find an answer let us first isolate those conditions under which agents find it in their interests to follow competitive behaviour. The work of Roberts and Postlewaite (1976) has established that if each agent holds only a small amount of resources relative to the aggregate available, then they will usually be unable to manipulate prices in any significant way and will act as price takers. It is the depth of the market that is important. This is also true when the commodity is information. If each agent is informationally small, in the sense that he either knows very little or what he does know is of little importance to others, then he loses little by behaving competitively (see Postlewaite and Schmeidler, 1986). On the other hand, if he is informationally important, as in the earlier example, he may have an incentive to behave non-competitively. The key is the size of the agent's resources, both real and informational, relative to the market.

The solution to market failure from non-competitive behaviour then seems to be to ensure that all agents are both resource and informationally small. Of course this must be accomplished through direct intervention, as in the anti-trust laws and the securities market regulations of the United States, and may not be feasible. For example, it may not be possible to correct this type of market failure by simply telling agents to behave competitively. In such an attempt, one would try to enforce a public policy that all firms must charge prices equal to the marginal cost of output. But, unless the costs and production technology of the firm can be directly monitored, a monopolist can easily act as if he were setting price equal to marginal cost while using a false cost curve. It would be impossible for an outside observer to distinguish this non-competitive behaviour from competitive behaviour without directly monitoring the cost curve. If the monopolist were a consumer whose preferences were unobservable, then even monitoring would not help. In general, market failure from non-competitive behaviour is difficult to correct while still retaining markets. We will hint at some alternatives below.

Expansion of the number of markets can also lead to violations of the third condition of the First Theorem. For illustration we consider three examples. The first and simplest of these is the case of increasing returns to scale in production. The classic case is a product which requires a fixed set-up cost and a constant marginal cost to produce. (More generally we could consider non-convex production possibilities sets.) If the firm acts competitively in this industry and if the price is above marginal cost, the firm will supply an infinite amount. If the price is at or below marginal cost, the firm will produce nothing. If the consumers' quantity demand is positive and finite at a price equal to marginal cost, then there is no price such that supply equals demand. Equilibrium does not exist. The real implication of this situation is not that markets do not equilibrate or that trade does not take place; it is that a natural monopoly exists. There is room for at most one efficient firm in this industry. Again it is the assumption of competitive behaviour which is ultimately violated.

The next example, due to Starrett (1972), involves an external diseconomy. Suppose there is an upstream firm that pollutes the water and a downstream firm that requires clean water as an input into its production process. It is easy to show that if such a diseconomy exists and if the downstream firm always has the option of inaction (i.e. it can use no inputs to produce no outputs at zero cost), then the aggregate production possibilities set of the economy when expanded to allow enough markets cannot be convex. (See Ledyard, 1976 for a formal proof.) If the production possibilities set of the economy is non-convex then, as in the last example, it is possible that a competitive equilibrium will not exist. Expansion of the number of markets to solve the inefficiencies due to external diseconomies can lead to a situation in which there is no competitive equilibrium.

The last example, first observed by Green (1977) and Kreps (1977), arises in situations of asymmetric information. Recall the earlier example in which one agent was fully informed about the state of the world while the other thought each state was equally likely. Suppose preferences and endowments in each state are such that if both know the state then the equilibrium prices in each state are the same. Further, suppose that if the uninformed agent makes no inferences about the state from the other's behaviour then there will be different prices in each state. Then no (rational expectations) equilibrium will exist. If the informed agent tries to make inferences the prices will not inform him, and if the uninformed agent does not try to make inferences the prices will inform him. Further, it is fairly easy to show that if a market for information could be created (ignoring incentives to hide information) the resulting possibilities set is in general non-convex. In either case there is no equilibrium.

Most examples of non-existence of equilibrium seem to lead inevitably to non-competitive behaviour. In our example of non-existence due to informational asymmetries, it is natural for the informed agent to behave as a monopolist with respect to that information. In the example of the diseconomy, if a market is created between the upstream and the downstream firm, each becomes a monopoly. If there is a single polluter and many pollutees, the polluter holds a position similar to a monopsony. The non-existence problem due to the fundamental non-convexity caused by the use of markets to eliminate external diseconomies is simply finessed by one or more of the participants assuming non-competitive behaviour. An outcome occurs but it is not competitive and, therefore, not efficient.

Market failure, the inefficient allocation of resources with markets, can occur if there are too few markets, non-competitive behaviour, or non-existence problems. Many suggested solutions for market failure, such as tax-subsidy schemes, property rights assignments and special pricing arrangements, are simply devices for the creation of more markets. If this can be done in a way that avoids non-convexities and ensures depth of participation, then the remedy can be beneficial and the new allocation should be efficient. On the other hand, if the addition of markets creates either non-convexities or shallow participation, then attempts to cure market failure from too few markets will simply lead to market failure from monopolistic behaviour. Market failure in this latter situation is fundamental. Examples are natural monopolies, external diseconomies, public goods and informational monopolies. If one wants to achieve efficient allocations of resources in the presence of such fundamental failures, one must accept self-interested behaviour and explore non-market alternatives. A literature using this approach, sometimes called implementation theory and sometimes called mechanism design theory, was initiated by Hurwicz (1972) and is surveyed in Groves and Ledyard (1986).

BIBLIOGRAPHY

Arrow, K. 1951. An extension of the basic theorems of classical welfare economics. In *Proceedings of the Second Berkeley Symposium on Mathematical Statistics and Probability*, ed. J. Neyman, Berkeley: University of California Press.

Arrow, K. 1969. The organization of economic activity: issues pertinent to the choice of market versus non-market allocation. In Joint Economic Committee, *The Analysis and Evaluation of Public Expenditures: The PPB System*, Washington, DC: Government Printing Office, 47–64.

Bator, F. 1958. The anatomy of market failure. *Quarterly Journal of Economics*, 351–79.

Coase, R. 1960. The problem of social cost. *Journal of Law and Economics* 3, 1–44.

Debreu, G. 1959. *Theory of Value: An Axiomatic Analysis of Economic Equilibrium*. Cowles Foundation Monograph No. 17, New York: Wiley.

Foley, D. 1970. Lindahl's solution and the core of an economy with public goods. *Econometrica* 38, 66–72.

Green, J. 1977. The nonexistence of informational equilibria. *Review of Economic Studies* 44, 451–63.

Groves, T. and Ledyard, J. 1986. Incentive compatibility ten years later. In *Information, Incentives, and Economic Mechanisms*, ed. T. Groves, R. Radner and S. Reiter, Minneapolis: University of Minnesota Press.

Hurwicz, L. 1972. On informationally decentralized systems. In *Decision and Organization*, ed. C.B. McGuire and R. Radner, Amsterdam: North-Holland.

Kreps, D. 1977. A note on 'fulfilled expectations' equilibria. *Journal of Economic Theory* 14, 32–43.

Ledyard, J. 1976. Discussion of 'On the Nature of Externalities'. In *Theory and Measurement of Economic Externalities*, ed. S. Lin, New York: Academic Press.

Muth, J. 1961. Rational expectations and the theory of price movements. *Econometrica* 29, 315–35.

Pigou, A. 1932. *The Economics of Welfare*. 4th edn, New York: Macmillan; New York: St Martin's Press, 1952.

Postlewaite, A. and Schmeidler, D. 1986. Differential information and strategic behavior in economic environments: a general equilibrium approach. In *Information, Incentives, and Economic Mechanisms*, ed. T. Groves, R. Radner and S. Reiter, Minneapolis: University of Minnesota Press.

Radner, R. 1968. Competitive equilibrium under uncertainty. *Econometrica* 36, 31–58.

Roberts, J. and Postlewaite, A. 1976. The incentives for price-taking behavior in large exchange economies. *Econometrica* 44, 115–27.

Scitovsky, T. 1954. Two concepts of external economies. *Journal of Political Economy* 62, 70–82.

Starrett, D. 1972. Fundamental non-convexities in the theory of externalities. *Journal of Economic Theory* 4, 180–99.

412

Marketing Boards

PETER BAUER

With trivial exceptions, marketing boards for agricultural products fall into two distinct categories: first, boards endowed by government with monopoly power in the sale of controlled products; second, marketing boards similarly endowed with monopsony power in the purchase of controlled products. The former function mainly in advanced countries, the latter in certain poor countries.

I. To be effective, monopolistic action in a particular country requires official support and enforcement because of the multiplicity of producers of standardized commodities and the availability of imports. Without such support, agricultural markets approximate the model of perfect competition of the textbooks.

Concerted action to raise farm prices was often tried during the interwar period, and occasionally even earlier. These attempts failed because of incomplete market control. In the early 1930s, farm prices declined sharply, partly as a result of the expansion of capacity, and partly as a result of the depression. Under the influence of political pressure and because of social considerations, many governments wished to arrest the decline of farm prices and incomes. In many instances fiscal considerations were thought to preclude direct subsidies. Again, prohibition or control of competing imports was of no avail to producers of some important perishable commodities such as liquid milk and main crop potatoes. State supported or organized monopolies, termed marketing boards, were among the instruments introduced for maintaining or raising farm prices and incomes in a politically and administratively practicable and politically painless manner. The boards set up under the British Agricultural Marketing Acts of 1931 and 1933 are examples of marketing boards effectively controlled by producer representatives (Astor and Rowntree, 1938; Bauer, 1948; Warley, 1967).

The methods used by marketing boards to raise returns to producers include the following: acreage restriction (as with hops and potatoes); direct and indirect restriction of the amounts producers may market (as with potatoes); and the exercise of discriminating monopoly power, with higher prices in sheltered

413

markets and lower prices in exposed markets (in milk, the liquid market and the market for processed products respectively).

The raising of prices and farm incomes are the objectives and principal effects of these marketing boards. Some other features of these boards and their operations may be of greater interest than this banal result. (a) The acreage restictions under the potato and hops schemes conferred windfall profits on the owners of land that had quotas attached to it. (b) The boards encouraged and supported cartels of processors and distributors, and also minimum resale and retail prices for the controlled commodities. These arrangements, an example that monopoly breeds monopoly, were *prima facie* surprising since they reduced the share of the prices paid by consumers that went to the farmers. The reasons behind them may have been a wish to placate distributors and processors, or to benefit the minority of producers who were also retailers. But it appears that the Milk and Potato Boards, at any rate, were also misled by inappropriate analogy with those manufacturers of branded goods who were practising resale price maintenance. (c) The boards, established to assist farmers at the time of a sharp fall in prices and incomes, were retained, and new ones created, in radically different postwar conditions – an example of the self-perpetuating character of organizations established by governments. (d) The system involved decisions at two levels, namely the boards and the individual producers. The former were faced with sloping demand curves. In the absence of production or marketing quotas, the individual producer faced a horizontal demand curve. With such quotas, the producer faced a demand curve which was horizontal up to the assigned quota and then became vertical (or nearly so).

II. Marketing boards of the second type by statute have the sole rights to buy the designated produce for exports. During World War II, marketing boards of this type were set up in the former British West African colonies for cocoa, palm oil, palm kernels and groundnuts, and subsequently for cotton. The produce was bought for the boards by merchants as their agents. During the war and early postwar years these agents bought the controlled produce for export on the basis of official quotas calculated according to their prewar performance. Agents who exceeded their quotas paid large penalties to those who had underbought, the settlement being effected through the boards. The declared purpose of these arrangements was to prevent a collapse in the local price of cocoa (feared because of shortage of shipping and the closure of major outlets, notably Germany) and to encourage the exports of the other crops (required by the loss of Far Eastern supplies).

These arrangements were anomalous. The British Government in any case had undertaken to purchase the entire exportable output at seasonally fixed prices, so that the market available to local producers was unlimited at those prices. Monopsony of export and the imposition of buying quotas were unnecessary to maintain the local price of cocoa, and deterred the production and exports of the other crops. The statutory monopsony *cum* quota system had been proposed in 1939 by a trade association of the major West African merchants. The quota system in effect provided statutory enforcement for their restrictive prewar marketing sharing agreements, which had limited success both because of breaches of the agreements and also because of the entry of new competitors. Buying quotas are easier to enforce where there is only a single official buyer, and where over-buying is effectively penalized by that buyer. The boards also did not admit new buying agents.

In the early postwar years the quota system was abandoned in the face of its unpopularity with influential local interests and of pressure by competitors. State export monopsony was, however, retained. It was also extended to other British colonies in Africa and also to Burma. The system was continued by the governments of the new independent successor states.

The principal reason officially advanced for maintaining state export monopsony was the need for stabilization in the sense of shielding producers from the damaging effects of short-period price fluctuations. Subsidiary reasons included the usefulness of maintaining and adapting for peacetime purposes organizations established during the war; and also the impossibility of returning to the many thousands of unregistered small-scale producers the large surpluses already accumulated by the boards. The latter explanations were transparent rationalizations for self-perpetuation. Thus, if it were true that the surpluses accumulated during the war by the boards could not be returned to the producers whose output had yielded the surpluses, this would be true equally of the accumulations of the successor organizations.

According to the British Government White Paper, *Statement on the Future Marketing of West African Cocoa*, Cmnd. 6950, 1946, the Cocoa Marketing Boards would prescribe seasonally fixed producer prices each year, thereby cutting the link between fluctuating world market prices and local producer prices. When world prices were high the board would make a surplus, with which it would support producer prices when market prices were low. In this way prices received by producers would be stabilized. The Cocoa White Paper stated emphatically that the board would not use its powers to underpay producers systematically and to build up increasing surpluses. The boards would act as agents and trustees for the producers, and would on no account become instruments of taxation in effect. Similar promises were made for other controlled crops.

These explicit and categoric pledges were soon broken. From their inception, the marketing boards have paid producers much less than the realized market prices. The level of taxation represented by the boards' policies has varied from time to time, and varied also between different crops. But for most products it has been extremely severe. The boards have withheld vast sums from the producers. Killick (1966) calculated that from 1939 to 1961 (when the Ghana Cocoa Marketing Boards ceased to publish annual reports) out of net export proceeds of £805 million, about £357 million, or 44 per cent, was withheld from producers. For all Nigerian marketing boards the corresponding figures from 1939 to 1962 were about £1096 million and £301 million, that is, about 27 per cent (Helleiner, 1964). Reliable series are not available for more recent years, but substantial underpayment of producers has continued, especially the systematic

415

underpayment of producers by the board in Ghana. (These calculations appropriately include the proceeds of local and export taxes, which served to siphon off directly part of the boards' surpluses.) For years on end, producers with very small annual cash incomes were taxed at rates applicable only to taxpayers in the highest income brackets in the UK. On the other hand, people with incomes far higher than those of the producers paid little or no direct taxes, and were indeed often directly subsidized by the funds of the marketing boards.

The incidence of this taxation was practically wholly on the producers. West African exports of vegetable oils and oil seeds and cotton are a very small part of world supplies, so that world prices are not affected by the boards' activities. Cocoa exports from Nigeria and Gold Coast Ghana were about 50–60 per cent of world exports in the late 1930s, but had declined to 25–30 per cent by the early 1980s as a result of the decline of exports from Gold Coast Ghana and the expansion of supplies elsewhere. Indeed, the systematic underpayment of producers has contributed to the decline of cocoa exports from Ghana, the virtual cessation of new cocoa plantings, and the decline in exports of palm produce from Nigeria. There was some smuggling of cocoa from Ghana to the neighbouring countries where prices were higher, but the distance of some of the principal producing areas from the frontiers, the activities of armed frontier guards and the bulky nature of the crop made smuggling difficult. The dearth of consumer goods in the cocoa areas in recent decades also suggests that smuggling was rather restricted. There was no scope for smuggling palm oil and palm kernels out of Nigeria. The decline of exports was the result of several factors, among which the underpayment of producers was almost certainly the most important.

Two sets of influences were behind the development of the marketing boards into instruments of taxation. The first was the difference in political effectiveness between the boards and the farmers. The boards were directed and administered first by British officials, and after independence by African politicians and officials. These groups have been much more powerful and articulate than the farmers; and the underpayment of producers suited their political and personal interests. The British civil servants derived prestige from the surpluses of the boards. Since independence, the reserves and revenues of the boards have served as financial power bases for African politicians. Through the boards they have the power to tax producers and prescribe their living standards. They also have the power to license processors and buying agents. These powers have been a major factor in politicizing life and exacerbating political conflict in countries where export monopsonies have operated.

The policies of the marketing boards are a conspicuous instance of the disparity in political effectiveness between the urban political elites and the unorganized and inarticulate rural population. The former largely control the political and administrative machinery, the media, and usually also key elements in the military. This discrepancy in political effectiveness is a familiar feature of the scene in less developed countries and is especially pronounced in Africa. In West Africa, notably Ghana and Southern Nigeria, the position of the urban political elites and their associates in the military, in the civil service, the media and in business, was reinforced by the removal of power and influence from the traditional tribal chiefs towards the end of colonial rule and in the early years of independence.

The second factor in the transformation of the marketing boards was the vagueness of the concept of stabilization, and the prevalence of simplistic notions about it.

Arising from the operation of the West African marketing boards, an extended academic discussion took place on issues in price or income stabilization for primary producers. This was initiated by Bauer and Paish (1952) and concluded by Helleiner (1964). In order to prevent price stabilization becoming the cloak for taxation, Bauer and Paish proposed a formula for setting producer prices by the boards which would smooth fluctuations while ensuring maintenance of contact with the trend of market prices, and thereby would clearly distinguish the smoothing of fluctuations from other objectives of policy. This article elicited several critical replies, the most significant by Friedman (1954). He argued that compulsory smoothing, even with a clearly defined formula to ensure maintenance with the trend, was unwarranted, as individual producers could always save part of their incomes in prosperity and draw on reserves in adversity. Friedman's article was an early application of his permanent income hypothesis. He also drew attention to various other disadvantages of compulsory smoothing schemes.

Bauer subsequently modified his position, partly in response to Friedman's position, and partly on the ground that in less developed countries a compulsory smoothing scheme was always liable to develop into an instrument of taxation, even in the face of specific assurances to the contrary. In fact, he and Yamey explained how a voluntary stabilization scheme could operate for small-scale agricultural producers (Bauer and Yamey, 1968).

Bauer and Paish (1952) also drew attention to major ambiguities in the concept of stabilization. Stabilization can refer to money prices, money incomes, real prices or real incomes. It can mean the establishment of maximum or minimum prices or incomes. To be meaningful, the concept needs to make clear the period over which a stabilization policy is to balance surpluses and disbursements. It needs to make clear whether numerous small changes represent more or less stability than a smaller number of larger discontinuous changes. The relation between open market prices and producer prices also has to be clarified.

Unless these ambiguities are resolved, stabilization becomes an empty omnibus expression, susceptible to widely different and conflicting interpretations, all of which can be invoked in support of any policy by an official monopsony. These ambiguities are exacerbated when there is a long-period tendency for prices to rise, as there has been in West African export prices since the war: the higher are the prices, the larger become the amounts necessary to maintain them at a given level, so that a particular accumulated reserve appears (or can be made to appear) to be insufficient as a reserve, and this then provides superficial justification for further accumulation of surpluses.

To have brought into the open the ambiguities of the concept of stabilization and the difficulties and dangers of price stabilization in practice may have been the most useful outcome of the protracted academic discussion about the West African Marketing Boards.

BIBLIOGRAPHY

Astor, Viscount and Rowntree, B.S. 1938. *British Agriculture*. London: Longmans & Co.
Bauer, P.T. 1948. A review of the agricultural marketing schemes. *Economica* 15, May, 132–50.
Bauer, P.T. 1954. *West African Trade*. Cambridge: Cambridge University Press. Revised edn, London: Routledge & Kegan Paul, 1963.
Bauer, P.T. and Paish, F.W. 1952. The reduction of fluctuations in the incomes of primary producers. *Economic Journal* 62, December. Reprinted in Bauer and Yamey (1968).
Bauer, P.T. and Yamey, B.S. 1968. *Markets, Market Control and Marketing Reform: Selected Papers*. London: Weidenfeld & Nicolson.
Friedman, M. 1954. The reduction of fluctuations in the incomes of primary producers: a critical comment. *Economic Journal* 64, December, 698–703.
Helleiner, G.K. 1964. The fiscal role of the marketing boards in Nigerian economic development, 1947–1961. *Economic Journal* 74, September, 582–610.
Killick, A.T. 1966. The economics of cocoa. In *A Study of Contemporary Ghana*: Vol. I, *The Economy of Ghana*, ed. W. Birmingham, I. Neustadt and E.N. Omaboe, London: George Allen & Unwin.
Report of the Committee Appointed to Review the Working of the Agricultural Marketing Acts. 1947. Ministry of Agriculture and Fisheries, Economic Series No. 48, London: HMSO.
Statement on the Future Marketing of West African Cocoa. 1946. Colonial Office, Cmnd. 6950, London: HMSO.
Warley, T.K. 1967. A synoptic view of agricultural marketing organizations in the United Kingdom. In *Agricultural Producers and their Markets*, ed. T.K. Warley, Oxford: Oxford University Press.

Market Places

POLLY HILL

It is usual to follow the *Final Report* of the British Royal Commission on Market Rights and Tolls (1891) by defining a market place as an 'authorized public concourse of buyers and sellers of commodities, meeting at a place more or less strictly limited or defined, at an appointed time', and to regard fairs, which meet far less frequently (commonly annually for a number of days in succession), as different types of assembly. While this definition broadly satisfies present purposes, some qualifications and additional emphases are required. First, the commodities (wares) must be on view so that corn exchanges and the like (and certainly stock exchanges) are disqualified; second, sellers must be quite numerous in relation to buyers, which disqualifies supermarkets as well as the small gatherings of women foodstuff vendors which are such a familiar feature of the West African scene; third, markets last for no longer than a day (or sometimes an evening), so that they constantly open and close; fourth, regular periodicity, which is most commonly based on the recognized local 'market week', is a fundamental feature; fifth, services (such as bicycle repair, food cooking or barbering) as well as commodities may be on offer; sixth, auction yards, as such, are disqualified, though sales by auction are not unknown in certain specialized market places; seventh, market places are 'public' concourses in the sense that potential buyers or onlookers may enter freely, not because they are necessarily publicly owned; eighth, taxation of sellers is usual, by means of tolls (on wares) or stall-rents; and ninth, it is the activities of the various participants (their organization) which defines the market, despite the usual emphasis on 'place'.

Traditionally, economists have displayed little interest in market places, as distinct from market principles, having condescendingly passed the subject to economic historians – see the entry on 'Market as Place of Sale' in the 1925 edition of *Palgrave's Dictionary of Political Economy*; their disdain has now become absolute in the sense that their exceedingly numerous publications on 'marketing' never include the 'place' in their indexes. This is odd since market

419

places, especially those handling livestock or wholesaling meat, fish, vegetables and other natural produce, are far from being defunct institutions in Europe; but the function of European retail markets is now so petty relative to that in the time of Samuel Pepys (when the only food shops in central London were grocers and bakers), and is so inherently uninteresting compared to that of the market place systems of the less developed world, that Europe is here ignored. (As for the United States, market places were always unimportant there.)

No disdain for history is implied by such an approach since many non-Western market places are very ancient. Cortés himself reported on the market place of Tenochtitlan, the capital city of the Aztecs, where 60,000 traders were said to assemble daily, the organization being generally familiar to Spaniards. Then, Ibn Battuta provided evidence for the existence of considerable market places over a large area of the Western Sudan in the mid-14th century; Pieter de Marees noted that every town on the Gold Coast in 1600 had its appointed market day; and in the mid-17th century Djenne, on the upper reaches of the Niger river, was accounted one of the great market places of the Muslim world. As for late Imperial China, the anthropologist, G.W. Skinner (1964, p. 5) emphasizes that the regularities in central-place hierarchies there had evolved over many centuries; his analysis of hierarchical market place systems (1964, 1965, 1977) is uniquely monumental.

Fortunately, two massive bibliographies testify to the importance of non-Western markets. These are Fröhlich (1940) on African markets, which lists 406 titles including much reference material of historical interest; and the three-part series of publications on world market places and fairs, in the major European languages, which has been issued by the International Geographical Union (1977, 1979, 1985) – it has now been discontinued. Although the latter series includes a fair number of titles on marketing rather than market places, and although some items are included more than once under different geographical headings, it is significant that no fewer than 45 per cent of the 2155 entries in the two earlier issues relate to the four regions of West Africa, Middle America, South Asia and the Andean Republics. West Africa with 418 titles (19 per cent) is much the best-documented region.

But the degree of documentation is not an entirely reliable indicator of the significance of market places which may happen to go unstudied in some regions. Possibly the most remarkable area of neglect is the Indian sub-continent, for it is only during the past few years that it has begun to seem likely that rural periodic market places there have long been much more important than the very unimpressive literature would suggest. It seems that in their intense preoccupation with land revenue systems the officials of the British Raj overlooked both market places and marketing generally, thus accurately reflecting the interests of contemporary economists whom they found so influential; and it is certain that independent India still remains firmly wedded to the former British approach, as in so many other socio-economic contexts affecting the countryside. In West Africa, on the other hand, where colonial administrations had been so fleeting and unimpressive compared to the Raj, and where anthropologists and travellers had long found market places fascinating, the end of colonialism was associated with an indigenous flowering of new-style historical studies, and modern research on market places has a thoroughly satisfying historical base (see Meillassoux, 1971). Nor did the deplorable 'Polanyi debate', an aberration which suddenly flourished in the 1960s, have any lasting influence there; Karl Polanyi knew little of the organization of pre-colonial West African economies and his basic notion that uncontrolled exchange in the market place was peculiar to 19th- and 20th-century industrialism seemed preposterous in a region where ordinary farmers had commonly bought chattel-slaves in public markets, for cash, in the 19th century and earlier.

Soon after geographers became the dominant students of Third World market places in the late 1960s, they began to search (as all intellectual leaders must) for a single theory of periodic marketing (Smith, 1978). But their search was in vain, for the functions of large rural periodic market places, which are the mainstay of all marketing systems, are very variable, both within and between regions. In some regions, most notably in late Imperial China, there is strict hierarchical ordering of market places of several levels, in accordance with the importance of their wholesaling function, grand city markets being the invariable apices. But Skinner was wrong in supposing (1964, p. 3) that the glorious structures he described were 'characteristic of the whole class of civilizations known as "peasant" or "traditional agrarian" societies', for in West Africa, for instance, the most important market in a region might be situated in the open countryside, serving as a link between different ecological zones, and there is not necessarily any close association between the 'level' of a market and the size of the settlement (if any) where it is situated. Owing to its vast size and to the exceptional longevity and stability of its society, China is typical only of itself. Elsewhere there has not necessarily yet been time for the population to distribute itself so appropriately in terms of central-place theory. Only a Sinologist could assert that a close relationship between population density and crop yields is 'virtually axiomatic' in traditional agrarian societies (Skinner, 1977, p. 283).

However, the basic distinction between rural periodic market places and daily markets *is* generally useful: the latter are always situated in cities or large towns and include a fair proportion of specialist traders who occupy permanent stalls or selling positions on most days; the former always include a considerable element of cultivators, or their wives, who sell their own produce – people who are also apt to be customers themselves, but who would not have time to come to market daily.

Christaller's central-place theory, involving the drawing of hexagons, certainly had much better application to late Imperial China than to its native Germany and this may be generally true of many developing regions where the strict assumptions on which it is based, among them a flat and featureless topography, are sufficiently satisfied; but despite the best efforts of the geographers, it is too early to be sure. Of course temporal as well as spatial factors have much exercised the geographers. But the debate as to whether, for example, the four-day market week is the 'mother' of the eight-day week or vice versa continues to be unresolved.

Skinner contended (see Hill, 1966) that market intensification in response to population growth always involves a reduction, usually a halving, in the length of the market week; Fröhlich's hypothesis was the converse, for he held that existent markets made way for new ones by lengthening their market schedules. Most writers consider that market weeks (which in any district are usually uniformly three, four, five, six, seven, eight or ten days long, though alternate-day markets occasionally occur) are economic rather than calendrical in origin, but this idea does not get us very far. Considering the widespread introduction of the European seven-day week for commercial and educational purposes, the persistence of non-seven-day market weeks in many parts of such regions as West Africa is most interesting.

Governmental attitudes to periodic market places vary greatly. In Mexico City they are said to be a well-established component of the retail structure, despite official efforts to eliminate them. In Papua New Guinea, by contrast, officialdom is endeavouring to introduce them for the first time. Indian planners emphasize the significance of urban regulated markets and despise the indigenous rural institutions, though their attitude must soon change. Kenya and Tanzania are presumably somewhat ashamed of the rarity of non-coastal markets until this century. Skinner reports (1965, p. 371) on the disastrous and unsuccessful attempt to dispense with markets in China in the late 1950s. As for city markets, everyone is apt to deplore the lack of storage facilities and the insanitary conditions in so many of them.

All attempts to formulate general theories on the relationship between market places and long-distance trading, whether or not involving caravans, are bound to fail. In some regions caravans link market places while in others they avoid them, if only because their transport-animals require adequate grazing – besides, they are themselves mobile markets following established routes. As for long-distance lorry-borne traders, they may avoid markets altogether, perhaps because they pick up their heavy loads of plantains or yams at the farms and sell them from urban sheds or lorry parks. By neglecting such considerations the geographers have strait-jacketed market studies and introduced false notions of urban–rural continua.

In earlier times when anthropologists, not geographers, ruled the roost, more emphasis was apt to be placed on the political, religious, recreational, sociological and other non-economic aspects of market places. But, again, there is much variation. In one region the market is the anonymous, safe, kinless area where men and maidens meet; in another, Islam forbids the nubile woman from displaying her covered body there.

The geographers' emphasis on space and time neglects the actors (the customers, trader, onlookers – many of them children) who bring the market to life. Their predecessors, the anthropologists, painted colourful descriptive pictures of the people and their wares, but few of them examined the traders as economic men or women, perhaps the most notable exception being S.W. Mintz in his numerous publications on Caribbean and Latin American traders. It is generally agreed that the sellers of any commodity, who in certain important regions are mainly women, arrange themselves in clumps in the market place, and that they commonly endeavour, usually unsuccessfully, to 'fix' the prices of potentially quantifiable wares on any particular day. Although competition is usually so pronounced that price-rigging is impracticable, the frequency of 'regular customer' relationships means that it is apt to be imperfect; besides, everyone knows that the standard measures (there is seldom any weighing) are commonly suspect – as in some southern Ghanaian markets where all the kerosene tins used for measuring maize have false bottoms inserted by blacksmiths working openly in the market.

The organization of cattle markets is exceptionally interesting, especially in West Africa; the indigenous systems involving landlords and brokers, who accommodate the traders and facilitate trading with the help of credit, may best be studied there; see Hill (1985).

One 'Polanyi-supporter' has affirmed that 'for most of history' man has lived with fixed-price markets, non-price-making market places and perhaps mostly with economic systems whose essential character must be established independently of orthodox economic theory. Maybe ... but such a period was the stone age of market place studies.

BIBLIOGRAPHY

Fröhlich, W. 1940. Das afrikanische Marktwesen. *Zeitschrift für Ethnologie.* (An English translation was published in 1982 by the International Geographical Union.)

Hill, P. 1966. Notes on traditional market authority and market periodicity in West Africa. *Journal of African History* 7(2), 295–311.

Hill, P. 1985. *Indigenous Trade and Market Places in Ghana 1962–4.* Jos Oral History and Literature Texts, University of Jos, Nigeria.

International Geographical Union. 1977, 1979, 1985. *Periodic Markets, Daily Markets and Fairs: a Bibliography.* 1st 2 issues ed. R.J. Bromley, University College of Swansea; last issue ed. W. McKim, Towson State University, Maryland.

Meillassoux, C. (ed.) 1971. *The Development of Indigenous Trade and Markets in West Africa.* International African Institute, London: Oxford University Press.

Skinner, G.W. 1964, 1965. Marketing and social structure in rural China. *Journal of Asian Studies,* Part I, 24(1), November 1964, 3–43; Part II, 24(2), February 1965, 195–228; Part III, 24(3), May 1965, 363–99.

Skinner, G.W. (ed.) 1977. *The City in Late Imperial China.* Stanford: Stanford University Press.

Smith, R.H.T. (ed.) 1978. *Periodic Markets, Hawkers and Traders in Africa, Asia and Latin America.* Vancouver: Centre for Transportation Studies, University of British Columbia.

Markets with Adverse Selection

CHARLES WILSON

Consider a market in which products of varying quality are exchanged. Both buyers and sellers rank products of different quality in the same way, but only the sellers can observe the quality of each unit of the good they sell. Buyers can observe at most the *distribution* of the quality of the goods previously sold. Without some device for the buyers to identify good products, bad products will always be sold with the good products. Such a market illustrates the problem of *adverse selection*.

Economists have long recognized that the problem of adverse selection can interfere with the effective operation of a market. However, the modern theoretical treatment of the problem began with a paper by George Akerlof, 'The Market for Lemons' (1970). As the title suggests, he considered a stylized market for used cars. The set of cars is indexed by a quality parameter q uniformly distributed between 0 and 1. For a car of quality q, he assumed that the reservation value of a buyer is $(3/2)q$ while the reservation value for a seller is just q. He then addressed the problem of determining the market price and the volume of trade in a situation where the number of potential buyers exceeds the number of sellers.

If both sides can observe the quality of cars in such a market, efficiency requires that all cars be exchanged and, if the market is competitive, cars of quality q are exchanged at a price of $(3/2)q$. Akerlof assumed, however, that buyers can observe only the *average* quality of a car for sale at any price p. Since, in this case, any seller with a car of quality p or less offers the car for sale, the average quality of the cars for sale at any price p is equal to $q/2$. Given this relation between price and average quality, buyers value the car offered for sale at only $(3/4)p$. Consequently, the only market clearing price is 0 with no transactions occurring at all.

Akerlof's example presents the most extreme consequence of the problem of adverse selection. In general, not all trade is eliminated. Nevertheless, the market allocation is almost always inefficient. Briefly, the reason is as follows. Since sellers offer any good for exchange whose value is less than the price, the value to the sellers of the *average* product offered for sale is generally lower than the price. In contrast, the uninformed buyers purchase the product to the point where the value to them of the average product offered for sale is equal to the price. Consequently, in any Walrasian equilibrium, the value of the *marginal* car to the buyer exceeds its value to the seller. Furthermore, all buyers purchase from the same pool of products. To the extent that some buyers are willing to pay more for products of higher quality, a second source of inefficiency results.

Akerlof's analysis was generalized by Wilson (1980). He showed that when the buyers have heterogeneous preferences, there may be multiple Walrasian equilibria which can be ranked by the Pareto criterion. His argument is based on the following observation. If the average quality of the goods offered for sale increases sufficiently with the price, some buyers may actually prefer to buy at higher prices. Consequently, even in the absence of income effects, the demand curve may be upward-sloping over some range of prices. If the demand and supply curves intersect more than once, multiple Walrasian equilibria result. Furthermore, since the supply curve must be upward-sloping, demand must also be higher at higher equilibrium prices. It then follows by revealed preference that some buyers must also be better off at these prices. In fact, if the buyers have a constant marginal rate of substitution between the quality of the car and the consumption of other goods, Wilson showed that every buyer prefers a higher equilibrium price to a lower equilibrium price. Since sellers always prefer to sell at a higher price, it follows immediately that higher equilibrium prices are Pareto superior to lower equilibrium prices. It is also possible to construct examples where a price floor is Pareto superior to any equilibrium price even if the excess supply is rationed at random.

Based on these observations Wilson went on to argue that, in the presence of adverse selection, market forces may not lead to a single price. In fact, the nature of the equilibrium will generally depend on the nature of the institution or convention used to set the price. Akerlof's analysis implicitly assumed some kind of Walrasian mechanism. That is, in equilibrium all goods are exchanged at a single price which clears the market. Suppose instead, that each buyer must announce a price and then wait for offers. Then, if any buyer prefers a price which is higher than the Walrasian price, an equilibrium may result with excess supply which must be rationed. To increase the average quality of the product, sellers may prefer a price which is so high that supply exceeds demand, so that some suppliers are unable to sell their product.

This idea has been used by Stiglitz and Weiss (1981) to explain credit rationing. They considered a competitive banking system in which the supply of loanable funds is an increasing function of the deposit rate. Each borrower requires the same amount of funds and is indistinguishable to the banks from any other borrower. However, because of the possibility of default, borrowers differ in the expected return banks will earn at any given interest rate. In this model the banks assume the role of the uninformed buyers in Akerlof's used car example and the borrowers assume the role of the informed sellers. Stiglitz and Weiss then demonstrated that for a robust class of parameters, the market equilibrium implies an excess demand for loans.

I will illustrate their argument with a simple example. Suppose there are two types of borrowers. Both types use funds B to finance an investment project with the same expected return. Each of the n low risk borrowers earns a zero return with probability $1/2$ and a return 2B with probability $1/2$. Each of the n high risk borrowers earns a zero return with probability $3/4$ and a return 4B with probability $1/4$. In order to borrow the funds, banks require that firms put up collateral $C = B/2$. Then, at any (gross) interest rate r, a borrower repays the loan only if his return exceeds $[r - (1/2)B]$. Otherwise, he defaults and the bank collects whatever the firm earns plus the collateral.

Now consider the demand curve for loans. So long as this expected return exceeds the interest rate, a borrower will stay in the market. However, because of the differences in their distributions, the two types have different reservation values. Low risk borrowers earn non-negative profits only when $r \leqslant 3/2$, while high risk borrowers earn non-negative profits so long as $r \leqslant 5/2$. Consequently, the demand for loans is $2n$B for $0 < r \leqslant 3/2$, nB for $3/2 < r \leqslant 5/2$, and 0 for $r > 5/2$.

Finally, consider the supply of loanable funds. Since a bank is equally likely to lend to either a low or a high risk borrower when $r \leqslant 3/2$, for $0 < r \leqslant 3/2$, the expected (gross) rate of return to a bank is $[3r + (5/2)]/8$. For $3/2 \leqslant r \leqslant 5/2$, only the high risk borrowers are serviced, resulting in an expected rate of return of $[2r + 3]/8$. Now suppose that the level of loans supplied by banks is $(16/13)n$B times the gross rate of return. Then we obtain a 'supply' curve of $n(16/13)$B$[3r + (5/2)]/8$ for $r \leqslant 3/2$ and $n(16/13)$B$[2r + 3]/8$ for $3/2 < r \leqslant 5/2$. Note that this supply curve is upward-sloping everywhere except at $r = 3/2$, at which point it falls discontinuously from $n(14/13)$B to $n(12/13)$B. Consequently, 'supply' is equal to demand at loan rate $r = 7/4$. At this loan rate, only high risk borrowers demand loans and the average rate of return to each bank is $13/16$.

Although an interest rate of $7/4$ clears the market, this is not the outcome we would expect if profit-maximizing banks could set their own interest rates, even in a competitive market. Since the interest rate is above $3/2$, the least risky borrowers have dropped out of the market. Consequently, by lowering the interest rate to $3/2$ and attracting the low risk borrowers, it is possible for a bank to raise its expected rate of return even though it earns a lower rate of return on each high risk borrower. In this example, any bank which lowers its interest rate to $3/2$ and attracts an equal number of both types of consumers will increase its expected rate of return to $7/8$. Since every borrower prefers the lower interest rate, the higher 'market clearing' rate is not sustainable. The result is an equilibrium rate of return with an excess demand for loans.

In his *Bell Journal* paper, Wilson suggested that a different equilibrium might emerge if the informed agents were the price setters. Refer back to the used car example. It is easy to show that the higher the reservation value of the seller, the smaller is the decrease in price he is willing to accept in order to increase his chances of finding a buyer. This observation suggests that it may be possible to sustain an equilibrium with a distribution of prices. Sellers of high-quality products announce high prices which attract only a few buyers. Sellers of low-quality products announce low prices which attract more buyers. Buyers are willing to purchase at both prices because the quality of the cars offered increases with the price. The quality of cars increases with the price because more buyers purchase at low prices than at high prices. This tradeoff between price and the probability of selling has also been exploited by Samuelson (1984) and others in the design of optimal mechanisms for allocating goods in environments with adverse selection.

Both of the non-Walrasian equilibria discussed above are the consequence of individual agents trying to exploit the relation between quality and price to avoid the problem of adverse selection. Indeed, the study of how agents try to compensate for the problems of adverse selection makes up a large part of the literature on markets with imperfect information. One of the most important ideas to come out of this line of research is the concept of market signalling first investigated by Michael Spence (1973). The idea is that sellers of higher-quality products will try to reveal themselves by undertaking some activity which is less costly to them than to sellers of lower-quality products. In his example, more productive workers signal their productivity by purchasing education. In product markets, firms use guarantees to signal product reliability. In credit markets, lenders use collateral to signal credit worthiness (Bester, 1984).

BIBLIOGRAPHY

Akerlof, G. 1970. The market for lemons. *Quarterly Journal of Economics* 84(3), August, 488–500.

Bester, H. 1984. Screening versus rationing in credit markets with imperfect information. University of Bonn Discussion Paper No. 136, May.

Samuelson, W. 1984. Bargaining under asymmetric information. *Econometrica* 52(4), July, 995–1005.

Spence, M. 1973. Job market signalling. *Quarterly Journal of Economics* 87(3), August, 355–74.

Stiglitz, J. and Weiss, A. 1981. Credit rationing in markets with imperfect information. *American Economic Review* 71, June, 393–410.

Wilson, C. 1980. The nature of equilibrium in markets with adverse selection. *Bell Journal of Economics* 11, Spring, 108–30.

Marxist Economics

ANDREW GLYN

By Marxist economics we mean the work of those later economists who based their methodology and approach on the work of Karl Marx. Excluded from discussion here is the enormous body of exegetical literature seeking to amplify the genesis of and development of Marx's own thinking (Rosdolsky, 1968). Before discussing three areas where the contribution of Marxists has been most striking and important, it is helpful to bear in mind certain general features of their approach which could be said to separate them off from other traditions in economic theory.

Marxist economists view the capitalist system as essentially *contradictory*, in the sense that its malfunctions derive in an essential way from its structure, rather than representing 'imperfections' in an otherwise harmonious mechanism. At the heart of this structure is the relationship between capital and labour, which is necessarily an exploitative one. The conflict which results has a crucial influence on the way the capitalist system develops in every respect, from the form of technologies developed to the pattern of state policies adopted. Capital accumulation, the motor of the system, cannot therefore be analysed simply in quantitative terms: the structural changes in the economy which it brings are influenced by, and in turn help to shape, relations between the classes. So while the underlying logic of capitalism has remained unchanged, its history can be divided into different periods characterized by particular sets of class relations, technologies, state policies and international structures.

If some of these ideas would seem practically self-evident to economists with any interest in economic history, this underlines the powerful confirmation which the past century has provided for many of Marx's central ideas. It cannot, unfortunately, be said that mainstream economic theory has caught up with this, hiding, under ever more powerful formal techniques, an unchanging conceptual superficiality in its approach.

The body of Marxist economics which underpins the approach of Marxist economists to the analysis of particular phases and aspects of capitalist development may be divided into three main parts: (1) the labour process; (2) value, profits and exploitation; (3) capital accumulation and crises. What follows represents a brief survey of debates around and developments of these aspects of Marx's work; it is necessarily narrowly 'economic' (excluding work on the theory of the state and of classes) and concentrates on theoretical debate rather than on historical application.

THE LABOUR PROCESS. Marx's most fundamental criticism of his Classical predecessors, and especially of Ricardo, was that they failed to analyse how the capitalist system emerged as a specific mode of production resulting from a particular historical process. The dispossession of previously independent producers led to a division of society into workers, with only their labour power to sell, and employers who owned and controlled the means of production. This ownership was the basis of the profit appropriated by the capitalists, for it gave them control over the process of production itself. It allowed the capitalist class as a whole to force the working class to work longer than was required to produce their means of subsistence. Marx paid special attention to this control over the labour process, analysing in great detail how the development of machinery qualitatively increased the depth of this control by literally taking the pace of work out of the hands of the workers. This stress on the process of production as a *labour* process is arguably the most important distinguishing feature of Marxist economics as compared with other schools, which analyse production solely in technical terms (Rowthorn, 1980, ch. 1).

It was not, however, until more than 100 years after the publication of Volume I of *Capital* that his analysis of capitalist control over the labour process was applied to subsequent developments. Harry Braverman's *Labour and Monopoly Capital* (1972) had as its central theme the striving of employers to separate the conception of tasks from their execution, in order to preserve and enhance their control over the process of work. Frederick Taylor's system of Scientific Management, for example, analysed the operations required of skilled machine tool operatives so that 'scientific' timings could readily be allocated for new types of work. Ford's introduction of the assembly line was similarly intended to force a certain pace of work. Subsequent writers have extended this analysis to describe systems of 'bureaucratic' control exercised in large modern corporations, where effort is secured by payment systems allowing a steady progression of earnings for loyal employees (Edwards, 1979).

This more recent work is a revision, as well as an extension, of Marx's own analysis. In his conception of 'modern industry', control over the pace of work was exercised by the machine itself, which carried out the operations on the materials automatically, leaving the worker as a simple machine minder who fed the machine and dealt with minor malfunctions. This pattern, which Marx saw in contemporary developments in the textile industry, has not become the universal one. For in many types of production the worker still carries out operations on the materials. This has made it necessary for the employers to attempt to gain control over the speed of work by mechanical contrivance (the production line which obliges the worker to carry out tasks at a set speed) or organizational means (scientific management). Moreover, it has been more recently argued that 'Fordist' systems of mass production, where there is a minute division of labour, are giving way to more flexible systems where workers perform a greater range of tasks (Aglietta, 1979). This reflects the trend towards more sophisticated consumer goods, which demand shorter production runs and more model changes, and also the problems of overcoming the employee dissatisfaction with mindless and repetitive work which exploded in a number of countries at the end of the 1960s.

Marx's fundamental insight remains, however, the inspiration of this whole body of work, focusing on an issue of tremendous contemporary significance as employers struggle with the necessity of restructuring production in the fiercely competitive conditions of the 1980s (see as an example Willman and Winch, 1985). Only very recently has mainstream economics begun to address the problem of controlling work, and even then, as argued by Bowles (1985), from a less compelling perspective.

VALUE, PROFITS AND EXPLOITATION. Critics of Marx, from Böhm-Bawerk (1896) onwards, have always contended that his theory of profits and exploitation was fatally flawed by his reliance on a simplistic 'labour theory of value' – that commodities exchange in proportion to the amount of labour time required to produce them. If the price of a commodity was determined directly by this 'embodied labour', then the wage would directly measure the labour time required to produce the goods which workers bought in order to maintain themselves (the *value of labour power* in Marx's terminology). Profit, being the difference between the value added by the worker and the wage, would similarly measure directly the excess of time worked over the value of labour power, that is the surplus value produced by the worker while under the employer's control. At the level of society as a whole, total profits would be a direct measure of the surplus labour performed by the whole working class, that is the time worked beyond that necessary to reproduce the means of subsistence. Marx's *rate of exploitation*, the ratio of surplus value to the value of labour power, would be directly reflected in the ratio of profits to wages. Marx's insistence that the source of profit was the capitalist's ability to control the labour process, and thus force the working class to perform surplus labour, would receive a clear expression.

Marx himself was quite aware that the assumption he employed in *Capital*, Volume I, that commodities exchange at their values, that is, in proportion to the labour required to produce them, was a simplification designed to highlight the overall relation between capital and labour. In Volume III he explains that this assumption will only hold when the *organic composition of capital*, that is the ratio between the value of outlays on machinery and materials (*constant capital*) and on wages (the value of variable capital), is equal across industries. Where the organic composition differs across industries, then the surplus value produced by workers in a particular industry would represent a greater or lesser rate of profit on total capital employed depending on whether the organic composition was low or high. But exchange in proportion to labour time would inevitably mean that the capitalists within an industry received surplus value equal to that produced by their workers. This is because the commodities they received in exchange would be of equal value to those produced, thus leaving a surplus value for the capitalists, after setting aside what was required to pay for constant and variable capital, just equal to the surplus value their workers produced. Accordingly, exchange in proportion to labour time would imply unequal profit rates across sectors, which is impossible under competitive conditions.

Marx's own solution was to propose that commodities exchange not at their values, but at their prices of production. These represented a modification or transformation of values in order to ensure equal rates of profit across sectors despite unequal organic compositions of capital. It was simple for him to show that such prices of production implied that industries with a high organic composition, and which therefore needed to appropriate more surplus value than their workers produced to compensate for the bigger outlays on constant capital, would have to have a higher than average ratio of price of production to value (and vice versa for low organic composition sectors). So Marx's solution to the transformation problem involved a simple redistribution of total surplus value away from labour-intensive industries.

As von Bortkiewicz (1906) was the first to point out, Marx's solution to the transformation problem was incorrect. When constructing his prices of production Marx adds the average rate of profit applied to the values of the inputs. But if commodities do not sell at their values then capitalists are not purchasing their inputs at their values but at their prices of production. So correct prices of production have to be calculated on the basis of a simultaneous transformation of inputs *and* outputs from values to prices of production. Marx was actually aware that this further step was necessary but thought, not unreasonably, that it would make no important difference. Unfortunately he was wrong.

For the 'correct' solution to the transformation problem makes it impossible to maintain Marx's equality between such value aggregates as surplus value and the total value of output on the one hand, and their price correlates, profits and total output in money prices. Much subsequent literature (see von Bortkiewicz, 1906, and the later generalization by Seton, 1957) concentrated on describing the circumstances under which at least one of the 'invariances' between the price and value systems would hold. It can be argued, however, following the Uno school of Japanese Marxists (see Itoh, 1980), that this search for numerical equality between surplus value and profit is wholly misconceived, stemming from Marx's failure to maintain consistently his Volume I distinction between the *substance* of value (labour time) and its *form* (money prices). Any attempt to force numerical equality is artificial and thus misleading.

Even so this does not dispose of the 'problem'. For the correct, simultaneous solution also makes the rate of profit on capital employed different from Marx's general rate of profit, calculated as the ratio of surplus value to the value of capital employed (see von Bortkiewicz, 1906, and Steedman, 1977). What might seem more damaging still is that the rate of exploitation in value terms is not in general equal to the ratio of profits to wages. So Marx's basic expression of the extent of capitalist domination does not find a direct reflection in the money aggregates.

This in fact does not damage Marx's theory at all. The ratio of profits to wages reflects the ratio of surplus product to the bundle of wage goods as manifested in the exchange process (aggregate wages must represent the price of production of all wage goods and aggregate profits the price of production of the surplus product). The rate of exploitation is the ratio of the work done to produce the two bundles. These two ratios will only be equal when the organic compositions in the sectors producing the wage goods and surplus products are equal. Clearly there is no theoretical necessity for this to hold, though empirical estimates by Woolf (1979) suggest that the deviation of relative prices from relative values for these bundles of commodities may be rather small.

This divergence between the form of exploitation (the ratio of profits to wages) and its real substance (the ratio of surplus value to the value of labour power) can be readily accepted. Using Sraffa's construction of a standard commodity to show what pattern of industries would ensure equality between the two ratios seems to add rather little (see Medio, 1972). Retreating to the rather grandly named Fundamental Marxian Theorem, that positive profits require positive surplus value (Morishima, 1973), also seems unnecessarily defensive in that it fails to explain clearly the relationship between the price and value dimensions. It is important to emphasize that this interpretation of the transformation problem does not establish the case *for* analysis in terms of values. It merely shows how the value categories can be reconciled with the surface phenomena of profits and prices.

Further controversy over the adequacy and usefulness of Marx's theory of value has revolved around two further issues. The whole 'transformation problem' assumed that the values of commodities can be unambiguously defined as the labour time socially necessary for the production of a commodity at prevalent degrees of mechanization, skill and intensity of work. But critics from Böhm-Bawerk onwards have disputed that different types of labour can be 'reduced' to simple labour (see Rowthorn, 1980, ch. 6). It has further been argued (Steedman, 1977) that, in situations of joint production, labour values may not be determinable at all. If the output of shepherds is mutton and wool, how can their labour be allocated between the two products? If the employers used the wool and the shepherds ate the mutton it would not be possible to divide the shepherds' total working day into the necessary labour worked to produce the means of subsistence and the surplus labour worked for the employers. More generally, where there are different methods of joint production, the standard method of deriving labour values can lead to their being negative. Negative surplus value has been shown to coexist with positive profits (Steedman, 1977), though not uncontroversially (King, 1982).

These criticisms have at least made Marxists accept that there are real analytical difficulties in drawing up consistent value schema. The riposte of some (e.g. Himmelweit and Mohun, 1981, drawing on the work of I. Rubin, 1928) that the whole project of deducing values prior to their reflection in market prices is a misguided 'neo-Ricardian' exercise has not found much favour. It seems to abandon any *quantitative* aspect to value theory, leaving simply a *qualitative* emphasis on understanding exchange as an exchange of labours (see Hilferding's reply in Böhm-Bawerk [1896]; Sweezy, 1942; Rubin, 1928).

The conceptual problems in formalizing value theory hardly differentiate it from other theoretical constructs. The most serious attack on it has come from those claiming that it is *redundant*, that it adds nothing to the conceptualization of equilibrium prices and profits based on physical quantities. This criticism goes back at least to Joan Robinson (1942), was formalized by Samuelson (1971) and re-emphasized by Steedman (1977). Following Sraffa (1960), it is argued that prices and profits can be derived directly from knowledge of the real wage and the requirements of labour and means of production required to produce commodities, and that values can only be derived from the same data. Thus it is said that it is unnecessary to go via values to reach profits (even assuming values can be unambiguously defined). This attack has confronted Marxists with the question – what precisely is it that values are designed to do?

The justifications for using labour as the central conceptual category, and thus analysing exchange and exploitation in terms of embodied labour time, have ranged from rather abstract statements of the fundamental role played by labour in Marx's whole theory of society (Shaikh, 1981), to the claim that working with values focuses the analysis on labour's part in production (Dobb, 1937). Sen (1978) points out that we naturally focus on the human contribution to production just as we focus on an artist's part in a sculpture. Indeed, critics of value theory never stop to question why they are perfectly happy to regard labour productivity as a vital concern (over time, across countries, etc.) but object to the concept of value (which is just the inverse of labour productivity). Certainly for those who accept the central role of the economic surplus produced by the working class in the development of society, and the relations on the factory floor as the key to the production of this surplus, then analysis in terms of labour time is clear and simple. If we want a vivid and forceful way of analysing the relation between capital and labour then labour time seems the obvious category to use. After all what capitalists make workers do is *work*.

ACCUMULATION AND CRISES. Marx's *Capital* was aimed not only at uncovering the basis of capitalist exploitation but above all at revealing capitalism's 'laws of motion'. Marx argued that competition between capitalists was fought out by their investing in new, more efficient techniques of production and that the economies of scale which this brought acted as a pressure forcing individual capitalists to accumulate (a very different conception from the neoclassical idea of accumulation as trading off present for future consumption – see Marglin, 1984). The outcome of this process was the increased concentration of industry (termed centralization by Marx) which was further accelerated by the development of the credit system. Many Marxist writers, from Hilferding (1910) to postwar Marxists (Mandel, 1962) have documented this trend, with the conclusion being drawn on occasions that the extent of monopolization was actually destroying the pressure to accumulate (Baran and Sweezy, 1966). This seemed to be contradicted, however, by the great boom of the 1950s and 1960s in Europe and Japan, and the spread of international competition which it brought.

For Marx the impact of accumulation, both on the working class and on profits, was dominated by its presumed labour-saving form. Marx argued that higher productivity required an increased volume of constant capital per worker (what later economists have called the capital–labour ratio). While this is not necessarily the case, since new techniques may economize on constant capital, subsequent experience has entirely vindicated Marx's view. What has been more controversial are the implications of this for employment, wages and the rate of profit.

A rising mass of constant capital per worker implies that employment grows more slowly than the capital stock. But whether or not this leads to a rising or falling *reserve army of labour* depends on the strength of accumulation, the rate at which technical progress is labour saving and the growth of the labour force. In the advanced countries at least, the trend has indeed been for the capitalist sector to overcome pre-capitalist sectors like peasant agriculture, but for those 'set free' to be absorbed into wage labour. It is important here to distinguish the impact of the trend of accumulation on employment (at full utilization of capacity), from periods of 'cyclical' unemployment, which may be of extended duration of course, resulting from the under-utilization of capacity during crises. The mass unemployment of the 1970s and 1980s in Europe, for example, is obviously due mainly if not wholly to the crisis of accumulation (that is, the lack of it), rather than to the form accumulation has been taking.

Despite periodic bouts of unemployment there has been a tendency for real wages to grow in line with labour productivity in the advanced countries, that is, for the profit share to be roughly constant over time or even to decline. Despite measurement complications concerning the treatment of self-employment, this suggests that Marx's rate of exploitation has not shown the tendency to increase which he expected would be ensured by the reserve army of labour. Some authors (Gillman, 1957, for example) have sought to verify a rising rate of exploitation by reference to Marx's concept of unproductive labour (supervisory staff, bank employees, etc.). If these workers are regarded as being paid out of surplus value, rather than as constituting a cost of production which reduces surplus value, and if their relative importance in the labour force has been rising (which it has), then a rising rate of exploitation is consistent with a rising share of wages in national income. But to argue that the surplus value available to the capitalists for accumulation has declined because, given the growth of productivity of productive workers, there has been a growth in the proportion of unproductive workers, does not seem to add much to the simpler idea that the growth of productivity of all workers has been insufficiently fast relative to real wages.

The rising trend of real wages has raised the issue as to whether Marx's concept of the value of labour power, dependent on the time required to produce the 'necessaries', is still valid. The usual answer has been for Marxists to stress the 'moral and historical' element in the value of labour power as defined by Marx. Periods of strong demand for labour and the development of trade unions have allowed a widening of workers' 'needs', including the provision of more extensive state services. The difficulties that employers have found in cutting real wages, and governments in seriously eroding the welfare services despite the mass unemployment in the 1970s and 1980s, have added conviction to the idea that the current standard of living is, socially, *necessary* (Rowthorn, 1980, ch. 7).

Marx argued that the trend towards a rising organic composition would allow the rate of exploitation to be increased, but would nevertheless lead to a falling *rate* of profit on total capital employed as outlays on constant capital would grow. Despite the fact that Marx regarded this Law of the Tendency of the Rate of Profit to Fall as the 'most important law of political economy' it played only rather a background role in the classic works of Marxism (Luxemburg, 1913; Hilferding, 1910). With the revival of interest in Marxist economics in the late 1960s it received prominence in the works of writers such as Mandel (1975). The main controversy has surrounded whether or not there is a fundamental tendency for the value of constant capital per worker to rise as the Law requires. Marx himself recognized that this was the outcome of a two-sided process. The increased mass of constant capital per worker tended to drag the value of capital up. On the other hand the productivity growth which was part and parcel of the process tended to reduce the value of constant capital per worker. Whether the value of constant capital per worker rises or falls depends on whether productivity grows slower or faster than the increased mass of capital per worker. Marx himself gave no convincing reasons why productivity growth should be the slower of the two, and it has long been argued that there is no such reason (Robinson, 1942; Sweezy, 1942; van Parijs, 1980). Attempts to argue that in some sense the rise in the mass of constant capital per worker is more fundamental and that there is a Law of the Tendency of the Rate of Profit to Fall even if it was manifested in an upward trend in the profit rate (Fine and Harris, 1978) have not been found convincing. Marxists who have attempted to provide empirical evidence in support of the Law have typically confused the mass of constant capital with its value: the capital–output ratio, which is the price correlate of the value of capital per worker, has not shown an upward trend.

If this objection makes a falling profit trend contingent on the strength of productivity growth (an empirical matter), the second line of objection (originated by Okishio, 1961) argues in fact that the techniques willingly introduced by capitalists will never, in and of themselves, result in a lower profit rate for the capitalist class. It can be shown that new techniques which raise the profit rate for the innovating capitalist will also imply, contrary to Marx's belief, a cost saving and thus a higher profit rate for the capitalist class. For the average profit rate to fall with the introduction of new techniques, therefore, there must have been, in addition, some increase in real wages. All this is not to say that the value of constant capital may not rise in some periods, and that it may not be associated with a falling profit rate (both were true of many countries in the early 1970s), but only that there must also be rising wages (as was also the case). It has been argued by Shaikh (1978) that oligopolists might not maximize the profit rate; but even if this were so it could not establish any necessity for the profit rate to fall.

Discussion of the Law of the Tendency of the Rate of Profit to Fall has emphasized the importance of the course of real wages for the development of capitalism. The two main schools of Marxist crisis theory have indeed placed real wages at the centre, but in very different ways. Underconsumptionist theorists (Luxemburg in the classic period, Sweezy amongst later writers) have argued that insufficient growth in real wages depresses the incentive to invest by restricting the market for consumer goods. As Tugan-Baranovsky (summarized by Sweezy, 1942) pointed out with the help of Marx's reproduction schemes, it is not possible to prove the *necessity* of a crisis of underconsumptionism from a rising rate of surplus value. As Marx explained, whether or not surplus value was realized depends entirely on capitalists' spending decisions (on investment and consumption). The capitalists could realize a growing share of surplus value provided they were prepared to invest more and more in the capital goods sector (Department I of Marx's reproduction schemes), even though this investment was destined just to produce more capital goods (Bukharin, 1924). So crises of underconsumption, which would arise when capitalists failed to increase their investment in line with the potential surplus value, rely on the behavioural assumption that capitalists will actually not keep up their investment spending. The most influential postwar analysis along these lines, Baran and Sweezy's *Monopoly Capital* (1966, which acknowledges its theoretical debt to Steindl, 1952), saw the growing monopolization of US capitalism enhancing the tendency for the share of surplus value to rise, while at the same time relaxing the pressure to invest.

It was something of an irony that just at the time that *Monopoly Capital* was written, Europe and Japan were enjoying a phenomenal boom. Many Marxist economists in these countries favoured an overaccumulation theory of crisis (Glyn and Sutcliffe, 1972; Rowthorn, 1980, chs 4–6; Itoh, 1980). The strength of the boom eroded the reserve army of labour and caused tight labour markets, rising wages and thus falling profits, inflation and a recession (Armstrong, Glyn and Harrison, 1984). Also emphasized by these theories has been the role of stronger trade unions in pressing for higher state welfare spending and the difficulties that full employment brought for employers attempting to reorganize production to increase productivity (Bowles, Gordon and Weisskopf, 1983).

Why these difficulties should lead to a crisis, rather than simply slower growth, again depends on the central question of capitalists' investment behaviour. Precisely why and when a fall in profits leads to a precipitate decline in investment is notoriously difficult to model. Japanese Marxists (Itoh, 1980) have made an important contribution by emphasizing the importance of the credit system in both prolonging a boom and initiating a collapse. Kalecki, who immortalized

Marx's insight in the dictum 'workers spend what they get, capitalists get what they spend', wrote near the end of his life that the determination of investment 'remains the great *pièce de résistance* of economics' (1971, p. 165).

The recuperative role of crises in restoring the conditions for renewed accumulation has always been stressed by Marxists. It is more plausible in the case of crises due to overaccumulation (where the problem is rising wages) than for underconsumption crises (where wages have been rising too slowly). Indeed, Keynesian policies of demand expansion seem designed to meet the latter, and political difficulties have to be put forward as blocking such an obvious solution (Baran and Sweezy, 1966). In crises of overaccumulation Keynesian policies are more likely to be used in reverse, in order to speed up the impact of unemployment in reducing labour's bargaining position over wages and productivity. Some French Marxists, known as the 'Regulation School' have recently emphasized the necessity for the whole pattern of institutions, state policies, technologies, etc. to be reformed if a major structural crisis is to be overcome (Aglietta, 1979; Boyer, 1979; de Vroey, 1984). Whether the microchip, decentralization of production, internationalization of production and capital markets, Japanese-style industrial relations, more freedom for market forces and so forth provide a new 'way out' for capitalism in the 1990s is currently under intense discussion.

If this review of Marxist economics has concentrated on debates about, revisions to and extensions of Marx's own ideas it is to emphasize that the days of Stalinist orthodoxy and dogmatic repetition of the texts are gone. Marxist economics is again making a forceful and imaginative contribution to the analysis of contemporary society.

BIBLIOGRAPHY

Aglietta, M. 1979. *A Theory of Capitalist Regulation*. London: New Left Books.
Armstrong, P., Glyn, A. and Harrison, J. 1984. *Capitalism Since World War II*. London: Fontana.
Baran, P. and Sweezy, P. 1966. *Monopoly Capital*. New York: Monthly Review Press.
Böhm-Bawerk, E. 1896. *Karl Marx and the Close of his System*. Ed. P. Sweezy, New York: Kelly, 1948. (First published in German.)
Bortkiewicz, L. von. 1906. On the correction of Marx's fundamental theoretical construction in the third volume of Capital. In Böhm-Bawerk (1948). (First published in German.)
Bowles, S. 1985. The production process in a competitive economy. *American Economic Review* 75(2), March, 16–36.
Bowles, S., Gordon, D. and Weisskopf, T. 1983. *Beyond the Wasteland*. New York: Anchor Press.
Boyer, M. 1979. Wage information in historical perspective: the French experience. *Cambridge Journal of Economics* 3(2), June, 99–118.
Braverman, H. 1972. *Labor and Monopoly Capital*. New York: Monthly Review Press.
Bukharin, N. 1924. *Imperialism and the Accumulation of Capital*. Ed. K. Tarbuck, London: Allen Lane, 1972. (First published in German.)
Dobb, M. 1937. *Political Economy and Capitalism*. London: Routledge & Kegan Paul.
Edwards, R. 1979. *Contested Terrain*. London: Heinemann.
Fine, B. and Harris, L. 1978. *Rereading Capital*. London: Macmillan.
Gillman, J. 1957. *The Falling Rate of Profit*. London: Dobson.

Glyn, A. and Sutcliffe, B. 1972. *British Capitalism, Workers and the Profit Squeeze.* Harmondsworth: Penguin.

Gough, I. 1979. *The Political Economy of the Welfare State.* London: Macmillan.

Hilferding, R. 1910. *Finance Capital.* London: Routledge & Kegan Paul, 1981. (First published in German.)

Himmelweit, S. and Mohun, S. 1981. Real abstractions and anomalous assumptions. In *The Value Controversy*, ed. I. Steedman et al., London: Verso.

Itoh, M. 1980. *Value and Crisis.* London: Pluto Press.

Kalecki, M. 1971. *Selected Essays on the Dynamics of the Capitalist Economies.* Cambridge: Cambridge University Press.

King, J. 1982. Value and exploitation: some recent debates. In *Classical and Marxian Political Economy*, ed. I. Bradley and J. Howard, London: Macmillan.

Luxemburg, R. 1913. *The Accumulation of Capital.* London: Routledge & Kegan Paul, 1951. (First published in German.)

Mandel, E. 1962. *Marxist Economic Theory.* London: Merlin.

Mandel, E. 1975. *Late Capitalism.* London: New Left Books.

Marglin, S. 1984. *Growth, Distribution and Prices.* Cambridge, Mass.: Harvard University Press.

Medio, A. 1972. Profits and surplus value. In *A Critique of Economic Theory*, ed. E. Hunt and J. Schwartz, Harmondsworth: Penguin.

Morishima, M. 1973. *Marx's Economics.* Cambridge: Cambridge University Press.

O'Connor, J. 1973. *The Fiscal Crisis of The State.* New York: St Martin's Press.

Okishio, N. 1961. Technical change and the rate of profit. *Kobe University Economic Review* 7, 85–99.

Parijs, P. van. 1980. The falling-rate of profit theory of crisis. *Review of Radical Political Economics* 12(1), Spring, 1–16.

Robinson, J. 1942. *An Essay on Marxian Economics.* London: Macmillan.

Rosdolsky, R. 1968. *The Making of Marx's Capital.* London: Pluto Press, 1977. (First published in German.)

Rowthorn, R. 1980. *Capitalism, Conflict and Inflation.* London: Lawrence & Wishart.

Rubin, I. 1928. *Essays on Marx's Theory of Value.* Detroit: Black & Red, 1972. (First published in Russian.)

Samuelson, P. 1971. Understanding the Marxian notion of exploitation. *Journal of Economic Literature* 9, June, 399–431.

Sen, A. 1978. On the labour theory of value. *Cambridge Journal of Economics*, June, 175–80.

Seton, F. 1957. The transformation problem. *Review of Economic Studies* 24, June, 149–60.

Shaikh, A. 1978. Political economy and capitalism. *Cambridge Journal of Economics* 2(2), June, 232–51.

Shaikh, A. 1981. The poverty of algebra. In *The Value Controversy*, ed. I. Steedman et al., London: Verso.

Sraffa, P. 1960. *Production of Commodities by Means of Commodities.* Cambridge: Cambridge University Press.

Steedman, I. 1977. *Marx After Sraffa.* London: New Left Books.

Steindl, J. 1952. *Maturity and Stagnation in American Capitalism.* Oxford: Blackwell.

Sweezy, P. 1942. *The Theory of Capitalist Development.* New York: Monthly Review Press.

Vroey, M. de. 1984. A regulation approach interpretation of the contemporary crisis. *Capital and Class* 23, Summer, 45–66.

Willman, P. and Winch, G. 1985. *Innovation and Management Control.* Cambridge: Cambridge University Press.

Woolf, E. 1979. The rate of surplus value, the organic composition of capital and the general rate of profit in the US economy 1947–67. *American Economic Review* 69(3), June, 329–41.

Mercantilism

WILLIAM R. ALLEN

As conventionally pictured, mercantilism was a long chapter of simple coherence in the history of European economic thought and national economic policy, extending from roughly 1500 to 1800. With diverse expositors and practitioners scattered far over space as well as time, it was intended to promote production and commerce of private entrepreneurs who benefited from and contributed to the consolidation, prosperity and power of nation-states, with foreign trade being the most strategic variable.

The mercantilist authors – typically in business and the professions in England, some of them government officials on the continent – were pamphleteering and proselytizing men of affairs, more characteristically advocates of self-promoting policies than dispassionate scholars, who shared certain perspectives and biases and concerns of economic purpose and practice. In their pragmatic, gain-seeking worldliness, they represent a sharp break with the preceding scholastic scholars of the medieval period; in their heavy reliance on an alliance between the business community and the regulating and subsidizing state, they differ greatly from the individualistic vision and thrust of the classical analysts who followed.

This conventional picture may be judged more right than wrong. But it provides problems to modern commentators. Indeed, it has presented so many problems to commentators for over two centuries that some now deny that the label of 'mercantilism' can be usefully employed in intellectual or economic history. If there was an identifiable chapter of mercantilism, it certainly was well scattered, but it was hardly one of simple coherence. And however explicable it may be deemed by some in its historical context, it provided only very modest advancement of economic theory.

I. Confronted by so many writers in so many places over so long a time, survey and assessment are facilitated by taking the English literature of the 17th century as most representative. England, along with France, was one of the two dominant nations of the time; it provided the period's major economic writing; and it was the central base of the succeeding classical thought, including the development

440

particularly of international trade theory. The remarkable 17th century – remarkable in the shaping of the dynastic national state and in the flourishing of political thought as well as of science and of art – is an appropriate focus. The previous century was still heavily touched by medievalism; the following century provided firm foundations of modern economics.

Still, do we have a subject? It appears 'beyond doubt' to Eli Heckscher (Coleman, 1969, p. 33) that 'it is admissible to speak of mercantilism as a policy and as a theory governed by an inner harmony'. D.C. Coleman (1969, p. 117) agrees partially with respect to theory but not at all with respect to policy – and particular policy-making was much more the mercantilistic concern than general theory-making. And A.V. Judges discards mercantilism as a historical category of 'coherent doctrine': lacking in actual history both 'creed' and 'priesthood', it is 'an imaginary system conceived by economists for purposes of theoretical exposition and mishandled by historians in the service of their political ideals' (Coleman, 1969, pp. 35, 58–9).

At any rate, the notion of a well-defined era of 'mercantilism' has been long, if not well, employed. And most of those who have used it 'for purposes of theoretical exposition' have included the following elements pertaining to the historical role, the theoretical tenets and the policy strategy of mercantilism.

The precepts and proposals of mercantilism were the economic component of state-building, providing much of the rationale and suggesting some of the procedures of national unification, seen especially in England, France and Spain. Men of trade sought the protection and the order essential for expansion of their activity, as well as monopolistic subsidization of their ventures from the crown. Men of government sought the material means of acquiring and consolidating domestic administrative authority and military strength for foreign excursions and colonization. Unification was to be achieved – but not easily or quickly – in the face of both the universalism of medieval thought and emotion (the Roman Catholic Church and the Holy Roman Empire) and the medieval physical particularism (small, largely self-sufficient political and economic units). Unification was a prerequisite both of power abroad and of wealth at home, with the wealth to accrue more to the throne and to the mercantile elite than to the populace at large.

Economic well-being and betterment were not defined in terms of or measured by the satisfying of revealed community consumption preferences. Nor was production commonly deemed highly important during the 17th century except as it led to an export surplus and compensatory inflow of precious metals. But accumulated wealth was vital to, as well as the result of, power. And wealth was intimately associated with specie. The better mercantilist writers in their better moments did not make wealth and specie synonymous. Wealth and specie were closely associated, however, and rising accumulation of gold and silver was taken as reflection of, even if it did not literally constitute, increasing wealth. More bullion could provide a convenient state reserve in an age prior to central banking and efficient taxation – 'money is the sinews of war' – and a form of private saving in an age which lauded thrift. At the same time, excessive hoarding of money by either government or citizens would depress prices and curtail employment. With later writers, the emphasis was increasingly on the circulation of money rather than simply on the held stock of money. More bullion and its expenditure would alleviate the commonly perceived 'scarcity of money' and serve to 'quicken trade'. A persistently rising and vigorously circulating money stock somehow would conduce prosperity, facilitate exchange and encourage employment. The mercantilists recognized that inflow of bullion would reflect an export balance of goods and services – there was no thought or hope that the export trade balance would be financed with capital outflow – and it seemed apparent that for a nation, as for an individual or a firm, prosperity stems from spending (importing) less than income (exporting). Writers were increasingly content to deal with a country's global trade balance, not requiring an export balance in each bilateral exchange relationship.

Nothing else could be really quite as good as gold. But England had no gold mines, and piracy on the Spanish Main by such 16th-century heroes as John Hawkins, Francis Drake and Walter Raleigh was an uncertain source of specie – thus the critical role of an ongoing export ('favourable') balance of goods and services in providing for an indefinite accumulation of bullion. But the gains from trade and the gain of power – each reflected in import of specie – were considered one-sided: what one nation acquired, the rest of the world must lose. The analysis of mutually advantageous exchange, based on the principle of comparative advantage, was not adequately formulated until the early 19th century. But at least there was the possibility of unilateral gain in foreign trade, the gain manifested in specie inflow, whereas domestic exchange did not directly yield national benefit, for, again, the profit of one party is counterbalanced by the loss of another.

The particular policy tactics of the mercantilists stemmed readily from their theoretical tenets. A desired export balance called for encouraging most exports (except machinery which could aid commercial competitors and armaments which could strengthen military opponents) and discouraging most imports (except raw materials and exotic items for re-export). Shipping and port services, as well as goods, were candidates for sale to foreigners. A strong navy was required, along with much commercial tonnage, merchant ships often being convertible into navy vessels. In order to have much to export and little reason to import, there must be much produced, with minimal domestic consumption. Increasing population was favoured as a source of labour and military manpower and a basis of large aggregate output. Wages, it was generally felt, where to be kept low to minimize production costs, avoid excessive consumption and spur greater effort by workers. The interest rate, too, should be low for small costs of production and of inventories, and low interest rates were associated with large stocks of money as well as with saving, although some advocated legally-specified interest rate ceilings. Land was to be utilized fully and well; mineral resources were to be exploited; fishing grounds were to be secured. The mercantilists shared some of the medieval distrust of monopoly, and in England they rarely advocated operations directly by the state; still, favoured organizations were paternalistically and variously subsidized at home and granted exclusive privileges in foreign endeavours. Colonies were potentially a source of demand for mother-country exports, tax revenues, military bases, raw materials, unusual products and gold; they were also a source of manpower or an outlet for excessive or otherwise unattractive people, depending on the perceived population problem.

II. Such a review, even though brief and general, does not completely hide all the inner strains and seeming contradictions within mercantilist thought. But it imposes a more systematic scheme than the original literature warrants, and it camouflages controversies and individual contributions.

Selling – both at home and abroad – was something of a mercantilistic end in itself. In a domestic context, vigorous commerce was not sought for the purpose of meeting the preferences of the citizenry in general, but much buying and selling would help to dispose of goods and to raise prices, both results possibly contributing indirectly to national wealth. Internationally, 'fear of goods' was intimately associated with a fondness of specie. Commodity imports were commonly rationalized only as a means of promoting exports – some relationship between exports and imports was acknowledged – but specie was a much superior means of financing exports.

The desire to attract specie had as its counterpart a dread of losing it, and in the mid-17th century there were prohibitions of specie export. Such prohibitions, a continuation of medieval policy, were gradually relaxed and then abandoned, partly because of recognized difficulties in enforcement. In addition, there developed, with continuing debate, the feeling or attitude – there was no rigorous conceptualizing – that some occasional foreign expenditure of specie would so facilitate commercial operations as ultimately to bring in a greater quantity. In particular, operations of government-sanctioned trading companies called for such overseas outlays. Thomas Mun provided the metaphor of the husbandman who immediately appears mad in casting seed-corn on the ground, but who at harvest proves the wisdom of his foresighted investment. The title of Mun's major book (written about 1628, published 1664), *England's Treasure by Forraign Trade, or the Ballance of our Forraign Trade Is the Rule of our Treasure*, indicates the appropriate causal emphasis: the balance of trade, not restrictions on specie flows or other foreign-exchange market manipulations, will determine the nation's treasure. Josiah Child later went a major step further than Mun: although he favoured a large and growing money stock and the export trade balance which provided it and the high and rising prices which resulted from it, he opposed government impediments to specie export which businessmen find convenient even if a particular expenditure offered no definite promise of an eventual greater reflux.

Not only was there some bowing to indirect and long-term considerations with respect to the ultimate objective of specie accumulation, but there can be seen some fumblings for a notion of an adjustment mechanism. Nothing was more stressed by mercantilist writers than the relations between the foreign-trade balance and the counter international flow of specie. Before the end of the 17th century, there was common recognition of some relation between changes in the amount of money and corresponding changes in prices. And there was some discernment of a relation between commodity prices and quantities of commodities bought, with even a nod to an idea of elasticity of demand. Further, some modern commentators purport to find a considerable number of 17th-century writers – Antonio Serra in Italy as well as Edward Misselden, Gerard de Malynes, Mun, Dudley North and John Locke in England – who more or less consciously sought to identify an automatic market mechanism of international adjustment. Yet the implications of changes in the money stock of different nations, and of resulting opposite changes in the prices of specie-gaining and specie-losing countries, for international demands and commerce, leading to a correction of trade imbalances and cessation of gold movements, were not grasped, exposited and appreciated until well into the 18th century. A systematic, self-contained model of price-induced equilibration of the trade balance was a product which finally found expression in a 1752 essay by David Hume.

If not all gold outflow was necessarily bad, and if net inflow might not persist forever, might the very wish for an indefinitely prolonged increase in gold accumulation be suspect? It would not be analytically easy to reconcile a permanent gold inflow with a mechanism of adjustment which would terminate the flow. And even some of the supposed early architects of the adjustment model did desire continued specie importation. Malynes, for example, who, it has been said in our time (Schumpeter, 1954, p. 365), 'saw ... nearly the whole' of the automatic mechanism, found that more money at home than in neighbouring nations means prices higher domestically than those abroad; and generally, but not invariably, he applauded higher prices, for they seemed to be associated with great demand, flourishing exchange and large business receipts, as well as favourable terms of international trade.

The relatively sophisticated Locke and Charles Davenant near the end of the 17th century seemed as enamoured of a persistent export balance of goods and concomitant specie inflow as were the relatively primitive Malynes and Mun in the first part of the century. Such an interest, if not preoccupation, had characterized mercantilistic literature since the 14th century. But the persisting doctrine of the desirability of a persistent export balance was not provided with a clear analytic base. If beneficial foreign trade is associated with a merchandise export balance, just what is the connection between the gains and the balance? Modern commentators have tried to infer what the original writings leave uncertain. Does the trade balance *measure* the gain from trade, or does the balance *constitute* the gain, or is the balance the sole *source* of the gain? J.A. Schumpeter explicitly denies that the mercantilists meant any of the three propositions – although he does not provide an alternative rationale he finds consistent with the literature; Jacob Viner finds appreciable merit in all those interpretations (Schumpeter, 1954, p. 357; Viner, 1937, pp. 16–17).

Perhaps the basic thrust of interpretation should be reversed. Instead of supposing that a growing population of low-paid, fully and effectively employed and assiduous labourers and subsidized producers and merchants were intended finally to generate an export trade balance and net specie inflow, maybe mercantilism makes more sense as a strategy using foreign trade as a device to keep the domestic economy stimulated. In this alternative conception of causal relations, national prosperity and strength remain the ultimate goal, but the export balance and its accompanying increase in the money stock was the critical *means*, with full employment being the major operational *end*. Especially among later writers, extending far into the 18th century, there is much said about employment. And there was suggestion of a modified balance of trade concept, in which the amounts to be compared are not so much the money values of goods and services exported and imported as the labour inputs embodied in those goods and services. Thus the objective was an export balance of domestic labour or employment, and exports were desired because of their direct effect on employment rather than because of their indirect stimulative effect through an increase in money. Some modern students who try to fit a systematic scheme to the welter of literature (e.g. W.D. Grampp, 1965, vol. 1, part 2) find that most of the policy prescriptions can be explained most simply and completely by assuming that full employment was the major mercantilistic goal.

The protectionist policies advocated by mercantilist authors are conspicuously consistent with emphasis on the 'balance of employment' argument, and protectionism was increasingly promoted with little or no reference to specie inflow and money expansion. Still, many mercantilists remained impressed with the importance of vigorous monetary circulation, and few embraced paper money as an adequate substitute for metallic money. If the amount of money remained important and if money meant specie, then concern with the foreign-trade balance could not be long or much suppressed.

Finding the final focus of economic policy in employment and production might help to resolve the complication of reconciling a 'favourable' trade balance with an ongoing increase in the money stock. So long as the balance persisted, specie would flow in, to be sure. But if increasing money results in increasing prices, and if quantities demanded are partial functions of prices, then domestic inflation from specie inflow, along with deflation abroad, would discourage commodity exports and stimulate imports, thereby correcting the trade balance. We have suggested that many mercantilists did relate changes in money directly to changes in prices; a few did not, and some did or did not, depending on what was convenient in a particular context. But even when the money–price relationship was acknowledged, it was only rarely related to issues of foreign trade; and when it was linked to foreign trade, it was commonly done so only to note the improvement in the terms of trade as a result of higher export prices. While high rising prices were not invariably sought, there should be sufficient money to avoid deflation, for falling prices were deemed a hindrance to economic activity and development.

Some modern commentators (e.g. Mark Blaug, 1985, p. 18) have suggested an escape from the adjustment conundrum. When the mercantilists sought a greater money supply and expenditure, perhaps they envisaged – with unrealistic presumptions of great factor mobility and general economic adaptability – not a higher price level, but a greater volume of transactions: in terms of the 'equation of exchange' (which the mercantilists did not formulate), a larger money supply and velocity of money is balanced by a larger trade balance or national output, with the price level little affected. But to the considerable extent that they actually did adopt a notion of the quantity theory of money – note the forceful presentation, in particular, of Locke – not only would the desired export balance tend to be corrected, but, in the context of domestic activity, a greater price level (P) implies a lower level of output (Q) for a given national income (PQ). This is an awkward consideration if one strives for an inflationary policy, through an export balance or otherwise, as a means of stimulating output and employment.

Mercantilism was oriented towards geopolitics as well as economics, and notions of the balance of trade fitted comfortably with those of the balance of power. It was commonly presumed that world wealth, on the one hand, and world power, on the other, were essentially given quantities, so an absolute increase in either for a country meant also an increase relative to, and at the expense of, the rest of the world. Still, while both wealth and power were of critical interest to the mercantilists, perhaps one was deemed largely the means to an end consisting of the other. And if wealth and power are related as a means and end, the most common interpretation by modern historians subordinates wealth to the more ultimate objective of power. As on many other issues, the ancient literature is not definitive. But it appears most reasonable to describe the basic mercantilistic position as one of considering wealth and power each to be vital, with the two being mutually dependent and harmonious in the long run. As concluded by Child, 'Foreign trade produces riches, riches power, power preserves our trade and religion' (Coleman, 1969, p. 76).

III. The difficulties of historians dealing with the mercantilists are not confined to exposition of the content of the literature. There is also the problem of assessment. It has been suggested that it is misdirected and unfruitful to evaluate mercantilistic analysis and action by criteria of modern theory: we are not to denigrate old writings although we may sometimes praise them as imputed precursors of the best of later theory. Adverse evaluation supposedly is inappropriate because historical literature is to be accounted for by the peculiar 'circumstances of the time'. A seeming corollary is that, if the economics of an era is inexorably explained and made manifest by those circumstances, then it could not have taken other form and is thereby justified. This mystic view does not explain disagreements among writers living in the same milieu, or the uncertain correlation of popularity of view with sophistication of analysis, or how correct conclusions can be conveyed by circumstances to chosen writers when adequate explanatory analytics are not conveyed. Obviously, circumstances of the time can suggest subjects of concern; certainly, they do not provide techniques and contents of analysis.

Many modern commentators have held that the mercantilists were men of considerable competence: the writers of the 17th century are purported to be rational, pragmatic observers of prevalent and pressing problems. We may grant most of this. But it does not follow that these men of affairs were good economists. While their interests at one level were wide in scope – one cannot get much broader than concern for national power and wealth in an age of emerging nationalism – their orientation and intent were not in explicating an economic system or elucidating an economic mechanism. The complaint here against mercantilist literature is not primarily that it was incomplete and consisted of bits and pieces. Rather, these bits and pieces were so scattered in subject and context, so frequently directed in *ad hoc* manner to special topics for immediate tactical reasons, so polemical in form and purpose, so undigested and unsystematized, that they not only failed to constitute, but barely even directly contributed to a conception of economic order and process.

To be sure, one can now discern in (or construct from) the writings something of an orientation and a perspective, a range of general policy priorities and grand communal objectives, a more or less common set of topics to discuss and problems to be resolved, an assorted body of typical biases, some recurring themes which a generalizing hindsight may now codify and even label 'theory'. But all this hardly composes a mode or engine of analysis, a developed tool-box of analytic constructs and techniques, a generally recognized and accepted body of mutually consistent, systematically derived and empirically testable hypotheses. The mercantilist writers may have provided an inelegantly formulated philosophy of sorts – 'essentially a folk doctrine', Viner (1968, p. 436) calls it – and they provided a transition from medieval thought to physiocratic and classical theory by shifting the arena of economics discourse from ethical preconceptions and preoccupations with justice to self-serving presumption and material progress, and by replacing a relatively static and constricted view of society and its prospects with a more expansive and optimistic perspective. But in neither the large nor the small, in neither the abstract nor the concrete did they provide an explanation of societal arrangement and procedure – a vital omission not merely illustrated by, but largely consisting in, their failure to provide an adequate price theory. Especially on the Continent, economic organization and discipline and guidance, resolution of competing community interests and harmonization of individual and collective aims, required private enterprise to be constrained and directed more by government than by an open-market price system.

BIBLIOGRAPHY

Allen, W. 1968. The position of mercantilism and the early development of international trade theory. In *Events, Ideology and Economic Theory: The Determinants of Progress in the Development of Economic Analysis*, ed. R. Eagly, Detroit: Wayne State University.
Blaug, M. 1985. *Economic Theory in Retrospect*. 4th edn, Cambridge: Cambridge University Press.
Coleman, D. (ed.) 1969. *Revisions in Mercantilism*. London: Methuen.
Grampp, W. 1965. *Economic Liberalism*. 2 vols, New York: Random House.
Heckscher, E. 1931. *Mercantilism*. 2 vols, London: Allen & Unwin, 1934.
Schumpeter, J. 1954. *History of Economic Analysis*. New York: Oxford University Press.
Spengler, J. 1960. Mercantilist and physiocratic growth theory. In J. Spengler, *Theories of Economic Growth*, Glencoe, Ill.: Free Press.

Viner, J. 1937. *Studies in the Theory of International Trade.* New York: Harper.
Viner, J. 1968. Mercantilist thought. In *International Encyclopedia of the Social Sciences,* New York: Macmillan and Free Press.

Monetarism

PHILLIP CAGAN

Monetarism is the view that the quantity of money has a major influence on economic activity and the price level and that the objectives of monetary policy are best achieved by targeting the rate of growth of the money supply.

BACKGROUND AND INITIAL DEVELOPMENT. Monetarism is most closely associated with the writings of Milton Friedman who advocated control of the money supply as superior to Keynesian fiscal measures for stabilizing aggregate demand. Friedman (1948) had proposed that the government finance budget deficits by issuing new money and use budget surpluses to retire money. The resulting countercyclical variations in the money stock would stabilize the economy, provided that the government set its expenditures and tax rates to balance the budget at full employment. In *A Program for Monetary Stability* (1960), however, Friedman proposed that constant growth of the money stock, divorced from the government budget, would be simpler and equally effective for stabilizing the economy.

In their emphasis on the importance of money, these proposals followed a tradition of the Chicago School of economics. Preceding Friedman at the University of Chicago, Henry Simons (1936) had advocated control of the money stock to achieve a stable price level, and Lloyd Mints (1950) laid out a specific monetary programme for stabilizing an index of the price level. These writers rejected reliance on the gold standard because it had failed in practice to stabilize the price level or economic activity. Such views were not confined to the University of Chicago. In the 1930s James Angell of Columbia University (1933) advocated constant monetary growth, and in the post-World War II period Karl Brunner and Allan Meltzer were influential proponents of monetarism. The term 'monetarism' was first used by Brunner (1968). He and Meltzer founded the 'Shadow Open Market Committee' in the 1970s to publicize monetarist views on how the Federal Reserve should conduct monetary policy. Monetarism gradually gained adherents not only in the US but also in Britain (Laidler, 1978)

449

and other Western European countries, and subsequently around the world. The growing prominence of monetarism led to intense controversy among economists over the desirability of a policy of targeting monetary growth.

The roots of monetarism lie in the quantity theory of money which formed the basis of classical monetary economics from at least the 18th century. The quantity theory explains changes in nominal aggregate expenditures – reflecting changes in both the physical volume of output and the price level – in terms of changes in the money stock and in the velocity of circulation of money (the ratio of aggregate expenditures to the money stock). Over the long run, changes in velocity are usually smaller than those in the money stock and in part are a result of prior changes in the money stock, so that aggregate expenditures are determined largely by the latter. Moreover, over the long run growth in the physical volume of output is determined mainly by real (that is, nonmonetary) factors, so that monetary changes mainly influence the price level. The observed long-run association between money and prices confirms that inflation results from monetary overexpansion and can be prevented by proper control of the money supply. This is the basis for Friedman's oft-repeated statement that inflation is always and everywhere a monetary phenomenon.

The importance of monetary effects on price movements had been supported in empirical studies by classical and neo-classical economists such as Cairnes, Jevons and Cassel. But these studies suffered from limited data, and the widespread misinterpretation of monetary influences in the Great Depression of the 1930s fostered doubts about their importance in business cycles. As Keynesian theory revolutionized thinking in the late 1930s and 1940s, it offered an influential alternative to monetary interpretation of business cycles.

The first solid empirical support for a monetary interpretation of business cycles came in a series of studies of the US by Clark Warburton (e.g. 1946). Subsequently Friedman and Anna J. Schwartz compiled new data at the National Bureau of Economic Research in an extension of Warburton's work. In 1962 they demonstrated that fluctuations in monetary growth preceded peaks and troughs of all US business cycles since the Civil War. Their dates for significant steps to higher or lower rates of monetary growth showed a lead over corresponding business cycle turns on the average by about a half-year at peaks and by about a quarter-year at troughs, but the lags varied considerably. Other studies have found that monetary changes take one to two years or more to affect the price level.

In *A Monetary History of the United States, 1867–1960* (1963b) Friedman and Schwartz detailed the role of money in business cycles and argued in particular that severe business contractions like that of 1929–33 were directly attributable to unusually large monetary contractions. Their monetary studies were continued in *Monetary Statistics of the United States* (1970) and *Monetary Trends in the United States and the United Kingdom* (1982). A companion National Bureau study *Determinants and Effects of Changes in the Stock of Money* (1965) by Phillip Cagan presented evidence that the reverse effect of economic activity and prices on money did not account for the major part of their observed correlation, which therefore pointed to an important causal role of money.

The monetarist proposition that monetary changes are responsible for business cycles was widely contested, but by the end of the 1960s the view that monetary policy had important effects on aggregate activity was generally accepted. The obvious importance of monetary growth in the inflation of the 1970s restored money to the centre of macroeconomics.

MONETARISM VERSUS KEYNESIANISM. Monetarism and Keynesianism differ sharply in their research strategies and theories of aggregate expenditures. The Keynesian theory focuses on the determinants of the components of aggregate expenditures and assigns a minor role to money holdings. In monetarist theory money demand and supply are paramount in explaining aggregate expenditures.

To contrast the Keynesian and monetarist theories, Friedman and David Meiselman (1963) focused on the basic hypothesis about economic behaviour underlying each theory: for the Keynesian theory the consumption multiplier posits a stable relationship between consumption and income, and for the monetarist theory the velocity of circulation of money posits a stable demand function for money. Friedman and Meiselman tested the two theories empirically using US data for various periods by relating consumption expenditures in one regression to investment expenditures, assuming a constant consumption multiplier, and in a second regression to the money stock, assuming a constant velocity. They reported that the monetarist regression generally fitted the data much better. These dramatic results were not accepted by Keynesians, who argued that the Keynesian theory was not adequately represented by a one-equation regression and that econometric models of the entire economy, based on Keynesian theory, were superior to small-scale models based solely on monetary changes.

The alleged superiority of Keynesian models was contested by economists at the Federal Reserve Bank of St Louis (see Andersen and Jordan, 1968). They tested a 'St Louis equation' in which changes in nominal GNP depended on current and lagged changes in the money stock, current and lagged changes in government expenditures, and a constant term reflecting the trend in monetary velocity. When fitted to historical US data, the equation showed a strong permanent effect of money on GNP and a weak transitory (and in later work, nonexistent) effect of the fiscal variables, contradicting the Keynesian claim of the greater importance of fiscal than monetary policies. Although the St Louis equation was widely criticized on econometric issues, it was fairly accurate when first used in the late 1960s to forecast GNP, which influenced academic opinion and helped bring monetarism to the attention of the business world.

Although budget deficits and surpluses change interest rates and thus can affect the demand for money, monetarists believe that fiscal effects on aggregate demand are small because of the low interest elasticity of money demand. Government borrowing crowds out private borrowing and associated spending, and so deficits have little net effect on aggregate demand. The empirical results of the St Louis equation are taken as confirmation of weak transitory effects. The debate over the effectiveness of fiscal policy as a stabilization tool has produced a large literature.

In their analysis of the transmission of monetary changes through the economy, Brunner and Meltzer (1976) compare the effects of government issues of money and bonds. If the government finances increased expenditures in a way that raises the money supply, aggregate expenditures increase and nominal income rises. Moreover, the increased supply of money adds to the public's wealth, and greater wealth increases the demand for goods and services. This too raises nominal income. The rise in nominal income is at first mainly a rise in real income and later a rise in prices. They compare this result with one in which the government finances its increased expenditures by issuing bonds rather than money. Again wealth increases, and this raises aggregate expenditures. As long as the government issues either money or bonds to finance a deficit, nominal income must rise due to the increase in wealth. Brunner and Meltzer therefore agree with Keynesians that in principle a deficit financed by bonds as well as by new money is expansionary. However, they show that the empirical magnitudes of the economy are such that national income rises more from issuing a dollar of money than a dollar of bonds.

POLICY IMPLICATIONS OF MONETARISM. Because monetary effects have variable lags of one to several quarters or more, countercyclical monetary policy actions are difficult to time properly. Friedman as well as Brunner and Meltzer argued that an active monetary policy, in the absence of an impossibly ideal foresight, tends to exacerbate rather than smooth economic fluctuations. In their view a stable monetary growth rate would avoid monetary sources of economic disturbances, and could be set to produce an approximately constant price level over the long run. Remaining instabilities in economic activity would be minor and, in any event, were beyond the capabilities of policy to prevent. A commitment by the monetary authorities to stable monetary growth would also help deflect constant political pressures for short-run monetary stimulus and would remove the uncertainty for investors of the unexpected effects of discretionary monetary policies.

A constant monetary growth policy can be contrasted with central bank practices that impart pro-cyclical variations to the money supply. It is common for central banks to lend freely to banks at times of rising credit demand in order to avoid increases in interest rates. Although such interest-rate targeting helps to stabilize financial markets, the targeting often fails to allow rates to change sufficiently to counter fluctuations in credit demands. By preventing interest rates from rising when credit demands increase, for example, the policy leads to monetary expansion that generates higher expenditures and inflationary pressures. Such mistakes of interest-rate targeting were clearly demonstrated in the 1970s, when for some time increases in nominal interest rates did not match increases in the inflation rate, and the resulting low rates of interest in real terms (that is, adjusted for inflation) overstimulated investment and aggregate demand.

The same accommodation of market demands for bank credit results from the common practice of targeting the volume of borrowing from the central bank. Attempts to keep this volume at some designated level require the central bank to supply reserves through open market operations as an alternative to borrowing by banks when rising market credit demands tighten bank reserve positions, and to withdraw reserves in the opposite situation. The resulting procyclical behaviour of the money supply could be avoided by operations designed to maintain a constant growth rate of money.

Brunner and Meltzer (1964a) developed an analytic framework describing how monetary policy should aim at certain intermediate targets as a way of influencing aggregate expenditures. The intermediate targets are such variables as the money supply or interest rates. (Since the Federal Reserve does not control long-term interest rates or the money stock directly, it operates through instrumental variables, such as bank reserves or the federal funds rate, which it can affect directly.) The question of the appropriate intermediate targets of monetary policy soon became the most widely discussed issue in monetary policy.

In recognition of the deficiencies of interest-rate targeting, some countries turned during the 1970s to a modified monetary targeting in which annual growth ranges were announced and adhered to, though with frequent exceptions to allow for departures deemed appropriate because of disturbances from foreign trade and other sources. Major countries adopting some form of monetary targeting included the Federal Republic of Germany, Japan and Switzerland, all of which kept inflation rates low and thus advertised by example the anti-inflationary virtues of monetarism. In the US the Federal Reserve also began to set monetary target ranges during the 1970s but generally did not meet them and continued to target interest rates. In October 1979, when inflation was escalating sharply, the Federal Reserve announced a more stringent targeting procedure for reducing monetary growth. Although the average growth rate was reduced, the large short-run fluctuations in monetary growth were criticized by monetarists. In late 1982 the Federal Reserve relaxed its pursuit of monetary targets.

By the mid-1980s the US and numerous other countries were following a partial form of monetary targeting, in which relatively broad bands of annual growth rates are pursued but still subject to major departures when deemed appropriate. These policies are monetarist only in the sense that one or more monetary aggregates are an important indicator of policy objectives; they fall short of a firm commitment to a steady, let alone a non-inflationary, monetary growth rate.

MONETARIST THEORY. Monetarist theory of aggregate expenditures is based on a demand function for monetary assets that is claimed to be stable in the sense that successive residual errors are generally offsetting and do not accumulate. Given the present inconvertible-money systems, the stock of money is treated as under the control of the government. Although a distinction is made in theory between the determinants of household and business holdings of money, money demand is usually formulated for households and applied to the total. In these formulations the demand for money depends on the volume of transactions, the fractions of income and of wealth the public wishes to hold in the form of money balances, and the opportunity costs of holding money rather than other income-producing assets (that is, the difference between yields on money and on alternative assets). The alternative assets are viewed broadly to include not only financial instruments but also such physical assets as durable consumer goods, real property, and business plant and equipment. The public is presumed to respond to changes in the amount of money supplied by undertaking transactions to bring actual holdings of both money and other assets into equilibrium with desired holdings. As a result of substitutions between money and assets, starting with close substitutes, yields change on a broad range of assets, including consumer durables and capital goods, in widening ripples that affect borrowing, investment, consumption and production throughout the economy.

The end result is reflected in *aggregate* expenditures and the average level of prices. Independently of this monetary influence on aggregate expenditures and the price level, developments specific to particular sectors determine the distribution of expenditures among goods and services and relative prices. Thus monetarist theory rejects the common technique for forecasting aggregate output by adding up the forecasts for individual industries or the common practice of explaining changes in the price level in terms of price changes for particular goods and services.

Monetarists were early critics of the once influential Keynesian theory of a highly elastic demand for money with respect to short-run changes in the interest rate on liquid short-term assets, which in extreme form became a 'liquidity trap'. Empirical studies have found instead that interest rates on savings deposits and on short-term market securities have elasticities smaller even than the $-\frac{1}{2}$ implied by the simple Baumol–Tobin cash balance theory (Baumol, 1952; Tobin, 1956).

In empirical work a common form of the demand function for money includes one or two interest rates and real GNP as a proxy for real income. A gradual adjustment of actual to desired money balances is allowed for, implying that a full adjustment to a change in the stock is spread over several quarters. The lagged adjustment is subject to an alternative interpretation in which money demand reflects 'permanent' instead of current levels of income and interest rates. This interpretation de-emphasizes the volume of transactions as the major determinant of money demand in favour of the monetarist view of money as a capital asset yielding a stream of particular services and dependent on 'permanent' values of wealth, income and interest rates (in most studies captured empirically by a lagged adjustment). Treatment of the demand for money as similar to demands for other asset stocks is now standard practice.

The monetarist view of money as a capital asset suggests that the demand for it depends on a variety of characteristics, and not uniquely on its transactions services. The definition of money for policy purposes depends on two considerations: the ability of the monetary authorities to control its quantity, and the empirical stability of a function describing the demand for it. In their study of the US Friedman and Schwartz used an early version of M2, which included time and savings deposits at commercial banks, but they argued that minor changes in coverage would not greatly affect their findings. Subsequently the quantity of transactions balances M1 has become the most widely used definition of money for most countries, though many central banks claim to pay attention also to broader aggregates in conducting monetary policy.

In view of the wide range of assets into which the public may shift any excess money balances, the transmission of monetary changes through the economy to affect aggregate expenditures and other variables can follow a variety of paths. Monetarists doubt that these effects can be adequately captured by a detailed econometric model which prescribes a fixed transmission path. Instead they prefer models that dispense with detailed transmission paths and focus on a stable overall relationship between changes in money and in aggregate expenditures.

In both the monetarist model and large-scale econometric models, changes in the money stock are usually treated as exogenous (that is, as determined outside the model). It is clear that money approaches a strict exogeneity only in the long run. The US studies by Friedman and Schwartz and by Cagan established that the money supply not only influences economic activity but also is influenced by it in turn. This creates difficulties in testing empirically for the monetary effects on activity because allowance must be made for the feedback effect of economic activity on the money supply. Econometric models of the money supply can allow for feedback through the banking system (Brunner and Meltzer, 1964b). Under modern systems of inconvertible money, however, the feedback is dominated by monetary policies of the central banks, and attempts to model central bank behaviour have been less than satisfactory. Statistical tests of the exogeneity of the money supply using the Granger–Sims methodology have given mixed results. Although the concurrent mutual interaction between money and economic activity remains difficult to disentangle, the longer the lag in monetary effects the less likely that the feedback from activity to money can account for the observed association. In the St Louis equation, for example, while the correlation between changes in GNP and in money concurrently could largely reflect feedback from GNP to money, the correlation between changes in GNP and lagged changes in money are less likely to be dominated by such feedback.

OPPOSITION TO MONETARY TARGETING. While monetarism has refocused attention on money and monetary policy, there is widespread doubt that velocity is sufficiently stable to make targeting of monetary growth desirable. Movements in velocity when monetary growth is held constant produce expansionary and contractionary effects on the economy. In the US the trend of velocity was fairly stable and predictable from the early 1950s to the mid-1970s, but money demand equations based on that period showed large overpredictions after the mid-1970s (Judd and Scadding, 1982). Financial innovations providing new ways of making payments and close substitutes for holding money were changing the appropriate definition of money and the parameters of the demand function. In the US the gradual removal of ceilings on interest rates that banks could pay on deposits played a major role in these developments by increasing competition in banking. In Great Britain the removal of domestic controls over international financial transactions led to unusual movements in money holdings in 1979–80. Germany and Switzerland also found growing international capital inflows at certain times a disruptive influence on their monetary policies.

The 'monetary theory of the balance of payments' (Frenkel and Johnson, 1976) is an extension of monetarism to open economies where money supply and demand are interrelated amoung countries through international payments. A debated issue is whether individual countries, even under flexible exchange rates, can pursue largely independent monetary policies. The growing internationalization of capital markets is often cited as an argument against the monetarist presumption that velocity and the domestic money supply under flexible foreign exchange rates are largely independent of foreign influences.

Uncertainties over the proper definition of money and instability in the velocity of money as variously defined led to monetarist proposals to target the monetary liabilities of the central bank, that is, the 'monetary base' consisting of currency outstanding and bank reserves. The monetary base has the advantage of not being directly affected by market innovations and so of not needing redefinitions when innovations occur. Monetarists have proposed maintaining a constant growth rate of the base also because it would simplify – indirectly virtually eliminate – the monetary policy function of central banks and governments. Some of the European central banks have found targeting the monetary base preferable to targeting the money supply, though not without important discretionary departures from the target.

Yet financial market developments can also produce instabilities in the relationship between the monetary base and aggregate expenditures. Economists opposed to monetarism propose instead that stable growth of aggregate expenditures be the target of monetary policy and that it be pursued by making discretionary changes as deemed appropriate in the growth of the base. This contrasts sharply with the monetarist opposition to discretion in the conduct of policy.

THE PHILLIPS CURVE TRADE-OFF. The inflationary outcome of discretionary monetary policy since World War II can be explained in terms of the Phillips curve trade-off between inflation and unemployment. Along the Phillips curve lower and lower unemployment levels are associated with higher and higher inflation rates. Such a relationship, first found in historical British data, was shown to fit US data for the 1950s and 1960s and earlier. The trade-off depends on sticky wages and prices. As aggregate demand increases, the rise in wages and prices trails behind, inducing an expansion of output to absorb part of the increase in demand. US experience initially suggested that any desired position on the Phillips curve could be maintained by the management of aggregate demand. Thus a lower rate of unemployment could be achieved and maintained by tolerating an associated higher rate of inflation. Given this presumed trade-off, policy makers tended to favour lower unemployment at the cost of higher inflation.

In the 1970s, however, the Phillips curve shifted toward higher rates of inflation for given levels of unemployment. Friedman (1968) argued that the economy gravitates toward a 'natural rate of unemployment' which in the long run is largely independent of the inflation rate and cannot be changed by monetary policy. Wages and prices adjust sluggishly to unanticipated changes in aggregate demand but adjust more rapidly to maintained increases in demand and prices that are anticipated. Consequently, the only way to hold unemployment below the natural rate is to keep aggregate demand rising faster than the anticipated rate of inflation. Since the anticipated rate tends to follow the actual rate upward, this leads to faster and faster inflation. This 'acceleration principle' implies that there is no permanent trade-off between inflation and unemployment. The existence of a natural rate of unemployment also implies that price stability does not lead to higher unemployment in the long run.

Monetarist thought puts primary emphasis on the long-run consequences of policy actions and procedures. It rejects attempts to reduce short-run fluctuations in interest rates and economic activity as usually beyond the capabilities of monetary policy and as generally inimical to the otherwise achievable goals of long-run price stability and maximum economic growth. Monetarists believe that economic activity, apart from monetary disturbances, is inherently stable. Much of their disagreement with Keynesians can be traced to this issue.

RATIONAL EXPECTATIONS. One version of the rational expectations theory goes beyond monetarism by contending that there is little or no Phillips curve trade-off between inflation and unemployment even in the short run, since markets are allegedly able to anticipate any systematic countercyclical policy pursued to stabilize the economy. Only unanticipated departures from such stabilization policies affect output; all anticipated monetary changes are fully absorbed by price changes. Since unsystematic policies would have little countercyclical effectiveness or purpose, the best policy is to minimize uncertainty with a predictable monetary growth.

This theory shares the monetarist view that unpredictable fluctuations in monetary growth are an undesirable source of uncertainty with little benefit. But the two views disagree on the speed of price adjustments to predictable monetary measures and on the associated effects on economic activity. Monetarists do not claim that countercyclical policies have no real effects, but they are sceptical of our ability to use them effectively. It is the ill-timing of countercyclical policies as a result of variable lags in monetary effects that underlies the monetarist preference for constant monetary growth to avoid uncertainty and inflation bias.

INTEREST IN PRIVATE MONEY SUPPLIES. Monetarism is the fountainhead of a renewed interest in a subject neglected during the Keynesian revolution: the design of monetary systems that maintain price-level stability. Scepticism that price-level stability can be achieved even by a constant growth rate of money however defined or of the monetary base has led to proposals for a strict gold standard or for a monetary system in which money is supplied by the private

457

sector under competitive pressures to maintain a stable value. While monetarists are sympathetic to proposals to eliminate discretionary monetary policies, they view such alternative systems as impractical and believe that a nondiscretionary government policy of constant monetary growth is the best policy.

ASSOCIATED VIEWS OF THE MONETARIST SCHOOL. Monetarism is associated with various related attitudes toward government (see Mayer, 1978). Monetarism shares with *laissez faire* a belief in the long-run benefits of a competitive economic system and of limited government intervention in the economy. It opposes constraints on the free flow of credit and on movements of interest rates, such as the US ceilings on deposit interest rates (removed by the mid-1980s except on demand deposits). The disruptive potential of such ceilings became evident in the 1970s when financial innovations, partly undertaken to circumvent the ceilings, produced the transitional shifts in the traditional money-demand functions that created difficulties for the conduct of monetary policy. Government control over the quantity of money is viewed as a justifiable exception to *laissez faire*, however, in order to ensure the stability of the value of money.

BIBLIOGRAPHY

Andersen, L.C. and Jordon, J.L. 1968. Monetary and fiscal actions: a test of their relative importance in economic stabilization. *Federal Reserve Bank of St Louis Review* 50, November, 11–24.

Angell, J. 1933. Monetary control and general business stabilization. In *Economic Essays in Honour of Gustav Cassel*, London: Allen and Unwin.

Baumol, W.J. 1952. The transactions demand for cash: an inventory theoretic approach. *Quarterly Journal of Economics* 66, November, 545–56.

Brunner, K. 1968. The role of money and monetary policy. *Federal Reserve Bank of St Louis Review* 50, July, 8–24.

Brunner, K. and Meltzer, A. 1964a. The federal reserve's attachment to the free reserve concept. US Congress House Committee on Banking and Currency, Subcommittee on Domestic Finance, April.

Brunner, K. and Meltzer, A. 1964b. Some further investigations of demand and supply functions for money. *Journal of Finance* 19, May, 240–83.

Brunner, K. and Meltzer, A. 1976. An aggregative theory for a closed economy. In *Studies in Monetarism*, ed. J. Stein, Amsterdam: North-Holland.

Cagan, P. 1965. *Determinants and Effects of Changes in the Stock of Money 1875–1960*. New York: Columbia University Press for the National Bureau of Economic Research.

Frenkel, J.A. and Johnson, H.G. (eds) 1976. *The Monetary Approach to the Balance of Payments*. Toronto: University of Toronto Press.

Friedman, M. 1948. A monetary and fiscal framework for economic stability. *American Economic Review* 38, June, 256–64.

Friedman, M. 1960. *A Program for Monetary Stability*. New York: Fordham University Press.

Friedman, M. 1968. The role of monetary policy. *American Economic Review* 58, March, 1–17.

Friedman, M. and Meiselman, D. 1963. The relative stability of monetary velocity and the investment multiplier in the United States, 1897–1958. In Commission on Money and Credit, *Stabilization Policies*, Englewood Cliffs, NJ: Prentice-Hall.

Friedman, M. and Schwartz, A.J. 1963a. Money and business cycles. *Review of Economics and Statistics* 45(1), Part 2, Supplement, February, 32–64.

Friedman, M. and Schwartz, A. 1963b. *A Monetary History of the United States 1867–1960.* Princeton: Princeton University Press for the National Bureau of Economic Research.

Friedman, M. and Schwartz, A. 1970. *Monetary Statistics of the United States Estimates, Sources, Methods.* New York: National Bureau of Economic Research.

Friedman, M. and Schwartz, A. 1982. *Monetary Trends in the United States and the United Kingdom: Their Relation to Income, Prices and Interest Rates, 1867–1975.* Chicago: University of Chicago Press.

Judd, J.P. and Scadding, J.L. 1982. The search for a stable money demand function: a survey of the post-1973 literature. *Journal of Economic Literature* 20, September, 993–1023.

Laidler, D. 1978. Mayer on monetarism: comments from a British point of view. In *The Structure of Monetarism*, ed. T. Mayer, New York: W.W. Norton & Co.

Mayer, T. (ed.) 1978. *The Structure of Monetarism.* New York: W.W. Norton & Co.

Mints, L.W. 1950. *Monetary Policy for a Competitive Society.* New York: McGraw-Hill.

Simons, H. 1936. Rules versus authorities in monetary policy. *Journal of Political Economy* 44, February, 1–30.

Tobin, J. 1956. The interest elasticity of transactions demand for cash. *Review of Economics and Statistics* 38, August, 241–7.

Warburton, C. 1946. The misplaced emphasis in contemporary business-fluctuation theory. *Journal of Business*, October.

Monetary Policy

DAVID E. LINDSEY AND HENRY C. WALLICH

The term *monetary policy* refers to actions taken by central banks to affect monetary and other financial conditions in pursuit of the broader objectives of sustainable growth of real output, high employment and price stability. The average rate of growth of the stock of money in circulation has been viewed for centuries as the decisive determinant of overall price trends in the long run. General financial conditions associated with money creation or destruction, including changes in interest rates, have also been considered for some time an important factor of business cycles.

In the modern era the bulk of money in developed economies consists of bank deposits rather than gold and silver or government-issued currency and coin. Accordingly, governments have authorized central banks today to guide monetary developments with instruments that afford control over deposit creation and affect general financial conditions. Central banks' actions are deliberately aimed at influencing the performance of the nation's economy and are not based on ordinary business considerations, such as profit. The guide-posts and degree of discretion central banks should use in implementing monetary policy remain controversial issues, as are questions of the coordination of monetary policy with fiscal policy and with policies abroad.

THE INSTRUMENTS OF MONETARY POLICY. The instruments available to central banks vary from country to country, depending on institutional structure, political system and stage of development. In most developed capitalist economies, central banks basically use one or more of three main instruments to control deposit creation and affect financial conditions. *Required reserve ratios* set minimum fractions of certain deposit liabilities that commercial banks and, in some countries, thrift institutions must hold on reserve as assets in the form of cash in their vaults or deposits at the central bank. *The discount or official rate* is the interest charged by the central bank for providing reserve deposits directly to the banking system either through lending at a 'discount window' or through rediscounting or purchases of financial assets held by banks.

Open market operations are the third instrument. They involve either outright or temporary purchases and sales, typically of government securities, by the central bank with the market in general. The central bank pays for a securities purchase by crediting the reserve deposit account of the seller's bank, which in turn credits the deposit account of the seller. The central bank receives payment for a sale of securities by debiting the reserve account of the buyer's bank, which in turn debits the account of the buyer. In this way, open market operations that alter the amount of securities held in the central bank's asset portfolio have as their counterpart a change in the nonborrowed reserves held by banks, that is, the reserves that do not originate through bank discount borrowings. The amount of these nonborrowed reserves also is changed by variations in other, noncontrolled items on the asset or liability side of the central bank's balance sheet, such as gold holdings that were important historically or the deposits of domestic and foreign governments that can vary considerably today. Still, central banks routinely monitor these items and can prevent them from having sizable undesired impacts on nonborrowed reserves by engaging in offsetting open market operations.

The sum of borrowed and nonborrowed reserves constitutes the total reserves available to the banking system. The central bank can exercise considerable control over these two sources of total reserve availability. Open market operations, as noted, provide for fairly close control of overall non-borrowed reserves. The level of the discount rate as well as other administrative procedures affect the amount of borrowed reserves. Given the interest rates on other sources of short-term bank funding, a change in the discount rate, or commonly in some countries in other lending terms and conditions, alters the incentives banks face to borrow reserves at the discount window. A discount rate increase, for example, would tend to induce banks to reduce their discount borrowing and turn to other sources of funds. Banks would attempt to replace the funds by borrowing reserves from other banks, or by issuing large-sized certificates of deposit, or even by selling liquid financial assets in secondary markets. These actions would transmit upward tendencies to the interest rates on these instruments.

The control by central banks over the availability of total reserves to private banks gives central banks at one remove a decisive influence over the availability of deposits to the public as well as over conditions in the money market. Given total reserves, the required reserve ratio sets an upper limit on the amount of deposits that can be created. In practice, this upper limit is not reached because private banks desire to hold a portion of total reserves not as required reserves but in the form of a cushion of reserves in excess of requirements. But since excess reserves are assets that typically earn no interest, unlike loans and investments, banks seek to hold them to minimal levels.

If reserves represent the lever central banks can use to control deposits, then the required reserve ratio represents the fulcrum. A given increase in the supply of total reserves has an amplified effect on deposits. This is the case whether it is brought about through an open market operation that tends to raise non-borrowed reserves or a cut in the discount rate that tends to raise borrowed reserves. Banks initially receiving the new reserves could immediately attempt to loan their surfeit of reserves to other banks, thus depressing the interest rate on overnight loans of reserves between banks. The easing of conditions in this market puts downward pressure on rates of other money market instruments, such as Treasury bills or large certificates of deposit. This general reduction in short-term interest rates encourages the public to hold more transactions and savings deposits, because the incentive to economize on such money balances is reduced by the narrower opportunity cost (in terms of foregone interest income) of holding low-return deposits instead of other interest-bearing assets. Deposits will rise, boosting required reserves, until required reserves have risen enough to exhaust all unwanted excess reserves, which necessitates an expansion in deposits that is some multiple of the original increase of reserves.

Required reserve ratios also represent a potentially active alternate instrument for varying supplies of money and credit. Changes in these requirements alter the amount of bank deposits that a given quantity of total reserves can support. However, reserve requirement variations are a blunt instrument at best, as even relatively small changes in them produce large effects on the amount of deposits that can be supported by reserves outstanding. Accordingly, central banks infrequently resort to changes in these required reserve ratios.

Some countries do not impose reserve requirements. In those cases, the central bank's liabilities to banks are represented by voluntarily held vault cash and clearing or working balances. These central banks can still use open-market-type operations to influence deposit creation and money market conditions by varying reserve supply relative to these voluntary demands for reserves. However, the relationship between reserves and deposits, which in these countries depends on the average of the banks' desired ratios of reserve assets to deposits of the public, is less predictable than is the case with binding reserve requirements.

Whether the banking system's vault cash and deposits at the central bank are held predominantly as required or voluntary reserves, total reserves plus currency outside banks represent the nation's total monetary base. This aggregate also is potentially controllable by the central bank. However, since currency has traditionally been supplied to meet the demands of the public, as a practical matter central banks have found it more advisable to exercise direct control over reserves than over the monetary base.

Variations in the supply of reserves relative to the demand for them, with associated impacts on the cost of reserves, other interest rates and the stock of money, are the initial channels through which most central banks of developed capitalist countries use their policy instruments to affect the macroeconomy. Some countries with less developed securities markets rely more heavily on policies focused on bank lending, including in some cases direct controls on bank credit through ceilings or reserve requirements against bank assets. The activities of these central banks in controlling aggregate credit and its allocation are conceptually separate from monetary policy *per se* and are not considered in this article.

THE DISTINCTIONS BETWEEN MONETARY POLICY, DEBT MANAGEMENT AND FISCAL POLICY. Monetary policy can be distinguished from debt management and fiscal policy. Debt management and monetary policy are similar only in the limited sense that both change the composition of the public's holdings of financial assets and the public's liquidity position through shifts between short- and longer-term assets. More liquidity is provided if the government shortens the average maturity of its outstanding debt. Similarly, if a central bank purchases government debt from a member of the public, liquidity is enhanced because the public has traded a less liquid security for a more liquid deposit. Nonetheless, an open market purchase by the central bank of government securities in effect retires the debt, by replacing securities outstanding in the hands of the banks or the public with bank reserves and associated public deposits, both of which earn no or below-market returns on the margin. The injection of this kind of reserve liability of the central bank from outside the private economy brings about widespread portfolio adjustments that lower market interest rates generally as an aspect of the expansion in money. A debt management operation of the federal government, by contrast, just replaces one security in the hands of the public with another, affecting the term structure of outstanding debt and possibly the term structure of interest rates but not the general level of interest rates.

Monetary policy is clearly distinguishable from fiscal policy because each affects the economy through a different route. Fiscal policy has a direct effect on spending through government outlays and a direct effect on income available for spending through tax rates. Fiscal policy also has a financial aspect because budgetary deficits or surpluses imply changes in government debt that presumably influence total credit demands and interest rates. (On the other hand, to the debatable extent that the public views government debt as entailing an ultimate tax liability, a larger government deficit indirectly would tend to encourage an equal and offsetting increase in private saving to finance future tax payments and hence discourage private spending.) In contrast to the direct spending and income effects of fiscal policy, the impact of monetary policy is wholly indirect and depends on the response of spenders and borrowers to the changes in monetary and financial conditions brought about by policy actions.

THE MACROECONOMIC EFFECTS AND OBJECTIVES OF MONETARY POLICY. Monetary policy responsibilities of central banks today go far beyond the role originally seen for central banks, which involved ensuring the stability of the banking system and the convertibility of deposits, especially in times of financial panics. Early in their history, central banks assumed the role of 'the lender of last resort', meaning that they would provide a source of funds for financially troubled banks to forestall liquidity crises. Subsequent experience indicated the need for central banks to provide an 'elastic currency' to accommodate seasonal variations in the demands for reserve assets. By doing so, central banks could avoid periodic reserve shortages that had disturbed market conditions and also, on occasion, confidence as well, giving rise to runs on banks. Deposit insurance, bank supervision with on-site examinations, and bank regulation ranging from circumscribing certain risky activities to setting minimum requirements for bank capital or certain bank assets or liabilities have also been introduced to help assure a stable banking system. In some countries, responsibility for many of these functions has been granted to other governmental agencies.

A major role for central banks in maintaining the safety and soundness of the financial system has continued to the present day, even though it has been joined in this century by a responsibility for overall macroeconomic stabilization. Macroeconomic stability requires a sound financial system; a weak financial system may not be able to withstand the effects of exogenous shocks to the economy or of restrictive policy actions that would be otherwise appropriate.

The dominant influence of monetary policy over time on the price level has traditionally elevated long-term price stability to a paramount position among the macroeconomic objectives of central banks. Under a gold standard, the world stock of gold historically provided a longer-term anchor to the world's average price level. But the commitment of central banks to buy and sell gold at a fixed price in terms of the domestic currency automatically gave rise to substantial inflows or outflows of gold to individual countries in the process of international adjustment. Large impacts on domestic economic activity and prices resulted in cyclical instability and sustained inflationary or deflationary episodes. The demise of the gold standard lessened the constraints on central banks in pursuing shorter-term domestic stabilization goals, but the discipline of the outstanding gold stock over long-term international price trends was also lost. In the modern era, central banks have been given the charge of exercising self-discipline in seeking the objective of longer-term price stability. Meanwhile, the widely recognized short-run impact of monetary policy on economic activity and employment has fostered increased emphasis on countercyclical objectives as well.

Over extended periods, the effects of monetary policy are concentrated almost wholly on nominal magnitudes, that is, those measured in terms of the monetary unit. As noted, central banks are able to control the nominal stock of bank reserves and, as one remove, the money stock. Average price trends become established as the nominal quantity of money interacts over time with the private sector's demand for real money balances, that is, the value of money after adjustment for the impact of inflation or deflation of prices. Thus monetary policy has considerable influence over the long run on the average price level. In addition, factors that affect demands for real money balances, such as financial innovation, and more generally, those that affect demands or supplies of aggregate output also play a role in price level determination.

The supply of output is determined in the long run mainly by real factors such as population growth, participation in the labour force, capital accumulation and productivity trends. Real values for wages, interest rates, and currency exchange rates also respond secularly to fundamental real forces. The influence of monetary policy over the level and trend rate of change of the nominal price level carries over indirectly as an influence on the nominal values of those other variables but not on their real values. The real values of wages, interest rates and exchange rates that are ground out by the market economy, interact over time with nominal price behaviour to determine their nominal values. In the very long run, then, a change in the nominal quantity of money will be neutral as all nominal prices and wages tend to adjust proportionally, *ceteris paribus*.

While the influence of monetary policy on the behaviour of real values is widely agreed to be minor over the long pull, it is also recognized that monetary policy can affect real variables significantly in a shorter-run cyclical context. Doubts about the effectiveness of expansive monetary policy under conditions of a domestic depression raised during the Keynesian revolution have since been largely resolved. The views of today's mainstream macroeconomists with regard to the impact of monetary impulses on real economic activity are not far from those expressed in the following passage from David Hume:

> Though the high prices of commodities be a necessary consequence of the encrease in gold and silver, yet it follows not immediately upon that encrease; but some time is required before the money circulates through the whole state and makes its effect be felt on all ranks of people. At first no alteration is perceived; by degrees the price rises, first of one commodity then another; till the whole at last reaches a just proportion with the new quantity of specie.... In my opinion, it is only this interval, or intermediate situation, between the acquisition of money and rise of prices, that the encreasing quantity of gold and silver is favourable to industry (David Hume, 'Of Money', 1752; reprinted in *Writings on Economics*, edited by Eugene Rotwein, Madison: University of Wisconsin Press, 1955).

The proposition that monetary policy actions necessarily have a short-run effect on real variables is not universally accepted. In the last decade, the macro rational expectations school has argued that changes in monetary policy may not alter real variables, even in the short run. If a policy-induced movement in the nominal money stock is expected by the public in advance, then the public will have the incentive to adjust accordingly the actual, as well as expected, levels of all nominal values. Such a public response in principle would neutralize even the short-run impact of the expected policy change on real variables.

This recent challenge to the traditional view concedes, though, that unexpected policy actions can alter real variables, if only temporarily. Unanticipated policy actions can cause the outcomes for various nominal, and thus real, magnitudes to diverge, at least for a time, from their expected values. But the rational expectations school stresses that the public will come to expect policy actions that respond systematically to economic developments. Only policy actions that were purely random, or based on information not shared by the public, would then be unexpected, in which case the scope for effective countercyclical policy would be greatly narrowed.

In recent years, however, considerable counterevidence has been marshalled to the view that only unexpected policy moves can affect real values. Most empirical studies suggest that even systematic and expected changes in the direction of monetary policy do not show through fully right away in nominal values but have short-run impacts on real economic values.

465

The evident lagged effects on nominal values have been explained by various frictions, adjustment costs and information imperfections. While prices may adjust minute-by-minute in auction markets, in other markets explicit or implicit longer-term contracts impart rigidities to nominal prices and wages, preventing a complete short-run adjustment to even expected changes in nominal policy variables. Costs of changing certain prices also can give rise to gradual adjustment of nominal magnitudes over time. In addition, the buffer role of inventories keeps even an expected change in nominal spending on goods and services from being felt by all producers simultaneously. Finally, because firms and workers get information about demands for their own goods and services more rapidly than information about economy-wide demands, they can misperceive as only local events what really are generalized phenomena ultimately affecting all nominal values. Economic agents can be induced in the short-run to change their real behaviour in supplying goods and services, rather than fully altering the nominal prices or wages they offer as would actually be called for by overall developments.

THE CHANNELS THROUGH WHICH MONETARY POLICY AFFECTS THE ECONOMY. Even though economists now better understand these general behaviour patterns, the precise channels through which monetary policy actions are transmitted to the economy at large and the specific variables that best indicate the stance of monetary policy remain unresolved issues. The immediate effects of changes in the instruments controlled by central banks on the supply and cost of reserves are clear. Both an open market purchase of government securities that raises nonborrowed reserves and a cut in the discount rate augment reserve availability relative to demands for excess and required reserves. This places interest rates on money market instruments under downward pressure. After that, an almost infinite sequence of 'ripple effects' ensues, and analysts still differ in sorting out the most important of these in affecting the economy. Their differing views reflect the complexity of the linkages between the modern financial system and economic activity and the alternative simplifications various schools have adopted in an effort to capture the essential elements.

The mainstream view derives from the Keynesian tradition and highlights induced movements in market interest rates across the maturity spectrum as the primary linkage between monetary policy actions and private spending. An 'easing' or 'tightening' of monetary policy is indexed by decreases or increases in market rates. Of course, the distinction between nominal and real interest rates is recognized; a change in market interest rates that simply compensates for an accompanying change in inflationary expectations may have minimal real economic effects.

These Keynesian channels of influence have been worked out in some detail, both theoretically and in large-scale econometric models. With an easing monetary policy action, for example, the initial fall in money market rates induces market participants to revise downward their expected levels of future short-term rates as well, causing a softening in long-term rates. Inflation expectations are thought to adjust sluggishly in lagged response to actual inflation and to be largely unresponsive to the monetary easing itself. Thus, any tendency for inflation expectations to rise and mute the decline in nominal longer-term rates is viewed as minor. More administered interest rates, such as the prime rate and consumer credit and mortgage rates also come under downward pressure over time, and credit terms and conditions tend to become less restrictive.

Spending in the interest-sensitive sectors, such as housing, consumer durables and business investment, are most affected at first, as lowered borrowing costs stimulate demand. Some second-round effects also begin to come into play. The associated increase in income and production further stimulates consumption and investment spending. Also, the fall in interest rates is mirrored by a rise in financial asset values, and this gain in wealth encourages even more consumption spending.

Prices come under delayed upward pressure in part because tighter labour markets reduce the unemployment rate, at least transitionally, below its 'natural' level consistent with the realization of wage and price expectations. Such a fall in unemployment is associated with an acceleration of wage rates. Higher capacity utilization may also boost price mark-ups over costs. As the actual inflation rate picks up, inflation expectations begin to increase as well, imparting a separate upward thrust to price and wage setting.

An internationally related channel can also become important, especially in countries with a significant external sector and flexible exchange rates. A more accommodative monetary policy action that reduces domestic interest rates is likely to diminish the demand for assets denominated in the home currency. Under flexible exchange rates, the resulting depreciation of the exchange value of the currency will lower export prices in world markets and raise import prices. These developments will work over time to bolster spending on net exports. But as the associated rise in import prices feeds through the domestic price structure, broad price indexes will also tend to move higher.

Monetarists adopt a somewhat different viewpoint, asserting that monetary policy stimulus is best measured by the growth of the money stock. A sustained speed-up in money growth after some lag leads to a temporary strengthening in real economic activity and even later to faster inflation. The process is set in motion because an injection of reserves supports more money than the public desires to hold given prevailing levels of real income, prices and interest rates. As the extra balances 'burn a hole in people's pockets', purchases of a wide variety of goods and services as well as financial assets are stimulated. Short-term market interest rates may fall initially, but more importantly, prices across a broad spectrum of financial and real assets are bid up, stimulating demand for and production of investment and consumer goods. Monetarists, like Keynesians, contend that in the long run the impact on real activity dissipates as the monetary stimulus becomes fully reflected in inflation. People end up needing the extra money just to carry out normal transactions at inflated prices, leaving no more extra stimulus to real spending.

GUIDES FOR MONETARY POLICY. With a wide variety of financial and non-financial measures affected in the process of economic adjustment to a monetary policy action, the question remains as to which variable represents the best indicator of the stance of policy, that is, the variable providing the most reliable indication of the future effects of monetary policy on the economy. Moreover, with policy decisions having lagged effects and policymakers necessarily uncertain about economic linkages and trends, such a variable presumably could also be used to keep policymakers' judgement from going astray by serving as an intermediate guide to monetary policy actions. An intermediate guide is a variable that the central bank would attempt to keep in line with a prespecified target, and thus it would need to be reasonably controllable by the central bank. The central bank would adjust the level of the intermediate target less frequently than the settings of the policy instruments.

Central banks over time have used, with evolving emphasis, alternative primary policy guides. Historically, the price at which gold or some other metal was convertible into the domestic currency played this role. Subsequently, market interest rates and foreign exchange rates received more emphasis as policy guides. In recent decades, targets for overall money and debt have been adopted in many industrial countries. Other candidates have been proposed, including the monetary base, indexes of commodity prices or the general price level, nominal GNP and real interest rates.

Unfortunately, both macroeconomic analysis and experience suggest that no single variable can consistently serve as a reliable policy guide, so no hard-and-fast answer as to the best one can be given that holds under all conditions. All variables beyond non-borrowed reserves and the discount rate are influenced by factors other than monetary policy actions, and it turns out that the degree of stimulus to the economy involved in movements in any of them will depend on the nature of the other factors at work. Summarizing the advantages and disadvantages of several variables demonstrates this dilemma.

Monetary aggregates represent collections of financial assets, grouped according to their degree of 'moneyness'. Narrow measures of money comprise currency and fully checkable deposits to encompass the public's primary transactions balances. Broader measures also include other highly liquid accounts with additional savings features. Sharp lines of demarcation separating the various aggregates are difficult to draw as the characteristics of various assets often shade into one another over a wide spectrum, especially in countries with developed, deregulated and innovative financial markets.

Monetary aggregates serve well as policy guides when the public's demands for them are stably related to nominal spending and market interest rates and have a relatively small interest sensitivity. Suppose, for example, that there is a cyclical downturn in total spending. If the central bank withdraws reserves from the system in order to maintain a given level of market interest rates in the face of falling demand for money, the money stock would decrease at a time when additional monetary stimulus is needed. If instead the central bank maintains the original level of reserves in order to keep the money stock at its target level, interest rates must fall. The less interest-sensitive is money demand, the more would interest rates have to decline to offset the depressing effect of reduced spending on the public's desired money holdings. Thus, by maintaining money at the target level, an easing of credit conditions and perhaps a depreciating foreign exchange rate over time would partially offset the original decline in spending, and moderate the cyclical downturn.

However, when the public's willingness to hold monetary aggregates given nominal spending and interest rates is undergoing an abnormal shift, movements in measures of the money stock provide misleading signals of monetary stimulus or restraint. Such shifts in money demand have occurred in response to financial innovations and deposit deregulation as well as varying precautionary motives on the part of the public. As a result, the properties of empirical relationships connecting the money stock to nominal spending and market interest rates have been altered – in some cases permanently. The precise nature of the impact is difficult to assess when the process is underway. For example, in the United States during the 1980s, the disinflation process interacted with sluggishly adjusting offering rates on newly deregulated transaction deposits to raise substantially the responsiveness of the demand for narrow money to changes in market interest rates. The sizable declines in market interest rates after the early 1980s enhanced the relative attractiveness of returns on interest-bearing fully checkable deposits, which are included in narrow money. Inflows into these accounts were massive, with a significant portion representing savings-type funds.

Faced with unusual money demand behaviour, the central bank would be best advised not to resist departures of money from target but instead to accommodate reserve provision to the shifting demands for money. It could do so by maintaining existing reserve market conditions. Otherwise, the very process of restoring the money stock to target would transmit the disturbance in money demand to spending behaviour and economic activity. The changing conditions in reserve and credit markets associated with returning money to target would be inappropriate for stabilizing spending. Central banks that rely on monetary aggregates as policy guides have interpreted such episodes as demonstrating the need for monitoring overall economic developments and making feedback adjustments to monetary targets in response to evident disturbances of money demand relative to income.

Market interest rates thus would serve as a better policy guide than monetary aggregates if the only disturbances were to the money demand relationship. In a realistic economic context, though, independent disturbances to the relation between nominal spending and market interest rates are also likely to occur. Collection lags for data on economic activity and uncertainties about the structure of behavioural relations in the economy and the permanence of disturbances make the appropriate reaction to unexpected pressures on interest rates and misses of money from target difficult to determine at the time. For example, suppose the central bank sees that an unanticipated rise in interest rates is needed to keep the money stock from overshooting its target. The reason could be an unexpected strengthening of inflation and nominal spending that is boosting money demand, or a surprise upward shift in money demand relative to spending, or some combination of the two. The source of overshoot of money from

469

target could prove self-reversing, or it could be only the beginning of a cumulative departure. Unless uncertainty about the money demand relationship is exceptionally severe, it might be safer for the central bank to permit some upward movement in nominal interest rates than for it simply to keep interest rates stable by fully accommodating reserve provision to the outsized money growth. The latter reaction would provide no counterweight at all to what later could prove to have been an inflationary upturn of nominal spending.

On the other hand, suppose spending had clearly weakened, and the central bank has responded by adding to reserve availability in the face of a very interest-sensitive demand for the targeted monetary aggregate. The resulting fall in interest rates has led to a sizeable overshoot of money from target. In this circumstance, it may turn out better for the economy if the central bank accepts the full overrun of money above target. With a highly interest-sensitive demand for money, only a small reduction in interest rates is implied by keeping money on target when spending turns down. This easing in financial conditions will provide only little offset to the weakness in economic activity, unless there is an upward adjustment to targeted money growth.

Relying more on interest rates as a policy guide will not necessarily resolve the problem of determining the appropriate central bank reaction to unexpected developments. The relationship between nominal values of spending and market interest rates is qualitatively less predictable and stable over time than the already loose underlying relation between their real values. Determining what level of real interest rates is associated with a given level of nominal interest rates is hampered because the public's inflationary expectations are difficult to measure. Longer-term real interest rates, which are thought to have the most powerful influence on many important components of real spending, are especially difficult to discern since the public's expectations of inflation over the distant future are the most obscure.

Central banks thus face considerable uncertainty about the real interest rate that would be implied initially by the choice of a particular level for the nominal interest rate. Also, unless the resulting level of real interest rates just happened to be consistent with full employment and a stable inflation rate, the implied real interest rate would tend to move over time in a destabilizing direction, as was originally pointed out by Knut Wicksell. Suppose the central bank maintained nominal interest rates over an extended period at a level that from the start yielded an overly stimulative real interest rate. Economic activity would press against the economy's productive and labour capacities, and inflation would tend to accelerate. But as inflation expectations adjusted upward in response to actual inflation, the real interest rate implied by the targeted nominal interest rate would be driven still lower. This fall in the real interest rate would add even more stimulus to nominal spending and inflation. Even so, growth of reserves and money would have to be continually accelerated to maintain the targeted nominal interest rate. An ever faster rise in nominal spending and inflation hence would result from pegging the nominal interest rate at too low a level. Those central banks emphasizing market interest rates as policy guides interpret such possibilities as requiring them to monitor overall monetary and economic developments and to make feedback adjustments over time in setting market interest rates.

Since the potential pitfalls of either monetary aggregates or market interest rates as policy guides have induced central banks to respond to more ultimate gauges of economic performance – such as nominal GNP, prices and unemployment – in setting intermediate targets, some observers have recommended that central banks should cut through the feedback process by simply targeting one of these ultimate objectives itself. But this approach has disadvantages beyond the fact that the particular objective variable to be selected is of course controversial. Any of these ultimate variables are affected by numerous forces outside the central bank's control, including domestic fiscal policy and foreign fiscal and monetary policies. Data on most of these variables are received with some delay and then subject to sizeable revisions. Finally, an attempt to convert an ultimate objective to a shorter-term policy target would risk unstable macroeconomic outcomes over time in light of the uncertainties and lags in the impact of money policy actions.

For these reasons, central banks have not believed that they can justifiably be held accountable for the near-term performance of the overall economy. Despite the problems of interpreting the various monetary and debt aggregates and interest rates which are more under their near-term control, central banks, as well as many other analysts, view the constellation of these financial variables taken together as offering a surer indication of the longer-term stance of monetary policy itself than current values of ultimate economic variables. While the disadvantages under some circumstances of guiding policy by any single financial measure argue against an overreliance on any one, the advantages of each under different circumstances are viewed as suggesting that, when taken in the context of broader economic developments as well, none can be completely ignored in the conduct, or assessment, of monetary policy.

Nevertheless, the long-run linkage between money growth and inflation, together with the traditional concern of central banks for price stability, give monetary aggregates a special position among these financial variables. Continuing to focus on average money growth over extended periods, while accounting for the influence of distortions to its demand behaviour, forces central banks to keep longer-term price objectives in mind in the process of adjusting policy actions in response to shorter-term financial and economic developments.

POLICY RULES VERSUS DISCRETION. Some critics of the discretion embodied in such a policy approach place even more weight on the longer-term consideration of providing a nominal anchor to the macroeconomy. They also interpret the difficulty of forecasting both economic developments and the impact of policy actions as implying that central banks should not even attempt to stabilize the economy over shorter periods of time through discretionary policy actions. Given the lags and uncertainties involved, they believe such flexibility in policy is likely to do more harm than good, despire the best of intentions.

These critics have recommended that monetary policy should be based on fixed rules rather than discretion. The most influential has been the proposal of the monetarists to maintain a low, constant money growth rate through thick and thin. These economists under the intellectual leadership of Milton Friedman, have argued that excessive money growth is the main cause of inflation and that variations in monetary growth historically have been responsible for the large cyclical fluctuations in real output. With constant money growth, self-correcting mechanisms would prevent macroeconomic shocks from having major, sustained impacts on economic activity.

The rational expectations school has added a new wrinkle to the case for policy rules. They believe discretion imparts an inflationary bias to monetary policy because central banks face an irresistible temptation over time to put aside announced long-term plans to maintain price stability in pursuit of short-term production and employment aims. If the public had adjusted price expectations to the central bank's announced intention to maintain price stability, then a temporary increase in money growth would surprise the public and cause a desirable, if short-lived boost to output and employment with little inflationary cost. But with rational expectations, the public would see through this temptation and expect such a policy action. Expectations of inflation would emerge in anticipation of the monetary stimulus, leaving only price increases but no output gains as the policy is implemented. Indeed, if the central bank did not undertake the expected stimulus after all, then output would instead be temporarily depressed. Given this dilemma, central banks would end up providing the monetary stimulus, even though it only validates ongoing inflation and has no output effects.

Following an invariant policy rule would avoid this problem, according to these advocates, by making an anti-inflation policy credible to the public. The public then would expect only policy actions consistent with price stability. This school supports a rule defined in terms of a fixed target for either money growth or the price level.

While monetarist views have affected central bank practice in recent decades, as evidenced by the enhanced reliance on monetary aggregates in actual policy making during the 1970s, central banks have shied away from the adoption of fixed money rules in light of the perceived advantages of policy flexibility. The abstract, even hypothetical, nature of the rational expectations argument has limited its influence. And the substantial disinflation worldwide from the early- to mid-1980s despite continued rapid growth of monetary aggregates appears to have weakened the case of both schools for policy rules.

COORDINATION WITH OTHER DOMESTIC AND FOREIGN POLICIES. The separate influences of domestic fiscal policy and foreign fiscal and monetary policies on macroeconomic outcomes at home raise the issue of coordination with domestic monetary policy. On the domestic side, a more expansionary fiscal policy involving enlarged government spending or reduced taxes, for example, may require that offsetting actions be taken to make monetary policy more restrictive.

Even if the policy mix is changed in such a way to keep overall employment, production and prices the same, nominal and real values of market interest rates and foreign exchange rates would be altered, as would the composition of aggregate output in terms of real consumption, investment and net exports.

The traditional view has been that after some point a shift in the policy mix toward more stimulative fiscal policy and more restrictive monetary policy becomes undesirable, since investment and net exports will have to be 'crowded out' by higher real interest rates and exchange rates to make room for larger government purchases or private consumption. A reduced pace of investment would retard capital accumulation and the economy's longer-term growth potential, while lowered net exports would harm export and import-competing industries. The increased government budget deficit would be associated with a larger deficit in the current international payments accounts, implying a faster build-up of both government and external debt. Repayments of both debts over time would become more burdensome for domestic residents by requiring a greater sacrifice of future consumption. If capital inflows were invested effectively, they could provide resources to make future debt-service payments, but if these funds simply helped to finance government budget deficits, they would not support private capital accumulation.

A more recently advanced 'supply side' view is that sizable reductions in marginal tax rates will encourage private saving, investment, work effort and entrepreneurship. The economy's growth potential will be increased sufficiently that a more restrictive monetary policy need not be adopted, even if government deficits are initially increased. Evidence drawn from the United States following sizable cuts in marginal tax rates early in the 1980s suggests, however, that the resulting incentive effects on the economy's potential growth rate are relatively minor.

In practice, fiscal policy has not proven to be as flexible a macroeconomic tool as monetary policy, for other social goals beyond countercyclical considerations, as well as legislative delays, have prevented prompt adjustment in spending programmes or tax laws in response to overall economic developments. This situation has placed monetary policy in the forefront in pursuing macroeconomic stabilization objectives. Monetary policy actions become most politically sensitive when fiscal policy is expansionary and private spending and wage and price decisions are causing the economy to overheat. The required turn to a more restrictive monetary policy engenders opposition to higher interest rates, particularly from sectors where employment and production are especially disadvantaged by upward movements in interest and exchange rates. Having monetary policy bear too much of the brunt of countercyclical policy restraint is to be avoided partly because the central bank may not practically be able to bear the political pressures, and partly because economic imbalances across sectors become more pronounced.

Difficulties of achieving the proper mix of monetary and fiscal policy are exacerbated when considered in a multi-country context. International policy coordination is not just an issue of meshing monetary policies, but of coordinating

473

overall macro policy mixes in general. It also covers a range of possible interactions among countries. A higher degree of policy coordination obviously becomes more necessary in a regime of fixed exchange rates or common trade areas, or to the degree that different countries have accepted common exchange rate objectives. But even without explicit exchange rate objectives, some international policy coordination may still yield benefits given the transmission of effects of policy actions. A general move to restrictive fiscal policy abroad, for example, would reduce foreign spending on domestic exports. Also, the fall in foreign interest rates can heighten the willingness of international investors to hold domestic financial assets; these higher asset demands would act to keep domestic interest rates lower than otherwise but raise the exchange rate, ultimately depressing further the domestic balance of trade. Self-reinforcing cycles can even occur in which more expansive fiscal policies abroad, with a rise in foreign interest rates, produce a depreciation of the exchange value of the domestic currency. The lower value of the currency then leads to higher domestic inflation and inflationary expectations, in turn possibly contributing to a further depreciation of the currency, depending on the domestic monetary policy response.

A process of international policy coordination is in the interest of interrelated nations. Closer coordination could, in principle, provide for a greater measure of stability in exchange markets, while maintaining some of the features of flexible exchange rates in cushioning international disturbances and in lessening the constraints on policy implied by automatic flows of international reserves under a fixed-rate system. But the interests and circumstances of sovereign nations may well diverge at times. This can occur either because of a somewhat different emphasis on the various ultimate economic objectives or because the countries are experiencing different stages of the business cycle. In such situations, scope for agreement about the appropriate pattern of macroeconomic policies across countries may be limited.

BIBLIOGRAPHY

Axilrod, S.H. 1985. US monetary policy in recent years: an overview. *Federal Reserve Bulletin* 71(1), January, 14–24.
Bank of England. 1984. *The Development and Operation of Monetary Policy, 1960–1983.* London: Oxford University Press.
Friedman, M. 1960. *A Program for Monetary Stability.* New York: Fordham University Press.
Goodhart, C.A.E. 1984. *Monetary Theory and Practice: The UK Experience.* London: Macmillan.
Lindsey, D.E. 1986. The monetary regime of the Federal Reserve System. In *Alternative Monetary Regimes*, ed. C.D. Campbell and W.R. Dougen, Baltimore: Johns Hopkins University Press.
McCallum, B.T. 1984. Credibility and monetary policy. In *Price Stability and Public Policy*, Kansas City: Federal Reserve Bank of Kansas City.
Poole, W. 1970. Optimal choice of monetary policy instruments in a simple stochastic macro model. *Quarterly Journal of Economics* 84(2), May, 197–216.
Wallich, H.C. and Keir, P.M. 1979. The role of operating guides in US monetary policy: a historical review. *Federal Reserve Bulletin* 65(9), September, 679–91.

Monopoly

EDWIN G. WEST

Irving Fisher (1923), once defined monopoly simply as an 'absence of competition'. From this point of view various attitudes to, or criticisms of, monopoly are connected with the particular vision of competition that each writer has in mind. To the neoclassical economist monopoly is the polar opposite to the now familiar 'perfect competition' of the textbooks. Modern writers in the classical tradition, on the other hand, complain that perfect competition neglects the *process* of competitive activity, overlooks the importance of time to competitive processes and assumes away transaction or information costs.

In effect, 'perfect competition' to the neoclassical economist implies perfect decentralization wherein exchange costs happen to be zero. But the modern critics insist that exchange is not costless. And for this reason competition can be consistent with a wide variety of institutions that are employed to accommodate time, uncertainty and the costs of transacting (Demsetz, 1982). Such arrangements include, for example, tie-in sales, vertical integration and manufacturer-sponsored resale price maintenance. Such price-making behaviour means that in the real world decentralization is imperfect. And it is imperfect decentralization that is embodied in the classical paradigm of *laissez faire*. Consequently many phenomena that are automatically treated by neoclassical writers as the absence of perfect competition or the presence of behaviour that *looks* monopolistic, are often viewed approvingly by those in the classical tradition.

It is widely believed that, historically, Adam Smith's *Wealth of Nations* provided the most sustained and devastating attack on monopoly. It is true that he speaks of 'monopoly' quite frequently, but typically he uses the term in a wide 18th-century sense to include all kinds of political restrictions. Monopoly under the modern meaning of a single uncontested firm was not Smith's usual target. He employed the term most often to refer to multi-firm industries enjoying statutory protection. Thus, 'the law gave a monopoly to our boot-makers and shoe-makers, not only against our graziers, but against our tanners' (Smith [1776], 1960, vol. 2, p. 153). Again, the whole system of mercantilism

475

was condemned as monopolistic: 'Monopoly of one kind or another, indeed, seems to be the sole engine of the mercantile system' (ibid., p. 129).

The Ricardians too were more concerned with general restrictions, and especially with the fixed supply of land. Ricardo's *Principles of Political Economy and Taxation* has only five pages out of 292 that discuss monopoly, while John Stuart Mill's *Principles of Political Economy* has only two out of 1004. Following the Ricardians, the development of Darwinian philosophy in the mid-19th century only served to reinforce the classical emphasis on the necessity, if not inevitability, of competition. It is true that the 'modern' and more rigorous theory of monopoly, showing equilibrium to be determined by the equality of marginal revenue with marginal cost, was introduced by Cournot in 1838. But it received very little attention until much later.

In America the classical *laissez faire* view of competition and imperfect decentralization prevailed at least to the end of the 19th century. When the Sherman Antitrust Act was passed in 1890, economists were almost unanimously opposed to it. Thus, despite his general disposition for widespread government intervention, the founder of the American Economic Association, Richard T. Ely (1900), firmly rejected the politically popular policy of 'trust busting'. In the late 1880s John Bates Clark similarly feared that antitrust laws would involve a loss of the efficiency advantages of combinations or trusts. Combination itself was often necessary to generate adequate capital and to insure against adversity during the depressing period of the business cycle. Other contemporary economists, including Simon N. Patten, David A. Wells and George Gunton, had similar views. The last argued that the concentration of capital does not drive small producers out of business, 'but simply integrates them into a larger and more complex system of production, in which they are enabled to produce wealth more cheaply for the community and obtain a larger income for themselves'. Instead of the concentration of capital tending to destroy competition, the reverse was true: 'By the use of large capital, improved machinery and better facilities, the trust can and does undersell the corporation' (Gunton, 1888, p. 385).

Consider now, and in contrast, the subsequent neoclassical approach which eventually involved the comparison of monopoly with what is said to be its polar opposite market structure of perfect competition. The method was gradually developed from the last part of the 19th century and ultimately, in the 1950s, reached the stage of empirical measurement of what was described as the social cost of monopoly. The most influential study has been that of Harberger (1954), whose basic argument can be summarized in terms of Figure 1.

Assume that long-run average costs are constant for both firm and industry and are represented by the line $M_c = A_c$. The perfectly competitive output would be at Q_c where M_c intersects the demand curve DD. If a monopolist were substituted, he could maximize profits by producing Q_m at price P. His monopoly profit, π, would be represented by the rectangle $ABCP$. The loss of consumers' surplus is measured by the trapezoid $AECP$. The part of this area represented by $ABCP$, however, is not destroyed welfare but simply a transfer of wealth from

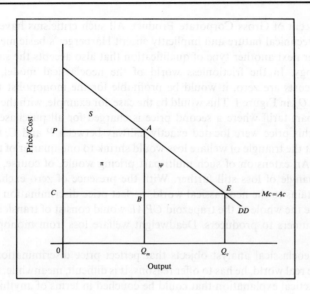

Figure 1

consumers to the monopolist. The net loss to society as a whole from the monopoly is given by the 'welfare triangle' *ABE*, denoted in Figure 1 by ψ. After making some heroic assumptions, in particular that marginal cost (M_c) was constant for all industries and that the price elasticity of demand was unity everywhere, Harberger estimated an annual welfare loss of \$59 million for the US manufacturing sector in the 1920s. This figure was surprisingly small since it represented only one-tenth of 1 per cent of the US national income for that period.

Subsequent writers have argued that Harberger's measure was a serious underestimate for statistical and other reasons. George Stigler (1956) objected that (1) monopolists normally produce in the range where elasticity is greater than unity; (2) some monopoly advantages become embodied in the accounted costs of assets, so leading to an underestimate in reported profits. Subsequent studies that allowed for Stigler's objections reported social costs of monopoly much higher than Harberger's. Thus D.R. Kamerschen (1966) reported an annual welfare loss due to monopoly in the 1956–61 period amounting to around 6 per cent of national income. D.A. Worcester, Jr. (1973), on the other hand, using *firm* rather than *industry* data, and assuming an elasticity of (minus) 2, reported a maximum estimate of welfare loss in the range of 0.5 per cent of national income for the period 1965–9. Focusing on the complaint that Harberger assumed the normal competitive profit rate to be represented by the actual average profit rate earned, whereas the latter itself contains a monopoly profit element, Cowling and Mueller (1978) reported that 734 large firms in the US generated welfare losses totalling \$15 billion annually over the period 1963–6, and this amounted

477

to 13 per cent of Gross Corporate Product. All such criticisms have obviously been of a technical nature and implicitly accept Harberger's basic methodology.

Consider next another type of qualification that also accepts the same central methodology. In the frictionless world of the neoclassical model, where all exchange costs are zero, it would be profitable for the monopolist to produce more than Q_m in Figure 1. This would be the case, for example, with the institution of a two-part tariff where a second price is charged for all purchases in excess of Q_m. If this price were located exactly halfway between P and C, it could be shown that the triangle of welfare loss would shrink to one-quarter of the existing size of ψ. An extension of such multi-part pricing would, of course, reduce the welfare triangle of loss still further. With the presence of zero exchange costs, which pertains to the neoclassical world, perfect price discrimination is possible. In this case the whole of the trapezoid $CPAE$ would consist of transferred wealth from consumers to producers. Deadweight welfare loss from monopoly would be zero.

If the neoclassical analyst objects that perfect price discrimination does not exist in the real world, he has to offer reasons. It is difficult, meanwhile, to conceive of any practical explanation that could be couched in terms of anything else but significant costs of exchange, such as positive information costs and risk. But such explanation undermines the 'purity' of the neoclassical model and points us back in the direction of the classical world of imperfect decentralization featuring real-world limitations on knowledge, and the existence of dynamic change under uncertainty.

It will be helpful now to describe classical analysis in terms of Figure 1. But first recall that, instead of the notion of perfect competition as a static long-term equilibrium, we start with the view of competition, espoused by Adam Smith and his successors, as a process of rivalry within a time dimension. In Schumpeter, for instance, competition is seen as 'a perennial gale of creative destruction'. It is the possibility of profit, of course, that drives the innovating entrepreneur. Without it the *laissez faire* model of decentralization would collapse. But once profits are obtained by a successful pioneer his operation is immediately copied by others, so that there is a constant tendency for entrepreneurial profit to be competed away. It is this focus on a continual series of short runs that distinguishes the analysis from that of 'perfect competition', which is always expressed in terms of the very long run.

Assume then the discovery of a new product, product X, by an entrepreneur who proceeds to offer Q_m of it at price P (see Figure 1). It is only academically true that he is restricting output compared with what potential rivals would produce if they possessed his knowledge and business acumen. But since, in reality, they do not, the only alternative to Q_m supply of product X is some positive quantity of conventional products that the factors were previously producing (the supply of X being zero). The result of his activity in producing X, therefore, is pure social gain, and this is measured in Figure 1 by the profit plus the consumer surplus S. The welfare triangle of social loss (ψ) does not exist. It can be expected that the entrepreneur's action will lead to the eventual entry of rivals. At this stage competition will lead to a lowering of price towards cost. This process will then involve a transfer of wealth from the original entrepreneur to consumers. But the latter's original and temporary profit is necessary to induce him to introduce the product at an earlier time than otherwise. It is this earlier introduction indeed that produces the social gains. So while such temporary profit may be described as proceeding from the market structure of 'imperfect competition', nevertheless, according to the Smithian/Schumpeterian analysis, the monopolies so described are necessary institutions, since economic growth would be much weaker without them. Indeed, society recognizes such logic when it grants temporary legal monopolies in the form of patents.

It is necessary now to examine the special place that is usually accorded to the phenomenon of what is called 'natural monopoly'. This is said to exist when it is technically more efficient to have a single producer or enterprise. The ultimate survival of such a single firm is usually the natural outcome of initial rivalry between several competitors. J.S. Mill ([1848], 1965, p. 962) appears to have been the first to use the adjective 'natural' and to use it interchangeably with 'practical'. Examples quoted by Mill included gas supply, water supply, roads, canals and railways.

In his *Social Economics* (1914) Friedrich von Wieser was probably the first to distinguish the modern from the classical doctrine of monopoly. The classical (and possibly also the Marxian) attribution to monopoly of the 'favoured' market position of capital over labour was incorrect. So was Ricardo's reference to the 'monopoly' of agricultural soil. The price of urban rents was a competitive price. A typical real monopoly for von Wieser consisted of what he called the 'single-unit enterprise', that was identical to the organization that Mill had previously identified as a 'natural monopoly'. The postal service was an excellent illustration:

> In the face of [such] single-unit administration, the principle of competition becomes utterly abortive. The parallel network of another postal organization, beside the one already functioning, would be economically absurd; enormous amounts of money for plant and management would have to be expended for no purpose whatever [von Wieser [1914], 1967, pp. 216–17].

The conclusion was that some kind of government control such as price regulation was required.

One must conjecture that von Wieser would have been astonished by the application (in the 1980s) to natural monopolies of the new theory of 'the contestable market'. According to its promulgators, this is a situation in which 'entry is absolutely free, the exit is absolutely costless' (Baumol, 1982). To such economists, even von Wieser's postal service is, at least conceptually, open to such market contestability (although the main example quoted by the new analysts has been that of airlines). The essence of a contestable market is that it is vulnerable to hit-and-run entry: 'Even a very transient profit opportunity need not be neglected by a potential entrant, for he can go in, and before prices change, collect his gains and then depart without cost, should the climate grow hostile' (Baumol, 1982, p. 4).

In effect, such new analysis is a theoretical development of the neoclassical concern with perfect competition and especially with its condition of free entry. Indeed, one writer prefers the term "ultra-free entry' to 'perfect contestability' (Shepherd, 1984). What is involved is not only the possibility of a new firm gaining a foothold (which is conventional 'free entry') but the ability to duplicate immediately and entirely replace the existing monopolist. The entrant can, moreover, establish itself before the existing firm makes any price response (the Bertrand–Nash assumption). Finally, exit is perfectly free and without cost. Sunk cost, in other words, is zero. Given these conditions, even the threat of entry (potential competition) may hold price down to cost. A government scheme of regulated prices might therefore be socially detrimental.

Although such theoretical innovation is challenging, it has given rise to considerable controversy concerning both the internal consistency of the theory and empirical support for it. The assumption of zero sunk costs has been the one that has come under most attack. It has been observed for instance that in most markets sunk costs are more obvious in the short run then in the long run; and this is by definition. With *any* element of sunk cost the existing firm has a proportionate potential pricing advantage over an entrant. But it is in the very short period that the pure contestability theory stipulates a zero-price response from the incumbent. Meanwhile, with respect to the question of the empirical basis for the theory, Baumol et al. concede that very little is available so far.

Doubts about the efficiency of government price regulation of natural monopolies have also been raised by Demsetz (1968).He has proposed that formal regulation is unnecessary where governments can allow 'rivalrous competitors' to bid for the exclusive rights to supply a good or service over a given 'contract period'. The appearance of a single firm may not imply monopoly pricing, because competition could have previously asserted itself at the franchise bidding stage. Monopoly *structure* therefore does not inevitably predict monopoly *behaviour*, although some element of the latter could appear if conditions, say of production, change during the period of the contract.

An ostensibly similar line of argument to that of Demsetz was offered by Bentham and Chadwick. Chadwick's investigation into water supply in London in the 1850s revealed circumstances of natural monopoly. But he argued that inefficiency was prevalent because the field was divided among 'seven separate companies and establishments of which six were originally competing within the field of supply, with two and three sets of pipes down many of the same streets' (quoted in Crain and Ekelund, 1976). Following Chadwick's recommendation, rivalry was channelled into what he called competition *for* the field and away from (costly) competition '*within* the field'. The same reasoning applied to the railways. Public ownership was advocated while management (operation) of the services was to be contracted out via a competitive franchise bidding process from among potential private enterprises.

It must next be recognized that very many monopolies, if not most, are *unnatural*; that is, they arise not from inexorable economic conditions but from man-made arrangements, usually through the exercise of political power. In these cases the monopoly is typically awarded by government but not usually with the intention of encouraging the introduction of a new product (as with patents). Instead, one supplier is granted the sole right of trading an existing product or service to the exclusion of all other suppliers. A natural state of competition is thus converted by fiat into one of (statutory) monopoly. In this case the classical analyst might see more potential relevance in Harberger's model of welfare loss from monopoly.

Where the monopoly right is granted by the government, and assuming that price discrimination is prohibitively costly, it would seem, again at first sight, that the monopoly rent or 'prize' to the successful producer could indeed be represented by a rectangle such as *ABCP* in Figure 1. But since the seminal writing of Tullock (1967), economists have come to recognize that the pursuit of such monopoly rents is itself a competitive activity, and one that consumes resources. Since Krueger (1974) this process has become known as 'rent seeking' and it frequently takes the form of lobbying, offering campaign contributions, bribery, and other ways of influencing the authorities to grant exclusive rights to production, rights that are then policed by the coercive powers of government.

Recent work has modified the conclusion that the value of resources used in pursuit of the rents would exactly equal the value of the rents. Some writers have urged that lobbying by consumers might to some extent offset that of potential monopolists such that a regulated price at a magnitude lower than *P* (but higher than *C*) in Figure 1 would result. In this case, of course, the expected rectangle of monopoly rent would be reduced and the producers collectively would not spend more than this in rent seeking.

Jadlow (1985) has reduced still further the expected magnitude of such monopoly rent rectangles by introducing a multi-period model wherein other rent seekers continue to compete for the valued monopoly prize while consumers, regulators and antitrusters continue their endeavours to eliminate the rents over a protracted period into the future. Since, therefore, instead of a one-time prize, the monopoly rent is viewed as the expected present value of a stream of rents over a series of future time periods in which uncertainty is present, there is likely to be a significant reduction of resources invested in rent-seeking activities.

It is usually implied by economists that the task of public policy with regard to monopoly is to eliminate monopoly profit by one means or another. The above analysis reveals, however, that the conventional measures of social losses via the welfare triangles, plus the rectangles of potential transfers that are partially 'eaten up' by resources devoted to rent-seeking, are predominantly applicable to monopolies that are politically bestowed. We are thus left with the conclusion that appropriate public policy (according to usual economic reasoning) involves government 'correcting for' something it has created itself. The direct way of solving such a problem, at least to the innocent, would be for the government simply to abstain from granting statutory monopoly privileges in the first place. The newer 'economics of politics', however, has produced reasons why the legislative activity of monopoly rent creation is inherent in the very structure of majority voting democracies. Indeed, some writers (Brennan and Buchanan, 1980) argue that the very institution of government is usually a monopoly. In so far as this is true, we face the paradoxical situation that the public policy prescribed in economics textbooks is one whereby monopoly in general is policed or controlled by an institution that is itself a monopoly.

BIBLIOGRAPHY

Baumol, W.J. 1982. Contestable markets: an uprising in the theory of industry structure. *American Economic Review* 72(1), March, 1–15.

Brennan, G. and Buchanan, J. 1980. *The Power to Tax: Analytical Foundations of the Fiscal Constitution.* Cambridge: Cambridge University Press.

Cowling, K. and Mueller, D.C. 1978. The social cost of monopoly power. *Economic Journal* 88, December, 727–48.

Crain, W.M. and Ekelund, R.E., Jr. 1976. Chadwick and Demsetz on competition and regulation. *Journal of Law and Economics* 19(1), April, 149–62.

Demsetz, H. 1968. Why regulate utilities? *Journal of Law and Economics* 11, April, 55–65.

Demsetz, H. 1982. *Economic, Legal, and Political Dimensions of Competition, Professor Dr F. de Vries Lectures in Economics.* Vol. 4, Amsterdam: North-Holland.

Ely, R.T. 1900. *Monopolies and Trusts.* New York: Macmillan.

Fisher, I. 1923. *Elementary Principles of Economics.* New York: Macmillan.

Gunton, G. 1888. The economic and social aspects of trusts. *Political Science Quarterly* 3(3), September, 385–408.

Harberger, A.C. 1954. Monopoly and resource allocation. *American Economic Association, Papers and Proceedings* 44, May, 77–87.

Jadlow, J.M. 1985. Monopoly rent-seeking under conditions of uncertainty. *Public Choice* 45(1), 73–87.

Kamerschen, D.R. 1966. An estimation of the 'welfare losses' from monopoly in the American economy. *Western Economic Journal* 4, Summer, 221–36.

Krueger, A.O. 1974. The political economy of the rent-seeking society. *American Economic Review* 64, June, 291–303.

Mill, J.S. 1848. *Principles of Political Economy.* Ed. W.J. Ashley. Reprinted, New York: A.M. Kelley, 1965.

Shepherd, W.G. 1984. 'Contestability' vs competition. *American Economic Review* 74(2), September, 572–87.

Smith, A. 1776. *An Inquiry into the Nature and Causes of the Wealth of Nations.* 2 vols, ed. E. Cannan, London: Methuen, 1960.

Stigler, G. 1956. The statistics of monopoly and merger. *Journal of Political Economy* 64, February, 33–40.

Tullock, G. 1967. The welfare costs of tariffs, monopolies, and theft. *Western Economic Journal* 5, June, 224–32.

von Wieser, F. 1914. *Social Economics.* Trans. A. Ford Hinrichs, New York: A.M. Kelley, 1967.

Worcester, D.A., Jr. 1973. New estimates of the welfare loss to monopoly, United States: 1956–69. *Southern Economic Journal* 40(2), October, 234–45.

National Income

WILFRED BECKERMAN

Although there are numerous complexities and ambiguities attached to this concept, and a variety of reasonable alternative ways in which it may be articulated in detail, national income corresponds basically to the income accruing to a nation by virtue of its productive activity. Some of the ambiguities, therefore, arise on account of different definitions of what constitutes a 'productive activity'. Hence, the best approach to the concept of national income is via the more widely used concept of 'national product', or one of its variants. Of these the most commonly used has been 'gross national product'.

The gross national product is the *unduplicated* value of what a nation produces. The qualification 'unduplicated' indicates that the value of the total output of the economy in question must be estimated without 'double counting'. That is to say, one must not count the value of goods that are used up in the production of other goods both when they are produced and then again in the value of the other goods in which they are subsequently embodied. For example, in a simple agricultural economy that produced only wheat which is then turned into flour and then into bread, it would be misleading to add the value of the wheat and the flour to the value of the bread since the latter already includes the value of the wheat and flour embodied in it. Thus one method of measuring the output of an economy is to measure the goods and services that cross 'the production boundary' – that is, pass from the productive sector to what is known as 'final demand', where the goods in question are not used up again in the production of other goods.

In other words, one way of estimating a country's gross national product (GNP) in any time period (say a year) is simply to add up the total of all the goods and services that enter into 'final demand'. Final demand is generally defined as comprising 'capital formation' (capital goods plus changes in stocks), private consumption (food, clothing, entertainment and so on), as well as public consumption (e.g. expenditure on schools, hospitals, defence, etc.). It is also necessary to add exports, since although these are not used by the population

483

of the economy in question they have been produced by them and give them claims on other countries. In the same way it is necessary to subtract imports because although these would be included in the value of the consumption and other expenditures of the nation in question they have not been produced by that nation but represent, instead, claims by other nations.

The particular classification of final demand set out above is not, however, the only classification that would be legitimate as a means of arriving at the same total. For largely historical reasons the millions of individual transactions entering into final demand are summarized in classes that reflect some 'model' of the way that economic activity is determined. Since national income accounting – at least in Britain (though less so in the United States) – grew up in close conjunction with the widespread adoption of Keynesian theory in British economic circles towards the end of the 1930s and, even more particularly, in conjunction with Keynes's influence, during World War II, on the quantification of the problem of how to reconcile available resources with the heavy claims on these resources, it was inevitable that the national accounting methods and conventions developed (largely under the direction of Richard Stone) were heavily influenced by the Keynesian model of income determination.

In particular, expenditures on final output were classified into those classes – notably government expenditure on goods and services, investment and exports – which, in the simplest possible Keynesian model, could be regarded as largely exogenous injections into the flow of income, and those – private consumption and imports – which were endogenously determined. These categories constitute the variables that appear in the most elementary of Keynesian macroeconomic models.

The influence of Keynes's concern with – amongst other things – the effect of financing the British war effort on the development of national accounting was mirrored in the shift in the focus of national accounting in the US away from its earlier primary concern with measuring 'national income' in the direction of measuring gross national product. The two concepts differ since the capital goods that are included in final demand do, in fact, get 'used up' in the production of other goods, if not in the same time period to which the estimate of national product or income refers. Hence, some deduction needs to be made in each time period to allow for the depreciation of the capital stock in that time period in order to arrive at the economy's *net* output. The resulting concept, which is often known as *net* national product (by contrast with *gross* national product), is thus equal to national income. This corresponds to the concept of 'income' when this is defined as the income available to any economy after it has set aside something to maintain capital intact. Thus whilst in any short period a country's gross national product measures the total amount of goods and services that it produces and could use up in that period, clearly it could not maintain that level of production and use of resources if it did not set aside a part of the output for maintaining its capital stock.

The shift of interest from national income to GNP was largely the result of the need to measure what an economy's production capacity would be in the short run considered relevant for wartime purposes – as distinct from what would be its longer-run sustainable level of output. Thus, for example, a classic exposition of national income analysis by one of the pioneers in the field (Simon Kuznets, 1933), showed the distribution of net national income by type of income received (wages, salaries and so on) but not the distribution of the total product by type of final demand, whereas a later well-known American work in the field (Gilbert and Jaszi, 1944) showed estimates of both and emphasized the important role of estimates of *gross* national product.

Whatever the merits of the particular classification system for final demand set out above and generally adopted, it illustrates the scope for ambiguity and for differences of opinion as to what constitutes final product (and hence should be included in GNP). For example, it is often claimed that some – or even most – public consumption really constitutes undesirable necessities rather than additions to final output, and hence ought to be treated as intermediate goods (or services) that are used up in the course of production in the same way that the wheat was used up in the production of bread. This might apply, for example to the services of the police, which – it is sometimes argued – should be treated as inputs into the productive process since without them there would be no organized economy, and hence their inclusion in final demand, under the heading of public consumption, is a form of 'double counting'. Similarly, it is often argued that various services, such as passenger transport, are really inputs into the system since they do not add to welfare, but are merely part of the costs that people incur in order to go to work.

Similarly, there is no sharp distinction between income that represents payments for productive activities (whether contributing directly to final output or to intermediate output) and payments that are regarded as merely transfers of income without the quid pro quo of any 'productive' activity being involved. Transfer payments such as old age pensions are an obvious example of the latter. But there are many others that are less obviously of one kind or another. In particular, in the Soviet bloc countries it is common to treat many services, such as entertainment or public sector activities or passenger transport and so on, as representing 'transfer payments' rather than payments made in exchange for productive activities that add to the national income.

Clearly, the dividing lines between what are really inputs into other productive activities, or what are not productive activities to begin with, and what adds to final economic welfare are arbitrary and it would not be logically impossible to arrive at the conclusion that all outputs are really just regrettable necessities and that net economic welfare is zero. Given the inevitable arbitrariness of the value judgements that have to be made in deciding exactly where to draw the boundary between final output and intermediate output, or between transfer payments and productive activities, it is not surprising that different countries adopt different conventions.

Through the activities of international organizations, notably the Organization for Economic Cooperation and Development and the United Nations, certain international standard conventions have been drawn up and are enshrined in

A System of National Accounts, known as SNA. The first version of this system, which was published in 1952 (UNO, 1952) was a development of the League of Nations Report on 'The Measurement of National Income and the Construction of Social Accounts', the design of which owed much to the work of Richard Stone. Subsequent revisions to the system have appeared from time to time and it has not been possible for all countries to adopt the latest conventions. In 1983 it was stated by the UN Statistical Office that only about 55 per cent of the 'market economies' (i.e. excluding 'centrally planned economies', which is a euphemism for Soviet bloc countries and a few other countries that adopt similar stances) have been able to adopt the latest standardized system in its entirety.

Furthermore, some countries – notably the Soviet bloc countries – prefer a different conceptual basis, usually known as the 'Material Product System' (MPS), which restricts the concept of national product to the production of goods and services related to the production, repair, transportation and distribution of *material* goods. Thus, it excludes non-material services such as public administration and defence, finance, education, health, personal services and the maintenance of what passes for law and order in most modern societies. French national accounting practice resembles Soviet conventions in many ways, no doubt partly because of its development in the early postwar years when national economic planning was extensively used in France. Also, French-speaking African countries have used what is known as the 'Courcier' system which is close to the MPS in many ways but which also includes a special method of treating the output of non-residents stationed in the country. (The details of the SNA and of the other systems are set out in various UN publications, notably recent issues of *A System of National Accounts*.)

However, it should not be thought that the only source of incomparability between the national income estimates of different countries is the scope for conceptual differences. It cannot be too strongly emphasized that any figure of GNP or of national income involves an enormous amount of estimation on the basis of what are often very shaky assumptions and inadequate data. As a result, national income estimates are frequently subject to very large revisions. For example, comparison of the estimates of the 1977 GNP for some countries as shown in the 1977 and the 1979 editions of the World Bank's *World Tables* show that the estimates of 1977 GNP were revised, between these two years, by over 30 per cent in Gambia and Ghana, by 25 per cent in Nigeria and by nearly 20 per cent in many other countries. It is also quite common for there to be more than one quasi-official set of estimates of GNP in the same country (e.g. estimates by the Central Bank as well as by the Statistical Services). In fact, even in statistically relatively very advanced and sophisticated countries, it is usually the case that different estimates of GNP are obtained by different methods – though by the same agency.

Among the other major conceptual variations on the basic theme is the difference between gross *national* product and gross *domestic* product. Roughly speaking, 'national product' is what is produced by normal residents of the country wherever they may happen to be providing their services (capital or labour), and 'domestic product' is what is produced by people who happen to be providing services (capital or labour) in that country, irrespective of their nationality and normal country of residence. In the latest version of SNA, domestic product is now defined as the value of all goods produced and services provided in a country by residents and non-residents without regard to its allocation among domestic and foreign claims, whereas GNP is the sum of the total domestic and foreign output of all the residents of a country including income received from abroad by residents for factor services rendered overseas and after subtracting transfers of income to abroad by residents of other countries. Everything turns, therefore, on the concept of 'residents', usually defined as including the *de facto* population of a country adjusted by adding the number of people abroad for less than one year and subtracting the people in the country for a similar duration. Thus, for countries where there is a large migrant labour force, or where a significant part of the capital stock is owned by overseas residents, there may be major differences between domestic product (roughly speaking, what is produced inside the geographical boundaries of the country) and national product (what accrues to the normal residents of the country as defined). For example, the ratio of GDP to GNP varies from 1.22 in Bahrain to 0.75 in Kuwait. In the latest revision of SNA the concept of GNP no longer appears and only GDP is indicated, but most countries still prepare GNP estimates and these are still reported in the estimates of international organizations. Indeed, it is widely accepted that for purposes of comparisons of the economic *welfare* of a nation, national product is probably more relevant than domestic product.

This does not mean that the GNP concept is a *good* indicator of economic welfare, let alone of welfare in some wider sense. Apart from the conceptual problems mentioned above, there are many other limitations on GNP as a measure of economic welfare, such as the failure to allow for externalities (e.g. the failure to include pollution, congestion and so on, as negative items); the difficulties involved in evaluating home-produced output or subsistence output which may be very important in poorer countries; the common failure to value the output of most public services in a welfare-oriented manner instead of in a cost-of-input manner; the failure to include the output of many public facilities and the failure to allow for many other non-market activities – of which housewives' services are one of the best-known examples; the failure to allow for differences in leisure or working conditions; and, above all, the failure to reflect the degree of equality in the distribution of the income.

Furthermore, special problems arise in making comparisons over time or between countries. In attempting to make comparisons of welfare on the basis of changes in national income over time, allowance obviously has to be made for changes in the price level. Thus what is required is an estimate of 'real' national income (or real GNP). And the comparison of price levels is not a simple matter for various reasons, such as changes in the quality of products or the variety of products available, as well as in the patterns of consumption. Similar problems arise in making inter-country comparisons of 'real' national income.

For it should not be assumed that exchange rates accurately reflect international differences in price levels or in 'purchasing power parities'. And, as between countries of vastly different standards of living, national customs, relative price structures and so on, it is not possible to obtain reliable and meaningful comparisons of 'real' national income, in spite of outstanding work carried out in this field by a team under the direction of Irving Kravis which follows a methodology originally laid down in 1954 by Gilbert and Kravis.

Of course, making welfare comparisons is not the main use to which national income estimates are put. They are used much more as indicators of the macroeconomic situation of a country – that is, the extent to which the economy is expanding or failing to do so, and the extent, therefore, to which other developments may be anticipated, such as tightness of the labour market, or balance of payments difficulties. This sort of macroeconomic analysis requires, of course, much more than aggregative estimates of total national income, and needs to be supplemented by a great deal of detail on the structure of GNP by sector, by type of product, by type of expenditure and so on. Indeed, the main development over the years has been not in the sophistication of the concept of total national income, but in the enormous increase in the complexity of detailed supporting tables. This has been accompanied by linkages between national income data and closely related statistical data, such as 'input–output' tables which show the interrelations between the inputs and outputs of different industries and other activities.

In recent years there has also been a move toward extending the disaggregation of national accounting in a direction that encompasses social accounting matrices designed to link the economic relationships with other forms of data concerning the social characteristics of different groups in the economy. All these developments have taken place in the context of a vastly increased complexity of economic models designed to explain economic behaviour and predict economic events. Unfortunately, in spite of the greatly increased computational power that is also now available, these efforts have so far met with very little success.

BIBLIOGRAPHY

Gilbert, M. and Jaszi, G. 1944. National product and income statistics as an aid in economic problems. *Dun's Review*. Reprinted in *Readings in the Theory of Income Distribution*, ed. W. Fellner and B.F. Haley, Philadelphia: Blakiston, for the American Economic Association, 1946.

Gilbert, M. and Kravis, I.B. 1954. *An International Comparison of National Products and the Purchasing Power of Currencies*. Paris: Organization of European Economic Cooperation.

Gilbert, M. et al. 1958. *Comparative National Products and Price Levels*. Paris: Organization of European Economic Cooperation.

Kravis, I.B., Heston, A. and Summers, R. 1982. *World Product and Income*. Baltimore: Johns Hopkins Press, for the World Bank.

Kuznets, S. 1933. National income. *Encyclopedia of the Social Sciences*. Reprinted in *Readings in the Theory of Income Distribution*, ed. W. Fellner and B.F. Haley, Philadelphia: Blakiston, for the American Economic Association, 1946.

UNO. 1952. *A System of National Accounts and Supporting Tables*. New York: United Nations Publications, Series F, No. 3.

National System

HENRY W. SPIEGEL

The term 'national system of political economy' stems from a filiation of American and German ideas that arose in opposition to the universalist character of classical economics and were designed to promote public policies serving the economic development of the nation. The development was visualized as one that would yield a balance of agriculture and industry and make the most of a country's potential economic strength. The term 'American system' occurs as early as 1787 in No. 11 of *The Federalist*, where Alexander Hamilton launches this appeal to his readers: 'Let the thirteen states, bound together in a strict and indissoluble Union, concur in erecting one great American system, superior to the control of all transatlantic force or influence and able to dictate the terms of the connection between the old and the new world.'

Hamilton's more detailed proposals regarding the ways and means to construct the American system can be found in his great state papers, written when he served as Secretary of the Treasury in President Washington's cabinet, and dealing with manufactures, a national bank and the public debt. With the help of these three instruments he wished to emancipate the new nation from the rural economy of its forefathers, one that Thomas Jefferson, Hamilton's great antagonist, attempted to preserve. Among Hamilton's specific devices to promote industrial development, bounties, or subsidies, stood out. Later writers emphasized protective tariffs rather than bounties.

These writers included Daniel Raymond, a Baltimore attorney, whose *Thoughts on Political Economy* of 1820, while not elaborating the notion of a national system in so many words, made a substantial contribution to the later interpretation of the term by introducing the concept of 'capacity' to produce goods, identified by him with national wealth. Raymond placed on government the duty of utilizing and enlarging this capacity by a policy of protection. His plea for protective tariffs was supported both by the infant-industry argument and the employment argument, in conjunction with which Raymond wrote explicitly of 'full employment'.

489

The next step in elaborating the concept of a national system was taken by Frederick List, the German writer and promoter, who in 1827 during his residence in the United States published *Outlines of American Political Economy*. Like Hamilton, List writes of the 'American system', which was to realize its potential with the help of tariff protection. This work was written and distributed at the behest of a Pennsylvania manufacturers association whose members clamoured for tariff protection. Composed ostensibly in the form of letters addressed to a leading protectionist, the work appeared serially in the *National Gazette* of Philadelphia and was reprinted by more than fifty other newspapers. When published in pamphlet form, it was distributed in 'many thousand' copies, as List later reported. It was sent to the members of Congress and was apparently helpful in securing the adoption of the Tariff Act of 1828.

In an abortive attempt to win a prize, in 1837 List wrote an essay in French on 'The Natural System of Political Economy', which remained, however, unpublished until 1927, when it was printed in French and German. An English translation appeared only in 1983. This work anticipates in a number of respects List's principal work, *National System of Political Economy*, in which the national-system doctrine reached its full flowering. This work was published in German in 1841; an English translation, sponsored by protectionist interests in the United States, appeared in 1856, and another one, published in England, in 1885. The work, while substantial enough in itself, was intended to be the first part of a larger project, which, however, was never completed. Of the English translations, the earlier one omits the preface, while the later one contains extracts from the preface but omits the introductory chapter that provides a summary of the work.

In the *National System,* List finds fault with the classics for a variety of reasons. He takes them to task for having constructed a system of thought that is permeated by individualism and cosmopolitanism but neglects the nation. According to List, the community of nations is not a homogeneous group but made up of members that find themselves at different stages of their development. List then goes on to construct a stage theory which visualizes progress from the agricultural stage to one in which agriculture is combined with industry, and to still another one in which agriculture, industry and trade are joined together. List tends to equate agriculture with poverty and low level of culture, whereas industry and urbanization bring wealth and cultural achievement. The classics, with their homogenized picture of the world which neglected national differences, would tend to perpetuate the underdeveloped status of the United States and continental Europe vis-à-vis the highly developed Britain. According to List, each stage, or each nation at its respective stage, requires a different set of economic doctrines, whereas the classics claimed universal validity for their doctrines.

At heart, List wanted to improve on Providence by turning all people into Englishmen. To allow the underdeveloped countries of his time to participate in the march toward higher stages, attention would have to be paid to their productive capacities. The development and utilization of these was a task that List placed squarely on national governments. In this connection List called for liberal political institutions, for the construction of what is now known as social overhead, especially in the form of transportation facilities, for balanced growth and for tariff protection for infant industries (not for agricultural products). List was willing to endorse the free-trade orientation of the classics as valid for the future, when all nations had utilized their potential and attained the most progressive stage. Then free trade would be combined with universal peace and a world federation.

There are a number of questions that List left unanswered. To begin with the most often heard objection to the infant-industry argument for protection, what tests are there to identify infant industries and to mark their eventual attainment of maturity, when protection presumably is to terminate? Moreover, List did not explain how the type of economic warfare that he envisaged would prepare the ground for universal peace. Nor did he show awareness of the likelihood that, once all nations had progressed to what he called the normal state, one nation would again get ahead of the others, perhaps for reasons of technological advances, a matter treated with so much insight by Hume in his analysis of the migration of economic opportunities.

List had been a protectionist of sorts already in his young years in his native Germany. His protectionist leanings came to the fore in the United States, where he encountered an even richer potential for economic development and where changing economic conditions were more rapid and conspicuous. Here List's strictures on the classics fell on fertile ground because so many features of their dismal science did not seem to fit into the American environment, especially Malthus's population doctrine and Ricardo's theories of subsistence wages, diminishing returns and free trade. Thus List's work coalesced with the works of native American critics of the classics, especially of Henry Carey, who developed theories of increasing rather than diminishing returns and of rising wages and profits and declared that each successive addition to the population brings a consumer and a producer. According to Samuelson, Carey's 'logic was often bad and his prolix style atrocious. But his fundamental empirical inferences seem correct for his time and place' (p. 1732). Beginning in 1848, Carey became an ardent exponent of protectionism. By this time List was dead and it is uncertain to what extent, if any, Carey was indebted to List's thought. Neither of the two developed his proposal for tariff protection in isolation but as parts of a wider system of thought, of a theory of economic development in the case of List and of a theory of a harmoniously ordered society in the case of Carey.

Among political leaders in the United States Henry Clay is often mentioned as an architect of the American system, in which the industrial east and the agrarian west were allied in a powerful union. He pleaded for such a system in a famous speech in 1824, in which he supported protective tariffs as instruments of industrial development. Later still, in 1870, Francis Bowen, an early teacher of economics at Harvard, would publish *American Political Economy*, in which he supported tariff protection, and which caused him to lose his teaching job in economics, the president easing him into the presumably less controversial field of history.

In Germany, List's ideas had a profound and lasting influence. He promoted the customs union, which by 1844 covered almost all of Germany, and agitated for railroad construction and tariff protection. The very name of economics in Germany, *Nationalökonomie*, conveys associations with List. Some German interpreters of the history of economics have compared List with Marx. Both had utopian visions of a society to come in the fullness of time. Both made much of a fusion of theory and practice and of economics and politics. Both are linked by their reputation as rebels who opposed the established order. It is an interesting trivium that in 1841 List turned down an offer to serve as the editor of a newspaper that was to be published under the name of *Rheinische Zeitung*, a post that Marx filled the following year.

List's thought has an affinity with the historical schools and institutional economists, who had ideas of their own about the possibility of universally valid economic doctrines. The word 'system', cleansed of its protectionist implications, continued to play a key role in the writings of such 20th-century German economists as Walter Eucken and Werner Sombart. An equally faint echo of the Hamiltonian idea can be discerned in the current usage of the word in conjunction with the study of comparative economic *systems*.

BIBLIOGRAPHY

Carey, H. 1858–9. *Principles of Social Science.* 3 vols, Philadelphia: Lipincott.

Conkin, P.K. 1980. *Prophets of Prosperity: America's First Political Economists.* Bloomington: Indiana University Press.

Dorfman, J. 1946. *The Economic Mind in American Civilization*, Vols 1–2. New York: Viking Press.

Hamilton, A. 1934. *Papers on Public Credit, Commerce and Finance.* Ed. S. McKee, New York: Columbia University Press.

Henderson, W.O. 1983. *Friedrich List: Economist and Visionary 1789–1846.* London: Cass.

Hirst, M.E. 1909. *Life of Friedrich List and Selections from His Writings.* London: Smith, Elder.

Samuelson, P.A. 1960. American economics. In *Postwar Economic Trends in the United States*, ed. R.E. Freeman, New York: Harper. Reprinted in *P.A. Samuelson, Collected Scientific Papers*, Vol. 2, ed. J.E. Stiglitz, Cambridge, Mass.: MIT Press, 1966.

Spiegel, H.W. 1960. *The Rise of American Economic Thought.* Philadelphia: Chilton.

Spiegel, H.W. 1983. *The Growth of Economic Thought.* Revised and expanded edn, Durham, North Carolina: Duke University Press.

Natural Selection and Evolution

SIDNEY G. WINTER

Important theoretical concepts tend to resist satisfactory definition (cf. Stigler, 1957). Such concepts are in the service of the expansive ambitions of the theories in which they occur, and must accordingly respond flexibly to the changing requirements for maintaining order in a changing intellectual empire. The term 'evolution' – obviously important in biology, but also in the physical and social sciences – provides a good illustration of this principle. A prominent biologist and author of a highly expansive treatise on biological evolution has the following to offer in his glossary:

> *Evolution.* Any gradual change. Organic evolution, often referred to as evolution for short, is any genetic change in organisms from generation to generation, or more strictly, a change in gene frequencies within populations from generation to generation (Wilson, 1975).

Note the abrupt and radical reduction in the breadth of the conceptual field from the first phrase of this definition to the last. The beginning connects the term to common discourse; the reference to gene frequencies at the end clearly brands the term as belonging to biology, but does not do much to explicate it. The layman is left wondering whether this is meant to cover what happened to the dinosaurs, and perhaps puzzled also as to whether 'gradual change' adequately captures the common features of organic evolution, cultural evolution and stellar evolution.

To the extent that biology 'owns' the concepts of natural selection and evolution, the meanings of these terms tend to be regarded as biology-specific. It then seems to follow that the application of evolutionary thinking in other realms falls under the rubric 'biological analogies', whence it is believed to follow, further, that the appropriateness of an evolutionary approach somehow depends on the closeness of the parallels that can be drawn between the situation in view and situations considered in biology.

493

The quest for close parallels is substantially impeded by the fact that a prominent feature of the biological scene, sexual reproduction, is, one might say, peculiar. Although asexual or haploid reproduction plays a significant role in biological reality, and this is suitably reflected in portions of biological theory, critics of 'biological analogies' tend to stress the question 'what is the analogue of genetic inheritance?' with sexual reproduction in mind. A persuasive case can be made that the inability to complete an analogy in this respect is not necessarily a bar to its utility. It is certainly true, nevertheless, that a great deal of biological theory cannot readily be adapted for use in non-biological arenas because the implications of sexual reproduction are so central to the analysis.

This essay puts forward a radical approach to these issues: it challenges biology's basic ownership claim to the concept of evolution by natural selection. An account of the basic framework of evolutionary analysis is set forth, and while this account attaches meanings to 'evolution' and 'selection' that are obviously strongly influenced by evolutionary biology, it adapts more readily to discussion of various types of cultural evolution than to biological evolution (at least to the extent that the latter involves sexual reproduction). Examples of the application of the evolutionary viewpoint to economics are then provided in discussions of two areas, the evolution of productive knowledge and the character of Economic Man.

THE FRAMEWORK OF EVOLUTIONARY ANALYSIS. Fundamentally, and in the most abstract terms, an evolutionary process is a process of information storage with selective retention. Consider, for illustrative purposes, the books in an undergraduate library. Such a library typically has many copies of some books. Given the hazards of loss, pilferage and wear and tear, as contrasted with the comparative constancy of much of the subject matter, the library will not infrequently order new copies of books it has long possessed.

Although each individual volume is informationally complex and in some respects unique, there are nevertheless 'types' of books, for example, volumes with the same author and title. Formally, 'same author and title as' is an equivalence relation on the set of books, and a relation of particular interest to librarians, students, professors and others. There are, however, a great many other equivalence relations: 'same publisher as', 'same Library of Congress classification as', 'same colour as' and so forth. In fact, given the complexity of the individuals (volumes) that make up the library, the possibilities for defining equivalence relations – which in effect describe alternative approaches to describing the library – are virtually endless.

Now consider the change in such a library over the course of a year – say, at successive annual inventory times when the academic year is over, no books are circulating and all those that are going to be returned have been returned. In terms of a hypothetical exhaustive description of the library, which for example would note every change in yellow highlighting and marginal question marks, the amount of change is enormous in the sense that it would take a great many bytes of information to describe it. A more practical approach to describing the change is to take one or more interesting equivalence relations and count members of equivalence classes at the two dates. For example, for each title-and-author the number of elements in that equivalence class and in the library at t could be counted and the result compared with the number in that same equivalence class and in the library at $t + 1$. While a librarian might be chiefly interested in accounting for the difference in the two numbers, an evolutionary theorist is more likely to divide the latter number by the former and call the result the (observed) 'fitness' of that title-and-author. (Of course, this can only be done provided the denominator is not zero.)

Proceeding along this line, it is possible to discuss how the library evolves (at the title-and-author level) by 'natural selection'. This term refers to the action of the complex collection of processes that are involved in the introduction to and disappearance from the library of individual volumes. The word 'natural' connotes the expectation that these processes cannot be entirely explained by reference to the intent of some individual actor who is effectively in charge of the whole situation – perhaps the head librarian. (Were this expectation not held, the evolutionary approach to understanding the library might well be abandoned in favour of an attempt to fathom the intentions of the controlling actor.)

As described thus far, the evolutionary approach to understanding the library may provide a useful framework, but it is not a theory. In particular, the notion of 'fitness' provides a purely tautological 'explanation' of how the library changes over time. (It is also only a partial explanation, first because of the problem of new acquisitions (zero denominators), but more fundamentally because it treats of a small structure of equivalence relations and does not aspire to complete description.) There is no difficulty in converting this framework into a genuine theory; for example, just assume that 'title and author fitnesses' are constant over time. This theory has abundant empirical content; unfortunately, it is false. A weaker version, substituting 'approximately constant' will fare very little better. The difficulty lies not in the construction of genuine theories with empirical content within such an evolutionary framework, but in producing successful ones. More specifically, some non-tautological propositions about theoretical fitness must be derived and turn out to be true of observed fitness. Whether the quest for such propositions proves successful depends on the equivalence relations chosen for study.

In the library example, the choice of title-and-author as the focal equivalence relation for the theory is a masterstroke of creative insight (or would be if it were not obvious). With title and author as taxonomic criteria, a great deal of detailed information about individual volumes is succinctly captured. Also, the fact that there are printers and publishers (and copyright laws) has strong implications for the precision of the 'inheritance' mechanism in this evolutionary system, and the selection mechanism has persistent features reflecting the existence and persistence of academic departments, professors, large enrolment courses, reading lists and library budget levels.

Detailed knowledge of the actual systems governing inheritance and selection would certainly be helpful to the evolutionary scientist seeking to understand the

495

library, but it is not essential. Once 'on to' the idea that 'same title and author' is an important relation to the larger context that affects the evolution of the library, the investigator can make progress without necessarily knowing the answers to a lot of questions about why this idea is fruitful.

So far as the formal, tautological structure of the evolutionary approach is concerned, the investigator could just as well be working with the equivalence classes induced by the relation 'same word appears as the first word on page fifteen'. The investigator can still count volumes and measure fitness, and it will still be true (*ex post*) that the fittest types come to dominate the library – or more precisely, that approximately equal fitness is a requirement for long-term coexistence in the library environment. It would be surprising, however, if interesting empirical regularities emerged from such an inquiry.

If the foregoing discussion of the evolution of the undergraduate library were an attempt at developing a biological analogy, it would be time to pull back the veil from the correspondences that have not been made explicit thus far. The equivalence classes of 'same title and author as' correspond to species. Different editions or printings of a given book correspond to genotypes because there are systematic differences among them, yet the differences are small compared to the differences between classes. Underlining, yellow highlighting, torn pages and the like are examples of phenotypic variation, which reflect the incidents and accidents encountered by an individual volume over its life cycle. The Library of Congress provides a readymade taxonomic structure to facilitate discussion of evolution above the 'species' level. Journals are apparently a different life form altogether, since the usual close association of title and author does not prevail.

One could just as well, however, take evolutionary bibliography as the prototypical evolutionary science and think of biology in terms of bibliographic analogies (setting aside, of course, the facts of history and the wide difference in degree of development of the two subjects). In this perspective, the key idea on which the power of the evolutionary approach is seen to rest is that of an equivalence class within which the elements (individuals) are close copies of each other in observable respects. The meaning of 'close' involves a contrast between small intra-class variation and large inter-class variation in the system of equivalence classes. Related fundamental ideas are the idea of counting or otherwise measuring the aggregate of elements in such an equivalence class at different points in time, plus the notion that, over time, new individuals appear in a previously existing class – implying that somewhere and somehow the capacity to produce new individual copies exists.

Biological species that reproduce sexually represent a complex variant of this basic evolutionary paradigm. The part of the process that involves the production of the most exact copies, the replication of chromosomes in the course of gameteogenesis, involves information that is a complete genetic description neither of the parent nor of the offspring. The concept of genetically identical individuals – individuals that are alike the way different copies of the same printing of a book are alike – is prominent in theoretical models, but because of the genetic complexity of individuals and the character of sexual reproduction the phenomenon is rare in the part of nature where sexual reproduction prevails. One consequence is that the concept of a 'species', which is so central to evolutionary biology, displays imperfectly resolved tensions between taxonomic criteria and reproductive (interbreeding) criteria. This difficulty is a peculiarity associated with the phenomenon of sexual reproduction. Perhaps it is in part a reflection of the fact that the major substantive problem of the origin of species is not conclusively solved, and it would be counterproductive to leave no flexibility in the definition of species while pursuing that important goal.

In any case, the contention here is that the empirical application of the framework of evolutionary analysis requires in general the development of a taxonomic system (or more formally, a system of equivalence relations on the set of individuals considered) to which generalized concepts of inheritance, fitness and selection can be applied.

EVOLUTION OF PRODUCTIVE KNOWLEDGE. Many prominent economists have endorsed some version of the idea that evolutionary principles, or biological science, provide intellectual models that economists would do well to emulate. Marshall's famous dictum that 'The Mecca of the economist lies in economic biology rather than in economic dynamics' (Marshall, 1920, p. xiv) is an obvious and important case in point. Thomas (1983) analyses with admirable thoroughness the origin, meaning and implications of this statement in the development of Marshall's thought, emphasizing the central importance of the idea of *irreversible* evolutionary change in economic life. Somewhat less well known, perhaps, is Schumpeter's statement that

> The essential point to grasp is that in dealing with capitalism we are dealing with an evolutionary process.... Capitalism, then, is by nature a form or method of economic change and not only never is but never can be stationary (Schumpter, 1942, p. 82).

In Schumpeter's case, too, irreversible change is probably dominant among the connotations of 'evolution', a term which he employed quite frequently.

Neither Marshall nor Schumpeter presented what the above discussion argues to be the key to the development of a predictive evolutionary science – a suggestion about how to interpret economic reality in terms of a system of equivalence relations that effectively breathes empirical content into generalized notions of inheritance and selection. Such a suggestion was advanced, albeit sketchily, by Thorstein Veblen in his paper, 'Why Economics is not an Evolutionary Science' (1898, pp. 70–71, emphasis supplied):

> For the purpose of economic science the process of cumulative change that is to be accounted for is the sequence of *change in the methods of doing things* – the methods of dealing with the material means of life.

Although perhaps not as a result of direct influence from Veblen, a similar proposal (emphasizing imitation of 'rules of behaviour') figures in the classic essay on evolutionary economics by Alchian (1950). The idea is featured more prominently in Winter (1971), and more prominently still, under the rubric of 'routines', by Nelson and Winter (1982). It is the evolutionary economist's answer to an important element in the critique of 'biological analogies' offered by Penrose (1952).

Evolutionary economics thus attaches central importance to a question that is not merely unanswered, but unasked in the context of orthodox economic theory: what are the social processes by which productive knowledge is *stored*? Certainly the concepts of production sets and functions do not seriously evoke this question, and even the bulk of the theoretical literature concerned with technical change disregards the issue as it probes the causes and consequences of things becoming 'known' that were formerly 'unknown'. From an evolutionary viewpoint, abstracting from the storage process in this fashion inevitably has a crippling effect on the effort to understand the appearance of new methods of doing things and the selective pressures to which innovations and innovators are subjected. In particular, the fact may be overlooked that the role of business firms as sources of innovations is intimately related to their social role as repositories of productive knowledge.

These themes cannot be explored in detail here. By way of illustration, however, consider one example of a method of doing things – the method of producing written text that resembles print, called 'typewriting'. There is an equivalence relation 'same (alphabet) keyboard as' on the set of machines used for this purpose, and an equivalence class called 'standard (QWERTY) keyboard'. There is a related human skill called 'touch typing', and an equivalence class of skilled typists 'trained on standard keyboard'. The early evolutionary history of these familiar phenomena has been nicely analysed and described by Arthue (1984) and David (1985). It stands as a warning against simplistic ascriptions of optimality to the outcomes of evolutionary processes. As David explains, the familiar arrangement of keys on the standard keyboard originated as an adaptive response to a particular technical problem – the problem of key jamming produced by typists typing on a machine vastly different from the modern typewriter (be it mechanical, electric, electronic, or a facet of the capabilities of a computer). In particular, the text being produced was invisible to the typist, and jamming of the keys was both hard to detect and serious in its consequences. After many decades of evolution, during which the typewriter itself has been radically transformed, the QWERTY keyboard survives and still performs its intended function of slowing typists down.

David argues convincingly that a central feature of the social process that replicates QWERTY over the generations, to the exclusion of alternatives that permit faster typing, is the complementarity between typewriters and skilled typists. Without machines with an alternative keyboard, nobody learns an alternative touch typing skill. Without a good supply of appropriately trained typists, a shift to alternative machines does not pay.

There are some interesting facets of this situation that Arthur and David do not touch upon. One reason that the supply of typists plays the role it does is that touch typing is a tacitly known skill. Although concerned with symbol production, it is not transferable from individual to individual by symbolic communication. One cannot give a lecture to a roomful of typists and thereby convert their skills from one keyboard to another. Typists do not know (in a conscious or articulable way) how they do what they do. As a matter of fact, the level of performance displayed by a highly skilled typist remains mysterious even upon scientific analysis, seemingly surprising bounds set by known facts of human neurophysiology (Salthouse, 1984). The tacit character of typing skill implies high switching costs; the high performance levels achievable even under the QWERTY handicap presumably reduce the incentives to switch (assuming the demand for typing services is price inelastic).

The social process that maintains the QWERTY typewriting method on a large scale is a complex and multi-faceted phenomenon, involving a host of factors traditionally regarded as economic, plus others, such as tacit knowledge, that have more recently entered the disciplinary lexicon. The story of this somewhat obsessive social memory is the story of an innovation; on the other hand, it is also a story of how success was precluded for a number of other innovative efforts. In both of its aspects, it has counterparts today. For them, as for QWERTY, understanding how and why methods of doing things *do not* change is fundamental to understanding how and why they *do* change.

ECONOMIC MAN: THE EVOLUTIONARY CRITIQUE. Economists are wont to regard themselves as hard-headed realists in their assessments of the world in general and of human nature in particular. The trained eye of the economist penetrates facades of pompous pretence, cunning deceit and impassioned demagoguery, discerning the rational pursuit of self-interest in martyr, merchant and murderer alike. Many such penetrating analyses contain, no doubt, an important element of truth. Arguably, the making of them is an important role played by economists and others in a free society. For the purposes of economic science, however, the model of the rational self-interested individual has serious limitations. When it is not a transparent caricature (the textbook consumer who cares only about consumption of goods and services), it is often an obscure tautology (with no definite limits set on what may affect 'utility' and hence choice).

From an evolutionary viewpoint, the key question is which, if any, of the various theoretically described subspecies of *homo economicus* might have been well adapted to the real environments that have shaped humanity. A realistic and *scientific* appraisal of human nature (and the degree and nature of the self-interest manifested therein) is an appraisal supportable by reference to the biological and cultural determinants of contemporary human behaviour and the evolutionary forces that have shaped those determinants. If, in a particular instance, the implications of such an appraisal turn out to be different from those of 'hard headed' economic analysis, then economics ought to change – presuming of course, that the objective in view is the advance of economic science.

Outside of the realm of human motivation, economists routinely (but often implicitly) make use of theoretical assumptions that are plainly not 'hard headed' but the reverse. The leading case in point is the assumption that society somehow

499

provides perfect and costless enforcement of contracts. A second case is disregard
of social networks (defined by various criteria) as determinants of transacting
patterns. One does not have to be imbued with an evolutionary viewpoint, but
only moderately experienced in the world, to acknowledge that economic analysis
based on such assumptions may yield a seriously distorted image of reality. Where
an evolutionary viewpoint comes in handy is in discussing how and why the
economy functions as well as it does in spite of the limitations of third party
contract enforcement, and the role that non-economic social relations may play
in making this possible.

To some extent, the errors introduced by excesses of hard and soft headedness
tend to cancel out. Markets perform sometimes well and sometimes poorly, and
economics has managed to discover a good deal about this matter in spite of
the fact that it has left entirely out of account two major categories of reasons.
The burdens of carrying along the two sets of errors have, nevertheless, been
heavy. It is important to leave them behind.

Progress is being made in doing so. As economics breaks out of the shell
formed by its first approximation assumptions, its relationships to other social
sciences and to biology become both more obvious and more fruitful. The
intertwined themes of the role of self-interest in behaviour and the bases of social
cooperation are fundamental not just in economics but in all of social science,
and in much of biology as well. Jack Hirshleifer, who has repeatedly and
insightfully emphasized the universality of these themes, recently proclaimed
that '*there is only one social science*' (1985, p. 53). For a 'generalized
economics' to serve as that one social science, economics 'will have to deal with
man as he really is – self-interested or not, fully rational or not' (ibid.,
p. 59).

Although it is probably premature to announce a contest to provide the best
name for unified social science – a contest that would no doubt evoke numerous
alternatives to 'generalized economics' – it does seem that many of the elements
are at hand for a move toward unification. Major contributions from a variety
of directions have vastly improved understanding of how cooperative behaviour
in general and exchange behaviour in particular can arise in spite of weak or
nonexistent institutional support. Some of these involve explicit use of the
evolutionary framework (e.g. Axelrod, 1984); some do not (e.g. Williamson, 1985).
All are at least potentially adaptable to a general multi-level evolutionary scheme
in which patterns reproduced by a variety of mechanisms are subjected to selective
pressure. Major difficulties, and major controversies, attend the problem of
characterizing the linkages between the levels. On this front too there is recent
progress, particularly the work of Boyd and Richerson (1985), who study the
interactions of biological and cultural evolution with the aid of a collection of
'dual inheritance' models. Such interactions have, of course, implications for the
understanding of human biology as well as for the study of culture.

In sum, natural selection and evolution should not be viewed as concepts
developed for the specific purposes of biology and possibly appropriable for the
specific purposes of economics, but rather as elements of the framework of a new

conceptual structure that biology, economics and the other social sciences can comfortably share.

BIBLIOGRAPHY

Alchian, A. 1950. Uncertainty, evolution and economic theory. *Journal of Political Economy* 58, June, 211–21.

Arthur, W.B. 1984. Competing technologies and economic prediction. *Options* (I.I.A.S.A., Laxenburg, Austria), April, 10–13.

Axelrod, R. 1984. *The Evolution of Cooperation.* New York: Basic Books.

Boyd, R. and Richerson, P. 1985. *Culture and the Evolutionary Process.* Chicago: University of Chicago Press.

David, P. 1985. CLIO and the economics of QWERTY. *American Economic Review* 75(2), May, 332–7.

Hirshleifer, J. 1985. The expanding domain of economics. *American Economic Review* 75(6), December, 53–68.

Marshall, A. 1920. *Principles of Economics.* 8th edn, London: Macmillan, 1953; New York: Macmillan, 1956.

Nelson, R. and Winter, S. 1982. *An Evolutionary Theory of Economic Change.* Cambridge, Mass.: Harvard University Press.

Penrose, E. 1952. Biological analogies in the theory of the firm. *American Economic Review* 42, December, 804–19.

Salthouse, T. 1984. The skill of typing. *Scientific American* 250(2), February, 128–35.

Schumpeter, J. 1942. *Capitalism, Socialism and Democracy.* 3rd edn, New York: Harper, 1950.

Stigler, G. 1957. Perfect competition, historically contemplated. In G. Stigler, *Essays in the History of Economics,* Chicago: University of Chicago Press, 1965.

Thomas, B. 1983. Alfred Marshall on Economic Biology. Paper presented to the History of Economics Society, May.

Veblen, T. 1898. Why economics is not an evolutionary science. In T. Veblen, *The Place of Science in Modern Civilization,* New York: Russell & Russell, 1961.

Williamson, O. 1985. *The Economic Institutions of Capitalism.* New York: Free Press.

Wilson, E. 1975. *Sociobiology: a New Synthesis.* Cambridge, Mass.: Harvard University Press.

Winter, S. 1971. Satisficing, selection and the innovating remnant. *Quarterly Journal of Economics* 85(2), May, 237–61.

'Neoclassical'

TONY ASPROMOURGOS

The term 'neoclassical' was first used by Veblen (1900, pp. 242, 260–62, 265–8) in order to characterize Marshall and Marshallian economics. Veblen did not appeal to any similarity in theoretical structure between the economics of Marshall and classical economics in order to defend this novel designation. Rather, he perceived Marshall's Cambridge school to have a continuity with classical economics on the alleged basis of a common utilitarian approach and the common assumption of a hedonistic psychology. Derivative from Veblen's usage, this meaning of the term subsequently gained some currency, particularly in the 1920s and 1930s; for example, in the writings of Wesley Mitchell, J.A. Hobson, Maurice Dobb and Eric Roll. It is evident that the emergence of this notion of Marshallian economics as a 'neoclassical' project also involved, at least in part, an acquiescence to Marshall's understanding of the continuity between his own economics and the classical tradition. Keynes (1936, pp. 177–8) also employed the term, though in an idiosyncratic manner, derivative from his notion of classical economics.

The use of the term with the meaning which became the accepted convention after World War II, extending it to embrace marginalist theory in general, can be traced to Hicks (1932, p. 84) and Stigler (1941, pp. 8, 13, 297). From what source they derived the term is not certain. It is highly unlikely that either of them coined it independently. Perhaps the likeliest source of Hicks's usage is Dobb's article, published as it was in the London School of Economics 'house journal'. Following Hamilton (1923), Dobb (1924, p. 68) writes that 'neo-classical' is not an entirely inappropriate term to describe Marshallian economics, 'for what the Cambridge School has done is to divest Classical Political Economy of its more obvious crudities, to sever its connection with the philosophy of natural law, and to restate it in terms of the differential calculus. The line of descent is fairly direct from Smith, Malthus, and Ricardo'. Hicks's article itself, or Veblen, are the most likely sources of Stigler's usage. Stigler refers to both of them. Hicks and Stigler were certainly more correct than Veblen in perceiving the unifying core of the marginalist theories to be, on the one hand, methodological individualism and, on the other, the marginal productivity theory of distribution deriving from the subjective theory of value. However, neither of them offered any significant defence for their (then) implicit view that the writings of the classical economists also can be characterized in terms of this theoretical approach. Subsequently this characterization – and the nomenclature for marginalism associated with it – has given way to a recognition of the sharp theoretical disjuncture between classical and marginalist economics. Stigler's usage, albeit hesitant, was probably as influential as his book. The term first gained wide currency in the debates on capital and growth in the 1950s and 1960s. It was no doubt also popularized by the extensive use made of it in Samuelson's textbook. From the third edition, Samuelson (1955, p. vi) presents the book as setting forth a 'grand neoclassical synthesis'.

BIBLIOGRAPHY

Dobb, M. 1924. The entrepreneur myth. *Economica* 4(10), 66–81.

Hamilton, W.H. 1923. Vestigial economics. *The New Republic*, 4 April.

Hicks, J.R. 1932. Marginal productivity and the principle of variation. *Economica* 12(35), 79–88.

Keynes, J.M. 1936. *The General Theory of Employment, Interest and Money.* London: Macmillan.

Samuelson, P.A. 1955. *Economics: An Introductory Analysis.* 3rd edn, New York: McGraw-Hill.

Stigler, G.J. 1941. *Production and Distribution Theories.* New York: Macmillan.

Veblen, T.B. 1900. The preconceptions of economic science III. *Quarterly Journal of Economics* 14, 240–69.

Neoclassical Synthesis

OLIVIER JEAN BLANCHARD

The term 'neoclassical synthesis' appears to have been coined by Paul Samuelson to denote the consensus view of macroeconomics which emerged in the mid-1950s in the US. To quote from the third edition of *Economics* (1955, p. 212):

> In recent years 90 per cent of American Economists have stopped being 'Keynesian economists' or 'anti-Keynesian economists'. Instead they have worked toward a synthesis of whatever is valuable in older economics and in modern theories of income determination. The result might be called neo-classical economics and is accepted in its broad outlines by all but about 5 per cent of extreme left wing and right wing writers.

Unlike the old neoclassical economics, the new synthesis did not expect full employment to occur under *laissez faire*; it believed however that, by proper use of monetary and fiscal policy, the old classical truths would come back into relevance.

This synthesis was to remain the dominant paradigm for another twenty years, in which most of the important contributions, by Hicks, Modigliani, Solow, Tobin and others, were to fit quite naturally. Its apotheosis was probably the large econometric models, in particular the MPS model developed by Modigliani and his collaborators, which incorporated most of these contributions in an empirically based and mathematically coherent model of the US economy. The synthesis had, however, suffered from the start from schizophrenia in its relation to microeconomics. This schizophrenia was eventually to lead to a serious crisis, under the challenge of the 'new classical macroeconomics' led by Lucas, Sargent and others, from which it has not yet emerged. I shall describe in turn the initial synthesis, the mature synthesis and the current crisis.

THE INITIAL SYNTHESIS. In retrospect, the postwar consensus view was a consensus about two main beliefs.

504

The first was that the decisions of the firms and of individuals were largely rational, and as such, amenable to study using standard methods from microeconomics. Modigliani, in the introduction to his collected papers, states it strongly:

[One of the] basic themes that has dominated my scientific concern [has been to integrate] the main building blocks of the General Theory with the more established methodology of economics, which rests on the basic postulate of rational maximizing behaviour on the part of economic agents ... (1980, p. xi).

The faith in rationality was far from blind: animal spirits were perceived as the main source of movements in aggregate demand through investment. For example, the possibility that corporate saving was too high and not offset by personal saving was considered a serious issue, and discussed on empirical rather than theoretical grounds.

This faith in rationality did not, however, extend to a belief in the efficient functioning of markets. The second main belief was indeed that prices and wages did not adjust very quickly to clear markets. There was wide agreement that markets could not be seen as competitive. But, somewhat surprisingly given the popularity of imperfect competition theories at the time, there was no attempt to think in terms of theories of price and wage setting, with explicit agents setting prices and wages. Instead, the prevailing mode of thinking was in terms of *tâtonnement*, with prices adjusting to excess supply or demand, along the lines of the dynamic processes of adjustment studied by Samuelson in his *Foundations*. The Phillips curve, imported to the US by Samuelson and Solow in 1960, was in that context both a blessing and a curse. It gave strong empirical support to a *tâtonnement*-like relation between the rate of change of nominal wages and the level of unemployment, but it also made less urgent the need for better microeconomic underpinnings of market adjustment. Given the existence of a reliable empirical relation and the perceived difficulty of the theoretical task, it made good sense to work on other and more urgent topics, where the marginal return was higher.

These twin beliefs had strong implications for the research agenda as well as for policy.

Because prices and wages eventually adjusted to clear markets, and because policy could avoid prolonged disequilibrium anyway, macroeconomic research could progress along two separate lines. One could study long-run movements in output, employment and capital, ignoring business cycle fluctuations as epiphenomena along the path and using the standard tools of equilibrium analysis: 'Solving the vital problems of monetary and fiscal policy by the tools of income analysis will validate and bring back into relevance the classical verities' (Samuelson, *Economics*, 3rd edn, 1955). Or one could instead study short-run fluctuations around that trend, ignoring the trend itself. This is indeed where most of the breakthroughs had been made by the mid-1950s. Work by Hicks (1937) and Hansen (1949), attempting to formalize the major elements of Keynes's informal model, had led to the IS–LM model. Modigliani (1944) had made clear the role played by nominal wage rigidity in the Keynesian model. Metzler (1951) had shown the importance of wealth effects, and the role of government debt. Patinkin (1956) had clarified the structure of the macroeconomic model, and the relation between the demands for goods, money and bonds, in the case of flexible prices and wages. There was general agreement that, except in unlikely and exotic cases, the IS was downward-sloping and the LM upward-sloping. Postwar interest rates were high enough – compared to prewar rates – to make the liquidity trap less of an issue. There was still, however, considerable uncertainty about the effect of interest rates on investment, and thus about the slope of the IS relation. The assumption of fixed nominal wages of Keynes and early Keynesian models had been relaxed in favour of slow adjustment of prices and wages to market conditions. This was not seen, however, as modifying substantially earlier conclusions. The 'Pigou effect' (so dubbed by Patinkin in 1948), according to which low-enough prices would increase real money and wealth, was not considered to be of much practical significance. Only activist policy could avoid large fluctuations in economic activity.

Refinements of the model were not taken as implying that the case for policy activism was any less strong than Keynes had suggested. Because prices and wages did not adjust fast enough, active countercyclical policy was needed to keep the economy close to full employment. Because prices and wages, or policies themselves, eventually got the economy to remain not far from its growth path, standard microeconomic principles of fiscal policy should be used to choose the exact mix of fiscal measures at any point in time. The potential conflict between their relative efficacy in terms of demand management, and their effect on the efficiency of economic allocation was considered an issue; but it was not considered a major problem, and nor was the fact that the market failure which led to short-run fluctuations in the first place was not fully understood or even identified.

The ground rules for cyclical fiscal policy were laid down in particular by Samuelson in a series of contributions (1951, for example). Countercyclical fiscal policy was to use both taxes and spending; in a depression, the best way to increase demand was to increase both public investment, and private investment, by taxes, so as to equalize social marginal rates of return on both. Where the synthesis stood on monetary policy is less clear. While the potential of monetary policy to smooth fluctuations was generally acknowledged, one feels that fiscal policy was still the instrument of predilection, that policy was seen as fiscal policy in the lead, with accommodating monetary policy in tow.

THE MATURE SYNTHESIS. For the next twenty years, the initial synthesis was to supply a framework in which most macroeconomists felt at home and in which contributions fitted naturally. As Lucas remarks in his critique of the synthesis, 'those economists, like Milton Friedman, who made no use of the framework, were treated with some impatience by its proponents' (1980). The research programme was largely implied by the initial synthesis, and the emphasis on the behavioural components of the IS–LM and its agnostic approach to price and wage adjustment; quoting from Modigliani, 'the Keynesian system rests on four basic blocks: the consumption function, the investment function, the demand and the supply of money, and the mechanisms determining prices and wages' (1980, p. xii). Progress on many of these fronts was extraordinary; I now summarize it briefly.

The failure of the widely predicted postwar oversaving to materialize had led to a reassessment of consumption theory. The theory of intertemporal utility maximization progressively emerged as the main contender. It was developed independently by Friedman (1957) as the 'permanent income hypothesis' and Modigliani and collaborators (1954 in particular) as the 'life cycle hypothesis'. The life cycle formulation, modified to allow for imperfect financial markets and liquidity constraints, was, however, to dominate most of empirical research. Part of the reason was that it emphasized more explicitly the role of wealth on consumption, and through wealth, the role of interest rates. Neither wealth effects nor interest rate effects on consumption had figured prominently in the initial synthesis.

Research on the investment function was less successful. Part of the difficulty just came from the complexity of the empirical task, the heterogeneity of capital and the possibility of substituting factors *ex ante*, but not *ex post*. Many of the conceptual issues were clarified by work on growth but empirical implementation was harder. Part of the difficulty came, however, from the ambiguity of the neoclassical theory about price behaviour, about whether firms could be thought of setting prices or whether the slow adjustment of prices implied that firms were in fact output constrained. The 'neo-classical theory of investment' developed by Jorgenson and collaborators is ambiguous in this respect, assuming implicitly that price is equal to marginal cost, but estimating empirical functions with output rather than real wages.

Research on the demand and supply of money was extended to include all assets. Solid foundations for the demand for money were given by Tobin (1956) and Baumol (1952), and the theory of finance provided a theory of the demand for all assets (Tobin 1958). The expectations hypothesis, which alleviates the need to estimate full demand and supply models of financial markets, was thoroughly tested and widely accepted as an approximation to reality.

In the spirit of the initial synthesis, work on prices and wages was much less grounded in theory than work on the other components of the Keynesian model. While research on the microeconomic foundations of wage and price behaviour was proceeding (Phelps, 1972, in particular), it was poorly integrated in empirical wage and price equations. To a large extent, this block of the Keynesian synthesis remained throughout the period the ad hoc but empirically successful Phillips curve, respecified through time to allow for a progressively larger effect of past inflation on wage inflation.

All these blocks, together with work on growth theory, were largely developed in relation with and then combined in macroeconometric models, starting with the models estimated by Klein. The most important model was probably the MPS–FMP model developed by Modigliani and collaborators. This model, while maintaining the initial IS–LM Phillips curve structure of its ancestors showed the richness of the channels through which shocks and policy could affect the economy. It could be used to derive optimal policy, show the effects of structural changes in financial markets,.... By the early 1970s the synthesis appeared to be have been highly successful and the research programme laid down after the war to have been mostly completed.

THE CRISIS. Since 1975, the neoclassical synthesis has been fighting for survival. While the initial crisis came from its failure to explain events, it was soon clear that the problem was deeper. The synthesis has been struggling with this problem since then.

The scientific success of the synthesis had been largely due to its empirical success, especially during the Kennedy and the first phase of the Johnson administrations. As inflation increased in the late 1960s, the empirical success and in turn its theoretical foundations were more and more widely questioned; the more serious blow was however the stagflation of the mid-1970s in response to the increases in the price of oil: it was clear that policy was not able to maintain steady growth and low inflation. In a clarion call against the neoclassical synthesis, Lucas and Sargent (1983) judged its predictions to have been an 'econometric failure on a grand scale'. But one cannot condemn a theory for failing to anticipate the shape and the effects of shocks which have never been observed before; few theories would pass such a test. As long as the events can be explained after the fact, there is no particular cause for concern. In fact, soon thereafter, models were expanded to allow for supply shocks such as changes in the price of oil. Models based on the synthesis so expanded, either analytical or empirical, are still successfully used to analyse and guide policy. It has become clear however that, while the models could indeed be adjusted *ex post*, there was a more serious problem behind the failure to predict the events of the 1970s. To quote again from the polemical 1983 article by Sargent and Lucas, 'That the doctrine on which [these predictions] were made is fundamentally flawed is simply a matter of fact.'

The 'fundamental flaw' is the asymmetric treatment of agents as being highly rational and of markets as being so inefficient in adjusting wages and prices to their appropriate levels. The tension between the treatment of rational agents and myopic impersonal markets had been made more obvious by the developments of the 1960s, and the representation of consumers and firms as highly rational intertemporal decision makers. It was further highlighted by the research on fixed price equilibria, which went to the extreme of taking prices and quantities as unexplained and solving them for macroeconomic equilibrium under non-market clearing. That research made clear, in a negative way, that progress could only be made if one understood why markets did not clear, why prices and wages did not adjust. That line of research has, as a result, largely disappeared in the United States although it is still very active in Europe.

The solution proposed by Lucas and others in the 'new classical synthesis' was and still is thoroughly unappealing to economists trained in the neoclassical synthesis. It was to formalize the economy as if markets were competitive and clearing instantaneously. The 'as if' assumption seemed objectionable on *a priori* grounds, in that direct evidence on labour and goods markets suggested important departure from competition; it also appeared to many to be an unpromising approach if the goal was to explain economic fluctuations and unemployment. Papers by Fischer (1977) and Taylor (1980) showed that one could replace the Phillips curve of inflation and unemployment by a model of explicit nominal price and wage setting and still retain most of the traditional results. But it was also clear that labour and goods markets were substantially more complex than was captured by these models. Thus, much of the recent research has turned to the microeconomic workings of labour and goods markets. This research covers work on the effects of insurance and asymmetric information, on efficiency wages, on monopolistically competitive and oligopolistic behaviour in goods markets. It has already made clear that most of the explanations proposed for price and wage behaviour have implications for other components of the model, that the separation made in the neoclassical synthesis between decisions about quantity and the behaviour of prices may often be misleading. This research is still, however, largely speculative and poorly integrated; a new synthesis is at best far on the horizon.

BIBLIOGRAPHY

Baumol, W.J. 1952. The transactions demand for cash. *Quarterly Journal of Economics* 66, November, 545–56.

Fischer, S. 1977. Long-term contracts, rational expectations, and the optimal money supply rule. *Journal of Political Economy* 85(1), February, 191–205.

Friedman, M. 1957. *A Theory of the Consumption Function*. New York: National Bureau of Economic Research.

Hansen, A. 1949. *Monetary Theory and Fiscal Policy*. New York: McGraw-Hill.

Hicks, J. 1937. Mr Keynes and the 'classics': a suggested interpretation. *Econometrica* 5, April, 147–59.

Lucas, R. 1980. Methods and problems in business cycle theory. *Journal of Money, Credit and Banking* 12(4), Part 2, November, 696–715.

Lucas, R. and Sargent, T. 1983. After Keynesian macroeconomics. In *After the Phillips Curve: Persistence of High Inflation and High Unemployment*, Federal Reserve of Boston.

Metzler, L. 1951. Wealth, saving and the rate of interest. *Journal of Political Economy* 59, April, 93–116.

Modigliani, F. 1944. Liquidity preference and the theory of interest and money. *Econometrica* 12, January, 45–88.

Modigliani, F. 1980. *Collected Papers*. Vol. 1: *Essays in Macroeconomics*. Cambridge, Mass.: MIT Press.

Modigliani, F. and Brumberg, R. 1954. Utility analysis and the consumption function: an interpretation of cross section data. In *Post-Keynesian Economics*, ed. K.K. Kurihara, New Brunswick, NJ: Rutgers University Press.

Patinkin, D. 1948. Price flexibility and full employment. *American Economic Review* 38, September, 543–64.

Patinkin, D. 1956. *Money, Interest and Prices*. New York: Harper & Row.

Phelps, E. 1972. *Inflation Policy and Unemployment Theory*. London: Macmillan.

Samuelson, P. 1951. Principles and rules in modern fiscal policy: a neoclassical reformulation. In *Money, Trade and Economic Growth: Essays in Honor of John Henry Williams*, ed. H.L. Waitzman, New York: Macmillan.

Samuelson, P. 1955. *Economics*. 3rd edn, New York: McGraw-Hill.

Taylor, J. 1980. Aggregate dynamics and staggered contracts. *Journal of Political Economy* 88(1), February, 1–23.

Tobin, J. 1956. The interest-elasticity of transactions demand for cash. *Review of Economics and Statistics* 38, August, 241–7.

Tobin, J. 1958. Liquidity preference as behavior towards risk. *Review of Economic Studies* 25, February, 65–86.

Neutral Taxation

ARNOLD C. HARBERGER

One can detect in the literature of economics two important lines of thinking on the subject of neutral taxation. One emphasizes economic efficiency (i.e. the elimination of deadweight loss) as the objective in terms of which the neutrality of taxation is defined. The other emphasizes the generality of a tax as itself imparting the quality of neutrality. Two examples, each with a long history in economic thinking, illustrated the main lines of the distinction.

On the one hand we have the taxation of land rents or land values. It builds on the notion (not precisely true in fact) that each piece or plot of land is totally fixed in supply, with the consequence that any tax levied upon it will ultimately be paid out of its pure economic rent.

On the other hand we have the relatively modern idea of a general tax on value added, the tax being applied at a uniform rate on all activities in the economy. Here there is no thought that the underlying resources are fixed in each activity; quite to the contrary, mobility among the various taxed activities is taken for granted for most of the resources on whose product the tax will fall.

It is easy enough by making artful assumptions to bring these two notions very close together. For example we can *assume* that no manmade improvements to the soil are possible, or alternatively that the tax assessors can always distinguish between 'the intrinsic and immutable qualities of the soil', on which tax is then duly assessed, and the manmade improvements thereon or accretions thereto, on which (under our convenient assumption) no tax is either assessed or paid. Similarly, we can *assume* for the value added tax that there are just three basic resources in the economy – land, labour and capital – and that each of them is fixed in supply. Therefore a uniform tax on the marginal product of any one of them will be neutral, striking the factor equally regardless of the end use to which it is applied, and leaving the factor (because of the assumed zero-elasticity of its supply) no untaxed haven (not even leisure) to which it might choose to escape.

The above assumptions make it easy to define neutral taxation for a dictionary. (Neutral taxation is taxation falling on something that is in completely inelastic supply, with the tax being so designed as not to affect resource allocation either within or among the affected categories or between them and the other activities not subject to the tax.) But it would probably not add much to the usefulness of the dictionary.

To be truly useful, I believe, a definition of neutral taxation should be able to throw away such artificial crutches as the two assumptions presented above. It should be able to live in the real world, where we know that the relevant supply elasticities are rarely zero, but where we do not feel at all sure about their magnitudes nor how they vary as between the short, middle and long run. It should be able to cope with reality that, for tax policy at least, the objects of tax do not have an independent essence as commodities; rather, a commodity subject to tax is whatever the tax law (including the regulations and practices followed in enforcing that law) defines it to be. And finally it should come to grips with the serious claims that can be made for considering equality (among the affected activities) in the applicable tax rate to be an attribute whose presence connotes neutrality and whose absence creates a presumption of non-neutrality.

Economics has come the farthest in responding to the first of the desiderata expressed above. Deadweight loss is a concept completely familiar to the discipline, as is the idea of minimizing the deadweight loss of raising a certain amount of tax revenue subject to given constraints. A clear line of thinking runs from Ramsey in the 1920s through Hotelling in the 1930s, Meade in the 1940s, Corlett and Hague and Lipsey and Lancaster in the 1950s, Harberger in the 1960s, to the modern writers on optimal taxation of whom Atkinson, Diamond, Dixit, Mirrlees and Stiglitz are a representative few. Flowing through this strand of thought are the related ideas (a) that uniform taxation is not always neutral; (b) that the special condition under which uniform taxation of a subset of commodities or activities minimizes the deadweight loss of raising a given amount of revenue from that subset, is met when the equilibrium quantity (or activity level) of *each* member of the taxed subset would respond in the same proportion to a (hypothetical) uniform tax on all goods or activities that are *not* in the taxed subset; and (c) that whenever the condition stated in (b) is *not* met then instead of uniform taxation the minimization of deadweight loss requires higher-than-average taxation on goods whose quantities would fall as a result of a (hypothetical) uniform tax on the uncovered group and lower-than-average taxation on those whose equilibrium quantities would rise most sharply.

The analysis underlying the above statements is straightforward, and one can even call economic intuition into play to explain the conclusion. If the tax authorities are denied the possibility of taxing certain goods or activities, then it can to some degree 'get around' the ban by putting higher taxes on those items within the taxable subset which are complements of those that cannot be taxed. In a similar vein, since one way of thinking of the resource misallocation that occurs when only a subset of activities is allowed to be taxed is that resources are 'artificially' shunted from the taxed to the untaxed subset, it seems quite plausible that the optimal patterning of tax rates within the taxed subset should entail taxing at somewhat lower-than-average rates those particular activities in which a percentage point increment of tax would lead to notably greater-than-average 'shunting' of resources to untaxed activities.

The line of reasoning just presented is persuasive – sufficiently so that some economists have been tempted to write off uniformity altogether as a plausible objective of tax policy. There remain many, however, who adhere to uniformity as a goal. Given the ease with which propositions (a) through (c) above can be derived, one should hope that most of those who hold to uniformity base their adherence on considerations extraneous to the derivation, say, of the Ramsey rule and other similar propositions in the literature on optimal taxation. The discussion that follows assumes so.

To build a case for uniformity in taxation in the face of the foregoing logic, one should (appropriately, I think) postulate that one is not dealing with two quite arbitrary categories of goods and/or activities, viz., the taxed subset and the untaxed subset. Instead, one should assume that the taxed subset, rather than being 'any arbitrary bundle', is so selected as to contain all the goods and activities that can plausibly and without unusual administrative or regulatory effort be brought into the tax net. One then proceeds to view the problem not as a simple analytical puzzle but as one of guiding or governing the interaction between the society's fiscal authorities and its members.

With this objective in mind, an advocate of uniform taxation might set up a quite different problem from that posed earlier. He might consider the 'disturbance' with which he is dealing to be a consumer changing his mind about how to spend his money or a worker changing his preference about where or for whom to work. A uniform-tax advocate would likely place a considerable value on the authorities' simply not caring about these various changes of mind.

When one solves the Ramsey problem one takes as given the tastes and preferences of economic agents and maximizes government revenue for a given aggregate level of the agents' welfare. Under the differentiated set of tax rates that emerges from this exercise, the maximizer is not indifferent to changes in tastes of the agents. The maximizer likes it when agents shift their tastes from low-taxed to high-taxed activities, and is disappointed by shifts in the other direction.

Something of the same thing occurs when uniform taxation is implemented. Here the 'good' event would be a shift in tastes that caused untaxed activities to contract and taxed activities to expand; the 'bad' event would be the opposite. But there would be a wide range of changes of tastes that would be neutral – these would cover shifts among commodities or activities within the sector subject to the uniform tax, and also shifts among activities in the untaxed sector. To the degree that the authorities are successful in extending the tax net over quite a wide range, it may turn out to be true that most changes in tastes simply lead to shifts in the composition of goods within the taxed group. This is the sort of scenario that would best fit the vision of an advocate of broad-based, uniform taxation and at the same time would (at least if changes in tastes within the taxed sector were frequent and important) create problems for proponents of Ramsey rule taxation.

Subtle overtones of a less technical nature also arise when Ramsey-rule taxation is compared to a broad-based, uniform levy. In Ramsey-rule taxation individuals are genuinely presented with incentives to shift their demand from high-taxed to low-taxed products, and workers are likewise motivated to shift their labour efforts from high-taxed to low-taxed activities. Both these incentives are counterproductive from the social point of view. Subtly hidden in the way the problem is framed is the assumption that people's tastes are given. The reality of the world is that tax laws change only rarely; once enacted, they stay in effect for long periods of time, over which economists can be certain that there will be important changes in the parameters of tastes and technology. The goal of having a tax system that is *robust* against these unknown future shifts in demand and supply is not capricious; it deserves to be taken seriously.

In a quite different vein, there arises the question of to what degree we want our choice of tax patterns to depend on parameters like elasticities of supply and demand about which our knowledge is very spotty and imperfect. Proponents of uniform taxation can fairly argue that their choice of such a form does not depend seriously on knowledge about the parameters of demand and supply. Economic theory assures us that the dominant force is substitution (in the sense that a tax on an activity will, other things equal, cause that activity to contract). There is thus a very strong presumption that broadening the coverage and lowering the rate of a uniform tax will reduce the deadweight loss associated with it (for given revenue yield). One can build policy on this basis without having any detailed knowledge of the parameters of supply and demand, without any particular hope of gaining anything more than a very patchy knowledge about them in the future, and indeed *with* an almost absolute assurance that whatever the relevant parameters might be now, they will undergo substantial changes in the future. If one believes that these conditions come close to describing our present and likely future state of knowledge about the relevant parameters, he will likely be predisposed toward uniform as against Ramsey-rule taxation.

The last line of argument favouring uniform taxation has to do with the interplay between equity and efficiency considerations in governing tax policy. The motivations that fall under the umbrella of 'equity' are too numerous and too varied to try to recount here. But nowhere among them can one find that it is fairer to tax more heavily factors of production that cannot flee to other activities or that it is more just to tax heavily those items whose demand happens to be less elastic. To tax salt more heavily than sugar simply and solely because it has a lower elasticity of demand is at least as capricious (from the standpoint of equity) as taxing people differently according to the colour of their eyes.

Ultimately, I believe, the issue of uniform versus Ramsey-rule taxation may turn out to be just one facet of much broader philosophical differences. Consider the philosophy of government that assigns to government the role of creating a framework of laws and regulations within which the private sector then is encouraged to operate freely. Under this philosophy a positive value is placed on the authorities' not caring about what private agents do (so long as they abide by the rules). It is a positive desideratum to create a tax system that is robust against changes in tastes and technology.

On the other side of the coin we have a philosophy of social engineering, in which the detailed tastes and technology of the society enter as data into a process by which the policy makers choose parameters such as tax rates and coverages so as to maximize some measure of social net benefit.

Each of these philosophies has had its own long trajectory within the profession of economics. Each has its representatives today. Each will surely be reflected in the literature of future decades. In my opinion, the future debate as to how the concept of neutrality in taxation should be reflected in real-world policy decisions will swirl around the subtle differences between the ways in which holders of these two philosophies view the world, between the roles they envision for government, and between the ways they see the science of economics interacting with government in the formation of policy.

BIBLIOGRAPHY

Atkinson, A.B. 1977. Optimal taxation and the direct versus indirect tax controversy. *Canadian Journal of Economics* 10, 590–606.

Atkinson, A.B. and Stiglitz, J.E. 1980. *Lectures on Public Economics*. New York and Maidenhead: McGraw-Hill (esp. Lectures 12–14).

Corlett, W.J. and Hague, D.C. 1953. Complementarity and the excess burden of taxation. *Review of Economic Studies* 21, 21–30.

Diamond, P.A. and Mirrlees, J.A. 1971. Optimal taxation and public production. I: Production efficiency: II: Tax rules. *American Economic Review* 61, 8–27, 261–78.

Dixit, A.K. 1970. On the optimum structure of commodity taxes. *American Economic Review* 60, 295–301.

Harberger, A.C. 1964. Taxation, resource allocation and welfare. In *The Role of Direct and Indirect Taxes in the Federal Revenue System*, ed. J.F. Due, Princeton: Princeton University Press.

Hotelling, H. 1938. The general welfare in relation to problems of taxation and of railway and utility rates. *Econometrica* 6, 242–69.

Lipsey, R.G. and Lancaster, K. 1956–7. The general theory of second best. *Review of Economic Studies* 24, 11–32.

Meade, J.E. 1955. *Trade and Welfare*. Vol. II: *Mathematical Supplement*. Oxford: Oxford University Press.

Mirrlees, J.A. 1976. Optimal tax theory: a synthesis. *Journal of Public Economics* 6, 327–58.

Mirrlees, J.A. 1979. The theory of optimal taxation. In *Handbook of Mathematical Economics*, ed. K.J. Arrow and M.D. Intriligator, Amsterdam: North-Holland.

Open Field System

DONALD N. McCLOSKEY

The open field system was the arrangement of peasant agriculture in northern Europe before the 20th century into scattered strips communally regulated but privately owned. The system shares features with much peasant agriculture worldwide, especially in its scattering of strips. Dissolved gradually by 'enclosure' (Turner, 1984), first in England and Scandinavia and later in France (Grantham, 1980), Germany (Mayhew, 1973) and the Slavic lands (Blum, 1961), it has been seen as an obstacle to agricultural development. The system is most thoroughly documented in England (Gray, 1915; Ault, 1972; Baker and Butlin, 1973; Yelling, 1977; and hundreds of local studies). The English case has long been disproportionately important because it has provided a rich set of myths for other cases of traditional agriculture and reform. (The Russian version, the *mir*, is important for the same reason; but its unique feature – the periodic redistribution of the strips among families – arose in the 18th century out of the need to pay taxes, not out of the ancient community of cousins.)

The scattering of strips within two or three large, unfenced (hence 'open') fields, perhaps a thousand acres each, implied common grazing on the stubble: fencing of the typical landholder's seven or so plots, an acre or so each, was otherwise too expensive. The common grazing implied in turn common decisions on what was to be grown and when. The grazing herd forced all the villagers to plant and harvest on a common schedule.

The word 'common' has led to a misunderstanding of the system by economists and geographers unfamiliar with the history (Hardin, 1968; Baack and Thomas, 1974; Cohen and Weitzman, 1975). The 'commons' famed in nursery rhyme and academic fantasy were the waste land suitable only for grazing, usually absent or tiny in the open field regions, and to be distinguished from the main fields, the ploughed lands grazed 'in common' after the harvest (confusingly named 'the common fields'). The 'common' grazing and 'common' cropping did not mean that cattle and sheep were socialized or that cultivation was accomplished in communal gangs. The commonness was in coordination, not in ownership;

516

in regulation, not in reward. Land, labour and capital were wholly private and rent-earning, not (as economists have imagined) 'common pools' or 'fisheries'. The inefficiency of open fields, therefore, was not the inefficiency of a primitive socialism but of an imperfect capitalism.

The inefficiencies of open fields arose from spillovers and lack of specialization (the loss of land in boundaries and the loss of time in commuting from strip to strip were unimportant). Court records of quarrels between neighbours, and the poetry of the time, speak eloquently of the inconvenience of propinquity. In *Piers Ploughman* (*c*1378) Avarice boasts 'If I go to the plough, I pinch so narrow/ That a foot's land or a furrow to fetch I would/ Of my next neighbour, take of his earth;/ And if I reap, overreach, or give advice to him that reap/ To seize for me with his sickle what I never sowed.' Three centuries later, after voluntary enclosure had narrowed the system (which anyway had not existed in highland areas), Thomas Tusser recommended 'several' (that is, consolidated) farming over 'champion' (that is, open field), because 'Good land that is several, crops may have three,/ In champion country it may not so be:/ .../There common as commoners use,/ For otherwise shalt thou not choose.' Although the open field village as a whole could introduce novelties, the lone villager bound by the decision of the commoners could not. The system lasted in the Midlands of England into the 18th century, the last of it dissolved slowly by special acts of Parliament. Arthur Young was typical of this latter age, and of historians looking back, in scorning the inefficiencies of the system, railing against 'the Goths and Vandals of open-field farmers'.

With a complete set of markets, as A. Smith, R. Coase, and K.J. Arrow have explained, the Goths and Vandals would have traded away their inefficiencies. An explanation of open fields must depend therefore on some trade being blocked. The oldest explanation, imagining a spirit of fellowship within the primitive Germanic community, asks 'Who laid out these fields? The obvious answer is that they were laid out by men who would sacrifice economy and efficiency at the shrine of equality' (Maitland, 1897). Evidence has accumulated since the 19th century that the fields in question were not laid out at once and the men laying them out did not worship at the shrine of equality. Yet even if they did, and did lay out the fields, they could have exchanged their scattered strips to achieve rational holdings later. An egalitarian explanation of *persistent* open fields depends therefore on a failure in the market for land. Here again, however, the evidence testifies to the contrary: villages in medieval England and in much of Europe had in fact a cheap and active market in parcels of land.

The same difficulty lies in the way of any other explanation of scattering. Scattering has been explained as arising also from egalitarian inheritance (Dovring, 1965), common ploughing (Seebohm, 1883), common grazing (Dahlman, 1980), scheduling of harvest work (Fenoaltea, 1976) and diversification of local risks (McCloskey, 1976). These depend on market failures respectively in land, ploughing services, grazing rights, labour and insurance. None of these is immune from the criticism, and few have faced it.

517

Insurance has been tested most thoroughly. The scattering of strips strikes the eye of an economist as diversification. Anthropologists, trained to take seriously the reasons proffered by their people, report the Hopi scattering corn lands to diversify against floods and Swiss peasants diversifying across altitudes. Furthermore, the amount of local variation in England was great: a wet year flooded clay lands in the valley while the chalk hills drained; infestations of insects and the paths of hailstorms were local. The portfolio that a peasant bought by having scattered strips can be calculated from medieval evidence of yields and modern evidence of agronomical experiments. The optimal number of plots proves to be roughly the same as the observed number.

The insurance argument, like the rest, can be criticized for ignoring a market, the market in this case for insurance (Fenoaltea, 1976). It may well be that scattering was a form of insurance, but most social institutions anyway have an element of insurance, more so in the 14th century than now. A peasant could insure by sharecropping, by entering an extended family, by taking loans from the landlord, by purchasing liquid assets, and by storing grain. At the margin, however, the return from each form of insurance would be the same as any other. The scattering of strips incurred costs of about 15 per cent of output. The one other form of insurance whose costs are easily calculable is storage of grain (McCloskey and Nash, 1984). A year's worth of grain storage in the 14th century cost 40 per cent of the value of the crop, largely because interest rates were 30 per cent a year (by 1600, after interest rates had fallen, the cost was only 15 per cent: enclosure proceeded apace). For insurance, at least, we have a measure of the great imperfection in its market and therefore an explanation of the persistence of open fields.

Precise conclusions aside, the recent explanations all agree on a picture of the medieval peasant differing sharply from the romantic one drawn by 19th-century German scholarship. The new picture is market-saturated (Popkin, 1979) and individualistic (Macfarlane, 1978); at any rate it is more so than the 'natural economy' once thought to prevail in medieval Europe and the 'moral economy' now thought to prevail in poor countries today.

BIBLIOGRAPHY

Ault, W.O. 1972. *Open-Field Farming in Medieval England: a study of village by-laws.* London: Allen and Unwin; New York: Barnes and Noble.

Baack, B.D. and Thomas, R.P. 1974. The enclosure movement and the supply of labor during the Industrial Revolution. *Journal of European Economic History* 3(2), Fall, 401–23.

Baker, A.H.R. and Butlin, R.A. (eds) 1973. *Studies of Field Systems in the British Isles.* Cambridge: Cambridge University Press.

Blum, J. 1961. *Lord and Peasant in Russia: from the Ninth to the Nineteenth Century.* Princeton: Princeton University Press.

Cohen, J. and Weitzman, M.L. 1975. Marxian model of enclosures. *Journal of Development Economics* 1(4), February, 287–336.

Dahlman, C. 1980. *The Open Field System and Beyond: a property rights analysis of an economic institution.* Cambridge: Cambridge University Press.

Dovring, F. 1965. *Land and Labor in Europe in the 20th Century.* 3rd edn, The Hague: Nijhoff.

Fenoaltea, S. 1976. Risk, transaction costs, and the organization of medieval agriculture. *Explorations in Economic History* 13(2), April, 129–51.

Grantham, G. 1980. The persistence of open field farming in nineteenth-century France. *Journal of Economic History* 40(3), September, 515–31.

Gray, H.L. 1915. *English Field Systems.* Cambridge, Mass.: Harvard University Press.

Hardin, G. 1968. The Tragedy of the Commons. *Science* 162, 13 December, 1243–8.

McCloskey, D.N. 1975. The persistence of common fields. In *European Peasants and Their Markets,* ed. W.N. Parker and E.L. Jones, Princeton: Princeton University Press.

McCloskey, D.N. 1976. English open fields as behavior towards risk. *Research in Economic History* 1, 124–70.

McCloskey, D.N. and Nash, J. 1984. Corn at interest: the cost and extent of grain storage in medieval England. *American Economic Review* 74(1), March, 174–87.

Macfarlane, A. 1978. *The Origins of English Individualism.* Oxford: Basil Blackwell.

Maitland, F.W. 1897. *Domesday Book and Beyond.* Cambridge: Cambridge University Press.

Mayhew, A. 1973. *Rural Settlement and Farming in Germany.* New York: Barnes and Noble.

Popkin, S.L. 1979. *The Rational Peasant: the political economy of rural society in Vietnam.* Berkeley: University of California Press.

Seebohm, F. 1883. *The English Community.* London: Longman & Co.

Turner, M. 1984. *Enclosures in Britain, 1750–1830.* London: Macmillan.

Yelling, J.A. 1977. *Common Field and Enclosure in England 1450–1850.* London: Macmillan.

Opportunity Cost

JAMES M. BUCHANAN

The concept of *opportunity cost* (or alternative cost) expresses the basic relationship between scarcity and choice. If no object or activity that is valued by anyone is scarce, all demands for all persons and in all periods can be satisfied. There is no need to choose among separately valued options; there is no need for social coordination processes that will effectively determine which demands have priority. In this fantasized setting without scarcity, there are no opportunities or alternatives that are missed, foregone, or sacrificed.

Once scarcity is introduced, all demands cannot be met. Unless there are 'natural' constraints that predetermine the allocation of end-objects possessing value (for example, sunshine in Scotland in February), scarcity introduces the necessity of choice, either directly among alternative end-objects or indirectly among institutions or procedural arrangements for social interaction that will, in turn, generate a selection of ultimate end-objects.

Choice implies rejected as well as selected alternatives. *Opportunity cost is the evaluation placed on the most highly valued of the rejected alternatives or opportunities.* It is that value that is given up or sacrificed in order to secure the higher value that selection of the chosen object embodies.

OPPORTUNITY COST AND CHOICE. Opportunity cost is the anticipated value of 'that which might be' if choice were made differently. Note that it is not the value of 'that which might have been' without the qualifying reference to choice. In the absence of choice, it may be sometimes meaningful to discuss values of events that might have occurred but did not. It is not meaningful to define these values as opportunity costs, since the alternative scenario does not represent a lost or sacrificed opportunity. Once this basic relationship between choice and opportunity cost is acknowledged, several implications follow.

First, if choice is made among separately valued options, someone must do the choosing. That is to say, a chooser is required, a person who decides. From this the second implication emerges. The value placed on the option that is not chosen, the opportunity cost, must be that value that exists in the mind of the individual who chooses. It can find no other location. Hence, cost must be borne exclusively by the chooser; it can be shifted to no one else. A third necessary consequence is that opportunity cost must be subjective. It is within the mind of the chooser, and it cannot be objectified or measured by anyone external to the chooser. It cannot be readily translated into a resource, commodity, or money dimension. Fourth, opportunity cost exists only at the moment of decision when choice is made. It vanishes immediately thereafter. From this it follows that cost can never be realized; that which is rejected can never be enjoyed.

The most important consequence of the relationship between choice and opportunity cost is the *ex ante* or forward-looking property that cost must carry in this setting. Opportunity cost, the value placed on the rejected option by the chooser, is the obstacle to choice; it is that which must be considered, evaluated, and ultimately rejected before the preferred option is chosen. Opportunity cost in any particular choice is, of course, influenced by prior choices that have been made, but with respect to this choice itself, opportunity cost is *choice-influencing* rather than *choice-influenced*.

OTHER NOTIONS OF COST. The distinction between opportunity cost and other conceptions or notions of cost is best explained in this choice-influencing and choice-influenced classification. Once a choice is made, consequences follow, and these consequences may, indeed, involve utility losses, either to the person who has made initial choice or to others. In a certain sense it may seem useful to refer to these losses, whether anticipated or realized, as costs, but it must be recognized that these choice-determined costs, as such, cannot, by definition, influence choice itself.

A single example may clarify this point. A person chooses to purchase an automobile through an instalment loan payment plan, extending over a three-year period. The opportunity cost that informs and influences the choice is the value that the purchaser places on the rejected alternative, in that case the anticipated value of the objects which might be purchased with the payments required under the loan. Having considered the potential value of this alternative, and chosen to proceed with the purchase, the consequences of meeting the loan schedule follow. Monthly payments must be made, and it is common language usage to refer to these payments as 'costs' of the automobile. The individual will clearly suffer a sense of utility loss as the payments come due and must be paid. As choice-influencing elements, however, these 'costs' are irrelevant. The fact that, in a utility dimension, post-choice consequences can never be capitalized is a source of major confusion.

Economists recognize the distinction being made here in one sense. With the familiar statement that 'sunk costs are irrelevant', economists acknowledge that the consequences of choices cannot influence choice itself. On the other hand, by their formalized constructions of cost schedules and cost functions, which necessarily imply measurability and objectifiability of costs, economists divorce cost from the choice process.

Essentially the same results hold for accountants, who normally measure estimated costs strictly in the *ex post* or choice-influenced sense. Those 'costs' estimated by accountants can never accurately reflect the value of lost or sacrificed opportunities. Numerical estimates could be introduced in working plans for alternative courses of action prior to decision, but such estimates of opportunity costs would be the accountant's measure of the values for projects not undertaken rather than the value of commitments made under the project chosen.

As suggested, choice-influencing opportunity costs exist only for the person who makes choice. By definition, opportunity costs cannot 'spill over' to others. There may, of course, be consequences of a person's choice that impose utility losses on other persons, and it is sometimes useful to refer to these losses as 'external costs'. The point to be emphasized is that these external costs are obstacles to choice, and hence a measure of foregone opportunities, only if the individual who chooses takes them into account and places his own anticipated utility evaluation on them.

OPPORTUNITY COST AND WELFARE NORMS. The source of greatest confusion in the analysis and application of opportunity cost theory lies in the attempted extension of the results of idealized market interaction processes to the definition of rules or norms for decision makers in non-market settings. In full market equilibrium, the separate choices made by many buyers and sellers generate results that may be formally described in terms of relationships between prices and costs. Under certain specified conditions, prices are brought into equality with marginal costs through the working of the competitive process. Further, the general equilibrium states described by these equalities are shown to meet certain efficiency norms.

Prices may be observed; they are objectively measurable. A condition for market equilibrium is equalization of prices over all relevant exchanges for all units of a commodity of service. From this equalization it may seem to follow that marginal costs, which must be brought into equality with price as a condition for the equilibrium of each trader, are also objectively measurable. From this the inference is drawn that, if marginal costs are then measured, 'efficiency in resource use can be established independently of the competitive process itself through the device of forcing decision makers to bring prices into equality with marginal costs.

The whole logic is a tissue of confusion based on a misunderstanding of opportunity cost. The equalization of marginal opportunity cost with price for each trader is brought about by the adjustments made by each trader along the relevant quantity dimension. The fact that the marginal opportunity costs for all traders are all brought into equalization with the relevant uniform price implies only that traders retain the ability to adjust quantities of goods until this condition is met. There is no implication to the effect that marginal opportunity costs are equalized in some objectively meaningful sense independently of the quantity adjustment to price.

Consider an idealized market for a good that is observed to be trading at a uniform price of $1 per unit. The *numéraire* value of the anticipated lost opportunity is $1 for each trader. But it is only as quantity is adjusted that the trader can bring the *numéraire* value of his subjectively experienced and anticipated utility sacrifice into equality with the objectively set price that he confronts. The anticipated value of that which is given up in taking a course of action is no more objectifiable and measurable than the anticipated value of the course of action itself. The two sides of choice are equivalent in all respects.

Independently of market choice, there is no means through which marginal opportunity costs can be brought into equality with prices. Hence, any 'rule' that directs 'managers' in nonmarket settings to use cost as the basis for setting price is and must remain without content. There is, however, a second equally important criticism of the welfare rule that opportunity cost reasoning identifies, quite apart from the measurability question. Even if the first criticism is ignored, and it is assumed that marginal opportunity cost can, in some fashion, be measured, instructions to 'managers' to use cost to set price must rely on 'managers' to behave, personally, as robots rather than rational utility-maximizing individuals. Why should a 'manager' be expected to follow the rule? Would he not be expected to behave so that marginal cost, that which he faces personally, be brought into equality with the anticipated value of the benefit side of choice? The fact that the 'manager' remains in a nonmarket setting insures that he cannot be the responsible bearer of the utility gains and losses that his choices generate. His own, privately sensed, gains and losses, evaluated either prior to or after choice, must be categorically different from those anticipated for principals before choice and enjoyed and/or suffered by principals after choice.

OPPORTUNITY COST AND THE CHOICE AMONG INSTITUTIONS. As noted earlier, in the absence of 'natural' constraints that predetermine allocation, the introduction of scarcity introduces the necessity of choice, either directly among ultimate 'goods' or indirectly among rules, institutions and procedures that will operate so as to make final allocative determinations. Opportunity cost in the second of these choice-settings remains to be examined. In a sense, the use of institutionalized procedures to generate allocations of scarce resources may eliminate 'choice' in the familiar meaning used above and is akin in this respect to the 'natural' constraints noted. Results may emerge from the operation of some institutional process without any person or group of persons 'choosing' among end-state alternatives, and, hence, without any subjectively-experienced opportunity cost. Despite the absence of this important bridge between cost and choice in the ordinary sense, however, values may be placed on the 'might have beens' that would have emerged under differing allocations. The patterns of these estimated value losses, over a sequence of institution-determined allocations, may enter, importantly, in a rational choice calculus involving the higher-level choice among alternative institutional procedures for allocation. In this higher-level choice, opportunity cost again appears as the negative side of choice even if 'choice' in the standard usage of the term is not involved in the making of allocations, taken singly.

Consider the following extreme example. There are two mutually exclusive thermostat settings for a building, *High* and *Low*. An institution is in being that uses an unbiased coin to 'choose' between these two settings each day. It is meaningful for an individual to discuss the potential value to be anticipated if the setting is *High* rather than *Low*, even if the individual does not make the selection, individually or as a member of a collective. The setting that is 'chosen' by the coin flip has consequences for individual utility and these consequences may be anticipated in advance of the actual 'choice'. So long as the institutional procedure remains in effect, however, with respect to a single day's selection, the anticipated value lost by one setting of the thermostat rather than the other cannot represent opportunity cost.

Suppose, now, that instead of the unbiased and equally weighted device, the institution in being is one that allows all persons in the building to vote, each morning, on the thermostat setting with the majority option 'chosen' for the day. Assume, further, that the group of voters is large, so that the influence of a single person on the expected majoritarian outcome is quite small. It is important to emphasize that, in this procedure, as with the coin toss, no person really 'chooses' among the alternative end-states. Each voter confronts the quite different, intra-institutional choice between 'voting for *High*' and 'voting for *Low*', with the knowledge that any individual has relatively little influence on the outcome. In the choice that he confronts, the voter cannot rationally take into account the anticipated losses from the ultimate alternatives, either for himself or for others, in any full-value sense of the term. The loss anticipated from, say, a *Low* thermostat setting may be estimated to be valued at $1000 for the individual. Yet if he considers himself to have an influence on the outcome of the voting choice only in one case out of a thousand, the expected utility value of the anticipated loss will be only $1 in terms of the *numéraire*. This $1 will then represent the *numéraire* value of the *opportunity cost* involved in voting for *High*.

Since these same results hold, with possibly differing values, for all voters, no one 'chooses' in accordance with fully evaluated gains and losses. 'Choices' emerge from the institutional procedure without full benefit–cost considerations being made by anyone, taken singly or in aggregation. In the relevant opportunity-cost sense, effective choice is shifted to that among alternative institutions. The results of the 'choices' made within an institution over a whole sequence of periods (over many days in our thermostat example) may, of course, become data for the choice comparison among institutions themselves. And, to the extent that the individual, when confronted with a choice among institutions, knows that he is individually responsible for the selection, the whole opportunity cost logic then becomes relevant at the level of institutional or constitutional choice. This result is accomplished, however, only if each person in the relevant community does, in fact, become the chooser among institutional rules. Only if, at some ultimate level of institutional–constitutional choice the Wicksellian unanimity rule becomes operative, hence giving any person potential choice authority, can the opportunity cost of alternatives for choice be expected to enter and to inform individual decisions.

SUMMARY. *Opportunity cost* is a basic concept in economic theory. In its rudimentary definition as the value of opportunities foregone as a result of choice in the presence of scarcity, the concept is simple, straightforward, and widely understood. In the analysis of choices made by buyers and sellers in the market place, the complexities that emerge only in rigorous definition of the concept remain relatively unimportant. But when attempts are made to extend opportunity cost logic to nonmarket settings, either in the derivation of norms to guide decisions or in application to choice within and among institutions, the observed ambiguity and confusion suggest that even so basic a concept requires analytical clarification.

BIBLIOGRAPHY

Alchian, A. 1968. Cost. *Encyclopedia of the Social Sciences*, Vol. 3, 404–15. New York: Macmillan.

Buchanan, J.M. 1969. *Cost and Choice*. Chicago: Markham. Republished as Midway Reprint, Chicago: University of Chicago Press, 1977.

Buchanan, J.M. and Thirlby, G.F. (eds) 1973. *LSE Essays on Cost*. London: Weidenfeld and Nicholson. Reissued by New York University Press, 1981.

Coase, R.H. 1960. The problem of social cost. *Journal of Law and Economics* 3, October, 1–44.

Optimum Currency Areas

MASAHIRO KAWAI

An optimum currency area refers to the 'optimum' geographical domain having as a general means of payments either a single common currency or several currencies whose exchange values are immutably pegged to one another with unlimited convertibility for both current and capital transactions, but whose exchange rates fluctuate in unison against the rest of the world. 'Optimum' is defined in terms of the macroeconomic goal of maintaining internal and external balance. Internal balance is achieved at the optimal trade-off point between inflation and unemployment (if such a trade-off really exists), and external balance involves both intra-area and inter-area balance of payments equilibrium.

The concept of optimum currency areas was developed in a context of the debate over the relative merits of fixed versus flexible exchange rates. Proponents of flexible exchange rates, such as Milton Friedman (1953), had argued that a country afflicted with price and wage rigidities should adopt flexible exchange rates in order to maintain both internal and external balance. Under fixed exchange rates with price and wage rigidities, any policy effort to correct international payments imbalances would produce unemployment or inflation, whereas under flexible exchange rates the induced changes in the terms of trade and real wages would eliminate payments imbalances without much of the burden of real adjustments. Such an argument in favour of flexible exchange rates left the general impression that any country must adopt flexible exchange rates irrespective of its economic characteristics. However, countries differ in many ways. The theory of optimum currency areas claims that if a country is highly integrated with the outside world in financial transactions, factor mobility or commodity trading, fixed exchange rates may reconcile internal and external balance more efficiently than flexible exchange rates.

The pioneering work by Mundell (1961) and McKinnon (1963) (in addition to Ingram, 1962), attempted to single out the most crucial economic properties to define an 'optimum' currency area. The subsequent work by Grubel (1970), Corden (1972), Ishiyama (1975) and Tower and Willet (1976) turned their

526

attention to evaluating the benefits and costs of participating in a currency area. Hamada (1985) studied the welfare implications of individual countries' participation decisions.

1. PROPERTIES OF AN OPTIMUM CURRENCY AREA

Price and wage flexibility. Price and wage flexibility, or lack thereof, was the central issue in the debate over fixed versus flexible exchange rates. Indeed, the assumed price–wage inflexibility was the basis for Friedman's argument in favour of flexible exchange rates and the later development of the optimum currency area literature. (It is appropriate to point out, however, that Friedman did not entirely dismiss the idea that a group of countries, such as the sterling area, may fix their exchange rates with one another and let the rates fluctuate jointly against the rest of the world; Friedman, 1953, p. 193.)

Consider an area which is made up of a group of regions (or countries), however they may be defined. Then it can be postulated that, if prices and (real) wages are flexible throughout the area in response to the changed conditions of demand and supply, the regions in the area should be tied together by fixed exchange rates. Complete flexibility of prices and wages would achieve market clearance everywhere and facilitate instantaneous real adjustments to disturbances affecting inter-regional payments without causing unemployment. The ultimate, real adjustment consists of 'a change in the allocation of productive resources and in the composition of the goods available for consumption and investment' (Friedman, 1953, p. 182). The required changes in relative prices and real wages accomplish such adjustment, so that inter-regional (i.e. intra-area) exchange rate flexibility becomes unnecessary. Connecting the regions by fixed exchange rates is beneficial to the area as a whole, because it enhances the usefulness of money (see section 2). External payments balance is maintained by the joint floating of the area's currencies against the outside world as well as by internal price–wage flexibility.

When prices and real wages are inflexible, however, the transition towards ultimate adjustment may be associated with unemployment in one region and/or inflation in another. In such an economy, exchange rate flexibility among the regions, as well as its substitutes, may partially assume the role of price-wage flexibility in the process of real adjustments to disturbances. The following measures of internal market integration have been proposed as substitution for exchange rate flexibility so as to warrant the establishment of a currency area.

Financial market integration. Ingram (1962) noted the smooth way in which a high degree of internal financial integration financed inter-regional payments imbalances and eased the adjustment process within the United States, or as between the United States and Puerto Rico. This suggests that a successful currency area might be tightly integrated in financial trading.

When an inter-regional payments deficit is caused by a temporary, reversible disturbance, capital flows can be a cushion to make the real adjustment smaller or even unnecessary. When the deficit is caused by a persistent and irreversible disturbance, though financial capital flows (apart from those induced by differentials in long-run real rates of return) cannot sustain the deficit indefinitely, real adjustment is allowed to be spread out over a longer period of time. The cost of adjustment is reduced by the additional help from price–wage flexibility and internal factor mobility both of which tend to be higher in the longer run. Also financial transactions strengthen the long-term adjustment process through a different channel, i.e., wealth effects. The surplus region accumulating net claims raises expenditures and the deficit region decumulating net claims lowers them, thereby contributing to real adjustment.

Thus, financial market integration lessens the need for inter-regional (i.e. intra-area) terms-of-trade changes via exchange rate fluctuations, at least in the short run. Considering the undesirable effects that exchange rate flexibility and the associated exchange risk may have, i.e., drawing a sharp line of demarcation between 'local' and 'generalized' financial claims (Ingram, 1962, p. 118) and thus separating regional financial markets, fixed exchange rates are preferred within the financially integrated area.

Factor market integration. Mundell (1961) argued that an optimum currency area is defined by internal factor mobility (including both inter-regional and inter-industry mobility) and external factor immobility. Internal mobility of factors of production can moderate the pressure to alter real factor prices in response to disturbances affecting demand and supply; hence the need for exchange rate variations as an instrument of real factor prices change is mitigated. In this sense factor mobility is a partial substitute for price–wage flexibility, partial because factor mobility is usually low in the short run. Therefore, it is more effective in easing the cost of long-run real adjustment to persistent payments imbalances than short-run adjustment to temporary imbalances, which is minimized by financial capital mobility.

Thus, factor market integration enables the fixed exchange rate system not to interfere with the maintenance of inter-regional payments balance, while increasing the usefulness of money inside the currency area. Internal balance (the optimum inflation–unemployment trade-off) can be secured by monetary and fiscal policy, and external balance relative to the rest of the world is achieved by the joint floating of the exchange rates.

Goods market integration. The apparent relative smoothness of longer-run inter-regional adjustment within the United States is often attributed to its internal openness. This suggests that a successful currency area must have a high degree of internal openness, i.e. extensive trading of products inside the area. 'Openness' for a given area is measured by such indicators as the ratio of tradable to nontradable goods in production or consumption, the ratio of exports plus imports to gross output, and the marginal propensity to import.

McKinnon (1963) raised the question whether an area with a certain degree of external openness should choose flexible exchange rates against other areas or join them to belong to a larger currency area. First, suppose the area is externally highly open so that tradables represent a large share of the goods produced and consumed. Then exchange rate flexibility vis-à-vis other areas is not effective in rectifying payments imbalances, because any exchange rate variation would be offset by price changes without significant impacts on the terms of trade and real wages. That is, the area is too small and open for expenditure-switching instruments to be potent, though wealth effects operate in the direction of restoring payments equilibrium. The by-product is an unstable general price level. Instead, the area would find it beneficial to assign expenditure-reducing policy to external balance and fixed exchange rates to price stability, provided the tradable goods prices are stable in terms of the outside currency. Second, when the area is relatively closed against the rest of the world, it should peg its currency to the body of nontradable goods so as to stabilize the liquidity value of money, and assign exchange rate flexibility to external balance. Exchange rate flexibility is effective because it brings about the desired changes in the relative price of tradable goods and real wages.

Thus, the optimal monetary arrangements of an internally open, externally relatively closed economy would be to peg its currency (or currencies jointly) to the body of internally traded goods – which are viewed as nontradables from the standpoint of the outside world – for price stability, and adopt externally flexible exchange rates for external balance. Splitting such an economy into smaller regions with independently floating currencies is not desirable, nor is attaching itself to the outside world to become part of a larger currency area.

Political integration. The analysis above demonstrates the case for a currency area when a given economy has a high degree of internal market integration for financial assets, productive resources or outputs. (Other properties such as product diversity (Kenen, 1969) and similarities in tastes for inflation–unemployment trade-offs have also been proposed as 'criteria' for optimum currency areas.) It is obvious that the smooth functioning of a currency area system rests on absolute confidence in the permanent fixity of exchange rates and unlimited convertibility of member currencies inside the area. This will require close coordination of national monetary authorities and perhaps even the creation of a supranational central bank. Surrendering the national sovereignty over the conduct of monetary policy to a supranational authority involves not only an economic but political processs as well. The recent experience of the European Monetary System indicates that, without commitment to reaching some form of political integration, managing a currency area as loose as EMS would not be easy. (EMS is a loose currency area or a 'pseudo-exchange-rate union' (Corden, 1972) because occasional currency realignments are allowed.)

2. BENEFITS AND COSTS OF CURRENCY AREA PARTICIPATION

For a complete welfare analysis of optimum currency areas, one would, ideally, like to examine how the entire world economy should be divided into independent currency areas to maximize global welfare. But constructing a general analytical framework for such a task is almost impossible. Thus, cost–benefit analysts such as Ishiyama (1975) and Tower and Willet (1976) focused on the more restricted question whether particular countries should join with one another to form a currency area. Each country is assumed to evaluate the benefits and costs of currency area participation from a purely nationalistic point of view. The price of such a restricted approach is that a 'nationally' optimum currency area thus determined may not coincide with the 'globally' optimum currency area.

Benefits. The single most important benefit a country may derive from currency area participation is that the usefulness of money is enhanced (Mundell, 1961; McKinnon, 1963: Kindleberger, 1972; Tower and Willet, 1976). Money is a social contrivance which simplifies economic calculation and accounting, economizes on acquiring and using information for transactions, and promotes the integration of markets. The use of a single common currency (or currencies rigidly pegged to one another with full convertibility) would eliminate the risk of future exchange rate fluctuations, maximize the gains from trade and specialization and, thus, enhance allocative efficiency. The usefulness of money generally rises with the size of the domain over which it is used. Money is inherently a public good.

Related to the above benefit is the fact that externalities are provided in several forms. First, currency area participation means that the participating country pegs its currency to the class of representative goods in the area. Hence, a financially unstable country can enjoy a high liquidity value of money by joining in a more financially prudent currency area. Secondly, a financially well-integrated currency area offers the domain of risk-sharing. An inter-regional payments imbalance is immediately accommodated by a flow of financial transactions, which enable the deficit country to draw on the resources of the surplus country until the adjustment cost is efficiently spread out over time. (There are other benefits arising from currency area participation, such as the reduction of official reserves and the elimination of speculative capital flows.)

Costs. The system of flexible exchange rates, in principle, allows each country to retain monetary independence. However, the system of fixed exchange rates requires unified or closely coordinated monetary policy, constraining the participating countries' freedom to pursue independent monetary policy. This loss of monetary independence is considered the major cost of currency area participation, since it may force the member countries to depart from internal balance for the sake of external balance. The cost is deemed large if the country has a low tolerance for unemployment and is subject to strong price and wage pressures from monopolistic industries, labour unions and long-term contracts. On the other hand the cost may be small if it faces a relatively vertical Phillips curve (as in the case of a small, highly open economy), because in such a case the country would not have much freedom to choose the best inflation–unemployment trade-off in the first place.

Calculus of participation. Currency area formation is a dynamic process. In the process towards more complete monetary integration, public confidence in the system will grow, some new benefits may emerge, the existing benefits may rise, and the costs may diminish. Thus, intertemporal balancing of the benefits against the costs is necessary. It can be postulated, therefore, that an individual country will decide to participate in a currency area if the expected (discounted value of future) benefit exceeds the expected (discounted value of future) cost.

Two remarks must be made in this calculus of participation. First, the country is assumed to compare two extreme exchange rate regimes, i.e. irrevocably fixed exchange rates and freely flexible exchange rates. However, from the viewpoints of maximizing national welfare (namely benefits minus costs), there will almost always be an optimal exchange market intervention strategy that allows some exchange rate flexibility and some changes in external reserves, and the polar cases of fixed and flexible exchange rates are unlikely to be optimal – see for example Boyer (1978), Roper and Turnovsky (1980) and Aizenman and Frenkel (1985).

Second, each country chooses the best exchange rate arrangement on the assumptions that its choice and policy would not affect the rest of the world, though it may condition its actions on the policies pursued by other countries. As a result, the 'optimum' currency area thus determined may not be 'globally' optimum. As is emphasized by Hamada (1985), when the important benefits of currency area formation exhibit public-good characters and externalities and the costs are borne by individual countries, the rational theory of collective action (e.g. Buchanan, 1969) suggests that individual countries' participation decisions tend to produce a currency area that is smaller than is 'socially' optimum. (However, if the public-bad character of the costs dominates the public-good character of the benefits, the resulting currency area based on individual calculations may well be larger than is globally optimum.) The proposed calculus of participation obviously neglects the possible strategic interactions among countries; there is no leader–follower relationship and no cooperation. The game-theoretic approach to optimal exchange rate arrangements has recently attracted economists' attention – see Hamada (1985), Canzoneri and Gray (1985) and papers in Buiter and Marston (1985).

3. WHAT HAVE WE LEARNED?

Several issues have been made clear in the course of the development of the optimum currency area literature and its cost–benefit application.

First, the choice of a flexible or fixed exchange rate regime is understood as one of the second-best solutions to friction-ridden economies (Komiya, 1971). If the markets for outputs, factors of production and financial assets were completely integrated on a worldwide scale, relative prices and real wages were perfectly flexible, and economic nationalism (which attempts to insulate a national economy from the rest of the world by way of artificial impediments to trade, capital flows and foreign exchange transactions) were absent, then the optimum currency area would be the whole world. In such a case, the real adjustment to payments imbalances would be extremely smooth, factor resources would be always fully employed, and the usefulness of money would be maximized. However, to the extent that the payments adjustment mechanism is impaired by market fragmentation and price–wage rigidities, a country may adopt flexible exchange rates as a second-best policy to attain internal and external balance. The optimum currency area literature has shown that measures of market integration (for financial assets, factor resources and goods) may partially, and more effectively, substitute the required role of price–wage flexibility than does exchange rate flexibility.

Second, the cost–benefit approach to optimum currency areas based on purely national interest is limited in the analysis of designing an optimum international monetary system. Given the degree of spillover effects and economic inter-dependence among closely integrated countries, the strategic behaviour on the part of national policy makers must be explicitly incorporated in order to deepen our understanding of the nature of 'globally' optimum currency areas and optimal international monetary arrangements.

As a final note it is interesting to observe that the two economists who advanced the theory of optimum currency areas, Mundell and McKinnon, now support fixed exchange rates. Mundell has been advocating a worldwide gold standard system and McKinnon (1984) a fixing of the exchange rates among three major industrialized countries (USA, West Germany and Japan). Thus they regard the world as a whole or the industrial core of western society as capable of establishing a currency area.

BIBLIOGRAPHY

Aizenman, J. and Frenkel, J. 1985. Optimal wage indexation, foreign exchange intervention, and monetary policy. *American Economic Review* 75(3), June, 402–23.

Boyer, R.S. 1978. Optimal foreign exchange market intervention. *Journal of Political Economy* 86, December, 1045–55.

Buchanan, J.M. 1969. *Cost and Choice*. Chicago: Markham.

Buiter, W.H. and Marston, R.C. (eds) 1985. *International Economic Policy Coordination*. Cambridge: Cambridge University Press.

Canzoneri, M.B. and Gray, J. 1985. Monetary policy games and the consequences of non-cooperative behavior. *International Economic Review* 36(3), October, 547–64.

Corden, W.M. 1972. *Monetary Integration*. Essays in International Finance No. 93, April, Princeton: International Finance Section, Princeton University.

Friedman, M. 1953. The case for flexible exchange rates. In M. Friedman, *Essays in Positive Economics*, Chicago: University of Chicago Press.

Grubel, H.G. 1970. The theory of optimum currency areas. *Canadian Journal of Economics* 3, May, 318–24.

Hamada, K. 1985. *The Political Economy of International Monetary Interdependence*. Cambridge, Mass.: MIT Press.

Ingram, J.C. 1962. *Regional Payments Mechanisms: The Case of Puerto Rico*. Chapel Hill: University of North Carolina Press.

Ishiyama, Y. 1975. The theory of optimum currency areas: a survey. *IMF Staff Papers* 22, July, 344–83.

Kenen, P.B. 1969. The theory of optimum currency areas: an eclectic view. In *Monetary Problems of the International Economy*, ed. R.A. Mundell and A.K. Swoboda, Chicago: University of Chicago Press.

Kindleberger, C.P. 1972. The benefits of international money. *Journal of International Economics* 2, September, 425–42.

Komiya, R. 1971. Saitekitsukachiiki no riron (Theory of optimum currency areas). In *Gendaikeizaigaku no Tenkai* (The development of contemporary economics), ed. M. Kaji and Y. Murakami, Tokyo: Keisoshobo.

McKinnon, R.I. 1963. Optimum currency areas. *American Economic Review* 53, September, 717–25.

McKinnon, R.I. 1984. *An International Standard for Monetary Stabilization*. Policy Analyses in International Economics 8, March, Washington, DC: Institute for International Economics.

Mundell, R.A. 1961. A theory of optimum currency areas. *American Economic Review* 51, September, 657–65.

Roper, D.E. and Turnovsky, S.J. 1980. Optimal exchange market intervention in a simple stochastic macro model. *Canadian Journal of Economics* 13, May, 269–309.

Tower, E. and Willet, T.D. 1976. *The Theory of Optimum Currency Areas and Exchange-Rate Flexibility*. Special Studies in International Economics No. 11, May, Princeton: International Finance Section, Princeton University.

Yeager, L. 1976. *International Monetary Relations: Theory, History, Policy*. 2nd edn, New York: Harper & Row.

Perfectly and Imperfectly Competitive Markets

JOHN ROBERTS

In the competition between economic models, the theory of perfect competition holds a dominant market share: no set of ideas is so widely and successfully used by economists as is the logic of perfectly competitive markets. Correspondingly, all other market models (collectively labelled 'imperfectly competitive' and including monopoly, monopolistic competition, dominant-firm price leadership, bilateral monopoly and other situations of bargaining, and all the varieties of oligopoly theory) are little more than fringe competitors.

Although it is not surprising that perfect competition should play a central role as a benchmark for normative purposes, the dominance of perfectly competitive forms of analysis in descriptive and predictive work is remarkable. First, economic theorists seem to be increasingly of the view that something like imperfect competition is the fundamental idea, in that perfect competition should be justified by deriving it from models where imperfectly competitive behaviour is allowed and, in particular, agents recognize the full strategic options open to them and any monopoly power they have. This view has led to a large volume of work over the last twenty-five years that, for the most part, suggests that perfect competition corresponds to an extremely special, limiting case of a more general theory of markets. Second, as the idea of perfect competition has been made more precise and the conditions supporting it have become better understood, it has become completely evident that no important market fully satisfies the conditions of perfect competition and that most would not appear even to come close. This is not to say that models should be descriptively accurate; the only way a map could approach descriptive accuracy would be for it to have a scale of 1:1, but such a map is useless. Still, it is striking that economists so consistently opt for a model with so little apparent descriptive value. Third, the received theory of perfect competition is a theory of price competition that contains no coherent explanation of price formation. That such a

534

fundamental incompleteness does not severely limit the value of the theory is striking.

Given all this, the dominance of perfectly competitive methods should probably be viewed as a reflection of the weakness of imperfectly competitive analysis. There is in fact no powerful general theory of imperfect competition. Instead, there is a myriad of competing partial equilibrium models of imperfectly competitive markets, and the only general equilibrium theories either rely on questionable assumptions or embody institutional specifications that are no more satisfactory than those associated with perfectly competitive analysis.

Despite the unsatisfactory state of both perfectly and imperfectly competitive market theory, recent work based on game-theoretic methodology holds promise of providing a more satisfactory theory of imperfectly competitive markets, of yielding better insight into why perfectly competitive analysis seems to work so well, and of unifying these theories.

PERFECT COMPETITION. The idea of perfect competition has many aspects: absence of monopoly power; demand and supply curves that, to the individual, appear horizontal; negligibility of an individual's quantities relative to aggregates; price-taking behaviour (with respect to publicly quoted prices); zero profits and equality of returns across all activities; prices equalling marginal costs and factor returns equalling the values of marginal products; and Pareto-efficiency of market allocations and the efficacy of the Invisible Hand. Stigler (1957) has traced the historical development of the idea of perfect competition essentially through the 'imperfect competition revolution' of the 1930s, noting the appearance of many of these features and documenting the increasing recognition of the stringency of the conditions that appeared to be necessary and/or sufficient for perfect competition. Together these include: large numbers; free entry and exit; full information and negligible search costs; product homogeneity and divisibility; lack of collusion; and absence of externalities and of increasing returns to scale.

The theory about which Stigler wrote still largely corresponds to what is presented in intermediate textbooks and probably to the way most economists think about perfect competition when doing applied work. Firms and consumers are treated as making quantity choices at given prices, because with large numbers, it is suggested, individual quantities are 'negligible' relative to the aggregate, upon which prices are assumed to depend. (These arguments derive from Cournot, 1838.) But how prices are determined is not modelled. This approach is justified by informal arguments that prices are actually set by individual agents, but that, with many agents on each side of the market, any individual would be unable to deviate significantly from the prices charged by others without losing all demand or being overwhelmed by buyers. This idea is connected to the work of Bertrand (1883), but is not supported by formal arguments showing that the outcome of such price setting would be perfectly competitive under the assumed structural conditions (large numbers, homogeneity, free entry, etc.).

When Stigler wrote, Arrow, Debreu and MacKenzie had already provided their path-breaking formal analyses of Walrasian general equilibrium, and within two years Debreu published *Theory of Value* (1959), which is still the standard treatment of this subject. In this theory, competition is given a behavioural definition. There is a given list of consumers and of firms and a given list of commodities. A single price for each good is introduced, and perfectly competitive behaviour is then defined. It involves each consumer selecting the net transactions that maximize utility, subject to a budget constraint defined under the assumptions that the consumer can buy or sell unlimited quantities at the specified prices and that the consumer's purchases do not influence the profits he/she receives. As well, each firm selects the inputs and outputs that maximize its net receipts, again given that the firm can buy and sell any quantities it might consider without influencing prices. Finally, equilibrium is a price vector and perfectly competitive choices for each agent at these prices aggregate to a feasible allocation, i.e. such that markets clear.

Three fundamental results are proved for this model. These give conditions on tastes, endowments and technology under which competitive equilibria exist (existence), equilibrium allocations are Pareto-optimal (efficiency), and, with an initial reallocation of resources, any Pareto optimum can be supported as a competitive equilibrium (unbiasedness). The efficiency and existence theorems together formalize Adam Smith's argument of the invisible hand leading self-interested behaviour to serve the common good, while the unbiasedness result indicates that the competitive price system does not inherently favour any group (capitalists, workers, resource owners, consumers, etc.). The non-wastefulness result requires few assumptions beyond those built into the structure of the model: it is enough that not all consumers are satiated. The existence theorem, however, involves much stricter conditions, including especially the absence of any increasing returns to scale. (This is also needed for the unbiasedness result.)

Many of the conditions arising in less formal treatments of perfect competition are embodied in Debreu's formulation. For example, the very definition of a commodity involves homogeneity, and divisibility is explicitly assumed. Strikingly, however, free entry and large numbers play no explicit role in this theory: all the theorems would hold if there were but a single potential buyer and seller of any commodity.

This numbers-independence property relies crucially on the theory being only an *equilibrium theory*, that is, one which specifies what happens only if behaviour is exactly as stipulated and prices are set at equilibrium, market-clearing values. No examination is offered of what would happen if prices were not at their Walrasian levels, nor indeed, of how prices are determined. Further, not even the famous story of a disinterested Walrasian auctioneer and *tâtonnement* (no trade at nonequilibrium prices) supports this equilibrium by giving a consistent model of price formation with rational actors. Instead there would be incentives to misrepresent demands, responding consistently to each price announcement by the auctioneer as if one had different preferences than actually obtain, with the object of effecting monopolistic prices and outcomes (Hurwicz, 1972).

The ability of an individual to manipulate price formation by an auctioneer does disappear once one moves to a model where individuals truly are negligible. Such a model was first introduced by Aumann (1964), where the set of agents is indexed by a continuum endowed with a non-atomic measure. This measure is interpreted as given the size of a group of agents in comparison with the whole economy. The absence of mass points implies that no individual's excess demands represent a positive fraction of the totals. Thus, any individual's withholding of supply affects neither the magnitude of excess demand (as measured on a per capita basis) nor, correspondingly, whether particular prices clear markets. Thus price-taking is fully rational if prices can be considered to be set by a disinterested auctioneer.

The infinite economy framework captures the large numbers, negligibility and (with an auctioneer) price-taking aspects of perfect competition. Infinite models also provide a setting where numerous other models of production and exchange agree with the Walrasian in their outcomes. However, infinite models clearly are an extreme abstraction, and the real issue is the extent to which they approximate finite economies. This question leads to consideration of sequences of increasingly large finite economies in which each individual becomes relatively small, perhaps with many others like him or her being present. The identification of perfect competition with such sequences of economies and the asymptotic properties of their allocations dates back to Cournot (1838) and Edgeworth (1881) and has become the basis of several major lines of research.

The most complete of these shows that the core converges to the Walrasian allocations (see Hildenbrand, 1974). However, recently attention has focused on the programme initiated by Cournot of obtaining perfect competition as the limit of imperfectly competitive behaviour and outcomes (see Mas-Colell, 1982).

There are three approaches to this problem. One, represented by Roberts and Postlewaite (1976), effectively takes some version of the auctioneer story as given and examines the incentives to respond to price announcements using one's true demands. Here it is shown that if the economy grows through replication or if the sequence of economies under consideration converges to one at which the Walrasian price is locally a continuous function of the data of the economy, then correct revelation of preferences and price-taking is asymptotically a dominant strategy. The second line of work builds more directly on Cournot's model. Agents select quantities and prices somehow arise to clear markets, with some agents (usually the firms) recognizing the impact of their choices on prices and others (consumers) taking prices as given. The central results here are due to Novshek and Sonnenschein (1978), who showed that the free-entry Cournot equilibria converge to the Walrasian allocations as the minimum efficient scale becomes small, provided that a condition of downward-sloping demand is met. Finally, the game-theoretic models of noncooperative exchange initiated by Shubik (1973) also lead asymptotically to Walrasian equilibria (see Postlewaite and Schmeidler, 1978). A significant feature of these game-theoretic models is that they explicitly treat out-of-equilibrium behaviour: the outcome of *any* pattern of behaviour is specified, not just what happens in equilibrium. This is an important advance. However, in these models, prices appear only as the ratio of the amount of money bid for a good to the amount of the good offered, and are not directly chosen by agents.

A complementary approach to perfect competition (Ostroy, 1980) relates to marginal productivity theory and to horizontal demands. Central to this approach is a no-surplus condition that, agent by agent, the rest of the economy would be no worse off if the agent's resources and productive capability were removed from the economy. No-surplus allocations correspond to the economy's having Walrasian equilibria at the same prices with or without any single agent (so demands are horizontal). An economy is defined as perfectly competitive if the no-surplus condition is met. This can happen with a finite number of agents, but typically it requires an infinity.

Thus, various pieces of formal theory capture most of the aspects of the intuitive notion of perfect competition, but this theory points to perfect competition being a limiting case associated with many agents in each market or the existence of close substitutes for each firm's output, as well as with properties of continuity of the Walras correspondence and downward-sloping demand. Also, this theory lacks models in which prices are explicitly chosen by economic agents. None of these results gives much reason for the success that economists have using perfectly competitive analysis.

IMPERFECT COMPETITION. Formal modelling of markets begins with Cournot's (1838) treatment of quantity-setting, noncollusive oligopoly. Cournot's model yields prices in excess of marginal cost, with this divergence decreasing asymptotically to zero as the number of firms increases. The 19th century saw two other important contributions to imperfect competition theory: Bertrand's (1883) price-setting model which, with constant costs, yields perfectly competitive outcomes from duopoly, and Edgeworth's (1897) demonstration that introducing capacity constraints into this model could prevent existence of (pure strategy) equilibrium.

Thus, even before the imperfect competition revolution, the theory of imperfectly competitive markets was subject to one of the standard complaints still made against it: that it consists of too many models that yield conflicting predictions. This complaint intensified with the proliferation in the 1930s and later of models of firms facing downward-sloping demands. These models usually capture some element of actual competition (or at least appear more realistic than the perfectly competitive alternative). However, it sometimes seems that one can concoct an imperfect competition model that predicts any particular outcome one might wish.

A second complaint against imperfectly competitive analysis is its lack of a satisfactory multiple market formulation.

The first significant contribution to a general equilibrium theory of imperfect competition was Negishi's (1961) model, with later contributions from numerous authors during the 1970s. Although these models differ on important dimensions, the basic pattern in this work involves supplementing the Arrow–Debreu multi-market model of an economy by allowing that some exogenously specified set of firms perceive an ability to influence prices. (These firms may or may not perceive the actual demand relations correctly.) Equilibrium is then a set of choices (prices or quantities) for each imperfect competitor that maximizes its perceived profits, given the behaviour of the other imperfect competitors and the pattern of adjustment of the competitive sectors (under Walrasian, price-taking behaviour) to the choices of the imperfect competitors.

This theory, as it stood in the mid-1970s, was obviously incomplete on several grounds. Most fundamentally, there was no explanation of why some agents should take prices as given while other agents, who formally might be identical to the price-takers, behave as imperfect competitors. Moreover, it then emerged that there were serious flaws in the crucial existence theorems that purported to show that the models were not vacuous.

These theorems obtained profit-maximizing choices for the imperfect competitors that were mutually consistent by use of fixed-point arguments based on Brouwer's theorem. To use these methods, the optimal choices of any one agent must depend continuously on the conjectured choices of the others. This role of continuity of reaction functions is analogous to that of continuity of demand functions in the Arrow–Debreu model. However, unlike the continuity of demand, continuity of reaction functions was not derived from conditions on the fundamental data of the economy. Rather, it was either directly assumed or obtained by supposing that the imperfect competitors' perceptions of demand yielded concave profit functions.

Roberts and Sonnenschein (1977) showed that this approach was problematic by displaying extremely simple, nonpathological examples in which reaction functions are discontinuous and no imperfectly competitive equilibrium exists. The source of these failures is nonconcavity of the profit functions, and no standard conditions on preferences ensure the needed concavity: it can fail with only a single consumer or when all consumers have homothetic preferences. (Note, however, that existence ceases to be a problem in general equilibrium Cournot models if the economy, including the number of imperfect competitors, is made large enough through replication.)

These problems with imperfect competition theory perhaps explain some of the popularity of perfect competition models. However, they also suggest two important, positive points. First, the multiplicity of models and the divergence in their predictions indicates that, at least in small numbers situations, institutional details are important. Economists, habituated to the use of perfectly competitive methods, typically are imprecise about such factors as how prices are actually determined, whether decisions are made simultaneously or sequentially, whether individuals select prices, quantities, or both, and what happens when agents' plans are inconsistent. These factors cannot be treated so cavalierly in dealing with imperfectly competitive models and probably ought not to be when actual markets are being analysed. Second, both the failure of existence in models of imperfectly competitive general equilibrium and the unexplained asymmetry of assumed behaviour in these models suggest that a simple grafting of imperfect competitors onto the standard Arrow–Debreu model will not yield a satisfactory theory. Rather, one ought to start afresh from the foundations with a more careful modelling.

STRATEGIC MODELS OF COMPETITION. An approach to both of these points is provided by the methods of the theory of noncooperative games and especially games in extensive form. Recent work using this approach has resulted in significant improvements in the partial equilibrium theory of imperfect competition, and there is reason to hope that these same methods can provide a satisfactory general equilibrium theory. Moreover, this approach also offers hope of ultimately yielding a unified theory of competition that would encompass both perfect and imperfect competition.

To model a market as a game in extensive form, one must specify the set of participants, the beliefs each has about the characteristics of the other agents, the order in which each acts, the information available to each whenever it makes a decision, the possible actions available at each decision point, the physical outcomes resulting from each possible combination of choices and the valuations of these outcomes by the agents. Thus, such a model involves a complete specification of a particular set of institutions. This aspect might be viewed as a drawback, but it is in fact a potential strength of these methods.

(Note that adopting this approach does not require that price formation be modelled by having prices be chosen by agents in the model. Indeed, Cournot's original model is a well-specified game, but price formation is not explicitly modelled. However, this framework does facilitate and encourage such a specification.)

Given a game, one next specifies a solution concept. In principle, there is great freedom in making this specification, but most researchers opt for the Nash equilibrium or some refinement thereof. Note that adopting the Nash equilibrium – that each agent maximizes his utility given the strategies of all other agents – does not rule out collusion if opportunities to coordinate and to enforce agreements are modelled as part of the game. Nor does it mean that the agents are acting simultaneously: the order of moves is part of the specification of the game, and the Nash equilibrium applies equally to simultaneous or sequential moves. To illustrate, the von Stackelberg solution corresponds to subgame-perfect Nash equilibrium in a game where the designated leader moves first and the follower observes the leader's choice before making its own. Finally, the Nash criterion does not restrict analysis to one-shot situations; it is equally applicable to models of repeated play.

When von Neumann and Morgenstern's (1944) treatise on game theory first appeared, there was hope among economists that these methods would unify and advance the analysis of imperfect competition. When these hopes were not quickly realized, many economists wrote off game theory as a failure. This position is still reflected in many intermediate textbooks. However, in the last decade these hopes have been revitalized by actual accomplishments of these methods.

The first contribution of this work has been to begin unifying the existing theory of imperfect competition. This has been done on one level by providing a common language and analytical framework in terms of which earlier work can be cast and understood. In this line, game theoretic treatments have made formal sense out of such ideas as reaction curves and kinked demand curves by obtaining equilibria of well-specified dynamic games that have these features. As well, various of the older theories that appeared to be in conflict have been shown to be consistent in that they arise from a common, more basic model. For example, the Cournot and the von Stackelberg solutions can both be attained as Nash equilibria in a single model where the timing of moves is endogenous. In a similar vein, the Cournot, Bertrand and Edgeworth models have been integrated by showing that equilibrium in a two-stage game where duopolists first select capacities and then compete on price yields the Cournot quantities.

A second contribution has been to provide models embodying aspects of imperfect competition that had been widely discussed in the industrial organization literature but previously lacked formal expression. The best example here is work showing how limit pricing, predatory pricing and price wars can arise as rational behaviour in the presence of informational asymmetries between competitors (see Roberts, 1986). Further examples include explanations of sales and other discriminatory pricing policies, the determination and maintenance of product quality, the use of capacity and other investments in commitment to deter entry, and the opportunities for and limitations on implicit collusion. This work is revolutionizing the field of industrial organization.

The third contribution has been to permit the analysis of realistic models of institutions for exchange that are actually present in the economy. The best-developed example of such work is that on auctions to sell a single object to one of many potential buyers (see Milgrom, 1986), but important work has also been done on multi-object auctions and other monopoly pricing institutions (including posted prices, priority pricing and nonlinear pricing), bilateral monopoly and bargaining, and bid-ask markets or oral double auctions. In this work, the rules of the institution being modelled, the distribution of information about tastes, costs, etc., held by the various participants, and the preferences of these agents together induce a game in extensive form. This game captures the full strategic options open to all the participants, specifying completely the prices and allocations resulting from any choice of actions. Thus, the Nash equilibrium of this game yields explicit predictions of the choices of prices and of the volume, timing and pattern of trade. Often these predictions are both remarkably tight and in agreement with observed behaviour.

This work is providing a more complete description and a clearer theoretical understanding of the operation of actual markets. Moreover, by providing detailed predictions of the outcomes of equilibrium behaviour under different institutions, it gives the basis for a theory of the choice among market institutions (see, for example, Harris and Raviv, 1981). Finally, it provides an approach to unifying the theories of perfect and imperfect markets and market behaviour. In this work, agents' behaviour is rationally strategic relative to the given economic situation. However, in particular environments this imperfectly competitive behaviour may be very close to perfectly competitive or may yield outcomes that are essentially competitive (see Wilson, 1986). By determining the situations in which this is true, we may finally understand when and why perfectly competitive analyses succeed.

BIBLIOGRAPHY

Aumann, R.J. 1964. Markets with a continuum of traders. *Econometrica* 32, 39–50.

Aumann, R.J. 1975. Values of markets with a continuum of traders. *Econometrica* 43, 611–46.

Bertrand, J. 1883. Théorie mathématique de la richesse sociale. *Journal des Savants* 48, 499–508.

Cournot, A. 1838. *Recherches sur les principes mathématiques de la théorie des richesses.* Paris: M. Rivière.

Debreu, G. 1959. *The Theory of Value.* New York: John Wiley & Sons.

Edgeworth, F.Y. 1881. *Mathematical Psychics.* London: P. Kegan; New York: A.M. Kelley, 1967.

Edgeworth, F.Y. 1897. La teoria pura del monopolio. *Giornale degli Economisti* 15, 13ff.

Harris, M. and Raviv, A. 1981. A theory of monopoly pricing schemes with demand uncertainty. *American Economic Review* 71, 347–65.

Hildenbrand, W. 1974. *Core and Equilibria of a Large Economy.* Princeton: Princeton University Press.

Hurwicz, L. 1972. On informationally decentralized systems. In *Decision and Organization*, ed. C.B. McGuire and R. Radner, Amsterdam: North-Holland.

Kalai, E. and Stanford, W. 1985. Conjectural variations strategies in accelerated Cournot games. *International Journal of Industrial Organization* 3, 133–52.

Kreps, D.M. and Scheinkman, J.A. 1983. Quantity precommitment and Bertrand competition yield Cournot outcomes. *Bell Journal of Economics*, 14, 326–37.

Mas-Colell, A. (ed.). 1982. *Non-cooperative Approaches to the Theory of Perfect Competition.* New York: Academic Press.

Milgrom, P.R. 1986. Auction theory. In *Advances in Economic Theory*, ed. T. Bewley, Cambridge: Cambridge University Press for the Econometric Society.

Negishi, T. 1961. Monopolistic competition and general equilibrium. *Review of Economic Studies* 28, 196–201.

Novshek, W. and Sonnenschein, H. 1978. Cournot and Walras equilibrium. *Journal of Economic Theory* 19, 223–66.

Ostroy, J. 1980. The no-surplus condition as a characterization of perfectly competitive equilibrium. *Journal of Economic Theory* 22, 183–207.

Postlewaite, A. and Schmeidler, D. 1978. Approximate efficiency of non-Walrasian equilibria. *Econometrica* 46, 127–37.

Roberts, J. 1986. Battles for market share: incomplete information, aggressive strategic pricing, and competitive dynamics. In *Advances in Economic Theory*, ed. T. Bewley, Cambridge: Cambridge University Press for the Econometric Society.

Roberts, J. and Postlewaite, A. 1976. The incentives for price-taking behavior in large exchange economies. *Econometrica* 44, 115–27.

Roberts, J. and Sonnenschein, H. 1977. On the foundations of the theory of monopolistic competition. *Econometrica* 45, January, 101–13.

542

Shubik, M. 1973. Commodity money, oligopoly, credit and bankruptcy in a general equilibrium model. *Western Economic Journal* 11, 24–38.

Stigler, G. 1957. Perfect competition, historically contemplated. *Journal of Political Economy* 65, 1–17.

von Neumann, J. and Morgenstern, O. 1944. *Theory of Games and Economic Behavior*. Princeton: Princeton University Press.

Wilson, R. 1986. Game theoretic analyses of trading process. In *Advances in Economic Theory*, ed. T. Bewley, Cambridge: Cambridge University Press for the Econometric Society.

Performing Arts

WILLIAM J. BAUMOL

In the past two decades a substantial international literature on the economics of the arts has accumulated. Aside from the importance of the cultural contribution made by the arts, interest in the subject among economists has been elicited by some special attributes of the economics of the arts which have proved interesting analytically and whose analysis has had significant applications outside the field. Notable is the 'cost disease of the performing arts' which has been proposed as an explanation for the fact that, except in periods of rapid inflation, the costs of artistic activities almost universally rise (cumulatively) faster than any index of the general price level. Another major theoretical issue with which the literature has concerned itself is the grounds on which public sector funding of the arts can be justified.

ORGANIZATION AND FUNDING. The structure of the performance industry is similar in many of the industrialized countries. The largest enterprise in terms of budget and personnel is the opera, followed, in rank order, by the orchestra, theatre and dance. The theatres are the only group that contains a substantial profit-seeking sector. All of the others, and many of the theatres as well, receive a substantial share of their incomes from government support and private philanthropy. The US, with its policy of tax exemptions, is probably the only country in which the share of private philanthropy is large, and there it exceeds the amount of government funding by a large margin. In many countries the bulk of such financing is provided by only a single agency, while in the US an arts organization whose application has been rejected by one funding source can usually turn to others for reconsideration.

The available statistical evidence suggests that demand for attendance is fairly income elastic but quite price inelastic, at least in the long run. This suggests that the widely espoused goal of diversity in audiences prevents ticket prices from rising more than they have, although fear that such rises will cause temporary but substantial declines in revenues and will reduce philanthropic or government support no doubt also plays a part.

In every country in which systematic audience studies have been carried out, the audience has been shown to be drawn from a very narrow range. It is far better educated than the average of the population, it has a far higher average income, it is somewhat older, and it includes a remarkably small proportion of blue-collar workers. Even free or highly subsidized performances affect this only marginally.

While total expenditures on ticket purchases have, of course, risen over the years, the pattern is modified substantially when corrected for changes in population, the price level and real incomes. Thus, in the US, the share of per capital disposable income devoted to admissions to artistic performances declined from about \$0.15 out of every \$100 in 1929 to about \$0.05 in 1982. The latter figure has been virtually unchanged throughout the period since World War II.

THE COST DISEASE OF THE PERFORMING ARTS. One of the special features of the economics of the performing arts that seems to colour their cost structure is their 'cost disease'. This condemns the cost of live performance to rise at a rate persistently faster than that of a typical manufactured good. An illustration comparing the costs of watchmaking and of musical performance over the centuries shows the reason. There has been vast and continuing technical progress in watchmaking, but live performance benefits from no labour-saving innovations – it is still done the old-fashioned way. Toward the end of the 17th century a Swiss craftsman could produce about 12 watches per year. Three centuries later that same amount of labour produces over 1200 (non-quartz) watches. But a piece of music written three centuries ago by Purcell or Scarlatti takes exactly as many person hours to perform today as it did in 1685 and uses as much equipment.

These figures mean that while one has to work just about as many hours to pay for a ticket to an opera today as one would have in similar jobs 300 years ago, the cost of a watch or of any other manufactured good has plummeted, in terms of the labour time we must pay for it. In other words, because manufactured goods have benefited from technological advance year after year while live performances have not, almost every year theatre and concert tickets have become more and more expensive in comparison with the price of watches. This phenomenon has been called 'the cost disease of live performance'.

To facilitate comparison with the discussion of the cost structure of the mass media that follows, it is helpful to describe the cost disease formally. Let

y_{it} = output of product i in period t

x_{kit} = quantity of input k used in producing i

AC_{it} = average cost of i in period t

w_{kt} = (real) price of k in period t

$\pi_{it} = y_i / \Sigma w_{kt} x_{kit}$ = total factor productivity in output i

* = rate of growth, i.e. for any function, $f(t)$

$f^* = \dot{f}/f$.

Then we have:

Proposition 1. Let y_{1t} and y_{2t} be two outputs produced by single product firms. Then, if $\pi_{1t}^{*} \leqslant r_1 < r_2 \leqslant \pi_{2t}^{*}$, so that output 1 may be called relatively 'stagnant' (and output 2 is relatively 'progressive'), the ratio of the average cost of output 1 to that of output 2, AC_{1t}/AC_{2t} will rise without limit.

Proof: By definition

$$AC_{1t}/AC_{2t} = \pi_{2t}/\pi_{1t}$$

so that

$$(AC_{1t}/AC_{2t})^{*} = \pi_{2t}^{*} - \pi_{1t}^{*} \geqslant r_2 - r_1. \qquad \text{Q.E.D.}$$

Here, of course, y_1 may be interpreted as the output of live performance and y_2 as the output of manufactured goods. It follows that the prices of manufactured goods can be expected to rise less quickly than those of concerts, dance or theatrical performances. Ticket prices must therefore rise faster than the economy's overall rate of inflation, since the latter is an average of the increases in the prices of all the economy's goods.

It is sometimes suggested that the mass media – film, radio, television and recording – can provide the cure for the cost disease, but recent analysis suggests that despite their sophisticated technology many of the mass media are in the long run vulnerable to essentially the same problem. As a matter of fact, the data indicate that the cost of cinema tickets and the cost per prime-time television hour have been rising at least as fast as the price of tickets to the commercial theatre. The explanation apparently lies in the structure of mass media production, which is made up of two basic components that are very different technologically. The first comprises preparation of material and the actual performance in front of the cameras, while the second is the transmission or filming.

Television broadcasting of new material requires these two elements in relatively fixed physical proportions – one hour of programming (with some flexibility in rehearsal time) must be accompanied by one hour of transmission for every one hour broadcast. However, since the first component of television is virtually identical with live performance on a theatre stage, there is just as little scope for technical change in the one as in the other, while the second component, on the other hand, is electronic and 'high tech' in character and constantly benefits from innovation.

Industries with this cost structure have been referred to as 'asymptotically stagnant'. The evolution of such an industry over time is characterized by an initial period of decline in total cost (in constant dollars) which *must* be followed by a period in which its costs begin to behave in a manner more and more similar to the live performing arts. The reason is that the cost of the highly technological component (transmission cost) will decline, or at least not rise as fast as the economy's inflation rate. At the same time, the cost of programming increases at a rate surpassing the rate of inflation.

If each year transmission costs decrease and programming expenses increase because of the cost disease that besets all live performance, eventually programming cost must being to dominate the overall budget. Thereafter, total cost and programming cost must move closer and closer together until virtually the entire budget becomes a victim of the disease, with the stable technological costs too small a fragment of the whole to make a discernible difference.

These results are encompassed in the following propositions:

Proposition 2. Suppose an activity, A, uses stagnant input x_1 and progressive input x_2 in fixed proportion v, so that $x_{2t} = vx_{1t}$. If w_{1t}, the unit price of x_{1t}, increases at a nonnegative rate no less than r_1 and w_{2t} increases at a rate no greater than r_2, where $r_2 < r_1$, then the share of total expenditure by A that is devoted to x_{1t} will approach the limit unity. Moreover, for any g such that $0 < g < 1$, there exists T such that for all $t > T$

$$1 \geqslant w_{1t}x_{1t}/(w_{1t}x_{1t} + w_{2t}x_{2t}) \geqslant 1 - g.$$

Proof: We are given

$$w_{1t} \geqslant a_1\, e^{r_1 t}$$

$$w_{2t} \leqslant a_2\, e^{r_2 t}, \qquad x_{2t} = vx_{1t}.$$

Then,

$$1 \leqslant \frac{w_{1t}x_{1t} + w_{2t}x_{2t}}{w_{1t}x_{1t}} = 1 + \frac{vw_{2t}}{w_{1t}} \leqslant 1 + (a_2/a_1)v\, e^{(r_2-r_1)t}. \qquad \text{Q.E.D.}$$

Along similar lines one can prove:

Proposition 3. Let A in Proposition 2 be supplied under conditions of perfect competition, and let its output, y_t satisfy $y_1 = ux_{1t}$ (u constant) and let its price be p_t. The p^* will approach that of the price of its stagnant input.

Corollary. The smaller the value of w_{2t}, i.e. the more progressive is the progressive input of A, the more rapidly will the behaviour of A's price approximate to that of its stagnant input.

GROUNDS FOR PUBLIC SUPPORT. Several economists have explored the grounds, if any, on which public support for the performing arts can be justified. They have examined all the usual criteria and found most of them weak. For example, income distribution concerns surely do not explain public financing of activities consumed largely by persons with incomes above the average. The beneficial externalities of attendance of the arts are not only difficult to document but are even hard to describe in the abstract. The same is true of the public good

547

properties of performance. The best that has been done is to argue (1) that they have an 'option value' – even those who do not care to attend, themselves, may want to keep the arts alive for their grandchildren; and (2) that they constitute a partially public good through their part in the educational process and the (national) pride they engender even in those who do not attend themselves (or the embarrassment they avoid among those who do not want to belong to a nation of philistines). In the last analysis, it is simply argued that the arts deserve support because they are 'merit goods' (to use Musgrave's term). But that amounts to substitution of nomenclature for analysis. What the discussion comes down to is that the evidence suggests strongly that the public considers the arts worth supporting, and that in a democracy the public has the right to support what it wants to. Welfare theory has little to contribute here.

The cost disease analysis has been used by administrators throughout the world as justification for support but, of course, the fact that an activity is under financial pressure is, by itself, no valid reason for public subvention, as economic theory shows so clearly. However, if support is decided upon on other grounds, the cost disease analysis does legitimately help to give guidance on the amounts it will be appropriate to provide. It also warns us of the dangers of underfinancing as a result of what W.E. Oates has called 'fiscal illusion'. The cost disease implies that the cost of performance will rise faster than the general price level. If so, when government support for the arts increases only marginally faster than the general price level, politicians are likely to conclude that, though they have increased the real level of support, the quantity and quality of activity the public is getting for its money is declining. Mismanagement and waste are then likely to be blamed and budgets may be trimmed, on those grounds, below the level that is called for by the public's actual preferences.

BIBLIOGRAPHY

Baumol, H. and Baumol, W.J. (eds) 1984. *Inflation and the Performing Arts.* New York: New York University Press.
Baumol, W.J. and Bowen, W.G. 1966. *Performing Arts: The Economic Dilemma.* New York: Twentieth Century Fund.
Blaug, M. (ed.) 1976. *The Economics of the Arts.* London: Martin Robertson.
Feld, A.L., O'Hare, M. and Schuster, J.M.D. 1983. *Patrons Despite Themselves: Taxpayers and Arts Policy.* New York: New York University Press.
Netzer, D. 1978. *The Subsidized Muse.* New York: Cambridge University Press.
Throsby, C.D. and Withers, G.A. 1979. *The Economics of the Performing Arts.* New York: St Martin's Press.

Periphery

IMMANUEL WALLERSTEIN

The term 'periphery' makes sense only as part of the paired antinomy 'core(centre)–periphery'. It refers to an economic relationship that has spatial implications. This pair of terms has long been used in the social sciences, but until recently it has been used metaphorically rather than spatially, and to refer to social and political rather than to economic phenomena. Palgrave's original *Dictionary of Political Economy* (1894–9) did not know the concept.

Nor is it merely an issue of semantics. It is not the case that some other reasonably similar concept had previously been used instead. The issue is more fundamental. Mainstream 19th-century economic thought – both classical and neoclassical economics, but to a very large extent Marxism as well – had no place in its theorizing for space, except as location that might affect the cost of a factor of production. Transport costs obviously affected total costs. And location might give a natural rent advantage. Geological deposits were where they were. Water sources that could be dammed for power were located in one place but not another. Space thereupon became one more theoretically accidental, exogenous variable which had to be taken into account in concrete economic practice but was in no sense intrinsic to the functioning of the economic system.

The classic formulation of this view is to be found in the theory of comparative costs. England and Portugal each had certain natural advantages, such that it followed that it was rational, to use Ricardo's example, for Portugal to exchange her wine for English cloth even though she was able to produce cloth more cheaply than England. In this example the Methuen Treaty never entered the discussion.

It is not that no one ever raised the issue as to whether the natural advantages were not the result of political and social decisions which themselves were integral to the processes of economic behaviour. There had long been, for example, a current of theorizing which justified protectionism. Friedrich List stands out as a leading spokesman of this view in the 19th century. The protectionists did argue in effect that comparative advantage was socially structured and that

549

therefore state policy could and should endeavour to transform inequalities. But there are two things to note about this current of protectionist thought. Firstly, it was always marginal to the leading centres of academic economics, and to the extent that its views were incorporated, state policy was once again relegated to the status of an exogenous variable. Secondly, the protectionist current did not challenge, indeed on the contrary it reinforced, a basic pillar of mainstream thought, the parallel and theoretically independent trajectories of a series of states (societies, economies), each of which was separately governed by the same economic laws.

In the interwar period, the worldwide depression in agricultural prices which dates from the early 1920s led to a revival of protectionist theorizing, particularly in those parts of the world which combined three features: a predominance of agricultural production; a small industrial sector; a reasonably large scholarly sector. The three areas which best matched this profile were eastern Europe, Latin America, and India and in all three zones such economic writings appeared. They had in fact, however, rather little impact on local policy and even less on world scholarship.

The situation changed in the post-1945 period. Although the general expansion of the world-economy was no doubt conducive to free trade ideology, the political emergence of the Third World led to some questioning of what in the 1970s would come to be known as 'the international economic order'. It is in this context that the concept of 'periphery' took shape, first of all in the work of Raúl Prebisch and his associates in the UN Economic Commission for Latin America (ECLA).

The original Prebisch thesis laid emphasis on the 'structural' factors which underlay what by the 1950s was being called 'underdevelopment'. Prebisch argued that peripheral countries were basically exporters of raw materials to industrialized core countries. He argued that there was a long-term decline of the terms of trade against raw materials exporters. Prebisch concluded that this relationship had two basic effects. It maintained the peripheral countries in a vicious cycle of lower productivity and a lower rate of savings than the core countries. And it made it impossible for them to retain the benefits of such increases in productivity as they might experience.

The explanation was 'structural', that is, that there were socio-political 'structures' that affected, even shaped the market, and thereby in (large) part determined advantage in the market. The industrialized countries had 'self-sustained' economies whereas the underdeveloped countries did not, since they functioned as peripheries to centres. The world market forces operated to maintain this undesirable 'equilibrium'. The policy implications were clear. Since the 'normal' operations of the market would only continue the same pattern, state action was required to alter it. The basic immediate recommendation was industrialization via import substitution. The long-run implication was, however, more fundamental. Unlike Ricardo's analysis, the Prebisch argument suggested that the pattern of international trade was established importantly, perhaps primarily, by political decisions and therefore could be changed by political will.

Or more generally, the determining framework for the 'world market' was more the overarching world political structure than vice versa.

This basic thesis was picked up and developed by a large number of economists and other social scientists, in Latin America to be sure, but in the Caribbean, in India and Africa as well. It also became the basic argument of a group of social scientists located in Europe and North America, although it should be noted that many of these were persons whose areas of research were in what was now being called the Third World. One of the first of this latter group was H.W. Singer, whose principal contribution was published in 1950, the same year as Prebisch's famous report. For this reason, this viewpoint is sometimes called the Prebisch–Singer thesis.

In time, the Prebisch thesis developed in the 1960s into a doctrine which was called *dependista*, because it emphasized the fact that peripheral areas were in a larger system within which they were 'dependent' as contrasted with more autonomous zones. The primary focus of criticism of the *dependistas* was a dominant mainstream model which was coming to be called 'modernization theory' or 'developmentalism'.

Developmentalism centred around the issue of how those *countries* which were 'underdeveloped' might 'develop'. Developmentalism made several assumptions. Some combination of traits of a country – there was much debate about what they were – led to development. All countries could develop in similar ways, were they to ensure the proper combination of traits – in this sense, the doctrine was melioristic. Development was a patterned process. The last assumption was often expressed as a stage theory. The single most influential expression of this last argument was W.W. Rostow's *Stages of Economic Growth* (1960). Developmentalism originated as an economic doctrine, but others soon began to suggest parallel processes of political development and social development. There was much discussion of the linkages among the various 'aspects' of development and hence much encouragement of so-called interdisciplinary analysis.

By the 1960s developmentalism had become a dominant and self-conscious mode of analysis in world scholarship, particularly in any discussion of the 'Third World' or the 'underdeveloped' countries. Prebisch had argued against classical free trade ideology. The main thrust of the 'second generation' of theorizers about the periphery – that of the *dependistas* of the 1960s – was directed against these 'developmentalists' even though many of them had already accepted the legitimacy of some state intervention in the economy. This second generation was still very largely Latin American – F.H. Cardoso, T. Dos Santos, Celso Furtado, Ruy Mauro Marini, O. Sunkel, R. Stavenhagen were major figures – but there were also Lloyd Best (Trinidad), Samir Amin (Egypt) and Walter Rodney (Guyana). All of these scholars attacked in one way or another the theory of modernization and in particular the assumption that Third World countries could 'repeat' European–North American patterns of development by copying in one way or another the policies, past or present, of the presumably 'successful' states.

The contribution of André Gunder Frank to this second-generation theorizing was that he spelled out two arguments which, while present in the work of his colleagues, had not been as clearly underlined, or as widely disseminated. The first argument is to be found in the slogan he coined, 'the development of underdevelopment'. This is the argument that underdevelopment is not undevelopment, a primordial pre-capitalist or pre-modern state of being, but rather the consequence of the historic process of worldwide development through the linked formation of core and periphery. It followed from this perspective that the further extension and deepening of the division of labour on a world scale led not to national development (as the developmentalists argued) but to the further underdevelopment of the periphery. The policy implications of the two perspectives therefore were directly opposed one to the other.

The second argument involved a critique not of modernization theorists but of so-called orthodox Marxists. To understand this critique we have to look at the history of Marxist theory. From about 1875 on there arose a version of Marxist theory which became predominant in the two major world organizational structures, the Second and Third Internationals, and which very largely reflected the theoretical input of the German Social-Democratic Party (c1875–1920) and the Bolsheviks, later Communist Party of the Soviet Union (c1900–50). Whether this version was or was not faithful to Marx's own theorizing is not under discussion here, and is irrelevant to the issue at hand.

Since both Internationals were oriented to the issue of obtaining state power, the *de facto* unit of economic analysis became the state, and, in this respect, there was no real difference with neoclassical models of economic development. Furthermore, under Stalin, a very strong stage model of 'modes of production' was delineated which paralleled structurally the Rostowian model, although the details were quite different.

In the period 1875–1950, the worldwide structure of capitalist development disappeared or became secondary in 'orthodox' Marxist theorizing except for a brief interval around World War I where momentarily such figures as Otto Bauer, Nikolai Bukharin, Rosa Luxemburg, and in part Lenin discussed these issues. By the 1920s all such discussion ceased, and by the 1950s Communist parties in Latin America (and elsewhere) were deriving very specific policy implications from the state-centred 'orthodox' theorizing. The reasoning went as follows. Feudalism as a stage comes before capitalism which comes before socialism. Latin America was still in the feudal stage. What was on the politico-economic agenda, and implicitly 'progressive', was national capitalist development. Ergo, Communist parties should enter into political alliances with the national bourgeoisie in order to further national development, postponing to a later date 'socialist revolution'.

The *dependistas* saw this analysis as leading to virtually the same policy results as the analysis of the modernization theory developmentalists. Since the late 1960s was also a period of increasing US–USSR political detente, they saw the theoretical 'convergence' as tied to a world-level political convergence which in turn was facilitated by the hitherto unremarked common underpinnings of analysis.

The *dependista* popularization of the concept 'periphery' was abetted by two theoretical works which claimed to be Marxist in economic theory yet challenged in each case a major strand in 'orthodox' Marxist economic theorizing. The first was Paul Baran's *Political Economy of Growth*, published in 1957, and which directly inspired many *dependista* authors. Baran modified the concept of *surplus* by introducing a distinction between 'actual' and 'potential' economic surplus, suggesting that the consequence of capitalism was not merely a particular allocation of actual surplus but even more importantly the non-creation of a potential surplus. This non-created potential surplus existed throughout the system but one major component was located in the 'backwardness' of underdeveloped countries.

The second challenge was in Arghiri Emmanuel's *Unequal Exchange*, published in 1969. Emmanuel's book launched a direct attack on the Ricardian theory of comparative advantage, noting that its assumption, the immobility of the factors of production, had never been seriously challenged, even by Marxists. Asserting that while capital is internationally mobile, labour has not been, Emmanuel argued that wages determine prices, and not vice versa. Given unequal wages (and immobile labour) internationally, international trade involves unequal exchange, since items priced identically and ensuring parity in rate of profit in fact encompass different amounts of labour. This theory thus challenges the idea that surplus is transferred only in the work process, and that space is irrelevant. The fact that frontiers are crossed is crucial to the theoretical explanation of unequal exchange.

Two other, initially separate intellectual debates entered the scene to complicate the issue further. In the late 1950s, Maurice Dobb and Paul Sweezy had a public debate (in which others then joined) about the so-called transition from feudalism to capitalism in western Europe in early modern times. They disagreed about many things: the time of the change, the motor of change, the geographical context of analysis, the very definition of feudalism and capitalism. What the debate accomplished was that it forced a reconsideration of the definition of feudalism, which was important, since many peripheral zones were being characterized as having 'feudal' characteristics. When in the late 1950s and 1960s a new debate arose on the nature of, indeed the existence of, an 'Asiatic mode of production', the debate widened. The more the debate widened, the more the distinction between what is internal and what is external (to the nation/state/ society) so fundamental to 'orthodox' Marxist thought, but also to neoclassical thought, came under challenge.

There was a second debate, purely political and far outside world academic circles. It was the obscure, seemingly esoteric debate between the Soviet and Chinese state apparatuses over the process of the hypothetical transition from socialism to communism. This too occurred in the 1950s. The issue was whether states would go forward in this hypothetical transition singly or collectively. This too implied a difference concerning the unit of analysis. The Chinese position had far-reaching implications which by the late 1960s were being called 'Mao-Zedong thought'.

It was in the 1970s that these strands of thinking about the 'periphery' and related topics came together. The term '*dependista*' disappeared. Some began to speak of 'world-systems analysis'. The core–periphery relationship was now being defined as the description of the axial division of labour of the capitalist world-economy. Core and periphery were now less linked locations than linked processes which tended to be reflected in geographical concentrations. These processes had as one major consequence the formation of states within the framework of an interstate system. One could think of the interstate system as the political superstructure of the capitalist world-economy. This world-economy was an historical social system, a socially created whole which developed in specific ways over its history. The overall structure was seen as defining the parameters within which the capitalist market processes occurred. As new geographical zones had been incorporated historically into this system, they had been for the most part 'peripheralized'. This meant that various worldwide mechanisms (political, financial and cultural) tended to make it profitable for individual entrepreneurs to segregate production processes spatially such that some zones had disproportionately high concentrations of peripheral processes – that is, processes with a high labour component and relatively low-cost labour – ensured by the involvement of wage-workers in these zones in usually reorganized household structures in which lifetime income returns from wage labour comprised a minority percentage of total real revenue.

While state policies could affect these relationships, the ability of any single state to transform the situation was constrained by its location in the interstate system and therefore depended significantly upon the changing condition of the balance of power. The interstate system varied in patterned ways between periods in which there was one hegemonic power and periods in which there was acute rivalry among several strong powers.

In addition, the ability of states to affect the processes of peripheralization was said to be a function of the cyclical rhythms of the world-economy, believed to alternate, once again in patterned ways, between periods of expansion and stagnation.

The regular cyclical rhythms and the alterations of the conditions of the interstate system led to some continuous but limited shifting in the economic roles of particular geographical zones within the system without necessarily changing the basic structuring of core–periphery relations.

Finally, it has been argued that the geographical concentration of different economic processes has been trimodal rather than bimodal, there having been at all times semiperipheral zones, defined as regions having a fairly even mix of core-like and periphery-like economic processes.

The concept 'periphery' thus has involved a basic theoretical criticism of 19th-century economic paradigms. It has not been spared counterattack from three main quarters: of course from the modernization/developmentalists under attack, most of whom have been basically Keynesians in their economic theorizing; but even more from so-called neo-liberals (the critique of P.T. Bauer has been the most trenchant), and from 'orthodox' Marxists.

The concept 'periphery' has served a polemical purpose in the last 20 years. To advance its utility, its proponents must now come to clearer terms about the functioning interrelations of the three antimonies of the capitalist world-economy:

core–periphery relations in the division of labour; A and B phases in the cyclical long waves; and periods of hegemony versus periods of rivalry in the interstate system.

BIBLIOGRAPHY

Amin, S. 1974. *Accumulation on a World Scale*. New York and London: Monthly Review Press.

Arrighi, G. 1983. *The Geometry of Imperialism*. Revised edn, London: Verso.

Baran, P. 1957. *The Political Economy of Growth*. New York: Monthly Review Press.

Bauer, P.T. 1972. *Dissent on Development*. Cambridge, Mass.: Harvard University Press.

Emmanuel, A. 1969. *Unequal Exchange*. New York and London: Monthly Review Press, 1972.

Frank, A.G. 1969. *Latin America: Underdevelopment or Revolution*. New York and London: Monthly Review Press.

Furtado, C. 1963. *The Economic Growth of Brazil*. Berkeley and Los Angeles: University of California Press.

Hilton, R. (ed.) 1976. *The Transition from Feudalism to Capitalism*. Revised edn, London: New Left Books.

Hirschman, A.O. 1958. *The Strategy of Economic Development*. New Haven and London: Yale University Press.

Hopkins, T.K. and Wallerstein, I. 1982. *World-Systems Analysis*. Beverly Hills: Sage.

Love, J.L. 1980. Raúl Prebisch and the origins of the doctrine of unequal exchange. *Latin American Research Review* 15(1), 45–72.

Prebisch, R. 1950. *The Economic Development of Latin America and its Principal Problems*. New York: United Nations.

Rostow, W.W. 1960. *The Stages of Economic Growth*. New York and London: Cambridge University Press.

Singer, H.W. 1950. The distribution of gains between investing and borrowing countries. *American Economic Review* 40(2), May, 473–85.

Wallerstein, I. 1974, 1980. *The Modern World System*. 2 vols, New York, San Francisco and London: Academic Press.

'Political Economy' and 'Economics'

PETER GROENEWEGEN

This article provides a survey of the origin of the term 'political economy' and its changes in meaning, emphasizing in particular its first modern usage in the 18th century, its demise from the end of the 19th century, when it was gradually replaced by the word 'economics', and its revival in a variety of forms, largely during the 1960s, which have altered its meaning from more traditional usage. What follows is therefore largely definitional and etymological, designed to indicate the lack of precise meaning associated with both the term 'political economy' and its more modern synonym, 'economics'.

The origin of words starting with 'econom' is Greek, from *oikos* meaning 'house' and *nomos* meaning 'law' in the sense appropriate to astronomy when it deals with 'the law and order of the stars' (Cannan, 1929, p. 37). The traditional meaning of *oikonomike* or economics, was therefore 'household management'. Aristotle (1962, p. 30) used it in this sense when analysing households as 'three pairs: master and slave, husband and wife, father and children'. This meaning persisted in moral philosophy until the middle of the 18th century, for example, in Hutcheson (1755) and Smith (1763, p. 141). The Latin *oeconomia* likewise meant management of household affairs and extended to management in general including orderly arrangement of speech and composition. The French *oeconomie* or *économie* took over this wider meaning of management from the Latin and when combined with *politique* it signified public administration or management of the affairs of state. Arthur Young (1770) applied this wider meaning in the title of a treatise on agricultural management. Using 'economy' as a synonym for 'thrift', 'frugality' and careful management of the finances of households and other organizations also derives from the Latin adaptation. 17th-century concern with nation-building gave the term 'public administration' a wider scope, and given developments in France under Henry IV and Richelieu it is not surprising that the term 'political economy' made its first appearance there. This first use is generally attributed to Montchretien (1615), but King (1948) indicates prior use in Mayerne-Turquet (1611). Because the relationship between state and economy it signified was so appropriate to the times, King suggests that other, perhaps earlier uses, may be found. Petty (1691, p. 181 and cf. 1683, p. 483) used the term in England. As Cannan (1929, p. 39) surmised, he could as well have used 'political economy' as 'political anatomy' to describe his analysis of the Irish economy, considering he used 'political arithmetick' for the art of making more precise statements on the political economy of nations, interpreted as their comparative strengths (cf. Verri, 1763, pp. 9–10, who speaks of the science of political economy in this manner). Cantillon (1755, p. 46) referred to an 'oeconomy' in the sense of an economic organism in which classes exist as interdependent units, but his book remained an 'Essay on Commerce'.

More precise formulations of political economy as a science of economic organization, though with continuing connotations of management, regulation and even orderly natural laws, are found in Physiocracy. Quesnay's early usage generally implies the traditional meanings, but in addition he applied the term to include discussions of the nature of wealth, its reproduction and distribution. This double meaning is particularly evident in his *Tableau économique*. It is therefore no accident that Mirabeau (1760) spoke of *économie politique* 'as if it consisted of a dissertation of agriculture and public administration as well as on the nature of wealth and the means of procuring it' (Cannan, 1929, p. 40). During the subsequent decades the second meaning became more dominant, the word 'science' was added to it (an innovation attributed to Verri, 1763, p. 9) and by the 1770s it almost exclusively referred to the production and distribution of wealth in the context of management of the nation's resources.

Sir James Steuart (1767) is the first English economist to put 'political economy' into the title of a book. Its introductory chapter explained that just as 'Oeconomy in general, is the art of providing for all the wants of the family', so the science of political economy seeks 'to secure a certain fund of subsistence for all the inhabitants, to obviate every circumstance which may render it precarious, to provide every thing necessary for supplying the wants of the society, and to employ the inhabitants ... in such a manner as naturally to create reciprocal relations and dependencies between them, so as to make their several interests lead them to supply one another with reciprocal wants' (1767, pp. 15, 17). Steuart's full title gave the subject matter to be covered: 'population, agriculture, trade, industry, money, coin, interest, circulation, banks, exchange, public credit and taxes'. In 1771 Verri published *Reflections on Political Economy*, the preface of which referred to a new department of knowledge called political economy. Although Smith did not use 'political economy' in his title the introduction and plan of his book refers to 'different theories of political economy' and at the start of Book IV he defined the term as 'a branch of the science of a statesman or legislator' with the twofold objectives of providing 'a plentiful revenue or subsistence for the people ... [and] to supply the state or commonwealth with a revenue sufficient for the public services' (Smith, 1776, pp. 11, 428). Elsewhere (1776, pp. 678–9) Smith indicated that he saw political economy as an inquiry into the nature and causes of the wealth of nations or, as the physiocrats had initially suggested, the science of the nature, reproduction, distribution and disposal of wealth.

The association of the science, political economy, with material welfare proved to be particularly hardy, as was its association with the art of legislation. Bentham (1793–5, p. 223) put the matter concisely when he argued, 'Political Economy may be considered as a science or as an Art. But in this instance as in others, it is only as a guide to the art that the science is of use'. Torrens (1819, p. 453) also called it 'one of the most important and useful branches of science' while James Mill (1821, p. 211) and McCulloch (1825, p. 9) defined it as a systematic inquiry into the laws regulating the production, distribution, consumption an exchange of commodities or the products of labour. 'Confounding' the art with the science was criticized by Senior (1836, p. 3) as being detrimental to its development, a position likewise taken by John Stuart Mill (1831–3) and which also reaffirmed its moral and social nature. In this influential essay, Mill (1831–3, p. 140) defined political economy as 'the science which traces the laws of such of the phenomena of society as arise from the combined operations of mankind for the production of wealth, in so far as those phenomena are not modified by the pursuit of any other object'. This position was more or less adhered to in his later *Principles* (1848, p. 21), when he defined its subject matter as 'the laws of Production and Distribution, and some of the practical consequences deducible from them ...'. Cairnes (1875, p. 35) condensed this to the statement that 'Political Economy ... expounds the laws of the phenomena of wealth.'

The middle of the 19th century saw two criticisms of this meaning of political economy. Marx (1859, p. 20) identified the study of political economy with a search for 'the anatomy of civil society' or, as Engels (1859, p. 218) put in his review of the book, 'the theoretical analysis of modern bourgeois society'. This preserved the name but criticized the scope and method of political economy. Others suggested the name be changed because it had become misleading. Hearn (1863) put forward *Plutology* or the theory of effects to satisfy human wants; MacLeod (1875) proposed 'economics', defining it as the 'science which treats of the laws which govern the relations of exchangeable quantities', a nomenclature of whose virtues he successfully persuaded Jevons (Black, 1977, p. 115). When in 1879 the Marshalls published an elementary political economy text, they called it *The Economics of Industry*. The new name of MacLeod and the Marshalls was favourably referred to in the second edition of Jevons's *Theory* (1879, p. xiv) because of convenience and scientific nicety (it matched mathematics, ethics and aesthetics) and Jevons's last published book (Jevons, 1905) bore the title *Principles of Economics*. Although Cannan (1929, p. 44) claimed Marshall (1890) induced acceptance of the new name, this only came with the later editions, and the change was not completed until the early 1920s (Groenewegen, 1985). Even then, Marshall (1890, p. 1) appeared to treat the two names as synonyms: 'Political Economy or Economics is a study of mankind in the ordinary business of life; it examines that part of individual and social action which is most closely connected with the attainment and with the use of the material requisites of well-being.'

Just as J.S. Mill (1831–3, pp. 120–1) had attempted retrospective codification of scope and method in the 1820s, so Robbins (1932, p. 16) redefined economics in its marginalist form as 'the science which studies human behaviour as a relationship between ends and scarce means which have alternative uses'. This did more than supply a meaning for the new term, 'economics'. It destroyed the view classical economists had of their science, as Myint (1948) clearly pointed out. Others (e.g. Knight, 1951, p. 6) complained that Robbins's definition neglected the link between economics and the 'individualistic or "liberal" outlook on life, of which "capitalism", or the competitive system, or free business enterprise, is the expression upon the economic side, as democracy on the political'. However, the major drawback of the Robbins definition was its irreconcilability with Keynes's work with its proof of the possibility of unemployment equilibrium and hence contradicting Robbins's requirement for the existence of an economic problem that resources have to be scarce. Modern mainstream definitions of economics (Rees, 1968; Samuelson, 1955, p. 5) have simply combined the Robbinsian resource allocation problem with the new economics of employment, inflation and growth developed from Keynes's work.

Robbins's definition also aimed to make economics a 'system of theoretical and positive knowledge' (Fraser, 1937, p. 30), preferring to reserve the older name, 'political economy' for applied topics such as monopoly, protection, planning and government fiscal policy, subjects included in his essays on political economy (Robbins, 1939). Although Schumpeter (1954) held a similar opinion he was careful to warn that 'political economy meant different things to different writers, and in some cases it meant what is now known as economic theory or "pure" economics' (p. 22). These views of political economy conflict with the pragmatic Cambridge outlook on economics, derived from Marshall's description of economics as 'an engine for the discovery of concrete truth', encapsulated by Keynes (1921, p. v) in his famous introduction to the Cambridge Economics Handbooks: 'Economics is a method rather than a doctrine, an apparatus of the mind, a technique of thinking which helps its possessor to draw correct conclusions.' This sentiment is concisely summarized by Joan Robinson's view of economics (1933, p. 1) as 'a box of tools'.

Marxists had never abandoned the older terminology of political economy. Dobb (1937, p. vii) defended 'political economy' against the new term 'economics' because its controversies 'have meaning as answers to certain questions of an essentially practical kind', associated with the 'nature and behaviour' of the capitalist system. Likewise, Baran (1957, p. 131) argued for a 'political economy of growth' because an 'understanding of the factors responsible for the size and the mode of utilization of the social surplus ... [is] a problem, not even approached in the realm of pure economics'. For the classical economists, use of the surplus had been a major research question. Political economy is therefore a very appropriate title for the endeavours of some contemporary economists to resurrect both practical and theoretical aspects of the classical tradition in what they describe as the surplus approach.

By the 1960s the radical libertarian right from Chicago and the Center for the Study of Public Choice appears to have appropriated the title 'political economy' for their wide application of Robbins's (1932) injunction that analysis in terms of '*alternatives*' is the key distinguishing feature of economics. This effectively replaced Robbins's question 'what is or is not economic in nature?' with the far wider one of 'what can economics contribute to our understanding of this or that problem?'. This opens up the way for an economics of 'family life, child rearing, dying, sex, crime, politics and many other topics' which some of its practitioners identify with Adam Smith's research agenda (McKenzie and Tullock, 1975, p. 3). Others continue to associate the term 'with the specific advice given by one or more economists ... to governments or to the public at large either on broad policy issues or on particular proposals' or, alternatively, as another term for 'normative economics' (Mishan, 1982, p. 13).

At the approach of the 21st century, both terms – 'political economy' and 'economics' – survive. During their existence, both have experienced changes of meaning. Nevertheless, they can still essentially be regarded as synonyms, a feature of this nomenclature reflecting an interesting characteristic of the science it describes. In its sometimes discontinuous development, economics or political economy has invariably experienced difficulties in discarding earlier views, and traces of old doctrine are intermingled with the latest developments in the science.

BIBLIOGRAPHY

Aristotle. *The Politics*. Trans. J.E. Sinclair, Harmondsworth: Penguin Classics, 1962.

Baran, P.A. 1957. *The Political Economy of Growth*. Harmondsworth: Penguin Books, 1973.

Bentham, J. 1793–5. *Manual of Political Economy*. In *Jeremy Bentham's Economic Writings*, ed. W. Stark, London: George Allen & Unwin, 1952.

Black, R.D.C. (ed.) 1977. *Papers and Correspondence of William Stanley Jevons: Correspondence 1873–78*. London: Macmillan for the Royal Economic Society.

Cairnes, J.E. 1875. *The Character and Logical Method of Political Economy*. London. Reprinted, New York: Kelly, 1965.

Cannan, E. 1929. *A Review of Economic Theory*. London: P.S. King & Son.

Cantillon, R. 1755. *Essay on the Nature of Commerce in General*. Ed. H. Higgs, London: Macmillan & Co., 1931.

Dobb, M.H. 1937. *Political Economy and Capitalism*. London: G. Routledge & Sons.

Engels, F. 1859. Karl Marx's 'A contribution to the critique of political economy'. *Das Volk*, Berlin, No. 14, August. In Marx (1859), 218–22.

Fraser, L.M. 1937. *Economic Thought and Language*. London: A. & C. Black.

Groenewegen, P.D. 1985. Professor Arndt on political economy: a comment. *Economic Record* 61, December, 744–51.

Hearn, W.E. 1863. *Plutology*. Melbourne: Robertson.

Hutcheson, F. 1755. *A System of Moral Philosophy*. Glasgow: Robert and Andrew Foulis.

Jevons, W.S. 1879. *The Theory of Political Economy*. 2nd edn, London: Macmillan; Preface in 4th edn, London, 1910.

Jevons, W.S. 1905. *Principles of Economics*. London: Macmillan.

Keynes, J.M. 1921. Introduction to Cambridge Economic Handbooks. In D.H. Robertson, *Money*, London and Cambridge: Cambridge Economic Handbooks.

King, J.E. 1948. The origin of the term 'political economy'. *Journal of Modern History* 20, 230–31.

Knight, F.H. 1951. Economics. In F.H. Knight, *On the History and Method of Economics*, Chicago: University of Chicago Press, 1963.

McCulloch, J.R. 1825. *Principles of Political Economy with Sketch of the Rise and Progress of the Science*. London: Murray, 1870.

MacLeod, H.D. 1875. What is political economy? *Contemporary Review* 25, 871–93.

McKenzie, R.B. and Tullock, G. 1975. *The New World of Economics: Explorations into the Human Experience*. Homewood, Ill: Irwin.

Marshall, A. 1890. *Principles of Economics*. 9th variorum edn, ed. C.W. Guillebaud, London: Macmillan, 1961.

Marshall, A. and Marshall, M.P. 1879. *The Economics of Industry*. London: Macmillan.

Marx, K. 1859. *A Contribution to the Critique of Political Economy*. Introduction by M. Dobb, London: Lawrence & Wishart, 1971.

Mayerne-Turquet, L. de. 1611. *La Monarchie Aristodémocratique; ou le Gouvernement composé et meslé des trois formes de légitimes républiques*. Paris.

Mill, J. 1821. *Elements of Political Economy*. 3rd edn, London, 1926. Reprinted in James Mill, *Selected Writings*, ed. D. Wisen, Edinburgh: Oliver & Boyd for the Scottish Economic Society, 1966.

Mill, J.S. 1831–3. On the definition of political economy; and on the method of investigation proper to it. Essay V in J.S. Mill, *Essays on Some Unsettled Questions of Political Economy*, LSE Reprint, London, 1948.

Mill, J.S. 1848. *Principles of Political Economy with some of their Applications to Social Philosophy*. In *Collected Works of John Stuart Mill*, ed. J.M. Robson, Toronto: University of Toronto Press, 1965.

Mirabeau, V.R., Marquis de. 1758–60. *L'ami des hommes ou traité de la population*. Avignon and Paris.

Mishan, E.J. 1982. *Introduction to Political Economy*. London: Hutchinson.

Montchrétien, A. de. 1615. *Traité de l'économie politique*. Ed. Th. Funck-Brentano, Paris: Plon, 1889.

Myint, H.L.A. 1948. *Theories of Welfare Economics*. London: Longmans, Green & Co.

Petty, Sir W. 1683. *Observations Upon the Dublin Bills of Mortality and the State of that City*. In *The Economic Writings of Sir William Petty*, ed. C.H. Hull. Reprinted, New York: Kelley, 1963.

Petty, Sir W. 1691. *The Political Anatomy of Ireland*. In *The Economic Writings of Sir William Petty*, ed. C.H. Hull. Reprinted, New York: Kelley, 1963.

Rees, A. 1968. Economics. In *International Encyclopaedia of the Social Sciences*, ed. D.L. Sills, New York: Macmillan, Vol. 4, 472–85.

Robbins, L. 1932. *An Essay on the Nature and Significance of Economic Science*. London: Macmillan. 2nd edn, 1935.

Robbins, L.C. 1939. *The Economic Basis of Class Conflict and Other Essays in Political Economy*. London: Macmillan.

Robinson, J.V. 1933. *The Economics of Imperfect Competition*. London: Macmillan.

Samuelson, P.A. 1955. *Economics*. 3rd edn, New York: McGraw-Hill. 7th edn, 1967.

Schumpeter, J.A. 1954. *History of Economic Analysis*. London: George Allen & Unwin.

Senior, N.W. 1836. *An Outline of the Science of Political Economy*. London: Unwin Library of Economics, 1938.

Smith, A. 1763. *Lectures on Jurisprudence*. Ed. R.L. Meek, D.D. Raphael and P.G. Stein, Oxford: Oxford University Press, 1978.

Smith, A. 1776. *An Inquiry into the Nature and Causes of the Wealth of Nations*. Ed. R.H. Campbell and A.S. Skinner, Oxford: Oxford University Press, 1976.

Steuart, J. 1767. *An Inquiry into the Principles of Political Economy*. Ed. A.S. Skinner, Edinburgh and London: Oliver & Boyd for the Scottish Economic Society, 1966.

[Torrens, R.] 1819. Mr Owen's plans for relieving the national distress. *Edinburgh Review* 32, October, Article XI.

Verri, P. 1763. Memorie storiche sulla economia pubblica dello sato di Milano. In *Scrittori Classici Italiani di Economia Politica*, Parte Moderna, Vol. XVII, Milan, 1804.

Verri, P. 1771. *Reflections on Political Economy*. Trans. B. McGilvray, ed. P. Groenewegen. Reprints of Economic Classics, Series 2, No. 4, Sydney: University of Sydney, 1986.

Young, A. 1770. *Rural Oeconomy, or Essays on the Practical Parts of Husbandry*. London.

Poverty

A.B. ATKINSON

Concern for poverty has been expressed over the centuries, even if its priority on the agenda for political action has not always been high. Its different meanings and manifestations have been the subject of study by historians, sociologists and economists. Its causes have been identified in a wide variety of sources, ranging from deficiencies in the administration of income support to the injustice of the economic and social system. The relief, or abolition, of poverty has been sought in the reform of social security, in intervention in the labour market, and in major changes in the form of economic organization.

Poverty today is most obvious – and has the most pressing claim on our attention – on a world scale. The unequal distribution of income between countries, and the disparities within countries, mean that there are large numbers of people in Africa, Asia and Latin America whose standard of living would be agreed by everyone to be poor. The World Bank has suggested that there is 'a global total of close to 1 billion people living in absolute poverty' (World Bank, 1982, p. 78), of whom about 400 million are thought to live in South Asia, about 150 million in China, and some 100 million in East/South-East Asia and Sub-Saharan Africa. At such levels of living, the risks of death through hunger or cold, and vulnerability to disease, are of a quite different order from those in advanced countries. This has manifested itself most urgently in the occurrence of famine. Whatever the immediate cause of such disasters, whether inadequate total supply of food or whether unequal distribution, the severity of the situation in areas such as the Sahel and Ethiopia is an indicator of the precariousness of survival in many low-income countries.

Such mass poverty in poor countries is quite different from poverty in advanced countries. The target of the American War on Poverty, launched in 1964, was the minority of Americans with incomes below a poverty line of $3000 a year for a family of four (in 1962 prices), which was many times the average income of India. The basis for the US official poverty line is to be found in a food consumption standard (the Department of Agriculture economy food plan), but

563

its level reflects the prevailing living conditions in that society. It might well be argued that concern with poverty in advanced countries, at a time when other countries face disaster, is unjustified and that the term 'poverty' cannot legitimately be applied. The parallel may be drawn with rearranging the deckchairs on the *Titanic* as the ship goes down. This does not, however, seem fully apposite. A closer parallel is with the position of those on ships steaming to the aid of the stricken vessel. The overriding objective should be to get to the rescue as rapidly as possible, but those on the rescuing ships should also be concerned that their steerage passengers do not die of exposure on the way. The relief of famine, and the redistribution of income to alleviate poverty on a world scale, should have priority, but the problem of poverty in advanced countries, defined in their terms, may legitimately come next on the list of concerns.

The fact that the term 'poverty' is being used in different senses highlights the need to clarify the underlying concept, and the discussion so far has touched on several aspects which need to be elaborated. After a brief historical review of studies of poverty in section 1, we examine some key conceptual issues. What is the indicator of resources which should be employed in measuring poverty? What is the underlying notion of poverty and how is it related to inequality? These issues are discussed in section 2. The determination of the poverty standard is a crucial question. Here we need to consider approaches based on such 'absolute' concepts as food requirements and those poverty scales which are explicitly 'relative'. We must consider the treatment of families with differing needs. These topics are the subject of section 3. Once we have established the extent of poverty, its causes become a central concern. Here we are led first to ask 'who are the poor?' This is examined in section 4. Is poverty concentrated in particular classes or particular sections of society? How far is it associated with particular stages of the life-cycle? The composition of the poor provides in turn a starting point for the investigation of the underlying causes of poverty, and an analysis of policies to combat poverty. These are the subject of section 5.

1. HISTORICAL REVIEW OF STUDIES OF POVERTY. The scientific study of poverty in the Anglo-Saxon world is usually taken to date from the investigations of Booth and Rowntree at the end of the 19th century. In Britain it is true that King and others had given estimates of the number of paupers; and that *The State of the Poor* by Eden (1797) contained a great deal of material collected from over 100 parishes and giving details of family budgets. Engels and Mayhew provided insight into the condition of the poor in urban England. But it was Booth's *Life and Labour* (1892–7) survey of London, started in the East End in the 1880s, that combined the elements of first-hand observation with a systematic attempt to measure the extent of the problem. Taking the street as his unit of analysis, he drew up his celebrated map of poverty in London.

The study of Rowntree (1901) was intended to compare the situation in York, as a typical provincial town, with that found by Booth in London, but his method represented a significant departure in that it was concerned with individual family incomes and in that he developed a poverty standard based on estimates of nutritional and other requirements. The development of survey methods was taken further by Bowley (1912–13) who pioneered the use of sampling in his 1 in 20 random sample of working-class households in Reading. A great many local studies were subsequently conducted, including Bowley's Five Towns survey in 1915, replicated in the early 1920s, and the new Survey of London Life and Labour published in the early 1930s. Rowntree himself repeated his survey of York in 1936 and 1950. The latter became the standard source of information as to the effectiveness of the post-1948 welfare state, with most commentators concluding that poverty had been effectively abolished in Britain by the combination of full employment and the new social benefits. Doubt began to be cast on this conclusion by the work of empirical sociologists and came to the fore with the publication of *The Poor and the Poorest* by Abel-Smith and Townsend (1965). This showed, using secondary analysis of a national survey, that in 1960 about two million people fell below the social security safety net level. This finding was confirmed in official estimates which began to be published by the Department of Health and Social Security in the 1970s, and by Townsend's own major survey (1979).

As in many fields, the United States entered later and has taken the subject further. The definition of a poverty line was attempted by Hunter in 1904 and this was developed in a series of studies, such as the 'minimum comfort' and other budgets produced for New York City. There was the 1949 report on low-income families by the Joint Committee on the Economic Report. It was not, however, until the 1960s that the problem of poverty received systematic study, with a few notable exceptions such as the work of Lampman (1959). *The Other America* by Harrington (1962) and *The Affluent Society* by Galbraith (1958) did much to arouse the attention of the public, politicians and academics. The 1964 report of the Council of Economic Advisers set out the $3000 poverty level, drawing heavily on the research of Orshansky (1965), and this was subsequently refined to form the official poverty line, which has been applied since that date (with modifications, such as the addition of alternative measures including the value of transfers in kind).

Similar studies have been carried out in many countries, and researchers have become increasingly interested in cross-country comparisons. The OECD made an early attempt at such comparisons and a more extensive exercise is being carried out in the Luxembourg Income Study. Any assessment of world poverty depends on the availability of information about the distribution of living standards within individual countries; and here both the World Bank and the International Labour Organization have made significant contributions. In some low-income countries, there has been extensive research on poverty, India being an example, where there has been a great deal of discussion as to whether poverty has increased or decreased over time. The ILO and the World Bank have also been influential in the widespread interest, reflected in the Brandt Report (1980), in the concept of 'basic needs', or a minimum set of specific goods and environmental conditions.

World of Economics

2. POVERTY: LIVING STANDARDS AND RIGHTS. Concern about poverty may take the form of concern about such basic needs: for example, food, housing and clothing. In this case, we can identify clearly the items of consumption in which we are interested. This approach leads to poverty being measured in a multidimensional way, where a family may be deprived in one but not other respects, although particularly serious will be situations where families suffer deprivation in several dimensions, or what is referred to typically as 'multiple deprivation'.

This approach is concerned with specific deprivation, but we may also seek to record disadvantage in a single index of living standards, such as total expenditure, a household being said to be in poverty if it has total expenditure below a specified amount. This is not, however, the approach followed in most studies of poverty in advanced countries, which record poverty on the basis of total *income*. Income may *understate* the level of living. A family may be able to dissave or to borrow, in which case its current level of living is not constrained by current income and expenditure may be the more appropriate index. (Although in the short run there may be a divergence between *consumption* and *expenditure*, as families use up stocks of goods, etc.) The level of living may exceed that permitted by income where the family is able to share in the consumption of others. An elderly person living with his or her children may benefit from their expenditure. Income may, conversely, *overstate* the level of living. This may happen where money alone is not sufficient to buy the necessary goods: where there is rationing, or unavailability of goods. It is also possible that people choose a low level of consumption. This latter reason has led to its being argued that income *should* be the indicator of poverty, since it is a measure of the opportunities open to a family and is not influenced by the consumption decisions made.

In considering the choice between income and expenditure, it is helpful to distinguish two rather different conceptions of poverty: that concerned with *standards of living* and that concerned with *minimum rights* to resources. On the former approach, the goal is that people attain a specified level of consumption (or consumption of specific goods); on the latter approach, people are seen as entitled, as citizens, to the minimum income, the disposal of which is a matter for them. In practice, the two notions are often confounded, but the distinction is important, and it has obvious implications for the choice of poverty indicator. Income is the focus of the rights approach, but its use on a standard of living approach must be seen as a proxy for consumption.

The reference to 'rights' raises the question of the relation between poverty and inequality. Here four different schools of thought may be distinguished. There are those who are concerned only with poverty, attaching no weight to income inequalities above the poverty line. There are those who attach weight to the reduction of inequality as a goal of policy but give priority to the elimination of poverty, so that we have a lexicographic objective function. There are those who are concerned about both goals and who are willing to trade gains in one direction against losses in the other. Finally, they are those who attach no especial significance to poverty, simply regarding it as a component of the wider cost of inequality.

566

In this context, reference should be made to the choice of *poverty measures*. Where poverty puts survival in doubt, it is natural to take as one's measure the proportion of the population at risk. Concern for minimum rights may also make the 'head count' the most relevant measure. But we may also be concerned, particularly on a standard of living approach, with the severity of poverty, in which case measures such as the poverty deficit (the total shortfall from the poverty line) may be more appropriate. One can indeed go further, as proposed by Sen (1976), and take account of the distribution of income within the poor population: for example, with the poverty index depending on the Gini coefficient for this distribution.

3. SETTING THE POVERTY LINE. The most straightforward approach to the determination of the poverty line is to specify a basket of goods, denoted by the vector $\mathbf{x}^*$, purchasable at prices $\mathbf{p}$, and to set the poverty standard as:

$$(1 + h)\mathbf{p} \cdot \mathbf{x}^*,$$

where h is a provision for inefficient expenditure or waste, or a provision for items not included in the list $\mathbf{x}^*$. This was in effect the method adopted by Rowntree, whose diet for Tuesdays was porridge for breakfast, bread and cheese for lunch, and vegetable broth for dinner. It was the method followed by Orshansky, where $\mathbf{x}^*$ represented food requirements and $h \, (= 2)$ made allowance for spending on other goods. This approach is often referred to as an 'absolute' poverty standard, and contrasted with a 'relative' approach that relates the poverty line to contemporary levels of living: for example the proposal of Fuchs in the United States that the poverty line should be one-half the median family income. It is sometimes suggested that the absolute standard is less problematic than the relative approach and less dependent on value judgements.

The term 'absolute' can, however, scarcely be used in the same sense as in the physical sciences and there is scope for a great deal of disagreement about where the line should be drawn. This is most evident in the case of the rights approach, where the determination of the minimum level of income is explicitly a social judgement, but it applies also to the standard of living approach. In the case of food requirements, where a physiological basis may appear to provide a firm starting point, it is in fact difficult to determine $\mathbf{x}^*$ with any precision. There is no one level of food intake required to survive, but rather a broad range where physical efficiency declines with a falling intake of calories and protein. Nutritional needs depend on where people live and on what they are doing. They vary from person to person, so that any statement can only be probabilistic: at a certain level of consumption there is a certain probability that the person is inadequately fed. Even if these problems could be resolved, there is the difficulty of the disparity between expert recommendations and actual consumption behaviour. The factor h is intended to allow for this, but the precise allowance will depend on the judgement of the investigator. Rowntree, for example, included an allowance for tea, which has little or no nutritional value but which formed a staple item of consumption.

567

In the case of non-food items, there is even greater scope for judgement. This applies whether we seek to include the goods in the vector $\mathbf{x}^*$ or whether we allow for non-food items via the multiplier h. For example, the procedure of Orshansky has been criticized as understating the proportion of income spent on food and hence overstating the value of h. More fundamentally, the role of goods in the determination of the poverty line needs reconsideration. The literature on 'household production' has pointed to the role of goods as an input into household activities, with the level of activities being our main concern rather than the purchase of goods as such. On this basis, if we denote the target level of activities by $\mathbf{z}^*$, and if there is an input–output matrix A, relating goods inputs to activity levels, then the necessary level of expenditure becomes:

$$Y = (1 + h)\mathbf{p}A\mathbf{z}^*.$$

The significance of this view is that poverty may be measured in absolute terms, in the sense that the vector $\mathbf{z}^*$ is fixed, but the required bundle of goods may be changing because the input–output matrix is affected by developments in the particular society. If the activity is 'attending school', then the demands in terms of clothing, books and equipment are quite different today from those of a century ago. This does not mean that there is no distinction between absolute and relative concepts. There is a clear difference in principle between taking the vector $\mathbf{z}^*$ as fixed and allowing it to be influenced by the living patterns of the rest of society, as in the work of Townsend (1979), who is concerned with the extent to which families can participate in the 'community's style of living'.

The notion of a fixed absolute poverty standard, applicable to all societies and at all times, is therefore a chimera. Nor is it evident that a poverty standard, once set, can be compared across time by simply adjusting by an index of consumer prices. In the case of both absolute and relative approaches, we have to face the problems of judgement. Here several lines of attack may be discerned. There are studies which take the *official* poverty standards as embodying social values, which seems natural on the minimum rights approach and which at least provides a measure of governmental performance. There are studies which base the poverty line on the views expressed in surveys of the population as a whole. In the United States, the Gallup Poll has regularly asked the question: 'What is the smallest amount of money a family of four needs to get along in this community?' These, and other approaches, will produce a range of poverty lines, and it seems unlikely that we can reach universal agreement. There are therefore strong reasons for recognizing such differences of view explicitly and using a *range* of poverty lines. This means that we may not be able to reach unambiguous conclusions – it may be that poverty will be shown to have increased according to one line but not according to another – but it will avoid a total impasse. In the same way, when making a comparison over time, we may want to compare 1950 with two alternative lines for 1980, one updated by the price index and the other adjusted to allow for rising real incomes, thus generating a 'confidence interval' around the 1980 estimate.

To this point, the poverty line has been discussed as though it were a single number, but families of different types and different sizes will receive different treatment. In Britain, for example, the social security safety net is typically some 60 per cent higher for a couple than for a single person. The relationship between the poverty lines for different family types is usually referred to as an *equivalence scale*. However, a prior question before the equivalence scales are determined is the choice of the *unit of analysis*. Here the distinction between the standard of living and rights approaches is important. In the latter case, the notion of rights must be essentially individualistic. The case for considering a wider unit must rest on there being within-family transfers which cannot be adequately observed. The family is taken when measuring poverty because we do not accept that a large number of those with zero recorded cash income are in fact without resources. At the same time, little is known about the distribution of income within the family. Certainly, it would be quite wrong to treat all married couples as having equal rights to the joint income. On a standard of living approach, the logical unit is that which shares consumption; and we may wish to go beyond the inner family to the household as a whole. This would take account of the fact that items of expenditure may have 'public good' characteristics for the family members. Again, however, it may be that there are unequal living standards within the household.

Several approaches have been adopted to the determination of the equivalence scales for different-sized units. Survey information about individual assessments of what is needed 'to get along' has been used for this purpose. More commonly, the basis has been sought for observation of actual behaviour. One of the early methods provides an illustration. By taking a commodity consumed only by adults (e.g. men's clothing), one can observe the level of income at which a family with one child, say, can attain the same level of consumption of that commodity as a family with no children. This method, and other more sophisticated implementations of the idea, have been the subject of considerable debate. The underlying difficulty is that one is assuming, in the example given, that preferences for the commodity are independent of family composition: the arrival of the child may mean that the couple go out less and spend less on clothing. With other methods based on observed consumption behaviour, identifying restrictions are similarly needed. At a more fundamental level, the ethical status of such scales is far from transparent. Not only is it impossible to draw conclusions about welfare levels with different family compositions, but also society may wish to modify the implied judgements: for example, to vary the parental evaluation to take account of the interests of the children.

4. THE COMPOSITION OF THE POOR. One of the main aims of those investigating poverty has been to establish who the poor are. Popular opinion is often coloured by vivid, but not necessarily representative, accounts of life below the poverty line. For this reason, the Council of Economic Advisers stressed at the start of the War on Poverty in the US that poverty should not be seen as a minority phenomenon: 'Some believe that most of the poor are found in the slums of the

central city, while others believe that they are concentrated in areas of rural blight. Some have been impressed by poverty among the elderly, while others are convinced that it is primarily a problem of minority racial and ethnic groups. But objective evidence indicates that poverty is pervasive ... the poor are found among all major groups in the population and in all parts of the country' (1964, pp. 61–2).

Poverty in advanced countries affects a minority in terms of numbers but it is not confined to specific marginal groups. At the same time, certain groups are much more at risk. In 1983, the poverty rate for blacks in the United States was nearly three times that for whites, and that for Hispanics was more than twice. Compared with the average, the rate for families with children is nearly double, and that for families with a female head is much higher. The evidence for other countries equally shows large differences in the incidence of poverty between groups: for instance, in Malaysia, recorded poverty among Malays is much higher than among the Indian or Chinese ethnic groups. The World Bank has argued that poverty in low-income countries is very much a rural problem; and the evidence from India shows poverty to be much higher in rural than urban areas.

If we seek to probe further into the composition of the poor, then the dynamics of poverty must be taken into account. Is poverty a largely transitory phenomenon, in that the families poor today will quite probably be above the poverty line next year? Is poverty associated with particular periods of the life cycle? Transitory poverty may occur for a variety of reasons. Income may be temporarily reduced because of ill-health or unemployment or because wages are cut. It may be a bad harvest. Families may split up, leaving one parent with the family responsibilities but inadequate income. The evidence from panel surveys, where the same families are interviewed on a continuing basis (as, for example, in the Michigan Panel Study of Income Dynamics), has shown the extent of mobility in the incomes and circumstances of the poor. A sizable fraction of those recorded as poor in one year are above the poverty line next year. This does not mean that their poverty is not a matter for concern, since low current incomes may impose severe hardship, but it means that these people do not constitute a permanent 'under class'.

Such mobility does however require careful interpretation. It may arise on account of the life cycle. In Rowntree's 1899 survey he found that the life of the labourer was marked by 'five alternating periods of want and comparative plenty', the periods of want being childhood, when he himself had children, and old age. The impact of such life-cycle factors depends on the extent to which income support is provided by state or private transfers. In this respect the situation in Britain has changed dramatically since 1899, with the introduction of state pensions, a large increase in private pensions, and the payment of child and other benefits. In other countries too there has been major growth in transfers: between 1960 and 1981 social expenditure as a percentage of GDP rose in the United States from 7 per cent to 15 per cent, in West Germany from 18 per cent to 27 per cent, and in Japan from 4 to 14 per cent (Institute for Research on Poverty,

1985). Transfers, and other programmes, such as health care, must have reduced the extent of life-cycle poverty. The incomes of the elderly in the United States, for example, are considered to have risen relative to those of the population as a whole. But there remains concern about certain stages of the life cycle, particularly among families with children; and while the poverty rate among the elderly in the US has fallen, that among the non-elderly has risen.

To the extent that poverty is a life-cycle phenomenon, this means that more people experience poverty at some point in their lives but that its duration is limited. At the same time, poverty at one stage of the life cycle may lead to poverty at a subsequent stage. Those who are hard-pressed when they are bringing up children may have little savings on which to draw in retirement. Those who grow up in low-income families may themselves be more likely to be below the poverty line, as was found in the follow-up in the 1970s of the children of the families interviewed by Rowntree in 1950 (Atkinson, Maynard and Trinder, 1983). Moreover, we should not lose sight of the fact that for some people poverty persists. Agricultural labourers, or farmers with small plots, may be in poverty even in 'good' years. Among industrial workers, there are those whose earnings are inadequate to support even themselves; there may be a problem of *low pay*. And the low paid may be more vulnerable to the transitory factors such as ill-health and unemployment.

5. CAUSES AND POLICIES. In 1913, R.H. Tawney argued for the restatement of the problem of poverty: 'the diversion to questions of social organization of much of the attention which, a generation ago, was spent on relief'. The problem of poverty, he said, was 'primarily an industrial one'. In terms of the composition of the poor described above, this means that the causes of poverty were sought not in the failure of income support but in the reasons why income was inadequate in the first place.

Tawney recognized the importance of personal factors in causing poverty, but laid principal stress on the position of groups and classes and their economic situation, factors which may equally be relevant today. Workers may be locked into low-paying industries where techniques and machinery need to be modernized; they may live in depressed regions to which private capital cannot be attracted. There may be a low level of unionization and employers may be able to hold wages down. These aspects, which have been emphasized in theories of 'segmentation' in the labour market, point to the need for government intervention. This may take the form of minimum wage legislation, to guarantee minimum levels of earnings, coupled with measures to offset any adverse effect on employment and to modernize the sectors or regions concerned. At a macro-economic level, the government has an important responsibility. Studies in the United States have identified unemployment as a much more serious problem than inflation for low-income groups. There can be little doubt, for example, that the recession of the 1980s has increased the incidence of poverty in advanced countries.

The counterpart of this structural explanation in the context of less developed, primarily agricultural economies is to be found in the role of land tenure and its distribution, and in the nature of labour and capital markets. Rural poverty is high among landless labourers and those farmers with small or unproductive holdings. Their difficulties may be intensified by the terms on which they have to borrow or purchase intermediate goods. Here too policy requires government intervention, whether to redistribute land holdings, or to facilitate the introduction of new methods, or to eliminate extortionate lending practices, or to provide non-farm employment. Measures such as land reform raise major political issues, and in both developing and advanced countries it can be argued that basic changes in the form of economic system are necessary to eradicate poverty. The World Bank has noted, for example, the role played by the Chinese food security policy in the reduction of poverty and the way in which it is tied into China's collective system.

The industrial explanation of poverty may be contrasted with the 'supply side' explanation which has seen low pay as attributable to workers lacking productive skills, because they have been unable to complete education or training. This 'human capital' interpretation leads in turn to the policy recommendation that training and educational programmes should be expanded, a proposal that is congruent with the goal of reducing inequality of opportunity. Education and training had a central role in the United States War on Poverty, with schemes such as the Job Corps and the Neighborhood Youth Corps. A characteristic of individual workers also identified in the United States is that of race. Discrimination may lead to otherwise equally qualified workers receiving lower pay, as where black workers were prevented from entering certain occupations. The civil rights legislation and the operations of the Equal Employment Opportunity Commission may have reduced the direct effect of discrimination (as well as the indirect effect via unequal opportunities in education etc.), but although the policy implications are clear in principle, experience suggests that they are not easily made effective.

Policies to improve job and earnings prospects must be central to the elimination of poverty, but they cannot succeed without complementary income maintenance provisions. The growth of transfers has not succeeded in providing a completely effective income guarantee for those without incomes from work or with additional needs. This is because of incomplete coverage, particularly where new needs develop, because of the inadequate levels of benefits (for example, those paid to people with poor employment records) and the incomplete take-up of income-tested benefits. In the last case, there is evidence that complexity or stigma deters families from claiming the transfers to which they are entitled, and hence they fall through the safety net.

To this end, proposals have been made for major reform of the transfer systems in advanced countries. One front-runner for many years in the United States has been the 'negative income tax', which would pay an income-related supplement using the income tax machinery. There are those reformers who would like to integrate fully the income tax and social security systems, as with the basic income guarantee scheme, where everyone receives a basic income and is then taxed on all income. Such a reform would mean that income maintenance largely ceased to be categorical: for example, there would not be separate treatment for the unemployed or the sick. An alternative would be to preserve the categorical nature of social insurance but to make the insurance benefits more extensive in their coverage and sufficient to avoid the necessity to depend on public assistance or other forms of means-tested benefits. In considering the feasibility of such reforms, one must have regard both to the arithmetic of the redistribution and to the reasons why they have not been enacted in the past. As the 'public choice' school of public finance economists has stressed, the actions of the government are themselves to be explained by economic and other motives. The reasons why governments have failed to enact successful anti-poverty policies is a subject of great importance.

The policies discussed in this section are solely concerned with the poverty *within* countries, and would do nothing to redistribute between countries. Indeed, some of the policies designed to help the low paid in advanced countries may actually have adverse consequences for low-income countries. The income transfers which rich countries have so far made are of minuscule size when viewed against the magnitude of the problem of world poverty, and there can be little doubt that redistribution on a world scale is of the highest priority.

BIBLIOGRAPHY

Abel-Smith, B. and Townsend, P. 1965. *The Poor and the Poorest.* London: Bell.
Atkinson, A.B., Maynard, A.K. and Trinder, C.G. 1983. *Parents and Children.* London: Heinemann.
Booth, C. 1892–7. Life and Labour of the People of London. 9 vols, London: Macmillan.
Bowley, A.L. 1913. Working class households in Reading. *Journal of the Royal Statistical Society* 76, June, 672–701.
Brandt, W. (Chairman). 1980. *North–South.* London: Pan.
Council of Economic Advisers. 1964. *Annual Report.* Washington, DC: Government Printing Office.
Eden, Sir F.M. 1797. *The State of the Poor.* London: Cass.
Galbraith, J.K. 1958. *The Affluent Society.* Boston: Houghton Mifflin.
Harrington, M. 1962. *The Other America.* New York: Macmillan.
Institute for Research on Poverty. 1985. Antipoverty policy: past and future. *Focus*, Summer.
Lampman, R.J. 1959. *The Low Income Population and Economic Growth.* Study Paper No. 12, US Congress Joint Economic Committee. Washington, DC: Government Printing Office.
Orshansky, M. 1965. Who's who among the poor: a demographic view of poverty. *Social Security Bulletin* 28(7), July, 3–32.
Rowntree, B.S. 1901. *Poverty.* London: Macmillan.
Sen, A.K. 1976. Poverty: an ordinal approach to measurement. *Econometrica* 44(2), March, 219–31.
Tawney, R.H. 1913. *Poverty as an Industrial Problem.* London: London School of Economics.
Townsend, P. 1979. *Poverty in the United Kingdom.* London: Penguin.
World Bank. 1982. *World Development Report, 1982.* New York: Oxford University Press.

Predatory Pricing

PAUL MILGROM

It has long been part of the popular folklore of business that firms sometimes engage in predatory actions against their competitors. For example, a firm might cut its price so low in some local market where it faces competition that neither the firm nor its competitor can earn a profit there. Such price-cutting would be called 'predatory' (by some) because it is inconsistent with short-run profit maximization by the firm and it appears to benefit the firm in the long run only by bankrupting or otherwise weakening its rival. Of course, predatory actions are not limited to pricing decisions – for example, a choice of store locations by a grocery chain too near its competitors could be predatory – but our discussion in this short note will focus on predatory pricing and the theoretical controversy surrounding it.

Theoretical interest in predatory pricing was high in the late 19th and early 20th centuries. Sharp price reductions were thought to be one of the tactics used by trusts and monopolies to consolidate their power. Perhaps the most famous early allegations of predatory pricing were those made by attorneys for the United States against John D. Rockefeller's giant Standard Oil trust. In one of the first successful applications of the Sherman Antitrust Act, US government lawyers claimed that Standard Oil Company had (among other unlawful practices) cut prices to unprofitable levels in selected local markets in order to drive the local competition out of business (*US* v *Standard Oil et al.*, 1911). Then, once the competition was gone, Standard Oil raised the price again to enjoy monopoly profits. Even apart from ethical considerations, such behaviour leads to inefficient resource use: the competitors' productive facilities lie idle and the monopolist's ultimate production level is inefficiently low.

After a period of dormancy, theoretical interest in predatory pricing was rekindled by an influential paper of John McGee (1958). McGee examined the court records of the Standard Oil case, and found that the evidence supporting a claim of predatory pricing was weak. More significantly, he argued on theoretical grounds that predatory tactics are unprofitable and therefore unlikely ever to be observed. So, regulations aimed at prohibiting such practices would serve only to restrict competition.

The arguments made by McGee and his followers (including Telser, 1966, Areeda and Turner, 1975, Bork, 1978, and Easterbrook, 1981), which dominated theoretical discussions of predatory pricing until the late 1970s, can be summarized as follows. First, when a successful predator seeks to enjoy the fruits of its newly gained monopoly by raising its price, it will soon face new entry. One possibility is that the old competitor will try again once the price has been increased. Even if it has no taste for another fight, its old plant still stands, and could be bought cheaply by a new entrant. New entry is therefore inexpensive and potentially profitable, so it is likely to occur – an outcome which would make the original predatory tactic unprofitable. Second, when a firm like Standard Oil with an 80 per cent market share in a local market cuts prices substantially to drive out a firm with a 20 per cent share, it suffers a large loss of revenues in 80 per cent of the market in order to gain the profits of only 20 per cent. That is unlikely to be a worthwhile exchange. Third, the predator has better strategies available, like buying out the competitor, which removes both the competitor and its plant from the market, achieving monopoly while making new entry less likely. Fourth, there is little reason for a competitor facing a price war to give up the fight and withdraw from the market. The predator, too, is suffering losses and can be expected to restore its prices to a profitable level soon. This knowledge will bolster the competitor and its creditors and investors through a difficult, but short-lived predatory episode.

For those who accepted these seemingly cogent arguments, the unavoidable conclusion was that legal restrictions aimed at blocking predatory activities or making them unprofitable are misguided, and only serve to restrict the legitimate activities of businessmen. The threat of legal sanctions can dissuade firms that achieve cost reductions from reducing prices. This harms consumers directly and weakens incentives for cost reduction. A prohibition against reducing prices in response to entry would only deprive consumers of one of the main benefits of entry and could also encourage collusive pricing practices. In short, restrictions aimed at eliminating the non-existent problem of predatory pricing would only interfere with the normal and desirable workings of competitive markets.

Theory notwithstanding, there is good evidence that predatory tactics have sometimes been adopted by overzealous competitors. For example, early in this century, ocean shipping cartels made use of 'fighting ships' that followed competitors' ships into port and undercut their prices (US Department of Justice, 1977). Predatory intent also seems to be the best explanation of some of the price wars that have occurred in local gasoline markets as well as among US coffee distributors following entry into some regional markets, and of the fierce price cutting in the computer peripheral equipment industry in the early 1970s, to name just a few events. Clearly, some key element was missing from the theories of McGee and his followers.

When a firm considers entering a market, it must base its decision on its expectations of profit from entry. It asks: Will the incumbent firm respond aggressively? If so, by how much will prices fall when we enter? Will our firm be able to produce cheaply enough to be profitable? Will there be enough demand to support another producer? The firm's expectations – the way it answers these questions – are pivotal in determining its entry decision. Now here is the crux of the matter: an incumbent firm can, by its actions, influence the expectations of a potential entrant.

The idea that a firm with market power might try to discourage a competitor by manipulating its expectations was introduced into the modern literature of industrial organization by Milgrom and Roberts (1982a), whose focus was on the problem of limit pricing. The idea was quickly adapted by Kreps and Wilson (1982) and Milgrom and Roberts (1982b) to explain episodes of predatory pricing. By responding aggressively to entry, a predator may be able to convince that entrant, or other potential entrants, that entry into its markets is unprofitable.

Thus, for example, a firm in an industry with rapid product change might cut prices sharply in answer to new entry in order to discourage the new entrant from continuing an active product development programme. Whether the entrant attributes its lack of profitability to its high costs, to weak market demand, to overcapacity in the industry, or to aggressive behaviour by its competitor, it will properly reduce its estimate of its future profits. If its capital has other good uses, this might lead it to withdraw from the industry. If not, it may nevertheless be dissuaded from making new investments in and developing new products for the industry. At the same time, other firms may be deterred from entering the industry. If *any* of these things happens, the predator benefits.

Notice that, according to this theory, predatory activities do not have to drive the competitor from the market to be successful. And, in contrast with McGee's theory, if they do succeed in driving a competitor out, new entry will not follow inevitably when the monopolist raises its price to enjoy the fruits of its actions: potential entrants may no longer expect to profit by entry. It is not even necessary for the predator to profit directly from its price cutting in the contested market in order for predatory pricing to be profitable. When Maxwell House resisted the introduction of Folger's brand coffee into some of its Midwestern United States markets, its pay-off came from Folger's decision to delay entry into the largest Eastern markets, such as the New York city market.

The new 'expectational' theories of predatory pricing differ in several important respects from the turn-of-the-century's 'drive the competitor into backruptcy' theories. First, expectational predatory behaviour can vary in its intensity, which makes it harder to identify than the 'bankrupt the competitor' kind of predatory act. Second, the social welfare cost of predatory pricing according to the new theories comes more from dynamic inefficiencies than static ones. To be profitable, predatory behaviour need not force the competitor's facilities to lie idle or lead to monopoly pricing in the contested market; it is sufficient to deter further investments and discourage new product development by competitors. Predation discourages innovators and entrepreneurs by leading them to expect low returns for their valuable efforts. In a growing industry or one with rapid technical change, the chilling of innovation and new investment entails even higher social costs than the static efficiency costs identified by the older theories. Third, expectational competition is not always a social bad: when two or more strong competitors battle to gain market share, demonstrating their commitment to their industry by cutting prices and introducing new products, the public benefits from vigorous competition.

The proper policy response to the threat of predatory price cutting is complex, because the facts are complex. It is true that excessive price cutting can discourage an innovative firm from making new investments, but it is also true that price cutting allows efficient firms to enjoy the benefits of their cost advantage and encourages inefficient firms to improve their efficiency or to curtail their production. The new theories do make one conclusion quite clear. Policymakers should be especially sensitive to predatory pricing in growing, technologically advanced industries, where the temptation to discourage entry is large and the costs of curtailed entry even larger.

BIBLIOGRAPHY

Areeda, P. and Turner, D. 1975. Predatory pricing and related practices under Section 2 of the Sherman Act. *Harvard Law Review* 88(4), 697–733.

Bork, R. 1978. *The Antitrust Paradox: A Policy at War with Itself.* New York: Basic Books.

Brook, G. 1975. *The US Computer Industry: A Study in Market Power.* Cambridge, Mass.: Ballinger.

Easterbrook, F. 1981. Predatory strategies and counterstrategies. *University of Chicago Law Review* 48(2), 263–337.

Kreps, D. and Wilson, R. 1982. Reputation and imperfect information. *Journal of Economic Theory* 27(2), 253–79.

McGee, J. 1958. Predatory price cutting: the Standard Oil (NJ) Case. *Journal of Law and Economics* 1, October, 137–69.

McGee, J. 1980. Predatory pricing revisited. *Journal of Law and Economics* 23(2), 289–330.

Milgrom, P. and Roberts, D.J. 1982a. Limit pricing and entry under incomplete information: an equilibrium analysis. *Econometrica* 50(2), 443–59.

Milgrom, P. and Roberts, D.J. 1982b. Predation, reputation and entry deterrence. *Journal of Economic Theory* 27(2), 280–312.

Telser, L. 1966. Cut-throat competition and the long purse. *Journal of Law and Economics* 9, October, 259–77.

US Department of Justice. 1977. *The Regulated Ocean Shipping Industry.* Washington, DC: Department of Justice.

Prisoner's Dilemma

ANATOL RAPOPORT

The game nicknamed 'Prisoner's Dilemma' by A.W. Tucker has attracted wide attention, doubtless because it has raised doubts about the universal applicability of the so-called Sure-thing Principle as a principle of rational decision.

The game is illustrated by the following anecdote. Two men, caught with stolen goods, are suspected of burglary, but there is not enough evidence to convict them of that crime, unless one or both confess. They could, however, be convicted of possession of stolen goods, a lesser offence.

The prisoners are not permitted to communicate. The situation is explained to each separately. If both confess, both will be convicted of burglary and sentenced to two years in prison. If neither confesses, they will be convicted of possession of stolen goods and given a six-month prison sentence. If only one confesses, he will go scot-free, while the other, convicted on the strength of his partner's testimony, will get the maximum sentence of five years.

It is in the interest of each prisoner to confess. For if the other confesses, confession results in a two-year sentence, while holding out results in a five-year sentence. If the other does not confess, holding out results in a six-month sentence, while confession leads to freedom. Thus, 'to confess' is a *dominating strategy*, one that results in a preferred outcome regardless of the strategy used by the partner. A dominating strategy can be said to be one dictated by the Sure-thing Principle. Nevertheless, if both, guided by the Sure-thing Principle, confess, both are worse off (with a two-year sentence) than if they had not confessed and had got a six-month sentence.

In this way, Prisoner's Dilemma is seen as an illustration of the divergence between individual and collective rationality. Decisions that are rational from the point of view of each individual may be defective from the point of view of both or, more generally, all individuals in decision situations where each participant's decision affects all participants.

Generalized to more than two participants (players), Prisoner's Dilemma becomes a version of the so-called Tragedy of the Commons (Hardin, 1968). It

578

is in each farmer's interest to add a cow to his herd grazing on a communal pasture. But if each farmer follows his individual interest, the land may be overgrazed to everyone's disadvantage. Overharvesting in pursuit of profit by each nation engaged in commercial fishing is essentially Tragedy of the Commons in modern garb.

Many social situations are characterized by a similar bifurcation between decisions prescribed by individual and collective rationality. Price wars and arms races are conspicuous examples. In the context of Prisoner's Dilemma, holding out would be regarded as an act of cooperation (with the partner, of course, not with the authorities); confession with noncooperation or defection.

Because the prescriptions of individual and collective rationality are contradictory, a normative theory of decision in situations of this sort becomes ambivalent. Attention naturally turns to the problem of developing a *descriptive* theory, one which would purport to describe (or to predict, if possible) how people, faced with dilemmas of this sort, actually decide under a variety of conditions.

As experimental social psychology was going through a rapid development in the 1950s, Prisoner's Dilemma became a favourite experimental tool. It enabled investigators to gather large masses of data with relatively little effort. Moreover, the data were all 'hard', since the dichotomy between a cooperative choice in a Prisoner's Dilemma game (C) and a defecting one (D) is unambiguous. Frequencies of these choices became the principal dependent variables in experiments on decision-making involving choices between acting in individual or collective interest. As for the independent variables, these ranged over the personal characteristics of the players (sex, occupation, nationality, personality profile), conditions under which the decisions were made (previous experience, opportunities for communication), characteristics or behaviour of partner, the payoffs associated with the outcomes of the game, etc. (cf. Rapoport, Guyer and Gordon, 1976, chs 9, 15, 18, 19).

Prisoner's Dilemma is usually presented to experimental subjects in the form of a 2×2 matrix, whose rows, C_1 and D_1, represent one player's choices, while the columns, C_2 and D_2, represent the choices of the other. The choices are usually made independently. Thus, the four cells of the matrix correspond to the four possible outcomes of the game: $C_1 C_2$, $C_1 D_2$, $D_1 C_2$ and $D_1 D_2$. Each cell displays two numbers, the first being the payoff to Row, the player choosing between C_1 and D_1, the second the payoff to Column, who chooses between C_2 and D_2. The magnitudes of the payoffs are such that strategy (choice) D of each player dominates strategy C. The decision problem is seen as a dilemma, because both players prefer outcome $C_1 C_2$ to $D_1 D_2$; yet to choose C entails forgoing taking advantage of the other player, should he choose C, or getting the worst of the four payoffs, should he choose D.

The experiments are usually conducted in one of three formats: (1) single play, where each player makes only one decision; (2) iterated play, in which several simultaneous sequential decisions are made by a pair of players; (3) iterated play against a programmed player, where the subject's co-player's choices are determined in a prescribed way, usually dependent on the subject's choices.

The purpose of a single play is to see how different subjects will choose when there is no opportunity of interacting with the other player. The purpose of iterated play with two bona fide subjects is to study the effects of interaction between the successive choices. The purpose of play against a programmed player is to see how different (controlled) strategies of iterated plays influence the behaviour of the subject, whether, for example, cooperation is reciprocated or exploited, whether punishing defections has 'deterrent' effect, etc. For an extensive review of experiments with a programmed player, see Oskamp (1971).

The findings generated by experiments with Prisoner's Dilemma are of various degrees of interest. Some are little more than confirmations of common sense expectations. For example, frequencies of cooperative choices in iterated plays vary as expected with the payoffs associated with the outcomes. The larger the rewards associated with reciprocated cooperation or the larger the punishments associated with double defection, the more frequent are the cooperative choices. The larger the punishment associated with unreciprocated cooperation, the more frequent are the defecting choices, and so on. As expected, opportunities to communicate with the partner enhance cooperation; inducing a competitive orientation in the subjects inhibits it.

Of greater interest are the dynamics of iterated play. Typically, the frequency of cooperative choice averaged over large numbers of subjects at first decreases, suggesting disappointment with unsuccessful attempts to establish cooperation. If the play continues long enough, average frequency of cooperation eventually increases, suggesting establishment of a tacit agreement between the players. The asymptotically approached frequency of cooperation represents only the mean and not the mode. Typically, the players 'lock in' either on the $C_1 C_2$ or on the $D_1 D_2$ outcome (Rapoport and Chammah, 1965).

Bimodality is observed also in iterated plays against a programmed player who cooperates unconditionally. Roughly one-half of the subjects have been observed to reciprocate this cooperation fully, while one-half have been observed to exploit it throughout, obtaining the largest payoff.

Comparison of the effects of various programmed strategies in iterated play showed that the so-called Tit-for-tat strategy was the most effective in eliciting cooperation from the subjects. This strategy starts with C and thereafter duplicates the co-player's choice on the previous play. Of some psychological interest is the finding that the subjects are almost never aware that they are actually playing against their own mirror image one play removed. In a way, this finding is a demonstration of the difficulty of recognizing that others' behaviour towards one may be largely a reflection of one's behaviour towards them. Escalation of mutual hostility in various situations may well be a consequence of this deficiency.

Perhaps the most interesting result of Prisoner's Dilemma experiments with iterated play is that even if the number of iterations to be played is known to both subjects, nevertheless a tacit agreement to cooperate is often achieved. This finding is interesting because it illustrates dramatically the deficiency of prescriptions based on fully rigorous strategic reasoning.

At first thought, it seems that a tacit agreement to cooperate is rational in iterated play, because a defection can be expected to be followed by a retaliatory defection in 'self-defence', so to say, by the other player with the view of avoiding the worst payoff associated with unreciprocated cooperation. However, this argument does not apply to the play known to be the last, because no retaliation can follow. Thus, D dominates C on the last play, and according to the Sure-thing Principle, $D_1 D_2$ is a forgone conclusion. This turns attention to the next-to-the-last play, which now is in effect, the 'last play', to which the same reasoning applies. And so on. Thus, rigorous strategic analysis shows that the strategy consisting of D's throughout the iterated play is the only 'rational one', regardless of the length of the series.

The backward induction cannot be made if the number of iterations is infinite or unknown or determined probabilistically. In those cases, provided the probability of termination is not too large, the 100 per cent D strategy is not necessarily dictated by individual rationality. The question naturally arises about the relative merit of various strategies in iterated play of Prisoner's Dilemma. This question was approached empirically by Axelrod (1984).

Persons interested in this problem were invited to submit programmes for playing iterated Prisoner's Dilemma 200 times. Each programme was to be matched with every other programme submitted, including itself. The programme with the largest cumulated payoff was to be declared the winner of the contest.

Fifteen programmes were submitted, Tit-for-tat among them. It obtained the highest score. A second contest was announced, this time with probabilistic termination, about 150 iterations being the expected number. The results of the first contest together with complete descriptions of the programmes submitted were publicized with the invitation to the second contest. This time 63 programmes were submitted from six countries. Tit-for-tat was again among them (submitted by the same contestant and by no other) and again obtained the highest score.

The interesting feature of this result was the fact that Tit-for-tat did not 'beat' a single programme against which it was pitted. In fact, it cannot beat any programme, since the only way to get a higher score than the co-player is to play more D's than he, and this, by definition, Tit-for-tat cannot do. It can only either tie or lose, to be sure by no more than one play. It follows that Tit-for-tat obtained the highest score, because other programmes, presumably designed to beat their opponents, reduced each other's scores when pitted against each other, including themselves. The results of these contests can be interpreted as further evidence of the deficiency of strategies based on attempts to maximize one's individual gains in situations where both cooperative and competitive strategies are possible. Moreover, the superiority of cooperative strategies does not necessarily depend on opportunities for explicit agreements.

Support for the latter conjecture came from a somewhat unexpected source, namely, applications of game-theoretic concepts in the theory of evolution (Maynard Smith, 1982; Rapoport, 1985). Until recently, game-theoretic models used in theoretical biology were so-called games against nature (e.g. Lewontin, 1961). A 'choice of strategy' was represented by the appearance of a particular genotype in a population immersed in a stochastic environment. Degree of adaptation to the environment was reflected in relative reproductive success of the genotype, i.e. statistically expected numbers of progeny surviving the reproductive age. In this way, the population evolved towards the best-adapted genotype.

In this model, adaptation depends only on the probability distribution of the states of nature occurring in the environment (e.g. wet or dry seasons) but not on the fraction of the population that has adopted a given strategy. When this dependence is introduced, the model becomes a genuine game-theoretic model with more than one bona fide player.

The model suggested by Prisoner's Dilemma appeared in theoretical biology in connection with combats between members of the same species, for example over mates or territories. Assuming for simplicity two modes of fighting, fierce and mild, we can see the connection to Prisoner's Dilemma by examining the likely result of evolution. In an encounter between a fierce and a mild fighter, the former wins, the latter loses. However, an encounter between two fierce fighters may impose more severe losses on both than an encounter between two mild fighters. With proper rank ordering of payoffs (relative reproductive success), the model becomes a Prisoner's Dilemma. Development of non-lethal weapons, such as backward-curved horns or behavioural inhibitions may have been results of natural selection which made lethal combats between members of the same species rare.

Iterated combats suggest comparison of the effectiveness of strategies in iterated play. Maynard Smith and Price (1973) observed a computer-simulated population of iterated Prisoner's Dilemma players, using different strategies, whereby the payoffs were translated into differential reproduction rates of the players using the respective strategies. In this way, the 'evolution' of the population could be observed. Eventually, the 'Retaliators', essentially Tit-for-tat players, became distinctly predominant.

A central concept in game-theoretic models of evolution is that of the evolutionary stable strategy (ESS). It is stable in the sense that a population consisting of genotypes representing that strategy cannot be 'invaded' by isolated mutants or immigrants, since such invaders will be disadvantaged with respect to their reproductive success. It has been shown by computer simulation that a population represented by programmes submitted to the above-mentioned contests evolved towards Tit-for-tat. It was, however, shown subsequently that Tit-for-tat is not an ESS in all environments.

In sum, the lively interest among behavioural scientists and lately many biologists in Prisoner's Dilemma can be attributed to the new idea generated by the analysis of that game and by results of experiments with it. The different prescriptions of decisions based on individual and collective rationality in some conflict situations cast doubt on the very meaningfulness of the facile definition of 'rationality' as effective maximization of one's own expected gains, a definition implicit in all manners of strategic thinking, specifically in economic, political and military milieus. Models derived from Prisoner's Dilemma point to a clear refutation of a basic assumption of classical economics, according to which pursuit of self-interest under free competition results in collectively optimal equilibria. These models also expose the fallacies inherent in assuming the 'worst case' in conflict situations. The assumption is fully justified in the context of two-person zero sum games but not in more general forms of conflict, where interests of participants partly conflict and partly coincide. Most conflicts outside the purely military sphere are of this sort.

Finally, Prisoner's Dilemma and its generalization, the Tragedy of the Commons, provide a rigorous rationale for Kant's Categorical Imperative: act in the way you wish others to act. Acting on this principle reflects more than altruism. It reflects a form of rationality, which takes into account the circumstance that the effectiveness of a strategy may depend crucially on how many others adopt it and the fact that a strategy initially successful may become self-defeating *because* its success leads others to imitate it. Thus, defectors in Prisoner's Dilemma may be initially successful in a population of cooperators. But if this success leads to an increase of defectors and a decrease of cooperators, success turns to failure. Insights of this sort are of obvious relevance to many forms of human conflict.

BIBLIOGRAPHY

Axelrod, R. 1984. *The Evolution of Cooperation*. New York: Basic Books.

Hardin, G. 1968. The Tragedy of the Commons. *Science* 162, 1243–8.

Lewontin, R.C. 1961. Evolution and the theory of games. *Journal of Theoretical Biology* 1, 382–403.

Maynard Smith, J. 1982. *Evolution and the Theory of Games*. Cambridge: Cambridge University Press.

Maynard Smith, J. and Price, G.R. 1973. The logic of animal conflict. *Nature* 246, 15–18.

Oskamp, S. 1971. Effects of programmed strategies on cooperation in the Prisoner's Dilemma and other mixed-motive games. *Journal of Conflict Resolution* 15, 225–59.

Rapoport, A. 1985. Applications of game-theoretic concepts in biology. *Bulletin of Mathematical Biology* 47, 161–92.

Rapoport, A. and Chammah, A.M. 1965. *Prisoner's Dilemma*. Ann Arbor: University of Michigan Press.

Rapoport, A., Guyer, M. and Gordon, D. 1976. *The 2 × 2 Game*. Ann Arbor: University of Michigan Press.

Property Rights

ARMEN A. ALCHIAN

PRIVATE PROPERTY RIGHTS. A property right is a socially enforced right to select uses of an economic good. A private property right is one assigned to a specific person and is alienable in exchange for similar rights over other goods. Its strength is measured by its probability and costs of enforcement which depend on the government, informal social actions and prevailing ethical and moral norms. In simpler terms, no one may legally use or affect the physical circumstances of goods to which you have private property rights without your approval or compensation. Under hypothetically perfect private property rights none of my actions with my resources may affect the physical attributes of any other person's private property. For example, your private property rights to your computer restrict my and everyone else's permissible behaviour with respect to your computer, and my private property rights restrict you and everyone else with respect to whatever I own. It is important to note that it is the physical use and condition of a good that are protected from the action of others, not its exchange value.

Private property rights are assignments of rights to choose among inescapably incompatible uses. They are not contrived or imposed restrictions on the feasible uses, but assignments of exclusive rights to choose among such uses. To restrict me from growing corn on my land would be an imposed, or contrived, restriction denying some rights without transferring them to others. To deny me the right to grow corn on my land would restrict my feasible use without enlarging anyone else's feasible physical uses. Contrived or unnecessary restrictions are not the basis of private property rights. Also, because those restrictions typically are imposed against only some people, those who are not so restrained obtain a 'legal monopoly' in the activity from which others are unnecessarily restricted.

Under private property rights any mutually agreed contractual terms are permissible, though not all are necessarily supported by governmental enforcement. To the extent that some contractual agreements are prohibited, private property rights are denied. For example, it may be considered illegal to agree to work

584

for over 10 hours a day, regardless of how high a salary may be offered. Or it may be illegal to sell at a price above some politically selected limit. These restrictions reduce the strength of private property, market exchange and contracts as means of coordinating production and consumption and resolving conflicts of interest.

ECONOMIC THEORY AND PRIVATE PROPERTY RIGHTS. A successful analytic formulation of private property rights has resulted in an explanation of the method of directing and coordinating uses of economic resources in a private property system (i.e. a capitalistic or a 'free enterprise' system). That analysis relies on convex preferences and two constraints: a production possibility and a private property exchange constraint, expressible biblically as 'Thou Shall Not Steal', or mathematically, as the conservation of the exchange values of one's goods.

For the decentralized coordination of productive specialization to work well, according to the well-known principles of comparative advantage, in a society with diffused knowledge, people must have secure, alienable private property rights in productive resources and products tradeable at mutually agreeable prices at low costs of negotiating reliable contractual transactions. That system's ability to coordinate diffused information results in increased availability of more highly valued goods as well as of those becoming less costly to produce. The amount of rights to goods one is willing to trade, and in which private property rights are held, is the measure of value; and that is not equivalent to an equal quantity of goods not held as private property (for example, government property). It probably would not be disputed that stronger private property rights are more valuable than weaker rights, that is, a seller of a good would insist on larger amounts of a good with weaker private property rights than if private property rights to the goods were stronger.

FIRMS, FIRM-SPECIFIC RESOURCES AND THE STRUCTURE OF PROPERTY RIGHTS. Though private property rights are extremely important in enabling greater realization of the gains from specialization in production, the partitionability, separability and alienability of private property right enables the organization of cooperative joint productive activity in the modern corporate firm. This less formally recognized, but nevertheless important, process of cooperative production relies heavily on partitioning and specialization in the components of private property rights. Yet, this method is often misinterpreted as unduly restrictive and debilitating to the effectiveness and social acceptability of private property rights. To see the error, an understanding of the nature of the firm is necessary, especially in its corporate form, which accounts for an enormous portion of economic production. The 'firm', usually treated as an output-generating 'blackbox', is a contractually related collection of resources of various cooperating owners. Its distinctive source of enhanced productivity is 'team' productivity, wherein the product is not a sum of separable outputs each of which is attributable to specific cooperating inputs, but instead is a non-decomposable, non-attributable value produced by the group. Thus, for something produced jointly by several separately

585

owned resources, it is not possible to identify or define how much of the final output value each resource could be said to produce separately. Instead, a marginal product value for each input is definable and measurable.

Whereas specialized production under comparative advantage and trade is directed in a decentralized process by market price and spot exchanges, productivity in the team, called the firm, relies on long-term, constraining contracts among owners who have invested in resources specialized to the group of inputs in that firm. In particular, some of the inputs are specialized to the team in that once they enter the firm their alternative (salvage) values become much lower than in the firm. They are called 'firm-specific'. In the firm, firm-specific inputs tend to be owned in common, or else contracts among separate owners of the various inter-specific resources restrict their future options to those beneficial to that group of owners as a whole rather than to any individual. These contractual restrictions are designed to restrain opportunism and 'moral hazard' by individual owners, each seeking a portion of each other's firm-specific, expropriable composite quasi-rent. Taking only extremes for expository brevity, the other 'general' resources would lose no value if shifted elsewhere. A firm, then, is a group of firm-specific and some general inputs bound by constraining contracts, producing a non-decomposable end-product value. As a result, the activities and operation of the team will be most intensively controlled and monitored by the firm-specific input owners, who gain or lose the most from the success or failure of the 'firm'. In fact, they are typically considered the 'owners' or 'employers' or 'bosses' of the firm, though in reality the firm is a cooperating collection of resources owned by different people.

Firm-specific resources can be non-human. Professional firms – in law, architecture, medicine – are comprised of teams of people who would be less valuable elsewhere in other groups. They hire non-human general capital, for example building and equipment. The contract, which defines 'hiring', depends on the specificity and generality, not on human or non-human attributes nor on who is richer. Incidentally, 'industrial democracy' arrangement are rare, because the owners of more general resources have less interest in the firm than those of specific resources.

THE CORPORATION AND SPECIALIZATION IN PRIVATE PROPERTY RIGHTS. In a corporation the resources owned by the stockholders are those the values of which are specific to the firm. The complexities in specialization in exercise of the components of property rights and the associated contractual restraints have led some people to believe that the corporation tends to insulate (e.g. 'separate') decisions of use from the bearing of the consequences, (i.e. control from ownership) and thereby has undermined the capacity of a private property system to allocate resources to higher market value uses. For example, it has been argued that diffused stock ownership has so separated management and control of resources from 'ownership' that managers are able to act without sufficient regard to market values and the interests of the diffused stockholders. Adam Smith was among the first to propound that belief. Whatever the empirical validity, the logical analysis underlying those charges rests on misperceptions of the structure of private property rights in the corporation and the nature of the competitive markets for control and ownership, which tend to restrain such managers. What individual managers seek, and what those who survive are able successfully to do in the presence of competition for control, are very different things.

An advantage of the corporation is its pooling of sufficient wealth in firm-specific resources for large-scale operations. Pooling is enabled if shares of ownership are alienable private property, thereby permitting individuals to eliminate dependence of their time path of consumption on the temporal pattern of return from firm-specific investments. Alienability is enabled if the shares have limited liability, which frees each stockholder from dependence on the amount of wealth of every other stockholder. The resultant ability to tolerate anonymity, that is, disinterest in exactly who are the other shareholders, enable better market alienability.

When voluntary separability of decision authority over firm-specific resources from their market value consequences is added to alienability, the ability to specialize in managerial decisions and talent (control) without also having to bear the risk of all the value consequences, enables achievement of beneficial specialization in production and coordination of cooperative productivity. Specialization is not necessarily something that is confined to the production of different end products; it applies equally to different productive inputs or talents. Voluntary partitionability and alienability of the component rights enable advantageous specialization (sometimes called 'separation') in (a) exercise of rights to make decisions about uses of resources and of (b) bearing the consequent market or exchange values. The former is sometimes called 'control' and the latter, 'ownership'. Separability enables the achievement of the gains from specialization in selecting and monitoring uses, evaluating the results, and bearing the risk of consequent future usefulness and value. Because different uses have different prospective probability distributions of outcomes, and because outcomes are differentially sensitive to monitoring the prior decisions, separability and alienability of the component rights permit gains from specialization in holding and exercising the partitionable rights.

Thus, the modern corporation relies on limited liability to enhance alienability and on partitionability of components of private property rights in order to achieve gains from large-scale specialization in directing productive team activity and talents. Rather than destroying or undermining the effectiveness of private property rights, the alleged 'separation' enables effective, productive 'specialization' in exercising private property rights as methods of control and coordination.

GOVERNMENT PROPERTY RIGHTS. It might be presumed that government property rights in a democracy are similar to corporate property with diffused stockholdings and should yield similar results. The analogy would be apt if each voting citizen had a share of votes equivalent to one's share of the wealth in the community, and if a person could shift wealth among governments, as one can among different corporations. If, for example, one could buy and sell land (as assets capturing essentially most of the value of whatever the government does in that particular state) in several different governments and could vote in each proportion to the value of the 'land', then government property would be closer to private property in its effects. But it is difficult to take that possibility seriously. The nature of government, public or communal property rights surely depend on the kind of government. Because these are so vaguely and indefinitely defined, attempts to deduce formally the consequences of resource allocation and behaviour under each have been hampered.

NON-EXISTENT PROPERTY RIGHTS. Not all resources are satisfactorily controlled by private property rights. Air, water, electromagnetic radiation, noises and views are some examples. Water under my land flows to yours. Sounds and light from my land impinge on yours. Other forms of control are then designed, for example, political or social group decisions and actions, though these other forms are sometimes employed for ideological or political purposes, even where private property rights already exist.

If these other forms permit open, free entry with every user sharing equally and obtaining the average return, use will be excessive. Extra uses will be made with an increased realized total value that is less than the cost added, that is, the social product value is not maximized. This occurs because the marginal yield is less than the average to each user, to which each user responds. So, use occurs to the point where the average yield is brought down to marginal cost, with the consequence that the marginal yield is less than the marginal cost – often exampled as excessive congestion on a public road or public park, or overfishing of communal, free-access fishing areas. The classic 'communal property' implication that apples on the public apple tree are never allowed to ripen is an extreme example of the proposition that property rights, other than private, reduce conformity of resource uses to market revealed values. Alternatively, if communal property rights mean that incumbent users can block more users, the resource will be underutilized as incumbents maximize their individual yield, which is the average, not the marginal. This results in fewer users. Though more users or uses would lower the average value to the incumbents and hence dissuade a higher rate of use, the addition to the total group value (of the extra use) exceeds the extra costs. Examples are public, low-tuition colleges that restrict entry to maximize the 'quality' of those who are educated – that is, to maximize the average yield of those admitted. Some labour unions (i.e. teamsters) are examples of similar situations.

A mistaken inference commonly suggested by the example of fishermen who overfish unowned lakes is that independent sellers with open access to customers will 'overcongest' in product variety and advertising to catch customers, with unheeded costs borne by other sellers. If, for example, Pall Mall cigarettes attract some customers from Camel, the loss to Camel is the reduced value of Camel-specific resources, not its lost sales revenue. General resources will be released from making Camels for use elsewhere with no social loss. But Camel-specific resources fall in value by the extent to which Pall Mall's product is better or cheaper. Camel's loss is more than offset by the sum of Pall Mall's increased net income plus the transfer gain to customers from lower prices or better quality. The loss to Camel is not from new entry itself, but from its incorrect forecasts of its earlier investment value. It is presumed here that mistaken forecasts should not be protected by prohibiting the unexpected future improvements. This differs from the overfishing case in that consumers, in contrast to fish, have property rights in what they pay and what they buy. If every fish had a separate owner or owned itself, none would allow it to be caught unless paid enough, and overfishing would not occur. One owner of all the fish is unnecessary; it suffices that each fish (or potential customer) be owned by someone who can refuse to buy. (Of course, unless the lake were owned, the lake surface might be overcongested with too many fishermen, each fishing to a lesser area, even if the fish were owned.)

Ownership of tradeable rights by customers is the feature that is missing in the overfishing, overcongestion case. Because rights to (or 'of') the fish or whales need not be bought, overfishing does not imply overcustomering where customers own rights to what the competing sellers are seeking. Otherwise, customers could be caught like fish, wherein sellers would be competing both to (1) establish property rights over the customers and to (2) possess those rights. Costly redundant competition for initial establishment of rights could be avoided simply by establishing customers' rights to themselves, as is in fact done. If the preceding seems fanciful, replace 'fish' with people and the lake surface with streets on which taxi-drivers cruise for customers. Excessive costs will be incurred in competition for use of unowned, valuable resources, in this case, the streets.

MUTUAL PROPERTY RIGHTS. 'Mutual' forms of organization are used apparently in order to sustain the maximum average per member, or to reserve for the incumbent members any greater group value from more members. Mutual private property, a form that has barely been analysed, does not permit anonymous alienability of interest in what are otherwise private property rights. A 'mutual' member can transfer its interest to other people only upon permission of the other mutually owning members or their agents. Fraternal, social and country clubs are examples. These activities have not typically been viably organized nor their services sold, as for example, in restaurants and health and exercise gymnasia. The intragroup-specific resources are themselves the members (erstwhile customers) who interact and create their social utility. More members affect each incumbent's realized utility in two ways: by social compatibility and by congestion. An outside, separate owner interested in the maximum value of the organization, but not the maximum average per member, could threaten to sell more memberships which, although enabling a larger total social value with more members, would reduce the average value to the existing members. This is an example of the earlier analysed difference between maximizing the average yield per input rather than the total yield by admitting more members, who while they would be made better off than if not admitted nevertheless reduce the average value to the incumbent members. In addition, the ability of newcomers to compensate incumbents for

589

any loss in the individual (average) value to incumbent members is restrained if the membership fee were to go instead to an outside owner of the club. To the extent that a pecuniary compensation, via an initiation fee, were paid to an outside owner and exceeded the reduction in their average individual and total group utility, newcomers would be admitted, and the outside owner would gain, but incumbent members would lose their composite quasi-rent of their inter-personal sociability. (It is not yet well understood why, aside from tax reasons, the mutual form occurs in savings and loans and insurance firms.)

TORTS, CONDITIONAL AND UNASSIGNED PROPERTY RIGHTS. Private property rights may exist in principle, but, quite sensibly, not be blindly and uncompromisingly enforced against all possible 'usurpers'. For example, situations arise in which someone's presumed private property rights do not exclude an 'invader's' use. Accidental or emergency use of some other person's private property without prior permission constitutes an example, and is sometimes called a 'tort'. Another possibility is that the property rights are so ill-defined that whether a right has been usurped or already belonged to the alleged 'usurper' is unclear. For example, my newly planted tree may block the view from your land. But did you have a right to look across my land? If the rights to views (or light rays) were clearly defined and assigned, we could negotiate a price for preserving the view or my putting up a tree, depending upon which was more valuable to the both of us and with payment going to whoever proved to have the rights. Or, while sailing on a lake, to escape a sudden storm and save my boat and life, I use your dock without your prior permission. Did I violate any of your rights, or did your rights not include the right to exclude users in my predicament? If such emergency action is deemed appropriate, then rights to use of the dock are not all yours, as you may have thought. Whereas in the tree and view case, where a prior negotiation might have avoided a 'tort' (except that initially we did not agree about who had what rights), in the emergency use of the dock, prior negotiation was unfeasible. If prior negotiation is uneconomic, rights to that emergency use 'should' and will exist if that use is the most valuable use of the resource under the postulated circumstances. And compensation may or may not be required to the erstwhile 'owner'. The principle underlying such a legal principle seems straightforward and consistent with principles of efficient economic behaviour. It suffices for present purposes merely to call attention to this aspect of economic efficiency underlying the law.

Rent

ARMEN A. ALCHIAN

'Rent' is the payment for use of a resource, whether it be land, labour, equipment, ideas, or even money. Typically the rent for labour is called 'wages'; the payment for land and equipment is often called 'rent'; the payment for use of an idea is called a 'royalty'; and the payment for use of money is called 'interest'. In economic theory, the payment for a resource where the availability of the resource is insensitive to the size of the payment received for its use is named 'economic rent' or 'quasi-rent' depending on whether the insensitivity to price is permanent or temporary.

To early economists, 'rent' meant payments for use of land; Ricardo, in particular, called it the payment for the 'uses of the original and indestructible powers of the soil' (Ricardo, 1821, p. 33). Subsequently, in recognition that a distinctive feature of what was called 'land' was its presumed indestructibility (i.e. insensitivity of amount supplied to its price), the adjective 'economic' was applied to the word 'rent' for any resource the supply of which is indestructible (maintainable for ever at no cost) and non-augmentable, and hence invariant to its price. In the jargon of economics, the quantity of present and future available supply is completely inelastic with respect to price, a situation graphically represented by a vertical supply line in the usual 'Marshallian' price–quantity graphs.

ECONOMIC RENT. The concept of 'economic rent' is graphically depicted by the standard demand and supply lines in Figure 1 with a vertical supply curve (quantity supplied invariant to price) at the amount X_r. At all prices the supply is constant. The entire return to the resource is an 'economic rent'. If the aggregate quantity of such resources may in the future be increased by production of more indestructible units of the resource in response to a higher price (but the amount available at any moment is fixed regardless of the rent for its services), the supply line at the current moment is vertical. The supply curve for future amounts slopes upward from the existing amount, as depicted by the line FF in Figure 1. The

591

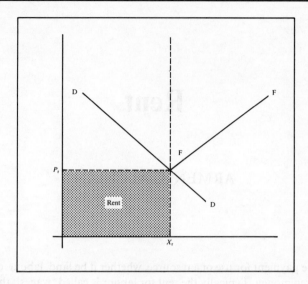

Figure 1

long-run rent would be P_r and the equilibrium stock would be X_r: at that equilibrium stock the 'market supply' (in Marshall's terminology) would be a vertical line. Thus, the supply of indestructible units would have depended on past anticipated prices about the present prices, but the supply of current units would be insensitive to the current price or rent. The return could be called 'economic rent', except that no convention has been developed with respect to the terminology for this situation of indestructible but augmentable resources.

QUASI-RENT. Closely related to 'economic rent' is 'quasi-rent', a term apparently initiated by Alfred Marshall (Marshall, 1920, pp. 74, 424–6). Because virtually every existing resource is unresponsive to a change in price for at least some very small length of time, the return to every resource is like an 'economic rent' for at least a short interval of time. In time, the supplied amount will be altered, either by production or non-replacement of current items. Yet, the fact that the amount available is not instantly affected by price led to the term 'quasi-rent', which denotes a return, variations in which do not affect the current amount supplied to the demander but do affect the supply in the future.

If a rental (payments) stream to an existing resource is not suffcient to recover the costs incurred in its production the durability of that existing resource will nevertheless enable the resource to continue to provide services, at least for some limited time. In other words, because of the resource's durability it will continue for some interval to yield services even at a rent insufficient to recover its cost of production, but sufficient for current costs of use including interest on its salvage value (which is its highest value in some other use). Any excess over those current costs is a 'quasi-rent'.

592

Quasi-rent resembles an 'economic rent' in that it exceeds the amount required for its current use, albeit temporarily – except that a flow of rents that did not cover all 'quasi-rent' would preserve it for only a finite future interval, after which the resource would be diminished until not worth more than its salvage value. If the resource received a payment exceeding all the initially anticipated and the realized costs of production and operation, it will have achieved a profit, that is, more than pure interest on the resource's investment cost. The question exists as to whether 'quasi-rent' means just that portion of the rent in excess of the minimum operating costs over the remaining life of the asset, or all the excess, including profits, if any. Convention seems still to be missing. Marshall seems to have excluded interest on the investment as well as any profits from what he called quasi-rents, so that any excess over variable costs of operation were partitioned into quasi-rents, interest on investment and profits (Marshall, 1920, pp. 412, 421, 622).

COMPOSITE QUASI-RENT. 'Composite quasi-rent' was another important, but subsequently ignored, concept coined by Marshall (Marshall, 1920, p. 626). When two separately owned resources are so specific to each other that their joint rent exceeds the sum of what each could receive if not used together, then that joint rent to the pair was called 'composite quasi-rent'. The two resources presumably already had been made specific to each other (worth more together than separately) by some specializing interrelated investments. Marshall cited the example of a mill and a water power site, presumably a mill built next to a dam to serve the mill, each possibly separately owned. One or both of the parties could attempt to hold up or extract a portion of the other party's expropriable quasi-rent. It is interesting to quote Marshall about this situation:

> The mill would probably not be put up till an agreement had been made for the supply of water power for a term of years; but at the end of that term similar difficulties would arise as to the division of the aggregate producer's surplus afforded by the water power and the site with the mill on it. For instance, at Pittsburg when manufacturers had just put up furnaces to be worked by natural gas instead of coals, the price of the gas was suddenly doubled. And the history of mines affords many instances of difficulties of this kind with neighbouring landowners as to rights of way, etc., and with the owners of neighbouring cottages, railways and docks (Marshall, 1920, p. 454).

A reason for attributing importance to the concept of 'composite quasi-rent' is now apparent. If it arises with resources that have been made specific to each other in the sense that the service value of each depends on the other's presence, the joint value of composite quasi-rent might become the object of attempted expropriation by one of the parties, especially by the one owning the resource with controllable flow of high alternative use value. To avoid or reduce the possibility of this behaviour, a variety of preventative arrangements, contractual or otherwise, can be used prior to making the investments in resources of which at least one will become specific to the other. These include, among a host of possibilities: joint ownership, creation of a firm to own both, hostages and bonding, reciprocal dealing, governmental regulation, and use of insurers to monitor uses of interspecific assets. This is not the place to discuss these arrangements, beyond asserting that without the concept of 'quasi-rent' and especially 'expropriable quasi-rent' – which Marshall called 'composite quasi-rent' – a vast variety of institutional arrangements would otherwise be inexplicable as a means of increasing the effectiveness of economic activity.

Though Marshall briefly mentioned similar problems between employers and employees, I have not found any subsequent exposition by him about the precautionary contractual arrangements and institutions that attempt to avoid this problem, which has become a focus of substantial important research on what is called, variously, 'opportunism, shirking, expropriable quasi-rents, principal–agent conflicts, monitoring, problems of measuring performance, asymmetric information, etc.'.

RICARDIAN RENT. The rents accruing to different units of some otherwise homogeneous resource may differ and result in differences of rent over the next most valued use, differences that are called 'Ricardian rents'. This occurs where the individual units, all regarded as of the same 'type' in other uses, are actually different with respect to some significant factor for its use *here*, though this factor, which is pertinent *here*, is irrelevant in any other uses. Examples of such factors can be location, special fertility, or talent that is disregarded in the other potential uses. For some questions the inaccurate 'homogenization' can be a convenient simplification, but for explaining each unit's actual rents it can lead to confusion and misunderstanding. The service value, hence rents, for the use of the services *here* may differ, though equal in every relevant respect elsewhere. Whether the specific use – uniqueness is created by natural talent or sheer accident, the special differences in use value *here* imply differences in payments, often called 'Ricardian rents' to distinguish them from differences in rents (prices) obtained because of monopolizing or unnatural restrictions on any potential competitors, which may lead to higher rents, called 'monopoly rents' for the protected resources.

DIFFERENTIAL RENTS. 'Differential rents' are another category representing rent differences in a sort of reverse homogeneity. Units of resource that are equal with respect to their value in use *here* differ among themselves in their values of use elsewhere. This can be represented graphically as in Figure 2. The differential rents of successive units are represented by the differences between the price line and the curve RR, which arrays the units from those with the lowest alternative use values to the highest, a curve labelled RR. The arrayed units are not homogeneous for uses elsewhere, so even if identical for use *here*, calling them successive units of the same good is misleading. They are not totally homogeneous; if they were, each unit would have the same as any other unit's use value and rent elsewhere. A curve like RR is equivalent to Marshall's particular expenses curve, which arrayed units according to each individual unit's cost of production, or use value elsewhere, from lowest to highest (Marshall, 1920, p. 810n). The

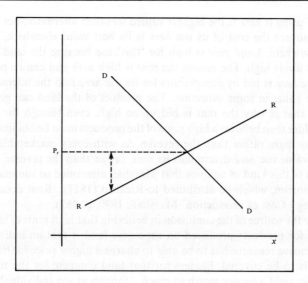

Figure 2

difference between price or rent *here* and the value on the RR curve is called 'producers' surplus' or 'differential rent'. In sum, 'Ricardian rents' indicate differences in rents to units that are equal in their best alternative use values, but different in their rent value *here*, while 'differential rents' are the premia to units that are the same value *here* but different in their best alternative use values.

It is worth digressing to note that an upward rising true supply curve, which reflects increasing marginal costs of production, is different from the RR curve. In the true supply curve the area between the supply curve and the price line does not represent any of the above-mentioned rents nor 'producers' surplus' (as it does with the RR curve). It is the portion of earnings of the supplier that exceed the variable costs and are applicable to cover the costs (possibly past investment costs) that are invariant to the rate of output. That area does not represent any excess of rental or sale value of units produced over their full costs, since only the variable costs are under the marginal cost curve. It represents the classic distribution of income to capital, if, for example, labour is presumed to be a variable input and capital a fixed input.

HIGH RENTS A RESULT, NOT CAUSE, OH HIGH PRICES. An earlier unfortunate analytic confusion occurred in the common misimpression that high rents of land made its products more expensive. Thus the high rent of land in New York was and is still often believed to make the cost of living, or the cost of doing business, higher in New York. Or higher rent for some agricultural land is believed to increase the cost of growing corn on that land. Proper attention to the meaning of 'demand' and 'costs' would have helped avoid that confusion. Demand *here* for some unit of resource is the highest value use of that resource if used *here*.

595

The cost of using it *here* is the highest valued forsaken alternative act elsewhere. For any resource the cost of its use *here* is its best value elsewhere, that is, its demand elsewhere. Land rent is high for 'this' use because the land's value in some other use is high. The reason the rent is high *here* and can be paid is that its use value *here* is bid by competitors for its use *here* into the offered rent and exceeds the value in some other use. The product of the land can get a higher price *here*; that is why the rent is bid up so high, even though the particular winning bidder then believes a high price of the products must be obtained because the rent was high, rather than the reverse. As with every marketable resource, its highest value use *here* determines its rent, rather than the reverse. It was the implication of this kind of analysis that Marshall attempted to summarize in the famous aphorism, which he attributed to Ricardo (1817): 'Rent does not enter into [Money] Cost of production' Marshall, 1890, p. 482).

Probably the source of the confusion in believing that high rents of land caused high prices for products produced on expensive land is that an individual user of that expensive resource has to be able to charge a higher price for the product, if the rent is to be covered. Bidders for that land compete for the right to the land that can yield a service worth so much – though to any individual successful bidder that rent has to be paid regardless of how well the successful bidder may be at actually achieving the highest valued use of the land. Hence it may appear to an individual bidder that the rent determines the price that must be charged, rather than, as is the correct interpretation, the achievable high valued use enables the high bid for the land for the person best able to detect and achieve that highest valued use.

FUNCTION OF RENT. Some people were aware of this bidding for the 'land' and concluded that the rent served no social purpose, since the land would exist anyway. But the high receipt resulting from competitive bidding for its uses serves a useful purpose. It reveals which uses are the highest valued and directs the land to that use. In principle, a 100 per cent tax on the land rent would not alter its supply (assuming initially that 'land' is the name of whatever has a fixed indestructible supply). This would be correct if in this case the 'owner' of the land had any incentive left to heed the highest bidder where the highest bid determines the rent. The assertion assumes that somehow the highest valued use can be known and that amount of tax be levied without genuine bona fide competitive bids for its use, a dubious if not plainly false proposition.

MONOPOLY RENT. Let the word 'monopoly' denote any seller whose wealth potential is increased by restrictions on other potential competitors, restrictions that are artificial or contrived in not being naturally inevitable. Laws prohibiting others from selling white wine, or opening restaurants, or engaging in legal practice are examples. It should be immediately emphasized that this does not imply nor is it to be inferred that all such restrictions are demonstrably undesirable. Nevertheless, the increased wealth potential is a 'monopoly rent'. Whether it is realized by the monopolist as an increase in wealth depends upon the costs of competing for the imposition of such restrictions. Competition for 'monopoly rents' may transfer them to, for example, politicians who impose the restrictions, and in turn may be dissipated by competition among politicians seeking to be in a position to grant such favours. The 'monopoly rents' may be dissipated (by what is often called 'rent-seeking' competition for such monopoly status of rights to grant it) into competitive payments for resources that enable people to achieve status to grant such restrictions. Those who initially successfully and cheaply obtained such 'monopoly' status may obtain a wealth increase, just as successful innovators obtain a profit stream before it is eliminated by competition from would-be imitators.

BIBLIOGRAPHY
Marshall, A. 1890. *Principles of Economics*. 1st edn, London: Macmillan.
Marshall, A. 1920. *Principles of Economics*. 8th edn, London: Macmillan; reprinted, 1946.
Ricardo, D. 1821. *Principles of Political Economy and Taxation*. 3rd edn, London: Dent Dutton, 1965.

Rent Control

KURT KLAPPHOLZ

Rent control, found the world over, is an arrangement under which a governmental agency prescribes the maximum rents private landlords may charge for accommodation, as the control is intended to benefit tenants. In Section I it is argued that rent control can help existing tenants, but only if it is accompanied by additional legal measures. Since the details of these legal measures change over time, and vary across areas, only examples can be provided to illustrate the argument. Yet, whatever these legal measures, rent control can not help *potential* tenants (except in unusual circumstances, e.g. when landlords expect it to be temporary). In Section II we examine why rent control leads to inefficiency.

I. Text-book treatments of price control in competitive markets stress that, for maximum price control to be effective, the ceiling price must be below the market price. This condition is necessary, but not sufficient. Consider a government enacting a law which stipulates a ceiling rent for specified kinds of accommodation, unaccompanied by any other legal provisions. Assuming landlords do not expect a future tightening of the law, its effects would be short lived. Tenants with unexpired leases would enjoy lower rents until their leases expired. What landlords did as leases expired would depend on other provisions of the law, for example, whether *all* tenancies, or only *existing ones*, for the class of accommodation defined were subject to the control. If the latter were the case, existing tenants could be offered new leases at market rents; if the former were the case, landlords would face a number of options, among them the sale of dwellings into owner occupation, the exercise of which would imply that rent control ceased to be effective. These examples suffice to show that the mere fixing of rent ceilings below the market clearing level cannot ensure the effectiveness of rent control. Additional measures are required.

The most obvious and usual measure is to accompany rent ceilings with security of tenure, i.e. with the tenants' right to remain in controlled dwellings for as long as rent control remains in force (a period inherently difficult to predict, for

598

political reasons), provided they pay the ceiling rent. Security of tenure is an implicit form of rationing, which renders legally null and void the expiry dates of previously signed leases. If the purpose of rent control were only the protection of existing tenants, then this measure, accompanied by effective prevention of harassment (Cullingworth, 1979, p. 68), would be sufficient to protect them at the expense of their landlords (a qualification of this is noted below, Section II).

However, sometimes rent control legislation also provides security of tenure for new tenants, as, for example, in the 1965 Rent Act in the UK. If this is done, rent control is viewed, not merely as an emergency measure, but as a '... long-term ... policy for the privately rented sector' (Cullingworth, 1979, p. 67). It is important to consider what effects such a policy has, in addition to the effects just described. This can not be done in the absence of additional information about the law, in particular, about the legality of landlords charging premiums (key money) for new tenancies. If landlords are permitted to charge key money then rent control might not prevent market-clearing for new tenancies (assuming that landlords do not expect a retro-active tightening of the law, involving, e.g., a requirement to refund key money). If a market persisted, would the total rental cost be the same as that in an uncontrolled market? The answer sometimes suggested is that the cost would be the same, as key money would approximate '... the discounted present value of the difference between the expected market rent and the controlled rent over the relevant period' (Cheung, 1979, p. 28). This appears to ignore two differences between these alternative situations. First, prospective tenants would find borrowing for premiums difficult, since a tenancy is 'poor' collateral, and, if the landlord were the lender, he could not evict the tenant for non-repayment of the loan. Second, for any given premium, the cost to the tenant and the benefit to the landlord would decrease with the length of the tenant's stay. With security of tenure (see below) any agreement on the term of the tenancy would be unenforceable. Landlords would know that tenants have an incentive to express an intention to stay for a short period dishonestly. Tenants would know that, should they wish to stay less long than they had originally intended, they would face bargaining problems with their landlords when wishing to terminate the tenancy (see below, Section II). These strategic considerations suggest that some mutually advantageous bargains would be inhibited, and that the outcome would not approximate the situation in which the duration of leases can be freely negotiated. It has been suggested that 'statutory law is powerless to suppress ...' the taking of key money, which can be easily 'disguised' (Cheung, 1979, p. 28). This cannot be true as a general statement unless it is qualified. UK statutory law (as consolidated in the Rent Act 1977, Section 126) appears to have suppressed exchanges of key money for residential tenancies, since otherwise the drying up of the supply of the latter – see below – would be difficult to explain (assuming that, with key money, a market would exist).

In the absence of premiums landlords will be unwilling to offer new tenancies for a class of accommodation to which rent control applies. Text-book treatments (e.g. Le Grand and Robinson, 1984, pp. 96–9) do not stress the differential effects of rent control on existing, as against potential, tenants, and thus omit an indispensable element in the explanation of the drying up of the supply of new tenancies. That element is the legal status of security of tenure for statutory tenants (*Baxter* v. *Eckersley* [1950], 480 at 485). The kind of legislation which prevailed, e.g., in the UK from 1965–80, greatly increased the actual and potential number of statutory tenants. Under that kind of law a new tenant, who might be willing to pay a rent in excess of that stipulated by the legislation, and to forego security of tenure, has no legally enforceable means of assuring a landlord that he will do so, since the legislation affords tenants legally inalienable protection. Under these circumstances, if a landlord granted a tenancy, he would have to rely solely on the tenant's word. Thus, if as was the case in the UK, the legal protection for new tenants is the same as that for existing ones, in general potential tenants will not be offered tenancies. It has been noted that 'had it been the long-term objective to kill off the private landlord, British housing policy has achieved a remarkable degree of success' (Cullingworth, 1979, p. 73). Moreover, neither existing tenants, nor the heirs who may inherit their tenancies, live for ever. When their dwellings become vacant landlords will not re-let them, but transfer them to other uses, e.g., owner occupation. In the 'long run' (which, in the case of housing, may be long indeed) the dwellings subject to rent control tend to disappear. Then potential tenants are harmed rather than helped by rent control (Whitehead and Kleinman, 1986, ch. 6.).

An equity effect of rent control, and a constitutional aspect related to it, must be mentioned. It would be a sheer fluke if the wealth transfers resulting from effective rent control conformed to any reasonable criterion of equity (Friedman, 1985, p. 460). Moreover, they do not appear in the budget and are not explicitly considered by the legislature.

II. Apart from the redistributive effects stressed in Section I rent control also has efficiency effects. One of these follows from the analysis in the previous Section, i.e., the disappearance of a service to new buyers who would wish to buy it in the absence of rent control. The extent of the resulting welfare losses depends on how close are the substitutes which remain outside control, which, in turn, depends on how comprehensively rent control is applied. To give an example, in the UK between 1965 and 1974, rent control with indefinite security of tenure applied to unfurnished accommodation only, so that furnished rented accommodation remained accessible to new tenants. In 1974 tenants of furnished accommodation were accorded the same protection as unfurnished tenants, with predictable results (Maclennan, 1978; Cullingworth, 1979, pp. 71–2). It may be surmised that welfare losses increased. The persistence of this inefficiency was explained in Section I. Other inefficiencies commonly attributed to rent control can be exhaustively grouped under two headings; (i) inefficiencies in the allocation of the existing housing, of which classic examples are the immobility of 'sitting' tenants and their excessive consumption of housing space (Olsen, 1972, pp. 1096–7); (ii) inefficient maintenance, including reconstruction, of that stock. These claims about the effects of rent control are of long standing (e.g. *Rent Control*, 1975), but the concepts which might help to explain them have been systematically introduced into economics much more recently. These concepts concern the relationship between legislative enactments, such as rent control, and the resulting changes in property rights and transactions costs.

We saw in Section I that the introduction of rent control implies a capital levy on existing landlords and a capital subsidy to existing tenants. Why should such a windfall transfer cause the inefficiencies just listed, i.e. why should it prevent the full exploitation of subsequent potential gains from trade? For example, it has been calculated that the losses to landlords from rent control in New York City were twice as high as the gains to their tenants, but what prevented the elimination of this inefficiency is not explained (Olsen, 1972). Why do existing tenants not make arrangements to transfer their tenancies to other tenants, who value them more highly, or why do they not give them up, by making appropriate arrangements with their landlords, who could then transfer the dwellings to higher valued uses?

To answer this question one needs to consider the incentives which rent control with security of tenure offers to the potential parties to the exchange, which requires us to take account of the more detailed legal specifications of the rent control legislation (Cheung, 1974, 1975, 1979).

At first sight rent control would not seem to impede transfers of tenancies from existing to new tenants, the latter paying premiums to the former, as analysed in Section I. However, this presupposes that the law allows existing tenants to accept such premiums, which is not the case, e.g., in the UK (*Farrell* v. *Alexander* [1977]). It also presupposes that existing tenants have the right to assign tenancies without requiring their landlords' consent, which is rarely the case (Friedman, 1985, p. 460). Once the landlord's consent is required, the division of premiums is not market-determined, but is the outcome of bilateral bargaining, which raises the cost of reaching agreement between the parties. It may be noted that, *purely on grounds of efficiency*, it would be preferable if landlords could not refuse consent to the re-assignment of a tenancy – assuming tenants were allowed to accept premiums.

As regards transfers between tenants and landlords, the bargaining costs are the same as those just discussed, and whether there is a systematic bias in the direction of transfers would depend on legal influences on components of transactions costs other than bargaining. To illustrate: if security of tenure is legally inalienable a landlord cannot frame a contract which obliges the tenant to vacate the dwelling for a consideration; by contrast, if the landlord wishes to sell the property to the tenant, the transaction is an ordinary conveyance. However, landlords can offer tenants financial inducements to leave, the money being transferred to the tenant by a stake holder *after* the former has vacated the premises. These considerations do not yield any general conclusions, and it seems that the direction of transfers will depend on the circumstances of the case.

Turning to the second group of inefficiencies it is also appropriate to ask why rent control should generate them. As regards sub-optimal maintenance, one popular answer is that landlords 'cannot afford' to maintain rent-controlled properties, but this is not a satisfactory answer (Ricketts, 1981, p. 509). The appropriate answer is that landlords certainly have no incentive to maintain the quality of the property at a level above that for which the tenant is just willing to pay the controlled rent. Indeed, the landlord might find it profitable to allow the property to deteriorate so far that the tenant quits voluntarily, leaving the landlord free to sell to an owner-occupier, unless the landlord can be legally prevented from allowing that degree of deterioration (Ricketts, 1981, p. 511). But this does not explain why tenants should not undertake adequate maintenance, since, by assumption, this would make them better off. Once again, we need to invoke the fact that, with rent control and security of tenure, both tenants' and landlords' property rights are less clearly specified than in their absence, making tenants' investment in maintenance more risky than it would be for landlords in the absence of rent control. Hence the *possibility* that rent control may even make existing tenants worse off (Ricketts, 1981, pp. 507–510).

As regards rebuilding, it is conceivable that landlords, if legally obliged to house their protected tenants at a standard stipulated by the authorities, might find it less costly to rebuild than to repair properties. In practice, this does not appear to happen. Landlords rebuild if, by so doing, they can free the building from rent control (Cheung, 1975). The question is whether the legal provisions of the rent control legislation would affect landlords' decisions regarding rebuilding. We consider only two possible legal provisions: (a) if the landlord can prove that he will rebuild, he has the right to evict his rent-controlled tenants without compensation (as was the case in Hong Kong over a certain period, Cheung, 1975); (b) the landlord may not evict tenants to re-build his property, unless he offers them 'equivalent' accommodation (as has been the case for statutory tenants in the UK since 1965 – *Hill and Redman's*, 1976, pp. 824–7, 899). One might be tempted to conclude at once that, under (a), there would not only be more reconstruction than under (b), but that there would be excessive reconstruction. This conclusion is suggested by the consideration that the private return to the landlord exceeds the social return, since the former includes a recoupment of the transfer conferred on the tenant by rent control. However, the conclusion is not yet warranted, since it ignores the incentives that tenants have to bribe landlords to forego excessive reconstruction. Nevertheless, taking these incentives into account does not vitiate qualitatively the initial, albeit unwarranted, conclusions, since, given the bargaining costs with tenants, the private returns to landlords from rebuilding are likely to exceed the social returns (Cheung, 1975). By contrast, under (b) the reverse seems likely, because of the costs imposed on landlords by having to establish that they are offering tenants equivalent accommodation.

BIBLIOGRAPHY

Baxter *v.* Eckersley. [1950] 1 KB 480.

Cheung, S.N.S. 1974. A theory of price control. *Journal of Law and Economics* 17, April, 53–71.

Cheung, S.N.S. 1975. Roofs or stars: the stated intents and actual effects of a rent ordinance. *Economic Inquiry*, April, 1–21.

Cheung, S.N.S. 1979. Rent control and housing reconstruction: the postwar experience of prewar premises in Hong Kong. *Journal of Law and Economics* 22, April, 27–53.

Cullingworth, J.B. 1979. *Essays on Housing Policy*. London: George Allen & Unwin.

Farrell v. *Alexander*. [1977] All E.R. 721, H.L. (E.).

Friedman, L.S. 1985. *Microeconomic Policy Analysis*. New York and London: McGraw-Hill.

Hill and Redman's Law of Landlord and Tenant. 16th edn, London: Butterworths, 1976.

Le Grand, J. and Robinson, R. 1984. *The Economics of Social Problems*. 2nd edn, London: Macmillan.

Maclennan, D. 1978. The 1974 Rent Act – some short run supply effects. *Economic Journal* 88, June, 331–40.

Olsen, E.O. 1972. An econometric analysis of rent control. *Journal of Political Economy* 80, November–December, 1081–1100.

Rent Act 1977. London: HMSO.

Rent Control – A Popular Paradox. 1975. Ed. F.A. Hayek et al., Vancouver: Fraser Institute.

Ricketts, M. 1981. Housing policy: towards a public choice perspective. *Journal of Public Policy*, October, 501–22.

Whitehead, C.M.E. and Kleinman, M.P. 1986. Private Rented Housing in the 1980s and 1990s. Cambridge, University of Cambridge Department of Land Economy, Occasional Paper 17.

Rent Seeking

GORDON TULLOCK

The term 'rent-seeking' was introduced by Ann O. Krueger (1974), but the relevant theory had already been developed by Gordon Tullock (1967). The basic and very simple idea is best explained by reference to Figure 1. On the horizontal axis we have as usual the quantity of some commodity sold, on the vertical axis its price. Under competitive conditions the cost would be the line labelled PP and that would also be its price. Given a demand curve, DD, quantity Q would be sold at that price. If a monopoly were organized, it would sell Q′ units at a price of P′.

The traditional theory of monopoly argued that the net loss to society is shown by the shaded triangle, which represents the consumer surplus that would have been derived from the purchase of those units between Q′ and Q, that are now neither purchased nor produced. The dotted rectangle, on the other hand, has traditionally been regarded simply as a transfer from the consumers to the monopolist. Since they are all members of the same society, there is no net social loss from this transfer.

This argument tends to annoy students of elementary economics (because they don't like monopolists), but until the development of the work on rent seeking it was nevertheless thought to be correct by most economists. Its basic problem, however, is that it assumes that the monopoly is created in a costless manner, perhaps by an act of God, whereas in fact real resources are used to create monopolies.

Most discussion of rent seeking has tended to concentrate on those monopolies that are government created or protected, probably because these are observed to be the commonest and strongest. It should be kept in mind, however, that purely private monopolies are possible – indeed, some actually exist. Concentration on government-created monopolies (or restrictions of various sorts that increase certain people's income) is probably reasonable, granted the contemporary frequency of such activities. Nevertheless, as we point out below there are certain significant areas where private rent seeking causes net social loss.

604

In the initial work both of Tullock and Krueger it was assumed that profit-seeking businessmen would be willing to use resources in an effort to obtain a monopoly, whether it was privately or government sponsored, up to the point where the last dollar so invested exactly counterbalanced the improved probability of obtaining the monopoly. From this it was deduced that the entire dotted rectangle (Figure 1) would be exhausted. Although this assumption is open to question (see Tullock, 1980), for the time being we will continue to assume that in effect there is no transfer from purchasers to the monopolist, but simply a social loss which comes from the fact that resources have been invested in unproductive activity, i.e. the negatively productive activity of creating a trade restriction of some sort. Theoretical reasons exist for believing that this assumption probably does not fit perfectly anywhere, but it is just as likely to overestimate as to underestimate the social cost; it will be discussed more thoroughly below.

To quote an aphorism frequently used in rent seeking: 'the activity of creating monopolies is a competitive industry.' For this reason it is anticipated that quite a number of people at any given time are putting at least some resources into an effort to secure a monopoly, only some of whom are successful. The situation is like a lottery, in which many people buy lottery tickets, a few win a very large amount of money and the rest lose, perhaps large or small amounts, depending on how much they have committed. In almost all existing lotteries, of course, the total investment of resources by the gamblers is considerably greater than the total payoff, whereas here it is still assumed that total resources committed to rent seeking equal the total monopoly profits.

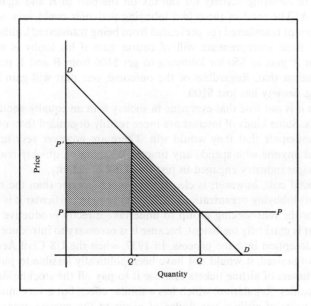

Figure 1

Thus the activity of creating monopolies could both absorb very large resources, particularly those resources that take the form of exceptionally talented individuals who devote their attention to this difficult and highly rewarded activity, and lead to considerable redistribution of wealth in the community. Suppose that ten different lobbyists go to Washington representing ten different associations, and each spends one million dollars over the course of a couple of years in the hope of influencing Congress to provide them with a monopoly. Only one of the lobbyists is successful and the monopoly turns out to have a present discounted value of ten million dollars. There is a substantial redistribution of resources from the unsuccessful lobbyists to the successful.

This substantial redistribution has occurred simultaneously with a considerable waste of resources in general, both because these highly intelligent people could otherwise be doing something of higher productivity and because the economy's use of resources has been further distorted by the creation of the monopoly. Further, although so far the discussion has been primarily about monopoly, actually very many possible interventions in the market process raise the same problem. A simple maximum or minimum price may have very large redistributive effects and the people who thus benefit may put considerable resources into receiving them. Of course there are many situations in which one lobbyist is pushing for a particular restriction and another lobbyist is pushing against it. The second activity is sometimes called 'rent avoidance', but it is costly and of course would not exist if there were not also rent seeking activity.

Another area is simple direct transfers. A tax on A for the purpose of paying B will lead to lobbying activity for the tax on the part of B and against it on the part of A. The total of these two lobbying activities could very well equal the total amount transferred (or prevented from being transferred), although one or other of these entrepreneurs will of course gain if his lobby is successful. Assume that A puts in $50 for lobbying to get $100 from B and B puts in $50 lobbying against that. Regardless of the outcome, one part will gain $50 from his lobbying. Society has lost $100.

Of course it is not true that everyone in society is in an equally good position to seek rents. Some kinds of interest are more readily organized than others and we would anticipate that they would win. There are however very many such interests and anyone who spends any time in Washington quickly realizes that there is a major industry engaged in just this kind of activity.

Actual social cost, however, is clearly very much greater than the mere cost of the various lobbying organizations in Washington. In particular it is normally necessary for the rent-seeking group to undertake directly productive activities in a way that is markedly inefficient, because it is necessary to introduce a certain element of deception into the process. In 1937, when the US Civil Aeronautics Board was organized, it would not have been politically feasible to put a direct tax on purchasers of airline tickets and use it to pay off the stockholders of the airline companies. Regulation, which has a similar effect, but a very much higher cost to the users of airlines per dollar of profit to the owners, was, however, politically possible. The necessity of using inefficient methods of transferring funds to the potential beneficiary, because the efficient methods would be just too open and above board, is often one of the major costs of rent seeking. The rent avoidance lobbyist would have had too easy a time if the proposal had been a tax on uses of airlines for the benefit of the stockholders.

Note that in this case the argument against rent seeking turns out also to be an argument against political corruption. Suppose you are in a society which has an exchange control system and that it is possible to buy foreign currency by bribing an official in the exchange control office. This is the kind of situation dealt with by Krueger (1974), who was able to obtain a measure of the total social cost in Turkey and India where the amounts of the necessary bribes were well known; the cost varied from 7 to 15 per cent of the total volume of transactions.

Traditionally economists have tended to view this kind of bribery as in itself desirable, because it gets round an undesirable regulation. However, it leads to rent seeking. In this case the rent seeking does not come from the users of the permits but from the competition to get into the position where you can receive the bribe. Throughout the underdeveloped world, large numbers of people take fairly elaborate educational programmes which have no real practical value for their future life and engage in long periods of complicated political manoeuvring in hope that they will be appointed, let us say, a customs inspector in Bombay. Since these young men have a free career choice presumably the expected returns from this career are the same as in any other. The difference is that a doctor, say, begins earning money immediately on completing medical school whereas the young man who has studied economics and is now trying to obtain appointment as customs inspector will have a considerable period of time in which he is not appointed at all. Indeed, there will probably be enough such candidates that he has only perhaps one chance in five of being so appointed. The total cost of the rent seeking is the inappropriate education and the political manoeuvring of the five people of whom only one is appointed.

So far we have assumed that the total cost of rent seeking is the present discounted value of the income stream represented by the dotted rectangle in Figure 1. This assumes a special form for the function which 'produces' the monopoly or other privilege. It must be linear, with each dollar invested having exactly the same payoff in probability of achieving the monopoly as the previous dollar (Tullock, 1980). Most functions do not have this form, instead they are either increasing or decreasing cost functions.

If the organizing of private monopolies, or of influencing the government into giving you public monopolies, is subject to diseconomies of scale, then total investment in rent seeking will be less than the total value of the rents derived even if we assumed a completely competitive market with completely free entry. When there are economies of scale the situation is even more unusual. Either there is no equilibrium at all or there is a pseudo-equilibrium, in which total investment to obtain the rents is greater than the rents themselves. This is called a pseudo-equilibrium because although it meets all the mathematical requirements for an equilibrium, it is obviously absurd to assume that people would, to take a single example, pay $75.00 for a 50–50 chance of $100.

Obviously, what is needed is empirical research, and an effort to measure the production functions appropriate to rent seeking. So far, however, no one has been able to develop a very good way of making such measurements. It seems likely that it would be easier to measure the costs of generating political influence than of private monopolies, if only because many of the expenditures used to influence the government appear in accounts in various places. The costs of private monopolies on the other hand, tend to be much more readily concealed. This does not mean that they do not exist.

The reader has no doubt been wondering what is wrong with rents and why we concern ourselves deeply with rent seeking. The answer to this is that the term itself is an unfortunate one. Obviously, we have nothing against rents when they are generated by, let us say, discovering a cure for cancer and then patenting it. Nor do we object to popular entertainers like Michael Jackson earning immense rents on a rather unusual collection of natural attributes together with a lot of effort on his part to build up his human capital. On the other hand, we do object to the manufacturer of automobiles increasing the rent on his property, and his employees increasing the rent on their union memberships, by organizing a quota against imported cars. All of these things are economic rents, but strictly speaking the term 'rent seeking' applies only to the latter. Its meaning might be expanded to seeking rents from activities which are themselves detrimental. The man seeking a cure for cancer is engaged in an activity which clearly is not detrimental to society. Thus we may observe immediately that activities aimed at deriving rents cover a continuum, but that the term 'rent seeking' is only used for part of that continuum.

The analysis of 'rent seeking' has been one of the most stimulating fields of economic theory in recent years. The realization that the explanation of the social cost of monopoly which was contained in almost every elementary text in economics was wrong, or at the very least seriously incomplete, came as quite a surprise. Revision of a very large part of economic theory in order to take this error into account is necessary. And history also needs to be revised. That J.P. Morgan was an organizer of cartels and monopolies during most of his life is well known, as is the fact that he received very large fees for this, fees which were part of the rent-seeking cost of generating these monopolies. It is possible to argue that as a stabilizing factor in the banking system, Morgan more than repaid to the United States the social cost of his monopolistic activities in industry. But that there was a very large rent-seeking cost is obvious. This cost is in addition to the deadweight cost of the monopolies.

To date, research on rent seeking has to a considerable extent changed our way of looking at things. We now talk of a great deal of government activity as rent seeking on the part of somebody or other. It was known that special interest existed, but we have traditionally tended to underestimate its cost greatly because we looked only at the deadweight costs of the distortion introduced into the economy. The realization that the actual cost is much greater socially, that the large-scale lobbying industry is truthfully a major social cost, is new, although presumably at all times anyone who thought about the matter must have realized that these highly talented people could produce more in some other activity.

BIBLIOGRAPHY

Buchanan, J., Tollison, R. and Tullock, G. (eds) 1980. *Toward a Theory of the Rent-Seeking Society*. College Station, Texas: Texas A and M University Press.

Krueger, A.O. 1974. The political economy of the rent-seeking society. *American Economic Review* 64, 291–303.

Tullock, G. 1967. The welfare cost of tariffs, monopolies, and theft. *Western Economic Journal* (now *Economic Inquiry*) 5, 224–32.

Tullock, G. 1980. Efficient rent seeking. In Buchanan, Tollison and Tullock (eds), 91–112.

Rhetoric

DONALD N. McCLOSKEY

Rhetoric is the study and practice of persuasive expression, an alternative since the Greeks to the philosophical programme of epistemology. The rhetoric of economics examines how economists persuade – not how they say they do, or how their official methodologies say they do, but how in fact they persuade colleagues and politicians and students to accept one economic assertion and reject another.

Some of their devices arise from bad motives, and bad rhetoric is what most people have in mind when they call a piece of writing 'rhetorical'. An irrelevant and inaccurate attack on Milton Friedman's politics while criticizing his economics would be an example, as would a pointless and confusing use of mathematics while arguing a point in labour economics. The badness does not reside in the techniques themselves (political commentary or mathematical argument) but in the person using them, since all techniques can be abused. Aristotle noted that 'if it be objected that one who uses such power of speech unjustly might do great harm, *that* is a charge which may be made in common against all good things except virtue itself'. Cato the Elder demanded that the user of analogy (or in our time the user of regression) be *vir bonus dicendi peritus*, the *good* man skilled at speaking. The protection against bad science is good scientists, not good methodology.

Rhetoric, then, can be good, offering good reasons for believing that the elasticity of substitution between capital and labour in American manufacturing, say, is about 1.0. The good reasons are not confined by syllogism and number. They include good analogy (production is *just like* a mathematical function), good authority (Knut Wicksell and Paul Douglas thought this way, too), good symmetry (if mining can be treated as a production function, so should manufacturing). Furthermore, the reasonings of syllogism and number are themselves rhetorical, that is, persuasive acts of human speech. An econometric test will depend on how apt is an analogy of the error term with drawings from an urn. A mathematical proof will depend on how convincing is an appeal to

610

the authority of the Bourbaki style. 'The facts' and 'the logic' matter, of course; but they are part of the rhetoric, depending themselves on the giving of good reasons.

Consider, for example, the sentence in economics, 'The demand curve slopes down.' The official rhetoric says that economists believe this because of statistical evidence – negative coefficients in demand curves for pig iron or negative diagonal items in matrices of complete systems of demand – accumulating steadily in journal articles. These are the tests 'consistent with the hypothesis'. Yet most belief in the hypothesis comes from other sources: from introspection (what would I do?); from thought experiments (what would they do?); from uncontrolled cases in point (such as the oil crisis); from authority (Alfred Marshall believed it); from symmetry (a law of demand if there is a law of supply); from definition (a higher price leaves less for expenditure, including this one); and above all, from analogy (if the demand curve slopes down for chewing gum, why not for housing and love too?). As may be seen in the classroom and seminar, the range of argument in economics is wider than the official rhetoric allows.

The rhetoric of economics brings the traditions of rhetoric to the study of economic texts, whether mathematical or verbal texts. It is a literary criticism of economics, or a jurisprudence, and from literary critics like Wayne Booth (1974) and lawyers such as Chaim Perelman (1958) much can be learned. Although its precursors in economics are methodological criticisms of the field (such as Frank Knight, 1940), censorious joking (such as Stigler, 1977) and finger-wagging presidential addresses (such as Leontief, 1971, or Mayer, 1975), the main focus of the work has been the analysis of how economists seek to persuade, whether good or bad (Klamer, 1984; Henderson 1982; Kornai, 1983; McCloskey; 1986). Econometrics has its own rhetorical prehistory, more self-conscious than the rest (Leamer, 1978), reaching back to the founders of decision theory and Bayesian statistics.

The movement has parallels in other fields. Imre Lakatos (1976), Davis and Hersh (1981) and others have uncovered a rhetoric in mathematics; Rorty (1982), Toulmin (1958) and Rosen (1980) in technical philosophy; and numbers of scientists in their own fields (Polanyi, 1962; Medawar, 1964). Historians and sociologists of science have since the 1960s accumulated much evidence that science is a conversation rather than a mechanical procedure (Kuhn, 1977; Collins, 1985). The analysis of conversation from scholars in communication and literary studies (Scott, 1967) has provided ways of rereading various fields (a sampling of these is contained in Nelson et al., 1987).

A rhetoric of economics questions the division between scientific and humanistic reasoning, not to attack quantification or to introduce irrationality into science, but to make the scientific conversation more aware of itself. It is a programme of greater, not less rigour and relevance, of higher, not lower standards in the conversations of mankind.

BIBLIOGRAPHY
Booth, W. 1974. *Modern Dogma and the Rhetoric of Assent.* Chicago: University of Chicago Press.

611

Collins, H.M. 1985. *Changing Order: replication and induction in scientific practice*. London: Sage.

Davis, P.J. and Hersh, R. 1981. *The Mathematical Experience*. Boston: Houghton Mifflin.

Henderson, W. 1982. Metaphors in economics. *Economics* 18(4), No. 80, Winter, 147–53.

Klamer, A. 1984. *Conversations with Economists: new classical economists and opponents speak out on the current controversy in macroeconomics*. Totowa, NJ: Rowman and Allanheld.

Knight, F. 1940. 'What is truth' in economics? *Journal of Political Economy* 48, February, 1–32.

Kornai, J. 1983. The health of nations: reflections on the analogy between medical science and economics. *Kyklos* 36(2), June, 191–212.

Kuhn, T. 1977. *The Essential Tension: selected studies in scientific tradition and change*. Chicago: University of Chicago Press.

Lakatos, I. 1976. *Proofs and Refutations: the logic of mathematical discovery*. Cambridge: Cambridge University Press.

Leamer, E. 1978. *Specification Searches: ad hoc inferences with nonexperimental data*. New York: Wiley.

Leontief, W. 1971. Theoretical assumptions and nonobserved facts. *American Economic Review* 61(1), March, 1–7.

McCloskey, D.N. 1986. *The Rhetoric of Economics*. Madison: University of Wisconsin Press.

Mayer, T. 1980. Economics as a hard science: realistic goal or wishful thinking? *Economic Inquiry* 18(2), April, 165–78.

Medawar, P. 1964. Is the scientific paper fraudulent? *Saturday Review* 1, August.

Nelson, J., Megill, A. and McCloskey, D.N. (eds) 1987. *The Rhetoric of the Human Sciences: papers and proceedings of the Iowa Conference*. Madison: University of Wisconsin Press.

Perelman, C. and Olbrechts-Tyteca, L. 1958. *The New Rhetoric: a treatise on argumentation*. Notre Dame: University of Notre Dame Press.

Polyani, M. 1962. *Personal Knowledge: towards a post-critical philosophy*. Chicago: University of Chicago Press.

Rorty, R. 1982. *The Consequences of Pragmatism: Essays*. Minneapolisis: University of Minnesota Press.

Rosen, S. 1980. *The Limits of Analysis*. New York: Basic Books.

Scott, R. 1967. On viewing rhetoric as epistemic. *Central States Speech Journal* 18(1), February, 9–17.

Stigler, G.J. 1977. The conference handbook. *Journal of Political Economy* 85(2), April, 441–3.

Toulmin, S. 1958. *The Uses of Argument*. Cambridge: Cambridge University Press.

Ricardian Equivalence Theorem

ANDREW B. ABEL

The Ricardian Equivalence Theorem is the proposition that the method of financing any particular path of government expenditure is irrelevant. More precisely, the choice between levying lump-sum taxes and issuing government bonds to finance government spending does not affect the consumption of any household nor does it affect capital formation. The fundamental logic underlying this argument was presented by David Ricardo in Chapter XVII ('Taxes on Other Commodities than Raw Produce') of *The Principles of Political Economy and Taxation* (1821). Although Ricardo clearly explained why government borrowing and taxes could be equivalent, he warned against accepting the argument on its face: 'From what I have said, it must not be inferred that I consider the system of borrowing as the best calculated to defray the extraordinary expenses of the state. It is a system which tends to make us less thrifty – to blind us to our real situation' (1960, pp. 162–3).

Another formulation of the question of debt vs. taxes arises in the determination of national income. The aggregate consumption function plays an important role in models of national income determination, and aggregate consumption is often specified to depend on contemporaneous aggregate disposable income and on aggregate wealth. The question is whether the public's holding of bonds issued by the government should be treated as part of aggregate wealth. If consumers recognize that these bonds, in the aggregate, represent future tax liabilities, then these bonds would not be part of aggregate wealth. If, on the other hand, consumers do not recognize, or for some reason do not care about, the implied future tax liabilities associated with these bonds, then they should be counted as part of aggregate wealth in an aggregate consumption function. Patinkin (1965, p. 289) recognized this question and specified that a fraction k of the stock of outstanding government bonds is to be treated as wealth. Under the Ricardian Equivalence view, k would be equal to zero; under the view that consumers ignore future tax liabilities, k would be equal to one. Bailey (1971) also examined the question of whether future tax liabilities affect aggregate consumption in a model of national income determination, though his formulation of the aggregate consumption function does not explicitly include aggregate wealth.

The question of whether government bonds are net wealth and the question of the effects of alternative means of financing a given amount of government expenditure are, in many contexts, basically the same question. For purposes of exposition, it is perhaps clearest to focus on one particular formulation of the question. The discussion below will focus on the question of the choice between current taxation and debt finance.

The underlying logic of the Ricardian Equivalence Theorem is quite simple and can be displayed by considering a reduction in current (lump-sum) taxes of 100 dollars per capita. This reduction in government tax revenue is financed by the sale of government bonds on the open market amounting to 100 dollars per capita. For simplicity, suppose that the bonds are one-year bonds with an interest rate of 5 per cent per year. In addition, suppose that the population is constant over time. In the year following the tax cut, the bonds are redeemed by the government. In order to pay the principal and interest on the bonds, taxes must be increased by 105 dollars per capital in the second year.

Now consider the response of households to this intertemporal rearrangement of their tax liabilities. Households can afford to maintain their originally planned current and future consumption by increasing their current saving by 100 dollars. In fact, the additional 100 dollars of saving could be held in the form of newly issued government bonds. In the second year, when the government increases taxes by 105 dollars to redeem the bonds, the household can pay the extra tax using the principal and interest on the bond. Thus, the originally planned path of consumption continues to be feasible after the tax change. In addition, since the originally planned path of consumption was chosen by the consumer before the tax change, it would continue to be chosen after the tax change since all relative prices remain unchanged. Therefore, household behaviour is invariant to the switch between tax finance and debt finance for a given amount of government spending.

The example above illustrates the fundamental insight that underlies the Ricardian Equivalence Theorem. Because the example is extremely simple, it is useful to point out which of the simplifying assumptions are fundamentally important for the result and which are merely for expositional clarity. In the example above, only lump-sum taxes were changed and it was assumed that the tax cut and the subsequent decrease fell equally on all consumers. Each of these assumptions is crucial for the result and will be discussed further below. The example made no explicit mention of the unpredictability of future taxes or future income, but the Ricardian Equivalence Theorem would hold in the above example even if future consumption is not known with certainty. It also would hold if the realized real interest rate on the government bonds is not perfectly predictable. Provided that in the first year the consumer adds 100 dollars of government bonds to his portfolio, he will be able to maintain precisely the same path of current and future consumption after the tax change as before the tax change.

In the basic example, the tax cut in the current year is financed by the issue of one-year government bonds. However, the invariance result continues to hold if the current tax cut is financed by the issue of N-year bonds. The argument is that once again each consumer uses the extra 100 dollars of disposable income in the first period to purchase 100 dollars of newly issued government bonds. If these government bonds pay interest in years before the bond is redeemed, then the government must increase lump-sum taxes in these years to service these bonds. Consumers who are holding the bonds and receive interest use the interest on their bonds to pay the increased taxes. Then, when the bonds mature after N years, each consumer uses the principal and final interest on these bonds to pay the higher taxes that are levied to redeem the debt. Once again, consumers can afford to maintain the originally planned path of current and future consumption and find it optimal to do so.

Having seen that the Ricardian Equivalence Theorem holds even if long-term bonds are issued to cover the current tax cut, it is natural to ask whether the invariance result continues to hold even if some or all of the currently living consumers die before the bonds are redeemed. The first answer to this question would appear to be that consumers who are alive during the tax cut, but who die before the newly issued bonds are retired, would have a reduction in the present value of their taxes and thus an increase in the present value of their disposable income. Equivalently, such consumers could afford to increase their current and future consumption. It is not necessary for these consumers to hold on to the extra bond which is issued in the first year because they will not have to use the bonds to pay for the future tax increase needed to redeem the bonds. Therefore, these consumers would tend to increase their current and future consumption, *ceteris paribus*.

If consumers are entirely self-interested, then escaping future taxes through death would invalidate the Ricardian Equivalence Theorem. However, Robert Barro (1974) presented an ingenious argument which extends the Ricardian Equivalence Theorem to cover the case in which consumers die before future taxes are increased to compensate for the current tax cut. Before discussing the substantive content of Barro's argument, it is interesting to observe that the term 'Ricardian Equivalence Theorem' apparently was first used by James Buchanan (1976) in a published comment on Barro's paper. Buchanan's comment begins by pointing out Barro's failure to credit Ricardo with the idea that debt and taxes may be equivalent and, indeed, the comment is titled, 'Barro on the Ricardian Equivalence Theorem'. Previously, Buchanan had referred to this result as the 'equivalence hypothesis' (1958, p. 118).

Barro postulated that consumers have bequest motives of a particular form which has been labelled 'altruistic'. An altruistic consumer obtains utility from his own consumption as well as from the utility of his children. Therefore, a consumer who is altruistic toward all of his children cares not only about his own consumption, but also indirectly about the consumption of all his children. Furthermore, if all of the altruistic consumer's children are also altruistic and care about the utility of their children, then the altruistic consumer cares indirectly about the consumption of all of his grandchildren. Provided that all consumers are altruistic, the argument can be extended ad infinitum with the important implication that an altruistic consumer cares, at least indirectly, about the entire path of current and future consumption of himself and all of his descendants.

Barro's insight that an intergenerationally altruistic consumer cares about the entire path of his family's consumption defuses the argument that consumers who escape future taxes through death will increase consumption in response to a current tax cut. For altruistic consumers, it does not matter whether they themselves, or their descendants, pay the higher taxes necessary to pay the principal and interest on the newly-issued bonds. In response to a 100 dollar tax cut in the current year, an altruistic consumer will not change his consumption but will hold an additional 100 dollars of government bonds. If the bonds are not redeemed until after the consumer dies, he will bequeath them to his children who can then use the bonds to pay the higher taxes in the year in which the bonds are redeemed, or else bequeath the bonds to their children if the bonds are not redeemed during their lifetimes.

It is important to note that the fact that a consumer leaves a bequest is not prima facie evidence that he is altruistic in the sense defined above. Bequests may arise as the accidental outcome of an untimely death or they may arise for motives other than pure altruism in the sense used by Barro. For instance, if the utility that a consumer obtains from leaving a bequest depends only on the size of the bequest, then he will not care about tax increases which may be levied on his children or his children's children. In this case the Ricardian Equivalence Theorem would not hold.

The argument that each current and future consumer in a family of intergenerationally altruistic consumers cares about his own consumption as well as the consumption of all of his descendants forever then raises the question of whether the government must ever pay off the newly-issued government bonds. If the government could roll over the principal and interest on this debt forever, so that it would never be necessary to increase future taxes, it would seem that a current tax cut financed by an issue of government bonds would reduce the present value of the taxes paid by the current and future members of the family and hence would lead to an increase in the family's consumption. The question of whether a current tax cut must be followed at some time by a tax increase depends on whether the interest rate is greater or less than the economy's growth rate. If the interest rate exceeds the growth rate, then it is impossible to roll over the principal and interest on the newly-issued bonds for ever. If the government attempted to do so by issuing new bonds, the stock of these bonds would grow in perpetuity at the rate of interest. If the rate of interest exceeds the economy's growth rate, then these bonds would not willingly be held in private portfolios. Alternatively, if the rate of interest falls short of the economy's growth rate – a condition which signals an inefficient overaccumulation to capital – then, as pointed out by Feldstein (1976), it is possible for the government to roll over the debt permanently, Carmichael (1982) has shown that in this case, the altruistic bequest motive will not be operative but that an altruistic gift motive from children to parents (which specifies that a consumer's utility depends on his own consumption and the utility of his parents) may be operative. If the gift motive is operative, then Carmichael argues that the Ricardian Equivalence Theorem will hold, despite the fact that government bonds may be regarded as net wealth.

Now that we have described a fairly general set of conditions under which the Ricardian Equivalence Theorem holds, it is useful to discuss several of the conditions that might lead to a violation of the Ricardian Equivalence Theorem. A clear overview of reasons why the Ricardian Equivalence Theorem may not provide an accurate description of the actual effects of debt finance vs tax finance is provided by Tobin (1980).

The Ricardian Equivalence Theorem requires not only that consumers be intergenerationally altruistic, but that their bequest motives be operative in the sense that consumers can bequeath whatever amount they choose subject to their budget constraint. To be more precise, it is possible that an altruistic consumer may like to leave a negative bequest to his children, but he is constrained from leaving a bequest less than zero. The fact that a consumer may want to leave a negative bequest does not necessarily violate the assumption that the consumer is altruistic. It may be that the consumer's children will all be so much wealthier than the consumer that, even though the consumer cares about the utility of his children, he could achieve higher utility by taking some of his children's resources and consuming then himself. Formal conditions which imply that altruistic consumers would like to leave negative bequests have been presented by Drazen (1978) and Weil (1984). Under these conditions, if the consumer is constrained from leaving a negative bequest, he will instead leave a zero bequest. In such cases, a tax cut which is followed by a tax increase after the consumer's death will reduce the present value of the taxes paid by the consumer and he will increase his consumption. In effect, the current tax cut helps the consumer to effect the desired negative bequest by giving him current resources and taking resources away from his descendants.

Another reason for departure from the Ricardian Equivalence Theorem is that policy often redistributes resources among families and that families may have different marginal propensities to consume out of income or out of wealth. For instance, suppose that the tax cut in the current year affects only one half of the consumers. More precisely, suppose that one-half of the consumers face a 200 dollar tax cut in the current year and the other half of the consumers have unchanged taxes in the current year. The government issues bonds in the amount of 100 dollars per capita and in the following period it redeems the bonds and pays the interest. For simplicity, suppose that the population is constant and that the interest rate on government bonds is 5 per cent per year. Then in the year following the tax cut, there is a tax increase of 105 dollars per consumer. Finally, suppose that this tax increase is levied on all consumers equally. In this case, the tax cut in the current year is clearly a redistribution of resources from the consumers whose taxes are unaffected to the consumers whose taxes are reduced in the current year. The recipients of the transfer will increase their consumption and the other consumers will reduce their current consumption.

617

The re-allocation of consumption across consumers may be viewed as a violation of the Ricardian Equivalence Theorem. Whether aggregate consumption rises or falls depends on the marginal propensities to consume of the recipients of the transfer compared to the marginal propensities to consume of the other consumers. If all consumers have equal marginal propensities to consume, then there will be no effect on aggregate consumption or capital accumulation. However, if, for instance, the recipients of the transfers have a higher marginal propensity to consume than the other consumers, then aggregate consumption would increase. It should be pointed out that in some sense, this example does not represent a violation of the Ricardian Equivalence Theorem, because it ignores the possibility that there might exist an insurance market for individual tax liabilities. If there were such a market, then consumers could have insured themselves against the redistribution of taxes. Such markets do not generally exist, but whether the Ricardian Equivalence Theorem holds may depend on the reason why these markets do not exist.

Uncertainty about the length of an individual consumer's lifetime is not, by itself, sufficient to violate the Ricardian Equivalence Theorem, although there are situations in which it will lead to a violation. For simplicity, consider consumers who each contribute 1000 dollars to a social security fund during their working life. At the end of the working life, suppose that some of the consumers die and that some survive and live in retirement for a certain period of time. Although the number of consumers who die at retirement may be predictable, the identities of those who will die and those who will survive are not predictable. The surviving retired consumers each receive an equal share of the social security fund (with accrued interest) to which they contributed while they were working. Each survivor's social security income is greater than the 1000 dollars (plus interest) which he contributed, because the fund contains the contributions plus interest of his peers who died at the end of the working life.

Now the question arises as to whether the introduction of this type of social security system affects consumption and capital accumulation or whether the Ricardian Equivalence Theorem implies that consumption and capital accumulation will be unaffected. To answer this question, it is useful to observe that this stylized social security system has the characteristics of an actuarially fair annuity. That is, consumers pay a premium when young (the social security tax) and receive a payment if they survive to old age. Furthermore, if all consumers face the same probability of dying, the rate of return to the survivors is equal to the actuarially fair rate of return. If there were a competitive annuity market, it would also supply annuities offering the actuarially fair rate of return. In this case, the social security would indeed have no effect on the consumption or capital accumulation of altruistic consumers. The reason is that workers who are taxed 1000 dollars are essentially forced to hold 1000 dollars of the publicly-provided actuarially fair annuity called social security; however, these consumers can afford to maintain their originally planned consumption and bequests by reducing their holdings of privately supplied annuities by 1000 dollars. This reduction in the holding of private annuities will be chosen by an individual consumer because it allows the consumer to re-establish his initial portfolio of annuities and other assets while maintaining his consumption unchanged. Thus, the Ricardian Equivalence Theorem holds in this example.

If the probability of surviving until retirement differs across consumers, and if individual consumers are better informed about their own survival probabilities than are insurance companies, then the funded social security system described above will have an effect on consumption and on capital accumulation. The reason is that if an insurance company offered annuities at a price that would be actuarially fair to the average consumer, it would suffer from what is known as 'adverse selection'. As a simple example, suppose that insurance companies know the average mortality probability but have no additional information about the mortality probabilities of individual consumers. If an insurance company offered annuities at a price that would be actuarially fair to the average consumer, then consumers who believe they are healthier than average would view these annuities as a bargain; consumers who believe they are less healthy (or engage in more dangerous activities) than average would view these annuities as overpriced because these consumers have a smaller chance of living to reap the rewards. As the healthy consumers would buy a disproportionately large share of annuities, they would, on average, inflict losses on the sellers of these annuities and would induce these sellers to charge a higher price for annuities. However, the social security system can supply its annuities at the actuarially fair price for the average consumer because a compulsory social security system is immune to adverse selection. That is, because the government can determine the amount of the publicly provided annuity held by each individual, it does not have to worry that a disproportionately large share of annuities are held by healthy consumers. Therefore, as shown in Abel (1986), the annuity offered by the social security system would yield a higher rate of return than private annuities, or equivalently, would be made available at a lower price to consumers. Because of the difference in the prices of the publicly provided and privately supplied annuities, consumers would not exactly offset the effects of social security by transacting in private annuity markets.

The basic argument underlying the Ricardian Equivalence Theorem is that it makes no difference whether the government issues debt in the amount of 100 dollars per capita or whether it collects taxes of 100 dollars per capita, since in the latter case consumers can borrow 100 dollars per capita to pay the higher taxes. In the former case, public borrowing is increased by 100 dollars per capita and in the latter case, private borrowing is increased by 100 dollars per capita. Under the appropriate conditions it makes no difference whether the borrowing is by the public sector or by the private sector. In order for the choice between debt finance and tax finance to have an effect, it must be the case that any changes in government borrowing cannot be fully offset by changes in private sector behaviour. Equivalently, there must be something that the government can do in credit markets that the private sector cannot do. For example, as shown above, if individual consumers would like to leave negative bequests, but are unable to do so, then a tax cut accompanied by an issue of government bonds allows at least some members of the current population to transfer resources from their heirs to themselves. This intergenerational transfer of resources permits some consumers to effect negative bequests which they were individually unable to effect. Another example of something the government can do that the private sector cannot do is provided by the discussion of adverse selection. Because of the compulsory nature of taxes, the government can avoid the adverse selection problem which private insurance companies would inevitably face.

The example in which adverse selection leads to violation of the Ricardian Equivalence Theorem was constructed to obey the strict set of rules demanded by strong adherents to the view that the choice between debt finance and tax finance is irrelevant. In particular, the following assumptions were maintained: (1) consumers have operative altruistic bequest motives so that they care about taxes after their death; (2) there is a complete set of competitive markets; and (3) only lump-sum taxes are changed. However, actual economies display several important departures from each of these assumptions. Violations of these assumptions are discussed below.

First, consumers may not have a bequest motive, either because they have no children or because they do not care about the welfare of anyone else. Even if consumers do have a bequest motive, it may not be operative as discussed above. Even if the bequest motive is operative, it may not be of the appropriate form for the Ricardian Equivalence Theorem to hold. If a consumer's utility depends directly on the size of the bequest he leaves rather than on the utility of his heirs, then a current tax cut followed by a tax increase on his heirs, would tend to raise the current consumption of the consumer. The reason is that he does not care about his heirs' utility *per se*. His bequest yields utility directly just as any other consumption good. As a result of the decrease in taxes he must pay over his lifetime, the consumer will have a higher level of lifetime income and can increase his own consumption and the bequest he leaves. If his own consumption and the bequest are both normal goods in his utility function, then he will choose to increase both of these.

Even if all consumers have operative altruistic bequest motives, a tax cut may increase current consumption. If all consumers have several children, but if each consumer cares about the utility of only one of his children, then there will be consumers in future generations whose utility is ignored by all current consumers. To the extent that future taxes are levied on these consumers, some part of future tax liabilities associated with a current tax cut will be ignored by current consumers. In this case, a tax cut would increase contemporaneous aggregate consumption.

A second type of departure from the strict set of assumptions is that there may not be a complete set of competitive markets. For instance, a young consumer with a high prospective income might like to borrow to increase his consumption when young with the intention of repaying the loan when his income is higher in the future. However, for a variety of reasons, it may simply not be possible for the young consumer to borrow the desired amount; if this is the case, the consumer is described as 'liquidity-constrained'. If the current tax is reduced, the liquidity-constrained consumer may choose to consume some portion, or even all, of the tax cut rather than save the entire tax cut. The reason is that the liquidity-constrained consumer would have liked to have borrowed to increase current consumption but was unable to do so. In effect, the current tax cut allows the consumer to borrow in order to increase current consumption. The current tax cut financed by an issue of government bonds can be viewed as the government borrowing on behalf of the consumer. Although this example makes it seem clear that a liquidity-constrained consumer would increase his current consumption in response to a current tax cut, some caution is required in interpreting this result. Unless the reason for the liquidity constraint is specified, one cannot determine what will be the effect of the tax cut. For example, suppose that a consumer is able to borrow some funds, but is liquidity-constrained in the sense that he would like to borrow even more funds. If his creditors determine how much they are willing to lend by looking at his ability to repay the loan, then, in response to the prospective tax increase accompanying the current tax cut, his lenders will reduce the amount they are willing to lend by the amount of the tax cut. In this case, the Ricardian Equivalence Theorem would continue to hold.

Another type of departure from complete competitive markets that could interfere with the Ricardian Equivalence Theorem is the absence of certain types of insurance markets. Chan (1983) and Barsky, Mankiw and Zeldes (1986) have recently argued that if there are no markets for insuring against unpredictable fluctuations in after-tax income, then a current tax cut could increase current consumption. The argument, which was outlined by Barro (1974, p. 1115) and Tobin (1980, p. 60) is that to the extent that individual tax liabilities are proportional to income, the tax system provides partial insurance against fluctuations in individual disposable income. Therefore, the increase in tax rates which follows a current tax cut will reduce the variability of future disposable income. The reduction in the riskiness of future disposable income reduces current precautionary saving which consumers undertake to guard against low future consumption. The counterpart of the reduction in precautionary saving is an increase in current consumption.

A third type of departure from the strict set of assumptions underlying the Ricardian Equivalence Theorem is that most taxes are not lump-sum taxes. Generally, taxes are levied on economic activities, and changes in these taxes provide incentives to alter the levels of these activities. Although the existence of distortionary taxes does not in all cases imply that the theorem is violated when applied to lump-sum tax changes, it does strain the interpretation of empirical tests of the Ricardian Equivalence Theorem that examine historical data on deficits and consumption.

As discussed above, there are many potential sources of departure from the Ricardian Equivalence Theorem, and ultimately the importance of these departures is an empirical question. The existing literature that attempts to test empirically whether the theorem holds has produced mixed results, some claiming to show that it holds, and others the opposite. In judging the empirical relevance of the Ricardian Equivalence Theorem, however, the important question from the viewpoint of fiscal policy formulation is not whether the theorem holds exactly but whether there are departures from it which are quantitatively substantial. Existing empirical work has not yet produced a consensus on this question.

BIBLIOGRAPHY

Abel, A.B. 1986. Capital accumulation and uncertain lifetimes with adverse selection. *Econometrica* 54(5), September, 1079–97.

Bailey, M.J. 1971. *National Income and the Price Level*. 2nd edn, New York: McGraw-Hill.

Barro, R.J. 1974. Are government bonds net wealth? *Journal of Political Economy* 82(6), November–December, 1095–117.

Barsky, R.B., Mankiw, G.N. and Zeldes, S.P. 1986. Ricardian consumers with Keynesian propensities. *American Economic Review* 76(4), September, 676–91.

Buchanan, J.M. 1958. *Public Principles of Public Debt*. Homewood, Ill.: Richard D. Irwin.

Buchanan, J.M. 1976. Barro on the Ricardian equivalence theorem. *Journal of Political Economy* 84(2), April, 337–42.

Carmichael, J. 1982. On Barro's theorem and debt neutrality: the irrelevance of net wealth. *American Economic Review* 72(1), March, 202–13.

Chan, L.K.C. 1983. Uncertainty and the neutrality of government financing policy. *Journal of Monetary Economics* 11, May, 351–72.

Drazen, A. 1978. Government debt, human capital and bequests in a lifecycle model. *Journal of Political Economy* 86, June, 337–42.

Feldstein, M.S. 1976. Perceived wealth in bonds and social security: a comment. *Journal of Political Economy* 84(2), April, 331–6.

Patinkin, D. 1965. *Money, Interest and Prices*, 2nd edn, New York: Harper & Row.

Ricardo, D. 1821. *The Principles of Political Economy and Taxation*. London: M. Dent & Sons, 1911. Reprinted, 1960.

Tobin, J. 1980. *Asset Accumulation and Economic Activity*. Chicago: University of Chicago Press.

Weil, P. 1984. 'Love thy children': reflections on the Barro debt neutrality theorem. Mimeo, Harvard University, October. Forthcoming in *Journal of Monetary Economics*.

Rising Supply Price

PETER NEWMAN

'Rising supply price' is a name that partial equilibrium theorists give to their encounters with general equilibrium reasoning. Such encounters must have occurred ever since economics began but for us the story begins in 1912 with Pigou, who asserted that:

> in industries of increasing returns the supply price is greater than the marginal supply price; in industries of diminishing returns the supply price is less than the marginal supply price ... . It follows that, other things being equal, in industries of increasing returns the marginal net product of investment tends to exceed, and in industries of diminishing returns to fall short of, the marginal net product yielded in industries in general (1912, pp. 176–7).

These conclusions led him to argue that taxes should be placed on decreasing returns industries and bounties on increasing returns industries. Assuming, what Clapham (1922) seriously doubted, that actual industries can be sorted into such boxes, this is a policy recommendation that appears remarkably specific in content and general in application.

For Pigou, a decreasing returns industry is one in which the expenses of producing $x + \Delta x$ units exceed those of producing x units by more than the expenses attributable directly to the Δx units; this is what excess of 'marginal supply price' over supply price means. However, since the proposed tax-subsidy policy only makes sense for the long run, replication of a plant of optimal size is always possible and at once rules out decreasing returns to scale in the physical sense. This makes it difficult to see how Pigovian decreasing returns industries can exist, unless the expansion in output from x to $x + \Delta x$ causes a rise in price of one or more of the resources used by the industry. Pigou was willing to admit this possibility.

But then, as Allyn Young gently pointed out in his review of Pigou's book, there is

A more serious difficulty when we inquire as to the precise content of the 'resources' which are devoted to the work of production .... Changes in the prices of product and of resources are the very essence of the situation. Increased prices for the use of land and the other factors in production do not represent an increased *using up* of resources in the work of production. They merely represent *transferences* of purchasing power (1913, p. 683, his italics).

Thus the rising supply price that accompanies expansion of the industry (as distinct from expansion of any one of its firms) is simply a consequence of increases in the rents of those resources that it uses relatively heavily. Barring net physical external diseconomies, it does not correspond to any increase in the use of real resources.

It took a long time for Young's fundamental point to sink in. In what was essentially the second, much enlarged and retitled, edition of his book, Pigou acknowledged that Young's cricitism was 'very important' but defended himself with the feeble argument that 'each [industry] ... is supposed to make use of only a small part of the aggregate resources of the country' (1920, pp. 934–6). Thus Frank Knight, who had been Young's graduate student at Cornell when the latter's review of Pigou appeared, felt called upon to point out once more the nature of the errors that Pigou was making. So effective was the famous article in which he did this (1924) that it has been reprinted many times, which Young's prior contribution never was, not even by Young himself in his collection (1927).

But that was welfare economics. In positive economics, Clapham's article of 1922 set off a controversy over increasing returns and competition which exploded like a string of firecrackers in the pages of the *Economic Journal* over the next ten years, until the books on imperfect competition by Chamberlin and Joan Robinson in 1933 brought it sputtering to a close. The controversy inevitably touched upon problems of 'rising supply price', but nowhere did it do so effectively save in an article by Roy Harrod, written in 1928 but not accepted and published until 1930 ('An egoistic footnote' in 1951, p. 159, fn2, attributed the delay to an unfavourable referee's report by Frank Ramsey). His argument went like this:

Let us call the proportion in which the factors of production A,B,C ... are mixed in use at the margin in national industry as a whole a:b:c: ... if an industry using the factors in the proportion of a + x:b:c: ... expands, it can only get increasing quantities of A at an enhanced price in terms of B, C .... No doubt by the law of substitution x will be reduced in consequence of the expansion of this industry; but not to zero ....

... it follows that every industry which uses an appreciable fraction of the factors of production, unless it be an industry using them at the margin in the proportions of a:b:c: ..., obeys the law of increasing supply price ....

This analysis seems to clear up the problem of the old classical distinction between agriculture and the manufacturing industries. If A is land, and a + x:b:c: ... the proportion in which the factors are mixed at the margin in agriculture as a whole. x/a is clearly large. Agriculture as a whole is thus markedly subject to increasing supply price (1930, pp. 240–41).

This is an explicit account of what Young merely sketched, though there is no evidence that Harrod had read Young's review. In the following year Viner (1931) published his much-reprinted codification of neoclassical partial equilibrium theory, in which without reference to either Harrod or Young he introduced the idea of 'pecuniary' economies and diseconomies, both internal and external. According to this classification, what have been discussed here so far are 'net pecuniary external diseconomies', which at that time Viner did not emphasize. However, almost twenty years later Viner added a Supplementary Note to the 1950 reprint of (1931), in which he felt

> ... it incumbent upon me, ... to avoid propagating serious error, to carry the analysis ... further ... by departing here from the traditional Marshallian pattern of assumptions to which the article adheres. The partial-equilibrium nature of the Marshallian assumptions leaves a wider range of possibilities to the long-run tendencies of costs for an expanding industry than is consistent with general-equilibrium analysis. I first saw this in 1938, and thereafter pointed it out to my students at the University of Chicago. But the first and, to my knowledge, still the only, analysis in print similar to what I have in mind is in Joan Robinson's excellent article, 'Rising Supply Price' ... [1941] ... which has not atrracted the attention which in my opinion it eminently deserves (Viner, 1951, p. 227).

In a further footnote, added to the 1951 reprint of the 1950 version, Viner also acknowledged Harrod's prior contribution in (1930). Joan Robinson's fine article is indeed the culmination of this whole line of reasoning, developing in much greater detail and in crystal-clear prose the mode of analysis that began with Harrod; but it is puzzling that Harrod (unlike Hicks, Marshall, Pigou, Robbins and Sraffa) is never mentioned, in spite of the striking similarities between the two analyses. An interesting sidelight is that, in a letter written soon after the appearance of her article and published in Robinson (1951, pp. 42–3), Keynes took a markedly general equilibrium approach to the problem.

Apart from relevant surveys of external economies by Ellis and Fellner (1943) and Chipman (1965, Section 2.8, pp. 736–49) there has been little further discussion of 'rising supply price', evidence perhaps that its nature is by now well understood. However, even as late as 1954, Scitovsky's well-received article with its Pigovian policy conclusions and remark that 'Pecuniary external economies clearly have no place in equilibrium theory' (1954, pp. 149, 146), showed that confusion still existed. Maybe each generation of partial equilibrium theorists has to learn the lesson anew.

BIBLIOGRAPHY

Arrow, K.J. and Scitovsky, T. (eds) 1969. *Readings in Welfare Economics*. Homewood, Ill.: Richard D. Irwin. Reprints Knight (1924) and Scitovsky (1954).
Boulding, K.E. and Stigler, G.J. (eds) 1951. *Readings in Price Theory*. Homewood. Ill.: Richard D. Irwin. Reprints Clapham (1922), Ellis and Fellner (1943), Knight (1924), Robinson (1941) and Viner (1931).

Chamberlin, E.H. 1933. *The Theory of Monopolistic Competition*. 6th edn, Cambridge, Mass.: Harvard University Press, 1948.

Chipman, J.S. 1965. A survey of the theory of international trade. Part 2. The neo-classical theory. *Econometrica* 33, 685–760.

Clapham, J.H. 1922. Of empty economic boxes. *Economic Journal* 32, 305–14.

Clemence, R.V. (ed.) 1950. *Readings in Economic Analysis*. Vol 2: *Prices and Production*. Cambridge, Mass.: Addison-Wesley. Reprints Viner (1931).

Harrod, R.F. 1930. Notes on supply. *Economic Journal* 40, 232–41.

Harrod, R.F. 1951. *The Life of John Maynard Keynes*. London: Macmillan.

Harrod, R.F. 1952. *Economic Essays*. London: Macmillan. Reprints Harrod (1930).

Knight, F.H. 1924. Some fallacies in the interpretation of social cost. *Quarterly Journal of Economics* 38, 582–606.

Knight, F.H. 1935. *The Ethics of Competition*. London: George Allen & Unwin. Reprints Knight (1924).

Pigou, A.C. 1912. *Wealth and Welfare*. London: Macmillan.

Pigou, A.C. 1920. *The Economics of Welfare*. London: Macmillan.

Robinson, J.V. 1933. *The Economics of Imperfect Competition*. London: Macmillan. 2nd edn, 1969.

Robinson, J.V. 1941. Rising supply price. *Economica* NS 8, 1–8.

Robinson, J.V. 1951. *Collected Economic Papers*. Oxford: Basil Blackwell. Reprints Robinson (1941).

Scitovsky, T. 1954. Two concepts of external economies. *Journal of Political Economy* 62, 143–51.

Viner, J. 1931. Cost curves and supply curves. *Zeitschrift für Nationalökonomie* 3, 23–46.

Viner, J. 1951. Reprint of (1931) in Boulding and Stigler (1951).

Young, A.A. 1913. Pigou's Wealth and Welfare. *Quarterly Journal of Economics* 27, 672–86.

Young, A.A. 1927. *Economic Problems New and Old*. Boston: Houghton Mifflin.

Scholastic Economic Thought

HENRY W. SPIEGEL

Scholastic economic thought, which flourished during the Middle Ages, differs in many respects from the economic thought of our own time. It was not positive or hypothetical but normative, directing the faithful to do certain things and abstain from doing others. Human weakness or wickedness would account for gaps between the norm and its fulfilment. Furthermore, scholastic economic thought did not generate rules that were uniformly applicable to *homo economicus*; instead there was a division among its addressees between the select few capable of abiding by the counsel of perfection and the general run of humanity that required a less exacting rule. Moreover, scholastic economic thought was not presented in systematic form but arose sporadically and incidentally in conjunction with other matters treating, perhaps, of sales, fraud or usury. It was not shaped by professional economists but by theologians and lawyers. It did not form an autonomous discipline but relied on precepts derived from theology, philsophy and law. A number of social ideals that are characteristic of modern times were alien to it, chiefly the ideal of progress; instead, stratified medieval society, which was organized more on the principle of status than of contract, looked for a golden age that was located in the past rather than the future. Scholastic economic thought was the thought of an age of faith whose overriding concern was the salvation of souls in the next world rather than this-worldly concern with reforms that might produce an earthly paradise. With man fallen and tainted by original sin, perfection was not of this world.

What scholastic economic thought had in common with modern and indeed with all economic thought was its function to cope with the central economic problem of scarcity. It did this in its own way, different from the way it was done at other times. The Greek philosophers counselled moderation that would reduce the demand for goods as the principal means to resolve the economic problem of scarcity. Modern economic thought attempts to resolve this problem by increasing the supply of goods. As for the medievalists, a case may be made to

627

the effect that their way to cope with the problem of scarcity was to impress upon the faithful the need to maximize charity and minimize sin.

Scholastic economic thought had its principal sources in the Bible, the writings of the Fathers of the Church, in Roman, canon and civil law, in the evolving theological tradition and, at a relatively late stage, in the writings of Aristotle, whose authority was high and who was referred to as 'the philosopher'. The scholastics typically employed a method of analysis in which a question was raised, a possible answer to the question discussed in detail, and after the reader was almost convinced, another answer discussed, again in detail and all with copious citations of authorities. The last answer provided was the one chosen by the writer in question.

A medieval theologian might set forth views about economics in a comprehensive *Summa* that covered the entire field of theology, or in a monograph devoted to a special topic. Of the highest authority were the *Summa* and other writings of Saint Thomas Aquinas (c1224–74), whose teachings were at first considered controversial but were eventually endorsed by the papacy to become the official Catholic doctrine.

Scholastic economic thought, though it was generated in a number of different countries, did not reflect national diversity but the universalism of a civilization integrated by the common faith. Thus, for instance, Saint Thomas left his native Italy to be educated at Paris and Cologne and teach at the University of Paris, then the centre of theological studies, just as the University of Bologna was the centre of legal studies. Scholastic economic thought also had a time dimension. As it grew and developed over a period of a thousand years, certain features came to the foreground while others receded into the background.

The scholastics were no egalitarians, but the practice of private charity, to which the faithful were exhorted and which they generously carried out, brought a levelling tendency into the medieval distribution of income and wealth. It did not, however, place an unduly heavy burden on the faithful, because they were under no duty to allow charitable donations to endanger their position in the hierarchically ordered society. Thus, while charity was highly commendable, no one had to impoverish himself on account of it. Austerity and asceticism were counsels of perfection addressed to the select few. Contrariwise, the wealthy were exhorted to practice not only charity but also liberality and munificence, that is, to use their riches generously and for some great and noble purpose.

At the end of the Middle Ages, with the coming of the reformers, the role of private charity declined because of the reformers' emphasis on faith rather than good works. The passing of the Elizabethan Poor Law in 1601 marks this change. It made poor relief a function of public authorities.

If the property owner is under a religious duty to practise charity, liberality and munificence, a sort of spiritual mortgage is placed on his property. The stewardship of wealth with which he is entrusted detracts from the absolute character of property rights such as prevailed in Roman Law. The medievalists distinguished between property and the use of property; they recognized private property as not being in violation of natural law but did not go so far as to consider it required by natural law. The latter interpretation would have done violence to the patristic tradition of the early Church, which had extolled the virtues of communal ownership. It was in effect a concession to this tradition that required a use of private property that would be conducive to the common good. Communal ownership was advised as a counsel of perfection to the spiritual elite.

Tradition, as embodied in the Bible, Greek thought and the teachings of the Fathers of the Church, also took a dim view of money making and trading. As time went on, attitudes became more permissive and reference was made to a distinction in the writings of Saint Augustine, who held that the trader must not be confused with trade, that is, that trading itself is morally neutral but may be corrupted by a sinful trader. It became recognized that the trader served a useful purpose, especially if he transformed or transported goods, stored them or took care of them. He was allowed a return that would cover his labour and expenses, including a premium for risk. Even pure profit could be legitimized by the trader's intention, that is, if he intended to use the profit for self-support or charity, or if he was motivated by the desire to perform business as a service to the public.

The enforcement of the charity requirement and of business ethics in general took place mainly in the agent's conscience rather than before a court of law. This was different in the case of the just price, another important concept in scholastic economics. Here there was the Roman Law tradition of *laesio enormis*, excessive violation, which originally had applied only to transactions in land at unduly low prices. Medieval practice expanded the rule to apply to any transaction where the buyer had been overcharged by more than 50 per cent of the just price, or where the seller had obtained less than 50 per cent of it. In cases involving these matters, recourse could be had to a court of law, civil or ecclesiastical, rather than only to the internal forum of the agent's conscience.

The just price was the market price prevailing at a certain place at a certain time, as estimated by a fair-minded person. The estimate might be expressed in the form of a range of prices rather than as a fixed amount. If the actual price deviated 'considerably' from the just price, restitution was owed. The just-price rule thus was stricter than the *laesio enormis*, reflecting, it was held, the greater strictness of divine law as compared with civil law. Justification for the just-price doctrine was found in the golden rule – do to others as you want them to do to you – as well as in the requirement of justice in exchange as set forth by Aristotle.

Some scholastic writers interpreted the just price as one covering labour and expenses. To others, a just price reflected a good's usefulness or its capacity to satisfy human wants. These interpetations have made it possible for later schools of thought to claim the scholastics as their forerunners. To some, the scholastics were exponents of a labour theory of value such as was held by the classical economists and Karl Marx. Others argued that the scholastics anticipated the utility approach to the theory of value that came into vogue late in the 19th century. Still others found the germ of a demand-and-supply theory in the just-price doctrine. Again others interpreted the just price as a competitive one. It may be noted that the scholastics were not familiar with the concept of competition ?nd had no word for it, the English word and its French counterpart, *concurrence*, making their appearance only in the 17th century. The scholastics were familiar, however, with monopoly, both the word and the concept, and condemned it in no uncertain terms. The word 'monopoly' can indeed be traced back to Aristotle, who uses it in the first book of his *Politics*, chapter 8. The scholastics were familiar also with monopolistic combinations, but had no word for oligopoly, a term that was introduced by Saint Thomas More in his *Utopia* of 1518 but which did not come into common usage until some four hundred years later.

If a price was regulated by a public authority, as was often the case, the regulated price was considered the just one. At times, the regulated price constituted a ceiling; at other times it served as a floor. Depending upon the circumstances, the regulated price either strengthened or weakened the conservative tendency of the medieval price system.

If the just price was meant to cover the labour and expenses of the seller, it would bring into the medieval price system a conservative tendency that resisted changes in the allocation of productive resources. In the modern market economy changing prices act as guide-posts that draw productive resources from certain employments and channel them into others. A price system that legitimizes only a price that covers the cost of production will tend to preserve the prevailing allocation of productive resources.

In the centre of scholastic economic thought stood the usury doctrine. During the Middle Ages, usury as an object of the Church's condemnation played a role comparable to such later targets as socialism in the 19th century and abortion and birth control in the 20th century. It was a matter of profound concern that occupied clerics and lawyers alike and gave rise to a voluminous literature. 'Usury', at that time, referred to the lender's intention to receive in return more than the principal of the loan, so that any interest was considered usurious. In modern usage, only exorbitant interest is called usurious.

The usury doctrine was compatible with the primitive economic conditions that prevailed in the early Middle Ages, when the typical loan was a consumption loan. Later on, the flourishing economies of the emerging cities and the requirements of commerce were accommodated by a number of exceptions from the strict usury doctrine which allowed interest or its equivalent on the strength of so-called extrinsic titles. One of the most important of these was the compensation granted to the lender on account of escaped gain. Such a compensation was legitimized only hesitatingly, but once it was established any businessman who employed productive capital funds in his enterprise could in good conscience claim interest on money he had lent out.

In the usury doctrine money is considered a measure with a fixed and stable value. If a lender received more money than he had given to the borrower, a different measure would prevail, an ostensibly obvious inequity. By the same token, a debasement of money would yield a different measure resulting from an action of the monetary authority – the prince – that was as damnable as usury itself. Throughout the Middle Ages, the debasement of the coin constituted indeed an ever-recurring problem that absorbed much of the attention of writers on monetary matters, comparable to the problem of inflation in modern times. Everybody was against it, but it was practised on a large scale.

A notable contribution to the theory of money was made by Jean Buridan, the 14th-century philosopher still famous for his conundrum of the ass that would starve between two equal bales of hay. In its terseness and conciseness Buridan's analysis of the nature of money in terms of the four causes of Aristotle's logic is a masterpiece that illustrates scholastic economic thought at its best. In his discussion of the *Ethics* of Aristotle, printed posthumously in Paris in 1489, Buridan has this to say: The material cause of money, from which it is made, is a rare commodity. Its efficient cause, which produces money, is the government. Its formal cause, which transforms the rare commodity into money, is the symbol of value that is inscribed on the coin. Its final cause, or purpose, is to be of service to man by serving as a medium of exchange.

The late scholastics also made significant contributions to the theory of prices. The quantity theory of money was a multiple discovery to which a number of writers contributed. While Jean Bodin is usually credited with a full-fledged statement of the quantity theory, the nucleus of the theory can be found in a manual on moral theology, with an appendix devoted to a discussion of usury, written by Martin de Azpilcueta, also known as Navarrus, who taught canon law at Toulouse and Salamanca. This manual was published in 1556, twelve years ahead of Bodin's *Reply to the Paradoxes of M. Malestroit*. The context within which Navarrus develops the quantity theory is a discussion of the legitimacy of profit earned as a result of disparities of the value of money in different countries. These disparities in the purchasing power of money reflect the relative scarcity of the two moneys. Money, according to Navarrus, is worth more where it is scarce than where it is plentiful. Where money is scarce, goods and services fetch low prices; prices are high where it is plentiful, as it is in Spain as a result of the inflow of precious metals from the New World.

The teaching of the scholastics forms the background of Max Weber's thesis of the Protestant or Puritan origin of capitalism, which has provoked a lively discussion since the beginning of this century. Weber's thesis, like Tawney's similar argument, fails to account for the flourishing economic life in the Italian cities, whose residents adhered to the old faith. As far as these are concerned, an idea recently advanced by the French economic historian Jacques Le Goff may be more to the point. In *The Birth of Purgatory* (1984) Le Goff develops the idea that Purgatory, a third place between Heaven and Hell, the notion of which was instilled in the minds of the faithful between 1150 and 1200, contributed to the birth of capitalism by making the salvation of the usurer possible (p. 305). Others have pointed out that what are known as Puritan attitudes can be found in earlier periods as well. For example, reference is made to the rule of Saint Benedict with its insistence on an austere way of life, discipline, clockwork regularity, hard work and poverty, which may have invited imitation (Hallam, 1976, pp. 28–49). Again others elucidate the complex relationships that connect the mendicant friars of the Middle Ages with the rise of an urban ideology favouring the commercial society (Little, 1978).

In North America, scholastic economic thought lingered on in the business ethics of the Puritan divines. An illustration is provided by the case of Robert Keayne, a Boston merchant who was castigated from the pulpit of the First Church in 1639 by the Puritan clergyman, John Cotton, for overcharging and other sharp practices. In his sermon, Cotton established the requirements of a just price and listed a number of other rules of proper business behaviour similar to the rules of the scholastics (see Hosmer, 1908, vol. 1, pp. 315–18). The just price continues to play a role in our own time in connection with such concepts as fair return and reasonable value, which are determined by regulatory commissions.

BIBLIOGRAPHY

For treatments of the period by outstanding economists see Joseph A. Schumpeter (1954, ch. 2) and Jacob Viner (1978, ch. 2), the latter being chapters of an unfinished work published posthumously and also available in book form. For a survey that treats not only the scholastics but Roman and canon law as well see Gordon (1975, pp. 122–272). For a textbook treatment with ample bibliography see Spiegel (1983, chs 3 and 4). For a collection of articles by the outstanding specialist of his time dealing with such topics as scholastic economics, the scholastic attitude towards trade and entrepreneurship, and monopoly theory, see de Roover (1958, 1967, 1976). For a work by an historian on the same subject, see Baldwin (1959). On usury see Noonan (1957) and Nelson (1969), the first the work of a legal historian, the second that of a sociologist, and both based on original sources. About Navarrus and other Spanish writers see Grice-Hutchinson (1978). For an English translation of a manual on business ethics see Nieder (1966), originally published in Latin in 1468 and authored by a lesser-known scholastic. See also Monroe (1924, chs 3 and 4) for translations from Saint Thomas Aquinas and Nicole Oresme.

Baldwin, J.W. 1959. The medieval theories of the just price. *Transactions of the American Philosophical Society* NS 49(4), 15–92.

de Roover, R. 1958. The concept of the just price. *Journal of Economic History* 18, December, 418–34.

de Roover, R. 1967. *San Bernadino of Siena and Sant'Antonio of Florence: The Two Great Economic Thinkers of the Middle Ages.* Publication No. 19 of the Kress Library of Business and Economics, Boston: Baker Library, Harvard Graduate School of Business Administration.

de Roover, R. 1976. *Business, Banking and Economic Thought in Late Medieval and Early Modern Europe.* Chicago: University of Chicago Press.

Gordon, B. 1975. *Economic Analysis before Adam Smith.* London: Macmillan.

Grice-Hutchinson, M. 1978. *Early Economic Thought in Spain, 1177–1740.* London: Allen & Unwin.

Hallam, H.E. 1976. The medieval mind. In *Feudalism, Capitalism and Beyond*, ed. E. Kamenka and R.S. Neale, New York: St Martin's Press.

Hosmer, J.K. (ed.) 1908. *Governor John Winthrop's Journal*, Vol. 1. New York: Scribner's.

Le Goff, J. 1984. *The Birth of Purgatory.* Chicago: University of Chicago Press.

Little, L.K. 1978. *Religious Poverty and the Profit Economy in Medieval Europe.* Ithaca: Cornell University Press.

Monroe, A.E. 1924. *Early Economic Thought.* Cambridge, Mass.: Harvard University Press.

Nelson, B.N. 1969. *The Idea of Usury*. 2nd edn, enlarged, Chicago: University of Chicago Press.

Nieder, J. 1966. *On the Contracts of Merchants*. Trans. C.H. Reeves, ed. R.B. Schumann, Norman: University of Oklahoma Press.

Noonan, J.T., Jr. 1957. *The Scholastic Analysis of Usury*. Cambridge, Mass.: Harvard University Press.

Schumpeter, J.A. 1954. *History of Economic Analysis*. New York: Oxford University Press.

Spiegel, H.W. 1983. *The Growth of Economic Thought*. Revised and expanded edn, Durham, North Carolina: Duke University Press.

Viner, J. 1978. Religious thought and economic society. *History of Political Economy* 10(1), Spring, 9–189. Published as *Religious Thought and Economic Society: Four Chapters of an Unfinished Work by Jacob Viner*, ed. J. Melitz and D. Winch, Durham, North Carolina: Duke University Press.

Scottish Enlightenment

JOHN ROBERTSON

Between 1740 and 1790 Scotland provided one of the most distinguished branches of the European Enlightenment. David Hume and Adam Smith were the pre-eminent figures in this burst of intellectual activity; and around them clustered a galaxy of major thinkers, including Francis Hutcheson, Lord Kames, Adam Ferguson, William Robertson, Thomas Reid, Sir James Steuart and John Millar. The interests of individual thinkers ranged from metaphysics to the natural sciences; but the distinctive achievements of the Scottish Enlightenment as a whole lay in those fields associated with the enquiry into 'the progress of society' – history, moral and political philosophy and, not least, political economy.

In the European context, Scotland's was a characteristically 'provincial' Enlightenment. Conscious of their membership of a wider movement, the Scottish thinkers cultivated connections with Paris, the Enlightenment's acknowledged metropolitan centre. But the Scottish Enlightenment is perhaps best understood when it is compared with the Enlightenment in France's provinces, or in the provincial states of Italy and Germany. The concern with economic improvement and its moral and political conditions and consequences was as urgent, for instance, in the distant Kingdom of Naples as in Scotland; and political economy was equally absorbing to the Neapolitan philosopher-reformers Genovesi and Galiani.

At the same time, the experience of Scotland in the 18th century was distinctive in a number of respects, which offered a particular stimulus to Scottish thinkers. First of all, there was the actual achievement of economic growth. Slow in coming, but increasingly perceptible, it gave Scottish thinkers an unusually direct acquaintance with the phenomena of development. Political change was also significant. The Union of 1707 with England was in no simple sense the cause of Scotland's economic growth (or the precondition of its Enlightenment). But the sacrifice of the nation's independent parliament for the opportunity of free trade with England and its empire highlighted the problem of the institutional conditions of economic development. Most dramatic of all were the changes in

634

religion and culture. The fierce, covenanting presbyterianism of the 17th century was dissipated, as the 'Moderate' group of clergy rose to power in the Kirk. The four universities of Edinburgh, Glasgow, Aberdeen and St Andrews were reformed, allowing professorial specialization; and around the universities fluorished a vigorous informal culture of voluntary clubs, most famous of which was the Select Society of Edinburgh. Together these changes secured for Scottish thinkers unprecedented intellectual freedom and social support; and they provided an object lesson in the importance of the moral and cultural as well as the material dimensions of progress.

Nothing in Scotland's comparatively successful provincial experience, moreover, inclined its Enlightenment in a very radical direction. It was not that the Scottish thinkers were complacent: on particular issues they were anxious to influence the leaders of Scottish society. But where in backward provinces like Naples, Enlightenment thinking was programmatic, even utopian, the thought of the Scottish Enlightenment was characterized by a relatively detached, analytic interest in the underlying mechanisms of society's development.

Against the background of Scotland's particular provincial experience, it was natural for the Scottish thinkers to study economic phenomena in the framework of a wider enquiry. There were three principal dimensions to that enquiry: the historical, the moral and the institutional.

The historical theory of the Scottish Enlightenment developed a line of argument from later 17th-century natural jurisprudence, a tradition made familiar to the Scots by its incorporation in the moral philosophy curriculum of the reformed universities. Discarding the older jurisprudential thesis of the contractual foundations of society and government, the Scots focused on the new insights of Pufendorf and Locke into the origin and development of property. According to Pufendorf, there had never been an original state of common ownership of land and goods; from the first, property was the result of individual appropriation. As increasing numbers made goods scarce, individual property became the norm, and systems of justice and government were established to secure it. What the Scots added to this argument was a scheme of specific stages of social development: the hunting, the pastoral, the agricultural and the commercial. At each of these four stages the extent of property ownership was related to the society's means of subsistence, and both shaped the nature and sophistication of the society's government. Different versions of the theory were offered by Adam Ferguson in his *Essay on the History of Civil Society* (1767) and by John Millar in his *Origin of the Distinction of Ranks* (1770), and underlay Lord Kames's investigations into legal history and William Robertson's historical narratives. The *locus classicus* of the theory, however, was Adam Smith's *Lectures on Jurisprudence*, delivered to his students in Glasgow in the early 1760s.

As Smith's exposition makes particularly clear, the stages theory of social development provided the historical premises for political economy. An explicitly conjectural theory – a model of society's 'natural' progress – it provided a framework for a comparably theoretical treatment of economic development as 'the natural progress of opulence'. By positing the systematic interrelation of

World of Economics

economic activity, property and government, with consequences which could be neither foreseen nor controlled by individuals, the theory also established the essential irreversibility of the development process. Short of a natural catastrophe, it demonstrated, the advent of commercial society was unavoidable.

The moral thought of the Scottish Enlightenment was closely related to the historical, sharing a common origin in 17th-century natural jurisprudence. Here the inspiration was the jurisprudential thinkers' increasingly sophisticated treatment of needs. These, it was recognized, could no longer be thought of primarily in relation to subsistence; with the progress of society, needs must be understood to cover a much wider range of scarce goods, luxuries as well as necessities. The potential of this insight was seen by every Scottish moral philosopher, but again it was Smith who exploited it to the full, in the *Theory of Moral Sentiments* (1759). Beyond the most basic necessities, Smith acknowledged, men's needs were always relative, a matter of status of emulation, of bettering one's individual condition. But it was precisely the vain desires of the rich and the envy of others which served, by 'an invisible hand', to stimulate men's industry and hence to increase the stock of goods available for all ranks.

Such an argument, however, had to overcome two of the most deeply entrenched convictions of European moral thought: the Aristotelian view that the distribution of goods was a matter for justice, and the classical or civic humanist view that luxury led to corruption and the loss of moral virtue. The Scots answered the first more confidently (but perhaps less satisfactorily) than the second. Following Grotius, Hobbes and Pufendorf, they defined justice in exclusively corrective terms, setting aside questions of distribution. On the issue of corruption, they were divided. Hume, who ridiculed fears of luxury, was the most confident; Ferguson, who defiantly reasserted the ideal of virtue, the least. Smith was closer to Hume in preferring propriety to virtue, at least for the great majority; but he showed that he shared Ferguson's doubts when he added, at the end of his life, that the disposition to admire the rich and the great did tend to corrupt moral sentiments. At a fundamental level, however, there was general agreement. As a consequence of the progress of society, the multiplication of needs was not only irreversible; it was the essential characteristic of a 'cultivated' or 'civilized' as distinct from a 'barbarian' society. And civilization, however morally ambiguous, was preferable to barbarism. With consensus on this, the moral premises of political economy were secure.

The definition of justice in simple corrective terms provided the starting point for the institutional dimension of the Scottish enquiry. The priority of any government, the Scots believed, must be the security of life and property, ensuring every individual liberty under the law. This, as Smith put it, was freedom 'in our present sense of the word'; and there was a general confidence that it was tolerably secure under the governments of modern Europe, including the absolute monarchies. In principle, individual liberty was a condition of a fully commercial society: its provision, therefore, was the institutional premise of political economy.

Few of the Scots took institutional analysis beyond this relatively simple, if vital, point; the theory of the modern commercial state was not a Scottish achievement. But Hume and Smith did get further than the rest, identifying and exploring a two-fold problem in the government of commercial society. Most urgently, they argued that it was necessary to limit the opportunities for governmental aggrandizement at the expense of 'productive' society, by confining government to the minimum necessary provision of justice, defence and public works. In the longer run, as the lower ranks of society acquired material and moral independence, it would also be necessary to satisfy their demands for an extension of citizenship and enlargement of political liberty. It was the responsibility of legislators, Hume and Smith believed, gradually to adapt institutions to meet these needs. Both outlined models by which legislators might proceed, Hume reworking the institutional concepts of the classical, civic tradition in his 'Idea of a perfect Commonwealth', Smith elaborating the principles of parliamentary sovereignty in his exemplary vision of British-American imperial union.

A large part of the originality of the Scottish Enlightenment's conception of political economy lay in this exploration of the historical, moral and institutional framework of economic activity. But of course the Scots also engaged directly in economic analysis; and one such work of analysis, Adam Smith's *Wealth of Nations* (1776), so outshone all others that it seemed to establish political economy as a science in its own right.

The Scots' attention naturally focused on growth. In contemporary terms, the issue was the means by which a poor country (such as Scotland) could best hope to catch up on a rich country (such as England). The alternatives, canvassed afresh by Hume in his *Political Discourses* (1752), were those aired in the Scottish debate before the Union, fifty years earlier: free trade to take advantage of the poor country's lower wages, or protection and credit creation to assist its manufactures. An optimist, Hume favoured the free trade alternative. Sir James Steuart countered in his *Principles of Political Economy* (1767) that rich nations would not permit free trade to their disadvantage, and that protection and credit creation were therefore essential. Unfortunately for Steuart, his arguments were simply ignored in the *Wealth of Nations*. Smith was agnostic about the prospects for poor countries; but he was unequivocal about free trade. The uninhibited expansion of the market was necessary, he explained, to achieve the maximum extension of the division of labour and the optimum allocation of capital, the twin motors of growth.

Smith's confidence in the powers of the market was the cornerstone of more than his explanation of growth. It shaped his entire presentation of political economy. In writing the *Wealth of Nations*, Smith consciously set himself to achieve the standards of simplicity, coherence and comprehensiveness which he associated with successful philosophical systems, and with the Newtonian philosophy in particular. What gravity was to Newton's astronomy, the market was to Smith's political economy. For the market was not simply the matrix of growth. It was also, he believed, the mechanism by which the fruits of growth were distributed, so that the unprecedented inequality of commercial society was offset by an equally unprecedented increase in the standard of living of even the lowest and poorest ranks. (As a means of improving the condition of the poor, in other words, the market was far more effective than any previous arrangement guided by the notion of distributive justice. It was the 'invisible hand' through which the vain desires of the rich were transformed into an increased stock of goods for all). In addition, the market could help to check the growth of unproductive government, since in Smith's view most institutions could be subjected to some degree to its disciplines. The market, in short, was cast in the *Wealth of Nations* as the hub of a complete, virtually self-sustaining economic system.

It was the systematic and comprehensive analysis which this faith in the market made possible, rather than simply the account of growth, which set the *Wealth of Nations* above any other work of Enlightenment political economy, Scottish or European. To be systematic and comprehensive had earlier been the ambition, at least, of Quesnay's *Tableau Economique* (1758–9), Genovesi's *Lezioni di Commercio* (1765) and Steuart's *Principles*; but the *Wealth of Nations* eclipsed them all. Its success, moreover, was such as to suggest that political economy had an identity all of its own. Smith himself did not admit such an implication, continuing to insist that political economy was but 'a branch of the science of a statesman or legislator': his own work in jurisprudence and moral philosophy left him disinclined to drop the wider intellectual framework in which political economy had been conceived. But when the single concept of the market made possible an analysis at once so extensive and so self-contained, it was at least plausible to suppose that what was being presented in the *Wealth of Nations* was a distinct, autonomous science of political economy.

Smith's death in 1790 coincided with the end of the Scottish Enlightenment. In Scotland, as throughout Europe, the French Revolution transformed the conditions and assumptions of intellectual life, while political economy had to come to terms with machinery. Within Scotland Dugald Stewart set himself to adapt the Enlightenment conception of political economy to these new circumstances; but his expansive, didactic approach had few imitators. Another Scot, Thomas Chalmers, took the lead in attaching political economy to newly urgent theological concerns, while in England Ricardo and his followers simply took a narrower view of the subject. Even so, it would be a mistake to see 19th-century classical political economy as a new departure. As the philosophical analysis of Hegel (who learnt much from Steuart) and the radical critiques of Marx and the early socialists pointed out, the historical, moral and institutional premises on which political economy rested were still those elucidated by the Scots. In any case, it was the Scottish Enlightenment, and specifically the *Wealth of Nations*, which had first shown how political economy might be presented as an independent science.

BIBLIOGRAPHY

Bryson, G. 1945. *Man and Society: the Scottish Enquiry of the Eighteenth Century.* Princeton: Princeton University Press.

Campbell, R.H. and Skinner, A.S. 1982. *The Origins and Nature of the Scottish Enlightenment.* Edinburgh: John Donald.

Hont, I. and Ignatieff, M. (eds) 1983. *Wealth and Virtue. The Shaping of Political Economy in the Scottish Enlightenment.* Cambridge: Cambridge University Press.
Medick, H. 1973. *Naturzustand und Naturgeschichte der bürgerlichen Gesellschaft.* Göttingen: Vandenhoeck and Ruprecht.
Phillipson, N.T. 1981. The Scottish Enlightenment. In *The Enlightenment in National Context*, ed. R. Porter and M. Teich, Cambridge and New York: Cambridge University Press.
Sher, R.B. 1985. *Church and University in the Scottish Enlightenment.* Princeton: Princeton University Press; Edinburgh: Edinburgh University Press.

Self-interest

D.H. MONRO

Two of the basic equations with which moral philosophers have been concerned are: (a) what are the fundamental principles of morality? and (b) why should we obey them? One tempting answer to the second question is: because obeying them is in your own interest. Tempting, because any other answer simply invites a further 'why?'. For example, 'why bother about helping others to get what they want?' clearly demands an answer. But 'why bother about getting what *you* want?', though of course it can be *asked*, hardly makes sense.

Self-interest as the answer to the second question, however, implies a similar answer to the first. Self-interest can only be a reason for obeying moral principles if those principles do always benefit us as individuals, so that the fundamental one becomes: Do whatever will enable you to satisfy your own desires. And this seems perverse, since most moralists tell us to consider others rather than ourselves. Self-sacrifice, we are told, is noble, and self-seeking base.

Thomas Hobbes answers this objection by pointing out that, while human desires are diverse, so that there is no common end, there is a single means common to all ends. They all require the cooperation of other people, or at least their non-interference. Everyone has an interest in maintaining a peaceful and harmonious society. Moral principles are simply the rules which everyone must follow in order to obtain such a society. We should obey them because obeying them makes for peace and security, and without peace and security no one has much chance of satisfying *any* desires. If morality requires us to consider others and not ourselves, it is for our own sakes in the long run.

To suppose that men imposed moral restraints on themselves for this reason might suggest a far-sightedness greater than most of us are capable of. Bernard Mandeville suggested that men are motivated less by this consideration than by vanity. Morality, he conjectured, came about through the artifice of a relatively few far-sighted men who, in order to make men useful to their fellows, spread the myth that man is somehow different from the other animals and shows his superiority by being able to conquer his desires. 'Moral Virtues', he says, 'are the Political Offspring which Flattery begot upon Pride' (Mandeville, 1724, vol. 1, p. 51). Part of Mandeville's purpose is to satirize the doctrine that no action is virtuous unless it involves self-denial. If that is true, he argues, then virtue does not exist, since all actions aim at some gratification, if only an increase in self-esteem. Civilization did not come about through self-denial, but through what moralists regard as moral weaknesses: avarice, vanity, luxuriousness, ambition and the rest. Hence his famous paradox: 'Private Vices, Publick Benefits.' In developing it he gives an example which has often been quoted: the many materials garnered from all over the world, and the toil and hardship endured by a multitude of workmen, in order to produce a scarlet coat. Even a tyrant, Mandeville says, would be ashamed 'to exact such terrible Services from his Innocent Slaves' merely for 'the satisfaction a Man receives from having a Garment made of Scarlet or Crimson Cloth'. Yet in pursuit of their own private ends men perform feats of endurance which neither their own benevolence nor the tyranny of others would drive them to (Mandeville, 1724, vol. 1, pp. 357–8). This passage has often been used to illustrate the efficiency and smooth working of a market economy; but, looked at in a slightly different way, it would really fit just as well into the first book of Marx's *Das Kapital*, which is full of atrocity stories about the sufferings of workers under capitalism.

Mandeville distinguishes between virtue and goodness. Virtue, in the sense of complete self-denial, is an illusion, since all actions spring from self-interest. It is not possible to subdue the passions, but only to set one passion against another. No action is completely virtuous, but (he seems to imply) it may be good, if it is useful to others. Mandeville, then, agrees with Hobbes that self-interest is the ultimate motive for all actions, but probably does not agree with his other thesis, that self-interest, as distinct from the general happiness, is ultimately the sole good.

The first of these two theses is ambiguous, because 'self-interest' is ambiguous, in more ways than one. If the thesis is that every action springs from some desire or other, including disinterested desires for the welfare of others, then it is probably a truism and in any case of very little interest. If it means that in every action the agent is aiming at his own greatest happiness in the long run ('enlightened self-interest' or 'cool self-love'), then it is significant but false. Actually Hobbes seems to mean something else again: that there are no altruistic or disinterested desires. Apparent altruism turns out on examination to be selfish or interested in the ordinary sense of those words, aiming perhaps at public acclaim or enhanced self-esteem.

It was argued against Hobbes that benevolence, the disinterested desire for the welfare of others, is as basic a part of human nature as self-interest. But, if there are two basic human instincts instead of one, which should we follow when they conflict? The stronger? But it would be rash to claim that benevolence is a stronger feature of human nature than selfishness. Shaftesbury and Hutcheson detected a third instinct, an innate moral sense which requires us to prefer benevolence to self-interest when they conflict. But why should we prefer *that* instinct? As an answer to the question 'why be moral?' this is hardly more satisfactory than to say (with other philosophers) that it is an eternal and immutable truth, known by intuition, that we should allow benevolence to prevail over self-interest.

David Hume and Adam Smith, while agreeing with Hutcheson in the main, try to make his position more plausible by going more deeply into the psychological sources of benevolence. An important one, they say, is sympathy, the tendency to enter into the joys and sorrows of others. Mandeville had regarded pity as a weakness, because it is a passion, though an amiable one: a self-indulgent desire to rid ourselves of a particular kind of uneasiness. Adam Smith insists that sympathy is disinterested, and suggests that 'that whole account of human nature ... which deduces all sentiments and affections from self-love ... seems to me to have arisen from some confused misapprehension of the system of sympathy' (Smith, 1759, p. 317).

Smith called attention to another tendency in human nature: the aesthetic delight in 'the fitness of any system or machine to produce the end for which it was intended', leading, very often, to the means being valued for its own sake, quite apart from the original end. (Smith would have understood the secretary of a home for unmarried mothers who said in an annual report: 'It would be a great pity if, after so much devoted work by so many people, this home had to close for lack of girls needing help'.) Although he regards this tendency as distinct from both self-interest and benevolence, consideration of it leads Smith to conclusions curiously like Mandeville's. One manifestation of it, he says, is the heaping up of riches far beyond the needs of the rich themselves:

> The rich only select from the heap what is most precious and agreeable. They consume little more than the poor, and in spite of their natural selfishness and rapacity, though they mean only their own conveniency, though the sole end which they propose from the labours of all the thousands which they employ be the gratification of their own vain and insatiable desires, they divide with the poor the produce of all their improvements. They are led by an invisible hand to make nearly the same distribution of the necessaries of life which would have been made had the earth been divided into equal portions among all its inhabitants; and thus, without intending it, without knowing it, advance the interest of the society, and afford means to the multiplication of the species (Smith, 1759, pp. 184–5).

It is clear from this that Smith, like Mandeville, sees that the actual consequences of actions may be quite different from those intended. The bees in Mandeville's fable intended merely to lead virtuous and abstemious lives; they did not foresee that this would lead to the ruin of dressmakers, milliners, lawyers, turnkeys, footmen, courtiers, cooks and many others, and eventually to the economic collapse of the hive. Mandeville concludes that public benefits flow from private vices; but obviously the practitioners of those vices are not thinking of the public benefit, but solely of their own gratification.

Adam Smith, in his other reference to the invisible hand, says that most individuals, in their economic transactions, neither intend to promote the public interest nor realize that they are doing so. 'He intends only his own gain, and he is in this, as in many other cases, led by an invisible hand to promote an end which was no part of his intention'. He adds that this is on the whole a good thing. 'By pursuing his own interest he frequently promotes that of the society more effectually than when he really intends to promote it. I have never known much good done by those who affected to trade for the publick good. It is an affectation, indeed, not very common among merchants, and very few words need be employed in dissuading them from it' (Smith, 1776, p. 456).

Nor is that all. It is not only that the pursuit of wealth or power leads the ambitious to promote the public interest while seeking only their own; the aesthetic tendency to value a means for its own sake causes them to have false notions about where their own real interests lie. The pleasures of wealth and greatness, which do not really add much to happiness,

> strike the imagination as something grand, and beautiful, and noble, of which the attainment is well worth all the toil and anxiety which we are so apt to bestow on it. And it is well that nature imposes upon us in this manner. It is this deception which rouses and keeps in continual motion the industry of mankind (Smith, 1759, p. 183).

But perhaps the most optimistic version of the theory of the invisible hand is put forward by T.H. Green. The actions of bad men, he says (at least when they are also powerful) are 'overruled for good'. There is, he tells us, nothing supernatural about this; it is simply one of the beneficient effects of living in society, and particularly in a nation-state. He gives Napoleon as an example:

> With all his egotism, his individuality was so far governed by the national spirit in and upon him, that he could only glorify himself in the greatness of France, and though the national spirit expressed itself in an effort after greatness which was in many ways of a mischievous and delusive kind, yet it again had so much of what may be called the spirit of humanity in it, that it required satisfaction in the belief that it was serving humanity. Hence the aggrandisement of France, in which Napoleon's passion for glory satisfied itself, had to take at least the semblance of a deliverance of oppressed peoples, and in taking the semblance it to a great extent performed the reality ... (Green, 1886, p. 134).

One may doubt whether the world's experience of dictators would yield much evidence of such overruling.

For Hobbes, moral principles ('laws of nature') are sociological laws about how men may cooperate peacefully. For Hume and Smith they are rather psychological truths about what men have come to approve, given their peculiar amalgam of dispositions (of which self-interest is merely one) and also the social need (which Hobbes had stressed) for some fixed standards of behaviour.

The psychological approach was also taken by the early Utilitarians. They were, however, less unwilling to found morality on self-interest, because the alternatives, 'intuition', 'the moral sense', 'natural law' and the rest, seemed to them to be merely an excuse for deifying one's own prejudices. 'Nature', Bentham said, 'has placed mankind under the governance of two sovereign masters, pain and pleasure. It is for them to point out what we ought to do, as well as to determine what we shall do' (Bentham, 1789, p. 11). These masters might have been expected to order each individual to pursue his own greatest happiness. But, according to Bentham, they set a different goal, the happiness of *everybody*. Bentham does not explain this transition.

Mill attempts to explain it, in a brief and much-criticized argument. Like Adam Smith, he appeals to the tendency for a means to become an end in itself. Virtue, he says, the desire to promote the general happiness, originally cultivated as a means to one's own happiness, comes to be aimed at for its own sake. From being a means to happiness, it has become a part of that happiness. G.E. Moore dismisses this contemptuously as a blatant failure to distinguish two very different things, a part and a means. Mill's argument may, however, be more subtle than that (Moore, 1903, pp. 71–2).

According to Hobbes, moral rules state the way men must behave if society is to be possible. Needing society, the individual accepts as his aim, not self-interest merely, but a compromise between his own interests and those of everybody else. He accepts the compromise because half a loaf is better than no bread. Consequently he feels obliged to subordinate his own interests to the compromise when they conflict. But he obeys moral rules only as a means, in order to induce others to obey them too. Having others obey them is his reward; obeying them himself is the price he pays. But it may be objected that we do not think of morality like that. We want to do the right thing for the sake of doing it. It would seem to follow from Hobbes's account that it would be more rational to be a successful hypocrite than a genuinely good person.

Consider, however, what happens once the compromise is accepted. Since society depends on that acceptance, society will take pains to inculcate in each new generation the importance of accepting it. To anyone so trained, the compromise will not be thought of *as* a compromise, but simply as the right thing to do. Moreover, he will feel uneasy at the prospect of attaining his personal ends in a way that could run counter to the compromise. In Mill's words, he comes to think of himself as a being who *of course* pays regard to others (Mill, 1863, p. 232). Conformity with morality, aiming at the general happiness, has become part of his private happiness and not just a means to it.

Mill's answer to the question 'what is the fundamental moral principle?' is: do whatever makes for the greatest happiness all round. His answer to the other question (why obey it?) is: because you have been socially conditioned to associate your own happiness with that of other people. If you had not been so conditioned, there would be no stable society, and your life would be miserable. Moreover (and Mill learned this from David Hartley rather than Hobbes) greater satisfaction is to be derived from our socially conditioned desires than from our primary or biological ones.

Later Utilitarians have not usually followed Mill in this. Henry Sidgwick, indeed, in spite of Bentham, founded the greatest happiness principle on a rational, self-evident intuition. Moral philosophers of other persuasions have either accepted some form of intuitionism or have argued (unconvincingly) that 'why be moral?' is a nonsensical question.

BIBLIOGRAPHY

Bentham, J. 1789. *An Introduction to the Principles of Morals and Legislation*. Ed. J.H. Burns and H.L.A. Hart, London: Athlone Press, 1970.

Green, T.H. 1886. *Lectures on the Principles of Political Obligation*. London: Longmans, 1941.

Hobbes, T. 1651. *Leviathan, or The Matter, Forme & Power of a Commonwealth, Ecclesiasticall and Civill*. Oxford: Clarendon Press, 1909; New York: E.P. Dutton & Co., 1934.

Hume, D. 1739. *A Treatise of Human Nature*. Ed. L.A. Selby-Bigge, Oxford: Clarendon Press, 1896.

Hume, D. 1751. *Enquiries Concerning the Human Understanding and Concerning the Principles of Morals*. Ed. L.A. Selby-Bigge, Oxford: Clarendon Press, 1902.

Hutcheson, F. 1728. *An Essay on the Nature and Conduct of the Passions, with Illustrations upon the Moral Sense*. Facsimile edn prepared by B. Fabian, Hildesheim: G. Olms, 1971.

Mandeville, B. 1724. *The Fable of the Bees, or Private Vices, Publick Benefits*. Ed. F.B. Kaye, Oxford: Clarendon Press, 1924.

Mill, J.S. 1863. *Utilitariansim*. In *Essays on Ethics, Religion and Society*, ed. J.M. Robson, Toronto: University of Toronto Press; London: Routledge & Kegan Paul, 1969.

Moore, G.E. 1903. *Principia Ethica*. Cambridge: Cambridge University Press.

Shaftesbury [A.A. Cooper], 3rd Earl. 1699. *An Inquiry Concerning Virtue or Merit*. Ed. D. Walford, Manchester: Manchester University Press, 1977.

Sidgwick, H. 1907. *The Methods of Ethics*. 7th edn, ed. E.E.C. Jones, London: Macmillan, 1962.

Smith, A. 1759. *The Theory of Moral Sentiments*. Ed. A.L. Macfie and D.D. Raphael, Oxford: Clarendon Press, 1974.

Smith, A. 1776. *An Inquiry into the Nature and Causes of the Wealth of Nations*. Ed. R.H. Campbell, A.S. Skinner and W.B. Todd, Oxford: Clarendon Press, 1976.

Shadow Pricing

RAVI KANBUR

When a businessman evaluates a project, he does it with a view to calculating the prospective profit from it. These calculations can be seen as taking place in two steps. At the first step, all the physical consequences of relevance to the businessman – the inputs to and outputs from the project – are assessed. At the second stage, these inputs and outputs are converted into costs and revenues, using *market prices*. It is natural that a private businessman should use the ruling market prices for costing inputs and for valuing sales, since these are the prices at which transactions take place and hence profit is generated.

Consider now the evaluation of a project by a government. Such evaluation will differ at each of the two steps referred to above. At the first step, the government will be interested in *all* of the repercussions of the project, however indirect. This is because it is the government rather than a private businessman concerned with his own narrowly defined activities. At the second step, the government will wish to use not the ruling market prices but prices which reflect social costs and social benefits, in order to calculate what might be termed social profit. These prices are referred to as *shadow prices*, or accounting prices (see Little and Mirrlees, 1974), and the name suggests that they are to be used in lieu of the actual market prices.

Market prices are what they are. But how are shadow prices to be calculated? Clearly they depend on the government's objective function and on the constraints it faces. The shadow prices should be such that the social profit from the project is positive if and only if the project increases the value of the government's objective function. In a general competitive equilibrium, if the government's objective is economic efficiency, then it can be argued that for a small project the shadow prices do in fact coincide with market prices. If the government's objective includes the pursuit of equity, but it has lump sum instruments to carry this out, then shadow prices still coincide with market prices. Basically the government should use redistributive lump sum taxation to pursue equity and use the project to pursue increases in aggregate economic welfare.

646

But if the government does not have a sufficient range of instruments to pursue effective redistribution without distortion it may be the case that, even with a full competitive equilibrium, shadow prices may differ from market prices. In addition to this, if the economy is not in a full competitive equilibrium, then the case for using shadow prices different from market prices can be argued strongly.

In programming terms, shadow prices are simply dual to the changes in the government's objective function. One justification for their use is the benefits of decentralization: local project evaluators are better equipped to analyse the physical consequences of a project, and this localized knowledge should be used in conjunction with centrally determined shadow prices to evaluate the social profitability of projects. But the real difficulties arise in specifying the objectives of the government and in specifying its constraints, and this is in turn related to who is thought of as doing the project evaluation.

The standard assumption is one of a unitary government with a given social welfare function – a benevolent dictator. But the reality is one where the project evaluator is either part of a government which is a coalition of interests, or the project evaluation is being done by an international agency which faces a government made up of conflicting and competing objectives. The logical procedure for an international agency should be clear – in evaluating a project it should incorporate a model of the political process to clarify the responses of various government instruments to the project. Sen (1972) gives an illuminating discussion of a project which requires importing an input on which there is already a quota – so that the border price of the input is very different from its domestic scarcity value. The Little and Mirrlees (1974) method of using border prices is predicated on the assumption that it is these prices which represent the transformation possibilities for the economy as a whole. But if the assessment of the political realities is such that this quota will not be removed by the government – because of the overriding influence of interest groups that benefit from the rents generated by the quota – then the domestic scarcity value should be used in costing the input.

Similarly, any project which alters significantly the distribution of income will have repercussions on the political process – and there will be attempts by groups who are adversely affected to restore their standard of living. Project evaluation in general, and shadow pricing in particular, should take these into account. Consider, for example, the shadow cost of labour. If the labour used on the project comes from the agricultural sector, and if this labour is a constraint on output, then agricultural output will fall. If government revenue depends on taxation of this output, this will fall too. If, in turn, government expenditure is a major source of non-agricultural (urban) incomes, then at constant fiscal deficit urban incomes will fall. This change in the distribution of income will be an important element in the shadow cost of labour. But suppose now that the political processes are such as not to allow a decline in urban living standards. Rather, government expenditure remains constant and the fiscal deficit increases. Now it is the increased burden on future generations which has to be taken into account. Either way, it should be clear that a model of the political process is crucial in specifying shadow prices even if the project evaluator (be it an international agency or a project evaluation unit within the government) is clear about what the objectives are. Braverman and Kanbur (1985) have provided a prototype analysis of how such constraints might be taken into account, in the specific context of projects in West Africa.

BIBLIOGRAPHY

Braverman, A. and Kanbur, S.M.R. 1985. Urban bias, present bias, and the shadow cost of labour for agricultural projects: the West African context. The World Bank, Mimeo.

Little, I.M.D. and Mirrlees, J.A. 1974. *Project Appraisal and Planning for Developing Countries*. London: Heinemann.

Sen, A.K. 1972. Control areas and accounting prices: an approach to economic evaluation. *Economic Journal* 82, Supplement, 486–501.

Social Cost

J. DE V. GRAAFF

The idea underlying the notion of social cost is a very simple one. A man initiating an action does not necessarily bear all the costs (or reap all the benefits) himself. Those that he does bear are *private* costs; those he does not are *external* costs. The sum of the two constitutes the *social* cost.

Behind this apparently straightforward statement lies a host of difficulties of definition, valuation and aggregation. They are considered in Section I. Section II discusses very briefly certain contexts in which, despite the ambiguities, the concept is often used.

I. PROBLEMS OF DEFINITION

Private cost is usually defined in opportunity-cost terms as the highest valued (or most preferred) option necessarily forgone. In practice this usually means no more than that the private cost of an object is the money paid for it. The definition works because the individual (or firm) is assumed to be optimizing. Every choice entails a sacrifice. There is always an option 'necessarily forgone'.

The external costs imposed on others by the initiator of an action are imposed on optimizing agents, so the definition works for them too. But it does not work for social cost because there is no reason to suppose that society is optimizing. Society may, without giving up leisure or anything else, be able to get more guns *and* more butter. Technically, this will be possible whenever it is operating 'within' (rather than 'on') its social production frontier – a situation as likely to be the norm as the exception. There would, in these circumstances, be no option forgone and therefore no cost.

If society does happen to be 'on' its production frontier, there is at least a cost. But its significance may depend on who bears it. Is butter forgone by A (who is rich) as important as that forgone by B (who is poor)? Can the two amounts simply be added together to get the cost to society?

The definition of social cost as the sum of private and external costs avoids the difficulty that society may not be optimizing but not the one that costs borne

649

by different people have to be added together. Nor does it avoid certain other difficulties. We shall discuss these under separate headings, starting with the least troublesome.

(1) *Scope of society.* If I build a house that obstructs my neighbour's view, but affects no one else, it is fairly clear that the external cost I impose on him is the only one to be added to my own in determining the cost of my action to society. He will suffer an immediate loss of amenity, which may or may not be easy to value, and a decline in the resale value of his property which, if the market functions as it should, will be a reasonable estimate of the loss to his successors in title.

In other situations the position may not be so simple. Pollution of the atmosphere, or of a common waterway, may affect several nations. Are we interested in the cost to *our* society, or to the world community? What of activities that may affect unborn generations? How is the cost to them to be estimated? If one is dealing with questions such as the social cost of nuclear energy, these matters may be very relevant.

We must be clear about the scope, in time and space, of the society in which we are interested before talking about social cost. When we are, we can proceed to the other difficulties.

(2) *Costs and benefits.* The external costs imposed on others by the initiator of some action need not all be positive. Some may be negative costs, or benefits. (If I paint my house bright yellow it may horrify Jones, but delight Smith.) It is largely a matter of convention whether we reckon these negative costs separately, and call them benefits, or set them off against the positive ones immediately, to arrive at a figure for *net* cost.

In Cost–Benefit Analysis the usual practice is to deal with the two categories separately, and then to weigh the one against the other. But in other branches of the subject it is common to reckon costs net of benefits. An example is the proposition, advanced in many standard texts, that *social cost excludes rent*. What is meant is that the increased rents earned by factors whose prices have risen in the face of increased demand for their services represent mere transfers of wealth, not costs to society.

If a project creates a demand for labour and other factors that results in higher wages and prices, these of course mean higher private costs for the entrepreneur who initiates it. But they are offset by negative external costs in the form of benefits to the factors (or their owners). The two balance out, so that when private and external costs are summed there is no net contribution to social cost. The increased rents enter into both private and external costs (with opposite signs), and – as the proposition says – not into the cost to society.

When costs borne by individuals are not costs to society it is often proper to call them *losses*, and their counterpart *gains*. If I own a shop next to yours and take away your trade by cutting prices, you will suffer a loss that is counterbalanced by the gain to consumers and my profit (if there is any) on the extra sales. Gains and losses due to price changes are not costs to society.

Implicit in the assertion that price changes do not give rise to social costs is the assumption that we are dealing with a closed economy. In an open economy, a movement in the international terms of trade may either impose real costs on nationals or enable them to earn rents at the expense of foreigners. Also implicit in the assertion is the assumption that the problems of measurement and aggregation have been solved.

(3) *Short and long run costs.* When measuring costs it is essential to state the time period under consideration. There is a tendency for most to be lower in the long run than in the short, and this applies with especial force to external ones. Injured parties are at first taken by surprise, but then will try to reduce costs imposed on them by adjusting their operations to the new circumstances. If the laws of society are such that they have a claim against the initiator of the activity that precipitated the external costs, the victims may succeed in getting him to modify his actions in a way that reduces the costs still further. Of course the *sum* of private and external costs (i.e. the social cost) may not be reduced to the same extent – but that is another matter.

An old example (Pigou, 1932, p. 134) can be adapted to illustrate the point. If sparks from a railway engine increase the probability of fire damage to crops planted by a farmer whose land the line traverses, a sudden doubling of the number of trains will impose additional external costs on him. Over time he may be able to mitigate these by planting evergreens near the line, or leaving a strip of land fallow. If the law allows, he may be able to sue the railway company for any damage actually caused, or claim compensation for loss of profit on land put to inferior use. This may eventually persuade the company to fit spark suppressors to the locomotives or reduce the number of trains. These factors all combine to make it probable that external costs will decrease with time.

In an example such as this, where only two parties are involved, negotiation might be expected to be a real alternative to legal action. The division of the gains would of course depend on the bargaining strength of the negotiators, which would in part by determined by their rights, but the outcome would be much the same: a reduction in the sum of private and external costs until a further reduction would bring about a greater reduction in benefits. As negotiation is always time-consuming, one would again expect the result to be a social cost that was lower in the long run than the short.

(4) *Aggregation.* When we add external costs to private costs to get social cost we are adding costs borne by different people. In the last resort this amounts to saying that, all else being equal, a cost of $10 borne by A represents a greater cost to society than one of $9 borne by B, no matter who A and B might be. There are really only two possible justifications for this procedure.

The first is along *utilitarian* lines, with full interpersonal comparability and an assumption that the marginal utility of money is the same to everyone. Lower social cost then represents a lower loss of aggregate satisfaction.

The second is in terms of *compensation tests* (Graaff, 1957, ch. 5). Very briefly, these tests use as a criterion of social desirability the possibility of those who benefit from some change being able to compensate those who lose by it, without themselves becoming losers. Obviously, the lower the sum of private and external costs, the greater the possibility of being able to compensate those who bear them.

Neither justification is entirely satisfactory. Utilitarianism still has its adherents, but few among them would lightly assume that the marginal utility of money was the same to rich and poor. And the *possibility* of compensation means very little unless the compensation is actually carried out. (What does it help to say that, although several men will starve, the cost to society is low, because they *could* be given sufficient food to prevent their starving?) If, on the other hand, the compensation is paid, price changes can lead to *reversals* of the sort analysed by Scitovsky (1941). The social cost of activity A may then be lower than that of B before compensation, higher after it. Choosing the activity with the lower cost entails a prior choice between two distributions of wealth. Otherwise we go round in circles.

II. APPLICATIONS

The principal application of the notion of social cost is in the field of Cost–Benefit Analysis. Valuation problems abound. How, for instance, does one value the cost of a human life, if the probability is that an extra one will be sacrificed when savings are made on safety or design specifications for a new highway? And how does one value other goods for which there are no markets? (In practice one uses prices in related markets; but these are what they are precisely because there are no prices for the goods one is trying to value!) Cost–Benefit analysts handle these matters with great skill, and if they were the only problems they had to contend with, would emerge with great credit.

But the theory also has to face the aggregation problems just mentioned. The utilitarian approach tends to use 'distributional weights' to indicate the analyst's rough assessment of differences in the marginal utility of money to different people. In this way $1 borne by a poor man can be made to contribute more to social cost than $2 borne by someone rich. It is almost fair to say that social cost then becomes what the analyst wants it to be.

Those who use the compensation-test approach tend to hope that price changes following hypothetical compensation would not be large enough to bring about embarrassing reversals. The matter cannot be disposed of that easily. Comparing social costs with social benefits to determine social choice is an exercise subject to all the impossibility theorems of Social Choice Theory. Reversals that give rise to intransitive choices can be expected unless our assumptions are rich enough to exclude them. Utilitarians recognize this when they boldly allocate distributional weights. Without a similar boldness those who base their analysis on the possibility of compensation leave the significance of the costs they calculate in considerable doubt.

Social cost theory has also been used in the analysis of *market failure*. Without too much regard for the niceties of definition, the older theory (Pigou, 1932) went something like this. Maximization of the national dividend requires the equality of marginal social costs and benefits. Optimizing behaviour in markets secures the equality of marginal private costs and benefits. Unless the two sets of costs and benefits coincide, market behaviour will not maximize the national dividend. Divergences between private and social costs (and benefits) are the cause of failure. Various measures are available to correct these divergences.

A more modern statement would be that a market fails when it clears without all mutually advantageous bargains having been struck. This is most likely to happen when a transaction affects parties other than those directly involved in its negotiation. The existence of these external costs and benefits entails a divergence between private and social costs and benefits. (This follows directly from the definition.)

The more modern version brings out the central problem. *Why* are the 'other parties' not directly involved in the negotiations? Even if they have no legal standing (which, if property rights are clearly defined, they may well have), they can never be worse off negotiating. The answer, of course, lies in *transaction costs*. Bargaining is a costly and time-consuming procedure, especially when large numbers of people are involved. In addition, to get full benefit from deals struck, it may be necessary to take expensive steps to exclude freeloaders. (I may make it worth my neighbour's while not to park in front of my house, but unless I can stop others using the vacant space it will help me very little.) Any analysis of market failure that does not explicitly recognize the role played by the costs of bargaining is severely flawed.

If bargaining were costless and without legal impediment, optimizing behaviour by market participants would automatically imply that all mutually advantageous bargains were struck. With zero transaction costs, market failure is impossible. This result, often attributed to Coase (1960), has been described as the Say's Law of Welfare Economics (Calabresi, 1968). But it might be fairer to reserve that accolade for the version of it that says that, if a bargain is *not* struck, it can only be because optimizing agents, in their wisdom, have decided that the transaction cost would exceed the benefit. It would be nice if the world were really like that.

A treatment of social cost that deals adequately with the costs of bargaining has not yet been developed. That, and the unsolved problems of aggregation, should make us wary of using the concept without the necessary circumspection.

BIBLIOGRAPHY

Calabresi, G. 1968. Transaction costs, resource allocation and liability rules: a comment. *Journal of Law and Economics* 11, April, 67–73.
Coase, R.H. 1960. The problem of social cost. *Journal of Law and Economics* 3(1), October, 1–44.

Graaff, J. de V. 1957. *Theoretical Welfare Economics*. Cambridge: Cambridge University Press.

Pigou, A.C. 1932. *The Economics of Welfare*. 4th edn, London: Macmillan; New York: St Martin's Press, 1952.

Scitovsky, T. 1941. A note on welfare propositions in economics *Review of Economic Studies* 9(1), 77–88.

Specie-flow Mechanism

WILLIAM R. ALLEN

The 'specie-flow mechanism' is an analytic version of automatic, or market, adjustment of the balance of international payments. In competitive markets with specie-standard institutions, behaviour will lead to national price levels and income flows consistent with equilibrium in the international accounts, commonly interpreted in this context to mean zero trade balances.

The classic exposition of the mechanism, for the better part of two centuries all but universally accepted, at least as a first approximation, was provided by David Hume in a 1752 essay, 'Of the Balance of Trade'. While it is appropriate to associate the essence of the model with Hume, all the ingredients of Hume's argument had long been available. There were even notable prior attempts to fit the analytic pieces into a self-contained model. Further, even if we give to Hume all the considerable credit due to his systematic, compact statement, his version is not the whole of the specie-flow mechanism; and the specie-flow mechanism is not the whole analysis of balance of payments adjustment.

Hume's presentation is a simple application of the quantity theory of money in a setting of international trade and its financing. With a pure 100 per cent reserve gold standard, and beginning with balance in the international accounts, a decrease in the money stock of country A results in a directly proportionate fall in its price level, which is also a decrease relative to the initially unaffected price levels of other countries; as country A's price level falls, consumer response, in Hume's account, will reduce A's imports and increase its exports; when the exchange rate is bid to the gold point, the export trade balance will be financed by gold inflow, which will raise prices in A and lower prices abroad until the international price differentials and net trade flows are eliminated. The line of causation runs from changes in money to changes in prices to changes in net trade flows to international movements of gold that eliminate the earlier price differentials and thereby correct the trade imbalance and stop the shipment of gold. In equilibrium, the distribution of gold among countries (and regions within countries) yields national (and regional) price levels consistent with zero trade balances.

655

This theory of trade equilibrium links with the Ricardian theory of production specialization. In a comparative advantage model of two countries, two commodities, and labour input, country A has absolute advantages of different degrees in both goods. To have two-way trade, the wage rate of country A must be greater than that abroad, within the wage-ratio range specified by the proportions of A's productive superiority in the two goods. Gold will flow until the international wage ratio yields domestic prices that equate total import and export values.

The conclusion that trade imbalances, and thus gold flows, cannot long obtain was in fundamental contrast to the mercantilistic emphasis on persistent promotion of an export balance and indefinite accumulation of gold. Still, the mercantilists decidedly associated gold inflows with export surpluses of goods and services; a good many writers had posited a direct relation between the money stock and the price level; similarly, it had been indicated that relative national price level changes would affect trade flows. However, while we should bow to such predecessors of Hume as Isaac Gervaise (1720) and Richard Cantillon (1734) and perhaps nod to Gerard de Malynes (1601) for attempts to construct adjustment models, Hume put the elements together with unmatched elegance and awareness of implication – and influence.

Hume's version was specifically a *price*-specie-flow mechanism, with the prices being national price levels (and exchange rates). Even as a price mechanism, the model has problems.

While it is reasonable to presume that price levels will move in the same directions (even if not in the same proportions) as the huge changes in the money stock envisioned by Hume, there remain questions of the impact on import and export expenditures. Vertical demand schedules in country A for imports and in other countries for A's exports would leave the physical amounts of imports and exports unresponsive to price changes. If, following Hume, we upset the initial equilibrium by a large decrease in money and thus in prices in country A, foreign expenditure on A's goods will fall proportionally with the fall in A's prices. The import balance of A will be financed with gold outflow, resulting in a further fall in A's prices and export value and an increase in prices abroad and in A's import expenditure. The gold flow, rather than correcting the trade flow, will increase the import trade balance of A when demand elasticities are zero (or sufficiently small). The import and export demand (and supply) elasticity conditions required for price (including exchange rate) changes to be equilibrating – conditions which are empirically realistic – came much later to be summarized in the 'Marshall–Lerner condition'. Under the most unfavourable circumstances of infinite supply elasticities and initially balanced trade, all that is required for stability is that the arithmetic sum of the elasticities of foreign demand for A's exports and of A's demand for imports be greater than unity.

Aside from the nicety of specifying elasticity conditions for stability, is it appropriate to couch the model in terms of diverging national price levels or of changes in a country's import prices compared to its export prices? Suppose country A has a commodity export balance, resulting perhaps from a shift in international demands reflecting changed preferences in favour of A's goods or imposition of a tariff by A or a foreign crop failure. As gold flows in, A's expenditures expand and prices are expected to rise. Prices of A's *domestic* goods (which do not enter foreign trade) do rise; but prices of *internationally* traded goods are affected little, if at all, for the increase in A's demand for such goods is countered by decrease in demand for them in gold-losing countries. Consumers in A, facing the domestic–international price divergence, shift to now relatively cheapened international goods (imports and A-exportables) from more expensive domestic goods, thus increasing import volume and value and also absorption of exportables. Producers in A shift out of international goods into domestic, thus reducing exports and expanding imports. Corresponding, but opposite, substitutions and shifts are diffused among the other countries. These respective domestic adjustments in consumption and production would continue until the gold flow ceases and the trade imbalance is corrected.

Substantial modern empirical research, however, is more supportive of Hume's changes in the terms of trade or of transitory divergences in relative prices of traded and non-traded goods than of the assumed invariant applicability of the equilibrium 'law of one price' commonly adopted in the modern 'monetary approach' to the balance of payments.

When gold flows into country A, portfolio equilibria of individuals and firms are upset, with cash balances now in excess. People try to spend away redundant balances. Expenditure rises and money income becomes larger. With greater income, demands for goods – including foreign goods – increase: at any given commodity price, quantity demanded has become larger. Import quantities and values rise. Changes in money give rise abroad to opposite portofolio adjustments and changes of income, thereby decreasing A's exports. In all this, there are some changes (upward in A and downward abroad) in prices of domestic goods and production factors, but the adjustment process entails income changes as well as price changes.

Some such role of changes in money income and demand schedules was noted – in different contexts and with different degrees of clarity and emphasis – by many writers in the 19th and early 20th centuries. But single-minded emphasis on income, with little or no explicit role for the money stock and prices, came only with application to balance of payments adjustment of the national income theory of J. M. Keynes. However, such application – with its regalia of marginal propensities and secondary, supplemental repercussions of multipliers – is not contingent on, or uniquely associated with, an international gold standard. Further, neglect of money in the foreign-trade multiplier analysis is a grievous omission. Equilibrium in the income model is characterized by equating of the flows of income leakages (saving, tax payments, imports) and income injections (investment, government expenditure, exports). But such equality of total leakages and injections permits a continuing trade imbalance. And a trade imbalance financed by a gold flow – or accompanied by money change generally – leads to further change in income; that is, income has not reached a genuine equilibrium.

The actual world, even with the classical gold standard in the generation prior to World War I, has not conformed well in institutions and processes with the construct of Hume. A world generally of irredeemable paper money and universally of demand deposits along with fractional-reserve banking and discretionary money policy – a world including the International Monetary Fund arrangement of indefinitely pegged exchange rates – has relied on selected adjustment procedures more than on automatic adjustment mechanisms. So Hume's model in its own terms is inadequate and in important empirical respects is even inappropriate. But it provided analytical coherency and expositional emphasis in an early stage of a discussion which continues to evolve.

BIBLIOGRAPHY

Blaug, M. 1985. *Economic Theory in Retrospect*. Cambridge: Cambridge University Press.

Darby, M. and Lothian, J. 1983. *The International Transmission of Inflation*. Chicago: University of Chicago Press.

Fausten, D. 1979. The Humean origin of the contemporary monetary approach to the balance of payments. *Quarterly Journal of Economics* 93, November, 655–73.

Rotwein, E. (ed.) 1970. *David Hume: Writings on Economics*. Madison: University of Wisconsin Press.

Yeager, L. 1976. *International Monetary Relations: Theory, History, and Policy*. 2nd edn, New York: Harper & Row.

Sports

JAMES QUIRK

Professional team sports leagues and amateur sports associations typically operate as cartels in input and output markets. While details differ from sport to sport, most professional leagues follow the pattern of baseball, whose institutional structure was first described in the seminal paper by Rottenberg (1956). There have also been studies of the National Football League (Neale, 1964), the Professional Golfers Association (Cottle, 1981), cricket (Schofield, 1982), English soccer (Bird, 1982; Sloane, 1971; Wiseman, 1977), the National Hockey League (Jones, 1969), Scottish soccer (Vamplew, 1982) and Australian football (Dabschek, 1975). The literature on amateur sports is less extensive, but includes some interesting work on US college athletics (Koch, 1973). Basic sources of background information include several Congressional studies (US Congress, 1952a, 1952b, 1957, 1972) and a Brookings volume (Noll, 1974a).

There is of course a widespread and growing public interest in sports (see Horowitz, 1974), which helps to account for the attraction of economists to studies of the industry, and especially of economists concerned with cartel behaviour. Moreover, professional sports leagues are among the few cartels for which detailed current and historical information on cartel rules and decision making is publicly available, along with a wealth of data on inputs, outputs, and financial measures such as attendance, ticket prices, television and radio revenues and sales prices of franchises. The ambiguous antitrust status of sports leagues has led to a long history of court cases in which even more information about the workings of the leagues has been made public.

Organized baseball in the United States was the first organization to develop a detailed set of rules governing the economic operations of a sports league, and subsequent organizations in football, hockey, basketball, soccer and other sports have simply adapted the baseball rules to their own situations. Cartel rules in each of these sports have evolved over time in response to competition from other leagues, the emergence of player unions, changes in legislation relating to the league, court cases and cheating by cartel members. There have been changes as well in response to technological innovations from within a league, such as the invention of the farm system by Branch Rickey, and Bill Veeck's discovery of tax sheltering from team ownership; or innovations from without, such as radio and commercial and pay television. Davis (1974) presents a history of the evolution of cartel rules in baseball in response to such factors.

Following the lead of organized baseball, in all professional sports leagues restrictions on input and output markets include the granting of monopoly rights to teams to present league games within designated geographic areas, and the adoption of gate-sharing rules and the sharing of television and radio receipts. There are also rules that regulate the entry of new teams into a league and govern the sale of existing teams or the transfer of a team from one geographic location to another. Of particular importance are the restrictions on player mobility through the so-called 'reserve clause' or 'option clause' ('retain and transfer' in English soccer) in player contracts, combined with waiver rules governing the disposition of veteran players and drafting rules governing rights to new players. As the reserve clause was interpreted in baseball for almost a century, a player signing his first contract with a team was bound to that team for the remainder of his playing career or until the contract was sold, in which case he was bound to the team buying the contract. Other sports placed a less stringent interpretation on the clause. Under pressure from competitive leagues, player unions and the courts, the restrictions on player mobility were weakened substantially from about 1975 on.

These league rules reduced the bargaining power of players in wage negotiations, created local monopolies, limited entry into the industry and redistributed the income of the cartel among the cartel members. Estimates of the monopsony effects of the reserve clause in baseball range from those by Scully (1974b), who found that player salaries in the late 1960s averaged only between 10 and 20 per cent of their net marginal revenue products, to Medoff's (1976) estimate that salaries during the same period were approximately 50 per cent of net marginal revenue products. These estimates were constructed from theoretical models relating player performance to team revenues, and can be compared with later data on the effects of the introduction of free agency on player salaries. Average salaries in baseball rose from $51,000 in 1976 to $76,000 in 1977, the first year under free agency (Hill and Spellman, 1983), and to $100,000 in 1978 (Lehn, 1982). During negotiations preceding the one-day baseball strike of 1985, it was reported in the press that the average salary for the 1985 season was $340,000.

Most if not all of the rules of sports leagues would be violations of the antitrust laws if adopted by other industries, but baseball has the benefit of an exemption from those laws through a Supreme Court decision (*Federal Baseball Club* v. *National League*, 1922), reaffirmed in *Curtis C. Flood* v. *Bowie K. Kuhn* (1972), while for other sports there have been exemptions for certain specific actions through Congressional legislation (e.g. AFL–NFL merger, 1966; joint negotiations over television contracts, 1961). When sports leagues have been attacked in the courts or Congress or in the public press because of such rules (or actions taken under the rules), the leagues' argument has been that in the absence of such restrictions on economic competition, rich teams or big-city teams would acquire a disproportionate share of the best players, resulting in an imbalance of competition on the playing field that would ultimately destroy the league. The validity of this argument has been a central topic in the literature on the economics of sports.

Rottenberg was the first to show its invalidity under the assumption of profit-maximizing owners, arguing that big-city team owners would have economic incentives to limit the quality of their teams (and so help to maintain a degree of competitive balance within the league) even if players were free to sell their services to the highest bidder in a competitive labour market. El Hodiri and Quirk (1971, 1974) presented a formal model of a sports league, in which the profit-maximization assumption was used to prove that, so long as player contracts can be freely bought and sold among team owners, the distribution of playing strengths in a league is the same under the 'reserve clause' as it would be under free competition for players; that big-city teams on average will be stronger than small-city teams; that the distributions of playing strengths is independent of the gate-sharing rules; and that the distribution is one that maximizes total profits for the league. Combined with rules for the drafting of new players according to reverse order of finish, the 'reserve clause' was shown to redistribute income from players to owners, and to redistribute income from big-city to small-city teams. Certain of the El Hodiri–Quirk results can be viewed as applications of the Coase Theorem.

The profit-maximization assumption was challenged by Davenport (1969), who argued that team owners also obtain utility from winning *per se*. Dabschek (1975), Schofield (1982), Sloane (1971) and Vamplew (1982) presented rather convincing evidence that the profit-maximization assumption does not hold in cricket or in British soccer or in Australian football, where few if any teams operate at a profit, instead being financed through contributions by their owners and supporters. (Since teams can always costlessly withdraw from a league rather than operate at a loss, survival of a team that loses money contradicts the profit-maximization assumption.) While this evidence weakens the economists' argument that the reserve clause is not needed to maintain competition on the playing field, the same studies also showed that leagues in these sports have survived over long periods despite a dominance by a few big-city teams that is even more pronounced than in US sports leagues. Taking a different tack, Canes (1974) showed that one of the beneficial effects of the reserve clause is that it restricts the level of team quality, which, from an allocative standpoint, would be excessive if a free market in labour services operated.

Empirical studies of the demand for sports contests indicate that certain sports – baseball (Noll, 1974b), English soccer (Bird, 1982) – are inferior goods, and that price-inelastic demands for sports contests are also observed. Estimation of the demand function for sports contests is subject to the two facts that the marginal cost of presenting a game is close to zero and that teams operate with fixed stadium capacities. Ignoring stochastic elements, these two facts argue for an observed elasticity of demand of unity, except for sold-out games. It is also clear that even when a sports league maintains a monopoly in its sport (historically the most common situation, providing some evidence for Neale's claim that sports leagues are natural monopolies), it is still subject to competition from leagues in other sports and from suppliers of other recreational services. Noll, among others, argues that this makes the price elasticity of demand for league contests higher in big-city than in small-city markets, thus limiting the monopoly power of big-city owners and increasing their incentives to field winning teams.

Because production relations are relatively simple in sports and data on inputs and outputs are readily available, a number of studies have been done on the relation between pay and performance in the various sports leagues, on managerial efficiency, and related matters (see Fort and Noll, 1984; Porter and Scully, 1982). Likewise, because of the same factors, questions relating to the existence of racial discrimination are somewhat easier to formulate and resolve in this industry than in others. The pioneering work in this field was the study on racial discrimination in baseball by Pascal and Rapping (1972), followed by work also on baseball by Scully (1974a) and later work on basketball (Vining and Kerrigan, 1978). This work provides rather strong evidence for the presence of discrimination in baseball, with the case less clear in basketball; on the other hand, those baseball owners who were the first to employ blacks benefited from this decision (Gwartney and Haworth, 1974).

Sports has proved to be a fertile field for other applied economic studies as well. Cassing and Douglas (1980) claimed to find evidence of a 'winner's curse' resulting from the free agency auction mechanism that operates in baseball. De Brock and Roth (1981) used the Nash bargaining model to explain the economic rationale underlying the union and management strategies in the baseball strike of 1980, one in which the management had strike insurance that paid $1 million per day for 50 days of a strike, following a two-week grace period. The strike was settled just as the insurance benefits were being exhausted. Lehn (1982) looked at the pattern of contracts that were signed under free agency in the context of the principal–agent model and the allocation of risk as between players and owners. As the principal–agent model would predict, a change from the reserve clause to the long-term contracts signed under free agency has led to a marked (25 to 33 per cent) increase in the time spent on the disability list by players under long-term contracts.

Koch's (1973) work on college athletics provides an almost textbook example of the problems which beset a cartel (the NCAA) with a large and diverse group of members, limited resources for policing and enforcing its regulations (which cover the recruiting, support and maintenance of academic standards of student athletes), and subject to outside competition from organizations such as the Amateur Athletic Union (AAU) and the US Olympic committee. He argues that in amateur athletics as in professional team sports, the economic theory of cartels provides a predictive as well as an explanatory framework for analysing the behaviour of the governing organization.

BIBLIOGRAPHY

Bird, P. 1982. The demand for league football. *Applied Economics* 14, 637–49.

Canes, M. 1974. The social benefits of restrictions on team quality. In *Government and the Sports Business*, ed. R. Noll, Washington, DC: Brookings.

Cassing, J. and Douglas, R. 1980. Implications of the auction mechanism in baseball's free agent draft. *Southern Economic Journal* 48(1), 110–21.

Cottle, P. 1981. Economics of the PGA Tour. *Social Science Quarterly* 62(4), 721–34.

Dabschek, B. 1975. The wage determination process for sportsmen. *Economic Record* 51, 52–64.

Davenport, D. 1969. Collusive competition in major league baseball: its theory and institutional development. *American Economist* 13(2), 6–30.

Davis, L. 1974. Self regulation in baseball, 1909–71. In Noll (1974a).

De Brock, L. and Roth, A. 1981. Strike two: labor–management negotiations in major league baseball. *Bell Journal of Economics* 12(2), 413–25.

El Hodiri, M. and Quirk, J. 1971. An economic model of a professional sports league. *Journal of Political Economy* 79, 1302–19.

El Hodiri, M. and Quirk, J. 1974. The economic theory of a professional sports league. In Noll (1974a).

Fort, R. and Noll, R. 1984. Pay and performance in baseball: modeling regulars, reserves and expansion. SS Working Paper, Caltech.

Gwartney, J. and Haworth, C. 1974. Employer costs and discrimination: the case of baseball. *Journal of Political Economy* 82(4), 873–81.

Hill, J. and Spellman, W. 1983. Professional baseball: the reserve clause and salary structure. *Industrial Relations* 22(1), 1–19.

Horowitz, I. 1974. Sports broadcasting. In Noll (1974a).

Jones, J. 1969. The economics of the National Hockey League. *Canadian Journal of Economics* 2, February, 1–20.

Koch, J. 1973. A troubled cartel: the NCAA. *Law and Contemporary Problems* 38(1), 135–50.

Lehn, K. 1982. Property rights, risk sharing, and player disability in major league baseball. *Journal of Law and Economics* 45, 343–66.

Medoff, M. 1976. On monopsonistic exploitation in professional baseball. *Quarterly Journal of Economics and Business* 16(2), 113–21.

Neale, W. 1964. The peculiar economics of professional sports. *Quarterly Journal of Economics* 78(1), 1–14.

Noll, R. (ed.) 1974a. *Government and the Sports Business*. Washington, DC: Brookings.

Noll, R. 1974b. Attendance and price setting. In Noll (1974a).

Pascal, A. and Rapping, L. 1972. The economics of racial discrimination in organized baseball. In *Racial Discrimination in Economic Life*, ed. A. Pascal, Lexington, Mass.: Heath.

Porter, P. and Scully, G. 1982. Measuring managerial efficiency: the case of baseball. *Southern Economic Journal* 48(3), 642–50.

Rottenberg, S. 1956. The baseball players' labor market. *Journal of Political Economy* 64, 242–58.

Schofield, J. 1982. The development of first class cricket in England: an economic analysis. *Journal of Industrial Economics* 30(4), 337–60.

Scully, G. 1974a. Discrimination: the case of baseball. In Noll (1974a).

Scully, G. 1974b. Pay and performance in major league baseball. *American Economic Review* 64(6), 915–30.

Sloane, P. 1971. The economics of professional football: football club as utility maximizer. *Scottish Journal of Political Economy* 18, 121–45.

US Congress. 1952a. House Committee on the Judiciary. Subcommittee on Study of Monopoly Power. Study of Monopoly Power, Part 6, Organized Baseball. Hearings. 82 Cong. 1 sess. Washington: Government Printing Office.

US Congress. 1952b. Organized Baseball. Report of the Subcommittee on Study of Monopoly Power. House Report 2002. 82 Cong. 2 sess. Washington: Government Printing Office.

US Congress. 1957. Antitrust Subcommittee. Organized Professional Team Sports. Hearings. 85 Cong. 1 sess. Washington: Government Printing Office.

US Congress. 1972. Professional Basketball. Hearing. 92 Cong. 1 sess. (Part 1) and 2 sess. (Part 2). Washington: Government Printing Office.

Vamplew, W. 1982. The economics of a sports industry: Scottish gate money football, 1890–1914. *Economic History Review* 48(3), 549–67.

Vining, R., Jr. and Kerrigan, J.F. 1978. An application of the Lexis Ratio to the detection of racial quotas in professional sports: a note. *American Economist* 22(2), Fall, 71–5.

Wiseman, N.C. 1977. The economics of football. *Lloyds Bank Review* 123, January, 29–43.

Terms of Trade

RONALD FINDLAY

The two most basic questions about international trade are: What goods will each country export? and What will be the ratios at which the exports of one country exchange for those of its trading partners?

The first problem is that of 'comparative advantage'; the second that of the 'terms of trade', which is the subject of the present contribution. David Ricardo, in chapter 7 of the *Principles*, gave a definitive answer to the first question and went a long way towards the solution of the second, though it was J.S. Mill and Alfred Marshall who eventually gave the complete answer.

In the following discussion it will be convenient to assume, for simplicity, that there is only a single good exported and imported, and sometimes even that there is only a single factor of production, such as labour of a given quality. In practice, of course, we would have to use index numbers for unit values and physical volumes of exports and imports, giving rise to all the familiar problems.

CONCEPTS AND DEFINITIONS. There are a number of alternative concepts and associated statistical measures of the terms of trade. The most prominent are listed below:

(i) The *commodity* or *net barter* terms of trade. This is by far the most common meaning of the term, and is usually what is meant when the expression is used without any qualifying prefix. In principle it is the relative price of the 'exportable' in terms of the 'importable', that is the number of units of the latter obtainable for each unit of the former. It has the dimensions of 'nine waistcoat buttons for a copper disc' in the words of Lewis Carroll's 'Song of the Aged, Aged Man' in *Through the Looking Glass*, words that D.H. Robertson (1952, ch. 13) used as the motto for a delightful essay on the terms of trade. In statistical practice the commodity terms of trade are calculated as changes in the ratio of an export price index to an import price index, relative to a base year.

(ii) The *gross barter* terms of trade is a concept introduced by Taussig. It is the ratio of the *volume* of imports to the *volume* of exports. It coincides with the commodity terms of trade when trade is balanced, that is, there are no international loans or unrequited transfers. A deficit in the trade balance would cause the gross barter terms to be more favourable than the commodity or net barter terms and vice versa. This should not, of course, be interpreted as a trade deficit being necessarily preferable to balanced trade, since the additional imports now may have to be paid for by future trade surpluses.

(iii) The *income* terms of trade, sometimes also referred to as 'the purchasing power of exports'. It corresponds to the commodity terms of trade multiplied by the volume of exports. This is equal to the volume of imports under balanced trade, and exceeds or falls short of it if there is a surplus or deficit respectively in the balance of trade. In other words, it is the level of imports in real terms that can be sustained by current export earnings.

(iv) The *single factoral* terms of trade. This refers to the marginal or average productivity of a factor in the export sector, evaluated in terms of the imported good at the commodity terms of trade. The concept is meaningful for any single factor or production taken separately, though it is sometimes defined in a non-operational fashion in the literature as referring to 'units of productive power'.

(v) The *double factoral* terms of trade. This is an attempt to go behind the international exchange of commodities to the productive factors that are 'embodied' in them. Thus, if units are chosen such that a unit of labour in England produces a unit of cloth, and a unit of labour in Portugal produces a unit of wine, commodity terms of trade of say five wine to one cloth would mean that a unit of English labour exchanges implicitly for five units of Portuguese labour in international trade.

The first three concepts of the terms of trade are all measurable in practice, subject to the usual index number problems. The commodity terms of trade are routinely calculated for most countries in the world by international agencies such as the UN, the World Bank and the IMF. The gross barter and income terms of trade have also been calculated for several countries.

The single factoral terms of trade, for any particular factor, can also be computed. Indeed it corresponds exactly to the concept of 'shadow prices' for primary inputs that has recently been developed in the literature on cost–benefit analysis in distorted open economies. Thus it could indicate what the value of a worker or an acre of land, engaged say in the coffee export sector, was worth in terms of imported food at the commodity terms of trade. This could serve as a valuable guide to resource allocation, by comparing it with what these resources could produce in the domestic food sector.

The double factoral terms of trade, however, is either misleading if it is computed for any particular single factor in a world of more than one scarce input, or non-operational if defined amorphously as applying to units of 'productive power'. The concept is regarded by more than one economist as fundamental, and no less an authority than D.H. Robertson, in the essay referred to, called it the 'true' terms of trade. Equally eminent authorities, such as Haberler (1955) and Viner (1937), have, however, been more sceptical.

The concept has recently come to the fore again, after many decades of neglect, in connection with the theories of A. Emmanuel (1972) on 'unequal exchange' in trade between high-wage and low-wage countries, a form of 'exploitation' of the latter by the former. It is possible to interpret Emmanuel as saying that it is only when the double factoral terms of trade are equal to unity that there is no unequal exchange. As Emmanuel himself acknowledges, however, his argument requires equal capital intensity in the export sectors of the trading partners. We may all agree with Robert Burns that 'a man's a man for a' that' in terms of dignity and spiritual worth. It is another thing to say that skill or physical capital, both accumulated at some cost, should count for nothing, and that the only 'fair' exchange is one that takes place according to the simple labour theory of value.

Furthermore, it is clear that the commodity terms of trade can improve while the factoral terms worsen and vice versa. Thus suppose initially that one day's labour in 'North' and 'South' produces a unit of steel and coffee respectively and that the commodity terms of trade was one steel for one coffee. Suppose now that one worker in the North produces three steel, while his counterpart in the South still produces only one coffee. Let the commodity terms of trade now be two steel for one coffee. The commodity terms have doubled in favour of the South, while its factoral terms have deteriorated to two-thirds instead of unity. Which situation would the South prefer?

FUNDAMENTAL DETERMINANTS. Ricardo did not determine the terms of trade explicitly in his analysis in chapter 7 of the *Principles*. He was only able to show that the equilibrium value would be between the comparative cost ratios of the two countries, specified by the linear technologies. It was John Stuart Mill who solved the problem by his numerical example of 'reciprocal supply and demand', later refined by Marshall through the geometric device of the 'offer curves' showing the excess supplies and demands of the two goods in each country as functions of the terms of trade, the equilibrium value of which would be determined by setting world excess supply equal to zero. Marshall demonstrated the possibility of multiple equilibria and also established a criterion for stability of equilibrium that is in use to this day, in the form of the so-called Marshall–Lerner condition that the sum of the import demand elasticities has to be greater than unity.

In modern terms it is the preferences of the consumers that have to be introduced to close the model. Once these are introduced the equilibrium value(s) of the terms of trade are determined as a function of these preferences, the labour endowments and the technical coefficients of production. The subsequent development of the literature has generalized Ricardo's analysis to any number of goods, factors and countries and to variable instead of fixed technical coefficients. The determination of the terms of trade is thus technically nothing other than that of finding the equilibrium vector(s) of relative prices for general equilibrium models in which there is a world market for tradeable goods and internationally mobile factors, and national markets for non-traded goods and internationally immobile factors.

In addition to constituting a central problem for the theory of international trade in its 'positive' aspect, the terms of trade plays if anything an even more critical role in the 'normative' dimension of evaluating the 'gains from trade'. It is crucial to keep these two facets of the terms of trade conceptually distinct, though of course they are both involved in almost every theoretical or policy problem. Another essential distinction is between the terms of trade as an *exogenously* determined parameter, as in the 'small' open economy models, and as an *endogenously* determined variable, the equilibrium value of which is altered by some change in circumstances or parameters, such as factor endowments, technology or tastes. Much confusion has been caused in the literature by failure to bear these basic distinctions in mind at all times.

In the realm of positive theory, the terms of trade generally appear in comparative statics exercises as the key dependent variable, upon which the effect of some exogenous shock is sought. As an example, consider the effect of a switch in the composition of home demand in favour of the imported good. At constant terms of trade this would create an excess demand for the imported good. Assuming Walrasian stability, this must lead to a deterioration of the home country's terms of trade for the world market to return to equilibrium.

The famous 'transfer problem' is another example of this sort of comparative statics exercise. The transfer of purchasing power, at constant terms of trade, would lead to an excess supply in the world market of the transferor's exportable, if the home propensity to consume this good is greater than that of the recipient country (the so-called 'classical presumption'). Thus the terms of trade of the transferor would deteriorate, given Walrasian stability, imposing a 'secondary burden' on the transferor.

Finally, we may consider the effects of economic growth, in the form of exogenous changes in factor endowment or technical innovations in either sector, a literature that was stimulated by Hicks's (1953) inaugural lecture on the 'dollar shortage'. Here again the analysis consists in finding the effect of the change on excess supply or demand at constant terms of trade, and thus obtaining the direction of movement in the terms of trade necessary to clear the market, assuming stability in the Walrasian sense.

WELFARE EFFECTS. All of these exercises in positive theory of course have welfare consequences for both trading partners. In the case of the two-country transfer problem the transferor is worse off, even if the terms of trade were to move in its favour, while the recipient is better off, even if the terms of trade were to turn against it. In the case of a shift in the composition of home demand towards imports the welfare of the trading partner will rise under normal conditions (made more precise in the next paragraph) as a result of this improvement in its terms of trade. If growth in one country creates an excess demand for imports at constant terms of trade, its passive partner will also benefit from the resulting increase in the relative price of its export.

In the last two cases a country experiences an *exogenous* improvement in its terms of trade, with no alteration in its own preferences, technology or factor endowment. Must its welfare necessarily increase as a result? The answer in general is yes, unless there are domestic distortions such as monopoly or monopsony in product or factor markets, exogenous wage differentials or real factor-price rigidities. A simple example of how it is possible for a country to experience a *loss* in welfare as a result of an *improvement* in its commodity terms of trade can be constructed as follows. Suppose that domestic production is completely specialized on the export good and that the real wage is fixed in terms of the imported good. At constant employment and therefore constant marginal physical productivity of labour in terms of the exported good the real wage would be lower in terms of the imported good because of the improvement in the terms of trade. This will induce a decline in employment and output until the marginal physical product of labour rises in the same proportion as the relative price of the imported good has fallen, so that the original level of the real wage is restored. The terms of trade improvement, given employment and output, increases welfare, but the contraction in these variables induced by the change in the terms of trade reduces welfare. This negative effect can clearly be sufficient to outweigh the positive effect of the terms of trade gain considered in isolation, since the counteraction can be very sharp if the marginal productivity of labour schedule is assumed to be sufficiently elastic.

Haberler (1955, p. 30), in a characteristically penetrating and judicious discussion of the subject, has stated that 'other things being equal an improvement in the commodity terms of trade does imply an increase in real national income'. As our analysis of the example in the previous paragraphs shows, however, even such a cautious formulation needs to be interpreted with care. It would obviously be a mistake to compound the welfare effects of an exogenous shift in the terms of trade with the direct welfare effects of some *independent* shock. In our example, however, the terms of trade change was the sole shift in the data, the contraction of employment and output being induced by this very change in the terms of trade itself.

When the change in the terms of trade is a *consequence* of some exogenous shock, such as a change in tastes, technology or factor endowment, it is clearly erroneous to infer the total change in welfare solely from the direction of change in the terms of trade. Technological progress in the export sector that deteriorates the terms of trade can obviously leave a country better off in spite of the deterioration, even though it would of course have been still better off if the terms of trade had remained unchanged. It is this sort of consideration that has led to the introduction of concepts such as the factoral terms of trade, since these measures could show an improvement even when the commodity terms of trade deteriorate. In general, however, it is a mistake to expect any single concept of the terms of trade to be an unambiguous indicator of changes in the gains from trade when there are shifts in the fundamental determinants of tastes, technology and factor endowments.

The welfare effects of such changes can be broken into two parts: first, the effect at unchanged terms of trade, and second the effect of the associated change in the terms of trade. The *net* effect on welfare may thus be positive or negative and need not correspond with the direction of the change in the terms of trade. Bhagwati (1958) established the possibility that the net effect on welfare of the country experiencing economic growth can be *negative*, a phenomenon that he terms 'immiserizing growth'.

Finally, we may consider the terms of trade as an objective of policy, when the country has some degree of monopoly power in international markets. The consideration of a rational policy maker, ignoring the possibility of retaliation, would be to restrict trade to such an extent as to equate at the margin the benefit resulting from the improvement in the terms of trade with the loss of welfare resulting from the decline in the volume of trade. This is the famous 'optimum tariff' argument, the level of which varies inversely with the elasticity of foreign demand for imports.

SECULAR TENDENCIES. In addition to comparative statics analyses of the type considered up to now, the literature also contains some more speculative hypotheses about secular tendencies in the terms of trade. In the Ricardian tradition capital accumulation and technical progress lead to a steady expansion in the supply of manufactures, while the supply of primary products is always constrained by the limited availability of 'land' and other natural resources. Ricardo's theorem for a closed economy – that growth would raise the relative price of food and therefore the rent of land until a 'stationary state' is approached – has been extended to the world economy in the form of a presumption that there would be a tendency for the terms of trade to move against manufactures and in favour of primary products. Keynes, Beveridge, Robertson and E.A.G. Robinson all took part in a long-running debate on this issue. The story that W.S. Jevons kept enormous stocks of coal in his basement is a bizarre manifestation of this phobia. W.W. Rostow (1962, chs 8 and 9) gives a very interesting review and analysis of this literature, which foreshadows the views associated more recently with the Club of Rome.

Discussions of the secular tendencies of the terms of trade since World War II, however, have been dominated by the view of Raúl Prebisch (1950) and Hans Singer (1950) that the historical record shows a long-run tendency for the commodity terms of trade of the less developed countries to deteriorate. The evidence was a series showing an apparent long-run improvement in Britain's terms of trade between 1870 and 1940. Theoretical reasons given for the alleged tendency have been lower income-elasticity of demand for primary products than for manufactures, technical progress that economizes on the use of imported raw materials and monopolistic market structures in the industrial countries combined with competitive conditions in the supply of primary products. The general consensus on the statistical debate that has arisen on this issue is that there has *not* been any discernible secular trend for the commodity terms of trade of the developing countries to deteriorate (see Spraos, 1980, for a recent summary and assessment of the evidence; Lewis, 1969, presents a very interesting alternative theoretical and empirical analysis of this problem).

The Prebisch–Singer hypothesis and the more general concerns of the ongoing

North–South dialogue have also spawned a number of so-called 'North–South' models, in which the interaction of an advanced industrial region with a less developed and structurally dissimilar, labour-abundant, primary producing region is studied in a dynamic context. The terms of trade play a key role in these models, since the growth rate of the South is linked to this variable through dependence on capital goods imported from the North. This and other analytical issues related to secular trends in the terms of trade are further discussed in Findlay (1981, 1984).

BIBLIOGRAPHY

Bhagwati, J. 1958. Immiserizing growth: a geometrical note. *Review of Economic Studies* 25, June, 201–5.

Emmanuel, A. 1972. *Unequal Exchange.* New York: Monthly Review Press.

Findlay, R. 1981. The fundamental determinants of the terms of trade. In *The World Economic Order: Past and Prospects,* ed. S. Grassman and E. Lundberg, London: Macmillan.

Findlay, R. 1984. Growth and development in trade models. In *Handbook of International Economics,* ed. R.W. Jones and P.B. Kenen, Amsterdam: North-Holland, Vol. 1, ch. 4.

Haberler, G. 1955. *A Survey of International Trade Theory.* Princeton: International Finance Section.

Hicks, J.R. 1953. An inaugural lecture. *Oxford Economic Papers* NS 5, June, 117–35.

Lewis, W.A. 1969. *Aspects of Tropical Trade 1883–1965.* Stockholm: Almqvist and Wiksell.

Prebisch, R. 1950. *The Economic Development of Latin America and its Principal Problems.* New York: United Nations.

Robertson, D.H. 1952. The terms of trade. Ch. 13 of *Utility and All That,* New York: Macmillan.

Rostow, W.W. 1962. *The Process of Economic Growth.* New York: Norton, chs 8 and 9.

Singer, H.W. 1950. The distribution of gains between investing and borrowing countries. *American Economic Review, Papers and Proceedings* 5, Supplement, May, 473–85.

Spraos, J. 1980. The statistical debate on the net barter terms of trade between primary commodities and manufactures. *Economic Journal* 90, March, 107–28.

Viner, J. 1937. *Studies in the Theory of International Trade.* New York: Harper Bros, ch. 9.

Tiebout Hypothesis

BRUCE W. HAMILTON

The essence of the Tiebout hypothesis is that there exists a mechanism for preference revelation regarding publicly provided goods so long as consumer-voters can choose among 'jurisdictions'. The obvious application – the one both Tiebout and his followers had in mind – is that of a large number of autonomous suburban jurisdictions providing those goods which are generally in the domain of local governments, such a primary and secondary education, police and fire protection, sewer and water provision.

Tiebout's basic insight is laid out in his famous 1956 paper. It is worth noting that he offered his model as an antidote to Samuelson's rather gloomy results on the economy's inability to 'find' solutions to the efficient provision of public goods. In Samuelson's (1954) public-goods world (previously laid out by Bowen, 1943) consumers do not find it in their interest to reveal their preferences for public goods, since preference revelation merely results in a larger payment and essentially no increase in actual provision. As a consequence, voting schemes generally produce a below-optimum level of public goods. But Tiebout has endowed his consumers with another preference-revelation mechanism – mobility. By moving to a jurisdiction with his preferred level of local public services, the consumer simultaneously reveals his preferences and ends up on his demand curve. So long as there is a sufficient variety of jurisdictions, all consumers can get on (or at least close to) their demand curves.

Tiebout's insight is disarmingly simple – if there are different jurisdictions in a metropolitan area which offer, say, different levels of education, then the high demanders will go to the jurisdiction which supplies better schools. But despite this simplicity, he displayed considerable care in his characterization of many aspects of the problem. In defining local public goods, he substitutes non-excludability for Samuelson's famous non-rivalry. He also discussed the behaviour of bureaucrats. And he recognized that his results would break down if there were interjurisdictional spillovers. In other words, his insight was much deeper than 'voting with your feet'.

672

The Tiebout model lay fallow for over a decade after its publication. Interest was finally sparked by the publication of Oates's (1969) study of the effects of local taxes and school expenditures on property values. Oates found that high taxes depressed property values (by approximately the present value of the high taxes) and that high expenditures raised property values by a comparable magnitude. The conclusion was obvious – consumers think about schools and taxes when making their location decisions. Tiebout's statement regarding consumer behaviour appeared vindicated. (As we will see, capitalization plays a far greater role in modern versions of the Tiebout hypothesis than providing empirical support for Tiebout's behavioural claims.)

After publication of Oates's paper, economists began to study the theoretical underpinnings of the Tiebout model with more care. An important weakness in Tiebout's original treatment is that of the pricing mechanism associated with the local public goods. He simply speaks loosely about jurisdictions with high expenditure and high taxes. But without further specification, there is a serious free-rider problem. Consider the case of a jurisdiction with a high property tax rate to finance high-quality schools. Low-income people (who would not buy much housing anyway) could move in, buy the housing they demand, and acquire their high-quality schools at less than cost. This problem was first addressed by Ellickson (1971), who noted that free riding is not a serious problem so long as housing and local public services are sufficiently strong complements. In such a world, stratification by public service demand is voluntary. But the conditions for voluntary stratification are very restrictive, and there is no reason to believe that they hold in general.

Then, in a simple but extreme model, Hamilton (1975) noted that free riding could be eliminated by careful use of zoning and building controls. A property tax, coupled with the right dose of zoning, becomes a lump-sum tax, or better yet, a price, with all its attendant efficiency properties. Citizens of a rich jurisdiction could safely tax themselves sufficiently to finance their demanded level of public services, secure in the knowledge that the zoning code would protect them from free riders.

There are two obvious problems even with the less restrictive (1976) version of this model. First, local public goods are assumed to be produced under constant returns to jurisdiction size – as contrasted with Tiebout's U-shaped average cost curve. And second – related to but stronger than the first – there are no impediments to jurisdiction formation. Given these assumptions the world is populated by perfectly stratified (according to public-service demand) jurisdictions in which taxes are equal to average cost. Since the metropolitan area offers a wide range of such jurisdictions, each of which provides services at average (equals marginal) cost, the consumer faces the same budget constraint that he would if local public services were marketed through department stores. The perfect-competition paradigm carries over completely. Note also that the tax instrument is of critical importance if the efficiency or even existence of a Tiebout equilibrium is to be achieved. Westhoff (1977) has analysed the Tiebout world in which the public sector is financed by an income tax (with no zoning or analogous restrictions on entry) and found that equilibria exist only under fairly extreme assumptions.

At this point it is worthwhile to reconsider the capitalization results obtained in Oates (1969), which found (among other things) property value premia in jurisdictions with high school expenditure. Upon reflection, it is clear that this capitalization effect is part of the price people pay for the privilege of consuming high-quality schools. Taxes cover the cost of providing these schools; the presence of capitalization effects implies that the demand price (for the marginal consumer) exceeds production cost. This in turn can be interpreted as evidence of excess demand for high-quality schools. In the flexible-communities model discussed above, this should give rise to high-expenditure community formation, which in turn should eliminate the capitalization effect. Under this interpretation the Oates capitalization effect is the Tiebout analogue to short-run profit in the competitive model.

When community formation is free, when public services are produced according to constant costs, and when stratification (either voluntary or by fiat) is perfect, the Tiebout model is a simple and elegant extension of the competitive model.

There are two major remaining complications of the Tiebout model, each representing a step toward realism and each casting at least some measure of doubt upon the efficiency and even the existence of Tiebout equilibrium. The first complication is the existence of incomplete stratification, possibly due to institutional restrictions on jurisdiction formation or increasing returns in the provision of public services, or to limitations on the ability of jurisdictions to prevent free riders. The second complication concerns the nature of the technology in a fundamental way. There is mounting evidence that the cost of providing many local public services is heavily influenced by characteristics of the jurisdiction's residents, indicating that these characteristice enter into the production function for the services. There has been a great deal of research on the first of these complications, but virtually none on the second. I discuss them in turn below.

If stratification by demand is perfect, and if everybody faces an average-cost (equals marginal cost) price, then local governments have virtually no role to play. Every electoral issue receives unanimous consent (or unanimous rejection). Jurisdiction size is a matter of indifference to current residents (as well as to the local officials). But once we remove the constant-cost and perfect-stratification assumptions we cannot ignore the role of the voting process. And we cannot be sure that migration behaviour of consumers is efficiency-enhancing. Suppose for example that jurisdictions have not achieved sufficient size to exhaust scale economies. A consumer migrating from jurisdiction A to jurisdiction B raises cost in A and reduces cost in B. With non-constant returns the welfare effects of migration are not strictly internal to the migrant. This of course removes the presumption of efficiency from any Tiebout equilibrium. But the presumption of existence is also weakened; depending upon the instruments available to local governments, they might wage war for migrants, manipulating their public-service offerings in efforts to slide down their average cost curves. An interesting set of 'failure' examples is contained in Bewley (1981). In the most interesting of his failure examples, there are fewer jurisdictions than there are desired consumption bundles – either by assumption or through invocation of increasing returns.

The objections raised by Bewley and others suggest the importance of looking at community formation, and at the diversity among communities which would be required to approximate adequately the range of choice envisioned in the Tiebout model. Do the various jurisdictions in our cities generally offer enough choice to satisfy the requirements of the Tiebout model? The first impediment to such diversity would seem to be increasing returns. And to address this we need to examine the range of goods offered by local governments. On such examination, it seems clear that the empirical case for or against Tiebout must be built on public education. Education absorbs almost half of aggregate local spending in the United States, and no other item accounts for more than about 10 per cent. In addition, much of the typical non-education budget is devoted to such things as sewer, water and street maintenance. Although a few decades ago people may well have shunned certain cities because of the state of their sewers, it seems highly unlikely that jurisdiction choice is based on 'shopping' for one's demanded level of sewer service today.

As regards education, the best available evidence suggests that any increasing returns to community size are dissipated at a population of about 10,000. This evidence comes from work by Bergstrom and Goodman (1973) and Borcherding and Deacon (1972), and results from an examination of the relationship between expenditure and community size. Both sets of results find per capita expenditure invariant with community size above about 10,000. The 'simplest' interpretation of this finding is that unit cost does not vary with population. But an alternative explanation is that demand is unit elastic with respect to price, in which case one cannot tell anything about scale economies by regressing expenditure on scale.

Despite doubts about the interpretation of the empirical results on scale economies in education, there is no evidence which clearly points to scale economies beyond some modest scale. In fact, the reason for doubting scale economies extends beyond evidence from the expenditure–scale regressions described above. In the presence of scale economies, large jurisdictions should have a cost advantage over small ones, which should be reflected in property values. The failure of capitalization studies to find such an effect lends support to the presumption of constant returns.

All of this means that we have no particular reason to believe that scale economies are an impediment to wide community choice. Of course it is still possible that jurisdiction variety fails to arise for some other reason. Henderson (1985), however, has examined the data on jurisdiction formation and has discovered, somewhat surprisingly, that jurisdiction formation in most urban areas approximates population growth.

In conclusion, the concerns over community variety and formation raised by Bewley and others need to be taken seriously. But the evidence for scale economies, and for insufficient community variety, is not fully convincing.

The next issue to be addressed concerns the nature of the production function for education. Suppose we accept the view expressed above that education is the only good for which Tiebout-sorting and provision are relevant. Further, we will accept the notion that education is produced under constant returns to community size. One fundamental question, which has not been addressed by any of the Tiebout modellers, remains to be addressed.

Suppose the technology for producing education contains child and parent characteristics as one of its arguments. Both the casual and published evidence for this is overwhelming. Casual support can be found by noting that per-pupil expenditure on education is frequently higher in central cities than in their suburbs; yet nobody thinks education quality is higher in central cities. The statistical evidence is at least as compelling. Whenever one regresses a measure of education output – say, test sources or annual improvements in test scores, characteristics of parents and peers have strong explanatory power. (Indeed, the embarrassing aspect of these studies is that measures of purchased inputs, such as class size and teacher characteristics, frequently have no explanatory power at all. See Hanushek, 1986, for a thorough review of the economics of schooling.) Then we cannot model the Tiebout world as a choice set of communities offering education at a certain price, waiting like grocers for households to purchase their wares. For the quality of education depends upon the characteristics of the households who arrive.

It is highly likely in such a world that voluntary Tiebout sorting is unstable, as those households with 'bad' production inputs chase those with 'good' inputs. The problem is that sorting according to quantity demanded is not the end of the story; stability may well require that we separate high demanders who are cheap to educate from high demanders who are expensive to educate.

A second problem arises when we consider efficiency. Much like the world with increasing returns, we now have two efficiency objectives to worry about. First, we continue to have the traditional Tiebout objective of satisfying a variety of demands with a variety of offerings. But we now have a second objective, namely minimizing cost. Depending on the nature of the technology, there may be large cost savings associated with (say) placing a few high-motivation children in each classroom. The performance gains (cost savings) achieved by the other students might more than compensate the increased cost of educating these children in a non-enriched environment. In such a world there are externalities associated with ability-mixing. As there seems to be no obvious mechanism for internalizing these externalities, we have no reason to anticipate that Tiebout sorting will lead to an efficient outcome, even under the most favourable assumptions on every aspect of the problem except the technology.

BIBLIOGRAPHY

Bergstrom, T. and Goodman, R. 1973. Private demand for public goods. *American Economic Review* 63, June, 280–96.

Bewley, T.F. 1981. A critique of Tiebout's theory of local public expenditures. *Econometrica* 49, May, 713–40.

Borcherding, T. and Deacon, R. 1972. The demand for the services of non-Federal Governments. *American Economic Review* 62, December, 891–901.

Bowen, H.R. 1943. The interpretation of voting in the allocation of economic resources. *Quarterly Journal of Economics* 58, November, 27–48.

Ellickson, B. 1971. Jurisdictional fragmentation and residential choice. *American Economic Review* 61, December, 334–9.

Hamilton, B.W. 1975. Zoning and property taxation in a system of local governments. *Urban Studies* 12(2), June, 205–11.

Hamilton, B.W. 1976. Capitalization of intrajurisdictional differences in local tax prices. *American Economic Review* 66(5), December, 743–53.

Hanushek, E.A. 1986. The economics of schooling. *Journal of Economic Literature* 24, September, 1141–77.

Henderson, J.V. 1985. The Tiebout Model: bring back the entrepreneurs. *Journal of Political Economy* 93, April, 248–57.

Oates, W.E. 1969. The effects of property taxes and local public spending on property values: an empirical study of tax capitalization and the Tiebout hypothesis. *Journal of Political Economy* 77(8), November–December, 957–71.

Samuelson, P.A. 1954. The pure theory of public expenditure. *Review of Economics and Statistics* 36, November, 387–9.

Tiebout, C. 1956. A pure theory of local expenditures. *Journal of Political Economy* 64, October, 416–24.

Westhoff, F. 1977. Existence of equilibria in economies with a local public good. *Journal of Economic Theory* 14, 84–112.

Time Preference

MURRAY N. ROTHBARD

Time preference is the insight that people prefer 'present goods' (goods available for use at present) to 'future goods' (present expectations of goods becoming available at some date in the future), and that the social rate of time preference, the result of the interactions of individual time preference schedules, will determine and be equal to the pure rate of interest in a society. The economy is pervaded by a time market for present as against future goods, not only in the market for loans (in which creditors trade present money for the right to receive money in the future), but also as a 'natural rate' in all processes of production. For capitalists pay out present money to buy or rent land, capital goods and raw materials, and to hire labour (as well as buying labour outright in a system of slavery), thereby purchasing expectations of future revenue from the eventual sales of product. Long-run profit rates and rates of return on capital are therefore forms of interest rate. As businessmen seek to gain profits and avoid losses, the economy will tend toward a general equilibrium, in which all interest rates and rates of return will be equal, and hence there will be no pure entrepreneurial profits or losses.

In centuries of wrestling with the vexed question of the justification of interest, the Catholic scholastic philosophers arrived at highly sophisticated explanations and justifications of return on capital, including risk and the opportunity cost of profit foregone. But they had extreme difficulty with the interest on a riskless loan, and hence denounced all such interest as sinful and usurious.

Some of the later scholastics, however, in their more favourable view of usury, began to approach a time preference explanation of interest. During a comprehensive demolition of the standard arguments for the prohibition of usury in his *Treatise on Contracts* (1499), Conrad Summenhart (1465–1511), theologian at the University of Tübingen, used time preference to justify the purchase of a discounted debt, even if the debt be newly created. When someone pays $100 for the right to obtain $110 at a future date, the buyer (lender) doesn't profit usuriously from the loan because both he and the seller (borrower) value the future $110 as being worth $100 at the present time (Noonan, 1957).

A half-century later, the distinguished Dominican canon lawyer and monetary theorist at the University of Salamanca, Martin de Azpilcueta Navarrus (1493–1586) clearly set forth the concept of time preference, but failed to apply it to a defence of usury. In his *Commentary on Usury* (1556), Azpilcueta pointed out that a present good, such as money, will naturally be worth more on the market than future goods, that is, claims to money in the future. As Azpilcueta put it:

> a claim on something is worth less than the thing itself, and ... it is plain that that which is not usable for a year is less valuable than something of the same quality which is usable at once (Gordon, 1975, p. 215).

At about the same time, the Italian humanist and politician Gian Francesco Lottini da Volterra, in his handbook of advice to princes, *Avvedimenti civili* (1574), discovered time preference. Unfortunately, Lottini also inaugurated the tradition of moralistically deploring time preference as an overestimation of a present that can be grasped immediately by the senses (Kauder, 1965, pp. 19–22)

Two centuries later, the Neapolitan abbé, Ferdinando Galiani (1728–87) revived the rudiments of time preference in his *Della Moneta* (1751) (Monroe, 1924). Galiani pointed out that just as the exchange rate of two currencies equates the value of a present and a spatially distant money, so the rate of interest equates present with future, or temporally distant, money. What is being equated is not physical properties, but subjective values in the minds of individuals.

These scattered hints scarcely prepare one for the remarkable development of a full-scale time-preference theory of interest by the French statesman, Anne Robert Jaques Turgot (1727–81), who, in a relatively few hastily written contributions, anticipated almost completely the later Austrian theory of capital and interest (Turgot, 1977). In the course of a paper defending usury, Turgot asked: why are borrowers willing to pay an interest premium for the use of money? The focus should not be on the amount of metal repaid but on the usefulness of the money to the lender and borrower. In particular, Turgot compares the 'difference in usefulness which exists at the date of borrowing between a sum currently owned and an equal sum which is to be received at a distant date', and notes the well-known motto, 'a bird in the hand is better than two in the bush'. Since the sum of money owned now 'is preferable to the assurance of receiving a similar sum in one or several years' time', returning the same principal means that the lender 'gives the money and receives only an assurance'. Therefore, interest compensates for this difference in value by a sum proportionate to the length of the delay. Turgot added that what must be compared in a loan transaction is not the value of money lent with the value repaid, but rather the 'value of the *promise* of a sum of money compared to the value of money available now' (Turgot, 1977, pp. 158–9).

In addition, Turgot was apparently the first to arrive at the concept of *capitalization*, a corollary to time preference, which holds that the present capital value of any durable good will tend to equal the sum of its expected annual rents, or returns, discounted by the market rate of time preference, or rate of interest.

Turgot also pioneered in analysing the relation between the quantity of money and interest rates. If an increased supply of money goes to low time-preference people, then the increased proportion of savings to consumption lowers time preference and hence interest rates fall while prices rise. But if an increased quantity goes into the hands of high time-preference people, the opposite would happen and interest rates would rise along with prices. Generally, over recent centuries, he noted, the spirit of thrift has been growing in Europe and hence time preference rates and interest rates have tended to fall.

One of the notable injustices in the historiography of economic thought was Böhm-Bawerk's brusque dismissal in 1884 of Turgot's anticipation of his own time-preference theory of interest as merely a 'land fructification theory' (Böhm-Bawerk, 1959, vol. I). Partly this dismissal stemmed from Böhm-Bawerk's methodology of clearing the ground for his own positive theory of interest by demolishing, and hence sometimes doing injustice to, his own forerunners (Wicksell, 1911, p. 177). The unfairness is particularly glaring in the case of Turgot, because we now know that in 1876, only eight years before the publication of his history of theories of interest, Böhm-Bawerk wrote a glowing tribute to Turgot's theory of interest in an as yet unpublished paper in Karl Knies's seminar at the University of Heidelberg (Turgot, 1977, pp. xxix–xxx).

In the course of his demolition of the Ricardo–James Mill labour theory of value on behalf of a subjective utility theory, Samuel Bailey (1825) clearly set forth the concept of time preference. Rebutting Mill's statement that time, as a 'mere abstract word', could not add to value, Bailey declared that 'we generally prefer a present pleasure or enjoyment to a distant one', and therefore prefer present goods to waiting for goods to arrive in the future. Bailey, however, did not go on to apply his insight to interest.

In the mid-1830s, the Irish economist Samuel Mountifort Longfield worked out the later Austrian theory of capital as performing the service for workers of supplying money at present instead of waiting for the future when the product will be sold. In turn the capitalist receives from the workers a time discount from their productivity. As Longfield put it, the capitalist

> pays the wages immediately, and in return receives the value of [the worker's] labour, ... [which] is greater than the wages of that labour. The difference is the profit made by the capitalist for his advances ... as it were, the discount which the labourer pays for prompt payment (Longfield, [1834] 1971).

The 'pre-Austrian' time analysis of capital and interest was most fully worked out, in the same year 1834, by the Scottish and Canadian eccentric John Rae (1786–1872). In the course of attempting an anti-Smithian defence of the protective tariff, Rae, in his *Some New Principles on the Subject of Political Economy* (1834), developed the Böhm-Bawerkian time analysis of capital, pointing out that investment lengthens the time involved in the processes of production. Rae noted that the capitalist must weigh the greater productivity of longer production processes against waiting for them to come to fruition. Capitalists will sacrifice present money for a greater return in the future, the difference – the interest return – reflecting the social rate of time preference. Rae saw that people's time-preference rates reflect their cultural and psychological willingness to take a shorter or longer view of the future. His moral preferences were clearly with the low time-preference thrifty as against the high time-preference people who suffer from a 'defect of the imagination'. Rae's analysis had little impact on economics until resurrected at the turn of the 20th century, whereupon it was generously hailed in the later editions of Böhm-Bawerk's history of interest theories (Böhm-Bawerk, 1959, vol. I).

Time preference, as a concept and as a foundation for the explanation of interest, has been an outstanding feature of the Austrian School of economics. Its founder, Carl Menger (1840–1921), enunciated the concept of time preference in 1871, pointing out that satisfying the immediate needs of life and health are necessarily prerequisites for satisfying more remote future needs. In addition, Menger declared, 'all experience teaches that we humans consider a present pleasure, or one expected in the near future, more important than one of the same intensity which is not expected to occur until some more distant time' (Menger, 1871, pp. 153–4; Wicksell, 1924, p. 195). But Menger never extended time preference from his value theory to a theory of interest; and when his follower Böhm-Bawerk did so, he peevishly deleted this discussion from the second edition of his *Principles of Economics* (Wicksell, 1924, pp. 195–6).

Böhm-Bawerk's *Capital and Interest* (1884) is the *locus classicus* of the time-preference theory of interest. In his first, historical volume, he demolished all other theories, in particular the productivity theory of interest; but five years later, in his *Positive Theory of Capital* (1889), Böhm-Bawerk brought back the productivity theory in an attempt to combine it with a time-preference explanation of interest (Böhm-Bawerk, 1959, vols I, II). In his 'three grounds' for the explanation of interest, time preference constituted two, and the greater productivity of longer processes of production the third, Böhm-Bawerk ironically placing greatest importance upon the third ground. Influenced strongly by Böhm-Bawerk, Irving Fisher increasingly took the same path of stressing the marginal productivity of capital as the main determinant of interest (Fisher, 1907, 1930).

With the work of Böhm-Bawerk and Fisher, the modern theory of interest was set squarely on the path of placing time preference in a subordinate role in the explanation of interest: determining only the rate of consumer loans, and the supply of consumer savings, while the alleged productivity of capital determines the more important demand for loans and for savings. Hence modern interest theory fails to integrate interest on consumer loans and producer's returns into a coherent explanation.

In contrast, Frank A. Fetter, building on Böhm-Bawerk, completely discarded productivity as an explanation of interest and constructed an integrated theory of value and distribution in which interest is determined solely by time preference, while marginal productivity determines the 'rental prices' of the factors of production (Fetter, 1915, 1977). In his outstanding critique of Böhm-Bawerk, Fetter pointed out a fundamental error of the third ground in trying to explain the return on capital as 'present goods' earning a return for their productivity in the future; instead, capital goods are *future* goods, since they are only valuable in the expectation of being used to produce goods that will be sold to the consumer at a future date (Fetter, 1902). One way of seeing the fallacy of a productivity explanation of interest is to look at the typical practice of any current microeconomics text: after explaining marginal productivity as determining the demand curve for factors with wage rates on the *y*-axis, the textbook airily shifts to interest rates on the *y*-axis to illustrate the marginal productivity determination of interest. But the analog on the *y*-axis should not be interest, which is a ratio and not a price, but rather the *rental price* (price per unit time) of a capital good. Thus, interest remains totally unexplained. In short, as Fetter pointed out, marginal productivity determines rental prices, and time preference determines the rate of interest, while the capital value of a factor of production is the expected sum of future rents from a durable factor discounted by the rate of time preference or interest.

The leading economist adopting Fetter's pure time-preference view of interest was Ludwig von Mises, in his *Human Action* (Mises, 1949). Mises amended the theory in two important ways. First, he rid the concept of its moralistic tone which had been continued by Böhm-Bawerk, implicitly criticizing people for 'under'-estimating the future. Mises made clear that a positive time-preference rate is an essential attribute of human nature. Secondly, and as a corollary, whereas Fetter believed that people could have either positive or negative rates of time preference, Mises demonstrated that a positive rate is deducible from the fact of human action, since by the very nature of a goal or an end people wish to achieve that goal as soon as possible.

BIBLIOGRAPHY

Bailey, S. 1825. *A Critical Dissertation on the Nature, Measure, and Causes of Value.* New York: Augustus M. Kelley, 1967.

Böhm-Bawerk, E. von. 1884–9. *Kapital ind Kapitalzins. Zweite Abteilung: Positive Theorie des Kapitales.* 4th edn. Trans. by G.D. Huncke as *Capital and Interest,* Vols I and II. South Holland, Ill.: Libertarian Press, 1959.

Fetter, F.A. 1902. The 'Roundabout process' in the interest theory. *Quarterly Journal of Economics* 17, November, 163–80. Reprinted in F.A. Fetter (1977).

Fetter, F.A. 1915. *Economic Principles,* Vol. I. New York: The Century Co.

Fetter, F.A. 1977. *Capital, Interest, and Rent: Essays in the Theory of Distribution.* Ed. M. Rothbard, Kansas City: Sheed Andrews and McMeel.

Fisher, I. 1907. *The Rate of Interest.* New York: Macmillan.

Fisher, I. 1930. *The Theory of Interest.* New York: Kelley & Millman, 1954.

Gordon, B. 1975. *Economic Analysis Before Adam Smith: Hesiod to Lessius.* New York: Barnes & Noble.

Kauder, E. 1965. *A History of Marginal Utility Theory.* Princeton: Princeton University Press.

Longfield, S.M. 1971. *The Economic Writings of Mountifort Longfield.* Ed. R.D.C. Black, Clifton, NJ: Augustus M. Kelley.

Menger, C. 1871. *Principles of Economics.* Ed. J. Dingwall and B. Hoselitz, Glencoe, Ill.: Free Press, 1950.

Mises, L. von. 1949. *Human Action: A Treatise on Economics.* 3rd revised edn, Chicago: Regnery, 1966.

Monroe, A. (ed.) 1924. *Early Economic Thought.* Cambridge, Mass.: Harvard University Press.

Noonan, J.T., Jr. 1957. *The Scholastic Analysis of Usury.* Cambridge, Mass.: Harvard University Press.

Rae, J. 1834. *Some New Principles on the Subject of Political Economy.* In *John Rae: Political Economist*, ed. R.W. James, Toronto: University of Toronto Press, 1965.

Turgot, A.R.J. 1977. *The Economics of A.R.J. Turgot.* Ed. P.D. Groenewegen, The Hague: Martinus Nijhoff.

Wicksell, K. 1911. Böhm-Bawerk's theory of interest. In K. Wicksell, *Selected Papers on Economic Theory*, ed. E. Lindahl, Cambridge, Mass.: Harvard University Press, 1958.

Wicksell, K. 1924. The new edition of Menger's *Grundsatze*. In K. Wicksell, *Selected Papers on Economic Theory*, ed. E. Lindahl, Cambridge, Mass.: Harvard University Press, 1958.

Trade Unions

HENRY PHELPS BROWN

When they formulated their classic definition of a trade union, Sidney and Beatrice Webb had in view the long struggle of groups of English workers to maintain associations that could stand up to employers and gain acceptance by the community. 'A trade union,' they said, 'is a continuous association of wage earners for the purpose of maintaining or improving the conditions of their working lives' (1894, p. 1). An economist starting from the assumption of the ultimate rationality of decisions is likely to see the trade union as a cartel or monopoly intended to maximize the benefits of its members. An intermediate view recognizes that men and women join trade unions for reasons that arise out of imperfections of the labour market. Because of the slow response of employment to lower labour cost, the job seekers in any one district will be confronted at a given time with a limited number of jobs: if then they exceed that number, even by one, and compete with each other by underbidding, the wage can be brought down to a limit set by bare subsistence or the level of support in unemployment.

But even suppose that the numbers of vacancies and applicants match exactly: then if the employer and an individual applicant cannot reach agreement on the rate for the job, so that for the time being the employer lacks a workman and the applicant has no job or pay, which is in the greater trouble? As Adam Smith said, 'In the long run the workman may be as necessary to his master as his master is to him; but the necessity is not so immediate.' The applicants here are evidently unable to move away readily to other employers: those with whom they are dealing are monopsonists or oligopsonists. Against this, they try to maintain a monopoly. They agree to hold out for a minimum in common. They want to keep up the price of their work by limiting the supply. They also want to safeguard their jobs against a drop in demand – they aim to establish a property in jobs. To these ends they define lines of demarcation, within which they have the sole right to work, or they allow only approved entrants, in limited numbers, to acquire certain skills, or to be recruited for certain purposes. The defensive object of preventing their rates being undercut or their labour being displaced by outsiders merges here into the calculated purpose of pushing up their earnings by restricting supply.

In modern Western economies, trade union membership has also been maintained or extended, especially among white collar workers; by the need to renegotiate the pay of all employees to compensate for changes in the cost of living; the addition of an improvement factor in real terms has also been regarded as defensive from the point of view of any one group, which would otherwise fall behind the others. Beyond these issues of the rate of pay and job security are those that arise at the place of work. People join trade unions to secure protection against discrimination and arbitrary treatment by management, and the negotiation and observance of a code governing discipline, grievance procedure, promotion, redundancy, the pace of work, and the like.

FACTORS AFFECTING MEMBERSHIP. These forces making for trade union membership have arisen and taken effect only in certain conditions. Where trade unions emerged, their form and function differed widely in different societies. In the Western democracies, the proportion of employees unionized has varied widely over time and between countries (Bain and Price, 1960); sometimes it has fallen even against the trend of economic growth, notably in the USA since the 1960s. In full employment, and in places where the individual had access to a number of alternative employers, or to natural resources like the American open frontier, he would feel able to fend for himself. The absence of observed falls in wage rates down the centuries (Phelps Brown and Hopkins, 1981) implies that custom and tacit understandings can maintain rates in the absence of overt trade unionism. Individuals whose qualifications, temperaments and entries into employment interest them in personal advancement are not likely to become trade unionists; but these factors deterring clerical, administrative and managerial employees from membership have been offset by the growth of offices in size and impersonality, and the need of staff to negotiate frequent salary rises to offset inflation. The ability of manual workers to form their own trade unions has depended upon leaders coming forward from their ranks who were literate, upright, and skilful in administration; the workers themselves must be able to keep up a subscription and have the discipline to sustain a stoppage. Where those conditions are lacking, as in much of the Third World, trade unions tend to be organized by outsiders, often a political party.

In all countries, the ability of trade unions to maintain themselves and function depends on the provisions of the law and their application in the courts: landmarks here were the immunity from civil liability conferred on British trade unions in 1906, and the promotion of trade unionism and collective bargaining by American legislation in the 1930s. Linked with this is the attitude of the employers: whereas those in France, Germany and the United States generally felt themselves justified, down to 1914 and sometimes later, in resisting trade unionism, many British employers had come to accept it as a means of stabilizing industrial relations. In the Soviet-type economies, discontent with the conditions of employment leading to combined action can result only in a political revolt: trade unions exist by name, but only to administer social benefits and maintain the control of the party within the establishment.

Trade unions thus have to be viewed in their local variety and historical setting. 'Where we expected to find an economic thread for a treatise,' the Webbs wrote in the Preface to their *History of Trade Unionism* (1894), 'we found a spider's web; and from that moment we recognized that what we had first to write was not a treatise, but a history.'

TRADE UNIONS AS MONOPOLIES. None the less, there are economic threads to be followed through. One is the effect of the trade union on the relative pay of its members. Here the theory of the monopoly power of the trade union directs attention to the elasticity of substitution between the members' labour and other factors of production, and to the elasticity of demand for the product. Substantially, much depends on the possibility of the labour being replaced by equipment, and of the trade union gaining control of this if it were introduced. It is in the firms and industries themselves most strongly placed in the market, and able to retain ample margins, that trade unions are likely to maintain levels of pay above those obtaining elsewhere for similar grades of labour. The employers concerned are thus paying what seems more than the supply price of labour to them, and the differences found in surveys in the rates paid even in adjacent firms suggest that this is so; the trade unions may be said to share in the monopoly power of the employers. They may also acquire monopoly power directly by restricting supply and by forcing demand.

Craft unions have restricted supply by limiting the numbers of apprentices; when a trade is being organized for the first time, attacks on non-members who are continuing to work for less than the union rate serve either to exclude or recruit them; and this shades into the general purpose of the rule that no one shall undertake work of a certain kind unless he or she holds a union card, which serves more for recruitment than for exclusion. The pre-entry closed shop provides the most complete control. A trade union that organizes all the existing workers in an industry has to reckon with the possibility of the market being invaded by the products of non-members newly employed elsewhere – except in those cases where of its nature the produce must be supplied in the place where it is consumed.

Trade unions force demand by rules preventing work being taken away from their members, such as compositors' work being done by advertisers, or builders' work by the makers of pre-fabricated components; by stopping other workers doing jobs in the territory to which they claim exclusive rights; and by resisting the application of labour-saving equipment to their own work. Many restrictive prices are intended to maintain or increase the input of labour per unit of output.

The monopoly power of a group of workers who form an essential link in a chain of production but account for a small part of the whole cost, appears great. Adam Smith instanced the half-dozen woolcombers who were needed to keep a thousand spinners and weavers at work. Marshall asked why the bricklayers of his day did not get 'an enormous rise' by pushing their own rate up. This power is in fact limited by the employer's powers of resistance. He may redesign process or product, so as to by-pass the labour in question; he may put the work out to subcontract, or import components; at the limit, he may move the whole operation to a location where the trade union is not in control. His resistance to a claim by the union will also be stiffened by his knowledge that other groups in his employ will have regard to relativities, and will base their own claims on concessions he makes to the union.

COLLECTIVE BARGAINING. The most widely available use of monopoly power is the pushing up of the rate of pay by bargaining, which leaves it to employers to restrict the supply by the limitation of the number they engage at the higher rate. If we consider in the first place a negotiation whose effects are largely confined to the immediate parties, bargaining power proper may be defined as the power to inflict loss by withholding consent. It is understandable that if two parties cannot agree upon the terms of an agreement to work together, they should suspend operations meanwhile. But this suspension is not a merely negative act, for it puts each party into difficulties. Workers are left without pay. Craft unions have often had funds from which to issue strike pay; other unions, needing to keep subscriptions low, pay none, but have sometimes been able to maintain long strikes none the less with the aid of contributions from other unionists and the public. There has been a risk of the vacant places being filled by disloyal members of the union, or by imported blacklegs who will be kept on when the dispute is settled. These difficulties increase the longer the stoppage goes on. But so do those of the employer. There is the immediate loss of profitable operation, and in some industries this cannot in the nature of things be made good by increased output when work is resumed. There is the likelihood that customers will resort to other suppliers meanwhile, and the possibility that some of them will never return. Firms that have been unprofitable, though on that account they cannot easily afford a rise, may not, however, be able to hold out against settling for one, because of their attenuated cash flow. The actual experience of increasing difficulty makes the parties willing to modify the terms for which they stood out when the stoppage began: there is convergence, and they reach agreement. Such at least is a natural interpretation of the observation that most stoppages have ended in a compromise. Reflecting on this, J.R. Hicks inferred (1932, ch. 7) that if the parties estimated each other's powers of resistance accurately beforehand, there would be no stoppage, but agreement would be reached at once on the terms reached only at the end of a stoppage that occurs when the parties do not know those powers, or misconceive them, and find out the facts by painful experience.

That most agreements are reached without a stoppage does not mean that bargaining power is not exerted. But more enters into the reaching of an agreement than bargaining power. The matter to be negotiated is the terms and conditions on which a joint activity is to be carried on by the parties in future, and this is not, like the price of a horse, to be haggled over between two people who may

687

never deal with each other again: the relation between parties who continue to be indispensable to one another is more nearly matrimonial. The parties are therefore open to influence by the thought of what is fair and reasonable in the terms on which they can work together. Trade unionists may be moved by the aim, not of receiving the greatest possible gain, but of obtaining what is justly due to them, or of righting a wrong. Where justice is at stake they will fight without weighing the cost against the gain.

Another consideration in their conduct of a negotiation is their determination to avoid subservience. They refuse to accept the force of the remark that the improvements in terms achieved by a strike will not make good the wages lost in the strike until after many years: for that is an argument to show that the employer's superior resources should always oblige the workers to accept his terms. Bargaining may turn again into warfare, in which trade unionists whose blood is up will make sacrifices according to no maximizing calculus, and will attack blacklegs with patriots' hatred for a traitor.

So far, the bargaining power of the trade union has been considered as if it were exerted by one of two parties facing each other in isolation; but the power of many unions is enhanced by the impact of their strikes on third parties and on the community. The third parties who are most likely to be disturbed by the stoppage of the employer's activity, and interested in his reaching an early settlement, are the firms who supply him with substantial parts of their own output, and those who depend on him for supplies that they cannot readily replace from stock or from other sources. A trade union that can withhold the supply of an essential product or service from a whole region can force the intervention of the government.

In 1893 the power of the English Miners' Federation to cut off much of the country's heat, light and inland transport brought about what was unthinkable a short time before – the intervention of Government to effect a settlement. When the French railwaymen went on strike the Government broke the strike by mobilizing them for military service. A strike of the British miners that threatened to bring the whole country to a halt in 1912 was settled by an Act of Parliament that gave the miners much of what they had claimed. Where the Government has to settle a national emergency dispute, it cannot force the trade unionists to resume work on terms that they reject as unfair and reasonable, but it can apply a substantial coercive force to the employers.

Control of essential supplies and services offered certain trade unions great power in this way, and the Triple Alliance of miners, transport workers and railwaymen was formed in Great Britain to exploit it; but the Government for its part built up a detailed organization, held in reserve against an emergency, for the maintenance of supplies. In the USA, the Taft–Hartley Act of 1947 provided that in a strike that creates a national emergency the President might take the business concerned into public possession for eighty days, during which the employees must return to work while a fact-finding board reported on the circumstances of the dispute. With the extension of trade unionism in the public sector and in services in Great Britain, the object of strikes has shifted from inflicting loss on the employer to demonstrating discontent by disrupting the activities of the community, and inflicting hardship on the parents of schoolchildren or on invalids or commuters.

TRADE UNIONS AND THE LAW. The bargaining power of trade unions depends upon legal privilege. Employers may refuse to recognize a trade union unless the law obliges them to do so. In a strike, labour is commonly withdrawn in breach of the individual worker's contract of employment; losses are usually inflicted on third parties. In the USA, employers were able to inhibit many forms of trade union action by obtaining injunctions against them from the courts, until the Norris–La Guardia Act of 1932. If those who suffer damages are able to bring civil actions to recover them, most strikes will be impossible: British trade unions have operated under the shelter of immunities that were given outright statutory form by the Trade Disputes Act 1906. Many strikes, again, will not be effective unless pickets are posted to turn back men and women who want to go on working, or stop supplies moving: the effectiveness of legal provisions designed to regulate picketing depends on the possibility and practice of enforcement. Not only the activities but the very existence of a trade union, as a combination in restraint of trade, are anomalous in a country whose common law protects the freedom of the individual to use his labour and property. In these countries the law has found a place for the trade union by way of large exception, rather than by the conferment of delimited rights.

The close bearing of the law on trade union activities has led the trade unions to bring pressure to bear on the legislature. The entering of representations on particular measures was the original purpose of the British Trades Union Congress, and the policy of the American Federation of Labour under Gompers. In later years the British trade unions have become the principal financial support of the Labour Party, and the American leadership has become associated with the Democratic Party. A main reason for association between European trade unions and a political party is the sharing of social principles and ideals, and in France and Italy different groups of trade unions are linked with different parties.

THE BARGAINING AREA. Bargaining power cannot be considered apart from the bargaining area within which it is exerted. What that area shall be in a given case is the outcome of historical factors. Sometimes the initiative in shaping the present area has been taken by employers, sometimes by trade unionists. American employers, perhaps because they were highly individualistic and competitive, have generally been loath to associate, even for the legitimate purpose of collective bargaining, and the plant contract has predominated. The British tradition has been that of the craft union that has tried to make one rate obtain for all engagements, and maintain it through times of slack trade; here the wider the front that could be held, the better, and trade union policy drew together the major employers of each district. Through World War I this extended to industry-wide bargaining. 'Putting a floor under competition' throughout an industry in that way was a step towards turning it into a cartel. It might seem to offer the trade unions concerned the opportunity to push up their pay as far as the elasticity of demand for the products of the industry would let them. The difference between wages in the 'sheltered' and 'unsheltered' industries in the interwar years suggests that some effect of that kind did come about, if only in resisting downward pressure. More positive effects are less likely because employers' resistance will be based on their expectation of price rises stimulating competition from fresh sources at home as well as abroad.

Ideally, trade unions use establishment bargaining (the plant contract) to combine central control of 'the rate for the job' in all establishments, with whatever extra benefits can be extracted from the profitability of particular firms; but in hard times the local or union branch may prefer job security to maintenance of rates, and make concessions. Whereas industry-wide agreements are limited to simple provisions capable of general application, the American plant contract is generally voluminous, and provides rules for all manner of working practices and procedures in the plant. The trade union can therefore undertake to submit any dispute arising during the currency of the contract to arbitration, as the arbitrator can interpret and apply the relevant rule to the facts of the case.

TRADE UNIONISM AT THE PLACE OF WORK. Whether or not the trade unionists working in an establishment negotiate their own agreement with management, they are concerned with issues arising within its walls. Such issues include allocation and pace of work; discipline; promotion; redundancies; and the processing of grievances. Under the law of the USA, the sole negotiating rights for all the manual workers of an establishment can be vested in one union; the officers of its local branch will then represent them on all these issues. In a British establishment the workers may belong to a number of unions, but the shop stewards elected by the members of the different unions come together in a council, which provides unified representation in meetings with management; its convenor may be wholly occupied with administrative business. Where the roots of trade unionism run back to handicrafts, the workshop is the arena in which the issues arise which bind the member to the union and over which sterner battles have been fought, as new machines and methods have come in, than have been caused by disputes about pay.

It has long been the aim of some trade unions in Europe, but not in the USA, to transcend the adversary system which opposed their members to management at the place of work. Many have sought to do this by a political revolution that would abolish capitalism, but equally in the social democracies, part of the case for nationalization has been that it would substitute public appointment for the irresponsibility of the private employer. Some trade unions have been more concerned with the substance of face-to-face relations, and the possibilities of workers' control and self-management. Interest has therefore attached to the statutory provision in the laws of some European countries, especially Germany, for works councils and the appointment of directors to represent the workers on supervisory boards. The general verdict on the German provisions is that the works councils – where the franchise extends to all employees, but the representatives are in practice the trade unionists – are greatly valued by the trade unions as a means of consultation and joint consideration of management issues; but the appointment of 'worker directors', though a mark of status whose removal would be resented, is not found to confer benefits that are actively felt.

THE IMPACT OF THE TRADE UNION ON PAY. Some estimate of the effects that the trade unions have taken can be made by comparing the behaviour of pay in periods of trade union activity and at other times. In a number of Western countries there was a rapid extension of membership, for example, in the years following 1890; in Great Britain membership doubled during World War I; in many Western countries, but not in the USA, membership rose again in the years of full employment after World War II. When such indications as these of trade union strength and activity are set against the economic record, certain inferences suggest themselves about the extent to which trade unions may have changed the course of events, at large and in detail.

It appears that their effect on the general level of money wage rates has been in part to reinforce the ratchet effect which stops those rates dropping back and which has long been present even in the absence of combination: the much smaller reductions of wages in the organized trades in the USA in the great depression of 1929–34 is particularly striking. Generally it was observed that when the falling phase of the eight-year cycle brought wage cuts, the trade union deferred them or even staved them off altogether. Correspondingly, in the rising phase trade unionists were able to get a rise earlier than unorganized workers in their place would have done. But it has not appeared that even widespread and solid trade unionism has been able to push up the general level of money wage rates in a hard market environment, that is, when employers generally have not been able to pass higher costs on in higher prices. The case has been different when the expectation of the employers, reinforced by the commitments of government, allow the negotiation of wage rises needed to keep the workers concerned in line with others, even though product prices must be raised in consequence: in these conditions associated with full employment the trade unions decide the course of the price level jointly with that of money wage rates.

The effect of trade unions on the level of real wages depends on their effect in the first place on productivity, or output per head, and then on their effect on distribution, or the share of output that accrues to the worker. That the 'restrictive practices' enforced by those unions whose control of employment is close enough serve to reduce productivity is evident from their nature, and from the willingness of managers to pay for their removal; but there are understandings about stints and working practices among unorganized workers too, and management must accept some understanding about these issues in any negotiated agreement with its workforce – the question is where the line shall be drawn. If changes in the strength of trade unionism have affected changes in productivity over time, it has been as only one among other and stronger influences: though the activity and spirit of the New Unionism in Great Britain were held responsible for the check to productivity that became conspicuous there at the beginning of the

20th century, the extension of trade union membership and of trade union activity at the place of work in the 1950s and 1960s occurred at a time when the rise of productivity was exceptionally fast and sustained.

The effect of trade unions on distribution is illuminated by the evidence from a number of countries of trends that have kept real wages proportionate to productivity, that is, to real output per head (Phelps Brown and Browne, 1968). Whatever the course of money wages, and whatever trade unions may have done at certain times to make them rise faster, the prices of products must have been adjusted so as to maintain a given ratio of wage to product; and in periods such as 1874–89 and 1923–37 in Great Britain, when money wages did not rise at all from end to end but productivity rose, the real wage was raised by a fall in prices. A further implication is that the proportionate division of the product between pay and profits has been constant. But this division, and the stability in the ratio of the real wage to productivity, has been subject to occasional displacement, in which that ratio has been raised. In depression and deflation, the power of the trade union to resist cuts compresses profit margins, and it appears that when the upheaval is sufficiently thoroughgoing, as after World War I, norms and expectations are permanently shifted, and the previous share of profits may never be restored.

Evidently the rise in the standard of living which has transformed the condition of the working population of the western world since 1850 seems to owe nothing directly to trade union pressure for higher wages. Trade unions appear to have taken more effect on distribution as anvil than as hammer. But these inferences from the behaviour of the general level of wages are compatible with substantial influence of the trade unions on the structure of pay. Particular groups may have gained by unionization. One effect of unionization is that it reduces the dispersion of rates for labour of the same type of grade, which otherwise is commonly wide, even in the same locality. Inquiries have also agreed in finding that unionization lifts the organized relatively to the unorganized. Collectively, this shows itself in the rise obtained when a group first bargains; but this is only an impact effect. There has been a cyclical pattern of variation between the wages of organized and unorganized workers, but not progressive divergence. Whether trade unions have changed the differential for skill depends on whether the skilled grades are organized and negotiate separately, or, if they belong to a general union, on their political influence within it. In Sweden in the 1950s and 1960s the pay structure was compressed by agreements made at the national level in pursuance of the egalitarian philosophy of the *Landsorganisationen*, the national trade union organization; but differentials were restored by wage drift on the shop floor. Statistical studies have shown that individuals who belong to trade unions earn substantially more than non-members when allowance is made for the factors making up personal earning capacity: the difficulty is to be sure that all such factors have been taken into account.

COST PUSH, STAGFLATION AND INCOMES POLICIES. The ability of trade unions to push up the general level of pay when employers are not constrained from raising prices became an engine of cost inflation in the 1960s, when trade unionists sloughed off the cautious expectations formed in harder times, and began raising their claims. Various forms of incomes policy were devised to persuade or require the trade unions to accept rises in money wages that did not outrun the prospective rise in productivity. But for the individual trade unionist, a rise in the money wage was equally a rise in the real wage at the time it was given; and experience showed that the tolerance of trade unionists for policies that required them to accept less than full compensation for rises in the cost of living, was limited. When in the 1970s recession brought back constraints on employers, the trade unionists' expectations and claims persisted, and the combination of unemployment and cost inflation was known as stagflation. It was widely recognized that in these circumstances an expansion of demand would be effective in reducing unemployment only if it was not used by trade unionists in jobs to push their pay up, and that it would therefore have to be accompanied by some form of agreement on restraint between the government and the trade unions.

BIBLIOGRAPHY
Bain, G.S. and Price, R. 1960. *Profiles of Union Growth*. Oxford: Blackwell.
Hicks, J.R. 1932. *The Theory of Wages*. 2nd edn, London: Macmillan, 1963.
Phelps Brown, E.H. and Hopkins, S.V. 1955. Seven centuries of building wages. *Economica* 22, August, 87. Reprinted in E.H. Phelps Brown and S.V. Hopkins, *A Perspective of Wages and Prices*, London and New York: Methuen, 1981.
Phelps Brown, E.H. and Browne, M.H. 1968. *A Century of Pay: the course of pay and production in France, Germany, Sweden, the United Kingdom, and the United States of America, 1860–1960*. London: Macmillan.
Smith, A. 1776. *An Inquiry into the Nature and Causes of the Wealth of Nations*. Ed. E. Cannan. Reprinted, London: Methuen, 1961; New York: Random House, 1965.
Webb, S. and B. 1894. *The History of Trade Unionism*. 2nd edn, London: Longmans, 1920.

Utopias

GREGORY CLAEYS

The word 'utopia' is derived from a Greek term meaning 'no place'. A utopia is a fictional account of a perfect or ideal society which in its economic aspect is usually stationary and often includes community of goods. Many proposals for social reform have included elements inspired by utopias, and most utopias at least tacitly plead for social change. There is no single utopian tradition and thus no unilinear relationship between 'utopia' and the history of economic thought. Insofar as the provision of a subsistence for mankind has been the aim of all forms of normative economic thought, however, the mode of thinking about perfect or harmonious societies termed 'utopian' has usually presented itself as the most comprehensive answer to the riddles offered by economic writers. Particularly in the modern period this has involved the use of science and technology to solve economic problems. In turn, the most ambitious plans to settle all economic difficulties have themselves often verged upon the utopian (in the sense of being particularly fanciful or unachievable). A clarification of this relationship requires distinguishing utopian thought from at least four related modes of speculation. In millenarianism, all social problems are disposed of through divine intervention, often in the form of the Second Coming of Christ, at which time a perfect society is founded. In the medieval English poetic vision described in the 'Land of Cockaygne' and similar works, all forms of scarcity are dissolved in a fantasy of satiety, where desires remain fixed while their means of satisfaction increase without labour and are consumed without effort. In arcadias, a greater stress is given to the satisfaction of 'natural' desires alone and to the equal importance of a spiritual and aesthetic existence. In what has been termed the 'perfect moral community' the necessity for a prior change in human nature and especially in human wants is also assumed and more attention is given to spiritual regneration as the basis of social harmony.

In all forms of ideal societies the problem of wants or needs is central. The utopian tradition has tended to accept the central tension between limited resources and insatiable appetites, neither ignoring the problem nor assuming

694

any essential change in human nature (Fuz, 1952, has termed 'utopias of escape' those which begin with the assumption of plenty, 'utopias of realization' those which presume scarcity as a starting point). Most utopias attempt instead to control the key forms of social malaise (crime, poverty, vice, war, etc.) which result from human frailty, giving greater stress to the best organization of social institutions rather than idealizing either nature (as in the Land of Cockaygne) or man (as does the perfect moral commonwealth), and relying upon designs fostered by human ingenuity rather than those derived from divine foresight. In economic as well as other aspects, utopias seek the perfection of a completely ordered and detailed social model rather than an interim solution to or partial reform of present disorders. In the imaginative grasp of possibility and presumptive omniscience of exactitude lies the charm and utility as well as the overperfectionist dangers of utopian schemes. Seeking at once to preserve the best of the past and to design an ideal future, utopias have themselves often served as models for judging the adequacy of the present as well as – particularly in the areas of science and technology – its logical linear development.

As a general rule the economic aspect of the utopian tradition can be understod as moving from a central concern with the maintenance of limited wants and (very often) a community of goods to solve problems of production and distribution, to a greater reliance upon the productive powers provided by science, technology and new forms of economic organization, with less strenuous demands being made for a denial of 'artificial' needs. In this sense the history of utopias mirrors both economic history and the history of economic thought insofar as the latter has legitimized that potential for satisfying greater needs for which scientific and technological developments have provided the chief basis. As mainstream liberal political economy came to relinquish the ideal of economic regulation in the 18th century, relying instead upon the development of the market to overcome scarcity, utopianism also shifted its emphasis away from the creation of virtue and towards that of organized superfluity and affluence, often in combination with centralized economic planning and organization. Technology has been presumed to have brought a diminution in the amount of socially necessary labour without the necessity for a concomitant reduction in wants. The inevitability of an extreme division of labour has also been supplanted by the vision of alternating forms of more interesting and creative employment in many modern utopias. Contemporary utopianism both builds upon the promises of technology, and remains critical of forms of social organization which fail to develop this potential or to curb its harmful excesses. No longer content to offer a transcendent image of possibility, modern utopianism is moreover committed to the problem of actualizing planned and ideal societies.

Though the utopian genre is usually dated from the publication of Thomas More's *Utopia* (1516), the proposal of a community of goods as a major element in the solution to economic disorder is much older. An important antecedent was Plato's *Republic* (*c*360 BC), in which the ruling Guardians alone shared their goods in common as a means of ensuring the least conflict between private and public interest. At the end of the 2nd century AD Plutarch wrote his life of the mythical Spartan legislator Lycurgus, who ended avarice, luxury and inequality by an equal division of lands, the replacement of gold and silver by iron coinage, and various sumptuary laws. Though Aristotle was an early and influential critic of Plato's communism, the idea that a community of goods was the ideal state of property survived in various forms in the early Christian era. The very ancient image of a mythical Golden Age of flowing milk and honey which appeared in Hesiod (c750 BC), Ovid, and the Stoic-influenced account of the Isles of the Blessed here found a counterpart in the imagery of Paradise and the Garden of Eden, and it was universally assumed that the institution of private property could only have resulted from the Fall and the expulsion of Adam and Eve from Paradise. Some community of goods existed among the Jewish sect of the Essenes, in the early Christian Church as well as later monastic movements, and there was later considerable debate as to whether the Apostles had intended this to hold amongst themselves or for all mankind. But early on the Church offered a robust defence of the naturalness of private property on the grounds that it produced greater peace, order and economic efficiency. Charity, however, and especially the support of the poor in times of necessity, was regarded as the duty accompanying the private ownership of goods on an earth intended by God to be sufficient for the sustenance of all.

This was the tradition which Thomas More, with one eye on Plato and another, perhaps, on the potential for the New World, was to overthrow. In More the possibility of secular, social improvement was revived and now recrafted in a new image of fantasy. Both at this time and later, rapid economic change in Britain was a key reason for the Anglo-centric character of much of the utopian tradition. No doubt angered by the effects of land enclosures on the poor, More gave to the Utopians not only equality but also plenty, six hours' daily work (and more dignity to their activity than had done the ancient utopias) and a rotation of homes every ten years and of town and country inhabitants more frequently. Public markets made all goods freely available while public hospitals cared for the sick. National plenty and scarcity were to be balanced by compensatory distribution, while the surplus was in part given away to the poor of other countries and in part sold at moderate rates. Iron was to be esteemed higher than silver or gold, while jewels and pearls were treated as mere baubles fit only for children. Needs were clearly fixed and limited to the level of comforts. With the conquest of the fear of want, greed was largely eliminated, while pomp and excess derived from pride alone were prohibited by law.

The mid-16th century saw a variety of radical Protestant attempts and plans to emulate the purported communism of the early Church (e.g. in the Hutterite Anabaptism of Peter Rideman), and a considerable augmentation to anti-luxury sentiments within a few of the Protestant sects. A preference for agriculture and hostility to luxury typifies most Renaissance utopias, for instance Johan Günzberg's *Wolfaria* (1621), Andreae's *Christianopolis* (1619) (in which a guild model was of some importance), Campanella's *City of the Sun* (1623) (in which slave labour was first abolished in a utopia) and Robert Burton's *Anatomy of Melancholy* (1621) which included a powerful attack upon avarice as well as a

696

national plan for land utilization, the management of economic resources by a bureaucracy, communal granaries and the public employment of doctors and lawyers. Francis Bacon's *New Atlantis* (1627) was less concerned with the details of economic organization than with the justification of the rule of scientists, and established a paradigmatic attitude towards technology often repeated in later utopias. Bacon also paid some heed to the dangers posed by novelties generally to social order, while Samuel Gott's *Nova Solyma* (1648) was more severe in its condemnation of luxury and intolerance of waste. Of the utopias of the English civil war period, two are particularly worthy of note. Gerrard Winstanley's *The Law of Freedom in a Platform* (1652) developed the Diggers' efforts to reclaim common land for the poor into a scheme for the communal ownership of all land which included universal agricultural labour to age 40. Public storehouses were to make all necessary goods freely available as needed, while domestic buying and selling and working for hire were prohibited. Gold and silver were to be used for external trade alone. Better known was James Harrington's *Oceana* (1656), which popularized the proposal for agrarian laws in order to prevent the predominance of the aristocracy and urged a limit upon dowries and inheritance for similar reasons.

The late 17th century occasioned a profusion of welfare or full-employment utopias in Britain (only in the following century would France see as rich a development of the genre). At this time schemes for practical, immediate social reform and utopias proper were often not far removed. It is in this period, too, that we begin to find a shift away from a concern with a limited demand and the satisfaction of only natural wants towards a conception of maximized production with the full employment of people and resources and a minimization of waste (goals to some extent shared by mainstream Mercantilism). Such aims are evident in, for example, *A Description of the Famous Kingdom of Macaria* (1641), where most legislation is concerned with regulating the production of wealth, Peter Chamberlen's *The Poore Man's Advocate* (1649), which included a detailed scheme for the joint-stock employment of the poor to be supervised by public officials, Peter Plockhoy's *A Way Propounded to Make the Poor in These and Other Nations Happy* (1659), which proposed the resettlement into communities of an elite of artisans, husbandmen and traders, and John Bellers's *Proposals for Raising a College of Industry* (1695), in which the wealthy would help to found communities where the poor were to support them while also providing a decent subsistence for themselves. In such plans, solutions to economic distress tended to focus increasingly upon isolated communities rather than the nation-state, and upon segments of the population rather than, for example, all the poor. It has been suggested (by J.C. Davis, 1981) that this implied a waning confidence in the ability of the state to tackle the problem of poverty, and certainly it seems evident that the Act of Settlement of 1662 transferred this burden to individual parishes and away from central government.

The period between 1700 and 1900 marks not only the great age of utopian speculation, but also the period in which economic practice and utopian precept become increasingly intertwined. In addition, it was here that a community of goods ceased to be the *sine qua non* of utopian ideas of property, and that the liberal view of the benefits of private property ownership itself was expressed in utopian form. This entailed a combination of utopian thought and the theory of progress, though in the genre as a whole the two are usually understood as contradictory. In both modern socialism and classical political economy, then, needs are perceived as virtually unlimited, and social harmony is contingent largely upon their fulfilment. The homage to *homo economicus* is usually understood to have begun in Daniel Defoe's *Robinson Crusoe* (1719), and was at its most exalted in Richard Cobden and John Bright's mid-19th-century claims about the universal peace which would be incumbent upon the global extension of free trade. One of its first serious challenges was in John Stuart Mill's acceptance after 1850 of the desirability of a steady-state economy in which further economic development was avoided. Many 18th-century utopias were devoted to the notion of progress (e.g. Mercier's *L'An 2440* (1770) and Condorcet's *L'esquisse d'un tableau historique des progrès de l'esprit humain* (1794)). In others the critique of commercial society took various forms, such as Swift's gentle satire in *Gulliver's Travels* (1726), where the Houyhnhnms showed great disdain for shining stones and distributed their produce according to need, or Rousseau's more biting castigation of civilization in his *Discours sur l'origine de l'inégalité* (1755). Similar criticisms were developed into the foundations of modern communism in the writings of Raynal, Mercier, Mably, Morelly, Babeuf and in Britain, Spence and Godwin. In many of these the Spartan model was of some importance, and luxury seen as a principal source of working class oppression as well as general moral corruption.

Though the entire utopian edifice was severely shaken by the pessimistic prognosis of Malthus's *Essay on Population* (1798), the first half of the 19th century witnessed the widespread foundation of small 'utopian socialist' ideal communities which aimed to bring utopian goals into practice, and which could be essentially communistical (Robert Owen, Etienne Cabet) or semi-capitalist (Charles Fourier). Other plans concentrated upon the nation-state and the beneficial development of large-scale industry (Saint-Simon), a pattern which was to become increasingly dominant as the potential role of machinery in creating a new cornucopia became evident. (Some disenchantment with this view occured later, however, for example in William Morris's *News from Nowhere* (1890), with its preference for rustic and artisanal virtues.) Considerably more attention came to be paid in the early 19th century (for example, by Owen and Fourier) to the disadvantages of too narrow a division of labour and the benefits of task rotation. In the middle of the century began the most compelling radical vision of the age in the works of Marx and Engels, whose plans qualify as utopian in the degree to which they inherited overly optimistic assumptions about human nature, technology and social organization in a future society in which private property and alienation were to be superseded. The last twenty years of the century found, at least in Britain and America, a virtually continuous outpouring of planned-economy utopias, of which the best known are Edward Bellamy's *Looking Backward* (1887), which included provisions for the abolition of money, equal wages and credit for all, and an industrial army, W.D. Howells's *A Traveller from Altruria* (1894), and H.G. Wells's *A Modern Utopia* (1905), which made some effort to incorporate a conception of progress into the ideal image of the future, and included a mixed rather than wholly publicly owned economy.

In the 20th century utopianism has faltered in face of some of the consequences of modernity, and speculation has often taken the form of the negative utopia or dystopia. In the most famous of these, George Orwell's *Nineteen Eighty-Four* (1948), both capitalist aggression and inequality and communist despotism were criticized, with a central thesis of the work being the prevention of the majority enjoying the benefits of mass production via the deliberate destruction of commodities in war. More satirical of the hedonist utopia is Aldous Huxley's *Brave New World* (1932), though Huxley's later *Island* (1962) is a positive utopia which criticizes the spiritual impoverishment of an overly-materialistic civilization. Late 20th century popular utopianism has included some works of science fiction, the libertarian speculation of Murray Rothbard and Robert Nozick (*Anarchy, State, and Utopia*, 1974), and the steady-state environmentalism of Ernest Callenbach's *Ecotopia* (1975). With the progressive extension of both machinery and the welfare state, utopias developing such themes optimistically have declined. To those sated with goods some of the attractions of the consumerist paradise have faded. Technological determinism has often seemingly rendered forms of economic organization unimportant. Two world wars and the spectre of nuclear catastrophe have dented confidence in human perfectibility, while half a century's experimentation with centrally planned communism has lent little credence to the view that this provides the surest path to moral and economic improvement. Nor is 'growth' any longer an uncritically accepted ideal even amongst those who have not yet experienced its effects. Nonetheless the utility of utopias to economic thought is undiminished, for they offer both illumination into important aspects of the history of economic ideas (especially in the areas of welfare and planning), as well as an imaginative leap into possible futures into which more positivist and empirically based thinking fears to wander. If 'progress' can be realized without 'growth', it will likely first persuasively appear in utopian form.

BIBLIOGRAPHY

Adams, R.P. 1949. The social responsibilities of science in *Utopia, New Atlantis* and after. *Journal of the History of Ideas* 10, 374–98.

Armytage, W.H.G. 1984. Utopias: the technological and educational dimension. In *Utopias*, ed. P. Alexander and R. Gill, London: Duckworth.

Boguslaw, R. 1965. *The New Utopians: A Study of System Design and Social Change.* Englewood Cliffs, NJ: Prentice-Hall.

Bowman, S. 1973. Utopian views of man and the machine. *Studies in the Literary Imagination* 6, 105–20.

Claeys, G. 1986. Industrialism and hedonism in Orwell's literary and political development. *Albion* 18.

Claeys, G. 1987. *Machinery, Money and the Millennium. From Moral Economy to Socialism.* Oxford: Polity Press.

Dautry, J. 1961. Le pessimisme économique de Babeuf et l'histoire des Utopies. *Annales Historiques de la Révolution Francaise* 33, 215–33.

Davis, J.C. 1981. *Utopia and the Ideal Society. A Study of English Utopian Writing 1516–1700*. Cambridge and New York: Cambridge University Press.

Eurich, N. 1967. *Science in Utopia*. Cambridge, Mass.: Harvard University Press.

Farr, J. 1983. Technology in the Digger Utopia. In *Dissent and Affirmation: Essays in Honor of Mulford Sibley*, ed. A.L. Kalleberg, J.D. Moon and D. Sabia, Bowling Green: Bowling Green University Popular Press.

Flory, C.R. 1967. *Economic Criticism in American Fiction, 1792 to 1900*. New York: Russell & Russell.

Fogg, W.L. 1975. Technology and dystopia. In *Utopia/Dystopia?*, ed. P.E. Richter, Cambridge, Mass.: Schenkman.

Fuz, J.K. 1952. *Welfare Economics in English Utopias from Francis Bacon to Adam Smith*. The Hague: Martinus Nijhoff.

Gelbart, N. 1978. Science in French Enlightenment Utopias. *Proceedings of the Western Society for French History* 6, 120–28.

Goodwin, B. 1984. Economic and social innovation in Utopia. In *Utopias*, ed. P. Alexander and R. Gill, London: Duckworth.

Gusfield, J. 1971. Economic development as a modern utopia. In *Aware of Utopia*, ed. D.W. Plath, Urbana: University of Illinois Press.

Hall, A.R. 1972. Science, technology and utopia in the seventeenth century. In *Science and Society 1600–1900*, ed. P. Mathias, Cambridge and New York: Cambridge University Press.

Hont, I. and Ignatieff, M. 1983. Needs and justice in the *Wealth of Nations*: an introductory essay. In *Wealth and Virtue: the Shaping of Political Economy in the Scottish Enlightenment*, ed. I. Hont and M. Ignatieff, Cambridge: Cambridge University Press.

Hudson, W. 1946. Economic and social thought of Gerrard Winstanley: was he a seventeenth-century marxist? *Journal of Modern History* 18, 1–21.

Hymer, S. 1971. Robinson Crusoe and the secret of primitive accumulation. *Monthly Review* 23, 11–36.

King, J.E. 1983. Utopian or scientific? A reconsideration of the Ricardian Socialists. *History of Political Economy* 15, 345–73.

Klassen, P.J. 1964. *The Economics of Anabaptism 1525–60*. The Hague: Mouton.

Krieger, R. 1980. The economics of Utopia. In *Utopias: the American Experience*, ed. G.B. Moment and O.F. Kraushaar, London: Scarecrow Press.

Landa, L. 1943. Swift's economic views and Mercantilism. *English Literary History* 10, 310–35.

Leiss, W. 1970. Utopia and technology: reflections on the conquest of nature. *International Social Science Journal* 22, 576–88.

Levitas, R. 1984. Need, nature and nowhere. In *Utopias*, ed. P. Alexander and R. Gill, London: Duckworth.

MacDonald, W. 1946. Communism in Eden? *New Scholasticism* 20, 101–25.

MacKenzie, D. 1984. Marx and the machine. *Technology and Culture* 25, 473–502.

Manuel, F.E. and Manuel, F.P. 1979. *Utopian Thought in the Western World*. Oxford: Basil Blackwell; Cambridge, Mass.: Harvard University Press.

Mumford, L. 1967. Utopia, the city and the machine. In *Utopias and Utopian Thought*, ed. F.E. Manuel, Boston: Beacon Press.

Novak, M. 1976. *Economics and the Fiction of Daniel Defoe*. New York: Russell & Russell.

Perrot, J.-C. 1982. Despotische Verkunft und ökonomische Utopie. In *Utopieforschung. Interdisziplinäre Studien zur neuzeitlichen Utopie*, ed. W. Vosskamp, Stuttgart: J.B. Metzlersche Verlagsbuchhandlung.

Pocock, J.G.A. 1980. The mobility of property and the rise of eighteenth-century sociology. In *Theories of Property, Aristotle to the Present*, ed. A. Parel and T. Flanagan, Waterloo: Wilfred Laurier University Press.

Sargent, L.T. 1981. Capitalist utopias in America. In *America as Utopia*, ed. K.M. Roemer, New York: Burt Franklin.

Schlaeger, J. 1982. Die Robinsonade als frühbürgerliche 'Eutopia'. In *Utopieforschung. Interdisziplinäre Studien zur neuzeitlichen Utopie*, ed. W. Vosskamp, Stuttgart: J.B. Metzlersche Verlagsbuchhandlung.

Schoeck, R.J. 1956. More, Plutarch, and King Agis: Spartian history and the meaning of *Utopia*. *Philological Quarterly* 35, 366–75.

Segal, H. 1985. *Technological Utopianism in American Culture*. Chicago: Chicago University Press.

Sibley, M.Q. 1973. Utopian thought and technology. *American Journal of Political Science* 17, 255–81.

Soper, K. 1981. *On Human Needs: Open and Closed Theories in Marxist Perspectives*. London: Harvester Press.

Springborg, P. 1981. *The Problem of Human Needs and the Critique of Civilisation*. London: George Allen & Unwin.

Steintrager, J. 1969. Plato and More's *Utopia*. *Social Research* 36, 357–72.

Taylor, W.F. 1942. *The Economic Novel in America*. Chapel Hill: University of North Carolina Press.

Thompson, N.W. 1985. *The People's Science. The Popular Political Economy of Exploitation and Crisis, 1816–34*. Cambridge: Cambridge University Press.

Welles, C.B. 1948. The economic background of Plato's communism. *Journal of Economic History* 8, 101–14.

Value Judgements

JOHN C. HARSANYI

THE CLAIM OF OBJECTIVE VALIDITY. One may define value judgements as judgements of approval or disapproval claiming objective validity. Many of our judgements of approval and disapproval do not involve such claims. When I say that I like a particular dish, I do not mean to imply that other people ought to like it too or that those disliking it are making a mistake. All I am doing is expressing my personal preference and my personal taste. (But an expert chef or an expert food critic may very well claim that his judgements about food have some degree of objective validity – in the sense that other gastronomic experts would tend to agree with his judgements. Of course, it is an empirical question whether his claim would be justified and, more generally, how much agreement there is in fact among expert judges of food.) Yet when I say that Hitler's murder of many millions of innocent people was a moral outrage, I do mean to do more than express my personal moral attitudes and do mean to imply that anybody who tried to defend Hitler's actions would be morally wrong.

In claiming objective validity, value judgements resemble factual judgements (both those dealing with empirical facts and those dealing with logical-mathematical facts). But they resemble judgements of personal preference in expressing human attitudes (those of approval or disapproval) rather than expressing beliefs about matters of fact, as factual judgements do. But this immediately poses a difficult philosophical problem: We can understand what it means for factual judgements to be objectively valid, i.e. to be true, or to be objectively invalid, i.e. to be false. They will be true if they describe the relevant facts as these facts actually are, and will be false if they fail to do so. But in what sense can judgements expressing human attitudes be objectively valid or invalid?

It seems to me that this can happen in at least two different ways. Such judgements can be objectively invalid either because they are contrary to the facts or because they are based on the wrong value perspective. Value judgements can be contrary to the facts in the following sense: When we form our attitudes, we do so on the basis of some specific factual assumptions so that our attitudes and our judgements expressing these attitudes will be contrary to the facts if they are based on false factual assumptions. Mistaken factual assumptions may vitiate both our value judgements about instrumental values and those about intrinsic values. Thus, if I approve of using A as a means to achieve some end B, I will do this on the assumption that A is causally effective in achieving B. Hence, my approval will be mistaken if this assumption is incorrect. Likewise, if I approve of A as an intrinsically desirable goal, I will do this on the assumption that A has some qualities I find intrinsically attractive. My approval will be mistaken if in fact A does not possess these qualities.

Another way a value judgement may be objectively invalid is by being based on a value perspective different from the one it claims to have. For example, I may claim that my support for some government policy is based on its being in the public interest, even though actually it is based on its being in my own personal interest. Or, I may praise a very undistinguished novel as a great work of art merely because it supports my own political point of view. When a person claims to base his value judgement on one value perspective though actually he bases it on another, he may simply be lying, being fully aware of not telling the truth. Another possibility is that he is unaware, or only half aware, of using a value perspective different from the one he claims to use. (Likewise, when a person is making a value judgement based on false factual assumptions, he may or may not be fully aware of the falsity of these assumptions.)

DISAGREEMENTS IN VALUE JUDGEMENTS. As we all know, disagreements in value judgements are extremely common and in many cases are very hard, or even impossible, to resolve. It seems to me that in most cases careful analysis would show that these disagreements about values are based on disagreements about the facts. Yet, they may be very hard to resolve because these factual disagreements may be about very subtle facts about which reliable information is very hard, or even impossible, to obtain. For instance, our value judgements about a person's behaviour will often crucially depend on what we think his motives are. Some observers may attribute very noble motives to him, while others may do the opposite. Yet, the available evidence might be consistent with either assumption. Other value judgements we make may hinge on our predictions about future facts. Thus, different economists may advocate very different economic policies because they have very different expectations on the likely effects of specific policies – even if their ultimate policy objectives are much the same. Yet, at the present stage of our knowledge about the economic system, we may be unable to tell with any degree of confidence which predictions are right and which are wrong.

Of course, we could avoid most of these disagreements if we refrained from making value judgements until we could ascertain with some assurance that the factual assumptions underlying the value judgements we want to make are correct. But this would require more intellectual self-discipline than most of us can muster. We have to act one way or another; and it is psychologically much easier for us to act if we can manage to entertain value judgements justifying our actions –

even if the factual assumptions underlying these value judgements go far beyond, or are even clearly inconsistent with, the available evidence.

Let me add that most disagreements in value judgements are not disagreements about what the basic values of human life actually are. Rather, most disagreements are about the relative weights and the relative priorities to be assigned to different basic values. Some individuals and some societies will learn from their experience – possibly based on a very idiosyncratic personal or national history – that things tend to work out best if value A is given far greater weight than value B is. Other individuals and other societies will reach very much the opposite conclusion on the basis of their experience. Once a given ranking of these two values has been adopted, it may be retained for a long time even when conditions change and make this ranking utterly inappropriate. For instance, an individual or a society that suffered a good deal from lack of individual freedom may be so preoccupied with political liberty as to neglect the need for social discipline – even under conditions that would make the need for social discipline paramount.

Besides disagreements about the facts, another source of value conflicts are philosophical disagreements about the correct value perspectives to be used in making various classes of value judgements. For instance, even if two people agree about all the relevant facts, they may still make conflicting moral value judgements if they disagree about the nature of morality and, therefore, disagree about the nature of the moral perspective to be used in making moral value judgements. (For instance, one individual may favour a utilitarian interpretation of morality (see, e.g., Harsanyi, 1977), while the other may favour an entitlement interpretation (see Nozick, 1974).) In the same way, disagreements about the nature of the aesthetic perspective to be used in making aesthetic value judgements may lead to disagreements about the artistic quality of various works of art.

VALUE JUDGEMENTS IN ECONOMICS. There was a time when many economists wanted to ensure the objectivity of economic analysis by excluding value judgements, and even the study of value judgements, from economics. (A very influential advocate of this position has been Robbins, 1932.) Luckily, they have not succeeded; and we now know that economics would have been that much poorer if they had.

After some important preliminary work in the 1930s and 1940s, mainly in welfare economics, a new era in the study of economically relevant value judgements has started with Arrow's *Social Choice and Individual Values* (1951). This book has shown how to express alternative value judgements in the form of precisely stated formal axioms, how to investigate their logical implications in a rigorous manner, and how to examine their mutual consistency or inconsistency. Arrow's book and the research inspired by it have greatly enriched economic theory not only in welfare economics but also in several other fields, including the theory of competitive equilibrium. It has given rise to a new subdiscipline called *public choice theory*, which is a rigorous study of voting and of alternative voting systems and which has made important contributions to the study of alternative political systems and of alternative moral codes and, more indirectly, to the study of alternative economic systems as mechanisms of social choice.

Of course, value judgements often play an important role in economics even when they are not the main subjects of investigation. They influence the policy recommendations made by economists and their judgements about the merits of alternative systems of economic organization. But this need not impair the social utility of the work done by economists as long as it is work of high intellectual quality and as long as the economists concerned *know* what they are doing, *know* the qualifications their conclusions are subject to, and *tell* their readers what these qualifications are. In particular, intellectual honesty requires economists to *state* their political and moral value judgements and to make clear how their conclusions differ from those that economists of different points of view would tend to reach on the problems under discussion. What is no less important, they should make clear how *uncertain* many of their empirical claims and their predictions actually are. This is particularly important in publications addressed mainly to people outside the economist profession.

BIBLIOGRAPHY

Arrow, K.J. 1951. *Social Choice and Individual Values*. New York: Wiley.

Harsanyi, J.C. 1977. Morality and the theory of rational behavior. *Social Research* 44, 623–56.

Nozick, R. 1974. *Anarchy, State and Utopia*. Oxford: Blackwell.

Robbins, L. 1932. *An Essay on the Nature and Significance of Economic Science*. London: Macmillan.

Value of Life

THOMAS C. SCHELLING

It is not identified lives but statistical lives – the reduction of some mortal hazard to some part of the population – whose value is our topic. But the prolongation of individual lives is getting increased attention, and it deserves some of ours before we get on with the main business.

'Our society values life', a California judge commented when he ordered force-feeding for a quadriplegic woman who wished to die and had asked the hospital's help in starving to death. Medical technology now provides, and medical institutions often require, procedures that prolong lives expensively and indefinitely even when the life is of dubious quality to the patient. These are procedures that the deciding institutions either cannot deny or will not permit to be withdrawn, and they are independent of any assessment of value of the life extension procured. In some cases rejoicing is unanimous when death mercifully terminates an effort to prolong life.

Even assessing the value of statistical lifesaving – reducing some small carcinogenic hazard – is not universally considered properly subject to a comparison of costs and benefits. In the US government there has been controversy whether the cost per life saved should be a consideration in occupational-safety decisions: even the courts have had difficulty construing the legislation to permit taking costs into account. Nor is it generally accepted that hazardous activities should always be relocated to less densely populated areas where fewer would be at risk. Marginal outlays per expected life saved vary among agencies by two orders of magnitude.

In economics, valuing life means the prevention of death, not the creation of people who might never have existed. The economics of overpopulation can draw an economist's attention, but nobody measures the welfare gain to sterile parents of a steady supply of births for adoption. Economies of scale to population size in a sparsely populated area are easy to handle; but the value of simply having more 'lives' – more people born to enjoy life – is rarely discussed in our profession. It is only philosophers (Parfit, 1984, pp. 351–454, 487–90), and few of them, who write about 'whether causing someone to exist can benefit this person'. Our topic is therefore asymmetrical. I confine this essay to the value of preventing deaths because that is what the subject has been, but we can hope that the next Palgrave may have a more symmetrical topic to pursue.

WORTH TO WHOM?

The first principle that ought to bear on what it is worth to save a statistical life – to reduce a mortal risk to some part of the population – is that there ought to be some person or collection of persons to whom it is worth something. To whom is it worth something to reduce the risk of death to some identified part of the population? We can begin with the people at risk. They may not be good at calculating risks and handling probabilities and expected values; they may give exaggerated emphasis to risks that are mysterious or sensational; but if they are susceptible, they care; and unless their attitude is wholly superstitious they are likely to recognize that reducing statistical risks to their own and their families' lives is worth paying for. What is at stake is not only life itself but grief and the permanent loss of parents, children and spouses.

Many of the people targeted for risk reduction will be financially responsible for others. The family has an economic interest in the parent's continued living. The importance of the parent's livelihood, in contrast to his living, will depend on the private and public insurance and other arrangements to care for his dependents.

Social and private insurance, charities, and all the claims that the deceased's family will exercise introduce another set of interests – all the people and institutions that are sources or recipients of transfers on account of the death. The fact that in one respect the transfers cancel out – the dependents of the deceased showing receipts equivalent to the public and private payments to them – does not make them uninteresting. The transfers change and broaden the answer to the question, to whom is it worth something that these deaths be prevented.

Transfers can go in either direction. Some of the current discussions of health policy neglect this important fact. It is often alleged that people who smoke impose costs on the health-care system and should be penalized through higher cigarette taxes or health insurance premiums. But the typical lung cancer victim enriches the society he leaves behind. The median age for lung cancer is 65 and most victims are dead within a year; the median male retirement age in the United States is about 63; a 65-year-old male victim loses an expected fifteen years of life. Discounting at 5 per cent, if he is without dependents he relinquishes upwards of $50,000 in social security benefits, and if he was at the median income level during his pre-retirement years he may relinquish a like amount in private pensions. His terminal illness inflicts a small fraction of that on the health insurers (and he will not be around to be hospitalized again later in life).

Lung cancer reminds us that our financial stakes in the continued living of those among us who are at risk can be positive or negative. Aggregating the financial interests, positive and negative, that different people may have in the demise or longevity of some segment of the population is simpler than distinguishing local and national tax-payer interests, occupational interests in shared retirement funds, or policyholder interests in the claims exercised on a life insurance company. For policy purposes the question of who has interest in reducing (or not reducing) some mortal risk may be as important as how big the algebraic sum of those interests is.

So far we have identified two sources of 'value' for enhanced survival, the 'consumer interest' of a family in its own survival and the externalities that take mainly the form of transfers to or from the consuming unit. Whether it makes sense to add up the transfers into a net figure and add that figure to the consumer's own value will depend on the purpose for which some calculation of worth is desired. If the purpose, for example, is to see whether there are enough votes to support a programme that may save lives there may be jurisdictional constraints on the components that go into one's estimate of worth.

There are other interests. One that has received attention is the Gross National Product that is lost when a person dies (Rice, 1967; Hartunian, Smart and Thompson, 1981, pp. 41–56). The 'value' of the lives lost in motorcycle accidents that could have been saved with helmets has been approximated by the discounted lifetime earnings of the kinds of people who die in motorcycle accidents – mostly young men without dependents. But is is difficult to identify anyone to whom this loss accrues. The motorcyclist dies and this piece of the GNP disappears, but so does the person who was going to consume most of it. The economy does not miss him. He could as well have moved to another country. We can of course consider the taxes he paid and the exhaustible public benefits that he consumed, but we did that already in considering those transfers. It is not worth anything to the economy to spare his life. (The point can be reduced to absurdity by observing that a modest extension of this methodology discovers that abortions in the United States are 'costing the economy' a quarter of a trillion dollars every year.)

CONCERN FOR OTHERS' LIVES

To this point I have looked at selfish interests. What about our compassionate interest in the longevity of fellow citizens, or our charitable interests in the lives of those who are especially at risk because their poverty exposes them to hazards? What is the government's obligation for the safety of its citizens and how should it assess the worth of a programme, regulatory or budgetary, that may save some expected number of lives?

The question especially arises because many of the activities that promise to reduce mortality are public goods. We can find motorcycle helmets, smoke detectors and seatbelts in the market, but if we want more effective treatment for coronary heart disease we have to expect publicly financed medical research to carry the burden. (The research, of course, does not have to be financed by our own government to benefit us, as rescue and regulation would.)

How should the government, then, evaluate the lifesaving consequences of an activity that requires budgetary outlays or imposes regulatory costs on its citizens? Take the question on two assumptions, first that all families share equally in the potential benefits and, second, that programmes discriminate in their benefits by age, wealth, occupation, health status, or geographical location. 'Sharing equally' could mean either of two things: equal reductions in some risk of dying, or equal extensions of life expectancy, the difference depending mainly on age. If we take families as the sharing units, age differences will average out somewhat (and we can avoid the questions whether or not to count a foetus as a child). For simplicity assume that if citizens share equally in the expected reduction of mortality they also share equally in the associated transfers. This assumption is certainly false and is introduced only to reduce the scope of this essay.

In a first approximation I see no reason why a legislator or administrator should not approach mortal-risk-reducing activities in the same way he approaches activities that raise productivity, save time, reduce annoyance, provide entertainment, or reduce the discomforts of nonfatal illness (Schelling, 1968; Mishan, 1971; Zeckhauser, 1975). Specifically, one considers how the beneficiaries value the reduced mortality compared with what they could have procured with lower taxes or prices. It is always the case that some citizens value these things differently from others even when they benefit equally; that is in no way peculiar to risk reduction.

A way in which mortal-risk reduction differs from other benefits is in the lesser likelihood that the beneficiaries of reductions in small risks can articulate what it is worth to them or even discuss it reasonably when the issue arises. Traffic lights that reduce congestion are more susceptible to public hearings to establish their money values than lights primarily intended to save children's lives. On the other hand there is an economy of information to be enjoyed in connection with lifesaving if the principle can be adopted that, where all the citizens share equally in the reduced mortality, all benefits will be measured proportionately to the lives saved. (Or, if people so choose, life-years saved; see below.) If lifesaving is valued identically for traffic lights, cancer research, and police protection, one good determination of the 'value of lives saved' can be used repeatedly within any jurisdiction in which the character of the population has not changed much since that determination was made. This kind of determination has rarely if ever been done in any jurisdiction, but the same can probably be said of the value of noise reduction. The problem is not in the theory.

The hard issues arise when the benefits are not shared equally, and especially when the beneficiaries of a risk-reducing activity will be poor, or the innocent victims of the location of some hazardous activity. The debate in this case is familiar. Economists usually argue that if the beneficiaries are going to pay for the activity, it is their valuations that should govern the decision. And even if it is difficult to penetrate their valuations it can be concluded that the poor will value risk reduction, compared to the other things that money will buy, less than the well-to-do.

709

It is only one step to the corollary that when the poor are to be provided greater safety at the expense of the well-to-do it should still be their privilege to request cash instead that they can spend as they please on other things they value more than the reduction in some life-threatening hazard. Institutionally, however, it is usually not the case that funds available for reducing mortal hazards can be transferred to procurement of whatever the beneficiaries want even more.

There is an argument here that economics cannot resolve. In the days when the *Titanic* hit an iceberg there were lifeboats for first class and tourist, steerage was expected to go down with the ship. The economic efficiency of that arrangement does not necessarily make it appealing; and even letting the poor travel cheaply on densely packed separate ships with no first class and no lifeboats can be objected to on grounds that are not easily dismissed by mere reference to economic efficiency.

SOME TECHNICAL ISSUES

Life vs. risk. Despite emphasis that our topic is *risk reduction*, there is temptation to talk about the value of a *life* saved. If an individual will pay annually (or forego in wages) $100 to reduce some mortal risk to himself from $1:10,000$ annually to $1:20,000$ – a reduction of $1:10,000$ – it is convenient to say that he 'values his own life' at $2 million. That sounds as if, confronted with certain death, he would come up with $2 million to stay alive. But that is not what we meant, and it does not follow from the small-risk calculation. (In particular, there would be income effects if the risk-eliminating payment rose from $100 to $100,000.) What we mean is that 20,000 identical individuals identically at risk would collectively pay $2 million for each yet unidentified averted death among themselves. A terminological proposal is suggested by the unit of measure in part-time hiring, the FTE, 'full-time equivalent'; we can say that our subject values reducing the risk to his own life at $2 million per FLE, 'full life equivalent'.

Years of life saved. 'Saving a life' by reducing some mortal risk means only prolonging it; death eventually ensues. An alternative to the worth per life 'saved' would be the worth per 'year of life' saved. And not all years are worth the same. Some index of 'quality-adjusted life-years' has been proposed. These approaches are alternatives: we can impute more value to young lives than old, or measure benefits in life-years to the same effect.

Insurance. The availability of life insurance should have a powerful influence on the value of risk reduction to the person who provides for a family. Just as one might make heroic and uneconomic investments in fire safety to protect a home or farm that represented all of one's assets if insurance were unavailable, extreme precautions against the risk of death might appear necessary for the young parents of triplets if life insurance could not be procured. Thus any of the institutions that insure the welfare of dependent survivors can help to avoid inefficient investments in longevity. Similarly, older people without dependants might make collectively inefficient investments in longevity out of wealth that they would lose if they died; life annuities are a contractual solution.

Risk and anxiety. The elimination of certain mortal risks, besides saving lives, can reduce anxiety. Fear can afflict those who survive as much as those who die, so it is not double counting to include reduced anxiety among the benefits. But anxiety or concern, according to some studies, is not proportionate to the risk (Starr and Whipple, 1980). Some of it appears due to the stimuli that remind people of the danger, for example stories of violence on the streets at night. Two policy questions result. One is whether governments might wisely and properly give disproportionate emphasis – pay more per life actually saved – where the risks generate extraordinary anxiety, on grounds that the anxiety is commensurate in its impact on welfare with the actual incidence of death. (This would be like weighing nonfatal illness along with the fatal.) The second is whether a responsive government should deploy its resources toward those risks that citizens express most concern about, even when the government has evidence that those concerns are based more on imagination that on fact.

There are two possibilities here. One is that citizens grossly exaggerate some risk – a food additive, radioactivity, night-time violence – and the government knows that the public is simply wrong. The other is that citizens have preferences that are not confined to the arithmetic of life expectancy and consider certain horrors – perhaps those that their minds insist on dwelling on – more worth eliminating than others.

Discounting. Many policies entail current investment in future safety or reduced future mortality. (The two are not the same: exposure to asbestos or radiation increases the likelihood of cancer some decades later.) The question of discounting arises: is a death averted twenty years hence, or a hundred, worth less than a death averted today? Again: 'worth' to whom? People today who would bear the cost of averting that death a century hence can be expected to be less interested than they would be in averting a death that could be their own or their families', i.e. a death today, just as people who might bear the cost of saving lives in some remote part of the world, not being potential beneficiaries, would have to think of it as charity, not personal safety, and might be less interested.

But many programmes for health and safety are charitably motivated, that is, the expenses are incurred by people who do not expect to benefit. Should they discount future lives saved? There are economic arguments for discounting not the 'lives' but the money value imputed to a future life saved by some expenditure today. (1) Money spent today to save lives in the future could be invested instead to yield a larger lifesaving budget when the time comes, saving more lives. (2) Technological progress may make lifesaving cheaper in the future; wait and take advantage of the lower prices. (3) There is uncertainty about what hazards may disappear in the interim or cease to be lethal, and some of today's outlay will have procured no benefit. (4) And people may be richer in the future and better able to spend their own money to save their own lives. If one does not discount lives saved, the first two arguments together imply a higher marginal productivity in future lifesaving, and that all lifesaving resources should be channelled toward future lives until the marginal costs of future lifesaving have risen to that of current lifesaving. That that is not done is probably evidence that people do discount future lives whether or not they realize that they do.

Implicit valuations. It is sometimes argued that we should look at the implicit valuations expressed in social policy to 'discover' what 'our society' considers lives to be worth. In the United States there are tens of thousands of coronary bypass operations per year at a cost of $25,000 each. Most are undertaken in the hope of prolonging life. Since this surgical technique has been around for only a decade the data on its contribution to life extension are indecisive but suggest that the contribution is at most a year. (Some studies dispute any positive contribution.) Americans apparently acquiesce in the procurement of extended life at $25,000 or more per year. At that rate an averted lung cancer in a 65-year-old is worth (discounted at 5 per cent) upwards of $250,000, a youthful motorcycle fatality upwards of $500,000. These may not be bad numbers; but they do not reflect any explicit determination that the cost of bypass surgery is a reasonable price to pay for the life extension that on average it produces.

Market evidence. Some investigators have examined the relation of wage differentials among occupations or industries to the risk differentials, as measured by accidental deaths and work-related fatal illnesses (Viscusi, 1983). Econometric analysis leads to estimates of implicit own-life FLEs – the income workers forego to work in safer occupations. In 1980 prices, implicit FLEs are obtained over the range from roughly one to five million dollars, with workers in the extremely risky occupations 'revealing' implicit FLEs under one million. The different estimates are partly due to different data and methodologies but probably reflect also individual differences in willingness to trade money against risk of death, and some consequent sorting into the more and the less risky occupations.

BIBLIOGRAPHY
Hartunian, N.S., Smart, C.N. and Thompson, M.S. 1981. *The Incidence and Economic Costs of Major Health Impairments.* Lexington: Lexington Books.
Mishan, E.J. 1971. Evaluation of life and limb: a theoretical approach. *Journal of Political Economy* 79, 687–705.
Parfit, D. 1984. *Reasons and Persons.* Oxford: Clarendon Press.
Rice, D. 1967. Estimating the costs of illness. *American Journal of Public Health* 57, 424–40.
Schelling, T.C. 1968. The life you save may be your own. In *Problems in Public Expenditure Analysis*, ed. S.B. Chase, Jr., Washington, DC: The Brookings Institution.
Starr, C. and Whipple, C. 1980. Risks of risk decisions. *Science* 208, 1114–19.
Viscusi, W.K. 1983. *Risk By Choice.* Cambridge, Mass.: Harvard University Press.
Zeckhauser, R.J. 1975. Procedures for valuing lives. *Public Policy* 23, 419–64.

Welfare Economics

ALLAN M. FELDMAN

In 1776, the same year as the American Declaration of Independence, Adam Smith published *The Wealth of Nations*. Smith laid out an argument that is now familiar to all economics students: (1) The principal human motive is self-interest. (2) The invisible hand of competition automatically transforms the self-interest of many into the common good. (3) Therefore, the best government policy for the growth of a nation's wealth is that policy which governs least.

Smith's arguments were at the time directed against the mercantilists, who promoted active government intervention in the economy, particularly in regard to (ill-conceived) trade policies. Since his time, his arguments have been used and reused by proponents of *laissez faire* throughout the 19th and 20th centuries. Arguments of Smith and his opponents are still very much alive today: The pro-Smithians are those who place their faith in the market, who maintain that the provision of goods and services in society ought to be done, by and large, by private buyers and sellers acting in competition with each other. One can see the spirit of Adam Smith in economic policies involving deregulation of industries, tax reduction, and reduction in government growth in the United States; in policies of denationalization in the United Kingdom, France and elsewhere, and in the deliberate restoration of private markets in China. The anti-Smithians are also still alive and well; mercantilists are now called industrial policy advocates, and there is an abundance of intellectuals and policy makers, aside from neomercantilists, who believe that: (1) economic planning is superior to *laissez faire*; (2) markets are usually monopolized in the absence of government intervention, crippling the invisible hand of competition; (3) even if markets are competitive, the existence of external effects, public goods, information asymmetries and other market failures ensure that *laissez faire* results in the common bad rather than the common good; (4) and in any case, *laissez faire* produces an intolerable degree of inequality.

The branch of economics called welfare economics is an outgrowth of the fundamental debate that can be traced back to Adam Smith, if not before. The theoretical side of welfare economics is organized around three main propositions. The first theorem answers this question: In an economy with competitive buyers and sellers, will the outcome be for the common good? The second theorem addresses the issue of distributional equity. and answers this question: In an economy where distributional decisions are made by an enlightened sovereign, can the common good be achieved by a slightly modified market mechanism, or must the market be abolished altogether? The third theorem focuses on the general issue of defining social welfare, or the common good, whether via the market, via a centralized political process, or via a voting process. It answers this question: Does there exist a reliable way to derive from the interests of individuals, the true interests of society, regarding, for example, alternative distributions of wealth?

This entry focuses on theoretical welfare economics. There are related topics in practical welfare economics which are only mentioned here. A reader interested in the practical problems of evaluating policy alternatives can refer to the wide literature on subjects such as consumers' surplus, cost–benefit analysis and the compensation principle.

I. THE FIRST FUNDAMENTAL THEOREM, OR LAISSEZ-FAIRE LEADS TO THE COMMON GOOD

'The greatest meliorator of the world is selfish, huckstering trade.' (R.W. Emerson, *Work and Days*)

In *The Wealth of Nations*, Book IV, Smith wrote: 'Every individual necessarily labours to render the annual revenue of the society as great as he can. He generally indeed neither intends to promote the public interest, nor knows how much he is promoting it.... He intends only his own gain, and he is in this, as in many other cases, led by an invisible hand to promote an end which was no part of his intention.' The philosophy of the First Fundamental Theorem of Welfare Economics can be traced back to these words of Smith. Like much of modern economic theory, it is set in the context of a Walrasian general equilibrium model, developed almost a hundred years after *The Wealth of Nations*. Since Smith wrote long before the modern theoretical language was invented, he never rigorously stated, let alone proved, any version of the First Theorem. That honour fell upon Lerner (1934), Lange (1942) and Arrow (1951).

To establish the First Theorem, we need to sketch a general equilibrium model of an economy. Assume all individuals and firms in the economy are price takers: none is big enough, or motivated enough, to act like a monopolist. Assume each individual chooses his consumption bundle to maximize his utility subject to his budget constraint. Assume each firm chooses its production vector, or input–output vector, to maximize its profits subject to some production constraint. Note the presumption of self-interest. An individual cares only about his own utility, which depends on his own consumption. A firm cares only about its own profits.

The invisible hand of competition acts through prices; they contain the information about desire and scarcity that coordinate actions of self-interested agents. In the general equilibrium model, prices adjust to bring about equilibrium in the market fo each and every good. That is, prices adjust until supply equals demand. When that has occurred, and all individuals and firms are maximizing utilities and profits respectively, we have a competitive equilibrium.

The First Theorem establishes that a competitive equilibrium is for the common good. But how is the common good defined? The traditional definition looks to a measure of total value of goods and services produced in the economy. In Smith, the 'annual revenue of the society' is maximized. In Pigou (1920), following Smith, the 'free play of self-interest' leads to the greatest 'national dividend'.

However, the modern interpretation of 'common good' typically involves Pareto optimality, rather than maximized gross national product. When ultimate consumers appear in the model, a situation is said to be *Pareto optimal* if there is no feasible alternative that makes everyone better off. Pareto optimality is thus a dominance concept based on comparisons of vectors of utilities. It rejects the notion that utilities of different individuals can be compared, or that utilities of different individuals can be summed up and two alternative situations compared by looking at summed utilities. When ultimate consumers do not appear in the model, as in the pure production framework to be described below, a situation is said to be *Pareto optimal* if there is no alternative that results in the production of more of some output, or the use of less of some input, all else equal. Obviously, saying that situation is Pareto optimal is not the same as saying it maximizes GNP, or that it is best in some unique sense. There are generally many Pareto optima. However, optimality is a common-good concept that can get common assent: no one would argue that society should settle for a situation that is not optimal, because if A is not optimal, there exists a B that all prefer.

In spite of the multiplicity of optima in a general equilibrium model, most states are non-optimal. If the economy were a dart board and consumption and production decisions were made by throwing darts, the chance of hitting an optimum would be zero. Therefore, to say that the market mechanism leads an economy to an optimal outcome is to say a lot. And now we can turn to a modern formulation of the First Theorem:

First Fundamental Theorem of Welfare Economics: Assume that all individuals and firms are selfish price takers. Then a competitive equilibrium is Pareto optimal.

To illustrate the theorem, we focus on one simple version of it, set in a pure production economy. For a general version of the theorem, with both production and exchange, the reader can refer to Malinvaud (1972).

In a general equilibrium production economy model, there are K firms and m goods, but, for simplicity, no consumers. Given a list of market prices, each firm chooses a feasible input–output vector y_k so as to maximize its profits. We adopt the usual sign convention for a firm's input–output vector y_k: $y_{kj} < 0$ means firm k is a net *user* of good j, and $y_{kj} > 0$ means firm k is a net *producer* of good j. What is feasible for firm k is defined by some fixed production possibility set Y_k. Under the sign convention on the input–output vector, if p is a vector of prices, firm k's profits are given by

$$\pi_k = p \cdot y_k.$$

A list of feasible input–output vectors $y = (y_1, y_2, \ldots y_k)$ is called a *production plan* for the economy. A *competitive equilibrium* is a production plan $\hat{y}$ and a price vector p such that, for every k, $\hat{y}_k$ maximizes π_k subject to y_k's being feasible. (Since the production model abstracts from the ultimate consumers of outputs and providers of inputs, the supply equals demand requirement for an equilibrium is moot.)

If $y = (y_1, y_2, \ldots, y_K)$ and $z = (z_1, z_2, \ldots, z_K)$ are alternative production plans for the economy, z is said to *dominate* y if the following vector inequality holds:

$$\sum_k z_k \geqslant \sum_k y_k.$$

Finally, if there exists no production plan that dominates y, y is *Pareto optimal*. (The notational conventions are very important for this model; note for example that $y_{11} + y_{21} + \cdots + y_{K1}$ represents an aggregate amount of good 1 produced in the economy, if positive, and an aggregate amount of good 1 used, if negative. Note also that some y_{k1}'s might be positive and some negative, and that the direction of the vector inequality is 'right' whether good 1 is an input, in the aggregate, or an output.)

We now have the apparatus to state and prove the First Theorem in the context of the pure production model:

First Fundamental Theorem of Welfare Economics, Production Version. Assume that all prices are positive, and that $\hat{y}, p$ is a competitive equilibrium. Then $\hat{y}$ is Pareto optimal.

To see why, suppose to the contrary that a competitive equilibrium production plan $\hat{y}_1, \hat{y}_2, \ldots, \hat{y}_K$ is not optimal. Then there exists a production plan $z_1, z_2, \ldots, z_K$ that dominates it. Therefore

$$\sum_k z_k \geqslant \sum_k \hat{y}_k.$$

Taking the dot product of both sides with the positive price vector p gives

$$p \cdot \sum_k z_k > p \cdot \sum_k \hat{y}_k.$$

But this implies that, for at least one firm k,

$$p \cdot z_k > p \cdot \hat{y}_k,$$

which contradicts the assumption that $\hat{y}_k$ maximizes firm k's profits.

II. FIRST FUNDAMENTAL THEOREM DRAWBACKS, AND THE SECOND FUNDAMENTAL THEOREM

'That amid our highest civilization men faint and die with want is not due to niggardliness of nature, but to the injustice of man.' (Henry George, *Progress and Poverty*)

The First Theorem of Welfare Economics is mathematically true but nevertheless objectionable. Here are the commonest objections: (1) The First Theorem is an abstraction that ignores the facts. Preferences of consumers are not given, they are created by advertising. The real economy is never in equilibrium, most markets are characterized by excess supply or excess demand, and are in a constant state of flux. The economy is dynamic, tastes and technology are constantly changing, whereas the model assumes they are fixed. The cast of characters in the real economy is constantly changing, the model assumes it fixed. (2) The First Theorem assumes competitive behaviour, whereas the real world is full of monopolists. (3) The First Theorem assumes there are no externalities. In fact, if in an exchange economy person 1's utility depends on person 2's consumption as well as his own, the theorem does not hold. Similarly, if in a production economy firm k's production possibility set depends on the production vector of some other firm, the theorem breaks down.

In a similar vein, the First Theorem assumes there are no public goods, that is, goods like national defence or lighthouses, that are necessarily non-exclusive in use. If such goods are privately provided (as they would be in a completely *laissez faire* economy), then their level of production will be sub-optimal. (4) The most troubling aspect of the First Theorem is its neglect of distribution. *Laissez faire* may produce a Pareto optimal outcome, but there are many different Pareto optima, and some are fairer than others. Some people are endowed with resources that make them rich, while others, through no fault of their own, are without. The First Theorem ignores basic distributional questions: how should unfair distributions of goods be made fair? And on the production side, how should production plans that give heavy weight to luxury items for the rich, and little or no weight to food, housing and medical care for the poor, be put right?

The first and second objections to the First Theorem are beyond the scope of this entry. The third, regarding externalities and public goods, is one that economists have always acknowledged. The standard remedies for these market failures involve minor modifications of the market mechanism, including Pigovian taxes (Pigou, 1920) on harmful externalities, or appropriate Coasian (Coase, 1960) legal entitlements to, for example, clean air.

The important contribution of Pigou is set in a partial equilibrium framework, in which the costs and benefits of a negative externality can be measured in money terms. Suppose that a factory produces gadgets to sell at some market-determined price, and suppose that, as part of its production process, the factory emits smoke which damages another factory located downwind. In order to maximize its profits, the upwind factory will expand its output until its marginal cost equals price. But each additional gadget it produces causes harm to the downwind factory – the marginal external cost of its activity. If the factory manager ignores that marginal external cost, he will create a situation that is non-optimal in the sense that the aggregate net value of both firms' production decisions will not be as great as it could be. That is, what Pigou calls 'social net product' will not be maximized, although 'trade net product' for the polluting firm will be. Pigou's remedy was for the state to eliminate the divergence between trade and social net product by imposing appropriate taxes (or, in the case of beneficial externalities, bounties). The Pigovian tax would be set equal to marginal external cost, and with it in place the gap between the polluting firm's view of cost and society's view would be closed. Optimality would be re-established.

Coase's contribution was to emphasize the reciprocal nature of externalities and to suggest remedies based on common law doctrines. In his view the polluter damages the pollutee only because of their proximity, e.g., the smoking factory harms the other only if it happens to locate close downwind. Coase rejects the notion that the state must step in and tax the polluter. The common law of nuisance can be used instead. If the law provides a clear right for the upwind factory to emit smoke, the downwind factory can contract with the upwind factory to reduce its output, and if there are no impediments to bargaining, the two firms acting together will negotiate an optimal outcome. Alternatively, it the law establishes a clear right for the downwind factory to recover for smoke damages, it will collect external costs from the polluter, and thereby motivate the polluter to reduce its output to the optimal level. In short, a legal system that grants clear rights to the air to either the polluter or pollutee will set the stage for an optimal outcome, provided that transactions are costless.

With respect to public goods, since Samuelson (1954) derived formal optimality conditions for their provision, the issue has received much attention from economists; one especially notable theoretical question has to do with discovering the strengths of people's preferences for a public good. If the government supplies a public judicial system, for instance, how much should it spend on it (and tax for it)? At least since Samuelson, it has been known that financing schemes like those proposed by Lindahl (1919), where an individual's tax is set equal to his marginal benefit, provide perverse incentives for people to misrepresent their preferences. Schemes that are immune to such misrepresentations (in certain circumstances) have been developed in recent years (Clarke, 1971; Groves and Loeb, 1975).

But it is the fourth objection to the First Theorem that is most fundamental. What about distribution?

There are two polar approaches to rectifying the distributional inequities of *laissez faire*. The first is the command economy approach: a centralized bureaucracy makes detailed decisions about the consumption decisions of all individuals and production decisions of all producers. The main theoretical problems with the command approach are that it requires the bureaucracy to obtain and act upon superhuman quantities of information, and that it fails to create appropriate incentives for individuals and firms. On the empirical side, the experience of Eastern European and Chinese command economies suggest that highly centralized economic decision making leaves much to be desired, to put it mildly.

The second polar approach to solving distribution problems is to transfer income or purchasing power among individuals, and then to let the market work. The only kind of purchasing power transfer that does not cause incentive-related losses is the lump-sum transfer. Enter at this point the standard remedy for distribution problems, as put forward by the market-oriented economist, and our second major theorem.

The Second Fundamental Theorem of Welfare Economics establishes that the market mechanism, modified by the addition of lump-sum transfers, can achieve virtually *any* desired optimal distribution. Under more stringent conditions than are necessary for the First Theorem, including assumptions regarding quasi-concavity of utility functions and convexity of production possibility sets, the Second Theorem asserts the following:

Second Fundamental Theorem of Welfare Economics. Assume that all individuals and producers are selfish price takers. Then almost any Pareto optimal equilibrium can be achieved via the competitive mechanism, provided appropriate lump-sum taxes and transfers are imposed on individuals and firms.

One version of the Second Theorem, restricted to a pure production economy, is particularly relevant to an old debate about the feasibility of socialism, see particularly Lange and Taylor (1939) and Lerner (1944). Anti-socialists including von Mises (1922) argued that informational problems would make it impossible to coordinate production in a socialist economy; while pro-socialists, particularly Lange, argued that those problems could be overcome by a Central Planning Board, which limited its role to merely announcing a price vector. This is called 'decentralized socialism'. Given the prices, managers of production units would act like their capitalist counterparts; in essence, they would maximize profits. By choosing the price vectors appropriately, the Central Planning Board could achieve any optimal production plan it wished.

In terms of the production model given above, the production version of the Second Theorem is as follows:

Second Fundamental Theorem of Welfare Economics, Production Version. Let $\hat{y}$ by any optimal production plan for the economy. Then there exists a price vector p such that $\hat{y}$, p is a competitive equilibrium. That is, for every k, $\hat{y}_k$ maximizes $\pi_k = p \cdot y_k$ subject to y_k being feasible.

The proof of the Second Theorem requires use of Minkowski's separating hyperplane theorem, and will not be given here.

III. TINKERING WITH THE ECONOMY AND VOTING ON DISTRIBUTIONS

The logic of the Second Theorem suggests that it is all right, perhaps even morally imperative, to tinker with the economy. And after all, is not tinkering what is done by policy makers and their economic advisers? How often do we choose between a *laissez faire* economy and a command economy? Our choices are usually more modest. When choosing among alternative tax policies, or trade and tariff policies, or antimonopoly policies, or labour policies, or transfer policies, what shall guide the choice? The applied welfare economist's advice is usually based on some notion of increasing total output in the economy. The practical political decision, in a Western democracy, is normally based on voting.

Applied welfare economics. The applied welfare economist usually focuses on ways to increase total output, 'the size of the pie', or at least to measure changes in the size of the pie. Unfortunately, theory suggests that the pie cannot be measured. This is so for a number of reasons. To start, any measure of total output is a scalar, that is, a single number. If the number is found by adding up utility levels for different individuals, illegitimate interpersonal utility comparisons are being made. If the number is found by adding up the values of aggregate net outputs of all goods, there is an index number problem. The value of a production plan will depend on the price vector at which it is evaluated. But in a general equilibrium context, the price vector will depend on the aggregate net output vector; which will in turn depend on the distribution of ownership or wealth among individuals. Economists have always agreed that if q^1 and q^2 are alternative aggregate net output vectors, and if p^1 and p^2 are the corresponding price vectors, then $p^1 \cdot q^1 < p^2 \cdot q^2$ has no welfare implications. Unfortunately they now also agree that if there are two or more individuals in the economy, even $p^2 \cdot q^1 < p^2 \cdot q^2$ may not signify q^2 is an improvement in welfare over q^1.

An early and crucial contribution to the analysis of whether or not the economic pie has increased in size was made by Kaldor (1939), who argued that the repeal of the Corn Laws in England can be justified on the grounds that the winners could in theory compensate the losers: 'it is quite sufficient [for the economist] to show that even if all those who suffer as a result are fully compensated for their loss, the rest of the community will still be better off than before'. Unfortunately, Scitovsky (1941) quickly pointed out that Kaldor's compensation criterion (as well as one proposed by Hicks) was in theory inconsistent: it is possible to judge situation B Kaldor superior to A and simultaneously judge A Kaldor superior to B. The Scitovsky paradox can be avoided via a two-edged compensation test, according to which situation B is judged better than A if (1) the potential gainers in the move from A to B could compensate the potential losers, and still remain better off, and (2) the potential losers could not bribe the gainers to forego the move.

Scitovsky's two-edged criterion has some logical appeal, but it, like the single-edged Kaldor criterion, still has a major drawback: it ignores distribution. Therefore, it can make no judgement about alternative distributions of the same size pie. And worse, as was pointed out by Little (1950), either criterion would approve a change that would make the wealthiest man in England richer by £1,000,000,000, while making each of the 1,000,000 humblest men poorer by £900. In Little's view, the applied welfare economist should adopt Scitovsky's two-edged criterion and *also* requires that the change from A to B not result in a worse distribution of welfare. Unfortunately, what constitutes a worse distribution is, as Little concedes, purely a value judgement – a matter of personal opinion.

Another important tool for measuring changes in the economic pie is the concept of consumer's surplus, which Marshall (1920) defined as the difference between what an individual would be willing to pay for an object, at most, and what he actually does pay. With a little faith, the economic analyst can measure aggregate consumers' surplus (note the new position of the apostrophe), by calculating an area under a demand curve, and this is in fact commonly done in order to evaluate changes in economic policy. The applied welfare economist attempts to judge whether the pie would grow in a move from A to B by examining the change in consumers' surplus (plus profits, if they enter the analysis). Faith is required because consumers' surplus, like the Kaldor criterion, has been shown to be theoretically inconsistent; see for example Boadway (1974).

In short, although the tools of applied welfare economics are crucially important in practice, theory says they must be viewed with suspicion.

Voting.

> 'A minority may be right, a majority is always wrong.' (Henrik Ibsen, *An Enemy of the People*)

In most cases, interesting decisions about economic policies are made either by bureaucracies that are controlled by legislative bodies, or by legislative bodies themselves, or by elected executives; in short, either directly or indirectly, by voting. The Second Theorem itself raises questions about distribution that many would view as essentially political: how should society choose the Pareto optimal allocation of goods that is to be reached via the modified competitive mechanism? How should the distribution of income be chosen? How can the best distribution of income be chosen from among many Pareto optimal ones? Majority voting is the most commonly used method of political choice in a democracy.

The practical objections to voting, the fraud, the deception, the accidents of weather, are well known. To quote Boss Tweed, the infamous chief of New York's Tammany Hall: 'As long as I count the votes, what are you going to do about it?' But let us turn to the theoretical problems.

The central theoretical fact about majority voting has been known since the time of Condorcet's *Essai sur l'application de l'analyse à la probabilité des décisions rendues à la pluralité des voix*, published in 1785: voting may be inconsistent. The now standard Condorcet voting paradox assumes three individuals 1, 2 and 3, and three alternatives x, y and z, where the three voters have the following preferences:

$$
\begin{array}{cccc}
1: & x & y & z \\
2: & y & z & x \\
3: & z & x & y.
\end{array}
$$

(Following an individual's number the alternatives are listed in his order of preference, from left to right.) Majority voting between pairs of alternatives will reveal that x beats y, y beats z, and, paradoxically, z beats x.

Recently it has become clear that such voting cycles are not peculiar; they are generic, particularly when the alternatives have a spatial aspect with two or more dimensions (Plott, 1967; Kramer, 1973). This can be illustrated by taking the alternatives to be different distributions of one economic pie. Suppose, in other words, that the distributional issues raised by the First and Second Theorems are to be 'solved' by majority voting, and assume for simplicity that what is to be divided is a fixed total of wealth, say 100 units worth.

Now let x be 50 units for person 1, 30 units for person 2 and 20 units for person 3. That is, let $x = (50, 20, 30)$. Similarly, let $y = (30, 50, 20)$ and $z = (20, 30, 50)$. The result is that our three individuals have precisely the voting paradox preferences. Nor is this result contrived; it turns out that *all* the distributions of 100 units of wealth are connected by endless voting cycles (see McKelvey, 1976). The reader can easily confirm that for any distributions u and v that he may choose, there exists a voting sequence from u to v, and another back from v to u!

The reality of voting cycles should give pause to the economist who studies or recommends tax bills. And it is most disturbing for the economist looking for a political basis for judging among alternative distributions.

IV. SOCIAL WELFARE AND THE THIRD FUNDAMENTAL THEOREM

How then might the distribution problem be solved? One potential answer is to assert the existence of a Bergson (1938) Economic Welfare Function $E(\cdot)$, that depends on the amounts of non-labour factors of production employed by each producing unit, the amounts of labour supplied by each individual, and the amounts of produced goods consumed by each individual. Then solve the problem by maximizing $E(\cdot)$. If necessary conditions for Pareto optimality are derived that must hold for any $E(\cdot)$, this exercise is harmless enough; but if a *particular* $E(\cdot)$ is assumed and distributional implications are derived from it, then an objection can be raised: why that $E(\cdot)$ and not another one?

De V. Graaff (1957) focuses Bergson's approach by analysing welfare functions of the 'individualistic' type: these can be written $W(u^1, u^2, \ldots, u^n)$ where u^i represents person i's utility level. Graaff makes clear that maximizing a too broadly defined $W(\cdot)$ simply rediscovers the conditions for Pareto optimality, whereas maximizing a too narrowly defined $W(\cdot)$ simply rediscovers the preferences of the economist who invents $W(\cdot)$! Thus a good $W(\cdot)$ is neither too broadly nor too narrowly defined; rather it captures some widely shared judgements about which distributions are desirable and which are not. Maximizing such a welfare function implies both Pareto optimality and an appropriate distribution of wealth. But can a good $W(\cdot)$ function be discovered? Graaff is optimistic that the members of society can agree on the degree of equality to be incorporated in $W(\cdot)$. However, $W(\cdot)$ must also incorporate assumptions about an appropriate horizon (do we include unborn children?), as well as attitudes towards uncertainty, time discounting, and so on. And on these issues, he believes it extremely unlikely that enough agreement can be found to build a $W(\cdot)$. So, at the end of an illuminating book on normative economics, Graaff recommends that we all try positive economics. Which still leaves us with the Bergson social welfare function dilemma: where do they come from?

In his classic monograph *Social Choice and Individual Values* (1963), Arrow brings together both the economic and political streams of thought sketched above. Arrow's theorem can be viewed in several ways: it is a statement about the distributional questions raised by the First and Second Theorems; it is a remarkable logical extension of the Condorcet voting paradox; and it is a statement about the logic of choice of Bergson welfare functions, and about the logic of compensation tests, consumers' surplus tests, and indeed all the tools of the applied welfare economist. Because of its importance, Arrow's theorem can be justifiably called the Third Fundamental Theorem of Welfare Economics.

Arrow's analysis is at a high level of abstraction, and requires some additional model building. We now assume a given set of alternatives, which might be allocations in an exchange economy, distributions of wealth, tax bills in a legislature, or even candidates in an election. The alternatives are written x, y, z, etc. We assume there is a fixed society of individuals, numbered $1, 2, \ldots, n$. Let R_i represent the preference relation of individual i, so $xR_i y$ means person i likes x as well as or better than y. A preference profile for society is a specification of preferences for each and every individual, or symbolically, $R_1, R_2, \ldots, R_n$. We shall write R for *society's* preference relation, arrived at in a way yet to be specified. R is, of course, a much modernized version of Bergson's $E(\cdot)$, appearing here as a binary relation rather than as a function.

Arrow was concerned with the logic of how individual preferences are transformed into social preferences. That is, how is R found? Symbolically we can represent the transformation this way:

$$R_1, R_2, \ldots, R_n \rightarrow R.$$

Now if society is to make decisions regarding distributions, it must 'know' when one alternative is as good as or better than another, even if both are Pareto optimal. To ensure it can make such decisions, Arrow assumes that R is *complete*. That is, for any alternatives x and y, either xRy or yRx (or both, if society is indifferent between the two). If society is to avoid the illogic of cyclical voting, its preference ought to be *transitive*. That is, for any alternatives x, y and z, if xRy and yRz, then xRz. Following Sen (1970), we call a transformation of individual preference relations into a complete and transitive social preference relation an Arrow Social Welfare Function, or more briefly, an Arrow function.

Anyone can make up an Arrow function, just as anyone can make up a Bergson function, or for that matter a judgement about when one distribution of wealth is better than another. But arbitrary judgements are unsatisfactory and so are arbitrary Arrow functions. Therefore, Arrow imposed some reasonable conditions on his function. Following Sen's (1970) version of Arrow's theorem, there are four conditions: (1) *Universality*. The function should always work, no matter what individual preferences might be. It would not be satisfactory, for example, to require unanimous agreement among all the individuals before determining social preferences. (2) *Pareto consistency*. If everyone prefers x to y, then the social preference ought to be x over y. (3) *Independence*. Suppose there are two alternative preference profiles for individuals in society, but suppose individual preferences regarding x and y are exactly the same under the two alternatives. Then the social preference regarding x and y must be exactly the same under the two alternatives. In particular, if individuals change their minds about a third 'irrelevant' alternative, this should not affect the social preference regarding x and y. (4) *Non-dictatorship*. There should not be a dictator. In Arrow's abstract model, person i is a *dictator* if society always prefers exactly what he prefers, that is, if the Arrow function transforms R_i into R.

An economist or policy maker who wants an ultimate answer to questions involving distribution, or questions involving choices among alternatives that are not comparable under the Pareto criterion, could use an Arrow Social Welfare Function for guidance. Unfortunately, Arrow showed that imposing conditions 1 to 4 guarantees that Arrow functions *do not exist*:

> *Third Fundamental Theorem of Welfare Economics*. There is no Arrow Social Welfare Function that satisfies the conditions of universality, Pareto consistency, independence and non-dictatorship.

In order to illustrate the logic of the theorem, we will use a somewhat stronger assumption than independence. This assumption is called N–I–M, or *neutrality–independence–monotonicity*: Let V be a group of individuals. Suppose for some preference profile and some particular pair of alternatives x and y, all members of V prefer x to y, all individuals *not* in V prefer y to x, and the social preference is x over y. Then for *any* preference profile and *any* pair of alternatives x and y, if all people in V prefer x to y, the social preference must be x over y. In short, if V gets its way in one instance, when everyone opposes it, then it must have the power to do it again, under other possibly less difficult circumstances.

A group of individuals V is said to be *decisive* if for all alternatives x and y, whenever all the people in V prefer x to y, society prefers x to y. Assumption N–I–M asserts that if V prevails when it is opposed by everyone else, it must be a decisive group. If the social choice procedure is majority rule, for example, any group of $(n + 1)/2$ members, for n odd, or $(n/2) + 1$ members, for n even, is decisive. Moreover, it is clear that majority rule satisfies the N–I–M assumption, since if V prevails for a particular x and y when everyone outside of V prefers y to x, then V must be a majority, and must always prevail. (Majority rule is just one example of a procedure that satisfies N–I–M: there are countless other procedures that also do so.)

Now we are ready to turn to a short version of the Third Theorem:

Third Fundamental Theorem of Welfare Economics, Short Version. There is no Arrow Social Welfare Function that satisfies the conditions of universality, Pareto consistency, neutrality–independence–monotonicity and non-dictatorship.

The logic of the proof is as follows: First, there must exist decisive groups of individuals, since by the Pareto consistency requirement the set of all individuals is one. Now let V be a decisive group of minimal size. If there is just one person in V, he is a dictator. Suppose then that V includes more than one person. We show this leads to a contradiction.

If there are two or more people in V, we can divide it into non-empty subsets V_1 and V_2. Let V_3 represent all the people who are in neither V_1 nor V_2 (V_3 may be empty). By universality, the Arrow function must be applicable to any profile of individual preferences. Take three alternatives x, y and z and consider the following preferences regarding them:

$$\text{For individuals in } V_1: \quad x \quad y \quad z$$

$$\text{For individuals in } V_2: \quad y \quad z \quad x$$

$$\text{For individuals in } V_3: \quad z \quad x \quad y.$$

(At this point the close relationship between Arrow and Condorcet is clear, for these are the voting paradox preferences!)

Since V is by assumption decisive, y must be socially preferred to z, which we write yPz. By the assumption of completeness for the social preference relation, either xRy or yPx must hold. If xRy holds, since xRy and yPz, then xPz must hold by transitivity. But now V_1 is decisive by the N–I–M assumption, contradicting V's minimality. Alternatively, if yPx holds, V_2 is decisive by the N–I–M assumption, again contradicting V's minimality. In either case, the assumption that V has two or more people leads to a contradiction. Therefore V must contain just one person, who is, of course, a dictator!

Since the Third Theorem was discovered, a whole literature of modifications and variations has been spawned. But the depressing conclusion has remained more or less inescapable: there is no logically infallible way to aggregate the preferences of diverse individuals. By extension, there is no logically infallible way to solve the problem of distribution.

Where does welfare economics stand today? The First and Second Theorems are encouraging results that suggest the market mechanism has great virtue: competitive equilibrium and Pareto optimality are firmly bound. But measuring the size of the economic pie, or judging among divisions of it, leads to the paradoxes and impossibilities summarized by the Third Theorem. And this is a tragedy. We feel we know, like Adam Smith knew, which policies would increase the wealth of nations. But because of all our theoretic goblins, we can no longer prove it.

BIBLIOGRAPHY

Arrow, K.J. 1951. An extension of the basic theorems of classical welfare economics. *Second Berkeley Symposium on Mathematical Statistics and Probability*, ed. J. Neyman, Berkeley: University of California Press, 507–32.

Arrow, K.J. 1963. *Social Choice and Individual Values*. 2nd edn, New York: John Wiley and Sons.

Bergson, A. 1938. A reformulation of certain aspects of welfare economics. *Quarterly Journal of Economics* 52, 310–34.

Boadway, R. 1974. The welfare foundations of cost-benefit analysis. *Economic Journal* 84, 926–39.

Clarke, E.H. 1971. Multipart pricing of public goods. *Public Choice* 11, 17–33.

Coase, R.H. 1960. The problem of social cost. *Journal of Law and Economics* 3, 1–44.

Graaff, J. de V. 1957. *Theoretical Welfare Economics*. Cambridge University Press.

Groves, T. and Loeb, M. 1975. Incentives and public inputs. *Journal of Public Economics* 4, 211–26.

Kaldor, N. 1939. Welfare propositions of economics and interpersonal comparisons of utility. *Economic Journal* 49, 549–52.

Kramer, G.H. 1973. On a class of equilibrium conditions for majority rule. *Econometrica* 41, 285–97.

Lange, O. 1942. The foundations of welfare economics. *Econometrica* 10, 215–28.

Lange, O. and Taylor, F.M. 1939. *On the Economic Theory of Socialism*. Minneapolis: University of Minnesota Press.

Lerner, A.P. 1934. The concept of monopoly and the measurement of monopoly power. *Review of Economic Studies* 1, 157–75.

Lerner, A.P. 1944. *The Economics of Control*. New York: The Macmillan Company.

Lindahl, E. 1919. Just taxation – a positive solution. Translated and reprinted in *Classics in the Theory of Public Finance*. ed. R.A. Musgrave and A.T. Peacock, New York: Macmillan, 1958.

Little, I.M.D. 1950. *A Critique of Welfare Economics*. Oxford: Oxford University Press.

Malinvaud, E. 1972. *Lectures on Microeconomic Theory*. Amsterdam: North-Holland.

Marshall, A. 1920. *Principles of Economics*. 8th edn, London: Macmillan, ch. VI.

McKelvey, R. 1976. Intransitivities in multidimensional voting models and some implications for agenda control. *Journal of Economic Theory* 12, 472–82.

Mises, L. von. 1922. *Socialism: An Economic and Social Analysis*. 3rd edn, trans., Indianapolis: Liberty Classics, 1981.

Pigou, A.C. 1920. *The Economics of Welfare*. London: Macmillan, Part II.

Plott, C.R. 1967. A notion of equilibrium and its possibility under majority rule. *American Economic Review* 57, 787–806.

Samuelson, P.A. 1954. The pure theory of public expenditure. *Review of Economics and Statistics* 36, 387–9.

Scitovsky, T. 1941. A note on welfare propositions in economics. *Review of Economic Studies* 9, 77–88.

Sen, A.K. 1970. *Collective Choice and Social Welfare*. San Francisco: Holden-Day.

Zero-sum Games

MICHAEL BACHARACH

Zero-sum games are to the theory of games what the twelve-bar blues is to jazz: a polar case, and a historical point of departure. A *game* is a situation in which (i) each of a number of agents (*players*) has a set of alternative courses of action (*strategies*) at his disposal; (ii) there are outcomes which depend on the *combination* of the players' actions and give rise to preferences by the players over these combinations; (iii) the players know, and know that each other knows, these preferences. (Strictly, such a situation is a game of *complete information* in *normal form*: these qualifications should henceforth be understood.) In the case which dominates the literature of zero-sum games there are two players, A and B say, each with a finite set of strategies, and their preferences can be represented by von Neumann–Morgenstern utilities. The preference structure can then be displayed in a *payoff matrix*, whose (i, j)th entry (u_{ij}, v_{ij}) give the expected utilities or *payoffs* of A and B respectively for A using his ith strategy and B using his jth. A game of this type in which $u_{ij} + v_{ij} = 0$ for all i, j is known as a *zero-sum matrix game* (henceforth simply *zero-sum game*). In a zero-sum game the players have exactly opposed preferences over strategy-pairs. Hence there is no scope for the pair of them to act *as* a pair – there is nothing for them to cooperate about. The theory of cooperative zero-sum games is thus an empty box; zero-sum games are noncooperative games, and each player must choose in uncertainty of the other's choice.

Figure 1 shows the payoff matrix of a zero-sum game ('The Battle of the Bismarck Sea'). As is conventional with zero-sum games, only the 'row-chooser's' payoff is shown. General Kenney (A) must decide whether to reconnoitre to the north, where visibility is poor (α_1) or to the south (α_2); the Japanese commander (B) whether to sail north (β_1) or south (β_2). Kenney's payoff is the expected number of days for which he will bomb the enemy fleet.

The theory of games was introduced by von Neumann and Morgenstern (1944) as part of the theory of rational action. It was to be the part that dealt with *social* contexts, in which the outcomes of concern to agents are radically dependent

	B's strategies	
A's strategies	β_1	β_2
α_1	2	2
α_2	1	3

Figure 1

on each other's decisions. In such contexts characterizing the rational is problematical, as von Neumann and Morgenstern were acutely aware. The central theoretical problem is to say what A and B will do if each does what is best for him. But what is best for A depends on what B *will* do, and so, in any answer, on what is best for B. We are entrammelled in regress. To this deep problem von Neumann and Morgenstern believed they had discovered a satisfactory answer in the special case of zero-sum games. It is this answer which has made zero-sum games famous.

The power of von Neumann and Morgenstern's proposal lies in their demonstration that over a wide class of zero-sum games each of two quite independent principles of rational action gives the same answer to the question of what the players should do – and an essentially determinate one. This high degree of coherence in the theory, the reciprocal support of its postulates, may perhaps have led to too charitable a view of their individual merits. The two principles of rational action are the Equilibrium Principle and the Maximin Principle. The Equilibrium Principle says that the strategies α^* and β^* are rational only if each is a *best reply* to the other, that is, α^* maximizes $u(\alpha, \beta^*)$ and β^* maximizes $v(\alpha^*, \beta)$, where $u(\alpha, \beta), v(\alpha, \beta)$ denote the payoffs of A and B respectively for the strategy-pair (α, β). 'Reply' here is metaphorical, for there is no communication. Such a pair is called a *noncooperative* or *Nash equilibrium* in game theory. Here, since $v(\alpha, \beta) = -u(\alpha, \beta)$, it is often called a *saddle-point*, for it locates a maximum of u over α and a minimum of u over β. The Equilibrium Principle has often been too casually accepted, but it has also been carefully defended (see e.g. Johansen, 1981). Von Neumann and Morgenstern saw with clarity that it can be no more than a necessary condition on rational choices by the players: *if* such choices exist they must, arguably, satisfy it, but some independent argument for this existence is needed (von Neumann and Morgenstern, 1974, section 17.3).

The Maximin Principle says that A should maximize over α the minimum over β of $u(\alpha, \beta)$ – he should 'maximin' u; and B should maximin v, or, what is equivalent, 'minimax' u. In other words, A should maximize his *security level*, where the security level of a strategy α is defined as $\min_\beta u(\alpha, \beta)$, the worst that α can bring him; and B should minimize his *hazard level* $\max_\alpha u(\alpha, \beta)$, the best that β can bring his adversary. This principle has been much criticized, and the qualified acceptance it has enjoyed owes something to its protective alliance with other elements of von Neumann and Morgenstern's theory. Their own arguments for it were suggestive rather than apodictic. It is claimed to express a rational caution in a situation in which a player has no valid basis for assigning probabilities to his opponent's decision. A second argument is also advanced, unworthy of them and justly attacked by Ellsberg (1956), according to which it is rational for A to choose by supposing he is playing the 'minorant game' associated with the payoff matrix: in this game A chooses first and B second in knowledge of A's choice (so that A is Stackelberg 'leader'). In *this* situation rock-hard principles of decision under certainty make it rational for A to maximin. But convincing reasons for A to assume that it obtains are missing.

In the Bismarck Sea game it is readily seen that the set of maximin strategy-pairs and the set of saddle-points are the same. This fact instantiates a general fact (Theorem 1): In a zero-sum game which has a saddle-point, a strategy-pair is a saddle-point if and only if it is a maximin pair. Theorem 1 expresses the agreement of the two principles of choice. They are also effectively determinate, for we also have (Theorem 2): In a zero-sum game with a saddle-point, all maximin strategies of one player yield the same payoffs when paired with a given maximin strategy of the other player.

The significance of these results is impaired by their limitation to games which have saddle-points. Plenty do not. Von Neumann and Morgenstern's response was to seek a modest enlargement of the strategy-sets of the players of an arbitrary zero-sum game which would ensure a saddle-point. The ingenious mode of enlargement they propose is to provide the players with roulette wheels. More formally, if a player has strategies $\alpha_1, \ldots, \alpha_m$ at his disposal, it is supposed that he also has the strategy 'with probability p_1 do α_1 and ... and with probability p_m do α_m', where $p_1 + \cdots + p_m = 1$. The original strategies $\alpha_1, \ldots, \alpha_m$ are called *pure* strategies and the new ones *mixed* strategies. Now it may be shown that (Theorem 3): In any zero-sum game, $\max_\alpha \min_\beta u(\alpha, \beta) \leqslant \min_\beta \max_\alpha u(\alpha, \beta)$, with equality if and only if the game has a saddle-point. So a strategy-set enlargement which raises A's highest security level is a move towards ensuring a saddle-point. Allowing A to 'mix' his strategies is a hedging device which has just this effect. The security level of a strategy α is what A would get from it against a prescient opponent. But even such a being can only adopt one strategy. Generally, mixing raises A's security levels since, whatever that strategy is, with some probability it fails to inflict maximal damage.

The success of von Neumann and Morgenstern's manoeuvre is recorded in what is the most celebrated theorem in game theory, the so-called Minimax Theorem: Every zero-sum (matrix) game with mixed strategies has a saddle-point. The Minimax Theorem duly yields, as desired, counterparts of Theorems 1 and 2 for the class of all 'mixed' zero-sum games. The early proofs of the Minimax Theorem employed fixed-point theorems, but it may also be proved by a constructive method based on the properties of convex sets (see e.g. Gale, 1951). The main lines of this method may be gleaned from Figure 2 for the case in which A has two pure strategies.

729

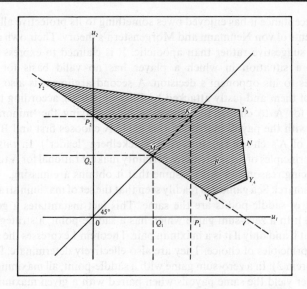

Figure 2

Let A's pure strategies be α_1, α_2 and B's be β_1, ..., β_n. Let $\mathbf{q} = (q_1, ..., q_n)$ denote the mixed strategy in which B does β_j with probability $q_j (j = 1, ..., n)$. Figure 2 shows a case in which $n = 4$. The axes measure A's payoffs to α_1, α_2 respectively. A vertex Y_j of the region R shows A's two payoffs if B chooses the pure strategy β_j, the other points of R his two payoffs against mixed strategies of B (e.g. the abscissa of the point N is $u(\alpha_1, \mathbf{q})$ for $\mathbf{q} = (0, 0, \frac{1}{2}, \frac{1}{2})$. At any point on a line like $P_1 K P_2$, B's hazard level is constant; hence B minimizes his hazard level at M (in other cases, not illustrated, the minimum-hazard point is along a side of a line of type $P_1 K P_2$ and at a *vertex* of R). At M, B is using the mixed strategy $\mathbf{q}^*(q^*, 1 - q^*, 0, 0)$, where $q^* = M Y_2 / Y_1 Y_2$; and A receives the payoff u^* say $(= O Q_1)$ whatever pure (or mixed) strategy he uses. The region whose north-east border is $Q_1 M Q_2$ and the region R are both convex. Consider their separating line ℓ – the extension of $Y_1 Y_2$. It may be written $p^* u_1 + (1 - p^*) u_2 = u^*$, where $0 \leqslant p^* \leqslant 1$. Then if $\mathbf{p}^*$ is the mixed strategy in which A does α_1 with probability p^* ($\mathbf{p}^*, \mathbf{q}^*$) is the claimed saddle-point. For on one hand since all A's strategies give the same payoff against $\mathbf{q}^*$, $\mathbf{p}^*$ maximizes it. On the other hand, since ℓ is the specified separating line, $p^* u_1 + (1 - p^*) u_2 \geqslant u^*$ for all (u_1, u_2) in R, that is, A's payoff from $\mathbf{p}^*$ is at least u^* for all the strategies available to B.

The Minimax Theorem establishes that the agreement of von Neumann and Morgenstern's two principles of rational choice holds in all zero-sum games provided players may mix their strategies. The mixability assumption, unfortunately, is far from innocuous. Not only may randomization be excluded by the rules of a game or by physical constraint, but the idea that rational players employ it threatens downright contradiction. For the pure strategy picked out by the wheel may have a lower security level than its alternatives, so that a maximinning agent has a motive to go back on his decision. This, moreover, he is in a position to anticipate.

It is worth considering briefly the empirical evidence about whether people play zero-sum games in the von Neumann–Morgenstern manner. The most important evidence is from laboratory experiments. Typically, the same situation is presented to the subjects in words, and they are invited to play a series of trials of the game for points or for small or fictitious reward: in some experiments subjects play against each other, in others against a programme. A fundamental difficulty is to make sure that subjects are solely motivated by the payoffs of the presented game, and do not 'import utilities', for example deriving utility from their opponents' payoffs. In most experiments subjects clearly have failed to choose in accordance with the theory, though sometimes a tendency has been noted for them to do so more nearly as trials progress. It should be noted that departure from saddle-point behaviour may be rational if it is rational to think that one's opponent is deviating from it. However, subjects have also typically failed to exploit programmed non-saddle-point play. They have declined, too, to avail themselves of randomizing facilities.

These experiments addressed an empirical question rather than the question to which von Neumann and Morgenstern claimed to have found an answer, that of how it is *rational* to act in zero-sum games. To the solution of the latter problem these authors made a revolutionary contribution which, however, did not dispose of it. Against the elegance, the formal satisfyingness and the pregnant originality of the von Neumann–Morgenstern theory must be set as yet unresolved doubts as to the adequacy of the pure theory of rational decision which it embodies.

BIBLIOGRAPHY

Colman, A. 1982. *Game Theory and Experimental Games.* Oxford: Pergamon.
Ellsberg, D. 1956. Theory of the reluctant duelist. *American Economic Review* 46, December, 909–23.
Gale, D. 1951. Convex polyhedral cones and linear inequalities. In *Activity Analysis of Production and Allocation*, ed. T.C. Koopmans, New York: Wiley.
Johansen, L. 1981. Interaction in economic theory. *Economie appliquée* 34(2–3), 229–67.
Von Neumann, J. and Morgenstern, O. 1944. *Theory of Games and Economic Behavior.* Princeton: Princeton University Press.

Contributors

Andrew B. Abel Robert Morris Professor of Banking, Professor of Finance and Economics, Wharton School, University of Pennsylvania. 'Dynamic effects of permanent and temporary tax policies in a q model of investment', *Journal of Monetary Economics* 9 (1982); 'Optimal investment under uncertainty', *American Economic Review* 73 (1983); 'Precautionary saving and accidental bequests', *American Economic Review* 75 (1985); 'Optimal Monetary Growth', *Journal of Monetary Economics* 19 (1987); 'Stock prices under time-varying divided risk: an exact solution in an infinite horizon general equilibrium model', *Journal of Monetary Economics* 22 (1988); 'Birth, death, and taxes', *Journal of Public Economics* 39 (1989).

Armen A. Alchian Emeritus Professor of Economics, University of California, Los Angeles. *University Economics* (with W.R. Allen, 1964); *Economic Forces at Work* (1977); *Exchange and Production* (with W.R. Allen, 1983).

William R. Allen Professor of Economics, University of California, Los Angeles. Vice President, Institute for Contemporary Studies. President, Western Economic Association; Vice President, Southern Economic Association. 'The International Monetary Fund and balance of payments adjustment', *Oxford Economic Papers* 15 (1962); 'Domestic investment, the foreign trade balance, and the World Bank', *Kyklos* 15(1962); *University Economics* (with A. Alchian, 1964); 'The position of mercantilism and the early development of international trade theory' in *Events, Ideology and Economic Theory: The Determinants of Progress in the Development of Economic Analysis*, (ed. R. Eagly, 1968); 'Economics, economists, and economic policy: modern American experiences', *History of Political Economy* 9 (Spring 1977); 'Irving Fisher, F.D.R., and the Great Depression', *History of Political Economy* 9 (1977).

Kenneth J. Arrow Joan Kenney Professor of Economics, Professor of Operations Research, Stanford University. John Bates Clark Medal, American Economic Association, 1957; Nobel Memorial Prize in Economic Science, 1972; von Neumann Prize of the Institute of Management Sciences and Operations Research Society of America, 1986. *Social Choice and Individual Values* (1951); *Essays in the Theory of Risk-Bearing* (1971); *The Limits of Organization* (1974); *Studies in Resource Allocation Processes* (with L. Hurwicz, 1977); *Collected Papers* (1983–5).

732

Tony Aspromourgos Senior Lecturer in Economics, University of Sydney. 'On the origins of the term 'Neoclassical'', *Journal of Economics* 10(3), (1986); 'Unemployment, economic theory and labour-market deregulation', *Australian Economic Papers* 26 (1987); 'The theory of production and distribution in Cantillon's *Essai*', *Oxford Economic Papers* 41 (1989); 'The logic of economic austerity', *Economic Appliquée* 42(1), (1989).

P.S. Atiyah QC, Professor of Law, Oxford University (1977–1988); Fellow, British Academy. *The Rise and Fall of Freedom of Contract* (1979); *Introduction to the Law of Contract* (1981); *Promises, Morals and Laws* (1981); *Essays on Contract* (1987); *The Sale of Goods* (1990).

A.B. Atkinson Tooke Professor of Economic Science and Statistics, London School of Economics. Fellow, British Academy. *Unequal Shares – Wealth in Britain* (1972); *Economics of Inequality* (1975); *The Personal Distribution of Income* (ed., 1979); *Lectures on Public Economics* (with J. E. Stiglitz, 1980); *Social Justice and Public Policy* (1982); *Poverty and Social Security* (1989).

Michael Bacharach University Lecturer and Fellow in Economics, Christ Church, Oxford. *Biproportional Matrices and Input–Output Change* (1970); *Economics and the Theory of Games* (1976); 'Some extensions of a claim of Aumann in an axiomatic model of knowledge', *Journal of Economic Theory* 37 (1985); 'A theory of rational decision in games', *Erkenntis* 27 (1987); 'Commodities, language, and desire', *Journal of Philosophy* 87 (1990).

Bela Balassa Professor, Johns Hopkins University. Consultant, World Bank. Doctor *Honoris Causa*, Sorbonne, Paris; External Member, Hungarian Academy of Sciences. *Toward Renewed Economic Growth in Latin America* (1986); *Adjusting to Success* (1987); *Changing Trade Patterns in Manufactured Goods* (1988); *Japan in the World Economy* (1988); *Comparative Advantage, Trade Policy, and Economic Development* (1988); *New Directions in the World Economy* (1989).

Francis M. Bator Ford Foundation Professor of Political Economy, JFK School of Government, Harvard University. Deputy National Security Advisor to President Lyndon B. Johnson, 1964–67; Distinguished Service Award, US Treasury Department; Guggenheim Fellow; Fellow, American Academy of Arts and Sciences. 'The simple analytics of welfare maximization', *American Economic Review* (March 1957); 'The anatomy of market failure', *Quarterly Journal of Economics* (August 1958); *The Question of Government Spending: Public Needs and Private Wants* (1960); 'Fiscal and monetary policy: In search of a doctrine', *Economic Choices: Studies in Tax/Fiscal Policy* (1982); 'The state of macroeconomics', in *Employment and Growth: Issues for the 1980s* (eds. Steinherr and Weiserbs, 1987); 'Must we retrench?', *Foreign Affairs* 68(2), (1989).

Peter Bauer Emeritus Professor of Economics, London School of Economics; Fellow, Gonville and Caius College, Cambridge; Fellow, British Academy; Life Peer. *The Rubber Industry* (1948); *West African Trade* (1954); *Dissent on Development* (1971); *Equality, the Third World and Economic Delusion* (1981); *Reality and Rhetoric: Studies in the Economics of Development* (1984); *Traders and the Development Frontier* (forthcoming 1991).

William J. Baumol Professor, Princeton and New York Universities. President, American Economic Association. *Superfairness: Applications and Theory* (1986); *Contestable Markets and the Theory of Industry Structure* (with J. C. Panzar and R. D. Willig, 1988); *Productivity and American Leadership: the Long View* (with S.A.B. Blackman and E.N. Wolff, 1989).

Contributors

Gary S. Becker University Professor of Economics and Sociology, University of Chicago. Honorary degrees from Hebrew University, Jerusalem; Knox College; University of Illinois, Chicago; W.S. Woytinsky Award; John Bates Clark Medal; Frank E. Seidman Distinguished Award in Political Economy; MERIT Award; John R. Commons Award; President, American Economic Association, 1987; Member, National Academy of Sciences; American Philosophical Society; American Academy of Arts and Sciences; National Academy of Education. *The Economics of Distribution* (1957); *Human Capital* (1964); *Economic Theory* (1971); *The Allocation of Time and Goods over the Life Cycle* (with G. Ghez, 1974); *The Economic Aproach to Human Behavior* (1976); *A Treatise on the Family* (1981).

Wilfred Beckerman Fellow, Balliol College, Oxford. *The British Economy in 1975* (with others, 1965); *Introduction to National Income Analysis* (1968); *The Labour Government's Economic Record, 1964–70* (1972); *In Defence of Economic Growth* (1974); *Slow Growth in Britain: Causes and Consequences* (ed. and contributor, 1979).

Olivier J. Blanchard Professor, MIT. Fellow, Econometric Society; Co-editor, *Quarterly Journal of Economics*. 'Speculative bubbles, crashes and rational expectations', *Economic Letters* (1979); 'Output, the stock market and interest rates', *American Economic Review* (1981); 'The production and inventory behaviour of the U.S. automobile industry', *Journal of Political Economy* (1983); 'Deficits, debt and finite horizons', *Journal of Political Economy* (1985); 'Hysteresis and European unemployment' in *Macroeconomics Annual* (ed. Stanley Fischer, 1986); *Lectures on Macroeconomics* (with Stanley Fischer, 1988).

Francine D. Blau Professor of Economics and Labor and Industrial Relations, University of Illinois, Urbana-Champaign. Research Associate, National Bureau of Economic Research, Cambridge Massachusetts. President 1991–92, Vice President, 1983–84, Midwest Economics Association; Executive Board Member, Industrial Relations Research Association, 1987–89. *Equal Pay in the Office* (1977); 'Race and sex differences in the quits of young workers', (with L. Kahn) *Industrial and Labor Relations Review* (1981); *The Economics of Women, Men, and Work* (with M. Ferber, 1986); 'Discrimination: Evidence from the United States', (with M. Ferber) *American Economic Review* (1987); 'Trends in Earnings Differentials by Gender: 1971–1982', (with A. Beller) *Industrial and Labor Relations Review* (1988); 'Black–white differences in wealth and asset composition', (with J. Graham) *Quarterly Journal of Economics* (1990).

Ester Boserup Honorary degrees in Economics, University of Copenhagen; in Human Letters, Brown University; in Agricultural Science, University of Wageningen. Foreign Associate, National Academy of Sciences, US. *Conditions of Agricultural Growth* (1965); *Woman's Role in Economic Development* (1970); *Population and Technological Change* (1981); *Economic and Demographic Relationships in Development* (1990).

James A. Brickley Professor of Economics, University of Rochester. 'The choice of organizational form: the case of franchising', (with F.H. Dark) *Journal of Financial Economics* 18(2), (1987); 'The market for corporate control: the empirical evidence since 1980', (with G.A. Jarrell and J.M. Netter) *Journal of Economic Perspectives* 2(1), (1988); 'Ownership structure and voting on anti-takeover amendments', (with R.C. Lease and C.W. Smith) *Journal of Financial Economics* 20(1–2), (1988).

James M. Buchanan Professor of Economics, George Mason University, Virginia. Nobel Memorial Prize in Economic Science, 1986. *The Calculus of Consent: Logical Foundations of Constitutional Democracy* (with G. Tullock, 1962); *Liberty, Market and State* (1986); *The Reason of Rules* (1984); *Economics: Between Predictive Science and Moral Philosophy* (with G. Brennan, 1988); *Explorations in Constitutional Economics* (1989); *The Economics and Ethics of Constitutional Order* (1991).

Phillip Cagan Professor of Economics, Columbia University. 'The monetary dynamics of hyperinflations', *Studies in the Quantity Theory of Money*, (ed. M. Friedman, 1956); *Determinants and Effects of Changes in the Stock of Money 1875–1960* (1965); *The Channels of Monetary Effects on Interest Rates* (1972); *Persistent Inflation* (1979); 'The uncertain future of monetary policy', *The Sixth Henry Thornton Lecture* (1984).

Steven N.S. Cheung Professor of Economics and Chair, University of Hong Kong; Fellow of Political Economy, University of Chicago. *The Theory of Share Tenancy* (1969); 'The structure of a contract and the theory of a non-exclusive resource', *Journal of Law and Economics* 13(1), (1970); 'The fable of the bees: an economic investigation', *Journal of Law and Economics* 16(1), (1973); 'A theory of price control', *Journal of Law and Economics* 17(1), (1974); *Will China Go Capitalist?* (1982); 'The contractual nature of the firm', *Journal of Law and Economics* (1983).

Gregory Claeys Lehrgebiet Auslandskunde und Anglistik, Hannover. 'Engels's *Outlines of a Critique of Political Economy* (1843) and the origins of the Marxist critique of capitalism', *History of Political Economy* 16(2), (1984); Industrialism and hedonism in Orwell's literary and political development', *Albion* 18 (1987); 'Justice, independence and individual democracy: the development of John Stuart Mill's views on society', *Journal of Politics* 49(1), (1987); *Machinery, Money and the Millennium. Labour and Civilization in Early British Socialism* (1987).

Robert D. Cooter Professor of Law, Universiy of California, Berkley; Olin Visiting Research Fellow, University of Virginia Law School 1988–89; Visiting Professor, University of Cologne Law Faculty May–July 1989; Guggenheim Fellowship 1985–86. *Law and Economics* (with T. Ulen, 1988); 'Economic analysis of legal disputes and their resolution', *Journal of Economic Literature* 27 (with D. Rubinfeld 1989); 'How to make custom into the common law of property for Papua New Guinea', in *Customary Land Tenure: Registration and Decentralization in Papua New Guinea* (ed. P. Larmour, 1989); 'Rawls's lexical orderings are good economics', *Economics and Philosophy* 47 (1989); 'Towards a market in unmatured tort claims', *University of Virginia Law Review* 75 (1989); 'Merit goods: some thoughts on the unthinkable', in *Rationality, Individualism, and Public Policy* (ed. G. Brennan and C. Walsh, 1990).

Ralf Dahrendorf Warden, St Antony's College, Oxford. KBE; Fellow, British Academy. *Class and Class Conflict in Industrial Society* (1959); *Society and Democracy in Germany* (1966); *Essays in the Theory of Society* (1968); *The New Liberty* (1975); *The Modern Social Conflict* (1988); *Reflections on the Revolution in Europe.*

Marcello de Cecco Professor of Monetary Economics, Universita di Roma; External Professor, European University Institute, Florence. 'The Origins of the Postwar Monetary System', *Cambridge Journal of Economics* (1977); *The International Gold Standard* (1984); *Changing Money* (ed., 1985); *A European Central Bank?* (ed., with A. Giovannini, 1989); 'Keynes revived' *Journal of Monetary Economics* (July 1990).

John Eatwell Fellow, Trinity College, Cambridge. *An Introduction to Modern Economics* (with J. Robinson, 1973); *Whatever happened to Britain?* (1982); *Keynes's Economics and the Theory of Value and Distribution* (ed., with Murray Milgate, 1983).

735

Contributors

Robert Eisner William R. Kenan Professor of Economics, Northwestern University. Fellow, American Academy of Arts and Sciences, Econometric Society; President, American Economic Association, 1988; Guggenheim Fellow, 1960. *Factors in Business Investment* (for National Bureau of Economic Research, 1978); 'A new view of the Federal Debt and deficits', (with P.J. Piper) *American Economic Review* 74(1), (1984); *How real is the Federal Deficit?* (1986); 'Budget deficits: rhetoric and reality', *Journal of Economic Perspectives* 3(2), (1989); *The Total Incomes System of Acounts* (1989); 'The real rate of national saving', *The Review of Income and Wealth* 37 (1991).

Allan M. Feldman Associate Professor of Economics, Brown University, Providence, R.I. *Welfare Economics and Social Choice Theory* (1980).

Ronald Findlay Ragnar Nurkse Professor of Economics, Columbia University. *Trade and Specialization* (1970); *International Trade and Development Theory* (1973); 'Relative prices, growth and trade in a simple Ricardian system', *Economica* 92(1), (1974); 'Relative backwardness, direct foreign investment, and the transfer of technology: a simple dynamic model', *Quarterly Journal of Economics* 92(1), (1976); 'The terms of trade and equilibrium growth in the world economy', *American Economic Review* 70 (1980); 'International distributive justice', *Journal of International Economics* 13 (1982).

David D. Friedman John M. Olin Faculty Fellow, University of Chicago Law School. *The Machinery of Freedom* (1971); 'An economic theory of the size and shape of nations', *Journal of Political Economy* (February 1977); 'Reflections on optimal punishment or should the rich pay higher fines?', *Research in Law and Economics* (1981); 'Efficient institutions for the private enforcement of law', *Journal of Legal Studies* (June 1984); *Price Theory: An Intermediate Text* (1986); 'Cold houses in warm climates and vice versa: a paradox of rational heating', *Journal of Political Economy* 95(5), (1987).

Ernest Gellner William Wise Professor of Social Anthropology, University of Cambridge. Fellow, British Academy. *Words and Things* (1959); *Muslim Society* (1981); *Nations and Nationalism* (1983); *The Psychoanalytic Movement* (1985); *Culture, Identity and Politics* (1987); *Plough, Sword and Book* (1988).

Andrew Glyn Lecturer, Corpus Christi College, Oxford. *British Capitalism, Workers and the Profit Squeeze* (with Bob Sutcliffe, 1972); 'The economic case against pit closures' in *Debating Colliery Closures* (ed. D. Cooper and T. Hopper, 1988); 'The diversity of unemployment experience since 1973' (with Bob Rowthorn) in *The End of the Golden Age* (ed. S. A. Marglin, 1989); *Capitalism since 1945* (with P. Armstrong and J. Harrison, 1991).

J. de. V. Graaff Formerly Emeritus Fellow, St John's College, Cambridge. *Theoretical Welfare Economics* (1957).

Christopher A. Gregory Senior Lecturer in Anthropology, Department of Prehistory and Anthropology, Australian National University. *Gifts and Commodities* (1982); *Observing the Economy* (with J. Altman, 1989).

Peter Groenewegen Professor of Economics, University of Sydney. Director, Centre for the Study of the History of Economic Thought, University of Sydney; Fellow, Academy of Social Sciences in Australia. *The Economics of A.R.J. Turgot* (1977); *Public Finance in Australia: Theory and Practice* (1979); *Everyone's Guide to Taxation in Australia* (1985); *Readings in Australian Taxation Policy* (ed., 1980); *Taxation and Fiscal Federalism: Essays* *in Honour of Russell Mathews* (ed., with G. Brennan and B. Grewal, 1988); *History of Australian Economics* (with B. McFarlane, 1990).

Bruce W. Hamilton Professor of Economics, Johns Hopkins University. 'Capitalization and intrajurisdictional differences in local tax prices', *American Economic Review* (1976); 'Wasteful commuting', *Journal of Political Economics* (1982); 'The flypaper effect and other anomalies', *Journal of Public Economics* (1983).

Arnold C. Harberger Professor of Economics, University of California at Los Angeles. Member, National Academy of Sciences of the United States; Fellow, Econometric Society, American Academy of Arts and Sciences. *Project Evaluation* (1972); *Taxation and Welfare* (1974); *World Economic Growth* (ed., 1985).

John C. Harsanyi Emeritus Flood Research Professor in Business Administration, University of California, Berkeley. Fellow, Econometric Society, American Academy of Arts and Science. Honorary Doctor of Science, Northwestern University. 'Games with incomplete information played by 'Bayesian' players', 1–3, *Management Science* 14 (1967–68); *Essays on Ethics, Social Behavior, and Scientific Explanation* (1976); *Rational Behavior and Bargaining Equilibrium in Games and Social Situations* (1977); *Papers in Game Theory* (1982); *A General Theory of Equilibrium Selection in Games* (with R. Selten, 1988).

Robert Hessen Senior Research Fellow, Hoover Institution, Stanford University; Lecturer in American Business History, Stanford Business School. *Steel Titan: The Life of Charles M. Schwab* (1975); *In Defense of the Corporation* (1979); 'Towards a new concept of corporations: a contractual and private property model', *Hastings Law Journal* (1979); *Does Big Business Rule America?* (ed., 1981); 'The modern corporation and private property: a reappraisal', *Journal of Law and Economics* (1983); 'Do business and economic historians understand corporations?', *Hoover Institution Working Papers* (1989).

Polly Hill Emeritus Reader in Commonwealth Studies, University of Cambridge; Emeritus Fellow, Clare Hall, Cambridge. *The Migrant Cocoa Farmers of Southern Ghana* (1963); *Studies in Rural Capitalism in West Africa* (1970); *Rural Hausa: A Village and a Setting* (1972); *Population, Prosperity and Poverty: Rural Kano 1900 and 1970* (1977); *Dry Grain Farming Families: Hausaland (Nigeria) and Karnataka (India) compared* (1982); *Development Economics on Trial: The Anthropological Case for a Prosecution* (1986).

Albert O. Hirschman Emeritus Professor of Social Science, Institute for Advanced Study, Princeton. Distinguished Member, American Economic Association; Member, National Academy of Sciences; Talcott Parsons Prize for Social Science; Festschrift (1986); numerous honorary degrees. *National Power and the Structure of Foreign Trade* (1945); *The Strategy of Economic Development* (1958); *Exit, Voice, and Loyalty* (1970); *The Passions and the Interests* (1977); *Essays in Trespassing* (1981); *The Rhetoric of Reaction* (1991).

Jack Hirshleifer Professor of Economics, UCLA. Fellow, American Academy of Arts and Sciences, Econometric Society; Vice-President, American Economic Association. 1979. *Water Supply: Economics, Technology and Policy* (with J.C. DeHaven and J.W. Milliman, 1969); *Investment, Interest and Capital* (1970); *Economic Behaviour in Adversity* (1987); *Price Theory and Applications* (1988).

Peter Howitt Bank of Montreal Professor of Money and Finance, Department of Economics, University of Western Ontario. 'Stability and the quantity theory', *Journal* *of Political Economy* 82 (1974); 'Activist monetary policy under rational expectations', *Journal of Political Economy* 89 (1981); 'Transaction costs in the theory of unemployment', *American Economic Review* 75 (1985); 'The Keynesian recovery', *Canadian Journal of Economics* 19 (1986); 'Business cycles with costly search and recruiting', *Quarterly Journal of Economics* 103 (1988).

Ravi Kanbur Director of Development Economics, Research Centre, Warwick University. 'How to analyse commodity price stabilization?', *Oxford Economic Papers* (1984); North–South interaction and commodity control', (with D.A. Vines) *Journal of Development Economics* (1985); 'Food subsidies and poverty alleviation', (with T. Besley) *Economic Journal* (1988).

Masahiro Kawai Professor, Institute of Social Science, University of Tokyo. 'Price volatility of storable commodities under rational expecations in spot and futures markets', *International Economic Review* 24(2), 1983.

Charles P. Kindleberger Emeritus Professor of Economics, Massachusetts Institute of Technology. D.Sc. (h.c.), University of Paris, University of Ghent; Honorary D.Sc., University of Pennsylvania. *The World in Depression, 1929–39* (1973); *Manias, Panics, and Crashes* (1978); *Financial History of Western Europe* (1984); *Keynesianism vs Monetarism and Other Essays in Financial History* (1986); *Historical Economics, Art or Science?* (1990).

Kurt Klappholz Reader in Economics, London School of Economics and Political Science. 'Methodological prescriptions in economics', (with J. Agassi) *Economica* (1959); 'Identities in economic models', (with E. Mishan) *Economica* (1962); 'Value judgements and economics', *British Journal for the Philosophy of Science* (1964); 'Economics and ethical neutrality', in *The Encyclopedia of Philosophy* (ed. P. Edwards, 1967); 'Equality of opportunity, "fairness" and efficiency', in *Essays in Honour of Lord Robbins* (ed. M. Peston and B. Corry, 1972).

John O. Ledyard Professor of Economics and Social Sciences, California Institute of Technology. Fellow, Econometric Society; President, Public Choice Society; Member, Executive Committee, Economic Science Association. 'Optimal allocation of public goods: a solution to the "free-rider" problem', (with T. Groves) *Econometrica* 45(4), (1977); 'The pure theory of large two candidate elections', *Public Choice* 44 (1984); 'The scope of the hypothesis of Bayesian equilibrium', *Journal of Economic Theory* 39, (1986); 'Allocating uncertain and unresponsive resources', (with J. Banks and D. Porter) *The Rand Journal of Economics* 20(1), (1989); 'Information Aggregation in Two-Candidate Elections', in *Contemporary Contributions to Political Theory* (ed. P. Ordeshook, 1989).

David E. Lindsey Member of the Board of Governors of the Federal Reserve System. 'Determining the monetary instrument: a diagrammatic exposition', (with S. Leroy) *American Economic Review* 68(5), (December 1978); 'Nonborrowed reserves targeting and monetary control', in *Improving Money Stock Control* (ed. L. H. Meyer, 1983); 'Short-run monetary control: evidence under a nonborrowed reserve operating procedure', (with H. Farr, G.P. Gillum, K.J. Kopecky and R.D. Porter) *Journal of Monetary Economics* 13 (January 1984); 'The monetary regime of the Federal Reserve System', in *Alternative Monetary Regimes* (ed. C.D. Campbell and W.R. Dougan, 1986); *Controlling Risk in the Payments System* (Report to the Task Force on Controlling Payments System Risk to the Payments System Policy Committee of the Federal Reserve System, Chairman 1988); *Economics* (with E.G. Dolan, 1990).

Donald N. McCloskey Professor of Economics and History, University of Iowa. *Essays on a Mature Economy: Britain after 1840* (ed., 1971); *Economic Maturity and Entrepreneurial Decline: British Iron and Steel, 1870–1914* (1973); *Enterprise and Trade in Victorian Britain: Essays in Historical Economics* (1981); *The Economic History of Britain, 1700–present* (ed. with R. Floud, 1981); *The Applied Theory of Price* (1982).

John J. McConnell Professor of Finance, Purdue University. Board of Directors, American Finance Association. 'Returns, risks and pricing of income bonds 1956–1976 (Does money have an odour?)', (with G.G. Schlarbaum); 'Valuation of GNMA mortgage-backed securities', (with K.B. Dunn) *Journal of Business* 54 (1981); 'The market value of control in publicly-traded corporations', (with R.C. Lease and W.H. Mikkelson) 2 (1983); 'Corporate capital expenditure decisions and the market value of the firm', (with C.J. Muscarella) *Journal of Financial Economics* 14(3), (1985); 'Corporate mergers and security returns', (with D.K. Dennis) *Journal of Financial Economics* 16(2), (1986); 'The determinants of yields on financial leasing contracts', (with J.S. Schallheim, R. Johnson and R.C. Lease) *Journal of Financial Economics* 19(1), (1987).

Edmond Malinvaud Professor, Collège de France. President, International Economic Association, 1974–7; President, European Economic Association, 1988. *Statistical Methods of Econometrics* (1966); *Lectures on Microeconomic Theory* (1972); *French Economic Growth* (with J.J. Carre and P. Dubois, 1975); *The Theory of Unemployment Reconsidered* (1977); *Théorie macroéconomique* (1981).

Burton G. Malkiel Chemical Bank Chairman's Professor of Economics, Princeton University. Former President, American Finance Association. *The Term Structure of Interest Rates* (1966); *Strategies and Rational Decisions in the Securities Options Market*, (with Richard Quandt, 1961); *Expectations and the Structure of Share Prices* (1982); *A Random Walk Down Wall Street* (1985).

Murray Milgate John L. Loeb Associate Professor of the Social Sciences, Harvard University. *Capital and Employment* (1982); *Keynes's Economics and the Theory of Value and Distribution* (ed., with J. Eatwell, 1983); *Critical Issues in Social Thought* (ed., with C.B. Welch, 1989); *Ricardian Politics* (with S.C. Stimson, 1991); *Laissez Faire* (1991).

Paul Milgrom Professor of Economics, Stanford University. Guggenheim Fellow; Fellow, Econometric Society, Institute of Advanced Studies in Jerusalem. 'A theory of auctions and competitive bidding', (with R. Weber) *Econometrica* 50 (1982); 'Limit pricing and entry under incomplete information: an equilibrium analysis', (with John Roberts) *Econometrica* 50 (1972); 'Predation, reputation, and entry deterrence', (with John Roberts) *Journal of Economic Theory* 27 (1982); 'Aggregation and linearity in the provision of intertemporal incentives', (with B. Holmstrom) *Econometrica* 55 (1987); 'Employment contracts, influence activities and efficient organization design', *Journal of Political Economy* 96(1), (1988); 'The economics of modern manufacturing: technology, strategy, and organization', (with John Roberts) *American Economic Review* 80(3), (1990).

David Hector Monro Emeritus Professor of Philosophy, Monash University. Fellow, Australian Academy of the Humanities, Academy of Social Sciences in Australia. *Argument of Laughter* (1951); *Godwin's Moral Philosophy* (1953); *Empiricism and Ethics* (1967); *The Ambivalence of Bernard Mandeville* (1975); *The Sonneteer's History of Philosophy* (1981); *Don Juan in Australia* (1986).

Peter Newman Emeritus Professor of Economics, Johns Hopkins University. *Costs in Alternative Locations: The Clothing Industry* (with D.C. Hague, 1952); 'The erosion of

Contributors

Marshall's theory of value', *Quarterly Journal of Economics* (1960); *British Guiana: problems of cohesion in an immigrant society* (1964); *Malaria Eradication and Population Growth* (1965); 'Some properties of concave functions', *Journal of Economic Theory* (1969).

Roger G. Noll Morris M. Doyle Centennial Professor in Public Policy, Department of Economics, Stanford University. 'The anticompetitive use of regulation: U.S. v. AT&T', (with Bruce Owen) in *The Antitrust Revolution* (ed. J. Kwoka, Jr. and L. White, 1988); 'Economic perspectives on the politics of regulation', in *Handbook of Industrial Organization* 5(2), (ed. R. Schmalensee and R. Willig, 1989); 'Structure and process, politics and policy: administrative arrangements and the political control of agencies', (with M. McCubbins and B. Weingast) *Virginia Law Review* (1989); 'Environmental markets in the year 2000', (with R. Hahn) *Journal of Risk and Uncertainty* (1990); 'Some implications of cognitive psychology for risk regulation', (with J. Krier) *Journal of Legal Studies* (1990); *The Technology Pork Barrel* (with L.R. Cohen, 1990).

Domenico Mario Nuti Professor of Economics, European University Institute, Florence; University of Siena. Formerly Fellow, Kings College, Cambridge (1965–79), Professor of Political Economy and Director of the Centre for Russian and East European Studies, University of Birmingham (1980–83). 'Perestroika: transition between central planning and market socialism', *Economic Policy* 7(3), (1988); 'Feasible financial innovation under market socialism', in *Financial Reform in Centrally Planned Economies* (ed. C. Kessides, T. King, M. Nuti and K. Sokil, 1989); 'Internal and international implications of monetary disequilibrium in Poland', *European Economy* 43, (1990); 'Crisis, reform and stabilisation in Central Eastern Europe: prospects and Western response', in *Transformation in Eastern Europe* (ed. J.-P. Fitoussi, 1990).

Mancur Olson Distinguished Professor of Economics, University of Maryland. Distinguished Fellow, US Institute of Peace, 1990–91; Fellow, American Association for the Advancement of Science, American Academy of Arts and Sciences; Honorary Fellow, University College, Oxford; Co-winner, American Political Science Association, Gladys M. Kammerer Award (for best book on US national policy – *The Rise and Decline of Nations*), 1983. 'Rapid growth as a destabilizing force', *Journal of Economic History* 23 (1963); *The Logic of Collective Action: Public Goods and the Theory of Groups* (1965); *An Economic Theory of Alliances* (with R. Zeckhauser, 1966); 'The marginal utility of income does not increase: borrowing, lending and Friedman–Savage gambles', (with M.J. Bailey and P. Wonnacott) *American Economic Review* 70 (1980); 'Positive time preference', (with M.J. Bailey) *Journal of Political Economy* 89(1), (1981); *The Rise and Decline of Nations: Economic Growth, Stagflation, and Social Rigidities* (1982).

B. Peter Pashigian Professor, Graduate School of Business, University of Chicago. Ford Foundation Fellowships; National Science Foundation and Chicago Board of Trade grants. 'Consequences and causes of public ownership of urban transit facilities', *Journal of Political Economy* (December 1976); 'The market for lawyers: the determinants of the demand for and supply of lawyers', *Journal of Law and Economics* (April 1977); 'The effect of environmental regulation on optimal plant size and factor shares', *Journal of Law and Economics* (April 1984); 'Environmental regulation: whose self-interests are being protected?', *Economic Inquiry* (October 1985); 'Why have some farmers opposed futures markets?', *Journal of Political Economy* (April 1988); 'Demand uncertainty and sales: a study of fashion and markdown pricing', *American Economic Review* (December 1988).

Edmund S. Phelps McVickar Professor of Political Economy, Columbia University. Member, National Academy of Sciences; Fellow, Econometric Society; Vice-President,

American Economic Association, 1983. *Studies in Macroeconomic Theory*, (2 vols, 1979); *Individual Forecasting and Aggregate Outcomes* (ed., with R. Frydman, 1983); *Political Economy: An Introductory Text* (1985); *The Slump in Europe* (with J.-P. Fitoussi, 1988); *Seven Schools of Macroeconomic Thought* (1990); *Recent Developments in Macroeconomics* (ed., 1991).

Henry Phelps Brown Professor of the Economics of Labour, London School of Economics and Political Science, 1947–68. Fellow, British Academy; MBE (mil.) 1945; KBE 1976. *The Framework of the Pricing System* (1936); *The Growth of British Industrial Relations* (1959); *A Century of Pay* (1968); *The Inequality of Pay* (1977); *The Origins of Trade Union Power* (1983); *Egalitarianism and the Generation of Inequality* (1988).

James P. Quirk Formerly Professor of Economics, California Institute of Technology. *Introduction to General Equilibrium Theory and Welfare Economics* (with R. Saposnik, 1968); *Intermediate Microeconomics* (1985); 'Choice of a Government discount rate: An alternative approach' (with K. Terasawa), *J.E.E.M.* (1990); *The Sports Business* (with R. Noll and R. Fort, 1991).

Anatol Rapoport Professor of Peace and Conflict Studies, University College, University of Toronto. Fellow, American Academy of Arts and Sciences; Lenz International Peace Research Award, 1975; Comprehensive Achievement Award, Society for General Systems Research, 1983; Harold J. Lasswell Award for Distinguished Scientific Achievement in Political Psychology, 1986; Honorary Doctor: of Human Letters, University of Western Michigan 1971; of Laws, University of Toronto 1986. *Fights, Games and Debates* (1960); *Prisoner's Dilemma* (with A.M. Chammah, 1965); *Mathematical Methods in the Social and Behavioral Sciences* (1983); *General System Theory* (1986); *The Origins of Violence* (1989); *Decision Theory and Decision Behaviour* (1989).

Melvin W. Reder Isidore and Gladys Brown Emeritus Professor of Urban and Labor Economics, University of Chicago Graduate School of Business. *Studies in the Theory of Welfare Economics* (1947); *Labor in a Growing Economy* (1957).

John Roberts Jonathan B. Lovelace Professor of Economics, Graduate School of Business, Stanford University; Professor of Economics (by courtesy), Department of Economics, Stanford University. Fellow, Econometric Society. 'On the foundations of the theory of monopolistic competition', (with H. Sonnenschein) *Econometrica* 45 (1977); 'Limit pricing and entry under incomplete information: an equilibrium analysis', (with P. Milgrom) *Econometrica* 50 (1982); 'Predation, reputation and entry deterrence', (with P. Milgrom) *Journal of Economic Theory* 27 (1982); 'An equilibrium model with involuntary unemployment at flexible, competitive prices and wages', *American Economic Review* 77 (1987); 'The economics of modern manufacturing: technology, strategy and organization', (with P. Milgrom) *American Economic Review* 80 (1990); *The Economics of Organization and Management* (with P. Milgrom, 1991).

John C. Robertson Fellow, Tutor and University Lecturer in Modern History, St Hugh's College, Oxford. 'The Scottish Enlightenment at the limits of the civic tradition' in *Wealth and Virtue: the shaping of political economy in the Scottish Enlightenment* (ed. I. Hont and M. Ignatieff, 1983); 'Scottish political economy beyond the civic tradition: government and economic development in *The Wealth of Nations*', *History of Political Thought* 4 (1983); *The Scottish Enlightenment and the Militia Issue* (1985); and several articles on the political thought and economy of David Hume, Adam Smith and other contributors the Scottish Enlightenment.

741

Contributors

Susan Rose-Ackerman Ely Professor of Law and Political Science, Yale University. *Corruption. A Study in Political Economy* (1978); *The Nonprofit Enterprise in Market Economics* (with E. James, 1986); *Knights, Raiders, and Targets: The Impact of Hostile Takeover* (ed., with J.C. Coffee and L. Lowenstein, 1988).

Murray N. Rothbard S.J. Hall Distinguished Professor of Economics, University of Nevada, Las Vegas; Vice President for Academic Affairs, Ludwig von Mises Institute, Auburn University. *Toward A Reconstruction of Utility and Welfare Economics* (1956); *Man, Economy and State: A Treatise on Economic Principles* (2 vols, 1962/70); *Panic of 1819: Reactions and Policies* (1962); *America's Great Depression* (1963); *Power and Market: Government and the Economy* (1970); Introductory essay, *Essays on Capital, Interest and Rent* (ed. F.A. Fetter, 1977).

Thomas C. Schelling Distinguished Professor of Economics and Public Affairs, University of Maryland, College Park. President, American Economic Association, 1991. *Strategy of Conflict* (1960); *Arms and Influence* (1967); *Micromotives and Macrobehavior* (1978); *Choice and Consequence* (1984).

Vernon L. Smith Regents' Professor of Economics and Research Director of the Economic Science Laboratory, University of Arizona. Founding President, Economic Science Association (1986–87); President, Public Choice Society (1988–90); Fellow, Econometric Society; President, Western Economic Association (1990–91). 'An experimental study of competitive market behavior', *Journal of Political Economy* (April, 1962); 'Economics of the primitive hunter culture with applications to pleistocene extinction and the rise of agriculture', *Journal of Political Economy* (July/August, 1975); 'Microeconomic systems as an experimental science', *American Economic Review* (December, 1982); 'Bubbles, crashes and endogenous expectations in experimental spot asset markets', (with G. Suchanek and A. Williams) *Econometrica* (September, 1988); 'Theory and individual behavior in first price auctions', *Journal of Risk and Uncertainty* 1 (1988); 'Designing 'smart' computer assisted markets: an experimental auction for gas networks', (with K.A. McCabe and S.J. Rassenti) *European Journal of Political Economy* (forthcoming).

Henry W. Spiegel Emeritus Professor of Economics, The Catholic University of America. Guggenheim Fellow (1945–46); Phi Beta Kappa, Pi Gamma Mu, Order of Artus. *Land Tenure Policies at Home and Abroad* (1941); *The Economics of Total War* (1942); *The Brazilian Economy* (1949); *Development of Economic Thought* (1952); *The Rise of American Economic Thought* (1960); *The Growth of Economic Thought* (3rd edn, 1991).

Hillel Steiner Senior Lecturer in Political Philosophy, University of Manchester. 'Individual liberty', *Aristotelian Society Proceedings* 75 (1975); 'The natural right to the means of production', *Philosophical Quarterly* 27 (1977); 'The structure of a set of compossible rights', *Journal of Philosophy* 74 (1977); 'Liberty and equality', *Political Studies* 29 (1981); 'Exploitation: a liberal theory amended, defended and extended', in *Modern Theories of Exploitation* (ed. A. Reeve, 1987); *An Essay on Rights* (forthcoming).

Lester C. Thurow Dean, Sloan School of Management, Massachusetts Institute of Technology. Fellow, American Academy of Arts and Sciences; Gerald Loeb Award, 1982; numerous honorary degrees. *The Economic Problem* (with R. Heilbroner, 1974); *Generating Inequality: The Distributional Mechanisms of the Economy* (1975); *The Zero-Sum Society: Redistribution and the Possibilities for Economic Change* (1980); *Dangerous Currents: The State of Economics* (1983); *The Zero-Sum Solution: Building A World-Class Economy* (1985); *The Deficits: How Big? How Long? How Dangerous?* (with D. Bell, 1986).

James Tobin Sterling Emeritus Professor of Economics, Yale University. Nobel Prize in Economic Science, 1981. *Essays in Economics* (3 vols, 1971/75/82); *The New Economics One Decade Older* (1974); *Asset Accumulation and Economic Activity* (1980); *Politics for Prosperity* (1987).

Gordon Tullock Karl Eller Professor of Economics and Political Science, University of Arizona; Foreign Service Officer (specializing in China). Leslie T. Wilkins Award, for 'The Outstanding Book in the Field of Criminology and Criminal Justice', by the Criminal Justice Research Center, Albany, NY (1982). *The Calculus of Consent: Logical Foundations of a Constitutional Democracy* (with J.M. Buchanan, 1962); *The Politics of Bureaucracy* (1965); *Autocracy*; *Economics of Income Redistribution*; *The New World of Economics: Explorations into the Human Experience* (with R.B. McKenzie, 1978); *The Organization of Inquiry*.

Immanuel Wallerstein Director, Fernand Braudel Center, SUNY-Binghamton. Doctor *honoris causa*, University of Paris, 1976. *The Modern World-System* (3 vols, 1974/80/89); *The Capitalist World-Economy* (1979); *Historical Capitalism* (1983); *The Politics of the World-Economy* (1984); *Geopolitics and Geoculture* (1991); *Unthinking Social Science: The Limits of Nineteenth-Century Paradigms* (1991).

Henry C. Wallich died 1988. Professor of Economics, Yale University, 1951–74; Member, Board of Governors of the Federal Reserve System, 1974–88; Assistant to the Secretary of the Treasury; Member, President's Council of Economic Advisors. 'Debt management as an instrument of economic policy', *American Economic Review* 36 (1946); *Monetary Problems of an Export Economy* (1950); *Mainsprings of the German Revival* (1955); 'Conservative economic policy', *Yale Review* 46(1), (1956); *The Cost of Freedom* (1960); *Monetary Policy and Practice* (1981).

Alan Walters Professor of Economics, Johns Hopkins University. *Money in Boom and Slump* (1968); *An Introduction to Econometrics* (1968); *The Economics of Road User Charges* (1968); *Noises and Prices* (1975); *Microeconomic Theory* (with R. Layard, 1978); *Britain's Economic Renaissance* (1986).

David R. Weir Associate Professor of Economics, Yale University. 'Life under pressure: France–England, 1670–1870', *Journal of Economic History* (1984); 'Rather never than late; celibacy and age at marriage in English cohort-fertility 1541–1871', *Journal of Family History* 9(4), (1984); 'Market and mortality in France 1600–1789', in *Death in the Social Order* (ed. Roger Schofield and John Walther, forthcoming).

Edwin G. West Professor of Economics, Carleton University, Ottowa. 'The theory of the second best: a solution in search of a problem', (with Michael Mckee) *Economic Inquiry* 19(3), (1981); 'Marx's hypothesis on the length of the working day', *The Journal of Political Economy* 92(2), (1983); 'Job signalling and welfare improving minimum wage hours', *Economic Inquiry* 26(2), (1988); 'Nonprofit organizations: revised theory and new evidence', *Public Choice* 63(2), (1989); *Adam Smith and Modern Economics: From Market Behaviour to Public Choice* (1990); 'Public education via exclusive territories', *Public Finance Quarterly* 18(4), (1990).

Charles A. Wilson Professor of Economics, New York University. Fellow, Econometric Society; Sloan Research Fellow. 'A model of insurance with incomplete information', *Journal of Economic Theory* 16 (1977); 'Anticipated shocks and exchange rate dynamics', *Journal of Political Economy* 87(3), (1979); 'An infinite horizon model with money', in

General Equilibrium, Growth and Trade (ed. J. Green and J. Scheinkman, 1979); 'The nature of equilibrium in markets with adverse selection', *The Bell Journal of Economics* 11(2), (1980); 'Equilibrium in dynamic models of pure exchange', *Journal of Economic Theory* 24(1), (1981); 'The war of attrition in continuous time with complete information', *International Economic Review* 29(4), (1988).

Robert Wilson Professor, Stanford Business School. 'A bidding model of "perfect" competition', *Review of Economic Studies* 4 (1977); 'Sequential equilibria', (with D. Kreps) *Econometrica* 50 (1982); 'Incentive efficiency of double auctions', *Econometrica* 53 (1985); 'Foundations of dynamic monopoly and the Coase conjecture', (with F. Gul and H. Sonnenschein) *Journal of Economic Theory* 39 (1986); 'Priority service: pricing, investment and market organization', (with H. Chao) *American Economic Review* 77 (1987); 'Efficient and competitive rationing', *Econometrica* 57 (1989).

Gordon C. Winston Professor of Economics, Orrin Sage Professor of Political Economy and Provost, Williams College. 'Addiction and backsliding: a theory of compulsive consumption', *Journal of Economic Behavior and Organization* (December 1980); *The Timing of Economic Activities: Firms, Households and Markets in Time-Specific Analysis* (1982); 'The economics of academic tenure: a relational perspective', (with M. McPherson) *Journal of Economic Behavior and Organization* (1983); 'Introduction' and 'Three problems with the treatment of time in economics', in *The Boundaries of Economics* (ed., with R. Teichgraeber, 1988); 'The time-shape of transactions', *Applied Behavioral Economics* (1989); 'Activities in time: a new approach to work and consumption', *Journal of Economic Behavior and Organization* (forthcoming).

Sidney G. Winter Chief Economist, US General Accounting Office, Washington DC; Professor of Economics and Management, Yale University, 1976–89. Fellow, Econometric Society, American Association for the Advancement of Science. 'Economic "natural selection" and the theory of the firm', *Yale Economic Essays* 4 (1969); 'Satisficing, selection and the innovating remnant', *Quarterly Journal of Economics* 85 (1971); 'Neoclassical vs. evolutionary theories of economic growth: critique and prospectus', (with R.R. Nelson) *Economic Journal* 84 (1974); 'An essay on the theory of production', in *Economics and the World Around It* (ed. S. Hymans, 1982); *An Evolutionary Theory of Economic Change* (with R.R. Nelson, 1982); 'Survival, selection and inheritance in evolutionary theories of organization', in *Organizational Evolution: New Directions* (ed. J.V. Singh, 1990).

G.D.N. Worswick Fellow and Tutor in Economics, Magdalen College, Oxford, 1945–65; Director, National Institute of Economic and Social Research, London, 1965–1982. Fellow, British Academy; President, Royal Economic Society, 1982–84. *The Economics of Full Employment* (contributor, 1944); *The British Economy 1945–50* (joint editor, 1952); *The British Economy in the 1950's* (joint editor, 1962); *The Uses of Economics* (ed., 1972); *Unemployment: A Problem of Policy* (1991).

Subject Classification

This classification by subject is meant simply to help readers who wish to read and study the essays in this volume according to field. It is therefore arranged into categories that are more or less standard in modern economics. An article may appear in two categories, if its subject matter crosses one of the rather arbitrary frontiers set up here.

History of Thought
Common Law
Malthus's Theory of
   Population
Monopoly
National System
'Neoclassical'
'Political Economy' and
   'Economics'
Scholastic Economic
   Thought
Scottish Enlightenment
Self-interest
Specie-flow Mechanism
Time Preference

Economic Doctrines
Chicago School
Economic Interpretation of
   History
Free Lunch
Interests
Keynesianism
Liberalism
Marxist Economics
Mercantilism
Monetarism
Utopias

Economic History
Agricultural Growth and
   Population Change
Bubbles
Continuity in Economic
   History

Counterfactuals
Economic Interpretation of
   History
Gold Standard
Hunting and Gathering
   Economies
Market Places
Open Field System
Trade Unions

Methodology and Philosophy
Counterfactuals
Economic Theory and the
   Hypothesis of Rationality
Entitlements
Equilibrium: an
   Expectational Concept
Equilibrium: Development
   of the Concept
Interpersonal Utility
   Comparisons
Rhetoric
Self-interest
Scottish Enlightenment
Value Judgments

Social Economics
Codetermination and
   Profit-sharing
Distributive Justice
Entitlements
Family
Gender
Gifts
Leisure

Poverty
Rent Control
Tiebout Hypothesis
Trade Unions
Value of Life

*Social and Political
   Organization*
Bribery
Bureaucracy
Coase Theorem
Common Law
Common Property Rights
Constitutional Economics
Law and Economics
Property Rights
Rent Seeking

*Welfare Economics and
   Public Finance*
Burden of the Debt
Coase Theorem
Distributive Justice
Interpersonal Utility
   Comparisons
Marketing Boards
Neutral Taxation
Ricardian Equivalence
   Theorem
Rising Supply Price
Shadow Pricing
Social Cost
Tiebout Hypothesis
Value Judgments
Welfare Economics

745

Index

Page span of each essay is given in italics after essay's name.

Index

748

Index

Index

Index

Index

Smith, A., and concept of equilibrium 228–11, 234; and constitutional economics 135–6; on economic development 635–6; on growth 637; and interests 351–4; and invisible hand 642–3; and monopoly 475–6; on needs 636; and political economy 556–8, 550; and rationality 201–2; and self-interest 642–3; and trade unions 684, 686; and welfare economics 713–15. *See also* classical economics, political economy, Scottish Enlightenment.

social choice, *see* value judgements, welfare economics.

social cost *649–54*; aggregation of 651–2; application of concept 652–3; and Coase theorem 653; and co-determination and profit sharing 70–72; and comparative advantage 100–101; concept of society 650; cost–benefit analysis 650–52; definition of 649–52; and economic integration 177–85; and international trade 651; and market failure 653; of monopoly 476–9; and rent 650; of rent control 600–601; in short- and long-run 651; and terms of trade 668–70; and transaction costs 653. *See also* compensation criterion, deadweight loss, externalities, Pareto criterion, rent seeking, shadow pricing, welfare economics.

social science 500.

social welfare functions 722–5.

specialization, in trade, and export-led growth 345–8. *See also* comparative advantage.

specie-flow mechanism *655–8*; and comparative advantage 656–7; and gold standard 327; and Hume 655–8; and Keynes 657; and Marshall–Lerner condition 656–7; and quantity theory of money 655.

speculation, *see* bubbles, financial intermediaries, sports *659–64*; cartels in 659, 662; monopoly in 660–61; profit maximization in 661; racial discrimination in 662; and trade unions 662. *See also* leisure.

stabilization, of agricultural prices and incomes 417–23; of hyperinflation 342–3.

static expectations, and cobweb theorem 58–9.

Steuart, J., and interests 351–2; and political economy 557; and Scottish Enlightenment 637.

sticky wages, and Keynes 287; and full employment 287.

Stigler, G. J., and Chicago School 45–6; and the history of the term 'neoclassical' 502–3; and perfect competition 535.

stocks, *see* dividend policy.

stock splits 214.

Stolper–Samuelson Theorem 104.

sunspot equilibria 207–11.

surplus value 431–6; and developing countries 553.

Sweezy, P. 436; on periphery 553.

tariffs, *see* economic integration.

targeting, of interest rates 452–3, 469–71; monetary 455–6, 468–71. *See also* fine tuning.

tastes, and Chicago School 47; and comparative advantage 102–3; and sexual discrimination in employment 299–301; and value judgments 702.

tâtonnement, see Walrasian auctioneer.

taxation, and capital gains and losses 37; and constitutional economics 140–41; distortionary, and Ricardian Equivalence Theorem 621; and dividend policy 170–71; and economic integration 185; and economic rent 511 and hyperinflation 341; marginal taxation rates and supply side 473; and marketing boards 415–17; and rent seeking 606; and tastes 513–15; and Tiebout hypothesis 673–4. *See also* distributive justice, neutral taxation, Ricardian Equivalence Theorem.

technology; and agricultural growth and population change 7–9; and bureaucracy 30; and communications 93–4, 97; and comparative advantage 99–100, 104; and competition and selection 112–15; and continuity in economic history 143–4; and economic integration 184; and evolution 498–9; and import substitution 347–8; and limits to growth 391; and Malthus's theory of population 401; and Marxist economics 429–35; and performing arts 545–7; Schumpeter on 112–15; and

terms of trade 669; and utopias 695. *See also* declining industries.

telecommunications, pricing of, 91–4. *See also* communications.

temporary equilibrium, *see* equilibrium.

tenure, agricultural, and population growth 9–10; security of, and rent control 598–603.

terms of trade *665–71*; different measures of 665–6; and economic integration 180–81; and exchange 237; and exploitation 667; Harberler on 669; long-run tendencies of 670; Marshall on 667; Mill on 667; and North–South economic relations 670–71; and optimal tariffs 670; and Prebisch–Singer hypothesis 670–71; Ricardo on 667; secular tendencies in 670; and shadow pricing 666; and technology 669; welfare effects of 668–70. *See also* comparative advantage.

Tiebout hypothesis *672–77*; and free riding 673; and returns to scale 674–6; and taxation 673–4.

time preference *678–83*; Böhm-Bawerk on 680–82; and efficient exchange 241; Fisher on 681; Menger on 681; and Mill 680; Rae on 680–81; and rent 681–2; and Turgot 679–80.

Tinbergen, J., and customs unions 178.

trade, direction of, and comparative advantage 99–100; and economic integration 177–84; and rationality 208. *See also* comparative advantage, import substitution and export-led growth, periphery, terms of trade.

trade unions *684–93*; bargaining areas of 689–90; and collective bargaining 687–9; impact on pay of 691–2; and inflation of 1960s and 1970s 692–3; and the law 689; membership of 685–6; as monopolies 686–7; and redistribution 692; and Adam Smith 684, 686; and sports 662; and S. and B. Webb 684; at workplace 690–91. *See also* codetermination and profit-sharing.

transaction costs, and bureaucracy 29; and Coase theorem 52–5; and rent control 601–2; and social cost 653.

transfer problem 668.

transformation problem 431–3.

transportation, and congestion 127–32; and market places 422.

transportation costs, and agricultural growth and population change 5–6; and bureaucracy 29–30; and economic integration 179; and periphery 549.

uncertainty, and Ricardian Equivalence Theorem 614, 618–19. *See also* expectations, information, risk.

underconsumptionist theory 436.

unemployment, *see* employment, full employment, inflation, inflation–unemployment trade-off.

uniform taxation, and neutral taxation 512–14.

Uno school 431.

urbanization, and agricultural growth and population change 5–7.

usury 630–31.

utilitarianism, and interpersonal utility comparisons 362; and law and economics 373–4; and self-interest 643–4.

utility, maximization of over time 507; and rationality 200–1. *See also* interpersonal utility comparisons, Pareto criterion.

utopias *694–701*; full-employment utopias 697; and *homo economicus* 698; and libertarianism 699; and Malthus 403; and Malthus's theory of population 698; and More 695–6; and Marx 698; and political economy 695; and private property rights 698; and scarce resources 694–7; and technology 695; utopian socialism 698.

value, subjective theory of value of firms 503. *See also* dividend policy, Marxist economics.

value-added tax 511.

value judgments *702–5*; Arrow on 704–5; disagreements in 703–4; in economics 704–5; objectivity of 702–3; and Robbins 704; and tastes 702.

value of life *706–12*; concern for others' lives 708–10; and cost–benefit analysis 706; and discounting 711–12; and

Index

externalities 707–8; and family 707–8; and government intervention 709; and gross national product 708; implicit valuations 712; and insurance 710–11; and risk 706–12; and scale economies 706.

Veblen, T., and history of term 'neoclassical' 502–3.

velocity of circulation, and monetarism 450–51, 455–6.

Verdoorn's Law 347.

Viner, J., and Chicago School 41–3; and comparative advantage 101; and economic integration 177–9; on rising supply price 625.

von Neumann, J., *see* game theory, von-Neumann-Morgenstern utility functions, zero-sum games.

von Neumann-Morgenstern utility functions 363.

voting, voting paradox 721–5; and welfare economics 720–22.

voting with your feet, *see* Tiebout hypothesis.

wage flexibility 287; and agricultural growth and population change 5; and optimum currency areas 527. *See also* full employment.

wage fund 102.

Walras, L., and concept of equilibrium 231–2; and rationality 205; Walrasian equilibrium and exchange 238–45. *See also* classical economics, equilibrium, perfect competition, Walrasian auctioneer.

Walrasian auctioneer 536–7; and relation of macroeconomics and microeconomics 395. *See also* Walras.

Webb, S. and B., and trade unions 684.

Weber, M., and bureaucracy 28; and economic interpretation of history 190–91.

Weitzman, M. L., and codetermination and profit-sharing 66–72.

welfare, *see* social cost, welfare economics.

welfare economics *713–26*; and Arrow 723–5; and Bergson 722; and Coase 718; compensation criterion 720–21; and competitive equilibrium 714–17; and externalities 717–18; First Fundamental Theorem of 714–18, 725; and government intervention 713–14; and Kaldor 720–21; and Keynesianism 368; and *laissez faire* 713–14, 720–21; and Lange 719; Lindahl prices 718; and Marshall 721; and mercantilism 713; Pareto optimality 715–17; and Pigou 717–18; and public goods 717–18; and redistribution 717–21, 727; and Samuelson 718; Second Fundamental Theorem of 719–22, 725; and Scitovsky 720–21; and Smith 713–15; social welfare functions 722–5; Third Fundamental Theorem of 722–6; and voting 720–22; and voting paradox 721–5. *See also* exchange; interpersonal utility comparisons, market failure, opportunity cost, social cost.

welfare state, and free lunch 285; and employment policy 290; and liberalism 387–8.

Wicksell, K., and criteria of economic efficiency 139; and constitutional economics 138–9; on gold standard 327–8; on interest rates 470.

women and economics, *see* discrimination in employment, family, gender.

zero-sum games *727–31*; and information 727; laboratory evidence of 731; and maximin principle 728–9; minimax principle 729–30; and Nash equilibrium 728; and rationality 272–31.

zoning 673.